LIFE AND HEALTH INSURANCE HANDBOOK

THE IRWIN SERIES IN RISK AND INSURANCE

EDITORS

EDISON L. BOWERS
The Ohio State University

DAVIS W. GREGG
The American College of Life Underwriters

BOILEAU, STALNAKER, & LUCK *Life Insurance Agency Financial Management*
BRAINARD *Automobile Insurance*
DICKERSON *Health Insurance* Revised Edition
DONALDSON *Casualty Claim Practice*
FOLLMANN *Medical Care and Health Insurance: A Study in Social Progress*
FRAINE *Valuation of Securities Holdings of Life Insurance Companies*
GREGG *Life and Health Insurance Handbook* Second Edition
GREIDER & BEADLES *Law and the Life Insurance Contract*
HABER & COHEN *Social Security: Programs, Problems, and Policies*
MAGEE & BICKELHAUPT *General Insurance* Seventh Edition
MAGEE *Life Insurance* Third Edition
MAGEE *Property Insurance* Third Edition
MCGILL *Legal Aspects of Life Insurance*
MCGILL *Life Insurance*
MEHR & CAMMACK *Principles of Insurance* Third Edition
MEHR & HEDGES *Risk Management in the Business Enterprise*
MYERS *Social Insurance and Allied Government Programs*
REDEKER & REID *Life Insurance Settlement Options* Revised Edition
SNIDER *Readings in Property and Casualty Insurance*

LIFE and HEALTH INSURANCE HANDBOOK

PLANNED AND EDITED BY

DAVIS W. GREGG, C.L.U.

President, The American College of Life Underwriters

WITH THE CO-OPERATION OF

ONE HUNDRED AND SIXTY-TWO OUTSTANDING AMERICAN INSURANCE AUTHORITIES

SECOND EDITION

1964

RICHARD D. IRWIN, INC.

HOMEWOOD, ILLINOIS

SECOND EDITION

First Printing, July, 1964

Library of Congress Catalogue Card No. 64–21026

PRINTED IN THE UNITED STATES OF AMERICA

To

MILDRED GRACE, CINDY, AND BILL

—a family offering continuing inspiration, and a family so typical of the precious relationships which are the foundation of life and health insurance the world over

PREFACE

Insuring human life values against risks to life and health is one of the major enterprises of our modern society. Premature death, disability, and superannuation are vital risks faced by every mortal man. Fortunately, most of the economic consequences of these major risks are subject to scientific treatment through the insurance mechanism with a resultant decrease in many of life's uncertainties.

The treatment of human life value risks is the principal responsibility of the life and health insurance business of the United States and Canada. The scope of the business—for all practical purposes only about 100 years old—has reached major proportions. In the neighborhood of 600,000 persons are directly involved as company employees, field underwriters, corporate buyers, regulatory personnel, and the like. About 1,600 life and health insurance companies operate in the United States and Canada. More than 130 million persons in the United States and Canada are covered by some form of life insurance, while substantially more (about 150 million) have some type of health insurance coverage. Approximately $24 billion, or about 5 per cent of the total national income of the two countries, is paid in premiums each year to this branch of insurance. Adding the $15 billion in social security contributions and the $4 billion in noninsured pension plan contributions gives a total of $43 billion, or about 9 per cent of the total national income, set aside annually to cope with life value risks.

Such is the scope of life insurance, health insurance, and pensions; such is the breadth of the field with which this *Life and Health Insurance Handbook* is concerned.

This second edition of the *Handbook* will serve as a comprehensive reference source on all major phases of life and health insurance, including the increasingly important field of pensions and profit sharing. It will serve as a highly practical tool for all insurance practitioners and such groups as lawyers, accountants, trust officers, and others vitally concerned from day to day with life and health insurance. Although designed as a handbook, it also provides an orderly, integrated volume of principles subject to textbook treatment by the serious student of life and health insurance.

A total of 162 outstanding insurance authorities have contributed to the *Handbook*, 82 serving as Contributing Authors and 80 as Consulting Editors. Each author has written his chapter within the carefully conceived master plan for the entire book and against a basic plan for each chapter. The volume is designed so that most chapters stand on their own, thus adding to the effectiveness of the *Handbook* as a reference tool.

The *Handbook* is divided into ten basic sections: Part I—Economic Bases of Life and Health Insurance; Part II—Individual Life Insurance and Annuities; Part III—Individual Health Insurance; Part IV—Group Life and Health Insurance; Part V—Pensions and Profit Sharing; Part VI —Business Uses of Life and Health Insurance; Part VII—Government Life and Health Benefits; Part VIII—Programing and Estate Planning; Part IX—Marketing Life and Health Insurance; and Part X—The Institution of Life and Health Insurance. An effort has been made to arrange the chapters within each Part in logical order for teaching and learning purposes. The Appendixes contain a variety of contracts, riders, forms, and other materials of practical value.

The basic objective of the Irwin Series in Risk and Insurance, initiated in 1949, has been to create insurance literature useful not only to college and university classes but also to the insurance business itself. From the beginning, the Editors were aware of the need for a comprehensive reference volume on insurance. Originally, it was conceived that a single handbook in insurance should be prepared but, as the design of the volume took shape, it became obvious that a one-volume work was not practicable. It was then decided that two handbooks would be published and, in 1958, preparation of the first edition of the *Life and Health Insurance Handbook* was begun. This volume, published in 1959, proved to be highly useful in the United States and in many foreign countries. Its success indicated the need for this subsequent revision and for the completion of its companion volume. The *Property and Liability Insurance Handbook,* planned and edited in conjunction with Professor John D. Long of Indiana University, will be published in 1965.

The first edition of this *Handbook* was based on the notion that an immense amount of intelligent and capable writing talent existed among insurance authorities, but that time and work pressures prevented most of them the opportunity to ponder and to articulate their thoughts. It was believed that limiting the writing assignment to a part of a volume would permit scores of able persons to make creative contributions to insurance literature. The validity of this thought is recorded on the pages of the first edition and of this current volume.

In the preface to the first edition, reference was made to the problems of inconsistent terminology. Hope was expressed that by the time the second edition was prepared it would be possible to improve insurance language. While some progress has been made through the efforts of the Commission on Insurance Terminology and its operating committees, and some of this progress is reflected in the terminology in this edition of the *Handbook,* much remains to be done. The reader is asked to have patience in regard to the terminological inconsistencies he will encounter.

It is believed that the language and thoughts are clear even though terminology used may differ among authors.

To acknowledge properly the help received from scores of able persons would require a very long preface indeed. It is hoped that the Contributing Authors and Consulting Editors, listed on subsequent pages, will feel great personal satisfaction in the wide use of their ideas. Such is the true compensation to any creative mind; my sincere gratitude to them seems small beside it.

Many very good friends have "walked the extra mile" in developing this edition and I am deeply grateful to them. G. Victor Hallman, my associate at the American College, and Joseph J. Melone, of the Wharton School of Finance and Commerce, were especially helpful not only as Consulting Editors but in their special assistance in reading galley proof for a number of the chapters. Their great knowledge and editorial skill added substantially to the quality of the chapters which had their attention. William T. Beadles, Kenneth Black, Jr., Robert M. Crowe, O. D. Dickerson, W. W. Dotterweich, E. J. Faulkner, J. F. Follmann, Jr., Herbert C. Graebner, G. Victor Hallman, William Harmelin, Jack C. Keir, Dan M. McGill, Robert W. Osler, J. Carlton Smith, J. Henry Smith, Armand C. Stalnaker, and Edmund L. Zalinski were especially helpful in refining the structure of the second edition. Others not named elsewhere who have given much appreciated help on the project are D. P. Cavanaugh, Gordon N. Farquhar, Karl W. Punzak, and Crampton Trainer of the Aetna Life Insurance Company; Robert M. Crowe of the American College of Life Underwriters; Arthur A. Windecker of the Equitable Life Assurance Society of the United States; H. W. B. Manning of the Great-West Life Assurance Company; M. Forrest Briggs, Richard A. Edwards, John P. Hanna, and James P. Quinn of the Health Insurance Association of America; Maryl Oldershaw of the Home Life Insurance Company; Milton Amsel, Paull M. Giddings, and Virginia Thompson Holran of the Institute of Life Insurance; J. L. Roueche of the Jefferson Standard Life Insurance Company; J. Edwin Matz of the John Hancock Mutual Life Insurance Company; Alden F. Jacobs of the Life Office Management Association; George P. Burke, Jr., Walter L. Grace, A. Peter Quinn, Jr., and Edward B. Sullivan, Jr. of the Massachusetts Mutual Life Insurance Company; George R. Berry, Frederick E. Boes, James S. Burke, Douglas S. Craig, Elles M. Derby, J. W. MacKinnon, LaRue S. Wagenseller, and Cecil G. White of the Metropolitan Life Insurance Company; Ralph Engelsman, Jr. of the Mutual Benefit Life Insurance Company; A. L. Lindley, Donald Rave, and J. M. Wickman of the Mutual Life Insurance Company of New York; David J. Pattison of the National Association of Life Underwriters; James S. Brock, Alden Guild, and Stuart J. Kingston of the National Life Insurance Company; John E. Kennedy of the New England Mutual Life Insurance Company; Howard H. Conley, Edward

A. Stoeber, Robert M. Wendlinger, and Saul A. Wilchins of the New York Life Insurance Company; Verne J. Arends of the Northwestern Mutual Life Insurance Company; James A. Carey of the Occidental Life Insurance Company of California; Harry G. Bubb, William Cunningham, Ben J. Helphand, and Ivan D. Pierce of the Pacific Mutual Life Insurance Company; Charles B. Strome, Jr. of the Provident Mutual Life Insurance Company; William Chodorcoff, Gerard G. Currall, Frank H. David, H. W. Hickman, William P. Lynch, and A. P. Morton of the Prudential Insurance Company of America; Robert C. Beetham of TIAA and CREF; and George E. Light of The Travelers Insurance Company.

Further, the contributions of the authors and editors of the first edition of this *Handbook* who have not participated in the second edition are thankfully acknowledged. Whatever the reason for their nonparticipation—whether retirement, change in structure of the volume, or some other factor—their previous help is greatly appreciated.

In an indirect but very real manner Dr. S. S. Huebner has served as the basic inspiration for this volume and for the other writing and editing I have done in my professional career. As a former teacher, and a long-time associate in American College work, his stimulation to creative endeavor has prevailed in an atmosphere of constant enthusiasm. How could anyone associated with him daily wish to do other than carry on his historic tradition?

In a related way, acknowledgment is made to Julian S. Myrick, Chairman Emeritus of the Board of Trustees of the American College; to Paul F. Clark, Chairman of the Board of the American College; to Charles J. Zimmerman, Vice Chairman of the Board of the American College; and to others on the College's Board of Trustees. This project, and other projects finished and yet to be finished, could never come to pass were it not for the determination of these men that the College will take its place among the outstanding educational institutions of the United States, that the College will give true educational leadership to life and health insurance, and that the officers of the College will devote as much time as possible to writing, research, and other such creative endeavors. Effective insurance literature comes into existence more easily in this kind of environment.

No person could possibly be blessed with more perfect publisher relationships. In every conceivable way, Richard D. Irwin, Inc. has made this project a happy one for all involved. Especially to Richard D. Irwin and Irvin L. Grimes goes warmest thanks for patience and understanding. Harry H. Bingham, Assistant to the Chairman of the Board, gave his personal attention to the editorial and production problems associated with the second edition. His wisdom, judgment, and immensely creative talents have added to the excellence of the final product and to the pleasure of the major task of revising the book.

Helen L. Schmidt, my colleague at the College, has carried the organization and administrative responsibility of the *Handbook* in a brilliantly effective manner. The realization that well over 2,500 letters have been exchanged with authors and editors within one year suggests that very unusual resourcefulness and ingenuity characterized her work. The additional fact that most of the *Handbook* work was carried on by both of us only during evening or weekend hours makes it even more remarkable. It is no exaggeration to say that this *Handbook* could not have been done without her; such is my appreciation to her.

In reflecting on the great amount of time devoted to this project and the resulting disruptions in normal family life, I must emphasize the truth in the thought that "They also serve who only stand and wait." My family's patience in permitting me the several hundred uninterrupted hours in my study has helped greatly in bringing this project to a successful close. So, to Millie, Cindy, and Bill, please forgive me. Let us be thankful that after these many months we all still have our life and health.

DAVIS W. GREGG

NEWTOWN SQUARE, PENNSYLVANIA
June, 1964

CONTRIBUTING AUTHORS AND CONSULTING EDITORS

LAURENCE J. ACKERMAN, Dean (retired), School of Business Administration, University of Connecticut, Storrs, Connecticut

DR. JOHN F. ADAMS, Assistant Vice President, Temple University, Philadelphia, Pennsylvania

EVERETT T. ALLEN, JR., Manager, Pension Plans Department, Provident Mutual Life Insurance Company, Philadelphia, Pennsylvania

THOMAS ALLSOPP, C.L.U., Senior Vice President, Prudential Insurance Company of America, Boston, Massachusetts

DAVID B. ALPORT, Vice President, Business Men's Assurance Company of America, Kansas City, Missouri

MORGAN H. ALVORD, F.S.A., Vice President, Connecticut General Life Insurance Company, Hartford, Connecticut

WILLIAM H. ANDREWS, JR., C.L.U., Manager, Jefferson Standard Life Insurance Company, Greensboro, North Carolina

JOHN C. ANGLE, F.S.A., Vice President and Actuary, Woodmen Accident and Life Company, Lincoln, Nebraska

JAMES A. ATTWOOD, F.S.A., Second Vice President, Equitable Life Assurance Society of the United States, New York, N.Y.

BRUCE BARE, C.L.U., General Agent, New England Mutual Life Insurance Company, Los Angeles, California

JOHN BARKER, JR., Senior Vice President, New England Mutual Life Insurance Company, Boston, Massachusetts

DONALD F. BARNES, Vice President, Institute of Life Insurance, New York, N.Y.

WILLIAM T. BEADLES, C.L.U., Professor of Insurance, Illinois Wesleyan University, Bloomington, Illinois

ORVILLE E. BEAL, C.L.U., President, Prudential Insurance Company of America, Newark, New Jersey

DR. JOSEPH M. BELTH, C.L.U., Assistant Professor of Insurance, Indiana University, Bloomington, Indiana

RAYMOND W. BENDER, F.S.A., Associate Actuary, Prudential Insurance Company of America, Newark, New Jersey

DR. KENNETH BLACK, JR., C.L.U., C.P.C.U., Chairman, Insurance Department, Georgia State College, Atlanta, Georgia

B. FRANKLIN BLAIR, F.S.A., Vice President and Actuary, Provident Mutual Life Insurance Company, Philadelphia, Pennsylvania

DAVID M. BLUMBERG, C.L.U., General Agent, Massachusetts Mutual Life Insurance Company, Knoxville, Tennessee

JOSEPH E. BOETTNER, C.L.U., President, Philadelphia Life Insurance Company, Philadelphia, Pennsylvania

WILLIAM J. BOWE, ESQ., Professor of Law, University of Colorado, Boulder, Colorado

L. M. CATHLES, JR., Vice President, Aetna Life Insurance Company, Hartford, Connecticut

DR. CHARLES C. CENTER, C.L.U., Professor of Commerce, University of Wisconsin, Madison, Wisconsin

EARL CLARK, C.L.U., President, Occidental Life Insurance Company of California, Los Angeles, California

DONALD D. CODY, F.S.A., Vice President, New York Life Insurance Company, New York, N.Y.

EDMOND H. CURCURU, Director of Education and Training, Life Office Management Association, New York, N.Y.

E. C. DANFORD, C.L.U., Vice President, Mutual Life Insurance Company of New York, New York, N.Y.

ARTHUR C. DANIELS, Vice President, Institute of Life Insurance, New York, N.Y.

DEANE C. DAVIS, President, National Life Insurance Company, Montpelier, Vermont

ROBERT DECHERT, ESQ., Dechert, Price and Rhoads, Philadelphia, Pennsylvania

DR. O. D. DICKERSON, C.L.U., C.P.C.U., F.C.A.S., Associate Professor of Insurance, Florida State University, Tallahassee, Florida

JOHN K. DYER, JR., F.S.A., Vice President and Actuary, Towers, Perrin, Forster and Crosby, Inc., Philadelphia, Pennsylvania

DR. ROBERT D. EILERS, C.L.U., Assistant Director, S. S. Huebner Foundation for Insurance Education, Philadelphia, Pennsylvania

COY G. EKLUND, C.L.U., Senior Agency Vice President, Equitable Life Assurance Society of the United States, New York, N.Y.

RALPH G. ENGELSMAN, Sales Consultant, New York, N.Y.

JARVIS FARLEY, F.C.A.S., First Vice President and Treasurer, Massachusetts Indemnity and Life Insurance Company, Boston, Massachusetts

E. J. FAULKNER, President, Woodmen Accident and Life Company, Lincoln, Nebraska

JOSEPH F. FOLLMANN, JR., Director, Information and Research Division, Health Insurance Association of America, New York, N.Y.

KENNETH C. FOSTER, C.L.U., Senior Vice President, Prudential Insurance Company of America, Newark, New Jersey

ERNEST W. FURNANS, JR., C.L.U., Associate General Counsel, Massachusetts Mutual Life Insurance Company, Springfield, Massachusetts

Charles E. Gaines, C.L.U., Director, Institute of Insurance Marketing, Southern Methodist University, Dallas, Texas

Harold W. Gardiner, C.L.U., Superintendent of Education and Field Training, Northwestern Mutual Life Insurance Company, Milwaukee, Wisconsin

Benjamin M. Gaston, C.L.U., Manager, North American Life Assurance Company, Philadelphia, Pennsylvania

Robert P. Gatewood, C.L.U., Robert P. Gatewood & Company, Washington, D.C.

Clyde F. Gay, Executive Vice President, John Hancock Mutual Life Insurance Company, Boston, Massachusetts

Lawrence B. Gilman, Vice President, John Hancock Mutual Life Insurance Company, Boston, Massachusetts

Herbert C. Graebner, C.L.U., Vice President and Dean, American College of Life Underwriters, Bryn Mawr, Pennsylvania

William D. Grant, C.L.U., President, Business Men's Assurance Company of America, Kansas City, Missouri

William C. Greenough, Chairman and President, Teachers Insurance and Annuity Association of America and College Retirement Equities Fund, New York, N.Y.

Miss Janice E. Greider, C.L.U., Associate Counsel, State Farm Life and Accident Assurance Company, Bloomington, Illinois

Alfred N. Guertin, F.S.A., Actuary, American Life Convention, Chicago, Illinois

Stanton G. Hale, President, Pacific Mutual Life Insurance Company, Los Angeles, California

G. Victor Hallman, C.L.U., Assistant Dean, American College of Life Underwriters, Bryn Mawr, Pennsylvania

James A. Hamilton, F.S.A., President, The Wyatt Company, Washington, D.C.

William Harmelin, C.L.U., Vice President, Business and Estate Planning Consultants, Inc., New York, N.Y.

Wm. Eugene Hays, C.L.U., General Agent, New England Mutual Life Insurance Company, Boston, Massachusetts

Charles G. Heitzeberg, C.L.U., Vice President, Mutual Benefit Life Insurance Company, Newark, New Jersey

Dr. Kenneth W. Herrick, C.L.U., C.P.C.U., Chairman, Insurance Department, Texas Christian University, Fort Worth, Texas

John A. Hill, C.L.U., President, Aetna Life Affiliated Companies, Hartford, Connecticut

Dr. Ronald C. Horn, C.P.C.U., Director of Educational Services, American College of Life Underwriters, Bryn Mawr, Pennsylvania

John M. Huebner, Senior Vice President, Penn Mutual Life Insurance Company, Philadelphia, Pennsylvania

DR. S. S. HUEBNER, President Emeritus, American College of Life Underwriters, Bryn Mawr, Pennsylvania

ROGER HULL, C.L.U., President, Mutual Life Insurance Company of New York, New York, N.Y.

ALEXANDER HUTCHINSON, C.L.U., Senior Vice President, Metropolitan Life Insurance Company, New York, N.Y.

DAVID A. IVRY, C.L.U., Professor of Insurance, University of Connecticut, Storrs, Connecticut

PAUL H. JACKSON, F.S.A., Associate Actuary, Aetna Life Insurance Company, Hartford, Connecticut

DR. DONALD R. JOHNSON, School of Business Administration, University of Miami, Coral Gables, Florida

RAYMOND C. JOHNSON, C.L.U., Executive Vice President, New York Life Insurance Company, New York, N.Y.

LAFLIN C. JONES, C.L.U., Vice President and Director of Markets Research, Northwestern Mutual Life Insurance Company, Milwaukee, Wisconsin

GEORGE R. JORDAN, JR., Executive Vice President, Southland Life Insurance Company, Dallas, Texas

HALSEY D. JOSEPHSON, C.L.U., General Agent, Connecticut Mutual Life Insurance Company, New York, N.Y.

D. E. KILGOUR, President, Great-West Life Assurance Company, Winnipeg, Canada

RAYMOND F. KILLION, F.S.A., Vice President, Metropolitan Life Insurance Company, New York, N.Y.

THOMAS H. KIRKPATRICK, F.S.A., Vice President and Actuary, Paul Revere Life Insurance Company, Worcester, Massachusetts

LAWRENCE G. KNECHT, ESQ., Kiefer, Waterworth, Hunter and Knecht, Cleveland, Ohio

KARL H. KREDER, C.L.U., Vice President, Metropolitan Life Insurance Company, New York, N.Y.

HARRY KRUEGER, C.L.U., General Agent, Northwestern Mutual Life Insurance Company, New York, N.Y.

R. J. LEARSON, Vice President for Group Insurance, Mutual Life Insurance Company of New York, New York, N.Y.

A. LESLIE LEONARD, C.L.U., C.P.C.U., Acting President, The College of Insurance, New York, N.Y.

M. ALBERT LINTON, F.S.A., Director, Provident Mutual Life Insurance Company, Philadelphia, Pennsylvania

JOHN L. LOBINGIER, JR., Assistant Secretary, Connecticut Mutual Life Insurance Company, Hartford, Connecticut

DR. JOHN D. LONG, C.L.U., C.P.C.U., Professor of Insurance, Indiana University, Bloomington, Indiana

ROBERT W. LORD, C.L.U., Vice President, Flitcraft, Inc., New York, N.Y.

JOHN K. LUTHER, C.L.U., Director of Training, Aetna Life Insurance Company, Hartford, Connecticut

WILLIAM B. LYNCH, ESQ., Pratte, Suckling & Lynch, Los Angeles, California

ROY A. MACDONALD, Managing Director, Life Office Management Association, New York, N.Y.

FRANK B. MAHER, Senior Vice President, John Hancock Mutual Life Insurance Company, Boston, Massachusetts

EDWIN H. MARSHALL, C.P.C.U., Vice President, Insurance Company of North America Companies, Philadelphia, Pennsylvania

JAMES R. MARTIN, C.L.U., Vice President, Massachusetts Mutual Life Insurance Company, Springfield, Massachusetts

DR. ARTHUR MASON, JR., C.L.U., Director of Insurance Research, Graduate School of Business Administration, Washington University, St. Louis, Missouri

JOHN F. MCALEVEY, ESQ., Assistant General Counsel, Health Insurance Association of America, New York, N.Y.

CHARLES B. MCCAFFREY, C.L.U., Consultant, Provident Mutual Life Insurance Company, Philadelphia, Pennsylvania

DR. DAN M. MCGILL, C.L.U., Executive Director, S. S. Huebner Foundation for Insurance Education, Philadelphia, Pennsylvania

BEN S. MCGIVERAN, C.L.U., Partner, The Seefurth & McGiveran Consulting Services, Milwaukee, Wisconsin

MICHAEL M. MCKENNY, C.L.U., Assistant Vice President, New York Life Insurance Company, New York, N.Y.

DR. ROBERT I. MEHR, Professor of Finance, University of Illinois, Urbana, Illinois

MEYER MELNIKOFF, F.S.A., Vice President, Prudential Insurance Company of America, Newark, New Jersey

DR. JOSEPH J. MELONE, C.L.U., C.P.C.U., Assistant Professor of Insurance, Wharton School of Finance and Commerce, Philadelphia, Pennsylvania

CLARENCE B. METZGER, C.L.U., Vice President (retired), Equitable Life Assurance Society of the United States, New York, N.Y.

JOHN H. MILLER, F.S.A., F.C.A.S., Executive Vice President, Monarch Life Insurance Company, Springfield, Massachusetts

MORTON D. MILLER, F.S.A., Vice President and Associate Actuary, Equitable Life Assurance Society of the United States, New York, N.Y.

WENDELL MILLIMAN, F.S.A., Milliman and Robertson, Inc., Seattle, Washington

PAUL S. MILLS, C.L.U., Executive Vice President and Managing Director, American Society of Chartered Life Underwriters, Bryn Mawr, Pennsylvania

EDWARD J. MINTZ, C.L.U., Field Consultant, New York Life Insurance Company, Salinas, California

STUART A. MONROE, C.L.U., General Agent, Mutual Benefit Life Insurance Company, Chicago, Illinois

ROBERT J. MYERS, F.S.A., Chief Actuary, Social Security Administration, Department of Health, Education and Welfare, Washington, D.C.

ROBERT R. NEAL, ESQ., General Manager, Health Insurance Association of America, Washington, D.C.

BLAKE T. NEWTON, JR., President, Institute of Life Insurance, New York, N.Y.

PAUL A. NORTON, C.L.U., Senior Vice President, New York Life Insurance Company, New York, N.Y.

CHARLES A. ORMSBY, F.S.A., Vice President, John Hancock Mutual Life Insurance Company, Boston, Massachusetts

DR. GRANT OSBORN, C.L.U., C.P.C.U., Director of Economic Research, American Medical Association, Chicago, Illinois

ROBERT W. OSLER, Consultant, Indianapolis, Indiana

W. SHEFFIELD OWEN, C.L.U., Vice President, Life Insurance Company of Georgia, Atlanta, Georgia

GERALD W. PAGE, C.L.U., General Agent, Provident Mutual Life Insurance Company, Los Angeles, California

WILLIAM K. PAYNTER, Vice President, Institute of Life Insurance, New York, N.Y.

FREDERIC M. PEIRCE, President, General American Life Insurance Company, St. Louis, Missouri

RAY M. PETERSON, F.S.A., Vice President and Associate Actuary, Equitable Life Assurance Society of the United States, New York, N.Y.

LORAN E. POWELL, C.L.U., Executive Vice President and Managing Director, Life Underwriter Training Council, Washington, D.C.

ROBERT K. POWERS, C.L.U., General Agent, Massachusetts Mutual Life Insurance Company, Spokane, Washington

CHARLES E. PROBST, F.S.A., Vice President, Provident Mutual Life Insurance Company, Philadelphia, Pennsylvania

G. FRANK PURVIS, JR., President, Pan-American Life Insurance Company, New Orleans, Louisiana

FREDRICK E. RATHGEBER, F.S.A., Senior Vice President and Actuary, Prudential Insurance Company of America, Newark, New Jersey

HARRY S. REDEKER, ESQ., Vice President and General Counsel, Fidelity Mutual Life Insurance Company, Philadelphia, Pennsylvania

JOSEPH H. REESE, SR., C.L.U., Reese Consulting Services, Inc., Rydal, Pennsylvania

CHARLES K. REID, II, C.L.U., Associate Director, Company Relations Division, Life Insurance Agency Management Association, Hartford, Connecticut

CHARLES F. B. RICHARDSON, F.S.A., Senior Vice President, Berkshire Life Insurance Company, Pittsfield, Massachusetts

Frederick C. Rozelle, Jr., C.L.U., Assistant Vice President, Old Colony Trust Company, Boston, Massachusetts

Charles H. Schaaff, C.L.U., President, Massachusetts Mutual Life Insurance Company, Springfield, Massachusetts

William H. Schmidt, F.S.A., Senior Vice President, Mutual Life Insurance Company of New York, New York, N.Y.

John Z. Schneider, C.L.U., Manager, Connecticut General Life Insurance Company, Baltimore, Maryland

Dr. Stuart Schwarzschild, C.L.U., Associate Professor of Insurance, Georgia State College, Atlanta, Georgia

William N. Seery, Vice President, The Travelers Insurance Company, Hartford, Connecticut

Charles A. Siegfried, F.S.A., Senior Vice President and Chief Actuary, Metropolitan Life Insurance Company, New York, N.Y.

Adon N. Smith, II, C.L.U., President, Adon Smith Associates, Inc., Charlotte, North Carolina

C. Carney Smith, C.L.U., Executive Vice President, National Association of Life Underwriters, Washington, D.C.

J. Carlton Smith, C.L.U., Educational Director, Southwestern Life Insurance Company, Dallas, Texas

J. Henry Smith, F.S.A., Underwriting Vice President, Equitable Life Assurance Society of the United States, New York, N.Y.

Bernhart R. Snyder, C.L.U., Assistant Director, Estate Planning Services, New England Mutual Life Insurance Company, Boston, Massachusetts

Armand Sommer, Vice President, Continental Casualty Company, Chicago, Illinois

Dr. Armand C. Stalnaker, C.L.U., Administrative Vice President, General American Life Insurance Company, St. Louis, Missouri

E. A. Starr, Second Vice President, Connecticut Mutual Life Insurance Company, Hartford, Connecticut

Walter W. Steffen, F.S.A., Vice President, The Lincoln National Life Insurance Company, Fort Wayne, Indiana

Leroy G. Steinbeck, C.L.U., Vice President, Life Insurance Company of North America, Philadelphia, Pennsylvania

E. James Stephens, C.L.U., Second Vice President, Massachusetts Mutual Life Insurance Company, Springfield, Massachusetts

Charles M. Sternhell, F.S.A., Vice President and Actuary, New York Life Insurance Company, New York, N.Y.

C. E. Stevens, Assistant Vice President, Insurance Company of North America, Philadelphia, Pennsylvania

Dr. John E. Stinton, C.L.U., School of Business, University of Colorado, Boulder, Colorado

Frank E. Sullivan, C.L.U., General Agent, American United Life Insurance Company, South Bend, Indiana

John S. Thompson, Jr., F.S.A., Vice President and Actuary, North American Company for Life, Accident and Health Insurance, Chicago, Illinois

Eugene M. Thoré, Esq., Vice President and General Counsel, Life Insurance Association of America, Washington, D.C.

John O. Todd, C.L.U., Special Representative, Northwestern Mutual Life Insurance Company, Evanston, Illinois

Leland T. Waggoner, C.L.U., Vice President-Sales, Home Life Insurance Company, New York, N.Y.

Christopher H. Wain, F.S.A., Associate Actuary, Prudential Insurance Company of America, Newark, New Jersey

G. N. Watson, F.S.A., Vice President and Director of Group Insurance, Crown Life Insurance Company, Toronto, Canada

Edwin E. Weller, Esq., Vice President and General Counsel, Provident Mutual Life Insurance Company, Philadelphia, Pennsylvania

Dr. C. Arthur Williams, Jr., Professor of Economics and Insurance, University of Minnesota, Minneapolis, Minnesota

James R. Williams, Vice President and General Manager, Health Insurance Institute, New York, N.Y.

J. Harry Wood, C.L.U., President, Home Life Insurance Company, New York, N.Y.

Benjamin N. Woodson, C.L.U., President, American General Life Insurance Companies, Houston, Texas

Dr. Edmund L. Zalinski, C.L.U., Executive Vice President, Life Insurance Company of North America, Philadelphia, Pennsylvania

Samuel L. Zeigen, C.L.U., General Agent, Provident Mutual Life Insurance Company, New York, N.Y.

Charles J. Zimmerman, C.L.U., President, Connecticut Mutual Life Insurance Company, Hartford, Connecticut

TABLE OF CONTENTS

PART VII. GOVERNMENT LIFE AND HEALTH BENEFITS

PART IX. MARKETING LIFE AND HEALTH INSURANCE

APPENDIXES

APPENDIX

INDEXES

LIST OF ILLUSTRATIONS

Figures

Tables

PART I

Economic Bases of Life and Health Insurance

Chapter 1

HUMAN LIFE VALUES— THE CONCEPT

BY S. S. HUEBNER

Economics has been defined as the "science of wealth," and insurance, as an applied division of economics, has as its fundamental mission the protection of wealth (values expressed in dollar valuation) in a scientific risk-bearing manner against loss from defined hazards to which the wealth is exposed. If the hazards relate to property values—tangible values like land, structures on the land, equipment within the structures, raw materials of manufacture, and finished goods—property and casualty insurance is used to insure the values. If the hazards relate to the human life values, life insurance, annuities, and health insurance are used to insure the values.

Origin of and Need for the Concept

The human life value concept had its origin in the thought that the human life value expressed in dollars constitutes the true basis for family and business life insurance, that life insurance as generally conceived in the early twentieth century did not observe this point of view, and that the life insurance business was handicapped by a number of fallacious economic views that required changing through a new realistic philosophy more in conformity with the thinking which prevailed in the property insurance area.

Until the late 1920's, life insurance was very generally regarded as a purely "death" proposition, without an explanation of what it was that really died. It seemed to be largely a matter of selecting a $2,000, $5,000, $10,000, $15,000, or $20,000 contract, without any very thoughtful dollar valuation of the insured life. Much consideration was given to the so-called *personal* estate (meaning property estate), overlooking substantially, or altogether, the *person* in that *personal* estate.

It was also very common in those days to stress the benevolent and altruistic concepts of life insurance, and to subordinate the profit motive of life insurance to the premium payor to such an extent as to give the decided impression that the family head had little prospect of benefiting personally. The "living values" of cash value life insurance, such as freedom of mind to venture, improved thrift, sound and profitable investment, better credit, greater vocational security, wise management of the human life value, and so forth, were minimized unduly. The insured, in other words, neglected his own life insurance advantages. He picked some figure like $2,000, $5,000, or $10,000, without having received much of a programing service, and therefore without any attempt at thoughtful appraisal of the money value of his life to his dependents.

There was also a strong disposition to argue that life insurance contracts, because of their actuarial foundation, were certain to meet their promises; that there could be no cheating of the policyholder, no matter what type of contract was purchased; that the buyer always received his money's worth; and that the greatest achievement for good was to market the largest possible volume of offered contracts. This view naturally led to emphasis upon sheer volume selling, to a substantial exclusion of "knowledge of subject matter involved" in the evaluation and analysis of a buyer's economic circumstances and true needs, and to a general failure to adopt the "professional attitude."

Meaning of the Human Life Value Concept

In 1924 the human life value concept was proposed as a philosophical framework for the analysis of basic economic risks faced by individuals. This concept has been widely accepted in life insurance circles and tends to change materially the views that life insurance is essentially a physical death proposition, that it cannot offer a profit motive to the premium payor, and that sheer volume selling, without emphasis upon adequate knowledge and professional attitude, is all that is really necessary. The concept means more than just a statement that a human life has an economic value. Rather, it involves the following six important concepts that life insurance service should contemplate:

1. *The human life value, expressed with a dollar valuation, should be carefully appraised and capitalized for insurance purposes.* It may be defined as the capitalized value of that part of the current earning power of the individual devoted to the support of family dependents (and sometimes the protection of business associates).

One simple method of appraising the economic value of a human life might be illustrated as follows: A, aged 35, has a gross annual income from his personal efforts of $12,000, and after deducting income taxes, his net income is $10,000. A uses $3,000 for his direct self-maintenance, thus leaving $7,000 of his earnings for the support of his wife and children. Assuming that A has a life expectancy of 33 years, but expects to retire at age 65, it is apparent that he can expect 30 more earning years.

On the assumption that his earnings, taxes, and distribution of income will remain approximately the same over the years, the economic value of A's life can be calculated by discounting at a reasonable rate of interest, say 3 per cent, the income flow of $7,000 per year for 30 years. At 3 per cent interest, $1.00 per year for 30 years is worth $19.60 today. Thus, $7,000 times $19.60 equals $137,200, which is A's economic worth to his family.

Obviously, many refinements could enter into a careful appraisal of A's human life value, but this illustration should emphasize the logic of appraising and capitalizing the values inherent in a human life.

From the broad social standpoint, at least a rough appraisal of the total human life values in our nation can be gained as follows: National annual income from wages and salaries in the United States amounts to about $300 billion. If we assume that on the average, one half of this income is devoted to family dependents—and that is very conservative—it follows that $150 billion should be capitalized at the assumed rate of 3 per cent interest. That would give us a total capitalized principal of $5 trillion, or about five times the total value of tangible property values in the United States. Owing to increasing population, this total of capitalized life values will continue to show a corresponding increase. Moreover, this total capitalized value needs to be maintained not only for dependents in case of the "premature death" of the breadwinner, but also for protection of children against the heavy burden of parental financial support following the "retirement death," by way of scientific liquidation through the annuity procedure.

Human life values in the United States, however, have a total money value much in excess of the $5 trillion already referred to. There should be added the money value of women in the household; the money value contributed (invested by parents) in the millions of young people by way of educational preparation in colleges, universities, and other preparatory institutions of learning; and human life values for strictly business purposes, for credit purposes, and for bequest purposes. Additionally, human life values also contribute heavily to income derived annually from interest, corporate profits, partnerships, and sole proprietorships. It may be safely concluded that human life values for all purposes amount to fully $9 trillion in the United States, or about ten times the nation's total property values.

2. *The human life value should be recognized as the creator of substantially all property values.* In other words, the human life value is the *cause,* and property values are the *effect.* Furthermore, the human life value motivates otherwise inanimate property into a productive force.

At present, annual income from interest, corporate profits, and sole proprietorships, after the payment of taxes, totals about $96 billion. Probably half of this huge amount, or $48 billion, is attributable to the human life value motivation of the property involved. If that assumption is correct, the capitalized total of this income at 3 per cent represents another $1.6 trillion.

3. *The family should be regarded as a business partnership from an economic point of view.* No doubt, it should also be viewed religiously, socially, and legally. But the time is long overdue when the family should be viewed as an economic institution, a decidedly sensible and realistic view. Moreover, the family should be regarded as man's first and most important business enterprise. It needs to be *organized originally, subsequently managed,* and its economic values *finally liquidated* in the same sensible manner that other business enterprises are organized, operated, and liquidated.

The business or professional vocation of the family head should be regarded as very important, but nevertheless as man's secondary business, to be pursued in the interest of giving the greatest advantages to the first business, the family business. A proper sense of responsibility on the part of the family head—the breadwinner—to his family is to be presumed, and there should be a proper recognition, far beyond present general acceptance by the public, of the wife's moral and religious rights, and a child's claim to adequate protection. Moreover, the family head—the insured—needs to recognize, far beyond present general acceptance, the outstanding creative functions of life insurance for his own personal advancement as an income producer, so that he may more adequately and advantageously support his family business, his first and most important business.

4. *The human life value should be regarded as constituting the principal link between the present and succeeding generations as regards protective benefits derived from life and health insurance.* Property values, on the contrary, are rather fleeting in character when successive generations are contemplated. With respect to the human life value, under this heading, three main thoughts should be borne in mind, namely, (*a*) the proper education and development of the children in the event of the family head's premature death or disability; (*b*) adequate advance preparation by way of systematic accumulation for the education and development of the children should the family head continue to live but not succeed personally in his hopeful wishing; and (*c*) the protection of the children against the burden of parental financial support following their parents' age of retirement.

5. *There should be applied to human life values the same fundamental principles of appraisal, indemnity, conservation of values, accounting, capitalization, accumulation of surplus, sound investment, credit, the last will and testament, and liquidation which have been applied so carefully to property values for so many decades.* These principles should by all means be applied to the organization, management, and liquidation of

the much larger and much more significant human life value. Many will be inclined to say: "Yes, but how?" The answer is found in life and health insurance, through which we can apply to our life value—our current earning capacity for others—all of the basic economic principles of organization, management, and liquidation which for decades we have as a matter of common sense applied to the organization, management, and liquidation of our property value possessions.

6. *The human life value is subject to loss of earning power through four serious hazards,* namely:

Premature death, or the "casket death."
Temporary disability (including expenses for medical and surgical care).
Total and permanent disability, or the "living death."
Compulsory retirement, or the "retirement death."
(There is a fifth hazard, namely, unemployment, with which we shall not be concerned.)

With respect to all the first four hazards referred to, there should be a proper sense of obligation on the part of the family head, as yet far beyond general acceptance, with respect to the wife's right and a child's claim in the family business partnership.

Health Insurance a Teammate of Life Insurance

Although the human life value concept originally was proposed in a life insurance environment, it obviously embraces all risks to the life value, including those of disability. The hazards of temporary and total disability, faced by all persons, have tremendous economic consequences. Accordingly, health insurance to protect against the loss of earning power and the costs of medical care is a natural teammate of life insurance.

Personal Current Earning Capacity Depends upon Certain Fundamental Characteristics of the Individual

The current earning power of the individual for the benefit of others, the very basis of life and health insurance, is essentially dependent upon six fundamental personal characteristics. They may be enumerated as (1) good character; (2) good health; (3) industry, or the willingness to work; (4) willingness to make a proper investment in the mind (with time, money, and effort) by way of education, training, and experience; (5) creative ability and judgment; and (6) the patience and commendable ambition, over a considerable period of time, to translate the economic dreams of the mind into tangible realities for the benefit of self, family, and mankind in general.

Nearly everybody will agree that good character is the main pedestal upon which all else in our economic career is essentially dependent. No one wants a lazy person in any line of economic endeavor. Good health is absolutely vital, and increasingly executives are recognizing the value of life conservation work, just as they have been accustomed to conserving their property assets against needless loss through loss-prevention activities. The investment in the mind by way of education and training is also vital, and was extolled by Benjamin Franklin about 175 years ago as the "investment above the ears," sure and dependable. Creative ability is apt to lead to very high current earning ability, since it differentiates economically the creative individual from the rank and file who complacently follow an economic "groove" trodden out by others, forgetting, as has been well said, that the difference between a "groove" and a "grave" is only about six feet. The sixth and last factor—patience and ambition over a long period of time to realize successfully the economic dreams of the mind—also represents creative ability of a different but nevertheless very high order, and sometimes has made empire builders.

These six factors are back of human earning capacity. Some persons unfortunately are without any of these factors to a worth-while degree. Many have only one or a few. Some have all and are very fortunate. These six factors, standing by themselves, rise much higher in significance than life and health insurance. They are the basis of life and health insurance, it is true, in that they are the basis of current earning capacity. But they are even more, in that they are the basis of economic life itself.

Economic Value of Human Life Contrasted with Other Values of Human Life

Originally, the human life value concept met with considerable opposition in certain well-meaning quarters. It seemed that the economic value concept of human life was in conflict with the "sentimental value" and the "spiritual value" conceptions of human life. Often, one heard about the awfulness of the idea of attaching a dollar value to a human life. Evidently, human life was classified in a category of values, for insurance purposes and otherwise, very different from the economic concept of values.

Yet, from the sentimental and spiritual points of view, there should be no objection to the economic use of dollar protection for dependent families when the facts clearly indicate the necessity and the religious and moral obligation of a family head to do so. Economically speaking, the application of a dollar program for family security welfare should be regarded as a great good, if wisely used.

The sentimental and spiritual views have their right for recognition, but the unfortunate economic happenings in American family life, attested to with precision by mortality and morbidity tables, certainly warrant the belief that recognition of the economic human life value concept is fully justified. In recent court decisions, huge verdicts running into thousands upon thousands, and sometimes several hundred thousands, of dollars in negligence cases involving total and permanent disability are being awarded ever increasingly in a matter-of-course way. One may wonder why, when the family head dies naturally or becomes disabled, he has seen fit to protect his family with less than two years' earning power, as is now the case with the average family in the United States.

There is no objection to such sentimental tokens as flowers and candy. Yet it would seem that the love of the wife for the husband, as well as the love of the children for the father when they have reached the age of discretion, will be greatly enhanced when they realize that all the cards have been placed on the economic table, and that the family head has given a firm economic financial foundation to the loved ones in his family, his first and most important business.

The Human Life Value Concept Based on Present and Future Earning Capacity

At the beginning of the working life of the individual, his current income may be very small. As the saying is by the groom in certain marriage ceremonies: "With all my worldly goods, I thee endow." The fact is that at that time, he may have no worth-while worldly goods in the property sense. Under such circumstances, "worldly goods" really means potential future earning capacity. That capacity should be recognized realistically and should be capitalized for the maximum amount obtainable for his human life value through life and health insurance. Under such circumstances, the *potential estate* is the all-important thing for family security. Yes, economically speaking, the potential estate through life insurance is even more important to the family business, for the time being, than the purchase of a home on the installment plan of payment. If death or disability occurs, the all-important thing is the dependable consummation of the potential estate in cash for family purposes.

As the family head increases his regular income in the course of time and the family standard of living keeps improving, it is essential that life and health insurance protection be increased correspondingly. Moreover, since about two out of every three family heads, starting at age 30, survive to the retirement age, it is highly essential in the great majority of instances that the life insurance should provide substantial retirement values for liquidation purposes on a life annuity basis for husband and wife, in order to protect the children against the heavy burden of parental financial support.

Life Values by Vocational Groups

The business worth of the human life can also be analyzed for the vocational groups which make up our economic life. Under this heading, the first concern is with the group in our economic system called wage and salary earners. Here, there almost always is a nearly total loss of income to family dependents in the event of death or disability of the family head. It is clear that in the overwhelming majority of cases the protection of the human life value asset of the family breadwinner should be the supreme objective for protection against loss of income to the family.

The professional and other expert vocations (where the chief asset is the good will of clients) resemble the previous classification of wage and salary earners. Although the availability of life and health insurance is greater in this group of our population, the life value from a current income point of view is usually much greater than the possession of accumulated property values. In these callings, although there is some property, regular income from the calling is largely associated with the continued patronage of clients, and that continuance is largely dependent on the continued effective working life of the practitioner who created the personal associations with his clients.

Then there are the vocations concerned chiefly with the fulfillment of long-running contracts. Here again, the life value of the contractor, for example, nearly always greatly exceeds the money value of the equipment used in the business venture.

Next comes the large agricultural group. Here, there is considerable property, but current income attributable primarily to personal ability and hard labor are determining factors. There are farmers and farmers; and the life value involved, depending upon agricultural ability, makes the great difference.

Finally, there is the large group of manufacturing, mercantile, and other industrial establishments. In these cases, much property seems apparent. Yet even here, the most extreme type that can be selected, a careful appraisal of values, between life values and property values in the light of all attending circumstances, will show that in the great majority of cases the monetary worth of the directing life values in the business greatly exceeds in importance the property values actually owned outright, i.e., after deducting the borrowed funds commonly prevailing in this group.

SELECTED REFERENCES

(See end of Chapter 2.)

Chapter 2

HUMAN LIFE VALUES—ROLE OF LIFE INSURANCE

BY S. S. HUEBNER

It is a strange anomaly that men should be careful to insure their houses, their ships, their merchandise, and yet neglect to insure their lives, surely the most important of all to their families, and more subject to loss.

—BENJAMIN FRANKLIN

Life Insurance Is Protector against All Forms of Death, i.e., Premature, Disability, and Retirement

Life insurance protects against all forms of economic death, namely, premature death or the "casket death," total and permanent disability or the "living death," and the compulsory "retirement death."

Protection against Premature Death. This form of economic death (namely, a physical death during the earning period of life prior to retirement from active work) occurs to about one out of three persons during the period from age 30 to age 65.

Such averages, however, although true *in general,* should not control the thinking of an *individual* breadwinner. To lessen the amount of family protection because the hazard strikes much less frequently than it does with respect to old-age retirement is sheer gambling with loved family dependents. The hazard of premature death will always remain one of the outstanding terrors to families in the overwhelming mass of cases. Life insurance is necessary to guarantee a potential estate of adequate size for the family in the event that the breadwinner does not live long enough to accumulate the estate through his own earnings and thrift.

Much is said of the some $720 billion of life insurance on the books of private life insurance companies in the United States. Yet, too often, we forget how little this really means from "economic," "moral," "religious," and "conscience" standpoints. Life insurance per family in the United States averaged in 1962 only about $11,400 in comparison with the annual personal income per family of $6,500, or about 21 months of income per family. Life insurance premiums annually amount to only about 3.8 per cent of total disposable personal income, and that has been the case for many years without appreciable improvement. This is certainly not what ought to be, in the light of the wife's right, a child's claim, and the family head's sense of family obligation and social responsibility. The average amount of life insurance per family does not represent more than a 10 per cent coverage of what should appear as meeting a full sense of obligation to the family, man's first and most important business.

Annual expenditures today for alcoholic beverages and tobacco total about one and a half times the nation's annual life insurance company premiums for life insurance and annuities combined. Comparatively speaking, the annual expenditures for television, radio, cosmetics, toys, sporting goods, and spectator amusements about equal annual private premiums for life insurance and annuities. Annual purchases of passenger automobiles and their operation and maintenance amounted in recent years to nearly twice the total annual premium income of United States life insurance companies for life insurance and annuities combined.

It is suggested that family budgets should be arranged into two distinct divisions, one relating to expenditures *for the present,* and the other to expenditures designed *to meet the future* as regards fundamental family obligations. This viewpoint, however, is far from general public acceptance today. Consultation with the average family head will show that present economic desires come first and family requirements for the future come last. The conversational account usually runs as follows: "I must have this, I must have that, and that, etc.; now tell me, in the light of my income, what is left to pay for an insurance program such as you suggest?" In other words, present desires supersede the basic family requirements for the future welfare of family dependents.

The public welfare suggests that strong emphasis should be placed upon the second part of the family budget in the interest of increasing the annual expenditure for life insurance protection beyond the meager 3.8 per cent of the average family's disposable income. In fact, during the past decade the increase in life insurance on the books of private insurance companies has scarcely kept pace with the inflationary increase in the current cost of living. Such a low percentage as 3.8 per cent of disposable income represents a strange sense of obligation—economically, morally, and religiously—under a system of private enterprise.

Total and Permanent Disability Insurance. Of all the forms of economic death, the "living death" is truly the most horrible. Still living, the victim is incapable of earning current income, and a loving family spends the family's nest egg for a "living death" which requires current living costs plus many additional maintenance and medical expenses. Despite this, the degree of insurance protection against this horror is even smaller than the existing protection against the premature physical death. Clearly, the need for greater coverage in this area is exceedingly vital in our economy. As some indication of the risk of "living death," the following conclusions are taken from a 1952 study:[1]

1. The chance of the occurrence of a long-term disability (lasting three months or longer) at age 30 is 2.7 times as great as the risk of dying. For ages 40 and 50, the chance is 2.3 and 1.8 times as great.
2. The average length of the disability case (three months or longer), depending on the age when disability occurred, lasted from four to 6½ years.
3. At age 35 the chance of experiencing total disability of three months or longer before age 65 is reached is about 33 per cent. The average length of the disability well exceeded five years. Moreover, nearly 30 per cent of all these total disability cases will be permanent.

Compulsory "Retirement Death." Economically speaking, this type of death has become considerably more important than the premature physical death, although the seriousness of the latter is not to be minimized by any means. But when we consider the compulsory "retirement death" hazard, we must realize that retirement happens twice out of three times starting at age 30. Moreover, while the population has doubled since 1900, the number of persons 65 years old and older has quadrupled. In the overwhelming mass of cases, both husband and wife are survivors at age 65; and in the great majority of instances the wife will be the ultimate survivor, since she has a longevity record a few years longer according to the mortality table, and also has an additional few years on the average because of her younger age than her husband's at the time of marriage.

There also remains the desirability of maintaining the appraised value of human life for life insurance purposes to the retirement death, preferably through long-term endowment insurance, so that the value may then be liquidated for old-age support in the form of a dependable annuity income for both husband and wife. This annuity income should be available to the end of the life of the last survivor of the two in the interest of protecting the children and their families against the heavy burden of parental financial support. Apparently, the joint-and-last-survivor annuity arrangement is desirable in many cases, since father and mother so generally are both alive at age 65 or 70. Moreover, the income under that arrangement should not be decreased when one of the parents happens to die, as is so often recommended in the interest of "marketing" the contract at a lower price because, as I have stated elsewhere: "The two old folks are, judging from longevity statistics, becoming older and older, and the last survivor, usually the widow, will be unable to care for herself alone in any efficient way, thus greatly increasing the expense incurred

[1] Robert A. Brown, Jr., "The Role of Disability Income Insurance in the Business Continuation Plan," *Journal of the American Society of Chartered Life Underwriters,* Vol. VII, No. 1 (Winter, 1953), p. 53.

during the period when both were alive and one could help the other."

The insurance-accumulated savings fund for old-age support, especially under long-term endowment insurance maturing at the retirement age, does much more than merely support the family against the absence of a decent investment estate at the time of premature death. Using my own case as an illustration, my premature death insurance originally protected just one family, namely, my own. Today, that insurance protects five families: my wife and myself in old age, and four additional families, namely, the four separate family units of my four children. "Protection against what?" a lot of people will ask. The answer is protection of the four families against being obliged to assume the heavy burden of parental financial support involved in the first family (the parents), which hazard, as has already been indicated, is increasing rapidly in both the number and the length of cases.

Much should also be said of the irresistible trend toward the use of the annuity concept. Annuities and pensions are the universal talk today for protection against the "retirement death." Total and permanent disability insurance should be regarded as an annuity for the "living death." And, as regards the "casket death," all the settlement options used, except the leaving of life insurance proceeds at interest, are annuity options of one kind or another.

Treatment of Life Values

Life insurance is the medium through which all the fundamental principles of organization, management, and liquidation commonly applied to property values can also be applied to the organization, management, and liquidation of human life values. Although reference has previously been made to some of these principles in a theoretical economic sense, the following headings under this chapter will refer to the principles in a more specific way.

Appraisal (Determining Values for Insurance Purposes). The definition of human life values for family appraisal purposes was discussed in Chapter 1. More specifically, it should be stated that families should use a budget plan to determine the proportion of total family income devoted to support of family dependents after deducting the portion applied to the support of the family head himself. The next question is to determine the capitalized amount for the benefit of the beneficiaries in event of the family head's death.

Next, it is important to plan the type of insurance contract to be used. Should it be term insurance originally, because the insured represents essentially a potential estate situation; or a higher premium contract, like straight life or limited-payment insurance; or a long-term endowment policy maturing at the retirement age of 65 or 70, to protect for old-age support and also to protect the children against the burden of parental financial support? From an underwriter's standpoint, *total family needs* should be considered for all of the family life, rather than only the one or two immediate needs at the time of solicitation. Likewise, the family head's obligation to family dependents should be emphasized. It is sad to see only about 10 per cent of human life values covered with life insurance today in the United States, when property values, in which owners seem to have great pride, are covered to about 80 per cent with fire insurance and to approximately 100 per cent with marine insurance.

Capitalization of Life Values. Capitalization of life values through cash value life insurance (straight life to long-term endowment) is entirely practical. In fact, such life insurance policies constitute a "callable sinking fund bond" issued against exhaustible human life values, just as such bonds have for many years been issued against exhaustible property values.[2] The bond consists of two complementary sides, a "sinking fund" side and a "callable" side. The sinking fund side starts very small at the beginning, say at age 30, and keeps on increasing until it accumulates to the face of the contract (say $50,000) at age 65; whereas the "callable" side (callable in the sense that the Almighty may prematurely call the insured) starts at nearly the face of the contract and keeps on decreasing, in the form of decreasing term insurance, until it reaches zero at the same time that the sinking fund reaches 100 per cent of the face of the contract. The two sides—the sinking fund side and the callable or decreasing term insurance side—move in opposite directions, at exactly the same rate, the sinking fund side moving ever upward and the callable side ever downward. At any time during the policy period the two sides added together equal the face of the contract. The callable side always equals the difference between the sinking fund accumulation and the face of the contract. When the sinking fund reaches the face of the contract, the callable side is reduced to zero, because no more decreasing term insurance is needed to protect the savings period. In other words, the full face of the policy has been realized, and insurance is no longer needed to protect the installment plan of thrift.

Accounting Principles. The "sinking fund" side of the callable sinking fund life bond represents the accounting principles of (1) the "sinking fund" created scientifically to meet definite anticipated future obligations of the insured, like old-age support and the higher education of the children; (2) the "emergency fund" to meet future unknown contingencies, such as unemployment and serious illness; and (3) the "depreciation fund" and "liquidation." The latter fund recognizes the exhaustible nature of the human life value at a fairly average age, like 65 or 70, and methodically accumulates a fund to equal the depreciation of the life value, so that it will be available for liquidation on a life annuity basis.

---

[2] S. S. Huebner, *The Economics of Life Insurance* (3d ed.; New York: Appleton-Century-Crofts, Inc., 1959), ch. vi.

The great majority of personal annuities today are created through the medium of life insurance, i.e., through its creative power of methodical accumulation of surplus through systematic thrift and sound investment. *The mission of life insurance is to create, and the mission of annuities is to liquidate what life insurance has created.* It should be added that the sinking fund side of the life insurance bond represents in an unexcelled manner the principles of accumulation of surplus and sound investment on the installment plan; likewise, the "callable" side can be made to represent the accounting principle of "obsolescence" of the human life value in the event of total and permanent disability.

The Creative Functions of Life Insurance to the Payor of the Premium

At one time, life insurance was generally purchased as a death proposition for the insured. For the responsible family head, there was no profit motivation to be emphasized to the insured. He was pictured as paying the necessary premium, usually more or less grudgingly, because all of the good services of life insurance were regarded as redounding to the so-called "beneficiary." To the insured, life insurance was a sort of philanthropy for family dependents, with no prospects for gain to the insurance premium payor himself.

In more recent years the idea has grown that life insurance is highly creative to the payor of the premium along at least four very important lines. These creative services of life insurance to the premium payor may be described as follows:

1. ***Elimination of Worry and Fear.*** Without the protective service of insurance the human traits of worry and fear are probably the greatest economic curses prevalent in our family and business life. They make many persons unwilling to undertake economic pursuit of real merit because death and personal disability seem to stand in the way of the otherwise profitable use of existing capital. Even as early as the sixteenth century, the British Parliament gave its permission to the practice of marine insurance because of its service in eliminating the devastating force of these two factors. But today the same service is equally desirable in the economic area served by life and health insurance.

Elimination of worry and fear leads directly to the stimulation of greater adventure, personal initiative, and greater productiveness. The latter creative result—greater personal productiveness—is particularly apparent in the field of business credit. Fire insurance is hailed as "the basis of credit." The same honor should also be accorded to life and health insurance. Not only does it protect the insured's existing capital in meritorious economic venture, but it also enables the insured to obtain commercial credit and, without fear or worry, to enlarge greatly the venture beyond the first limit made possible by the insured's existing—nonborrowed—capital.

2. ***Greater Creation of Estates by Premium Payors through Systemized Thrift and Sound Investment.*** The factors of thrift and investment are of greatest significance to all families and business pursuits in our financial life. Unless obtained previously through inheritance from others, or from the earnings derived from owned property personally accumulated, capital must first be accumulated through personal thrift through an installment plan before it can be invested for financial return from interest, dividends, and rent. There must be thrift before there can be investment. While both factors are very important financially, it may be said, comparatively speaking, that thrift is more vital than investment in our financial life. Thrift is the cause—the creator—of that which is invested, while investment is the result of human thrift. At the close of 1962, the investment of legal reserve life insurance companies in the United States totaled $133.3 billion. Nearly all of this huge total, amounting to probably one tenth of the total property valuation in the United States, was saved by the policyholders of these companies. It should also be noted that the annual increase of this huge fund amounted to $6.5 billion for 1962. Thrift becomes semicompulsory when viewed as a self-assumed moral obligation by the family head.

Unfortunately, thrift is retarded very generally by three outstanding causes, namely, (1) laziness and failure to labor and save consistently, (2) lack of a system or plan, and (3) inability to keep that which may have been saved. All of these handicaps become much less important when the family head—the insured—realizes the great services of legal reserve life insurance to himself as the premium payor. He realizes more and more the importance of continuing and increasing his life insurance coverage for protection of his dependents. He also strengthens his determination not to lapse his insurance under any circumstances. He is greatly strengthened in his belief that a family head owes his dependents a high sense of self-assumed financial obligation because of his own life value, which might be lost at any time through death or disability, and which should therefore be adequately insured, just as is his property estate.

Furthermore, the life insurance reserve is protected against unwise speculation and loss from an investment standpoint. The life insurance business's investment portfolio is unsurpassed by any other large investment business's portfolio for solvency and the largest return on a nonspeculative basis. During the appalling depression of the 1930's, the average annual loss to the total life insurance portfolio of the United States legal reserve companies did not amount to one tenth of 1 per cent of the total reserve value of all the policies. For 1930–32, the worst years of the depression, the actual loss amounted annually to only 90 cents per $1,000 of the total reserve values.

3. ***Life Insurance Serving as Property Insurance.*** From an economic standpoint, insurance may be classified under two broad divisions,

namely, *life insurance,* used to insure human life values, and *property insurance,* used to insure property values. Life insurance, however, is unique, in that it also serves as property insurance in many instances. The following main examples may be mentioned, and the payor of life insurance premiums, if he is the owner of property, should know that his life insurance serves him greatly in protecting his property estate as "property insurance":

a) Loss to the property estate through social, legal, and economic demands at the time of the insured's death, such as funeral costs, last-illness expenses, probate and other court costs, and post-mortem taxes (inheritance and estate taxes).

b) Through the death of the owner, loss of business and professional *good will* acquired through years of efficient service and appreciated friendship.

c) Loss of unmarketable assets through death of the owner, such as investment in the cost of education, training experience of the practitioner, and the cost of educating employees and advertising during the formative years of a business or professional enterprise.

4. ***Life Conservation Efforts.*** When the insured understands the financial importance of the great creative functions of life insurance to himself (as premium payor), he will want to undertake a new highly creative service in the area of life insurance, namely, *conservation of life.* Just as properties are constantly inspected in the interest of loss prevention, it is equally important to inspect regularly and frequently the human life against the risk of death or disability.

Such life conservation inspections should appeal as even more important from a loss-prevention standpoint, because of the much greater life values involved for American families than is the case in the property area. In fact, life conservation efforts constitute the most sensible investment the insured can make for himself and his dependents. If discovered in time, nearly all the killing ailments can be cured or at least effectively controlled. Serious ailments should be fought in their incipiency, and time of discovery is the essence of the problem. What greater economic investment can be envisioned than the determination to "keep a healthy person healthy" and thus assure the continuance of the creative functions of life insurance to the premium payor and his family, while living and healthy?

Life Insurance as a Life Will

The need for the use of both life wills and property wills should be apparent. Elsewhere the statement is made that:

The capitalized worth of that portion of personal earnings devoted to family support constitutes the larger part, and often substantially all, of the great majority of personal estates. The life insurance policy is a will—the insured being the testator and the beneficiary the devisee—by the terms of which we may bequeath to our loved ones the money value of the economic forces within us, just as we employ property wills to leave to them our material possessions.[3]

Wives and children, with respect to the human life value of the insured, should be regarded as "heirs" in a life will and not as so-called "beneficiaries." When I die, my wife and children do not benefit from my life insurance to the extent of a penny. They obtain only what they were already enjoying, namely, my life value, expressed as my earning force as I developed it while living with my family. Not even all of that financial value can be realized through life insurance.

Life insurance enables me to bequeath this value to my family heirs, under my life will, just as under my property will I bequeath to them my tangible property assets. My heirs obtain under life insurance only what they already had while I was living. If they are "beneficiaries" under my life insurance, they "benefit" only because of the creative function of life insurance to the insured has enhanced the human life value of the insured by improving his earning power, and he has had the wisdom to capitalize that increased earning power and leaves the insurance as a bequest to his wife and children, i.e., his heirs.

Advantages of the Life Will. As compared with the property will, it is important to note certain advantages of the life will. These advantages may be listed as follows:

1. The life insurance will is simple and unambiguous.
2. It leaves little or no chance for legal disputes.
3. Its terms are carried out without the requirement of probate court action.
4. Prompt payment is made to the beneficiaries.
5. There are no attorneys' fees, executors' fees, court costs, or publicity.
6. There may be inheritance and estate tax advantages.
7. The life insurance estate is a self-administered estate.

In addition to the above advantages, life insurance also serves as a creative supplement to the property will. Nearly always, the maker of a property will finds it difficult to have his dependable assets, which he has for bequest purposes, equal the total bequests he desires to leave to his heirs. After careful thought, for example, he feels he should leave $100,000, although his available assets for his bequest purposes total only $75,000. This shortage of $25,000 can be overcome immediately with new life insurance of $25,000 on the life of the testator. The desired additional assets of $25,000, in other words, are created immediately as soon as the new life insurance premium is paid and thereafter maintained.

The Definite and Detailed Naming of So-Called "Beneficiaries." Usually, in the case of property wills the testator consults his attorney to make sure that all of his heirs covered by the will are fully and properly

[3] Huebner, *op. cit.*, p. 207.

named. He gives the subject much thought, because he knows that the definite and detailed naming of his heirs is all-important. He is anxious to have a proper naming of his primary heirs and other special heirs, and usually is also advised to name a residuary legatee.

If such care is exercised in drafting property wills, then certainly the same common sense should be given to the so-called "beneficiary clause" in life insurance contracts, since it constitutes a life will. The family head, if he assumes his family obligations justly, should name in detail his family dependents—his first heirs, his secondary heirs, and possibly other classes of heirs. The so-called "beneficiary clause" in life insurance is the very heart of the life insurance protection program. It constitutes a life will to heirs with respect to the human life value of the family head, and in the overwhelming number of families the life value greatly exceeds the property value of the estate.

Proper Administration of Insurance Proceeds. Under property wills, provision is often made to conserve the bequest against unnecessary loss through unwise investment, needless spending, and foolish administration. If that is done in the field of property wills, then certainly the same precautionary care should be exercised in life wills by providing for administrative protection by the insurance company against the unnecessary loss of insurance proceeds through foolish spending, unwise investment, or unskilled management in other ways. Insurance companies grant many so-called "settlement options" designed to protect the wife, children, and other dependents. An example would be income to the widow for life and then to the children for specified periods, and the like. Such settlements can meet various changing circumstances occurring after the death of the testator, but under conditions of control by the insurance company agreed upon before the insured's death.

In many instances, arrangements may also be entered into, usually through the medium of trust companies, to protect the insurance proceeds with discretionary trust arrangements. Life insurance settlement options are definite and nondiscretionary, whereas trust companies may offer a discretionary service for the insurance proceeds left in trust with them. This means that the trustee, just as in the case of the property trustee, may exercise this discretionary service with reference to the use of the insurance proceeds in the event of unforeseen difficulties. Under normal circumstances, the life insurance trust may be sufficient to meet current expenditures, but may become woefully insufficient because of such happenings as several serious sicknesses in the family within a short period of time, an extraordinary increase in the cost of living, an extraordinary rise in the cost of higher education, and the like. In such cases the trustee may exercise his discretion as to the wisdom of allowing funds to be used as desired.

SELECTED REFERENCES

HUEBNER, S. S. *The Economics of Health Insurance.* Rev. ed. Bryn Mawr, Pa.: American College of Life Underwriters, 1963.

HUEBNER, S. S. *The Economics of Life Insurance.* 3d ed. New York: Appleton-Century-Crofts, Inc., 1959.

HUEBNER, S. S. *The Professional Concept in Life Underwriting.* Rev. ed. Bryn Mawr, Pa.: American College of Life Underwriters, 1963.

HUEBNER, S. S., and BLACK, KENNETH, JR. *Life Insurance.* 6th ed. New York: Appleton-Century-Crofts, Inc., 1964.

Chapter 3

HUMAN LIFE VALUES—ROLE OF HEALTH INSURANCE

BY EDWIN J. FAULKNER

"The most considerable hazard by far that confronts the individual is that loss resulting from accident and sickness to himself and his family." This evaluation was offered by Dr. C. A. Kulp, one of the most objective and best-informed students of insurance. A growing and now nearly universal appreciation of the omnipresence and severity of the hazard of disability is in large part responsible for the rapid growth of health insurance in the United States since 1933.

The Hazard of Disability

All men seek good health and long life. Except for death itself, mankind probably fears nothing more than disability. Illness and injury are with us always, a hazard from which none is exempt. Despite the tremendous and increasing effort by society to prevent or to cure the ills that afflict the human race, considerable disability seems to be inevitable. In such a situation, means to alleviate the financial consequences of illness and injury are desirable. Voluntary health insurance has come to be the predominant method in America for protecting people against the economic losses that disability entails.

Disability is variable, not absolute. It is affected by a person's age, character, occupation, financial status, location, physique, and temperament. It varies from the complete disability of the wholly paralyzed victim of a cerebral hemorrhage to the minor irritation of the mild hay fever sufferer. The condition that would be wholly debilitating for the infant or the aged person may be only an annoyance to the healthy adult. A hand injury that would prevent a concert violinist from engaging in his occupation would not prevent the banker from going to his countinghouse. The person of vigorous physique carries on in spite of minor affliction, whereas his frail brother takes to his bed with the same illness. The affluent or the person who "enjoys poor health" will be disabled by conditions that would not disable the individual who "can't afford to be sick," or who has a more rugged outlook on life.

Disability can never be a purely personal, individual thing. Modern man lives in an organized society. Its prosperity depends on the productiveness of its members. He who can work and earn not only supports himself and his family, but contributes to the well-being and progress of his community. Ill health can change the individual from a producer to a large-scale consumer. In the absence of provision for meeting the financial consequences of disability, the disabled person as a nonproducing large-scale consumer becomes a burden on all society. Because of its high cost and universality, disability and the means of its alleviation are of great concern to nearly every segment of the population.

Earning Ability as a Capital Asset

The cost of disability is composed of two principal elements. One is the loss of earned income or productiveness by the disabled person; the other is the expense that accrues in the provision of care made necessary by the disability. Both elements of cost are susceptible to reasonably accurate measurement. The concept of earning ability as a capital asset is as basic to health insurance as it is to life insurance. (See Chapter 1.) The human life has a value which can be expressed in terms of dollars. Those dollars are the capitalized value of the individual's ability to earn an income. For most individuals and families the breadwinner's earning ability is the most important—often the only significant—asset of the family. The capital value of the human life can be destroyed by (1) premature natural death—dying too soon—and (2) disability due to sickness or violent injury—the "living death." Through life insurance the individual can guarantee that his dependents will receive the discounted capital value of his life if he should die prematurely. In the same way, health insurance permits the individual to guarantee for himself and his dependents the value of his earning power and indemnification for unusual expenses if he should suffer serious illness or accident.

Health Insurance and Life Insurance

The complementary nature of life and health insurance is increasingly recognized. Originally a "casualty" insurance line, today approximately three quarters of the health insurance business of insurance companies is underwritten by life insurers or their affiliates. Essentially, both life insurance and health insurance are "income protection," the former projecting the earning capacity of the insured person beyond the grave, the latter providing a continuing income and paying medical expenses when the insured person is disabled.

Dr. S. S. Huebner has delineated the kinship of life and health insurance, pointing out that both belong in the category of human life value insurance (as distinct from property value insurance) and both aim to protect against the absence of current earned income, either permanently or temporarily.[1] Elements of health insurance have long been incorporated in the life insurance contract, e.g., the waiver-of-premium benefit to assure the continuance of the life insurance during periods of prolonged disability of the premium payor, and the permanent and total disability benefit to provide an income when the insured person becomes totally and presumptively permanently incapacitated. Health insurance, whether provided in a separate contract or written in conjunction with life insurance, is a protector of the insured person's life insurance as well as a safeguard against dissipation of the property estate when disability destroys earning capacity and heavy medical expenses are incurred.[2]

Extent of Disability and Its Cost

Although the hazard of disability is universal, it varies in its incidence and the burden of its impact. Many surveys have been made to determine the extent of disability. Their results vary according to their methodology, the definition of disability, and the time when the survey is made. Variously, they have showed that something between 1½ per cent and 5½ per cent of the population are disabled at any one time. This means that in the United States, from 2½ million to 8½ million people are injured or ill at all times.[3] On the average, each person suffers one substantial and recognized sickness per year. About one half of these sicknesses are disabling to the extent that the person is unable to engage in his daily routine of work, school, or other activity. Expressed on an annual basis, the days of restricted activity (days when customary daily activities are restricted because of illness or injury) amount to 15.9 days per person.[4] Bed disability days per person per year amount to 5.5. The Research Council for Economic Security has estimated that 3 per cent of the working population is constantly afflicted with illness of four or more weeks' duration.[5] In 1960, there were 6,876 recognized hospitals in the

---

[1] S. S. Huebner, *The Economics of Health Insurance* (rev. ed.; Bryn Mawr, Pa.: American College of Life Underwriters, 1963), pp. 4–8.

[2] Since life and health insurance are the alternate sides of the same coin, constituting the field of human life value insurance, it is appropriate that the program of the American College of Life Underwriters should be concerned with both lines. The Chartered Life Underwriter (C.L.U.) designation can properly be interpreted to mean chartered "human life value" underwriter in recognition of the importance of health insurance to any well-programed insurance estate.

[3] Lewis I. Dublin, *The Facts of Life from Birth to Death* (New York: Macmillan Co., 1951), p. 80.

[4] United States Department of Health, Education and Welfare, "Health Statistics," *U.S. National Health Survey* (Washington, D.C.: U.S. Government Printing Office, 1957), p. 4.

[5] Research Council for Economic Security, *Prolonged Illness—Absenteeism* (Chicago, 1957), p. 12.

United States providing a total of 1,658,000 beds. More than 24 million admissions were made to these hospitals in 1960, and the average daily number of persons in all United States' hospitals was 1,415,000. On the average, each year, one out of every ten people in the United States is a hospital bed patient.[6]

In 1960, aggregate private expenditures for health care amounted to $19.5 billion, of which $16.5 billion represented direct payments to physicians, dentists, nurses, and other practitioners, to hospitals and nursing homes, and for medicines and appliances. In addition, local, state, and federal governments spent an estimated $5.6 billion for health services in 1960.

The average amount spent by the American family for medical care is about 4 per cent of its budget. There is, of course, a wide variation in individual cases according to income level and the incidence of disability. Health care costs have risen precipitously since World War II because of (1) the amazing scientific progress of medicine, which has involved far wider use of expensive facilities and highly specialized personnel; (2) the greater familiarity with health care methods, inspiring greater utilization of them; (3) the more widespread ability of people to secure better health care because health insurance and general prosperity have removed financial impediments to care; and (4) the impact of inflation. From 1957 to 1963 the Bureau of Labor Statistics Consumer Price Index rose from 100.0 to 106.6, but the health care element of the Index rose to 116.8. The increase in medical care costs from the end of World War II to 1957 was even more marked.

The Insurability of Disability Costs

Risk may be eliminated, assumed, or transferred. Elimination of risk is to be preferred to its transference; but with disability, complete elimination of risk is not yet a possibility. Until Ponce de Leon's "Fountain of Youth" is discovered, provision for the effects of disability will be necessary. Most people are unable to assume the risk of disability because of its universality and high cost. Few have the resources out of which to withstand prolonged loss of income or to pay the heavy expenses of health care. So most people transfer the risk of disability through insurance.

The purpose of insurance is to substitute certainty for uncertainty. The individual transfers his highly uncertain risk of loss to an insurer. The insurer, by pooling a multitude of individual risks, is able to achieve the relative certainty of a predictable loss for the entire insured group, though it cannot foretell which members of the group will be afflicted. The hazard of disability conforms practically, though not perfectly, to

[6] Bureau of the Census, United States Department of Commerce, *Statistical Abstract of the United States: 1962* (83d ed.; Washington, D.C.: U.S. Government Printing Office, 1962), pp. 74–87.

the specifications of insurability. The desirable characteristics of an insurable hazard are:

(1) It must be represented by a group of exposure units sufficiently large and homogeneous to permit accurate prediction of average loss by application of the law of large numbers; (2) it must produce a loss definite in time and place . . . ; (3) it must produce a loss that is accidental in the basic sense of the expression; the loss to the insured must be fortuitous, unexpected and unpredictable in time and place . . . ; (4) it must produce a loss that does not visit all or a large section of the insured group at the same time; that is, there should be no incalculable catastrophe hazard. . . .[7]

Disability as an Insurable Risk

The hazard of disability afflicts all mankind. Within a practical framework of risk classification, the hazard is one that permits sufficiently accurate prediction of loss to be susceptible to use of the insurance technique. Health claims are less predictable and precise than death claims, but are still subject to approximate measurement. Though, to a degree, the hazard insured is affected by subjective considerations (in man the psyche cannot be separated from the soma), most illness and injury are unpredictable and not likely to be induced by the insured. The impact of disability varies from time to time and place to place, affected by epidemics and catastrophic accidents. Yet, if sufficiently large numbers of widely separated individuals are insured, the disability insurer is reasonably secure against a total catastrophe.

Thus, while the hazard of disability has proved to be insurable, it has required underwriting ingenuity to conform the coverage to sound and fundamental insurance principles. While, for most, bodily injuries arising from accidents are unforeseen, fortuitous, and unpredictable, self-inflicted injuries are not unknown. The great majority of people seek to avoid illness and, once ill, to terminate disability as promptly as possible. But others, whether for reasons of temperament or because they prefer to enjoy the benefits of insurance rather than to work, may feign disability or malinger. So the underwriter must safeguard the enterprise by selecting for insurance only those who can be assumed on the basis of reputation, past history, and economic prospects to prefer not to enjoy the insurance benefit. It has been well said that any insurance benefit the enjoyment of which is not necessarily inconsistent with the desires of the insured is foredoomed to underwriting failure.

Contractual Safeguards and Deductibles

In conforming the health insurance arrangement to broad insurance principles, the underwriter not only relies on astute selection of the risks

---

[7] C. A. Kulp, *Casualty Insurance* (3d ed.; New York: Ronald Press Co., 1956), p. 10.

to be insured, but establishes contract conditions as a protection against antiselection. Typical is an exclusion clause that denies benefits if disability is incurred because of illness existing at the time the insurance becomes effective. It is no more possible in health insurance to insure the disabled person than it is in fire insurance to insure the burning house. To discourage those who anticipate early disability from securing insurance, the contract sometimes incorporates a probationary or waiting period which eliminates from eligibility for benefits disability commencing within 15 or 30 days of the contract date. Such waiting periods were once uniformly used. Recently, more and more insurers have written their contracts to provide that sickness insurance benefits, like those for accident, shall be effective immediately on the date of the contract to cover sickness commencing thereafter. In eliminating the safeguard of the waiting period, the insurer places its reliance heavily on careful risk selection procedures.

An important consideration in the sound underwriting of health insurance is the use of the deductible provision. This eliminates from the category of payable benefits losses that are routine, recurrent, and trifling. Since nearly all persons incur some health care expense or suffer a few days of disability almost every year, to provide benefits covering such loss requires the insurer to collect the dollars that will inevitably be returned to the insured and, in addition, the relatively substantial sum necessary to the administration of claims for small amounts. Provision for minor health care costs is better made in the family budget than through insurance. By eliminating from coverage the small loss, the insured's premium dollar is conserved to provide protection against the really insurable risk—that of the large, costly, and unpredictable disability. With the substantial and continuing increase in the costs of health care which is directly reflected in the charge that must be made for health insurance, intelligent use of the deductible is not only a sound economy but, for those with limited purchasing power, makes possible ownership of reasonably adequate protection.

Coinsurance or Percentage Participation

Coinsurance or percentage participation is an important device used by insurers to align the interests of insured and insurer. In health insurance the coinsurance clause requires that the insured bear some part of every element of the loss.[8] For instance, if the contract is one to reimburse medical expense, the insured may be required to pay 20 per cent of the expense, with the insurer bearing 80 per cent of it. Since it is unwise to

---

[8] "Coinsurance" as used in property insurance has a distinctly different meaning and purpose. In property insurance the coinsurance clause seeks to encourage coverage of the insurable value by scaling down the indemnity payable for loss if the amount of the insurance is less than a specified percentage of full value.

tempt the insured to malinger by providing him with a loss-of-time benefit the equivalent of his earned income, it is the practice of insurers to apply the percentage participation principle to loss-of-time benefits by refusing to insure them to an amount in excess of 80 per cent of the insured's average earned income after income taxes. By underwriting ingenuity and conformance of contract provisions to fundamental insurance principles, the hazard of disability is insured successfully.

The Usages of Health Insurance

1. ***Income Replacement.*** The primary function of health insurance is income replacement. For most people, inability to work means cessation or drastic reduction of income. Health insurance indemnifies the insured against this loss. Personal and family expenses continue during disability, and without the means out of which to defray them, the individual and family become a burden on society. Health insurance to replace income is regarded as primary because it keeps the family intact, puts bread on the table, and maintains a roof over the family's head. Insurers have made great progress in improving the disability income benefit. Formerly issued in modest amounts for relatively short durations, benefits are now widely available for total disability in amounts approaching after-tax earned income. In addition, formerly onerous requirements of house confinement as a condition to sickness benefit payment have been eliminated for the most part. Also, the duration of benefits has been extended to five years, 10 years, age 65, or for life, and the contracts have been made available on a guaranteed renewable or noncancellable basis to age 65.

2. ***Reimbursement of Medical Expense.*** The rapid growth of health insurance to meet the costs of health care has tended to obscure the basic income-replacement function of health insurance. The costs of care in a serious illness or injury are spectacular; and for this reason, probably, many people are impelled to buy medical expense coverage before insuring their income against cessation because of disability. The interest of doctors and hospitals in the spread of health insurance to defray the costs of their services is an obvious and motivating factor in the great expansion of this kind of coverage. Not only are the financial problems of the insured and his family diminished when health insurance provides the funds out of which to pay the costs of health care, but the financial problems of the doctor and hospital are also abated. Care paid for by insurance proceeds is a principal source of income for most hospitals. A substantial part of physicians' income is derived directly or indirectly from insurance benefits. Medical expense insurance is available on many different plans. Insurance company contracts usually provide cash benefits to reimburse the insured person for incurred medical, hospital, and

miscellaneous health care costs subject to the specific limits stated in the contract. Buyers may select from contracts that schedule the benefits to be paid for each specific kind of expense or the broad unallocated type of coverage exemplified by major medical expense insurance, which reimburses for nearly the entire spectrum of expense without limit as to particular types of expense, subject to an over-all maximum amount and deductible and coinsurance provisions.

3. ***Stimulus to Adequate Health Care.*** While facilities are available to provide treatment for the indigent person, lack of personal means causes many people to defer seeking needed health care. When such funds are available through insurance, the financial obstacle to early and adequate treatment is removed and the way opened to speedier recovery. No small factor in restoring the insured to good health is the relief from financial worry provided by adequate insurance protection. Peace of mind imparted by the existence of a sound insurance program helps relieve the high tension of modern living and the fear of insecurity that in and of themselves cause or intensify illness.

4. ***Maintenance of Credit.*** Disability changes the income producer into a large-scale consumer. Without the income provided by health insurance, the disabled person's credit crumbles. Recognizing that disability is a principal reason for default in the payment of obligations, creditors look with great favor on adequate plans of health insurance. Purchase of expensive consumers' goods items on the installment plan has become a feature of American life. The installment loan almost always has to be paid out of earned income. When disability strikes down the breadwinner without insurance, the payments due on the automobile, the refrigerator, or the television set are not made. To prevent delinquencies of this kind, creditors offer plans of health insurance with benefits payable in the amount of the installment loan obligation when the insured is disabled. While consumer credit health insurance is more widespread than health insurance applied to protect mortgage loan obligations, this use is also becoming popular.

5. ***Safeguard of the Insurance Estate.*** Health insurance insures other insurance. In times of emergency the benefits of the health insurance contract provide the funds out of which life insurance and property insurance may be maintained. The principal sum or accidental death benefit provision of the health insurance contract constitutes a kind of life insurance limited to the sudden death of the insured by accidental bodily injuries.

6. ***Business Insurance.*** Health insurance has many important uses of financial value to business enterprises. Originally thought of as the principal support of the individual and family during the disability of the breadwinner, health insurance now plays significant roles as business

key man insurance and business and professional overhead expense indemnity. When the sole proprietor, the business partner, or the corporation key man is disabled, the enterprise is confronted not only with the loss of his services but with the necessity of continuing his compensation while hiring a replacement. For some businesses, such a financial burden, long continued, can be bankrupting. By arranging adequate health insurance on the key personnel, the enterprise transfers this risk of loss to the insurer. Increasingly, health insurance also is a vital factor in providing the financial means for implementing buy-and-sell agreements that become effective in the event of prolonged disability of one of the parties.

Business and professional overhead expense insurance has been developed to reimburse the entrepreneur or professional man during periods of disability for office overhead expenses such as rent, utilities, and employees' wages, which continue even though he cannot serve his clientele.

Health insurance also serves businesses as an important means of improving and solidifying good employer-employee relations. Freed of worry over the costs of disability, employees tend to be more productive. An adequate health insurance program is an important inducement by which businesses attract and hold the services of skilled and talented people.

7. ***Health Conservation.*** Many lines of insurance find their most important contribution in the prevention of the hazard underwritten. The inspection service of steam boiler and machinery insurers is the most significant benefit they provide. Health insurers are conscious of the importance of doing all that can be done to abate disability. They encourage their insureds and the general public to be safety-conscious and to take timely measures to prevent or cure illness. The nature of the health hazard is such, however, that except by supporting and encouraging medical research and public education in health care matters, insurers, for the most part, can do little to prevent illness and injury. The preventative services of health insurance will expand only as medical science progresses. The insurers' role in prevention is one of supporting the educational work of the public health service, doctors, and hospitals. Without infringing on individual prerogatives, the insurer cannot coerce the insured in health care matters.

Forces Stimulating the Growth of Health Insurance

When men lived a simple pastoral life, reliance for the necessities could be placed on one's own brain and brawn. But as men began to live together in communities, each contributing the product of his special talent or skill, absolute independence was replaced by interdependence. The Industrial Revolution accelerated the urbanization of our population and stimulated increased vocational specialization. At the same time, new and considerable hazards of injury and ill health arose as a result of people living together in crowded environments. With urbanization and industrialization, the self-sufficiency of the individual and the family unit declined. The former simple arrangements that had sufficed to provide care for the disabled person were no longer adequate in a highly complicated modern society. Men's innate craving for security demanded the development of socioeconomic mechanisms as a replacement for the individual independence that had been lost. In some countries, the state stepped in to provide for those who were disabled. In the United States, where the tradition of individual initiative was still strong, entrepeneurs, sensing a need, established and promoted voluntary health insurance.

The need for collective security, such as provided by insurance, became greater as the science of medicine progressed. The profession of medicine discovered how to prevent or to cure many of the infectious diseases that afflicted the young. In the first half of the twentieth century the expectation of life in America almost doubled. More and more people now live into the middle and older ages, when they are especially susceptible to the prolonged degenerative diseases. The scientific progress of medicine has resulted in techniques requiring use of costly equipment and highly trained and expensive personnel. Coincident with these medical advances, there has come into being a greater appreciation of the importance of early and adequate health care. All of these forces have tended to make losses due to disability greater because of the rising cost of treatment. Concurrently, since 1933 in the United States, heavy income taxes and rising living costs have inhibited the ability of most people to accumulate liquid savings out of which to pay for the expenses of disability. The penchant for mortgaging current income through installment payments has conspired to reduce the ability of the majority of people to defray disability expense out of current income.

Since the problem of disability is social as well as individual, it is natural that organized groups in the community have become concerned with the provision of adequate insurance against the effects of disability. Organized labor, operating through its unions, has made the provision of health insurance a bargaining objective. Government, which has always had the responsibility for the care of the indigent, has developed greater interest in health insurance. In some areas, it has moved in to make provision not only for the prevention of disability through public health measures but for the alleviation of its effects through the requirement of workmen's compensation benefits, compulsory cash sickness plans, payment of social security benefits to certain classes of permanently disabled persons, and a variety of other programs. Physicians, hospitals, and insurers, all of whom have a natural interest in disability and its effects, have served as important instruments of general education to develop a wider appreciation of the importance of owning adequate voluntary health insurance.

Advantages of Voluntary Health Insurance

The American system of voluntary health insurance is unique. It not only performs the necessary service of providing funds out of which income may be continued during disability, defraying the heavy expenses of illness, and maintaining the disabled insured's credit, but it accomplishes these purposes without imposing severe restrictions on the individual or society. The keen competition that exists in the health insurance business has been productive of an enormous variety of different contracts and different benefits. In no field of insurance is there a greater variety of insurers in terms of organization or type of benefit. The principal division of the business, between insurers providing cash benefits and plans offering service benefits, has encouraged wholesome competition and stimulated improvement of all plans in the public interest. This has given the prospective insured the opportunity to pick and choose the type and amount of benefit best suited to his personal needs.

While routine and recurrent expense is better budgeted than insured, the hazard of severe and prolonged disability imposes costs that for most people can be met only out of an adequate health insurance program. Budgeting, saving, or self-insuring for the costs of such disability is beyond the competence of the majority of people. Voluntary health insurance preserves for the individual free choice of physician and hospital. Insurance companies, whose function is to finance the costs of health care rather than actually to provide such care, do not interfere with the relationship between the patient and his physician or hospital. By supplying the financial means for securing care, insurance companies help preserve the traditional freedom of choice which is a cornerstone of the private practice of medicine. Compulsory systems of insurance necessarily imply controls by government, not only as to those who receive the benefits but also as to those who provide the health care services. Such controls are resisted vigorously by the medical profession as resulting in an inferior quality of medical care. A major contribution of voluntary health insurance is the support that it provides to the system of private enterprise in the United States.

SELECTED REFERENCES

DUBLIN, LEWIS I. *The Facts of Life from Birth to Death.* New York: Macmillan Co., 1951.

FAULKNER, EDWIN J. *Health Insurance.* New York: McGraw-Hill Book Co., Inc., 1960.

FOLLMANN, J. F., JR. *Medical Care and Health Insurance.* Homewood, Ill.: Richard D. Irwin, Inc., 1963.

"Hospital Statistics," *Journal of the American Hospital Association,* Vol. XXXI, Part 2 (August, 1957).

HUEBNER, S. S. *The Economics of Health Insurance.* Rev. ed. Bryn Mawr, Pa.: American College of Life Underwriters, 1963.

KULP, C. A. *Casualty Insurance.* 3d ed. New York: Ronald Press Co., 1956.

RESEARCH COUNCIL FOR ECONOMIC SECURITY. *Prolonged Illness—Absenteeism.* Chicago, 1957.

UNITED STATES DEPARTMENT OF COMMERCE, BUREAU OF THE CENSUS. *Statistical Abstract of the United States: 1962.* 83d ed. Washington, D.C.: U.S. Government Printing Office, 1962.

UNITED STATES DEPARTMENT OF HEALTH, EDUCATION AND WELFARE. "Health Statistics," *U.S. National Health Survey.* Washington, D.C.: U.S. Government Printing Office, 1957.

PART II

Individual Life Insurance and Annuities

Chapter 4

CONTRACTS—TERM INSURANCE

BY WILLIAM T. BEADLES

The earliest life insurance policy of which any known record exists was dated June 18, 1583, and provided insurance upon the life of William Gybbons for a period of twelve months from the date of underwriting. Many policies written during the 1700's provided protection for a period of only six months.

Nature of the Coverage

The above-mentioned policies were all term insurance, which, as the name indicates, gives protection for only a definite and limited period of time. If death occurs during the term for which the policy is written, the proceeds are payable to the beneficiary. If the insured survives the term, the policy expires. In this event, the insured has received the full value for which he paid his premiums. Throughout the entire term, he has known that his death at any time during that period would result in the insurer paying the policy proceeds to the beneficiary. This is the protection which he purchased.

Kinds of Term Insurance

It is possible to have about as many different forms of term insurance as there are identifiable terms or periods of time following the issuance of the policy. Among the more common forms are one-year term; two-, three-, four- and five-year term; 10-year term; 20-year term; and term to age 60 or 65. Some insurers issue what is called a term expectancy or a life expectancy contract, although there is no uniformity in the use of these names. The expectancy policy continues in force for the period of the insured's expectation of life as determined by the mortality table in use at the time the policy was issued.[1] At all ages, according to the Com-

[1] Technically, the term "expectation of life" is completely without meaning in relation to any one person. It has significance only to large numbers of insureds of a given age. In other words, mortality tables do not show the life expectancy of any particular person.

missioners 1958 Standard Ordinary Mortality Table, the expectation of life is to an age beyond 65.

At the other end of the scale, preliminary or initial term insurance is available for periods as short as a month. This insurance is usually restricted to situations in which it is desired to put insurance in force immediately, with the policy having an effective date, as far as future premiums are concerned, of one or more months in the future.

Term Riders

Term insurance is available also in the form of riders, which are attached to permanent insurance or endowment policies.[2] The protection afforded by the rider continues only for a stipulated period of time. Frequently, the rider is integrated into the basic contract and does not appear separately.

The most widely used is the decreasing term rider. For the period during which the rider is effective, the protection decreases each year (sometimes every month) in accordance with a predetermined schedule. More often than not, decreasing term insurance, when available, is in the form of a rider. Many insurers do not offer a decreasing term policy by that name. Many do sell a mortgage protection policy which may be only decreasing term insurance, although sometimes it is integrated with a small basic permanent policy.

The greatest use of decreasing term insurance is found in connection with the family income policy. Decreasing term insurance is an integral part of this popular contract. Occasionally, a straight decreasing term policy is called, although quite incorrectly, a "family income policy."

Increasing term insurance has come to be used more widely in recent years. The amount of insurance payable in the event of the death of the insured rises steadily each year. This type of coverage seems to be available only as a rider and not as a separate policy.

The principal use for this increasing term rider is in those policies which promise to return the premiums or cash values, in addition to the proceeds, if the insured dies within the term. Such a rider could be added to any policy, although it is usually integrated into the basic policy and does not appear separately. The operation of this return premium rider is quite simple. There is enough term insurance the first year to equal one annual premium. During the second year the term insurance increases to equal two annual premiums. It continues to increase in this manner for whatever period the return premium feature is to be effective.

The latest example of the use of an increasing term rider is in those

[2] Although endowment policies do not represent "permanent" insurance, this phrase will be used hereafter whenever reference is made to any form of insurance other than term.

policies which promise to pay a death benefit equal to the face plus the cash value of the policy if death occurs prior to a certain age.

Level term riders also are available. Probably the most common example is found in the family maintenance policy, which comprises an integrated basic policy plus a level term rider. This rider provides a level amount of insurance protection throughout its term, in addition to the coverage afforded by the basic policy.

Renewable Term Insurance

Term insurance expires automatically if the insured is living at the end of the policy term. In order to overcome this disadvantage to the insured who may need to have his coverage continue for a longer period, most companies provide one or more term policies which are renewable at the option of the insured. No term policy is renewable unless the contract so states. If it is renewable, the insurer must renew at the request of the insured, regardless of his insurability status.

Other things equal, a nonrenewable term policy will carry a smaller premium than will a renewable one, since under the latter the insurer may be forced to continue on the risk for people whose insurability would not be acceptable for a new policy.

When a policy is renewed, it carries the premium of a new policy issued at the attained age. If the insured is still insurable at standard rates, the renewable feature is of no particular value, since he could continue his protection by buying a new policy at the same rate. If, however, he is no longer a standard risk, or if he is uninsurable, then the renewable feature may be of great value if he needs to have the protection continue.

Different companies have different restrictions upon the number of times a policy can be renewed. Among the relatively few companies which issue one-year renewable term, some will renew for nine years, others for nineteen, and still others will renew each year to age 60, 64, or even 69. There is much greater uniformity in practice relative to five-year renewable term policies. Most of the companies will renew this policy to age 60, 64, or 65. With a few exceptions, the protection cannot extend beyond age 65.

Convertible Term Insurance

A second important feature of most term contracts is convertibility. This gives the insured the right to convert his policy to any form of permanent insurance which the company is issuing at the time of conversion. Although most term policies are convertible, it should be noted that any given one is convertible only if the contract so stipulates.

Frequently, there will be certain restrictions upon the conversion privilege. The most common is that which sets a date prior to the expiration of the term, by which time the conversion must be effected. A ten-year term policy thus might be convertible at any time prior to the end of its eighth year. Where such restrictions exist, their purpose is to avoid some of the adverse selection which might otherwise occur by reason of a deterioration in the health of the insured just prior to the expiration of the term policy.

It should be mentioned that decreasing term policies are characterized by somewhat different conversion features. In the first place, they are seldom convertible for the original amount of the decreasing term policy; instead, conversion is in relation to the amount of insurance in force at the time of the conversion. Many insurers will permit the conversion of decreasing term policies to an amount of permanent insurance equal to a percentage, say 75 per cent, of the amount of insurance then in force. Obviously, this means that decreasing term is convertible only on the attained-age basis.

It should be noted that the insurer must convert when requested to do so by the insured within the time limits set by the policy. It makes no difference what the state of health of the insured is; if his term policy is convertible, he may exercise that privilege simply by asking for conversion and by following one of the two procedures outlined below.

Most convertible policies may be converted either currently or retroactively, that is, either as of the attained age of the insured or as of the date of issue of the original term policy or some intermediate date. Conversion as of the attained age is the simpler of the procedures and is the one which is more widely used. Here the insured indicates his desire to convert to, say, a straight life contract. The term policy is canceled; the straight life is issued; and the insured pays premiums henceforth at the current rate for his present age. In other words, although he does not have to make a new application or prove insurability, if he is insurable the result is the same as if he had canceled his term policy and had made a new application for his straight life policy. It is when he is no longer a standard risk, or is uninsurable, that the conversion privilege becomes of greatest value to him.

Retroactive conversion (to the age of original issue) is a little more complicated, since the insured is asking the company to convert to a policy which carries the same premium he would have paid had he taken the permanent policy at the original date of the term contract. Assume a ten-year term policy issued at age 25, the insured now being age 32, and suppose that he wishes to convert retroactively to a straight life policy. The insured will find his premium on the new policy will be the same as if he had taken it out originally at age 25. Although the contract is dated back to the earlier age, the policy form may be either the one which the insurer is currently issuing at the time of the conversion or the form which was being issued at the time of the original application. There is no uniformity of practice in respect to this procedure. The contractual provision in the term policy prevails. It should be added that some companies restrict retroactive conversion to a date not more than three or five years earlier than the current date on which the conversion is being effected. Since the insured in this example has been paying only the term premium for the past seven years, a financial adjustment must be made if he is now going to receive a straight life policy with all of the guaranteed values as of the end of its seventh year. The payment which the insured must make is calculated in various ways. One procedure is to determine the difference between the gross premiums for the term policy, minus dividends received, and the net amount which would have been paid for the policy into which the conversion is being made. To this is added interest compounded at, say, 5 per cent for each year the term policy was in force. Many companies, on the other hand, simply ask for the payment of the difference in the reserves or cash values of the two policies, sometimes with a charge of 5 per cent of the difference.

Fundamentally, the financial adjustment in connection with this retroactive type of conversion is aimed at putting both the insurer and the insured into approximately the same financial situation as if the permanent policy had been acquired originally. The result is that the insured has had the protection thus far for a smaller annual outlay and still is in a position to acquire a permanent policy with the advantage of the lower premium rate as of the date of original issue.[3]

A study of over twenty thousand term policies issued by five life insurance companies showed that over 50 per cent were converted. The same study showed that over 95 per cent of all conversions were effected on the attained-age basis. The results of this study appear in the June, 1964, issue of the *Journal of Risk and Insurance.*

Several companies issue term policies which are nonrenewable but which are automatically convertible. If the insured does not choose to convert earlier, the policy converts to some preselected form of permanent insurance at the expiration of its original term. These policies are typically issued for one, two, three, four, or five years. Their significance seems to lie in the fact that the insured does not have to take any positive

[3] One little-recognized possible advantage of converting retroactively is illustrated as follows. Assume a five-year term policy issued at age 30 for $1,000, and suppose that it is converted at age 33 to a straight life policy, as of the original age of issue. In one company a cash payment of $42.03 is required to make the conversion. The annual premium for the rest of life is $20.59 instead of $22.55, which is the straight life rate at age 33 and the rate which would be paid if the policy were converted as of the attained age. The savings on all future gross premiums is $1.96 a year, which is equal to 4.7 per cent of the "investment" required to effect the conversion retroactively. In addition, all of the nonforfeiture values are three years ahead of what they would have been had the conversion been made at the attained age. If one can make the necessary payment, retroactive conversion may have very real advantages to the insured.

action in order to get his insurance converted. The conversion is automatic.

It should be obvious that from the viewpoint of the insured, the ideal term policy is one which is both renewable and convertible. This is true even though the right to renew or convert makes the policy cost a little more. These rights give the insured the greatest possible flexibility in connection with this insurance and help offset the most serious defect of the term coverage, namely, the fact that the term, and the accompanying protection, will expire if the insured outlives it. The danger in relying upon term insurance is that the need for insurance may not vanish at the expiration of the original term. Therefore, if the policy is both renewable and convertible, the insured is in a position to continue his protection, regardless of his insurability status.

Sales Suggestions for Conversions

The alert life underwriter tries to show his term policyholders the advantages of conversion. One underwriter who sold more than $1.1 million of term insurance in one year (that was less than 50 per cent of his production for that year) also converted, in that year, over $700,000 of term insurance he had sold in previous years.

Perhaps the most powerful way to present the advantages of conversion is to compare the additional annual premium (assuming conversion at the attained age) with the additional values which result from that larger premium. The term policy already involves a certain premium. The converted policy will have a higher premium. Find the difference between the two. The term policy will have no cash value at the end of its term. Therefore, the cash value of the policy into which conversion was made, at the end of that same period, will represent the difference in cash values of the policies. The annual difference in premium is then compared with the difference in cash value at the end of the term. By using the compound interest table which shows the amount of $1.00 per annum in advance, it is possible to find the rate of compound interest which the difference in premiums will earn as a result of the conversion. This calculation can be based upon either the guaranteed cash values or those values plus the estimated dividend accumulations.

One such illustration shows an annual difference in rate of $9.89 between a 15-year term and a straight life, both nonparticipating contracts and both issued at age 30 for $1,000. The guaranteed cash value of the straight life was $209.37 at the end of 15 years. The interest table showed that this difference in premium would have to be compounded at approximately 4½ per cent to equal the guaranteed cash value. Similar calculations for participating policies have shown that the difference in premium earns approximately 5 per cent compound interest. Furthermore, this earning was income tax-free during its period of accumulation!

One well-known writer has said: "A man has holes in his head if he owns term insurance and saves money in any medium other than life insurance." Where else can a man save and invest in a completely nonspeculative manner and have a return of 5 per cent compound interest with no current income tax liability?

If the person who holds term insurance also owns permanent insurance which has been in force for a longer period of time, there is an additional sales approach which can be made. The same financial advantages of converting can be demonstrated. If the client's answer is that he cannot afford the extra premium at the present time, the life underwriter proposes that the annual increase in the cash value of the permanent policy be borrowed and that amount used to convert as much term insurance as it will. Suppose that the cash value increased $50 this year. Suppose also that the difference in rate between the term policy and the one into which it is proposed to convert is $12.50 per $1,000. This means that $4,000 could be converted without increasing the annual outlay for premiums. There is, of course, an interest charge while the loan is in effect.

Other underwriters have been successful with another variation of the plan to convert without increasing the annual premium outlay of the insured. This requires conversion of a part of the term policy on the anniversary of the policy when the first dividend is payable. Of course, this will work only with participating policies. If the total dividend is used to help pay the increased cost arising from conversion, one company shows that approximately 20 to 25 per cent of the entire term policy can be converted into straight life without any increase in the annual premium the insured had paid. By adding the dividend on all of the term insurance to the premium saved on the portion which was converted, the annual outlay is not increased.[4]

Term Policy Features

There are very few differences in the contract provisions of term policies as compared with permanent ones. (See Appendix D for specimen individual life insurance contract.) About the only fundamental differences are in the nonforfeiture values and the dividend options. Term policies of fifteen years or less typically will not have any nonforfeiture values. Longer term policies do have some cash values, although

[4] One rate book shows a "quantity reduced" premium of $83.80 for $10,000 of ten-year term at age 28. The first-year dividend is $29.20. If $2,000 is converted, the term premium which is saved on that amount is $16.76. This makes a total of $45.96 available for the conversion ($29.20 plus $16.76). At age 29, when the conversion takes place, the gross premium for $2,000 of ordinary life is $46.10. Thus the net cost of the $2,000 ordinary life and $8,000 term would be just 14 cents more than the gross premium would have been on the $10,000 term without any conversion. The point is that the conversion is effected by spending only 14 cents more than the annual gross premium for the original term policy.

they usually start later than do those in permanent policies issued at the same age, rise for a few years, and then always decline to zero by the end of the policy term. Normally, there is no dividend option to provide for paid-up additions.

The waiver-of-premium clause, when operative in connection with a term policy, produces a unique and little-known benefit. In event of the total disability of the insured, as defined in the policy, the waiver operates in the usual manner to the end of the policy term. At that time, the term policy is converted into permanent insurance, a straight life policy, with the new, higher premiums continuing to be waived, with dividends being paid if the policy is a participating one, and with the regular nonforfeiture values being available.

Higher Mortality on Term Insurance

A significant fact about term insurance is that experience shows a higher rate of mortality among term insureds than for those who have permanent insurance. Company experience varies greatly, although all show essentially the same conclusion to a greater or less degree.

An actuarial report from one large company stated that "the mortality under term policies of large amount was nearly half again as great as that under life and endowment insurance."

Another study in a large company compared the term mortality experience with the entire experience of the company over the same period. This showed 18 per cent higher mortality by amounts of insurance for those who were insured under five-year term, and 11 per cent higher for the first five years of those insured under ten-year term.

Another company showed 13 per cent higher mortality for five-year convertible but nonrenewable term as compared with standard, medically examined business for the same years of issue and observation.

It has been suggested in recent years that because of better underwriting, particularly in connection with policies for large amounts, the spread between the mortality rates for term and permanent insurance is decreasing. This may be the situation in specific companies; however, there is little reason to believe that any significant change has yet taken place in the aggregate.

The *Transactions of the Society of Actuaries,* 1959 Reports, present findings of intercompany studies of the mortality on policies for large amounts, defined as policies with a face amount of at least $50,000. Based on experience on issues of 1934 through 1957, for 1953 to 1958 anniversaries, the total exposure for these policies was over $43 billion and showed $201 million death claims on 2,959 lives. On the basis of this experience the study concluded that (1) the mortality on term plans was significantly higher than that for the permanent plans, in the aggregate; (2) except for ages 10–19, mortality ratios were below 100 per cent at all ages for permanent policies, and were greater than 100 per cent at all ages for term—representative figures for permanent plans were from a low of 79 per cent to a high of 98 per cent, compared with a low of 109 per cent and a high of 157 per cent for the term plans; (3) as compared with permanent plans, term plans did not show more favorable mortality at any duration; and (4) excess mortality was apparent in term for all classifications by amount of insurance—for permanent plans the mortality ratio for different amount classifications from $50,000 and up to $1 million ranged from 72 per cent to 94 per cent, while term policies in the same amount classifications showed ratios from 119 per cent to 144 per cent.

Many different factors may help to account for the higher mortality under term insurance. It is generally believed that a person who knows that he is in poor health, although still insurable, will be inclined to select a plan of insurance which carries the lowest premium—term.

Renewable term offers a further possibility for adverse mortality experience. Here, too, it is felt that the healthier lives will be inclined to convert to permanent plans, to purchase permanent insurance with another insurer, or to let their policies lapse. Those who have become uninsurable can obtain continuing insurance only by converting or by renewing; and, of course, renewing is the cheaper of these alternatives. This helps to explain why renewed term insurance tends to have higher mortality.

Many companies are more strict in their underwriting requirements for applicants for term plans than for permanent insurance. These companies frequently will decline to issue term and offer instead some permanent form. This situation by itself tends to improve term mortality. When term shows a higher mortality, in spite of this practice, the conclusion must be that very fundamental forces are at work.

Further evidence of the inherently higher mortality under term insurance is furnished by many studies of the extra mortality experienced in connection with policies which go under the extended term nonforfeiture option. Twenty-seven companies showed, over a twelve-year period, a 26 per cent higher mortality among these policies than that experienced on standard permanent insurance over the same years. One large company's studies showed, over an eight-year period, a 41 per cent higher mortality on extended term insurance than its ultimate experience on standard policies issued during the same years.

Premiums

Since term insurance is basically an "if" type, which promises to pay only if the insured dies within the term, its rate will always be less than any "when" insurance, which promises to pay whenever the insured dies. Likewise, it will be less than that for any endowment insurance, which promises to pay if the insured dies within the term or if he is living at the expiration of the term. Since only death benefits are paid, and only for those deaths which occur within the term, there is no building-up of substantial cash values or reserve liabilities. When a term policy expires, there is no reserve; there are no cash values. In regard to annual outlay, term insurance is always the cheapest form of life insurance which may be purchased by any person.[5]

Advantages and Disadvantages to the Insured

The preceding analysis indicates the greatest advantage of term insurance. It involves the smallest possible annual outlay. Any person who finds himself in need of life insurance and without sufficient free funds to purchase the amount needed on a permanent basis will find term insurance particularly attractive. Whatever the sum of money which is available for life insurance, it will always purchase a larger amount of term insurance than of any other kind. The result is that many young families find themselves with a greater amount of protection than would be possible otherwise, simply because of the availability of low-premium term insurance.

However, it is possible to overemphasize the cost aspect of term insurance. Actually, it is low in cost only if the insured dies during the term of the policy protection. If the insured survives, then the term insurance will prove to have been the most expensive form of life insurance which could have been purchased—expensive, that is, in regard to total cost. This makes term insurance both the cheapest and the most expensive form of insurance. Since the low-outlay aspect has been considered, the following analysis will show that term is the most expensive, if the insured survives the term.

Assume a person aged 30 (the exact age makes no difference), who decides that he needs an additional $10,000 of life insurance for just the next 10 years. This appears to be an ideal situation for the use of a 10-year term policy. There are, however, other methods by which he could secure protection for this period. For example, he could buy a straight life policy (any policy other than term will do), pay premiums on it for 10 years, and then surrender it for its tenth-year cash value. If these two methods are to be compared, it will be necessary to cash in the straight life policy, since the term policy would expire automatically at the end of 10 years.

With either policy, the insurer promises to pay $10,000 to the beneficiary should the insured die within the 10-year period. As we have set up the situation, in either case the insured has no further protection after the original period. In other words, the purpose of the insured is to buy 10-

[5] Since every permanent insurance contract can be looked upon as a combination of term insurance plus a savings fund, it is well to note that the cost of the term insurance portion of a permanent contract is nearly always less than what an equal amount of term insurance would cost when purchased separately. This is largely due to the lower mortality which is experienced under permanent policies as compared with that from term policies.

year protection with one or the other of these policies. In nearly every instance the cost of the protection for the 10-year period will be less with the straight life contract, as the following typical illustrations will show.

One company's rate for 10-year term at age 30 is $8.97 per $1,000. This is a gross premium, for $10,000, of $897.00 over the 10 years. Its rate for straight life at the same age is $22.48, or $2,248.00 gross premium for the 10 years. The latter policy has a guaranteed cash value of $1,637.30 at the end of the 10 years. The cost of the straight life, then, is $2,248.00 minus $1,637.30, or $610.70, as compared with $897.00 for the term. This saving of $286.30 ignores the effect of dividends and also interest on the difference in premiums.

If the dividends on the above policies are considered, the difference is more striking. The net cost of the term is brought down to $534.40, while that of the straight life becomes $72.80, a saving over the 10-year period of $461.60.

The purist may want to consider interest on the difference in premiums each year as part of the cost of purchasing the straight life instead of the term policy. On the other hand, failure to consider the interest can be based upon the assumption that there is no reason to believe that the insured would have saved and invested the small difference in premiums each year.

Another feature of term insurance which should be considered carefully by the prospective purchaser is that it is only temporary protection. Even though the policy may be renewable, there is always an ultimate time limit beyond which all protection ceases unless the conversion right is available and exercised. If temporary protection is all that is needed, then term insurance can fill the bill completely and at the lowest annual outlay. The basic problem in this connection is that temporary needs have an almost universal tendency either to continue beyond the originally anticipated term or, if they vanish as planned, to be replaced by some other need. In either of these situations, reliance upon temporary protection may be disastrous.

If the policy is renewable, it may be continued in force at a higher premium at each renewal date. At the younger ages the premium does not increase greatly at each five- or 10-year interval. After the so-called "middle" ages are passed, the rates begin to jump significantly, so much so that it is quite possible that the insured will find his term premium much higher than what he would be paying had he purchased a straight life policy originally.[6]

---

[6] In addition to the higher premium, the net outlay may even be more for the term, as the following example shows. It is assumed that a person aged 20 purchases both a five-year renewable term contract for $10,000 and a straight life policy for the same face amount. Using current rates, dividends, and cash values of one participating insurer, it is assumed that dividends are used to reduce the premiums and that

The final point for the insured to consider is that term insurance usually has no built-in values, such as cash or loan values, as does permanent insurance. This is a result of the nature of term insurance and of its low premium rate. These so-called "built-in" values, which require more in terms of annual outlay, are present in all permanent policies.

"Buy Term and Invest the Difference"

One theory which has received wide publicity over recent years is the advice to the insured to buy term insurance and to invest separately the difference between the premium for the term and the premium for the same amount of permanent insurance. If the insured dies during the term, the beneficiary under the term policy will have not only the insurance proceeds but also whatever amount there is in the separate investment fund. If the total annual payment had been used to buy permanent insurance of the same face amount, then at death the beneficiary will have only the insurance proceeds.

This advice may be good for some people; however, it has certain aspects which need to be considered carefully. It was pointed out earlier that if a person knows that he is going to die within the next five years, then five-year term will be the cheapest form of insurance for him to buy. The same conclusion applies here. If death occurs within the term, there is no question that a greater amount can be provided for one's beneficiary by buying term and "investing the difference" rather than by putting the same total premium into permanent insurance.

It should be pointed out that the "difference" which is thus invested carries few of the advantages which are inherent in the investment portion of the permanent insurance contract. Each premium for permanent insurance can be considered as being divided into two parts. One part pays for term protection for the amount at risk in the contract, and the balance of the premium is put into a "savings fund" which is then invested. Thus the insured who buys permanent insurance finds himself, in each succeeding year, paying for a steadily decreasing amount of term insurance. The investment portion of the permanent contract is featured by safety of principal, guaranteed rate of compound interest, nonfluctuation in value, creditor protection, ready marketability at par, guaranteed loan values with the loan never callable while the policy is in force, and no income tax on the interest as it is compounding. Most important, perhaps,

---

the term contract is renewed at each succeeding five-year interval, through age 60. Then, at age 65, it is seen that the total net payments for the term insurance amount to $5,063.20, as compared with total net payments to age 65 of $3,245.00 for the straight life policy. The straight life policy required $1,818.20 less net payments than did the term! In addition, although the term policy had no cash value at age 65, the straight life policy had a guaranteed cash value of $6,506.30 at age 65. Significant to this comparison is that the term policy expires at age 65, while the other policy may be kept in force by continued payment of premiums or under one of the nonforfeiture options.

is the fact that the investment in the permanent contract can be taken at maturity in the form of a guaranteed life income. No other separate investment has all of these features.

M. Albert Linton used the average rates of ten mutual companies for a straight life contract and for comparison chose the lowest rates available for one-year renewable term insurance. The latest of his studies, based upon 1963 rates, values, and dividends, showed that the separate investment fund would have to earn 4.78 per cent compound interest, net after all expenses and taxes, in order to equal the return on the investment portion of the straight life premium.[7] This 4.78 per cent was for a policy taken out at age 35 and carried to age 65. The corresponding net return required if the policies were taken out at ages 45 and 55 and carried to 65 was 5.17 per cent and 6.37 per cent, respectively.

No comparison of the investment in the permanent life insurance contract with that of a separate fund is complete without reference to the semicompulsory nature of the former. This results in part from the fact that the protection and the investment elements are tied together inseparably in the permanent contract, so that one cannot be discontinued without giving up the other. This provides an additional incentive to continue the program, an incentive which is not present when the protection and savings are completely separate.

The decision to buy term and invest the difference or to put the entire amount into permanent insurance should be made only after full consideration has been given to all of the possibilities. The above analysis shows, however, that it is most unlikely that the separate investment can equal the results obtained from the investment portion of the permanent life insurance contract, particularly when the effect of income taxes on the income from the separate investment fund is taken into consideration.

SELECTED REFERENCES

Huebner, S. S., and Black, Kenneth, Jr. *Life Insurance.* 6th ed. New York: Appleton-Century-Crofts, Inc., 1964.

Linton, M. Albert. *How Life Insurance Can Serve You,* ch. iii. New York: Harper & Bros., 1958.

McGill, Dan M. *Life Insurance,* ch. iii. Homewood, Ill.: Richard D. Irwin, Inc., 1959.

Mehr, Robert I., and Osler, Robert W. *Modern Life Insurance,* ch. iii. 3d ed. New York: Macmillan Co., 1961.

National Underwriter Company. *Who Writes What?* 22d ed. Cincinnati, 1963.

[7] See Chapter 20 on "Life Insurance as an Investment," by M. Albert Linton.

Chapter 5

CONTRACTS—WHOLE LIFE

BY C. ARTHUR WILLIAMS, JR.

Whole life insurance, unlike term insurance, provides permanent protection. The insurer promises to pay the face value of the contract *when* the insured dies, not *if* the insured dies within a stated period. The first whole life insurance contract with a fixed face amount was issued in England in 1762 by the Society for the Equitable Assurance of Lives and Survivorships. At the present time, whole life contracts or modifications of these contracts represent about 45 per cent of the amount of life insurance in force.[1] If credit insurance and group insurance, which are largely term insurance, are excluded from consideration, whole life contracts represent almost 70 per cent of the amount of insurance in force.

Types of Whole Life Contracts

Whole life contracts can be divided into two major types: (1) the straight life contracts and (2) the limited-payment life contracts. The promise of the insurer to pay the face amount upon death is the same for both types of contracts. The major difference between the two categories is the premium payment period.

Under policies in the first class, the premiums are payable for the remainder of the insured's life. The terms "straight life," "ordinary life," and "continuous-premium whole life" are used interchangeably to denote this type of contract. The term "ordinary life" is used most frequently but is apt to create some confusion because "ordinary insurance" is also used to denote that branch of insurance which is neither credit insurance, group insurance, nor industrial insurance.[2] The term "straight life" is used in this chapter.

---

[1] Institute of Life Insurance, *Life Insurance Fact Book* (New York, issued annually).

[2] The Committee on Life Insurance Terminology of the Commission on Insurance Terminology is concerned at the time this chapter is written with the possibility of eliminating the term "ordinary" from life insurance language. Its recommendation is that the term "ordinary" is inappropriate and confusing, and that generally life insurance should be classified as "individual" or "group." See Davis W. Gregg, "Is Life Insurance Really 'Ordinary'?" *Journal of the American Society of Chartered Life Underwriters,* Vol. XVII, No. 3 (Summer, 1963), pp. 197–202.

Under policies in the second class, the premiums are payable for the remainder of the insured's life or until the expiration of a stated period, if earlier. Examples are a 20-payment whole life policy, more commonly known as a 20-pay life contract, a 30-payment life contract, and a paid-up-at-65 contract. An extreme example in this category is the single-payment life contract, under which the insured pays only one premium at the beginning of the policy period.

The differences in the level annual premium outlays for a straight life contract, a paid-up-at-65 contract, and a 20-pay life contract are indicated in Table 5–1, which presents the nonparticipating premium rates charged

TABLE 5–1

NONPARTICIPATING PREMIUM RATES PER $1,000 CHARGED MALES BY A LEADING INSURER FOR SOME REPRESENTATIVE $10,000 CONTRACTS

Age	Five-Year Term	Straight Life	Paid Up at 65	20-Pay Life	Endowment at 65	20-Year Endowment
25.......	$ 5.13	$13.56	$15.78	$22.94	$ 19.63	$43.98
35.......	6.58	18.82	22.97	29.03	28.90	44.89
45.......	10.88	27.79	37.65	37.65	47.86	47.86
55.......	22.05	41.78	80.21	50.27	103.37	55.14

by one leading insurer.[3] For comparison purposes, premium rates are also presented for five-year renewable and convertible term insurance, an endowment-at-65 policy, and a 20-year endowment policy. The table also indicates the effect of the age at issue upon the various premium rates.

Females pay lower rates than the ones presented in Table 5–1 for males. For example, the premium rates for a female aged 35 are $5.78 for five-year term insurance, $16.96 for straight life insurance, $21.24 for paid-up insurance at 65, $26.98 for 20-pay life insurance, $28.12 for an endowment at 65, and $44.48 for a 20-year endowment.

The premium rates also depend upon the face amount of the insurance policy because this insurer, like most others, recognizes in its premium rate structure that many of its expenses do not increase proportionately with the amount of insurance purchased. For example, the premium rates per $1,000 of this insurer, for a male aged 35 for a $5,000 contract would be $19.62 for straight life insurance, $29.83 for 20-pay life insurance, and $45.89 for a 20-year endowment. The corresponding premium rates per $1,000 for a $20,000 contract are $18.42, $28.63, and $44.49. This particular insurer uses a continuous plan under which the premium rate per

[3] Nonparticipating premium rates are presented in order partly to offset the effect of dividends. The participating premiums charged at age 35 by a leading insurer are $22.77 for straight life insurance, $27.37 for paid-up insurance at 65, $34.18 for 20-pay life insurance, $32.51 for an endowment at 65, and $48.70 for a 20-year endowment.

$1,000 decreases with each additional dollar of insurance.[4] Other insurers use a "band" approach. To illustrate, the insurer may charge one premium rate for policies with a face amount of less than $5,000, a lower rate for policies with a face amount of at least $5,000 but less than $10,000, an even lower rate for policies with a face amount of at least $10,000 but less than $25,000, and the lowest rate for policies with a face amount of $25,000 or more. A person considering the purchase of $9,000 of insurance from this insurer would find that for a small additional premium, or even a reduced premium, he can obtain $10,000 of protection because the premium rate for a $10,000 contract is substantially less than the rate for a $9,000 contract, which is subject to the same rate as a $5,000 policy. Instead of grading premiums by size of policy, some insurers have chosen to achieve the same effect by grading dividends on their participating insurance.[5]

The Level Premium Concept

Under a straight life insurance contract the insured pays a level premium rate for the rest of his life. If one-year term policies were issued which were renewable for life, these term policies would provide the same protection in case of death as the straight life contract, but the premium rate would increase each year. Table 5–2 compares the net level premium rate that would be paid for straight life insurance issued at age 35 with the net premium rates that would be payable at selected ages for the yearly renewable term insurance.[6]

It is clear that up to age 60, in this illustration, the total net premiums paid for the term protection would be much less than the total net premiums paid for the straight life contract. After this age, the yearly renewable term rate increases so rapidly that at age 73 the total net premiums paid for the yearly renewable term contract would exceed the total net premiums paid for the straight life protection. The rapid increase in the annual rates at advanced ages explains why it is not feasible to issue term

---

[4] In this instance, this reduction is accomplished by charging as the premium a policy fee of $8.00 plus a fixed-base premium rate for each age times the amount of insurance in thousands. For example, the premium for a $10,000 straight life insurance policy issued to a male aged 35 is $8.00 + ($18.02 × 10) = $188.20. The resultant premium rate per $1,000 is $18.82.

[5] The major difference between the two approaches is that the gradation in the initial premiums is guaranteed, while the gradation of dividends is not. On the other hand, proponents of graded dividends argue that it is easier to adjust inequities which may appear through the dividend structure.

[6] The net premium is based only upon expected mortality experience and interest earnings. The gross premium is the net premium plus an expense loading. The mortality and interest assumptions here are the 1958 CSO Mortality Table, using continuous functions and 2½ per cent interest.

Net premium rates are used in the illustration in order to eliminate the complicating effect of expense loadings and because actual gross premium rates for term insurance at the advanced ages are not available.

policies renewable for life. In practice, the increase would have to be even greater than indicated in Table 5–2 because only those insureds in poor health would be likely to renew their term policies. Consequently, one advantage of the level premium method of payment is that if the need for protection is permanent, and if the insured lives to an advanced age, the net premiums paid for the protection will be less than if yearly renewable term rates had been charged. This is true even after allowance is made for the fact that the extra premium dollars paid in the early years might have been invested elsewhere at a reasonable rate of return.[7]

TABLE 5–2

NET PREMIUM RATES PER $1,000 OF STRAIGHT LIFE INSURANCE ISSUED AT AGE 35 AND YEARLY RENEWABLE TERM INSURANCE AT VARIOUS AGES (1958 CSO Mortality Table, 2½ Per Cent Interest)

Age	Straight Life	Yearly Renewable Term
35	$18.28	$ 2.48
40	18.28	3.49
45	18.28	5.28
50	18.28	8.22
55	18.28	12.84
60	18.28	20.09
65	18.28	31.36
70	18.28	49.18
75	18.28	72.47
80	18.28	108.63
85	18.28	159.17
90	18.28	225.35
95	18.28	346.94

A much more important advantage of the level premium method is that a savings or investment element is created which is not part of a yearly renewable term contract. As already noted, the net level premiums exceed the cost of protection (based on the assumed mortality and interest rates) in the early years of the straight life contract. On the other hand, the expense loading in the gross premium is not large enough to pay the very high first-year expenses. As a result, the gross premium less the first-year expenses may be (and probably will be) less than the cost of the protection. After the first year, however, the expense loading is more than sufficient to pay expenses and provide a margin for contingencies. The gross premium paid the second year will therefore exceed the cost of protection and the necessary provision for expenses and contingencies in that year. If the remainder of the second-year gross premium exceeds the deficiency in the first-year gross premium accumulated at a specified rate of interest for one year, the difference is accumulated by the insurer at

[7] See Chapter 20 on "Life Insurance as an Investment," by M. Albert Linton.

the specified interest rate for one year. This accumulated amount is known as the cash value and is available to the insured upon request.[8] Moreover, if the insured dies, this cash value is part of the face value paid to his beneficiary. If the second-year gross premium, less the cost of protection and necessary provision for expenses and contingencies in that year, is less than the accumulated deficiency in the first year's premium, that deficiency is reduced, and the reduced amount is accumulated for one year at the specified rate of interest. The same procedure is followed during the third, fourth, and following years. Cash values usually become available no later than the end of the second year.

As stated above, when the insured dies, the cash value is part of the face amount paid to his beneficiary. Because the pure protection element in the policy (called the net amount at risk) is thus less than the face amount of the policy, the cost of the pure protection is less than it would be for a yearly renewable term contract of the same face amount as the straight life contract.

Except for insureds less than nine years of age, the mortality rate increases each year, thus tending to increase the cost of the pure protection. However, once there is a cash value, this cash value increases each year, thus reducing the pure protection element and reducing its cost over what it would be if the protection were for the full policy face. Initially, the increases in the mortality rate will probably be the dominant factor, and the cost of the pure protection will increase. The cost of the pure protection and the necessary provision for expenses and contingencies may in fact exceed the gross level premium during some years, but the assumed interest earnings during those years are always sufficient to produce a continuous increase in the cash values. Eventually, the decreasing amount of pure protection becomes the dominant element, and the cost of the pure protection begins to decline. If the assumed mortality rates are those in the 1958 CSO Mortality Table (and this has been the assumption in this illustration), at age 100 the cash value is the face value of the policy, and the cost of the pure protection for deaths during the preceding year is zero. This must be the case because under this table it is assumed that a person aged 99 will die before reaching age 100. Therefore, on the basis of the usual actuarial assumption that death benefits are paid at the end of the year, the face value must be on hand at age 100 for each insured who is aged 99 at the beginning of the year.

Straight life insurance, then, may be considered to be a combination of decreasing term insurance (the pure protection element) and an increasing savings or investment element which equals the face value at age 100.

Other forms of whole life insurance may be viewed in the same way,

[8] Some insurers do not charge the entire first-year expenses against the first gross premium. As a result, cash values may become available at the end of the first year.

except that the savings element will be more important and the cost of pure protection correspondingly less because the higher premiums are level over a period which may be less than the whole of life. Table 5–3 makes it possible to compare the actual cash values under the three whole life contracts for which premium rates were presented in Table 5–1. Note first that the cash values are zero at the end of the first year, for the reason indicated in the preceding discussion. Note secondly that the

TABLE 5–3

CASH VALUES PER $1,000 INSURANCE PROVIDED UNDER THREE NONPARTICIPATING WHOLE LIFE CONTRACTS ISSUED BY A LEADING INSURER TO AN INSURED AGED 35

End of Policy Year	Straight Life	Paid up at 65	20-Pay Life
1	....	....	....
2	$ 3	$ 9	$ 20
3	19	28	45
4	36	48	70
5	53	68	96
10	141	174	236
15	235	290	394
20	335	418	574
25	427	546	632
Age 65	517	690	690
Age 100	1,000	1,000	1,000

cash values under the limited-payment contracts continue to grow after the last premium has been paid because the interest on the cash value exceeds the cost of the pure protection and expenses. Thirdly, after the last premium has been paid on the paid-up-at-65 contract, the cash value is the same as that under the 20-pay life contract, which has a shorter premium payment period. Fourthly, the cash value under all three contracts at age 100 is the face value of the contract.

Flexible Provisions in Whole Life Contracts

Certain provisions in whole life insurance contracts make them highly flexible. (See Appendix D for specimen individual life insurance contract.) These provisions are also found in endowment contracts, but some of the provisions, such as the nonforfeiture options and the conversion privilege, provide more flexibility under whole life contracts.[9]

The nonforfeiture options provide a great deal of flexibility. If the insured should at any time wish to discontinue paying premiums, he may surrender the policy for its cash value or request that the insurance be

[9] For example, extended term insurance under an endowment policy cannot extend beyond the period of the endowment. Also, conversion from an endowment policy to a whole life policy without evidence of insurability is seldom, if ever, allowed.

continued as an equivalent amount of paid-up insurance or extended term insurance. The paid-up insurance option would provide permanent insurance protection of a reduced amount, while the extended term insurance option would continue the face amount of insurance (less outstanding policy loans and plus dividend credits) in force for some limited term.

This flexibility is increased when the insurer permits the insured to receive the cash surrender value according to the terms of one of the settlement options. For example, the insurer may permit the insured to withdraw the cash value in the form of a monthly income for the insured and his wife as long as they both shall live, with a reduced amount continuing for the lifetime of the survivor. An important feature of such options is that the conversion is made at net rates. Most insurers permit the withdrawal of the cash value according to the terms of some settlement option, either explicitly in the policy or as a matter of practice.

Dividend options, where available, provide even further flexibility because the dividends may be used, among other things, to convert the policy to a paid-up policy at an earlier date.

The loan provision also adds to the flexibility of the policy. Because of this provision, the insured may borrow some or all of the cash value at any time.

Finally, whole life policies usually permit the insured, without evidence of insurability, to convert the policy to some other contract with a larger savings element. This right provides the greatest flexibility when the whole life contract is a straight life contract because the range of alternatives is greatest.

Uses of Straight Life Insurance

Because straight life insurance provides permanent protection, combines savings with pure protection, and has so many flexible features, it has many uses. In fact, for most families, this policy is more satisfactory than any other basic form. It should be emphasized, however, that the most satisfactory contract depends upon individual needs and preferences, and that some combination of basic forms, such as those described in Chapter 8, may be the most appropriate contract.

Straight life insurance provides permanent insurance protection at the lowest annual cost. Consequently, it is a useful way for insureds to provide the necessary lifetime protection against such needs as probate costs and estate taxes. For the same reason, straight life insurance may be a convenient way for an insured to leave a legacy to some person or organization, regardless of the date of death.

Straight life insurance is also useful if the insured wishes to accumulate a savings fund for retirement or any other purpose without sacrificing too much protection against premature death losses. Straight life insurance provides less protection than term insurance, which has practically no savings element. On the other hand, straight life insurance provides more protection than limited-payment policies and endowment policies, which place more emphasis on the savings element than the straight life insurance contract does. This characteristic of straight life insurance makes it attractive to persons in lower income groups who cannot afford to pay sizable premiums for the protection they need or desire, but who wish to accumulate some savings as part of their insurance protection. This characteristic may also attract persons in higher income groups who desire to accumulate some savings in conjunction with their protection program, but who have alternative uses for some of their savings and who therefore wish to purchase low-cost permanent insurance.

The following illustration compares the straight life insurance contract with term insurance and higher annual premium policies in more concrete terms. A person aged 35 may purchase from the insurer whose rates were presented in Table 5–1 about $16,200 of straight life insurance for an annual premium of $300. This is less protection than he could obtain under a five-year renewable term policy, where the same premium would provide about $50,000 of protection. However, by purchasing the straight life contract, the protection is permanent if the insured so desires and the premium will not increase. A cash value also is available for emergencies, and, at age 65, for example, the insured may elect to withdraw the cash value of about $8,400 (assuming the nonforfeiture values in Table 5–3 apply) or to receive this cash value in the form of a monthly income of about $48.00 as long as he and his wife shall live, with $32.00 being paid to the survivor for life.[10] On the other hand, at 65, his protection needs may continue, but at a reduced amount. In such a case, he may, without further premium payments, have the insurance continued as about $12,200 of paid-up protection (assuming that at age 65 the paid-up insurance amount is $750 per $1,000 of insurance). In the event that his needs may have decreased in time rather than in amount, he may elect to have the face amount of protection continued as extended term insurance for some specified period, in this case fourteen years and nineteen days.[11]

A paid-up-at-65 policy purchased with the $300 annual premium would provide only about $12,000 of protection, but more savings. For example, at age 65 the cash value would be about $9,000.[12] However, the

[10] This assumes that the wife is the same age as the husband and that the monthly income per $1,000 of cash value is $5.67, with $3.78 being paid to the survivor. Other settlement options, of course, may also be available.

[11] This option may be especially attractive to persons in poor health because the face amount of the policy, minus any loans and plus dividend credits, will be continued in force without further payment of premiums.

[12] Straight life insurance may provide more savings at age 65 than relatively short-term limited-payment insurance purchased with the same annual premium because of the longer premium payment period. For example, a $300 annual premium would

insured usually has the right to increase the savings element by converting the straight life contract to a higher premium one. In short, a straight life policy enables the insured to compromise between varying objectives and to adapt his insurance program to new needs and desires.

This adaptability may also prove useful when a need that appeared to be limited in time extends, in fact, beyond that time. An insured with straight life insurance need not be concerned about underestimating the time period during which he will need the protection because the protection period extends until death. If the insured lives to the end of the period for which protection is needed and then surrenders the policy, he may even find that the cost of the protection was less with straight life insurance than it would have been with term insurance.

The principal limitation of straight life insurance arises out of one of its strong points. Because the straight life contract enables the insured to compromise between varying objectives, it is not as satisfactory as some other policy when the insured definitely wants to give primary emphasis to any one of these objectives. For example, term insurance may be more appropriate when the insured definitely wants to maximize the amount of insurance available for a given premium. Endowment insurance may be more satisfactory if the insured wishes to emphasize the savings element by providing a smaller amount of protection for a given premium. Needs change, however, and the straight life contract may still be the best in the long run, since it offers the maximum amount of protection, with some savings, on a permanent basis.

Straight life insurance is sometimes criticized on the ground that premiums *must* be paid for life. This, of course, is not true, as has already been demonstrated. A related criticism is that while a person who wishes to discontinue premium payments after he retires at, say, age 65 may do so, the price is a reduction in the amount of his protection. In many instances, this situation poses a most difficult decision for the insured. One way to avoid this problem would be to convert his straight life insurance to a paid-up-at-65 contract prior to his retirement.

Uses of Limited-Payment Life Insurance

Limited-payment life insurance contracts emphasize savings more than straight life contracts. They also make it possible for the insured to stop paying premiums at the expiration of a certain period without any reduction in the amount of the protection for life. Therefore, these contracts are useful in situations where either of these two features is important. Some examples follow.

The paid-up-at-65 contract is attractive when the insured wants

purchase only $10,300 of 20-pay life insurance from this insurer, with a cash value at 65 of less than $7,200.

permanent protection but does not want the premiums to continue beyond the end of his normal earning period. This contract also provides a larger savings element than straight life insurance, as already demonstrated; and at the younger ages the additional premium is slight, as shown in Table 5–1.

Policies with shorter payment periods may prove useful when a person's earning career or the most important part of his earning career covers a relatively short time. If the insured can purchase an adequate amount of protection under a policy with premium payments limited to this short period, he has the advantage of knowing that his insurance program will be completed at the end of that time and that a sizable savings component is accumulating. Furthermore, under current laws the interest credited by the insurance company each year on the savings component is not taxable in the year in which it is credited. However, if the insured cannot purchase an adequate amount of limited-payment insurance to meet his protection needs, he may be better off with a straight life contract because he can buy more insurance and later take advantage of the nonforfeiture insurance options.

Limited-payment contracts are often used as gifts because the premium payments can be completed within a stated period. The gift may be made for estate planning purposes. For example, a ten-pay life contract may be purchased with the income from a short-term reversionary trust. There are tax advantages to such an arrangement if the grantor is in a high tax bracket and the policy is not on his life because the trust income will be taxed at the lower rates applicable to the trust.

Because, as noted above, interest credited on the savings component of an insurance policy is not taxable in the year in which it is credited, limited-payment contracts may also be used to great advantage by persons in the upper income tax brackets to accumulate savings and to provide protection in case of death.

Single-premium contracts are especially useful when the insured is in a very high income tax bracket and therefore gains considerably from the tax-free accumulations. These contracts are also attractive as gifts and as a way of investing some unexpected income.

The principal limitation of limited-payment contracts is that they are suitable only when the insured's primary need is clearly savings. Many insureds who buy limited-payment contracts underestimate their protection needs. In addition, many of these insureds place too much emphasis on the fact that premiums cease at the end of a certain period. They may be better able to continue paying premiums at the end of that period than at the beginning. However, an insured with a limited-payment contract generally cannot lengthen his premium payment period except by proving insurability and buying a new contract.

Modified Life and Graded-Premium Contracts

Insurers often issue a whole life contract called a modified life contract, for which the premiums are not level over the premium payment period. Instead, the premium is lower than the level premium during the early years of the premium payment period and, in order to be actuarially equivalent, greater thereafter. The lower premium during the early years, however, is always greater than the term insurance premium would be for those years. For example, one insurer issues a participating "modified five" contract for which the premium for a $10,000 contract issued to a male aged 35 is $140.10 for the first five years and approximately double this amount, or $270.20, thereafter. A comparison of the cash values under this contract with the cash values under a straight life policy issued by the same insurer would reveal that the cash values under the modified contract are much less during the first five years, but the difference gradually decreases and disappears at age 100.

A graded-premium contract is a slightly different contract with non-level premiums. The premium increases each year during the early years of the contract (usually five years) and remains the same after that time. The initial premium is less than the equivalent level premium at the age of issue, while the final premium is more. The other premiums are usually less than the equivalent level premium. For example, one insurer which charges $220.80 for a participating $10,000 straight life insurance policy issues a participating graded-premium life policy for which it charges $120.50 the first year, $144.60 the second year, $168.70 the third year, $192.80 the fourth year, $216.90 the fifth year, and $231.00 the sixth and following years. As in the case of modified life contracts, the cash values are less than those of a level premium contract except at age 100.

Modified life and graded-premium life contracts are useful compromises between straight life insurance and convertible term insurance. The premium is less than that for straight life insurance in the early years. On the other hand, the insured is accumulating some cash values, he need not decide to convert term insurance or act upon this decision, and the premium increase is not so great as it would be with convertible term insurance. However, the premium does increase either annually for a period or at the end of some period, and the insured should be made clearly aware of this fact. Presumably, his income will increase over the years and the increasing premium will not be a financial burden, but this may not be the case.[13]

---

[13] Some insurers have used participating modified life and graded-premium contracts partly as a competitive tool to offset the appeal of lower nonparticipating initial premiums. Because dividends usually increase as the policy gets older, they may offset part of the premium increase.

Preferred Risk Contracts, "Specials," and the Gradation Principle

Many insurers, especially since World War II, have issued one or more of their whole life contracts (usually the straight life contract or a paid-up-at-85 contract) as a "preferred risk" or "special" policy at reduced rates. For example, the insurer whose premium rates were presented in Table 5–1 charges a premium rate of $23.15 per $1,000 for a $10,000 "executive special" contract issued to a male aged 35. This contract combines $10,000 of twenty-year term insurance with $10,000 of straight life insurance.

"Preferred risk" was the more popular term for these policies as long as they were issued only to persons meeting superior underwriting standards and as long as this was the major justification for the reduced premium. Today the term "special" is more frequently used because the insured is not always required to meet superior underwriting standards. Moreover, other factors, to be noted below, are usually more responsible for the reduced premium than expected mortality savings.

Specials are usually issued with high minimum amounts. For example, the special straight life contract noted earlier is available only in amounts of $10,000 or more. When preferred risk policies and specials were introduced, gradation of premiums or dividends by size did not exist because state antidiscrimination statutes cast doubt on the legality of this practice. These statutes prohibited discrimination between individuals of the same class and equal expectation of life, and it was not clear whether policies of the same size constituted a separate class as required by these laws. Preferred risk policies and specials provided insurers with a legal method for reducing the expense loading in the premium rate applicable to larger policies. Preferred risk policies were legal because standard lives and preferred lives had different life expectancies. Specials were legal because the type of policy sold as a special was not available on any other basis. In May, 1956, however, the National Association of Insurance Commissioners approved the gradation principle; and since then, state insurance departments have held that policies of the same size may constitute a separate class. Gradation of premiums or dividends is now a very common practice, and specials have become less important.

In addition to the minimum-amount requirement and (possibly) selective underwriting, the reduction in premiums for some specials may also be justified by one or more of the following factors: (1) a reduction in the agent's commission rate; (2) a requirement that premiums be paid annually; (3) reduced cash values; (4) a reduction in the number of settlement options or in the amounts available under a settlement option; (5) dividends payable only if the insured survives a specified period and terminates his policy at the expiration of that time; (6) a reduction in policy services, such as the right to receive the cash value according to the terms of one of the settlement options; and (7) anticipated lower lapse rates because of the economic and personal characteristics of insureds buying specials.

SELECTED REFERENCES

HUEBNER, S. S., and BLACK, KENNETH, JR. *Life Insurance.* 6th ed. New York: Appleton-Century-Crofts, Inc., 1964.

MACLEAN, JOSEPH B. *Life Insurance,* ch. ii. 9th ed. New York: McGraw-Hill Book Co., Inc., 1962.

MCGILL, DAN M. *Life Insurance,* ch. iv. Homewood, Ill.: Richard D. Irwin, Inc., 1959.

MEHR, ROBERT I., and OSLER, ROBERT W. *Modern Life Insurance,* ch. iv. 3d ed. New York: Macmillan Co., 1961.

Chapter 6

CONTRACTS—ENDOWMENT

BY KENNETH BLACK, JR.

Endowment insurance provides for payment of the face amount of the policy upon the death of the insured within a specified period, and also for the payment of the face amount at the end of the period *if the insured survives.* For example, a 10-year endowment policy for $25,000 face amount would pay the face amount to named beneficiaries at any time the insured might die during the 10-year period and would pay the face amount, usually to the insured, at the end of the 10-year period should he survive. Like whole life forms, an endowment policy is a combination of savings and protection, but with greater emphasis on the savings feature.

NATURE OF ENDOWMENT INSURANCE

Endowment Concepts

There are two concepts of endowment insurance, i.e., the mathematical concept and the economic concept.

Mathematical Concept. The insurance company makes two basic promises under endowment insurance that are exactly opposite in nature. First, it promises to pay the face amount in the event the insured dies during the endowment period. Second, it promises to pay the face amount in the event the insured survives to the end of the endowment period. The first promise is identical with that made under a level term policy for an equivalent amount and period. The second represents a different concept, that of the "pure endowment."

Just as a company may actuarially estimate how many out of a certain group will die by a given age, it can also estimate the number who will live to attain a certain age. A *pure endowment* is defined as a contract which promises to pay the face amount only if the insured is living at the end of the period specified, nothing being paid in case of prior death. A pure endowment contract is rarely sold separately, since few individuals are willing to risk the loss of all premiums paid in the event of death before the end of the endowment period. To provide a death benefit during the endowment period, only term insurance for this period need be added. Thus, endowment insurance, structurally, may be said to be a combination of two elements: (1) level term insurance, and (2) a pure endowment.

Economic Concept. The above analysis is correct and convenient for purposes of mathematical computation, but another and perhaps more logical and meaningful analysis of endowment insurance has been developed. The economic concept of endowment insurance divides an endowment insurance policy into two parts, namely, *decreasing term insurance* and *increasing investment.* The investment part of the contract is not considered—and in fact is not—a pure endowment, all of which is lost in case of death before the end of the term. Rather, it is a savings type of accumulation which is available at any time, after the first year or two, to the insured through surrender of the policy or exercise of the loan privilege. This investment feature is supplemented by term insurance, which is not, however, level term insurance for the face of the policy throughout the term of the contract. Instead, it is insurance for a constantly decreasing amount, which, when added to the investment accumulation at the date of death, will make the amount payable under the policy equal to its face. The insurance portion of the contract, therefore, is for a decreasing amount, being greatest in the early years of the contract and gradually decreasing throughout the term.

Thus, if at a particular time a $1,000 endowment policy has an investment accumulation of $150, the insured will be protected against death by $850 of decreasing term insurance; but when the investment accumulation reaches $900, there will remain decreasing term insurance for only the difference between the $1,000 face and $900, or $100. Finally, when the investment portion of the contract reaches 100 per cent of the face of the policy at the time of its maturity, the decreasing term insurance will have declined to zero.

Table 6–1 shows the reserve values (investment element) and corresponding net amounts at risk (insurance element) under a thirty-year endowment policy issued at male age 35. A study of Table 6–1 shows that at any particular time the accumulated savings fund when added to the amount of decreasing term insurance will always equal the face of the contract. Upon death, the company pays to the beneficiary the face amount of the policy, which is made up of (1) the investment accumulation, and (2) decreasing term insurance equal to the difference between the investment accumulation and the face of the contract. The purpose of the decreasing term insurance is always to equal that portion of the policy which the policyholder intended to save if he had lived, but which he failed to accumulate because of premature death.

The economic analysis of endowment insurance is equally applicable to all forms of permanent life insurance. Whole life contracts are also endowment insurance arrangements, although they are not customarily viewed in that manner. They are investment policies to a stated extent. It is all a matter of the degree to which the installment investment plan is emphasized. As the reserve value element—the investment element—of the contract increases, the death protection—the decreasing term insurance element—correspondingly decreases. In the case of a whole life policy, the decreasing term insurance is reduced to zero at age 100,[1] when the investment side reaches 100 per cent of the face of the contract.

TABLE 6–1

$1,000 Thirty-Year Endowment Insurance, Male Aged 35
(1958 CSO Table, 2½ Per Cent Interest)

End of Policy Year	Reserve Value	Net Amount at Risk	End of Policy Year	Reserve Value	Net Amount at Risk
1	.....	$1,000.00	16	$ 432.29	$567.71
2	$ 25.04	974.96	17	465.85	534.15
3	50.63	949.37	18	500.13	499.87
4	76.73	923.27	19	535.19	464.81
5	103.35	896.65	20	571.08	428.92
6	130.49	869.51	21	607.88	392.12
7	158.13	841.87	22	645.66	354.34
8	186.31	813.69	23	684.51	315.49
9	215.03	784.97	24	724.56	275.44
10	244.30	755.70	25	765.94	234.06
11	274.15	725.85	26	808.82	191.18
12	304.56	695.44	27	853.40	146.60
13	335.57	664.43	28	899.91	100.09
14	367.18	632.82	29	948.67	51.33
15	399.41	600.59	30	1,000.00	.....

Note: Reserve values based on the Commissioners Reserve Valuation Method—Curtate Functions.

It might be worthwhile to note the rationale for the economic concept of life insurance contracts, and the reason why permanent life contracts have not always emphasized the increasing investment–decreasing term insurance concept. In the early days of the business, there were no nonforfeiture values under life insurance contracts. If an individual was forced to cease premium payments under his contract, no return of any sort was available to him as a contractual right. The contract promised to pay in the event of the occurrence of death or survival to a certain age, but if the contract was dropped prior to the occurrence of these contingencies, all premiums were considered fully earned, and the reserve or savings element was forfeited.[2] Actuaries, in calculating reserve values,

[1] The exact "whole life" period would depend on the mortality table upon which the contract was based. In the case of the 1958 CSO Mortality Table, the terminal age is 100.

[2] Some companies did allow a cash value, but even here the policy usually contained no provision for them, so that the policyholder had no *right* to any surrender value. The values, when allowed, were small and generally were granted only if application was made within a short period after lapse. Until 1861, there was no *legal requirement* as to the allowance of a surrender value in any form, and no *legal requirement* for a *cash* surrender privilege until 1906.

also base their calculations on the mathematical concept of endowment insurance. They find it more feasible to work with pure endowment and mortality factors on a $1,000 basis rather than on the constantly changing amounts which the economic analysis involves. It was reasonable, then, to consider the mathematical interpretation as the proper explanation.

With the increasing emphasis on the living values in life insurance, and because it is easier for the layman to understand, the economic analysis of all permanent forms of life insurance has become increasingly accepted as the more meaningful explanation. Both the mathematical and the economic concepts are sound, as one is the actuarial equivalent of the other. They are simply two different ways of looking at, and of analyzing, the same thing.

Endowment Insurance Policies

Types. An examination of the contracts issued by different companies shows many variations in the use of the endowment insurance principle. Such policies may be made payable in 10, 15, 20, 25, 30, or more years, or the length of the term may be so arranged as to cause the policy to mature at certain ages, such as 60, 65, 70, and others. When written for a short term, the purpose of the policy usually is to combine immediate protection with heavy savings. If written for a long term, or to mature at an advanced age, the object is usually to combine death protection with provision for old age. It should be noted that for a person aged 45, a 20-year endowment and an endowment at 65 are exactly equivalent, the endowment period being 20 years in both cases.

Some companies offering "specials" with favorable premium rates also issue an "endowment at 85" in addition to a straight life policy. This enables them to avoid offering two straight life policies at different premium rates, which could be considered discriminatory by the state insurance departments. From a financial standpoint, however, an endowment at 85 is essentially the same as a straight life policy issued at the same age. A few companies offer "double endowments" and "semiendowments," under which the amount payable in the event of *survival* is twice or half that paid in the event of *death.*

The term "endowment" is also sometimes applied to "retirement income" contracts. Under such contracts the amount payable on survival is greater than the face amount, and the amount payable on death is the face amount or the cash value, whichever is greater.

Most companies also issue "juvenile" endowments, which mature at specified ages, usually corresponding with the age when the child is to attend college. A return-of-premium benefit is offered which provides for the return of premiums in the event of the child's death before reaching the endowment age. An extra benefit frequently added to juvenile endowments is a payor rider. Upon the death or disability of the premium payor of the policy, usually the father, the payor rider provides that premium payments shall cease, the policy becoming fully paid for in the event of death, or premiums are waived during the parent's disability.

Premiums Charged for Endowment Policies. Endowment contracts usually are paid for by premiums continuing throughout the policy period; but if desired, they may be paid on a limited-payment plan. For example, a 30-year endowment policy may be paid up in 20 years, or an endowment at age 65 may be paid up in 20 years. Since the company's liability under an endowment insurance policy involves not only the payment of its face upon death during the endowment period but also the payment of the full amount of the policy upon survival of the period, it follows that the annual premium on such policies is necessarily higher than that charged for a straight life policy. An examination of Table 6–2 of non-

TABLE 6–2

ANNUAL PREMIUM RATES FOR $1,000 ENDOWMENT INSURANCE

Age	10-Year Endowment	15-Year Endowment	20-Year Endowment	25-Year Endowment	30-Year Endowment	Whole Life Rate
20	$100.30	$63.57	$45.97	$35.04	$28.03	$13.74
25	100.33	63.63	46.12	35.29	28.41	15.79
30	100.44	63.85	46.47	35.80	29.13	18.37
35	100.73	64.29	47.12	36.72	30.39	21.65
40	101.16	64.91	48.08	38.12	32.27	25.65
45	102.09	66.14	49.85	40.49	35.29	30.98
50	103.72	68.17	52.57	44.00	40.02	37.90
55	105.10	70.11	56.42	50.46		47.01
60	107.42	76.58	65.30			59.18

participating rates shows this difference to be particularly significant when the endowment period is a short one. The significant difference indicated here is due chiefly to the necessity for accumulating more rapidly the investment portion of the endowment policy in order to have it equal the full face value at the end of the policy term.

The cash value of a $10,000 straight life policy issued at age 35 is $3,320 after the policy has been in force 20 years; for a whole life policy on the 20-payment plan, the twentieth-year cash value would be $6,250. A $10,000 20-year endowment policy issued at age 35, however, must, according to its definition, have a value of $10,000 at the end of the 20-year period. The difference between this value and the values noted for the other two policies must be obtained by the company through a higher premium.

In the case of participating policies, the gross premiums will be somewhat higher, subject to reduction through dividend distributions.

FUNCTION OF ENDOWMENT INSURANCE

In General

Broadly, the endowment insurance contract serves as an effective way to accumulate a specific sum of money over a period of time, with the savings program protected by insurance against the contingency of premature death. Such a contract, functionally, serves three purposes: (1) as an incentive to save, (2) as an investment, and (3) as a hedge against the savings period being cut short by death.

Incentive to Save. Endowment insurance is advanced as a method of systematic savings in that it provides for the laying-away of a moderate sum each year with a view to having the accumulations available at the end of a fixed period. Many people, for one reason or another, find it difficult to sustain a savings program even though they earn good incomes. For such persons an endowment policy generally turns out to be a means of forcing thrift, since the semicompulsory nature of the premium compels them to do that which, if left entirely to their own option, would remain undone. By requiring the payment of specific sums at regular intervals during a period of years, endowment insurance enables one to save a worthwhile sum, whereas haphazard methods of saving seldom achieve this result. It should also be emphasized that in many instances the difference between the premium for an endowment insurance policy and for a life insurance contract requiring a smaller payment is saved only because of the voluntarily assumed sacrifice of paying the higher rate. Endowment insurance, therefore, represents a means of using the by-product of one's earnings—the small sums otherwise wasted in needless expenditures—for the accumulation of a competence.

As an Investment. Endowment insurance also furnishes the advantage of a safe plan of investment. The accumulating sums are kept fully invested, and the sums are credited annually with a guaranteed interest rate.[3]

Since the endowment contract, particularly one of short term, is basically an investment contract, the question of yield is of some interest to the policyholder. Several methods have been advanced for computing the yield on an endowment insurance contract. A mistaken approach regards the *entire* premium as the contribution to the savings account and ignores the fact that part of the premium goes for insurance protection, part for expenses, and part for savings. This naturally produces an unrealistically low yield on the insured's "investment."

[3] In a nonparticipating contract the rate of interest guaranteed by the contract is credited, and the company's investment experience has no direct bearing on the position of the individual policyholder. In a participating contract the guaranteed rate is credited annually to the contract, but additional earnings may be credited through the dividend medium.

Another method treats the investment element of the premium as the difference between the full premium for the endowment insurance policy in question and the premium for a level term policy with the same face and term as the endowment. This method results in a higher yield than the true yield, since the insurance protection, the amount at risk, under an endowment contract is *not level* but is *decreasing* in nature.

The only proper method of calculating the yield on an endowment contract is to deduct from each annual premium the cost of one-year term insurance for the net amount at risk and to ascertain the rate necessary to accumulate the remainders to equal the face of the policy at the maturity date. This method, while correct, involves laborious calculations.[4]

Hedging against Saving Period Being Cut Short by Death. The attainment of a specific savings and investment objective requires the time necessary to earn and save. Life insurance affords the only known method of protecting a person against the possibility of not being able to accumulate the desired amount because of premature death. Were it not for the uncertainty of life and the inability of most people to carry out their resolution to adhere to a definite plan of saving, the accumulation of a specific fund could readily be accomplished by the deposit of certain sums at regular intervals. But as has been pointed out, the effort to save a fixed amount is confronted by the danger of death before there has been time to save the desired amount.

Endowment insurance is designed to protect the individual against this danger. Let us assume that it is the purpose of a person aged 25 to accumulate $20,000 during the next 40 years. The accomplishment of this purpose might be attempted by a single program involving two parts. The two-part program includes the saving and investing of a certain amount periodically plus the securing of insurance protection against the possibility of the saving period being cut short by death, through the purchase of a life insurance policy.

It is also clear that the same result can be accomplished by the purchase of a $20,000 40-year endowment policy maturing at age 65. In the event the insured dies before age 65, the face amount of $20,000 is payable immediately. If the insured survives to age 65 and has paid the premiums required under the contract, it will also mature for the face amount of $20,000. Thus the insured's effort at thrift is hedged against premature death, the chief danger attached to any plan of savings which is not hedged with a life insurance policy.

Specific Uses

The endowment insurance contract can be applied to any need for funds which are to be saved over a period of time. For example, funds for

[4] See Chapter 20, "Life Insurance as an Investment," by M. Albert Linton.

education, old age, debt retirement, and other purposes can be accumulated through the purchase of an appropriate endowment insurance contract.

Educational Funds. One of the most popular uses of endowment insurance contracts is to accumulate funds for the higher education of children. The contract may be written on the life of a parent or the child. As mentioned earlier, if the insurance is written on the life of the child,[5] it is advisable to attach a so-called *payor clause,* which provides that premiums are to be waived in the event the premium payor named in the clause should die or become disabled.

The contract is usually written to mature at the age the child is expected to enter college. If the child is three years old and is expected to be ready for college at age 18, for example, a 15-year endowment would appear to be appropriate. Most companies will not write an endowment for less than 10 years; but by increasing the face amount properly, the cash value of a 10-year endowment can be made to approximate the desired amount at shorter durations.[6]

The settlement plan is usually set up to meet the needs of the typical college student. It may be arranged so that the proceeds are to be paid in equal monthly installments over a four-year period, with no payments to be made during the usual vacation period. Other patterns of payment may be arranged, however.

Old Age. Another important use of endowment insurance is to provide funds for retirement purposes. Endowment insurance, if the term is so selected as to make the policy mature at or near anticipated retirement (e.g., 60, 65, or 70), serves as an excellent method of accumulating a fund for support in old age. Many who oppose endowments maturing at earlier ages because of their greater premium per $1,000 are ardent supporters of long-term endowments maturing at an age when a man's earning capacity usually ceases and when he normally expects to retire from actual work.

Relatively few individuals succeed in laying up a decent competence by the time retirement age is reached. Most people are confronted, therefore, with two contingencies: (1) an untimely death may leave their families unprotected; and (2) in case of survival until old age, they may lack the means of proper support. Both of these contingencies may be conveniently provided for by a long-term endowment. If death should

[5] It should be noted that consideration should not be given to insuring the lives of children until the father or other income producer has an adequate life insurance program. Since few men have an adequate program, it is generally desirable to place the insurance on the life of the parent even when the objective is to accumulate funds for educational purposes. If the child dies, the funds will not be needed. If the parent dies, the proceeds may be used for educational purposes or perhaps food and shelter, depending upon the circumstances.

[6] For example, at age 10, a $5,000 10-year endowment has a cash value of $3,865 at the end of eight years. If the amount desired at the end of eight years is $5,000, this can be accomplished by purchasing a 10-year endowment with a face amount equal to $6,463.

occur at any time during the term, the insurance proceeds go to the family. In the event the insured survives to old age, when the need for insurance for family protection in the usual sense has largely or altogether passed, he will himself receive the proceeds of the fund which his prudence and foresight enabled him to accumulate. The proceeds may be used for his own support and comfort, through the settlement options available in his contract, through the use of the trust facilities of a bank, or otherwise.

Other Purposes. Endowment insurance also may be utilized to accumulate a fund for other specific purposes such as a grant to a college, hospital, or church, or to finance a long-awaited trip abroad.

Misuse of Endowment Insurance

The above discussion has indicated the usefulness of endowment insurance, but it can be and has been misused. It is essentially a savings plan with insurance to protect the savings program against premature death. Its primary purpose is *not* to provide protection. Due to the heavy savings element, the premiums are the largest of any life insurance plan but provide the smallest amount of protection for each dollar of premium paid. Consequently, endowments should not be used where there is a great need for protection.

Most men have limited funds available and need a life insurance program with emphasis on the protection element. Therefore, the purchase of endowment insurance, particularly with a short term, may soak up available funds without providing the amount of needed protection. Younger men with no responsibilities frequently purchase endowments and then later, when their responsibilities increase, find they are not able to purchase additional protection since their limited funds are already committed to high-premium endowments. It may be possible to exchange an endowment contract for a lower premium, whole life contract at a later date; but where such a privilege is permitted, by contract right or by company practice, it is necessary to furnish evidence of insurability. This is not always possible.

It is important to note that the endowment insurance policy is subject to the limitations of term insurance as far as protection is concerned. It normally should not be recommended to cover a need which is permanent or could run beyond the term of the endowment.

As in all uses of insurance, it is important to relate the product to the need. Thus, for certain needs, an endowment policy has its limitations in the way it solves the problem. The only basis on which any contract should be criticized is that it fails to provide the optimum combination of investment and protection in the situation for which it has been recommended or is being used.[7] It is important to remember, however, that the

[7] It should be noted that even here it is not the contract, but the use of the contract, which should be criticized.

lower premium forms of permanent insurance have greater flexibility to permit adjustments to meet changing circumstances. Therefore, younger persons, who may have need for large amounts of protection which only life insurance can provide, and who face changing circumstances, should consider using straight life or some other form of low-premium, permanent life insurance. On the other hand, if the objective is specifically the accumulation of a fund for a specific purpose, and if there is a need to have decreasing insurance during the period of accumulation, the endowment insurance contract is the proper vehicle, and perhaps the only proper one.

SELECTED REFERENCES

HUEBNER, S. S., and BLACK, KENNETH, JR. *Life Insurance.* 6th ed. New York: Appleton-Century-Crofts, Inc., 1964.

MACLEAN, JOSEPH B. *Life Insurance.* 9th ed. New York: McGraw-Hill Book Co., Inc., 1962.

MCGILL, DAN M. *Life Insurance.* Homewood, Ill.: Richard D. Irwin, Inc., 1959.

MEHR, ROBERT I., and OSLER, ROBERT W. *Modern Life Insurance.* 3d ed. New York: Macmillan Co., 1961.

Chapter 7

CONTRACTS—ANNUITIES

BY ROBERT I. MEHR

The annuity has been called the "upside-down application of the life insurance principle." While this description is not strictly accurate, it does serve as a springboard for a discussion of annuities. This concept is based on the notion that the purpose of life insurance is the scientific creation of an estate, whereas the purpose of the annuity is the scientific liquidation of an estate. Under a life insurance contract the estate is created at death. Under the annuity contract the estate is fully liquidated by death. Reduced to its ultimate simplicity, the idea can be expressed by comparing the nature of the two types of agreements. In exchange for his premium the purchaser of life insurance expects his insurer to pay his beneficiary a specified sum upon his death. For his premium the purchaser of an annuity expects his insurer to pay him a periodic income as long as he lives. Thus, under a life insurance contract the insurer *starts* paying upon the death of the insured, whereas under an annuity contract the insurer *stops* paying upon the death of the insured.

THE ANNUITY PRINCIPLE

The important aspects of insurance are twofold: the reduction of uncertainty and the sharing of losses. The uncertainty facing the purchaser of an annuity is the length of his life. Although the insurance company does not know how long any given individual will live, it does know how to apply the law of large numbers to the experience of a given group of annuitants so as to approximate the actual result for that group. Therefore, when the savings or investments of a large number of individuals are combined into a group or joint account, each member can be paid an annual or monthly amount actuarially calculated to assure that no one will outlive his capital, yet the capital will be paid out and not hoarded. Thus, uncertainty is reduced, and losses (the costs of "living too long") are shared. The amount of periodic income drawn by each member of the group is determined not only by his contribution but also by his age, sex, and type of annuity contract purchased. The older a person is when his annuity income begins, the greater will be his periodic payments per dollar of contribution. A man will draw more periodically than a woman of the same age per dollar of contribution. And if the annuitant is willing to have his payments terminated at his death, he will receive a higher periodic income than if he insisted on a guaranteed minimum number of payments. Where the rating formula considers the physical condition of the annuitant, more will be paid per period to the unhealthy annuitant than to the healthy one.

The periodic income paid under an annuity contract is composed of three parts: principal, investment income, and a survivorship or insurance benefit. The amount allocated to each part from any given periodic payment can be computed easily. For purposes of illustration, assume an annuity of $1,000 a year issued to a man aged 65, first payment one year from date of issue. Assume further that the cost of the annuity is figured on the basis of 3 per cent interest and the 1949 Annuity Table. The net single premium for this annuity under these assumptions would be $11,013. If the annuity were purchased one year later (age 66), the net single premium would be $10,611. Thus, in the first year, $402 of the original capital would have been liquidated in the case of the annuity purchased at age 65.

The breakdown of the *first* $1,000 periodic payment into principal, interest, and survivorship benefit can be accomplished as follows:

Initial investment at age 65 (net)	$11,013.00
Interest assumed (3 per cent)	+ 330.39
Total amount available	$11,343.39
Annuity payment	− 1,000.00
Amount remaining without survivorship benefit	$10,343.39

Note that the net cost of the annuity at age 66 would be $10,611.00, but that only $10,343.39 is available. How is the deficiency of $267.61 made up? Not all of the 65-year-old annuitants will survive the one-year period to collect their first $1,000.00. Those who die will release their investment to be spread among the survivors. Each survivor's share will amount to $267.61, which is the deficiency in the fund available at the beginning of the second year.

Thus, for this annuity at age 65, the first annuity payment of $1,000.00 breaks down as follows:

Interest income	$ 330.39	($11,013.00 at 3 per cent)
Capital liquidation	402.00	($11,013.00 − $10,611.00)
Survivorship benefit	267.61	($10,611.00 − $10,343.39)
Total	$1,000.00	

Each successive year the survivorship benefit will increase, and the interest income and amount of capital liquidation will decrease. For example, the annuity payment for the second year will consist of:

Interest income	$ 318.33	($10,611.00 at 3 per cent)
Capital liquidation	401.00	($10,611.00 – $10,210.00*)
Survivorship benefit	280.67	($10,210.00* – $9,929.33†)
Total	$1,000.00	

* $10,210.00 is the cost of the annuity at age 67.
† $9,929.33 is the amount remaining from the initial fund plus interest after the $1,000.00 payment is made.

The division of payment for each successive year can be worked out using the method applied above. The formulas for each part are as follows:

Interest income = Net single premium at the beginning of the year times the interest rate assumed
Capital liquidation = Net single premium at the beginning of the year minus net single premium one year later
Survivorship benefit = Net single premium one year later minus (net single premium at beginning of the year plus interest minus annuity payment)

CLASSIFICATION OF ANNUITIES

Up to this point, we have been concerned with the annuity in its simplest form, the single-premium life annuity contract. Under this contract the insurance company promises to pay a given amount each period (monthly, semiannually, and so forth) to the annuitant during his lifetime in exchange for a single premium which immediately becomes the property of the company, no part of which is returnable in the event of the annuitant's death.

The single-premium life annuity contract, however, does not meet the economic or psychological needs of most annuity purchasers. Some buyers want to pay for their retirement annuities through a series of level annual premiums during their preretirement years. Some do not like the idea of having no further part of their premiums returnable to their estates in the event of early death following retirement. A few purchasers would like to have the annuity payments contingent upon the lives of more than one person. Also, some would like to have the payments expressed in units other than dollars. Because of the variety of interests among annuity customers, a number of variations in annuity forms has developed.

Anyone looking at the wide array of different types of annuities available in the market could become completely baffled without a systematic method of classifying them. Annuities may be classified on at least five different bases: method of paying premiums, disposition of proceeds, date benefits begin, number of lives covered, and units in which pay-out benefits are expressed. These classifications, however, are not mutually exclusive, since every annuity will fall into all five classes. Figure 7–1 is a useful device for viewing the annuity types as a unit.

Method of Paying Premiums

Annuities may be purchased with either a single premium or through a series of installment premiums.

Single-Premium Annuities. An annuity purchased by one lump sum is known as a single-premium annuity. Frequently, life insurance cash values or death proceeds are distributed as an annuity. Here the lump-sum proceeds are used, in effect, to purchase a single-premium annuity at

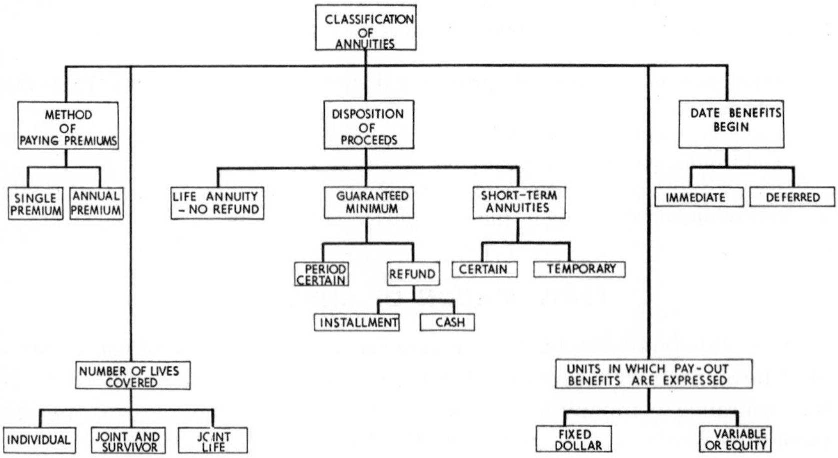

FIG. 7–1. Classification of annuities.

net rates. Aside from its use as a method of liquidating life insurance proceeds, the single-premium annuity is frequently used in pension and profit sharing plans to fund the retirement benefit at the time an employee retires. Otherwise, there are not too many people whose circumstances are such as to make them candidates for single-premium annuities.

Annual-Premium Annuities. By far the most popular type of annuity in the individual field is the annual-premium annuity. Here the premiums are paid in periodic installments over the years prior to the date on which the annuity income begins. This type of annuity is a flexible instrument. It is usually written as a savings contract during the period of accumulation. The net premiums, accumulated at interest, are not forfeited either at death or on surrender during this period. Consequently, the death of the annuitant or the surrender of the annuity during the accumulation period does not increase the benefits of the remaining annuitants. Whenever the annuitant wishes to cease paying premiums, he may select a paid-up annuity for a reduced amount or withdraw the surrender value. If he should die before the contract passes from the accumulation to the liquidation period, his beneficiaries are entitled to a death benefit equal to the cash value of the contract or the amount of premiums paid in, whichever is higher. The contract has one further flexible feature. Usually, the annuitant may elect to have his income payments started earlier or postponed until later, with the proper actuarial adjustment in the amount of the benefit. The annual-premium annuity appeals to one who wishes to use the annuity instrument as a vehicle for estate accumulation as well as for estate liquidation. And by its use, he is guaranteed an annuity income in the future at today's annuity rate. With longevity rates increasing, this guarantee could prove valuable.

Disposition of Proceeds

Annuities may be classified further on the basis of the time at which benefits stop. Under this classification there are four types of annuities: the life annuity—no refund, the guaranteed minimum annuity, the annuity certain, and the temporary life annuity.

The Life Annuity—No Refund. Under the life annuity—no refund, the annuitant is paid an income throughout his lifetime. Upon his death, there is no further equity in the contract, regardless of how few benefit payments have been received. This is the purest form of life annuity and offers the annuitant the largest income payment per dollar of purchase price. No financial arrangement can equal the straight life annuity in providing the largest, and at the same time certain, dollar income for life.

This contract, which is commonly called a straight life annuity, is used frequently in the field of group annuities but not so often in individual annuities. Annuitants in many cases fail to understand the insurance principle involved in annuities. If they are willing to sacrifice their unused principal at their death for the benefit of the other annuitants who survive them, they in turn will benefit from the release of similar funds by those whom they survive. The benefit of survival is greatest in the straight life annuity. Be this as it may, few annuitants want to run the risk of fully dissipating their principal in the event of early death following retirement.

Guaranteed Minimum Annuities. To meet the psychological and economic objections to the straight life annuity, two forms of guaranteed minimum annuities have been developed: period certain and refund. Refund annuities may be broken down further into installment refund and cash refund.

Under a *life annuity, period certain* contract, the annuitant is promised an income for life but is guaranteed a minimum number of payments, such as 120 or 240. If the annuitant dies before the minimum number of guaranteed payments has been made, the payments are continued to his beneficiary for the remainder of the stipulated (certain) period. If the annuitant survives the guaranteed payment period, the benefits continue until his death. For example, if the annuitant owning a 120 months' guarantee dies after five years (60 months), his beneficiary will continue to receive the benefits for 60 months, or she may choose instead to take the commuted value. If the annuitant lives beyond the 120 months, he will continue to collect payments until his death; following the death of the annuitant, his beneficiary will not be entitled to anything.

The cost of the period certain guarantee depends upon the age of the annuitant when benefits commence. For example, a 120 months' guarantee for a female aged 65 would cost between 5 and 6 per cent more than a no-refund annuity. At age 55, the difference in cost would be between 1 and 2 per cent more for the guarantee, whereas at age 45 the difference would be less than 1 per cent.

A *refund annuity* may be either an installment refund or a cash refund annuity. An *installment refund annuity* promises to continue the periodic payments after the death of the annuitant until the combined benefits paid to the annuitant and his beneficiary have equaled the purchase price of the annuity. A *cash refund annuity* agrees, upon the death of the annuitant, to return in cash the difference between benefits drawn and the purchase price paid by the annuitant. If the annuitant himself lives long enough to collect the purchase price in income payments, then upon his death all benefits and values terminate. For example, a $1,000-a-year installment refund annuity would cost about $15,350 for a woman aged 65. If she died after having received six annual installments, her beneficiary would be entitled to ten more installments, making the total pay-out $15,350, which is the purchase price of the annuity. If this were a cash refund annuity, the cost would be about $15,700. In the event of the annuitant's death after having received six payments ($6,000), her beneficiary would be entitled to collect $9,700 in cash, thus completing the total pay-out of $15,700. When the refund is made in cash instead of installments, interest on the decreasing principal not yet paid is sacrificed by the company. Therefore, the cash refund annuity is more expensive than the installment refund. If this were a life annuity—no refund, the cost would have been only about $13,450.

The choice between a guaranteed minimum annuity and a life annuity—no refund depends upon two considerations: (1) the age at which the annuity payments are to start, and (2) whether there is a need to provide for dependents in the event of the early death of the annuitant. The difference between the cost of a guaranteed minimum annuity and a life annuity—no refund is so insignificant for annuities commencing at early ages that it is uneconomic to purchase the life annuity—no refund. However, at later ages the straight life annuity has significant cost advantages and should be given serious consideration unless there is a need for a refund to provide for dependents in the event of early death. Actually, annuities of any type beginning at early ages seem to be uneconomic, since the return on a safe, direct, interest-bearing or dividend-yielding security is apt to be about as good, without the cost of capital liquidation. For example, at age 30, female, an annuity of $100 annually guaranteed for fifteen years would cost about $2,600. This amounts to a return of about 3.8 per cent, with part of it consisting of a return of principal. The would-be annuitant would not have to look very far today to find a safe direct investment yielding around 4 per cent. The low survival benefits at early ages account for the relatively low income from annuities at these ages.

The Annuity Certain. The annuity certain is a contract which provides the annuitant a given income for a specified number of years, independent of his life or death. Upon the termination of these years, the payments cease. Life expectancy is in no way a factor. Therefore, following the prior death of the annuitant, the payments continue to the end of the stipulated period. This form of annuity is commonly used as a method of paying out life insurance proceeds to a beneficiary under the fixed-period or fixed-amount options. For example, the insured might wish to use the $10,000 proceeds of a life insurance policy to pay his beneficiary an annuity certain of $179 a month for five years. If the beneficiary dies before he has received the income for five years, the payments continue to a secondary beneficiary until the end of the five-year period. The discounted value of these payments often is the method of settlement made with the secondary beneficiary.

Temporary Life Annuities. Temporary life annuities are similar to the annuity certain except that payments cease upon the death of the annuitant. A 10-year temporary life annuity will provide monthly payments for 10 years or until the prior death of the annuitant. These annuities are not popular and therefore are rarely seen. Their uses are limited. One use is to provide an income to fill a gap until an income from another source becomes available. For example, a widow aged 52, with no dependent children, might purchase a 10-year temporary life annuity to provide herself an income until her social security benefits start at age 62, 10 years hence.

Date Benefits Begin

Benefits may be payable immediately after the contract is purchased, or they may be deferred until a number of years later.

The Immediate Annuity. The immediate annuity is purchased with a single premium, and benefits begin at the end of the first income period. For example, under certain interest and mortality assumptions, a man aged 65 could purchase a nonparticipating immediate annuity of $100 a month for slightly under $14,500. The monthly benefit will begin one month after purchase. If benefits are to start at the beginning of the first income period, the annuity is called an *annuity due*. The annuity due is used when life insurance proceeds or cash values are converted into life annuity payments, as, for example, under the life income settlement option. With the exception of settlement options under life insurance contracts, few immediate annuities are purchased on an individual basis. On a group basis, however, immediate annuities are used in connection with deposit administration and immediate participation guarantee plans in pension administration.

The Deferred Annuity. The deferred annuity may be purchased with either a single premium or an installment premium. The benefit payments begin at the end of a given number of years or at optional ages established in the contract. Thus, for example, a man aged 44 might purchase, with a single premium of about $9,200, a $100-a-month installment refund annuity to begin at age 65. Or he might purchase the annuity for a series of twenty-one annual premiums of slightly more than $600. If a benefit is payable upon death during the accumulation period, the annuitant may shorten the deferred period, if he wishes, by accepting a smaller annuity. At age 55, for example, he could accept an annuity of about $59 a month if he has a single-premium deferred annuity, or one of about $36 a month if his annuity is an annual-premium annuity. An age 50 starting date would reduce the annuities to about $47 and $16, respectively.

The deferred period may also be lengthened under some deferred annuity contracts. A limitation usually restricts the extension to a given maximum age or to a given maximum number of years beyond the maturity date. In annual-premium deferred annuities, where an extension is allowed, the contract usually provides that no premiums shall be payable on or after the maturity date. An extension of the deferred period produces, of course, a higher annuity payment.

Under the annual-premium deferred annuity, if the annuitant wishes to discontinue his premium payments before the annuity matures, he may do so by agreeing to accept a smaller annuity at age 65. To illustrate, in the above case the annuitant can discontinue premium payments at age 54 and take a paid-up deferred annuity at age 65 of about $55 a month. If he discontinues premium payments at age 59, his paid-up annuity would amount to about $77 a month.

Deferred annuities have two periods: the deferred period and the liquidation or pay-out period. Minimum guarantees can be made available in one of these periods, in both, or in neither. For example, assume a single-premium deferred annuity of $100 a month commencing at age 65, issued at age 25, male. The cost of this annuity would be only about $3,500 if it were written without any guaranteed minimums, that is, if no death benefits were payable during either the deferred period or the period of liquidation. If the annuity guaranteed a return of the premium or cash value, if greater, upon death during the deferred period but was written on a life income only—no refund basis during the period of liquidation, the cost would be about $4,500. But if the annuity not only guaranteed a return of premium or cash value at death during the deferred period but also guaranteed a minimum of 120 payments during the period of liquidation, the cost would increase to about $4,900. It is customary, in writing deferred annuities on an individual basis, to guarantee a refund at death during the deferred period. Whether there is to be any guaranteed minimum during the period of liquidation, and, if so, the nature of any guarantee, is left to the discretion of the annuitant. Frequently, this guarantee feature is flexible, and the annuitant can make his choice at any time before the annuity commences. Of course, the higher the guaranteed minimum selected, the lower will be the amount of each annuity payment. In the group field, it is more common to find pure deferred annuities, that is, annuities written with no death benefits before retirement. Also in the group field, single-premium deferred annuities are common, whereas most individual annuities are annual-premium deferred annuities.

Number of Lives Covered

The usual annuity covers only one life. Situations do arise, however, when it is desirable to make annuity payments contingent upon several lives. The most popular type of annuity covering more than one life is the joint-and-last-survivorship annuity. Under this contract, income is payable throughout the joint lifetimes of two or more annuitants and continues throughout the lifetime of the last survivor. Sometimes the contract will provide for a reduction in income payments upon the death of the first annuitant, say a one-third reduction, with two thirds continuing to the survivor. For example, a man aged 65 and a woman aged 63 could purchase a joint-and-last-survivorship annuity in the amount of $100 a month for about $20,000. This contract will pay $100 a month as long as either of them is alive. If it is felt that two cannot live as cheaply as one, the couple could arrange to have $115 a month paid during their joint lifetimes and $77 a month during the lifetime of the survivor. In this example, this can be done without any change in premium. Commonly, joint-and-last-survivorship annuities are written on two lives—usually husband and wife —in order to guarantee income to both as long as either may live.

A type of annuity not frequently written is the joint life annuity. This annuity contract provides for payments which continue throughout the joint lifetime of two people but cease upon the death of the first. This type of annuity is valuable when there is an independent income sufficient to support one member of the family but insufficient for both.

Units in Which Pay-out Benefits Are Expressed

Annuities under this classification are of two types: fixed and variable. The terms "fixed" and "variable" have reference to dollars and not to purchasing power. The fixed-dollar annuity, sometimes referred to as the conventional annuity, guarantees the annuitant a fixed, minimum number of dollars during each pay-out period. The variable annuity expresses its promise in terms of a fixed number of units, the dollar value of which fluctuates periodically according to the experience of the company. In some variable annuity plans, these fluctuations are limited to investment experience only, whereas in others they include mortality and expense experience as well.

If the annuitant wishes a guaranteed fixed-dollar income and is willing to accept the risk of decreased purchasing power brought on by inflation, then he will purchase the fixed-dollar annuity. If he does not want to rely on the stability of the dollar and is willing to have his money income fluctuate in the hope that as a result his real income will fluctuate less, he will purchase a variable annuity.[1]

As stated, the various types of annuities described in this chapter are not mutually exclusive. For example, every annuity will have characteristics from each class. To illustrate, there can be a single-premium immediate joint-and-last-survivorship refund fixed-dollar annuity, or an annual-premium deferred life annuity—no refund variable annuity, or any other combination taking one characteristic from each of the five classes.

THE ANNUITY POLICY

The annuity policy itself is a simple instrument. It states that the company will pay the designated annuity to the annuitant and that the payment will be subject to the provisions in the document which constitutes the entire contract. The contract then presents certain information about the annuitant: his date of birth, sex, and age last birthday. This information is necessary to determine the premium. The policy also sets forth certain information about the annuity itself: maturity date, amount of the annuity, maturity value, death benefit table of guaranteed values, amount of the premium, premium due dates, and whether the contract is participating.

The annuity contract contains an ownership clause and provisions for change in ownership, as customarily found in life insurance policies. Other clauses typical of life insurance policies found in the usual annuity contract are those dealing with the grace period for paying premiums, incontestability, deferment of payment of cash values, policy loans, consideration, and beneficiary designation and change.

The contract has the customary assignment clause found in life insurance policies: "The company shall not be charged with notice of any assignment of any interest in the contract until the original assignment or a certificate copy has been filed with the company at its home office.

[1] Variable annuities are discussed in detail in Chapter 42. The various forms of group annuities are discussed in Chapters 39 and 40.

The company assumes no responsibility as to the validity or effect of any assignment and may rely solely on the assignee's statement as to the amount of his interest." Not all annuity contracts are assignable. In order to qualify for special treatment granted by the federal income tax law to certain qualified individuals, the annuity must be nontransferable. The typical misstatement-of-age clause found in the annuity policy is: "If the annuitant's age or date of birth as recorded has been misstated, the amount of the annuity payments under the contract shall be such as the premium would have purchased at the correct age or date of birth. Any overpayments by the company will be deducted from the payment or payments next succeeding correction of age."

Annuity contracts written on a participating basis offer the owner the options of using the dividend to buy paid-up additions or of applying it toward the payment of the premium rather than taking the dividend in cash. Where a death benefit is available, the annuity contract will usually contain a number of settlement options similar to those found in life insurance policies. A waiver-of-premium benefit in the event of disability and an accidental death benefit, also similar to those written with life insurance, may be found as riders to some annuity contracts.

USES OF ANNUITIES

The principal use of the annuity is to arrange an income for old age. When a man reaches that stage in life when he can no longer earn his living, he must live off earnings he has accumulated from the past. Unless that fund is large enough to provide a sufficient income from interest and dividends alone, it will have to be liquidated to supplement the periodic income. As the principal is reduced, income will decline, making it necessary to liquidate the fund at an increasing rate if a steady periodic payment is to be maintained. The fund eventually will expire. If the liquidator expires before the fund, there will be no problem. There is, however, a real risk that the fund will expire before the liquidator, leaving an old man without an income. It is the function of the annuity to protect against this risk.

The fundamental purpose of an annuity is to provide a vehicle for the scientific liquidation of capital. It is to assure a person an income he cannot outlive, an income well in excess of that to be derived from investing the cost of the annuity in safe, interest-bearing or dividend-yielding securities. The application of the annuity principle can be used to liquidate an estate created through life insurance contracts, investments in stocks and bonds, savings accounts, or the annuity contract itself. As long as there is a fund available for liquidation, the annuity principle is available to liquidate it scientifically.

Because of high prices, high taxes, and relatively low net yields on safe investments, today more people than ever are faced with the problem of capital creation, not with the idea of preserving it to pass it along to heirs, but to finance a livable income for their old age by liquidating it systematically through the annuity principle. For example, a young man aged 35 who can save \$50 a month toward his retirement would find that at a liberal 3 per cent net return compounded annually after allowances for income taxes and investment expenses, he would have accumulated about \$30,000 at age 65. This amount would yield a retirement income of about \$100 a month, assuming a 4 per cent return on the investment fund after retirement. If the same \$50 a month were put into an annual-premium retirement annuity, the guaranteed monthly income at retirement would be about \$150, an increase of 50 per cent over the direct investment plan.

Even when a person has amassed a fortune large enough to provide a livable income from investment return alone, he may well find a use for the annuity. The substitution of an annuity income for a direct investment income can free some capital for other uses without reducing the amount of the income. For example, it takes a capital sum of \$100,000 to provide an income of \$4,000 a year at 4 per cent interest. An income of \$4,000 a year, however, can be provided at age 65, male, by means of a single-premium life annuity, for about \$50,000, one half of the amount needed under the direct investment plan. Some or all of the released capital can be used by the annuitant to finance a philanthropic interest close to his heart or to pass on to his heirs while he is living and at a time when it might do them the most good. It stands to reason that a live man would gain more enjoyment than a dead man in seeing his money put to some social good. Also, the donor will have the satisfaction and pleasure of seeing his heirs put to good use the money he has accumulated for them. In addition, living gifts may have some tax advantages over transfers at death.

Annuities have certain tax advantages which might appeal to some investors. Assume that the investor referred to above purchases the \$4,000 annuity at age 65. How will these payments be taxed? According to the annuity tables put out by the United States Treasury Department, the life expectancy of a male aged 65 is 15 years. Since this is an annual annuity rather than a monthly annuity, the regulations require that this expectancy factor be adjusted downward by 0.5. This makes the adjusted expectancy period 14.5 years, and the expected return \$58,000 (14.5 × \$4,000). The purchase price of \$50,000 represents 86.2 per cent of the expected return. Therefore, 86.2 per cent of each \$4,000 annuity payment is viewed by the Internal Revenue Service as a return of invested capital, and only 13.8 per cent is considered taxable income. Thus, in this example, only \$552 is reportable as income, whereas the entire \$4,000 would be subject to income taxation under the direct investment plan. Where the investor is in high surtax brackets, the annuity can have a real income tax advantage.

Purchase of the annuity for $50,000 also reduces the gross estate for estate tax purposes. If the taxable estate before the annuity was purchased had a value of $100,000, the federal estate tax would amount to $20,700. Since the purchase of the annuity would reduce the taxable estate to $50,000, such a purchase would also reduce the federal estate tax liability to $7,000. The resulting tax savings is $13,700. So, in effect, the investor is able to purchase an annuity costing $50,000 for only $36,300.

The deferred annuity also has income tax advantages during the period of accumulation. The investment earnings are not reportable as income during the year earned. Instead, they act to reduce the purchase price of the annuity in calculating the exclusion ratio for income tax purposes at the time of distribution. The effect of this procedure is to postpone the tax until the period of retirement when income is likely to be lower, the retirement income credit may be available, and the double exemption is allowed.

LIMITATIONS OF ANNUITIES

For psychological—and sometimes economic—reasons, old people do not like to use up their capital in providing themselves a retirement income. They like to leave some of it behind for their heirs. Some are content to live on an income well below that to which their savings entitle them in order that they may conserve their estates. They do not look to the annuity as a method of increasing their old-age income because the annuity liquidates rather than conserves their assets. Frequently, elderly people are so concerned with passing on property to their children that they become dependent for a part of their support on the very children for whom they are denying themselves. These children might well be better off if their parents would purchase an annuity and thus have an adequate independent income without outside help. An annuity at ages past 60 generally will more than double the income available from direct investments of a conservative nature. Nevertheless the fact that annuities involve the expenditure of capital is one of their limitations.

In any discussion of the limitations of annuities, there must be a clear separation between the fixed-dollar annuity and the variable annuity. Since a separate chapter is devoted exclusively to the variable annuity, this discussion will confine itself to the fixed-dollar annuity. While in some quarters the fixed-dollar annuity is still looked upon as a safe means for arranging a dependable retirement income, in others there is an increasing awareness of the dangers involved in tying long-range investment programs to a fixed number of dollars. Unlike the units used in weights and measures, the dollar has not proved itself to be a dependable measuring rod. The dollar fluctuates in value so widely that it becomes impossible for anyone to determine how many dollars will be needed in the future to cover his retirement income needs. Although the annuity has the advantage of safety insofar as the financial risk is concerned, it leaves its holders miserably exposed to the purchasing power risk. Of course, if price levels decline, the annuitant has gained by accepting this risk. But if, on the other hand, price levels rise, as is likely to be the case, the annuitant has lost part of the security he thought he had purchased.

Recent trends in the purchase of individual annuities reflect the declining interest on the part of nongroup buyers in annuities. During the past ten years, when most other segments of the life insurance business were experiencing a major growth, individual annuities declined both in the number in force and, except for 1962, in the amount of annual income guaranteed. Activity of several companies and their agents in developing and selling annuities to employees of Section 501(*c*)(3) organizations and of public schools as a tax shelter has to some extent given some renewed interest in individual annuities. Activities growing out of the Keogh-Smathers Act have also extended the interest in individual annuities, but the new interest is limited only to these two tax-sheltered markets.

While Americans do not use individual annuities to the extent that the Scotch, French, and others do, they make greater use of the annuity options made available under life insurance policies in the settlement of both cash values and proceeds.

SELECTED REFERENCES

Crobaugh, Clyde J. *Handbook of Insurance,* Vol. I. Englewood Cliffs, N. J.: Prentice-Hall, Inc., 1949.

Huebner, S. S., and Black, Kenneth, Jr. *Life Insurance.* 6th ed. New York: Appleton-Century-Crofts, Inc., 1964.

Mehr, Robert I., and Osler, Robert W. *Modern Life Insurance.* 3d ed. New York: Macmillan Co., 1961.

Research and Review Service of America, Inc. *The R & R Advanced Underwriting and Estate Planning Service,* Vol. III, Sec. 19, pp. 47–56. Indianapolis. Loose leaf service.

Chapter 8

SPECIAL POLICIES

BY HERBERT C. GRAEBNER

Although there are only three basic types of life insurance policies—term, whole life, and endowment—many additional special policies are available. Structurally, these contracts are special because (1) they combine two or more of the basic three types or combine some of them with annuity contracts, (2) they place special emphasis on settlement arrangements, or (3) they offer a special type of premium payment arrangement.

Because these special policies are designed to satisfy a particular insurance need, they do not offer the same degree of flexibility as do the basic policies. Indeed, in some situations, well-informed life underwriters have discovered that separate basic contracts enable the policyholder to obtain all the benefits of the special contract without sacrificing flexibility. It is important for the life underwriter to have a clear understanding of the components of a special policy so that he can explain and recommend its use to clients whose interests are best served with such a contract.

The special policies described in this chapter are given different names by different companies. Some companies also attempt to gain additional product differentiation by making certain minor variations. Because of these variations, it is difficult to make accurate cost comparisons among similar policies offered by different companies.

Descriptions of special policies will be limited to those most commonly offered, excluding such popular contracts as juvenile and family policies, since they are described elsewhere in this *Handbook*. Special policies will be classified as follows: (1) those policies where primary emphasis is on the special mixture of protection and investment, (2) those policies where the primary emphasis is on unique settlement arrangements, and (3) those policies providing for unusual premium payment plans. The policies described should be regarded as illustrative of the kinds of variations that exist rather than as a complete listing.

PROTECTION AND INVESTMENT COMBINATION

Double or Triple Protection Policies

Double or triple protection policies provide an amount of insurance which is twice or three times the face of the policy until a given age, such as age 65, or for a specified period of time, such as 20 years, after which the amount of insurance is reduced to the face of the policy. For example, a common form is $20,000 of insurance for 20 years and $10,000 thereafter. An illustration of the double protection policy is presented in Figure 8–1.

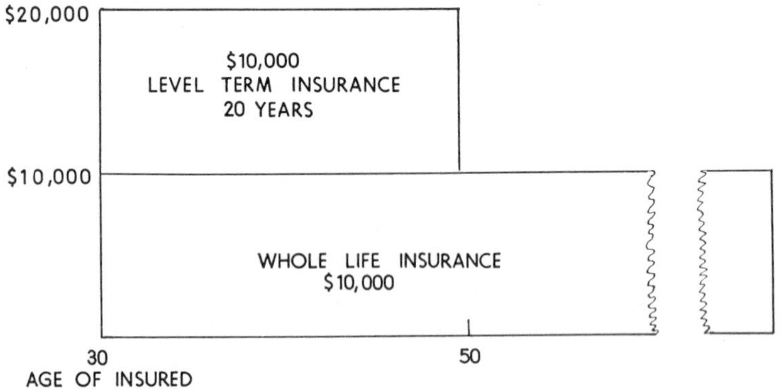

FIG. 8–1. Double protection policy, 20-year, issued at age 30. Pays $20,000 if death occurs during first 20 years and $10,000 if death occurs after age 50.

If such a policy were issued to a person aged 45, it might be called "double protection for 20 years" or "double protection to age 65."

Structurally, this type of policy is a combination of permanent insurance and level term insurance. In the illustration above, there is $10,000 of permanent insurance plus $10,000 of 20-year term insurance. If this were triple protection, the amount of the term insurance would be $20,000, or double the amount of permanent coverage. This coverage may be provided by a special integrated policy or as a term rider to a whole life or endowment policy. If written as a special policy, the premium may be level for the premium-paying period of the policy; whereas if the coverage is written as a rider, the premium will be reduced at the end of the term coverage. The term insurance usually is convertible into permanent insurance, subject to the usual limitations. Likewise, the usual settlement arrangements are available on both the permanent and the term insurance. This tends to give more flexibility to this special policy as compared to the family maintenance policy, to be described later in this chapter.

The double or triple protection policies afford extra protection at low premium outlay for a period of time when the additional protection may be needed. The chief weakness of this type of policy is that it may be misunderstood. The policyholder may confuse the amount of coverage offered by the term portion of the policy with permanent protection and become upset when the term portion expires and his protection is reduced to the face of the policy. This might be particularly disappointing to the insured if, at the expiration of the term coverage, there is still a need for the original insurance protection. A full explanation of the policy provisions at the time the policy is delivered, including a complete description of the face of the policy and periodic service calls by the underwriter, are the surest ways of reducing the possibility of client dissatisfaction.

Family Maintenance Policy

The family maintenance policy is also a combination of permanent insurance and level term insurance. It differs from the double and triple protection policies in that if death occurs during the term period, the proceeds of the term coverage are paid out in monthly payments and, unless otherwise provided, the payment of the proceeds of the permanent portion is deferred until all monthly term payments have been made. This deferral makes possible a smaller amount of term coverage than would be needed if the permanent insurance proceeds were not deferred, since interest will be earned on the permanent insurance while the proceeds of it are held by the company.

Typically, this policy provides for monthly payments equal to 1 per cent of the permanent insurance for the period from death to the end of the term coverage, followed by payment of the face amount. For example, a 20-year, 1 per cent family maintenance policy issued at age 30 in the amount of $10,000 would pay $100 per month for 20 years from death, if death occurred prior to age 50, and then $10,000 under the permanent insurance.[1]

In Figure 8–2, it is seen that this policy consists of $10,000 of whole life insurance, payment on which is deferred for 20 years after death, if death occurs during the 20-year family maintenance period, and term insurance in the amount of $15,060. Assuming the same interest as shown in the figure, it would take $18,975 of term insurance to assure 240 monthly payments of $100. However, because the whole life portion of the policy is held at interest for 20 years and at 2½ per cent yields $2.06 per month per $1,000, the amount of $20.60 per month is available toward the $100 per month. The amount of term insurance that is needed is reduced to $15,060, since this will produce $79.40 per month for 20 years. The usual

[1] In addition to 1 per cent family maintenance policies, there are also 2 per cent and 3 per cent policies available, under which the monthly payment is $20 or $30 per $1,000 of permanent insurance.

settlement arrangements are available for the permanent insurance. The family maintenance policy, like the double protection policy, may be written as a separate policy or as a rider to an existing policy.

Under the family maintenance policy, just as in the case of the double or triple protection policy, there is the danger of misunderstanding on the part of the insured. When his term portion expires, he may feel that he is

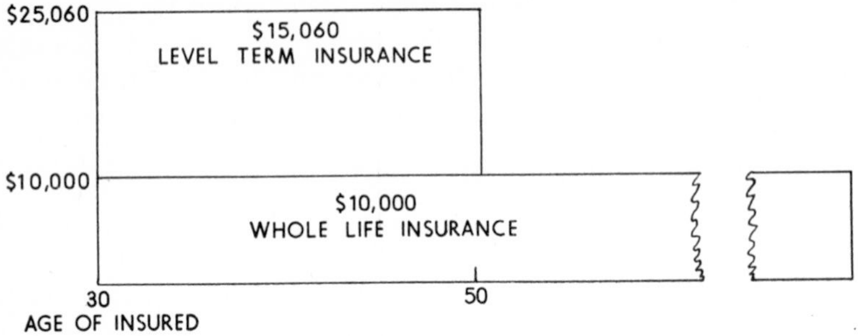

FIG. 8–2. Family maintenance policy, 20-year, issued at age 30, $10,000, 2½ per cent interest. Pays $100 per month for 20 years from date of death if death occurs prior to age 50, and then $10,000 from permanent insurance.

getting less than he paid for, even though his premiums are decreased after the term protection is eliminated. This again calls for complete disclosure and explanation on the part of the underwriter.

Family Income Policy

The family income is perhaps the most popular of all the special policies. Structurally, it combines permanent life insurance with a decreasing amount of term insurance. Its benefits differ from those of the family maintenance policy in that the monthly income payments are made only until the term period of the policy has expired. For example, assume a 20-year family maintenance policy issued on A's life at age 40, and a 20-year family income policy issued on B's life, also at age 40. In the event both died at age 50, monthly payments from the term part of the policy would be made under A's policy for 20 years; whereas in B's policy, monthly payments would be for only the unexpired portion of the 20-year term, which would be 10 years. In each policy, extra benefits are payable in the form of monthly income if the insured dies while the term portion is in force. In the family maintenance policy, these payments continue for 20 years from the date of death; in the family income contract, they are available only from the date of death to the end of the originally stipulated family income period. Obviously, in both cases, at the expiration of the income period the face of the permanent insurance would be payable.

Because all monthly income payments from the term part of the policy cease at the conclusion of the term period in the family income policy, the amount of protection needed to supply these monthly payments decreases until, at the conclusion of the term period, it becomes zero. This is illustrated in Figure 8–3, which shows that if death occurred in the first

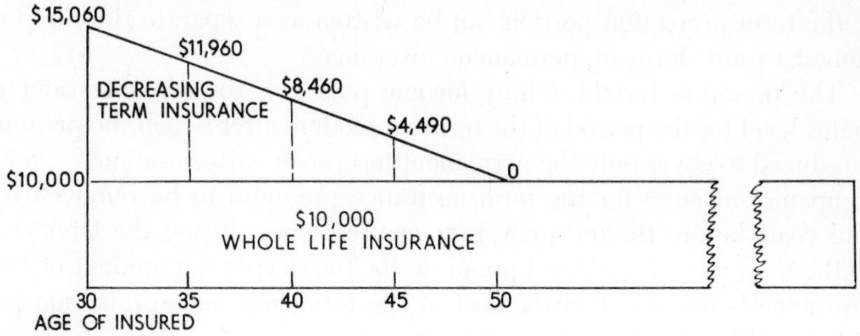

FIG. 8–3. Family income policy, $10,000, $100 per month for 20 years, issued at age 30, 2½ per cent interest.

year of the policy at age 30, the company would be obligated to make monthly payments of $100 for the remainder of the entire 20-year period, and then pay the $10,000 of whole life proceeds.[2] Again, because payment of the whole life portion is deferred for 20 years, the monthly interest earned per $1,000 is $2.06, or $20.60 on the $10,000. The amount of term insurance needed to pay $79.60 ($100 minus $20.60) for 20 years is $15,060. If death should occur at age 45, the amount of term insurance needed is that amount which will produce monthly payments of $79.60 for five years. In Figure 8–3, this is shown as $4,490 of term insurance.

Subject to the rules and limitations of the insuring company, the beneficiary may elect to have the proceeds of the whole life part of the policy paid in a lump sum or according to one of the settlement options offered by the company. The arrangement to be selected should depend upon such factors as the age of the beneficiary at the conclusion of the monthly income payments provided by the term insurance and the needs of the beneficiary. The client's life underwriter should be called upon to offer guidance to the family at this time.

Some family income policies provide for an additional lump-sum payment if death occurs during the term period. For example, this lump sum might be $150 per $1,000 of face amount. Such payment usually is provided by an additional amount of term insurance protection, since it does not reduce the proceeds paid under the whole life portion of the policy. Another variation offered by some companies calls for payment of the proceeds of the whole life portion of the policy immediately upon death, followed by the monthly income payments. In such a policy,

[2] In addition to 1 per cent family income policies, there are also 2 per cent and 3 per cent policies available under which the monthly payment is $20 or $30 per $1,000 of permanent insurance.

obviously, the amount of term insurance will be increased, since interest earned on proceeds held will not be available to meet part of the monthly income promised on the term part of the policy.

The family income policy can be written as a single integrated policy, or the term protection portion can be written as a separate rider and attached to any form of permanent insurance.

The premium for the family income policy or the separate rider remains level for the period of the term protection, after which the premium is reduced to cover only the permanent insurance part of the policy. Some companies arrange for the term insurance premium to be removed several years before the term coverage expires, since during the later years of the term period, the level premium for the decreasing amount of term insurance is greater than the cost of the term insurance protection provided in this period.

Companies may add three benefits—waiver of premium, disability income, and the accidental death provision—to the family income policy. When this is done, the additional benefits provided by the disability income and the accidental death provisions normally are added only to the permanent insurance part of the policy. The waiver-of-premium benefit often is added to both. Some companies will also permit conversion of a part of the term protection to a form of permanent insurance within a limited period without requiring evidence of insurability. The insured may provide for commutation of the proceeds by the beneficiary at his death. Most companies also will permit commutation of the proceeds at the request of the beneficiary to provide cash immediately.

The advantage of the family income policy is that it provides maximum income protection when this is most needed, at a minimum cash outlay because of the use of decreasing term insurance. As in the case of the family maintenance policy, there is the danger of confusion in the minds of the insured and his beneficiaries, since the protection provided under the term portion is of limited duration. Great care should be exercised by life underwriters to avoid misunderstandings about the length and the amount of protection provided for under family income policies.

Retirement Income Policy

The retirement income policy—which may have a variety of names, such as endowment annuity, insurance with annuity, retirement endowment, and income endowment—is a combination of a retirement annuity contract and decreasing term insurance. Under the retirement annuity part of the policy, provision is made for a lifetime income to the policyholder and also to his wife if he desires. The amount needed to annuitize is accumulated over a period of years. The decreasing term insurance during this accumulation period makes it possible for the death benefit during the early years of accumulation to be considerably larger than the mere return of annuity premiums or the cash value, whichever is larger. The term insurance, for example, may be arranged to provide a death benefit equal to $1,000 for each $10 of monthly income provided by the annuity. However, companies often offer policies carrying larger death benefits for each $10 of monthly income. The amount of term insurance decreases as the cash values of the annuity increase. When this cash value equals the face amount of the insurance, the insurance part of the policy is eliminated.

Figure 8–4 illustrates how decreasing term insurance is combined

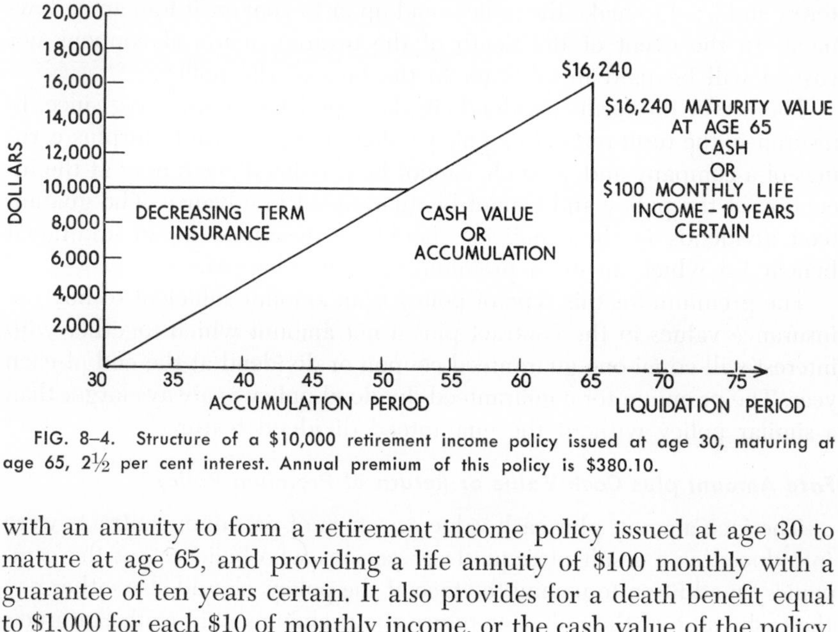

FIG. 8–4. Structure of a $10,000 retirement income policy issued at age 30, maturing at age 65, 2½ per cent interest. Annual premium of this policy is $380.10.

with an annuity to form a retirement income policy issued at age 30 to mature at age 65, and providing a life annuity of $100 monthly with a guarantee of ten years certain. It also provides for a death benefit equal to $1,000 for each $10 of monthly income, or the cash value of the policy, whichever is the larger, if death occurs during the accumulation period. From the illustration, it can be seen that the decreasing term insurance is zero when the cash value of the policy equals the death benefit. If the death benefit is greater than $1,000 for each $10 of annuity income, the term insurance would continue for a longer period. Obviously, the premium for a retirement income policy is greater than the premium for a retirement annuity contract. Likewise, the larger the death benefit, the higher the premium. Retirement income policies may be written to mature at earlier ages than 65. The maturity value of the retirement income policy may be taken in cash or in accordance with the options available under a retirement annuity, including a joint and survivorship annuity. The death benefits may be received in a lump sum or under the usual settlement options.

Retirement income policies are offered by practically all life insurance companies. They are commonly used in connection with individual policy pension trust plans and are often used in other types of pension plans.

Guaranteed Dividend Policy

Guaranteed dividend policies are sometimes called guaranteed investment or coupon policies. They combine a special savings feature with life insurance. They are nonparticipating policies under which a specified sum, called an annual dividend is guaranteed. Coupons upon which the amount of each annual dividend is stated usually are attached to the policy. Such coupons can be cashed each year or accumulated at compound interest and used to make the policy paid up or to convert it into an endowment. In the event of the death of the insured, matured coupons not cashed will be paid in addition to the face of the policy.

The use of the term "dividend" in these policies is confusing since, in insurance, the term refers to a policy's share in the divisible surplus earnings of a company and, as such, cannot be predicted accurately at the inception of the policy and cannot be guaranteed in advance. The guaranteed dividends in these policies should be described as an additional benefit for which an extra premium must be charged.

The premium for this type of policy is an amount sufficient to buy the insurance values in the contract plus a net amount which together with interest will equal one guaranteed coupon or dividend at the end of each year. The premium for a guaranteed dividend policy is always larger than a similar policy without the guaranteed dividend feature.

Face Amount plus Cash Value or Return of Premium Policy

The face amount plus cash value or return of premium contracts were introduced as a result of requests of persons who believe that the companies, in addition to paying the face of the policy, should also either pay the cash value of the policy or return the premiums paid at the insured's death. For example, the policy may provide that the death benefit will be increased by an amount equal to the gross premiums paid if death occurs during the first 20 years of the policy. This is accomplished by adding to the basic policy an amount of term insurance that increases during the 20-year period. At the conclusion of the term protection, the premium is reduced to the gross premium of the basic policy only.

Some companies provide policies that promise to pay the face plus the cash value regardless of when death occurs. In such cases, the policy consists of two whole life policies, one of which provides for payment of the face amount of the policy, with the other providing for payment of the increasing cash value. Although the amount of insurance protection increases each year, the premium for the policy is level throughout the life of the contract.

PRIMARY EMPHASIS ON SETTLEMENT ARRANGEMENTS

Life Income Policy

The life income policy is payable only in the form of income rather than in a lump sum. Payments are guaranteed for a specified period and for the remaining lifetime of the beneficiary, following the death of the insured. Payments will be made whether the beneficiary survives the period or not. This feature distinguishes the life income policies from the survivorship annuity policies, to be described later. In the life income policy, if the beneficiary survives the period specified in the policy, which may extend for 20 years, the payments will continue for the remaining life of the beneficiary. Should the beneficiary not survive the insured or not survive for the entire period guaranteed in the policy, the remaining installments will be paid to the contingent beneficiary.

Structurally, the life income policy consists of (1) the principal sum required to provide the specified minimum number of payments guaranteed, and (2) the sum required to provide for the payments, if any, in the event the beneficiary lives beyond the guaranteed period. The value of the first part will depend upon the length of the guaranteed period, which is customarily for 10, 15, or 20 years, and the amount of the monthly benefit. This sum can be provided by any form of whole life insurance. The second part of the coverage depends upon the amount of each payment and the age of the beneficiary, and is a deferred survivorship annuity, which will be described later in this chapter.

If the beneficiary does not survive the insured, the survivorship portion of the policy will terminate, but the whole life portion will continue in effect to protect the contingent beneficiary for the guaranteed payments. The premium in such a situation will be reduced at the beneficiary's death by the amount of the survivorship annuity cost. The beneficiary designation with respect to the survivorship annuity cannot be changed, but the designation for the guaranteed period payments may be changed.

When the life income policy is based on an endowment policy, it can be made to provide income either upon the insured's death or upon his reaching a certain age when the endowment would mature. In case the insured survives, the endowment would furnish the sum required to provide the payments during the guaranteed period, and the deferred survivorship annuity would provide the payments beyond the guaranteed period. Because of the endowment feature, this policy would be expensive but would provide excellent protection for an entire family.

Survivorship Annuity Policy

Although called an annuity, the survivorship annuity policy is really life insurance with the distribution of the proceeds being annuitized.

Under the policy the company agrees to pay a specified life income to a designated beneficiary only if the beneficiary should survive the insured. If the beneficiary predeceases the insured, which is the usual expectation, since in situations where this policy is appropriate the beneficiary is usually much older than the insured, the policy is terminated, and no benefit payments are made. Furthermore, payments to the designated beneficiary cease upon the beneficiary's death without any guaranteed period of payments.

The amount of life insurance at any particular time, sometimes called the "insurance value," is the sum needed to provide a specific life income to the beneficiary at his or her attained age. The amount of insurance under a survivorship annuity policy declines as the beneficiary grows older while the policy is in force, because the present value of an immediate life annuity declines with each increase in age. The amount at risk is determined by the size of the benefit payments and the age of the beneficiary. The policy does not permit a change of beneficiary designation. Since the death of the insured establishes the date when income payments begin, the companies require that the insured furnish evidence of insurability. No medical examination is required of the beneficiary because death of the beneficiary relieves the company of all obligations under the policy. Premium payments cease at the death of the insured or at the prior death of the beneficiary. The policy has no cash or loan values, but after a prescribed number of premiums have been paid, companies will permit the reserve to be used to provide a paid-up survivorship annuity. The amount of the annuity payments would, of course, be less than the plan would provide if premium payments would be continued. For an additional premium, companies may provide double benefit payments if the death of the insured is caused by accident. It is also possible to provide for waiver of premiums if the insured should become disabled.

There are two main advantages of this type of policy. One distinct advantage is its low cost when the age difference between the insured and the beneficiary is large, with the insured the younger. This low cost is due to the nature of the protection provided, there being a high probability that the beneficiary will predecease the insured. If this occurs, as was indicated above, no benefits are payable. The second advantage of this policy is that it provides a life income of a fixed amount for the beneficiary, regardless of the age of the beneficiary at the time of the insured's death. The survivorship annuity policy is useful for a son to guarantee a specific life income to an aged parent should the son predecease his parents. Life income can be provided at low cost without seriously jeopardizing the protection program the son has created for his wife and children.

The chief disadvantage of the survivorship annuity policy is its lack of flexibility. It provides income only to the specific person originally designated as beneficiary in the policy. The policy is not appropriate for a husband to use for the protection of his wife and young children, first, because the general proximity of the ages of the husband and wife makes the rate much higher and, second, because there would be no residual benefits to the children upon the death of the widow.

In the discussion of the life income policy, reference was made to a deferred survivorship annuity policy. This is a modification of the survivorship annuity policy, in that a waiting period after the death of the insured is established before the income payments to the beneficiary begin. If the beneficiary does not survive the waiting period beyond the death of the insured, no payments are made by the company. This deferred type of policy has the appeal of being much lower in cost than the straight survivorship annuity. The deferred survivorship annuity policy is recommended by some life underwriters to provide for the widow's life income. They suggest that the widow's income during the family-raising period and prior to the beginning of the payments under the deferred survivorship annuity policy be provided by proceeds of life insurance policies. As was described earlier, the life income policy can be used to provide both coverages in one policy.

Income and Principal Policy

The income and principal policy provides that at the death of the insured the primary beneficiary will be paid a life income of a specified amount, and the face of the policy will be payable to a secondary beneficiary upon the death of the primary beneficiary. In the event the primary beneficiary predeceases the insured, the face of the policy will be paid directly to the secondary beneficiary upon the death of the insured.

The specific purpose served by this policy is to provide for the lifetime needs of one beneficiary and to have the face of the policy ultimately distributed to a secondary beneficiary. These objectives can, of course, be accomplished also by leaving the proceeds of life insurance with the company under the interest option, with the interest to go to the primary beneficiary as long as he or she lives, and the face of the policy to a secondary beneficiary upon the death of the primary beneficiary. The weakness of this solution is that it would take a very large amount of life insurance for the interest income to be adequate for the needs of the primary beneficiary.

The income and principal policy guarantees a higher rate of interest on the proceeds held at interest than the rate at which such proceeds are usually held. This, of course, reduces the amount of insurance required to provide the larger income needed. This policy is in reality a combination of whole life insurance and a survivorship annuity. The whole life insurance policy proceeds furnish the funds that will eventually be paid to the secondary beneficiary upon the death of the primary beneficiary. The survivorship annuity provides the additional amount needed to increase the income from the use of the interest option on the whole life policy to the amount of insurance promised for the primary beneficiary under the income and principal policy. This added protection will increase the premium by an amount that will depend upon the age of the insured and the primary beneficiary.

If the primary beneficiary dies before the insured, the survivorship annuity ceases, with a corresponding reduction in the premiums to that in effect for the whole life portion of the policy. Upon the death of the insured, in these circumstances, the proceeds of the whole life policy are payable to the secondary beneficiary.

If the income and principal policy promises income to the primary beneficiary for a specified period of years rather than for life, the extra income required to meet the higher interest assumption is provided by additional whole life insurance instead of the survivorship annuity. To a certain extent, the income and principal policy may be misleading, since the insured may believe that his beneficiary will receive a larger return than is being earned by the company. This policy does not appear to be widely issued at the present time.

PRIMARY EMPHASIS ON PREMIUM PAYMENT ARRANGEMENTS

Modified Life Policy

The objective of the modified life policy is to make it easy for a person to acquire an amount of life insurance at a lower premium outlay for the first several years, such as three or five. This can be arranged by using some form of term insurance for the first few years and then starting a whole life insurance policy, or by using whole life insurance and redistributing the premiums, allocating smaller amounts in the first three or five years and higher premiums thereafter.

When term insurance is used, there are several possibilities. One type provides term insurance for the first three or five years and then whole life insurance, with the ultimate premium based upon the attained age of the insured. Another type uses decreasing term insurance, with increasing whole life insurance after the first year until at the sixth year the policy becomes a full whole life policy. Under this plan the premium increases for each of the first five years and then remains level thereafter.

In the cases where term insurance is not used in the modified life policies, the modification is brought about by redistributing the premiums, thereby charging less in the preliminary period and more in the later period. There are certain accepted limits within which the redistribution of the premiums is practicable. These limits are, on the one hand, the regular level premium at age of issue and, on the other hand, the premium for term insurance with automatic conversion to a permanent plan. The greater the excess of the rate during the first three or five years over the term rate, the smaller will be the level premiums for the balance of the life of the contract. These policies have cash and other nonforfeiture values during the first three or five years, but these values are less than those that would be available if the full level premium had been paid.

The modified life policy is meant for persons who feel that they are not able to afford the purchase of permanent insurance at regular rates at a particular time, but who expect that their financial status will improve within the next three or five years. Participating policies with modified premium patterns are often sold on a basis of anticipating that the dividends being paid by the time the premium increases will be sufficient largely or entirely to cover the increase in premium. Some life underwriters believe that these policies overcome the sales resistance of many prospects who seem to have unbounded expectations of higher incomes in the future or who think that higher premiums will be easier to pay in the future.

SELECTED REFERENCES

HUEBNER, S. S., and BLACK, KENNETH, JR. *Life Insurance*. 6th ed. New York: Appleton-Century-Crofts, Inc., 1964.

MACLEAN, JOSEPH B. *Life Insurance*. 9th ed. New York: McGraw-Hill Book Co., Inc., 1962.

MCGILL, DAN M. *Life Insurance*. Homewood, Ill.: Richard D. Irwin, Inc., 1959.

MEHR, ROBERT I., and OSLER, ROBERT W. *Modern Life Insurance*. 3d ed. New York: Macmillan Co., 1961.

Chapter 9

FAMILY AND JUVENILE POLICIES

BY FREDRICK E. RATHGEBER

THE FAMILY POLICY

The idea behind the family policy is to make available in a single life insurance contract a modest amount of protection on all members of the family. This policy makes it possible to accomplish a number of important objectives. These include concentrating most of the premium dollar on the father's life where it is most needed, providing insurance adequate to cover last expenses of other family members without the expense of issuing and administering separate policies, and "insuring the insurability" of present and future dependent children at the lowest possible cost. Upon expiry of the child's term insurance, the child has the privilege of obtaining a new policy without evidence of insurability.

Early family policies were essentially separate policies on family members jacketed together for billing purposes and hence known as "rubber band" policies. Modern family policies realize most of their savings by basing premiums, reserves, and nonforfeiture values on the husband's age only and by dispensing with all records of the number and ages of children except the policy application itself.

The family policy has achieved greater public acceptance than any other innovation in life insurance in the last decade. Why does this policy have such unique appeal? Probably it is because the family is the basic unit in American life today, and this policy is specifically designed to meet the insurance needs of the family. For new families, in particular, it forms an excellent foundation on which their whole insurance program may be built.

Benefits Provided by a Typical Policy

Most companies will issue policies providing multiples of up to, say, three times the following unit benefits.

Death Benefits. *Head of Family (Usually the Husband, but It May Be the Wife in Some Companies).* The plan is almost always cash value insurance such as straight life, life paid up at age 65, endowment at age

65, or endowment at age 85. The amount of insurance is often $5,000 per unit, but smaller amounts such as $3,000 are also sold, especially in connection with debit policies (premiums for which are collected in the home, usually on a monthly basis). Often, an accidental death benefit is included.

Spouse. The policies of many companies provide term insurance expiring when the head of the family reaches age 65 or 85, or after twenty years. A pure endowment benefit is sometimes provided at the expiry of the term. The amount of term insurance is usually $1,000 or $1,250 where the ages of the husband and wife are the same. If the ages are different, the amount of the spouse's term insurance is obtained from a table so constructed that the mortality cost at the spouse's actual age produces approximately the same mortality cost, on the basis of experience mortality, as if the ages were the same. Thus, where the wife is younger, her amount of insurance is greater; and where she is older, it is less than the amount of her insurance where there is no difference in age. There has been a trend toward providing insurance on the wife's life similar to that on the husband's life. Most companies also issue policies insuring only one parent to meet the situation where the spouse is dead, uninsurable, or already adequately insured, or where divorce or separation has occurred.

Covered Children. The plan is term insurance expiring at a specified age, such as 21 or 25, but generally no later than the end of the premium payment period for the policy. Children born after the policy is issued are usually included automatically as soon as they are two weeks old. The amount of insurance is generally $1,000 on each covered child. The benefit is often reduced during all or part of the first year of life.

Supplementary Benefits. At the death of the head of the family, all unexpired dependents' term insurance usually becomes fully paid up. Some companies include a benefit which waives premiums for the entire policy if the head of the family becomes totally and permanently disabled. Several companies include accidental death benefits on the head of the family and on the spouse, and in addition provide benefits for loss of eyesight or limbs on all dependents. At the expiry of each dependent's term insurance a conversion privilege is usually available. The spouse may convert her insurance to a permanent policy for the same amount. Children may usually convert to permanent insurance of up to five times the amount of their term insurance. The converted policies are issued at premium rates for the attained age at the time of conversion.

Nonforfeiture Values. Cash values must at least equal the statutory minimum requirement, considering the actual ages of the husband and wife. The statutory minimum is not increased because of the children. The usual extended insurance and reduced paid-up options are included in most policies but generally apply only to the head of the family. Some companies provide a short period (up to ninety days but never more than the term of extended insurance on the head of the family) of extended insurance on the dependents to protect the family in case of inadvertent lapse. No charge is made for this benefit if the policy is later surrendered for cash.

Provision when Wife Predeceases Husband. There are two common policy provisions to meet the situation where the wife dies during her husband's lifetime and before the expiry of her insurance. One of these provides for a reduction in premium and in cash value. The other provides $1,000 per unit of term insurance on the husband's life to be provided by that portion of the premium previously required to provide the wife's insurance.

Riders. Many companies permit the addition of riders providing additional insurance on the head of the family. These riders are similar to the family income, decreasing term, and level term riders which may be added to individual policies.

Technical Aspects

Premium Rates. Net premiums are usually calculated for adult benefits in the same way as for individual policies. The husband and the wife are assumed to be the same age, and the premium does not vary with the number or ages of the children; thus the husband's age determines the premium. In calculating the children's premium, assumptions are made as to the number and ages of the children. These assumptions regarding the children's insurance will have very little effect on the final policy premium because their insurance is term insurance subject to extremely low juvenile mortality rates.

The loading formulas used to compute gross premiums are similar to those for individual policies, but allowance must be made for additional expenses in underwriting and in processing claims.

Where premiums are payable for the head of the family after the expiry of the dependents' term insurance, the premium is usually reduced.

Application. A special application form is usually required. The information requested concerning the head of the family is similar to that requested on the application for an individual policy. In addition, such information as name, birth date, and health history is required for the spouse and each child to be covered.

Underwriting. In underwriting the head of the family, the standards used for individual policies apply. Many companies also issue policies at substandard rates based on the expected mortality of the husband. Where an accidental death benefit is included automatically, applicants whose occupation or physical condition would normally require a slight extra premium for such a benefit are usually accepted at regular rates, but the premium may include a loading based on the expected proportion of such applicants.

Dependents are generally accepted at standard rates if they may be expected to experience mortality of up to about 150 per cent of standard. To keep costs to a minimum, streamlined methods are used. Underwriting is almost entirely nonmedical, although attending physicians' statements are obtained where warranted by health histories. If the spouse would not qualify for an individual policy in the 150 per cent class without a medical examination, the family policy application is likely to be rejected. Where a child fails to qualify, the policy is usually issued with an endorsement excluding the child from coverage. Since the premium is independent of the number of children, it is not reduced because of the exclusion. The child may be included in the policy at a later date on presentation of evidence of insurability.

An eligible child is generally defined as a "child, stepchild, or legally adopted child" under a certain age (such as age 18). Policy forms are usually worded to cover "children named in the application" and those "acquired after the date of the application." Many companies permit only children living in the applicant's household to be named in the application (with certain routine exceptions such as children at boarding school), since the company must rely on the applicant for information as to the health and medical history of all members of the family.

Reinstatement. Applications for reinstatement are underwritten in a manner similar to that for issue. A special form is used to obtain information concerning any change in health of any family member. The reinstatement does not, of course, create any liability of the company on account of any member of the family who has died between the dates of lapse and reinstatement.

Form of Policy and Policy Provisions

Family Policies and Family Riders. Most companies issue family policies on forms quite similar to those used for individual policies. Some companies issue riders containing benefits similar to those described above for the spouse and children. A few companies permit the rider to be attached to either new or existing policies on the life of the head of the family.

Ownership and Control. In most policies the head of the family is the owner during his lifetime. At his death, ownership passes to his spouse or, if she is dead, as may be provided in the policy. For example, ownership may pass to each covered child individually, or jointly to the covered children.

Beneficiary Provisions. Most policies contain a standard provision designed to fit the majority of family situations. Insurance payable on the death of an adult is usually paid to the spouse, if living, otherwise to the estate of the deceased. Insurance payable on the death of a child is usually paid to the head of the family, if living; otherwise to the spouse, if living; otherwise to the estate of the adult member who died last.

While a standard provision such as that described above is usually included automatically, most companies allow the designation of another individual as beneficiary, provided a legitimate insurable interest exists.

Most policies include wording such as "the spouse named in the application." Even after divorce and remarriage, therefore, the spouse at the time of issue of the policy continues to be insured and, unless a change of beneficiary has been made, is the one to whom benefits are payable. In the event of divorce or legal separation, some companies permit a new beneficiary to be named at the request of the head of the family. Companies which use the spouse's premium to purchase additional term insurance on the head of the family after the spouse's death are usually willing to make the same transfer, by endorsement, after divorce or legal separation.

JUVENILE INSURANCE

A considerable amount of insurance is written on the lives of children, reflecting the popularity of juvenile policies in the United States.

Although the probability of a child's dying at a young age is relatively small, and no one would be dependent on the child for financial support, there are, nevertheless, numerous expenses which usually arise when death does occur. Doctor bills, hospital bills, and funeral expenses often reach substantial proportions.

Insurance on the child can also be regarded as contributing to his financial security, since it may be used to help pay for his higher education or may provide funds for his going into business.

Although most men are aware of the need for life insurance when they marry, not all of them can qualify for a policy. By becoming insured as a child, a person has a minimum amount of protection, almost always at standard rates, in the event that some physical impairment develops which might affect his insurability in the future. Where the person continues to be insurable, a policy bought during his youth can make him insurance-conscious and form the basis of his ultimate insurance program. He will also have the benefit of the lower premium rate applicable to his earlier age.

Agents find little resistance to these arguments among parents who want nothing but the best for their children. Most companies make the sale of a juvenile policy contingent on the existence of a reasonable amount of insurance on the life of the breadwinner. When selling a juvenile policy, a skillful agent has a good opportunity to convince the parent of the need for enlarging his own insurance program.

Although juvenile insurance serves the above very useful purposes, it should be noted that similar results are sometimes achieved by different means. For example, a family policy will provide, usually at a lower cost, the desired insurance protection plus a conversion privilege which guarantees the child a standard policy of a substantial amount. Where an educational savings fund is required, endowment insurance on the life of the breadwinner is usually preferable, since it is at his death rather than the child's that the greater financial need will arise. The agent should try to determine from the particular circumstances which type of insurance will be most satisfactory.

Types of Policy

Most regular forms of insurance other than term insurance are available at juvenile ages. Endowments maturing at ages 18 or 20 are particularly popular. Term insurance, preferred risk policies, and plans with very high minimum amounts are unsuitable. For a relatively small extra premium, most companies offer an additional benefit which waives all future premiums, or all premiums to a stated age such as 21 or 25, on the death or total and permanent disability of the applicant for the insurance (usually the father). This often is referred to as the payor benefit.

Special juvenile policies are also offered. The most popular of these is a contract with level premiums payable to age 65 or beyond, but with a varying amount of insurance. The amount of insurance provided by one unit of this plan before age 21 is usually $1,000 plus an amount approximating the accumulation of the total premiums paid. After age 21, one unit provides $5,000 of insurance. Multiples of these benefits are also available. These policies, which are sometimes called "jumping juveniles," have a well-founded sales appeal. The amount of insurance in the early years of life is low; at age 21, when there is usually an increased need for coverage, the amount of insurance takes a substantial jump; because of the large ultimate amount, the premium is quite high, and fairly large cash and loan values are built up, a circumstance which may prove helpful when the bills for education arrive.

Coverage in the First Year of Life

Even though modern medical skill and care have greatly reduced infant mortality, current United States population statistics show that of every 100,000 children born, more than 2,500 die before reaching age one. After the first year, mortality rates decline rapidly. The chance of dying in the second year of life is less than 10 per cent of that of dying in the first year. Not until about age 65 does the mortality rate again climb to its age zero level. Of the deaths occurring before age one, a large portion happen in the early days of infancy.

In order to keep the cost of insurance in the first year at a reasonable level, many companies restrict the benefit during all or part of the first year of life to 25 or 50 per cent of the ultimate amount of insurance. An increasing number of companies make no restriction on the amount of insurance but require that the child be at least one or two weeks old when the application is completed.

Underwriting

Amount of Insurance. *Statutory Limitations.* Fear that substantial amounts of insurance on the lives of children would be an incentive to murder gave rise to statutory restrictions on the amount of insurance which could be written. To meet these restrictions, policies limiting the amount of insurance in the early years were introduced.

Most such statutes were repealed many years ago, but a New York statute placed a fairly restrictive limit on the amounts of juvenile insurance until 1957. A 1957 amendment of the New York law permits a total of $5,000 of insurance on any child, regardless of the amount of insurance on the applicant's life. In Canada, the statutory limitations on insurance on the lives of children were repealed as of March 10, 1960 in Quebec, and as of July 1, 1962 in all the other provinces.

In Relation to Other Insurance. The New York law permits the issuance of more than $5,000 of insurance, provided the total amount of insurance in force on the child is not more than 25 per cent (below age 4½) or 50 per cent (ages 4½–14½) of the amount in force on the applicant. In order to protect themselves against speculation, many insurers apply a similar rule to applications for substantial amounts at juvenile ages in all states. A typical rule might require that the person supporting the child carry on his own life (if insurable) two or three times the amount of insurance applied for on the child's life. Such requirements are sometimes referred to as "times rules." Also, if the amount applied for on a child seems out of line with what is carried on other children in the family, a careful investigation is usually made before the insurance is issued.

In most companies the total amount of insurance permitted on a juvenile life is substantially smaller than the adult limit.

Insurable Interest. While it is difficult to demonstrate more than a small financial interest in the continuance of a child's life, family relationship is usually regarded as sufficient evidence of insurable interest.

Physical Condition of the Child. Since most juvenile applications are for amounts within the companies' nonmedical limits, a medical examination is generally not required. Birth at normal term, reasonable weight at birth (particularly in the case of multiple births), and normal growth and mental development are usually regarded as evidence of insurability. It is a sound underwriting rule to require that the agent see the child awake. Children with minor impairments may be accepted at a slight extra premium, but children with severe impairments are uninsurable.

Applicant's Waiver-of-Premium Benefit. This benefit is underwritten nonmedically in almost all cases unless the policy is very large. An applicant who would require a small extra premium if he applied for a policy on his own life may be accepted at standard rates for this benefit. If the possibility of a serious impairment is indicated on the nonmedical declaration, this benefit is usually not available.

Ownership and Control

Policies on the lives of children under 15 (16 in Canada) are usually issued on the application of an adult who has an insurable interest in the child. This practice protects the insurer, since children are not legally competent to make contracts.

While many states have statutes requiring the written consent of the person insured, an exception is usually made for children under 15 (16 in Canada). However, it is common practice among insurers to require the child's signature, as well as the applicant's, if the child is old enough to write.

The provisions concerning ownership and control differ from those in adult policies. Under a typical arrangement, ownership passes from the applicant to the insured when the insured attains age 21. If the applicant dies before the insured attains age 21, ownership passes to the beneficiary, if living, otherwise to the insured.

Many other arrangements are possible. Where, for example, the policy is a gift to the child or is purchased with the child's own funds, ownership may be vested immediately in the insured. If the policy is part of a trust, ownership may be vested in the trustee.

SELECTED REFERENCES

DAVIS, MALVIN E. "The Family Insurance Policy," *Journal of the American Society of Chartered Life Underwriters,* Vol. XI, No. 4 (Fall, 1957), pp. 303–10.

LIFE INSURANCE AGENCY MANAGEMENT ASSOCIATION. *The Family Life Insurance Policy.* Company Practices Study, Research Report 1957–57, File 116. Hartford, Conn.

MACNAUGHTON, DONALD S. "The Family Policy," a paper read before the Association of Life Insurance Counsel, May 5, 1958, at White Sulphur Springs, West Virginia.

SARNOFF, PAUL E. "The Valuation of the Family Policy," *Transactions of the Society of Actuaries,* Vol. X (1958), pp. 25–31.

Chapter 10

PROBABILITY, MORTALITY, AND MONEY CONCEPTS

BY CHARLES M. STERNHELL

Take a set of mortality rates, an interest rate, a dash of probability theory and compound interest theory, mix well, add an appropriate loading for expenses—and the result will be an actuarially sound premium rate for a life insurance contract. Of course, this recipe will produce a satisfactory result only if the ingredients are of the highest quality, and only if the blending is carried out with the necessary mathematical precision. The purpose of this chapter is to analyze the various ingredients called for by the recipe, and to explain the process by which they are blended into the final product.

PROBABILITY THEORY

A writer on insurance once said: "There is nothing more uncertain than life and nothing more certain than life insurance."[1] Obviously, an insurance company has no way of determining when any particular one of its policyholders will die. Yet, if the company is insuring a large enough number of policyholders, it can predict with a high degree of accuracy the mortality experience for the group as a whole. Who will die in a given year is a matter of complete uncertainty; how many will die is a matter of near certainty.

The phenomenon just described has been most commonly referred to as "the law of averages" or "the law of large numbers." This law, which is the very foundation of the insurance concept, is derived from the mathematical theory of probability. A complete exposition of this theory and proof of the law of large numbers are clearly beyond the scope of this chapter. However, an elementary knowledge of probability theory is

[1] Miles Dawson, *The Business of Life Insurance* (New York: Barnes & Co., 1911).

helpful in understanding and appreciating the actuarial calculation of premium rates and the operation of the law of large numbers.

The theory of probability had a somewhat tainted origin, having developed as a result of efforts to apply mathematics to certain gambling problems. In French society during the middle of the seventeenth century, gambling was a very popular and fashionable sport. An inveterate gambler, the Chevalier de Mere, consulted a famous French mathematician, Blaise Pascal, on some questions connected with various games of chance. This led to further correspondence between Pascal and some of his mathematical friends, principally Pierre Fermat. It was this correspondence which led eventually to the theory of probability as we know it today.

Definition of Probability

We all have some idea as to the meaning of the term "probability." We make statements such as "it probably will rain today," or "there is a good chance that the Dodgers will win the pennant this year," or "there is not much chance of winning the Irish Sweepstakes." The theory of probability attempts to sharpen this general kind of statement by deriving a numerical measure of the chance that a particular event will occur. The numerical measure, or number, that we associate with an event is called the "probability" of that event.

Suppose that a coin is tossed and we are interested in the probability that it will turn up "heads." From general observation of the coin, it would not appear that a head is any more or less likely than a tail; and we would expect that in the long run, heads will occur about half the time. It is natural, then, to assign the number 1/2 as the probability of heads. Similarly, we would expect that the toss of a single die would result in the number 2 about one sixth of the time, as each of the six numbers on the die is just as likely to come up as any other. Hence, we assign the number 1/6 as the probability of tossing a 2. If we are interested in the probability of an even number when a single die is tossed, we note that there are three favorable results, 2, 4, or 6, out of the six equally likely total possible results. Hence, we would assign the number $3/6 = 1/2$ as the probability of an even number. These few simple examples lead to the following more formal definition of probability:

Definition of Probability. If an experiment must result in one of n equally likely cases, and if the event A includes m of these cases, then the probability of the event A is equal to the fraction m/n.

Stated less carefully, but perhaps more understandably, the probability of an event is equal to the number of favorable cases divided by the total number of cases, provided all cases are equally likely. It is apparent from this definition that the probability of any event is a number between 0 and 1, with 0 meaning impossibility and 1 meaning certainty.

Rules of Probability

For combining probabilities, there are two simple rules that enable us to calculate the probabilities of more complicated events than those illustrated so far. These rules are called the "addition rule" and the "multiplication rule."

Addition Rule. If *A* and *B* are two mutually exclusive events, the probability that *at least one* of these two events occurs is equal to the sum of their respective probabilities. ("Mutually exclusive" means that the occurrence of one of the events precludes the possibility of the other.)

As an example of the addition rule, consider the drawing of a card from a standard deck of 52 cards. The probability of drawing an ace is 4/52. The probability of drawing a red king is 2/52. Therefore the probability of drawing either an ace or a red king is equal to

$$4/52 + 2/52 = 6/52 = 3/26$$

Multiplication Rule. If *A* and *B* are two independent events, the probability that *both* these events occur is equal to the product of their respective probabilities. ("Independent" means that the occurrence or nonoccurrence of one of the events does not affect the chance of the other event occurring.)

To illustrate the multiplication rule, let *A* be the event that a head occurs when a coin is tossed, and let *B* be the event that a 6 occurs when a die is tossed. The probability of heads on the coin is 1/2, and the probability of a 6 on the die is 1/6. Therefore, the probability of a head on the coin *and* a 6 on the die is equal to

$$1/2 \times 1/6 = 1/12$$

The calculation of more complicated probabilities usually requires the use of both the addition and multiplication rules. For example, suppose that Mr. A and Mr. B both fire at a target. The probability that A hits the target is given as 1/3, and the probability that B hits the target is given as 3/5. What is the probability that the target is hit exactly one time?

To solve this problem, we note that the desired result can occur in two mutually exclusive ways: (1) A hits the target, and B misses; and (2) B hits the target, and A misses. We note further that the probability that A misses the target is 2/3 (i.e., $1 - \frac{1}{3}$) and the probability that B misses the target is 2/5 (i.e., $1 - \frac{3}{5}$). The answer to the problem is then calculated as follows:

Probability that A hits *and* B misses:
$$1/3 \times 2/5 = 2/15 \text{ (multiplication rule)}$$
Probability that B hits *and* A misses:
$$3/5 \times 2/3 = 6/15 \text{ (multiplication rule)}$$
Probability that target is hit exactly once:
$$2/15 + 6/15 = 8/15 \text{ (addition rule)}$$

Law of Large Numbers

If a coin is tossed a large number of times, we expect that the proportion of heads obtained will be close to 1/2, which is the probability that a single toss results in heads. As more and more tosses are made, we expect that the proportion of heads will get closer and closer to 1/2.

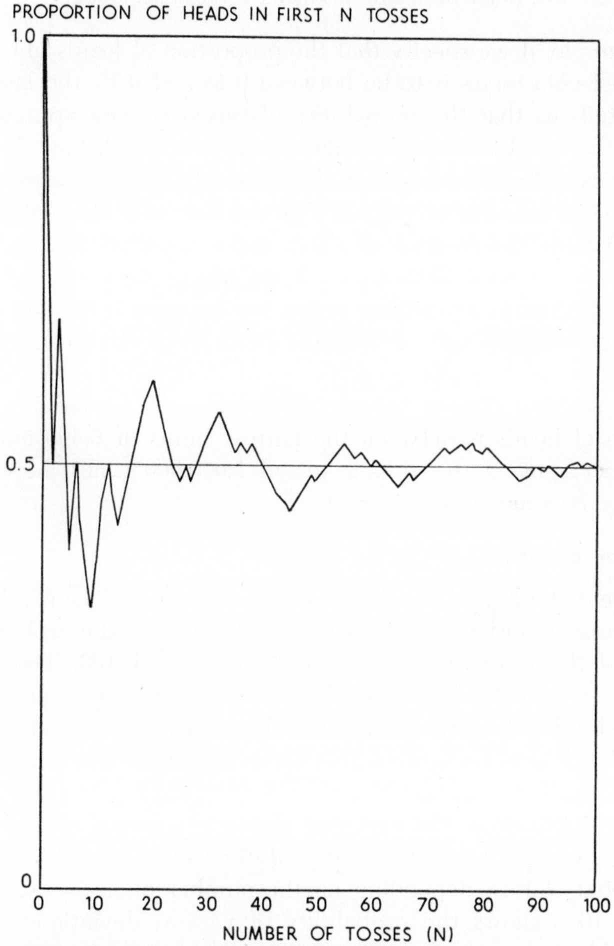

FIG. 10–1. Proportion of heads in sequence of one hundred coin tosses.

Figure 10–1 is a chart showing the results obtained by tossing a coin 100 times. It clearly shows the tendency of the proportion of heads to "settle down" at 1/2 as the number of tosses increases. Of course, there is no absolute guarantee that this will happen. For example, it is entirely possible that 100 tosses of a coin will result in 100 heads. The law of large numbers tells us, however, that as the number of tosses increases, the probability of a proportion of heads very much different from 1/2 becomes extremely unlikely. Following is an accurate statement of the law of large numbers in nontechnical language:

Law of Large Numbers. If p is the probability of success for a particular experiment, and more and more trials of the experiment are performed, the probability approaches certainty that the actual proportion of successes obtained will be close to p *within any specified degree of accuracy.*

For example, if we specify that the proportion of heads obtained in a sequence of coin tosses is to be between 0.45 and 0.55, the law of large numbers tells us that the probability of this occurring approaches certainty as the number of tosses increases. For example, on the basis of mathematical calculations, we can determine that the probability that the proportion of heads lies between 0.45 and 0.55 is 24.6 per cent if a coin is tossed 10 times, 72.9 per cent if a coin is tossed 100 times, and 99.9 per cent if a coin is tossed 1,000 times. If we specify that the proportion of heads is to be within a narrower range, say between 0.499 and 0.501, the law of large numbers tells us that the probability of this occurring also approaches certainty as the number of coin tosses increases still further. For example, if a coin is tossed 1,000 times, the probability that the proportion of heads is between the narrow limits of 0.499 and 0.501 is only 7.2 per cent. If the coin is tossed 1,000,000 times, however, this probability becomes 95.5 per cent.

Distribution of Insurance Claims

Suppose that a hypothetical life insurance company insures the lives of a certain number of persons in a single year, and that the probability that any one of the insureds will die in that year is 1/100. The insurance company will expect a certain number of claims (namely, 1 per cent of all the insureds), but its actual claims may be more or less than the expected number. The law of large numbers tells us that if the number of insureds is large enough, the actual claims will very likely show only a small relative deviation from the expected claims. By means of the theory of probability, we can calculate the probabilities of various deviations from the expected claims, depending on the number of insureds.

Figure 10–2 shows the probability of various deviations where the number of lives insured is 1,000, 10,000, and 100,000. If as few as 1,000 lives are insured, there is a good chance that actual claims will be relatively high or low compared to expected claims. This is indicated by the fact that in the "1,000 lives insured" section of the chart the bars in the left and right sections are almost as large as the bars in the center. Where 10,000 lives are insured, the bars are more prominent in the center of the chart, and there is more assurance that actual claims will be relatively

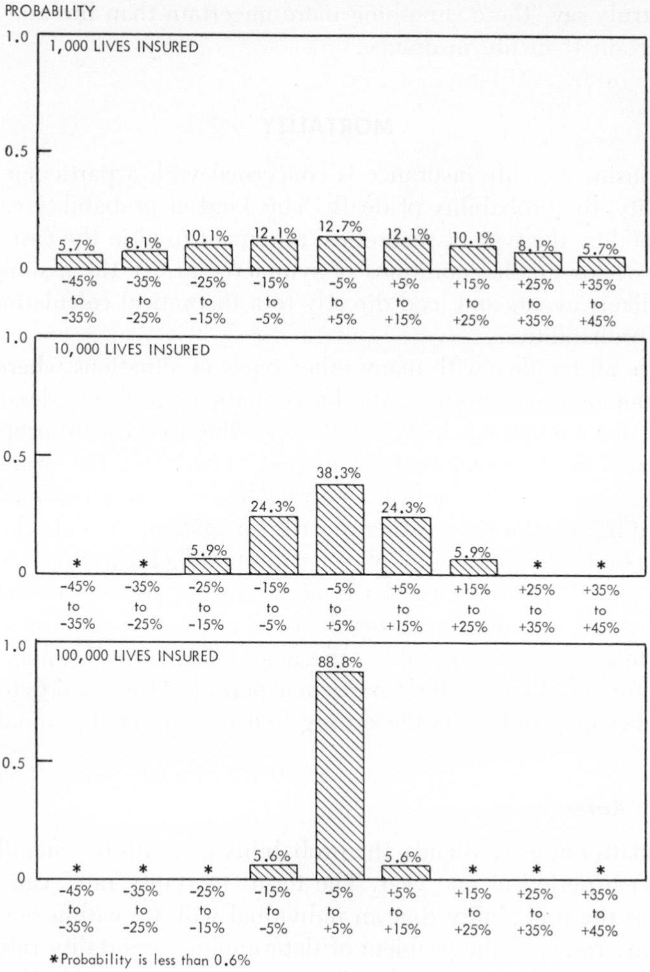

FIG. 10–2. Variation of actual claims from expected claims (for selected numbers of lives insured for one year where probability of death in that year is 0.01).

close to expected claims. The bottom section of Figure 10–2 shows that if 100,000 lives are insured, it is very likely that actual claims will be relatively close to expected claims.

In particular, Figure 10–2 shows that the probability of actual claims being within 5 per cent of expected claims is 12.7 per cent if 1,000 lives are insured, 38.3 per cent if 10,000 lives are insured, and 88.8 per cent if 100,000 lives are insured. Although not shown in the chart, the probability of actual claims being within 5 per cent of expected claims is greater than 99.99 per cent if 1,000,000 lives are insured.

Thanks to the theory of probability and to the law of large numbers, we can truly say "there is nothing more uncertain than life and nothing more certain than life insurance."

MORTALITY

The business of life insurance is concerned with a particular kind of probability, the probability of death. This kind of probability cannot be determined by the type of theoretical argument used in the case of coins or dice, where simple conditions of symmetry justify the assumption of equally likely events and lead directly to a theoretical calculation of the desired probabilities.

We are all familiar with many other types of situations where probabilities cannot be deduced on the basis of theoretical considerations. In many of these situations, however, it is possible to estimate probabilities on the basis of statistical analyses of past experience. For example, the probability that it will rain on a particular day in a given city can be estimated from historical weather records for that city. We also know that the probability that a baseball player will obtain a hit in his next time at bat can be estimated on the basis of his recent batting average.

Similarly, the solution to the problem of estimating the probability of death is to analyze past mortality experience. This means keeping track of a large number of people for a particular period of time and determining the number of people who die during that period and the number who survive.

Mortality Rates

As a matter of convenience, the probability of death is generally measured over a period of one year. The term "mortality rate" can then be defined as the probability that an individual will die within one year.

In many respects, the problem of determining a mortality rate is very similar to that of calculating a batting average. Let us assume that we are following a closed group of 1,000 people for a period of five years. Each person alive at the beginning of a year represents one "time at bat" and each death represents a "hit." The mortality rate for this group of people would be calculated in exactly the same way as we calculate a batting average, that is, by dividing the number of "hits" by the number of "times at bat."

This calculation is illustrated as shown in Table 10–1.

The average annual mortality rate for this group of 1,000 people over the five-year period would be 0.01022 (i.e., 50 ÷ 4,890). Another way of expressing this average annual mortality rate is to say that 10.22 out of each 1,000 people alive at the beginning of a year are expected to die within one year.

While this example illustrates the basic concept underlying mortality rates, it is an oversimplification of the actual problems involved in the determination of mortality rates. For example, in many cases people enter or leave the group under observation during the year and have to be counted as fractional "times at bat." In addition, the probability of death

TABLE 10–1

SIMPLE ILLUSTRATION OF MORTALITY RATE CALCULATION

Year	Number of People Alive at Beginning of Year ("Times at Bat")	Number of Deaths During Year ("Hits")
1	1,000	10
2	990	15
3	975	10
4	965	5
5	960	10
Total	4,890	50

depends on many factors, such as age, sex, occupation, state of health, and many others, and the actuary must determine mortality rates that will reflect these factors. The analysis of mortality experience is a far more complex problem than might appear at first glance, and requires considerable care and judgment on the part of the actuary.

Factors Affecting Mortality Rates

The first step in planning a mortality study is to specify the purpose for which the mortality rates are to be calculated. This will determine the particular group to be studied, the time period during which the group is to be observed, and the detailed classifications of the data that will be used in computing the actual mortality rates. Among the more important factors that must be considered are the following:

1. *General Population versus Insured Lives.* People who purchase life insurance policies are generally in the higher economic and social classes, receive a higher level of medical care, are judged to be in satisfactory health at the time they are insured (by the insurance company either through a medical examination or through other sources of information); as a result, they experience lower mortality than the population as a whole. *Mortality tables used by life insurance companies are practically always based on the mortality experience of insured lives rather than on the mortality experience of the population as a whole.*
2. *Life Insurance versus Annuity Mortality.* People who purchase annuity policies usually believe themselves to be in excellent health and expect to live a long time. Apparently, their judgments are quite good, on the average, because the mortality of persons who purchase annuity policies is substantially lower than the mortality of persons insured under life

insurance policies. A mortality table suitable for use in connection with life insurance policies would be entirely inappropriate for use in connection with annuity policies.

3. *Standard versus Substandard Insurance.* An insurance company underwrites all applications for new individual insurance policies, that is, it makes a judgment as to the degree of risk it will assume if it approves the application. If the applicant has a serious medical impairment, engages in a hazardous occupation or recreation, or appears in any other way to be subject to an extra mortality hazard, he is offered a substandard policy at an extra premium, or, in rare cases, is declined for insurance. It is obvious, then, that a mortality study must carefully distinguish between those who have been insured at an extra premium and those who have been accepted at standard rates.
4. *Age.* Age is one of the most significant factors affecting mortality. The probability of death is relatively high at birth, decreases to a low at about age 10, and then generally increases throughout the remainder of life. A mortality study invariably requires classification of the data by age.
5. *Sex.* Men may be stronger than women, but the fair sex exhibits mortality rates that are well below the corresponding rates for men. If a company charges the same premium rates for men and women, it would use mortality rates that represent an averaging of male and female mortality experience. However, many companies have recently introduced lower premium rates for women, reflecting their better mortality experience; and in these cases, separate studies of male and female mortality experience are required.
6. *Effects of Selection.* Because applicants for insurance are examined either medically or through other sources of information, mortality rates of insured lives are unusually low for a period of about five years after a policy is issued. For many purposes, it is desirable to have a mortality table that reflects the level of mortality reached after this initial period. Such a table is referred to as an "ultimate" mortality table, as it represents the ultimate level of mortality reached after the effects of the initial selection process have worn off.
7. *Period of Observation.* Because mortality has been improving regularly with advances in medical science and a generally higher quality of medical care, the period of observation must be a fairly recent one if it is to represent current mortality levels. It must also be a long enough period to include a sufficient body of data to produce statistically reliable results. If the period selected embraced any abnormal events such as a war, an epidemic, or an economic depression, the mortality rates derived from the study may be distorted unless steps are taken to adjust for the abnormality. For example, deaths resulting from an act of war are generally excluded from a mortality study.

The decisions that were made in the construction of the 1958 Commissioners Standard Ordinary Mortality Table (referred to as the 1958 CSO Table) provide a specific illustration of the foregoing considerations. This table was based on the mortality experience of lives *insured* under *standard ordinary* policies in fifteen large companies. It is an *ultimate table,* excluding experience during the first five policy years. The table is based on mortality experience during the period between 1950 and 1954 policy anniversaries, as this period provided a large volume of homogeneous data and was representative of recent experience. War deaths arising from the Korean War were excluded. The table is based on *combined male and female* experience, but the new legislation that accompanied the introduction of the table officially recognized lower female mortality by permitting, for females, the use of an age not more than three years younger than the actual age of the insured.

The completion of a mortality study along the lines described will produce observed mortality rates for each age based on the average experience of the companies included in the study. Two further steps are now required before these mortality rates can be used as the basis of a mortality table such as the 1958 CSO Table.

The observed mortality rates will normally not grade smoothly by age because of statistical fluctuations and will have to be adjusted by mathematical techniques (referred to as "graduation") to produce a set of mortality rates that grade smoothly by age and that are reasonably close to the observed rates.

The second step is to add appropriate "mortality margins," i.e., safety factors that reflect the margins required to cover the range of individual company variations in mortality rates, to these average experience mortality rates in order to produce mortality rates that will be "safe" for use by all companies in the industry.

Mortality Tables

A mortality table generally shows mortality rates for each age. Each mortality rate represents the probability that a person at that exact age will die during the following year.

In order to facilitate calculations involving the probability of dying or surviving during a period of years, two additional columns are usually included in the mortality table. These columns are designated as the "number living" and the "number dying."

Table 10–2 shows the 1958 CSO Mortality Table, an important modern table.[2] Column 1 of Table 10–2 shows the number of persons reaching each year of age out of 10 million persons starting at age zero. The figure of 10 million is an arbitrary one selected for convenience and is referred to as the "radix" of the table. Column 2 shows the number of persons dying

[2] It is not the purpose here to discuss exactly how life insurance companies use mortality tables. That will be done in later chapters. However, to illustrate the method by which premiums are calculated, the CSO Table will be used. Actually, the table is used by life insurance companies to calculate the reserve which they are required to hold by law and it is not used to calculate gross premiums.

TABLE 10–2

1958 COMMISSIONERS STANDARD ORDINARY MORTALITY TABLE

Age	(1) Number Living	(2) Number Dying	(3) Mortality Rate per 1,000	Age	(4) Number Living	(5) Number Dying	(6) Mortality Rate per 1,000
0	10,000,000	70,800	7.08	50	8,762,306	72,902	8.32
1	9,929,200	17,475	1.76	51	8,689,404	79,160	9.11
2	9,911,725	15,066	1.52	52	8,610,244	85,758	9.96
3	9,896,659	14,449	1.46	53	8,524,486	92,832	10.89
4	9,882,210	13,835	1.40	54	8,431,654	100,337	11.90
5	9,868,375	13,322	1.35	55	8,331,317	108,307	13.00
6	9,855,053	12,812	1.30	56	8,223,010	116,849	14.21
7	9,842,241	12,401	1.26	57	8,106,161	125,970	15.54
8	9,829,840	12,091	1.23	58	7,980,191	135,663	17.00
9	9,817,749	11,879	1.21	59	7,844,528	145,830	18.59
10	9,805,870	11,865	1.21	60	7,698,698	156,592	20.34
11	9,794,005	12,047	1.23	61	7,542,106	167,736	22.24
12	9,781,958	12,325	1.26	62	7,374,370	179,271	24.31
13	9,769,633	12,896	1.32	63	7,195,099	191,174	26.57
14	9,756,737	13,562	1.39	64	7,003,925	203,394	29.04
15	9,743,175	14,225	1.46	65	6,800,531	215,917	31.75
16	9,728,950	14,983	1.54	66	6,584,614	228,749	34.74
17	9,713,967	15,737	1.62	67	6,355,865	241,777	38.04
18	9,698,230	16,390	1.69	68	6,114,088	254,835	41.68
19	9,681,840	16,846	1.74	69	5,859,253	267,241	45.61
20	9,664,994	17,300	1.79	70	5,592,012	278,426	49.79
21	9,647,694	17,655	1.83	71	5,313,586	287,731	54.15
22	9,630,039	17,912	1.86	72	5,025,855	294,766	58.65
23	9,612,127	18,167	1.89	73	4,731,089	299,289	63.26
24	9,593,960	18,324	1.91	74	4,431,800	301,894	68.12
25	9,575,636	18,481	1.93	75	4,129,906	303,011	73.37
26	9,557,155	18,732	1.96	76	3,826,895	303,014	79.18
27	9,538,423	18,981	1.99	77	3,523,881	301,997	85.70
28	9,519,442	19,324	2.03	78	3,221,884	299,829	93.06
29	9,500,118	19,760	2.08	79	2,922,055	295,683	101.19
30	9,480,358	20,193	2.13	80	2,626,372	288,848	109.98
31	9,460,165	20,718	2.19	81	2,337,524	278,983	119.35
32	9,439,447	21,239	2.25	82	2,058,541	265,902	129.17
33	9,418,208	21,850	2.32	83	1,792,639	249,858	139.38
34	9,396,358	22,551	2.40	84	1,542,781	231,433	150.01
35	9,373,807	23,528	2.51	85	1,311,348	211,311	161.14
36	9,350,279	24,685	2.64	86	1,100,037	190,108	172.82
37	9,325,594	26,112	2.80	87	909,929	168,455	185.13
38	9,299,482	27,991	3.01	88	741,474	146,997	198.25
39	9,271,491	30,132	3.25	89	594,477	126,303	212.46
40	9,241,359	32,622	3.53	90	468,174	106,809	228.14
41	9,208,737	35,362	3.84	91	361,365	88,813	245.77
42	9,173,375	38,253	4.17	92	272,552	72,480	265.93
43	9,135,122	41,382	4.53	93	200,072	57,881	289.30
44	9,093,740	44,741	4.92	94	142,191	45,026	316.66
45	9,048,999	48,412	5.35	95	97,165	34,128	351.24
46	9,000,587	52,473	5.83	96	63,037	25,250	400.56
47	8,948,114	56,910	6.36	97	37,787	18,456	488.42
48	8,891,204	61,794	6.95	98	19,331	12,916	668.15
49	8,829,410	67,104	7.60	99	6,415	6,415	1,000.00

during each year of age out of the original 10 million. The figures in columns 1 and 2 are computed as follows:

(*a*) Number living at age zero:	10,000,000 (radix)
(*b*) Mortality rate at age zero:	0.00708
(*c*) Number dying between age zero and age one:	(*a*) × (*b*) = 70,800
(*d*) Number living at age one:	(*a*) − (*c*) = 9,929,200
(*e*) Mortality rate at age one:	0.00176
(*f*) Number dying between age one and age two:	(*d*) × (*e*) = 17,475
(*g*) Number living at age two:	(*d*) − (*f*) = 9,911,725
(*h*) And so forth.	

Many probabilities can be easily computed from the mortality table shown in Table 10–2. The probability that a person aged zero will survive to age 15 is obtained by noting that of the 10,000,000 persons starting at age zero, 9,743,175 reach age 15; hence the probability is 9,743,175/10,000,000 = 0.97432. Similarly, the probability that a person aged five will survive to age 85 is 1,311,348/9,868,375 = 0.13288.

The probability that a person aged 20 will die between the ages of 85 and 86 is equal to 211,311/9,664,994 = 0.02186, since the table shows that 211,311 persons will die between ages 85 and 86 out of the 9,664,994 who are alive at age 20. A final illustration is the probability that a person aged 10 will die before age 65. Table 10–2 shows that of 9,805,870 persons living at age 10, only 6,800,531 survive to age 65. Hence, there will be 3,005,339 (i.e., 9,805,870 − 6,800,531) deaths prior to age 65, and the probability that a person aged 10 will die before reaching age 65 is 0.30648 (i.e., 3,005,339/9,805,870).

Expectation of Life

According to the 1958 CSO Table, the expectation of life at age zero is 68.3 years. This figure is computed from the mortality table by finding the total number of years lived by all 10,000,000 persons starting at age zero, and dividing that number by 10,000,000 to obtain an "average number of years lived per person," more commonly referred to as the expectation of life. The total number of years lived is obtained by noting that 70,800 persons will die between ages zero and one and live one-half year, on the average; that 17,475 persons will die between the ages of one and two and live 1½ years, on the average; and so on throughout the remainder of the table. We then combine these results to obtain the total number of years lived by all persons, namely:

$$(70{,}800 \times \tfrac{1}{2}) + (17{,}475 \times 1\tfrac{1}{2}) + (15{,}066 \times 2\tfrac{1}{2}) + \ldots$$
$$+ (18{,}456 \times 97\tfrac{1}{2}) + (12{,}916 \times 98\tfrac{1}{2}) + (6{,}415 \times 99\tfrac{1}{2}) = 682{,}966{,}865 \text{ years.}$$

Dividing this figure by 10,000,000, we obtain the figure of 68.3 years for the expectation of life at age zero.

The expectation of life for a person at an age other than zero would be computed in similar fashion. For example, the expectation of life for a person aged 50 is 23.63 years, obtained as follows from the figures in Table 10–2:

$$(72{,}902 \times \tfrac{1}{2}) + (79{,}160 \times 1\tfrac{1}{2}) + (85{,}758 \times 2\tfrac{1}{2}) + \ldots$$
$$+ (18{,}456 \times 47\tfrac{1}{2}) + (12{,}916 \times 48\tfrac{1}{2}) + (6{,}415 \times 49\tfrac{1}{2}) = 207{,}052{,}871 \text{ years.}$$
$$207{,}052{,}871 \text{ years} \div 8{,}762{,}306 = 23.63 \text{ years}$$

The expectation of life is a convenient index of the general mortality level indicated by a particular mortality table and is useful in comparing the mortality levels of different tables.[3] However, the expectation of life is an average figure and, as such, cannot be used to determine the life expectancy of a particular individual. Similarly, the expectation of life cannot be used by the actuary in his calculations of premium rates, reserves, and other values. Because of the importance of interest earnings, the actuary also must take account of the exact time when each premium dollar will be received and each benefit dollar will be paid. This leads directly to the subject of the next section, "Money Concepts."

MONEY CONCEPTS

Straight life insurance policies call for a level premium to be paid throughout life. Because the rate of mortality generally increases with age, the level premiums are greater than the amount of death benefits paid in the early years and less than the amount of death benefits paid in the later years. The excess funds generated in the early years will be needed in the later years to augment the level premiums paid at that time. These funds that a life insurance company holds do not remain idle, but are invested to produce a return to the company in the form of "investment income" or "interest earnings" that are used to reduce the cost of insurance to policyowners.

Interest earnings are a very important source of income to life insurance companies, as evidenced by the fact that they accounted for about one fifth of all income received by United States life insurance companies during 1962.[4] It is obvious that the calculation of a premium rate must take account of interest. The means of doing this rests on the theory of interest.

Accumulated Value of Money

Anyone who works with interest theory soon develops a concept of money at work very similar to the picture of a snowball growing in size as it rolls through the snow. He thinks of each dollar as something that grows and grows as it passes through time into the future. For example,

---

[3] See Appendix E for death rates and expectation of life under various mortality and annuity tables.

[4] Institute of Life Insurance, *Life Insurance Fact Book* (New York, 1963).

consider a dollar that is deposited in a bank at a 3 per cent interest rate, compounded annually. This means that at the end of one year the bank will credit $0.03 interest, and the depositor will have $1.03 in his account. If that amount is left on deposit for another year, the bank will again credit 3 per cent interest, but this time on the larger amount of $1.03. Hence the interest credited at the end of the second year will be 3 per cent of $1.03, or $0.0309, and the amount on deposit will have grown to $1.0609 ($1.00 + $0.03 + $0.0309). Table 10–3 shows the results of continuing this process for 50 years.

TABLE 10–3

GROWTH OF $1.00 LEFT ON DEPOSIT AT 3 PER CENT INTEREST COMPOUNDED ANNUALLY

Year	(1) Amount on Deposit at Beginning of Year	(2) Interest Credited 3% × (1)	(3) Amount on Deposit at End of Year (1) + (2)
1	$1.0000	$0.0300	$1.0300
2	1.0300	0.0309	1.0609
3	1.0609	0.0318	1.0927
4	1.0927	0.0328	1.1255
5	1.1255	0.0338	1.1593
6	1.1593	0.0348	1.1941
7	1.1941	0.0358	1.2299
8	1.2299	0.0369	1.2668
9	1.2668	0.0380	1.3048
10	1.3048	0.0391	1.3439
15	1.5126	0.0454	1.5580
20	1.7535	0.0526	1.8061
25	2.0328	0.0610	2.0938
30	2.3566	0.0707	2.4273
35	2.7319	0.0820	2.8139
40	3.1670	0.0950	3.2620
45	3.6715	0.1101	3.7816
50	4.2562	0.1277	4.3839

The rapid growth of a dollar at 3 per cent interest is apparent—it has doubled in 25 years and more than quadrupled in 50 years. While these may seem like long periods of time, many life insurance contracts are in force for over 50 years. For this reason, the rate of interest is a very important ingredient in the calculation of premiums, and a difference of as little as one percentage point in the interest rate will affect the premium rate significantly. Figure 10–3 compares the accumulated value of $1.00 for several different interest rates and shows the importance of a one percentage point differential in the interest rate.

Discounted Value of Money

Table 10–3 shows that $1.00 accumulates to $1.8061 at the end of 20 years at 3 per cent interest. Hence, $0.5537 at 3 per cent interest accumulates to $1.00 at the end of 20 years ($0.5537 × 1.8061). We say, then, that "under a 3 per cent interest assumption, $0.5537 today is equivalent

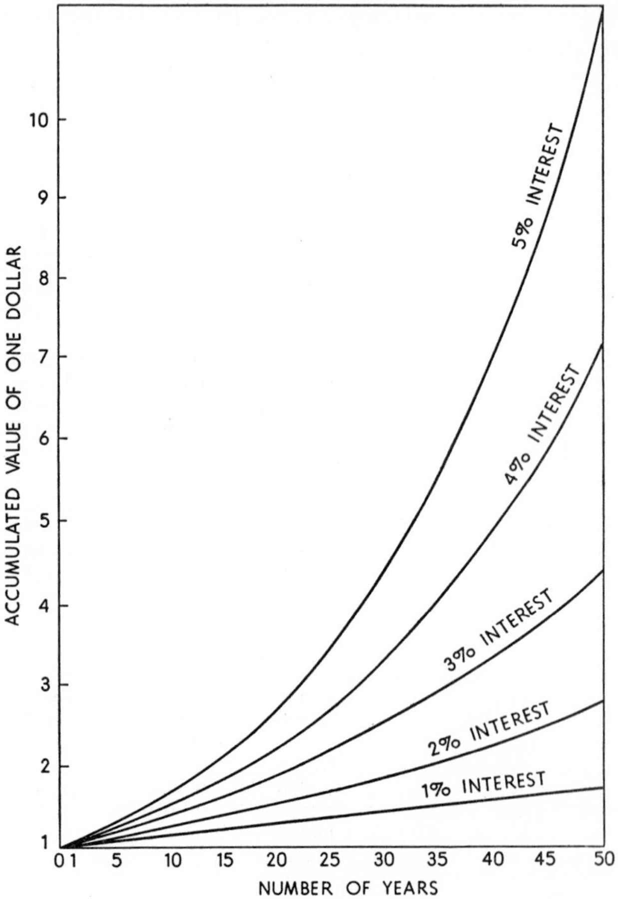

FIG. 10–3. Accumulated value of $1.00 at end of various years at selected interest rates.

to $1.00 in 20 years," or "the discounted value of $1.00 payable in 20 years, at 3 per cent interest, is $0.5537." Discounting is the reverse process of accumulating. When we think about accumulating a dollar deposited now, we picture the dollar growing as it moves into the future; when we think about discounting a dollar payable in the future, we picture the dollar shrinking as it comes back to the present. Table 10–4 shows the

TABLE 10–4

DISCOUNTED VALUE OF $1.00 PAYABLE AT THE END OF VARIOUS YEARS AT SELECTED INTEREST RATES

Year	Interest Rate				
	1 Per Cent	2 Per Cent	3 Per Cent	4 Per Cent	5 Per Cent
1	$0.9901	$0.9804	$0.9709	$0.9615	$0.9524
2	0.9803	0.9612	0.9426	0.9246	0.9070
3	0.9706	0.9423	0.9151	0.8890	0.8638
4	0.9610	0.9238	0.8885	0.8548	0.8227
5	0.9515	0.9057	0.8626	0.8219	0.7835
6	0.9420	0.8880	0.8375	0.7903	0.7462
7	0.9327	0.8706	0.8131	0.7599	0.7107
8	0.9235	0.8535	0.7894	0.7307	0.6768
9	0.9143	0.8368	0.7664	0.7026	0.6446
10	0.9053	0.8203	0.7441	0.6756	0.6139
20	0.8195	0.6730	0.5537	0.4564	0.3769
30	0.7419	0.5521	0.4120	0.3083	0.2314
40	0.6717	0.4529	0.3066	0.2083	0.1420
50	0.6080	0.3715	0.2281	0.1407	0.0872

discounted value, for several interest rates, of $1.00 payable at various times in the future.[5]

Annuities

An annuity is a series of payments made at certain specified intervals. Usually, the payment is a constant amount, and the intervals are regular, as, for example, $10 payable at the end of each month for five years, or $2,000 payable at the end of each year for ten years. The annuity payments may be certain, or they may be contingent on a particular person being alive. The former are called "annuities certain"; the latter are called "life annuities." The theory of annuities plays an important role in actuarial calculations because the premium payments for a life insurance policy constitute an annuity *to* the insurance company.

Consider an annuity certain of $1.00 per year, payable at the end of each of the next five years. This annuity is not worth $5.00 today because each of the dollars payable in the future is worth less today; that is, each must be discounted back to the present. The amount of discount will, of course, depend on the rate of interest. Figure 10–4 illustrates the method of calculating the discounted value of an annuity at 3 per cent interest. Each of the discounted values shown in Figure 10–4 can be found in Table 10–4 under the 3 per cent column. The sum of the discounted values, $4.5797, is the discounted value of the entire annuity, or, as it is frequently called, the present value of the annuity.

[5] See Appendix F for selected compound interest and discount functions.

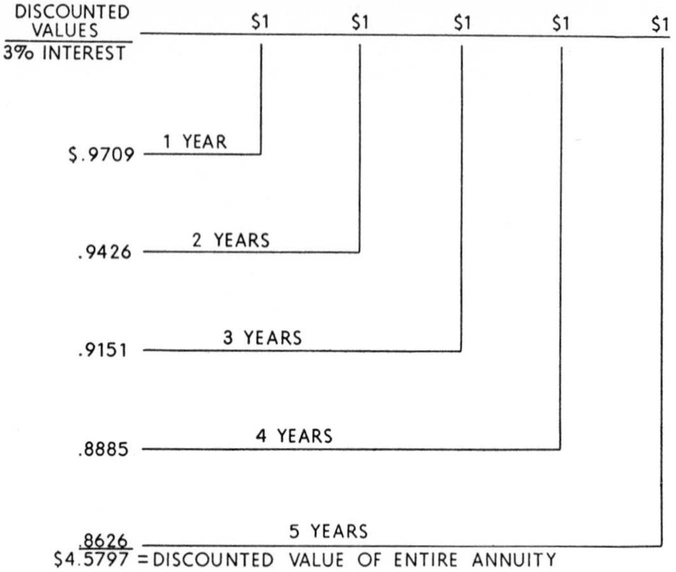

FIG. 10–4. Computation of discounted value of an annuity certain at 3 per cent interest.

Another way of interpreting the present value of an annuity is to note that if the $4.5797 were deposited in a bank at 3 per cent interest, and $1.00 were drawn from the account at the end of each year for five years, the account would end up at exactly zero when the last dollar was drawn. The way this would work out is shown in Table 10–5, which is sometimes referred to as an amortization schedule.

Frequently, it is necessary to find the amount of regular periodic payment which is provided by a single sum of money. For example, we might want to determine the payment which could be made at the end of each of the next five years, in exchange for a single sum of $1.00 paid now, if money is worth 3 per cent. From calculations already made in this

TABLE 10–5

AMORTIZATION SCHEDULE FOR AN ANNUITY AT 3 PER CENT INTEREST

Year	(1) Amount on Deposit at Beginning of Year	(2) Interest Credited 3% × (1)	(3) Amount on Deposit at End of Year before Annuity Payment (1) + (2)	(4) Annuity Payment at End of Year	(5) Amount on Deposit at End of Year after Annuity Payment (3) − (4)
1	$4.5797	$0.1374	$4.7171	$1.00	$3.7171
2	3.7171	0.1115	3.8286	1.00	2.8286
3	2.8286	0.0849	2.9135	1.00	1.9135
4	1.9135	0.0574	1.9709	1.00	0.9709
5	0.9709	0.0291	1.0000	1.00	0.0000

section, we know that a single sum of $4.5797 would provide, at 3 per cent interest, a $1.00 payment at the end of each of the next five years. For a single sum of $1.00, then, the annual payment provided would be equal to $1.00 ÷ 4.5797, or $0.2184.

COMBINATION OF MORTALITY AND INTEREST

Interest theory tells us that a dollar payable at a specified time in the future is worth less than a dollar now. This is true even if the future payment of the dollar is a certainty, and we call the process of obtaining the present value of the dollar "discounting for interest." Suppose now that the payment of the dollar in the future is not a certainty, but that it depends on some insured being alive at that time. It is apparent in this case that discounting for interest alone is not sufficient. It is necessary to reduce the present value of the future dollar still further, reflecting the probability that the insured will be alive to pay it. This is referred to as "discounting for mortality."

For example, suppose a dollar is payable in 10 years if a person now aged 80 is alive at that time. From Table 10–4, we know that discounting for interest at a 3 per cent rate reduces the present value of the future dollar to $0.744. From the mortality table (Table 10–2), we note that the probability that a person aged 80 will live 10 years is 468,174/2,626,372 = 0.178. Discounting for mortality only, we would say that the present value of the future dollar is $0.178. However, it is necessary to discount for both interest and mortality, and we find the present value of the future dollar to be $0.744 × 0.178 = $0.132.

If we ignore expenses and calculate the net premium rate for a life insurance policy, the present value of all future premiums will be equal to the present value of all future benefits, where the present values are obtained by discounting for both interest and mortality. In the form of an equation, this reads:

Present value of future premiums = Present value of future benefits

The way in which this equation works out is illustrated in Table 10–6 for a $1,000 whole life policy issued at age 80.

Column 1 shows the level net annual premium[6] which is paid at the beginning of each year if the insured is then alive. Columns 2 and 3 show the discounts for interest and mortality, while column 4 shows the present value of each future premium payment. The figures which appear on the line for attained age 90 are those used in the illustration earlier in this section. The total of $835.30 at the bottom of column 4 is the present value of all future premiums.

---

[6] The method of calculating this premium will be covered in the next chapter.

Column 5 shows the benefit payable (per survivor) in each future year. For example, the proportion of survivors who die between ages 90 and 91 is 0.22814, which is obtained from column 3 of Table 10–2. Since the death benefit is $1,000, the benefit per survivor is $1,000 × 0.22814 = $228.14, the figure which appears in column 5 of Table 10–6 on the line for attained age 90. The figures in column 6, the discounts for interest, are slightly smaller than the corresponding figures in column 2 because

TABLE 10–6

$1,000 Whole Life Policy Issued at Age 80

(Based on 1958 CSO Mortality Table and 3 Per Cent Interest)

Attained Age	Premiums				Benefits			
	Level Annual Premium (1)	Discount for Interest (2)	Discount for Mortality (3)	Present Value of Premium (4) [(1) × (2) × (3)]	Death Benefit (per survivor) (5)	Discount for Interest (6)	Discount for Mortality (7)	Present Value of Benefit (8) [(5) × (6) × (7)]
80........	$147.72	1.0000	1.0000	$147.72	$109.98	0.9709	1.0000	$106.78
81........	147.72	0.9709	0.8900	127.64	119.35	0.9426	0.8900	100.12
82........	147.72	0.9426	0.7838	109.14	129.17	0.9151	0.7838	92.65
83........	147.72	0.9151	0.6826	92.27	139.38	0.8885	0.6826	84.53
84........	147.72	0.8885	0.5874	77.10	150.01	0.8626	0.5874	76.01
85........	147.72	0.8626	0.4993	63.62	161.14	0.8375	0.4993	67.38
86........	147.72	0.8375	0.4188	51.81	172.82	0.8131	0.4188	58.85
87........	147.72	0.8131	0.3465	41.62	185.13	0.7894	0.3465	50.64
88........	147.72	0.7894	0.2823	32.92	198.25	0.7664	0.2823	42.89
89........	147.72	0.7664	0.2263	25.62	212.46	0.7441	0.2263	35.78
90........	147.72	0.7441	0.1783	19.60	228.14	0.7224	0.1783	29.39
91........	147.72	0.7224	0.1376	14.68	245.77	0.7014	0.1376	23.72
92........	147.72	0.7014	0.1038	10.75	265.93	0.6810	0.1038	18.80
93........	147.72	0.6810	0.0762	7.67	289.30	0.6661	0.0762	14.68
94........	147.72	0.6661	0.0541	5.32	316.66	0.6419	0.0541	11.00
95........	147.72	0.6419	0.0370	3.51	351.24	0.6232	0.0370	8.10
96........	147.72	0.6232	0.0240	2.21	400.56	0.6050	0.0240	5.82
97........	147.72	0.6050	0.0144	1.29	488.42	0.5874	0.0144	4.13
98........	147.72	0.5874	0.0074	0.64	668.15	0.5703	0.0074	2.82
99........	147.72	0.5703	0.0024	0.20	1,000.00	0.5537	0.0024	1.33
	Present value of premiums = $835.30*				Present value of benefits = $835.30*			

*Totals adjusted by $0.03 (premiums) and $0.12 (benefits) to correct for rounding differences.

we have assumed that the death benefit is paid at the end of the year, whereas the premiums are paid at the beginning of the year; hence the death benefits are discounted one more year than the premiums. Column 7 is the same as column 3, and column 8 shows the present value of each future benefit. The total of $835.30 at the foot of column 8 is the present value of all future benefits, and is precisely the same as the present value of all future premiums.

Table 10–6 shows that the net premium (disregarding any loading for expenses) reflects a blending of probability, mortality, and interest theory.

Each of these ingredients has been included in its proper place and has been combined with the other ingredients according to a precise mathematical recipe. The result is that, based on given assumptions as to mortality and interest, an insurance contract represents an equal exchange between the insured and the company. The present value of future benefits is the insured's expectation, while the present value of future net premiums is the company's expectation; it is the actuarial blending process which makes these two expectations precisely equal.

SELECTED REFERENCES

LARSON, ROBERT E., and GAUMNITZ, ERWIN A. *Life Insurance Mathematics.* New York: John Wiley & Sons, Inc., 1951.

TODHUNTER, ISSAC. *History of the Mathematical Theory of Probability from the Time of Pascal to That of Laplace.* New York: Chelsea Publishing Co., 1949.

Chapter 11

PREMIUMS—NET AND GROSS

BY JAMES A. ATTWOOD

A life insurance company collects premiums in exchange for promises to make payments upon death and survival under various forms of life insurance and annuity contracts. Whether a company gains, loses, or breaks even on its promises depends upon the adequacy of the premiums collected by the company in relation to the experience which actually occurs. Premiums must be large enough not only to cover a company's basic promises, but also to meet its expenses and other financial requirements.

Since premiums to be collected are determined in advance, future experience must be estimated in calculating premiums. Such estimates are based upon past experience and expected future trends. The assumption is made that past experience, adjusted for probable changes, provides a reasonable estimate of future experience. Experience fluctuates from year to year, both because of changing conditions and because of chance fluctuations. The reliability of past experience is enhanced when it is based upon a large body of experience. The chances of wide experience fluctuations are reduced when the results of past experience are applied to insurance for a large number of persons. Standard mortality tables usually include a specific mortality contingency margin. This is both a provision for unforeseen fluctuation in mortality and a factor for possible variation in mortality rates among various companies.[1]

UNDERLYING FACTORS AND ASSUMPTIONS

The Mortality Table

The mortality table is the basic tool used to measure probable future experience as to death and survival. Mortality rates are based upon past experience. The "number living" and "number dying" columns, which are derived from the mortality rates of a mortality table, convert past experi-

[1] See Chapter 10 for analysis of probability, mortality, and money concepts involved in pricing life insurance.

ence into a useful form. Although hypothetical in themselves, these columns are used to derive various proportions, or probabilities. For example, the proportion of persons now a certain age who will die within one year, or within any number of years, can be estimated. Also, the proportion of persons now a certain age who will survive to another age can be estimated.

In this chapter the Commissioners 1958 Standard Ordinary Mortality Table will be used in numerical illustrations. This is the mortality table prescribed in most states for minimum valuation and nonforfeiture standards for policies issued after January 1, 1966. In practice, this table is *not* used directly to determine premium rates. In the case of nonparticipating premiums, the table used will be one constructed from a company's own experience or a table representative of the company's experience. Also, it is a table that includes the effect of lower mortality in early policy years resulting from underwriting selection. Further, it is usually a table without margins for fluctuations in experience such as are contained in the 1958 CSO Table. In the case of participating insurance, some companies use tables constructed in a manner analogous to those used for nonparticipating insurance. Others use the table specified for statutory uses, but with certain adjustments in other premium factors to produce a desired level of premium rates.

Basic Premium Factors

There are three basic factors involved in the calculation of premiums—mortality, interest, and expenses. The calculation of premiums requires assumptions as to probable future experience with respect to each of these basic factors. Since contracts issued by life insurance companies may extend for long periods of time, these assumptions must be conservative. The premium rates produced must be adequate to assure the financial soundness of the company. On the other hand, they cannot be so high that they discourage the purchase of the company's contracts.

There is greater conservatism in premium rate assumptions for contracts issued on a participating basis than for those issued on a nonparticipating basis. Nonparticipating premiums are based on the expected future experience, with a planned margin for profit and contingencies. Participating premiums are purposely set at levels higher than the company expects will be necessary. The margin in the premium is returned to policyholders in the form of dividends. Thus, premiums for nonparticipating contracts must be established on the basis of more realistic assumptions, and the balance between adequacy and competition is much finer. Under nonparticipating contracts the cost of insurance to the policyholder is determined directly by the premium rates charged; under participating insurance the premiums charged, less dividends paid, determine the cost of insurance.

Calculation of Premiums

The premium charged by a life insurance company, and that paid by the policyholder for the promises made, is called the *gross premium.* Conceptually, there are two basic steps in calculating gross premiums. First, the factors of mortality and interest are combined to produce what is called the *net premium.* Second, the gross premium is derived from the net premium by adding a factor called "loading." Loading is the provision for expenses. It also usually includes a provision for contingencies, a margin for future dividends in the case of participating insurance, and a margin for profit in the case of a stock company.

In the case of nonparticipating insurance, the net premium provides for the benefit payments only. This is because the mortality table used includes the effect of underwriting selection and contains no margins as are contained in a standard mortality table like the 1958 CSO Table. No part of the net premium theoretically is available for expenses and contingencies. As previously indicated, a table without the effect of selection included, and with a margin, may be used in the case of participating insurance. Such margins supplement the loading under participating insurance premiums and are available for the payment of expenses and dividends, as well as providing a margin for contingencies.

In illustrating how premiums are calculated, it will be assumed that premiums are paid at the beginning of the policy year and that death benefit payments are made at the end of the year of death. These assumptions simplify the explanation; often, they are made in actual practice to simplify calculations. The first step will be to examine the calculation of net premiums, following which the various types of loading formulas used to develop gross premiums will be described. For convenience, the Commissioners 1958 Standard Ordinary Mortality Table and 2½ per cent interest will be assumed as the mortality and interest basis for the net premiums in the numerical illustrations used throughout this chapter. This is the basis used today by a number of life insurance companies for newly issued participating contracts. It is not so used for nonparticipating insurance. Although the assumptions vary, the method of calculation of net premiums is the same whether the policy is participating or nonparticipating.

The calculation of premiums made in this chapter is intended solely to illustrate the basic principles involved. In practice, methods are much more refined. The determination of the loading is the most complicated part of the calculation. It is made up of a number of different expense factors, each intended to represent a particular class of expenses. In addition, factors for fluctuations in experience, for dividends, and for profit may be added. All of these factors must be considered in light of the margins available in the assumptions used for determining the net premium. The methods of determination of these factors are beyond the scope of this chapter.

The determination of premium rates is often closely related to the fixing of nonforfeiture benefits, especially for nonparticipating insurance. In practice, it is customary to develop asset share calculations to produce the amount of funds anticipated at various points in the policy's duration to make sure that the cash values are properly, but not redundantly, covered. Adjustments in the preliminary loading formulas or in the cash values themselves may be made if the interrelationship is not satisfactory. This process will be described further in Chapter 13. In participating insurance, refined analysis of expenses and their distribution finds its expression in the distribution of dividends; accordingly, the premium-loading formulas may not be as complicated as for nonparticipating premiums.

Both net and gross premium rates vary according to amount of insurance, kind of policy, and the age of the person insured. Also, some companies charge different premium rates for men and women, this being almost universal with respect to annuity contracts. Insurance companies which offer life insurance to persons classified as substandard charge different premiums to these persons than to those classified as standard. In the calculations that follow, no distinction is made as to sex, and the premiums illustrated are for persons classified as standard.

THE NET SINGLE PREMIUM

Life insurance may be purchased by a single premium, by annual premiums, or by premiums paid more frequently than annually. Periodic premiums may be payable for life or for a limited period of years, depending upon the terms of the policy. The calculation of the net single premium is the first step in the calculation of premiums paid on any basis.

One-Year Term Insurance

Consider the net single premium for the promise of an insurance company to pay $1,000 if a person aged 35 dies within one year. This is a one-year term insurance contract, and the $1,000 will be paid only if death occurs within the one-year term of the contract. To calculate the premium for such a policy, it is necessary to estimate the probability that the $1,000 will be paid. Since it is assumed that the premium will be paid at the beginning of the year and the benefit, if it becomes payable, will be paid at the end of the year, the premium collected will be available for investment and thus earn interest for one year. The steps in the calculation of the net single premium are as follows:

1. According to the 1958 CSO Table, out of 9,373,807 persons living at age 35, 23,528 are expected to die before reaching age 36. The propor-

tion of deaths expected is 23,528 divided by 9,373,807. The probability of death is also 23,528 divided by 9,373,807, or 0.00251.

2. If $1,000 is needed at the end of the year for deaths which occur during the year, the amount needed at the beginning of the year for each such payment is the discounted or present value of $1,000 payable at the end of one year. The present value of 1 payable at the end of one year (at 2½ per cent interest) is 0.975610. Thus, the present value of $1,000 payable at the end of one year (at 2½ per cent interest) is $1,000 times 0.975610, or $975.61.
3. The net single premium is obtained by multiplying the probability of death during the year by the present value of the $1,000 benefit, that is, 0.00251 times $975.61, or $2.45.

This calculation of the net single premium for a one-year term insurance contract issued to a person aged 35 may be summarized as follows:

$$\frac{23{,}528}{9{,}373{,}807} \times \$1{,}000 \times 0.975610 = \$2.45$$

Or, stated in words, the net single premium for a one-year term insurance policy equals the probability of death during the one-year term, times the face amount, times the present value of 1 payable at the end of one year.

Five-Year Term Insurance

The basic principles of calculation of the net single premium for a five-year term insurance contract are the same except that instead of dealing with the cost of one year's insurance, the total of the separate costs of five years' insurance must be used. The probability of death during the various years of insurance, multiplied by the amounts of insurance, with the application of appropriate present value factors, will give the cost of insurance for the various years of insurance, and the total of these will give the net single premium for the contract. For example, the calculation of the net single premium for a five-year term insurance contract of $1,000 issued to a person aged 35, using the 1958 CSO Table and a 2½ per cent interest factor, would be as follows:

$$\frac{23{,}528}{9{,}373{,}807} \times \$1{,}000 \times 0.975610 = \$\ 2.449$$

$$\frac{24{,}685}{9{,}373{,}807} \times \$1{,}000 \times 0.951814 = 2.507$$

$$\frac{26{,}112}{9{,}373{,}807} \times \$1{,}000 \times 0.928599 = 2.587$$

$$\frac{27{,}991}{9{,}373{,}807} \times \$1{,}000 \times 0.905951 = 2.705$$

$$\frac{30{,}132}{9{,}373{,}807} \times \$1{,}000 \times 0.883854 = \underline{2.841}$$

$$\text{Net single premium} = \$13.09$$

The net single premium for a five-year term insurance policy is less than the total of net single premiums which would be paid for five one-year term insurance policies (sometimes called yearly renewable term insurance). This is explained in part by the fact that under a five-year term insurance policy the company earns interest on the second, third, fourth, and fifth years' cost of insurance for more than one year. Under yearly renewable term insurance, the cost of each year's insurance earns interest for one year only.

There is another factor in the comparison of the net single premium for a five-year term insurance policy with five yearly renewable term insurance premiums. Under the renewable term alternative, premiums are not collected for the balance of the five years from those who die during the five-year period. Under the five-year term insurance alternative, the single premium is collected from all persons—those who live and those who die—and this reduces the premium charged. This is shown clearly in the probability involved in the third year of insurance in the above calculation. This (26,112 divided by 9,373,807) represents the probability that a person aged 35 will die between ages 37 and 38. The net single premium for the third year of insurance under the yearly renewable term insurance alternative involves the probability that a person aged 37 will die between ages 37 and 38 (that is, 26,112 divided by 9,325,594). This latter probability is greater than the former, as is true in all years except the first, and this explains further the higher total premium for the yearly renewable term alternative.

Whole Life Insurance

Under a whole life insurance contract, the insurance company promises to pay the face amount on death whenever it occurs. Since death is a certainty, the payment of the face amount is a certainty. Only the time of payment is uncertain. In effect, a whole life insurance contract is a term insurance policy with the last year of insurance starting at the last age of the mortality table (age 99 in the 1958 CSO Table).

The net single premium for a whole life insurance contract is calculated in the same manner as that for a term insurance contract with the last year of insurance starting at the last age of the mortality table.

Endowment Insurance

Under an endowment insurance contract, the insurance company promises to pay the face amount on death if it occurs during the term covered, or at the end of such term if the person survives to that time. Endowment insurance is a combination of term insurance and a payment at the end of the term if the person survives. A payment contingent on survival to the end of a term is called a *pure* endowment. The net single premium for an endowment policy is, therefore, the sum of that for a term insurance contract and that for a pure endowment.

The net single premium for a pure endowment is based upon the probability of survival, the face amount, and the appropriate present value factor for the interest rate assumed. For example, the net single premium for a five-year pure endowment of $1,000 issued to a person aged 35, using the 1958 CSO Table and 2½ per cent interest, would be calculated as follows:

$$\frac{9{,}241{,}359}{9{,}373{,}807} \times \$1{,}000 \times \$0.883854 = \$871.37$$

That is, out of 9,373,807 persons living at age 35, 9,241,359 are expected to survive five years to age 40. The proportion of persons surviving and, therefore, the probability of a person aged 35 surviving to age 40 is 9,241,359 divided by 9,373,807. This probability times the present value of $1,000 payable at the end of five years at 2½ per cent interest (that is, $1,000 times 0.883854) gives the net single premium for the five-year pure endowment of $1,000 issued to a person aged 35. Adding the net single premium of $871.37 for a five-year pure endowment to the net single premium of $13.09 previously obtained for a five-year term insurance contract produces a net single premium of $884.46 for a five-year endowment insurance contract of $1,000 issued to a person aged 35.

Annuities

Under a whole life annuity contract the insurance company promises to pay a specific amount each year (or at other specified intervals) during the life of the annuitant. Premiums for annuity contracts are based upon mortality tables derived from the mortality experience of annuitants. Because of the decided historical trend toward improved mortality in past decades, annuity premiums are usually calculated with a specific provision for projected continued improvement of mortality in future years. The net single premium for an annuity is calculated as the sum of a series of pure endowments, each based upon a probability of survival, the amount of the payment, and an appropriate present value factor.

An annuity may be purchased with annuity payments starting one payment interval after purchase (an immediate life annuity), or with payments starting later (a deferred life annuity). The net single premium for a deferred life annuity is calculated as the sum of a series of pure endowments, with the first payable at the end of the deferment period, and with each payment based upon a probability of survival, the amount of the payment, and an appropriate present value factor. The net single premium for a whole life annuity with annuity payments guaranteed for a minimum stated period ("period certain") is calculated as the sum of the net single premium for a series of five annual payments not dependent upon probability of survival, and the net single premium for a five-year deferred whole life annuity where payments begin after five years and are dependent upon the probability of survival.

NET LEVEL PREMIUMS

Few policies are purchased by single premiums. Annual or more frequent premium payments are usual. The large size of the single premium and the desire to spread the premium over a period of years are the principal reasons that lead to the use of annual, semiannual, quarterly, or monthly premiums for the purchase of life insurance policies.

Annual Premiums

The net annual level premium is determined by a somewhat more complex calculation than that required for the net single premium. The calculation of the net single premium is the first step in the calculation of the net premium paid on any other basis. As previously shown, the net single premium is equal to the present value of probable future benefits to be paid under the insurance or annuity contract. Once the amount of the net single premium is known, the amount of the net annual level premium is determined as that level amount which, if paid annually, satisfies the following equation:

$$\begin{array}{c}\text{Present value of}\\ \text{net annual}\\ \text{level premiums}\end{array} = \begin{array}{c}\text{Net}\\ \text{single}\\ \text{premium}\end{array} = \begin{array}{c}\text{Present value of}\\ \text{probable}\\ \text{future benefits}\end{array}$$

Since annual premiums under a whole life insurance contract are paid at the beginning of each year, provided the insured survives to such date, a series of such annual level premiums is, in effect, a life annuity. Although it differs from a conventional immediate annuity in certain respects (e.g., it starts on the date of purchase rather than one year later), such a series of annual premiums has a present value which can be determined in the same way as the present value of a series of conventional annuity payments. Thus, the net single premium for a whole life insurance contract divided by the present value of a series of annual life annuity payments of 1 (first payment starting on date of purchase) gives the net annual level premium for such a contract.

The net annual level premium for a 20-payment whole life contract or a 20-year endowment insurance contract is calculated in a similar manner, except that premiums are not paid for life but rather for a limited period. The net single premium for such a contract is divided by the present value of a series of annual annuity payments of 1 starting on the date of purchase and continuing at the beginning of each year for 20 years (rather than for life, as in the earlier example), provided the insured survives to such date. (Such an annuity is called a temporary life annuity due.)

The net annual level premium for a term insurance contract is equal to the net single premium for such contract divided by the present value of a temporary life annuity due of 1 per year starting at the date of purchase and payable for the term of the policy. The total of all net annual level premiums for a term insurance policy is greater than the net single premium for two reasons: (1) Less interest is earned when premiums are paid on a annual-premium basis, and (2) the full number of annual premiums is collected only from those policyholders who survive the entire term of the policy.

Numerical Illustration

Consider the net annual level premium for a five-year endowment insurance contract of $1,000 issued to a person aged 35. Using the 1958 CSO Table and a 2½ per cent interest factor, $884.46 was previously determined as the net single premium for such a policy.

The annual premiums for this policy are paid immediately and at the beginning of each of the next four years. The present value of a series of five annual annuity payments of 1, starting at age 35, using the 1958 CSO Table and a 2½ per cent interest factor, would be as follows:

$$\frac{9{,}373{,}807}{9{,}373{,}807} \times 1 \times 1.000000 = 1.0000$$

$$\frac{9{,}350{,}279}{9{,}373{,}807} \times 1 \times 0.975610 = 0.9732$$

$$\frac{9{,}325{,}594}{9{,}373{,}807} \times 1 \times 0.951814 = 0.9469$$

$$\frac{9{,}299{,}482}{9{,}373{,}807} \times 1 \times 0.928599 = 0.9212$$

$$\frac{9{,}271{,}491}{9{,}373{,}807} \times 1 \times 0.905951 = \underline{0.8961}$$

$$\text{Present value} = 4.7374$$

The net annual level premium for the contract is equal to the net single premium for the contract divided by the present value of a series of annual annuity payments of 1 starting on the date of purchase. For a five-year endowment insurance contract of $1,000 issued to a person aged 35, the net annual level premium (using the 1958 CSO Table and 2½ per cent interest factor) is $884.46 divided by 4.7374, or $186.70.

GROSS PREMIUMS

Loading is the amount added to the net premium to produce the gross premium. When realistic mortality and interest assumptions are used to calculate net premiums, the loading is designed to cover all the operating expenses of an insurance company except investment expenses. Investment expenses are deducted from gross investment income and thus are reflected in the assumed interest rate rather than in the loading factor. In addition, loading usually includes margins for contingencies and, in the case of a stock company, margins for profit. Under participating policies, margins for future payment of dividends are included.

Types of Expenses

Noninvestment expenses of an insurance company include sales and issuance expenses, continuing administrative expenses, general overhead, and expenses of handling benefit payments. These expenses may be classified into three groups for purposes of developing a loading formula: (1) expenses that are a function of size of premium, such as commissions and state premium taxes; (2) expenses that are a function of amount of insurance, such as medical examinations and inspection reports; and (3) expenses that are a function of number of policies, such as administrative expenses and general overhead.

Distribution of Expenses

Sound life insurance practice requires an equitable distribution of an insurance company's expenses among policyholders. Some expenses vary by size of premiums, and others do not vary by size of premiums. The distribution of all expenses as a certain percentage of premiums would be disadvantageous to contracts with higher premiums and those issued at higher ages. Conversely, distribution of all expenses as a certain constant amount per $1,000 of insurance is disadvantageous to contracts issued at lower ages and on lower premium forms of policies.

Expense distributions expressed as a certain percentage of the premium plus a constant amount per $1,000 of insurance are generally considered to be more equitable. Expenses in dollar amounts increase as the premium increases, recognizing expenses which increase as the size of the premium increases. Expenses as a percentage of premium decrease as the premium increases, recognizing expenses which do not vary by the size of the premium. Other distributions, such as a certain percentage of the premium for the particular policy plus a certain percentage of the premium for a whole life policy, are also sometimes used.

Determining the Loading

As mentioned previously, the determination of the loading is a complex process. It includes consideration of the expenses distributed to the particular contract; any desired margins for contingencies, dividends, and profit; the conservatism of the assumptions used for calculation of the net premiums; and the nonforfeiture benefits to be provided. A trial-and-error process, often involving asset share projections, is utilized to produce the best-fitting loading formula. This is the formula which can be applied to predetermined net premiums to produce the desired level of gross premiums, taking all pertinent factors into consideration.

Loading formulas for participating policies may be designed with greater approximation, since inadequacies can be overcome by dividend adjustments. Loading formulas for nonparticipating policies must be more realistic, since there is not a later opportunity to adjust the premiums charged.

Varying Premiums by Size of Policy

Until the mid-1950's, it was considered impractical, and illegal in some states, to vary the gross premium rate by the amount of insurance. The universal practice was to charge the same gross rate per $1,000, regardless of face amount. Expenses which remained constant by policy were converted to expenses per $1,000 of insurance on the basis of an average-sized policy. Since the 1950's, the grading of premium rates by amount of insurance has become the general practice.

This has been accomplished by one of two approaches, both of which have the effect of varying the constant loading by the size of the policy. One system, called the "band" system, involves a gross premium of, say, $20 per $1,000 of insurance if the policy is in the $2,000 to $4,999 band; a premium of, say, $18 per $1,000 of insurance if the policy is in the $5,000 to $9,999 band; and so on. The other device, called the "policy fee" system, involves a gross premium expressed as the sum of a rate per $1,000 of insurance and a policy fee of a certain dollar amount. For example, a rate of $16.50 per $1,000 of insurance plus a policy fee of $7.00 would result in a gross premium rate of $89.50 (or $17.90 per $1,000) for a $5,000 contract under the policy fee system.

Fractional Premiums

Theoretically, net fractional premiums (i.e., premiums more frequent than annual) could be calculated on an exact basis, but this would require mortality tables based on time units shorter than one year. This is impractical, so fractional premiums are computed on an approximate basis. Often the gross annual premium is increased by some percentage, and the result is divided by the number of fractional premiums during the year. For example, in computing semiannual premiums, the gross annual premium may be increased by 3 per cent and the result divided by two.

The sum of fractional premiums during a year exceeds the annual premium for the year for a number of reasons. First, the collection of more premiums per year involves greater expense. Second, fractional premiums obviously involve a loss of interest. Furthermore, where a company does not refund the pro rata portion of an annual premium paid during the year of death, fractional premiums involve a loss of premiums in the year of death.

Current practice of many companies is to calculate premiums on the basis of a full year's premium in the year of death and to increase the level of fractional premiums appropriately to recognize that fractional premiums cease at death.

SELECTED REFERENCES

BASSFORD, J. R. "Premium Rates, Reserves, and Non-Forfeiture Values for Participating Policies," *Transactions of the Actuarial Society of America,* Vol. XLIII (1942), p. 328.

CAMMACK, E. E. "Premiums for Non-Participating Insurance," *Transactions of the Actuarial Society of America,* Vol. XX (1919), p. 379.

GUERTIN, ALFRED N. "Price Planning," in DAN M. MCGILL (ed.), *Life Insurance Sales Management.* Homewood, Ill.: Richard D. Irwin, Inc., 1957.

HUEBNER, S. S., and BLACK, KENNETH, JR. *Life Insurance.* 6th ed. New York: Appleton-Century-Crofts, Inc., 1964.

MACLEAN, JOSEPH B. *Life Insurance.* 9th ed. New York: McGraw-Hill Book Co., Inc. 1962.

MCGILL, DAN M. *Life Insurance.* Homewood, Ill.: Richard D. Irwin, Inc., 1959.

Chapter 12

POLICY AND OTHER INSURANCE RESERVES

BY WILLIAM H. SCHMIDT

Basic Concepts

The life insurance business is an important economic force because of the large amount of assets that it accumulates and is continuously investing. Most of the assets of a company are needed to provide the backing for the company's financial guarantee that it will be able to meet its contractual obligations. These obligations are measured by the policy reserves and other insurance reserves.

Policy reserves and the assets behind them arise because, under the level premium approach, the premiums paid in the early policy years usually exceed the death claims in those years. These "overpayments" in the early years are accumulated and invested in order to offset the effect of the increasing mortality costs in the later years.

Actually, policy reserves have significance only in the aggregate. For example, if a company sells only $1,000 one-year term policies, it should have a reserve of $1,000 for each person who will die during the next year and needs no reserve at all for those who will not. Since it cannot know in advance the identity of the individuals in each category, it uses the death rates shown in a mortality table to determine the amount which must be paid to the families of policyholders who die. This amount, when related to each $1,000 policy purchased, is known as the reserve per $1,000 policy. It is also known as the average reserve per $1,000.

Thus, the average reserve is merely a convenient device for permitting a company to determine the extent of its liabilities *under certain given assumptions*. If the assumptions are changed, the reserves may be increased or decreased. On the other hand, the assets of a company are more readily and objectively determined. Accordingly, the surplus to policyholders (i.e., the difference between assets and liabilities) is affected significantly by the assumptions that underlie reserve computations.

To establish a uniform and objective basis for ascertaining a company's surplus, Massachusetts in 1858 passed a law empowering its commissioner of insurance to establish minimum reserve standards. The traditional actuarial calculations for premiums and reserves assume that level annual premiums will usually be paid. For this reason the commissioner promulgated "net level premium" reserves, based on the "Combined" or "Actuaries" Table of Mortality and 4 per cent interest, as a minimum standard. Other methods of computing reserves are now permissible, but these will be discussed later.

Thus, the mortality table and the rate of interest to be used in the calculation of policy reserves must be determined by a company pursuant to state law. The statutes specify certain tables and rates of interest for various types of policy, annuity, and other contracts for use as minimum standards, and such laws usually give the insurance commissioner authority to approve other tables. The insurance company, therefore, is not completely free in its choice of standards for determining the value of its liabilities. In this respect, the situation is different from the freedom available to the company in the choice of mortality and interest standards used in the calculation of premiums.

Level Premium Reserves

As was shown in Chapter 11, "net premiums"[1] have traditionally been computed using the following assumptions: (1) that premiums, usually level, will be paid annually at the beginning of each policy year; (2) that interest will be earned on all monies at a certain annual interest rate (e.g., 2½ per cent per annum); (3) that deaths will occur in accordance with an assumed mortality table; (4) that all death claims will be paid by the insurance company at the end of the policy year in which death occurs; (5) that no portion of the annual premium is refundable in the event of death during the policy year; and (6) that all living persons will keep their policies and pay premiums in accordance with the terms of the policy. For reserve purposes, the mortality table used is one specified as appropriate by the applicable state laws, i.e., the Commissioners 1958 Standard Ordinary Mortality Table, generally referred to as the 1958 CSO Table.

Other assumptions can be made. Death claims are usually paid when proofs of death are received, premiums are often paid other than annually, and the unearned portion of a premium is refunded at death by some companies. Such assumptions cause minor variations in the individual policy reserve, but these technicalities are beyond the scope of this chapter. Then, too, not all policyholders continue to pay premiums for the duration of the contract. In such instances a "nonforfeiture value" is usually available (see Chapter 13).

[1] "Gross" premiums, in contrast to "net" premiums, have a specific margin added to allow for expenses. (Cf. Chapter 11.)

To illustrate how a reserve is computed, the traditional assumptions will be made in the calculation of the reserve for a five-year endowment policy issued to a man aged 35. (Mortality and interest assumptions will be the 1958 CSO Table and 2½ per cent interest.) Very few five-year endowment policies are issued, but this example illustrates the principles involved with a minimum of arithmetic. The net annual premium for this policy is $186.70, for a $1,000 benefit payable at the end of five years or at the end of the year of death, if death occurs within the five-year period.

The individual policy reserve can be computed in either of two ways: *retrospectively* or *prospectively*. Both methods produce the same result. However, variations of the net level premium approach to reserves can best be visualized if both the retrospective and the prospective methods are understood.

The Reserve Calculated Retrospectively

The retrospective method of calculation looks backward and asks: "What has happened to the premiums since the policy was issued? As a result, what is the company's reserve liability with respect to each $1,000 of insurance?" For example, under the 1958 CSO Table, at age 35, 9,373,807 persons would pay an aggregate net premium of $1,750,061,000, on which 2½ per cent interest would be earned during the year, bringing the fund to $1,793,813,000. Payment of 23,528 death claims would reduce the fund by $23,528,000, leaving $1,770,285,000, or $189.33 per $1,000 of insurance still in force. This is the average policy reserve at the end of the first policy year.

The calculations for all five policy years are shown in Table 12–1.

The Reserve Calculated Prospectively

The prospective method of calculation looks forward and asks: "Taking into consideration the premiums we expect to collect in the future, how much money should we have on hand now for each $1,000 policy currently in force in order to permit us to meet our obligations as they fall due?"

If 9,373,807 individuals now aged 35 each purchase a $1,000 five-year endowment, 9,350,279 will still be alive after one year. The present value at this point of all the *future* benefits in each policy is $906.33, and the present value at this point of the four remaining net premiums of $186.70 each is $717.00, taking interest and future deaths into account. The difference, $189.33, is a measure of our reserve obligations per $1,000 policy.

The complete calculations are shown in Table 12–2.

Initial, Terminal, and Mean Reserves

The above examples show the calculation of the *terminal* reserve of a policy, i.e., the reserve at the *end* of each policy year. The *initial* reserve,

TABLE 12–1

Calculation of Reserve by the Retrospective Method, Five-Year Endowment for $1,000

1958 CSO Table, $2\frac{1}{2}$ Per Cent—Male Aged 35
Net Premium $186.69698

(1)	(2)	(3)	(4)	(5)	(6)	(7)	(8)	(9)	(10)	(11)
			In Thousands of Dollars							
Year	Number Living	Number Dying	Net Premiums Paid	Total Fund	Interest on (5)	Fund + Interest	Death Claims	Endowment	Total Reserves	Reserve per $1,000 Policy
1.	9,373,807	23,528	$1,750,061	$1,750,061	$ 43,752	$1,793,813	$23,528	. . . .	$1,770,285*	$ 189.33
2.	9,350,279	24,685	1,745,669	3,515,954	87,899	3,603,853	24,685	. . . .	3,579,168	383.80
3.	9,325,594	26,112	1,741,060	5,320,228	133,006	5,453,234	26,112	. . . .	5,427,122	583.59
4.	9,299,482	27,991	1,736,185	7,163,307	179,083	7,342,390	27,991	. . . .	7,314,399*	788.91
5.	9,271,491	30,132	1,730,959	9,045,358	226,134	9,271,492	30,132	$9,291,360*	. . . .	1,000.00

Explanation of column headings:
(4) $186.69698 × (2).
(5) (10) at end of previous year + (4).
(6) (5) × $2\frac{1}{2}$ per cent.
(7) (5) + (6).
(8) $1,000 × (3).
(9) (7) − (8); at end of fifth year.
(10) (7) − (8) − (9).
(11) (10) ÷ [(2) − (3)].
* There are slight rounding differences in these figures between the prospective and retrospective methods.

TABLE 12–2

CALCULATION OF RESERVE BY THE PROSPECTIVE METHOD, FIVE-YEAR ENDOWMENT FOR $1,000

1958 CSO Table, 2½ Per Cent—Male Aged 35
Net Premium $186.69698

(1) End of Year	(2) Number Living	(3) Value of $1,000 at Death or at End of Five Years if Living	(4) Present Value of All Future Benefits (in Thousands)	(5) Total Premiums Payable (in Thousands)	(6) Present Value of $1.00 per Annum in Advance	(7) Present Value of Future Premiums (in Thousands)	(8) Total Reserve (in Thousands)	(9) Reserve per $1,000 Policy
1	9,350,279	906.33043	$8,474,442	$1,745,669	3.840452	$6,704,158	$1,770,284*	$ 189.33
2	9,325,594	928.80071	8,661,618	1,741,060	2.919170	5,082,450	3,579,168	383.80
3	9,299,482	951.88602	8,852,047	1,736,185	1.972673	3,424,925	5,427,122	583.59
4	9,271,491	975.60974	9,045,357	1,730,959	1.000000	1,730,959	7,314,398*	788.91
5	9,241,359	1,000.00000	9,241,359	....	....	....	9,241,359*	1,000.00

Explanation of column headings:
(4) (2) × (3).
(5) $186.69698 × (2).
(6) From 1958 CSO 2½ per cent tables. This figure is an "annuity due" which includes an immediate payment of $1.00, as well as the discounted value, allowing for both mortality and interest, of any required future annual payments of $1.00.
(7) (5) × (6).
(8) (4) − (7).
(9) (8) ÷ (2).
* There are slight rounding differences in these reserves between the prospective and retrospective methods.

i.e., the reserve at the *beginning* of each policy year, is the sum of the terminal reserve at the end of the previous policy year, plus the net annual premium payable at the beginning of the current year. The theoretical reserve at any point during the policy year is approximated by interpolating between the initial and the terminal reserve. All of these are, of course, average reserves.

In order to obtain the total policy reserve liabilities of a company as of December 31, the date of its annual statement, it is usual to assume that all of its policies have been issued evenly throughout the year. This is equivalent, on the average, to the assumption that all policies were issued on July 1. Accordingly, each of the policies in force is multiplied by the appropriate *mean* reserve, i.e., the mid-point between the initial and the terminal reserve. The combined mean reserves of all policies in force represent the aggregate reserve liabilities of the company.[2]

Reserve Bases Other than Net Level Premiums

The reserve basis just described assumes that a constant premium is available annually for reserve purposes. The premium actually charged, the "gross" premium, is usually equal to this "net annual premium," plus an additional level amount which consists principally of an allowance for expenses.

However, relatively heavy expenses are in fact incurred in the first policy year. After deducting these expenses from the gross premium, the balance left does not equal the net annual premium. Hence, to set up the traditional net level premium reserve in the first year, a life insurance company must transfer funds from its surplus. Most of the younger companies (and some older ones) avoid this strain on their surplus funds by using one of several modifications in calculating policy reserves.

All of the modifications assume that some of the initial net premium can be used to pay excess expenses, but that future net premiums must be increased to enable all of the policy benefits to be paid.

Full Preliminary Term Method

The full preliminary term reserve method assumes that the entire first-year net premium can be used to pay expenses, except for the one-year term premium needed to meet the first year's death claims. All the future net premiums are then increased by a constant amount so that the present value of all such increases is equal to the decrease in the first-year net premiums.

At age 35, for example, the net annual premium for a $1,000 whole life

---

[2] The reserve liabilities thus calculated assume that all premiums are payable annually and have been collected. Under actual conditions, an offsetting asset item must be computed, i.e., "net premiums deferred and uncollected."

policy (1958 CSO 2½ per cent) is $17.67. Under the full preliminary term method, only the one-year term premium of $2.45 is needed during the first year, but an increased net premium of $18.34 must be assumed in all future years.

Modified Preliminary Term Reserves

The full preliminary term method, in other words, provides an additional first-year expense allowance equal to the excess of the full net annual premium over the one-year term net premium. For whole life and other relatively low premium contracts, this is reasonable. For certain higher premium policies, however, the resulting expense allowance is too large. Historically, state statutes have limited this allowance, and several methods have been used to meet this situation. The one in most common use today was developed by the National Association of Insurance Commissioners for use under the Standard Valuation Law.

The *Commissioners Reserve Valuation Method* is the same as the full preliminary term method for policies with premiums not greater than the 20-payment life premium at the same age. For policies with premiums higher than the 20-payment life premium, the expense allowance, amortized by increasing net premiums after the first, is equal to the allowance for a 20-payment life policy.

The above approach is merely a variation of earlier methods. The *Illinois Standard* is the same as the Commissioners Reserve Valuation Method except that in the case of policies with net premiums higher than 20-payment life net premiums, the expense allowance must be amortized within the first 20 years if the premium payment period is greater than 20 years. The *Canadian* method is less liberal. The expense allowance cannot exceed that for a whole life policy, but is amortized over the premium-paying period. The *Ohio* and *New Jersey* methods are other variants of less importance than the above. The "select and ultimate" reserve method was another and earlier attempt to solve the problem of level premiums and nonlevel expenses. All of these methods, except the Commissioners Reserve Valuation Method, are now only of historical interest in the United States.

Effect on Reserves of Changes in Assumptions

The size of the individual policy reserve depends upon the assumptions inherent in its computation. For policies other than term, all reserve bases lead ultimately to the same point, i.e., $1,000 at the end of the contract period.

Change in Interest Rate. It can readily be appreciated that, under given mortality assumptions, an increase in the interest rate assumed (e.g., from 2½ to 3 per cent) will reduce the required net annual premium. The fund is assumed to earn interest at a higher rate, and the amount of death claims is identical. Looking at the situation "retrospectively," collecting the full 2½ per cent net annual premium will result in a fund more than sufficient to meet the policy benefits on a 3 per cent assumption. For example, the 1958 CSO 2½ per cent net annual premium for a whole life policy on a male aged 35 is $17.67, 8.4 per cent greater than the corresponding 1958 CSO 3 per cent premium of $16.29. Thus, two and one-half per cent reserves are higher than 3 per cent reserves. The percentage difference, however, is not uniform by policy duration. The percentage difference is greatest when the policy has many years to run. It gradually diminishes and at the termination of the contract the reserves are identical. Table 12–3 illustrates these points clearly.

TABLE 12–3

COMPARISON OF TERMINAL RESERVES PER $1,000 FACE AMOUNT
Whole Life (Male), Age 35

	Net Annual Premiums
1958 CSO 2½ Per Cent	$17.67
1958 CSO 3 Per Cent	16.29

Years in Force	Terminal Reserves		Difference as Per Cent of 3 Per Cent Reserve
	2½ Per Cent	3 Per Cent	
5	$ 81.05	$ 74.72	8%
10	167.90	156.29	7
15	259.12	243.48	6
20	352.54	334.23	5
25	445.78	426.20	5
30	535.77	516.21	4
35	618.77	600.25	3
40	692.16	675.36	2
45	757.75	743.20	2
50	811.36	799.12	2
55	857.35	847.43	1
60	905.46	898.40	1
65*	1,000.00	1,000.00	0

*At this duration, under the 1958 CSO mortality table, the last surviving policyholders are assumed to die. Any survivors, in general practice, will be offered the death benefits as an endowment payment.

For the average company's aggregate reserves, the effect of a change in interest rate has been found to be remarkably predictable. For a reasonably mature policy portfolio, a change of one half of a percentage point in the interest rate assumed in the reserve calculations will change aggregate reserves by approximately 5 per cent, i.e., the percentage change in aggregate reserves will be ten times the percentage point change in the assumed interest rate. This fact was recognized by the United States Treasury in the development of the Life Insurance Company Income Tax Act of 1959. One of its calculations requires a revaluation of the company's reserves, using the current over-all interest rate (or a five-year average rate) on all of the company's assets as the valuation interest rate. The use of the above "ten times" rule of thumb is written into the statute and applied to the policy reserves of all companies so as to revalue them on an interest rate based on investment experience.

Change in Mortality Table. The effect of a change in mortality on individual policy reserves is not so predictable. Given the same rate of interest, a table with a lower inherent mortality will produce lower net annual premiums. However, the size of the reserve depends more upon the steepness of the mortality rate curve of the underlying mortality table than upon the actual mortality rates. This is illustrated in Table 12–4.

TABLE 12–4

COMPARISON OF TERMINAL RESERVES PER $1,000 FACE AMOUNT

Whole Life (Male), Age 35

	Net Annual Premiums
American Experience Table, 3 per cent	$21.08
1958 CSO Table, 3 per cent	16.29

Years in Force	Rate of Mortality per 1,000 Lives		Terminal Reserves	
	American Experience Table	1958 CSO Table	American Experience Table, 3 Per Cent	1958 CSO Table, 3 Per Cent
5	9.79	3.53	$ 68.16	$ 74.72
10	11.16	5.35	146.01	156.29
20	18.57	13.00	327.58	334.23
30	40.13	31.75	522.92	516.21
40	94.37	73.37	698.21	675.36
50	235.55	161.14	844.01	799.12
60	1,000.00	351.24	949.70	898.40
Age 96		400.56	1,000.00	910.79
Age 100				1,000.00

It can be seen from Table 12–4 that the curve represented by the 1958 CSO Table mortality rates is below that of the American Experience Table mortality rates at all points, but it rises more steeply at the upper ages. The net annual premiums on the 1958 CSO Table are lower, as is to be expected. However, the reserves for the first twenty-five years are greater under the 1958 CSO Table than under the American Experience Table. To repeat, then, the effect of a change in the mortality table on the aggregate reserves of a life insurance company cannot be readily ascertained.

Other Changes in Assumptions. In the section on *net level premium reserves* above, the traditional assumptions of annual premiums paid at the beginning of the year and death claims paid at the end of the year were used for explanation. However, it was also mentioned that other assumptions could be made. The monetary tables of net premiums, reserves, basic values, and nonforfeiture benefits published by the Society of Actuaries for the 1958 CSO Table were computed on two bases:

1. "Curtate" functions, which assume that premiums are paid annually and that death claims are paid at the end of the year; and
2. "Continuous" functions, which assume that premiums are paid continuously throughout the year and that death claims are also paid continuously as they occur.

Table 12–5 shows for selected years the difference in terminal reserves based on these assumptions. The difference is explained quite easily by

TABLE 12–5

COMPARISON OF TERMINAL RESERVES PER $1,000 FACE AMOUNT

Whole Life (Male), Age 35

	Net Annual Premiums
Curtate	$17.67
Continuous	18.28

Years in Force	Terminal Reserves	
	Curtate	Continuous
5	$ 81.05	$ 82.81
10	167.90	171.53
15	259.12	264.74
20	352.54	360.17
25	445.78	455.44
30	535.77	547.38

general reasoning. On the average, deaths occur approximately in the middle of the policy year. Under the assumptions involved in the "continuous" functions, the beneficiary not only receives the $1,000 approximately six months earlier, but the insured has paid only one half of an annual premium. Because each "continuous" death claim is therefore "worth" somewhat more than $1,000, it follows that each "continuous" reserve must be somewhat larger than the corresponding "curtate" reserve.

Other Insurance Reserves

Reserves must also be established for several additional types of coverages offered. Reserves that are merely "net single premiums" (i.e., the present value of future benefits) are computed for all contracts on which no further premiums will be received. The principal examples of these are: (1) single-premium life and endowment policies, (2) individual life annuities, (3) paid-up life and endowment policies, and (4) supplementary contracts issued to beneficiaries in lieu of a lump-sum benefit. Similarly, when a policyholder becomes disabled, "disabled life" reserves of the single-premium type are computed to provide for the payment of the disability benefits on his life insurance policy (for either waiver of premium alone, or the combination of waiver of premium and disability income). Single-premium reserves must be established to cover premium payments under the "payor" or "premium protection" benefit on juvenile and family policies when the applicant has died.

Reserves of the level premium type are held during the premium-paying period for additional coverages such as (1) the accidental death benefit, (2) waiver of premium, (3) disability income, (4) level term riders, and (5) increasing term riders.

The calculation of terminal reserves for decreasing term policies and riders, on the other hand, frequently produces negative results. In other words, the net annual premiums charged are often not sufficient, *under the mortality table assumed,* to provide the benefits in the early years. In such cases, no credit is taken for the fact that the present value of future premiums is in excess of future benefits (because the policyholder can always stop paying premiums). The negative terminal reserve is taken as zero, and the mean reserve becomes simply one half of the net annual premium.

"Deficiency" Reserves

Actual mortality experienced and interest rates earned are usually more favorable than the conservatively assumed mortality and interest rates used for valuation. Therefore, some companies, particularly those selling nonparticipating insurance, may find themselves able to justify a gross annual premium lower than the net annual premium needed under the valuation standard they use. The gross premium, using realistic interest and mortality assumptions, can provide for commissions and other expenses as well as the expected actual mortality. In this situation, many states require that an additional "deficiency" reserve be set up immediately. The basic rule is that the net premium cannot be assumed to be larger than the gross premium.

While the necessity for this reserve requirement can be debated, the justification is readily apparent if we consider the reserve from the "prospective" point of view. The usual prospective reserve (under either the level premium or the modified preliminary term methods) can be considered as the difference between the present value of future benefits and the present value of future net annual premiums.

If the gross premium is *less* than the net annual premium, the present value of future premiums is thus clearly overstated; and the reserve is, to the extent of the difference, understated. The "deficiency" is overcome by setting up a special reserve equal to the present value of the excess of the net annual premium over the gross premium.

This deficiency reserve requirement has caused a significant strain in the surplus of new life insurance companies and was one of the major forces that led to the preparation and promulgation of both the 1941 and the 1958 CSO Mortality Tables as valuation standards. In each instance, the change permitted the reduction of the net premiums used in valuation to a more realistic level based on then current mortality experience.

Company Reserves as a Measure of Solvency

In the light of the foregoing, it is suggested that the true financial health of a life insurance company cannot be determined merely by looking at its annual report.[3] From an actuarial point of view, the basic test of a company's solvency is whether or not it has sufficient sound assets to equal its liabilities under a "gross premium" reserve calculation. Such a calculation would be made prospectively, based on (1) an estimated mortality table closely equivalent to the individual company's experience; (2) realistic interest and expense assumptions, both for the present and for the foreseeable future; and (3) the fact that future premiums received will be the *gross* premiums less the anticipated expenses. In a solvent, well-managed company, these "gross premiums less the anticipated expenses" generally will be greater than the net premiums.

This is a complex calculation; and in practice, it is rarely made. The *minimum* valuation standards of the various regulating bodies are intended to produce aggregate reserves in excess of a gross premium valuation through the use of: (1) mortality tables with some margin for extra mortality, and (2) a maximum interest rate less than the yield expected to be received by the company over the long term on its investments. After January 1, 1966, the minimum standard for new policies in most states will be the Commissioners Reserve Valuation Method, using the 1958 CSO Table and 3½ per cent interest (3 per cent in New York).

Summary

In summary, then, it can be said that the policy and other insurance reserves are a measure, in the aggregate, of the liability of the company with respect to its contractual future guarantees. Allowance is made, of course, for expected future premiums. Valuation standards are set by the various regulatory authorities, with the result that the reserves are computed on bases which are, generally, slightly conservative. In addition to the reserves for the basic policy benefits, reserves are also held against the liabilities created by the many supplemental coverages which are attached to or arise out of the contract provisions.

---

[3] See Chapter 73, "Company Annual Statement."

SELECTED REFERENCES

HUEBNER, S. S., and BLACK, KENNETH, JR. *Life Insurance.* 6th ed. New York: Appleton-Century-Crofts, Inc., 1964.

JORDAN, C. W. *Life Contingencies.* Chicago: Society of Actuaries, 1952.

MACLEAN, JOSEPH B. *Life Insurance.* 9th ed. New York: McGraw-Hill Book Co., Inc., 1962.

MCGILL, DAN M. *Life Insurance.* Homewood, Ill.: Richard D. Irwin, Inc., 1959.

Chapter 13

NONFORFEITURE VALUES AND POLICY LOANS

BY CHARLES F. B. RICHARDSON

Life insurance on the level premium basis is quite unlike most other forms of insurance because the risk of death increases rapidly with age, and because the premium remains level over an extended period of time. Under a level premium life insurance policy the premium in the early years is more than is necessary to cover mortality costs; and in the later years, it is less than is necessary to cover mortality costs. The excess of the premiums in the early years is accumulated to provide sufficient assets to offset the deficiency in the premiums in the later years. The so-called "nonforfeiture provisions" define the equity to which the policyholder is entitled in the event the policy is terminated other than by death. Nonforfeiture values are available in various forms, as may be elected by the policyholder.

Historical Development of Nonforfeiture Legislation

In the early days of life insurance in this country, a policy contained no provision for the payment of an amount representative of the insured's equity on termination of the policy prior to maturity, although in practice many companies voluntarily granted cash values or other forms of benefit upon termination of the policy. However, such values were usually allowed only if applied for soon after default in payment of the premium.

The first nonforfeiture law was enacted in Massachusetts in 1861. It required companies operating in that state to provide for extended term insurance for the period determined by application of 80 per cent of the reserve on the policy computed on the Combined Mortality Table at 4 per cent. The requirement that this law apply to all companies operating in the state is perhaps the first instance of extraterritorial regulation in this country. The law was changed in 1877 to apply only to domestic companies. Note that the law did not require a guaranteed cash value, but simply a continuation of coverage for a specified period. The law was defective in that the 20 per cent deduction from the reserve applied to the reserve less any indebtedness, so that the deduction varied with the amount of indebtedness. Also, the amount of coverage continued was the full face amount, whereas the coverage should have been reduced by the amount of indebtedness. If the insured died during the term period, the company could deduct from the face amount the unpaid premiums accumulated at 6 per cent interest. In 1900 the law was further amended to require guaranteed cash values, the forerunner of similar requirements in other states following the Armstrong Investigation.

New York did not enact a nonforfeiture law until 1879. It required a nonforfeiture benefit, upon demand within six months, in the form of either reduced paid-up insurance or extended term insurance. The amount of the benefit was obtained by applying the reserve according to the American Experience Table at 4½ per cent to purchase the coverage at the "published rates" of the company. Under such an arrangement, the benefits could be reduced substantially by using excessive premium rates. It is understood that the requirement that benefits be requested within six months after lapse was strictly enforced. The law was later amended to require that the value of the benefit granted be at least two thirds of the reserve; but by modern standards, these were still inadequate benefits, especially at the longer policy durations.

During the period from 1879 to 1906, competition gradually forced more liberal attitudes on the part of the companies. Many other states enacted legislation similar in principle to the New York law; but prior to 1906, in most states, there was still no statutory requirement for guaranteed cash values. In practice, however, many companies allowed cash values; and some of them, around the turn of the century, began including guaranteed cash values in the policy.

In 1906, following the famous Armstrong Investigation in New York, there were enacted laws which remained substantially unchanged for nearly forty years. These laws varied somewhat in the several states, but typically they contained several basic provisions. The laws required that the policy show the reserve basis, and a minimum basis was prescribed in the law. After payment of premiums for three years, the policy was required to guarantee a cash value equal to the reserve, less a deduction not exceeding $25 per $1,000 of face amount. Further, the policyholder could elect to take an equivalent value in the form of reduced paid-up or extended term insurance. Tables of these guaranteed values had to be shown in the policy. Although only one of the alternative options was required, nearly all companies included both in the policy; and in the great majority of cases, extended term was the automatic option if no election was made.

These laws applied to policies issued in each of the states. However, in 1940, New York amended its statute to require compliance by *all* companies operating in New York, rather than by domestic companies only, another example of extraterritorial supervision.

Concepts Underlying Current Nonforfeiture Value Practices

In 1939, in order to conduct a study of nonforfeiture provisions, the National Association of Insurance Commissioners appointed a committee which rendered its report in 1941. This report, made after a thorough, professional study by a most competent committee headed by Alfred N. Guertin, recommended far-reaching changes in the existing laws. These changes were enacted by most states around 1948. To understand the so-called "Standard Nonforfeiture Law" which resulted from this study, it is necessary to consider some of the defects of the laws enacted in 1906 and in subsequent years.

The amount a company can afford to pay in cash upon termination of a policy must take account of a large number of factors. First, the expenses incurred in the first policy year, including compensation of the agent and manager, medical fees, and the expense of policy issue, are much higher than the provision for expenses, called "loading," contained in the first year's premium. These excess expenses are, in fact, amortized over a period of years from loading in subsequent premiums, and the company has to make an immediate investment from its surplus to put a new policy on its books.

Second, the cash value bears no necessary relationship to the reserve. The mortality assumed in the reserve basis, which must contain safety margins, is a legal standard designed to be reasonably conservative and ignores the effect of selection on the mortality during the early policy years. The asset share, on the other hand, which determines the cash values that can be allowed, is computed on realistic assumptions as to mortality and other factors, and the mortality assumed is entirely different from that involved in the legal reserve basis.

Third, guaranteed cash values are available upon demand, irrespective of financial conditions. Experience has proved that surrender rates are much higher in periods of economic depression than in prosperous times. It is possible that the company might have to sell assets in a depressed market to meet a high demand for cash values, although this is unlikely because the cash inflow of an established company generally exceeds the cash outflow by a substantial amount. However, the payment of cash values does reduce the amount of funds the company can invest, and the company may be deprived of favorable investment opportunities that may exist under depressed economic conditions. The existence of cash values available on demand also requires the company to keep a certain portion of its assets in liquid form, with consequent reduction in yield, the cost of which may properly be charged against those who surrender their policies.

The rationale of the minimum legal requirements for nonforfeiture values was stated as follows in the Guertin Committee report:

It is fundamental in business relationships that contracts, other than insurance, which are terminated prior to their normal termination date, shall involve no loss to the party to the contract who is willing to continue the contract, and the party effecting discontinuance shall bear whatever loss is involved as a result of the termination of the transaction. It is stated elsewhere in this report that, in the case of life insurance, full forfeiture upon lapse is repugnant to the public interest and that it should be the policy of the state to establish a basis whereby the purchaser may recover in some form the unabsorbed part of the payments already made. However, it cannot be regarded as proper public policy to insist that the party to the contract who is willing to continue shall be made to suffer loss through the inability or lack of desire of another to continue his contract.

Equity, therefore, would appear to demand, as a general principle, that an insurance company transacting any type of insurance, as one contracting party, shall be left in as favorable a position following the termination of a policy by a policyholder as it was prior thereto, and equity does not demand that the seceding policyholder shall be in as favorable a position after termination as he was prior thereto.[1]

The technical process used by the actuary to determine the proper level of cash values is known as an asset share calculation. This is an *a priori* calculation involving forecasting of actual expected experience as to mortality, interest, expenses, and lapse rates, quite independent of statutory limitations or requirements. Stated in oversimplified terms, the policy is credited with premiums expected to be paid each year, less expected expenses as incurred, less the expected cost of mortality on a modern table, less anticipated dividends; and the balance is accumulated at an interest rate assumed to be realistic for the long term. Lapse rates also are frequently taken into account, any excess of the cash value over the asset share on lapses being charged against the fund each year. From this accumulation, certain charges must be made for the items discussed above and also for a reasonable contribution to the surplus funds of the company. This last item is necessary because each new policyholder receives the protection of the surplus funds existing in the company when he enters the insured group, and therefore should leave a modest contribution to such funds if he terminates.

The Standard Nonforfeiture Law, passed about 1948 in most states, resulted from the recommendations in the Guertin Committee report. In brief, the major changes in this law, enacted to correct defects in the earlier statutes, were as follows:

1. The basis for determining the minimum nonforfeiture values was changed to take proper account of the high first-year expenses and of the

---

[1] National Association of Insurance Commissioners, *Reports and Statements on Nonforfeiture Benefits and Related Matters* (Chicago: Actuarial Society of America and American Institute of Actuaries, 1942), pp. 43–44.

fact that such expenses vary quite substantially by plan and age of issue. It also took account of the fact that these expenses are amortized over renewal policy years. The old law used a constant deduction from the reserve of $25 per $1,000 of insurance, irrespective of plan, age, or duration, and produced cash values that were too low in some areas and too high in others. Moreover, the maximum permissible deduction did not decline in the later policy years, as would have been proper.

2. The formula for determining the minimum value was established on a basis independent of the reserve basis used by the company. Under the old laws a company using a weak reserve basis (e.g., the minimum reserves permitted by law) had lower minimum statutory cash values than a company using a strong reserve basis. The minimum values also were independent of whether the company used preliminary term or net level reserves.

3. The new law required that reduced paid-up or extended insurance values be granted at any duration if the formula produces a value, whereas the old law did not require such values until the end of the third policy year. The result is that nonforfeiture values are now required in the second year in many cases, and in the first year for some plans and ages.

4. Cash values are not required until premiums have been paid for three years. However, in practice, cash values are generally allowed by the companies at whatever duration the law requires that paid-up or extended insurance values be granted.

5. In computing minimum extended term insurance values equivalent to the cash value, the new law recognized the higher mortality experienced on such coverage.

NONFORFEITURE VALUES (OPTIONS)

The three types of nonforfeiture values required by statute will now be examined in some detail, covering the more important characteristics of each of the nonforfeiture options.

Cash Surrender Values

The mathematical process used to determine the minimum cash values under the Standard Nonforfeiture Law involves a process similar in principle to that involved in computing reserves, a subject treated in Chapter 12. Net level premium reserves are computed by deducting the present value of future net premiums from the present value of estimated future claims. In order to take account of the large first-year expenses relative to the loading in the first year's premium, the adjusted premium method provided in the standard nonforfeiture legislation makes allowance for a specified amount of excess first-year expenses in determining statutory *minimum* cash values. This is done by employing an adjusted premium sufficient to amortize the specified excess first-year expenses over the premium-paying period of the policy. The *minimum* cash value is found by deducting the present value of the adjusted premiums from the present value of expected future claims, on the basis of mortality and interest rates prescribed in the law.

Many companies allow cash values higher than the legal minimum. This can be done either (1) by using a rate of excess first-year expenses lower than the maximum allowed by law, or (2) by amortizing the excess first-year expenses over a period shorter than the premium-paying period of the policy. (Many companies amortize these expenses over 10 or 20 years.) Frequently, both these methods are combined to provide values larger than the legal minimum. In defining the basis of the cash values guaranteed in the policy, it is a common practice to refer in the policy to nonforfeiture factors, which are net premiums increased by amounts necessary to amortize the excess first-year expenses.

The level of cash values a company can afford to grant depends on many factors, including premium rates, dividends, expense rates, and many other items of a technical nature.

After the bank holiday and the government moratorium on the payment of cash values and policy loans in the financial crisis of 1933, most state laws were amended to permit the company to defer payment of cash values for three or six months. The Standard Nonforfeiture Law makes such a provision mandatory rather than permissive, and the period is six months, although companies rarely invoke this "delay clause."

Extended Term Insurance

As mentioned earlier, extended term insurance was the first type of nonforfeiture benefit used in the United States. The net cash value is applied as a single premium to purchase term insurance for the face amount of the policy, plus any dividend additions, less any indebtedness, for as long a period as the available cash value will purchase. When this provision becomes effective, any supplementary benefits, such as disability benefits, accidental death benefits, and term riders are cancelled. If the policyholder desires to resume payment of premiums while extended term is in effect, the company may require evidence of insurability, although in practice such evidence is generally not required if there is a long period of unexpired term remaining.

Some people do not understand why, under the extended term provision, the *amount* of coverage must be reduced by the amount of indebtedness rather than the period of time. An example should explain the reason. Suppose a person in very poor health has a policy for $10,000 which has a loan value of $6,000. If he takes the maximum loan and later dies, the net sum payable is $4,000. Suppose, however, he takes the $6,000 loan, and then exercises the extended insurance option. If the extended term coverage were for the full face amount, he would obtain total coverage of \$16,000 by exercising the option, but he would be covered for a shorter period of time. It is quite clear that this would subject the insurance company to a severe degree of antiselection and would be a most unsound procedure.

In the case of an endowment policy, the cash value, after a few years, is more than sufficient to purchase term insurance to the maturity date. Under these circumstances the balance of the cash value is used to purchase a pure endowment, payable only if the insured survives to the maturity date.

Before the enactment of the standard nonforfeiture laws in the late 1940's, the laws of most states required that the term insurance be purchased on the basis of the net single premium on the company's reserve basis. The Guertin Committee studied the mortality under extended term insurance and found it to be substantially higher than that under premium-paying policies. In connection with extended term calculations, therefore, the Standard Nonforfeiture Law permits the use of a special mortality table reflecting higher mortality than that under the mortality table used in reserve calculations.

Reduced Paid-Up Insurance

This option provides that the cash value is applied as a net single premium to purchase a fully paid-up policy for a reduced amount payable at the same time as the original policy. If there is a policy loan, some policies provide that only the net cash value is applied and that the loan is repaid at the time the option is selected. Others provide that the gross cash value be used to purchase a larger amount of paid-up insurance and that the policy loan be continued.

The cash value of the reduced paid-up policy is the reserve for a paid-up policy for the reduced face amount and therefore increases from year to year.

In the case of limited-payment life and endowment policies, the amount of paid-up insurance bears roughly the same proportion to the original face amount as the number of premiums paid bears to the number payable. For example, under a twenty-payment life policy the reduced paid-up insurance in the fifteenth year would be roughly three fourths of the original face amount. On straight life policies issued at the younger ages, the amount of paid-up insurance is generally greater than the amount of premiums paid. However, this is not true for the higher issue ages, because a larger part of the premium has been used to cover the cost of insurance in the early years of the contract.

When the original policy is participating, the reduced paid-up policy nearly always continues to be participating. On the other hand, extended term insurance is almost always nonparticipating, because any dividends that might be paid would be very small and not worth the administrative expense of handling.

In the absence of an election by the policyholder, and in the absence of the automatic premium loan provision, most standard policies issued today provide that extended term insurance is the automatic option that goes into effect in the event of a default in premium payments. Under substandard insurance, the reduced paid-up policy option is generally provided.

RELATED VALUES

Policy loans and automatic premium loans are features of the policy which arise out of the statutory cash value provisions. Although they are not, technically speaking, nonforfeiture options, they are important policy provisions which should logically be considered in conjunction with the options.

Policy Loans

State insurance laws require that long-term level premium policies provide for loans upon demand (subject only to the statutory provisions for deferral up to six months) up to the amount secured by the cash value of the policy, subject to interest at a guaranteed rate. This requirement came into existence during the legislative activity in the various states following the Armstrong Investigation, although some companies did allow policy loans prior to that time.

The maximum rate of interest the company may charge on policy loans varies in the several states from 5 per cent in arrears to 6 per cent in advance, the latter rate being equivalent to 6.38 per cent in arrears. The laws of a few states prescribe no maximum interest rate on policy loans. Prior to 1939, the rate generally charged was 6 per cent, but in that year the New York law was changed to provide a maximum rate of 5 per cent in arrears on new policies, and this applied to both domestic and out-of-state companies. Many authorities consider that even 6 per cent is not an excessive rate, for the following reasons:

1. The rate is guaranteed for the life of the policy, which could extend for a period as long as fifty years or more.
2. A policy loan is available upon demand, irrespective of economic conditions, and the loan cannot be called by the company.
3. Policy loans typically are of small average amounts, in most companies only a few hundred dollars; and the expense of administration is high, generally from ½ per cent to 1 per cent, depending on the average size of loan. Therefore, a gross rate of 5 per cent becomes nearer 4 per cent net of expenses. There have been many occasions in the past when the companies could invest funds at a substantially higher rate after investment expenses.

4. These loans are repayable in whole or in part at any time. In practice, however, the majority of policy loans are not repaid prior to surrender, maturity, or death, at which time they are deducted from the proceeds or cash value payable.
5. When market interest rates are higher than the rate charged on policy loans, the policyholder can borrow his equity and reinvest it at a higher rate elsewhere. This creates a cash drain upon the company and reduces the amount of money available for investing upon favorable terms. In this sense the borrowing policyholder gains an advantage at the expense of those who do not borrow. The lower the guaranteed rate, the more likely it becomes that such a situation will occur.

Frequently, market conditions are such that loans can be obtained at a lower rate of interest by borrowing from a bank on security of the policy. There are, however, several disadvantages in making such loans. Some banks are not interested in making small loans. They may change the rate of interest or call the loan. They may not allow partial repayment of small amounts, as the insurance company will permit. The procedure for negotiating the loan is more complicated and generally takes more time than the simple procedure involved in dealing with the insurance company. However, the use of life insurance contracts as collateral for bank loans is a common practice.

Automatic Premium Loans

Many policies contain an automatic premium loan provision under which, if a premium is not paid within the grace period, it is automatically advanced as a loan, provided the cash value is sufficient to cover the premium. Subsequent unpaid premiums are similarly advanced until the cash value is exhausted. The laws of Montana and Rhode Island require the inclusion of such a provision, which must be effective unless the policyholder elects another option.

Usually, this provision is not an automatic option but must be elected by the policyholder either at the time the policy is issued or at a later date.

While premiums are being advanced under this provision, all other provisions of the policy remain in effect, and no evidence of insurability is required if the policyholder elects to resume payment of premiums. Dividends continue to be paid, and any supplementary benefits such as waiver of premium, double indemnity, or term insurance riders (which terminate when extended term insurance or reduced paid-up insurance becomes effective) remain in force.

The main advantage of the provision is that it prevents inadvertent lapse of the policy, which sometimes occurs if the policyholder is away from home or ill, or is short of funds when the premium notice arrives. The disadvantage is that once the policyholder starts to use the provision, he may get out of the habit of paying premiums in cash, with the result that the policy may eventually terminate when the cash value becomes exhausted.

If the automatic premium loan provision is in operation instead of the extended term insurance provision, the period of coverage is generally somewhat longer, although the net amount payable on death gradually decreases because of the increasing loan. In the later policy years, particularly on participating policies where dividends are used to reduce premiums, extended term is likely to give a much shorter period of coverage than automatic premium loan. The chief advantage of the automatic premium loan provision lies in the fact that insurability is preserved and full coverage can be restored at any time.

On substandard policies, the extended term insurance provision is generally not available, particularly if the rating is high. The election of the automatic loan provision in such cases gives the policyholder more substantial immediate coverage upon default in payment of premiums than would be provided by the reduced paid-up insurance provision which would otherwise become effective.

A few companies have attempted to overcome the disadvantage of this provision by limiting the operation of automatic premium loans to two successive years, or a limited number of premiums, after which the extended term benefit becomes effective unless the premium is paid in cash. In the latter case, the automatic loan provision would again become effective in the event of a subsequent default.

SELECTED REFERENCES

HOSKINS, J. E. "Asset Shares and Their Relation to Nonforfeiture Values," *Transactions of the Actuarial Society of America,* Vol. XL (1939), p. 379.

NATIONAL ASSOCIATION OF INSURANCE COMMISSIONERS. *Reports and Statements on Nonforfeiture Benefits and Related Matters.* Chicago: Actuarial Society of America and American Institute of Actuaries, 1942.

RICHARDSON, CHARLES F. B. "Guaranteed Cash Surrender Values under Modern Conditions," *Transactions of the Actuarial Society of America,* Vol. XXXIX (1938), p. 237.

SHEPHERD, B. E. "Natural Reserves," *Transactions of the Actuarial Society of America,* Vol. XLI (1940), p. 463.

Chapter 14

DIVIDENDS AND THEIR USE

BY ARTHUR MASON, JR.

A policy providing that the insurance company will return annually to the policyholder premiums in excess of those needed to pay current costs is termed a "participating" policy. The amount to be returned is determined annually and is called a "policy dividend," a term brought to the United States from Europe, where it was used long before life insurance existed in North America.[1] Although participating policies and dividends have been associated primarily with mutual insurance companies, many stock companies offer participating policies and dividends.

The Nature of the Dividend

The insurance company, in computing the rate to charge a participating policyholder throughout the premium-paying period, intentionally overestimates its future needs for funds. The amount of funds needed necessarily must be sufficient to meet current obligations, to permit the accumulation of funds for future obligations, and to maintain the solvency of the company. The purpose of the overcharge in a participating premium is twofold. First, it provides additional margins in case the costs prove to be higher than anticipated, margins which can be drawn upon rather than drawing upon surplus funds of other policyholders. The second reason for the overcharge is that, by this method, the policyholder is able to buy life insurance at what will prove to be the actual cost, through his overpayment and subsequently his receipt of a refund called a dividend which can be determined after the actual cost is known. The contrast with this is the purchase of life insurance on a nonparticipating basis where the policyholder pays a fixed premium each year regardless of what costs prove to be. These guaranteed premiums may prove to be more or less than was needed to meet the actual cost of providing the insurance protection.

[1] A policy dividend is distinguished from dividends paid to stockholders of stock life insurance companies. The latter are similar to dividends to stockholders of any other corporation.

The excess of the actual over the expected results under participating policies becomes, in a sense, surplus. Each year, companies must decide how much of the surplus is to be retained and how much distributed to policyholders. The amount to be retained for additional protection of the policyholder is to some extent a matter of opinion. However, many states have statutes dealing with the maximum amount that may be retained and providing for distribution of surplus in the form of dividends.

Sources of Dividends

In general, three factors contribute to surplus and to the amount of the dividend for a given policy in a given year. These are mortality, loading, and investment yield.

Mortality Element. The contribution the mortality element makes toward dividends depends on the relationship between actual death claims and mortality rates as indicated by the mortality tables used as the basis for premium calculations. The better the actual mortality experience in relation to the expected, the greater the contribution of this element. Conversely, the poorer the actual experience, the smaller the contribution made by the mortality element to dividends.

Whether a gain is incurred or a loss sustained is dependent on a variety of factors, one of which is the mortality table used. The tables often contain a contingency or safety factor to compensate for excessive death rates that might occur. If death rates are normal or below normal, savings result, and a factor emerges as a part of the dividend. A second factor is the underwriting practices of the company. The company that is more liberal in determining the insurability of an applicant at a given premium should have a less favorable mortality experience than the company which is more stringent in its underwriting practices. A third factor is the period of time the policy has been in force. During the early policy years, favorable mortality experience results from the effect of recent selection. The generally declining trend in death rates in recent years has also produced favorable mortality experience. Finally, a contribution to surplus may result from favorable morbidity experience of those policies containing waiver-of-premium or disability income benefits.[2]

Loading Element. In computing premiums, liberal estimates of costs of operation are included in the loading. This results in expense savings. Also, the incidence of expenses is not level over the life of the policy even though the loading is level throughout the premium-paying period. Initially, costs of selling and issuing the policy usually exceed the loading; but in later years, expenses are lower. Hence a contribution to surplus exists.

The contribution of the loading element in the second and subsequent

[2] Technically, favorable morbidity experience should be considered as a fourth element (in addition to mortality, loading, and investment elements), but it is arbitrarily included at this point of the discussion for convenience.

years is a function of the period of time over which the company amortizes the excess first-year costs and the actual costs of operation as they are affected by general economic conditions and improved techniques of operation. The various state laws fix minimum nonforfeiture values at such levels that a company properly conducting its business will have margins to amortize the first-year costs. The period may be selected by the company.

Investment Element. An insurance company assumes, in computing premiums, that a certain rate of return will be earned on the assets offsetting its reserve liabilities. These rates of interest may or may not be the same as the rates used in calculating reserves. Investment earnings in excess of assumed earnings determine the contribution to surplus from this source.

The contribution of the investment element to the dividend will be different for each kind of policy, age of the insured at issue, and length of time the policy has been in force. The excess investment earnings will be apportioned in accordance with the reserves on the particular policy.

In addition to excess investment earnings, the company may enjoy capital gains or sustain capital losses from the sale of assets. If either occurs, it will have an additional impact on the contribution the investment element makes toward dividends. It will normally appear as an adjustment to the interest factor in the dividend formula. However, since life insurance companies generally experience few investment losses, this aspect of the investment element is relatively insignificant in dividend computations.

Distribution of Surplus

The surplus arising from favorable experience under participating policies should be distributed equitably among those policyholders. Ideally, each policyholder should receive a dividend consisting of the net contribution by his policy to surplus. Practically, the complexity of determining the contribution of each element by individual policies does not make this possible.

As in other aspects of life insurance, the procedure is to group the policyholders into classes and seek approximate equity among classes and among policyholders within classes. The elements making up surplus are each evaluated, and the approximate proportion of each element contributed by the class is allocated to the class. These amounts are distributed as dividends to the policyholders in the class responsible for them. The technique used to accomplish this equitable distribution of surplus is the "dividend formula."

Annual Dividends

For most of the twentieth century, it has been the practice of American companies to pay dividends annually on the anniversary date of the policy.[3] This practice stems primarily from laws enacted in the early 1900's calling for such a distribution.

Terminal Dividends

In addition to annual dividends, some companies pay a "terminal" dividend. The circumstances under which a terminal dividend is paid vary among companies. Terminal dividends are paid most often when the policy matures as an endowment or is surrendered.

The arguments for the payment of such a dividend are: (1) Companies do not distribute all surplus annually, but accumulate a portion of surplus in order to increase their financial strength and the protection afforded the policyholders; (2) it permits more equitable treatment than is possible under annual distribution under certain conditions, such as returning funds retained to strengthen reserves; (3) it preserves equity on cash settlements when surplus has been retained for settlement option losses; and (4) it provides a means of reducing losses caused by early withdrawals.

Special Distribution of "Dividends"

In recent years, contracts calling for special distributions of "dividends" have made their reappearance. In some cases, they are of a deferred dividend type, in which distributions are made less frequently than annually except when a death claim arises, and then a proportional distribution is made. In most instances, a twenty-year period is used. In other cases, the distribution may be made from only one of the three sources, and then there are conditions precedent to such a distribution. For example, the distribution of the special dividend may occur only after the capital stock life insurance company pays a dividend to its stockholders.

Many kinds of special dividends exist. They are normally found in the policies of some relatively new life insurance companies. These companies have included special dividend provisions in their policies to make them more attractive to the prospective buyer of insurance. Such special dividend distribution plans are not permitted in a number of states.

Dividend Options

Four dividend options are generally available to policyholders, including cash, premium credits or reduction of premiums, purchase of paid-up additions, and accumulation at interest. (See Figure 14–1.) In addition, many companies are now offering a fifth option, under which a part of the dividend is used to buy one-year term insurance.

The policyholder selects the dividend option at the time the policy is purchased. This selection usually remains in effect until a change is made.

[3] Some policies issued in Canada by Canadian companies provide for a dividend distribution every five years rather than annually.

Apportionment of Dividends. Upon payment of premiums to the end of the second policy year as they become due and payable in accordance with the terms hereof, and at the end of the second and each subsequent policy year, this policy while in force will be credited with such share of the surplus funds of the Company as may be apportioned hereto by the Directors, such apportioned shares being designated herein as dividends.

If the death of the insured occurs after the first policy year, and while this policy is in force, such post-mortem share of surplus as may be apportioned by the Directors will be included in the proceeds of the policy.

How Dividends May Be Used. At the option of the insured, while this policy is in full force, dividends will be (1) paid in cash, or (2) applied in reduction of premiums, or (3) used to purchase participating paid-up additions, payable with the sum insured, or (4) held by the Company to accumulate subject to withdrawal by the insured on demand. The insured may surrender paid-up additions which will have a value equal to the net single premium therefor at the then attained age of the insured, which value shall be not less than the dividends used to purchase such additions. Dividend accumulations will be credited at the end of each policy year with interest at such rate, not less than two per cent, as may determined by the Directors. Outstanding dividend accumulations will be paid in cash in the event of surrender of the policy, or will be added to the amount payable under the policy if it becomes a claim by death or matures as an endowment, or will be payable to the insured in one sum as of the date to which premiums have been paid in the event that extended term insurance becomes effective. If the insured has elected that dividends be applied in reduction of premuims and a premium due on the date on which a dividend is payable remains unpaid at the expiration of the grace period, the dividend will be automatically used to pay in full the premium shown by the policy under the next more frequent interval of payment, if any, for which such dividend may be sufficient, and any balance of dividend will be paid in cash; subsequent premiums on this policy shall be payable in accordance with such method of payment unless a written request for change shall be made. If no election is operative on any anniversary, the dividend due on that anniversary will be held by the Company to accumulate unless otherwise required by law.

Policy Fully Paid for or Matured for Face Amount. At the end of any policy year, if a request is made therefor and a release is given, satisfactory to the Company, this policy will be (1) endorsed as fully paid for, subject to any indebtedness hereunder, provided dividend accumulations, or the value available on surrender of paid-up additions, or both, together with the cash value of the policy, shall equal the net single premium at the then attained age of the insured for a fully paid-up policy of the same kind and amount; or (2) paid as an endowment less any indebtedness hereunder, provided such aggregate amount shall equal the face amount of the policy.

FIG. 14–1. A typical dividend provision. From sample policy of Institute Life Company available from Institute of Life Insurance.

If no selection is made, most companies will accumulate at interest or, in more recent instances, will apply to the purchase of paid-up additions. The policyholder may elect an option or change to another option during the time the policy is in force, although it is the practice of some companies to require the insured to show evidence of insurability satisfactory to the insurer in order to change to either the paid-up additions or the one-year term insurance options.

Cash Dividends

Under this option, the insurance company sends to the policyholder a check for the amount of the dividend on the anniversary date of the policy.

This option is commonly selected where the policy is paid up and the policyholder can make other uses of the dividend. From an insurance viewpoint the dividend may be used to pay a portion or all of the annual premium on other life insurance presently owned or to be purchased. Also, in the event the policyholder has a policy loan outstanding, the dividend provides money for a systematic repayment of the loan.

Premium Credits or Reduction of Premiums

The policyholder may elect to use his dividends to reduce future premiums. The insurance company will apply the dividend as part payment of the next premium only if the remainder of that premium is received before the grace period expires. The dividend also may prevent the policy from lapsing in the event the policyholder fails to pay his premium. For example, some companies will use the dividend to pay the premium on a quarterly rather than an annual basis, provided the dividend is sufficient.[4]

A young married man with dependents who needs to increase the amount of his life insurance, but whose income may be inadequate to do so, may find the premium credit option most beneficial. By applying the dividends to future premiums, the net annual outlay for a larger amount of life insurance may be within his means.[5] Similarly, an older person with a continuing need for life insurance but whose income declines as he approaches or reaches retirement may be able to keep his annual outlays for life insurance within his financial means by election of this option.

From time to time, temporary situations may arise which dictate the use of the premium credit option. Disability, unemployment, or unexpected major expenses may occur, and the use of the dividend as a

---

[4] Usually, these companies will apply the automatic premium loan provision, if elected by the insured, before changing to a more frequent payment interval for which the dividend is sufficient.

[5] An alternative solution to this young man's problem might be to buy nonparticipating insurance.

premium credit may be the only way to reduce the premium outlay short of terminating the policy. When the situation has changed, the policyholder may again change the dividend to one more appropriate for his needs at that time.

Dividends to Accumulate on Deposit

The effect of this option is to create a savings fund that accumulates at a minimum guaranteed rate of interest stated in the policy. The policyholder, having created this savings fund, has the right to withdraw a portion or all of it at any time. However, once withdrawn, it cannot be replaced. This dividend option provides the policyholder the greatest degree of flexibility for meeting changing needs without changing the dividend option.

The dividends held by the insurance company accumulate on a guaranteed compound interest basis which adds to the attractiveness of this option. Also, such accumulated dividends share in any interest earnings in excess of the guaranteed rate that is apportioned by the directors of the company.

When the policyholder wants to apply the dividend accumulations to a specific use, he must make his wishes known to the company in writing. If he desires the company to use the fund for periodic premium payments when he fails to pay them, he must notify the company in writing. The company can do this if the accumulation is large enough to cover the premium due. Furthermore, the company can change the premium-paying period to a more frequent one in the event the fund is not adequate to pay the premium due, but this change can be made only if the accumulation is sufficient to pay a fractional premium; it cannot be used as a partial payment unless the remainder of the premium is received by the company prior to the expiration of the grace period.

The policyholder also may use the accumulated dividends, when of sufficient amount, either to pay up the policy or to mature it as an endowment. A policy is paid up when the cash value (less any indebtedness) plus accumulated dividends equals the net single premium at the attained age for the policy. To mature as an endowment, the sum of the cash value (less any indebtedness) and accumulated dividends must equal the face amount. In the use of accumulated dividends in either manner, the insured need not restrict the use of accumulations prior to the time when they are applied to pay up the policy or mature it as an endowment. Once the dividend accumulation is applied to one or the other of these uses, it loses its separate identity. If the insured dies prior to withdrawing or applying the accumulation, the face amount of the policy, less any indebtedness, plus accumulated dividends, is paid. Similarly, if the policy is surrendered prior to its becoming paid up or maturing, the cash value and accumulated dividends are paid to the policyholder.

This dividend option has important applications in business insurance situations as well as in personal situations. A policy on a key employee for the protection of the business may, when supplemented by dividend accumulations, provide all or a portion of retirement benefits for the employee. Similarly, a deferred compensation plan funded by insurance and dividend accumulations can provide a larger sum than would otherwise be available.

The accumulation option, although offering a high degree of flexibility, has lost some of its popularity among policyholders due to its federal income tax status. The interest earned on dividend accumulations is reportable by the insurance company as interest income to the policyholder. Now that the company must file information returns with the Internal Revenue Service, many policyholders are switching from this option to others, such as purchase of paid-up additions, and converting outstanding accumulations to paid-up additions.

Purchase of Paid-up Additions

Under this option, the dividend is used to buy for the policyholder additional paid-up insurance of the same kind as the policy he owns. Thus, if the policyholder has a straight life insurance policy, he accumulates paid-up additions of straight life insurance. The dividend is used each year as a single premium to buy additional insurance at the insured's attained age. During the period when the option is operative, a series of single-premium policies is purchased.

The amount of life insurance purchased in a given year is a function of the insured's attained age, the amount of the dividend, and the kind of policy. The amount of additional paid-up life insurance purchased by each dollar of dividend decreases as the insured becomes older because the single premium for a straight life policy for a fixed amount of insurance increases as a person becomes older. At a given age, the same dollar amount of dividend will buy a larger paid-up straight life policy than paid-up endowment policy because the maturity date of the endowment policy is earlier. Stated differently, given the same age, the single premium for an endowment policy will always be larger than that for a straight life policy. If a person owned two policies of the same type but received different amounts of dividends, the policy paying the larger dividend would provide the greater amount of paid-up addition. Analysis of the effects of these three factors on the amount of paid-up additions may be complicated by the lack of comparability that these illustrations assume.

The paid-up additions option is normally selected at the time the policy is issued. If the option is chosen later, companies generally will not require evidence of insurability from the insured. However, if an existing accumulation of dividends is to be converted, evidence of insurability is required if the amount is substantial.

Paid-up additions have all the features of the policy from which they arose. If the basic policy has cash values, so also have the paid-up additions. As usual, the cash values may be obtained by surrendering the policy or may be borrowed. Generally, if the paid-up additions are surrendered, the cash values will be equal to the net single premiums at the attained age and in no event less than the dividends used to purchase such additions. The paid-up additions may be assigned, or they may be paid out as part of the policy proceeds under settlement options. Most companies automatically pay the proceeds of the paid-up additions under the income option selected by the policyholder for the basic contract.

This dividend option provides the policyholder with a long-range program for increasing the amount of life insurance owned, usually at net premiums.[6] Present life insurance may be inadequate to meet the policyholder's needs in either personal or business situations, and the purchases of life insurance through paid-up additions form an important supplement to the original amount of insurance. On the other hand, present life insurance may be adequate; but the insured, in anticipation of increased needs for life insurance, may select this option to provide a systematic increase in his life insurance. The paid-up additions option is particularly valuable to the policyholder who becomes uninsurable.

One-Year Term Insurance

Under this relatively new option (sometimes called the "fifth dividend option") now offered by many companies, the dividend buys additional one-year term insurance typically equal to the cash value of the policy. Each year on the policy anniversary date, a one-year term contract is bought for that year. Any remaining portion of the dividend, after buying the term insurance, may be accumulated or paid out to the policyholder.

This option is advantageous when the policy has a loan against it but the insured desires to maintain the full face amount of insurance or as close to the full face amount as is possible. Any indebtedness is subtracted from the face amount payable at death; however, the term insurance is payable in addition to this net amount. Whether the total amount paid as a death benefit is equal to, less than, or more than the face amount of insurance is dependent upon the amount of indebtedness, the amount of dividends, and the age of the insured.

This option is commonly used in split-dollar plans. Under such a plan, the amount of the insurance benefit for the employee's beneficiaries declines as the cash value increases. By selecting the one-year term option, the employee may maintain the full face amount as the death benefit for his beneficiary or beneficiaries.[7]

If the policyholder has combined a decreasing term insurance rider of

---

[6] For a distinction between net and gross premiums, see Chapter 11, "Premiums—Net and Gross."

[7] For further information on split dollar arrangements, see Chapter 60, "Split Dollar and Related Plans."

the family income type with a base plan of permanent insurance, he may find this option useful. The annual reduction in the amount of insurance provided by the rider is offset, in part, by the one-year term insurance.

This option, like paid-up additions, is normally selected at the time the policy is purchased. Election of this option at a later date usually requires evidence of insurability satisfactory to the company.

Summary

Selection of the proper dividend option requires the same attention as that required for proper selection of the amount of insurance and the type of policy. The choice is one of the policyholder's many rights. As with many of his other rights in the policy, the most appropriate selection will give him the maximum benefit from his life insurance—during his lifetime, upon death, or at retirement.

SELECTED REFERENCES

GUERTIN, ALFRED N. "Price Planning," in DAN M. MCGILL (ed.), *Life Insurance Sales Management,* pp. 116–63. Homewood, Ill.: Richard D. Irwin, Inc., 1957.

KRUEGER, HARRY, and WAGGONER, LELAND T. (eds.). *The Life Insurance Policy Contract.* Boston: Little, Brown & Co., 1953.

MACLEAN, JOSEPH B. *Life Insurance.* 9th ed. New York: McGraw-Hill Book Co., Inc., 1962.

MACLEAN, JOSEPH B., and MARSHALL, EDWARD W. *Distribution of Surplus.* Actuarial Study No. 6. Chicago: Actuarial Society of America, 1937.

MCGILL, DAN M. *Life Insurance.* Homewood, Ill.: Richard D. Irwin, Inc., 1959.

Chapter 15

IMPORTANT CONTRACT PROVISIONS

BY KENNETH W. HERRICK

Contract provisions are subject to state regulation and control, with most states requiring the inclusion of certain so-called "standard provisions." The exact wording of the standard provisions is not prescribed by law; hence, they are not actually "standard" in the sense that variations in phraseology are precluded. Approval of policies by the regulatory authorities is necessary, and the result is that all policies must contain the standard provisions in substance, although wording more liberal to policyowners than that employed in the statutes can be used.

Some of the more important standard provisions as well as *some* other important contract provisions are the subject of this chapter. Provisions quoted herein can only be cited as typical, since insurers are not required to employ uniform terminology. In this chapter, as elsewhere in this section, reference is confined to the individual branch of life insurance as distinct from group life insurance.

Grace Period

Any premium after the first may be paid not more than thirty-one days after the date upon which such premium becomes payable, during which grace period the policy will be continued in full force. If death occurs within the grace period, the premium, if unpaid, will be deducted from the amount payable hereunder.

The purpose of the grace period is to protect policyowners against unintentional lapsation, occurrence of which allows the insurer to require satisfactory evidence of insurability as a condition precedent to reinstatement. Provision for a grace period of at least one month is required by most states, and insurers prefer to state the specific number of days to avoid any misunderstanding regarding the exact duration of the grace period. If death occurs during the grace period prior to premium payment, the insurer is entitled to deduct the premium due from the proceeds ordinarily payable to the beneficiary. Most companies deduct only a monthly or a quarterly premium, especially when the contract provides for refund of the balance of premium in case of death.

In states requiring insurers to send policyowners a premium notice, the objective of the grace period is accomplished anyway; and as a matter of practice, companies send out premium notices even when not required to do so by statute. Be that as it may, a grace period is generally required and thus provides insureds with the comforting knowledge that if they are a little late in paying a premium, nothing is lost.

There is generally nothing in the law to prevent insurers from stipulating that interest will be charged on late premiums paid during the grace period or that when death occurs during the grace period, interest on the premium due as well as the premium itself will be charged against the policy proceeds. However, as a matter of practice, insurers do not provide for a loss of interest charge in this clause. Loss of interest during the grace period, as well as the thirty-one days of "free" insurance afforded those who lapse their policies and do not reinstate, is a cost borne by all premium payers in the form of a slightly higher premium than would be necessary if the grace provision could be omitted.

Incontestable Clause[1]

Inclusion of an incontestable provision in the life insurance policy contract is mandatory in most states. A common form of the provision is as follows:

> This policy shall be incontestable after it has been in force during the lifetime of the insured for a period of two years from the date of issue except for default in premium payment.

The purpose of the clause is to prevent the insurer, after a certain period of time (commonly two years), from denying a claim either on the basis of statements contained in the application or on grounds of concealment.

Death of an insured typically takes place many years after the policy was obtained. If, at the time of death, insurers were allowed to challenge the validity of a claim on grounds of misstatements in the application or concealment, the beneficiary would be at a decided disadvantage. The deceased insured (the one with firsthand knowledge of the facts) could not help the beneficiary. In addition, the beneficiary is frequently in great need of money and not in a position to command the same caliber of legal talent available to insurers. The advantage to the insurer inherent in this situation is eliminated when death occurs after expiration of the contestable period. Litigation is all but precluded, since none of the

---

[1] See Chapter 16 for further discussion of basic legal concepts underlying the incontestable clause.

insured's statements can be used as a basis for contesting the claim. Prompt payment of death proceeds is greatly facilitated by the existence of this clause.

The incontestable clause has the practical effect of making a fraudulent contract a valid contract at the end of the contestable period, since it has generally been held that the time limit specified precludes use of "fraud" as a defense by the insurer after the period has expired. This is an exception to the law that agreements in contracts to disregard fraud are against public policy and hence void. The incontestable clause thus does permit applicants for insurance to take advantage of insurers. However, insurers have some measure of protection, since they can initiate contests during the contestable period, and they do have time in which to verify statements contained in an application. In the entire field of contract law, the clause is unique to life insurance contracts, and there is no generally accepted legal explanation for it.

The unique nature of the incontestable clause has resulted in some legal confusion centering on what constitutes a "contest." The majority of courts have held that action to enforce contract terms is not a contest. Consequently, if, for example, the policy excludes death as a result of war and the insured is killed as a result of war, the insurer is simply complying with contract terms in not paying the death claim. The insurer, in so doing, is not contesting. Action to rescind a contract does constitute a contest and is not permitted after the contestable period has expired. Thus, correct legal interpretation does not prevent insurers from enforcing contract terms at any time—for example, those contained in the suicide or misstatement-of-age clauses—but it does prevent insurers from attempting to rescind a policy after the contestable period.

Though not included in the written terms of the insurance contract, common law is a part of all contracts. Thus, courts have held it to be against public policy for insurers to pay a claim when there was no insurable interest at the inception of the policy. The same ruling has prevailed in cases where someone other than the named insured took the physical examination and obtained the policy.

Entire Contract Clause

This policy and the application therefor, a copy of which is attached hereto, constitute the entire contract between the parties. All statements made by the insured in applying for this policy shall, in the absence of fraud, be deemed representations and not warranties, and no statement made by or on behalf of the insured shall avoid this policy or be used in defense of a claim hereunder, unless it is contained in said application and a copy thereof is attached to this policy when issued.

An entire contract clause is mandatory in most states; and in addition, some states require a statement similar to that contained in the second sentence quoted. The purpose of the first sentence is to prevent insurers from making their charter or bylaws a part of the policy contract. The objective of the second sentence is to make it unnecessary that statements by the insured be literally true so long as they are substantially correct. The distinction between warranty and representation is a tenuous one. In essence, a warranted statement must be literally true regardless of its materiality; if not true, the contract is voidable. A representation must be both untrue and material to make a contract voidable. By "material" is meant that the fact is of sufficient importance to have caused the insurer to reject the applicant or else to have taken different underwriting action on the application if it had known the truth.

Actually, despite the statement that the policy and the application constitute the entire contract, they do not constitute the entire contract. Statutory law and case law both are a part of the contract. Insured and insurer cannot by mutual agreement waive any provision required by law to be included in a policy. Moreover, case law rulings will be read into contracts. For example, courts have ruled that beneficiary murderers are not to receive death proceeds, and such decisions will prevent payment to a beneficiary though the contract itself says the beneficiary will receive the death proceeds. The entire contract clause does not apply to actions taking place after the policy is issued. For example, riders may be attached to a policy, beneficiaries may be changed, and so forth.

Misstatement-of-Age Clause

If the age of the insured has been misstated, the amount payable shall be such as the premium paid would have purchased at the correct age.

A provision similar to the one quoted above is required by most states. The purpose of the clause is to provide for an equitable settlement in cases where the insured's age has been misstated. The premium paid for a given amount of life insurance is dependent upon the age of the insured at time of issue. The older a person is, the less insurance a given premium will purchase. The misstatement-of-age clause provides that should the correct age of the insured differ from the age given in the application used to determine the premium, the amount of insurance will be adjusted to the amount the premium actually paid would have purchased at the insured's correct age at issue. For example, assume that the annual premium for a $10,000 policy was $200 if taken out at age 30 and $250 if taken out at age 34, and a person age 34 misstated his age as 30 and thus paid $200 for the $10,000 policy. Upon the insured's death, the beneficiary would receive $8,000 (the amount of insurance which $200 would have purchased for a person aged 34 at time of issue). When the correct age has been overstated, the proceeds paid upon death will exceed the face amount stated in the policy.

When an error in age is discovered by the insurer during the lifetime of the insured, the adjustment made generally depends upon whether age has been overstated or understated.[2] If age has been overstated, the insurer usually refunds the difference in reserves. However, under the usual misstatement-of-age provision, the insured, at his option, seemingly could insist on such additional insurance protection as would be purchased by the full premium at his correct age. Conversely, if the age has been understated, the choice of alternatives lies with the insurer. Usually, the insurer will charge the difference in reserves; but at the insurer's option, it can insist that the insured accept such reduced insurance as the premium paid would purchase at the correct age.

If the insured anticipates that there may be difficulty in establishing his correct age because of the unavailability of suitable records attesting thereto, he should seek an agreement in writing from the insurer "admitting" his age for purposes of the insurance policy. Insurers are willing to make agreements in these cases upon submission of the available evidence. This arrangement will avoid delay in payment of death proceeds at time of death which otherwise might be encountered.

The misstatement-of-age clause is not subject to the incontestable clause, for this is not a contest of the policy but an application of the exact terms of the policy specified to cover the situation which has developed.

Suicide Clause

If within two years from the date of issue the insured shall die by suicide, whether sane or insane, the liability of the company hereunder shall be limited to payment in one sum of the amount of premiums paid.

All states permit, but do not require, insurers to include a provision regarding death by suicide similar to or more favorable to the insured than that quoted above, and insurers generally include one. The purpose of the clause is to protect insurers from adverse selection and to prevent acquisition of insurance from serving as an inducement to suicide. The intent is to exclude claims when the insured takes the policy with suicide in mind; and with few exceptions, this objective can be accomplished by limiting the suicide exclusion to the first year or two after issue, because few people would buy a life insurance policy with intent to commit suicide and then wait two years to do it. Deaths by suicide are incorporated in the mortality tables; thus, it is not necessary to exclude suicides other than those where the policy is taken with suicide in mind. Nor is it desirable to penalize innocent beneficiaries unnecessarily. Consequently, a reasonable waiting period provides the practical solution to the problem.

An accepted definition of suicide is voluntary and intentional self-destruction. Courts are in general agreement that the taking of one's own

[2] Some companies also cover misstatement of sex, too, since it is used in rate determination.

life while insane is an accident and thus not intentional. In order to exclude all deaths resulting from self-destruction, insurers employ the words "sane or insane." When an insurer seeks to deny a claim on grounds that it is excluded by the suicide clause, the burden of proof is on the insurer, since a presumption against suicide is recognized by law.

The incontestable clause does not apply to the suicide clause, because here again there is no contest of the policy but merely an application of the policy terms to cover the contingency which has arisen. In fact, when the time cited in the suicide clause is equal to or shorter than the time limit in the incontestable clause, which is commonly the case, there is no possibility of disagreement on this point.

The majority rule is that reinstatement does not reopen the suicide period, because reinstatement does not result in a new contract but is simply restoration of an existing policy. Where courts have held that reinstatement does result in a new contract, then the time would logically start all over again.

Reinstatement Clause

About two thirds of the states require that a reinstatement clause be included in life contracts, and whether required by statute or not, insurers universally employ such a clause in their policies. The purpose of the clause is to provide an equitable means of restoring an insured to his original position when he has unintentionally lapsed his policy. A representative clause reads as follows:

> This policy may be reinstated within five years after the date of premium default if it has not been surrendered for its cash value. Reinstatement is subject to (1) receipt of evidence of insurability satisfactory to the company, (2) payment of all overdue premiums with interest from the due date of each at the rate of 5 per cent per annum, and (3) payment or reinstatement of any indebtedness existing on the date of premium default with interest from that date.

State statutes generally require the insurer to provide for reinstatement during a three-year period, but terms more liberal than those required by law can be used by insurers, and a five-year period is commonly employed in practice.

The phrase "evidence of insurability satisfactory to the company" has raised some legal questions as to its exact meaning. Today, there is little question that "insurability" encompasses more than just good health.[3] Occupation, habits, financial condition, and other selection factors are included in the determination of "insurability."

The legal interpretation of the phrase "satisfactory to the company" has also caused some problems. The majority opinion on this point is that there must be a sound and logical reason on the part of the insurer for

[3] *Kallman* v. *Equitable Life Assurance Society*, 248 AD 146, 288 NYS 1032 (1936).

finding the applicant uninsurable. The insurer cannot "act arbitrarily or capriciously but . . . evidence which would be satisfactory to a reasonable insurer is all that is necessary."[4]

The type of proof of insurability required is generally dependent upon the length of time the policy has lapsed. Many insurers require no proof if reinstatement is sought within thirty-one days after the end of the grace period. If reinstatement is sought within six months, a simple statement by the insured that he is in good health may be all the insurer will require. Reinstatements involving longer time periods generally require a physical examination. The insurer needs to insist upon some proof if it is adequately to protect itself against adverse selection.

On participating policies, some insurers give a dividend credit, in determining the payment to reinstate, equal to the dividends that would have been paid the insured had he actually paid his premiums when due. The payment to reinstate a term policy (which has no nonforfeiture options) is simply the current premium.

What about the status of the incontestable and suicide clauses when a policy is reinstated? The majority of courts have ruled that the incontestable period starts all over again with reinstatement, but only with reference to statements made by the applicant to reinstate the policy. On suicide, the majority view is that the time period specified in the contract does not begin anew with reinstatement; hence a suicide after reinstatement would be covered. Although the preceding statements represent the "majority rules," some courts have made decisions to the contrary.

When an insured reinstates, the effect is to restore his original contract. On occasion, insurers have attempted to place limitations on reinstated policies that were not in the original policies, e.g., a war clause or an aviation clause. When challenged, insurers have generally been defeated in court on this point. Insurers have also generally been prevented from deleting some coverage, such as disability income or the accidental death benefit, from the reinstated contract that was in the original policy.

When an insured has a choice of reinstating his policy or buying a new policy to replace his lapsed policy, it is generally to his advantage to reinstate. Reinstatement avoids incurring acquisition costs again, and additional acquisition costs are reflected in lower nonforfeiture values. In addition, it may be that the original policy contains terms more favorable to the insured than can be obtained in policies currently being issued.

Ownership Clause

An ownership clause is not mandatory, and there is a lack of uniformity among insurers in practice on this point. If the applicant is also the insured and he names a revocable beneficiary, then the applicant-

[4] *Kennedy* v. *Occidental Life Insurance Company*, 18 Cal.(2d) 627, 117 P.(2d) 3 (1941).

insured has complete control over the policy and is its owner. There are a number of valuable rights which the owner of a life policy can exercise, and to reduce the possibility of a dispute over who is the owner many companies employ an ownership clause similar to the one that follows:

> All privileges of ownership under this policy are vested in the owner named in this policy. Where used in this policy, "owner" means such owner, his successor, or transferee. "Privileges of ownership" means the right, before the death of the insured and without the consent of any beneficiary, to change the beneficiary one or more times; to receive every benefit and exercise every option, right, and privilege provided in this policy or allowed by the company to the owner; and to assign, transfer, or agree to any modification of this policy or any interest therein.

Where the owner is to be other than the insured, some companies issue an "ownership form" policy which emphasizes the rights of the owner in the policy by employing the word "owner" throughout the contract. Here again, the objective is to minimize the possibility of misunderstandings and disputes. This form of policy may also have more sales appeal in situations where the owner is other than the insured.

Assignment Clause

An assignment is the transfer of some or all incidents of ownership, and the owner of a life insurance policy has this right as a matter of law. Thus, there is no necessity to provide this right in the life contract itself, but an assignment clause is universally employed primarily for the purpose of delineating the insurer's responsibilities in the event the policy owner exercises his right to assign the policy. The wording of a typical clause is as follows:

> The company shall not be charged with notice of any assignment of any interest in the policy until the original assignment or a certified copy has been filed with the company at its home office. The company assumes no responsibility as to the validity or effect of any assignment and may rely solely on the assignee's statement as to the amount of his interest. All assignments shall be subject to any indebtedness to the company on this policy.
>
> The interest of any beneficiary shall be subordinate to any assignment, whether the assignment was made before or after the designation of beneficiary, and the assignee shall receive any sum payable to the extent of his interest.

The requirement that the insurer must be notified of an assignment relieves the insurer of responsibility where notice is not given, but the assignment is still valid between the owner and the assignee—the contracting parties. Since the insurer is not a party to the assignment transaction, it is not required to be responsible for the validity of the assignment.

Despite the fact that the assignment clause clearly stipulates that the assignee's rights are superior to those of the beneficiary, some courts may hold to the contrary. Where the beneficiary is the insured's estate, the assignee's prior right has been unquestioned. Thus, some insurers follow the practice of having the insured make his estate beneficiary prior to making an assignment, to avoid possible legal complications.[5]

War Clause

War clauses can be classified as either "result" or "status" types, although the varied phraseology employed in war clauses has often produced litigation over attempts to brand a clause as a result or status type. The status type excludes death while the insured is in military service outside the home areas, regardless of the cause of death, and a number of states no longer will permit this type of clause to be used. The result type excludes only deaths as a result of war, and it is favored by the majority of insurers. War clauses are rather lengthy and vary considerably among insurers; hence, none is quoted here. A few states specifically stipulate the wording that must be used in a war clause.

War clauses cannot be inserted into existing policies, and insurers seldom employ them on new contracts except when war has been declared or the danger of war is particularly imminent. Then they are generally placed in policies being issued to persons especially subject to the war peril. At the cessation of hostilities, insurers commonly cancel war clauses. The alternative to use of war clauses is for insurers to decline applications from those subject to the war peril or to charge an extra premium for this protection. Neither of these alternatives has proven satisfactory in the past.

War clauses have been the source of much litigation. The result type, although more liberal to the insured than the status type, has been the source of more legal battles, due to difficulty encountered in interpreting the phrase "death as a result of." The status type, since it excludes death while in military service regardless of cause, is very restrictive from the point of view of the insured. The terms "in military service" and "war" as utilized in war clauses have also raised onerous legal questions. Whether or not the "Korean action" constituted "war" within the meaning of the term as used in the life insurance contract has been decided both ways, although a majority of courts have held that the hostilities in Korea did constitute "war" as contemplated by use of that word in the contract. Modern war clauses preclude this type of dispute by employing more inclusive language, i.e., "war, declared or undeclared."

When an insured whose policy contains a war clause is killed as a result of war, the premiums paid plus interest are paid to the beneficiary. A minority practice is to pay the reserve on the policy. Some war clauses call for suspension or termination of total disability and double indem-

---

[5] See Chapter 56 for further discussion of assignments.

nity provisions in policies. Other insurers exclude total disability or death as a result of war rather than suspending or terminating these benefits in time of war.

Policy Change Clause

Many insurers grant insureds the right to change the existing permanent insurance policy to another permanent insurance policy type, subject to certain conditions. Even when not specified in the policy, insurers generally permit insureds to change plans. A typical change-of-plan clause may read as follows:

> This policy may be changed on any policy anniversary date, without medical examination, to another policy for the same face amount of insurance on any other form in use by the company at date of issue of this policy upon payment of the difference in reserves on the policies, provided the term of the insurance be not increased or the premium rate diminished, and that evidence of insurability satisfactory to the company (including good health) may be required if the new policy is to contain a disability benefit or an accidental death benefit. The premiums, values, and reserves of the new policy will be the same as if the new policy had been issued originally on the new plan.

In essence, policy change clauses commonly provide for changes to higher premium plans for the same or a smaller face amount of insurance without requiring satisfactory evidence of insurability. Generally, conversion to a higher premium plan can be accomplished by paying the insurer the difference in the reserves on the two plans and then paying the premiums for the new plan as they fall due.

Typically, a change to a lower premium plan, when permitted by the insurer, results in a refund to the insured of the difference in the reserves on the two plans, with the insured paying premiums for the new plan as they fall due. Satisfactory evidence of insurability is generally required before an insured is permitted to change to a lower premium plan.

Payor Clause

The payor clause is an optional endorsement for an additional premium offered by most insurers in connection with juvenile insurance. In the event of the premium payor's death or total disability, premiums on the policy are waived until the insured juvenile reaches age 21 or 25. (Death alone may be covered instead of death and total disability.)

The purpose of the clause is to help prevent lapses on juvenile policies because of the death or total disability of the premium payor. The premium for this coverage depends on the premium for the juvenile policy and the respective ages of the insured and the premium payor. On a twenty-year participating endowment policy issued on the life of a child aged five, parent aged 30, coverage for both death and total disability and until the child reaches age 25, a typical premium would be $3.65 per annum per $1,000 of insurance. This additional premium would cease when the child reached age 25.

SELECTED REFERENCES

GREIDER, JANICE E., and BEADLES, WILLIAM T. *Law and the Life Insurance Contract.* Homewood, Ill.: Richard D. Irwin, Inc., 1960.

HERRICK, KENNETH W. *Total Disability Provisions in Life Insurance Contracts.* Homewood, Ill.: Richard D. Irwin, Inc., 1956.

KRUEGER, HARRY, and WAGGONER, LELAND T. (eds.). *The Life Insurance Policy Contract.* Boston: Little, Brown & Co., 1953.

MEHR, ROBERT I., and OSLER, ROBERT W. *Modern Life Insurance.* 3d ed. New York: Macmillan Co., 1961.

REIDY, DANIEL J. "Trends in Life Insurance Law," *Insurance Lecture Series,* Second Lecture. Storrs: School of Business Administration, University of Connecticut, Spring, 1953.

Chapter 16

BASIC LEGAL CONCEPTS

BY JANICE E. GREIDER

A life insurance contract must meet the same basic legal requirements as any other contract. As an insuring agreement, it is also governed by other legal principles which relate specifically to insurance contracts. These include special rules concerning concealment, misrepresentation, and warranty, and have resulted in the extensive use of the doctrines of waiver and estoppel by the courts. The incontestable clause is closely related to these concepts but represents a complete departure from principles long recognized in general contract law. These basic legal concepts will be discussed in this chapter.

THE FORMATION OF A CONTRACT

Insurance requires a valid contract in the general sense of the word. This is ordinarily achieved in life insurance, as with any other contract not under seal, when competent parties express mutual assent to a promise or promises, with legally adequate consideration. If a form is required by law, that form must be followed, and there must exist neither a statute nor a court decision declaring such contracts illegal.

Competent Parties

As a basic principle, everyone is presumed to be capable of making a valid contract. However, certain classes of people have only limited contractual power. These include insane persons, intoxicated persons, married women (though their limitations have largely been removed), and persons who have not reached the required legal age (*minors* or *infants*). The most important of these in any consideration of the life insurance contract are minors.

In most states the age at which one attains contractual capacity is 21. In some states, by statute, a girl of 18 is of legal age, and in other states the limitations of minority are removed if one is 18 and married. The typical age, however, is 21.

The contracts of a minor are generally said to be "not void but voidable." This means that they may be carried out according to their terms if both parties wish. With a few exceptions, however, a minor may avoid any contract he has previously made—that is, declare it ineffective—at any time during his minority or within a reasonable length of time thereafter. The result is that an adult contracting with a minor is bound by the contract; the minor ordinarily is not.

In the absence of legislation to the contrary, a life insurance contract applied for and issued to a minor is subject to this same general rule. If the minor wishes, he may carry it out as if he were an adult, but at any time until he attains his majority and for a reasonable time after that, he has the privilege of disaffirming the contract. In most jurisdictions, he may recover all the premiums he has paid.

Many of the states have enacted statutes removing the limitations of minority with respect to life insurance contracts applied for by minors who have attained a specified age, typically 15 or 16. Frequently, the beneficiary is required to be the minor himself or someone closely related to him.

Mutual Assent

Mutual assent is ordinarily achieved when one party makes an offer or proposal which is accepted by the other. In life insurance the application is traditionally considered to be an offer. However, it is not an offer in the legal sense of the term unless the initial premium accompanies it. In that case the application and the premium constitute the offer, which is accepted when the company issues a policy as applied for. If the policy is issued other than as applied for, the company is considered to have rejected the offer and made a counteroffer. The counteroffer must then be accepted by the applicant before a contract will have been completed.

If the premium is not paid at the time of the application, the application is only an invitation for an offer. The offer is made when the company issues and delivers a policy to the applicant, and it is accepted when the applicant pays the initial premium.

The practice of issuing a conditional or binding receipt when the initial premium is submitted with the application presents a special set of circumstances. In form, the receipt acknowledges receipt of the initial premium; but as most commonly used, it also provides that the insurance applied for will become effective at an earlier date than would otherwise be the case, provided certain conditions are met. These receipts are differently worded, the circumstances differ, and court decisions on the subject are not always reconcilable. Generally, however, the receipts fall into three groups, although one, the true "binding" receipt, is not widely used.

One type of receipt provides that insurance will become effective as of the date of the receipt (or of the medical examination, if one is required) if the proposed insured is found to have been insurable as of that date. This is sometimes referred to as the insurability type of receipt. Another type provides that insurance will become effective only if the application is approved, although it may then become effective as of the date of the receipt. This is sometimes called the approval type of receipt. It might be noted, however, that because the language of these various receipts is not always clear, it is sometimes difficult to determine into which of these two general categories a given receipt actually falls.

A few companies use a true "binding" receipt, which makes the insurance effective immediately on an interim basis, subject to the right of the company to decline the application and terminate the insurance if the proposed insured is found not to be insurable.

The importance of these differences becomes apparent when the death of the proposed insured occurs prior to the date the application is approved or declined in the home office. Under the insurability type of receipt the application will be considered even after the death of the insured. If he is found to have been insurable as required, the insurance will have been effective on the date of his death, and the claim will be payable. Under the interim type of receipt, insurance is effective *until* the application is declined. Under the approval type of receipt, however, insurance does not become effective until the application is approved. In this case, therefore, coverage may not have been effective even though the proposed insured was, in fact, insurable on the date the receipt was given. Consequently, this type of receipt in particular has been involved in a substantial amount of litigation.

Unless a conditional receipt has been issued, delivery of the policy is ordinarily required. In such cases, it is of course important to determine what constitutes delivery. Generally speaking, delivery is accomplished whenever the company takes definite action to place the policy out of its legal control. This is done if the policy is manually handed over to the policyholder; however, it is also accomplished constructively when a policy is mailed to the applicant or when it is mailed to the soliciting agent for delivery, if no further action is to be taken except to make such delivery.

Consideration

Consideration may be defined as the price given or asked in exchange for a promise. It is a technical requirement, growing out of the fact that the law will not generally enforce a promise unless the promisee has given something of value in exchange for it. Life insurance policies frequently state that the insurance is granted "in consideration" of the application and payment of the premiums. This is generally held to mean payment of the initial premium. In the language of the law, this is adequate consideration. It puts the insurance into effect and thus is the price the promisor bargained for and was willing to accept.

Form Required by Law

Although most states do not specifically require that the life insurance contract be in writing, they do require that policy forms be filed with a regulatory official of the state before being used. In practice, therefore, a written policy is essential.

Insurable Interest Required

As a matter of public policy, certain insurable interest requirements must be met or the contract will be void. Thus, the presence of an insurable interest is of major concern in any consideration of the life insurance contract.

INSURABLE INTEREST

An insurable interest is one of the most basic of all requirements in insurance. Without it, the contract is a mere wagering agreement; with it, it is a contract whose social and economic importance is so generally acknowledged that it has an almost unique position in the business world.

In property insurance, one is generally considered to have an insurable interest if he has a reasonable expectation of profit or gain from the continued existence of the property or loss from its destruction. However, the term has a somewhat broader meaning in connection with life insurance.

In life insurance, there are two major situations: (1) the situation where one applies for insurance on his own life, and (2) the situation where he applies for insurance on the life of someone else. It is sometimes said that everyone has an unlimited insurable interest in his own life. Alternatively, it is said that the insurable interest requirement does not apply in this situation. Regardless of the reason, an application for insurance on one's own life does not usually present a question.

When one applies for insurance on the life of another for his own benefit, however, he must have an insurable interest in the life of that person. This means an expectation of benefit from the continued life of that person, but not necessarily a pecuniary benefit. The general rule is that the love and affection growing out of a close relationship by blood or marriage is sufficient. Thus a wife has an insurable interest in the life of her husband; a husband, in the life of his wife.

In the absence of a close relationship of this kind, the applicant must show an insurable interest of a pecuniary nature—that he has a risk of actual monetary loss from the death of the person whose life he wishes to insure. Business relationships furnish the clearest examples of this. The employer, for instance, has a definite risk of loss from the death of a key employee. A creditor has a risk of loss resulting from the death of his debtor.

If an insurable interest is present at the time a life insurance contract is formed, the validity of the contract will not be affected by the fact that it may have vanished before the proceeds become payable. This may be contrasted with the property insurance rule, which holds that the insurable interest must be present at the time of loss.

MISREPRESENTATION, CONCEALMENT, AND WARRANTY

Insurance contracts differ from the majority of business contracts in one very basic sense—the exchange of values. Most business contracts are commutative agreements, which provide for the exchange of relatively equivalent values. Insurance contracts, however, are aleatory in nature, which means that they may involve the exchange of widely varying values. Proceeds are frequently paid under policies on which only a very few premiums have been paid, for it is of the essence of insurance that no one knows when the contingency insured against will happen with respect to any individual risk. The handling of risk, therefore, is essential to the business of insurance, and several legal principles are derived from this fact.

When the early contracts of marine insurance were formed, in the days when underwriters frequented the coffee shops of eighteenth-century England, the risk to be assumed was evaluated almost entirely in reliance on information furnished by the applicant. Often the ship was far away and could not be inspected. In any case, it was the owner who was best acquainted with the condition of the ship, the circumstances of the voyage, and other matters which vitally affected the degree of risk involved. As a result, insurance was early declared to be a contract of the highest good faith, and the insurer was held to be entitled to rely upon the information submitted to him. Legal concepts relating to concealment, misrepresentation, and warranty, therefore, as they applied to insurance, were first developed in connection with marine insurance. In any consideration of their application to the life insurance contract, it is important to bear this fact in mind.

Concealment

The early marine insurance contracts were made between businessmen. The buyer was interested in the most favorable rate he could obtain, and the underwriters were entitled to a fair description of the risk. It was reasonable to require a full disclosure of all facts material to a consideration of the risk. The applicant's failure to disclose such information, therefore, was considered fraudulent, and the insurer was justified in avoiding the contract.

For several reasons, this principle was modified in this country as it applied to the life insurance contract. For one thing, life insurers ordinarily require completion of a detailed application form and a medical examination. Thus the applicant would seem to be justified in assuming that the insurer has asked for all the information it deems material to a consideration of the risk. Consequently, the rule in this country is that concealment of a material fact in connection with the application for a life insurance contract will justify the rescission of the contract, and hence denial of a claim, only if it is fraudulent—that is, made with intent to deceive. In other words, the applicant has a duty to volunteer information only when to withhold it would amount to bad faith.

Representations and Warranties

The terms "representations" and "warranties" both refer to statements made by the applicant in the process of forming an insurance contract. A warranty is a statement made by the insured which is contained in and made a part of the contract itself and which must be true in every respect or the contract will be voidable by the insurer. Thus the owner of a ship might warrant its classification. The insurer is entitled to rely upon this information, and if it is not literally true, the contract can be avoided. The parties must intend that a statement be a warranty, however, and it must be included as a part of the contract.

Representations, on the other hand, are statements made by the applicant at or before the time the contract is formed. They are made to influence the insurer to accept the risk, and they may or may not be a part of the contract. False representations will justify the insurer in avoiding the contract, but only if they concern matters material to the risk. The test of materiality is whether, knowing the truth, the insurer would have declined the application or accepted it only on different terms.

Representations are liberally construed by the courts. This means that they need only be substantially true. Warranties, by contrast, must be literally true, or the contract will fail.

Special Statutes

Many of the states have enacted laws modifying the harshness of the law of warranties. With respect to life insurance, the distinction between warranties and representations has been abolished entirely in some states. In others, warranties are defined and their legal effect limited in such a way that their effect is much the same as that of representations. The New York Insurance Law, for instance, provides as follows: "All statements made by, or by the authority of, the applicant for the issuance, reinstatement, or renewal of a policy of life, accident or health insurance or annuity contract shall be deemed representations and not warranties, anything in such policy, contract or application to the contrary notwithstanding."[1]

WAIVER AND ESTOPPEL

The special statutes noted above helped to modify the harsh operation of the doctrine of warranty. In the courts, two other devices were frequently utilized—the doctrines of waiver and estoppel. These concepts are highly technical, and they have not always been clearly differentiated. However, they have been frequently used in connection with problems arising out of the life insurance contract to bring about a more equitable solution than would be permitted by the strict application of the insurance rules of concealment and warranty.

Waiver

Waiver has been defined as "an intentional relinquishment of a known right."[2] Thus a company may have the right to declare a policy void for breach of a condition specifically set forth in the contract. If, knowing of the breach, an authorized officer of the company expresses an intention not to enforce the right, the right is said to have been waived. It cannot afterward be revived except by another agreement.

Estoppel

Estoppel is a different concept, but the result is much the same. Under an estoppel the company is precluded from relying on an otherwise available defense because of previous action taken. Technically, this is an equitable estoppel, which has been defined as follows: "The principle is that where one party has by his representation or his conduct induced the other party to a transaction to give him an advantage which it would be against equity and good conscience for him to assert, he would not in a court of justice be permitted to avail himself of that advantage."[3]

Thus, where a general agent delivered a life insurance policy with knowledge that the insured had recently been injured in an automobile accident, the company was held estopped to rely on the policy provision that no liability would exist "unless and until the policy be delivered,

---

[1] New York Insurance Law, Sec. 142, par. 3.

[2] William R. Vance, *Handbook on the Law of Insurance* (3d ed. by Buist M. Anderson; St. Paul: West Publishing Co., 1951), p. 479.

[3] *Union Mutual Life Insurance Company* v. *Wilkinson,* 13 Wall 222, 20 L. ed. 617 (1872).

and the first premium paid during the lifetime and sound health of the insured."[4]

THE INCONTESTABLE CLAUSE

As the business of life insurance grew, it became evident to insurers as well as courts and legislatures that the strict marine doctrines of concealment and warranty were not appropriate in life insurance. Unlike marine agreements, the life insurance contracts were not made and enforced between businessmen. In life insurance, disputes ordinarily arose only after the insured had died. Thus the best witness was unavailable, and the beneficiary often knew little, if anything, about the circumstances surrounding the application. Often, premiums had been paid over many years in reliance on a contract only to have its validity challenged on highly technical grounds at the time the benefit was payable. The result was a growing distrust of life insurers generally, on the part of the insuring public.

As a means of assuring the public of the good faith of the insurers, therefore, the companies themselves, in the second half of the nineteenth century, began to include in their policies provisions which declared that the contract would not be disputed or contested as to matters relating to its issuance after it had been in force a specified period of time. The standard provisions law, adopted by many of the states after the Armstrong Investigation in New York in 1905, specifically required an incontestable provision; and today, it is included in the life insurance contract as a matter of course.

The present New York law requires an incontestable provision, as follows:

> A provision that the policy shall be incontestable after it has been in force during the lifetime of the insured for a period of two years from its date of issue, except for nonpayment of premiums and except for violation of the conditions of the policy relating to military or naval service; and at the option of the insurer, provisions relating to benefits in the event of total and permanent disability, and provisions which grant additional insurance specifically against death by accident or accidental means may also be excepted.[5]

Companies may use their own wording if it is equally liberal. Thus a typical clause today might read as follows: "This policy shall be incontestable after it has been in force during the lifetime of the insured for two years from the date of issue."

---

[4] *Musette* v. *Monarch Life Insurance Company*, 309 Ill. App. 224, 32 NE(2d) 1004 (1941).

[5] New York Insurance Law, Sec. 155, 1(*b*).

Interpretation and Development

Originally, the statute did not include the words "during the lifetime of the insured," and it was generally believed that death of the insured during the contestable period stopped the running of the clause. In 1918, however, an Illinois Supreme Court decision[6] held that in such a case the clause continued to run. Unless a court action was initiated, therefore, the policy became incontestable at the end of the period.

This decision was followed by other courts, and in 1921 the National Association of Insurance Commissioners recommended the inclusion of the phrase "during the lifetime of the insured." When this wording is used, any defense available to the company if the insured dies during the period continues to be available, even though suit is not brought until the period expires.

At first, the original law was not generally thought to apply to provisions for disability benefits, although they were not specifically excepted from its operation. Later, court decisions held that the incontestable clause applied also to any disability benefits granted in connection with the policy. In 1922, therefore, the National Association of Insurance Commissioners recommended an amendment permitting exceptions for disability benefits and benefits in the event of death by accidental means. Today, however, the New York Insurance Law requires that provisions for disability benefits be incontestable after three years.

When the Clause Starts Running

According to the statute, the contestable period runs from the date of issue of the policy. Where different dates are concerned, however, this may not always be true. For instance, the policy date may be different from the issue date, and the date the first premium is paid may be different yet. Since ambiguities are interpreted in favor of the policyholder or beneficiary, if the insurance actually becomes effective on a date prior to the date of issue, the contestable period has sometimes been computed from the earlier date. Nevertheless, when the policy is dated back six months to obtain the benefit of a lower age and lower premium, it has been held that the contestable period runs from the date of issue and not the effective date of the coverage.[7]

The Meaning of a "Contest"

Some of the early life insurance policies provided that nonpayment of premiums made the policy *void ab initio*, that is, void from the begin-

---

[6] *Monahan* v. *Metropolitan Life Insurance Company*, 283 Ill. 136, 119 NE 68 (1918).

[7] *Forrest* v. *Mutual Benefit Life Insurance Company*, 195 Misc. 12, 86 NYS(2d) 910, affirmed 275 App. Div. 939, 89 NYS(2d) 488 (2d Dept. [1949]).

ning. It was necessary, therefore, to except nonpayment of premiums from the otherwise general effect of the clause. Today, nonpayment of premiums does not have that legal effect, but the wording remains. As a result, there has been some confusion with respect to the meaning of the word "contest."

It is very generally accepted that a life insurance policy is not contested when the insurer denies a claim on the grounds that the insured took his own life within the suicide period or that the death was for other reasons a risk not assumed under the terms of the policy. It is contested only when the validity of the contract itself is challenged. This is clearly stated in a case which arose out of a dispute concerning the approval of an aviation exclusion rider by the then Superintendent of Insurance of New York. The Superintendent disapproved the rider, stating that it conflicted with the statutory provision requiring an incontestable clause. Justice Benjamin Cardozo said:

> The provision that a policy shall be incontestable after it has been in force during the lifetime of the insured for a period of two years is not a mandate as to coverage, a definition of the hazards to be borne by the insurer. It means only this, that within the limits of the coverage the policy shall stand, unaffected by any defense that it was invalid in its inception, or thereafter became invalid by reason of a condition broken.[8]

In order to comply with the requirement for a contest within the contestable period, a court action must be commenced by the company. This may be for the purpose of canceling the policy during the lifetime of the insured or as a defense to a claim after his death.

Reformation

Courts generally permit a contract to be reformed to carry out the intention of the parties if a mutual error has been made. There have been instances when the insured has contended that the incontestable clause prevents the insurer from having the policy reformed. It is generally held, however, that reformation is not a contest of the policy and thus is not prevented by the incontestable clause.

Relationship to Other Policy Provisions

The incontestable clause is not generally held to apply to misstatements of age, and adjustments on that basis may be made even after the period has expired. In fact, there has been little controversy on this point. This has been explained on the basis that the age adjustment was well established prior to the introduction of the incontestable clause.

Suicide. At one time the incontestable clause and the suicide clause were sometimes considered to be in conflict. Ordinarily, the two periods

---

[8] *Metropolitan Life Insurance Company* v. *Conway*, 252 NY 449, 169 NE 642 (1930).

run concurrently for a period of two years from the policy issue date. The suicide clause, however, like the aviation exclusion, merely defines the risk the insurer is willing to assume. Denial of a claim because the insured's death resulted from suicide within the suicide period, therefore, is not a contest of the policy.

Reinstatement. After a contract of life insurance has become incontestable, it not infrequently happens that it lapses and is reinstated. This ordinarily requires a reinstatement application, and the insured is required to furnish evidence of insurability satisfactory to the company. The legal effect of the incontestable clause under these circumstances has been differently interpreted. The majority rule is that the incontestable clause applies to the reinstatement agreement just as it did to the original formation of the contract. That is, the reinstatement contract may be contested during the same length of time as the policy itself.

Two other rules have occasionally been followed. One is that after the incontestable period has once expired, the policy never again becomes contestable for any reason whatsoever, including reinstatement. The other is that the reinstatement application is contestable at any time, and the incontestable clause has no application to it. The majority rule is generally considered to effect a reasonable compromise between these two extreme views.

Incontestability and Fraud

As a general rule, fraud is said to vitiate a contract. In the early cases, therefore, the incontestable clause was sometimes held not to apply if fraud was involved. Today, the clause is generally held to bar a defense of fraud[9] as well as any other defense going to the validity of the contract. In fact, the incontestable clause has sometimes been criticized because it permits a fraudulent contract to be enforced after the expiration of the contestable period.

As a matter of fact, this is not quite the effect of the clause. Occasionally, a fraudulent contract will be enforceable, but the clause does not so much condone fraud as limit the time in which the company may discover the fraudulent conduct and take appropriate action to cancel the contract. There are also a few exceptions, even after the period has run. Thus, if the application for the insurance was a part of a criminal conspiracy or against public policy, or if someone other than the insured took the medical examination, these facts may be brought out as a defense in spite of the incontestable clause, and so may lack of an insurable interest at the inception of the contract, as a general rule.

The purpose of the incontestable clause is to assure that after a

---

[9] The rule is different in Canada, where the contract is contestable because of fraud at any time. See Chapter 79, "Important Variations in Canadian Life Insurance."

specified period the policyholder may rely upon the company to carry out the terms of the contract, regardless of irregularities at the time of application which may later be discovered. The fact that in giving this assurance the company may occasionally be precluded from interposing a defense based on fraud is generally considered justified by the sense of security given policyholders and beneficiaries by reason of the clause.

SELECTED REFERENCES

GREIDER, JANICE E., and BEADLES, WILLIAM T. *Law and the Life Insurance Contract.* Homewood, Ill.: Richard D. Irwin, Inc., 1960.

KRUEGER, HARRY, and WAGGONER, LELAND T. (eds.). *The Life Insurance Policy Contract.* Boston: Little, Brown & Co., 1953.

VANCE, WILLIAM R. *Handbook on the Law of Insurance.* 3d ed. by Buist M. ANDERSON. St. Paul: West Publishing Co., 1951.

Chapter 17

RISK SELECTION

BY JOHN M. HUEBNER

Selection Philosophy

Were an insurer to issue policies of the same amount and plan on every person in the country *and* be certain that all policies would remain in force, there would be no need for risk selection as it is known in individual life insurance today. The insurer's mortality experience would vary, of course, because of the influence of factors beyond its control, such as wars, epidemics, and progress in medicine and public health, but the adequacy of the premiums to be charged could be determined without considering the effects of selection against the insurer.

Such selection, often called antiselection or adverse selection, appears whenever the individual or group insured has freedom to buy or not to buy, to choose the amount or plan of insurance, and to persist or to discontinue as a policyholder. It is a reflection of the composite judgment of the buyers. One illustration can be found by contrasting the mortality experience of a company among, say, its 65-year-old male insurance purchasers who have been examined physically and carefully chosen, with its experience among 65-year-old male annuity buyers who have not been examined or otherwise selected. The mortality will invariably be higher among the insured lives. Persons tend not to buy annuities unless their judgment forecasts long life. Conversely, among insurance applicants the group will always contain a number for whom protection seems an "excellent investment."

An insurer charging the same price to all persons regardless of age, health, or exposure to accident hazards or other factors affecting longevity must expect inevitably to insure a higher than normal distribution of older persons, of those in various stages of impaired health, and of those for whom the probability of accident is high. Since this result will be reflected in the cost to all, the better risks tend not to join, or to drop out, and the cycle of selection against the insurer will be accelerated.

Risk selection by an insurer, therefore, is the science of classifying into groups those applicants of the same age who can be expected to produce mortality experience reasonably in accord with the premium charged so that each group bears its fair share of the over-all costs.

In theory, there can be as large a number of such groups as the insurer wishes; but in practice, too many groups will cause serious administrative problems, while too few will cause the insurer to suffer competitive disadvantages. Since the classification of "substandard" risks, those impaired sufficiently to require extra premiums, will be treated in the next chapter, it is sufficient here to note that the great majority of risks, approximately 90 per cent, fall within the standard or normal classification of most companies. This class will contain some risks better than normal, together with others expected to produce extra mortality not greater than roughly 25 per cent above normal, the upper limit of the standard class being dictated largely by competition.

Insurable Interest

Fundamental to the soundness of any insurance contract is the existence of an insurable interest; if it is lacking, or insufficient, speculation or gambling enters. Briefly, the person who is to benefit under the contract must stand to benefit from the continued life of the insured or expect to suffer loss by his death. This interest is usually a monetary one, and a prudent insurer will take care that the risk of loss is not *entirely* covered by insurance.

In most cases of individual life insurance, the insurable interest is obvious. It can become subtle and delicate, however, where the monetary interest is minor or nonexistent. For example, an insurer is apt to look askance at an application for insurance on the life of an older, dependent relative (burial insurance) because the purchaser will not suffer loss by the relative's death. He will be relieved of a financial obligation. However, quite a different case is presented by a parent's purchase of insurance on the life of his child. Here again, there is no monetary insurable interest in the sense of loss to the parent by the death of the child, since the obligation to support and educate which terminates upon the child's death greatly outweighs the expenses occasioned by death. But where the amount of insurance sought bears a reasonable relationship to that carried by the parent, and where it is consistent with the family status and with the amounts sought or carried on all other children or all other sons, the pattern is not one of insurance *on* the child for the parent's benefit, but rather is one of insurance *for* the child. The child's own future needs justify the purchase; it is the start of *his* insurance estate.

In any case where the insurable interest is not obvious, the agent can save much time and trouble by presenting to the insurer with the application a full explanation of the background of the sale, the need for the insurance, and the problems and solutions involved.

FACTORS IN SELECTION

The principal factors of selection include age, sex, build, family history, personal medical history, physical condition, occupation, aviation, habits, and finances. Each of these factors will be discussed briefly.

Age

While some factors affecting mortality are wholly or largely independent of the applicant's age (certain accident hazards, for example, of which the aviation passenger hazard is one), others are directly associated with age. Many physical impairments, particularly those of the degenerative type, are more likely to appear with the passage of time. Hence the percentage of applicants who will not qualify for standard insurance is higher among the older age groups than among the younger age groups.

As a result, insurers tend to exercise greater precautions in underwriting older age groups. There usually will be an upper age limit for nonmedical insurance, such as 40 or 45. Special examination requirements such as electrocardiograms, chest X rays, and laboratory studies will be called for more frequently. And since the older age groups contain fewer natural buyers of insurance (the need for protection tends to decrease with age), these groups will contain more speculative risks. Some companies will not write life insurance above age 65. In recent years, a number of companies have raised their top age limit to 70, while a few go even higher. At these ages, however, a high substandard and declined rate is to be expected.

Sex

Rates of mortality among females are now lower at all ages than among males. This lower mortality was not reflected in the cost of insurance until recently because women tended to buy smaller policies with proportionately higher administrative costs. However, within the last few years a number of companies have graded premiums by size of policy or have reflected the relationship between size of policy and costs in their dividend scales. Most companies now reflect the lower mortality among women by a lower gross premium or larger dividends.

Build

Probably no single factor in selection has been studied, restudied, and refined through the years as intensively as build. For our purposes, however, these fundamental principles are adequate:

1. Underweight is today of little consequence even at the younger ages (where it was once viewed seriously because of the tuberculosis, influenza, and pneumonia hazards) unless it is suspected of being caused

by infection, malnutrition, or some other impairment of health. At the younger ages, 25 to 30 per cent underweight may not bar an applicant from standard insurance, while even more extreme percentages may be acceptable at the older ages.

2. Overweight, even in moderate degree, brings with it extra mortality. However, it is the practice among many companies to treat a given percentage of overweight more leniently at the younger ages than at the older.
3. Charges for mortality from overweight may vary with body measurements where the degree of overweight is substantial. Generally, abdominal girth exceeding the measurement of chest expanded will increase mortality, while the large chest–small abdomen picture is more favorable.
4. The effect of overweight, even in moderate degrees, is increased by a number of related factors, such as elevated blood pressure, albumin or sugar in the urine, and family histories of certain types. The effect of certain "combinations of impairments" is greater than the sum of the impairments taken separately.

Family History

Even in the absence of any impairment in an applicant, his family's record of longevity and its freedom from or susceptibility to certain diseases is a factor in his classification. Where reliable records indicate a family of high resistance or tough stock, this alone may improve expected mortality by as much as 15 per cent, making the normal risk better than normal, and possibly being enough to bring into the standard class some risks otherwise just outside.

Histories of general lack of longevity are usually not of sufficient consequence to remove normal unimpaired applicants from the standard class, but family histories of multiple cardiovascular-renal deaths under age 60 or multiple cases of diabetes may well cause the insurer to examine or test them exhaustively. If such a family history relates to an applicant who is overweight, or whose blood pressure is borderline, or who shows signs of an impairment related to the family strain, standard insurance may be refused.

Personal Medical History

An extremely important factor in selection is the personal medical history of the applicant, which should include in detail all recent consultations with or treatments by any physician or practitioner, whether or not stated to be for reasons of importance. More detailed inquiry is made regarding the nervous, respiratory, digestive, genitourinary, and circulatory systems. Past infections of certain types, hospitalizations, surgical operations, heart studies, X-ray studies, and injuries are recorded.

The importance of careful development of a medical history cannot be overemphasized. Many diseases impair the functions of vital organs in ways not readily determinable by a necessarily limited life insurance examination. Many diseases have a characteristic of recurrence, but leave no telltale marks during periods of remission. It is not an exaggeration to say that in some age groups, medical history is more important to proper classification of a risk than physical examination.

It is fundamental that the utmost good faith prevail between the parties to a life insurance contract, and almost nowhere is this principle more pertinent than in developing the personal medical history. An applicant who cuts corners or glosses over his history only casts doubt on his reliability in other respects. Much time and trouble will be saved if the examiner or agent is careful to obtain accurately the names and addresses of attending physicians, together with authorizations to those the company may wish to consult for greater detail regarding complaints, symptoms, findings, and diagnosis than the applicant may be able to give.

Physical Condition

In addition to the applicant's height, weight, and body measurements, which have been discussed previously, the examining physician will check for abnormalities of the nervous system, lungs, and heart, and will record heart rate and rhythm, blood pressure, and the results of a urinalysis. He also will check for deformities or loss of limbs, for impairments of sight or hearing, and for the results of past surgery. An agent developing a case nonmedically will usually be limited to recording build and measurements and his observations regarding deformities, loss of limbs, and other defects; but within these limits, his obligation to give accurate information is as great as the examining physician's.

Even in the absence of pertinent history, applicants for larger amounts, particularly in the older age groups, may be examined physically in greater detail than has been described above. Most companies require that the examiner send a specimen of the applicant's urine to the home office or other central laboratory for microscopic examination when the amount of insurance requested reaches a certain limit. Similarly, most require special heart studies for large amounts of insurance. Such special tests are not routine requirements in smaller cases because of the costs.

Occupation

Accident hazards, health hazards, and environmental hazards may, singly or in combination, increase the mortality of certain occupational groups. Most of the accident hazards and health hazards are fairly obvious—falls, fires, explosions, and falling bodies or material, and dusts, poisons, infections, heat, and radiation are a few. Safety engineering and industrial health measures have reduced the extra mortality from these causes substantially.

The hazard of environment is less obvious. It is sometimes the companion and result of poor economic status. The unskilled laborer, even in nonhazardous industries, tends to be subject to extra mortality, partly because of his lower living standards, but probably also because he is not well equipped to meet the problems of life. Somewhat different environmental hazards may apply to some occupations in the liquor industry and the amusement industry. Yet others pertain to gamblers.

Former occupational exposure to a health hazard may not be ignored solely because of a change to nonhazardous work. Long exposure to dusts or poisons may have done damage which is not outwardly apparent. For example, a stonecutter of fifteen years' experience becomes the proprietor, an executive. Proper selection will require careful physical examination.

Some individuals will present hazards arising not from their usual occupations but from hobbies, avocations, or part-time occupations, and these hazards may require careful consideration. For example, businessmen may race automobiles or skin-dive. Interest in sky diving has increased. Farmers in some parts of the country work part time as loggers.

Aviation

The period since the close of World War II has been marked by tremendously increased interest in civilian aviation and by great improvement in the mortality experience among both passengers and crew members. At present, most companies accept within their standard classifications all commercial air-line passenger hazards (domestic and foreign, scheduled and nonscheduled), and, similarly, all military aviation passenger risks. Only rarely will other types of passenger hazards be significant.

Commercial pilots, usually exposed for a greater number of hours than any passenger, and sometimes, as in cases of student instructors and crop dusters, engaged in the more hazardous types of flying, will range from standard to classifications calling for substantial extra premiums.

It is quite general practice today to accept within the standard class all commercial air-line pilots flying scheduled passenger routes with at least one terminal in the United States. Pilots of scheduled cargo routes and of nonscheduled or charter flights vary in class from standard up, depending upon the stability of the air line, its equipment, maintenance, and personnel standards, and the routes covered.

Private pilots with good records generally qualify as standard if they are mature, experienced, and fly not more than 150 to 200 hours per year. Youth, inexperience, greater annual exposure to risk, or an unfavorable accident record will probably disqualify such pilots for standard insurance.

In cases of both commercial and private pilots, where a company accepts them as standard, there may be limitations as to plan or amount of insurance. Military pilots and crew members are rarely, if ever, accepted as standard.

Habits

The word "habits," when used in risk selection, refers to the applicant's habits with regard to the use of alcohol or drugs. Almost no impairment is more difficult of accurate appraisal, because of the breadth of variations from "normal" behavior, and because accurate information is difficult to obtain. Assessment of information requires a high degree of underwriting judgment.

Generally speaking, those who drink socially, in a healthy environment, in moderation, and with controlled behavior do not present a selection problem and are eligible for standard insurance. Applicants who become intoxicated occasionally or more often, those who never become intoxicated but drink steadily and freely, and those who drink rarely but to stupefaction for two or three or more days at a time, present varying degrees of extra hazard. The *quantity* of alcohol consumed is only part of the problem. The "spread" of its use is equally important, as is the character of the user's drinking associates and environment. Pugnacious or abusive behavior involves additional hazards. A tendency to drive recklessly after drinking requires no comment; the classic combination of alcohol and gasoline is already too well known.

Experience indicates that the quite prevalent opinion that excess mortality among habits cases is lower in the younger age groups does not appear to be sound.

Moreover, reformed drinkers must be underwritten or classified with great care. Even where the reform has been of substantial duration, there is the hazard of relapse and the question of impairment of health before reform. Applicants who have taken treatment or a "cure" will probably be classified more severely than those who have reformed without help. While the efforts of Alcoholics Anonymous are reported favorably from time to time, risk selectors do not yet have reliable information justifying preferential consideration.[1]

Finances

Throughout the years, many rules of thumb have been constructed to determine the proper limit of insurance on a life. One assumes that the portion of a man's earned income not needed for personal expenses and premiums be capitalized conservatively over his remaining earning life. Another, the so-called "20 per cent rule," permits an amount of insurance on any plan equal to the amount of whole life insurance which can be purchased by 20 per cent of the insured's earnings. These rules are arbitrary, but they do reflect attempts to determine the economic value of the

---

[1] Those who wish to pursue the study of habits mortality further should refer to the Lincoln National Life Insurance Company's study published in the *Proceedings of the Home Office Life Underwriters Association,* Vol. XXX, 1948.

insured's remaining lifetime. Both will permit larger amounts on younger lives than upon older lives with comparable earned incomes, but their lack of precision is obvious if, for example, the present incomes of students or medical interns with bright futures are used. The insured's prospects must be considered, and judgment cannot and should not be eliminated. The risk appraiser, however, remembering that premium dollars are sacrifice dollars, will beware of the applicant who under all the circumstances seems "too unselfish." There may be speculation.

Different problems are presented by cases involving income from investments alone. The need for an adequate degree of liquidity at death to settle estate taxes and prevent forced sales, and the need to supply beneficiaries with funds to pay inheritance taxes, are legitimate needs, but any pattern which suggests that the earlier death occurs the better off the beneficiary heirs will be creates the suspicion of speculation.

SOURCES OF INFORMATION

Application

The application is the primary source of information concerning the applicant's identity, age, marital status, and past, present, and contemplated occupations. It also develops pertinent information regarding proposed travel or change of residence, military status, aviation experience and intentions, and the total amount of insurance carried, pending, and contemplated. In addition, it serves to instruct the insurer as to the amount, plan, and other details of the policy desired, including the beneficiary arrangement and ownership.[2]

The application is usually completed by the agent, who will find that extra care will be repaid many times over in time and trouble saved.

Whenever the agent is dealing with an adult applicant, he should be sure to obtain residence and business addresses covering at least five years and should obtain all such addresses for that period. The individuals or agencies inspecting the risk may waste much time if they do not have this information, and that wasted time delays underwriting action.

The agent also should be as specific as possible in describing the occupation. Not all occupational titles indicate precise duties. The term "warehouseman" may be used to describe a shipping clerk or a freight handler. The duties of laboratory workers may range from those completely nonhazardous to those involving the handling of bacteria, poisons, or radioactive substances. The term "sales engineer" may cover demonstrators of heavy equipment or explosives, while the term "painter" does not indicate whether the individual paints the interiors of homes or

---

[2] See Appendix B for illustration of typical application form, including medical examiner's report.

structural iron work and bridges. In all such cases, of which these are a few examples, the risk appraiser must have complete facts.

If the applicant is in military service, his rank and branch of service may not constitute adequate information. If, for example, he is a diver, submariner, or flight surgeon, these facts should be disclosed. Agents will find that it is helpful to give the insurer as much information about the risk as they know or can reasonably obtain.

Medical Examination

The medical examination usually consists of two parts: a series of statements and answers to the examining physician regarding the applicant's personal and family histories, and a record of the examining physician's physical findings.[3]

The examiner should not hesitate to give detail. Medical directories are always somewhat out of date, and unless the correct addresses of attending physicians are given, a waste of time may result. As simple a matter as the full correct name of an attending physician is sometimes overlooked, but an insurer may have difficulty identifying the correct Dr. Smith in a large metropolitan area.

In practice, considerable delay can be avoided if the agent or examiner makes certain that authorizations to attending physicians are signed because, as a general principle, processing of the case through the insurer's selection machinery cannot proceed without the necessary authorizations.

Nonmedical Cases

Nonmedical underwriting, in which no medical examiner is used and the applicant's family history, medical history, build, and habits are recorded by the agent, has come into increasingly widespread use in recent years as a convenience to applicants and agents and because of rising costs of medical examinations.

The insurer expects the saving in examination cost to offset any higher mortality cost arising from physical defects or conditions which a medical examination would have disclosed. This saving is a nonrecurring item, and since the rate of mortality increases with the insured's age, the saving will offset a greater degree of extra mortality at the younger ages than at the older ages. Accordingly, the amount of insurance an insurer will write on any one life on a nonmedical basis scales downward as the age of the applicant increases; and as noted previously, most companies currently have established a top nonmedical age limit of 40 or 45.

While the privilege of submitting cases on a nonmedical basis is a great convenience, particularly in areas where prompt medical examinations are difficult to arrange, it imposes on the agent increased respon-

[3] See Appendix B for detailed questions in medical examiner's report as required by one company.

sibility for care and integrity in developing the required selection information. Agents who value their time properly will find substantial rewards flowing from the reliability of the information they give, and care and completeness on their part will eliminate inquiries and delay.

Medical Information Bureau

The Medical Information Bureau makes possible an exchange of information among life insurance companies similar to the exchanges of credit information by credit bureaus and other organizations in commerce. Its purpose is to permit life insurance companies to have before them as many of the relevant facts as possible when making underwriting decisions. The companies can thus guard the interests of existing policyholders against imposition and fraud. The information made available through the MIB chiefly concerns medical facts, both favorable and unfavorable, about a small percentage of those persons who apply for life insurance.

This information and its use are strictly limited by the rules of the organization. The MIB record does not indicate the action that was taken in regard to any application for insurance. The rejection or rating of a case is not recorded, nor is the amount of insurance issued.

The information is used primarily as an indication of what to look for and as a supplement to each company's own independent underwriting investigation.

The fact that a report has been made on an individual does not mean that his application was refused or rated; nor does it mean that on subsequent applications to other companies, he will be rejected or rated. The underwriting practices of the member companies are not identical, and one company may accept a risk that another company has rated or declined.

Every precaution is taken to see that MIB information is kept in a confidential manner. All reports are made in code form. Each member company is required to have a physician as medical director, and full responsibility must be assumed by the company for the reporting and care of the information.

Inspection

Insurers rely upon reports from their own investigating staffs, upon professional inspection agencies, and upon credit and claims bureaus for information rounding out their picture of the risk insofar as health, finances, business reputation, personal reputation, personal habits, and hobbies or avocations are concerned.[4] The practice of inspecting risks rarely causes resentment, but this may sometimes occur when the applicant, usually a woman, is surprised to learn that an investigation has

---

[4] See Appendix C for specimen life and health inspection report forms.

been or is being made. Most experienced agents avoid this problem by advising applicants that an investigation will be made as a regular practice.

Options to Purchase

A recent addition to the product line of many companies is a supplementary agreement variously called "guaranteed insurability agreement," "insurability option," or "option to purchase additional insurance," by which an insured, for a small extra premium, can assure himself of the right to purchase additional insurance in the future without then submitting evidence of insurability. These agreements have proved very popular with young men and with parents and grandparents who are buying insurance for their children or grandchildren. The agreements issued by different companies vary in detail, but a quite general pattern has been established.

They provide a series of option dates, usually policy anniversaries at three-year intervals from insuring ages 25 to 40, on each of which the policyowner may purchase a stated amount of additional insurance merely by exercising his option. An option expires if it is not exercised on the option date, but subsequent options are not lost by failure to exercise a prior option.

Generally, such agreements can be attached only to policies of a minimum size, such as $5,000, and will not be issued to permit the purchase of more than, say, $10,000 or $15,000 of insurance on any single option date.

More recently, a number of companies have extended such agreements to accelerate a male insured's next fixed-date option to the date of his marriage, or to the date of birth of a child of his marriage or the date of a legal adoption.[5]

SELECTED REFERENCES

HOME OFFICE LIFE UNDERWRITERS ASSOCIATION. *Proceedings of the Home Office Life Underwriters Association and the Occupational Committee,* Vols. I–XLIV (1930–63). Volumes X, XX, and XXX of the *Proceedings* contain ten-year indexes of subject matter.

HUEBNER, S. S., and BLACK, KENNETH, JR. *Life Insurance.* 6th ed. New York: Appleton-Century-Crofts, Inc., 1964.

MACLEAN, JOSEPH B. *Life Insurance.* 9th ed. New York: McGraw-Hill Book Co., Inc., 1962.

MCGILL, DAN M. *Life Insurance.* Homewood, Ill.: Richard D. Irwin, Inc., 1959.

SHEPHERD, PEARCE, and WEBSTER, ANDREW C. *Selection of Risks.* Chicago: Society of Actuaries, 1957.

SOCIETY OF ACTUARIES. *1951 Impairment Study.* Chicago, 1954.

[5] See Appendix D for specimen agreement form.

Chapter 18

INSURING SUBSTANDARD RISKS

BY WILLIAM D. GRANT

Although approximately 90 per cent of those who apply for life insurance qualify at standard rates, it is important that every effort be expended to provide insurance on some basis for those who cannot. Their need for insurance is as great as, if not greater than, the need of those in the standard group.

The practice of issuing life insurance subject to an extra premium is almost as old as modern life insurance. In the United States, it had its beginning prior to the start of the twentieth century, but it was not until after the publication of the Medico-Actuarial Investigation in 1910 that very many companies were willing to issue such policies.

Definition

The substandard or extra-premium group is made up of lives which are expected to produce a mortality rate higher than that of the normal, or standard, group. A 1962 study shows that the reasons for the extra-premium classification are heart disease, 30 per cent; weight problems, 20 per cent; other physical impairments, 24 per cent; hazardous occupations, 18 per cent; and other reasons, 8 per cent.

Individuals may be classified as substandard risks on the basis of a number of factors, such as the following:

Past Medical History. Any past ailment or disease of the important organs of the body may produce a definite increase in the mortality rate needed to provide insurance. An individual with a history of high blood pressure but with a current normal reading, or a history of tuberculosis that is arrested, may, after careful medical examination, be offered life insurance at an increased rate.

Present Physical Condition. Similarly, defects and disabilities found to be present currently also may be considered with a mortality rating higher than normal. If an applicant for insurance is found to have a heart murmur, a poorly functioning gall bladder, or albumin in the urine, while not eligible for insurance at regular rates, he may be insured on an extra-premium basis.

Hazardous Occupations. Many individuals who apply for insurance work in occupations where there is a greater possibility of accidents, or in some cases where, because of dust or moisture, their health may be affected. Those individuals working at unusual heights, such as structural steel workers, or those in occupations that require working in underground mines or tunnels, should be considered on the basis of the extra hazard involved. Other individuals may need a rating higher than normal because of participation in hobbies such as motorcycle or automobile racing.

Habits and Morals. Still another, and perhaps a more difficult, group to evaluate includes those individuals who use drugs or intoxicants to excess. In this same group should be considered those who operate on the fringe or completely outside the legal bounds of the community, and those who cannot or who refuse to conform to the moral pattern accepted by society. It is doubtful that any company would accept for life insurance a person addicted to the use of drugs. However, where the individual has been cured of drug addiction, insurance at higher than normal rates may be offered. On the other hand, companies do find it possible to accept on an extra-premium basis carefully selected cases who are currently using alcohol to excess.

Treatment of Substandard Risks

Once the home office underwriter or risk appraiser has determined the extent to which a risk is substandard, there remains the problem of determining the extra premium which should be charged. The type of charge made is, to some extent, dependent on the nature of the impairment or hazard involved. Many different methods of rating substandard risks have been employed by companies at various times. The following methods are among those more frequently encountered.

Multiple-Table Extra Premiums. Premiums varying by plan and age at issue are calculated on a mortality basis which reflects the expected percentage increase over standard mortality. The difference between these premiums and premiums calculated on the basis of standard mortality is charged as an extra premium.

In theory, the extra premium so obtained is appropriate when the underwriter expects the substandard mortality rates to be a multiple of standard mortality rates for a period at least equal to the duration of the coverage.

A common practice of many companies is to set up a number of mortality classes and assign a substandard risk to the appropriate class, determined by the severity of the impairment. These mortality classes may be designated by letters of the alphabet or, in some companies, by numerals, as illustrated in Table 18–1. The column headed "Range" indicates the approximate limits of the percentage of extra mortality expected by the home office underwriter which can appropriately be assigned to each substandard class.

As an illustration of the incidence of this type of extra premium by age and plan, Table 18–2 shows the standard rate and the extra premiums charged by one company.

TABLE 18–1

TABLE OF SUBSTANDARD MORTALITY CLASSIFICATIONS

Table (Designated by Letters of Alphabet)	Table (Designated by Numerals)	Mortality	Range
A.	1	125%	125–145%
B.	2	150	146–165
C.	3	175	166–190
D.	4	200	191–215
E.	5	225	216–240
F.	6	250	241–275
H.	8	300	276–325
J.	10	350	326–375
L.	12	400	376–450
P.	16	500	451–500

TABLE 18–2

TABLE OF ILLUSTRATIVE EXTRA-PREMIUM RATES

AGE	STRAIGHT LIFE				20-YEAR ENDOWMENT			
	Standard Rate*	Extra-Premium Table			Standard Rate*	Extra-Premium Table		
		2	4	6		2	4	6
20.	$10.56	$ 2.52	$ 4.47	$ 6.27	$43.00	$ 1.16	$ 1.99	$ 2.81
30.	14.86	3.51	6.30	8.87	43.86	1.70	2.99	4.29
40.	22.03	5.26	9.62	13.71	45.91	3.02	5.55	8.10
50.	34.00	8.09	15.18	21.92	51.14	5.69	10.86	16.07
60.	54.11	12.71	24.53	36.07	63.27	11.06	21.60	32.20

* Exclusive of size discount factor.

The generally smaller extra premiums charged on a twenty-year endowment as compared to those charged on straight life are due to the smaller over-all amount at risk under the endowment plan. However, at the older ages the extra premiums for the two plans tend to converge, since effectively there is less and less difference between the benefits under the two plans as the age at issue increases.

Since this method of charging extra premiums assumes a constant percentage increase in mortality at all ages, it will provide margins for an increasing number of extra deaths with policy duration. This is true because the mortality rate increases with age. This method of assessing an extra premium is appropriate, therefore, for those impairments for which the extra number of deaths may be expected to increase with duration. One example of such an impairment is abnormally high blood pressure. This method is also used in connection with some occupational hazards, but it is not appropriate when the extra hazard is expected to be a temporary one.

Because of the direct relationship of the extra premium to the extra hazard involved, the multiple-table extra-premium system is probably the most common method employed in establishing the appropriate premium for substandard risks. Another factor bearing heavily on the greater use of this particular method is that it simplifies home office administrative procedures.

Flat Extra Premium. On some risks, the underwriter assesses an extra premium of a flat dollar amount per thousand of insurance. This extra premium may be on either a temporary or a permanent basis. This type of extra premium constitutes a specific charge to cover an expected extra number of deaths. The extra mortality associated with certain occupations is frequently handled by flat extra premiums, normally in the range of $2.50 to $10.00 per $1,000.

A permanent flat extra premium is appropriate when the number of expected extra deaths tends to increase somewhat with policy duration. This is true because a compensating effect offsetting the increasing hazard is produced by the decreasing amount at risk as the reserve accumulates. Hence a given flat extra premium will provide for extra deaths increasing more sharply with duration when applied to a high-premium plan than when applied to a lower premium plan, such as term insurance.

These characteristics of the permanent flat extra premium make it appropriate for occupations where accident is the chief cause of extra mortality. Experience has demonstrated that there is a gradual increase in the incidence of accidents with increasing age. As a person grows older, his reactions slow, and he may be less alert to the dangers around him. Theoretically, at least, it would also be appropriate to increase the flat extra premium charged for an extra accident hazard with increasing age at issue; however, this refinement is rarely met in practice.

These same characteristics also help to explain why a lower flat extra premium is sometimes charged for the same risk in connection with an endowment policy with a rapidly increasing reserve than would be the case in connection with a straight life or term policy.

Despite the fact that the flat extra-premium method provides margins for extra mortality where the accidental deaths increase with duration, this method also is used for hazards which are relatively constant or even decrease slightly with the passage of time. In assessing the amount of extra premium to be charged for hazards of this type, the underwriter should take due cognizance of the average amount of risk.

The permanent flat extra premium frequently is used to provide for the extra hazard encountered in certain occupations, such as structural steel workers, bartenders, and coal miners. It is also used in many cases in connection with physical impairments, such as blindness and deafness.

When temporary flat extras are imposed, the same extra premium may be applicable to the entire temporary period, or the initial extra premium may be gradually reduced. Temporary flat premiums are suitable when the impairment or situation produces rapidly decreasing extra mortality or when the extra hazard is temporary in nature.

Temporary flat extras which reduce with age are particularly appropriate for military aviation risks. One company has adopted the following scale of extra premiums for certain classes of military aviators:

Under age 30	$11.25
Ages 30 to 39, inclusive	5.65
Age 40 and over	2.80

As the pilots attain the age specified, the extra premium is automatically reduced.

Liens. This method consists of delivering the policy subject to a lien. The lien will vary in term or amount, or both, according to the nature of the impairment. In case of death during the term of the lien, the amount of the lien still outstanding will be deducted from the face amount of the policy. In theory, most types of impairment can be covered equitably by this method. However, it has not been generally popular with prospective policyowners and is not widely used.

Theoretically, this method is particularly well suited to a decreasing mortality, such as the military aviation risk described above. It would have the practical advantage of avoiding the premium reductions incident to the temporary decreasing flat extra premiums which are now more commonly used. A further advantage is that the insured does not pay an extra premium, and if he outlives the period of the lien, he is henceforth in essentially the same position as if he had originally been a standard risk.

This method has the practical disadvantage that the lien is normally at its maximum during the early policy years, when the need of the beneficiaries for protection is greatest. A substantial decrease in the amount payable at the time a claim is presented, due to deduction of the lien from the face amount of insurance, is certainly a source of severe disappointment to the beneficiary and may lead to bad public relations for the insurance company.

For these reasons, as well as the fact that the laws of various states now prohibit the issue of lien policies as such, this method of treating substandard risks has fallen into disuse in the United States. It is still in general use in Canada and Great Britain, however.

Rate-Up in Age. This method was used rather extensively in the past but is no longer widely used. It consists of charging the substandard risk the rate applicable to a standard risk a specified number of years older. The policy is issued at the higher age and generally provides for cash values and dividends to be the same as for a standard risk at that age.

The margins for extra deaths provided by this method increase rather rapidly with age. They do not, however, coincide very closely with the extra deaths experienced for most impairments. Furthermore, the dividends and cash values at the rated-up age are probably in excess of what should be allowed if due cognizance is taken of the incidence of mortality. The survival of this method is no doubt due to its convenience and understandability rather than to its adequacy in reflecting the true incidence of substandard mortality.

Quite recently, however, the method has been used in reverse in a number of companies to reflect the lower mortality experienced on female risks as compared with males. This could be said to constitute a form of superstandard underwriting.

With the adoption of the 1958 CSO legislation, the insurance laws of all states now permit or will permit the cash values and reserves for policies issued to women to be the same as those for policies issued to men up to three years younger.

Most companies now offer insurance to women on a more favorable basis than to men; however, the methods employed vary rather widely. Some companies have adopted the three-year age setback for gross premiums, reserves, and cash values; others have adopted special tables of gross premiums for women with or without an age setback in cash values or reserves.

As part of its continuing mortality study, the Society of Actuaries is now accumulating separate data on the mortality of insured women. The emerging results of the study should demonstrate the validity of the age setback approach, or, alternatively, may demonstrate that separate mortality tables for women are desirable.

Other Methods. Closely related to the multiple-table method is the practice of simply multiplying the gross premium by the expected mortality expressed as a percentage of standard. For example, a risk assessed at 150 per cent of standard would pay 150 per cent of the gross premium. This approach is appropriate when the result is a reasonable approximation of the result which would have been obtained if the multiple-table method had been used.

It will be observed from the extra premiums used to illustrate the multiple-table method that the total premium charged does not increase proportionately with the extra mortality expected. This is due to several factors, but among the more important are the fact that the loading in the standard premium does not need to be increased proportionately as the charge for extra mortality is increased and the fact that that portion of the gross premium which constitutes primarily an investment element does not need to increase as mortality increases.

For insurance benefits where the loading is relatively low and where the investment element is relatively small, the gross premium consists mainly of the benefit charge. Since this charge should increase proportionately to the extra risk, it is appropriate to rate such benefits as short-term supplements, double indemnity, and waiver of premium by simply charging multiples of the gross premium. Thus, double indemnity and waiver-of-premium ratings are frequently 1¼, 1½, and 2 or more times the standard premium. Family income supplements also are sometimes rated in this manner.

Another approach frequently used is to limit the plan or amount which will be issued. Occasionally, the underwriter is willing to issue a higher premium form or a policy for a fairly moderate amount, but is not willing to issue term insurance or a policy for a large amount. Such a decision may be justified for impairments for which the initial amount of extra mortality is low, such as moderate overweight. An endowment contract may well have matured before the extra mortality becomes a serious factor. It therefore may well be issued standard, whereas a straight life contract would of necessity require an extra premium.

A limitation on the amount which will be offered frequently reflects the fact that there remains a large degree of uncertainty as to the appropriate rating for a particular hazard. In view of the likelihood of large fluctuations in the mortality experience of a company issuing substandard business, most companies limit the amount of highly substandard issues they will retain, often reinsuring all of it.

Occasionally, a company will set up special dividend classes for slightly impaired risks for which the future effect of the impairment is not clearly understood. The policy is issued standard, and dividends are based on the actual experience of the class. Obviously, the classes should be large enough to yield average experience. With the limited extent of the impairments which may be handled by this method, it is difficult if not impossible to maintain reasonable homogeneity within the classes. Consequently, treatment of the individual members of the class may be inequitable.

Dividends, Cash Values, and Nonforfeiture Benefits

Dividends on substandard policies are, for practical reasons, generally identical to dividends on standard issues, except when special dividend classes are used. Most companies offer the same scale of cash values on standard and substandard policies except when the rate-up-in-age method is used. Cash values for policies which are rated up in age generally are at the rated age. This may result in some inequity, in that surrendering policyholders may receive a larger cash value than that to which they would be equitably entitled if the true incidence of substandard mortality had been taken into account.

Extended term insurance is not generally provided in substandard policies except on those policies issued at very low ratings. Otherwise, nonforfeiture benefits are usually identical with standard issues. Usually, reduced paid-up insurance is the nonforfeiture provision included automatically in substandard life insurance contracts.

Basis for Rate Calculations

Various sources of data are employed by life insurance companies in compiling their underwriting manuals, i.e., the quantitative evaluation of specific impairments and hazards. As examples of such sources, there have been the several medical impairment studies, the latest of which was completed in 1951; the *1959 Build and Blood Pressure Study;* various clinical reports; governmental publications; reports of the Committee on Aviation of the Society of Actuaries; and reports by the large insurance companies of their own experience.

Current Practices

The field of substandard underwriting cannot remain static. New developments in medical treatment, as well as changes in the mortality levels of different groups, require constant revision in the evaluation of various impairments and hazards.

Some companies are currently experimenting in the field of underwriting highly substandard risks. Although many underwriters still prefer to decline risks evaluated at more than 500 per cent of standard mortality, risks of up to 1,000 per cent of standard are accepted by companies experimenting in this field.

Other underwriters are seeking an answer to the problem of removing part or all of the extra rating when the substandard risk subsequently improves. One approach has been to use temporary ratings for a wide range of impairments for which experience has shown decreasing extra mortality with duration. Presumably, the automatic reduction in the extra premium will tend to reduce requests for re-evaluation of the risk as the policyowner's condition improves. On the other hand, some risks will become more substandard. Since no increase can be made in the scale of premiums for which the contract was originally issued, the choice of impairments for which this method is appropriate is a crucial one. The future experience on policies issued on this basis will be observed with interest.

A few companies have recently adopted scales of substandard extra premiums based on the multiple-table method but providing that the extra premiums will be continued for only a limited number of years or to a specified age. This approach has the advantage from the insured's point of view of limiting the period during which extra premiums are payable; from the company's point of view, it has the advantage of accelerating to some extent the receipt of the funds needed to underwrite the extra hazard. It will also be of interest to observe the extent to which this method of charging extra premiums will be adopted by life insurance companies generally.

Through careful study, and by experimentation, much progress has been made in insuring an ever-increasing number of persons. As the experience of companies has improved, lower ratings have been made available for impaired risks. Many individuals are today accepted at standard rates who not too many years ago were charged an increase in rate.

Any consideration of insurance on substandard lives must be based on the theory of insuring large groups of lives. Many of those insured at increased rates will outlive persons accepted at standard rates. This cannot be considered as an indication, however, that the principle of accepting impaired risks at an increase in rate is in error, for it is only by the insuring of large numbers that the insurance company can expect to obtain an average experience.

A number of companies do not, even at the present time, retain substandard risks on their own account. Many of these companies reinsure their substandard business with life reinsurance companies which accept this class of business as a professional service and can therefore obtain a large enough volume of substandard business from many sources to obtain satisfactory experience.

Of course, companies which insure substandard risks cannot determine in advance which individuals insured will die at a given time. However, they can, by applying the proper rates of mortality, and by insuring a sufficiently large number of such lives, obtain a reasonably stable and satisfactory mortality experience.

There naturally will be some exceptions to substandard classifications, and a number of persons will die either sooner or later than expected according to the mortality class to which they were originally assigned. The legend of the declined or highly rated individual who lives to serve as pallbearer for all his friends who were insured at standard rates is not, therefore, living proof that the principle of insuring impaired lives is in error.

Tremendous progress has been made during the past fifty years in the facilities available to insurance companies in selecting and classifying risks for life insurance. In the early days, it was required that each applicant appear before the medical director and his staff for evaluation.

From those days the insurance industry has progressed on through the innovation of nonmedical selection for limited amounts to the use of many modern testing devices of medical science, such as the X ray, electrocardiogram, various blood tests, and urine reports.

Practically all companies now require, in addition to the usual medical examination and urinalysis, a chest X ray and/or an electrocardiogram when the amount of insurance reaches the higher figures. The exact amount usually varies with the age of the applicant, with the amounts requiring these special tests declining at the older ages. Reports from family doctors, or other doctors who may have treated or been consulted by the applicant, are extremely important to the insurance company.

The improvement in medical facilities in most parts of the United States has made it possible for most of our citizens to avail themselves of proper medical attention and care. The proper evaluation of medical reports requires careful attention to place the individual in the proper mortality group along with others found to have the same medical background. As the family doctor is treating the individual as a patient and therefore evaluates his findings from a clinical point of view, so also must the insurance underwriter use similar care and judgment in properly interpreting the effect this medical history may have in producing an increase in mortality.

Removing Substandard Ratings

The theory of substandard insurance would indicate that once an individual is placed in the proper mortality group, he will remain there for the duration of his policy contract. However, the individual who has been issued a rated policy may apply at some later date for additional insurance in another company or the same company and find that he can qualify for insurance on a more favorable basis. In such instances the usual reaction is to request a reduction in the rate being paid for the existing insurance.

It is doubtful that a company can successfully retain a policy in force on a substandard basis when the insured can at a later date purchase insurance at a more favorable rate. Even though the removal of, or a reduction in, rating is selection against the company, since there is no opportunity to increase ratings on insureds whose condition causing the rate-up has deteriorated, most companies follow the practice of reconsidering substandard cases. If the company does not reduce the rate on such cases, the insured will surely surrender or lapse his insurance in favor of insurance at more favorable rates in another company. Most companies, therefore, calculate their substandard premiums on the assumption that mortality rates may be adjusted on those persons who at a later date qualify for insurance on a more favorable basis.

Ratings charged for hazards which may be of a temporary nature, such as occupational hazards or for residence, usually may be removed when the condition which required the rating has been removed.

If the rating is based on an occupational hazard, the company may require information regarding the new occupation and other circumstances involved in the change. Favorable consideration usually may be given when the insured can demonstrate that the change is to be on a permanent basis. Thus the individual who has been engaged in manual labor requiring a rate increase would be given favorable consideration if, through increased training, he has been promoted to a supervisory position or other work where the accident hazard did not exist. In cases where the insured's health may have been adversely affected, the company usually requires satisfactory medical evidence before agreeing to a rate reduction. A time period of from one to two years usually is required to indicate to the company that the change is permanent rather than temporary. When the company has obtained sufficient proof that the hazard no longer exists and is not likely to recur, the rating is removed, and premiums are adjusted, usually retroactively to the date of the change of occupation or residence.

Importance of Insuring Substandard Risks

To the Insuring Public. Although only about 5 per cent of all new policies issued are on a substandard basis, the insuring of substandard risks renders an important service to the public, in that it makes life insurance protection available to a large number of persons who otherwise would be left without it.

As previously indicated, much progress has been made during the past fifty years in insuring substandard life insurance risks. As current experience improves and new investigations are completed, it is the responsibility of insurers to make available insurance for an increasing number of individuals and to offer more favorable rates in instances where experience has indicated that more favorable rates can be offered.

The decreased rate of declined cases indicates that life insurance is now available to all except those subject to such excessive rates of mortality that a premium would be required beyond their ability or willingness to pay.

To the Agency Force. In order to provide their agency force with underwriting service on a par with that offered by other companies, practically all companies avail themselves of the excellent underwriting facilities available from the various professional reinsurers and thus issue substandard business. The degree to which these professional reinsurers' services are required will vary somewhat with the size of the issuing company and the experience of its own underwriting staff. A young company with a modest amount of business written and perhaps an inexperienced underwriting staff may wish to reinsure all of its substandard business. As the company grows and its underwriting staff becomes more seasoned, an increasing proportion of its substandard business will be passed on by its own underwriters and retained at its own risk.

Since a percentage of all risks who apply for insurance do not qualify at standard rates, the companies are eager to classify properly all risks in the classification to which their own medical histories would indicate they belong. In connection with the handling of substandard risks, therefore, it is a general practice to obtain as much information as possible about the impairment and the applicant's physical condition.

Agents can be very helpful in determining the proper classification for each risk by co-operating in obtaining reports, statements, or examinations asked for by the company. When the agent explains to his client that this information is needed in order to consider his application on the most favorable basis possible, and that it is not a method of seeking a way to refuse coverage, the client is more apt to co-operate.

The proportion of substandard business written by an agent may be as much as 10 per cent of his annual volume and thus constitutes an important source of earnings for him over the course of a year. As experience and skill are gained by the agent in this type of business, he is able to place an increasing volume of rated cases, with his income benefiting accordingly. He is also able to render an important service to his clients.

From the Industry's Point of View. In fairness to all policyowners, it is essential that insurance be provided at rates in line with the mortality risks undertaken. As it should be the intention of every company to issue insurance at standard rates to as many persons as possible, so also should the companies use all means possible to see that each individual pays the proper rate for his life insurance.

Through the issuance of substandard insurance to those persons who cannot qualify at regular rates, the companies provide an important public service. Frequently, individuals are unaware of unfavorable physical factors until these are found through examinations for life insurance. Perhaps in this respect the insurance industry has helped awaken the public to the desirability of having periodic physical examinations.

SELECTED REFERENCES

HOME OFFICE LIFE UNDERWRITERS ASSOCIATION. *Proceedings of the Home Office Life Underwriters Association and the Occupational Committee.* Vols. I–XLIII (1930–62).

HUEBNER, S. S., and BLACK, KENNETH, JR. *Life Insurance.* 6th ed. New York: Appleton-Century-Crofts, Inc., 1964.

INSTITUTE OF LIFE INSURANCE. *Life Insurance Fact Book.* New York, published annually.

MACLEAN, JOSEPH B. *Life Insurance.* 9th ed. New York: McGraw-Hill Book Co., Inc., 1962.

SHEPHERD, PEARCE, and WEBSTER, ANDREW C. *Selection of Risks.* Chicago: Society of Actuaries, 1957.

SOCIETY OF ACTUARIES. *1951 Impairment Study.* Chicago, 1954.

SOCIETY OF ACTUARIES. *1959 Build and Blood Pressure Study.* Chicago, 1959.

Chapter 19

ANALYZING CONTRACTS AND COSTS

BY ROBERT W. LORD

When a man buys life insurance, he is buying a very special type of financial service evidenced by an impressive document known as a life insurance policy. This document has little intrinsic value, but the property, security, and service it represents are highly significant to the policyholder and his beneficiaries. The price he has to pay for life insurance is also important. Hence the subjects of contract analysis and cost analysis are of significance to purveyors and users of the life insurance service.

CONTRACT ANALYSIS

Because every person's insurance needs differ at least in some detail from every other person's, it could be argued that each life insurance policy should be individually written for the insured it is to cover. From a practical standpoint, however, standard policy forms as offered by most companies today can be adequately fitted to insurance needs if (1) the agent is capable, (2) his company offers a sufficient variety of coverages, and (3) his company provides flexible settlement arrangements for the time during which the proceeds will be paid out after the contract terminates by death or surrender.

Minimum Standards Required by Law

Every company, however flexible in its policy provisions, must have a basic set of clauses in its contracts, and these standard provisions—or provisions more favorable to the policyholder—must be included. The usual standard provisions are as follows:[1]

[1] See Index for more extensive analysis of these provisions in various chapters.

1. A *grace period* for the payment of premiums.
2. An *incontestable clause* that states that after the policy has been in force for a given time, it shall be incontestable except for nonpayment of premiums.
3. A statement that the policy and the application constitute the *entire contract* between the insured and the company.
4. A clause regarding *misstatement of age.* If the age of the insured has been misstated, the premium is applied to purchase insurance of the amount which would have been provided by the correct rate.
5. A clause defining the nature of the policy's *participation in surplus* (dividends) if the policy is a participating one.
6. A description of the options available if premiums should be unpaid at a time when the policy has been in force long enough to have a *nonforfeiture* value.
7. A clause defining the right to borrow the *loan value* of the policy, and a table of loan values.
8. Tables showing *installment payments* where proceeds are payable in this fashion.
9. A clause defining the rights of the insured with regard to *reinstatement* of the policy after lapse.

Provisions other than the standard provisions vary widely and often help to distinguish a company from other companies.

Examination of a typical policy will reveal what information and provisions can be disregarded in comparing contracts and with what the conscientious life underwriter must concern himself in order to fit life insurance to his client's needs. This discussion refers to currently issued policies; but in general, it will also apply to an analysis of older policies.

Less Significant Items of Contract Comparison

Contract items of little significance in comparing the products offered by various companies are the name of the insured, his age at issue, the policy date, the face amount, and, in most cases, the kind of insurance. These are, however, of prime importance in programing.

The amount of the rate book *premium* per $1,000 is one valid item of comparison, especially if the companies concerned are nonparticipating. This subject will be considered later.

In most cases, naming the *beneficiary* and contingent beneficiary is not a matter of comparison between companies. Some classes of beneficiaries cannot be elected in the policies of some companies, and the agent should refer to a handbook if he is in doubt. In general, however, there is no significant problem in the naming of beneficiaries.

More Significant Items of Contract Comparison

The first page of a policy indicates whether the policyholder is entitled to share in *distributions of surplus,* that is, whether the policy is "participating." In the absence of a statement that the contract is participating, it is a nonparticipating policy. The advantages and disadvantages of each type of contract have to be examined in the light of the desires and needs of the prospect. In most cases, the comparison is probably never made, with the purchaser relying more on the confidence he has in the life underwriter than upon his own knowledge of the contract recommended or the company the underwriter represents.

The *optional modes of settlement* can be of great importance in the comparison of policy provisions and the selection of a company.[2] Most companies offer a considerable range of settlement options.

Usually, a prospect can have his wishes accommodated by the options available in most companies. He can then choose among the available policies on the basis of considerations other than settlement options. In some instances, however, the insured may wish a settlement not available in the options allowed by a given company. In an instance like this, the selection of a company may turn on the settlement options available, if all other factors are equivalent.

A second way in which settlement options have an effect on selection of a company is in the *amounts of income* available in one company when compared with those in another, based on the same amount of proceeds. Where these income amounts are particularly favorable, they may influence a decision. Also to be considered is the interest rate currently being paid by companies on funds held under settlement options. A consideration of these factors, however, properly belongs in the discussion of cost later in this chapter.

Loan and surrender values may vary considerably among companies. United States life insurance companies and a number of Canadian companies use either the Commissioners 1941 Standard Ordinary Table of Mortality (1941 CSO Table) or the 1958 CSO Table for ordinary life insurance, but differences in the rate of interest assumed in calculation of premiums, reserves, and cash values, and other factors, make for variation in surrender and loan values among companies. Use of the 1958 CSO Table is mandatory by January 1, 1966, in the United States.

A conscientious life underwriter should bear in mind that although the insured may never expect to borrow on his policy or surrender it for cash, the existence of such privileges may prove of real value in adverse times. The cash and loan values in life insurance are part of the assets of the insured, and they are highly liquid.[3] Life underwriters therefore customarily take these values into consideration when comparing contracts.

Disability provisions vary substantially from company to company. The agent and the insured should ask themselves the following questions in analyzing the disability feature:

---

[2] See Chapter 57 for extensive analysis of settlement options.

[3] Despite the fact that companies reserve the right to defer payment for periods up to six months, this right has rarely, if ever, been exercised.

1. Does the disability clause provide waiver of premium and monthly income, or waiver of premium alone?
2. If income is provided, how much per month?
3. Does the disability clause provide for payment of the proceeds in installments during disability?
4. How long a waiting period is required?
5. After the waiting period is over, what retroactive benefits are available?
6. What is the age "deadline" before which disability must commence?
7. Are premiums waived for life during the continuance of disability?
8. What constitutes disability—inability to engage in any occupation for compensation or profit? Or is the definition less strict?
9. What are "recognized disabilities"? While these are probably blindness, or the loss of use of hands or feet or their dismemberment, the clauses of companies should be compared on these points.
10. Is the disability clause incontestable? If so, after how long?
11. What kinds of disability are excluded from payment? Most companies exclude from coverage disability arising from suicide attempt, war, and felony.
12. Are women offered waiver-of-premium coverage at higher rates than men? May they have disability income?

An important difference in the way companies handle the waiver-of-premium disability benefit is that most companies charge a separate premium for the benefit, making it optional, while a few companies provide the benefit in all standard policies (that is, those without an extra premium for health or occupation) and include the cost of the benefit in the regular premium. In the latter case, the disability coverage is mandatory, and the cost is spread over the premium-paying period of the policy. Where the benefit is charged for separately, the premium for the benefit is discontinued at the age when the benefit terminates. This difference in the method of charging for the benefit, however, has no effect upon the clause itself.

Some companies offer disability clauses that provide for both waiver of premium and income during disability, as well as clauses that provide only for waiver of premium. Other companies offer only the waiver of premium. The combination clause costs substantially more than a pure waiver-of-premium clause.[4]

Another valid point of comparison between companies' policies is the *change-of-plan* clause. One clause may be considerably more favorable to the policyholder than another, and well worth a small extra cost.

In calculating premiums, the assumption usually is made that the entire premium is paid at the beginning of the year. However, many policyholders choose to pay premiums semiannually, quarterly, or monthly. Thus, if an insured should pay the first quarterly premium of the year, for example, and then die before paying the second quarterly pre-

[4] See Chapter 22 for analysis of life insurance disability riders.

POLICY ANALYSIS

Aviation: No restrictions in policy; some restrictions in double indemnity benefit. No extra premium where only aviation activity is as passenger on regular scheduled airline flights but double indemnity benefit may be denied. Commercial airplane pilots and crew members will be considered standard for limited amount. Certain private pilots taken for limited amount with extra premium. Also use aviation rider to restrict liability for certain aviation hazards.

Cash Values: After one full year's premium in most cases; payment may be deferred six months, but if deferred thirty days or more interest is allowed on amount payable. After three years the cash value never differs from the reserve by more than 2½% of the sum insured and is equal to the full reserve at the end of the premium paying period or, for participating policies, at the end of twenty years if earlier.

Change of Plan: No provision but practice is to change at any time to higher or lower premium form. Evidence of insurability may be required in some cases.

Disability Benefits: After 6 months' disability, before age 60, premiums will be waived retroactively 1 year: Recognized disability 1; restriction 6. Contestable.

Dividends: Annually, end of the first year; not dependent upon payment of subsequent year's premium; dividends may be taken: (1) in cash, (2) to reduce premium (automatic), (3) to purchase participating paid-up additions, (4) to accumulate at interest of not less than 2%* (withdrawable at any time). May be used to reduce number of premiums or hasten maturity of policy. Post mortem dividend is paid.

Double Indemnity: Death within 90 days before age 65 doubles face amount of policy, provided death did not occur as a result of 50, 53, 54, 55, 56, 57, 58, 59, 60, 61, 62, 64, 67, 69.†

Incontestability: After policy has been in force during the lifetime of the insured for two years.

Loan Values: To the amount which with interest will not exceed the cash value for the end of the current policy year; after one full year's premium in most cases; at 5% interest not paid in advance; loan may be deferred six months; policyholders may repay loan at any time and may retain policy after endorsement.

Nonforfeiture Provisions: Policy provides for cash; automatic nonpar extended insurance with cash values; paid-up insurance (participating in par policies) with cash and loan values; fractional premium increases values proportionately, grace period 31 days without interest. Automatic premium loan available upon request.

Premiums: May be paid annually, semiannually (multiply annual by .51), quarterly (multiply annual by .26), or monthly (multiply annual by .0875); in event of death no further premiums are required for fractional parts of a year.

Reinstatement: Within 5 years, unless previously surrendered, upon evidence of insurability, and by payment of arrears in premiums and payment or reinstatement of indebtedness with 5% compound interest.

Reserve Basis: Commissioners 1958 Standard Ordinary Mortality Table, interest of 2½%, nonpar, 2¾%, full level premium. Annuities: Standard Table (1942 modification) 2%.

Restrictions: On residence, no restrictions; on occupation, no conditions; on travel, no restrictions; suicide, sane or insane within two years, liability limited to premiums paid in cash.

Settlement Options: Mode (1).‡ Interest on proceeds of at least 2%.‡ Mode (2). Regular installments until proceeds and interest (2% guaranteed‡) are exhausted. Mode (3). Installments for fixed period on annual, semiannual, quarterly or monthly basis. (2% int. guaranteed).‡ Mode (4). Life Inc. with period certain. All interest payments and all payments under settlement options for a fixed period of years increased by excess interest earnings of the company.† See back of book for complete figures, **Settlement Option Tables A, H, 27.**† Apply to cash values.

Women: Accepted on same basis as men (limit $200,000) except as follows: Disability 7W (Waiver only) issued to women. Disability before age 55. Special rates, ages 10 through 50. Limit $25,000.

* Present rate on dividend accumulations, 3 per cent, or the guaranteed rate if higher.

† These keyed references are to standard tables appearing in the comparative rate book but omitted here because of space limitations.

‡ Present rate on installments, 3 per cent, or the guaranteed rate if higher.

FIG. 19–1. Policy analysis page from a comparative rate book. This exhibit shows the most important clauses of the company's policies in condensed form for easy comparison with clauses of other companies. Copyright Flitcraft, Inc., *Flitcraft Compend*. Used by permission.

mium, the balance of the year's premium would technically be "owed." As a general rule, companies do not deduct this premium for the balance of the year from the proceeds paid at the death of the insured. Furthermore, some companies return that portion of the premium applying to the part of the current premium period following the death of the insured. Such practices must be charged for, so a policyholder can expect to pay a little more for a policy in a company that follows one or both of these practices.

Policy provisions may be analyzed in a condensed form for comparative purposes. Figure 19–1 shows how this is done for a company in a comparative rate book.

Replacing Older Policies

Sometimes an insured considers discontinuing a contract he already has in favor of buying a new one, or the idea may be suggested to him. In such a case, it is appropriate for him to compare the policy provisions of the old contract with the provisions in the new policy, using the method described above as a guide. There have been some changes in the principles used to calculate premiums and cash values in the last few years, and in addition, the rate of interest earned by life insurance companies has changed considerably. Therefore, one should compare premiums, dividends (both actual and projected), and cash values between the older policy in force and the new policy contemplated.

If the insured should take a new policy and give up an old contract which has been in force for several years, he will find that:

1. His premium is usually higher on account of the older age, if for no other reason.
2. It will usually be some years before his dividends will be as large under his new contract as they are under his old policy, if his policy is participating.
3. Cash values will be nonexistent or small for several years in the new policy.
4. As a general rule, cost or value will never overtake an older policy prior to maturity.
5. The policyholder will have to wait one or two years before the new contract is incontestable, and the suicide clause will begin to run anew.
6. The settlement options will probably be less favorable under the new policy than under the old, especially in the case of the life income options.
7. If his old policy was issued many years ago, say in the 1920's, it very likely has a disability income clause very favorable to the insured, chargeable at a rate that companies cannot offer today.

Because of all these considerations, an insured should use caution before thinking seriously of replacing an old policy with a new one. Experience shows that replacement is seldom advantageous to the insured or his beneficiaries.

COST ANALYSIS

A person is served best when he buys life insurance suited to his needs, with the advice of a competent life underwriter, in a good company, and at reasonable cost. Life insurance should fit the needs of the policyholder and his family. Unless the amount is adequate, the insurance is the kind that is needed, the beneficiary designation is correct, the settlement options are employed as they should be, and perhaps the whole is coordinated with social security benefits, the insurance will not do what it should for the insured and his family. It is only at this point that the subject of cost should assume significance.

Cost Comparisons

For fair comparisons, policies of different companies should be similar in kind, size, and policy provisions, or as nearly so as possible. Then the contracts can be compared on the basis of (1) premiums, (2) cash values, (3) dividends, and (4) amounts guaranteed under settlement options.

The comparison may use the dividends paid on policies issued some years ago ("histories") so as to indicate performance during the past 10 or 20 years. Or the comparison may use "projections" of the current dividend scale on policies currently being issued—preferably the very ones being considered by the prospective policyholder. These projections indicate what will happen if conditions affecting cost remain unchanged during the next 10 or 20 years. Neither method is necessarily better than the other, and both may well be employed in making a choice of policies.

A Cost Formula

A simple general formula is used in comparing payments and cost figures involving premiums, cash values, and, in the case of participating policies, dividends. This is: what the policyholder pays the company, less what the company returns to him in dividends, gives *net payments;* what the policyholder pays the company, less what it returns in dividends and cash value, gives *net cost.* In other words:

Premiums
minus Dividends (if participating)
Net payments (Average yearly payment is arrived at by dividing net payments by number of years in period considered)
minus Cash value (including surrender dividend, if any)
Net cost (Average yearly cost is arrived at by dividing net cost by number of years in period considered)

Certain assumptions are made in the formula. Since most insureds are living at the end of 10 or 20 years after the policy was put in force, it is assumed that the insured is living at the end of these periods.[5]

Graded Premiums

As in other lines of business, the purchaser who buys more "units" of the life insurance product—in this case more thousands of dollars of face amount—normally obtains a lower price per unit. Some costs to a life insurance company do not increase with the size of the policy, and most companies can pass on this saving in the form of a discount on currently issued ordinary policies. This gradation by size is accomplished by several methods: (1) charging one premium rate per $1,000 face amount for policies of a certain size range ("band")—for example, one premium rate per $1,000 for face amounts of $1,000 to $4,999, a lower rate for face amounts of $5,000 to $9,999, a still lower rate for $10,000 to $19,999, and so on; (2) deriving the total premium by multiplying a "basic premium" for the age and plan by the number of thousands of face amount and adding a flat "policy fee" for the entire contract; (3) making a flat extra charge per $1,000 for small-sized policies, with a maximum, however, which amounts to the use of a policy fee in the case of medium-sized and larger policies; (4) having two series of policies—those under $5,000 face amount and those over that figure, for example, with no direct relationship in premiums, but with each series using one of the above methods of grading by size.

Because of variation in method of grading by size among companies, there is a tendency in comparative rate literature to base premiums, dividends, net payments, and costs on figures per $1,000 for $10,000 contracts, with a formula given for deriving other face amounts. A reasonably valid comparison between companies can then be made for $10,000 policies. However, a person considering buying insurance should ask for a comparison based on the policy size he is considering, with payments and costs adjusted accordingly. It should be noted that a comparison is not valid if figures per $1,000 in the lowest size group in one company in method (1), (3), or (4) are compared with figures in another company for a different size group, or if only basic premiums are compared and varying policy fees are neglected in method (2).

---

[5] This "traditional" method of cost calculation has been the subject of criticism because it fails to take interest into account, it disregards the actual net amount of protection in a policy, and its results are inapplicable at every duration other than 20 (and/or 10) years. On the other hand, the method has the important attribute of simplicity. Attempts have been made to develop cost calculation methods that overcome some or all of these weaknesses. See Selected References on this subject at the end of this chapter.

A few participating companies have extended the benefit of gradation by size to old policyholders as well as new by grading dividends on policies issued in the past.

Some companies now issue policies resembling straight life with large minimum amounts. These are frequently paid up at age 90 or 95, or endowment at age 90 or 95, with a minimum of $25,000 or more, often with no further discount per $1,000 for policies larger than the minimum.

Rates for females are often lower than for males of the same age, whatever the system for grading premiums by size, because of favorable female mortality.

Net Cost Comparison

A complete net cost comparison shows what happens if at the end of the period the insured (1) continues the contract (net payments), or (2) surrenders the contract (net cost). The policy is considered "surrendered" at the end of 10 or 20 years because this is one way of giving weight to the cash values of the policies, which may differ considerably among companies. Very few policies actually are surrendered at these durations.

The reader may be cautioned that although many comparisons emphasize net cost rather than net payments, both are important. Net payments are important because a policy which has been in force 10 or 20 years will probably be maintained in force until the death of the insured, or the maturity of the policy if it is an endowment. In the case of net cost, sometimes called "surrendered net cost," the net cost figure is important because it gives weight to the valuable cash and loan emergency values of life insurance.

It should be remembered, too, that lower net cost may be largely a result of higher net payments. The company has more money to work with, and this in turn produces a higher cash value and lower net cost. This is an added reason why both net payments and net costs should be considered in their proper relationship. It is obvious that the mathematical exercise does not permit the actual enjoyment of net cost unless the insured terminates the contract, or unless the contract, by its terms, matures.

Cost Exhibits

A cost exhibit is shown in Table 19–1. (Figures are representative but cannot be identified with any company.) Two policies are indicated—a straight life and a 20-payment life, both nonparticipating contracts. Summaries are shown for 10 and 20 years.

Because these contracts are written on a nonparticipating basis and do not pay dividends, the exhibit involves only premiums, cash values, and the resulting cost. Although these figures are published as "projections" of nonparticipating policies being issued today, 10 or 20 years from now

TABLE 19–1

MALE NONPARTICIPATING NET PAYMENTS AND NET COST EXHIBIT*

1964 Guaranteed Costs (Nonparticipating) per $1,000 for $10,000 Policies—1958 CSO 3 Per Cent

	Straight Life					20-Pay Life				
10-Year Summary										
Age	25	30	35	45	55	25	30	35	45	55
Premiums	$ 13.41	$ 15.85	$ 18.99	$ 27.92	$ 41.95	$ 22.29	$ 25.14	$ 28.62	$ 37.49	$ 49.47
Ten premiums	134.10	158.50	189.90	279.20	419.50	222.90	251.40	286.20	374.90	494.70
Cash value	89.00	113.00	139.00	196.00	258.00	183.00	209.00	237.00	293.00	340.00
Net cost	41.00	45.50	50.90	83.20	161.50	39.90	42.40	49.20	81.90	154.70
Average cost	4.10	4.55	5.09	8.32	16.15	3.99	4.24	4.92	8.19	15.47
20-Year Summary										
Twenty premiums	269.20	317.00	379.80	558.40	839.00	445.80	502.80	572.40	749.80	989.40
Cash value	233.00	278.00	324.00	427.00	514.00	460.00	515.00	575.00	690.00	793.00
Net cost	36.20	39.00	55.80	131.40	325.00	14.20†	12.20†	2.60†	59.80	196.40
Average cost	1.81	1.95	2.79	6.57	16.25	0.71†	0.61†	0.13†	2.99	9.82

* Because dividends are not paid on nonparticipating contracts, concise summaries make the net payments and net cost picture clear. Copyright Flitcraft, Inc., *Flitcraft Compend*. Used by permission.

† Return over cost.

the same figures can serve as actual histories of the contracts, since all the figures are guaranteed.

Premiums are shown on each of the contracts at five representative ages. These premiums also serve as the average yearly payment because no dividends are involved. The average yearly payment shows the yearly outlay to the policyholder if the contract is continued at the end of 10 or 20 years.

The net payments and net cost exhibit shown in Table 19–2 is for 10- and 20-year projections from a comparative rate book for participating straight life and 20-payment life. Dividends are expected to be paid over the next 10 and 20 years. Projections of dividends (all based on the present scale) are shown annually for the first 10 years, followed by dividends for the fifteenth and twentieth years. Dividends are expected to be paid in the years where no figures appear, but are omitted to conserve space.

The summary shown in Table 19–2 uses the cost formula referred to above. Note that the 10 years' premiums, less dividends for 10 years, give net payments, following which the average yearly payment is shown. Then the tenth year cash value is subtracted from the net payments figure, leaving net cost. Finally, the net cost figure is divided by the number of policy years to give an average yearly cost during the first 10 years.

Table 19–2 also shows the twentieth policy year summary for the same contracts.

Occasionally, a summary shows a figure for a surrender dividend (also called a "terminal" or "termination" dividend), although the illustration in Table 19–2 does not contain one. The surrender dividend is paid to the withdrawing policyholder, and sometimes to the beneficiary of a policyholder who dies, provided the policyholder has continued the policy the required number of years. Many companies, perhaps having paid a somewhat larger dividend annually through the years, do not pay a surrender dividend.

Sometimes the summary figures for projections are followed by illustrations of results if dividends are left with the company to accumulate at interest and then later used to pay premiums, to pay up the policy earlier than guaranteed, or to mature the policy as an endowment. Two projections are involved here, one for the cash dividend and the other for the interest rate which will be paid in the future on dividends left with the company.

In the projections shown in Table 19–2, only the premiums and cash values can be said to be guaranteed. In general, the dividend figures, and those they affect, will correspond to the dividends actually paid in the future only if present conditions affecting dividends remain unchanged, so that the present scale of dividends is continued. The company warns its

Male Participating Net Payments and Net Cost Exhibit*—XYZ Life Insurance Company

(Present Dividend† Scale and Values per $1,000—1958 CSO 2½ Per Cent per $1,000 for Policies of $10,000)

	Straight Life					20-Pay Life			
Age	25	30	35	45	55	25	35	45	55
Premiums	$ 17.35	$ 20.02	$ 23.44	$ 33.60	$ 59.28	$ 29.31	$ 35.86	$ 45.31	$ 60.19
Dividends:									
Year 1	1.04	1.29	1.69	3.04	6.15	1.39	2.34	3.98	4.55
2	2.05	3.14	4.22	6.12	6.49	2.01	3.05	4.67	5.24
3	2.28	3.56	4.58	6.43	6.81	2.54	4.53	6.25	5.44
4	2.52	3.88	4.66	6.75	7.14	2.93	4.91	6.85	5.69
5	2.78	4.15	4.99	7.08	7.50	3.29	5.28	7.21	6.06
6	3.04	4.42	5.17	7.40	7.81	3.70	5.59	7.57	6.69
7	3.33	4.65	5.48	7.66	8.25	4.21	5.96	7.94	7.35
8	3.61	4.89	5.72	7.95	8.86	4.51	6.24	8.29	8.37
9	3.92	5.20	6.00	8.23	9.31	4.84	6.60	8.62	9.45
10	4.20	5.52	6.23	8.50	10.12	5.32	6.92	9.06	11.02
15	5.42	6.57	7.52	9.72	13.92	7.04	8.66	10.73	14.07
20	6.59	7.66	8.69	10.69	17.40	8.66	10.50	12.69	18.07
Summary—10 Policy Years									
Ten premiums	173.50	200.20	234.40	336.00	592.80	293.10	358.60	453.10	601.90
Total dividends	28.77	40.70	48.74	69.16	78.44	34.74	51.42	70.44	64.42
Net payments	144.73	159.50	185.66	266.84	514.36	258.36	307.18	382.66	537.48
Average payments	14.47	15.95	18.57	26.68	51.44	25.84	30.71	38.27	53.75
Cash value	125.18	147.76	172.53	228.70	307.00	232.03	285.02	336.96	505.96
Net cost	19.55	11.74	13.13	38.14	207.36	26.33	22.16	45.70	31.52
Average cost	1.95	1.17	1.31	3.81	20.74	2.63	2.22	4.57	3.15
Summary—20 Policy Years									
Twenty premiums	347.00	400.40	468.80	672.00	1,184.60	586.20	717.20	906.20	1,296.00
Total dividends	109.36	121.71	136.39	183.38	271.28	172.35	200.82	243.87	210.84
Net payments	237.64	278.69	332.41	488.62	913.32	413.85	516.38	671.35	1,085.16
Average payments	11.89	13.25	16.63	24.43	45.67	20.69	25.82	35.56	54.26
Cash value	275.42	317.01	361.17	454.66	576.00	524.93	633.63	740.90	832.72
Net cost	13.01‡	39.32‡	28.76‡	33.96	337.32	111.08‡	117.25‡	69.55‡	252.44
Average cost	0.65‡	1.96‡	1.44‡	1.70	16.87	5.55‡	5.86‡	1.48‡	12.62

* This exhibit shows the dividends and resulting net payments and net costs if the present dividend scale should be continued throughout 20 years of the contracts shown which are currently being issued. Copyright Flitcraft, Inc., *Flitcraft Compend*. Used by permission.

† Dividend illustrations are based on the current dividend scale and are not to be construed as guarantees or estimates of future dividends or results.

‡ Return over cost.

agents and others using the figures that they are neither estimates nor guarantees.

Dividend Histories

Table 19–3 shows dividend histories on contracts issued 20 and 10 years ago. The policies shown are straight life, 20-payment life, and 20-year endowment, each at issue ages 25, 35, and 45. In the 20-year history exhibit, following the premiums, the dividends are shown year by year (in this particular case, none was paid the first year). The summary follows the formula discussed above. These policies were issued on the American Experience Table of Mortality with 3 per cent interest assumed on reserves.

In the 10-year exhibit, 1941 CSO 2¼ per cent policies are shown, with premiums, dividends year by year, and a 10-year summary.

Problems of Cost Comparison

It is debatable as to what is the best way to compare costs of life insurance policies. Faced by the number of methods involved—projections on 10- and 20-year bases or histories, average yearly payments, or average yearly costs—it is no wonder that a person may be confused.

The principle of participating insurance being what it is, there is no simple way of decreeing that one particular method of determining costs is the best and only one which should be used. Dividend histories show what a company actually has done in the past and is doing presently for old policies. New policyholders today will be old policyholders tomorrow. Company policy and company management do not usually change drastically in a business such as life insurance. Ranged against immutable histories of contracts, however, is the fact that the policyholder is considering buying a policy *now.* So current earnings and the distribution thereof may prove a more accurate indication of the performance to be expected in the future. Each method has its points.

A majority of cost comparisons between companies are on the basis of projections of the present scale of dividends. The company which is ultraconservative in its present dividend scale is at a disadvantage if this is the only basis used. For this reason, it may be worth while to compare a company's projections in the past with its actual performance.[6]

The potential purchaser trying to make a decision between two policies, where sizable amounts of insurance are involved, may do well to look

---

[6] In its monthly magazine, *Flitcraft Courant,* Flitcraft does this annually for 10-year projections on straight life and for 20-year straight life projections and histories. It is of interest that for some years the 10-year studies have shown that projections 10 years earlier were generally conservative when compared with actual dividend histories on the same policies, with the companies generally delivering higher dividends than their projections. The recent 20-year comparison studies involve only a few companies, but show not much difference, on the whole, between projections and histories.

at projections, histories, and a side-by-side comparison of a projection for a policy issued some years back and the dividends actually paid on the contract. If the policyholder wishes to provide monthly income for his beneficiary, it will be well for him to take into account the amounts of guaranteed settlement options and the excess interest credited, both currently and in the past. Relatively low net cost on more than one basis is excellent; *no one company is best on every cost basis at all ages at issue.*

In most cases an exhaustive examination into cost is not necessary or desirable, lest a more important consideration in buying insurance be overlooked, namely, the functional value of life insurance as related to the buyer's total needs. Also, the interplay of premiums, dividends, and changes in the amounts of year-by-year dividends—both "projected" and actual—is so complex that comparative results between companies on a 10-year basis may be considerably different from those on a 20-year basis. Furthermore, the disparities will probably be even greater if calculations are made over a period longer than 20 years, such as from issue to age 65.

Further Considerations on Cost

A number of additional considerations must be borne in mind when attempting to compare costs of contracts. For a perfectly fair comparison to be made, everything except net payments or net costs must be precisely the same. This is manifestly not going to be the situation in any instance. No two policies are precisely the same.

It must be recognized that policies issued by different companies differ and that qualified life underwriters may offer somewhat differing programs to their clients. Given a situation, however, where these partly intangible factors are all of a high quality, one should try to make comparisons of more tangible matters, such as policy provisions and rates, on as nearly equivalent a basis as possible. Differences in policy contracts which make one more favorable to the policyholder than another make a difference in over-all cost to a company. Liberal provisions which are worthwhile may entail substantial cost, although the additional cost is rather intangible and likely to be forgotten in the "net cost" comparison.

There is sometimes no problem assuring oneself that the contracts considered are of the same kind in each company. For example, 20-payment life policies are pretty much the same in all companies. Straight life, however, has so many variations that often two slightly dissimilar things have to be compared. There is more than an imaginary benefit involved in a contract endowing at age 85 instead of age 100, as straight life does, since according to the mortality table a few more insureds will be living at the lower age to collect the face amount of insurance themselves. Other variations are life paid up at 85, 90 and 95, and endowment

TABLE 19-3

Actual Dividend Histories of Participating Policies*

20-Year Actual Dividend Histories of Policies Issued in 1944 per $1,000, American Experience 3 Per Cent

End of Year		Straight Life			20-Pay Life			20-Year Endowment		
Age		25	35	45	25	35	45	25	35	45
Premiums		$ 20.14	$ 26.35	$ 37.08	$ 30.12	$ 36.22	$ 45.73	$ 48.46	$ 50.11	$ 54.41
1945	1	....	....	....	....	....	....	....	....	....
1946	2	3.67	4.24	4.39	3.12	3.68	3.89	3.37	4.17	4.72
1947	3	3.91	4.44	4.67	3.40	3.94	4.23	3.62	4.35	4.91
1948	4	4.16	4.72	5.07	3.77	4.32	4.72	4.06	4.76	5.38
1949	5	8.22	9.39	9.87	7.70	8.69	8.93	7.98	9.16	10.37
1950	6	4.68	5.24	5.92	4.48	5.03	5.73	4.87	5.47	6.28
1951	7	4.94	5.49	6.35	4.83	5.36	6.24	5.25	5.79	6.71
1952	8	5.21	5.73	6.78	5.18	5.71	6.74	5.67	6.16	7.17
1953	9	5.49	5.98	7.21	5.54	6.04	7.25	6.04	6.48	7.59
1954	10	5.76	6.24	7.64	5.89	6.40	7.74	6.44	6.88	8.05
1955	11	5.71	5.82	6.50	5.49	5.66	6.39	5.37	5.67	6.46
1956	12	5.63	5.73	6.43	5.35	5.52	6.27	5.14	5.46	6.29
1957	13	5.53	5.56	6.36	5.20	5.31	6.15	4.89	5.20	6.12
1958	14	5.53	5.56	6.36	5.20	5.31	6.15	4.89	5.20	6.12
1959	15	5.53	5.56	6.36	5.20	5.31	6.15	4.89	5.20	6.12
1960	16	5.53	5.56	6.36	5.20	5.31	6.15	4.89	5.20	6.12
1961	17	5.53	5.85	7.18	5.74	5.93	6.35	5.06	5.44	6.12
1962	18	5.53	5.88	7.20	5.80	6.01	6.42	5.29	5.66	6.26
1963	19	5.56	6.48	9.09	6.42	6.67	7.54	6.62	6.89	7.42
1964	20	5.62	6.55	9.18	6.54	6.82	7.71	6.96	7.21	7.73
Summary—20-Year Histories										
Twenty premiums		402.80	527.00	741.60	602.40	724.40	914.60	969.20	1,002.20	1,088.20
Dividends, 20 years		101.74	110.02	128.92	100.05	107.02	120.75	101.30	110.35	125.94

Cash value, 20 years	230.50	327.58	441.35	504.59	609.92	723.24	1,000.00	1,000.00	1,000.00
Net cost, 20 years	70.56	89.40	171.33	2.24†	7.46	70.61	132.10†	108.15†	37.74†
Average yearly cost	3.53	4.47	8.57	0.11†	0.37	3.53	6.61†	5.41†	1.89†

10-Year Histories of Policies Issued in 1954—CSO 2¼ Per Cent

End of Year	Straight Life			20-Pay Life			20-Year Endowment		
Age	25	35	45	25	35	45	25	35	45
Premiums	$ 21.35	$ 28.46	$ 39.88	$ 33.63	$ 40.77	$ 50.75	$ 51.31	$ 53.52	$ 58.52
1955 1	2.78	3.81	5.67	3.11	4.14	5.95	3.59	4.48	6.14
1956 2	2.93	4.02	6.01	3.35	4.42	6.34	3.95	4.84	6.57
1957 3	3.07	4.24	6.26	3.57	4.72	6.64	4.29	5.22	6.91
1958 4	3.49	4.94	6.94	4.17	5.57	7.43	5.15	6.22	7.77
1959 5	3.65	5.22	7.14	4.41	5.90	7.66	5.50	6.61	8.03
1960 6	3.82	5.45	7.45	4.65	6.19	8.00	5.86	6.96	8.39
1961 7	4.27	6.01	8.21	5.27	6.88	8.83	6.69	7.78	9.27
1962 8	4.59	6.33	8.68	5.66	7.27	9.33	7.21	8.23	9.77
1963 9	5.05	6.84	9.44	6.36	7.98	10.21	8.21	9.15	10.75
1964 10	5.55	7.38	10.23	7.03	8.69	11.09	9.16	10.04	11.70

Summary—10-Year Histories

Ten premiums	213.50	284.60	398.80	336.30	407.70	507.50	513.10	535.20	585.20
Dividends, 10 years	39.20	54.24	76.03	47.58	61.76	81.48	59.61	69.53	85.30
Net, 10 years	174.30	230.36	322.77	288.72	345.94	426.02	453.49	465.67	499.90
Average yearly payments	17.43	23.04	32.28	28.87	34.59	42.60	45.35	46.57	49.99
Cash value, 10 years	137.32	180.28	233.26	260.94	306.12	348.89	438.87	436.58	431.68
Net cost, 10 years	36.98	50.08	89.51	27.78	39.82	77.13	14.62	29.09	68.22
Average yearly cost	3.70	5.01	8.95	2.78	3.98	7.71	1.46	2.91	6.82

* This exhibit shows dividends, net payments, and net costs on policies issued in the past. Copyright Flitcraft, Inc., *Flitcraft Compend*. Used by permission.

† Return over cost.

at 90. Cash values will be a little higher; but on the other hand, net payments will also tend to be higher on contracts endowing at the younger age.

It is of more importance in comparing like contracts to take into consideration the minimum amounts for which the policies will be issued. If one company is offering a policy with a minimum such as $15,000 or $25,000, the prospective purchaser should ask if the competing company also has such a higher minimum policy with which it can be compared.

The next consideration, and a most important one, is a comparison of the benefits offered in the two contracts which are being compared. How to make this comparison was the subject of the first part of this chapter.

Although allied to the subject of comparison of policy benefits, the handling of the disability and double indemnity or accidental death benefit may well be mentioned specifically. Usually, waiver of premium is desired. Where this is the case, the charge for waiver should be added to the annual premium, the average yearly payment, and the average yearly cost in the projection or history. Sometimes, waiver is included automatically by one company and not by another; so, to make comparisons fair, the waiver charge should be added to the premium which does not already include it. It should be noted that adding the cost of waiver does not make for a completely valid comparison with the company that automatically includes waiver, because of the difference in the period over which the cost is spread.

Where double indemnity is desired, the charge for this benefit should be added to the basic premium rate, average yearly payment, and average yearly cost.

CONCLUSION

In analyzing life insurance policy provisions and the cost of contracts, the advice of a competent life underwriter is invaluable. There is no substitute for his knowledge and experience. Furthermore, the most valuable policy that a prospect can buy is the one that fills his needs and accomplishes what he would wish to do if he were sure he could live to carry out his desires. The emphasis in comparing policies should, therefore, be on contract provisions. A fair consideration of the factor of cost, however, can aid the underwriter and the prospective policyholder in arriving at an intelligent decision.

SELECTED REFERENCES

BELTH, JOSEPH M. "The Cost of Life Insurance to the Policyowner . . . A Single Year Attained Age System," comments and author's reply regarding this paper; and "The Replacement Problem in Life Insurance . . . with

Special Emphasis on Comparative costs," *Journal of Insurance*, Vol. XXVIII, No. 4 (December, 1961), pp. 23–31; Vol. XXIX, No. 3 (September, 1962), pp. 424–29; and Vol. XXX, No. 1 (March, 1963), pp. 81–96.

FLITCRAFT, INC. *Flitcraft Compend.* New York, 1964.

FLITCRAFT, INC. *Settlement Options.* New York, 1964.

NATIONAL UNDERWRITER COMPANY. *Little Gem.* Cincinnati, 1964.

SOLBERG, HARRY J. "A Method for Consumer Valuation of Life Insurance Policies by Type," *Journal of Finance*, Vol. XVII, No. 4 (December, 1962), pp. 634–45; and comment and author's reply in Vol. XVIII, No. 4 (December, 1963).

Chapter 20

LIFE INSURANCE AS AN INVESTMENT

BY M. ALBERT LINTON

The general statement that the rates at which people die increase with age is not news. However, what may be news to many is that these increasing rates cause an investment element to be introduced into the types of life insurance making up the greater part of such insurance owned in this country.

Nature of Permanent Life Insurance

The typical policyholder prefers a kind of life insurance upon which the premiums do not increase from year to year. In order that this may be accomplished, he pays more in the early years of the policy than is necessary to meet expenses and to pay claims in those years. Later on, when the death rate has risen, the reverse is true. He will be paying less than he would have to pay under a policy taken at his advanced age.

What is it that makes this plan operate satisfactorily? It is that during the early years of the policy the excess of the premiums paid over the charge for current insurance protection is invested in a fund which builds up through successive additions of principal and interest. As the numbers of deaths increase with the advancing ages of the policyholders, interest on the fund is drawn upon to render unnecessary any increase in the premiums to take care of the claims. Steadily, the fund increases under each policy maintained in force until, at the extreme old age beyond which no one is assumed to live, there is in the accumulated fund the exact amount required to pay the policy in full. Under a mortality table in common use, this age is 100. Of course, only an exceedingly small number of policyholders survive to collect their policy monies in this way. The deaths of all the others occur at times when the accumulated funds are less than the face of the policies.

Under the plan, the company finds the money to pay such death claims from two sources. First, there is the accumulated fund. Suppose that under a $10,000 policy the fund amounts to $6,000. The $6,000 is thus used. Second, it draws upon what may be called its "mortality funds" to obtain the additional $4,000 required to make up the total claim of $10,000. With this explanation, one realizes why a policy of the kind under consideration can be described as a combination of protection and investment.

These principles underlie all policies covering the entire span of life—known as whole life policies—whether payable by premiums which continue during the entire period the policy remains in force or by premiums limited to a given period, such as 30, 20, or 10 years. The same principles apply also to so-called "endowment" policies. This kind of policy provides that if it is maintained in force over a given period, say to age 65, it "matures"—that is, becomes payable for its full face value. Furthermore, if the policyholder should die during the period before it matures, the policy also becomes payable for its full face value. Insurance on the whole life or endowment plans is known in insurance parlance as "permanent" or "cash value" life insurance.

In this chapter, the principal analysis will be of a straight life policy, which is a whole life policy with premiums payable as long as the policy remains in force. The first area of analysis will have to do with the characteristics of the accumulated fund—that is, the investment aspects of the policy.

Characteristics of Accumulated Fund

Everyone owning a straight life policy knows that it provides for guaranteed cash values which increase steadily year by year as premiums continue to be paid. These cash values are based upon the accumulated fund previously described. They are the tangible evidence of the investment elements in the premiums being paid.

What are the characteristics of these cash values, viewed as investments? For example, how safe or secure are they? How available are they in the event of emergency? If one desires to use them as security for loans, what are the conditions under which the loans may be made, including, of course, the rate of interest that will be charged? What rate of interest return may be expected upon the investment? In what ways does the plan differ from regular savings plans?

The security underlying a life insurance cash value in a well-established company is extremely high. First, it is based upon a diversity of investments. A contract with $5,000 cash value in a company owning one thousand separate investments would be the equivalent of the policyowner having $5.00 invested, on the average, in each of these investments. Moreover, these investments are in themselves of a conservative type with substantial margins of safety. This means not only that the risk of loss is small but that the fluctuations in market values are likely to be within a narrow range. This is an important reason why life insurance companies are able to guarantee the availability of cash and loan values. They could not do so if their investments were in securities subject to wide fluctuations in market values. In a well-established company, therefore, a policyowner need have no worry about the security of his invested savings.

The loan privilege guaranteed in the life insurance policy has important unique features. In the first place, it contains, when issued, a series of guaranteed loan values set out for each year the policy remains in force. This is not found in any bond, stock, or mutual fund share. In the second place, the rate of interest at which the loan can be obtained is also guaranteed in the policy. Under normal conditions, that is a convenience but not of special value. Under conditions of tight money or depression, it is extremely valuable. A recently purchased policy probably guarantees a borrowing rate of 5 per cent. No such provision is found in a bond, stock, or mutual fund share.

The granting of the loan provided for in a life insurance policy requires no statement of the policyowner's financial condition. The usual lender requires this, since, if the market value of the property behind the loan should decline, he wants to be sure the borrower can make good any deficiency. Moreover, the life insurance loan cannot be called by the company.

The ready availability of life insurance cash and loan values in periods of emergency is one of their most valuable characteristics. In times of prosperity, this ready availability is not unique. Many other forms of investment have it. However, in times of economic adversity when money is tight and market values are collapsing, the situation is very different. Then the right to withdraw or to borrow the amount of the cash value as guaranteed in the policy is of the greatest value. This was demonstrated in the prolonged, deep depression of the 1930's, when the guaranteed cash and loan values of life insurance saved great numbers of families and businesses from disaster. The amount of cash which can be realized on a stock, bond, or mutual fund share will depend upon the condition of the market at the time. Obviously, with a depressed market, tragic losses may be suffered by persons selling securities for cash needs.

A life insurance company sends out regular notices of the premiums as they are about to fall due. This is also done under other types of investment involving regular periodic payment plans. Such mild compulsion is a helpful factor in helping to maintain the plan intact. Under the life insurance policy, however, the interruption of the program may have collateral effects upon the protection side of the contract. The policy was probably taken out in the first place to protect the family in the event of the untimely death of the breadwinner. Anything interfering with that program or reducing its protection is likely to be of concern to the policyholder and his family. Consequently, the urge to maintain the regular periodic payments under the life insurance policy is likely to be stronger than the urge to do the same under a plan involving merely the accumulation of savings in another type of investment. Such a plan may be interrupted by the attractiveness of some tangible thing, such as a new car, a household appliance, or a more expensive than usual vacation.

This greater incentive to maintain the life insurance plan provides a valuable element of stability to the life insurance company in times of economic adversity. Under such conditions, there are always substantial segments of the population who have sufficient incomes to pay life insurance premiums. Consequently, there is a continual flow of premium income which includes investment elements to be added to the accumulated funds. These elements, which normally would be invested, provide the current funds to meet the demands for cash and loan values. Therefore, the need to sacrifice choice investments by forced sale to meet such demands is greatly reduced, and the opportunity to buy at attractive prices is present even in bad times. This is another reason why the life insurance companies can safely guarantee cash and loan values in their policies.

The Investment Return

What about the interest return on the investment or savings element in life insurance premiums, or, to put it in a way that is too often forgotten or overlooked, what must an investment or savings program yield if it is to duplicate what can be realized through the medium of life insurance? Because of the dual nature of the life insurance policy, involving both protection and saving, the answer cannot be arrived at readily. As previously described, the life insurance policy is, in effect, a combination of an increasing investment or savings fund plus a supplemental mortality fund which in the event of death provides the amount that must be added to the accumulated fund to produce the face amount of the policy. Therefore, it follows that the amounts that must be drawn from the mortality fund decrease as the accumulated fund increases.

In seeking an answer to the rate-of-interest question, the analysis must show how the life insurance policy may, in effect, be duplicated by establishing an investment fund and supplementing it with renewable term insurance bought in the open market on which the amount of the term insurance will decrease as the investment fund accumulation increases. Assuming that the amounts to be invested in each program are equal, the figure we are seeking is the net rate of compound interest that must be earned on the investment fund so that at the end of a given period, such as twenty years, the fund will equal the twentieth-year guaranteed cash value of the life insurance policy. In all of this discussion, it is important to remember that the build-up of the life insurance cash value over the years is not subject to income tax.

Recently, the author had occasion to have these calculations made for straight life policies. The procedure is complicated, but is greatly facilitated by the use of electronic computers. To provide a broad base, the figures for ten mutual companies were employed, using their 1963 dividend scales. The term insurance costs were obtained by using the relatively low renewable term insurance premiums of a company that shortly before had adopted rates based upon the new mortality table that will soon be used by all United States life insurance companies.

Taking a straight life policy at age 35, it was found that 4.78 per cent *net* would have to be realized on the separate investment fund, on which the interest is taxable as ordinary income each year, if it were to accumulate at the end of twenty years to the twentieth-year guaranteed cash value of the straight life policy. To realize 4.78 per cent net after income taxes and expenses, a much higher rate must be realized on a gross basis.

TABLE 20–1

INVESTMENT RETURN REQUIRED TO EQUATE WITH INCREASING LIFE INSURANCE CASH VALUES—POLICIES PURCHASED AT SELECTED AGES

Age	Return Required	
	Net	Gross: 50 Per Cent Income Tax Bracket
25	4.80%	9.60%*
35	4.78	9.56 *
45	5.17	10.34
55	6.37	12.74

* On each of the policies issued at ages 25 and 35, the cash value at the end of the twenty-year period is greater than the cost of the policy over the same period. Therefore, if the policy were not continued but surrendered for cash, there would be a taxable gain. Taking this into account for a policyowner in the 50 per cent bracket, the required returns for policies issued at ages 25 and 35 become 8.80 and 9.16 per cent, respectively.

For example, if a man were in a 32 per cent income tax bracket, the gross rate would have to be 7.03 per cent, year after year, on a compound interest basis. For a man in a 42 per cent bracket, the corresponding gross rate would be 8.24 per cent; and for the 50 per cent tax bracket, it would be 9.56 per cent.

These are impressive figures. They make life insurance men and women enthusiastic about their product as a savings medium. Even if there were no other advantages, life insurance could be sold on the basis of interest return alone, as against a combination of term insurance and separate investment.

Similar calculations were also made using $10,000 straight life policies taken at ages 25 and 45, each carried for 20 years, and for age 55, carried for 10 years. The results are as shown in Table 20–1.

Looking at the rates in Table 20–1, one may wonder how they can be valid, since the companies on their own invested assets are not earning rates that high. The answer lies in the relatively high cost of term insurance bought under a separate policy compared with the cost of the term insurance charged by the company against the straight life policy. If there are two programs side by side involving the same outlay, year after year, the one that has to pay the larger amount for term insurance will have less left over for investment. Therefore, it must realize a relatively high rate of return on the smaller sum to do as well in accumulating funds as does the program that has larger amounts for investment but earns a somewhat lower rate of return.

To make this clearer, assume that a fund of $10,000 is to be accumulated over a twenty-year period. If A invests $323 a year at 4 per cent net compound interest, he will accomplish his purpose. On the other hand, if B has only $288 a year to invest, he must realize 5 per cent net. Thus the person who tries to duplicate a life insurance policy through term insurance and separate investment finds himself in a position similar to that of B.

The next question is: Why is the cost of renewable term insurance purchased under a separate policy relatively expensive? The answer is twofold. First, combining the investment and protection elements results in savings which are reflected in the lower cost of the term or protection element. Issuing and maintaining a separate term insurance policy involve expenses that are reduced when the term insurance is combined with the savings element in a straight life policy.

The second reason for the higher cost of separate term insurance is that the mortality under renewable term insurance tends to be relatively high. The reason is that as successive renewals of the policy occur, each at a higher premium rate than the preceding one, healthy lives are likely to drop out. If they continue to need insurance, they take it on a level premium plan where the premiums do not increase. The result is that as time goes on, the cost of protection of impaired lives in the term insurance group tends to increase. This naturally leads to higher mortality costs. No such conditions operate in the case of the term insurance element in a straight life policy, where the over-all cost to the policyholder tends to decrease or, in the case of nonparticipating insurance, to remain level. This analysis explains why the term insurance costs in a combined policy are a bargain as compared with the cost of term insurance purchased under a separate policy.

Calculations similar to the ones producing the previously described equivalent earning rates have been made at several different times, beginning with 1927. As might be expected, the figures have varied with conditions in the long-term investment market. The highest rates were found in 1927, when the yield on long-term high-grade bonds was 4.65

per cent and the life insurance return at age 35 was 5.36 per cent. It was lowest in 1949, when the bond yield was 2.65 per cent and the life insurance yield 3.34 per cent. The bond yield in 1963 was 4.19, and, as has been shown, the corresponding return at age 35 was 4.78 per cent.

The figures from the various computations show that the life insurance method of saving has been favorable as compared with the rates on conservative investments. The advantage for life insurance is, of course, much greater than the differences between the life insurance returns and the bond yields because the life insurance rates are *net*, whereas income taxes and expenses must be deducted from the bond yields to obtain their net rates.

The foregoing analysis reveals the striking advantage of combining the two elements of protection and saving in the one life insurance contract. There are other advantages as well.

Other Advantages of the Single Contract

An advantage of permanent life insurance is the speed with which the proceeds of a life insurance policy go to work for the protection of the beneficiary. In the usual course, the separate investment fund would pass through the estate. The settlement of an estate takes time, perhaps a year or more. It involves court costs, legal fees, and frequently other forms of hampering red tape. If the will is contested, the proceedings may drag out over a long period, to the added expense and discomfort of those entitled to the funds.

Another advantage of the life insurance investment, as already pointed out, is that one knows just what its value will be in the future. In the case of a separate fund invested in bonds, stocks, or mutual funds, one does not know. Death may occur, or a serious emergency may arise, and the amount the separate fund would realize at forced sale could be embarrassingly low. That was indeed the case in countless instances in the 1930's. Of course, the reverse may be true. The value of the separate fund may be high. One has to balance that possibility against the possibility of a low value and its consequences, and then reflect upon the guaranteed features of the life insurance policy.

Life insurance has been granted preferred status in the laws of many states. For example, the policy proceeds often are exempt from the claims of the insured's creditors. The proceeds of life insurance at death generally are exempt from federal income tax. Likewise, the proceeds are exempt from state income taxes in most states having such taxes. In most states, life insurance policy proceeds are wholly or partially exempt from inheritance or estate taxes. These unique advantages have been granted by legislators who recognize the special value of life insurance as a protector of the family. Many legislators have utilized life insurance as the main protection of their own families.

Finally, the life insurance policy contains provisions whereby the policy proceeds may be applied, at guaranteed rates stated in the policy, to provide annuity incomes to beneficiaries. This has consistently proved to be a valuable privilege. The policy proceeds may become payable at a time when the rates charged for separate annuity policies—such as would have to be purchased by the separate fund—would be relatively high.

"Paying Interest on My Own Money" Fallacy

A review of the service of life insurance as an investment should also include an answer to a question that at times has puzzled policyholders. It is this: "Since the money represented by the loan value of my policy is 'my money,' why should I have to pay interest on the amounts I may borrow under the policy?" To see clearly why interest is charged, recall that the guaranteed loan values increase from year to year. A part of these increases results from interest earned on the funds in the hands of the company. Also, if the insurance is on the participating plan, the dividends the policyholder receives usually involve the excess of the interest earned above that assumed in the original computation. Therefore, it follows that if funds earning interest are withdrawn and paid to the policyholder, these two features of the policy could not be maintained if the withdrawn funds did not continue to earn interest. The only way to maintain the two features is to seek from the policyowner an additional sum of money at least equal to the interest which otherwise would have been earned by the company had the loan not been in effect.

In Summary

Millions of policyholders buy their life insurance primarily for the protection of their families. They frequently do not realize the numerous favorable investment aspects of their policies. Permanent life insurance renders a unique and exceedingly valuable investment service. Strangely enough, it all developed from the invention of a plan to cover the steadily increasing risk of death by a type of insurance calling for level rather than increasing premiums.

SELECTED REFERENCES

HUEBNER, S. S. *The Economics of Life Insurance.* 3d ed. New York: Appleton-Century-Crofts, Inc., 1959.

LINTON, M. ALBERT. *How Life Insurance Can Serve You.* New York: Harper & Bros., 1958.

PART III

Individual Health Insurance

Chapter 21

INDIVIDUAL DISABILITY INCOME INSURANCE

BY JOHN H. MILLER

The earning power of the head of the family, which is the principal asset of the great majority of families, is constantly at the risk of being reduced or lost completely by reason of a disabling injury or sickness. Protection of personal earning power by health insurance is therefore basic to any plan of individual or family security. Disability income insurance or, as it is sometimes called, loss-of-time insurance, fills this need.

History and Present Extent of Coverage

The development of disability insurance, which may be traced from the European guilds and the British friendly societies, commenced in the United States in 1850, when policies were first offered providing income benefits in the event of accidental injury. After an earlier abortive attempt to insure against disease, the next development occurred in the 1890's, when policies were offered covering disability from certain specified diseases as well as from accidental cause. As a result of the gradual liberalization of these early policies, by the advent of the twentieth century, broad forms covering substantially all diseases were being offered. A typical policy at that time provided benefits for total disability from the first day with a limit of one year on the maximum duration for which benefits would be continued if caused by sickness or two years if caused by accident. Liberalizations continued to be made until by the twenties, many policies provided lifetime disability benefits. Severe underwriting losses occurring during the economic depression starting in 1929 proved that some companies had gone too far in liberalizing benefits and had permitted many policyholders to become overinsured. A general retrenchment in benefits and underwriting practices occurred during the thirties. Since World War II, the trend has again been toward liberalization of policy benefits and underwriting practices, but limitations are generally observed with respect to the maximum period of disability for which indemnity will be paid, and the amount of indemnity issued is generally kept within reasonable relationship to the earnings of the insured.

It is estimated that over 14 million people are protected by disability income policies issued on an individual policy basis.[1] Altogether, more than 43 million people are estimated to have some form of protection against loss of income. This total, in addition to individual health policies, includes disability benefits provided by group policies, formal sick leave plans, union-administered plans, and employee mutual benefit associations.

Insuring Agreement and Other Provisions

The disability income policy must specify the type or scope of disability for which benefits will be paid, the periodic payments to be made, when the benefits will start and how long they will continue, and the specific policy exclusions.

Although earlier policies frequently covered disability resulting only from accident, the emphasis today is on policies that cover losses resulting from both accident and sickness. A typical insuring clause reads: "The company hereby insures the person named against loss resulting (1) directly and independently of all other causes from bodily injuries caused by accident which occurs while this policy is in force (herein called 'such injuries'); or (2) from sickness or disease contracted and commencing while this policy is in force (herein called 'such sickness')."

It should be noted that, subject to a statutory or voluntary time limit, pre-existing conditions are excluded by the insuring agreement. This is necessary to protect the company against adverse selection from individuals already suffering from an active or incipient disorder. The effect of this restriction is to keep the cost of insurance reasonable for honest individuals seeking protection for the unknown accident or sickness.

Some policies also contain a probationary period, usually applicable only to sickness benefits, requiring that loss occur more than 15 or 30 days after the policy date. This provision is designed primarily to avoid antiselection when exposure to some communicable disease has occurred. With relatively few such diseases prevalent today, this restriction is gradually disappearing.

The rate of income is usually expressed as a weekly or monthly benefit. Unless the income is to be paid for the full duration of disability, the policy will contain an indemnity limit, that is, a maximum period of time for which benefits will be paid during any one continuous period of disability—for example, two years. The indemnity limit may be the same for disability caused by accidental injury as for disability caused by sickness,

---

[1] Health Insurance Institute, *Source Book of Health Insurance Data, 1962* (New York, 1963).

or longer for accident disability. In some policies, benefits for disability caused by accident are payable as long as the insured remains disabled.

Most policies mention one or more causes of disability which are excluded. Typical exclusions, or risks not covered, are disabilities resulting from war or any act of war, from aviation if acting as a pilot or crew member, or from self-inflicted injury.

While there is no standard or statutory form of policy in health insurance, the legislation of most states includes the Uniform Individual Accident and Sickness Policy Provisions Law, which requires the inclusion of certain policy provisions and also specifies a number of optional provisions.[2]

Definition of Disability

Some of the earlier policies of disability insurance, as well as disability provisions in life insurance policies, provided for the payment of lifetime benefits if the insured was totally disabled from performing the duties of *his* occupation. Because of abuses by insureds who claimed total disability as the result of a minor injury that interfered with the pursuit of a highly specialized occupation but did not substantially impair their earning power, use of this definition in disability provisions of life insurance policies was prohibited by the standard provisions recommended in 1929 by a special committee of the National Convention of Insurance Commissioners. Health insurance policies which had included the "his occupation" definition without limitation were generally revised to provide that only for the first one or two years would disability be defined as inability of the insured to perform the duties of his occupation; thereafter, it would be defined as inability to perform the duties of any gainful occupation. This latter type of definition provides a period of rehabilitation during which the disabled person can adjust to a new occupation, if necessary. Many disability policies define disabilty of any duration as inability to engage in gainful occupation. In either case, it is now customary to qualify the words "gainful occupation" by language such as "for which the insured is reasonably fitted by education, training, and experience."

Confining and Nonconfining Disability

Some policies distinguish between confining and nonconfining disability where the cause of disability is sickness. While relatively few policies currently issued contain a "house-confined" restriction, those which do usually provide for the payment of lifetime benefits as long as the insured is confined to his house and regularly treated by a doctor. In

[2] See Chapter 27 for an analysis of contract provisions in individual health insurance policies.

other cases, full benefits are paid for a period of up to one year if the disability confines the insured to his house or to a hospital. When the insured ceases to be so confined but is still totally disabled for any gainful occupation, he will receive benefits at half the regular rate of indemnity, subject, in some cases, to a shorter limit, such as twenty-six weeks.

In recent years, there has been a tendency to liberalize the "house confinement" clause due to abuses brought about by strict interpretations. House confinement generally has been extended to include confinement to the home premises and visits to the doctor's office or a hospital. Even with such liberalizations, the value of such a clause to the policyholder is questionable. There are chronic diseases that result in total disability but do not require house confinement. Under such provisions, it is difficult for the insured to evaluate the extent of his protection, as it will depend on the nature of his disability.

Partial Disability

In addition to providing a stipulated weekly or monthly indemnity during total disability, many policies provide for payment of income at a reduced rate, such as 40 or 50 per cent of the full rate, for a limited period of time, often six months, if as a result of an accident the insured is prevented from performing one or more of the important daily duties of his occupation. In some policies, particularly those with an indemnity limit of five or ten years, partial disability due to sickness is also indemnified if it immediately follows a period of total disability. The partial disability benefit is not particularly appropriate in a policy insuring an employee, but a self-employed person often resumes his work on a part-time basis before complete recovery, in which case the partial disability benefit provides a supplementation of the reduced earnings which such part-time effort produces.

Long- and Short-Term Indemnity Limits

The length of the indemnity period is a matter of great importance to both the insurer and the insured. The tremendous losses which companies suffered during the depression years following 1929 under life insurance disability income benefits and noncancellable disability policies arose almost entirely from policies that paid benefits for the entire duration of disability. Under such policies the insured is likely to become a disability pensioner when he contracts a serious chronic disease. If his disability income is payable for life in an amount approximating the net income after taxes which he could hope to earn by returning to gainful employment, and if the disease or impairment from which he suffers is incurable, his urge for security may persuade him to cling to his status as a disabled person rather than to endeavor to overcome his disability by taking advantage of the modern techniques of rehabilitation which have enabled many severely impaired people to become self-supporting again.

The individual whose policy provides disability income with an indemnity limit of one or two years is in a very different situation. While he is assured of an income for the indemnity limit specified if his disability continues that long, he also knows that he must strive toward recovery or rehabilitation. His motivation is very different from that of the man who is insured under a life disability benefit. Since only a very small percentage of disabilities last for more than one year, the policy with an indemnity limit of one or two years offers complete protection for the great majority of disabilities without giving the insured an incentive to become a disability pensioner. For this reason, the insurance company can offer a much larger rate of income, both in absolute amount and in relation to the insured's earnings, under a policy with a one- or two-year indemnity limit than with a long indemnity limit.

A combination of a short-term policy for a very substantial monthly indemnity with a long-term policy paying benefits to age 65 at a considerably smaller monthly rate is considered by some to form a well-rounded program. The insured is then adequately protected against disability for up to one or two years, and also has some basic protection for the unusual but disastrous disability which results in years of complete incapacity.

Ancillary Benefits

The disability benefit may be the sole benefit in a health insurance policy, or it may be contained in a comprehensive policy also including one or more of the following benefits: accidental death or dismemberment indemnity; hospital, surgical or medical expense benefits; and additional benefits for special risks. Alternatively, these benefits may be available as riders to be attached to a disability income policy.

Elimination Period

The elimination period in disability insurance is akin to the deductible in automobile collision insurance. It is a period (such as seven, 30, 60, or 90 days, or even up to one year) at the beginning of the disability during which no benefits are payable. The elimination period permits the insured to minimize the cost of his disability insurance by personally assuming the risk of income loss caused by disability for an initial period of days or months during which his other resources are sufficient to meet his living expenses.

A second purpose of the elimination period is to avoid the expense of claims administration with respect to the short claims which fall entirely within the elimination period. Since a certain amount of expense must be incurred in the processing of any claim, however small, it is not economically sound to provide insurance against minor losses. The money saved through the use of a moderate elimination period can be applied either to purchase a larger monthly indemnity than the insured could otherwise afford or to extend the indemnity limit to provide payments over a longer maximum period.

The elimination period can also be used to advantage in arranging disability income to complement, without duplication, short-term benefits provided by group insurance, employers' wage continuance plans, or state cash sickness benefits.

Renewal Provisions

Health insurance policies differ widely not only as to the benefits but also as to the provisions and guarantees, if any, respecting the renewal of the policy.

Cancellable or Commercial Policies. The earliest form of health insurance policy provided that renewal was at the option of the insurer and that, between renewal dates, the insurer could cancel the policy by giving written notice and refunding the pro rata unearned premium. Over the years, there has been a trend toward the elimination of the cancellation provision but with reservation of the right of the insurer to refuse renewal on any premium due date. Some policies of the cancellable or commercial type have not specified any age of termination, and the insurer has used its right of refusing to renew as a means of terminating policies upon the insured's retirement or reaching some selected age.

Under the uniform law, the insurer must give five days' written notice of cancellation. When the insurer retains the right of cancellation, the insured also has the privilege of canceling after the original term of the policy. On cancellation by either the insurer or the insured, the pro rata premium must be returned.

Noncancellable Policies. Early in the century, policies were introduced which omitted the cancellation privilege and which gave the insured the right of renewal up to a specified age limit, subject only to the timely payment of premiums specified in the policy. Some of these policies were modeled after the more liberal cancellable policies containing no indemnity limit and promising benefits as long as the insured remained disabled. Very severe underwriting losses were sustained under this type of policy because the insurers did not have adequate statistical data for the determination of rates; they did not make allowance for the very liberal judicial interpretations of the definition of disability; they did not adequately guard against overinsurance, either through policy provisions or by underwriting practice; and in writing a disability benefit for life in large amounts, they made it attractive to many policyholders to become disability pensioners.

Other companies offered noncancellable policies subject to an indemnity limit, while some used an aggregate or collective limit which applied to all disabilities cumulatively from the time of issue of the policy. The unlimited policy was discontinued because of poor underwriting results, and the aggregate policy has generally been supplanted by the type incorporating a maximum benefit period for each disability. Only the last-mentioned form has survived the test of time. During recent years, an increasing number of companies have commenced the issuance of noncancellable disability income policies with indemnity limits varying from one to ten years or with benefits payable up to age 65.

Adjustable-Premium Guaranteed Renewable Policies. Another type of renewal provision guarantees the right of renewal subject only to timely payment of premiums until a specified termination date, with the insurer reserving the right to adjust premiums not on the individual policy but for any underwriting class. An underwriting class is usually considered to be a group of insureds of the same occupational classification, the same sex, and the same age or age group at issue. This type of renewal provision was first introduced in hospital and surgical policies in recognition of the fact that the claim cost is not only a function of insurable contingencies such as the incidence of accident or disease, but is also affected by price trends or changes in the value of the dollar. Since disability income benefits are paid in fixed dollar amounts, as contrasted to the reimbursement of expenses incurred under certain medical expense coverages, the same rationale for the adjustable premium is not applicable to the disability income policy. However, some insurers, not wishing to incur the full risk of noncancellable underwriting, have used this provision in disability income policies.

Prorating Provisions

Of the optional provisions previously mentioned, the following provide for proration of benefits under various circumstances. Many policies do not contain any of these prorating provisions, and probably no policy contains all of them. Their uses and purposes are briefly described below.

Change of Occupation. Premium rates for health insurance policies providing disability benefits are generally based upon an occupational classification. If an insured under a policy which provides for this type of proration suffers a disability after having changed to a more hazardous occupation than that which he followed at the time of applying for the policy, his benefits may be reduced to that proportion of the stated benefits which the premium rate for the original occupation bears to the premium rate for the new and more hazardous occupation.

Other Insurance. One of the optional provisions stipulates that if one or more policies previously issued by the insurer to the insured result in aggregate indemnity in excess of a specified limit of indemnity, the excess insurance shall be void. Another form, not appropriate for guaranteed renewable or noncancellable policies and rarely used in other types, provides for prorating if insurance is carried with another insurer and not disclosed to the insurer which issued the policy containing this provision.

Average Earnings Clause (Relation of Earnings to Insurance Clause). Since the purpose of disability income insurance is to provide a benefit in replacement of earnings lost as a result of the insured's inability to work, the benefit payable should be less than the net earnings of the insured after deduction of income taxes and business or occupational expenses. When a policy is issued on a noncancellable basis, the insurer incurs the risk that before the termination of the policy at age 65 or other stipulated age, the insured's earnings may decline to the point where the original indemnities represent overinsurance. There is also the possibility that the insured may purchase additional insurance after issue of the original insurance. As a protection, the insurer may employ the average earnings clause, which provides that if, at the time disability commences, the indemnities exceed the average earnings of the insured over the preceding two years, the indemnities will be reduced pro rata to such amount, but in no event to less than $200 per month or the monthly indemnity of the policy, if less.

In the prorating provisions mentioned above, except for the one relating to change of occupation, the insurer is required to refund the premium paid for any insurance invalidated by reason of such provision. Under the average earnings clause complying with the laws in effect in 1963, the refund of premiums is limited to the two years preceding disability.

Nonoccupational Policies

It was mentioned that most disability policies are rated on the basis of occupational classification and that some contain clauses prorating benefits in the event of a change to a more hazardous occupation. A variation is the so-called "nonoccupational" policy, which excludes the payment of any indemnity for disability resulting from an accident arising out of or in the course of the insured's occupation or employment. Policies of this type are usually issued at the same rate, regardless of the insured's occupation. They are designed particularly for insuring workers subject to workmen's compensation benefits.

Selection of Risks

The underwriting of health insurance involves the same considerations as apply to life insurance, that is, the occupation of the applicant, any indication of moral hazard, his habits, financial status, physical condition and medical history, family history, habitat, environment, and reputation.

The relative importance of these factors is not the same in health insurance as in life insurance, largely because disability is not a precisely determinable condition. The insured's attitude toward contracts, his sense of responsibility, and his reaction to illness all have a great deal to do with the amount of disability he will claim. The nature of the insured's employment, the stability of his income or earnings, and the relationship of earnings to the amount of indemnities payable will also have an important bearing on whether he will terminate a disability claim as soon as possible or be inclined to malinger.

It is important to recognize the difference between life insurance and disability insurance in respect to the insured's motivation. With rare exceptions, the insured has a deep urge for self-preservation which works in favor of the insurance company with respect to life insurance. While most people also wish to avoid sickness, many are in no hurry to terminate their disability income after sickness has occurred, particularly if they have no real interest in their employment or occupation.[3]

Treatment of Substandard Risks

More attention is being given to the risk who does not measure up to the qualifications of the standard risk but who is able to carry on in full-time employment despite some impairment to his health. In some situations, such as a history of allergy or of hay fever, an unrestricted policy may be offered at the standard premium if the elimination period is long enough to exclude the disabilities likely to arise from such a cause. In other conditions, the risk can be accepted subject to a waiver or impairment rider, which provides that the policy will not cover any loss caused by a named disease or resulting from a physical impairment occurring with respect to a designated part of the anatomy. The use of an impairment rider permits an insurer to offer protection against all the other hazards to health by excluding the cause or causes of disability which have already manifested themselves. As a rule, the regular premium is charged when an impairment rider is attached to a policy, although in some circumstances it may be necessary to use both the impairment rider and an extra premium.

Another method of substandard underwriting is the issuance of an unrestricted policy subject to an increased premium, with the amount of the increase reflecting the extra hazard indicated by the medical history or condition. This type of substandard underwriting is more difficult in connection with health insurance than it is in life insurance, where it has been so highly developed. If the disease or impairment is one which would normally be considered to be disabling, the insured might be able to submit a disability claim at almost any time he wished to do so, even

[3] See Chapter 26 for an analysis of risk selection in individual health insurance.

though he had previously been carrying on his work despite his impaired health.[4]

Administration of Benefit Payments

The successful underwriting of disability benefits requires not only careful selection of risks but effective administration of applications for benefit payments. The subjective elements of disability which create problems for the underwriter also affect the work of the claims adjuster. The proper payment of claims requires the conscientious discharge of responsibilities by both parties to the contract. The insured has the responsibility of giving the company prompt notice of the occurrence of an accident or the commencement of a sickness which may be expected to result in a payment under the policy. It also is his duty to submit proof of loss, authorizing any hospital reports or medical statements which the company requires, and to do so within the time limits specified in the policy. It is also the duty of the insured to obtain proper and adequate medical care and to follow the recommendations of his physician. The company, on its part, should process all papers promptly, determine its liability under the policy terms objectively, and make prompt payment of all benefits due the policyholder.

In determining whether disability exists and how long it continues, the company will have as evidence the claimant's own statement, the statement of his doctor, and the record of absence from his business or place of employment, with such corroboration as may be obtained through an inspection report. Experience studies indicating the average length of disability from various diseases or kinds of accident will be helpful in judging whether the period of disability claimed is reasonable.

If the policy has not been long in force, a careful check is made to determine the date of origin of the disability or, if an accident was the cause of loss, the date of the accident. This is necessary since pre-existing conditions are not covered by individual disability policies. However, under either the incontestable clause or the "time limit on certain defenses" provision which modern policies contain, a claim cannot be ruled out on the ground of pre-existence if the policy has been in force for more than three years or such shorter period as may be named in the policy.

In the event of evidence of pre-existence, a company may have two alternative courses to pursue: to declare the policy void from date of issue on the basis of misrepresentations, or to deny the claim on the ground that the origin of the condition predated the issuance of the policy.

After a disability claim has been admitted, the insurer must obtain periodic proof of the continuance of disability until the insured has

[4] See Chapter 26 for further analysis of the treatment of substandard risks in individual health insurance.

recovered or until payments have been made for the indemnity limit of the policy.

Trends and Prospects

Since the depression of the thirties, the development of individual health insurance has been in the direction of more comprehensive policies with fewer exclusions, with conditions and provisions more liberal to the insured, and with greater clarity of expression.

The market for individual disability income policies has been somewhat narrowed by the tremendous growth in group disability income insurance and its availability to groups which, because of their character or small size, were formerly not considered for group underwriting. Despite the extension of group underwriting, the establishment of compulsory cash sickness programs in four states, and the inclusion of permanent total disability benefits in the social security program, the public generally is still seriously underinsured with respect to loss of income because of disability. In particular, the self-employed and those whose living costs substantially exceed any group benefits available to them need this fundamental form of income insurance for their personal and family security. With continued increases in living standards and the increasing desire for economic security, the outlook for further growth of disability income insurance is very favorable.

SELECTED REFERENCES

DICKERSON, O. D. *Health Insurance.* Rev. ed. Homewood, Ill.: Richard D. Irwin, Inc., 1963.

FARLEY, JARVIS. "A 1940 View of Non-cancellable Disability Insurance," *Proceedings of the Casualty Actuarial Society,* Vol. XXVII (1940–41), p. 18.

FAULKNER, EDWIN J. *Health Insurance.* New York: McGraw-Hill Book Co., Inc., 1960.

HART, WARD VAN B. "Recent Developments in Commercial Accident and Health Insurance," *Proceedings of the Casualty Actuarial Society,* Vol. XXI (1934–35), p. 291.

MILLER, JOHN H. "The Development of Individual Health and Accident Insurance," *Journal of the American Society of Chartered Life Underwriters,* Vol. VI, No. 1 (December, 1951).

SOCIETY OF ACTUARIES. *Health Insurance Provided through Individual Policies.* (Edwin L. Bartleson, principal contributor.) Chicago, 1963.

Chapter 22

LIFE INSURANCE RIDERS—DISABILITY AND ACCIDENTAL DEATH INSURANCE

BY CHARLES A. ORMSBY

Several forms of individual health insurance have long been associated with individual life insurance, being provided as additional or supplementary coverages through riders or endorsements to individual life insurance contracts. The most popular forms of such coverages are disability income, disability premium waiver, and accidental death (or double indemnity). These supplementary coverages are health insurance benefits which create special drafting, underwriting, administrative, and claims problems. Whereas life insurance protection is, relatively speaking, easily defined because death is certain, definite, and rarely excluded from coverage, it is by no means a simple task to state definitively the conditions under which disability and accidental death benefits are payable. Complications are introduced by the multiplicity of terms to be clarified and by the need to spell out a variety of exceptions and exclusions in setting proper limits to the scope of these supplementary coverages.

The disability income rider, which is attached to about 5 per cent of life insurance policies currently being issued, is intended to provide regular cash income, usually monthly, to insured persons disabled under the contract. The hazard of total and permanent disability has been referred to as the "living death," in that the disabled person frequently is economically dead, because his earning power is destroyed, yet he is faced with many of the costs of normal living plus certain additional costs.

The disability premium waiver rider provides for waiver of the premiums falling due during a period of total and permanent disability under the contract. This is the most prevalent type of disability coverage presently combined with life insurance, appearing in about half of the policies issued by many companies.

DISABILITY INSURANCE

Disability insurance as an important part of a life insurance contract was developed originally to protect the insured against loss of earning power through injury or sickness which would make it impossible for him to continue paying premiums on his life insurance. Initially, the disability clause granted insurance for waiver of premium payments only in the event of total and permanent disablement.

While virtually all life insurance companies have over the years since its introduction offered premium waiver coverage, many also developed and extended this type of coverage by adding income payments (initially annual and later monthly) to the premium waiver and by broadening the definition of total and permanent disability to include many disabilities of a temporary nature.

Historical Development (United States)

It was as early as 1877 that the fraternal organizations in this country introduced disability insurance through a benefit which provided that half the life insurance would be payable in the event of the total and permanent disability of the member, and the balance of the face amount on the member's death.

Among the life insurance companies, the Fidelity Mutual was the first (1896) to offer a disability benefit, providing for waiver of premiums or, at the option of the insured, settlement of the insurance by annuity payments. This was followed by the adoption in 1906 of waiver-of-premium coverage by The Travelers Insurance Company of Hartford; and shortly thereafter (about 1910), underwriting of the premium waiver benefit became general.

In 1913, some companies extended their disability clause to include a provision for income payments in the form of payment of the policy's face amount in equal annual installments over a fixed period of years, such extension also providing that any unpaid balance of the face would be payable upon death before the expiration of the installment period. Only a relatively small volume of life insurance was issued with this "installment-reducing face" form of disability coverage.

About 1915 the first policy was issued with disability income benefits that did not reduce or affect the death benefit and premium waiver benefits. This more liberal form soon replaced the installment-reducing face type. The new form underwent a few changes over the next five years (for example, from annual to monthly disability benefits), and from about 1920 to 1932, the standard disability income benefit was a monthly income of $10 per $1,000 of life insurance combined with premium waiver for the entire contract.

In the early 1920's, the disability clause underwent noteworthy changes which were to have far-reaching effects on subsequent experience. About 1921, many companies introduced the 90-day clause to eliminate the difficulty of determining whether an admittedly total disability was also permanent. Without some presumption as to what total disabilities should be classified as permanent, there can frequently be doubt and honest differences of opinion as to whether a legitimate claim exists. Under the 90-day clause, a total disability can be established as "permanent" for claim purposes after it has existed for a mimimum of 90 days, even though such disability may be admittedly temporary.

The cash benefits of disability coverage were also liberalized in the 1920's by the retroactive payment of income benefits upon completion of the 90-day elimination period. A few companies also adopted a provision under which the income payments increased after disability had continued for a stated period (for example, after five and again after ten years of continuous disability).

It will be noted that the foregoing liberalizations, particularly the 90-day clause, materially added to the coverage (and hence to the cost) of disability insurance. The introduction of the 90-day waiting period brought within the meaning of the insuring clause total disabilities which were temporary. This innovation radically changed the nature and the cost of disability income protection.

In the late 1920's, the companies began to experience heavy financial losses on these disability benefits, which prompted them to institute strong corrective measures. Among the reasons cited for the unfavorable experience are:

1. Inadequacy of the premiums charged, due at least partly to lack of an appropriate experience table.
2. Overinsurance, stemming partly from underwriting approval of amounts excessive in relation to earned income and partly from the curtailed incomes of the ensuing depression.
3. Yielding to competitive pressures in coverage, underwriting, and claims administration.
4. Unexpected liberalizations by the courts of the benefits intended by the companies.

The main corrective measures adopted (about 1930) were:

1. Lengthening of the elimination period from 90 days to 120 days (generally increased to six months in 1932).
2. Substantial increases in premium rates.
3. Raising of underwriting standards.
4. Elimination of the retroactivity of income benefits.
5. Replacement of lifetime benefits in some companies with benefits not payable beyond age 65 and payment of the face amount at that terminal age if still disabled.

The serious loss situation, which had arisen prior to the depression, was aggravated by the poor economic conditions of the thirties. As a result of the large losses already suffered and the prospect of still further reverses, most of the companies abandoned the disability income field in the early thirties. A few reduced the unit benefit from $10.00 to $5.00 per month, lengthened the elimination period to six months, increased premiums again substantially, and adopted more stringent underwriting practices.

Since 1950, there has been a noticeable but only modest revival of interest among the life insurance companies in the issuance of disability income as an adjunct to life insurance. However, the underwriting continues to be conservative, and only a small percentage of the life policies of such companies are issued with the disability income feature. A highly pertinent recent development has been the increasing availability of noncancellable disability income policies and loss-of-income protection in individual and group health insurance contracts.

Studies of Disability Experience

Up to 1926, at which time the Actuarial Society of America reported on the joint disability experience of twenty-nine American and Canadian companies, the only generally acceptable basis for calculating premiums and reserves for disability benefits was Hunter's Disability Tables. These tables, showing the rates of disability and the mortality among insured lives, were derived largely from the experience of the fraternal societies. It was to be expected that the insurance companies' own disability experience would be less favorable than that of the fraternal societies because of the close surveillance given a disabled brother by the other members, who were quick to recognize malingering.

The data of the 1926 Report were subdivided as follows:

Class 1: Policies without a 90-day clause
Class 2: Policies with a 90-day clause in companies with a strict claims admission practice
Class 3: Policies with a 90-day clause in companies with a liberal claims admission practice

The rates of disability and average claim values experienced under Class 3 policies were adopted by most companies as the basis for premiums for new contracts and for reserves under all policies with the 90-day clause.

The tables of the 1926 Report, often with modifications, remained in general use until the publication of the *1952 Disability Report* of the Society of Actuaries. The 1952 Report is a far-reaching statistical study of premium waiver with a six-month waiting period and of disability income benefits combined with waiver coverage in five separate benefit classes, as follows:

Benefit 1: "Total and permanent" (no presumptive clause)
Benefit 2: 90-day presumptive clause with nonretroactive income and waiver
Benefit 3: 90-day presumptive clause with retroactive income and waiver
Benefit 4: 120-day clause with retroactive waiver and nonretroactive income
Benefit 5: Premium waiver with six-month waiting period

The results are shown separately for the periods 1930–35, 1935–39, 1939–46 (disabled lives only), and 1946–50. The period 1935–39 has been widely used by the companies as the morbidity basis of premium rates for waiver coverage. Generally, the companies have used the death and recovery rates among disabled lives of all four periods combined for rate-making purposes.

Tables 22–1, 22–2, and 22–3 show, respectively, comparative disability rates (that is, the number out of one thousand persons at a given age becoming totally and permanently disabled in a year), relative claim values (that is, the value at time of disability of future payments), and illustrative net annual premiums for decennial ages 20 through 50.

It will be noted from the tables of illustrative values that the disability rates (from data provided for study by larger life insurance companies) were much higher than those in Hunter's Tables, that the rates

TABLE 22–1

ILLUSTRATIVE RATES OF DISABILITY PER 1,000

Age	Hunter's (No 90-Day Clause)	1926 Report		1952 Report, 1935–39, Benefit 2
		Class 1	Class 3	
20	0.52	1.53	4.35	2.44
30	0.56	1.44	4.05	3.26
40	0.83	1.62	4.73	5.43
50	1.70	2.48	7.60	11.69

TABLE 22–2

ILLUSTRATIVE CLAIM VALUES (3 PER CENT), $10 MONTHLY INCOME

Age	Hunter's (No 90-Day Clause)	1926 Report		1952 Report, 1935–39, Benefit 2
		Class 1	Class 3	
20	$623	$433	$246	$355
30	955	656	356	425
40	966	671	431	500
50	876	642	449	580

TABLE 22–3

ILLUSTRATIVE NET ANNUAL PREMIUMS (3 PER CENT) FOR $10 MONTHLY INCOME, COVERAGE AND PREMIUMS TO AGE 60, LIFETIME BENEFITS

Age	Hunter's (No 90-Day Clause)	1926 Report		1952 Report 1935–39, Benefit 2
		Class 1	Class 3	
20	$0.80	$1.30	$1.99	$ 3.10
30	1.07	1.54	2.51	4.40
40	1.48	1.85	3.30	6.70
50	2.20	2.36	4.48	10.70

were increased greatly by the 90-day clause, and that the claim values were less than Hunter's because the greater number of deaths and recoveries reduced the average cost per claim in the companies' experience. Claims under the 90-day clause were more numerous but of shorter average duration.

Principal Rider Provisions for Disability Insurance

The publication of the 1926 Report pointed up the need for more uniformity among the companies in their disability provisions, so that data could be obtained for standard disability tables of greater practical value. After more than a year of study, the National Convention of Insurance Commissioners (now the National Association of Insurance Commissioners) promulgated in 1929 a set of standard provisions (effective on July 1, 1930). These so-called "standard" provisions (some required, some optional, and others prohibited) were adopted by ruling or otherwise in a number of states, including New York, and have led to a high degree of uniformity among the companies in their disability provisions.

The (1) insuring clause, (2) definition of total disability, and (3) exceptions and exclusions of a typical rider for disability insurance might read as follows:

1. The company agrees, subject to the terms and conditions of this rider and the policy, to waive the payment of premiums and to pay the disability monthly income specified on page 1 upon receipt at its home office of due proof of the insured's total disability at that time and that (*a*) the total disability began before the policy anniversary nearest the insured's sixtieth birthday while the policy and this rider were in full force and (*b*) the total disability has been continuous for at least six months.[1]
2. Total disability means (*a*) the incapacity of the insured to engage in any occupation or employment for remuneration or profit as a result of bodily injury or disease or mental disease, or (*b*) the total loss by the insured of the sight of both eyes or of the use of both hands or of both feet or of one hand and one foot.
3. No premiums will be waived and no disability monthly income will be paid:
   a) If the total disability results from a bodily injury sustained or a disease contracted before the payment of the first premium for this benefit;
   b) If the total disability has ceased or the insured's death has occurred prior to receipt of due proof of total disability;
   c) If the due proof of total disability is not received within one year after the earliest of (i) the due date of the first of any unpaid premiums; (ii) the lapse or termination, expiry, or maturity of the policy; (iii) the policy anniversary nearest the insured's sixtieth birthday; or (iv) receipt at the company's home office of written notice of claim;

[1] Waiver is retroactive, but income benefits are not.

d) If the total disability results wholly or partially from (i) willfully and intentionally self-inflicted injury or (ii) service in an armed force of any international organization, or any country or combination of countries at war, whether declared or undeclared.

The phrase "in any occupation or employment" in the above definition of disability is not, in practice, interpreted literally. A strict construction would eliminate all but a few extreme forms of disability. In general, the companies provide benefits whenever the insured is unable to work at his usual occupation or at another occupation for which he can reasonably be considered suited by education, training, or experience.

The rider provisions pertaining to (4) written notice of claim, (5) beginning of benefits, (6) proof of continuance of disability, and (7) maturity of the policy might read as follows:

4. Written notice of claim may be filed with the company to determine the beginning of the period for which benefits are provided, but no benefit will commence until the required due proof of total disability is received. In any case in which written notice of total disability is filed more than one year after total disability began, benefits will commence as if written notice had been filed within one year if it is shown that it was not reasonably possible to furnish written notice to the company sooner and that it was furnished as soon as was reasonably possible.
5. Premiums will be waived for the period commencing with the policy month following (*a*) the date total disability began or (*b*) the date one year before written notice of claim is received, whichever month is later. The portion of any premium paid for a part of the period for which premiums are waived will be refunded. The disability monthly income will commence on the day after six months of continuous total disability, or on the day six months prior to the date written notice of total disability is received, whichever is the later, and will be payable to the owner only at monthly intervals and for completed months of total disability. Interest on any indebtedness to the company under the policy may be deducted from income payments.
6. The company shall have the right to require proof of the continuance of total disability from time to time during the first two years following receipt of due proof. After two years, proof will be required not oftener than once a year. As part of any proof, the insured may be required to be examined by a medical examiner designated by the company at its expense.
7. On the policy anniversary nearest the insured's sixty-fifth birthday, the policy will be matured by payment of a terminal disability payment, if any, and the surrender value of the policy if (*a*) the policy has not previously terminated or matured, and (*b*) the disability monthly income was payable during the policy month preceding that anniversary, and (*c*) the insured's total disability has been continuous to and including that anniversary. The terminal disability payment will be equal to the amount, if any, by which the sum insured exceeds the policy cash value on the policy anniversary nearest the insured's sixty-fifth birthday. This maturity payment shall be in place of all future benefits otherwise payable and will discharge the company from all liability under the policy and this rider.

Underwriting of Applicants for Disability Income

One valuable lesson learned from the poor experience of the thirties is that underwriting applicants for disability benefits on the basis of information that is appropriate for life insurance can be unsound. The major causes of death (cardiovascular-renal diseases and cancer) are not the same as the major causes of disability (tuberculosis, nervous disorders, insanity, accidents). A failure to guard against overinsurance by requiring an element of self-insurance or coinsurance as a deterrent to claims and malingering can result in excessive losses.

The underwriter knows that many of the factors which affect mortality also affect the rate of disability. However, the difference between life and disability risk selection is often one of emphasis, because factors which may be very important as a cause of death may be of little consequence as a cause of disability.

Financial. The financial factor is by far the most important in underwriting disability income insurance. Since the purpose of the coverage is to replace partially the earning power lost by disability, it is highly important that total income benefits should be well below normal earned income, and such income should not be subject to serious fluctuations. The insured should be required to bear a part of the risk so that he will have sufficient financial incentive to return to work promptly upon recovery. Earlier, it was the practice of the companies to issue amounts of disability income as high as 75 per cent of earned income, without sufficient allowance for a possible subsequent reduction. Currently, 50 per cent of earned income is considered a more realistic maximum, combined with an over-all limit of possibly $500 or $600 of monthly income in all companies.

In guarding against overinsurance, financial underwriting must also recognize the tax-free aspects of income benefits and the fact that any income from investments may be continued during a period of disability. Disability income benefits under individual or group health insurance contracts, salary continuance benefits available through the employer, and disability income benefits under federal OASDI must also be considered.

Occupational. Since there are physical and, in some instances, nervous or mental hazards associated with many occupations, the occupation of the applicant is an important factor in disability underwriting.

The members of the learned professions, such as doctors, dentists, engineers, and lawyers, have been satisfactory risks for disability benefits. One likely reason for this is the initial selection to be associated with the disciplines imposed by the long and intensive periods of education and training. Coupled with this initial selection is the acceptance on the part of members of these professions of high standards of habits and social behavior. Members of the learned professions also enjoy a relatively high degree of economic security and stability.

Similar characteristics are found in other occupations requiring considerable training and skill. In general, the experience has been favorable among those in the clerical and technical occupations involving steady work with regular business hours and stable remuneration on a fixed salary basis.

Sound occupational underwriting requires that consideration be given not only to the applicant's present occupation but also to his previous occupations and possible changes in the future.

Physical. Disability underwriting requires attention to essentially the same physical factors that are important in life insurance selection. Those markedly overweight or with greatly elevated blood pressure are obviously not good disability risks. Asthma, arthritis, and a number of other diseases tend to increase the hazard of disability without appreciably affecting the mortality hazard.

A history of neurasthenia or of other nervous disorders raises the probability of a higher rate of disability but does not greatly increase mortality. There is also the likelihood here of claims which are not only costly but also difficult to handle administratively because of the subjective aspects.

Other Considerations. The moral hazard is of prime importance in underwriting disability insurance, for disability itself can be feigned, and the duration of true disability can be prolonged unnecessarily through malingering. Consequently, any applicant of questionable habits or morals would not be eligible for disability insurance.

From a selection point of view, perhaps the best issue ages for disability benefits are from 25 to 45. At ages under 25, success in an occupation and occupational stability are more difficult to assess. Less is also known about habits at the younger ages. At ages above 45, antiselection is present to a much greater degree because of physical impairments and because of proximity to the period of normal decline in earning power.

Many companies offer their disability insurance to male lives only. In the relatively few companies where females are also considered, this coverage is underwritten with more conservative limits and is usually restricted to female applicants who are single and self-supporting.

Underwriting of Applicants for Disability Premium Waiver

Since the extent of the moral hazard to be guarded against in underwriting disability insurance varies roughly in direct proportion to size of benefit, it is common practice to be less strict in the underwriting of waiver-of-premium coverage by itself. As a matter of fact, in many companies the request for waiver coverage is, with a few exceptions, granted with life insurance whenever the applicant is standard for the latter. The premium waiver coverage is accorded this relatively liberal treatment because the size of the benefit is ordinarily such that the insured is not likely to feign total disability in order to qualify and is not likely to be tempted to malinger once disability has been established.

While in most instances the underwriting of premium waiver differs substantially from that of disability income because of the much smaller financial incentive, there are occasional requests for premium waiver where there is substantial moral hazard. These often involve policies for large amounts on a high-premium form. The underwriter knows that a large amount of premium waiver can provide about as much incentive for antiselection as disability income and thus must be underwritten just as carefully.

A few companies have adopted the practice of automatically including premium waiver in standard life insurance policies. Their experience has been at least as favorable as that of the companies which underwrite this supplementary benefit separately.

ACCIDENTAL DEATH BENEFITS

Riders providing for additional benefits in the event of death by accident have been variously designated as "double indemnity," "additional indemnity," and "accidental death benefits." For many years, the most commonly used designation was "double indemnity," to denote the doubling of the amount payable. Companies originally would not offer such coverage for amounts in excess of the face amount of the policy. Strictly speaking, the term "double indemnity" is no longer applicable now that the companies under many circumstances are willing to issue amounts of accidental death benefits which may be a multiple of the policy's face (as much as four times in some instances).[2]

Since the primary purpose of life insurance is to provide for replacement of part of an individual's earning power on death, it would seem that the specific cause of death would be unimportant and that the amount of insurance needed should be governed by the economic value of the insured and his responsibilities to his dependents. It may therefore be argued that accidental death benefits have no necessary place in a sound insurance program and that whatever funds are available for insurance should first be applied to purchase adequate amounts of regular life insurance. However, it is clear to the companies that the average buyer of life insurance is attracted by the small amount of premium required to increase materially the total amount payable to his

[2] A few companies also provide in their riders for twice the amount of the accidental death benefit if the accidental death occurs while the insured is a passenger in a public conveyance operated by a common carrier for passenger service.

beneficiary should he die accidentally. Whatever the reasons or motives, a high percentage of life insurance in force and being issued today includes accidental death benefits. Perhaps a partial explanation for this is provided by the fact that according to the experience of American and Canadian life insurance companies, accidents in recent years have become the third most important cause of death (after cardiovascular-renal diseases and cancer). At ages under 30, accidents are the major cause of death.

Historical Development (United States)

It was in 1877 that the United States Mutual Accident Association introduced the concept of double indemnity by offering under its accident policies twice the benefits in the event death was caused by a railroad accident. In 1904, the Fidelity Mutual became the first life insurance company to offer a double indemnity benefit covering accidental deaths in general. About 1918, many of the larger companies adopted an accidental death benefit clause similar to the one in common use today.

Unlike disability income, the accidental death benefits rider has been profitable to the companies since its introduction, with the result that there have been relatively few problems in rate making and in underwriting. Policy wording and conditions in practice have been such that the courts over the years have tended to interpret the accidental death provision liberally but, for the most part, fairly.

Principal Policy Provisions for Accidental Death Benefits

The (1) insuring clause, (2) definition of accidental deaths, and (3) exclusions and exceptions of a typical accidental death benefits rider might read as follows:

1. The company agrees, subject to the terms and conditions of this rider and the policy, to pay an accidental death benefit to the beneficiary upon receipt at the company's home office of due proof of the accidental death of the insured which directly shows that (*a*) death resulted solely from an accidental bodily injury, and (*b*) death occurred within 90 days after the bodily injury, and (*c*) both the injury and the death occurred (i) on or after the policy anniversary nearest the insured's fifth birthday and (ii) before the policy anniversary nearest the insured's seventieth birthday, and (iii) while the policy and this rider were in full force.
2. The phrase "accidental death" means death resulting directly and solely from
   a) An accidental injury visible on the surface of the body or disclosed by an autopsy, or
   b) A disease or infection resulting directly from an accidental injury as described and beginning within 30 days after the date of the injury, or

  c) An accidental drowning.

3. No benefit will be payable under this rider if the insured's death results, directly or indirectly, or wholly or partially, from
   a) Any infection or bodily or mental infirmity or disease existing before or commencing after the accidental injury, except a disease or infection as provided in the definition of "accidental death";
   b) Intentionally self-inflicted injury while sane, or self-inflicted injury while insane;
   c) Participation in an assault or a felony;
   d) Travel, flight, or descent in or from any kind of aircraft which is being operated for any training purpose, or which the insured is aboard to perform specific duties, whether applicable to the operation of the aircraft or not;
   e) War, whether declared or undeclared;
   f) Service in an armed force of any international organization, or any country or combination of countries at war, whether declared or undeclared.

Another provision peculiar to the accidental death benefits rider reserves to the company the right and the opportunity to examine the insured's body and to perform an autopsy, unless forbidden by state law, at any time within thirty days after receipt of due proof of the insured's accidental death. This right may be valuable in resisting unfair claims.

As is true of disability benefits, in most states the accidental death benefits rider may be contestable at any time. As a practical matter, however, misrepresentations in the application with respect to this benefit are rare and generally not highly significant.

There has been considerable discussion over the years by the companies and the courts as to the validity of the distinction between "death resulting from accidental means" and "accidental death." Death may be regarded as resulting from accidental means if in the act preceding the injury something unusual, unforeseen, or unexpected occurs which causes the injury resulting in death. On the other hand, death may be considered accidental if it is the undesigned, unforeseen, unexpected result of even an intended act, whether the means be accidental or not. Clearly, then, a provision for "accidental death" is broader than one for "death resulting from accidental means." An example sometimes cited to illustrate the distinction between these two terms is that of death which occurs while the insured is being operated on under an anesthetic, which is considered the cause of death. The result may be accidental, but the means are not.

Because of the practical difficulties the companies have encountered over the years in attempting to observe a workable distinction between accidental death and death due to accidental means, many companies have discontinued the use of the word "means" in this connection and now simply require that death be due to accidental bodily injuries.

Underwriting

The problems of underwriting accidental death benefits are minimized by the exclusions and exceptions in the rider and by terminating the coverage at age 65 or 70. Originally, coverage was provided for life (or prior termination or maturity of the policy). Since the accidental death rate increases rapidly in later life, a fact which was not fully appreciated at first, coverage for life may mean troublesome claims at the older ages and relatively high claim rates.

The characteristics of individuals presenting an extra risk of accidental death include certain physical impairments, hazardous occupations, aviation activities, poor habits or morals, dangerous avocations or sports, poor driving records, and general proneness to accidents.

Physical. Applicants with physical impairments who are nevertheless eligible for standard life insurance are usually also acceptable for accidental death coverage at standard rates. Accidental death benefits at regular rates are also granted for many physical impairments where the life rating is not severe. Good examples are those who are assigned only mild ratings for overweight or elevated blood pressure.

The presence of organic heart disease, markedly elevated blood pressure, or other impairments of the circulatory system may preclude approval for accidental death coverage. Physical impairments which limit the applicant's mobility (for example, defective vision or hearing) obviously concern the underwriter. Diabetes may contribute to fatal results from injuries not otherwise serious.

Occupational. Occupations may involve health hazards, accident hazards, or both. Those that involve only health hazards may be eligible for standard accidental death coverage (for example, workers in abrasives, glass, and textile industries).

Applicants engaged in occupations involving an accident hazard frequently qualify for standard life insurance but are rated for accidental death. Illustrations are truck drivers, construction workers, and electrical workers. There are also occupations which require a rating for both the life and the accidental death coverages.

Other. Poor morals or serious criticisms of habits will require a heavy rating or outright rejection. A record of reckless driving or a clear indication of a proneness to accidents may also be sufficient reason for declination.

The underwriter has to exercise special care in considering requests for large amounts of accidental death benefits. There is ample evidence that claim rates are distinctly higher for the larger amounts. Part of this is a manifestation of antiselection. Another contributing factor may be the additional incentive the claimant may have to argue that death was accidental.

It is current practice of the companies generally to observe issue limits (depending upon the size of the company and its reinsurance facilities) and over-all participation limits in offering this supplemental coverage. The latter limit in some companies is now $150,000 (total amount in all companies) and as much as $200,000 in others.

Rates of Accidental Death

In the early years, the rates of accidental death for premium charges were derived from (1) the experience of health and accident companies with principal-sum accident benefits, and (2) a study of life insurance claims where death was due to an accident within the terms of the accidental death rider. Companies generally charged a flat premium, regardless of age, of $1.00 or $1.25 per $1,000, even where coverage was for life. This involved the false assumption that the rate of accidental death would be about the same for all ages.

A suitable table of rates of accidental death for premiums and reserves was provided by the Intercompany Accidental Death Table, published in 1934 by the Actuarial Society of America in a report of the experience of a group of companies covering the years 1926 to 1933. The most recent such table was published in 1959 by the Society of Actuaries, based on the period from 1951 to 1956, and is now being used generally for premiums and reserves.

Table 22–4 compares the rates of accidental death and the net

TABLE 22–4

ILLUSTRATIVE ACCIDENTAL DEATH RATES AND NET PREMIUMS

Age	Accidental Deaths per 1,000		Net Premiums per $1,000 for Ordinary Life (Coverage to Age 70—3 Per Cent)	
	1934 Report	1959 Report	1934 Report	1959 Report
15	0.88	0.48	$0.73	$0.52
20	0.75	0.75	0.71	0.49
25	0.56	0.49	0.71	0.46
30	0.44	0.39	0.77	0.46
35	0.50	0.39	0.86	0.49
45	0.68	0.43	1.10	0.56
55	1.12	0.52	1.43	0.67
65	1.72	0.81	1.81	0.88
75	2.80	1.71	...	...

premiums of these two investigations at several ages. It will be noted that for ages 20 and over, accidental death rates decrease by age (up to age 30 in the prior experience and now up to age 35) and then increase with age each year for life.

Some of the more noteworthy findings of the 1959 Report are:

1. Accidental death rates have changed markedly since the last study, both as to their general level and as to their incidence by age. It appears that motor vehicle and aircraft accidents have played a major role in changing the shape of the curve.
2. The pattern of improvement in the accidental death rate has been almost the reverse of that for total mortality. For accidental death rates the greatest reduction has been at the older ages, while the reduction in life insurance mortality rates has been greatest at the younger ages, with relatively little reduction at the advanced ages.
3. The wide variation among the companies in the rates experienced is particularly noteworthy. The ratios of actual deaths to those expected by a previous table ranged from 50 per cent to 169 per cent by amount of claim.
4. The distribution of deaths by cause has changed more than slightly since the period covered by the earlier table. For example, motor vehicle accidents accounted for 38 per cent of the deaths in the previous study, compared with 55 per cent of the claims in the present report. One cause which generated a consistent excess by amounts over policies was aviation deaths.
5. For issue ages 20 through 64, the insurance accidental death experience is less than half the population experience. This is additional confirmation of the importance of the underwriting standards.

SELECTED REFERENCES

ACTUARIAL SOCIETY OF AMERICA. *Joint Investigation of Experience of American and Canadian Companies with Reference to Total and Permanent Disability Benefits.* Report of Committee on Disability Experience. New York, 1926.

ACTUARIAL SOCIETY OF AMERICA. "Mortality under the Accidental Death Benefits in Life Insurance Policies," *Transactions of the Actuarial Society of America,* Vol. XXXV (1934), pp. 381–419.

HERRICK, KENNETH W. *Total Disability Provisions in Life Insurance Contracts.* Homewood, Ill.: Richard D. Irwin, Inc., 1956.

HUNTER, ARTHUR, and PHILLIPS, JAMES T. *Disability Benefits in Life Insurance Policies.* Chicago: Society of Actuaries, 1932.

LAIRD, JOHN M. "Double Indemnity," *Transactions of the Actuarial Society of America,* Vol. XXXIII (1932), pp. 183–90, 199–208.

MACLEAN, JOSEPH B. *Life Insurance.* 9th ed. New York: McGraw-Hill Book Co., Inc., 1962.

SHEPHERD, PEARCE, and WEBSTER, ANDREW C. *Selection of Risks.* Chicago: Society of Actuaries, 1957.

SOCIETY OF ACTUARIES. "Experience under Accidental Death Benefit Provisions in Ordinary Insurance Policies between 1951 and 1956 Policy Anniversaries," *Transactions of the Society of Actuaries,* Vol. X, Part II, No. 2 (1958), pp. 45–78.

SOCIETY OF ACTUARIES. "Experience under Certain Ordinary Disability Benefits between the 1930 and 1950 Anniversaries," *Transactions of the Society of Actuaries,* Vol. IV, Part II, No. 2 (1953), pp. 70–180.

Chapter 23

INDIVIDUAL MEDICAL EXPENSE INSURANCE

BY JOHN S. THOMPSON, JR.

The first form of individual health insurance provided either a lump sum or installment payments to persons disabled by accident or sickness. In recent years, however, disability income insurance has been overshadowed by the growing importance of insurance covering the expenses incurred for medical treatment of injury and sickness. Insurance on losses in this category, which may be referred to as "medical expense insurance," is designed primarily for coverage on some or all of the following kinds of expense:

1. Hospital charges for room and board, general duty nursing care, and other hospital services and supplies;
2. Fees for medical care or treatment by physicians, surgeons, and private duty nurses; and
3. Expenses incurred for other necessary medical and health care services and supplies, including dental care, nursing home care, medicines, and prosthetic appliances.

Although it is possible to describe insurable medical expenses in only three classes, modern-day medical practice has become so complex that each of these three classes is extremely broad. It is not surprising, then, that the various forms of medical expense insurance that have been developed in recent years differ widely with respect to the types of medical expenses that they cover and in their basic underwriting characteristics.

Medical expense insurance has developed on both an individual and a group basis. This chapter is concerned only with individual medical expense insurance.[1]

Development

The earliest form of hospital coverage, introduced prior to 1910, was generally issued as an adjunct to disability income insurance and pro-

[1] See Chapters 33 and 34 for analysis of group medical expense insurance.

vided for a 50 or 100 per cent increase in the monthly disability benefit during hospital confinement. The payment of the increased benefit during hospital confinement was generally limited to the first ninety days of the period of confinement. Since this form of hospital coverage was a "fixed benefit" payable during confinement in a hospital, without regard to the actual medical expenses of the insured, it could be regarded as a kind of disability income benefit rather than as insurance for medical expenses.

It was not until the depression years of the 1930's that medical expense insurance was first developed as a kind of insurance distinctly different from disability income insurance. Since that time, this new form of insurance has shown vigorous growth in both group and individual forms. The growth in individual medical expense insurance is indicated by the data in Table 23–1, which show the rapid increase in the number of persons

TABLE 23–1

NUMBER OF PEOPLE WITH MEDICAL EXPENSE PROTECTION UNDER INDIVIDUAL POLICIES IN INSURANCE COMPANIES

(000 Omitted)

End of Year	Hospital Expense Insurance	Surgical Expense Insurance	Regular Medical Expense Insurance
1940	1,200	850	. . . .
1945	2,700	1,800	200
1950	17,296	13,718	2,714
1955	26,706	22,445	6,264
1960	32,902	28,209	8,902
1961	33,874	30,402	10,117
1962	36,061	31,443	10,974

Source: Health Insurance Institute.

covered under the three important forms of individual medical expense policies over the past 20 years.

The increasing importance of medical expense insurance stems from improvements in coverage and the great advances achieved in medical science over the past 30 years. The improving quality of medical care has led to a preoccupation among the insuring public with all matters relating to health care. More importantly, however, the increasingly complex nature of medical care has resulted in substantial increases in the cost of such care. Consequently, the increasing utilization of medical facilities and their increasing cost have made it highly desirable for the insuring public to have a financing mechanism to assist them in the orderly budgeting of medical expenses. Medical expense insurance has been found to be eminently suited to fill this need.

Forms of Medical Expense Insurance

Medical expense policies, as currently written, may be put into two broad categories. The first of these is the so-called "basic coverages," under which benefits for hospital confinement begin with the first day of hospital confinement, and surgical coverages with the first dollar of professional fees for a surgical procedure. Typically, these basic coverages are subject either to a very small deductible or to no deductible. Benefits under basic coverages contain limitations on each element of medical expense, and are said to be on the "allocated" basis.

The second category of medical expense policies is that of "major medical" coverage. Major medical policies do not cover the first dollar of expense. Instead, they are designed to protect against the infrequent but financially catastrophic loss that occurs when sickness or injury requires a long period of hospital confinement or costly surgical or medical treatment. To accomplish this result, benefits under major medical policies are subject to a "deductible," in order to eliminate small losses for which most families can budget. Also, benefits under a major medical expense coverage are not on the allocated basis, except to a very limited extent. Instead, a broad class of expenses is covered subject to a deductible provision, to a coinsurance or percentage participation sharing of the risk, and usually with a single maximum benefit applicable to total benefits for each accident or each period of sickness.

Hospital Expense Benefit

The benefits payable under the hospital expense benefit are of two kinds: (1) the daily hospital benefit, and (2) the miscellaneous hospital expense benefit.

The purpose of the daily hospital benefit is to pay for hospital charges for room, board, general nursing care, and other routine services covered by the hospital's per diem charge. The daily hospital benefit is sometimes provided on a fixed benefit basis with a specified daily hospital benefit payable for each day of confinement, without regard to actual hospital charges. More commonly, the daily hospital benefit is on the "expense incurred" or "reimbursement" plan, with benefits equal to hospital charges for room, board, and general nursing care up to the stated daily hospital benefit limit. In either case, a limit is usually placed on the number of days of hospital confinement during each period of sickness or injury for which the benefit is payable. The limit on the compensable period of confinement for each period of hospitalization at first was generally a relatively short period, such as 30 days. Today, however, limits of 90, 120, or even 365 days are common.

The miscellaneous expense benefit, which is almost always on the expense-incurred basis, covers charges for hospital services and supplies not within the scope of the hospital's per diem charge. The use of the operating room, laboratory services, anesthetics, and drugs are examples of the types of hospital services and supplies that would be covered by the miscellaneous expense benefit, provided they are necessary for treatment and prescribed by the attending physician. As in the case of the daily hospital benefit, individual policies almost always specify an overall or maximum limit on the miscellaneous expense benefit payable for each period of hospital confinement. The maximum benefit is generally expressed as a multiple of the daily hospital benefit, such as 10 or 15 times the daily benefit. However, several variations of this approach have been used. One of these is to specify a maximum payment for each type of service. For instance, maximum benefits of $25 for use of the operating room and $15 for anesthetics, with appropriate limits for other hospital services, may be set. Another variation is to grade the maximum benefit for miscellaneous expenses by period of confinement. A variation of this type currently in use provides a limit of six times the maximum daily hospital benefit for a confinement that lasts only one day, seven times for a confinement of two days and increasing to 20 times the maximum daily benefit for confinements of fifty-one days or more.

Individual policies are generally so drafted that the hospital expense benefit is payable only if the patient is confined to the hospital as an in-patient. In some cases, a minimum period of confinement, such as 24 hours, is a further condition to receipt of benefits. These conditions may prevent use of the hospital for minor diagnostic treatment where there is no real sickness or injury and for out-patient services in general.

Some policies provide an "emergency accident benefit" which covers the cost of emergency treatment in a hospital as an out-patient within 24 or 48 hours after the time of the accident causing the injury. The maximum emergency accident benefit is usually two or three times the daily hospital benefit of the policy. One argument against providing the emergency accident benefit is that the average benefit payment is small and consequently the insurer's claims administration expense is relatively large in relation to the amount of benefit paid. On the other hand, a benefit of this kind is sound if it tends to reduce the number of hospital confinements in those cases where the insured can be treated as an out-patient.

It has become quite common to write individual hospital expense policies to provide for a small deductible, such as $25 or $50, to be applied to the sum of benefits otherwise payable for each illness or each accident. A deductible, even a relatively small one, enables the insurer to increase the benefits provided by each dollar of premium. This is accomplished by eliminating entirely the claims involving only a small amount of expense that would be covered in the absence of the deductible; claims rates and claims administration expense are thereby reduced.

Surgical Expense Benefit

This benefit pays for surgical procedures, subject to a schedule of limits on the benefit payable for each type of operation. Limits vary with the nature of the operation and are intended to bear a close relationship to the average fee charged by doctors for the listed operations in the areas where the covered persons reside. For example, in a schedule providing a maximum benefit of $250, $15 may be the limit specified for correcting the fracture of a finger, $125 for an appendectomy, $175 for removal of a gall bladder, and $200 for removal of a kidney. A condensed surgical schedule taken from a popular individual basic medical expense policy is shown in Table 23–2.

TABLE 23–2

SCHEDULE OF MAXIMUM AMOUNTS PAYABLE FOR SELECTED SURGICAL OPERATIONS UNDER $250 MAXIMUM LIMIT PLAN

Operation	Maximum Benefit Payable
Abscesses (other than breast)—incision and drainage	$ 10
Benign tumors—removal by surgery	15–$150
Biopsy	10– 50
Cystoscopy—with surgical procedure	50
Fistulectomy—single	75
Fracture of radius or ulna	100– 200
Hemorrhoidectomy:	
External	25
Other than external	75
Herniotomy—single	100
Hysterectomy	175
Lacerations of skin—suture and repair of	15
Tonsillectomy, with or without adenoidectomy:	
Child under 12 years of age	30
Other covered persons	50

It is naturally impracticable to name or even to anticipate all of the many operations that may be performed. Consequently, policies generally list only those operations which occur most frequently. The policy generally states that the maximum benefit for any unlisted operation shall be determined on a basis consistent with the limits in the schedule for comparable operations, subject to the over-all schedule maximum. Surgical schedules usually specify maximum benefits for as many as one hundred operations or more, in order both to cover the more common procedures and to provide a sufficiently broad base for determining consistent maximum benefits for unlisted operations.

The maximum surgical expense benefit for a surgical procedure is generally intended to apply to the total professional fees involved, including those of any assistant surgeon, and to the expense of postoperative care. Coverage for the cost of anesthetics and their administration has been handled in a variety of ways. In some cases, policies provide for a specific allowance for this item. It has been more generally covered, however, in the miscellaneous hospital expense benefit, even though in most hospitals it is not regarded as a hospital charge but is billed separately by a professional anesthetist. Another benefit sometimes found in surgical expense coverage provides for the cost of treatment of tumors by X ray or radium. This benefit may be provided by the surgical schedule or, alternatively, may be covered in a separate schedule.

In-Hospital Medical Expense Benefit

The term "medical expense benefit" is sometimes used in a narrow sense in health insurance to refer to coverage on charges by doctors for services other than those in connection with surgical procedures or post-operative care. (This coverage also is called "regular medical benefit" and "doctor fee" benefit.) In the field of individual medical expense insurance, coverage of doctor fees of this kind is generally found only in major medical policies and policies covering accidental injuries on a blanket basis. In basic coverages, benefits for doctor fees are generally provided only for such fees incurred during a period of hospital confinement and then only if no surgery is performed. A benefit of this type is frequently referred to as the "in-hospital medical expense benefit." A provision for this benefit recognizes that even if no surgery is performed during a period of hospital confinement, a patient normally requires professional medical services, so that it is reasonable to provide insurance coverage for doctors' fees in such cases. The amount of benefit provided for such fees is typically equal to the doctor's actual charges for professional services but no more than a specified limit, such as $3.00 for each day of confinement, subject to a limit on the number of days for which the benefit is payable.

Nursing Expense Benefit

Some policies provide a benefit for nursing care required in connection with the treatment of injury or sickness. Such a benefit, like the hospital expense benefit and the in-hospital medical benefit, is subject to limitations on the daily rate of benefit and the maximum period for which it is payable. Typically, the coverage is written to provide only for care by a private duty registered nurse other than a member of the insured's immediate family.

Coverage for nursing fees is generally included in blanket accident and major medical expense policies, since the intent in these forms is to cover the broadest possible range of medical expenses. The nursing fees benefit has also been written with the basic coverages, but its use as a part of basic hospital and surgical policies has been relatively uncommon.

Nursing Home Care Benefit

A recent development of considerable interest is the nursing home care benefit, which is designed to cover the expense incurred as a result of confinement in a skilled nursing home. Interest in this form of coverage has stemmed from the increasing importance of nursing homes in comprehensive medical care.

One of the important considerations in the development of nursing home care coverage is the increasing volume of medical expense coverages at the older ages, both through policies issued at the advanced ages and through policies providing lifetime coverage issued at the younger ages. Since the majority of the patients in nursing homes are over age 65, it is only natural that the nursing home care benefit has become important in the development of medical expense coverages at the older ages. A second and perhaps more important factor in the growing interest in the nursing home care benefit has been the increasing cost of medical care, especially in the case of hospital care. This has led to a search for forms of coverage that will promote the use of medical facilities, such as nursing homes, that are less costly than the intensive care normally associated with general hospitals.

The nursing home care benefit is such a recent development that it is still in its experimental stages. Consequently, no standard pattern of benefit structure has yet emerged. As currently written, however, it is generally coupled with coverage for hospital confinement and so written that confinement in a nursing home is covered only where such confinement follows a period of hospital confinement.

The amount of benefit for confinement in a nursing home is generally defined in much the same way as the hospital daily benefit. Under this approach, the amount of benefit is equal to actual charges for confinement in the nursing home but no more than a specified amount, such as $5.00, for each day of confinement, subject to a limit on the number of days for which the benefit is payable.

Blanket Accident Benefit

The blanket accident benefit was developed during the 1930's to provide comprehensive coverage of medical expenses resulting from treatment of accidental injuries. The benefit under this form of coverage is equal to actual charges for hospital confinement, nursing fees, physicians' and surgeons' fees, and charges for drugs, medicines, and appliances, provided they are required for treatment of the injury. Medical expenses are generally covered only if incurred during a specified period, such as one year, following the date of the accident causing the injury, and are subject to a stated maximum benefit, typically $1,000, although higher limits have been used. This form of coverage is in marked contrast to that of the basic hospital, surgical, and medical expense benefits, in that benefits payable for each type of expense are not subject to special limitations. Instead, an over-all maximum benefit applies to the total benefits for all types of expense combined. Underwriters have felt justified in using this approach on the ground that accidental injuries are entirely beyond the control of the insured, and in the treatment of accidental injuries, it is seldom that unnecessary or "elective" medical services are obtained.

Major Medical Expense Insurance

The major medical expense benefit was developed in the early 1950's, largely as a result of an increasing realization that the allocated basic hospital, surgical, and medical expense benefits often pay the cost of minor injuries or sickness which, in many instances, the insured could have met without the use of insurance, but are inadequate in paying the very large bills that may result from serious accident or prolonged sickness. Major medical was developed to meet the need for protection against a broad range of catastrophic medical expenses. Some of the earlier major medical policies were limited to expenses incurred in the hospital, a form of coverage which is sometimes referred to as major hospital expense. While major hospital expense coverages are still issued, most major medical expense policies do not require hospital confinement in order that the insured may qualify for benefit.

The major medical expense benefit is usually subject to a deductible, typically $200 to $1,000. This means that no benefit is payable until covered medical expenses for the accident or sickness have exceeded the deductible amount. There may be a limit on the period of time, such as ninety days, during which expenses must be incurred in order that the deductible may be satisfied. In most individual major medical policies, the benefit is based on the expenses incurred because of a single accident or illness, and is limited to expenses incurred during a stated period, such as two years following the date of the accident or the inception of the sickness. After the stated period has elapsed, the deductible must again be satisfied before further benefits are payable.

The "each illness" approach to the definition of covered expenses requires that where two or more separate illnesses occur during a benefit period, expenses incurred in connection with each of these illnesses be segregated. The occasional claims administration problems encountered under the "each illness" approach have been avoided by combining all eligible expenses incurred in each calendar year or policy year, without regard to the cause underlying each item of expense. Under this approach the benefit is based on the amount by which total eligible expenses incurred during the year, whether a policy year or a calendar year, exceed the deductible amount. Most individual major medical policies are based on the "each illness" approach; the "calendar-year" or "policy-year" deductible is found principally in group major medical insurance.

The deductible amount eliminates from coverage those injuries and sicknesses which require only relatively minor medical treatment and for which medical expenses can generally be easily budgeted without hardship. As a result of the application of the deductible amount, claims frequencies are reduced, and the average benefit per claim is increased. Both the reduction in claims frequencies and the increase in the average benefit tend to reduce the cost of claims settlement in relation to benefit payments. Consequently, use of a deductible tends to increase the proportion of the premium that may be devoted to policy benefits. In addition to the reduction in expense rates, the application of a deductible amount tends to eliminate duplication with basic coverages.

Major medical policies usually provide for coinsurance or percentage participation on the part of the insured. This is accomplished by providing that benefits will be a percentage, such as 75 or 80 per cent, of the amount by which eligible expenses exceed the deductible. This provision gives the insured a financial interest in medical expenses incurred on his behalf, so that he will tend to avoid seeking unnecessary or unduly expensive medical care.

A practice that has developed in recent years in the drafting of major medical coverages is to provide for "inside limits," which are intended to impose reasonable limitations on certain covered expenses. They also serve to increase the insured's participation in the cost of his own medical care, when the cost of treatment exceeds the inside limit. The most common of these inside limits is a limit on the daily rate charged by the hospital for room, board, and general nursing services. Limitations on professional fees for surgery are also becoming quite common through the use of surgical schedules. These inside limits may be viewed as setting an upper limit that may not be exceeded if charges for medical services are to be "reasonable." Coverages like major medical, providing benefits for a broad range of eligible medical expenses, invariably require that expenses be "reasonable" and "customary." Accordingly, it is quite logical that the policy define "reasonable" in terms of an upper limit.

The total benefits payable under a major medical policy usually may not exceed a maximum benefit of from $5,000 to $15,000, or even more. A maximum benefit may apply to all benefits payable during each benefit period and to the aggregate benefits payable under the policy for all benefit periods combined resulting from the same or related causes. Under calendar-year deductible plans, the maximum benefit applies to the sum of all benefits payable under the policy during the calendar year, without regard to the cause of individual claims.

As noted above, the application of the deductible amount tends to eliminate duplication of coverage where the insured has basic hospital-surgical coverages. This makes it possible to supplement a policy providing for basic coverage with major medical insurance for the applicant who wishes to have insurance protection against catastrophic losses in addition to his basic coverage.

Comprehensive Medical Expense Insurance

Some companies have experimented with a new form of coverage which has been called "comprehensive medical expense insurance," combining in one policy the benefits of basic hospital-surgical coverages and those of major medical coverages. This form of insurance is much like major medical insurance, but with a very low deductible, such as $50. In some forms, basic hospital, or hospital and surgical, charges are covered in full without a deductible or, in some cases, without coinsurance or percentage participation on the part of the insured. Comprehensive medical expense insurance has been written most widely under group contracts where insurance on large groups, under controlled conditions, can be issued. Very little of this form of insurance has been issued under individual policies, and experience has so far been too limited to indicate whether it can be satisfactorily underwritten on an individual basis.

Term of the Policy

Disability income insurance can be soundly underwritten to cover only one who is both able to work and actually engaged in gainful employment. As a result, disability insurance is almost invariably written to expire at an age, generally 65, approximating normal retirement age. Medical expense insurance, on the other hand, can be written without regard to whether or not the persons insured are in gainful employment. Furthermore, a need for medical care coverage continues throughout life. As a matter of fact, it can be argued that the need for such protection actually increases with advancing age, since earned income normally declines after retirement, which is the very time when the need for health care frequently increases. For these reasons, it has become quite common to write medical expense policies to provide for lifetime coverage.

In addition to lifetime coverage with premiums payable for life, a few companies have experimented with individual medical expense policies that become fully paid up at a stated age, such as 65 or 70, with the result that the insured may purchase lifetime coverage with premiums payable only during his productive years. In view of the rapidly increasing cost of insurance under the more comprehensive types of coverage like major medical insurance, limited-payment lifetime coverage has so far been written only with basic coverages. In addition, it is customary to set special limitations on benefits payable for hospital confinement and surgical operation fees after the policy becomes fully paid up. The need for such limitations follows from the uncertainties surrounding future levels of insurance costs under this form of coverage.

Probationary Period

Some individual medical expense policies provide that benefits will not be paid for expenses arising from sickness commencing during the first thirty days (or other specified period) following the policy date. The purpose of this "probationary period" is to minimize the number of borderline cases where it is difficult to establish the date of commencement of the sickness. It also serves as a deterrent to persons who are aware of a medical impairment and seek insurance coverage on losses which are practically certain. In addition to this form of probationary period, which is found in individual health insurance policies of all forms, the benefits payable under a medical expense policy with respect to specifically named surgical procedures may be subject to a longer probationary period, such as six months. Disorders subject to these special probationary periods are generally of the type for which treatment may be deferred at the insured's election. "Elective" or "postponable" procedures may occur, for instance, in the case of herniotomy or tonsillectomy.

Definition of Hospital

Since a substantial proportion of benefits under basic medical expense policies depends on confinement in a "hospital" as an in-patient, it is essential that both the insured and the insurer agree to the meaning of "hospital." This is accomplished by including a definition of the word "hospital" in the policy. One such definition is as follows:

> Hospital means an institution operated for the care and treatment of sickness and injuries and having facilities for diagnosis, twenty-four-hour nursing service, and, except in the case of a hospital primarily concerned with the treatment of chronic diseases, major surgery. The term "hospital" does not include an establishment that is, other than incidentally, a place for rest, a place for custodial care, a place for the aged, a place for drug addicts, a place for alcoholics, a nursing home, or a hotel.

While shorter definitions are frequently used, it is clear that an objective definition of "hospital" will avoid many troublesome questions that might arise when the insured is confined in a nursing or convalescent home.

Successive Periods of Hospitalization

Since benefits under hospital expense coverages are payable only during a fixed maximum period of hospital confinement, it is necessary to describe in the policy how the maximum benefit period applies in the event of two or more separate periods of confinement. This is accomplished by specifying that successive periods of confinement, resulting from the same or related causes, will be considered to be a single confinement unless separated by a specified period of recovery.

Exclusions

It has been customary, in writing medical expense policies, to exclude from coverage claims arising from intentionally self-inflicted injuries, air travel except as a passenger, and losses resulting from war. These exclusions are common to practically all forms of individual health insurance. There are also certain exclusions unique to individual medical expense policies. Some of the more important of these special exclusions are the following:

1. ***Governmentally Operated Hospitals.*** This exclusion applies to services and facilities provided by a hospital owned or operated by the United States government for the treatment of members or ex-members of the armed forces. This exclusion is desirable because such services are available to persons entitled to them without charge.

2. ***Cosmetic Surgery.*** It is apparent that cosmetic surgery is "elective" and is generally not required as a result of injury or sickness. Correction of congenital anomaly in infants and surgery required as a result of injury normally would be covered.

3. ***Expenses Not Associated with Injury or Sickness.*** Eyeglasses and hearing aids or their prescription or fitting are generally not covered under major medical policies or other policies that cover the cost of medical services not supplied by a hospital. Likewise, dentures and dentistry are generally not covered, except to the extent that they may be required as a result of injury within a stated period following the date of the accident causing the injury.

These exclusions are consistent with the basic principles that health insurance policies should cover only actual losses and only those losses that result directly from injury or sickness.

Risk Selection

The selection of risks for medical expense insurance involves much the same considerations as those that affect the underwriting of applicants for other forms of personal life and health insurance. Benefits under health insurance policies, however, including medical expense coverages, are not subject to the same objective determination as those of life insurance, but instead are to some degree subject to election by the insured. The nature of the risk assumed under health insurance coverages leads to adverse selection against the insurer. In some cases a person who knows, or suspects, that he may require medical treatment in the future may attempt to purchase medical expense insurance in order to defray the cost of the probable future treatment. This form of adverse selection may involve fraudulent concealment on the application or may be accomplished because of ignorance of basic insurance principles. One of the principal defenses against the form of adverse selection that is encountered in applicants who are in poor health, in addition to the "probationary" period, is the so-called "pre-existence" exclusion. This exclusion is generally accomplished in the insuring clause by stating that the policy covers only injuries occurring or sickness contracted and commencing after the policy date. It may also be accomplished by a specific exclusion stating that the policy does not cover any injuries occurring or sickness contracted prior to the policy date. In either case the effect is the same.[2]

[2] See Chapter 26 for analysis of risk selection in individual health insurance.

Summary

The growth of medical expense insurance and its rapid development as an important means of financing health care attest to the present importance of this line as a fully fledged partner of individual life and disability income insurance. This growth has been achieved during a period when medical science and practice have been undergoing many important changes, and in competition with other systems for financing health care.

Dramatic results have been accomplished both in the volume of medical expense coverage distributed and in the expansion of the scope of coverage under modern forms of insurance. These accomplishments have been due to a willingness to experiment with new coverages and to a continuous search for improved methods of providing personal insurance. Advances are now being made in the area of coverage for dental care and nursing home care. With continuing efforts in these directions, medical expense insurance will achieve even more important objectives in the health care needs of the nation.

SELECTED REFERENCES

DICKERSON, O. D. *Health Insurance.* Rev. ed. Homewood, Ill.: Richard D. Irwin, Inc., 1963.

FAULKNER, EDWIN J. *Health Insurance.* New York: McGraw-Hill Book Co., Inc., 1960.

PHILLIPS, JAMES T. "Some Considerations in the Development of an Individual Accident and Sickness Program," *Transactions of the Society of Actuaries,* Vol. VI (1954).

SOCIETY OF ACTUARIES. *Health Insurance Provided through Individual Policies.* (Edwin L. Bartleson, principal contributor.) Chicago, 1963.

Chapter 24

LIMITED AND SPECIAL RISK CONTRACTS

BY ARMAND SOMMER

LIMITED POLICIES

The definition of a limited policy in most states is patterned after the suggested definition developed by the National Association of Insurance Commissioners: "A limited policy is one that contains unusual exclusions, limitations, reductions, or contains such a restrictive nature that the payments or benefits under such policy are limited in frequency or in amounts."

Another way of identifying limited health insurance policies is the usual overprint found on the cover of the policy, as follows:

THIS IS A LIMITED POLICY—READ IT CAREFULLY

A more generic definition would be that limited policies are accident and health insurance contracts (1) that provide coverage for the general hazard of disability but whose benefits are small or restricted in duration, or (2) that provide broad coverage of a specified hazard to which people are subject generally.

Examples of limited policies are the automobile accident policy, the newspaper accident policy, the aviation accident policy, the polio and dread disease policy, and the limited accident and health insurance policy.

Automobile Accident Policy

The automobile accident policy is one of the best-known limited policies. Its period of greatest popularity was in the 1920's, but it is still issued by many companies. The most popular form is one that has a premium of $10 a year and covers (1) from $1,000 to $5,000 for accidental death; (2) $100 monthly income for total disability; and (3) hospital, medical, and surgical expenses varying from blanket reimbursement to specified amounts for specified services.

Payment of these benefits is conditioned upon injury to the insured while either driving or riding in an automobile, or being run over or struck down by an automobile. These policies are issued with little effort at risk selection, and many of them will insure the drivers of commercial vehicles as well as passenger automobiles.

Newspaper Accident Policies

In the middle 1920's, a travel-accident type of accident insurance was offered by some few newspapers. Using one leading newspaper as an example, any reader of the newspaper could fill out a coupon and buy an accident policy for a premium of $1.00 per year. There was no subscription obligation on the part of the policyholder, and this accident insurance was offered by the newspaper as a public service to its readers. The response of the public was so favorable that a few years later the beginning of newspaper accident insurance, as it is administered today, was introduced.

The newspaper accident policy is available only to subscribers of the newspaper and is renewed as long as the policyholder continues to purchase the newspaper on a subscription basis. The premium is collected monthly by the newspaper carrier. This is the plan in vogue today, and a very substantial volume of this type of accident insurance is sold, with most of the leading newspapers of the country using the plan as a combination of a public service and the means of obtaining and continuing subscribers.

A typical policy issued by one of the leading newspapers is a "travel, aviation, polio, and pedestrian accident policy." This policy pays $7,500 of accidental death benefits for the wrecking of a public passenger elevator in which the insured is riding or by the wrecking of any of the following public passenger vehicles operated by a common carrier: a railroad car drawn by steam, diesel, or electric power; a steamship; an electric street railway car; an electric interurban car; an elevated railway car; a subway car; or a taxicab operated by an incorporated company.

The policy pays smaller amounts for accidental death for more frequent types of travel accidents and pays weekly indemnity of $10 a week for fifteen weeks for specified accidents. There are other benefits in the policy, including $500 on essentially a blanket basis for poliomyelitis. The premium charged to the subscriber includes a 25-cent advance before the policy is issued and 10 cents monthly. The policy has no age limits either to new policyholders or for renewals, but benefits for accidental death are reduced 50 per cent when the insured is over 70 years of age.

There is a definite trend toward more liberalization in the newspaper accident field, and some policies are available which give limited benefits for many more types of accidental injuries. A recent development is the freeway accident insurance policy for newspaper subscribers. A typical policy pays $10,000 for accidental death and dismemberment or loss of sight sustained by the wrecking of a motor vehicle on specified freeways. The policy also contains accumulations, and after five years of continuous renewals the $10,000 becomes $16,500. The premium cost is $1.00 a year.

Aviation Accident Policy

Aviation accident insurance, while considered a "limited" policy, actually is very complete coverage of injuries sustained in aviation accidents. The most popular of all aviation accident policies is the so-called "aviation ticket policy" or "aviation trip policy."

In the early 1940's, air-line trip insurance coverage was restricted to a maximum of $5,000 for accidental death and dismemberment, and was limited to trips within the continental United States and a portion of Canada. The maximum period of coverage at that time was seven days. Early in 1945 the aviation ticket policy benefits were increased from $5,000 to a maximum of $25,000 for accidental death without any increase in basic rates. The rate at that time was 25 cents for each $5,000, or $1.25 for $25,000. The time limit was extended to twelve months.

This policy originally was sold by the air-line agents over the counter to outbound passengers. The increase in volume of air passenger traffic and the increasing work load of the air-line ticket agents at the airport ticket counters caused the insurance sales to become an undue burden on the time of the air lines' personnel, and they asked that another method of sales be devised. The first step in this direction was the creation of the electrical vending machines, which were installed in 1946. These machines restricted the sale of the policies to domestic travel only and were good for round trips completed within thirty days of the date of policy issuance.

In September, 1948, the first insurance booth was opened at the New York International Airport. Booths were introduced in order to provide coverage for international passengers and because of the belief that there was a good market for a personalized service. Most major airports now have one or more insurance counters.

In March, 1952, the air-line trip policy benefits were increased again to a maximum of $50,000 at the same premium base, the $50,000 policy costing $2.50. At this time the vending machine policies were liberalized so that both booth and machine policies were giving the broad coverage.

Starting with 1954, accidental death and dismemberment coverage of $6,250 for each 25 cents of premium was provided, with a maximum of 10 units, or $62,500 (premium $2.50), in one company. Today the aviation ticket policy pays for accidental death and dismemberment, and includes a blanket medical reimbursement benefit for 5 per cent of the accidental death amount. In 1960 the rates were still further reduced. The prevailing rate was set at 25 cents for each $7,500 of accidental death and dismemberment, with a maximum of 10 units, or $75,000, in any one company. The coverage for blanket medical reimbursement remains 5 per cent of the accidental death benefit, or $3,750 for the maximum of $75,000.

The policy pays for scheduled air-line passenger travel anywhere in the world. Some ground coverage is also provided by including benefits for injuries on the premises of the airport and while riding in vehicles controlled or "franchised" by the air lines or airport. The coverage is granted under these policies for a continuous round trip if completed within a year. A recent development is that some companies have broadened the coverage to include common carrier accidents on the same basis as aviation benefits during the effective period of the aviation insurance. The common carrier coverage is restricted to the United States only.

Many air travelers carry year-round aviation and other travel accident protection, but will supplement this coverage by ticket insurance whenever they travel by passenger airplane.

Polio and Dread Disease Insurance

Polio insurance is one of the universally known limited policies. The policy pays a total of $5,000 and, in some instances, as high as $10,000 for practically all expenses of medical-surgical-nurses' fees, hospitalization, and some types of special devices necessary to the polio patient.

The policy, generally issued on an individual basis, carries a premium of $5.00 annually for the individual and $10 annually for the entire family. This policy first came into prominence during a severe polio epidemic, and it was accepted with open arms by the insuring public. Although it is termed a "limited policy," it is actually full coverage of expenses due to polio. The low premium and broad coverage of a widely feared hazard made a widespread and favorable impression on the public. The rates and coverage on the policies being renewed today have not been changed by some companies, whereas other companies have added additional "dread disease" with no extra cost.

The original polio policy has evolved into the more modern "polio and dread disease" policy by inclusion under the typical polio policy coverage for specified diseases such as diphtheria, scarlet fever, leukemia, smallpox, encephalitis, spinal meningitis, and tetanus.

Today, because of immunization with Salk and Sabin vaccines, the polio hazard is greatly lessened. Many original buyers of polio insurance have retained their coverage, but relatively little polio or dread disease coverage is being sold.

Limited Health Insurance

The so-called "limited health policy" was one of the first limited policies to be widely sold. It was really limited in every sense of the word: It covered only rare diseases and unlikely accidents, including being "gored by a bull."

The policy was aggressively sold in the early days of health insurance, as it required a comparatively small premium and some of the benefits, particularly for accidental death, were spectacularly large. Today the policy is still offered by some companies but has been so changed that in most instances, it pays some small benefits for almost any type of accident or sickness. This kind of coverage does not represent an important segment of health insurance today but is mentioned here primarily because of its historical interest. No doubt, these policies did very little to build confidence in health insurance, but they introduced the concept of this coverage to many people, and many policyholders were paid claims in times of need.

Economic Significance of Limited Policies

Limited policies of the type which give very little basic coverage have relatively little inherent economic value. It is a fact that they have provided the insured with all of the benefits he was willing to pay for and have served a useful educational purpose. Then, too, many persons who would not buy any other type of accident and health insurance have bought these limited policies. Through this introduction to sickness coverage, the purchaser has eventually realized the need for full coverage and has purchased a program of disability income and medical expense insurance. In addition, under the most limited and restricted policies, many claims have been paid which have been helpful to those who needed money during disability, or to the family in the event of accidental death.

With reference to the "better" type of limited policy, it may be said to have had a decided economic value. Polio insurance, for example, with its $5,000 or $10,000 blanket medical expense coverage, has been a financial lifesaver to the family of the polio sufferer. The payment of all medical expenses for the unfortunate sufferer has been a vital help to the policyholder, and millions of dollars have been paid in polio claims at the time of greatest need.

Likewise, aviation accident insurance has been helpful in the rapid development of the aviation industry. Although plane crashes are infrequent, psychologically and financially this protection is desirable. Many business travelers purchase aviation insurance automatically and would perhaps hesitate to use passenger plane service if they were not assured of financial protection to their families if the rare but sudden crash should occur.

Attitude of Regulatory Officials

The various state regulatory officials have taken considerable interest in the supervision of limited policies in the last few years. In the heyday of the limited policy, there were many abuses that reflected unfavorably on the entire business. Vaudeville comedians, cartoonists, and radio performers had fun with ancient gags about limited benefits and "the small print" in the policies. Through the evolution of the business and the sincere desire of the companies to give value received for their policies, limited policies today are on a relatively satisfactory basis.

State insurance officials frown on policies which are misleading and which offer doubtful benefits. They watch loss ratios as a guide to the equity of these policies to the buyer. Although the companies themselves have taken the lead in discontinuing limited policies of dubious value, the state insurance departments continue to analyze this type of insurance carefully. The make-up of the policy must show restrictions in large print; and as mentioned previously, all limited policies have to be overprinted on the face with the phrase: "THIS IS A LIMITED POLICY—READ IT CAREFULLY."

Many limited policies are excellent values and favorable to the buying public. The state insurance departments have co-operated wholeheartedly in approving and encouraging this better type of limited policy.

Future of Limited Policies

Limited policies have a Dr. Jekyll and Mr. Hyde future. The complicated policies with very little basic value probably will disappear from the market or will be so changed that they will not be widely sold. However, many limited policies would seem to have a relatively bright future. For example, it would seem that with the great future of the aviation industry, it is likely that aviation accident insurance is destined for tremendous growth. Limited policies relating to specific diseases may well have a bright future. For example, experiments have been made with cancer policies, but so far, the sales have not been great. If the inherent difficulties in the underwriting and sale of cancer policies could be conquered, there could be as great a sale and demand for cancer coverage as there was for polio coverage in epidemic years.

With reference to polio insurance, which had phenomenal growth in years past, it seems likely that vaccines will so minimize the incidence of polio that the polio policy will no longer be sold in large volume.

As needs develop, as new ways of life inspire new coverages, it seems almost certain that many limited policies not available today will be introduced and successfully marketed.

SPECIAL RISK POLICIES

So-called "special risk policies" do not have the same precise meaning to all health insurance companies. The term is used by companies in many different ways. There is no legal definition of the term "special risk" as applied to health insurance.

Special risk policies might be considered to include:

1. Policies offering coverage for unusual and unconventional sets of circumstances.
2. Policies offering coverage on a pioneering and experimental basis for high-loss hazards previously not insurable.
3. Policies offering coverage for "everyday occurrences" which previously did not come under the province of health insurance.

From the standpoint of the type of policy, special risk policies fall into two classes, namely, an individual or group policy contract similar to other health insurance lines, and a manuscript policy. Most insurable situations are of the nature that they will fit into a conventional pattern; consequently, there can be a printed form which takes care of these insurable requests. Rather frequently, however, in the special risk field the coverage will be of such a nature that no conventional pattern fits the plan and there are not a sufficient number of these unusual situations to warrant printing a policy. In these instances, a manuscript or individual legal document (policy) is made up by the insurance company. These manuscript policies are typewritten rather than printed.

The special risk field has inherent flexibility, and any definition today could be incomplete tomorrow. The scope of special risk underwriting depends upon the imagination, ingenuity, and technical know-how of the home office agency, underwriting, and actuarial departments.

Special Policies to Cover Very Unusual Situations

Special risk policies may be written to cover very unusual situations. For example, the following types of situations have called for a coverage which has been written.

Flagpole Sitter. A merchandising association, for publicity purposes, placed a man on a high flagpole in Milwaukee with the promise that he would stay on this flagpole until the Milwaukee Braves baseball team won seven games in a row. A policy was issued in the amount of $25,000 to cover accidental death should this occur to the flagpole sitter as a result of the project.

Automobile Racing on Ice. An automobile race was staged in Alaska on a track of solid ice. This was a dramatic automobile-racing danger, but a special risk policy was issued for accidental death and medical reimbursement for all of the participants.

Diving—Sunken Ships. Divers whose under-ocean activities are in connection with sunken ships have very special hazards. The unusual diving depths that may be necessary, and the rummaging-around in the ship to recover objects from the interior, present both a real and a psychological danger. Special risk coverage for death, dismemberment, and medical expense has been issued to these divers.

Human Fly. In one of Olson & Johnson's theatrical shows, a "human fly" walked up the wall, across the ceiling, and down the other wall. A special risk policy was issued covering accidental death or medical expenses in this unusual situation.

Steeple Jacks. Steeple jacks, and those who paint church towers, present a hazard that could not be underwritten in the regular way. Policies in substantial amounts for death, dismemberment, and medical reimbursement are available through special risk underwriting.

Speed Record Test. A specially designed automobile, "The Spirit of America," broke the world's speed record on the Bonneville salt flats in Utah in 1962. This was a hazardous undertaking; but the driver and others participating in the speed test were issued a policy covering $25,000 for accidental death or dismemberment, $25,000 for permanent and total disability, and $10,000 for medical expense.

Student Accident and Sickness Insurance

The entire field of student accident, or student accident and sickness, coverages has an interesting and ever-changing historical life. It started out basically as a method of selling low-priced individual policies to students by the so-called "group" approach to the school. In the beginning the policies covered accidental death for a nominal sum such as $1,000, with medical reimbursement usually up to $500 for accidental injuries. With the inclusion of sickness insurance and expansion to the colleges and universities, student insurance has become a more important and more stabilized form of special risk insurance.

The student insurance for colleges and universities is becoming widespread and is assuming considerable importance. Basically, this type of student insurance could be classified under group coverages, but it is still considered in the special risk category.[1]

For many years, the student was neglected in his economically undesirable position between two types of insurance coverage. He may cease to be a dependent under the family medical expense plan and is not yet ready to enter the business world; therefore, no streamlined, low-priced coverage was available to him prior to student insurance. Student accident and sickness insurance has become the answer.

The following are the outlines of the coverage of two typical plans: (1) a relatively limited plan, and (2) a comprehensive plan. The benefits are the same under both plans 1 and 2, as follows: blanket accident medical reimbursement, up to $10,000; accidental loss of life, $1,000; accidental dismemberment, loss of sight, up to $10,000.

Plan 1 covers a student (*a*) while engaged in school activities during

[1] Chapter 35, on "Group Accident and Related Plans," discusses student insurance and certain other forms of special risk insurance under the category of blanket and franchise insurance.

the entire nine-month school year; (*b*) on school premises while attending classes during the hours and on the days when school is in session, including lunch and recess periods; (*c*) while traveling between the student's residence and school to attend classes or a school-sponsored activity; (*d*) while traveling with other students as a supervised group to or from a school-sponsored activity; (*e*) while participating in school-sponsored and -supervised activities during school hours; (*f*) in school-sponsored and -supervised social or nonsocial extracurricular activities after school hours or on days when school is not in session; and (*g*) in school-sponsored and -supervised athletics, except for interscholastic football, hockey, soccer, or lacrosse.

Plan 2, the comprehensive plan, covers the student for twenty-four hours a day for a twelve-month period.

The college and the insurance company, via the agent or broker, arrange the insurance on either a compulsory or a voluntary basis for the students. In most instances, the coverage is voluntary, with the students having the option of buying the policy.

There is an increasing trend toward including the premium for student health insurance as part of the fee system, making purchase by the student mandatory. The benefits and type of coverage are dovetailed with whatever services are available in the infirmary or clinic operated by the school or college. There is usually a restriction in the policy that services rendered by the infirmary, infirmary employees, or salaried physicians for the college are not covered under the policy. There is no individual risk selection in the student college coverage; every student is eligible.

There is today enough actuarial experience so that the rates can be calculated from actual data. Inasmuch as the coverage comes under the group category, administration and other expenses are low. Student insurance, therefore, is sound coverage and appeals to the buyer because it gives unusually good insurance value. It should be added that there are many variations in student coverage and rates. In the past, rates for student insurance have been so competitive that companies have encountered large underwriting losses. Today, there are many variations in rates and coverages in attempting to offer the student a rate compatible with what he, or the parents, can afford to pay and still stay within the limits of sound underwriting.

Test-Piloting an Airplane

With the airplane experimentation in the jet and rocket fields, both commercial and military development has been greatly assisted by the availability of coverage for persons testing these new and constantly changing types of apparatus. Special risk policies are now available to pilots testing these planes. Many of the test flights have to be attempted under hazardous conditions, and it has been a boon to the aviation industry that special risk policies can be issued for large amounts for accidental death, dismemberment, and medical reimbursement.

Another special risk policy in this category is available. In crop spraying the aviator travels at a very low altitude; hence, the hazard is severe. Special risk coverage is available with substantial benefits for accidental death, loss of income, and medical expense reimbursement.

Camp Insurance

From a coverage standpoint, camp health insurance may be divided into three categories:

1. Blanket accident-medical reimbursement for injuries to an enrollee of the camp, with some forms of sickness occasionally included.
2. Tuition refund, in which the enrollee may not be ill or injured but, because of an epidemic or other cause, the entire camp is closed. If the camp is closed, unexpired tuition is returned by the camp to the parents of the enrollee, and the camp is reimbursed by the insurance company.
3. The enrollee's parents can purchase tuition refund accident and health insurance. Even though the camp is not closed, if the student has to return home because of an accident or illness, the unexpired tuition of the enrollee is returned to the parents.

Sports Insurance

Sports insurance is becoming an important type of special risk insurance. The policy covers accidental death, dismemberment, and, in many instances, reimbursement for medical expenses resulting from accidental injury in the event that the injury is caused by a particular sport in which the insured is participating. For example, each member of many softball, professional baseball, and semiprofessional teams may be covered as a unit. Some of the major league teams are covered in high amounts for both the baseball hazard and traveling between cities.

Football teams of colleges, high schools, and grade schools may be covered, usually for medical reimbursement and accidental death. Other types of sports coverage available are for those who ski or play hockey, polo, soccer, and basketball.

Although the hobby of hunting comes under a special category, it could be considered under sports coverage. Hunters' insurance pays substantial accidental death, dismemberment, and medical reimbursement if the policyholder is killed or injured while hunting.

Youth Groups

Boy Scouts, Girl Scouts, and other similar organizations can purchase coverage for the entire group. A typical policy would be $1,000 for accidental death and dismemberment and $1,000 for medical reimbursement which covers the members while participating in any sponsored activity of the organization. The usual premium is $1.00 per member per year, and if the group purchases this type of insurance, it is mandatory for every member to purchase the coverage.

Charter Flight Insurance

A new type of coverage is now offered which protects the insured whenever he is prevented from making a chartered flight on the scheduled date of departure because of sickness or injury. Also, if, due to sickness or injury, he is unable to make the return flight on the scheduled date, he will be reimbursed for the specified cost of the return flight. A typical example is a plan that pays up to $500 when disability causes the insured to miss the entire trip or the return scheduled flight. The limit of coverage is the actual cost incurred.

Economic Significance of Special Risk Policies

When the Liberian government employed a United States engineering firm for major work in the economic development of the country, the special risk policy protecting these men was of extreme importance to employees working in Liberia. Further, when the United States government sends men all over the world in connection with certain scientific experiments, they have available to them a "tailored" special risk policy providing for a combination of medical expense disability income and accidental death benefits.

Without camp insurance in the special risk field, the financial soundness of children's camps would be greatly threatened. Aviation would, of course, grow and prosper and would continue scientific experimentation; nevertheless, the fact that special risk coverage offers test pilot insurance and other types of policies has been of help to the aviation industry. Certainly, aviation travel by the public has been enhanced by the various types of special risk and aviation policies.

State regulatory officials have co-operated in the special risk field. Often a manuscript policy is necessary because of the unconventional nature of the special risk coverage. Also, special risk policies may require coverage immediately. Any delays that might be encountered because of filing of manuscript policies might result in the policy being approved after the contingencies for which insurance was obtained are completed. The close co-operative relationship between the various companies and the state insurance departments has permitted speed and flexibility in these situations.

If pioneering were to stop in special risk coverage, the development of the present special risk facilities would halt. However, special risk underwriting will continue to pioneer, and any coverage that can be practically underwritten will be attempted in this field.

UNDERWRITING AND ACTUARIAL BACKGROUND OF LIMITED AND SPECIAL RISK POLICIES

The underwriting and actuarial background of limited and special risk policies is more of a philosophy than a science. In the pioneering of any of these coverages, the rates are figured by comparing, as far as possible, similar types of coverage and using what experience and statistics are available. These data are then oriented to the new coverage with whatever judgment factors must be used on account of the dearth of available statistics. Often the coverage is so new that no insurance experience is available and statistics have to be used from any available source.

As the coverage grows in amount of premiums written and in length of time on the market, experience kept by the companies may eventually become sufficient to compute a sound rate. For example, in the pioneering of polio insurance, there were few, if any, figures available from an insurance standpoint. There were morbidity statistics for polio. These statistics were helpful, but when the early policies were offered, there were so many "unknowns" in the polio insurance hazards that the judgment factor was more important than the statistics. As an aside, it is interesting to note that the early polio rates were too low; and in the epidemic years that followed, it was necessary to raise the rates.

Polio might be a good example to consider from an underwriting standpoint also. The companies had to adopt the philosophy that to issue polio coverage and restrict it in an epidemic region would defeat the purpose of the insurance. A brave philosophy was necessary so that in epidemic areas, polio insurance could be purchased. The only safeguards that could be required from a practical standpoint were that coverage should not be granted to anyone who had polio at the time of the application, and the approval of polio coverage should be postponed for those who were unduly exposed to polio at the time of the application. These two underwriting requirements were accomplished by (1) establishing a delay, usually from three to ten days, between the time of the application and the effective date of the coverage; and (2) including a question in the application such as: "Has any member of your family had polio within the last 90 days?"

From this brief description of the actuarial background and underwriting requirements of polio insurance, it is apparent that the philosophy of the company underwriting the risk was more important than any body of underwriting requirements based on experience or statistical data.

In the special risk field, where unusual projects are insured, the actuarial and underwriting approach is secondary to a basic company concept. It has been truthfully said that any hazard could be insured if the rate were high enough and enough people purchased the coverage. Many of these special risk projects, however, are the one-of-a-kind variety, and the insurance company must apply the theory of combining many of these plans for their eventual profit or loss. Many of the projects are actually close to a gamble with very little statistical foundation. The rates must therefore be computed by a combination of the judgment factor with whatever studies can be made on the hazards of the particular coverage.

As experience develops on these unusual situations, there is enough similarity so that in time judgment may be backed by actual experience. For example, automobile racing on ice could be rated by applying an extra premium loading on automobile racing on the various race tracks. Originally, there was some statistical background for the injuries and deaths in automobile racing, so that some experience was available when the first racing policy was offered. The loading factor for automobile racing on ice would be a judgment factor combined with whatever statistics might be available for other, somewhat similar hazards.

Underwriting, like rate making, is individual. Judgment is based on whatever experience may be available. Usually, the underwriting and rate making for an entirely new coverage or situation are undertaken at the same time. All of the hazards are weighed, and the rate is made on the particular plan. When the next plan of a similar nature is submitted to the company, both underwriting and actuarial judgment must be combined to compare it with the previous experience.

In summary, rate making in both limited and special risk coverages starts out as a combination of judgment, meager experience, and statistical information. As experience develops, more and more actuarial science can be used in the rate making on these coverages.

SELECTED REFERENCES

DICKERSON, O. D. *Health Insurance.* Rev. ed. Homewood, Ill.: Richard D. Irwin, Inc., 1963.

FAULKNER, EDWIN J. *Health Insurance.* New York: McGraw-Hill Book Co., Inc., 1960.

KULP, C. A. *Casualty Insurance.* 3d ed. New York: Ronald Press Co., 1956.

MAGEE, JOHN H., and BICKELHAUPT, DAVID L. *General Insurance.* 7th ed. Homewood, Ill.: Richard D. Irwin, Inc., 1964.

MEHR, ROBERT I., and CAMMACK, E. E. *Principles of Insurance.* 3d ed. Homewood, Ill.: Richard D. Irwin, Inc., 1961.

MILLER, JOHN H. "The Development of Individual Health and Accident Insurance," *Journal of the American Society of Chartered Life Underwriters,* Vol. VI, No. 1 (December, 1951), p. 5.

SOMMER, ARMAND. *Manual of Accident and Health Insurance.* Philadelphia: Spectator Co., 1928.

Chapter 25

PREMIUMS AND RESERVES

BY T. H. KIRKPATRICK

Individual health insurance policies cover a variety of risks, each involving different probabilities of loss. To determine premiums and reserves for these policies, it is first necessary to consider the nature of these probabilities and to evaluate them. This is not a simple task. Usually, it is assumed that future results will follow past experience. From existing data, an experience table is developed. This table is constructed in such a way that the underlying probabilities are expressed in a form that simplifies the calculations. Some of the several ways of constructing these tables and calculating premiums and reserves will be explained in this chapter.[1]

There are two types of premiums, *net* and *gross*. Net premiums take into account claims costs only. Gross premiums also include expenses and margins for contingencies and for dividends or profit.[2]

Reserves are of two general types, *active life* and *disabled life*. Active life reserves are like life insurance reserves. Disabled life reserves are of two types—those for accrued and those for unaccrued benefits. The former will be exactly determined in a short time when the claims are reported and processed. Any type of estimate of this reserve can be easily compared with the exact amount and the method of estimating it refined to give better values for the future. On the other hand, reserves for unaccrued benefits involve the probabilities inherent in the risk. Theoretically, these reserves are determined from mathematical formulas which include these probabilities. Any other determination is an approximation and justifiable by its simplicity and practical results.

Active life reserves arise when part of the early premiums must be set aside and accumulated to meet later costs. If premiums can be freely changed or the policy canceled or not renewed by the insurer, the only

---

[1] Many of the underlying principles developed in Chapter 10 on "Probability, Mortality, and Money Concepts," by Charles M. Sternhell, are equally applicable in health insurance.

[2] Net and gross premium concepts in individual life insurance are covered in Chapter 11.

liability is the unearned premium. More frequently, however, individual health insurance policies are issued as long-term contracts with level premiums. For the benefits provided, claims costs generally increase with attained age. This results in premiums and reserves which are similar in theory to those of life insurance policies, and the same principles and techniques may be used to determine them.

NET PREMIUMS

Progressing from the simplest to the most difficult formula, net premiums and reserves can be determined as follows:

1. If the benefit provides a fixed payment in the event of loss within a single year, and the probability of loss is the same for all policyholders, irrespective of age or other characteristics, the net premium is calculated by multiplying the fixed payment by the probability. At any time, the only liabilities are the unearned premiums or unpaid claims. Air-trip insurance, for example, falls into this category.

2. If the annual claims cost varies with a single factor, such as age, it is necessary to analyze the experience and determine the probability of claim for each attained age. If premiums are to be on a one-year term basis, they are determined by multiplying the probability of loss for each age by the amount payable. There is a different premium for each age. It is not necessary to accumulate any part of the premium from age to age. This arrangement would apply if health insurance were sold on a yearly renewable term basis.

3. When the risk increases with age, the use of level premiums gives rise to active life reserves. The theory is the same as that for life insurance. A level premium and its resulting reserve can be calculated, using the same methods as for life insurance, by simply replacing the annual mortality cost with the annual claims cost. Most health insurance policies currently issued fall into this category, or the extension described in the next paragraph.

4. For loss-of-time benefits and occasionally for hospital and major medical benefits, additional flexibility is desired so that premiums for different elimination periods and benefit periods can be calculated from the same table. The experience table must then be constructed to show the number disabled for each day during the entire benefit period. For example, for 100,000 lives exposed at age *X*, the experience table would show those disabled for each day of disability. This arrangement of data is known as a *continuance table*.[3] The results for age 35 are somewhat as shown in Table 25–1.

---

[3] The question of whether the term "continuance table" should be limited to those already disabled is unsettled. Perhaps there are two types of continuance tables—an exposure continuance table and a claims continuance table.

If the claims follow Table 25–1, then, of 100,000 lives, at age 35, exposed for one year, 4,954 will be disabled for a continuous period of at least 32 days due to a disability commencing during the year. Some of these will recover or die on the thirty-third day, so that only 4,731 will be disabled for at least 33 days.

TABLE 25–1

CONTINUANCE TABLE AT AGE 35 SHOWING NUMBER DISABLED AT STATED DURATIONS
(Per 100,000 Lives Exposed)

Day	Number Disabled	Day	Number Disabled	Day	Number Disabled
1...........	32,900	31.........	5,192	757........	137
2...........	31,380	32.........	4,954	758........	136
3...........	29,540	33.........	4,731	759........	135
4...........	27,490	34.........	4,521	760........	134
etc..........	.....	etc..........	....	etc..........	...

Similar figures are obtained from the experience for other ages. In practice, quinquennial age groups are used. A complete table will show for each quinquennial age group the number disabled for each day of disability for which benefits are provided.

The annual claims cost for each age is calculated by discounting the amount payable for each day of disablement for the benefit period. This can best be explained by considering the following example:

The net level premium is required for a loss-of-time policy issued at age 35, guaranteed continuable to age 65, as follows:
Amount: $100 monthly ($3.29 per day)
Elimination Period: Thirty days
Maximum Benefit Period: Two years for any one disability
Assumed Interest: Three per cent
Mortality: 1958 CSO Table

First, it is necessary to choose an experience table. For this example, the continuance table described above will be used. From this table, it is possible to calculate the probabilities of disablement for each of the days of the benefit period.

The next step is to determine the *annual claims cost* for each year of age. This is done by discounting at interest the amount payable for each day of disablement after the elimination period for the benefit period. Since the continuance table shows only those who have survived and continue to be disabled, i.e., recoveries and deaths having been deducted, mortality has already been taken into consideration. Thus, the experience table shows that of 100,000 lives exposed at age 35, 5,192 will be disabled for a continuous period of at least 31 days. This period represents the first day of coverage after the end of the elimination period. The probability of disability for this period at age 35 can be shown as $\frac{5,192}{100,000}$. The amount payable for this day of disablement then would be \$3.29 (the daily amount of coverage) $\times \frac{5,192}{100,000}$. This amount is discounted at the assumed rate of interest for 31 days to obtain the present value at the date of commencement of disability. Therefore, the present value of the benefit payable for the thirty-first day is $\frac{5,192}{100,000} \times \$3.29 \times \left(\frac{1}{1+i}\right)^{31/365}$, where i is the assumed interest rate. Similarly, the present value of the benefit payable for the thirty-second day is $\frac{4,954}{100,000} \times \$3.29 \times \left(\frac{1}{1+i}\right)^{32/365}$, and so on, with the present value of the benefit payable for the seven hundred sixtieth day (the last day of the maximum benefit period) being $\frac{134}{100,000} \times \$3.29 \times \left(\frac{1}{1+i}\right)^{760/365}$. The sum of these amounts is the annual claims cost for year-of-age 35.[4]

This summation technique to obtain the annual claims cost is an important concept in the calculation of health insurance premiums. The most important point in this discussion for the nonactuarial reader is an understanding of the nature of the process which is used to determine the premium rather than a knowledge of the specific actuarial formula used in calculating the premium.

The annual claims cost for all ages from 35 to 64, inclusive, are similarly determined. The level premiums and active life reserves can now be calculated, using the same methods as for life insurance. It is assumed that all claims commence in the middle of the policy year, and that the annual claims cost is discounted at interest and mortality to determine the present value of future benefits. To determine the level annual premium, the present value of future benefits (the single premium for the policy) is divided by the life annuity for the premium-paying period.[5]

---

[4] The actuarial formula which shows the annual claims cost for year of age 35 is as follows:

$$S_{35} = \$3.29 \left\{ \frac{5,192}{100,000} v^{31/365} + \frac{4,954}{100,000} v^{32/365} + \cdots \frac{134}{100,000} v^{760/365} \right\}$$

$$v = \frac{1}{1+i}, \text{ the interest discount factor}$$

This S formula simply adds together the present value of the benefits expected to be payable for the various days of disablement.

[5] The actuarial formulas at age 35 are as follows:

Where the annual claims cost can be directly obtained without the necessity of using a continuance table, net premiums and reserves are obtained by simply discounting at interest and mortality the annual claims cost.

Waiver-of-premium benefits are frequently provided. The premiums for them are calculated as if they were loss-of-time benefits of an amount equal to the net premium, plus the expenses to be incurred while premiums are being waived, during the period for which these benefits are provided.

RESERVES

Active Life Reserve

When a policy is issued with level premiums, *the present value of future net premiums is equal to the present value of future benefits.* Where the annual claims cost increases with attained age, then, after the date of issue, *the present value of future benefits is greater than the present value of future net premiums. The difference is the active life reserve.* The same reserve would have been obtained by accumulating that part of the net premium which had not already been paid in claims.

The active life reserve can be calculated by taking the present value of the difference between the attained-age and issue-age premiums. Consider two people now aged 45. One bought a policy ten years ago; the other purchases his policy now. Both have the same future benefits. The only difference is that one will continue to pay the age-35 premium and the other the higher age-45 premium. Equality is established by the reserve which is equal to the present value of this difference. This is the tenth-year terminal reserve on a policy issued at age 35.[6]

Where coverage is only provided for a short period, such as one year, the terminal reserve is zero. It is assumed, however, that policies are issued uniformly throughout the year, and a mean reserve represents the liability of the company on the valuation date. The mean reserve is equal to one half the net premium. In the event that one of these policies terminates, there is usually a refund of all or a part of the gross premium.

---

a) The single premium is $A = \sum_{t=0}^{29} S_{35+t} \frac{D_{35+t+\frac{1}{2}}}{D_{35}}$.

b) The net level annual premium is $P_{35:\overline{30|}} = \frac{A_{35:\overline{30|}}}{\overset{\infty}{\bar{a}}_{35:\overline{30|}}}$,

where D_x is the usual life insurance present value factor $v^x l_x$.

[6] The actuarial formula is as follows:

$$ {}_tV_{x:\overline{y-x|}} = (P_{x+t:\overline{y-x-t|}} - P_{x:\overline{y-t|}})\overset{\infty}{\bar{a}}_{x+t:\overline{y-x-t|}} $$

where y is the age to which the policy can be continued.

To meet this eventuality, the insurance departments require a minimum reserve of all or a part of the gross unearned premium. Historically, health insurance was developed as a casualty coverage, and the establishment of a gross unearned premium reserve was a natural consequence. Many companies, particularly those with cancellable policies, use the gross unearned premium approach and establish reserves for this type of policy on this basis.

Disabled Life Reserve

A *disabled life reserve* arises whenever a claim is incurred and the amount payable in the future depends upon future contingencies. For example, under a loss-of-time policy, a claim is considered as incurred when disability commences. Future amounts payable are dependent upon the continuance of total disability. *The disabled life reserve is the present value of the remaining benefits which the claimant may expect to be paid on his claim.* Contrariwise, if the amount is fixed as soon as the claim is incurred, disabled life reserves do not arise. The accidental death benefit is an example of the latter.

For each claim, the amount of the reserve depends upon the duration of disability already completed. It is therefore necessary to determine on the valuation date the distribution of disabled lives by duration of disability before applying the appropriate type of actuarial formula. This can be done in either of two ways:

1. ***By Analysis of Open Claims.*** The distribution of claims on the valuation date is determined directly from the actual claims open on the valuation date. They are sorted by duration of disability. The present value of future benefits is obtained by the summation method in the same way as was done in determining premiums, except that the starting point for each claim is the duration of disability as of the valuation date. For example, if the claimant had already been disabled six months, the summation process would start with those then disabled as represented by the experience table, and future benefits would be discounted to this starting point. The number and amount of incurred but unreported claims are estimated from past experience; or alternatively, the calculation of this reserve can be deferred for a short period until most of the unreported claims have been reported.

2. ***From the Continuance Table.*** If claims follow the continuance table, as assumed, then the distribution on the valuation date of claims by duration of disability can be determined. It is assumed that disabilities commence uniformly on each day during each year of age, 1/365 of the total for each day. The number remaining disabled on the valuation date is obtained by multiplying the number for each day of the benefit period by the appropriate probability that disability will continue to the valua-

tion date. The result is the expected number disabled for one day, two days, three days, and so forth, up to the maximum period of disability for which benefits are payable. The present value of expected future benefits for each duration is calculated by the summation formula already explained. The total of the expected number disabled for each day, multiplied by the appropriate present value factor, gives the *total disabled life reserve.*

Other Claims Reserves

On the valuation date, there are unreported claims. If time permits, calculation of the claims reserves can be held in abeyance until most of these claims are reported. If not, the lag in claims experienced in the previous year or two is analyzed to determine the amounts involved. They consist of amounts already accrued on the valuation date and the unaccrued benefits which are to be added to the disabled life reserve. Usually, simple factors are developed from experience and applied to the premiums in force or, in the case of unaccrued benefits, to the disabled life reserve. The amounts can be affected by miscellaneous factors such as an epidemic just before the valuation date, irregularity in mail deliveries, or the manner in which the days of the week fall at the valuation date. Normally, the reserves have margins which are sufficient to cover these variations.

Reserve for Claims in Course of Settlement. Usually, the company keeps the books open until all claims are processed and paid up to the valuation date. It only takes a day or two to do this. If this is not done, there is a liability for the amount involved.

Reserve for Accrued Benefits Not Yet Due. For both reported and unreported claims, there are accrued benefits not yet due. For example, a monthly disability income payment is expected to be due fifteen days after the valuation date. One half of a month's payment has already accrued. The amounts involved are quite small, and a simple estimate arrived at by reviewing the company's business by type of coverage will indicate the appropriate amount.

Reserve for Resisted Claims. Claims resisted are usually set up as a liability for the full gross amount which is expected to be payable.

Reserve for Future Contingent Payments. Reserves for future contingent payments result from policy provisions which give rise to future liabilities under a variety of circumstances. Usually, they provide that even if a policy lapses, a claim may still occur—for example, as a result of the right of reinstatement without evidence of insurability. Typically, the amounts involved are small, and the liability is determined as a matter of judgment and experience. An important exception is where maternity claims are payable if pregnancy commences while the policy is in force.

In this case, either (1) nine months' premiums for maternity benefits are carried as a premium reserve, or (2) nine months' maternity payments are carried as a claims reserve.

Deficiency Reserve

Individual health insurance policies are subject to relatively high lapse rates. After a block of business has been in force for some time, say 20 years, antiselection develops as the result of lapsation. The few remaining policies in force experience a claims rate substantially higher than expected. If it is found that for the claims level now reached, the present value of future benefits, less the active life reserve, exceeds the present value of future gross premiums, less future expenses, then a *deficiency reserve* of this amount should be established. The present values include interest, mortality, and lapse factors. Otherwise expressed, future gross premiums, plus the active life reserve, should be sufficient to pay future claims and expenses. Any deficiency should be set up as a reserve.

Total Reserve

Having determined the tabular reserve factors by plan, year of issue, and age, these factors are applied to the policies in force on the valuation date to obtain the total reserve. This total is based on averages and should not be allocated to any specific policy or policies. However, reserves on a one- or two-year preliminary term basis are sometimes used. This has the added advantage of reducing the new-business strain. As for life insurance policies, mean reserves apply on the assumption that policies are issued with annual premiums payable uniformly throughout the year. For other modes of premium payment, the unpaid net premiums for the balance of the policy year can be carried as an asset. Alternatively, the active life reserve can be reduced or more directly calculated as the midterminal reserve, plus one half the net premium, for the actual mode of premium payment.

Practical Considerations

Certain practical problems arise in the determination of premiums and reserves for other than loss-of-time benefits, some of which are as follows:

1. ***Hospital Benefits.*** It is helpful to construct experience tables, with the benefits broken down into (*a*) daily hospital benefits, (*b*) hospital extras, and (*c*) maternity benefits. Separate tables are prepared for males, females, and children. Where several benefit periods are to be used, annual claims costs for each may be determined from existing experience, or a continuance table may be constructed. Annual claims costs for maternity benefits decrease with attained age. Usually, however, the benefits are relatively small, and when combined with others in the policy, positive

reserves are produced. Claims reserves for maternity benefits require special treatment. They can be calculated by estimating the benefits which will be paid as a result of pregnancies existing on the valuation date. Alternatively, the premiums for maternity benefits for a nine-month period can be held in a premium reserve.

2. ***Surgical Benefits.*** The experience table for surgical benefits is constructed from experience on the same surgical schedule. Separate tables may be used for males, females, and children. A table of frequencies for the various surgical procedures can be developed. These frequencies can be used to evaluate the cost of a variety of surgical schedules.

3. ***Major Medical Benefits.*** The principal problems result from the experimental nature of major medical coverage and a rising trend in claims rates. Insurers are frequently changing the benefits, with the result that it is difficult to obtain data which reflect the claims rates to be expected in the future. To allow for the rising trend in claims costs, premiums and reserves may be calculated from a series of tables showing claims costs increasing by duration.

VERIFICATION OF CLAIMS ASSUMPTIONS

The assumption has been made that the claims cost for any policy follows an experience table. Premiums and reserves can therefore be mathematically determined. In practice, this is frequently not the case. Accordingly, the experience for various blocks of business must be kept under continuous scrutiny; and from time to time, adjustments are made in the experience tables so that they will in fact represent future results. The following methods are used for this purpose:

1. *Loss Ratios*

A loss ratio is simply the *ratio of claims to premiums.* Usually, it is calculated on an incurred basis. It is easily prepared. It can be used to locate blocks of business requiring more detailed analyses. The important age factor is, however, obscured. Loss ratios on recently issued policies are usually very low. These ratios alone can be misleading and must be supplemented with other methods.

2. *Actual to Expected*

From experience tables the expected claims costs are calculated with extensive breakdowns by plan, age, occupational class, and so forth. These are compared with the actual amounts paid for each subgroup to be analyzed. The results are expressed in simple ratios. They are reliable. They are quite feasible with electronic equipment. All subgroups of a company's business can be monitored by this method.

3. *New Experience Tables*

Another approach requires a complete analysis of the actual experience and the development of new experience tables. It requires a large amount of data to obtain significant results on which complete experience tables can be constructed. It takes time to accumulate the data, which is a serious limitation. It is sometimes only practical to develop new experience tables from intercompany experience. Once new tables have been constructed, net premiums and reserves can be recalculated. New tables are usually required to justify a change in the valuation standard.

GROSS PREMIUMS FOR NONCANCELLABLE POLICIES

Gross premiums must be *adequate, consistent, equitable, and salable. Adequacy* is obtained by basing premiums on a sound forecast of future results; *consistency,* by applying the theoretical formulas uniformly; *equity,* by basing premiums on realistic claims costs and with practical limits on expenses; and *salability,* by balancing the final gross premiums to a level which makes them competitive.

Premium scales usually show premiums for each plan by age at issue, sex, and occupational class. Occasionally, a residence factor is also included. In the calculation of gross premiums, any number of factors can be considered. Only the most important ones, however, are included in the agent's rate manual.

Basic Elements Affecting Premiums

The basic elements affecting gross premiums for health insurance policies are (1) claims, (2) expenses, (3) termination rates, and (4) interest and mortality.

Claims. In practice, it is quite difficult to find experience tables which forecast future claims costs. Claims rates change. Past experience does not necessarily represent future expectations. The characteristics of the policy for which premiums are being calculated usually differ from those reflected in the existing table. Frequently, only a single table exists, whereas theoretically a whole family of tables is required. A good deal of judgment is required in deciding on the table to be used. The future financial risk should be considered, and what future action can be taken if future claims are underestimated. In any event, a table must be decided upon so that the mathematical calculations can be made.

Expenses. Expenses generally follow the same pattern as applies to life insurance policies. In general, first-year costs exceed first-year income. The resulting first-year deficit is amortized from renewal premiums. Both direct and indirect expenses are analyzed and classified on a per policy and percentage-of-premium basis. They are divided between first-year and renewal expenses. To check this analysis, these charges are applied to a block of policies—for example, the expected sales for a year—and the results compared with the total expenses expected to be incurred on these policies.

Termination Rate. Lapses of individual health insurance policies are usually about 150 per cent of those for life insurance policies. For non-cancellable loss-of-time policies, lapse rates decrease rapidly with duration. Hospital, surgical, and major medical policies characteristically have about the same first-year lapse rates as loss-of-time policies, but renewal lapse rates tend to be substantially higher. A realistic table showing lapse rates by duration is constructed from the experience of in-force policies. Alternatively, the table can show the rates at which policies are continued, i.e., persistency rates.

Interest and Mortality. Interest and mortality are not very important. Reserves are relatively small as compared with those for similar life policies. Usually, an interest rate of from 2½ to 3½ per cent is used. Mortality can be based on the 1958 CSO Table.

Methods of Calculation

Having decided upon the claims cost, expenses, termination rates, interest, and mortality to be used, gross premiums can be calculated using either a *Cammack-Jenkins type of formula* or the *Hoskins asset share method.* The former emerges from the underlying relationship that the present value of future gross premiums, less expenses relating thereto, equals the present value of future claims and claims expenses. Interest, mortality, and persistency are included in the present value factors. The asset share method develops a fund supported by an assumed premium from which claims and expenses are paid as incurred. The balance in the fund at the end of, say, twenty years, must equal the active life reserve. The assumed premium is adjusted to the true gross premium so that this balance is achieved.

The asset share method is also quite valuable in testing variations in assumptions. Upper and lower limit results can be tested. Contingency or other miscellaneous factors can be inserted into the premium calculation and their results measured.

Theoretical gross premiums have to be reviewed to make sure they are salable. If not, the factors entering into the calculations must be reviewed. Expenses may have to be reduced. For example, many companies pay a lower first-year commission on hospital business as compared with loss-of-time policies. Lapse assumptions will change with the quality of the business written. Claims costs are related to underwriting standards.

PRACTICAL PROBLEMS IN RATE MAKING

Lack of Experience Data

There is a very limited amount of published data. What is available may be useful for reserves but not for premiums. Experience will vary between companies even for the same policies. An experience table of some kind is essential, and the following are some sources:

1. ***Papers and Committee Reports of the Society of Actuaries.*** Group insurance experience from papers and reports of the Society of Actuaries can be adapted to measure the risk under individual insurance policies.

2. ***Blue Cross/Blue Shield Experience.*** Blue Cross/Blue Shield data are seldom available directly, but are occasionally analyzed and published by individuals.

3. ***Published Studies Sponsored and Financed by Organizations Interested in the Subject.*** The Health Information Foundation is a sponsor of experience studies. The cost of medical care for the aged is an example of a subject studied.

4. ***Government Statistics—Federal, State, and Provincial.***

5. ***Suppliers of Medical Care.*** Both doctors and hospitals publish statistics which are sometimes helpful.

6. ***Casualty Insurance Company Statistics.*** Casualty insurance company statistical data cover automobile accident rates, workmen's compensation claims rates, and the like.

Adaptation of Table to Specific Policy

Even after statistics are located, it is necessary to modify them to make them applicable. Are they up to date? Will the lives insured be better or poorer risks? What will be the degree of selection against the company? Are claims to be handled more or less strictly than the experience? The result is that the existing data are frequently adjusted before being used in the experience table on which the premiums are to be based.

Practical Limits on Expenses

A low-cost policy can only carry a relatively small per policy expense. Where the risk can be carried by the policyholder in his budget, a relatively high percentage of premiums must be returned in claims. Accordingly, it is necessary to check that the expenses are within the practical limits which the policyholder is willing to pay. If not, the method of selling and administering the policy must be changed so that the expenses will meet this requirement. This may be done in a variety of ways—for example, through mass marketing and simplified underwriting, policy issuance, and record keeping.

Conservative versus Realistic Assumptions

In the calculation of premiums, assumptions must be made regarding future claims costs, future expenses, and future persistency rates. The most likely results can be assumed, or conservative assumptions can be chosen. In the first case, margins must be included for variations from the expected, whereas variations from conservative assumptions are favorable to the insurer.

Provision for Catastrophes

It is necessary to consider the financial results of catastrophic changes in the level of claims. What would be the amount of the loss to the insurer if there were a persistent increase in claims rates due to inflation, a general change in the attitude of the public toward early retirement, or wholesale lapsation of policies? Fortunately, even such adverse changes can be kept within permissible loss limits, largely due to the fact that through lapsation the company's risk continuously decreases and the lower renewal expense rates permit a substantial increase in claims rates before a group of existing policies becomes unprofitable. The premium guarantees, of course, have an important effect on the whole problem. Model office calculations can be made with various assumptions as to the volume of sales, lapses, and claims rates, and in this way the limits of financial loss for any policy can be estimated and catastrophic hazards evaluated.

Completion of Premium Schedules

The amount of work involved in calculating a complete set of gross premiums is very great. Time can be saved by only calculating premiums for pivotal ages. Other ages are obtained by interpolation. Minor differences in plans are approximately calculated. Premiums are first obtained for the most important occupational class, and a simple formula is used to obtain premiums for other classes.

SUBSTANDARD PREMIUMS

Because of the subjective nature of total disability, it is doubtful if substandard loss-of-time insurance can be generally issued. However, for certain impairments and for other benefits the extra risk is measurable, and substandard insurance is possible. The practice generally followed is to set up substandard classes on the basis of extra premiums of, say, 125 per cent, 135 per cent, and so forth, up to the highest class of, say, 200 per cent of the standard premium. Impaired risks are assigned to these classes on a "best judgment" basis. Experience statistics have not yet emerged. Ultimately, each substandard class will develop its own experience table, and premiums and reserves can be based on them.

REGULATION

The regulation of health insurance is under the jurisdiction of the state insurance departments. Several states have adopted the NAIC recommendation that minimum reserves be established on the basis recommended in the Task Force 4 Report.[7] A few states require premiums to be filed. Approval of premiums is required in one state. Premiums must also meet the general rules that they be nondiscriminatory and reasonable in relation to benefits.

SELECTED REFERENCES

BARNHART, E. PAUL. "Some New Tables for Major Medical and Disability Benefits," *Transactions of the Society of Actuaries,* Vol. XIII (1961), Part 1, p. 497.

BARTLESON, EDWIN L., and OLSEN, JAMES J. "Reserves for Individual Hospital and Surgical Expense Insurance," *Transactions of the Society of Actuaries,* Vol. IX (1957), pp. 334 and 404.

DORN, LOWELL M. "New York Life Morbidity Experience under Individual and Family Major Medical Policies," *Transactions of the Society of Actuaries,* Vol. XV, No. 42 (1963), p. 275.

HOSKINS, J. E. "A New Method of Computing Non-Participating Premiums," *Transactions of the Actuarial Society of America,* Vol. XXX (1929), p. 140.

JENKINS, WILMER A. "Non-Participating Premiums Considering Withdrawals," *Record of the American Institute of Actuaries,* Vol. XXI (1932), p. 8.

MILLER, MORTON D. "Gross Premiums for Individual and Family Major Medical Expense Insurance," *Transactions of the Society of Actuaries,* Vol. VII (1955), p. 1.

SOCIETY OF ACTUARIES. *Health Insurance Provided through Individual Policies.* (Edwin L. Bartleson, principal contributor.) Chicago, 1963.

SOCIETY OF ACTUARIES. *Reports of Mortality and Morbidity Experience,* p. 70. Chicago, 1952.

---

[7] *1957 Proceedings of the National Association of Insurance Commissioners* (Chicago), Vol. II, p. 319.

Chapter 26

RISK SELECTION AND SUBSTANDARD RISKS

BY DAVID B. ALPORT

PURPOSE OF SELECTION

There are several basic purposes to be served by the risk selection process in individual health insurance. First, if experience is to be satisfactory, a number of risk selection factors must be carefully considered so that the applicants can be classified properly. Just as in life insurance, the purpose of risk selection in health insurance is to obtain a large group of insureds in common classifications so that the risk of disability for each individual does not vary to any great degree from the average of the classification. Thus the appropriate premium can be charged for the individual insureds in these broad risk groupings.

Risk selection also aims at avoiding situations where there is anti-selection, or selection against the insurance company, by the applicant. For example, when information concerning poor health, pending surgery, or exposure to some contagious disease is not disclosed in the application for insurance, selection against the company occurs.

Another reason for risk selection is to determine that the applicant is not attempting to profit from his purchase of insurance. Applying for an amount of daily room and board benefit under a hospital policy which exceeds the cost of facilities in local hospitals, or applying for an amount of disability income benefit in excess of an individual's "take-home" pay, are examples of a source of possible profit from the purchase of health insurance. The existence of such sources of possible profit may give rise to moral hazard and excessive claims.

RESPONSIBILITY OF THE FIELD UNDERWRITER

The field underwriter plays an important role in the selection of risks for health insurance. He makes the primary selection of health risks, and the ultimate company experience, favorable or unfavorable, mirrors the care exercised by him and the other field underwriters in this regard.

When health insurance is sold according to the prospect's needs, and all questions on the application are asked the applicant and his answers recorded in detail, the home office underwriter can be much more effective in selecting and properly qualifying the risks his company assumes.

On the other hand, if the field underwriter permits the prospect to assume that he should at least "get his premium dollars back," minimizes the importance of complete answers to the questions on the application, and records only the minimum of medical history, an unfavorable experience will inevitably follow.

The field underwriter, therefore, has a dual responsibility: one to his client, and one to his company. He must provide the home office underwriter with all available details to permit proper classification of the risk. To do otherwise will only disappoint his clients when benefits cannot be allowed because of an undisclosed history or a pre-existing condition. He has the additional responsibility of making certain that the benefits and limitations are fully explained to the client and that the benefits are those which best fulfill the particular needs of that client.

The agent is an underwriter in the most literal sense. He has an opportunity to appraise the applicant in person and to see his home surroundings, his family, and even his place of employment. As the agent completes the application, he has an opportunity to evaluate the manner in which the answers are given by the applicant. If there is a hesitancy in answering, a vagueness in giving details, the agent can probe further. Indeed, he has a responsibility to make certain that full information is passed along to the home office underwriter. The agent truly is a field underwriter and should obtain complete answers to the questions on the application and record them exactly as given. He should not attempt to interpret the answers on the application, as that is the job of the home office underwriter.

FUNCTION OF THE HOME OFFICE UNDERWRITER

There appears to be a natural tendency for those in good health to delay purchasing health insurance and for those already impaired or in poor health to attempt to obtain it. The function of the home office underwriter or risk appraiser is to counter this tendency to select against the company. To achieve this result, the lines of communication between the field and home office underwriters should always be open for cooperative two-way messages, either written or verbal.

There are several final courses of action which may be taken by the home office underwriter with respect to an application for insurance. He may approve the coverage for issuance as applied for, offer the coverage with an increase in premium, offer the coverage with an impairment waiver, modify the coverage or plan applied for, or make a decision that a policy cannot be issued at all.

From the various sources available to him, the home office underwriter collects the information he needs to evaluate the factors affecting selection. The sources of information and the factors affecting selection are essentially the same as those involved in life insurance. The factors which affect mortality also affect morbidity, but in varying degrees. As a result, certain sources of information are not utilized in health underwriting to the same extent as in underwriting life insurance.

Risk selection in health insurance is complicated because of the inadequacy of morbidity data. The paucity of reliable morbidity information often results in the judgment factor in underwriting assuming a major role. Also, risk selection in health insurance is somewhat different than in life insurance because of the greater uncertainties of frequency and amount of health insurance benefit payments.

The home office underwriter develops a skill in evaluating the possible morbidity experience to be expected. He learns to analyze the various factors in order to develop, as it were, a word picture of the proposed insured.

With plans which are renewable at the option of the company, the home office underwriter may again have an opportunity to review the risk in the light of later developments concerning the insured's medical history or physical condition. The underwriter thus can evaluate the insured's continued insurability for coverage under his policy.

SELECTION FACTORS

The principal selection factors in individual health insurance include age, occupation, income and finances, build, family history, personal medical history and physical condition, habits, moral hazard, environment, and other insurance holdings. Each of these factors will be analyzed briefly.

Age

The relationship between age and morbidity is not as clearly defined for most health insurance coverages as is the relationship between age and mortality in life insurance. Nevertheless, morbidity does increase with advancing age. Companies provide for this increase in benefit payments with advancing age by charging premiums which increase with age.

In the case of guaranteed renewable and noncancellable forms, rates generally are shown for each age. On policies which are renewable at the option of the insurer, rates are usually given for five-year age group brackets. However, some companies show rates for each age above age 35 for policies which are renewable at the option of the insurer.

With increasing age the average individual experiences the degenerative disabilities usually associated with older ages, as well as a lengthening of the period of time required for recuperation. These factors are recognized by higher premium rates and, in many cases, more limited benefits. From an underwriting point of view, a longer and more varied history of disabilities is to be anticipated with increasing age, and more careful investigation is required to classify the applicant properly.

Just as there are relatively fewer deaths in the younger age groups, sickness is less frequent at the younger ages than at the older ages. On the other hand, persons in some of the younger age groups show a higher incidence of accidents than almost any other cause of disability; automobile accidents in particular take a heavy toll.

Age also is an important factor in many of the other risk selection factors which are discussed in this chapter.

Occupation

Health insurance plans providing benefits for accidental injuries and providing twenty-four-hour coverage, or so-called "on-the-job" coverage, are rated according to the insured's occupation. The reason for this is twofold: the hazards of accident and sickness imposed by the nature of the occupation, and the varying periods of absence from the occupation due to disability that can be expected.

Fine lines of occupational classifications are involved, ranging from sedentary office workers to underground miners. Those whose duties are primarily limited to office work, for example, would not ordinarily be prevented from performing their duties by a relatively minor injury, such as an injured hand. Yet this same injury could result in a period of total disability for one whose normal duties required the use of both hands, such as an assembler of appliances. Individuals in both these occupations could perhaps continue at least a portion of their duties with a back sprain which would completely disable a worker whose duties require handling, lifting, or carrying heavy objects, or operating heavy equipment such as bulldozers. A school teacher or an office worker could continue to carry on most of the important duties of his occupation even though he might be required to walk on crutches, or to carry an arm in a sling. However, a surgeon would be totally disabled if he were to have a hand bandaged due to even a relatively minor injury. A minister or a lecturer would be disabled if he had a continuing throat ailment affecting his ability to speak.

Health conditions and safety measures in industry have improved materially in recent years, but there are some occupational classifications which still must be considered to involve a health hazard. Occupations in flour mills, quarries, or chemical plants, where there is danger of inhaling dust or fumes, require special recognition in setting rates for occupational classification. Also, where health insurance policies providing benefits for loss of time are involved, the permanence, stability, and regularity of the employment are important considerations.

In selecting risks, the home office underwriter must recognize these occupational hazards and determine the proper occupational classification in each case. Usually, companies have occupational listings for the guidance of their underwriters, and the most general practice is to classify the individual according to his most hazardous daily duty.

The most common occupational classification listings today are AAA, AA, A, B, and C.

Class AAA: Includes the least hazardous occupations involving clerical and office duties, and a certain number of office occupations involving relatively light duties and no obvious hazards (environment or accident).

Class AA: Includes occupations involving more than office duties and a minimum risk of occupational injury, together with certain occupations in which disability is of more than average frequency or duration.

Class A: Includes occupations involving light manual labor and/or use of light machinery, entailing a slight risk of occupational injury. Working conditions must be favorable with no exposure to heavy machinery, dust, extreme temperature, high voltage, harmful chemicals, and the like.

Class B: Includes occupations involving heavy manual labor and/or use of heavy machinery, with considerable exposure to occupational injury, as well as occupations in which environment presents a hazard.

Class C: Includes those engaged in unusually hazardous occupations.

There are only a few extrahazardous duties that are not insurable because of the applicant's occupation. Hazardous avocations and sports activities also are deserving of close scrutiny in the selection of risks.

Income and Finances

The applicant's financial picture in selecting health insurance risks is regarded somewhat differently from risk selection in life insurance. In life insurance, the economic value of the individual's future earnings is a guidepost in selection. In health insurance, the earned income to be replaced by disability income coverage is the criterion to be used.

When other disability income coverage is owned, the dangers of overinsurance should be considered. There should be adequate incentive for the insured to return to work, to discourage malingering.

Other factors which determine the amount of disability income to be issued are the fact that a certain part of the employee's salary is withheld to pay taxes, and that, during employment, he has certain work expenses that are not present during disability. By establishing an underwriting limit of disability insurance which will be issued as a percentage of the applicant's earned income, and also establishing a flat amount as the top limit, all of these conditions can be properly recognized.

Companies formerly used a graded scale of percentages starting at about 80 per cent of incomes under $2,000 and grading this down to around 50 per cent for incomes above $6,000. The more popular and current formula, which is quite generally followed, is to insure for 50 per cent of the earned income plus $50. For example, if an individual's salary is $800 per month, the maximum coverage he could apply for and receive would be $450 of monthly indemnity, or, in other words, 50 per cent of his income plus $50.

The maximum amount of coverage usually issued by any one company ranges from $600 to $1,000 per month, regardless of the applicant's income. However, most companies will permit a separate, somewhat higher maximum of insurance to be in force in all companies; this generally runs from $800 to $1,500 per month. Income from rents or investments that would continue regardless of the health of the insured should not be considered in establishing the total coverage limit in all companies.

In considering risks for hospital and medical expense coverage, the applicant's financial status serves as the home office underwriter's index to the type of accommodations that individual might require in the event of hospitalization, surgery, or other medical attention. Most current contracts providing benefits for hospital and medical expenses limit benefits payable to the actual expenses incurred.

Build

The applicant's build is a primary factor in the numerical system of underwriting for life insurance. While the numerical system is not so readily applicable to selection of risks for health insurance, the home office underwriter recognizes the possible effect that build will have on morbidity.

Overweight contributes to abnormal morbidity experience. It may affect the length of time for recovery from ailments and the propensity of the applicant for certain ailments. The saying of our grandfathers that it takes "a lean horse to run a long race" is not an old wives' tale insofar as man is concerned. For example, individuals who are overweight are more prone to the development of diabetes and hypertensive cardiovascular disease in all its manifestations. Also, the individual with a normal or somewhat undernormal build generally tends to combat respiratory infection and acute infectious diseases much better than does the overweight individual.

In years gone by, it was believed that the underweight individual was more prone to the development of tuberculosis, but time and observation have proved this to be a fallacy. Marked underweight, however, must be considered in risk selection. Most underwriters have "build tables" from which they can determine limits of acceptability.

Family History

In the selection of risks for life insurance, the longevity of the applicant's family may be considered as a guide to the applicant's longevity. In considering risks for health insurance, however, family history is taken into account only in those situations where heredity plays a part.

Histories of family susceptibility to certain disorders, such as coronary artery disease or hypertensive cardiovascular disease in parents or siblings, should be looked at with apprehension. While diabetes is not hereditary, there does seem to be a tendency for the disease to be transmitted from the maternal side. There does not seem to be any particular significance when there is a history of malignancy in the parents or siblings of the applicant. It is questionable whether or not there is any particular significance to a history of nervous disorders in the applicant's family.

In general, it may be said that family history does not play an important part in underwriting health insurance.

Personal Medical History and Physical Condition

The fact that the major portion of most health insurance applications is devoted to the medical history and physical condition of the applicant attests to the importance of these factors in risk selection. Satisfactory morbidity experience depends mostly on the tendency toward recurrence of past disorders, as well as on the likelihood of hospitalization, medical treatment, or disability as a result of the present physical condition of the applicant.

Many disabilities which have little or no effect on mortality, even when there is a high ratio of recurrence, require careful classification of the applicant for health insurance, or may even disqualify him for health insurance. For example, histories of hay fever, hernia, tonsillitis, hemorrhoids, and allergies affect the underwriting of health insurance, while standard life insurance usually is offered in cases with such histories.

Other impairments, such as diabetes and epilepsy, may lend themselves to offers of substandard life insurance but prevent offers of health insurance coverage because of the extent to which they aggravate and complicate other relatively minor disabilities. The underwriter must also determine whether a given impairment in the medical history might recur or serve as a basis for related disabilities or impairments.

Personal medical history is one of the most difficult factors about which to obtain complete information. The field underwriter should develop skill in questioning the applicant concerning past medical treatment and illnesses.

The home office underwriter must seek the assistance of the medical director in developing his knowledge of those conditions which are of a recurrent nature. The flexibility of the health insurance contract and the use of impairment waivers enable the home office underwriter to provide insurance protection in many cases where the client has a history of a condition which may cause a disability or other loss in the future.

Since the majority of health insurance applications are considered without requiring a medical examination of the applicant, the home office underwriter does not get as complete a picture of the physical condition of the applicant as does the underwriter in the selection of life risks who has the benefit of a medical examiner's report. Therefore, the application is the most useful tool in health insurance underwriting for developing this information.

Physical condition refers not only to any deformity or crippling condition of the applicant, but also to any health abnormality existing at the time of the application, as opposed to a history of illness or injuries.

Conditions such as epilepsy, impaired hearing or eyesight, or other central nervous system impairments increase the probability of accidental injuries, since these disabilities affect co-ordination and reflex actions. Other conditions, such as diabetes, frequently turn a minor injury into a serious disability. It can be seen, therefore, that poor health may cause or intensify an injury and also may cause a much longer period of disability than would otherwise have existed.

Additionally, some physical impairments lend themselves to malingering for those individuals who are so disposed. Perhaps the most obvious disability of this type is the back sprain or strain, which not only is easy to suffer by those so inclined, but also is difficult to disprove.

Habits

Addiction to drugs or excessive use of alcohol not only contributes to degeneration of health but also may be a contributory cause of accidental injuries. Not infrequently, those individuals whose character or reputation is questioned because of either of these habits present moral hazards as well. Therefore, caution must be used in accepting any of these risks even for substandard health insurance.

Applications for health insurance frequently contain questions about the applicant's habits. An answer indicating questionable habits requires further investigation. Usually, however, this information comes from an inspection report. With all information available, the underwriter must determine if standard rates can apply in these cases.

Moral Hazard

A health insurance authority, in commenting on moral hazard, says: "No single factor equals it in importance in determining the acceptability of a risk and in no insurance line can underwriting results be affected more adversely and unfairly than in health insurance."[1] Unfortunately, indications of such a hazard may not be readily apparent or easily discovered. If it appears at all, it may present itself in the form of criticism of personal reputation.

Moral hazards range from falsification or withholding of important information, exaggeration of disabilities, and general lack of integrity to illegal activities or association with criminal elements. Because the facts are often so nebulous and hard to ascertain, moral hazard is one of the most difficult factors to underwrite.

Malingering is a form of moral hazard in health insurance that the home office underwriter must constantly consider. It is extremely difficult for a doctor to know when his patient actually suffers pain other than when the patient tells him that he has a pain. A headache is something that cannot be seen; it is felt only by the person who suffers from it. A disability suffered by one person may not keep him from carrying on his daily duties, whereas another person might be totally disabled with the same symptoms. Malingering by not returning to work when disability has ended, or by staying in the hospital an extra day following recovery from surgery, is a moral hazard which increases claims costs and affects the experience of any group of risks.

When moral hazard is present, there is danger of poor experience not only as a direct result of the hazard but also indirectly because of the attitude such an individual has toward the conventions of society. Misrepresentation and dishonesty can be expected in such cases.

Environment

Environment refers to the daily surroundings of the applicant. Are they conducive to good health and well-being, or do they present a problem that could bring on nervous disorders, worry, or even poor health? Is the applicant obliged to associate with persons not in good health or who suffer from contagious diseases? Does he have proper sleeping accommodations, or are there crowded and unsanitary conditions in the home? Does the home environment indicate that hospitalization would be necessary for the treatment of a minor condition? Is he living in an area that is improperly ventilated or damp? These are factors that should be considered in determining the acceptability of the risk for insurance.

Although environment often is assumed to refer only to the immediate living conditions of the applicant, it also includes a much wider area. For example, certain occupations, because of their nature, such as pool hall attendants or tavern employees, could place the applicant in a bad environment if they are conducive to the carrying-on of illegal or questionable operations.

[1] Edwin J. Faulkner, *Health Insurance* (New York: McGraw-Hill Book Co., Inc., 1960), p. 327.

Other Insurance (Overinsurance)

The type and amount of other coverage owned by the applicant is an important factor in underwriting health insurance. The problem of overinsurance, which, for example, may be created by issuing disability income benefits in excess of usually accepted underwriting limits, not infrequently creates a moral hazard. In addition, reimbursement from two or more contracts providing duplicate medical expense benefits will result in a profit to the insured if the sum reimbursed by insurance exceeds the actual charges incurred by the insured.

Because it is important to guard against overinsurance, it is vital for successful risk selection to have full knowledge of all existing health insurance policies on the applicant, including information on the amounts and types of benefits.

Most applications ask about other health insurance owned by the applicant, and this is another point where the field underwriter can be most helpful in getting complete data. If an applicant owns a sufficient amount of hospital benefits to provide him with daily accommodations in the hospital in his area, any additional amount of hospital coverage might provide him with an incentive to malinger or to abuse the benefits provided in the policy. When an individual is insured for too large a percentage of his earned income, his desire to return to work in the event of a disability may be lessened. This causes unfavorable claims experience which not only is bad for the company but also may work a hardship on other policyowners to the extent that the company might find it necessary to increase rates on policies in certain classes where this is permitted by the policy terms.

Many employers today provide certain sick leave pay for their employees, so many individuals will not suffer a loss of income during the early days of a disability. A policy with a seven-day elimination or waiting period can be owned for a lower premium than one providing first-day coverage. Therefore, if sick pay is continued by the employer for 15 or 30 days or longer, savings in premium can be passed along to those policyholders who purchase insurance to provide benefits beginning with the sixteenth or thirty-first day, or even a later day of disability. This fitting of the plan to the applicant's needs allows the applicant to use the premium savings for the purchase of more adequate or broader health insurance protection, or to provide additional life insurance or other needed coverages.

SOURCES OF INFORMATION

Application

There is little doubt that the application is the most important source of underwriting information in individual health insurance. In many instances the application is the only document completed and provides the only evidence of insurability considered. As a result, it is very important that the field underwriter obtain complete answers to all questions on the application. When properly and fully completed, the application provides the home office underwriter with a word portrait of the applicant.

The applicant is usually asked when he was last attended by a physician, the nature of the illness, the duration of the illness, and whether or not he has recovered without any residuals of the illness. The name and address of the attending physician are usually requested. Many applications ask for reports on all illnesses or injuries suffered during the last five years and also may ask for the name of the personal or family physician.

There are questions on the application about any history of disease of the heart, lungs, kidneys, high or low blood pressure, rheumatism, and many of the other diseases which are quite common.

The occupation and duties of the applicant are stated on the application. A statement of any other insurance owned by the applicant also is included. Another usual question is whether or not the applicant has ever been declined, postponed, cancelled, or offered a modified policy by another insurance company.

With the continued increase in hours of leisure time enjoyed by so many individuals, a recent trend has been to inquire into any activities of the applicant in hazardous avocations or sports.

These queries on the application help to develop that information which the underwriter must have to consider all the factors of insurability. It is the home office underwriter's responsibility to determine if additional information, such as an attending physician's report, a medical examination, or an inspection report, is needed.

Attending Physician's Statement

The attending physician's statement also plays an important part in risk selection. Without it, there is no doubt that some people would obtain health insurance without being eligible for it according to the insurer's underwriting standards. Others who are eligible might be deprived of coverage on suspicion of medical problems.

The applicant's personal physician has a more intimate knowledge of his medical history than can be obtained from any other source. Without the benefit of these attending doctors' reports, it is doubtful if satisfactory morbidity experience could be obtained. For example, attending physicians' statements regarding "routine checkups" are particularly revealing. Unfortunately, some applicants report an illness for which they have received medical treatment as a "physical checkup." Also, when an individual is attended by a physician, he does not always learn the exact nature of his disability, or his lack of understanding of medical terms may prevent him from repeating accurately what the doctor told him. The attending physician's statement usually will reveal the true nature of the applicant's condition in these cases.

If the applicant indicates a history of past medical treatment, he is asked to give the name of the physician who has the medical records and to give his signed permission for the physician to give the insurer information from these records. Reports thus obtained describe the illness, its significance, its treatment and prognosis, and verify and supplement the health history statements made by the applicant.

Most underwriters use uniform attending physicians' blanks prepared through the co-operation of the medical profession and the insurance industry. Such a blank provides the doctor with space for giving a record of his treatments of the applicant for the period during which the individual was his patient.

Medical Examination

As stated previously, most health insurance policies are written on a nonmedical basis. However, medical examinations are frequently obtained in cases originally submitted on a nonmedical basis in order to obtain a direct check on the current condition of a reported impairment.

It is common practice to obtain a medical examiner's report when policies providing long-term disability income benefits for sickness are applied for, or if the plan of insurance is noncancellable or guaranteed renewable and disability income benefits for sickness extend for longer than two years. Some companies require medical examinations for all health insurance plans if the amount of monthly indemnity exceeds $200 and if the applicant is over a certain age, such as 45.

The home office underwriter usually reserves the right to ask that an applicant be examined in any case where it is believed that a medical examination would assist in determining the individual's eligibility for the coverage applied for.

Inspection Reports

Inspection reports generally are ordered when the amount of monthly disability income benefits exceeds $200 per month, or when the principal sum exceeds $5,000, and usually in connection with guaranteed renewable and noncancellable plans. These reports also are obtained whenever there is a possibility of improper conduct by the applicant or excessive use of alcohol or drugs. They are of great benefit in supplying details of occupational duties. In addition, data on the applicant's medical history and physical condition which were not given on the application quite often are developed. The applicant's reported income on applications for disability income coverage may or may not be confirmed, and the report may disclose an unusual number of applications in other companies, indicating possible speculation.

Inspection reports are provided by organizations whose business is to make investigations and credit reports. The ordinary inspection report covers such items as finances, health, general reputation, habits, morals, and community standing.

Investigation by these commercial reporting agencies provides an impersonal compilation of the impressions of friends, neighbors, and business associates about the applicant. If there is any criticism of habits or morals, it normally is obtained from this source. As a third-party investigation, it is assumed to be a reliable cross check of the applicant.

SUBSTANDARD HEALTH INSURANCE

The development of the writing of individual health insurance on substandard risks has not kept pace with substandard underwriting in life insurance due to a dearth of morbidity statistics. In connection with life insurance selection, the home office underwriter has the benefit of the results of mortality studies developed through medico-actuarial investigations and study. These results provide information about the possible effect of certain medical histories on mortality. By means of rating tables developed from these studies, the home office underwriter can readily determine the extra mortality to be expected in a group of risks having certain medical histories. He then can indicate in his approval of the risk the table rating necessary to increase the mortality factor in the premium sufficiently to enable the company to provide insurance coverage for the applicant.

In health insurance, however, where certain medical histories or physical impairments exist, the home office underwriter generally must use impairment waivers if the risk is to be accepted. For example, an individual with a history of rheumatism would receive a policy in which there is an endorsement that the policy will not provide any benefits if the individual suffers a loss caused by or contributed to by rheumatism or arthritis. Such a waiver generally covers broad conditions or areas of coverage; therefore, if more than one unrelated condition is involved, the case usually is declined because the use of more than one waiver would strip the policy of its intended purpose of providing needed coverage.

However, in considering the practices of writing business on a substandard basis, it should be pointed out that substandard insurance can take many forms in the health insurance business other than the use of impairment waivers. For example, a policy may be offered on a different basis from that originally applied for in certain cases. An individual who has a condition that might cause him to have numerous small claims could be offered insurance with benefits beginning with the eighth, sixteenth, or thirtieth day of disability. This would provide insurance that otherwise could not be issued if the policy were to have first-day coverage. It also follows that in those cases where the condition is one that might cause a long period of disability, the maximum duration of benefits under the policy could be limited to, say, twelve months or even less.

More recently, companies have experimented with various plans for providing full coverage to many substandard risks by using practices similar to those applied in substandard life insurance. One of the plans used is to state in the policy that an extra premium is charged because of a qualified condition. Also, it would be provided that benefits will not be paid for disability caused by the qualified condition for a stated period. A qualified condition, for example, might be a heart and circulatory disorder. After the policy has been in force for the stated period, benefits would be paid if disability occurs thereafter due to the qualified condition. In addition, the duration of coverage for the qualified condition might be limited to from one- to six-month periods of disability during the lifetime of the contract. Coverage of all other conditions would, of course, be on a standard basis. In this way, a risk who otherwise would be declined can have protection against everything, including the impaired condition (after the stated period).

However, the basic life insurance approach to substandard insurance, that of increasing the premium by a sufficient amount to enable the company to offer the applicant full coverage, is becoming the most popular method.

Some conditions themselves create an extra hazard over and above the fact that they are of a recurrent nature. In these cases, it is still necessary to charge an extra morbidity premium as well as to issue the policy with an impairment waiver. For example, with a history of severe neuritis or repeated attacks of stomach ulcers, there is a great chance of frequent recurrence and a possibility that a longer convalescence period for other conditions might result, this longer period being contributed to by the waivered condition. To cover this possibility, an extra premium charge as well as the impairment waiver is necessary.

Conditions which may involve elective surgery, such as hernia, appendicitis, tonsillitis, and several others, in which the corrective surgery can be postponed until coverage is arranged for, are still written only with an impairment waiver. If extra premiums were to be charged for such risks, they would have to be equal to the benefit provided by the policy.

This experimentation with substandard underwriting in health insurance has accomplished two things. First, it has enabled the companies to reduce dramatically the number of risks to whom it was necessary to decline to issue coverage. And second, it has resulted in providing full coverage in other cases formerly necessitating the eliminating of coverage for an impairment by means of a waiver. Also, standard nomenclature has been developed as a basis for morbidity studies should the companies decide to pool their information and the results of their experimentation.

It will be many years, however, before any of these studies can have a meaningful value to the home office underwriter. Today, educated guesses are still necessary in many cases to determine the amount of extra morbidity involved in order to fulfill the obligation to try to provide insurance when at all possible.

SELECTED REFERENCES

CASEY, WILLIAM J. *Health Insurance Desk Book,* Sec. XXIII. New York: Institute for Business Planning, Inc., 1962.

FAULKNER, EDWIN J. *Health Insurance.* New York: McGraw-Hill Book Co., Inc., 1960.

HEALTH INSURANCE ASSOCIATION OF AMERICA. *Compendium on Risk Selection for Individual and Family Accident and Health Insurance.* New York, 1959.

MACDONALD, ROY A. *The Underwriting of Substandard Accident and Health Insurance.* Cincinnati: National Underwriter Co., 1951.

MILLER, STANFORD, and BROWN, ROBERT D. *Health Insurance Underwriting.* Chicago: Eastern Underwriter Co., 1962.

SOCIETY OF ACTUARIES. *Health Insurance Provided through Individual Policies,* ch. iv, "Underwriting." Chicago, 1963.

TILTON, EARLE B., and YOCHEM, DONALD E. *A Guide to Health Insurance Underwriting.* Indianapolis: Research & Review Service of America, Inc., 1961.

Chapter 27

IMPORTANT LEGAL CONCEPTS AND CONTRACT PROVISIONS

BY JOHN F. McALEVEY

A distinguishing feature of health insurance is its great diversity of contract forms. In part, this diversity reflects the multiplicity of insuring organizations providing coverage. Health insurance is a highly competitive field and the coverage is written by all types of insurers, including life insurance companies, specialty health insurance companies, and casualty insurance companies.

It is impossible to generalize about many areas of the health insurance business, and this is no less true of the contract. There are few "standard" practices in the business. The health insurance operations of life companies and casualty companies are often vastly different, reflecting the manner in which the company conducts its other lines of business. Similarly, the monoline or specialty health insurers have yet other methods of operation. Among the various companies, there are also widely varying concepts of the business or social function to be performed by health insurance. All of these variables reflect themselves in the policy, the type of application, and the company attitude about common problems of operation.

This chapter is concerned with the general legal principles involved and the more significant policy contract provisions of individual and family insurance contracts issued by private insurance companies.

Contract Principles Applicable

The contract of individual or family health insurance is a legal document subject to the usual law of contracts, except as modified in the case of insurance contracts generally. Most of the elements of contract law, including those relating to offer and acceptance, consideration, mutuality, and capacity to contract, are fully applicable. Also, many of the basic legal concepts applicable to individual life insurance contracts are fully applicable to individual health insurance contracts.[1]

Formation of Contract

When health insurance was concerned primarily with accident coverage and was written chiefly by casualty insurance companies, the making of an oral application and the issuance of the policy by the field agent or branch office was commonplace. Today the only categories of individually purchased health insurance marketed in this fashion are statistically inconsequential limited policies and travel accident policies.

Most health insurance is written today only after the forwarding by the agent of a written and signed application to the home office of the insurer, where it is subjected to varying degrees of underwriting, depending on the type of contract and the amount of insurance applied for. For economic reasons, most underwriting, especially on hospital, surgical, and medical contracts, is done almost entirely on the basis of the written application.

As in life insurance, the agents do not have the authority to bind the company. Many applications used in health insurance are unique in that the portion of the form which indicates the type of insurance applied for, the amount of the policy, and the other details of the policy, is not considered to be a part of the application as this term is used in the policy and statutes. It has long been the practice with many companies for this information to be entered by the agent in a separate space so that it does not appear over the applicant's signature. Thus, the health insurance application is primarily a health questionnaire designed to elicit the basic underwriting information.

The insurance laws provide that a copy of the application must be attached to or reproduced on the policy form as it is issued if the application is to become a part of the contract. If the application is not included, the insurer will be precluded from using any misstatement therein as the basis for resisting a claim or voiding the contract at any future time. This is true even if the misrepresentation or misstatement was material and was discovered before the expiration of the "time limit on certain defenses" provision or the "incontestable" provision, as the case may be.

This seemingly hard doctrine is not designed to protect the fraudulent, as may appear at first glance, but to insure accuracy in the completion of the application. The insurer can preserve its rights by the simple expedient of attaching a copy of the application to the policy. This, in turn, provides the insured with a copy of the statements and representations

---

[1] See Chapter 16 for discussion of basic legal concepts as applied to individual life insurance, and Chapter 15 for important contract provisions in individual life insurance.

exactly as relied on by the insurer. If the agent, who usually fills out the application in conjunction with the prospective insured, did not enter the information accurately, the insured has a second and better opportunity to discover this when the policy arrives. The temptation to either the agent or the prospect to falsify the information contained on the application is thus substantially reduced.

The tender of the application and the first premium, or part thereof, is an offer on the part of the prospective insured to contract. The issuance of the contract initially sought is an acceptance of the applicant's offer by the insurer. On the other hand, the issuance of a modified contract, such as for a modified benefit or amount, for example, constitutes a counteroffer by the insurer. This counteroffer then may be accepted by the applicant.

The written application is, therefore, the first step in the effectuation of a contract, and it later becomes an integral part of the contract by reason of the physical attachment of a copy of the application to the contract.

POLICY CONTRACT

The Insuring Clause

A critical paragraph of every insurance contract is the insuring clause. In health insurance, this clause almost invariably will define the risk as *loss* as a result of accident or sickness. The mere occurrence of an accident or sickness since the date of issuance of the policy is not enough. A loss must occur. It also must occur in the manner specified, i.e., it must be an accidental bodily injury or a sickness contracted after the probationary period, and must occur within the policy period. Quite often, some of the more important limitations on the coverage also are set forth in the insuring clause.

The Benefit Clause

The paragraphs listing the benefits payable usually follow the insuring clause. As recently as twenty years ago, the health insurance business was conducted largely with prepackaged benefit policies. Today, however, the schedule type of policy is very common.[2] This type of policy provides a method for writing different benefit levels and different benefit combinations with one policy form. This is accomplished by listing all the available coverages on the policy form and then indicating which coverages are

[2] A "schedule-type policy" in this sense should be distinguished from a "surgical schedule." The latter is a list of surgical procedures giving relative values, according to a base figure, for most of the common types of operations. Surgical schedules will be contained even in contracts with a narrative benefit clause. Since no surgical schedule can list all possible operative procedures, the policy will also provide that unlisted procedures will be recognized on a relative basis.

operative for the particular policy, depending upon the needs and desires of the insured. In this way, the individual or family contract can be tailored to different benefit combinations and benefit levels. The explanation of the contingencies which will adversely affect the payability of each of the benefits, either as to type of loss or as to character or circumstances of the loss, is required to be printed either directly with the benefit clause to which they apply or, if not so printed, they must be set forth under a common caption reading "exceptions and reductions."

Exceptions and Reductions

While exceptions and exclusions from coverage are much less numerous today than formerly, the nature of health insurance is such that if insurers are to fulfill their proper social function, there will always need to be some limitations on coverage. It is a waste of premium money, for example, for the policyholders of a private insurer to allow themselves, in effect, to be taxed twice for the use of a government facility—once as members of the taxpaying public and again as holders of a health insurance policy. For this and other reasons,[3] most health insurance contracts exclude coverage for hospital confinement in government facilities.

Most hospital, medical, and surgical insurance policies also exclude payment for injuries which are covered under workmen's compensation, because of the obvious duplication of benefits.

However, other formerly common exclusions, such as private flying, for example, are now typically used selectively as riders to the contract, as a result of the initial underwriting process, instead of appearing in the printed form of the policy. This permits greater flexibility and selectivity by the insurer. Travel abroad also is not generally an exclusion today, but continued or extended residence abroad may stop the running of benefits under a loss-of-time contract because of the difficulty of determining the continuance of an extended disability.

Pre-existing Conditions

There is no specific exclusion in most individual health insurance contracts for pre-existing conditions, that is, impairments of health which existed at the time the insurance was applied for. The exclusion of such conditions is automatically effected by the language of the insuring clause, which, by providing coverage only for accidents and illnesses occurring after the effective date, does not cover those which occurred before that time.

---

[3] In Veterans Administration hospitals, for example, the period of confinement in most instances is longer than the confinement period for the treatment of the same ailment in a nongovernment hospital.

UNIFORM POLICY PROVISIONS

The law applicable to the drafting and approval of policy provisions for individual health insurance contracts in every state is the Uniform Individual Accident and Sickness Policy Provisions Law,[4] or corresponding legislation. The Uniform Individual Accident and Sickness Policy Provisions Law was recommended to the states by the National Association of Insurance Commissioners in 1950.

While the companies have almost free rein under this statute in drafting the language they will use in the benefit provisions, the insuring clause, and other miscellaneous parts of the contract, the law prescribes certain other provisions which must appear in all contracts of individual health insurance. These are referred to as required or mandatory statutory provisions. The law also specifies certain optional statutory provisions. These optional statutory provisions cover things about which the contract may be silent, but if the subject matter is covered in the policy, the optional provisions prescribe the nature of the policy provisions which can be used.

It should be noted that the 1950 recommendations of the National Association of Insurance Commissioners was for a uniform law. While the provisions prescribed in that law are often referred to as the "uniform provisions" to distinguish them from the old "standard provisions" of the 1912 Standard Provisions Law, this is not an entirely accurate description. The law does contain a certain presumption that the provisions will be used in the words and in the order of the statute, but it also permits a certain flexibility in their use, subject to the approval of the regulatory authority in each state. The statutes uniformly state that companies may "substitute for one or more of such provisions corresponding provisions of different wording approved by the commissioner which are in each instance not less favorable in any respect to the insured or the beneficiary." Even "required" provisions which are inappropriate or inapplicable to the coverage provided may be omitted. There is, however, considerable uniformity in the use of these "uniform provisions."

The basic purpose of these "uniform provisions" is to minimize the opportunity for denial of claims or avoidance of the policy by the insurer through the use of unreasonable, arbitrary, or restrictive procedural policy provisions.

Required Statutory Provisions[5]

The *entire contract* provision provides that the policy and its attached papers constitute the entire contract. No changes can be made in the

[4] See Appendix H.

[5] Not all of the uniform provisions will be mentioned here because some are so plainly and explicitly written as to require no comment, e.g., the "legal actions" and "unpaid premiums" provisions. All are contained in full in Appendix H.

contractual relationship unless they are appropriately endorsed on or attached to the contract. No agent can change or modify the contract. The legal consequences noted above of the attachment, or nonattachment, of a copy of the application are here given legal effect in the contract itself. Note, however, the apparent exception governing applications for reinstatement, as described later.

The *time limit on certain defenses* provision is divided into two paragraphs, (*a*) and (*b*). The (*a*) paragraph is given in two versions. The required minimum version of paragraph (*a*) places a three-year limitation on the right of the company to contest a claim or attempt to void the policy because of any misstatements, "except fraudulent misstatements," in the application.

The second or alternative version of paragraph (*a*), captioned "incontestable," makes no reference to fraud after the three-year period, and is restricted in use to noncancellable and guaranteed renewable, or guaranteed renewable, contracts. Superficially, an incontestable provision would seem to provide greater protection to the insured than a simple "time limit on certain defenses" provision and hence to qualify for use as "different language . . . not less favorable." To allow the word "incontestable" to be featured in a contract which is not guaranteed renewable for a period of years, however, might create an illusion of protection which did not exist; hence, it is prohibited.

Many persons do not see too much practical difference in the two versions because they regard the burden of proof in the case of a fraudulent misstatement (the only defense which survives the three-year limit in the first version) to be so high as to be impracticable. An offset to preserving this as a possible future defense in the first version is the extending of the expiration of the contestable period under the "incontestable" version by any length of time during which the insured was disabled during that period.

Part (*b*) of the "time limit on certain defenses" provision cuts off the general defense of pre-existing condition. After the running of the three-year period, any condition, unless specifically excluded by name or specific description, is conclusively presumed not to have been pre-existing.

In a number of states the statutory time period in one or both paragraphs of this provision is two years instead of the originally recommended three years. Almost all companies have now adopted two years as their contract norm, regardless of the availability of the three-year period.

Part (*b*) is sometimes omitted from accident-only contracts on the ground of nonapplicability. This modification has been approved by some insurance departments and opposed by others.

A *grace period* of from seven to thirty-one days is provided in all contracts. As in life insurance, the coverage continues in force through the grace period; hence, it constitutes, as to the individual, free insurance for the additional period, although any claim paid because of an occurrence during the grace period usually will result in the premium being paid as a deduction from the claim.

The grace period is inoperative, however, if the insurer has taken nonrenewal action and has given written notice of nonrenewal within the requisite period of time before the premium due date.

The statutory *reinstatement* provision provides that reinstatement shall be accomplished automatically if the insurer accepts a late premium without requiring an application for reinstatement. If an application is required, then the procedure is similar to an original application and may be subjected to a reunderwriting, including the attachment of a waiver or impairment rider as a condition of reinstatement. Accidents which occurred during the period of lapse, or sickness beginning less than ten days after reinstatement, are excluded as pre-existing.

Whether the "time limit on certain defenses" provision runs anew as to the statements in an application for reinstatement is an open question. The Uniform Law is silent. Unlike the situation in life insurance, there is no *right* to reinstatement in health insurance. Nor does the company need to reinstate at the same benefit level or on the same terms as originally. Hence the analogy to a new contract is strong.

The "entire contract" provision notwithstanding, the insurer is not required to attach to the policy a copy of the application form used in the request for reinstatement. Yet the statute is clear that for some (unspecified) time the statements in the application for reinstatement can be used to contest a claim. Section 5 of the Uniform Law acknowledges this by providing that the insurer, upon receipt of a written request therefor from the insured, his beneficiary, or assigns, must supply a copy of the reinstatement application within fifteen days. If the insurer does not comply, it loses its right thereafter to utilize the application for reinstatement in any legal action based on the contract or its renewal. The better and more prevalent view is that the same two- or three-year period as is provided in the case of the original application should govern the contestability of the reinstatement application.

The *notice-of-claim* provision requires the insured to give the insurer notice of a claim within twenty days of the occurrence or commencement of the loss; but the time is not inflexible—the notice may be "as soon thereafter as is reasonably possible." In the loss-of-time contracts, the insurer also may require a continuing notice of disability every six months during a claim which may run for two years or more.

The *claim forms* provision states that upon receipt of a notice of claim, the insurer must co-operate by promptly supplying the forms on which the proof of loss is to be submitted. If the insurer should neglect to do this, the insured has the right to make a submission of the requisite proof in any form he chooses.

Proof-of-loss forms are required to be returned within ninety days; but again, a rule of reason is applied. Lateness can be excused on reasonable grounds, although the insurer need not accept any proof later than one year from the date it was first required.

The *time of payment of claims* provision requires the insurer to pay other than periodic benefits "immediately" in one lump sum. Periodic benefits are required to be paid at least monthly.

Under the *payment-of-claims* provision the insurer is required to respect beneficiary designations on death benefits. In the absence of a designation, the amounts are payable to the insured's estate. Optionally, the insurer may include in the contract either or both of two additional facility of payment clauses permitting payment of up to $1,000 to any relative by blood or marriage, and the payment of hospital, surgical, or medical benefits directly to the providers of care. This latter provision allows such a payment to be validly made even without an assignment from the insured, although the insured can block a direct payment to the providers of care by filing a written statement of instruction not to do so.

A *physical examinations and autopsy* provision provides the insurer with reasonable examination rights to the insured's person, alive or dead, although autopsy is not permitted to insurance companies in some states.[6]

The contract is required to contain a *change-of-beneficiary* provision to make clear the insurer's requirements. The uniform language provides that an irrevocable designation of beneficiary may be made, but this language is optional, and an insurer may choose not to permit irrevocable designations. As in life insurance, if it is not irrevocable, the designation can be changed by the policyholder at any time without the named beneficiary's knowledge or consent.

Optional Statutory Provisions

Change of occupation is the first of the optional statutory provisions. Its principal use is in loss-of-time contracts, but it is illustrative of the careful allowance which must be made for the many variable factors in most health insurance coverages. The premium rates for loss-of-time contracts are usually based on an occupation classification manual which grades employments by the degree of hazard involved. Under this provision, if the insured switches to a more hazardous occupation after the contract is written, his benefit level will be reduced in the event of a loss to the amount of insurance which the premium paid would have purchased if his new occupation had been stated. If, however, he has moved in the other direction on the occupational classification scale, no more than the policy amount will be paid, but the unearned premium, represented by the difference between the premium actually paid and the

---

[6] Massachusetts, Mississippi, Oklahoma, and South Carolina.

reduced rate which would have been paid if the company had been advised of the new occupation, will be refunded to the insured.

Misstatement of age operates in a fashion similar to the change-of-occupation provision and for the same purpose. It requires that the insured's correct age be related to the premium paid and that the benefits be adjusted accordingly. Neither the company nor the policyholder can profit from a misstatement.

Other Insurance and Overinsurance Provisions

Highly significant optional statutory provisions pertain to other insurance and overinsurance. The 1950 Uniform Individual Accident and Sickness Policy Provisions Law, as presently on the statute books of most states, contains four optional provisions which were intended to provide insurers with protection against overinsurance as a result of multiple contracts owned by the same insured. For a number of reasons, these provisions failed of their purpose and fell into disuse almost immediately. The provisions include one captioned "other insurance in this insurer," two captioned "insurance with other insurers," and one captioned "relation of earnings to insurance."

The *other insurance in this insurer* provision addressed itself to a problem which, for the most part, can be controlled by underwriting. An exception is where the company is engaged in writing limited or machine-issued types of contracts or is attempting to service a marginal market through mass-enrollment techniques which do not permit individual underwriting. An example of the first instance is aviation trip insurance. An example of the second would be the various company experiments in extending health insurance coverage to the aged.

The *insurance with other insurers* provisions in their present form have failed to meet their purpose for either the optionally renewable or the noncancellable types of insurance. In the optionally renewable type of coverage the insurer (and the agent of the insurer) with such a provision in the policy would be at a serious competitive disadvantage compared with an insurer whose contract did not reduce or prorate benefits because of other insurance. In noncancellable or guaranteed renewable policies, if the first insurer were given notice of other insurance once its contract was issued, the first insurer could neither terminate its own contract nor apply proration in the case of other contracts of which it has been given notice. Therefore, the "insurance with other insurers" provisions would not be effective in connection with noncancellable or guaranteed renewable policies.

The *relation of earnings to insurance* provision, which may be used in noncancellable or guaranteed renewable policies, has the defect of allowing full replacement of income without regard to the substantial difference between stated income and take-home pay and the nontaxability of health insurance benefits under the federal tax laws. Since total replacement of income is not desirable as a matter of underwriting policy, this provision is obviously inadequate.

From December, 1959 to December, 1963, the National Association of Insurance Commissioners and the Health Insurance Association of America worked on the problem of devising substitute provisions to cope with the subject of overinsurance. This resulted in the recommendation by the National Association of Insurance Commissioners of three new provisions to replace the previous four.[7]

Each of the new provisions is entitled "overinsurance," and all adaptions of any, or all, of these provisions which subsequently appear in health insurance contracts will bear that caption.

The new provisions are not yet approvable[8] in most states, but an effort to secure the necessary amendments to the 1950 Uniform Individual Accident and Sickness Policy Provisions Law will be made in 1964 and 1965. It is expected that the new provisions will be generally approvable by the latter part of 1965. The business has great hope that, unlike their predecessors, there will be no disadvantage and some advantage to the use of the new provisions and that consequently they will be widely adopted. The rationale behind these, as behind the former provisions, is that no one should be allowed to make a profit out of health insurance. Giving effect to this ideal, however, is not so simple.

The first of the newly recommended provisions constitutes only a minor modification of one of the alternative versions of the present Section 3(*B*)(3) of the Uniform Law. This is to eliminate any ambiguity concerning the applicability of the provision to all policies of similar coverage in the same insurer. As noted previously, most insurers, unless engaged in writing certain specialty business, can control overinsurance in their own companies by underwriting and have little need for the provision in its old or new form.

The new replacement provision for the two present "insurance with other insurers" provisions provides for the proration of benefits with other individual health policies which also contain the new provision. In the event the "other valid coverage" does *not* contain the new provision, however, the new provision makes the policy contract in which it appears excess insurance over the contract or contracts covering the same loss but not containing the new provision. While use of any of the new provisions is optional, it is hoped that the opportunity thus obtained to become excess will overcome the previous reluctance of insurers to use proration provisions.

Further to insure that the operation of the provision can work no

---

[7] The text of the new provisions and related explanatory material from the NAIC proceedings is contained in Appendix I.

[8] As of July, 1964.

hardship because of any narrow definitions of allowable expenses under the several contracts, "allowable expense" is defined as "110 per cent of any necessary, reasonable and customary item of expense which is covered, in whole or in part, . . . under this policy or under any other valid coverage." Provision is also made for recouping overpayments by the insurer if the insured failed at the time of claim to make the proper disclosure of other coverages which would bring the provision into play.

The new *overinsurance* provision for loss-of-time benefits is open (within limits)[9] as to the percentage of "earned income" which the insurer may specify as the limit of its coverage. It also contains language making a contract with the new overinsurance provision excess over any contract or contracts without the provision. The minimum amount below which this or other contracts cannot operate to reduce the loss-of-time benefits payable (if sufficient coverage exists to provide that amount without proration) is raised to $300 from the present $200.

The *cancellation* provision still appears as an optional uniform provision in the insurance codes of most states. For practical purposes, however, it can be discounted today as an object of study. From a formerly common provision, it has been relegated to a position of small importance in little more than a decade. Most health insurance contracts today are limited in the renewal underwriting action which the insurer may take. Cancellation within a term for which a premium has been paid is no longer an accepted practice in the business, and this has been fortified by amendments to the policy provision law in several states[10] expressly providing that cancellation cannot occur during the policy term and that the insurer may retire from a risk only at the policy anniversary date.

Even more restrictive than this is the New York law,[11] which expressly denies to the insurer the right to decline renewal of hospital, surgical, or medical contracts after two years from the date of issue and before the age limit or date or time period of coverage specified on the ground of deterioration of health. The law enumerates several grounds on which termination by the insurer will be permitted, such as fraud, moral hazard, overinsurance, and discontinuance of the type or class of contract.[12]

---

[9] All of the intricacies of the new provisions cannot be developed in the space available in this text. The interested reader is urged to read the full text in Appendix I.

[10] E.g., New Mexico (1953), North Carolina (1955), Ohio (1956), Oklahoma (1955), and South Carolina (1956).

[11] New York Insurance Law, Sec. 164–6.

[12] Other variations on the theme of mandatory noncancellability include the North Carolina statute, which states that the company cannot retire from a risk without giving an extended notice of the intention to cancel, the notice period varying from one month to two years, and a Georgia statute that renewal cannot be declined by the insurer unless it has paid back to the insured in benefits, or tendered, a stated percentage of the amount paid in premiums during the lifetime of the contract.

SUPERIMPOSITIONS ON THE HEALTH INSURANCE CONTRACT

In addition to the language needed to effectuate a legal and unambiguous contract, and the language required of all insurers by the Uniform Policy Provisions Law, other statutory and regulatory additions to the contract are encountered in some states. Limited policies, for example, are required to be so labeled "across the face of the policy and the filing back in contrasting color from the text of the policy and in outline type not smaller than eighteen points" with the words: "THIS IS A LIMITED POLICY—READ IT CAREFULLY."[13]

Another contract addition is the requirement, now made statutory in some ten states, of a 10-day period during which the policyholder has the right to examine the contract and return it for a full refund if not satisfied. The existence of this right must be called to the policyholder's attention by one of several specified methods. It can be written into the contract as a separate provision on the first page and separately captioned; it can be in a sticker or notice attached to the first page of the policy; or in some states, it can be included in a "welcome" letter to the new policyholder. Since there is no value to the 10-day inspection period once the 10 days have expired, permanent affixation to the policy has not been required.

THE NATURE OF THE CONTRACT ON RENEWAL

The metamorphosis of health insurance from a casualty-oriented coverage to a personal line more akin to life insurance is by no means complete. One of the vexing problems to result from this is the nature of the contract on renewal. It is clear that the noncancellable and guaranteed renewable health insurance contracts are continuing obligations for the period of time stated. In this respect, they are similar to most life insurance policies.

The still common term contract of health insurance, however, is superficially similar to term contracts in other lines of insurance. In most states, the insurer has the option of declining to renew it at least at each anniversary date and in some states even within the term. The insurer also could impose new conditions unilaterally on renewal; yet, for all of this, the business has thus far been successful in maintaining that it is not a term contract in the sense of its fire and casualty cousins. Established law with respect to other term contracts is that the contract is subject at renewal to the law at the time of renewal. The justification for the exception for health insurance is based on the demonstrable fact that, unlike property coverages, it cannot as either a practical or a legal matter be

[13] National Association of Insurance Commissioners, *Official Guide for the Filing and Approval of Accident and Health Policies* (3d ed.; Chicago, 1947).

switched with impunity from one carrier to another at the renewal period. The health of the insured may have deteriorated so that he would not be acceptable to another company as a new risk. The legislatively prescribed "time limit on certain defenses" provision, with its beneficial results after two or three years, would never come into being if the contract ran anew on renewal, and many probationary periods before certain parts of the coverage became fully effective would never be satisfied. Accumulations might also be in jeopardy. This uniqueness of the health insurance contract on renewal is typical of the legal problems still to be resolved in the health insurance field.

SELECTED REFERENCES

DICKERSON, O. D. *Health Insurance.* Rev. ed. Homewood, Ill.: Richard D. Irwin, Inc., 1963.

MCALEVEY, JOHN F. *The Uniform Individual Accident and Sickness Policy Provisions Law.* Insurance Department Rulings Bulletin 495. Bureau of Accident and Health Underwriters, New York, 1952.

MCBRIDE, C. J. *Uniform Individual Accident and Sickness Policy Provisions Law—Analysis and Effect on Policy Drafting.* Insurance Department Rulings Bulletin 393. Bureau of Accident and Health Underwriters, New York, 1951.

NATIONAL ASSOCIATION OF INSURANCE COMMISSIONERS. "The Reinstatement Provisions: Statement of Interpretation by the Health Insurance Association of America," *Proceedings of the National Association of Insurance Commissioners,* Vol. II (1963), p. 514.

NATIONAL ASSOCIATION OF INSURANCE COMMISSIONERS. "Sixth Status Report on Overinsurance," *Proceedings of the National Association of Insurance Commissioners,* Vol. II (1963), p. 498.

O'REGAN, F. J. "The Time Limit on Certain Defenses and Incontestable Provisions," *Proceedings of the American Bar Association,* Section on Insurance, Negligence and Compensation Law, 1957, p. 103.

PART IV

Group Life and Health Insurance

Chapter 28

NATURE AND DEVELOPMENT OF GROUP INSURANCE

BY CHARLES E. PROBST

Group insurance has existed only for a half century, yet it is a major form of personal security and represents a significant portion of all life and health insurance written. United States life insurance companies alone provide group life insurance for more than 50 million persons, and the total number of persons covered under some form of group health insurance, including Blue Cross and Blue Shield plans, is well over 100 million. Further, it is estimated that the total premiums paid for group insurance in 1963 approximated $6.1 billion.

Group insurance most commonly covers persons who are active on a continuous, full-time basis in the operations of an enterprise, organization, or one of its units. The employer-employee relationship has always been considered the most suitable to group insurance. However, group insurance is extended to a number of other types of relationships.

Related Coverages

While group insurance accomplishes many worth-while social purposes, it should be distinguished from government-sponsored security programs, generally referred to as social insurance. Under social insurance, not only are the groupings of individuals and the objectives of the insurance oriented to the needs of society, but also the sources of revenue often are not derived directly from those eligible to receive the benefits. In addition, social insurance often has recourse to the taxing powers of governmental units. Group insurance, on the other hand, depends for its financing upon premiums which are paid either by the individuals to whom the benefits are payable or by the employer of these individuals, or partly by each. Interestingly enough, the element of compulsory coverage may be present both in group insurance and in social insurance. However, this aspect is much more prominent in the latter, while in many group coverages participation is elective.

Another form of coverage to be distinguished from group insurance is known as blanket insurance. Under group insurance the individuals in the covered group are clearly defined; in fact, the names are on record and can be accounted for as they enter or leave the insured group. Their eligibility for the insurance is based upon a continuous and active relationship in the group. In blanket insurance the policy is issued to cover an indefinite, changing group of people, generally only temporarily exposed to one particular hazard or a narrow range of hazards. An example is travel insurance, or trip insurance, in which case the insurance carrier agrees to accept risk on certain individuals temporarily exposed to the hazards of travel or to those of only a specific trip or type of transportation.

Franchise insurance is another form of personal coverage which should be distinguished, in the technical sense, from group insurance. The name "franchise insurance" is generally used in connection with health insurance. Under franchise insurance, individual contracts are issued to each insured person, but the carrier selects the individual risks by some modification of individual underwriting rules, recognizing that a number of like contracts are being written simultaneously on persons having some type of group relationship under circumstances which reduce individual selection. The coverage is essentially individual insurance and is considered in the same context as group insurance only because it is mass-marketed like group insurance and enjoys certain expense reductions because of mass underwriting and mass marketing.

For life insurance coverages the form of insurance paralleling franchise insurance is generally known as "wholesale" or "employee" life insurance. Wholesale life insurance and franchise health insurance are commonly utilized to insure small groups (less than ten employees) which do not qualify for group insurance under the laws of the particular state or perhaps under the underwriting rules of the particular company. However, large groups are sometimes covered on this basis for various reasons, including the fact that the group laws of the particular state in which the group is situated do not permit the qualification of the group, or the characteristics of the group are such that they justify some modification of individual underwriting but do not justify group underwriting.

Wholesale insurance does not include the mass issue of regular individual policies of life or health insurance, such as occurs in the pension trust or the employee profit sharing and salary savings areas. In these instances, a standard individual policy form is generally used, and the contract is between the insured person and the insurance company. The "guaranteed issue" principle represents a modification of standard individual insurance underwriting rules, but the differences in marketing technique are sufficient for these forms not to be considered franchise insurance.

Terminology

Group insurance has been so successful and so popular that the name "group" has been applied to practically every type of personal insurance coverage issued on a mass basis. In the foregoing paragraphs a differentiation has been made between group and blanket, franchise, wholesale, and guaranteed issue, but even retirement plans written on a group basis are sometimes referred to as group insurance. Group retirement plans are more correctly identified as group annuity plans or group pension plans. In this chapter, therefore, group insurance describes only group life and group health insurance. Group life insurance includes coverage for death benefits together with any disability features, such as waiver of premium.

Group health insurance includes the wide range of coverages for accidental death or loss of income resulting from either accident or sickness, as well as the various hospital, surgical, and other medical care type of expenses. Although accidental death and dismemberment insurance (the group counterpart of double indemnity or additional death benefits in individual policies) is often issued in conjunction with a group life policy, it is also issued separately or as a part of other health coverages and is generally considered to be a health insurance coverage.

The terminology of group health insurance is somewhat confusing. This is largely due to the very rapid development of this broad field and the resultant difficulty in producing any uniform nomenclature either for the coverages or for the various concepts essentially described in the policy provisions. For example, short-term disability income insurance was the first type of group health coverage to gain wide acceptance. It was variously known as group "accident and sickness" insurance, group "disability" insurance, group "weekly indemnity" insurance, and group "accident and health" insurance. This caused little difficulty when there were only a few forms of health coverages in existence. However, as coverages encompassing reimbursements for hospital expenses, surgical expenses, and many other medical care benefits were developed, it was recognized that these, too, might be titled accident and sickness, accident and health, and the like. Attempts to define the terminology more clearly were undertaken by various insurers, but no defined set of terms has universal acceptance as yet. In 1958, the Commission on Insurance Terminology of the American Risk and Insurance Association took the first step in attempting to clarify terminology in this broad field. It recommended that these coverages be referred to by the generic term "health insurance," and the term is being rapidly adopted. However, the annual statement blanks prescribed by the state supervisory authorities use the words "group accident and health insurance."

Eligible Groups

Group insurance is most commonly issued where an employer-employee relationship exists. A master policy is issued to the employer (corporation, proprietorship, or partnership), covering individuals who are regular full-time employees of the enterprise. This basic concept has expanded to include groups where two or more employers are brought together through some common interest, such as a labor contract or membership in an employer trade association; to employees (of any number of employers) who belong to a common labor union (or unions) or a professional or craft association; and in the field of credit, to borrowers having loans from a common creditor, and other group relationships. Both the laws of a particular state and the underwriting practices of the insurers determine the availability of this insurance to the various groups.

Types of Group Insurance Coverage

Among the more significant types of group life insurance coverage are group term, group permanent, group creditor, and dependents group.

Group Term. Group term insurance on the one-year renewable term basis is by far the most widespread. Basically, this coverage pays a death benefit of a stipulated amount for each class of insured individuals. It is usually available with a waiver-of-premium feature in the event of total and permanent disability, and sometimes with a disability income feature in lieu of a premium waiver provision.

Group Permanent. The group permanent (or "nonterm") plans of group life insurance can be divided roughly into group paid-up plans and level premium group permanent plans. Under group paid-up plans, certain portions of the employees' contributions are used to buy units of paid-up insurance, dependent upon the age and amount of insurance for the class to which the employee belongs. The difference between the accumulated amounts of paid-up insurance which is purchased and the scheduled total amount of insurance for each employee is made up by supplemental purchases of group term insurance which diminish as the group paid-up amounts increase. The level premium group permanent plans are close counterparts of the more common forms of permanent individual insurance, and accumulate reserves and nonforfeiture values in the same manner. Level premium group permanent forms have been less attractive than group paid-up coverages because the latter are accorded more favorable and less confusing tax treatment by the Internal Revenue Service.

Dependents Group. Dependents group life insurance can be offered in many states and is issued in conjunction with group insurance for the insured members on the lives of their eligible dependents. The general practice is to issue a fixed schedule with a uniform death benefit for the wife and another stipulated amount (usually smaller than the wife's benefit) payable on the death of each dependent child of the insured individual. In terms of both coverage in force and economic importance, dependents group life coverages are less significant than the coverage of group members themselves.

Group Creditor. Group creditor life insurance covering the lives of borrowers from a common creditor provides death benefits, generally in the amount of the unpaid indebtedness on the death of the borrower. This protection can cover short-term debts such as monthly repayable bank loans, can be extended to cover the unpaid balances of long-term mortgages, and, in some states, can be extended to cover other types of indebtedness, provided there is a regular plan for repayment of such indebtedness. (Group creditor health insurance is also available in most states to pay the borrower's monthly installments falling due while he is totally disabled.)

Group Health Insurance

Group health insurance includes a great variety of forms, some of which might be considered primary coverages and others of a supplemental nature. Included within the primary coverages would be disability income insurance and the principal forms of medical expense insurance. The supplemental coverages would include accidental death and dismemberment, travel accident, supplemental accident, diagnostic expense, physicians' attendance, radiation therapy, polio and dread disease, and dental expense.

Disability Income Insurance. Disability income insurance indemnifies the insured individual for loss of income due to disability. The short-term form of this coverage usually provides protection for periods no longer than fifty-two weeks. Long-term disability income benefits are also available with benefits payable to age 65 or for lesser periods.

Medical Expense Insurance. Medical expense insurance includes a number of different forms of coverage against expenses incurred by the insured member and his eligible dependents for medical care.

1. Hospital expense insurance reimburses for expenses incurred in a hospital, such as daily room and board charges plus miscellaneous, or ancillary, charges.
2. Surgical expense insurance reimburses for expense of surgical procedures.
3. Comprehensive medical expense insurance covers a broad range of expenses or charges without schedules or inside limits, using the principle of deductibles to screen out the very small expenses and percentage participation (coinsurance) to give the insured a financial interest in the amount of service required. Broad categories of expenses, such as hospi-

tal expenses, surgical expenses, physicians' attendance and diagnostic expenses, drugs, and nursing services are reimbursed with few limitations. The result is a single plan covering the areas of both the basic type of coverage and the major or catastrophic medical expense coverage under one reimbursement formula.

4. Major medical expense insurance reimburses for expenses incurred over and above the types of expenses contemplated in the basic hospital and surgical plans. It is designed to reimburse a large part of the additional expense incurred when the more basic types of medical care insurance are not broad enough to cover the applicable charges or when benefits under the basic types of insurance have been exhausted.

Accidental Death and Dismemberment Insurance. Accidental death and dismemberment insurance provides additional indemnity if the insured individual dies as a result of an accident. The dismemberment feature is a stipulated indemnity (usually at one half the amount for accidental death) for accidental loss of certain members of the body, that is, eyes, arms, legs, or combinations of these members.

Travel Accident Insurance. Travel accident insurance, a more limited form, covers loss of life (and usually the loss of limbs or eyes) of insured individuals while traveling.

Supplemental Accident Insurance. Supplemental accident insurance covers additional expenses, usually in the hospital and surgical categories, when such expenses are incurred as a result of an accident. This coverage normally pays over and above the hospital and surgical expenses otherwise reimbursed, and therefore supplements these coverages for accident conditions only.

Diagnostic Expense Insurance. Diagnostic expense insurance reimburses for the expense of diagnostic procedures not covered under hospital expense insurance or physicians' attendance insurance. Insurance may cover the expense of X rays used in diagnosis or, in addition, laboratory tests or other diagnostic procedures.

Physicians' Attendance Insurance. Physicians' attendance insurance reimburses for expenses incurred as a result of visits to a physician or for physicians' calls or for treatment other than surgery.

Radiation Therapy Expense Insurance. Radiation therapy expense insurance covers the cost of radiation for therapeutic purposes and differs from diagnostic expense insurance in that it covers *treatment* by radiation.

Polio and Dread Disease Insurance. Polio and dread disease insurance covers expenses incurred, generally at much higher maximum limits than basic coverages, with respect to certain specified diseases or lists of diseases which are quite often serious and involve long and expensive treatment. Since the coverage is limited to only certain specified diseases or causes, its scope is limited, but the maximum amounts of reimbursement are substantial.

Dental Expense Insurance. Dental expense insurance covers expenses incurred in connection with dentistry. This is a relatively new group coverage and is still somewhat in the experimental stage. It is currently being offered both as a basic benefit and as a comprehensive benefit covering a wide area of expense, but with deductibles and percentage participation by the insured.

Basic Characteristics of Group Insurance

Several characteristics of group insurance may be delineated as significant in the group-insuring process, including group underwriting or selection of risks, group administration, the master policy and certificate, group marketing, and group rating.

Group underwriting is unique. It is based on the concept that if groups of persons enter an insurance pool with sufficient homogeneity to the average group, and if the plan of insurance can be so drawn as to preclude selection against the insurance pool by the individual as to amounts of insurance, types of benefits, and similar characteristics, and if the participation by those in the group is sufficiently high, then the pool as a whole should develop a relatively stable and measurable cost that can be assessed equitably against the members of the group.

In group selection the determination of the benefit structure and amounts of insurance for each class within the group is extremely important. Equally important is the selection of the classes and the rules which determine eligibility of the classes. Whereas the effect of individual selection is the underwriting problem of individual insurance, the establishment of the plan and the requirement of a continued high participation in each class are the very essence of group selection. Group selection should be every bit as rigorous and careful in choosing groups with characteristics appropriate for the insurance pool, and in matching an appropriate plan to the group, as that exercised in selecting an individual risk, and its plan of insurance, for an individual life insurance pool.

Group administration is designed for simplified and efficient recording of individuals' insurance and group premium payments and for prompt settlement of individual claims. A master policy is issued to the group, and the individual is usually furnished with a certificate evidencing his coverage. This certificate is a simplified extract of the important provision of the master policy (the master policy provisions govern all transactions—the certificate is "unofficial"). Thus the insured individual has a summary statement of the significant features of his insurance coverage. The record of insured individuals is maintained either by the insurer, with the policyholder (or other administrator) submitting periodical records of changes in the insured individuals, or by a "self-accounting" procedure, whereby only the master policyholder maintains a continuous record of the individuals insured, subject to audit by the insurer. Premiums are usually determined by applying the premium rate to the running total of insurance in force and are remitted in one sum to the insurer. Claims forms are most commonly submitted by the master policyholder, together with any supporting statements required from physicians, the claimant, or others. Thus, much of the administrative work becomes a normal part of the clerical routine of the master policyholder, eliminating much of the cost of premium collection, coverage records, and claims transactions between the insurer and each insured individual. The result is a substantial reduction in cost.

The device of issuing the master policy to the group policyholder permits negotiations on contract provisions to be carried on by a limited number of parties. Since these provisions include definitions of the coverages intended for the insured individuals, the classes of individuals eligible for insurance, the conditions under which insurance commences and ceases, the schedule of benefits, and many other provisions, the consummation of the contract essentially between two parties is a great advantage over individual negotiations. Even the certificates or individual descriptions of coverage given to the persons insured are usually delivered by the group master policyholder at the place of work or by some other convenient channel.

Group marketing is accomplished through a regular insurance agent or a broker, with the insurance carrier supplying salaried technical sales assistance in the field to assist the broker and the policyholder in selecting, installing, and administering the details peculiar to group insurance. Commission scales reflect the reduced amount of personal contact and service to the individual insured, and thus the selling procedure is less complicated and less expensive than if individual effort were needed to sell an insurance coverage to each member of the insured group. It should be recognized, however, that group coverage with respect to the individual is standardized and is designed to provide basic benefits and not to substitute for insurance tailored to the complete individual need of the insured persons.

Group insurance actuarial science applies its techniques to characteristics of the groups and to the plans of insurance designed for the various groups. The statistics are aimed at developing data which will give premium rates applicable to age distributions and average ages, industry hazards, schedules of insurance, percentage of risk on females, employee income variations within the group, and differences in costs by geographical location (for medical expense coverages). An important actuarial-underwriting function is the experience rating of groups, which is usually done each year on the policy anniversary. This involves a survey of the claims experience of each group and a redetermination of the rate for the ensuing year. Experience rating is accomplished by weighing the experience of the group and that of the insurance pool of which it is a member. Dividends or experience refunds, if any, are determined for individual groups through rating techniques.

Group insurance is also characterized by continuous developments and innovations. Larger employers or other group policyholders look for ways to recruit and keep desirable employees, and hence exert pressures on group insurance carriers to improve and expand their benefit plans. Many advances have resulted from these incentives and pressures. In medical care coverages the range of benefits in the hospital, surgical, and medical fields has constantly expanded, with ventures into the field of dental expenses being the most recent. The length of time over which benefits are payable for earnings lost during disability has been constantly increased, and long-term disability benefit periods of five years, ten years, and lifetime are now common. Mortgage insurance on long-term mortgage debt was introduced where formerly only short-term debts were insured.

HISTORY AND GROWTH

The first group policy was issued by the Equitable Life Assurance Society covering employees of the Pantasote Leather Company, effective in June, 1911. Prior to this time, negotiations between Montgomery Ward and Company and the Equitable Life Assurance Society apparently had brought the idea to the fore, and a policy on Montgomery Ward was also issued by the Equitable with an effective date of July 1, 1912. Both of these policies provided only group term life insurance. The New York State Insurance Department approved the Pantasote group contract on June 3, 1911. In the next few years a number of similar policies were written by other insurers.

By 1917 the National Convention of Insurance Commissioners found group life insurance problems of sufficient moment to propose a "model bill" which served as a recommended legislative blueprint for regulation of group life insurance in the various states. This model legislation embodied a "definition" of group life insurance which, by spelling out types of groups and classes of eligible employees, had the effect of prohibiting issuance to those groups not mentioned. In addition, the model bill set forth certain "Standard Provisions" that group life policies issued in a state should contain for the protection of the insuring public.

Laws regulating the issuance of group insurance passed by the various states have followed this two-part format. In 1946, the National Association of Insurance Commissioners promulgated a new model bill which recognized four basic groups for group life insurance: employer groups, creditor groups (policy issued to a creditor to insure the lives of his debtors for the amount of the unpaid debt), labor union groups, and trusteed groups. In the latter case the trustee could act for two or more employers in the same industry or for two or more unions, or for funds created jointly by employers and unions.

It should be recognized that the bills recommended by the National Association of Insurance Commissioners were not necessarily adopted by the states in the exact form promulgated. Naturally, the states are free to enact their own versions of the model bill or to pass entirely different types of regulatory statutes. For example, coverage of associations of certain employees, professional people, and other types of relationships are permitted in a number of states. Also, from the time of the original 1917 promulgation, which was drawn to include only groups of 50 or more employees, it became common to permit groups of 25 or more. More recently, the minimum has been set at 10 employees, and even smaller groups are now permitted in a few states.

TABLE 28–1

GROUP LIFE INSURANCE IN FORCE IN THE UNITED STATES
(000 Omitted)
(Includes Creditor Groups)

Year	Number of Master Policies	Number of Certificates	Amount
1915	0.3	120	$ 100,000
1925	12.0	3,200	4,247,000
1935	19.0	6,788	10,283,000
1945	37.0	13,049	22,436,000
1955	116.0	54,605	113,671,000
1962	240.0	89,041	241,098,000

Source: Institute of Life Insurance.

The dramatic growth of group life insurance, as shown in Table 28–1, reflects both the rapid expansion of American industry in general and the growing consciousness of the value of insurance protection. However, certain special factors which also affected group health insurance produced a rapid expansion of both group life and group health insurance beginning in the early 1940's.

Under date of November 7, 1920, the *Proceedings of the Casualty Actuarial and Statistical Society of America* published a paper by James D. Craig entitled "Group Health Insurance," which described coverages providing weekly income for loss of time due to sickness contracted or injuries sustained. Craig described the coverage as "foreign to occupation accidents and full health. . . ." He discussed the development of premium rates for this coverage, referring to the table known as the Manchester Unity 1907 Experience, which had been published in Great Britain. Thus, it is evident that by the time of the Craig paper, the idea of group disability income coverages had gained sufficient acceptance to elicit discussions of underwriting practices, premium rates, and coverage provisions.

The most recent, spectacular growth of group insurance has been in the field of hospitalization and surgical and medical care. These plans began as hospitalization plans and plans to reimburse for surgeons' fees only. Gilbert W. Fitzhugh, at a June, 1934, meeting of the American Institute of Actuaries, reported on a survey of these plans. He indicated that in 1927, in Brattleboro, Vermont, the Thompson Benefit Association for Hospital Service launched a plan to cover "surgical hospitalization, including surgeons' and special hospital charges, up to a maximum of $300, except that the member paid the first $30 of expenses. If hospitalization is necessary for some reason other than an operation, one half of such charges are paid [after the first $30]." Fitzhugh reported that in 1930 the total membership in the plan was about 550, including dependents. In 1929, Baylor University Hospital in Dallas, Texas, introduced a group hospitalization plan for a local teachers' society on a group prepayment basis. This plan was later extended to other groups in the Dallas area and was the forerunner of the current Blue Cross associations.

In the early 1930's, during the years of the Great Depression, the need to preserve the solvency of local hospitals in the face of uncollected patients' bills led to formation of several local "prepayment" societies. Both groups and individuals were enrolled. With the advent of these plans the possibility of insuring hospital and medical care expenses on a nationwide basis became evident; and it was natural for insurance companies, with large facilities, both regional and nationwide, for the pooling of experience and for the enrolling of members, to enter this field. Throughout the 1930's a slow expansion of this coverage, sold mostly to employers, began to take place.

At that time, it appeared that group health insurance was to enjoy a steady but modest growth in the fields of disability income and minimum basic hospital benefits and surgical benefits. However, Table 28–2 shows a dramatic growth not only in these basic coverages but in the medical expense and major medical expense categories. As in the case of group life insurance, certain factors described below acted to accelerate greatly the growth of group health coverages.

In the 1940's, several factors acted to accelerate all types of group insurance at a dramatic rate. During World War II, a period of strict economic controls, government "wage freezes" led employers to compete vigorously in the labor market by offering fringe benefit programs to attract and keep their work forces. Group insurance of all kinds was a natural area in which to compete. Consequently, group life insurance, disability income, and many plans of hospital, surgical, and medical coverages were developed and installed.

Immediately after World War II, the famous Inland Steel decision by the Supreme Court of the United States, which held that pensions and other employee fringe benefits are subject to the collective bargaining process, brought organized labor fully into the group insurance picture.

Coincident with the rapid expansion of group health coverages, rapid advances in medical science made the prepayment and pooling of medical care costs by the insurance mechanism a virtual necessity, at least for a minimum floor of protection for most workers. The group device was aided in its development by the fact that employers have become increasingly willing to share in the cost of experimental types of

TABLE 28–2

NUMBER OF PEOPLE WITH INSURANCE COMPANY GROUP HEALTH INSURANCE PROTECTION IN THE UNITED STATES
(000 Omitted)

Year	Disability Income	Hospital Expense	Surgical Expense	Regular Medical Expense	Major Medical Expense
1940.....	Not recorded	2,500	1,430	.....	.....
1945.....	7,135 (1946)	7,800	5,537	335	.....
1950.....	15,104	22,305	21,219	5,587	96 (1951)
1955.....	19,171	39,029	39,725	20,678	4,759
1960.....	20,970	55,218	55,504	35,802	25,608
1962.....	22,313	59,153	59,787	40,012	35,053

Source: Health Insurance Institute.

coverages and in the expansion of the more established types of group insurance.

The growth of major medical insurance has been the most recent major impetus to growth of group health insurance. In 1949, the Liberty Mutual Insurance Company issued a contract of "major medical group insurance" to the Elfun Society, an organization of management personnel of the General Electric Company. This concept of lumping all covered medical expenses arising from a given condition or medical situation, and treating the combined total of such expenses under a "deductible and coinsurance" formula led insurers to further experimentation in the field of comprehensive reimbursement of most types of medical expense. Many variations of this basic concept have been developed and are in widespread use today.

Thus, in a period of a little more than ten years a virtual explosion of group coverages was brought about by these successive waves of pressures and incentives.

SELECTED REFERENCES

GREGG, DAVIS W. *Group Life Insurance.* 3d ed. Homewood, Ill.: Richard D. Irwin, Inc., 1962.

HEALTH INSURANCE INSTITUTE. *Source Book of Health Insurance Data.* New York, published annually.

INSTITUTE OF LIFE INSURANCE. *Life Insurance Fact Book.* New York, published annually.

PICKRELL, J. F. *Group Health Insurance.* Homewood, Ill.: Richard D. Irwin, Inc., 1961.

Chapter 29

GROUP TERM LIFE INSURANCE

BY WENDELL MILLIMAN

Characteristics of Group Insurance

The principal characteristics of group insurance which distinguish it from individual insurance relate to the nature of the contract and the relationships between the parties, the selection process, and the cost of the insurance.

The Contractual Relationship. A group insurance contract, by its very nature, insures several individuals. An individual life insurance contract, on the other hand, covers only a single individual (or an individual and members of his family). The individuals insured under a group insurance contract are not parties to it. It is a contract between the insurer and a policyholder for the benefit of a group of individuals having a defined relationship to the policyholder (e.g., an employer-employee relationship).

Furthermore, a group insurance contract is a continuing contract. It must provide for periodic additions to the group of insured lives as additional individuals qualify for the insurance, and for the termination of insurance on individuals as they leave the eligible group.

The Selection Process. Any sound plan of insurance must be based on a system which will keep those who know that they have a better than average chance of benefiting from the insurance from taking undue advantage of that knowledge. We know this process of combating adverse selection on the part of applicants as the "selection process."

Individual insurance policies are offered to the public at large. No one insurance company can expect to sell insurance policies to more than a small proportion of its potential market. Furthermore, an applicant may, within wide limits, select the amount of insurance for which he will be insured. The applicant for individual insurance usually knows if he has some physical condition or is exposed to some occupational hazard which might materially affect the risk he is asking the insurance company to assume. Under these circumstances the insurance company must, in order to obtain risks compatible with its premiums, follow a selection process which will guard against self-selection on the part of the applicants for insurance. This is done by use of health questionnaires, medical examinations, and inspection reports. Each risk is thereby evaluated as an individual on the basis of the information developed, and a substandard applicant either is offered insurance subject to an extra premium or is rejected.

Evidence of insurability is seldom required from the individuals eligible for insurance under a group policy. This is possible because the group of eligible individuals constitute a definitive group, and the relationship which makes them members of the group (for example, employees of a common employer) is normally of substantially greater importance to them than the insurance for which they are eligible as members of that group. In most situations, this relationship results in the group of eligible lives being, from a health standpoint, at least as good as would be obtained by random selection from the public at large. Under these circumstances, the insurer can predict with reasonable accuracy the level of mortality which can be expected in the group.

Cost of the Insurance. The cost of group insurance is normally lower than the cost of individual insurance. This is primarily the result of the fact that the costs of selling and administering group insurance require a smaller percentage of the insurance premiums than is required to sell and administer individual insurance. Also, most forms of individual insurance have premiums level over a period of time, and a part of earlier years' premiums is reserved for higher later insurance costs as the insured gets older.

The cost of the group insurance to the insured individual, where he contributes toward the cost, is reduced even further by virtue of the fact that the group policyholder, particularly where the policyholder is the employer of the persons insured, usually bears a substantial proportion of the cost of the insurance.

It will be seen that the nature of the relationship that binds the separate individuals into a group is all-important. A proper relationship is essential to successful group selection. Likewise, a strong relationship is necessary in order that the policyholder may be in a position to enroll individuals as they become eligible for the insurance, and so that he can be relied upon to handle the many administrative details required to make a group insurance program work smoothly and economically.

Origin of Group Life Insurance

Group life insurance appears to have developed as the natural outgrowth of the mutual benefit association movement of the latter part of the nineteenth century and the early part of the twentieth century. Through the medium of group life insurance, the risk-bearing capacity and experience of life insurance companies were used in providing life insurance protection for groups of employees, thereby accomplishing the main objective of mutual benefit associations.

While group life insurance was first issued to cover employees of a single employer, almost from the start consideration was given to the issuance of group insurance to cover other types of groups. Furthermore, some of the early group insurance contracts were issued on a level premium basis; yet, over 90 per cent of the group life insurance in force is on a term insurance basis. Both at its inception and later, the predominant form of group life insurance has been group term life insurance issued to cover the employees of a single employer. The first group credit life insurance policy was issued in 1926. This form of group term life insurance has proved to be popular and currently accounts for over 13 per cent of all group life insurance in force.

Growth of Group Term Insurance

The rate of growth of group term life insurance in the United States continues to be more rapid than that of any other form of life insurance. This is illustrated by the increasing percentages, set forth in Table 29–1,

TABLE 29–1

GROUP LIFE INSURANCE AS PERCENTAGE OF TOTAL LIFE INSURANCE IN FORCE IN THE UNITED STATES
(Selected Years, 1945–62)

Year	Per Cent
1945	14.8%
1950	21.8
1955	30.5
1960	34.3
1962	35.7

of the total life insurance in force in the United States which has been provided on a group basis.

Uses of Group Term Life Insurance

An employer, in establishing a plan of group insurance, is concerned primarily with providing this protection during the period of employment. The cheapest form of protection is, of course, term insurance. The very characteristics which bind groups of people together in a manner which makes group insurance practical also make it feasible to issue life insurance to these groups on a term insurance basis. The two primary areas in which group term life insurance has been found practical are:

1. To provide for temporary replacement of earnings in the event of the death of an employee. The insurance may be provided under a contract

issued to the common employer, or to a labor union, or to the trustees of a trust fund established as the result of collective bargaining between a union and an employer or employers.

2. To provide, for an individual with outstanding installment indebtedness, repayment of part or all of the remaining debt in the event of his death. The insurance may be provided under a contract issued to a bank or other lending institution to cover unsecured loans repayable in installments, or to a dealer to cover installment sales.

A third use which deserves notice is that of providing insurance upon the lives of dependents (spouse and children) of employees. Substantially all the conditions which make term insurance a feasible form for providing group life insurance protection for employees of an employer apply to group life insurance for dependents of employees. Despite this fact, the growth in popularity of this form of group life insurance has been limited.

In all these situations, there is a steady stream of lives coming into the group to replace the lives that are leaving the group. The new lives, in general, are younger than the terminating lives, which tends to keep the average age of the insured lives from increasing. This is a vital factor, since, as a result, the cost of group coverage tends to remain relatively constant. It should be noted, however, that when insurance is continued on employees after they have retired from active employment, the average age of the insured group tends to increase for a great many years until a point of stability is reached.

Underwriting and Legal Requirements

The insurance laws of most states contain statutory definitions of group life insurance. These statutory definitions impose certain limitations and restrictions on the issuance of group life insurance. Many, but not all, of these limitations are basic underwriting requirements which would be required for the sound operation of group insurance even if they were not imposed by law. (See Appendix J for NAIC Model Group Life Insurance Bill, including definition and standard provisions.)

Important underwriting requirements which are found in statutory definitions of group life insurance are:

Insurance Incidental to Group. The very essence of group insurance is to be found in the fact that the group of individuals to be insured are bound together as a group by some strong interest other than that of obtaining the insurance. Such a relationship is to be found in practice as the result of the employer-employee relationship and the union-member relationship, and frequently in the case of debtor-creditor relationships involving debts repayable in installments. These relationships are recognized in all statutory definitions of group life insurance.

Proposals are frequently made that group life insurance be made available to less cohesive groups, such as fraternal societies, veterans' organizations, and professional societies. The statutes of a number of states permit issuance of group life insurance to these and similar types of groups. A substantial volume of group life insurance has been written within recent years to provide coverage for members of professional societies and for employees of members of trade associations. In general, however, the absence of a strong common interest, as well as the absence of a central administrative agency and of a source of funds to enable the group policyholder to share in the cost of the insurance, has limited the success of such extensions of the field of group life insurance.

Nondiscriminatory Classifications. Statutory requirements, underwriting judgment, and, in the case of employer-employee groups, good personnel practices, all require that the classes to be insured must be determined by nondiscriminatory classifications. The statutory requirement, in the case of employer-employee groups, is that the classes of eligible employees must be determined by conditions pertaining to their employment. For instance, employees with less than sixty days of employment could be excluded, or coverage could be restricted to employees employed in specified locations. In the case of a policy issued to a labor union, the eligible classes may be determined by conditions pertaining to employment, or to membership in the union, or both. Corresponding requirements apply to creditor and other types of group life insurance.

High Proportion Must Be Insured. In order to avoid selection on the part of those eligible which would adversely affect the insurance risk, a high proportion of the eligibles must be covered. The usual statutory definition of group life insurance requires that when the employer pays the entire cost of the insurance (noncontributory group life insurance), all employees in the eligible classes must be insured. For practical reasons, participation by as few as 75 per cent of the eligible employees is normally allowed, both by statutory definition and underwriting requirements, in cases where the employees share in the cost (contributory group life insurance).

Amounts Precluding Selection. Statutes and underwriting judgment again both require that the amounts of insurance must be determined by a plan which precludes individual selection. Under employer-employee groups the amounts of insurance are commonly graded in proportion to earnings so as to provide for one or two years' earnings as a death benefit during active employment. Some group contracts base benefit levels on the employee's position within the firm or on his length of service. While in the past, under most group life policies, the insurance has been either substantially reduced or terminated when an employee was retired, there is a trend toward the continuation of more substantial amounts of insurance after retirement.

Sharing of Cost. Under noncontributory plans the policyholder pays the entire cost of the insurance. Under contributory plans, in order to maintain a high participation, the cost of the insurance must be attractive to those eligible for the insurance. This may be accomplished if the policyholder shares in the cost. The usual statutory definition for employer-employee groups requires that the employer must share in the cost, but does not specify the share he must pay. By common practice, supported by rulings of some state insurance departments, employee contributions have been limited to 60 cents a month per $1,000 of insurance, a level of contributions which has proved to be quite generally attractive to eligible employees.

The following factors contribute to keeping the balance of the cost, which must be met by the employer, at moderate levels:

1. The low selling and administrative costs which are characteristic of group insurance.
2. The fact that the premiums are on a term insurance basis, with coverage generally being terminated or reduced at retirement.
3. The fact that the group is automatically so constituted that the administrative details can be economically administered by the employer.

Limitation of Amounts. An important legal limitation, which is not based upon generally accepted underwriting requirements, is that of many states limiting the amount of group life insurance which may be issued on the life of an individual. The most common limitation prohibits the issuance of a group policy "which provides term insurance on any person which . . . exceeds $20,000 unless 150 per cent of the annual compensation of such person from his employer or employers exceeds $20,000, in which event all such term insurance shall not exceed $40,000 or 150 per cent of such annual compensation, whichever is the lesser." Some important states impose no limitation upon the amount of group term life insurance, while other states have limitations ranging up to a flat $100,000. These limitations represent an attempt to prevent group life insurance from invading what many believe to be the proper field of individual life insurance.

The fact that there are no such limits in several of the most populous states, and that these limits are not retroactive to contracts which were made before their enactment, has considerably restricted the effectiveness of this effort to limit amounts of group life insurance. Moreover, insureds with offices or plants in one or more liberal states can apply benefit levels in other areas on the basis of the laws of that date if the group plan is established therein.

The federal Revenue Act of 1964 limited, for the first time, the amount of group term life insurance on an individual which may be paid for by the employer without giving rise to taxable income to the employee. Under the terms of this Act, the cost of the first $50,000 of such insurance is tax-free. Contributions towards premiums, whether for coverage up to $50,000 or for excess coverage, may be subtracted from the cost (determined on a basis prescribed by regulations) of insurance over $50,000 otherwise taxable to the covered employee. It is not yet apparent what the effect of this change in tax treatment will have on the popularity of large amounts of group life insurance.

Master Contract, Certificates, and Booklets

The relationships under a group insurance plan are usually evidenced by three classes of documents—the group policy (sometimes called the master contract), certificates of insurance issued to individuals insured under the group policy, and announcement booklets.

Master Contract. The group policy sets forth the contractual relationship between the employer (or other policyholder) and the insurer. It is a continuing contract, which may outlive any of the lives insured under it. Accordingly, in addition to provisions paralleling those of individual insurance contracts, relating to such things as the consideration, the amount of benefit, and when and to whom the benefit is payable, it contains various administrative provisions. Among other things, these provisions determine who is eligible to become insured, how and when they may become insured, and how and when their insurance will terminate. (See Appendix K for specimen group life insurance master policy.)

Individual Certificates. The statutes of many states require that a certificate be issued to each insured person summarizing the pertinent provisions of the group policy, identifying his beneficiary, and giving the amount of his insurance protection. A group insurance certificate is merely evidence of insurance under the group policy and is not itself a life insurance policy. A special form of certificate is required in some states under a group creditor's policy. (See Appendix L for specimen group life employee's certificate.)

Announcement Booklets. It is customary, at the time a group insurance plan is installed, to give to each eligible employee an announcement booklet. These booklets are designed to summarize the benefits and to tell the employees how they may become insured. Normally, these booklets are written more as sales and public relations documents than as legal instruments. Because of the absence of technical detail, they are frequently referred to in explaining and administering the plan.

Benefits Provided

The primary benefit provided under a group term life insurance policy is the payment of the amount of insurance in case an insured individual dies while his insurance under the policy has been continued in force on a premium-paying basis. Premiums for term insurance are calculated to cover only the current claim costs; consequently, there are no accumulating equities under group term life insurance of the type which give rise to nonforfeiture values under level premium insurance. However, since premium payments with respect to an employee's insurance may be terminated for reasons beyond his control, group life insurance policies contain various provisions designed to continue the insurance protection under certain conditions beyond the date of termination of premium payments. In addition, the policy permits an employee, upon termination of his group insurance, to convert part or all of this insurance into an individual life insurance policy. In general, these provisions are designed to prevent an insured employee from being deprived of his insurance protection through termination of his insurance, intentionally or otherwise, while he is in poor health.

Provisions for Continuing Protection

The usual provisions for continuing protection beyond the date of termination of premium payments under the group insurance policy are as follows:

Conversion Privilege upon Termination of Employment. Under this provision, an employee is given the right to secure continuance of his insurance protection under a permanent form of individual policy issued at his attained age and without evidence of insurability, provided that he makes application for such insurance and pays the required premium within 31 days after termination of employment.

Conversion Privilege upon Termination of the Group Policy. A similar conversion right is given upon termination of the master policy, but usually only to employees who have been insured for at least five years. The maximum amount which may be converted under this provision is normally $2,000 and may be even less if the employee becomes eligible for group life insurance under another policy issued or reinstated within 31 days after termination of the old group policy.

Thirty-One-Day Continuation of Protection. Protection somewhat similar to that provided by the grace period under individual life insurance policies is provided under group life insurance policies upon termination of the insurance due either to termination of employment or to termination of the master policy. The usual provision continues the life insurance protection which an individual is entitled to convert for a period of 31 days following termination of premium payments for his group life insurance.

Waiver-of-Premium Provision. The conversion right and the 31-day free death benefit provision give substantial protection in many situations. However, on occasion, premium payments are discontinued and group life insurance is terminated on an employee whose active employment has terminated due to total disability. Not all such employees convert their insurance. In order to furnish a proper safeguard to the rights of such employees, most group life insurance policies contain a waiver-of-premium provision. A typical waiver-of-premium provision will continue the insurance in effect if (1) the employee was under age 60 at the date of commencement of his total disability, (2) his total disability commenced before termination of his insurance and of the group life insurance policy, (3) the total disability was continuous from the date of termination of insurance to the date of death, and (4) proof of total and continuous disability is presented to the insurance company at least once every twelve months.

Cost of Group Life Insurance[1]

In much the same manner as individual insurance, group insurance is frequently sold with the expectation of premium refunds or dividends. In the purchase of group insurance, as much or more attention is given to the expected net cost of the insurance as is given to the initial gross premium cost.

Net Costs and Retention. The net cost of group term life insurance is simply the difference between gross premiums paid by the policyholder and the dividends or premium refunds, if any, returned by the insurance company. The "retention" of an insurance company is the balance of this net cost after provision for incurred claims; that is, the retention is the amount available to the insurer for expenses, for contingency reserves, and for profit. It is, of course, possible that claims will exceed premiums, with the result that the insurer will have no retention. The smaller the number insured, the greater is the chance that this situation will occur in any given period of time. In the case of groups insuring enough lives to justify assuming some stability in claims rates, "costs" of competing insurers are frequently compared on the basis of what retentions could be expected to be under hypothetical patterns of future claims experience.

Gross Premiums. Premiums for group term life insurance are based on a scale of one-year term premium rates contained in the policy. This scale is usually guaranteed for only one year at a time. An average monthly premium rate is computed from this scale at the beginning of the policy year, based on the distribution of insurance in force by attained ages. This average premium rate is then used for each monthly premium statement throughout the year. At the end of the policy year the average may be recomputed from the same scale, or a new scale (higher or lower) may be used, or the initial average rate may be continued in effect.

Minimum Initial Premium Scales. The insurance laws of New York, Maine, Michigan, Ohio, and Pennsylvania establish minimum initial premium rates for group life insurance. The New York law is designed to regulate the minimum premium rates to be charged during the first policy year of any group life insurance policy issued by any life insurance company authorized to do business in New York, regardless of where the

---

[1] See Chapter 36, "Group Premiums and Experience Rating," for further discussion.

business may be issued. An insurer is, however, free to reduce premium rates at the end of the first policy year. Since most of the largest writers of group life insurance are licensed in New York State, this has had the effect of establishing minimum initial premium rates for the great bulk of the group life insurance issued in the United States.

Continuing Insurance on Retired Lives

It is often—and correctly—said that an individual should not rely upon group insurance as part of his permanent insurance estate. Unfortunately, however, group insurance is frequently an important part of an individual's total life insurance. If this insurance is lost due to loss of employment, particularly when this occurs at retirement age, the individual may find—despite his right to convert to individual insurance—that he cannot afford to replace the lost group insurance.

Many employers, because of this problem, provide for the continuation of insurance upon retired employees, but for a reduced amount. This practice results in a gradually increasing amount of insurance upon the older, retired employees, with resultant increases in the cost of the insurance. When the effect of continuation of insurance on retired employees upon costs has not been explained in advance, the employer may be shocked when the full effect of this practice shows up in his premiums.

A number of methods have been adopted for meeting part or all of the cost of continuation of insurance on retired lives by premium payments during an employee's working years. Most of these approaches are, of course, forms of permanent insurance and will be discussed in the following chapter. One method of dealing with this problem deserves mention in this chapter. This is a "deposit administration" type of arrangement, under which the employer establishes a special fund, usually with the insurance carrier, to finance these costs. The fund may be created through employer contributions, through employee contributions, or from dividends or refunds on the basic group term policy, plus, of course, interest earnings on such funds. The amounts accumulated in such a fund are not allocated to the purchase of paid-up or level premium insurance for individual employees, as in the case of the various forms of group permanent insurance. Instead, they are used to cover the term insurance premiums as they fall due for retired employees.

This approach permits the employer to anticipate the probability of termination of employment prior to retirement, and to avoid the expenses involved in establishing and terminating records of accumulating equities for the employees who do not stay in service until retirement. Apparently, if no employee acquires an irrevocable right in such a fund, the employer payments into the fund do not constitute taxable income to the employees.

SELECTED REFERENCES

GREGG, DAVIS W. *Group Life Insurance.* 3d ed. Homewood, Ill.: Richard D. Irwin, Inc., 1962.

ILSE, LOUISE WOLTERS. *Group Insurance and Employee Retirement Plans.* New York: Prentice-Hall, Inc., 1953.

MILLIMAN, WENDELL. *Is Group Insurance for You?* New York: North American Reassurance Co., 1958.

Chapter 30

GROUP PAID-UP AND GROUP PERMANENT LIFE INSURANCE

BY PAUL H. JACKSON

From its origin in 1911 until perhaps the mid-1940's, group life insurance was almost universally underwritten on the yearly renewable term basis. The remarkable growth of group insurance and the rapid expansion of pension plans in recent years have resulted in a broadening of the concepts of employee welfare programs to the point where real concern for the pensioner is now commonplace. Group term insurance is still the finest and most efficient means for providing a death benefit to a group of actively working employees. The efficiency of term insurance is a direct result of the absence of permanent insurance equities, but this very absence has also been responsible for major problems which have been brought into sharper focus with the increasing attention being given to pensioners and their special problems.

BACKGROUND

Reasons for Development of Permanent Plans

An employee who leaves his employment is given the right to convert his group life insurance to an individual policy without medical examination at the standard premium for the employee's attained age. At typical retirement ages the cost of a converted policy usually ranges from $70 to $80 annually for each $1,000 of insurance converted. The combination of a high premium rate and a sharply reduced income has forced most retiring employees to drop their group life insurance, even though in all too many instances it is the only life insurance protection they carry. This area of employee dissatisfaction is minimized if the employee can accumulate paid-up insurance equities in realistic amounts during his active employment.

Employees insured under contributory term plans are frequently disappointed to learn when they terminate employment that even though they may have contributed for their group life insurance for many years, they have nothing to show for their past contributions. Since the usual employee contribution of 60 cents per month per $1,000 exceeds the attained-age cost of group term insurance below age 45 where most of the voluntary terminations occur, this grievance does have some theoretical justification. This area of employee dissatisfaction is minimized to the extent that provision is made for the accumulation of nonforfeiture benefits in the form of paid-up insurance or cash that can be taken with the employee when he withdraws from the group.

Most employers have come to recognize the difficulty in terminating group life insurance completely when an employee reaches retirement age. When insurance must be cancelled, the active employee has just one more reason why he should resist retirement. While many of the reasons for continuing insurance on retired employees may be based upon sentiment, the principal reason for not continuing the insurance is the very high premium required for term insurance at advanced ages. If full insurance could be continued for pensioners at small cost, almost everyone would be in favor of it. To the extent that some group life insurance coverage for pensioners is desirable and some realistic limit on employer cost must be imposed, it may become necessary to ask the employee to contribute a larger than usual amount for his coverage in order to have the desired insurance amount after retirement. Ideally, any employee contribution should be restricted to his active working years, so that he can get his share of the cost out of the way before retirement and avoid encumbering his pension income.

Where group life insurance is continued for retired employees on a yearly renewable term basis, many different factors can affect the employer's promise to continue the coverage. There may be a change in company policy, such as a severe cost-cutting program instituted when profits are low. A company may go out of business, sell out to a successor organization, or merge. There may be a change in union leadership, bargaining strategy, or ultimate welfare goals. Most of the pensioners will not understand all of these factors fully; and if they did, they would probably strongly prefer to be insured against loss of their group insurance after retirement by having it entirely paid for prior to their retirement date. Further, from the employer's standpoint, sound cost accounting principles require the full funding of each pensioner's death benefit over his productive working years, and this necessitates some form of prepaid permanent insurance for the pensioner. The life span of every industry, let alone of each individual company, is characterized by a period of healthy growth, followed by prosperous maturity, declining fortune, and, finally, economic death. If a business organization is not willing or able to guarantee the promises it makes to its employees and pensioners in the more prosperous periods of growth and maturity, and pay for that guarantee then, it will probably never be able to live up to all of those promises thereafter.

In each of these major problem areas an increase in the amount of term insurance for active employees merely intensifies the problem, and perhaps this implies a natural limit to the amount of pure term insurance beyond which some permanent insurance becomes a necessity. In any event, the problem of providing pensioners with reasonable amounts of insurance at reasonable employer cost and on a funded basis cannot be solved without some form of permanent insurance.

Basic Types of Permanent Plans

In recent years a number of different group life insurance plans involving permanent insurance have been developed. These plans are usually classified under two general headings—group paid-up and group permanent life insurance.

Group paid-up insurance is a form of group life insurance under which the employee's contributions are applied each month to purchase units of paid-up insurance, just like single-premium whole life insurance. The paid-up insurance becomes a part of the employee's scheduled amount of insurance, and the balance of his coverage is made up of term insurance. Repeated contributions by the employee result in repeated purchases of paid-up insurance. As the paid-up insurance accumulates, the term insurance required to make up the full scheduled amount decreases accordingly. At any time after termination of employment the paid-up insurance can be surrendered for a cash value that is guaranteed to be at least as great as the total amount contributed by the employee.

Group permanent life insurance consists in essence of a collection of individual policies of permanent life insurance that are tied into a single master contract with group underwriting and administrative simplifications. Coverage is generally provided on a yearly renewable term basis until the employees meet an age or service requirement, at which time all or part of the employee's insurance is changed to a plan of whole life insurance, limited-payment life insurance, or single-premium life insurance. A single plan of permanent insurance would normally be offered under a given group contract, and the amounts of insurance would be scheduled so as to preclude individual selection. The employee is usually given a separate certificate of insurance for his original amount of permanent insurance and for any subsequent increase in permanent insurance. A level premium is required for each separate issue of permanent insurance from its effective date to the end of the premium-paying period. Cash and paid-up insurance values are accumulated in much the same fashion as under individual policies of life insurance, and all or part of these equities can be made available to the terminating employee, depending on the vesting provisions in the plan.

Tax Ruling on Permanent Insurance

The course of development of permanent forms of life insurance on a group basis was affected considerably by a ruling of the Commissioner of Internal Revenue (Mim. 6477, February 23, 1950) that all insurance provided "on a typical level premium form is considered a permanent form and all of each premium paid with respect to an employee under such a form, less any employee contributions on account of the premium, is required to be included in the income of the employee for the year in which the premium is paid." The ruling further went on to state:

> Where a portion of the insurance is provided by units of paid-up insurance on a typical single premium form or is on a typical level premium form, and the balance is provided on a typical current term form, with separate premiums specified in the policy for each portion, only the paid-up or level premium insurance is considered a permanent form and all of each premium paid for paid-up level premium insurance with respect to an employee under such a plan, less any employee contributions on account of such premium, is required to be included in the income of the employee for the year in which the premium is paid. Thus if each premium for paid-up or level premium insurance for an employee is provided from employee contributions on account of it, no premiums are considered paid by the employer for a permanent form of insurance under such a plan.[1]

Because of the employee income tax liability under group permanent insurance and the administrative difficulty in determining and reporting the amount of additional income subject to tax, these level premium forms have lost a great deal of their attractiveness; and for the most part, their use has declined substantially in recent years. This tax ruling also affects the design of the group paid-up plans because, if employer money is used for the purchase of paid-up insurance, it becomes taxable as income to the employee insured. This makes it imperative, at least from a practical standpoint, that the entire premium for the purchase of paid-up insurance be derived from employee contributions.

GROUP PAID-UP INSURANCE

Under a plan of group paid-up insurance, each employee who joins and remains in the plan is covered for an insurance amount in accordance with the schedule of insurance in the group master policy. Each month, in order to remain in the plan, the employee must contribute an amount

[1] It is important to note that this tax ruling applies only to permanent plans of group life insurance which are not qualified with the Internal Revenue Service as pension plans. Where, for example, a group permanent plan involves retirement income policies and the plan has been qualified with the Internal Revenue Service as a pension plan, a completely different set of tax rulings applies. Accordingly, a distinction is usually drawn between group permanent life insurance plans and group permanent pension plans. The group permanent pension plans are closely related to individual policy pension trusts and will be described in Chapter 38.

determined by his classification in the schedule of insurance, and this contribution is applied to purchase paid-up insurance. The amount of paid-up insurance purchased by a particular contribution depends upon the employee's age at the time the contribution is made. At any given time a part of the total insurance for each of the employees will consist of the accumulated paid-up insurance that has already been purchased by his contributions. Each month the employer purchases a complemental amount of term insurance, so that the employee's coverage always adds up to the desired scheduled amount. Table 30–1 shows the amounts of paid-up insurance purchased by an employee, entering a typical paid-up plan at age 35, who is insured for $1,000 of life insurance and who is contributing $1.00 monthly.

TABLE 30–1

ILLUSTRATIVE AMOUNTS OF PAID-UP INSURANCE AND TERM INSURANCE FOR FIVE YEARS BEGINNING AT AGE 35

Age	Contributions during Year	Amount of Paid-up Insurance per $1.00 of Contribution	Paid-up Insurance Purchased	Accumulated Paid-up Insurance Owned by Employee	Term Insurance Purchased by Employer	Total Insurance
35........	$12.00 ×	$2.75 =	$33.00	$ 33.00	$967.00	$1,000
36........	12.00 ×	2.68 =	32.16	65.16	934.84	1,000
37........	12.00 ×	2.62 =	31.44	96.60	903.40	1,000
38........	12.00 ×	2.55 =	30.60	127.20	872.80	1,000
39........	12.00 ×	2.49 =	29.88	157.08	842.92	1,000

If the employee in this example terminated his employment at the end of the five-year period, he would continue to be insured for $157.08 of paid-up insurance for life without further payment of premiums. He could, then or later, elect to surrender his paid-up insurance for its cash value, which would be at least equal to his total contributions of $60. Further, he could, within thirty-one days, elect to convert the $842.92 of group term insurance to an individual policy of life insurance.

The Cash Surrender Provision

The employee's right to surrender his paid-up insurance for cash is subject to one important restriction, namely, that he must have terminated his employment with the employer. The chief reason for this restriction is that if cash values were made available whenever an employee ceased to contribute for paid-up insurance for any reason, the participating employees would be sorely tempted from time to time to withdraw from the plan to secure the immediate use of their accumulated cash value. If the plan is to accumulate reasonable amounts of paid-up insurance by the time employees retire, it is clear that continuous participation is necessary, and thus the cash value cannot be freely available while employment continues. Moreover, no employee contributions could be diverted to purchase paid-up insurance equities unless the employer agreed to assume the entire cost of the term insurance, and most employers are unwilling to take on this added cost if the purpose of the plan can be defeated by the capricious withdrawal of cash by the participating employees.

When a group master policy is terminated, the individuals then insured do not have the right to surrender their paid-up insurance for cash until their employment subsequently terminates because otherwise the accumulation of increasing potential cash values would merely generate increasing demands on the part of covered employees for the lapse or replacement of the master contract. These restrictions on cash values are vitally necessary for the insurance companies underwriting group paid-up plans because they minimize the danger of mass surrender during periods of economic depression when asset values may be extremely depressed. Further, they make it possible for an employer to maintain the plan on a permanent basis despite the fact that over any substantial number of years, brief periods are almost certain to occur where employees experience a pressing temporary need for ready cash.

One fundamental requirement of the paid-up plan is that there be a steady and continued accumulation of employee-bought paid-up insurance. This accumulation might be seriously disrupted by layoffs, strikes, leaves of absence, and absences from work due to sickness or injury. To minimize the effect of such temporary employment conditions, the paid-up plan typically provides that cash surrender values will not be available during the first year of such temporary absence unless the employee has completely terminated his employment relationship to the extent that he no longer has the right to return to work on a preferential basis.

Contribution Rates

The standard paid-up plan provides for employee contributions of $1.00 monthly for each $1,000 of scheduled insurance. This standard $1.00 rate will result in about half of an employee's insurance being paid up at the end of twenty years' contributions. Because of the relatively high rate of contribution, the schedule of insurance would normally be based on the employee's earnings, although it could provide a flat amount for all employees, or an amount varying by job classification or length of service. The considerations involved in designing a suitable schedule of insurance for a plan of group paid-up insurance are essentially no different from what they are for a plan of conventional term insurance.

While the contributions are normally set at $1.00 monthly per $1,000 of insurance, the level of contributions depends upon a number of important considerations. First, the level of contributions must exceed some absolute minimum amount per employee; otherwise the employee will never accumulate a worth-while amount of paid-up insurance. Second, the contributions should be reasonably related to the scheduled amount of insurance. The employee's paid-up coverage should not compare unfavorably with an individual policy of insurance on a level premium plan, such as straight life or whole life paid up at 65. For this reason, employee contribution rates seldom exceed $1.50 monthly per $1,000 except perhaps for contribution rates that apply only to those employees who first enter the plan at the older ages, say after age 50. Third, the employee contributions must be reasonably related to the employee's rate of earnings. In general, the contributions should not exceed perhaps 3 per cent of earnings if favorable participation is to be secured. For each group the level of acceptable employee contributions is, of course, affected by the amount of employee income that is required for other welfare, pension, or savings programs. Finally, the level of contributions should be set high enough so that adequate amounts of paid-up insurance will be accumulated by the time the employees retire. In particular, where some minimum death benefit is desired for pensioners, the contribution must be high enough so that the employee who enters the plan after the effective date will accumulate more paid-up insurance than that minimum by the time he retires.

Within this general framework, it has been found that employee contributions should probably not fall below $1.00 monthly per $1,000 of insurance for insurance amounts up to perhaps one and a half times earnings, or $20,000. Further, the contributions should not fall below $2.00 monthly for each $1,000 of pensioner insurance desired. Of course, the contributions for paid-up insurance need not be determined by using a fixed rate, such as $1.00, for each $1,000 of insurance under the plan. One possible variation is to set the contributions at $1.00 for each $1,000 of insurance in excess of some basic amount, such as $1,000 or $2,000, in order to make the contributions for the lower paid employees more attractive. Another variation is to grade the rate of contribution from $1.00 for employees entering the plan under age 45 to perhaps $2.50 for employees entering over age 55, in order to enable the older entrants to accumulate more paid-up insurance.

Combination Term and Paid-up Plans

Where employment turnover is very high, it becomes both fruitless and expensive to keep the records on contributions for the many employees who quit work after a short period of service and then withdraw a small amount of cash. It is therefore occasionally desirable to use a relatively long probationary period for the paid-up portion of the coverage and provide conventional contributory term insurance during this preliminary period. As an example, combination term and paid-up plans have been developed which, under a single group master contract, provide that an employee will become insured upon employment for a specified amount of term insurance for which he must contribute at the rate of 60 cents monthly per $1,000, with this contribution being applied by the employer as a partial offset to the cost of the term insurance under the plan. Upon the completion of perhaps five years of service or, alternatively, upon the attainment of age 35 or 40, the employee would enter the paid-up portion of the plan, under which he would continue to be insured for the same scheduled amount of insurance, but at a monthly contribution of $1.00 per $1,000, with his contributions thereafter being applied to purchase paid-up insurance for him.

These plans have the advantage that the initial cost to the employer is lower than the initial cost of a standard paid-up plan because the contributions for term insurance from the group not yet eligible for paid-up insurance continue as an offset to employer cost. Further, when the paid-up portion of the plan is restricted to the longer service, older employees whose rate of voluntary withdrawal is usually much lower than for the group as a whole, the value of the paid-up contributions in reducing employer cost is substantially increased because each unit of paid-up insurance will, on the average, offset the employer-bought term insurance for a longer period.

Since these plans are more complicated to underwrite, explain, and administer, the use of special preliminary term insurance periods under paid-up plans is usually restricted to larger groups where the rate of employment turnover is abnormally high and is concentrated at the young ages or in the short-service group.

Pensioner Guarantees—Provision for Past Service Benefits

On the effective date of a typical group paid-up plan, the employees who are below age 45 can be expected to accumulate 50 per cent or more of their final insurance in the form of paid-up insurance by retirement age. The employees who are within a few years of retirement will be able to accumulate only nominal amounts of paid-up insurance. It is frequently desirable for the employer to agree to provide some minimum amount of pensioner insurance for the older employees who are insured on the effective date of a paid-up plan. For example, for those employees who keep their paid-up insurance in force after retirement, the employer might agree to continue to purchase sufficient additional term insurance so that the total of the term insurance and any paid-up insurance that has been purchased will equal $1,000—or perhaps, alternatively, 25 or 50 per cent of the amount of insurance in force at retirement. This minimum amount is frequently graded down on the basis of length of service at retirement. Another alternative is to credit the employee with 1 or 2 per cent of his insurance for each year of past service on the effective date of the plan as the flat amount of term insurance the employer will continue after his retirement in addition to any paid-up insurance purchased. Naturally, the more generous the provision for retired employees, the greater the financial obligation taken on by the employer, and the greater his future cost. It is important to keep in mind that each $1,000 of life insurance to be continued for an employee retiring at age 65 is equivalent to a lump-sum cash payment of about $700.

The general objective in designing a fully funded paid-up plan is to make sure that all employees under a given age at installation of the plan or hired in the future will accumulate the desired pensioner death benefit in the form of paid-up insurance by the time they retire. This means that any extra benefits that may be granted on account of past service on the effective date of the plan should not be greater than the amount of paid-up insurance the employee would have purchased if the paid-up plan had been in force continuously since the date of his employment. If greater past service pensioner benefits are desired, greater employee contributions are probably necessary. Any past service provision should, of course, be restricted to those employees insured on the effective date of the plan who remain continuously insured until their retirement date. Employer liability for pensioners' term insurance is then restricted to a closed initial group of employees.

Comparative Costs—Term Plans versus Paid-up Plans

The provision of insurance for retired employees under group term plans necessarily implies that the total cost of the insurance, even assuming a completely level active working force indefinitely in the future, will exhibit a continuous and gradual increase as more and more retired employees are added to the benefit rolls. The eventual cost of the pensioners' insurance will depend upon the amount of benefit continued for them as well as on those employment characteristics of the group which determine the number of employees that can be expected to retire each year.

For a typical industrial group, including both hourly and salaried employees, about 1¼ per cent of the active working group could be expected to reach normal retirement age each year in the stable situation where employment remains level. Naturally, the pensioner group will be increased by this 1¼ per cent who retire and be decreased by the number of pensioners dying. As long as the annual retirements exceed the annual pensioner deaths, the number of surviving pensioners will continue to increase until the leveling-off point is reached where there are as many pensioners dying each year as there are retirements. This implies that the number of pensioners dying each year must eventually stabilize at about 1¼ per cent of the number of active employees. By way of contrast, in a typical group of active employees, only about one half of 1 per cent could be expected to die in one year, so that in the long run, there will probably be about two and one-half times as many deaths among the pensioner group as there are among the active employees.

Further, where insurance amounts are based on earnings, job classification, or length of service, the employees reaching retirement age tend to have a substantially higher average amount of insurance than the younger active employees, so that if the full amount of insurance is continued, the total amount of pensioner death claims might well stabilize at between three and four times the total amount of death claims on active employees. It is this imbalance in cost that makes the continuation of pensioner insurance impractical under term plans unless the pensioners' amounts are relatively small, say 10 to 20 per cent of the active amount.

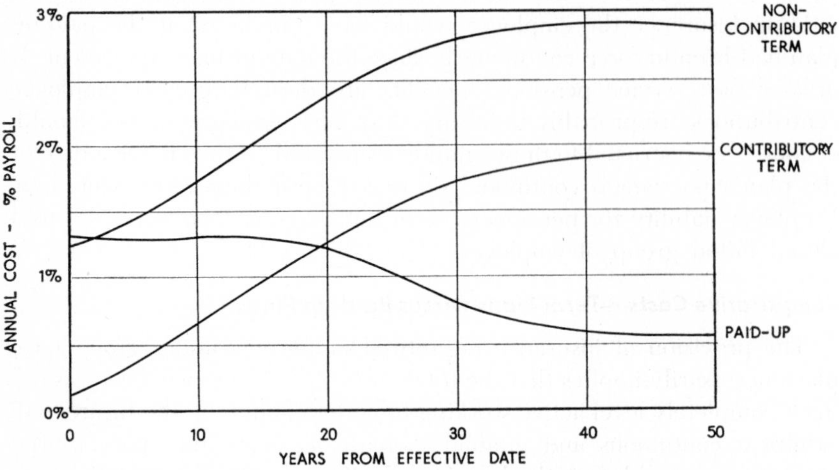

FIG. 30–1. Cost trends for continuing life insurance on retired employees under noncontributory group term, contributory group term, and group paid-up insurance.

Under plans of group paid-up insurance the increase in the cost of insuring retired employees is severely dampened by the accumulation of greater paid-up amounts by each successive wave of pensioners. As an example, the provision of a minimum of 25 or 50 per cent of the insurance for retired employees will eventually involve no employer cost under a paid-up plan because no supplemental term insurance will be required for those pensioners retiring after the plan has been in force about twenty years. Further, the cost of insuring the active employees decreases from the outset because of their accumulating paid-up insurance.

Figure 30–1 illustrates the general trend in employer cost that would be expected to follow a decision to continue 50 per cent of the insurance for retiring employees. Separate cost patterns are shown for noncontributory group term insurance, group term with 60-cent contributions, and group paid-up insurance with $1.00 contributions. The graphs are based on an insurance schedule equal to 150 per cent of annual earnings, a constant number of active employees, and an employment turnover rate of 23 per cent.

Advantages of Funding

Under group term plans a substantial part of the total employer cost will eventually be required for the pensioners' coverage. As to any particular year, the number of pensioners insured and the cost of their insurance will, of course, be independent of whether business conditions are good or bad. Thus, in bad times, when the employer is decreasing his working force and cutting his active payroll, the cost of pensioner life insurance increases as a percentage of annual payroll, much as an item of fixed overhead might. In good business years, when the active working force is expanding, the cost of pensioners' insurance would, of course, decrease as a percentage of payroll. Under paid-up plans, this "fixed overhead cost" is continuously being reduced by the paid-up accumulations, and the point is eventually reached where all of the costs are for active employees. Thus the cost of a paid-up plan would tend to rise and fall in a fashion much more closely parallel to the changes in payroll and other labor costs.

Sound cost accounting requires that a realistic portion of the employer's cost of a pensioner's life insurance should be allocated as an additional cost of labor to each of the years in which he was a member of the active work force. Where continued insurance is promised for retired employees, management has accepted a certain contingent liability each year for the cost of pensioner insurance for each of the actively working employees. The liability is, of course, contingent on the particular employee's neither dying nor withdrawing from service prior to normal retirement age. Under term insurance plans the employer's cash outlay in any particular year is just sufficient, after adding employee contributions, to provide for the current protection in that year, and nothing is paid for the contingent liability for pensioner insurance. Under paid-up plans the employer, by waiving the immediate offset of employee contributions, increases his cash outlay to an amount more nearly approximating the true incurred cost of insurance, including this contingent liability for pensioner term insurance.

The paid-up plan represents a practical solution to the management problem of providing group life insurance coverage for pensioners as well as active employees on a basis whereby, in the long run, employer costs after retirement are eliminated. For each new employee the cost of the continuing insurance is paid for during the employee's productive working years, a basic requirement of the sound financing of pensioners' benefits. The paid-up plan is a popular contributory insurance program, and its adoption by an employer may anticipate and divert demands on the part of the employees for noncontributory insurance protection. By adopting a paid-up plan, the employer with a contributory term program may merely be accepting the full cost of term insurance a few years in advance of the date it would otherwise have been forced upon him, while at the same time continuing to enjoy the many advantages of contributory plans as well as the cost advantage resulting from the accumulation of employee-bought paid-up insurance.

The group paid-up plan is the most efficient means of providing a funded pensioner death benefit that is nonforfeitable prior to retirement, and in the typical case the cost of giving cash values or paid-up insurance to the terminating employees is more than covered by the increase in employee contributions from 60 cents to $1.00. The paid-up plan is flexible and can be tailored to fit the specific requirements of each employer. Further, the group paid-up plan is a modern and popular coverage, and its adoption may give the employer one more small advantage over other firms competing for personnel in the same employment market. In the long run, the value of any benefit plan depends upon the sound design of the program and the employee appreciation the program develops. The employee appeal of group paid-up insurance is clearly demonstrated by the participation of about 95 per cent of eligible employees in the typical paid-up plan.

Under the paid-up plan an employee is given the opportunity to purchase insurance on a permanent and guaranteed basis at lower cost and with higher cash values and paid-up amounts than are generally available when purchasing life insurance under individual policies. The accumulating paid-up insurance tends to offset the problems caused by the high premium cost of converted policies at the older ages by reducing the amount of insurance that needs be converted. The employee's paid-up insurance can be surrendered for a cash value at any time after he terminates employment, so that it can be diverted by the ex-employee to other personal needs, such as funds to tide an ex-employee over a temporary period of unemployment, or as a drawing account for the pensioner who incurs catastrophic medical expenses. Group paid-up insurance further answers one of the traditional objections to contributory group insurance, namely, that the older employee has nothing to show for many years' contributions he has made to the plan. Group paid-up insurance is popular with employees because the employee does not have to "die to win" and each participant can visualize himself collecting something under the plan.

The Market for Group Paid-up Insurance

Group paid-up plans are suited for employee groups with low to average employment turnover—for example, salaried employees. For those groups with relatively high employment turnover, say in excess of 25 per cent per year, it may be necessary to use a combination term and paid-up plan. Paid-up plans are most successfully sold where there is a need for insurance protection for retired employees. Group paid-up insurance should probably not be suggested where the amounts of group term life insurance are inadequate. For such cases, any additional employer or employee money should first be used to provide additional amounts of current protection. Only when active employees are insured for adequate amounts of group term life insurance does it become reasonable to divert some premium money for the funding of pensioner death benefits.

For the larger insurance risks the purchase of group paid-up plans is usually based on financial considerations involving actuarial projections of the future cost of various group paid-up plans and group term insurance plans for each of the pensioner benefits being considered. For smaller cases the plan is generally purchased solely on the basis of the employee appeal of a money-back guarantee and an accumulating personal equity in the group insurance program.

Typical Underwriting Requirements

The group paid-up plan is made available today by almost every major group-writing company. Many companies require a minimum of 50 insured employees before they will underwrite this coverage, some require 100 lives or more, and a few will provide group paid-up insurance for certain types of groups as small as 10 lives. Within limits, however, the number of lives to be insured is of less importance than the relative permanence of the business and the facilities the employer has at his disposal for the administration of the plan. By way of example, a 25-life bank is probably a better paid-up prospect than many 50- and 100-life groups with minimum accounting facilities.

The maximum amount of insurance permitted for any one employee is generally greater than under policies of group term life insurance because of the favorable effect on the experience of the plan that can be expected from the accumulation of substantial amounts of paid-up insurance. Most companies would require a minimum of perhaps $1,000 in total annual paid-up premiums in addition to the term premium for the plan and a minimum contribution from any employee of $1.00 per month. The group paid-up coverage is thus currently available to a broad group of prospects with a minimum amount of restriction.

GROUP PERMANENT LIFE INSURANCE PLANS

The group permanent life insurance plans currently being issued fall into two general classes—those plans based on single-premium life insurance purchased when an employee retires from service and those based on whole life insurance plans that require level premiums either for life or to age 65. The single-premium plans provide for the insurance of all active employees on a conventional yearly renewable term plan with a special contract provision and premium table for the single-premium purchases to be made when employees retire. The amount of single-premium coverage is simply the amount of insurance being continued after retirement, and the purchases are usually made on an individual basis as each employee actually retires. The purpose behind this plan is to pay for the entire cost of the retiring employee's continuing coverage on the date he retires rather than have the cost stretched out over his remaining future lifetime on a term insurance basis. The single-premium plan thus enables an employer to reflect, as a current operating cost, the entire value of the insurance gift he is making to the retiring employee in the year the liability for pensioner insurance ceases to be contingent and becomes instead a reality.

The 1950 tax ruling referred to earlier clearly requires that if the insurance is nonforfeitable, the retiring employee must include the entire single premium with his taxable income in the year the premium is paid, whether or not the insurance can be surrendered for a cash value. The combination of a relatively high single premium paid by the employer, together with perhaps a 20 per cent income tax paid by the employee to the federal government, results in a total employer-employee expenditure that may well approach the total face amount of insurance being provided. Because of this serious tax disadvantage, the plans providing fully vested coverage are used infrequently today and are set up on an "employee pay all" basis, or else special steps are taken to minimize the tax impact.

Straight life and limited-payment life plans are occasionally used to fund, prior to the date of his retirement, the amount of insurance to be continued for a retiring employee. A typical plan might provide that the expected pensioner benefit for employees over age 50 will be insured under a program of life paid up at 65, and the balance of the coverage over age 50 and all insurance under age 50 will remain on a yearly renewable term basis. These plans can be viewed as a modification of the single-premium plan under which the single premium has been spread back over the last 10 or 15 years of active employment. The excess of the level premium for the life-paid-up-at-65 coverage over any contributions made by the employee is taxed as income to the employee unless the coverage is nonvested.[2] For this reason, some group permanent plans designed to fund the pensioner benefit provide that the employee's cover-

[2] The 1950 Revenue Bureau ruling taxes only that form of permanent insurance that is vested, i.e., that the employee can take with him as a matter of right in the event of termination of employment or cancellation of the group master policy. If the insurance is nonvested, no tax is required until the insurance vests, at which time the entire value of the insurance becomes taxable as though a single premium had just been paid to purchase it.

age will be forfeited without value to the employee if he terminates employment, if he is removed from the list of eligible pensioners, or if coverage under the group master contract is discontinued. The employees' and pensioners' benefits under plans of this type, as well as the certificates of insurance, are thus exactly the same as they would be under a plan of group term life insurance.

The laws of a number of states limit the amount of term insurance that can be issued to any one employee under a policy of group life insurance. Where the law specifically limits only the amount of term insurance, the amount of permanent life insurance is obviously not subject to the group maximum limitation, and this advantage, under special circumstances, may well outweigh the tax problem. Further, plans of this type almost invariably provide that the employees' coverage will be forfeitable at all times, both before and after retirement.

Employer premiums for these plans are deductible as business expenses for tax purposes under the usual rule for deducting premium payments for plans of group life insurance where the employer is not directly or indirectly a beneficiary under the plan. These plans usually provide that the reserves released when an employee's permanent coverage terminates will be applied as an offset to the next employer premium due under the plan and thus reduce the employer's deduction for that period.

Term Plans with Special Reserves

Although not, strictly speaking, a form of group permanent insurance, the tax complications introduced by the 1950 tax ruling have resulted in the occasional financing of pensioners' insurance under conventional yearly renewable term plans by means of nonvested deposit funds. Under this arrangement, either the employer pays a specific extra premium, or the insurance company allocates all or a part of any group life dividends into a "pensioner continuation fund." The annual interest credited to the fund and the annual deposit are intended to be the source of premium payments for the retired employees' coverage in future years. Many of these special funds are informal, in the sense that no specific contract provision is made for their accumulation or use. Most are based on the accumulation of employer dividends rather than a specific premium. The coverage for the active and retired employees is conventional yearly renewable term insurance, in the sense that it is subject to discontinuance at any time by the employer without value to the employee.

If the employer payment to a pensioner continuation fund is made on a freely recoverable basis, the question arises as to whether that payment constitutes a necessary and reasonable business expense in the year the payment is made (or the year the dividend is left with the insurance company). Presumably, from an accounting standpoint the deposit represents nothing more than a premium paid in advance if the employer can recover it at will. If the fund is not recoverable by the employer, there may be a tax problem for the retired employee, although payment of term premiums only from the fund during retirement years gives a "nonvested" aspect to the fund. Further, on a nonrecoverable and informal basis, it is frequently not clear just what happens to the fund if the employer should decide to transfer his coverage to another insurance carrier. Despite the many problems involved, this type of arrangement has been used more and more frequently, probably because the program can be set up with a minimum of added administrative detail.

Unfortunately, there are no specific tax rulings that clarify the tax picture for either the nonvested group permanent plans or the pensioner continuation funds. In actual practice, these plans have been restricted to relatively large groups with perhaps five hundred or more employees; apparently, these approaches are not practical for the smaller groups. In any event, these plans constitute another current and interesting method of adding permanent insurance and reserves to conventional yearly renewable term insurance.

SELECTED REFERENCES

Espie, R. G. "Group Life Insurance with Paid-up Values," *Transactions of the Society of Actuaries,* Vol. VII, No. 18 (1955).

Gregg, Davis W. *Group Life Insurance.* 3d ed. Homewood, Ill.: Richard D. Irwin, Inc., 1962.

Chapter 31

CREDIT LIFE AND HEALTH INSURANCE

BY KENNETH C. FOSTER

Consumer debt based on installment loans or installment purchases has become an accepted part of the average family's economic life. Homes, automobiles, furniture, and appliance purchases today are frequently financed over a period of time by payments from future income. The growth of consumer credit has continued to the point where the amount of outstanding installment indebtedness at the end of 1963 was approximately $51 billion.

With heavy debt on the family's shoulders, death or disability of the wage earner creates a financial crisis. Moreover, death of a debtor may mean a financial loss to those making loans or selling goods on credit. These various interests are insurable risks and have given rise to the growth and development of credit life and health insurance.

Nature of Credit Life and Health Insurance

Credit life insurance is defined as that form of insurance under which the life of the borrower of money or purchaser of goods is insured in connection with a specific loan or credit transaction. Credit health insurance is that form of insurance under which indemnity is provided for payments becoming due in connection with a specific loan or credit transaction while the borrower of money or purchaser of goods is disabled as a result of accident or sickness.

Both credit life and credit health insurance are generally available to all lending institutions or vendors providing services or selling goods on an installment basis. The principal ones are banks, sales finance companies, credit unions, small loan companies, department stores, furniture and appliance dealers, and motor vehicle dealers.

The classes of indebtedness to be insured under a policy depend upon the type of creditor through which the coverage is issued. For example, a group policy issued to a bank might specify as the classes: personal loans, both secured and unsecured; direct loans for the purchase of motor vehicles, furniture, appliances, equipment, and other commodities; and obligations for consumer goods sold through an installment or conditional sales contract originated by a dealer vendor and discounted to the bank. A group policy issued to a sales finance company or to a vendor would normally specify the same classes of indebtedness except for personal loans.

Depending upon the creditor's business, certain other classes of indebtednesses may be insured under arrangements appropriate to the special problems involved. These include home modernization loans, residential mortgage loans, mobile home loans, some commercial loans, revolving credit accounts, mutual fund share purchases, and educational loan plans. When the indebtedness is of long duration, the insurance is sometimes provided under different arrangements than those used for shorter duration indebtedness of five years or less.

The rapid postwar growth of credit life insurance is evidenced by the fact that in 1947 it constituted less than 1 per cent of the total life insurance in force in the United States and reached about 6 per cent in 1962. In the ten-year period 1952–62 the actual amount increased from $6.5 billion to $38 billion, an increase of about 500 per cent. Credit health insurance, while a comparatively new product, has also grown substantially. Over the five-year period 1947–52, written credit health insurance premiums increased from $32.4 million to $50 million, an increase of about 65 per cent.

Group credit life insurance accounts for about 84 per cent of the total credit life in force. About 65 per cent of the gross premium for credit health insurance is written under group policies.

Although some credit insurance is written on an individual policy basis, the bulk of credit insurance is provided through group insurance policies, as may be seen from the statistics above. The two methods of providing credit insurance differ in form but not in substance. Therefore, this chapter is devoted mainly to a discussion of group credit insurance, but includes a separate reference to the individual policy approach. Furthermore, because credit insurance involves two entirely different risks (death or disability), each will be considered separately in this chapter.

GROUP CREDIT LIFE INSURANCE

The group insurance policy is issued to the creditor and insures the lives of his debtors. There is no direct contract between the insurance company and the debtor. To inform the debtor of his insurance coverage, he is furnished a certificate describing the life insurance protection he has with respect to his indebtedness. In this connection, it should be noted that the arrangement among the insurer, the creditor, and the debtor is analogous to the arrangement which exists among an insurer, an employer, and an employee in the usual group context.

As credit life insurance is ancillary to the credit operation, the essence of which is the indebtedness, group insurance is a well-suited vehicle for providing coverage. The creditor, through whom insurance is provided, performs somewhat of an underwriting function when making loans or granting credit. Since credit underwriting has some elements in common with insurance underwriting, his credit investigation helps to screen out persons who would not be considered good insurance risks.

Benefits

Group credit life policies provide that the insurance company, in the event of the death of the debtor, will pay the remaining insured balance of the indebtedness to the creditor as beneficiary. The benefits must be used toward the discharge of the indebtedness. The policies are usually written on a decreasing term basis, so that each insured debtor is covered for an amount of life insurance equal to the amount of his indebtedness. As the indebtedness is being repaid in installments, the amount of insurance on his life reduces correspondingly. Provision is made for the insurance to terminate if an account becomes delinquent and remains so for a specified period, unless the policyholder (the creditor), if permitted to do so under the terms of the policy, elects to continue premium payments on delinquent indebtedness up to the maximum period stated in the policy (usually six months beyond the original maturity date of the indebtedness).

Group insurance policies generally limit the amount of insurance per life to a specified maximum. (See also the section entitled "Legal and Underwriting Requirements.") Where the initial indebtedness exceeds the maximum provided under the policy, the debtor normally is insured for that maximum until the indebtedness is reduced to the level of the maximum. After that point the insurance reduces as the indebtedness reduces.

Another less common method may be employed for determining the amount of insurance when the indebtedness exceeds the maximum specified under the group policy. Under this method the debtor is insured for an amount equal to the actual amount of indebtedness, reduced in the proportion which the maximum provided under the policy bears to the original amount of indebtedness. For example, assuming that a man borrows $4,000 and is covered under a policy specifying a $3,000 maximum, his amount of insurance always equals three fourths of his outstanding indebtedness. Under this method the amount insured always bears the same relation to the actual indebtedness as the ratio determined at the origin of the indebtedness.

Most group credit life policies cover types of indebtedness that are repayable in periodic installments over a duration not normally exceeding 60 months. When group credit life insurance is provided to insure real estate mortgagors, indebtednesses with durations of as much as thirty-five years may be covered, depending upon the legal maximums of the various states.

Several states now permit group credit life coverage on obligations repayable in one payment. The maximum period of indebtedness is usually limited to 18 months, with a right to extend for a further period of six months for renewal or refinancing.

Premium Rates

Premium rates for group credit life insurance are seldom based on age distributions of individual debtors because age data are not readily available in the credit operation. For this reason a flat premium rate is normally used. This contrasts with employer-employee group life coverage, where, although a flat rate is used for premiums and only a flat contribution rate may be required of employees, the premium rate is based on a table of rates by age and an age distribution of amounts on individual insureds.

There is considerable variation in the premium rates used by the many insurers who underwrite this coverage as they set rates to achieve their own sales, underwriting, and financial objectives. However, premium rates are subject to acceptance and approval of many of the state insurance departments under the laws and regulations governing credit insurance. Additional discussion of the effects of these laws and regulations is contained in the section of this chapter entitled "Credit Insurance Controls."

Group credit life insurance premiums are usually paid monthly by the creditor to the insurer and are determined in either of two ways. Under the most common method the premium is based on the amount of outstanding insured indebtedness on each monthly premium due date and a monthly premium rate. For example, if the creditor's volume of outstanding insured indebtedness on a monthly premium due date is $1 million and the applicable rate is 60 cents per month per $1,000 of outstanding balance, the total premium due the insurer from the creditor for that month is $600.

Under the other method the creditor pays the insurer, on each monthly premium date, a single premium for each indebtedness which became insured during the month just elapsed. This single premium provides coverage for the full scheduled term of indebtedness. For example, the single-premium rate corresponding to the outstanding balance rate of 60 cents per $1,000 cited above would be 39 cents per $100 of initial indebtedness, repayable in 12 monthly installments. (See Table 31–1.)

It should be noted that, for a given indebtedness, under the outstanding balance method the creditor remits a premium to the insurer on each monthly premium due date that the indebtedness exists during its term, while under the single-premium method the creditor pays the total premium in one sum.

Table 31–1 shows the total gross cost of group credit life insurance for an initial $100 loan repayable in 12 equal monthly installments. It illustrates the gross cost over the full term of the loan corresponding to a 60-cent monthly rate per $1,000 of outstanding balance.

In renewal years the premium rate applicable to group credit life insurance may be adjusted to reflect the actual experience under the

TABLE 31–1

GROSS COST OF GROUP CREDIT LIFE INSURANCE FOR AN INITIAL $100 LOAN REPAYABLE IN TWELVE EQUAL MONTHLY INSTALLMENTS

Month	Amount Outstanding	Premium per $1,000 at 60 Cents
1	$100.00	6.0 cents
2	91.67	5.5
3	83.34	5.0
4	75.00	4.5
5	66.67	4.0
6	58.34	3.5
7	50.00	3.0
8	41.67	2.5
9	33.34	2.0
10	25.00	1.5
11	16.67	1.0
12	8.34	0.5
Total cost per $100 initial loan		39.0 cents

policy. This practice corresponds to the setting of renewal rates for other forms of group insurance. Group credit life insurance is usually participating or subject to experience credits.

The foregoing deals with premium payments the creditor makes to the insurer. Inasmuch as the insurance protects the debtor as well as the creditor, the creditor may require the debtor to pay all or part of the cost of the coverage. The amount a debtor is required to pay is referred to as the charge for insurance. This charge is usually made as a single sum and is included in the amount of the credit transaction. Any such charge made to a debtor may not be more than the premium or premiums to be paid by the creditor to the insurer as computed at the time the indebtedness is incurred.

Legal and Underwriting Requirements

Group credit life insurance is written in most states under the terms of specific provisions of the insurance laws permitting such coverage. Insurance laws vary from state to state, but all have the effect of regulating group credit life insurance so that coverage is provided on a sound underwriting basis. Limitations which may be present in insurance laws are:

1. The maximum amount of insurance per individual insured debtor is usually $5,000 or $10,000. The insurance may not exceed the indebtedness.
2. The maximum durations of installment loans, other than mortgage loans, eligible for group credit life insurance are limited by a few states to five years. Maximum durations for mortgage loans range up to thirty-five years.
3. The coverage may be issued only if debtors enter the eligible group at a rate of at least one hundred per year. The purpose of this requirement is to obtain an average exposure by a continual flow of new insured debtors.
4. Where the cost of the insurance is absorbed by the creditor, all debtors in the eligible classes of indebtedness are automatically insured at the time the indebtedness is created.
5. Where the debtor pays all or part of the cost, the coverage is provided only to those debtors who elect to be insured. Where less than 75 per cent of eligible debtors elect the coverage, the insurance company must reserve the right to request evidence of insurability for each new eligible debtor.

In addition to statutory requirements, certain underwriting requirements are imposed by most insurance companies writing group credit life insurance. The major requirements are:

1. The creditor's portfolio of eligible classes of indebtedness must meet a minimum volume requirement and must be expected to produce a minimum number of debtors to be insured.
2. A limit on the maximum amount of insurance that may be provided on the life of a debtor is specified.

The purpose of establishing a minimum total indebtedness and a minimum number of debtors to be insured is to assure that there will be enough new entrants into the group to counteract the effects of individual selection against the plan.

Another purpose of the minimum case size is to assure that there will be sufficient premium income to provide for claims and administrative expenses connected with providing the coverage. For example, the insurance company may require that a creditor have an amount of loans outstanding of at least $25,000 in the eligible classes before the policy can be issued. It is not necessary to insure the amount of indebtedness outstanding on the date the policy is to be effective—this is optional with the policyholder—but in any event the amount is considered as a condition to underwriting the policy.

The requirement governing the maximum amount of insurance on the life of any one debtor is in addition to the statutory maximums. Insurance companies normally limit the maximum amount and make it depend upon the volume of loans eligible for insurance. Table 31–2 shows typical limitations for coverage of other than mortgage loans. Maximums for mortgage loan coverage are usually those imposed by the law of the state where the group policy is issued.

In addition to the statutory and underwriting norms described above, age limitations and evidence of insurability requirements are sometimes used as underwriting safeguards. Age limitations, if used, usually preclude coverage of debtors aged 65 or more at the time of indebtedness or aged 66 or more on the scheduled maturity date of the indebtedness. Evidence of insurability requirements range from a simple test of the debtor's employment status to a medical examination.

TABLE 31–2

TYPICAL SCHEDULE OF MAXIMUM AMOUNTS OF GROUP CREDIT LIFE INSURANCE ON THE LIFE OF ANY ONE DEBTOR

Outstanding Balance on Classes of Indebtedness to Be Insured	Maximum Amount of Insurance on the Life of Any One Debtor
Less than $500,000	$ 5,000
$500,000 but less than 600,000	6,000
600,000 but less than 700,000	7,000
700,000 but less than 800,000	8,000
800,000 but less than 900,000	9,000
900,000 and over	10,000

These safeguards may be used when a case includes classes of indebtedness such as loans for home modernization or mobile homes, commercial loans, and education loan plans.

Administration

As is true of other forms of group insurance, the administration of group credit life insurance is kept simple. A certificate or statement of insurance for the debtor is completed by the policyholder (creditor) and shows such items as the name of the insured, account number, and amount of insurance. The policyholder maintains insurance information with the credit transaction records necessary to the credit operation. Insurance company representatives make a regular periodic audit of the policyholder's records to assure proper administration of the insurance program in accordance with the terms of the group policy and with the requirements of state law or regulations. The policyholder submits both a check for the premium on each premium due date and a simple form which shows the basis for his premium calculation.

Claim handling is also relatively simple. A transcript of the death certificate, or a doctor's certificate of death, is submitted to the creditor, who determines from his records the amount of insured outstanding indebtedness and completes a claim form. Claim payments in many cases are made to the creditor through a draft drawn upon the insurance company by the creditor. In other cases, he may receive a direct payment from the insurance company. The claim form and evidence of death are forwarded to the insurance company.

GROUP CREDIT HEALTH INSURANCE

Credit health insurance, like credit life insurance, provides insurance protection which is directly related to the amount of indebtedness. It is designed to protect the insured debtor by paying to the creditor the amount of the debtor's monthly installments which accrue while he is indebted to the creditor and totally disabled. Normally, a debtor is considered to be totally disabled when he is unable, because of sickness or injury, to perform any work or engage in any business for remuneration or profit.

Benefits

Credit health insurance benefits are payable for disabilities which begin while the debtor is insured if he remains continuously disabled for a specified period. The specified period, sometimes called the qualification period, usually is 14 or 30 days. Benefits may be payable retroactive to the first day of disability (the first day of the qualification period), in which event the policy pays for disability of the debtor during the qualification period as well as for disability which continues after the qualification period. When benefits are not retroactive, the policy pays only for continuous disability after the qualification period.

Benefits are usually determined as of the debtor's monthly installment due date according to one of two methods.

One method, referred to as the pro rata method, pays the debtor's total monthly payment if he has been disabled for the full payment period, or pays one thirtieth of the monthly payment for each day of continuous disability during the payment period if he has been disabled for less than the full payment period.

A second method, referred to as the monthly installment method, pays benefits equal to the debtor's full monthly payment if he has completed the qualification period and has continued totally disabled to the monthly payment due date.

Under either method, disability benefits continue while the insured debtor remains totally disabled, but not beyond the scheduled maturity date of the indebtedness.

Premium Rates

As is true with group credit life insurance, premiums for credit health insurance may be paid in either of two ways. The first method is the single-premium method, under which the rate is expressed per $100 of initial insured indebtedness and the total premium is paid in one sum. Under the second method, premiums are paid monthly on the basis of a rate per $1,000 of insured outstanding balance.

As an illustration, the single-premium rates charged by one company for a plan of nonretroactive benefits following a thirty-day qualification period are 89 cents per $100 for a 12-month indebtedness, $1.24 for a 24-month indebtedness, and $1.52 for a 36-month indebtedness.

Again, for illustrative purposes, the monthly outstanding balance rates charged for the same type of plan are $1.37 per month per $1,000 for a 12-month indebtedness, 99 cents for a 24-month indebtedness, and 82 cents for a 36-month indebtedness.

In renewal years the premium rates applicable to credit health insurance may be adjusted to reflect the actual experience under the policy. This corresponds to the setting of renewal rates for other forms of group insurance. As is the case with group credit life insurance, group credit health insurance is normally participating or subject to experience credits.

Legal and Underwriting Requirements

In addition to the legal and underwriting requirements described under group credit life insurance, the following apply to group credit health insurance:

1. The amount of periodic indemnity is defined as the original amount of indebtedness divided by the number of periodic payments to be made by the debtor. As underwriting safeguards, the credit health policy usually provides a maximum amount which the periodic indemnity may not exceed, and limits the total disability benefit payable in respect of a disabled debtor's indebtedness. These limitations sometimes depend upon the size of the case.
2. The policy may contain a provision which excludes payment of benefits for disability resulting from a condition which disabled the insured debtor within a period of time, usually six months, immediately preceding the date the debtor became insured. This exclusion is sometimes modified to allow benefits for such disabilities if the debtor has been free of disability on account of the condition for a stated continuous period of time after becoming insured. This period is usually six months.
3. Disabilities caused by pregnancy and those resulting from acts of war are excluded from benefit.
4. The policy may require an eligible debtor to be gainfully employed as a condition precedent to becoming insured.

Administration

As group credit health insurance is frequently provided together with group credit life insurance, its administration is similar to that of the credit life. However, although death claims under the life insurance may be paid by the creditor drawing a draft on the insurer, claim payments under the health insurance are usually processed and paid directly by the insurer. Claim payments are generally made monthly to the creditor as the beneficiary, and are then credited to the debtor's account in lieu of his monthly payment. Because of the eligibility requirements normally present under a credit health program and the variations in the plans, proper claims administration of the coverage requires the experience and services of the insurer.

INDIVIDUAL CREDIT LIFE AND HEALTH POLICIES

Credit insurance is provided under an individual policy issued to the debtor directly by the insurer as well as under a master group policy issued to the creditor, with a certificate describing the coverage being issued to the debtor. The laws of most states governing credit life insurance provide that the amount of insurance must not exceed the amount of the indebtedness, so that individual credit life, as well as group credit life, is usually decreasing term insurance. In some states, two types of individual policies are permitted: decreasing term and level term.

Under the decreasing term type the amount of insurance reduces on a basis consistent with the scheduled repayment of the indebtedness. The creditor is the beneficiary, and the scheduled amount of insurance equals the amount of the unpaid debt at any time, unless the insured debtor is in default or has prepaid part or all of his indebtedness. Under the level term type the initial amount of insurance remains constant throughout the period of indebtedness. Because under level term the amount of insurance at death usually exceeds the amount of indebtedness, the creditor is designated as the *primary* beneficiary. A *second* beneficiary, normally the estate of the debtor, is designated by the insured to receive any amount payable in excess of the amount necessary to discharge the indebtedness at death.

The benefits provided by individual policies are determined at the issuance of the policy. Therefore, under the decreasing term form of individual coverage, if the loan balance outstanding is reduced through an acceleration of payments, the insurance continues to reduce in accordance with the original schedule of the indebtedness, so that the amount of insurance may exceed the actual unpaid balance. Many states, however, require that the insured be given the option of terminating the insurance in exchange for a refund of the unearned premium in the event of complete prepayment of the loan. By the same token, if the account becomes delinquent, no adjustment is usually made to reflect the fact that the indebtedness exceeds the amount of insurance. Both decreasing term and level term individual credit life insurance provide coverage for the duration of the original period of indebtedness.

Credit health insurance coverage provided the debtor under an individual policy is normally identical with that provided under a master group policy from the standpoint of plans and benefits. Also, as in group insurance, premium rates vary, and depend upon the waiting period and duration of indebtedness.

Aside from the format, there are few essential differences between the protection provided under the group and individual policy bases of credit life and health insurance. On either basis, coverage is mass-marketed through creditors who provide lending and debt services to the public, and the insurance protection is complementary to the indebtedness, regardless of the form used.

The group master policy plus the certificates of insurance, taken together, cover the same ground as the individual insurance agent agreement (which the creditor, acting as intermediary, executes) and the individual policies.

The insurance risk is the same on either basis. As the insurance company's concern is not for the insurability of any individual debtor, group underwriting techniques are employed under the individual policy approach to creditor insurance.

CREDIT INSURANCE CONTROLS

Because credit insurance during the postwar years was rapidly becoming an important segment of the insurance industry, the National Association of Insurance Commissioners, through appointed committees, examined credit insurance practices, and in 1957 authored a Model Bill for consideration of and adoption by the various state legislatures. The bill was intended to serve as a uniform standard for the guidance of insurers in properly conducting the business of credit insurance, and for the guidance of insurance supervisory authorities in governing credit insurance. A primary objective of the bill was to correct certain abuses in some areas in the credit life and health insurance fields which had resulted from the debtors' inferior status in the creditors' bargaining process. Principally, the abuses were:

1. Overcharging—requiring debtors to pay higher insurance charges than warranted by the benefits provided, and
2. Lack of disclosure—failure to inform debtors of their insurance coverage and its cost.

The bill, known as the "NAIC Model Bill to Provide for the Regulation of Life Insurance and Credit Accident and Health Insurance," was revised in December, 1960, to reflect more accurately and to clarify certain aspects of credit insurance control. This bill does not set rate standards to control overcharging but, in effect, requires that benefits be reasonable in relation to premiums, as discussed later on.

To date, 30 jurisdictions have enacted specific credit insurance legislation patterned substantially after the NAIC Model Bill. The insurance departments of 21 of these jurisdictions have promulgated credit insurance regulations to implement the intent of the law. The insurance departments of nine additional states have promulgated regulations under authority granted them by regular insurance laws other than specific credit insurance laws. Thus, as of 1964, there are 39 jurisdictions with laws and/or regulations controlling credit life and/or health insurance. These control measures apply equally to group and individual credit insurance.

Although the laws and regulations impose requirements which must be met by insurers, a principal objective is protection of the debtor's interests. The principal features of credit insurance control established to achieve this objective are:

1. Disclosure—requires that the insured debtor receive evidence of his insurance. Certificates must be furnished under group coverage; policies under individual coverage.
2. Charge for insurance—the charge to the debtor must not exceed the premium paid by the creditor to the insurer.
3. Refunds—a requirement that the debtor receive, in cash or as a credit to his indebtedness, a refund of the unused portion of the insurance charge if his insurance terminates.

Probably the most important aspect of credit insurance control is that of the charge to the debtor. The Model Bill provides that the insurance supervisor may disapprove insurance forms (policies, certificates, and the like) if the benefits are not reasonable in relation to the premium charge. To give meaning to this provision, and to provide further guidance to insurance departments, the NAIC, in December, 1959, adopted the following resolution: "The Committee in executive session recommends to all insurance supervisors that a rate for Credit Life or Credit Accident and Health producing a loss ratio of under 50% should be considered to be excessive."

This bench mark for controlling premium rates and, consequently, charges to debtors has been promulgated by 13 states in their regulations. Ten of these states, in addition, have promulgated premium rate standards for the guidance of insurers which prima facie meet the 50 per cent loss ratio criterion. Five states have promulgated premium rate standards without the 50 per cent bench mark. One state has promulgated a minimum loss ratio other than 50 per cent, and premium rate standards accordingly. The promulgations of the various states have taken various forms. For example, such states as New Jersey and New York have promulgated premium rate standards which depend upon the size of the case, the rates varying from 44 cents per $100 of initial indebtedness repayable in 12 monthly installments for large cases to 64 cents per $100 of initial indebtedness repayable in 12 monthly installments for very small cases. Most of the other states that have promulgated standards for premium rates have established rates ranging from 60 cents to 75 cents per $100 of initial indebtedness repayable in 12 monthly installments for cases of all sizes.

Although, at the present time, only 16 states have promulgated maximum premium rates, it is expected that additional states will adopt rates based on realistic appraisals of the credit insurance risk as determined from credible statistics.

COMPENSATION

Compensation for the sale of group credit life and health insurance is usually paid to the writing representative (who must be a licensed agent or broker) on a basis similar to that used for other forms of group insurance. A scale of commission rates is applied to the particular group policy. A decremental scale is used so that as the premium increases, the commission, as a percentage of premium, decreases. The commission may vary from 20 per cent of premiums on the smallest case to less than 1 per cent on a large case. Commission payments are usually limited to a period of ten policy years, even though new debtors continue to become insured under the policy after that period.

Under group insurance the master policy is issued to the creditor, who is eligible for dividends and/or rate credits when earned, based on the experience of the group.

Under the individual policy approach, agency agreements are usually made between the insurance company and the creditor whereby the creditor or a representative of the creditor becomes the agent of the insurance company. Compensation to the creditor, acting as agent, may range up to 65 per cent of the full premiums paid on each individual policy issued to a debtor.

CONCLUSION

Credit life and credit health insurance designed to meet the financial needs of debtors and creditors has continued to develop as an important segment of the insurance industry. Its expanded use in connection with all types of consumer debt, as well as its phenomenal growth, is indicative of its acceptance by the public using the debt services available to finance the purchase of goods and services.

SELECTED REFERENCES

CADE, A. J. "Fundamental Issues of Consumer Credit Insurance," *Insurance Law Journal,* No. 385 (February, 1955), pp. 76–93.

DOWNEY, F. R. "Insurance in Installment Credit Transactions," *Insurance Law Journal,* No. 423 (April, 1958), pp. 256–63.

DOWNEY, F. R. *Report on Insurance Charges in Consumer Credit Transaction to Leffert Holz, Superintendent of Insurance.* Albany: State of New York, 1957.

DUNBAR, E. A. "Credit Insurance—Use by Licensed Lenders," *Insurance Law Journal,* No. 402 (July, 1956), pp. 443–58.

INSTITUTE OF LIFE INSURANCE. *Life Insurance Fact Book.* New York. Published annually.

JACOBSON, J. B. *An Analysis of Group Creditors Insurance.* Newark: Prudential Insurance Co., 1955.

KEDZIE, D. P. *Consumer Credit Insurance.* Homewood, Ill.: Richard D. Irwin, Inc., 1957.

MORS, W. P. "Consumer Installment Credit Insurance," *Insurance Law Journal,* No. 400 (May, 1956), pp. 299–318.

NATIONAL ASSOCIATION OF INSURANCE COMMISSIONERS. *NAIC Model Bill to Provide for the Regulation of Credit Life Insurance and Credit Accident and Health Insurance, as Revised December 1960.* Adopted by the Subcommittee on November 28, 1960. New York, n.d.

NATIONAL ASSOCIATION OF INSURANCE COMMISSIONERS. *Study on Credit Life and Credit Accident and Health Insurance.* New York, 1957.

UNITED STATES CONGRESS (SENATE). *The Tie-in Sale of Credit Insurance in Connection with Small Loans and Other Transactions.* Report of the Subcommittee on Antitrust and Monopoly Legislation of the Committee on the Judiciary, 83d Congress, 2d session. Washington, D.C.: U.S. Government Printing Office, 1955.

WHITTAKER, E. B. "Group Creditors Life Insurance," *Journal of the American Society of Chartered Life Underwriters,* Vol. VII (June, 1953), pp. 219–24, 254.

Chapter 32

GROUP DISABILITY INCOME INSURANCE

BY J. HENRY SMITH

The purpose of group disability income insurance is to provide limited indemnity for income lost during disability caused by accident or sickness. Using group insurance principles, a weekly or monthly payment is provided, frequently in an amount determined by the individual's normal rate of pay. Payments start after a fixed minimum period of absence from work and continue during disability up to a fixed maximum time limit. Most policies have a benefit duration limit not often greater than twenty-six weeks and are classed as "temporary" disability income insurance. In recent years, some policies have been written with much longer benefit periods, and they are popularly known as "long-term" policies. Where the characteristics of these two forms differ in important respects, they are treated separately in this chapter.

HISTORY AND DEVELOPMENT

Like group life insurance, this form of protection for employees was developed to meet needs arising as the American scene shifted from an agrarian to an industrial economy. Protection of the pay check against the hazards of illness and injury, as well as old age and death, became more and more important as this transition progressed. Previously, European workers had attempted to meet this need through the formation of guilds or fraternal societies. In America, so-called "establishment funds," providing small cash payments in the event of sickness or accident, made their first appearance during the 1880's. Toward the end of the nineteenth century, increasing concern for injured employees led to the strengthening of the employer liability laws, and many employers turned to the insurance companies for protection against adverse court decisions in accident cases. For this purpose, workmen's collective insurance was introduced around 1896 in the form of a rider to employers' liability policies. Such riders covered accidents (sometimes both occupational and nonoccupational), but left unsolved the problem of disability of the worker through illness.

This problem was given serious consideration in the Montgomery Ward and Company negotiations which led to the introduction of group life insurance in 1911. Montgomery Ward met the problem by an arrangement with a casualty insurance company for a more comprehensive workmen's collective policy providing benefits in the event of sickness as well as accidents. Many industrial firms followed that example. About 1915, however, a few of the insurance companies began to experiment with an idea borrowed from the group life insurance plan, and group disability income insurance, much as we know it today, came on the scene. Around 1919, group disability income insurance became widely available from a number of insurance companies. Thereafter the market for workmen's collective insurance quickly declined as workmen's compensation laws gained momentum and the group-writing companies promoted group disability income policies.

TABLE 32–1

GROUP DISABILITY INCOME INSURANCE IN THE UNITED STATES, 1935–62

Year	Number of Policies	Number of Persons Covered	Premiums
1935	6,200	2,000,000	$ 26,000,000*
1940	13,300	3,840,000	48,000,000*
1945	23,059	5,928,000	125,000,000*
1950	175,780	15,104,000	272,300,000
1955	226,920	19,171,000	510,000,000
1960	281,180	20,970,000	707,000,000
1962	346,660	22,313,000	757,000,000

* Includes premium for accidental death and dismemberment protection.
Source: Health Insurance Association of America.

Statistics as to the growth of group disability income insurance are available only for the period since the mid-1930's, although by that time the coverage was well established. Table 32–1 gives an idea of the growth since then.

The importance which this form of insurance has achieved may also be measured by benefits paid. It is estimated that in 1962 the total of such payments in the United States amounted to well over $600 million.

Starting during World War II and accelerating thereafter, labor agreements often contained disability wage continuance provisions, many of which were implemented by group temporary disability income policies. This accounts for much of the growth shown in Table 32–1 after 1940. Spectacular increases occurred in the year 1950, however, at the time the New York Compulsory Disability Benefits Law became effective. The number of persons covered in the nation increased by nearly 50 per cent in that year alone.

The trend in volume of insurance in force (roughly measured by premiums in Table 32–1) has also been influenced very largely by the trend of wages and by inflation, inasmuch as the amounts of benefits are usually related to earnings. The increase in number of policies over the years was importantly affected by a progressive reduction in size of groups acceptable for insurance, a trend which was enormously influenced by the various state compulsory disability benefit laws. The California law applies to employers having one or more employees. The New York and New Jersey laws originally applied to those employing four or more; but subsequently, New York extended its requirements to one or more. Many companies undertook to insure the smallest groups under these laws, even though these laws were effected only a few years after many companies decided to reduce their minimum size requirement from the original 50 to 25 employees in a group.

Even in those states which have not adopted compulsory disability insurance laws, the insurance companies have gradually reduced the minimum size of group they will undertake for temporary disability income benefits. Today an employer of 10 persons is considered large enough by most companies; some go even lower.

Almost all the coverage is in the class of "temporary" income benefits. Since most disabilities do not run more than a few weeks, the temporary form is adequate in a very large proportion of disabilities. There remains, however, a serious need for more extensive group insurance protection against long-term disabilities. In the past, insurance companies have found it difficult to administer long-term or total and permanent disability insurance; therefore, they have been hesitant to undertake it under group health policies. Nevertheless, in recent years, they have been experimenting with new types of plans for this purpose. These are now achieving widespread interest. The actual coverage figures are not yet large and are not even separately available, but there is reason to believe that this form of insurance is now enlarging rapidly and will show significant expansion in the next few years.

BENEFIT PROVISIONS

Scope of Coverage

Temporary Disability Income Policies. A typical group temporary disability income policy defines the contingencies against which the individual is insured in the following terms: "If the employee shall become wholly and continuously disabled as a result of nonoccupational accidental bodily injuries or nonoccupational sickness, and thereby be prevented from performing any and every duty pertaining to his employment, the company will pay. . . ." Various companies use different versions of this insuring clause; but generally speaking, this quotation illustrates the nature of the protection commonly afforded.

It will be noted that partial disability is not covered; but on the other hand, the test of disability lies in the phrase "and thereby be prevented from performing any and every duty pertaining to his employment." In actual practice the question of eligibility for the benefit hinges on the question of whether the individual can perform his usual duties. Sometimes a somewhat more restricted phraseology is used, in terms of whether the individual can engage in any employment for compensation, thus seemingly excluding a case where the individual cannot do his usual work but can engage in some light occupation. In practice, however, most companies administer this form of insurance on the basis of whether the individual is prevented from engaging in his usual work.

The determination of whether the individual is unable to work usually rests on certification by a physician. Policies generally stipulate that benefits are not payable for a period of absence from work unless the employee is under the care of a physician during that absence, and in practice a statement as to the nature and severity of disability is required from the physician.

Most group temporary disability income policies limit protection to nonoccupational causes of disability. This results in coverage generally complementary to workmen's compensation; in fact, the determination of whether a disability had a nonoccupational or an occupational cause usually hinges in practice on whether compensation benefits are payable. In some instances, however (for example, where workmen's compensation payments are relatively low), the group policy may be written to cover all causes, omitting the word "nonoccupational" from the insuring clause quoted above. In such policies the amount payable in the event of an occupational accident is a supplement to compensation and is carefully controlled so that the combination of compensation and group payments is properly related to earnings.

Although a strict reading of the insuring clause of the usual group disability policy would seem to rule out payments for absences from work because of pregnancy or childbirth, it is customary to treat such absences as if they are caused by sickness. Special provisions are included, however, as to the amount or duration of payment, as indicated later. Where the policyholder so desires, the policy may be written with a specific exclusion prohibiting payments in case of maternity.

Long-Term Disability Income Policies. Long-term disability income policies are still somewhat experimental, and there are many variations in provisions. They often make a distinction in defining covered contingencies between disability which prevents pursuit of the individual's usual occupation and disability which prevents any work for compensation. A frequent provision uses the so-called "his occupation" definition with respect to the initial period of disability and requires that after disability has continued for a substantial period of time, such as two years, further payments will be conditioned on disablement preventing any employment. The purpose here is to provide a period of disability income to replace normal earning power, and to recognize that after a significant period of time the individual, if able, may be expected to reorient himself in any occupation he can follow. If he is not able to engage in any occupation, the payments continue up to the stated number of months provided by the policy.

Unlike temporary income policies, most long-term income policies provide coverage of both nonoccupational and on-the-job accidents, supplementing workmen's compensation insurance in the latter case. As to maternity, however, long-term income policies usually do not provide benefits.

Period of Benefits

Temporary Disability Income Policies. In the case of accidents, some policies provide that benefits will be payable beginning with the first day of absence from employment. Others call for a waiting period of three days of absence, and still others use seven days. For sickness, it is almost universal to require some waiting period. Three days are sometimes used, but the most common period is seven days.

Except where the accident coverage starts on the first day, the two waiting periods are often of the same length—either three days or seven days. In isolated cases, some other period, such as five days, is used; and in a few, a relatively long period, such as 14 or 30 days, is specified because salary continuance or other temporary provision has been made for the initial part of the absence.

The federal income tax law in effect between 1954 and 1964 had some influence on the provisions of new plans. Where benefits were paid for by the employer, the law permitted employees to exclude from their taxable income those benefits (not exceeding $100 a week) payable from the first day for accident, the seventh day for sickness, or the first day of hospitalization. Some group policies were written with corresponding waiting periods. The 1964 tax law introduces further complications, including a lengthening of the seven-day taxable period to 30 days for non-hospitalized absence in certain circumstances. The new form of the law seems too complicated to be directly reflected in the provisions of new plans.

These waiting periods serve the primary function of reducing the cost of the insurance, because they eliminate payments in a great many trivial disabilities for which the individual has no great need for indemnity, and they eliminate payment for a few days in the longer disabilities. Obviously, there is saving in both the claims payments and, perhaps of equal importance, the disproportionate expense of handling many very small claims. Another important function of the waiting period is to minimize the tendency for the insurance to encourage unwarranted absence from work, as will be discussed later in this chapter.

Once payments begin under a disability policy, they continue as long as the employee remains unable to work, until the end of the maximum period of benefits specified in the policy. This period varies from group to group, but commonly runs for either 13 or 26 weeks. Earlier plans mostly used a 13-week limit; but in recent times, particularly where the specifications are set by union bargaining, the 26-week limit has become more frequent. In a few instances a short limit such as 10 weeks is used; on the other hand, some plans permit payments as long as 52 weeks, but these are rare. Almost universally, the limit is the same for accident and sickness.

In most policies the provision as to the maximum period of payment refers to each separate disability; therefore, a full maximum payment may be made more than once for a particular person. In some instances, however, policies are written with a cumulative maximum disability limit. For example, it may be provided that no more than 26 weeks of benefit payments will be allowed during any one 12-month period, regardless of the number or causes of absence. This type of limit appears in policies written to conform to the minimum requirements of some of the state compulsory disability insurance laws. Also, this form of limit was common some years ago as a special provision applicable to older employees, such as those over age 60, but it is not widely used for that purpose today.

Recurring disabilities create problems both as to the waiting period for benefits and as to the maximum benefit period. A typical solution is to provide that successive periods of disability will be considered as one period if separated by less than two weeks of active employment, unless the second disability can be shown to be due to unrelated causes.

Except in cases where the policy excludes coverage of maternity absences, a special limitation on the duration of benefits is customarily used with respect to pregnancies and childbirth. Under this limitation the period of payment usually will not exceed six weeks, although a longer or shorter period may be used if the policyholder so desires. In some policies, it is provided that on cessation of work because of pregnancy, the maximum benefit computed for the specified period is payable in a lump sum.

Long-Term Disability Income Policies. Provisions of long-term group policies take a variety of forms. Often, they are used as supplements to temporary disability income plans or to uninsured wage or salary continuance plans, and sometimes to disability annuities under pension plans.

In order to integrate benefits with such plans, the long-term policy usually has a long waiting period, during which the individual must be disabled before payments start. A waiting period equal to the benefit period under the temporary benefit plan (or salary continuance plan) is common and thus could be, say, six months in duration. Even where the long-term plan is not a supplement to another plan but stands alone as the only disability benefit, it is likely to have a substantial waiting period, such as 30 or 90 days.

Also, there is a wide variation in the maximum duration of benefits under long-term policies. Some policies have a maximum as short as two years; some provide benefits until the individual reaches normal retirement age; and a few have a lifetime benefit, at least for accidents. Probably the commonest provisions are five years, ten years, and to age 65. Some policies may use different maximums for different classes of employees, such as those having different periods of service.

The choice among these possibilities depends on the other provisions the employer (sometimes acting under a bargained agreement) may make for disability protection and on what is deemed appropriate, considering costs, the nature and duration of employment, and other such factors.

Amounts of Benefit

Temporary Disability Income Policies. There are various ways of determining the amount of disability income. In all of them the comparison of the benefit to normal earnings is an important underwriting consideration. Furthermore, inasmuch as the primary purpose of the insurance is to replace compensation lost because of disability, it is common for the policy to provide amounts of benefit graded according to wages or salaries. In some cases the amount is expressed as a fixed percentage of the employee's pay, subject to some maximum amount and possibly to some minimum amount. This percentage does not often exceed 66⅔ per cent and is seldom less than 50 per cent.

In many cases the policy contains a schedule of salary groupings, with an amount of insurance fixed for each group. For example, a schedule like the following might be used:

Normal Weekly Earnings	*Weekly Benefit*
Less than $50	$30
$50 but less than $70	40
$70 but less than $90	55
$90 but less than $110	65
$110 and over	75

In still other cases the amount of insurance may be determined according to the title or occupational classification of the employee. This type of schedule is not preferred by insurers because it does not necessarily maintain a proper relationship between the amount of indemnity and the amount of compensation. Furthermore, it is often difficult to arrive at occupational groupings which are precise, definite, and properly differentiated.

In a number of cases, particularly where the specifications for insurance are set by union bargaining, the amount of weekly benefit is the same for all persons covered under the policy. For example, it might be provided that the benefit is $60 a week for all. This type of plan is satisfactory where there is a fairly homogeneous group of wage earners covered, but it is usually carefully underwritten to be sure that the amount provided bears a satisfactory relationship to the extremes of pay reported in the group. In many instances a special clause is included, stating that the fixed amount will be modified, if necessary, so that the benefit payable will not exceed some fixed percentage, such as 66⅔ per cent, of the employee's normal earnings.

Amounts of weekly benefit are not usually written in excess of $100 a week, although some plans in recent years have gone beyond that figure. In general, group temporary disability income policies are not used to provide high amounts of indemnity for the higher paid personnel of an employer, even though a few somewhat experimental policies have been issued for this purpose.

Where the group policy provides for different amounts of insurance for different classes, or where it provides a fixed percentage of pay, it also calls for an automatic change in the amount of insurance when the employee's pay or insurance classification changes, subject, however, to the further provision that if the employee is not actively at work, any increase in the insurance may not be effective until he returns.

Group Long-Term Disability Income Policies. Under group long-term disability income policies the amount payable (usually payable monthly rather than weekly) is determined according to the same principles outlined above, but some additional considerations enter the picture. One of them is that this form of benefit has been used to a considerable extent for higher paid employees and therefore the maximum amount which is provided often runs to a considerably higher figure than for temporary benefits. Many plans have a maximum benefit of $800 or $1,000 a month, and some are known to provide amounts as high as $2,000 a month.

As a limiting factor, however, considerable care is taken in underwriting long-term benefits to assure that the amount is significantly less than the individual could earn (net after taxes) if he were working. In terms of gross pay, companies do not generally want to provide a benefit much greater than 50 per cent of the normal earnings, although 60 per cent is often used. This matter is of added importance in long-term benefits because of the high amounts involved and their favored income tax position. Benefit payments purchased by employee contributions are not taxable at all; those paid for by the employer may be taxable during the first part of disability (as defined in the tax law) but not for the longer durations except as to amounts exceeding $100 a week. This is of great advantage, especially to high-paid people whose income tax rates are high and sharply progressive.

A further limiting factor on the amount of benefits is the extent to which the individual may be entitled to disability income from other sources. There are many such sources which may be taken into account, including workmen's compensation, the social security benefit, veterans' pensions, employer's pension plan disability benefits, and even individually purchased disability income policies. Except for workmen's compensation, these other sources of income are not usually considered important (and are not taken into account) in determining benefits for temporary disability income plans. For long-term benefits, however, the large amounts and extensive durations of payment require "integration" of the different forms of benefits in order to avoid making the total of disability payments too attractive as compared with normal earnings. The sharply graded income tax is an important consideration here, for disability benefits have important tax advantages as compared with salary or wages. Therefore the usual procedure is to provide that benefits from the other described sources will serve to reduce the long-term amounts payable under the group policy.

Limitations

Usually, temporary disability income benefits are limited to nonoccupational causes of disability, although in some instances where the state workmen's compensation law is thought to be inadequate, the group policy may provide supplementary occupational benefits. The long-term disability income policies, however, nearly always provide coverage for occupational causes because the benefit levels often are substantially greater than workmen's compensation. The policy is written in such a manner as to make the two benefits supplementary; the amount of group insurance payable is reduced (through the "integration" clause) by the amount of workmen's compensation benefit payable.

Otherwise, limitations on benefits under group policies are remarkably few. Unlike many policies issued to individuals, group policies do not usually contain any exclusion of disabilities having a cause predating the insurance, except in some instances of very small groups and some classes of long-term policies. Furthermore, group policies do not usually exclude many of the causes (such as alcoholism, drug addiction, or nervous and mental diseases) which are often excluded in other forms of health insurance. It is customary, however, to exclude both self-inflicted injuries and sickness or injury sustained outside the continental limits of the United

States and Canada, or to provide that no payment will be made during disability while the insured is outside that area. The breadth of coverage so obtained in group insurance is one of its valuable assets; simplified claims administration and better policyholder relationships are the result.

OTHER MAJOR POLICY PROVISIONS

In general, the provisions of a group disability policy, aside from the benefit provisions, follow those of the usual group insurance pattern. Included are the standard clauses dealing with the scope of the contract, certificates to be issued to employees, assignments, the payment of premiums, the right to examine the claimant, and the like. There are special provisions which deal with the notice and proof of claims; usually, these require that notice of claim be furnished within some period such as 20 days after disability begins, and proof of claim must be presented within some period such as 90 days after termination of the period of disability for which claim is made. These requirements are relaxed when it is shown that the claimant could not reasonably comply with the time requirements.

Most group disability policies are technically terminable by the insurer on any policy anniversary date, although the provision to this effect is scarcely ever brought into play. In addition, it is usually stipulated that the policy may be terminated by the insurance company, like other forms of group insurance, when the number covered drops below some stated minimum or percentage (usually 75 per cent) of those eligible.

Because of the nature of the insurance, the policy provision dealing with the termination of the insurance of individuals when they cease work is somewhat stricter than is used for group life insurance. It is not customary to permit continuance of the protection following termination of active work, at least not for any extensive period of time. This is consistent with the basic purpose of the insurance, in that when wages cease because of termination of employment, there is no further proper use for the insurance, inasmuch as it is intended to replace income lost through illness or accidents. Furthermore, experience has shown that disability insurance is likely to result in adverse experience for the insurer with respect to individuals who have no regular employment because the tendency is for such individuals, if insured, to submit claims for conditions that would not normally be disabling, or for spurious or exaggerated causes, and to prolong claims beyond their normal or proper duration.

UNDERWRITING

Broadly speaking, the usual principles of group insurance underwriting are applied in group disability income insurance. There is no individual screening of risks, but dependence on the average health composition of a group produces a sound insurance venture when premiums are properly computed.

Special Underwriting Considerations

There are, however, some features of group underwriting which take on special emphasis in this form of protection. One of these is that, in general, it is desirable to guard against unstable industries and those where employment is erratic or periodic. Whenever layoffs or interruptions in employment are to be expected in unusual degree, care must be taken because experience has shown that individuals will take advantage of the insurance to the extent that it becomes a kind of unemployment benefit. Feigned or imaginary illnesses, or those which the employee disregards in regular employment, become the causes of lengthy disability claims when unemployment is prevalent. Malingering is a real hazard, and it is exaggerated when those insured lose their source of livelihood.

Underwriters have been very cautious, therefore, in insuring groups with unstable employment and those with periodical shutdowns. In the latter category are school teaching and such seasonal industries as food canning, summer amusements, and resort operations. For the periodical industries, it is sometimes provided that protection ceases—and even benefit payments for those disabled cease—when the regular period of employment comes to an end, to be resumed when employment starts up again.

The effect of economic conditions on the financial experience under group disability policies has been keenly illustrated twice in the last thirty years. The Great Depression of the 1930's brought much unemployment, and soon the trend of claims under these policies turned upward. There could be no doubt that to some extent, disability insurance was being used as a form of unemployment compensation. Again, in the later years of World War II the opposite condition—overemployment—brought trouble. The demands for war production required industrial hiring of marginal workers, older people, and those on the fringe of the labor market, many of whom were poor insurance risks. Furthermore, long overtime and the strain of the era brought exhaustion which encouraged people to take what amounted to long vacations at the expense of the insurance plan. In both of these periods, mounting losses were partly offset by increasing premiums and resorting to restrictive measures, but the real solution awaited a return to more normal employment conditions.

In the underwriting process, careful attention is given to the provisions of the policy having to do with the waiting period and the maximum duration of benefits. The waiting period is an important tool in controlling claims experience. Particularly in those situations where irregular employment might tend to stimulate both more and higher claims, a lengthy waiting period during sickness before payments begin may be helpful in obtaining satisfactory results. Also, in irregular and unstable employment, it is important to limit the coverage to those who are employed for a substantial minimum period, such as six months.

Experience has shown that unless it is substantially disadvantageous to the employees to take off a day or two now and then, an unduly high absence rate will be experienced. If the insurance plan were to pay a substantial indemnity for one- or two-day absences, human nature would take advantage of it. The history of disability insurance is replete with warnings of this sort, and some controls are needed. Also, underwriters are usually careful in approving benefit provisions with long maximum periods of disability in cases where employment conditions suggest that caution is in order.

There has been some experimentation in the past with provisions calling for retroactive payments on completion of the waiting period. For example, a policy might provide that when the individual reached the fourth day of illness, payments would begin retroactive to the first day. In general, this type of provision proved unwise—the temptation to malinger to get the bonus payment at the end of the waiting period was so strong that poor results were obtained. As a consequence, this type of provision is seldom used today, unless it be where the benefits are supplemental to workmen's compensation.

Relationship of Benefits to Wages

Also, for the purpose of safeguarding the insurance against undue frequency and duration of claims, the underwriter is cautious with respect to the relationship of the amount of disability benefit which the policy will pay in relation to the individual's normal wages. If the benefit is allowed to approach the individual's normal full "take-home" pay, he will be encouraged to rely on the insurance rather than to maintain steady employment. In these days of high income taxes, this becomes a somewhat intricate problem. The benefit should be related not to gross income, but to net after taxes, having in mind the favorable position of benefits under income tax laws.

For these reasons, it is common to construct the benefit formula in such a way that the amounts will not exceed 50 or 60 per cent of gross pay (excluding overtime and bonus payments and such), or even less in some cases. This has been a difficult underwriting principle to maintain in some instances where union bargaining has tended to establish a uniform weekly benefit regardless of wages. Experience during poor economic times, however, has conclusively demonstrated the wisdom of maintaining a moderate relationship between benefits and normal wages.

For long-term disability benefit cases, some additional considerations come into play, as indicated earlier in the section dealing with amounts of benefit.

Co-operation of Employer Needed

The group insurance principle rests heavily on co-operation by the policyholder. It is needed for satisfactory administration of the insurance in all respects. In group disability insurance, however, it is particularly important in the matter of claims administration. While the establishment of a claim depends on the facts of the individual's state of health to the extent that they are ascertainable and certified by a physician, it has been conclusively demonstrated over the years that the attitude of the employer as to absences of employees has a significant influence on the frequency and duration of claims payments. Lax employment practices and lack of follow-up of employees with minor disabilities can have a seriously adverse effect on the financial experience under a group disability policy.

This need for co-operation on the part of the employer and for control measures leads most underwriters to feel that the employer should participate in financing the insurance. A financial stake in dividends which may be payable under the policy in the event of good experience will encourage a co-operative and helpful attitude in the administration of the benefits. Many insurance companies decline to insure cases in which the employees pay the whole premium.

Associations and Other Entities as Policyholders

While the bulk of group insurance is purchased by employers separately, acting on behalf of their employees, a substantial number of policies have been issued to other entities. A simple example is that of a labor union or a professional association purchasing insurance to cover its members. A wide variety of types of entities has been tried out for various forms of group insurance over the years.

As for group disability insurance, however, the companies are usually hesitant to undertake policies not issued to employers because, as has been noted, success in this form of coverage is likely to rest heavily on a rather closely integrated employment relationship. Association groups do not usually permit the close control on which disability insurance relies. Those associations which are accepted for group disability insurance usually have certain safeguards and underwriting restrictions intended to compensate for the lack of a direct employer-employee relationship.

One major exception exists, however, in the form of a trade association or trusteeship which acts as the policyholder and administrator of group insurance bargained collectively with a union for all its members in an industry or area. A great deal of group insurance, including disability benefits, has been issued in this way in recent years. Nevertheless, even for such cases, care must be taken to see that the usual employment controls operate to protect the ever-present "moral hazard" in disability insurance.

GROUP DISABILITY INSURANCE UNDER COMPULSORY LAWS

Chapter 54 of this *Handbook* describes existing compulsory disability insurance laws and indicates how private insurance is utilized in connection with them. It will suffice here to point out certain special problems that arise in this connection.

In setting up a group plan under one of these laws, it is necessary to conform to the legal specifications as to benefits, policy provisions, and so forth. For this purpose, special policy forms are needed, and benefit provisions must be especially prepared to take into account those requirements which vary from the ones usually found in group plans.

In California and New Jersey the most important problem in underwriting this kind of business stems from the fact that the insurance companies are in competition with state insurance funds, which use a different fundamental principle. According to the law, employers are automatically insured in the state fund unless they choose to provide greater than statutory benefits through insurance companies. These state funds charge premiums on a basis that might be described as somewhat "socialized," inasmuch as the rate of premium, initially at least, is a fixed percentage of payroll regardless of the composition of the group. In New Jersey, some variation is gradually introduced through moderate experience rating, but the degree of variation is not so great as private insurance customarily uses.

Sales and administrative expenses and taxes encountered by the private carriers, but not by the state funds, make for difficult competition, particularly in the many cases where the premium rate for the state fund is relatively low. Furthermore, in both California and New Jersey the state funds possess very large reserves (initially obtained from unemployment compensation taxes paid by employees) which contribute substantial backing and annual income. In general, the companies have been up against a very difficult situation in California and a somewhat uncertain situation in New Jersey.

Furthermore, in California the fundamental differences between the state fund and insurance companies have recently been the basis of state action resulting in near disaster for the companies' interests. In order to protect the state fund against having to carry an undue proportion of poor risk groups, the law provides that voluntary plans carried by insurance companies may not be unduly limited to better risks only. This provision and its implementation have lately been made so restrictive and onerous that after long struggle the companies have had to relinquish most of their group coverage under this law. This result is regrettable from most viewpoints, including that of the public in general, for now the advantages of variety and competition provided by the insurers are no longer available in California.

The situation is different in New York, in that there is no comparable state operation. The only public insurer in New York operates very much like the usual insurance company. This law operates in a manner similar to the usual workmen's compensation law; it merely requires the employer to provide insurance however he wishes, subject to certain standards. The insurance companies have found it a much more satisfactory system than the others.

The compulsory law in Rhode Island provides monopolistic state insurance, and the benefits are sufficiently high to permit practically no opportunity for private insurers to write additional or supplementary benefits for the bulk of employees. If such additional benefits were attempted, they would be either so small in amount as to be uneconomical to administer or would produce the overinsurance which is so fatal in disability coverage. In effect, California has now reclassified itself in much the same status.

ACCOUNTING AND CLAIMS ADMINISTRATION

As far as record keeping, premium collection, and accounting are concerned, group disability insurance follows the pattern used for group life and other forms of group insurance.

Systems used in the administration of claims also follow those for other forms of group health insurance. In disability insurance the key to the claim is the physician's certification, giving the cause and his opinion as to the individual's inability to work. In most instances the system calls for further corroboration by the employer, who attests to the individual's eligibility for benefits under his plan and gives pertinent facts from the employment records. It is common to have employers indicate their concurrence in the validity of the claim.

For temporary disability income plans, benefit payments are usually made every two weeks, with renewed medical and employer certification as to the continuing disability. In the usual course of events, not many problems arise in these operations. It is found, however, that continued care must be taken to avoid malingering, particularly when employment is slow. Of course, there are some spurious claims to be denied, although these are generally few in number. The lack of restrictions and limitations in group policies makes for relatively simple claims operations.

Although long-term disability income benefits are generally paid monthly, the administration of long-term claims generally follows the same pattern as for temporary income plans. However, the fact that benefits are frequently large in amount and extend over a long period of time necessitates a more extensive and continued investigation of the validity of claims. In addition to the information furnished by the claimant, the attending physician, and the employer, there is need for independent investigation. Also, because of the long-term nature of the claims, insurance companies are concerned with the possibility of rehabilitation of the claimant in order that he may return to his normal role in society; sometimes they make special settlement arrangements to aid in financing rehabilitation.

Recurrent Claims

An important point occurs in a claim settlement in the event that recovery is followed by recurrence of disability. A decision must be made as to whether the individual must again complete the waiting period before benefits are resumed, and as to whether the first period of payments will be counted in determining how long benefits may be paid with respect to the second absence. The insurance companies, after much experimentation, have devised various pragmatic rules to handle these problems. One of these, which is common in temporary income policies, is illustrated by a provision reading: "Successive periods of disability separated by less than two weeks of continuous active employment with the employer shall be considered as one continuous period of disability unless they arise from different and unrelated causes." This type of rule sometimes results in connecting several absences. Where more than two weeks intervene, or where the two disabilities do not arise from the same or related causes, the second disability is treated as a new one, with no reference to the prior disability.

For long-term plans the same principle is used as to recurrent claims, except that a three-month rule (rather than the two weeks used in temporary income plans) is used to connect recurrent claims for the same or related causes.

SELECTED REFERENCES

Dickerson, O. D. *Health Insurance.* Rev. ed. Homewood, Ill.: Richard D. Irwin, Inc., 1963.

Faulkner, Edwin J. *Health Insurance.* New York: McGraw-Hill Book Co., Inc., 1960.

Ilse, Louise Wolters. *Group Insurance and Employee Retirement Plans,* pp. 1–45, 159–89. New York: Prentice-Hall, Inc., 1953.

McCahan, David (ed.): *Accident and Sickness Insurance.* Philadelphia: University of Pennsylvania Press, 1954.

Pickrell, J. F. *Group Health Insurance.* Homewood, Ill.: Richard D. Irwin, Inc., 1961.

Chapter 33

GROUP MEDICAL EXPENSE INSURANCE—INSURANCE COMPANY

BY CHARLES A. SIEGFRIED

Medical expense insurance refers to various types of insurance plans which undertake to provide monetary benefits to reimburse the insured, in whole or in part, for expenses incurred for various kinds of medical services. Some plans apply only to a specific kind of medical expense, such as hospitalization or surgery; others are broader in scope. Medical expense insurance may be provided through the mechanism of group insurance or individual insurance. This chapter deals only with group plans.

Nature

As the name suggests, group plans are those which insure groups of persons. The most common type of group are the employees of a single employer. Other types of groups for insurance purposes include the members of a labor union, the employees of two or more employers in the same industry, and employees of an association of employers. Generally speaking, the groups which may be insured for medical expense insurance are the same as those which may be insured for other types of group insurance. The definition of the types of groups that may be insured is a subject of the insurance laws of most states. Generally, a legally qualified group must consist of not less than 10 employees, although in some states the law either contains no specified minimum number or authorizes a lower number than 10.

Insurance may be provided for employees alone (or other members of the insured class), or for such persons and their dependent wives and children. Only in very unusual circumstances would coverage be provided for dependents alone. In some cases, coverage might be extended to a broader classification of dependents.

Group medical expense insurance is an outgrowth of group life insurance and group disability (loss-of-income) insurance, and the administrative and other mechanisms used are either identical with or closely follow those associated with the earlier forms. An important advantage of group medical expense insurance is that it can be established and administered efficiently as a part of a broad program of employee benefits.

The costs of a group medical expense insurance program may be provided by contributions of employees alone or by their employers alone, or they may be shared in various proportions or ways. Under some plans, for example, the cost of the insurance for employees may be borne by the employer, and that of the insurance for dependents by the employees. Under many programs the contributions of employees are for a broad package of benefits, including group medical expense insurance, with no specific separation for the components.

Group medical expense insurance may have a variety of objectives. The monetary benefits provided may be established at a level which aims to "break the back" of the bill for the medical services covered. In other words, it may not aim to pay the full bill or substantially the full bill. Some plans, on the other hand, aim to pay the full cost of certain expenses, such as, for example, hospital expenses for semiprivate room accommodations up to seventy days. Generally speaking, the objective is to produce a practical and desirable result with the funds that are available for purchasing the insurance, recognizing that the need and desire for medical expense insurance is in competition with other needs and desires. Among the features of group medical expense insurance are its flexibility in meeting a broad range of needs and its adaptability in the light of differing views as to how much money should or can be applied for it.

Development

A definitive history of group medical expense insurance would reveal experiments and plans going back many years. However, the principal developments leading to the current situation had their origins in the early 1930's. An impressive aspect of this history is the vigor and extent of the growth that has occurred in a relatively short span of years.

Group medical expense insurance up until about 1950 was largely occupied with benefits related to expenses for hospital confinement and surgery. This is understandable, since such expenses are important items in those cases where medical bills are the cause of considerable inconvenience financially and of actual hardship. Then, also, the development of this insurance has been influenced substantially by efforts of hospitals and physicians and community leaders to find sound, orderly methods for dealing with the financial aspects of hospital and surgical care.

Since about 1950, great strides have been made in developing much broader medical expense insurance plans. These plans generally undertake to deal with practically all varieties of medical expense and are usually constructed so as to be especially helpful in dealing with cases where very large expenses have been incurred. These plans are gaining in popularity and acceptance, and are viewed by many as providing a sound, comprehensive approach to the problem of financing the medical care costs of illnesses and accidents.

In the evolutionary development that has been occurring in the field of group medical expense insurance, plans have been developed dealing with other specific types of expense. Usually, these plans were designed to supplement hospital expense or surgical expense plans. In this category, there are plans providing benefits for various types of X-ray or laboratory services, or for the costs of doctors' visits under various circumstances, or for a broader range of medical expenses which may be incurred for certain specific diseases—polio, for example. These plans are of interest because they illustrate the nature of the efforts which have been made to gain experience soundly and to widen the range of expenses that can appropriately be made the subject of medical expense insurance.

TABLE 33-1

NUMBER OF PERSONS INSURED UNDER INSURANCE COMPANY GROUP MEDICAL EXPENSE PLANS, 1940, 1957 AND 1962

TYPE OF MEDICAL EXPENSE INSURANCE	NUMBER OF PERSONS INSURED*		
	1940	1957	1962
Hospital expense	2,500,000	48,439,000	59,153,000
Surgical expense	1,430,000	48,955,000	59,787,000
Regular medical expense	No record	28,317,000	40,012,000
Major medical expense	Not written	12,428,000	35,053,000

* Based on estimates made by the Health Insurance Council of persons covered under group plans issued by insurance companies. The figures do not include persons covered under Blue Cross or Blue Shield plans.

Table 33-1 indicates the broad categories of group medical expense insurance as underwritten by insurance companies and the growth that has taken place in the United States since 1940.

Group Hospital Expense Insurance

Most hospital expense insurance deals separately with the expense of room and board charges and the expenses for other hospital services—such as charges for laboratory services, drugs, dressings, X rays, and the like. Under some plans a fixed number of dollars of benefit are payable for each day of confinement on account of room and board, irrespective of what the actual charge may be. Such an amount would almost always be set at a level not to exceed the actual charge. Most plans being underwritten today are on the basis of paying the actual charges up to a specified maximum. Under other plans the benefit for room and board may be indefinite as to amount, being equal to the hospital's actual charge but not to exceed the charge for a room in a specified classification, e.g., semiprivate. Daily room and board benefits are payable for each day of confinement up to a specified maximum duration. In the early days a 31-day limit was customary; currently, most plans have a 70- or 120-day maximum, while some have a 365-day maximum.

With respect to charges for specified hospital services other than room and board, the customary plan undertakes to pay the cost of the actual charges up to a specified maximum amount. In the early plans a maximum of five or 10 times the daily benefit for room and board charges was common. Under more recent plans, somewhat higher maximums are commonly used, such as 20 times or a specified dollar amount—$200, for example—with further provision for paying a specified percentage (e.g., 75 per cent) of charges above the amount to an over-all maximum for these services of, say, $1,500. Some plans in effect today have no specific limit for the amount of specified hospital services covered by the plan.

Plans usually provide some special limitations with respect to maternity benefits. This reflects, in part, thinking as to how the available funds can be most usefully applied for the benefit of the persons covered, and partly a consideration of reasonable limits on the obligations of the plans for dealing with maternity cases. Most plans cover only pregnancies having their inception while the individual is insured. Generally speaking, many plans limit maternity benefits for room and board and benefits for special services combined to 10 times the daily room and board benefit.

Hospital expense insurance plans generally aim to deal only with the expenses in cases requiring actual hospital confinement. To this end, there is usually a requirement that a person be confined at least eighteen hours in order to qualify for benefits, although this is not usually required if treatment is for emergency care due to an accident or if a surgical operation is performed.

Group Surgical Expense Insurance

Surgical expense insurance provides reimbursement for the charges made by physicians for surgical procedures. Benefits are usually specified in a schedule naming the operation covered and the maximum reimbursement for the operation. In constructing such schedules, thought is given to the relative value of different operations; but views differ widely, and many different kinds of schedules have been used over the years. The schedules are necessarily brief, and provision is made that the maximum payment for unlisted procedures will be determined on a consistent basis. The maximum benefit payable varies fairly widely, the more common plans currently having a maximum of $300.

Table 33–2 shows the maximum amounts of reimbursement provided for thirteen common operations under a recently developed schedule which has a $300 over-all maximum. Based upon results of a recent inter-insurance company study, the operations listed would account for about

37 per cent of all claims costs for surgical benefits (exclusive of obstetrical claims) for a group of employees with personal and dependent coverage.

The amount of reimbursement under most plans is not intended to indicate what the physician's charge will or should be in a particular case.

TABLE 33–2
SCHEDULE OF MAXIMUM AMOUNTS PAYABLE FOR SELECTED SURGICAL OPERATIONS UNDER $300 MAXIMUM-LIMIT PLAN

Operation	Maximum Benefit Payable
Abscesses (other than breast), superficial incision and drainage	$ 7.50–$25.00
Appendectomy	110.00
Benign tumors, superficial, removal by surgery	10.00– 20.00
Biopsy, gland muscle or superficial tissue	10.00– 30.00
Cholescystectomy	175.00
Cystoscopy, diagnostic, with ureteral catherization	35.00
Fistulectomy, single	65.00
Fracture of radius, close	50.00–100.00
Hemorrhoidectomy:	
External	25.00
Other than external	80.00
Herniotomy, single	110.00
Panhysterectomy	180.00
Lacerations of skin, suture and repair of	7.50– 30.00
Tonsillectomy, with or without adenoidectomy	40.00

While insurance companies and Blue Shield organizations have been active over the years in developing surgical schedules, the work of medical societies in this field must also be recognized. In 1956 the California Medical Association developed a Relative Value Schedule (revised in 1960) for the guidance of physicians in establishing fees for various kinds of services; surgery; visits to the office, home, or hospital; radiology; and laboratory. Medical societies in other areas have devised relative value schedules to fit their local needs and patterns of medical care, so that there were approximately fifteen in use in 1963. A relative value schedule is not a fee schedule in the sense that dollar amounts are shown, but merely shows the value of one procedure in relation to another. For example, one procedure might be valued at 20, another at 35, and a third at 50. The individual doctor would determine the level of his fees by applying a factor of his own choice to the relative values. Thus, he might decide to use a factor of $5.00, which would make his fees $100, $175, and $250, respectively, for the procedures mentioned.

Relative value schedules have been used by the group underwriting insurance companies in developing surgical schedules for particular groups. Thus, schedules which have gained widespread acceptance, such as the California Relative Value Schedule, have been used in conjunction with factors appropriate to the area involved.

In a few areas, special plans have been developed in co-operation with certain medical groups under which a prepared schedule of benefits is accepted by participating surgeons as the full fee for insured persons whose incomes do not exceed specified amounts.

This has been carried one step further recently under certain plans from which the usual specific schedule of allowances has been omitted. Provision is made to pay benefits equal to the fee actually charged, provided that the fee charged by the surgeon is reasonable and customary for the income level of the employee, and with the further provision that if the income of the employee exceeds a certain limiting amount (say, $7,500), the maximum benefit allowed will be the fee that would have been charged if the employee's income had been at the limit.

Group Plans Providing Benefits for Other Specified Types of Medical Expenses

Experience gained with hospital expense and surgical expense insurance plans has encouraged the development of other forms of coverage, with the aim of extending the scope of medical expense insurance. A variety of different plans are available. Some plans aim at providing benefits for specific kinds of expense, e.g., the cost of diagnostic X-ray examinations and laboratory tests when these services are rendered outside a hospital and are not covered by a hospital expense insurance plan. Other plans undertake to provide reimbursement of physicians' fees other than surgeons' fees. Such plans may cover such fees only in case of physicians' visits while the insured is confined in a hospital, or they may be broader and cover home and office visits.

Some plans, recognizing that the benefits available under plans previously described are limited to modest amounts, aim to provide a much more substantial level of benefits in cases of severe illness. In this category are various kinds of polio expense coverage and so-called "dread diseases" insurance. Under a dread disease plan, benefits are provided for expenses incurred for certain specified diseases which, though occurring infrequently, might involve large costs.

Group Major Medical Expense Insurance

Major medical expense insurance is the name which is given to plans which provide benefits on account of all or most types of medical expense and which aim to give a substantial amount where expenses are especially large because of the duration or severity of the case. Such plans may be of a "supplemental" variety as an adjunct to a basic plan of hospital-surgical expense benefits. Alternatively, the plan may be a "comprehensive" type, providing benefits for the less severe cases as well as the more severe ones, and dealing with all types of expense as a whole.

Where the plan is of the supplemental type, there is usually a "corridor" between it and the basic benefits, i.e., an unreimbursed amount of expense above the part covered by the base plan benefits. The corridor expenses are the responsibility of the insured. Expenses above this corridor are covered by the plan, and plans usually pay 75 per cent, 80 per cent, or, less frequently, 85 per cent of such expenses. The corridor expenses not covered by the plan are usually referred to as a "deductible." The amount is often a uniform flat amount such as $100, or may be a percentage of annual earnings such as 1 per cent. The separation of expenses into a proportion (expressed as a percentage) covered by the plan and a part which the insured must pay himself is referred to as "percentage participation" or "coinsurance." This has the valued effect of giving the insured a continuing interest in the amount of expenses incurred and, on the other hand, keeps the cost of the insurance at a more acceptable level than otherwise would be possible.

Under a comprehensive plan the arrangements might be as follows: The first $25, $50, or $100 of expense would not be covered. After that level the plan would pay 75 per cent, 80 per cent, or, less frequently, 85 per cent of expenses. After the deductible, some portion of the expenses might be paid in full, with the percentage participation or coinsurance provision becoming applicable only with respect to expenses above the paid-in-full area.

In figuring the benefits under a major medical expense insurance plan, the period of time used as a basis may be either a calendar year or a period of not more than twelve months measured from the time expenses were incurred for a particular period of illness. Some plans relate the benefits to each separate period of disability or cause of disability.

Usually, a major medical expense insurance plan will not undertake to cover dental bills (except where they are caused by an accident), eyeglasses, or health checkups. Because duplication of benefits leads to excessive utilization of services or excessive charges, some plans do not undertake to cover expenses for which benefits are paid under some other plan. Generally speaking, reasonable provisions are included to assure that the most effective use is made of the insurance and that improper charges or unnecessary utilization of services are guarded against. This is particularly important because the maximum benefits for any one individual may be very substantial, running up to $5,000, $10,000, or even more.

Risk Selection

The primary objective of risk selection is to insure groups which will yield an average spread of risk. While there are a number of factors to be considered in risk selection, a very important one is the plan of benefits offered to the group.

In recent years, many changes have been occurring in medical practice, and the cost of medical services has been steadily rising. How to provide reasonable and effective safeguards against unnecessary care or unnecessarily costly care, and against waste and inefficiency generally, is an important consideration in the construction and administration of medical expense benefit plans. There is growing evidence that the type and amount of insurance benefits available appreciably affects the utilization and cost of medical services. These conditions make many purchasers thoughtful of plan specifications.

Premium Rates

The insurance company, in setting premium rates, has as its purpose the determination of an initial rate that is consistent with prior general experience with groups similar to the particular group being rated. Initial premium rates are usually applicable for only the first contract year; thereafter the insurance company adjusts the rates on all but certain small group cases very largely in the light of the experience of the particular group. Many employers prefer to have the costs of the insurance on their employees determined by the experience of their particular groups; this gives them the opportunity to try out new ideas and improve administration, and this makes for more effective utilization of available funds for their own plans.

In conformity with group insurance practice generally, the premium rates are set at a level which will be sufficient to provide the expected amount of benefit payments which will be incurred, the cost of premium and other taxes and other expenses of administration, and a margin to cover the fluctuations in claims that normally occur, as well as unforeseen contingencies. The cost of the insurance under participating policies is affected by premium refunds or "dividends" that may be declared in the light of the emerging actual experience. The same type of adjustment in cost is accomplished under nonparticipating policies of stock insurance companies by means of retrospective rate credits.

The premium rates charged for group medical expense insurance are based on experience which has been built up since the early experimental plans. This experience has demonstrated that the costs of such insurance are substantially influenced by the following factors: sex, age, earnings level, geographical variations in charges for medical services, and environmental factors pertaining to the community or the employed group. However, in actual practice, premium rates for other than major medical coverage generally reflect only the proportion of females insured for personal coverage, while major medical premium rates commonly recognize all of the above factors.

There are so many possible variations in plan specifications and factors affecting the rates that it is not practicable to set forth illustrative premium rates for all the types of medical expense insurance referred to in this chapter. However, Tables 33–3 and 33–4 furnish some helpful rough indications of the level of premiums for the given set of specifications for (1) a major medical expense insurance plan of the "comprehensive" type and (2) a basic hospital-surgical plan supplemented by a major medical expense insurance plan.

Coverage for Older Age Persons

One of the important developments in group medical expense insurance has been the enlarged provision of medical care for older age persons. Group insurance has few restrictions on account of age for active employees. Prior to 1950, however, medical expense coverage was provided only infrequently on retired employees and their dependents. Since that time, there has been a tremendous growth in the number of group plans providing such coverage either by continuation under the group plan for the same or a modified plan, or by conversion to an individual plan of insurance.

The most recent development in the provision of medical care for older age people is the so-called "65" plans, developed first in Connecticut and later in Massachusetts and New York. Other areas are in the process of developing such plans. These plans are offered by joint associations of insurance companies to all persons over age 65 in the area on a mass enrollment basis, and provide basic hospital and surgical expense and major medical expense coverage on a group basis without health examination or other evidence of insurability. The offering of these plans to the public was made possible by special enabling legislation in each state. These plans make available broad coverage for many persons who could not otherwise obtain coverage.

Coverage for Dental Expenses

Most of the medical expense plans do not provide reimbursement for expenses incurred in connection with dental work except to a very limited extent, such as when required because of an accident. In recent years, insurance companies have commenced underwriting group dental insurance plans which provide benefits for a wide range of dental expenses. The benefit formula under many of the plans is similar to the major medical benefit formula and includes an initial deductible amount and a percentage participation or coinsurance feature. There are some who feel that the expansion in this area will be substantial in the next decade and perhaps even match the rapid growth of major medical expense insurance in the 1950's.

TABLE 33-3

ILLUSTRATIVE GROUP MAJOR MEDICAL EXPENSE INSURANCE PLAN OF COMPREHENSIVE TYPE, INCLUDING PREMIUM RATES

BRIEF DESCRIPTION OF PLAN

Expenses covered—reasonable and customary charges for necessary service:	
Type A expenses	Hospital room and board (limited to semiprivate charge), special hospital services, surgical fees.
Type B expenses	Physicians' fees other than surgery, X rays, and other types of diagnostic services out of hospital, drugs and medicines, professional ambulance service, registered nurses, artificial limbs and eyes.
Benefits:	
For each individual covered during calendar year	For Type A expenses: Employee pays first $25, plan pays next $225 in full, plan pays 75 per cent of excess. For Type B expenses: Employee pays greater of first $50 or 1 per cent of earnings (reduced by any expenses applied toward $25 deductible under Type A), plan pays 75 per cent of excess. For maternity—Type A and Type B expenses: Normal delivery, $150; Caesarean section, $225; miscarriage, $75. Where there are severe complications, plan pays 75 per cent of additional medical expenses incurred because of such complications.
Maximum benefits	$5,000 in any calendar year; $5,000 aggregate.
Principal expenses not covered	Dental care (except due to accident), eyeglasses, health checkups, expenses paid by government or other employer plan.

ILLUSTRATIVE GROSS MANUAL PREMIUM RATES*

Estimated Average Semiprivate Room and Board Charges Applicable in Area Where Plan Operates	Initial Monthly Premium for Insured Employee Only	Initial Monthly Premium for Dependents
$15.00	$4.86	$ 9.95
20.00	5.58	11.24
25.00	6.33	12.02

* These rates would apply to a small group case. For the smallest cases, these premiums would be increased up to 5 per cent. For larger group plans the gross premium rate may be reduced by as much as 15 per cent. These rates would apply to a group with the following characteristics:

1. All employees covered; less than 30 per cent earning $5,000 or more; less than 7 per cent earning $10,000 or more.
2. Normal age distribution among employees.
3. Average medical care costs apply for area involved.
4. Thirty-one per cent to 40 per cent of benefits cover female employees.

TABLE 33–4

ILLUSTRATIVE GROUP MAJOR MEDICAL EXPENSE INSURANCE PLAN SUPPLEMENTING A BASIC PLAN, AND PREMIUM RATES

BRIEF DESCRIPTION OF PLAN

Basic plan benefits:

A. Hospital benefits.................. Hospital care in semiprivate accommodations up to 120 days, special services of $200 + 75 per cent of next $2,400.

B. Surgical benefits................. Benefits up to $300 in accordance with a specified schedule, depending on type of operation.

(See below for maternity benefits.)

Major medical expense insurance—reasonable and customary charges for necessary service:

A. Type of expenses covered.......... Hospital room and board (up to $25), special hospital services, and surgical charges not covered by basic plan. Physicians' fees other than surgery, X rays, and other types of diagnostic services out of hospital, drugs and medicines, professiona, ambulance service, registered nursesl artificial limbs and eyes.

B. Benefits........................ Employee pays first $100 (or 1 per cent of annual earnings) of expense above that covered by basic plan. Plan pays 75 per cent of excess. Maximum benefits $5,000 in any calendar year; $10,000 aggregate.

Maternity benefits................. Normal delivery, $150; Caesarean section, $225; miscarriage, $75. Where there are severe complications, plan pays 75 per cent of additional medical expenses incurred because of such complications.

Principal expenses not covered under major medical expense insurance....... Expenses covered under basic plan. Dental care (except due to accident), eyeglasses, health checkups, expenses paid by government or other employer plan.

ILLUSTRATIVE GROSS MANUAL PREMIUM RATES*

Estimated Average Semiprivate Room and Board Charges Applicable in Area Where Plan Operates	Initial Monthly Premium for Insured Employee Only			Initial Monthly Premium for Dependent		
	Hospital-Surgical and Maternity Expense	Major Medical Expense	Total	Hospital-Surgical and Maternity Expense	Major Medical Expense	Total
$15.00............	$4.20	$1.12	$5.32	$ 9.04	$1.65	$10.69
20.00............	4.80	1.12	5.92	10.11	1.63	11.74
25.00............	5.31	1.11	6.42	11.14	1.62	12.76

* These rates would apply to a small group case. For the smallest ones, these premiums would be increased up to 5 per cent. For larger group plans the gross premium rate may be reduced by as much as 15 per cent. These rates would apply to a group with the same characteristics as shown in Table 33–3.

SELECTED REFERENCES

CHAMBER OF COMMERCE OF THE UNITED STATES. *Major Medical Expense Insurance*. Washington, D.C., 1957.

DICKERSON, O. D. *Health Insurance*. Rev. ed. Homewood, Ill.: Richard D. Irwin, Inc., 1963.

FOLLMANN, J. F., JR. *Medical Care and Health Insurance*. Homewood, Ill.: Richard D. Irwin, Inc., 1963.

FOLLMANN, J. F., JR. *Voluntary Health Insurance and Medical Care—Five Years of Progress, 1952–1957*. New York: Health Insurance Association of America, 1958.

HUEBNER, S. S. *The Economics of Health Insurance*. Rev. ed. Bryn Mawr, Pa. American College of Life Underwriters, 1963.

NEW YORK STATE INSURANCE DEPARTMENT. *Voluntary Health Insurance and the Senior Citizen*. Albany, 1958.

PICKRELL, J. F. *Group Health Insurance*. Homewood, Ill.: Richard D. Irwin, Inc., 1961.

SERBEIN, OSCAR N., JR. *Paying for Medical Care in the United States*. New York: Columbia University Press, 1953.

Chapter 34

GROUP MEDICAL EXPENSE INSURANCE—BLUE CROSS AND BLUE SHIELD

BY O. D. DICKERSON

In the broad sense of the term, "medical expense insurance" refers to all the types of insurance which protect against the expenses of medical care. Medical expense insurance policies may be divided into six major categories: hospital, surgical, medical, dread disease, major medical, and comprehensive.

Medical expense insurance is provided by insurance companies, hospital and medical associations, and a variety of other insurers loosely classed as "independent." This chapter will be confined to a discussion of the coverages provided by the hospital and medical associations, commonly referred to as "Blue Cross" and "Blue Shield," respectively.

Hospital Service Associations

Although the federal government provided hospital protection for seamen as early as 1798, voluntary plans date from 1880 in Minnesota, and insurance companies offered coverage (usually as a rider to an income replacement contract) beginning around 1910, the real impetus to the growth of modern hospital insurance was the Baylor University Hospital Plan, which began operations late in 1929. The first groups enrolled were schoolteachers, then newspaper and bank employees. The experiment soon gained national attention. Since a primary objective was to facilitate the hospitals' collection of bills due, the ensuing depression led to widespread interest in the device on the part of the hospitals. Soon, plans developed in other communities, at first on an individual hospital basis, but shortly including most or all of the hospitals in the community. Eventually, many plans were extended to a state-wide basis. By 1933 the American Hospital Association approved these plans in principle and began to encourage their formation and to develop standards. In 1936, it established the Commission on Hospital Service, later named the Blue

Cross Commission and now the Blue Cross Association. This Association is the national co-ordinating agency.

Most hospital associations are organized under special legislation which exempts nonprofit hospital service corporations from the provisions of the state insurance laws, sets certain standards, and recognizes the organizations as charitable and benevolent institutions exempt from most state and local taxes, including state insurance premium taxes. All but eight states now have such laws. The initiative for the organization of the plans usually came from the hospitals, and some of the state laws require that the majority of the directors be administrators or trustees of "member hospitals." Usually, the general public and the physicians of the area are represented on the board, but hospital personnel tend to dominate. Frequently, the board is self-perpetuating.

The hospital association contracts with insured "subscribers" to provide specified hospital expense protection, and with its "member" hospitals to provide these services to the insured patients. The contracts with the hospitals specify the method of payment by the Association on the basis of an agreed per diem amount, the actual charges billed or a portion thereof, or on a cost basis. The last method is the most common. Costs may include allocations of overhead, including depreciation, interest, contingency reserves, nurses' training, and care of the indigent, but sometimes may not include all these items, resulting in a "discount" to Blue Cross.

Sometimes the hospitals guarantee the financial obligations of the Association. Even where no formal guarantee is found, the hospitals are in effect the ultimate risk bearers. The schedule of payments by the Association to its member hospitals is always subject to renegotiation, and it is extremely unlikely that the hospitals would let the fund become insolvent. Just as the schedule of payments may be reduced in the event of high utilization, it might be increased in the event of low utilization. Historically, this has not been a problem, but schedules have been periodically raised to reflect increased costs of hospital operation. Currently, the rapid rise in hospital costs has created a serious problem for the hospitals and Blue Cross. Renegotiation of hospital contracts directly affects the Blue Cross claims costs, and premiums must be increased to cover increased claims costs. It is difficult for Blue Cross to keep pace with the demands of member hospitals for more adequate reimbursement, since continued substantial rate increases lead to strong objections from the insured public and insurance commissioners are reluctant to approve substantial increases.

Seventy-seven United States Blue Cross plans have been approved by the American Hospital Association. Seventy-five of these are members of the Blue Cross Association. Four Canadian plans maintain associate membership. At the close of 1962, about 61 million persons were enrolled in the American plans. This represents about 40 per cent of those covered by hospital insurance sold in this country. The plans have contracts with over six thousand member hospitals, or about 90 per cent of the hospitals in this country. Each plan operates in a limited area, which ranges from a single city to about one and one-half states. Plans overlap in only one area, North Carolina.

National co-ordination is achieved through several means. The American Hospital Association administers the trade-mark license agreement, handles the approval program, and co-ordinates relations between the hospitals and Blue Cross. The Blue Cross Association is a membership corporation made up of the various plans and represents them in activities related to enrollment, government, and mutual operating programs. It supervises the national advertising program, represents its members in the enrollment of employee groups on a national basis, and contracts with the United States government on behalf of the plans participating in the Medicare program for dependents of uniformed services personnel and in the federal employees' group insurance program. It has established Health Service, Inc., a wholly owned stock casualty insurance company, to act as underwriter for benefits for national employee groups which cannot be provided by the local associations. This is one means by which it is possible for a large firm to provide its employees in many locations with uniform coverage despite the differences among local plans. The company usually underwrites only coverage in excess of the benefit levels of the local plans.

Because each plan operates within a limited area through contracts with local member hospitals, the Inter-Plan Service Benefit Bank has been established by the plans to facilitate the handling of claims for subscribers hospitalized outside the area of the "home" plan. This enables the subscriber to receive the benefits of the plan in the area in which he is hospitalized through its arrangements with local member hospitals. The Bank serves as a clearinghouse for charges and credits of the "host" and "home" plans. For hospitalization in hospitals not under contract to any Blue Cross plan, most plans provide cash allowances toward the cost of hospitalization. When an insured subscriber changes his residence, transfer from plan to plan is facilitated by an Inter-Plan Transfer Program. This provides uniformity of treatment and prevents temporary lapse of coverage.

Medical Service Associations

Although insurance or prepayment for medical care can be traced back at least to 1655 in Montreal and some industrial plans operated in the United States in the 1880's, the major development in this field has been in this century. Insurance companies first issued surgical coverage in 1903 and medical expense in 1910. County medical societies sponsored plans in the

Northwest in the 1920's, but the Blue Shield movement really dates from the establishment of the California Physicians' Service on a state-wide basis in 1939. Plans soon developed in Michigan, New York, North Carolina, Pennsylvania, and other areas. The American Medical Association had been studying the problem throughout the 1930's and, from time to time, resolutions were adopted setting forth guiding principles for constituent society plans. The AMA established its Council on Medical Service (and Public Relations) in 1943. This Council conducts studies and disseminates information regarding medical plans. The AMA did much to encourage the formation of plans and issued a "Seal of Acceptance" for approved plans from 1946 to 1954. The National Association of Blue Shield Plans is the national co-ordinating association. Its governing body is a board of directors to which representatives are elected, 22 on a district basis and 11 at large. Five of the 33 directors are appointed by the AMA. At least 19 must be physicians.

Nationwide coverage is provided by a stock insurance company, Medical Indemnity of America, Inc. This is similar to Health Service, Inc., which performs a similar function for Blue Cross; and through a joint operating agreement, each assumes a portion of the risk written by the other.

The American Medical Association lists 76 voluntary medical prepayment benefit plans in operation in the United States and 10 in Canada. Seventy-two of the United States plans have been approved by state or county medical societies, and four are affiliated or co-ordinated with Blue Cross, but not medical-society-approved. Seventy-nine plans (including six Canadian and one Jamaican) belong to the National Association of Blue Shield Plans, and not all of these use the Blue Shield or similar insignia. While it is not technically correct, the term "Blue Shield" often is used to designate the entire group.

About 48 million persons in the United States and 2.8 million in Canada and Jamaica are covered by the seventy-nine plans reporting to the National Association of Blue Shield Plans, Inc. About four million persons are covered by the other United States plans, including those affiliated with Blue Cross, a total of about 52 million in this country and more than two million in Canada. The United States plans cover about 26 per cent of the eligible population, and provide 37 per cent of the surgical and 47 per cent of the regular medical expense protection provided by all voluntary insurers.

Organizationally, these plans are more heterogeneous than Blue Cross. There are four general methods of organization: special or general enabling legislation, underwriting by regular insurance companies, and provision of supplementary benefits in Blue Cross coverages. Most of the plans organized under special or general legislation enjoy a tax-exempt status as nonprofit organizations, as, of course, do the Blue Cross-affiliated plans. In a few states, stock or mutual insurance companies have been organized by the medical profession in order to avoid the need for special enabling legislation. The plans operated by Blue Cross generally make use of a rider attached to the hospital insurance certificate which provides a cash benefit according to a schedule for various surgical and medical procedures. The hospital association is the insurer.

The plans organized under special or general legislation are nonprofit associations whose boards of directors or trustees are elected in a variety of ways. On the average, about two thirds of the board members are physicians, so that the medical profession is in a position to exercise control. Contracts with participating physicians may provide for a scaling of fees when the association faces financial stringency, but it is doubtful if the physicians can be said to be the ultimate risk bearers in the sense that the hospitals are for Blue Cross, since a physician may withdraw from the plan or, in most circumstances, bill the patient directly for fees in excess of Blue Shield benefits. Usually, the Blue Shield and Blue Cross organizations in an area work very closely together. Frequently, the Blue Cross organization handles administration, enrollment, record keeping, and claims administration for Blue Shield on some type of reimbursement basis.

HOSPITAL COVERAGES

Hospital coverage is provided by the Blue Cross associations. The coverage includes expenses for room and board and for "hospital extras," usually on a service rather than a cash benefit basis.

Service Benefits

The provision of hospital coverage in the form of service benefits rather than in the form of cash benefits is an outstanding characteristic of the Blue Cross plans. Payment is made by the association directly to its member hospitals according to a scale agreed upon in advance. The insured patient deals directly with the hospital, and is billed only for the excess, if any, of his charges over the coverage of the insurance contract. Frequently, the only charges billed to the patient will be for miscellaneous services, such as telephone calls, which are not covered by the contract.

Room and Board

The room and board benefit is the basic coverage of a hospital insurance contract. It includes the services of general duty "floor" nurses. The typical Blue Cross coverage provides for semiprivate accommodations for a specified period on a full-service basis. A semiprivate room may contain anywhere from two to eight beds, with four the most common. A ward is any accommodation with more beds than a semiprivate room. Where coverage is on a ward or semiprivate basis, the usual contract provides an agreed dollar allowance toward the cost of more expensive accommodations.

In 1960, 64 per cent of Blue Cross subscribers had full-service room and board benefits on a semiprivate basis, 7.8 per cent on a ward basis, and 21.8 per cent were covered by plans providing for dollar maximums, similar to insurance company coverages. Plans covering 6.4 per cent of subscribers included deductible or percentage participation provisions. The proportion of subscribers on a full-service basis varied from a high of 100 per cent in the Middle Atlantic states to a low of 9 per cent in the New England states.

The number of days of full-service or full-cash allowance provided by Blue Cross plans in 1961 ranged from 21 to 365 days under the most widely held certificates, with the most common limits being 70 to 120 days (about 40 per cent for 70 days and 20 per cent for 120 days), followed by 21 and 30 days (about 10 per cent of plans each). For the most comprehensive certificates the number of days range from 21 to 730 days, or unlimited, with the most common limits being 70 to 120 days (about 16 per cent for 70 days and 50 per cent for 120 days), followed by 365 days (13 per cent of plans) and 730 days (5 per cent of plans.) Table 34–1

TABLE 34–1

BLUE CROSS CERTIFICATE BENEFITS, ROOM AND BOARD AND DAYS OF FULL BENEFITS, AS OF DECEMBER 31, 1960

(Per Cent of Total Membership in Each Payment Category)

	Group	Direct Payment	Total
Room, board, and general nursing:			
Semiprivate (two or more beds)	70.9%	42.1%	64.0%
Ward	7.7	8.1	7.8
Coinsurance or daily deductible	4.2	13.4	6.4
Dollar allowances	17.2	36.4	21.8
Days—full benefits:			
365 or more	3.8	0.6	3.0
120 to 180	49.3	20.7	41.9
70–100	21.7	28.9	23.6
50–60	4.3	5.0	4.4
40 or less	20.9	44.8	27.1

Source: Letter from William R. Nightingale, Director of Technical Services, Blue Cross Association.

shows the distribution of enrollees by payment category in 1960.

About 5 per cent of plans impose shorter limits during the first one or more years of membership. Such deductions range from four to 39 days. In two plans, five years of membership are required to attain full coverage, and two years are required in two others. The more comprehensive certificates of these plans provide full immediate coverage.

Hospital Extras

Hospitals provide many services in addition to basic room and board and general nursing. All Blue Cross plans make provision for some of these extra expenses. Most plans provide full service coverage of operating room use, dressings and casts, oxygen, laboratory fees, drugs, anesthesia, and basal metabolism and electrocardiogram tests. Some include blood and plasma; and a few, radium and X-ray therapy. While many plans provide these coverages on a full service basis, a substantial proportion impose limits as to the cost of services which will be covered by a schedule of maximum amounts for the various services. Table 34–2

TABLE 34–2

BLUE CROSS PLANS HAVING COVERAGE OF SPECIFIED HOSPITAL EXTRAS UNDER MOST WIDELY HELD CERTIFICATE, UNITED STATES, 1961

Expense Item	Per Cent with Full Coverage	Per Cent with Cash Allowance	Per Cent with No Coverage
Drugs	88%	12%	0%
Laboratory	85	12	3
Operating room	100	0	0
X ray	42	28	30
Anesthesia	68	5	27
Oxygen	93	5	2
Dressings and casts	98	2	0
Basal metabolism	89	3	8
Electrocardiogram	78	5	17
Intravenous solutions	57	8	35
Blood and plasma administration	87	4	9
Radium therapy	13	4	83
X-ray therapy	11	3	86

Source: Letter to the author from William R. Nightingale, Director of Technical Services, Blue Cross Association, February 16, 1962.

shows the proportion of plans covering various types of hospital extra expense and the basis of payment.

Maternity Benefits

The typical Blue Cross plan includes maternity benefits for a limited amount after the subscriber has been covered for a probationary period of six to 18 months, usually nine or 10.

One third of the plans provide full-service maternity benefits for a limited number of days, 31 per cent provide full-service benefits without limiting the days, and 28 per cent pay a stated reimbursement amount, under the most prevalent certificates. Unlike insurance company group plans, coverage is not extended for nine months after the policy ceases to cover, probably because of the ease of transferring to nongroup coverage. About 26 per cent of plans impose a limit of ten days' benefit, about 7 per cent have a flat $75 limit, 13 per cent have a flat $80 limit, 5 per cent have a seven-day limit, and the balance show little uniformity.

Exclusions

About half the Blue Cross contracts provide limited benefits and one quarter provide full benefits for nervous and mental conditions, while the remaining quarter exclude them. For alcoholism and drug addiction, limited benefits are provided by 22 per cent of the plans, regular benefits by 38 per cent, and the remaining 40 per cent exclude them. Tuberculosis is covered in full by 24 per cent of the plans, limited by 43 per cent, and excluded by 33 per cent. Venereal diseases are covered in full by 72 per cent of the plans, limited by 3 per cent, and excluded by 20 per cent. Quarantinable diseases are covered in full by 81 per cent of the plans, limited by 2 per cent, and excluded by 17 per cent. Only 2 per cent of the plans exclude pre-existing conditions, while 29 per cent cover them without a waiting period. The remaining 59 per cent of the plans impose waiting periods. Tonsilitis or adenoiditis requires such a probationary period in about 60 per cent of the plans, and appendicitis requires a probationary period in a few of the plans.

The services of physicians and private nursing are not covered by Blue Cross plans. Benefits for physicians' services are offered by Blue Shield. Often, iron lung and antibiotics are not covered or are drastically limited. Most plans do not cover admissions for primarily diagnostic services, treatment obtained or obtainable without cost from government hospitals, or occupational injuries which would (presumably) be covered by workmen's compensation. Out-patient services are usually excluded or limited to emergency accident care or minor procedures, and are limited in amount. Admission to the hospital as a regular patient is usually required in order to qualify for other than this quite limited coverage.

SURGICAL AND MEDICAL COVERAGES

Coverage of surgical and medical expenses is provided by Blue Shield and other medical-society-approved plans and by a few Blue Cross organizations. Where provided by Blue Cross, it must be on a cash benefit basis, with payment made directly to the insured. However, some Blue Cross plans provide certain medical services on a service basis. In other plans, coverage may be on a full-service basis, according to a schedule of benefits for various procedures, or on some combination of the two bases.

Service Benefits

Like Blue Cross, Blue Shield emphasizes service benefits. However, the situation is more complicated. Instead of dealing with a few dozen hospitals, a Blue Shield plan must deal with hundreds of physicians, most of whom have long been conditioned to charging patients in accordance with "ability to pay." Thus, while the service benefit approach is implemented, in that the association pays directly to participating physicians, for many, if not most, subscribers the physician may charge additional amounts directly to the patient. Medical association plans may be classified into three categories: full service, partial service, and cash benefit plans.

Full service plans provide complete coverage of the procedures included. The participating physicians agree to accept the benefits provided by the plan in full settlement of their charges. Cash benefit plans provide a schedule of benefits for various procedures, but the physician is not limited by this schedule and may charge the patient whatever he wishes. Except for the detail of direct payment to the physician, these plans do not differ materially from the typical insurance company policy. Indeed, the benefits under an insurance company contract may be assigned to the physician by the patient, if desired.

Partial service plans are a combination of the other two approaches. Full service coverage is provided for subscribers of lower income groups, while the higher income subscriber is covered according to a schedule of cash allowances and must bear any additional amounts of expense himself. The income ceilings for full service coverage in such plans average $5,200 for an individual and $7,500 for a family. Of the plans reporting to the National Association of Blue Shield Plans, 11 offer full service benefits, 51 offer partial service benefits, and 15 offer cash benefits. In March, 1963, plans offering full service benefits represented 6 per cent of total Blue Shield enrollment, partial service plans represented 70 per cent, and 24 per cent of enrollment was in the cash benefit plans. National data as to the proportion of subscribers under partial service contracts who are entitled to full service benefits are lacking.

Surgical Benefits

All Blue Shield plans involve a schedule of fees for various procedures. In the full service plans, this appears only in the agreement between the association and the participating physicians. In the other plans, it appears in the contracts with the individual subscribers, although a low-income subscriber in a partial service plan is not concerned with it. The schedule is comparable to that provided in insurance company policies. It lists a variety of procedures, including the common surgical operations, and treatment of fractures and sprains; and sometimes it includes diagnostic procedures and home, hospital, and office calls. The latter, of course, are properly medical—not surgical—coverage, but Blue Shield plans usually include both under the same contract.

Maternity benefits are usually scheduled the same way as other benefits, but may be subject to a limit even where other procedures are covered on a full service basis. The usual limits are from $50 to $150 for normal delivery, with $75 the most common provision. Usually, twice this amount is payable for a Caesarean section. A probationary period for maternity coverage, usually of at least nine months, is almost universal.

Medical Benefits

All Blue Shield plans offer some coverage of basic medical fees, and about 90 per cent of Blue Shield membership is covered for such benefits. About two thirds of the plans provide coverage on an in-hospital basis only, while the remainder extend coverage to home and office visits as well. In about 30 per cent of the plans which provide medical benefits, this coverage is optional with the insured. In the others, it is part of all basic packages. Most of the partial service plans provide in-hospital medical expense only. Coverage of home and office calls is more common in the full service plans; but frequently, there is some type of limit. This may involve an exclusion of the first one or two calls per sickness or injury, or a limit on the maximum number of calls. In the in-hospital medical coverage, most plans pay higher amounts for calls during the first few days of hospitalization. Many also offer higher allowances for cases requiring extraordinary care.

Exclusions

The usual basic contract excludes the type of service covered under other hospitalization policies, as well as care available under government law (such as workmen's compensation), care available in government facilities (such as Veterans Administration hospitals), drugs and medication, cosmetic surgery for other than necessary improvement of function, appliances, and nursing services. Other services which often receive reduced benefits, compared to others, include dental services (generally restricted to oral surgery), mental and nervous conditions, tuberculosis, alcoholism, and drug addiction. Also, services for obstetrics, pre-existing conditions, tonsillectomy, and adenoidectomy generally are covered only after a probationary waiting period of from six to twelve months. Similar waiting periods are occasionally applied for other conditions such as hernias, hemorrhoids, and female disorders.

MOVEMENT TOWARD MAJOR MEDICAL COVERAGE

Until recently, Blue Cross and Blue Shield plans have not provided coverage comparable to the major medical expense policies written by insurance companies or the comprehensive plans offered by many of the "independents" and some insurance companies.

Dread Disease Benefits

Thirteen Blue Shield associations now issue dread disease policies. These are usually provided as a rider extending the coverage of the basic

Blue Shield surgical-medical plan. In some cases the coverage is issued jointly with the Blue Cross plan. The typical plan covers ten "dread diseases": poliomyelitis, leukemia, diphtheria, scarlet fever, smallpox, tetanus, spinalmeningitis, encephalitis, tularemia, and rabies. The typical policy covers to a maximum of $5,000, sometimes allocated as to type of expense and sometimes subject to a two-year maximum period. The types of expense covered are quite broad and about the same as in insurance company plans.

Blue Cross and Blue Shield Extended Benefits

Extended benefit arrangements in Blue Cross and Blue Shield plans represent responses to the same need that led insurance companies to the development of major medical and comprehensive coverages. However, except for 11 plans offered in conjunction by Blue Cross and Blue Shield, benefits are limited to the hospital area or to the medical-surgical area. Moreover, some of the combination plans do not cover such items as blood and plasma, expensive drugs, or nursing services, which insurance company major medical and comprehensive policies cover like other eligible medical care expenses.

Forty-two Blue Cross plans offer extended benefit programs, either alone for hospital benefits only or in conjunction with Blue Shield to include medical-surgical benefits. Twenty of these resemble insurance company major medical contracts, in that they include provisions for deductibles and percentage participation; 22 represent extensions of the basic hospital contract.

Illustrative of the latter approach is the extended benefit program of the Colorado Hospital Service. It provides for extending the basic hospital coverage from 120 days to either 240 or 610 days, except in cases of pulmonary tuberculosis or nervous and mental diseases. Major-medical-type coverage also is available from the Colorado plan.

A fairly typical Blue Cross–Blue Shield extended benefit program following the major medical approach is described below. There are separate deductibles for Blue Shield and Blue Cross. Fifty dollars each is typical. A choice of upper limits is provided.

Blue Cross master medical endorsement pays 80 per cent of the following charges after the basic contract benefits expire and the deductible is satisfied:

1. Hospital room and board up to $25 per day.
2. All hospital ancillary services.

Blue Cross master medical endorsement pays 80 per cent of the following charges after the deductible has been satisfied:

3. In-hospital services for a registered nurse or licensed practical nurse for private duty nursing care (not related to the subscriber by blood or marriage).

4. Services of a registered nurse in the home for private duty nursing care (not related to the subscriber by blood or marriage).
5. Physical therapy treatment other than as provided in the basic contract.
6. Rental of an iron lung or other durable equipment required for temporary therapeutic use.
7. Crutches, splints, casts, and other such prosthetic appliances.
8. Drugs and medicines requiring a written prescription and dispensed by a licensed pharmacist, other than as provided in the basic contract.
9. Emergency ambulance service to nearest hospital.

Blue Shield master medical endorsement pays 80 per cent of the following charges after the basic contract benefits expire and the deductible is satisfied:

10. Services of physicians, including specialists, for surgical and nonsurgical care; for treatment of fractures and dislocations, including such care in a hospital, in the home, and in the physician's office, except that for outpatient physician's care for mental and nervous disorders, payments by Blue Shield will be limited to 50 per cent.

With a corridor deductible and percentage participation clause, contracts of this type resemble insurance company major medical contracts quite closely, except that they may not cover certain types of expense. Twenty Blue Cross and 19 Blue Shield plans offer benefits of this type, but not necessarily in conjunction with each other.

Eleven plans which depart from the insurance company approach are offered in conjunction by Blue Cross and Blue Shield. Benefits generally are extended without a corridor deductible, and percentage participation generally is applied only to certain types of benefit which are subject to abuse. As of May, 1963, 48 Blue Shield plans offered some form of extended benefit or major medical coverage, and it is estimated that six million persons are covered under these programs. As of December 31, 1962, 4.7 million Blue Cross enrollees had major-medical-type coverage, and 1.6 million had extended benefit-type coverage.

BLUE CROSS–BLUE SHIELD OPERATION

Primary and Dependents' Coverage

Blue Cross and Blue Shield plans always offer dependents' coverage optionally at an extra premium. A certificate issued to the primary insured indicates whether such coverage is included. About 60 per cent of total enrollees are dependents. Dependents' coverage has been increasing at a rate even greater than that of primary coverage.

Enrollment

Blue Cross and Blue Shield originally emphasized group enrollment. Their major selling efforts have continued to be directed toward employee groups. However, they generally have permitted members who have left their groups to continue coverage on an individual basis, usually at a higher rate. This continuation of coverage is facilitated by the fact that the "Blues" look upon group enrollment in a slightly different light than insurance companies. The individual subscriber is issued a certificate which frequently is the policy, since often there is no group master policy. This operation is somewhat comparable to what the insurance companies class as franchise insurance.

Individual subscribers are solicited continuously by many associations, while many open their books to new enrollees for a week or two at a time once or twice a year. Thus, they hope to limit adverse selection. In addition to those who enroll as individuals or leave an insured group, individual enrollments arise from termination of dependent status by aging of children, divorce, and death of the primary insured. Conversion is usually permitted in all these instances. Most plans also permit conversion to an individual basis when the subscriber retires. Generally, the underwriting requirements are more liberal than those of insurance companies, especially for group conversions and the higher ages. This is a corollary of the Blues' concept of nonprofit community service.

Rating

Generally, the Blues have practiced community rating. This means that there is little attempt to relate the rate for a group to its own loss probability. Except for differences due to variations in coverage and the amount of dependent coverage, all groups are charged the same. Similarly, individual rates are constructed on a broad base, with only the most major classifications as to coverage of spouse and children. The number of children is not considered; and often, there is no charge for children above the charge for husband and wife with maternity coverage. While this is in accord with their concept of community service, it makes the Blues vulnerable to the competition of insurance companies who may "pick off" the better groups by more scientific rating procedures. However, for the last twenty years, the Blues have been making more and more use of various forms of experience rating.

THE PLACE OF THE "BLUES"

Share of the Market

Currently, the Blues have 40 per cent of the hospital insurance market (as measured by number of individuals covered), 37 per cent of the surgical market, 47 per cent of the basic medical, and about 12 per cent of the major medical and extended benefit market. The major competing type of insurer, insurance companies, has 56 per cent of the hospital market, 58 per cent of the surgical, 45 per cent of the basic medical, and 86 per cent of the major medical and extended benefit business. Independent plans have 4, 5, and 8 per cent of the hospital, surgical, and medical markets, respectively.

The Blues pioneered in this area, and their early efforts resulted in a tremendous growth of voluntary private insurance against medical care expenses. However, the insurance companies, which started later, have grown faster, and their relative share of the market still seems to be increasing.

Distinctive Characteristics of the Blues

The characteristics which distinguish the Blue Cross and the Blue Shield associations are community sponsorship, control by the purveyors of service, nonprofit operation, service benefits, community rating, and provision of first-dollar benefits. None of these is completely their province; but in combination, these characteristics present a distinctive pattern. Some are competitive advantages; some are of dubious value in the market place.

The close relationship with the purveyors of service—the physicians and hospitals, respectively—gives an advantage, in that the associations can purchase services for insured members at wholesale rates. Claims administration is facilitated, since the purveyors think of it as "their" plan. This attitude should also contribute toward controlling excessive utilization. However, a good case can be made that the participation of a third party in financing contributes more to sound claims procedure than does the unrestrained conscience of the purveyors of care, i.e., physicians and hospital representatives.

Most of the Blues are legally recognized as nonprofit organizations. This confers major tax advantages over their competitors, even over many of the equally nonprofit mutual insurance companies. However, this is often associated with pressure for increased participation of representatives of the community or general public in the controlling bodies of the associations. If this community aspect is pushed too hard, it may result (as in some instances it has) in considerable public furor over rate changes.

The provision of service benefits facilitates claims settlement and tends to minimize moral hazard by making it almost impossible for a claimant to profit on his loss. However, a claimant may have another policy from which he collects cash benefits. Some plans attempt to control this by devices such as subrogation clauses. The insurance companies recently have developed uniform claim forms which simplify claims procedure and facilitate the assignment of benefits. This is almost the equivalent of service benefits, as far as the method of claims payment is concerned, but the benefits may not cover the entire amount of the physician's bill.

Community rating was discussed above. This may constitute a competitive disadvantage to the Blues in some instances and subject them to adverse selection.

Largely as a result of the activities of the Blues, first-dollar coverage has become traditional for hospital and surgical coverages. However, the extremely rapid growth of major medical coverage seems to indicate that the public can be educated to the need for high upper limits in preference to first-dollar coverage. If the medical care dollar is limited, as it probably is, a growing awareness of this principle may result in a major shift to contracts providing more adequate coverage subject to a small deductible. Much of the problem of cost stems from their adherence to first-dollar coverage, but it seems certain that the Blues will participate in such future developments and remain an important part of the medical care picture for the foreseeable future.

SELECTED REFERENCES

American Medical Association. *Voluntary Prepayment Medical Benefit Plans*. Chicago, 1963.

Becker, Harry (ed.). *Financing Hospital Care in the United States*. 3 vols. New York: McGraw-Hill Book Co., Inc., 1954–55.

Blue Cross Association. *Blue Cross Guide*. Annual. Chicago, 1963.

Dickerson, O. D. *Health Insurance*. Rev. ed. Homewood, Ill.: Richard D. Irwin, Inc., 1963.

Eilers, R. D. "The Fundamental Nature of Blue Cross and Blue Shield," *Journal of Insurance*, Vol. XXIX, No. 3 (September, 1962), p. 385.

Eilers, R. D. *Regulation of Blue Cross and Blue Shield Plans*. Homewood, Ill.: Richard D. Irwin, Inc., 1963.

Follmann, J. F., Jr. *Medical Care and Health Insurance*. Homewood, Ill.: Richard D. Irwin, Inc., 1963.

Levine, Sol; Anderson, Odin W.; and Gordon, Gerald. *Non-Group Enrollment for Health Insurance*. Cambridge: Harvard University Press, 1957.

MacDonald, Donald L. "Blue Cross Troubles: A Price of Delusion," *Weekly Underwriter*, November 17, 1956, p. 1134.

MacIntyre, Duncan M. *Voluntary Health Insurance and Rate Making*. Ithaca: Cornell University Press, 1962.

Serbein, Oscar N., Jr. *Paying for Medical Care in the United States*. New York: Columbia University Press, 1953.

Somers, Herman M., and Somers, Anne R. *Doctors, Patients, and Health Insurance*. Washington, D.C.: Brookings Institution, 1961.

Chapter 35

GROUP ACCIDENT AND RELATED PLANS

BY EDWIN H. MARSHALL

The chapter title "Group Accident and Related Plans" is intended to embrace a heterogeneous collection of insurance coverages which have developed for the most part since World War II. These forms of insurance are not technically group insurance in the conventional sense. On the other hand, they are far more similar to group insurance than to individual insurance.

Most of these plans provide coverage for accidental injuries or death, although some few of them provide coverage for sickness. Travel accident insurance is an important coverage. Accident insurance for special hazard types of situations, such as atomic energy operations and guided missile construction, is another type. Accident coverage, and sometimes sickness coverage, for school students, campers, stock car racers, civil defense workers, and other such groups are further examples.

Regulated as Blanket or Franchise Insurance

The various forms of coverage analyzed in this chapter generally are not written under the authority of the group section of state insurance laws. Instead, most such coverages are regulated as "blanket insurance" or "franchise insurance" under the appropriate sections of the insurance laws among the states. Blanket insurance is that type of coverage which justifies group-type insurance but does not meet all the requirements of regular group insurance. For example, it is either uneconomical or impractical to issue certificates of insurance to all members of many groups, such as all participants in a one-day soapbox derby, but these persons can be covered under a blanket policy. In many cases the type of group differs from that allowed under the group section of the law, as, for example, sports teams or units of civil defense workers. Or the insurance may be limited to a specific hazard, such as air travel.

A Model Blanket Accident and Sickness Insurance Bill promulgated by the Health Insurance Association of America defines as blanket insurance coverage under a contract issued to:

1. A transportation company covering passengers;
2. An employer covering employees, dependents, or guests with reference to specified hazards;
3. A school or college covering students, teachers, or employees;
4. A religious, charitable, recreational, educational, or civic organization covering members or participants defined by specified hazards incident to activities or operations;
5. A sports team, camp, or sponsors thereof covering members, campers, employees, officials, or supervisors;
6. A volunteer fire department, first-aid, civil defense, or other such volunteer organization covering members or participants defined by reference to specified hazards incident to activities or operations;
7. A newspaper or other publisher covering its carriers;
8. An association or labor union covering members or participants defined by reference to specified hazards incident to activities or operations; and
9. Any other risk or class of risks which in the discretion of the commissioner may be properly eligible for blanket accident and sickness insurance.[1]

Franchise insurance offers individual policies to members of groups at reduced cost. This coverage is designed to permit some of the savings and advantages of regular group insurance, even though all the principles of group insurance are not present. The savings are achieved through the central-source collection of premiums and the reduced sales effort due to the sponsorship of that central source. Usually, the client is given a selection of coverages and benefits not offered under the rigid classification system of group insurance, and a required percentage of participation is relaxed.[2]

GROUP ACCIDENT INSURANCE

Certain risks are dramatized in the minds of employees and their families either because such risks are indeed extremely hazardous or because people regard them so. Air travel, business trips to foreign lands, exposures to hazardous industrial research, experimentation with new instruments of warfare, and other such situations are experiences that cause people to feel that they have moved beyond the general possibility of an accident.

Employees exposed to these dramatized hazards frequently want substantial benefits, particularly accidental death coverage, added to their basic employee benefit insurance program. Employers have been recep-

---

[1] See Appendix M for wording of Model Blanket Accident and Sickness Insurance Bill.

[2] See Appendix N for wording of Model Franchise Accident and Health Insurance Bill recommended by Health Insurance Association of America.

tive to providing additional amounts of insurance to protect employees against these hazards.

This form of coverage also acts to fill one or two gaps which often exist in the coverage provided in other employee benefit insurance plans, including such hazards as war and flying in aircraft of other than standard commercial air lines.

Of course, from the standpoint of the economic loss in the death of an employee from some special hazard, there is no more lost because of death by accident than would be by death in some more conventional manner. However, in the same way that the accidental death or double indemnity coverage in individual life insurance has been popular, the additional benefits provided under these group-type accident coverages are relatively inexpensive and provide needed additional coverage when loss through these special hazards occurs.

Group Travel Accident Insurance

Each employer will have his own ideas as to what travel accident hazards should be insured and to what extent. Among the wide range of coverages for the travel accident hazard are the following:

1. ***Commercial Airline Only.*** Commercial airline insurance covers all accidents which occur while an employee is traveling on business in any aircraft operated by a commercial airline.

2. ***Broad Aircraft.*** Broad aircraft insurance covers business travel accidents occurring on private aircraft as well as on airlines. It thus adds coverage when an employee is called upon to fly in one of the some 38,000 aircraft operated by business concerns for the use of their employees and guests. Also, an employee may occasionally be required to fly in a chartered aircraft in order to reach some town not served by an airline.

3. ***Public Conveyance.*** Public conveyance insurance covers business travel aboard any public conveyance, not just air travel. Railroad, airline, bus, taxi, streetcar, ship, ferry—all these modes of transportation are covered. Some firms lean toward this choice; they feel that employees who travel by rail or other public transportation are entitled to the same protection as granted to those who go by air.

4. ***All Public Conveyance, Including Broad Aircraft.*** All public conveyance insurance is merely the broadening of the public conveyance coverage to include private aircraft flying in industrial or chartered planes, that is, a combination of (2) and (3) above.

5. ***All Conveyance.*** All conveyance insurance is primarily intended for adding automobile travel to the public conveyance coverage. As is well recognized, much business travel is by automobile, with its attendant hazards, and many concerns feel that this coverage is as important as that for aircraft and other means of public transportation.

6. ***All Travel outside a Given Area.*** This insurance provides broad protection while traveling on business, 24 hours a day, for all accidents occurring during a trip, on or off the travel conveyance. It covers injury or death due, for instance, to hotel fires, and all other accidents unrelated to the travel conveyance. Frequently, buyers wish to cover only what they consider an actual out-of-town trip. So they will want the coverage to apply only when the employee travels outside the city of employment, or perhaps beyond its twenty-five-mile radius. In this way, local, daily business travel is excluded.

7. ***All Travel.*** All travel insurance is the same 24-hour business travel coverage as in (6), but without area restriction. It covers any and all business travel off the firm's premises, even a ten-minute trip. It is important to recognize that most firms have now gravitated to this "all travel" coverage choice. Over half of all new group travel policies issued are now in this category or (6) above.

8. ***Foreign Travel.*** Foreign travel insurance covers travel to foreign countries. The hazards of hot and cold war spots all over the world make it desirable that war risk exposure be included in this coverage.

Special Risks Accident

Special risks accident coverage is needed by many industrial firms and other organizations for employees exposed to special occupational hazards. Some examples of the kind of hazards for which accident insurance has been developed are:

Atomic energy operations
Guided missile construction or testing
Electronic research
Testing of experimental aircraft
Testing of aircraft instruments
Television tower maintenance
Chemical research
Speed and endurance tests
Offshore oil exploration
Munitions manufacture or transportation
Submarine testing
News correspondents and photographers
Geological surveys
Aerial pipe-line and power-line inspections
Disaster emergency crews
Underwater diving—construction or salvage
Bank guards and messengers

This list is not intended to be complete. New special risk exposures are being developed constantly. Many require temporary coverage only, as, for example, the protection desired by a corporation for its employees while piling up sandbags on a levy along the Mississippi during flood conditions.

Types of Benefits

Group accident benefits typically fall into three general categories: (1) death and dismemberment, (2) weekly indemnity for loss of income, and (3) medical expense reimbursement.

Death and Dismemberment. A death and dismemberment benefit is the most popular in group accident insurance. The very nature of the hazards covered by the insurance leads to thoughts of a fatal accident. Also, the employee may have adequate amounts of disability income and medical expense coverage in other group insurance provided by his employer or under some uninsured salary continuance program provided by the employer. When the employee is exposed to a variety of special hazards, however, he often looks to the employer to provide an additional death and dismemberment sum, and the employer often wishes to provide this extra coverage. The typical benefit amounts are usually sizable, with limits ranging from $25,000 to $100,000, based on classification.

Disability Income Weekly Indemnity. Disability income weekly indemnity can be payable up to a maximum of one, two, or five years of disability, commencing with the first day. Or the benefit period can be of such length that aggregate payments will equal the death benefit named in the policy. Any of these choices may be written, with a deductible period ranging from one week to one year. A one-year deductible will, in many cases, eliminate any important overlap with salary continuance plans or other group coverages. A not unusual combination of benefits might be a $25,000 death benefit and $150-a-week disability income, commencing after one year and then payable until the $150 payments total $25,000.

Medical Expense Reimbursement. The medical expense reimbursement benefit is quite important if there is no other applicable insurance, or if other insurance is inadequate. Where unlimited medical expense coverage is provided under workmen's compensation and a broad group medical expense program exists, it might be well to eliminate any medical expense reimbursement benefit under the group accident policy. When the medical expense reimbursement benefit is included, it normally is written on a blanket basis, ranging from $500 to $5,000 top limit.

Benefit Formulas

Several approaches are possible in determining the amount of benefit. The simplest system, but probably the least satisfactory, is to provide the same amount for all employees. This gives no recognition to differences in need based on standards of living and income. It is common, therefore, as in most other group insurance, to have various classifications to reflect need. These classifications may be established on the basis of position, such as Class I, Executive Officers; Class II, Department Heads; Class III, All Other Employees. The classifications may be set up on the basis of salary, such as Class I, over $15,000; Class II, $5,000 to $14,999; and Class III, below $5,000.

A popular variation is in amount of insurance expressed as a percentage of income; e.g., the death benefit might be twice the annual salary, with a minimum of $10,000 and a maximum of $50,000; the weekly benefit at a level of, say, 60 per cent of salary, with a minimum of $50 a week and a maximum of $250 a week. The medical expense benefit might also be keyed indirectly to salary by having the limit equal to $100 for each $1,000 of accidental death benefit. By this popular method, benefits vary in amount according to income without the necessity of establishing a classification system.

Premiums

A variety of premium bases may be offered for the particular benefit program selected. For the travel exposures the choices include a charge per person or per number of trips, or a percentage of fares expended for travel. For special risks exposures the premium base may be the number of hours or days of exposure per person insured. In truth, the premium base is flexible and a subject of negotiation between insurer and insured.

Almost always, the entire premium is paid by the employer. By its very nature, group accident insurance gives recognition to an extra or unique exposure to accident, and most employers feel that it is their responsibility to provide and pay for the needed insurance protection.

Although guidelines exist for the underwriter for the establishment of the premium for many classes, such as air-line travel (e.g., 50 cents per $1,000 accidental death and disability per person or one half of 1 per cent of air-line fares expended for each $5,000 of insurance), many risks are so unusual or the coverage and benefits so tailor-made that the premium determination comes down to underwriting judgment. For example, a rate for newspaper correspondents sent to Viet Nam, the Congo, and other world trouble spots, or the rate for test pilots of an aircraft manufacturer who are to test-fly a newly developed supersonic aircraft, can be established only by judgment.

It also follows that in the field of group accident underwriting, premiums are not normally subject to experience rating, retrospective rating, or retention treatment. In this field, many risks will have no losses, and some risks will have losses that will wipe out premiums for a hundred years. Obviously, true insurance principles must apply, with the pool of premiums contributed by all insured risks used to meet the extreme needs of those which suffer the catastrophic losses. Rates for the classification with credible amounts of like exposure are modified periodically to reflect the fluctuations of experience on the classification as a whole and to reflect the pressure of competition.

Underwriting

Underwriting in the travel accident and special risks field seldom involves examination of health conditions or moral factors with respect to the employee group being considered for insurance. The underwriter's main responsibility is to be certain, with experience as his best guide, that he has received proper description of the hazards to be insured and a complete revelation of the exposure units. He must be certain that the amounts of insurance are reasonable but, at the same time, be prepared to take millions of dollars of risk for very minor sums where the risk is calculably small. He must look for protection to the accumulated premium volume of many risks to withstand the infrequent but catastrophically large losses.

The single most important principle for the underwriter to understand is that he is dealing with catastrophe risk. Under normal circumstances, absence of loss for several years on a single risk is no more justification for a reduction in premium than would several large losses (such as employees killed on a scheduled air-line flight) be justification for a rate increase on a particular risk. The underwriter must underwrite a book of business as a whole; and even here, he must look at a period of years and not be influenced greatly by fluctuation in experience on that book created by one or two major catastrophes or the absence of such catastrophes.

Voluntary Franchise Accident Insurance for Employee Groups

The previously described blanket accident insurance coverages have led to the more recently developed voluntary franchise accident insurance for employee groups. Perhaps the two most important reasons for the development were (1) the almost insatiable desire for high limits of death benefit for exposure to the accident dangers of hazardous occupations and modern high-speed transportation, and (2) a desire for protection to cover off-the-job travel and other accident hazards.

In general, most employers feel that they have met their obligation to the employee with the more limited blanket accident insurance. Hence, the voluntary coverage is offered to the employee through the medium of payroll deduction and fully at his own expense.

Briefly, voluntary franchise accident insurance offers to employees of a common employer amounts of insurance ranging from $5,000 to $100,000. Higher limits are sometimes negotiated. It covers all accidents, twenty-four hours a day, whether occupational or nonoccupational. The employee may select the benefit amount and may also insure his wife, usually for a smaller sum. No fixed percentage of employee participation is required, and all who apply during the enrollment period are accepted, regardless of health history.

Accidental death benefit only, or accidental death and dismemberment, can be provided. A total and permanent disability income benefit may be included at an additional premium charge. Air coverage is usually limited to air-line travel, but can be extended if there is a corporate aircraft. Frequently, however, coverage on the employer-owned aircraft is already provided in high limits by employer-purchased seat-accident or admitted-liability insurance.

The cost of voluntary franchise accident insurance is low, due to mass marketing or the quasi-group approach.

BLANKET INSURANCE FOR NONEMPLOYEE GROUPS

Many groups other than those of an employer-employee or association nature are covered under blanket insurance for accidental death and dismemberment, disability income indemnity, and medical expense reimbursement. For the most part, these groups consist of persons who have a common interest of membership in, or who participate in the activities of, a special group or team.

In most cases the relationship of the group is impermanent or transitory in nature, such as campers, or the group relationship is limited in strength or importance, as in the case of volunteer civil defense workers. Because of the nature of the relationship, it is rarely desirable to provide full-coverage insurance programs. Further, because of the limited nature of the group relationship, the group normally is not a desirable vehicle for a permanent program. Consequently, insurance issued for such miscellaneous groups usually is limited either to the short period of group relationship or to the common hazards shared, or to both. More often than not, the insurance is for accident benefits only, rather than accident and sickness benefits. However, for campers and students in private schools, both accident and sickness benefits have a proper place.

In considering the desirability of blanket insurance covering the entire group as contrasted to individual insurance, it is important to realize that in many of these types of groups the blanket approach provides coverage more advantageously than the individual approach; and in many cases, it provides protection when individual insurance would not be available. For example, a football-playing student is a poor individual risk, but he is acceptable as a small element in the total school body. Another example is a stock car racer, who becomes a desirable risk only when he is part of a group large enough to provide a spread of risk and some stability of experience. Still another example would be a civil defense worker. For such a person, reasonable insurance limited to his civil defense activities can be provided quite inexpensively on a group basis, whereas it might be prohibitively expensive on an individual purchase basis.

Among the more common types of groups covered are students, camps, sports teams, youth groups, volunteer public worker groups, and social or fraternal groups; and, shifting to the nature of the activity itself, a great variety of special events are covered.

Students (Public and Parochial Schools)

Most public and parochial elementary and high schools now offer all parents an opportunity to purchase an accident policy covering their sons and daughters while on school premises and while engaged in school-related activities. The principal benefit is typically $3,000 of medical expenses, with a small accidental death benefit included.

Students (Private Schools and Colleges)

Many students in private schools and colleges live on the campus; and, typically, a blanket policy provides broad benefits, both accident and sickness, and covers twenty-four hours a day, whether or not an accident or sickness is related to school activities. Most plans are tailor-made so as to be integrated with the type and degree of health facilities provided by the school. Some schools require enrollment in the plan at registration, while others offer it on a completely voluntary basis. Obviously, the higher the percentage of participation, the sounder the plan.

Camps

This classification includes day and boarding camps, and private and organizational camps. Normally, all campers are required to be included in a blanket policy of accident insurance. Many camps require sickness insurance as well. Coverage is limited to activities during the camp season, and travel to and from the camp. Medical expense benefits are of the basic type, with accidental death coverage supplementary. In addition, tuition refund insurance is often written, providing for the return to the parent of the tuition paid in the event a child is forced to withdraw from camp because of epidemic, flood, injury, or sickness.

Sports Teams

Sports teams usually find it desirable to arrange blanket policies of accident insurance for all participants while practicing for or participating in team activity. High school football, basketball, hockey, and other physical contact teams are examples of teams that are covered. School authorities usually insist that insurance be in force before they will permit a student to participate. Junior teams, such as Little League baseball, carry accident insurance on the young participants and their coaches as well.

Accident insurance on sports teams places the principal emphasis on a blanket accident medical expense benefit, sometimes with a small deductible, and will frequently include a small accidental death or dismemberment benefit.

Youth Groups

Youth groups generally find blanket accident insurance on their members a desirable relief for the adult supervisors. Groups such as Boy Scouts, Campfire Girls, DeMolay, 4-H Clubs, Blue Birds, Girl Scouts, Rainbow Girls, Job's Daughters, Future Farmers of America, and YMCA have blanket policies, usually optional at the local level, with benefits concentrated in the medical expense reimbursement area.

Volunteer Public Worker Groups

Groups such as civil defense workers, auxiliary police, volunteer firemen, Red Cross volunteers, and others, because of the hazardous risks they face in their duties, are often protected by blanket accident insurance while participating in the activity of the group.

In addition to blanket medical expense benefits and accidental death or dismemberment benefits, the groups may provide disability income benefits, because their membership usually comes from employed adults.

Organizational Groups

Other organizations of a social or fraternal nature also find that a blanket accident insurance policy covering the group activity encourages membership and prevents needless criticism in the event of injuries. Types of organizations that consider such coverage desirable are Lions Clubs, Junior Chamber of Commerce chapters, Exchange Clubs, Kiwanis Clubs, Chambers of Commerce, church groups, and other businessmen's and service groups.

Special Events

Sponsors of special events, such as soapbox derbies, bowl games, picnics, conventions, charity bazaars, and other short-term events, secure blanket accident insurance covering the participants or the public who may be injured as a result of the event. The variety of such special events is unlimited. Premiums are established by the insurer based upon judgment.

Underwriting and Rate Making

Some classifications among the nonemployee groups involve little or no underwriting selection among risks of the same class. For example, junior sports teams like Little League teams are accepted without underwriting. In such classes, the underwriting skill comes in the design of the plan of insurance, the determination of the classification of risks to be used, and the establishment of the rate to be applied to all risks within each classification.

For example, many underwriters have found that a deductible must be used to eliminate the small, insignificant losses which mean little economically to the claimant, but in the aggregate put an intolerable burden on the experience for the classification.

Rates for these classifications are established from experience and the natural operation of competitive forces.

Other nonemployee groups, such as the students of private schools or colleges, involve a considerable degree of underwriting skills on a risk-by-risk basis. The medical facilities available at each school, the attitude of the school authorities toward the insurance, the make-up of the student body, including factors such as sex and economic background, and rural versus urban origins—all are important in evaluating the risk. The prior insurance experience is also sought in every case by the underwriter.

From this analysis comes the establishment of a rate for the particular school based on a system of debits and credits from established guide rates.

Renewal underwriting plays an important role as well, as the underwriter has the opportunity to correct his original errors with changes in rates based on experience and redesign of the insurance plan to avoid abuses that may appear.

Nonemployee groups, then, fall into two basic underwriting classes: (1) the classes which are underwritten solely on a class basis and (2) those which require careful risk-by-risk underwriting skill.

SELECTED REFERENCES

DICKERSON, O. D. *Health Insurance.* Rev. ed. Homewood, Ill.: Richard D. Irwin, Inc., 1963.

FAULKNER, EDWIN J. *Health Insurance.* New York: McGraw-Hill Book Co., Inc., 1960.

Chapter 36

GROUP PREMIUMS AND EXPERIENCE RATING

BY DONALD D. CODY

The organization of an insurance company, the conduct of its business, and its methods of pricing are similar to those in industry generally. Because of differences in nomenclature and the intangible nature of the insurance product, this similarity has not generally been recognized. As a result, pricing of the group insurance product has had an air of mystery which has hampered public understanding of the methods of determining initial premiums, renewal premiums, retrospective rate credits, and dividends. The whole concept of insurance pricing should be considered in the same perspective as pricing in production and service industries producing, distributing, or servicing tangible products.

The Group Insurance Product

Group insurance provides death benefits, disability income benefits, medical expense benefits, and dental expense benefits to groups of employees. These benefits, along with pensions, are recognized as fringe benefit additions to the wages of employees, and employers purchase them with the same care as they make other expenditures. Employers choose their carriers on the basis of quality of the product, level of pricing, and ability to perform long-range service functions.

Because group insurance is part of the warp and woof of personnel relationships, the design of the group product is concerned not only with pricing and design of benefits but also with a complex of human relationships. For instance, carriers are concerned with the relationships of the employer with his employees, including bargaining with his unions. Carriers usually deal with the employer through an agent, a broker, or an actuarial consultant. And the employer and the employees are involved with doctors, hospitals, and other providers of medical care in the sensitive areas of quality of care and fee making.

Because of this complex of relationships, group product design not only involves the pricing and design of benefits, which are familiar topics in connection with individual policies, but also includes a system design covering procedures at the sale and installation of a group case and the month-to-month activities during the continuance of the case. Each group case differs from other group cases in greater or lesser degree.

General Theory of Pricing in Group Insurance

The pricing of group insurance is important in a highly competitive market. Since insurance companies have virtually unlimited capacity to produce with the existing home office and field organizations, this market is essentially a buyer's market. Pricing is important both at time of sale and at time of each renewal, for many group cases face competitive bids at each renewal as employers seek to obtain better pricing or more extensive service.

Group insurance premiums, adjusted for retrospective rate credits or dividends, must be large enough in aggregate for the whole group line to cover incurred claims, expenses, commissions, taxes, risk charge, and profit.[1] Claims constitute the cost of material in a general business sense. The expenses and taxes are similar to the corresponding items in general business. The risk charge recognizes the insurance risk on each policy—a charge sufficient in the aggregate for the whole group insurance line over a period of years to cover unanticipated losses on high-claim cases. The risk charge is greater on small cases as a percentage of premium than on large cases. The profit charge finances the expansion of the insurance company, provides for growth of contingency reserves, and, in stock companies, also compensates the owners for use of their capital. The formulation of risk and profit charges varies from company to company.

In coverages like group paid-up life insurance and group permanent insurance, premiums, of course, must also provide for the development of actuarial reserves to provide for the future payment of benefits. However, most group insurance is on the one-year term basis, and the price is set at a level to cover claims, expenses, taxes, risk charge, and profit.

EXPERIENCE RATING

Group insurance coverages are experience-rated both with respect to expenses and with respect to claims. This experience rating is not done solely at the option of the insurance company but is required also by the demands of a competitive market.

In the absence of experience rating, individual companies could restrict themselves to specific geographical areas and to classes of policy-

[1] Net investment income earned on group funds is another pricing factor but will be introduced later in the analysis.

holders which are known to have low levels of claims and low expenses. However, most insurance companies operate in a wide geographical area, offering their product to essentially all employed groups. Operation over such a broad spectrum of policyholders necessitates experience rating so as to meet the competition of specialty companies and self-insurance.

Also, group insurance is usually offered without individual evidence of insurability, and there are wide variations in claims characteristics from group to group. Large employers with good claims experience naturally seek carriers with experience rating, so that their costs will reflect their better claims experience. Conversely, those with bad experience would seek out companies without experience rating.

The question naturally arises as to how Blue Cross/Blue Shield in many areas operates without experience rating in this competitive market. Blue Cross/Blue Shield, however, in a particular area is essentially a franchise operation, with no competition by any other carrier operating in the same manner. Blue Cross/Blue Shield has contracts with doctors and hospitals, and has charges made to it in accordance with cost determination formulas, giving cost advantages not available to the general population, including the part of the population insured by insurance companies. The price advantage, together with the predilection of many people to the guaranteed full-payment benefits offered by some plans, permits Blue Cross/Blue Shield to operate successfully in a wide segment of the medical expense market without experience rating. However, in many areas, Blue Cross/Blue Shield is being forced into experience rating with sizable employers for the same reasons that insurance companies themselves experience-rate.

Experience Rating of Expenses

In the determination of premiums, retrospective rate credits, and dividends, insurance companies make a careful cost accounting of expenses, recognizing the various activities connected with each group policyholder at issue and during the continuance of the group contract. This cost accounting recognizes such expenses at issue as commissions and salaried sales costs, issuance of contract, certificates and announcement booklets, and installation of the billing and claims systems. During the continuance of the contract, recognition is taken of taxes, commissions, cost of billing, claims payment expenses, and expenses of activities with broker, agent, and employer. It is evident that while many of these expenses are independent of size of case, others depend upon number of employees, amount of premiums, number and type of claims, level of commissions, and effort expended in dealing with the employer. In determining initial and renewal premium rates, the variations of these expenses are reflected by premium rate variations of as much as 20 per cent between the largest and the smallest employers. In retrospective rate credits and dividends, a more refined formulation of these expenses is made.

Experience Rating of Claims

Usually, claims costs are reflected partially by recognizing the average level of claims in the whole class of policyholders for each type of group insurance and partially by recognizing the actual claims on each case. The claims of small policyholders will vary considerably in each case from year to year; and little, if any, attention is paid to actual claims in such instances. In cases with several thousand lives, claims vary less widely as a percentage of premium from year to year, and a high degree of recognition is given to the group's own experience. In fact, in determining dividends or retrospective rate credits on such large cases, the claims charge used by most companies is equal to the group's actual claims incurred, without any recognition of average claims in the class of cases. Between the smallest and largest cases, there is a blend, as illustrated below.

The formulas for experience rating of claims to be charged to a particular group take a number of forms, but those in most general use fall into two general types. A fundamental criterion for all formulas is that the aggregate of claims charges realized must be equal to the aggregate of actual claims incurred for each year over all groups.

***Type 1* (*Risk-Averaging Formula*).** This type of formula calculates the claims charge as a weighted average of (1) actual claims on the case and (2) average claims on the class of cases. The claims charge as a percentage of premium (called loss ratio charged) can be expressed as follows:

$$\frac{K}{P} = \frac{yC}{P} + (1 - y)k, \text{ where for each coverage on each case}$$

P = Annual premium earned

K = Claims charge $\left(\frac{K}{P}\right)$ = Loss ratio charged

C = Actual incurred claims $\left(\frac{C}{P}\right)$ = Actual loss ratio

k = Average ratio of claims to premiums on class of coverage

y = Credibility factor varying by coverage and dependent on volume of exposure, as measured by number of lives or amount of premium (larger for larger numbers of lives or larger premium)

In determination of dividends or retrospective rate credits, the formula is applied to the experience of the policy year, and the credibility factor (y) might be as shown in Table 36–1. Thus, in a group with five hundred lives, six tenths of the claims portion of its life insurance dividend would be determined by its own claims experience. It should be noted that the premium P is rerated also on an experience basis, so that the average claims level kP reflects past experience as well.

TABLE 36–1

CREDIBILITY FACTORS FOR GROUP INSURANCE DIVIDENDS BY SIZE OF GROUP

Size of Group (Lives)	Life Insurance	Medical Care and Short-Term Disability Insurance
100	0.0	0.2
200	0.2	0.5
300	0.3	0.8
500	0.6	1.0
1,000	1.0	1.0

The same type of formula may be used to determine renewal rates, except that the values of C and P reflect experience over a longer period of time than one year, the experience for the latest year being usually weighted more heavily than for prior years. Claims for past years must be adjusted to reflect typical trends in claims levels. Premiums for past years must be adjusted to a level consistent with present rates. Similarly, the credibility factor (y) reflects the number of life-years of exposure in past years. The credibility factor (y) is usually lower in renewal rate determinations than in dividend determinations, and typically might be as shown in Table 36–2.

TABLE 36–2

CREDIBILITY FACTORS FOR GROUP INSURANCE RENEWAL RATING BY SIZE OF GROUP AND LENGTH OF PERIOD INSURED

Size of Group (Lives)	Life Insurance		Medical Care and Short-Term Disability Insurance	
	One Year	Five Years	One Year	Five Years
100	0.00	0.25	0.20	0.65
500	0.25	0.60	0.75	0.80

Type 2 (Risk Charge Formula). This type of formula, used only in connection with dividends or retrospective rate credits, utilizes an additional risk charge, R, where R depends on type of coverage and is larger as a percentage of premium, the smaller the case.

Here the claims charge K is in this form:

$$K = C + R$$

R is realized only on those cases where actual claims, C, are less than premiums earned after provision for expenses, commissions, taxes, normal risk charge, and profit. Hence the level of R on each case must be adjusted so that the aggregate of R over all cases on which R is so realized is equal to the aggregate excess of claims incurred over premiums (adjusted for expenses, commissions, taxes, normal risk charge, and profit) on all other cases.

It is usual for all coverages under a group policy to be experience-rated together, and for premiums for all coverages to be treated as a combined premium so as to obtain more stability from offsetting random variations in the various coverages. The larger the premium, the lower is the risk charge made by the insurance company as a percentage of premium, in recognition of the greater stability which accompanies larger numbers of lives and coverages. The employer thus enjoys a lower cost from the combination of coverages.

The manner in which insurance companies apply these concepts of experience rating of expenses and claims to renewal premiums, retrospective rate credits, and dividends will be referred to later.

TRENDS IN CLAIMS COSTS

Claims trends are slowly downward on life insurance due to improving vitality, better public health, and more effective industrial accident control. On disability income insurance, claims reflect the characteristics of the employer and his employees; trends are not common, but economic conditions will cause significant change in claims levels from time to time. Premium making is not too difficult on these coverages.

Group medical expense insurance is an entirely different problem. Utilization of medical facilities is slowly increasing with changing attitudes of the public and doctors. The hospital has become a community facility, accepted without fear by the public and freely used by doctors. Drugs are prescribed and purchased in expensive profusion. Medical care is primarily a personal service function, and its cost has increased with the inflation of the dollar and with mounting industrial productivity, both of which factors have increased salaries, wages, and fees of medical personnel. Costs of hospital buildings, costs of expensive therapeutic and diagnostic equipment needed for the new medical and surgical techniques, and costs of teams of specialists have been going up year by year. Some relief will develop in these costs with better regional planning of hospital locations and specialties, and with improved hospital management. Also, there is some unnecessary utilization of facilities, and such abuse can be reduced in time by education and control. However, by and large, increasing costs of medical care reflect better medical care by better trained personnel using better facilities for more and more people legitimately needing such care.

Between 1951 and 1961, national expenditures for medical care increased from about $10 billion to $21 billion and from 4.1 per cent of disposable personal income to 5.7 per cent. In the same period the price index for medical care items increased about 3.5 per cent a year, while the general price index moved up only by about 1.5 per cent a year. Surgeons' fees moved up about 2 per cent a year, drugs moved up about 1 per cent a year, and general practitioners' fees increased about 3.5 per cent a year. The hospital cost index was the most volatile part of the medical care index, moving up about 7 per cent a year. In New York City, for instance, semiprivate room and board charges increased from an average of about $12 a day in 1951 to $24 a day in 1961.

The effect of these inflationary forces on premium rates is about 8 per cent a year on major medical coverages, 5 per cent a year on hospital coverages with dollar maximums, and 2 to 3 per cent a year on doctors' fees coverages.

In the section on renewal premiums, further reference will be made to the effects of claims cost trends.

INITIAL PREMIUM RATES

Life Insurance

The initial premium rates for group life insurance for all companies licensed in New York are based on a minimum standard promulgated by the New York State Insurance Department for use in the first policy year. Companies licensed in New York must recognize this minimum standard extraterritorially in all states. The states of Maine, Michigan, Ohio, and Pennsylvania have the same minimum standard applicable just to groups within these states. The mortality basis of these rates is the 1960 Commissioners Standard Group Table, developed from intercompany group experience with an aggregate of nearly 60 million years of lives exposed. The net premium rates are loaded for expenses by a formula which broadly recognizes the level of expense by size of case. The rates vary by 20 per cent between the largest and smallest cases. Table 36–3 shows these rates at decennial ages.

Companies not licensed in New York State usually use somewhat lower rates outside of Maine, Michigan, Ohio, and Pennsylvania, but the majority of large companies are licensed in New York, so that most new cases are issued with CSG rates.

Accidental Death and Dismemberment Insurance

The initial premium rates for this coverage and other group health coverages are determined by each company independently. Claims costs are available from intercompany experience developed by the Society of Actuaries. In the long run, the average loss ratios for this coverage are relatively stable and tend to decrease slowly with the reducing occupational accident hazards. In some industries with serious accident hazards, higher premiums are used where benefits are paid for both occupational and nonoccupational losses. The typical premium is 6 cents per month per $1,000 for nonoccupational coverage, or for nonoccupational and occupational coverage in industries without accident hazard. In industries with the greatest accident hazard, the premium can run three to five times this level where there is occupational coverage.

TABLE 36-3

COMMISSIONERS STANDARD GROUP (CSG) LIFE RATES
(PER $1,000)
(Illustrated for Decennial Ages Only)

Age	Monthly
20	$ 0.23
30	0.27
40	0.45
50	1.06
60	2.51
70	5.81
80	12.83

Adjustments: (1) To the aggregate premium determined from the above rates, $0.20 per $1,000 is added, with a maximum of $8.00 per group. (2) The aggregate premium determined by (1) is reduced by the following percentage reductions, shown only for selected premium sizes:

Aggregate Monthly Premium before Reduction	Percentage Expense Reduction
Under $ 200	0%
$ 400– 450	5
800– 1,000	10
10,000– 15,000	15
60,000 and over	20

Short-Term Disability Income

Companies generally rely heavily upon intercompany experience, compiled by the Society of Actuaries, as a basis for initial premium rates for short-term disability income coverage. A typical monthly premium rate on an all-male group for a benefit period of twenty-six weeks, with benefits starting on the first day in the case of accident and on the eighth day in the case of sickness, is 71 cents per $10 weekly indemnity prior to the application of any expense reduction factors. Rates depend on the percentage of females and on the presence of maternity benefits. Claims levels on this coverage on small groups run about 70 per cent of premiums on the average and higher on large groups. The claims levels, however, vary from group to group with different economic conditions and different labor relations.

Traditionally, premiums on this coverage do not reflect the variation of risk with age. However, considerable variation in the risk by age exists, running, in the case of nonmaternity coverage, from less than 50 per cent of the average risk for employees under age 30 to more than 300 per cent of the average risk for employees over age 65.

Long-Term Disability Income

Long-term disability income is a relatively new coverage in the group insurance field. It is similar to short-term disability income coverage but typically has a six-month waiting period, and benefits run for five years, for ten years, or to age 65. With little or no mature group experience as yet, premiums generally are based upon experience under disability features of individual life insurance policies, and upon experience under personal disability income policies, with recognition of the fact that these experiences are primarily on self-employed individuals. The group risk is on wage or salaried employees, and is more favorable. Claims on this type of coverage will vary considerably with economic conditions and can also be expected to vary from year to year even more than life insurance claims on particular cases. Premium rates depend upon distribution of benefits by age and sex.

Medical Expense Insurance

Reference has been made to the annual increases in medical care costs, especially in hospital costs. Premium rates for new cases must be increased on the average about 3 to 5 per cent a year on medical expense policies providing typical hospital, surgical, and doctors' fees coverages. The average annual increase in major medical expense rates is about 8 to 10 per cent. Similar percentage increases apply also to premiums for hospital coverages which provide for semiprivate room and board charges without a dollar-per-day maximum, or which provide large amounts of benefits for hospital extras.

Information as to claims levels comes from the experience of each individual company, from intercompany data compiled by the Society of Actuaries, and from data compiled by such organizations as the American Hospital Association and the Department of Health, Education and Welfare of the federal government.

Premium rates for hospital insurance are made up of two parts: a rate per dollar of room and board charges, which is usually independent of geographical area, and a rate for extra charges, which depends upon geographical area. Premium rates for surgeons' and doctors' fees coverages are generally independent of geographical area. Except for groups with unusual numbers of high-age employees, and except for retired lives, usually no account is taken of variation in medical care costs by age on base plan coverages. The reason is that for typical plans (including dependents' coverage) the cost by age is relatively level as a result of the higher costs of maternity benefits at the lower ages, which offset the lower nonmaternity costs at such ages. As in the case of short-term disability income and long-term disability income coverages, higher rates apply to females than to males.

Major medical expense rate making is a great deal more complicated. Data compiled by the Society of Actuaries and individual companies appearing in the *Transactions of the Society of Actuaries* have been in sufficient detail to permit the use of formulations reflecting all the various pertinent factors, such as the following:

1. Costs vary by geographical location, the range of variation being about 170 per cent from the least expensive to the most expensive area.
2. Costs vary by age over a range of 500 per cent from the lowest to the highest ages.
3. Costs vary as between males and females.
4. Costs vary by level of income of the employee over a range of about 300 per cent.
5. Various deductible and coinsurance factors, and variations in benefit design and coverage, affect costs.
6. The maternity benefits are usually under a separate insurance clause and reflect the higher cost of maternity benefits for young age groups as opposed to older age groups.

Premiums for liberal medical care benefits may amount to as much as $25 a month for each employee with a family.

Dental Care Insurance

Group dental care insurance is a new form of coverage which has as yet been adopted by only a few employers and labor-management trustee plans. Claims estimates for premium purposes are based upon the experience of a number of pioneering service plans, labor-management trustee plans, and data compiled by the American Dental Association. Costs of procedures in local areas have been compiled by county and state dental societies. Benefits have been expressed in the form of either schedules or some blanket benefit formula, such as 60 per cent of actual charges after an annual deductible of $50 per person (or $150 per family), with a benefit maximum per year of $500 per person. The premium is higher in the first year of coverage due to the costs of cleanup procedures. Annual premiums per family are quite high, running from $50 to $100 a year, depending upon the level of benefits and the level of charges in an average cost area for an average age and income group. Premiums are dependent upon a number of factors in addition to the benefit design, such as the geographical area (range of two to one), percentage of females (range of 1.15 to one), distribution of ages (range of 2.5 to one), and the level of income (range of two to one), the ranges reflecting differing utilization and dental fee patterns.

The effect of the existence of insurance on the utilization and charges, and the trends in dental care costs with time, are as yet unrevealed.

Recognition of Expenses by Size of Case in Premiums

Group health insurance premiums at issue are subject to reductions by size of aggregate premium running up to 17 per cent and more from the smallest to the largest cases. Reductions broadly reflect the decreasing percentage of premium required for expenses as the case grows in size.

Rating of Transfer Cases

Since group insurance is experience-rated, carriers usually take account of experience with the previous carrier in their underwriting of a prospective case which is in the market for transfer of carriers. The technique of setting rates for such a case is identical with that for determining renewal rates. This is a very important underwriting safeguard in health insurance coverages, especially medical expense coverage, because an unwary carrier would otherwise accumulate an undue proportion of high claims cases at inadequate rates.

RENEWAL RATING OF GROUP CASES

As has been noted, experience rating has application in the determination of premium rates on renewal, and in the determination of dividend and retrospective rate credits at the end of each policy year. The premium rate established at the renewal of a group policy is determined to provide adequately, after dividends or retrospective rate credits, for claims charges, expense charges, commissions, taxes, risk charge, and profit charge during the coming policy year. First-year and renewal premiums must be adequate in the aggregate, after dividends or retrospective rate credits, to cover these items for the whole group business of the insurance company.

On a particular case, it is easy, by cost accounting methods, to determine the portion of the premium rate needed for expenses, commissions, taxes, risk charge, and profit charge. The more important problem is to determine the portion needed to cover the claims charge for the coming year.

As indicated in the general discussion of experience rating, the claims charge (Type 1) is determined by a blend of average experience on the class and actual experience on the case, the blend being such that on the smaller cases, where random fluctuations are most likely, greater emphasis is put upon the experience of the class of cases. On the other hand, in the larger cases, more and more emphasis is put upon the actual experience of the cases. On life insurance, accidental death and dismemberment insurance, and long-term disability income insurance, greater emphasis is put upon class experience for a case of a particular size than is true for medical expense insurance and short-term disability income insurance, where chance fluctuations of experience are likely to be smaller.

Because of the trend in medical care costs, the expected claims for the coming year are calculated on the basis of the experience-rated claims plus a trend factor of the size indicated in the earlier discussion of medical expense cost trends. In addition, on the more fully experience-rated cases, companies add a further experience fluctuation factor of the order of 5 to 10 per cent to take care of unusual random fluctuations in the claims on the particular case. This fluctuation factor is necessary because medical care costs in particular areas move in unusual jumps; for instance, hospitals are more likely to increase their charges every other year rather than every year. There can also be sudden changes in pattern of utilization of facilities on particular cases.

In the event that the actual claims charge is lower than the expected claims charge provided for by projecting the experience of the previous year with the use of trend and fluctuation factors, the insurance company reflects the excess premium in a dividend or retrospective rate credit.

The continual increase in medical expense premiums has made the group insurance market quite chaotic. However well informed policyholders may be from newspapers and personal experiences as to the increase in medical care costs, it seems difficult for them to appreciate the need for insurance companies to keep their premiums in line with the increasing costs. This has led to high lapse rates of group insurance policies as employers move from carrier to carrier. These lapses have also increased the cost of conducting the group insurance business because with each lapse the costs of reselling and reinstalling the group case fall upon group policyholders generally.

It is usual for life insurance and short-term disability income premiums to be rerated somewhat below the level of initial premium rates, except where experience is worse than average.

DIVIDENDS AND RETROSPECTIVE RATE CREDITS

Mutual life insurance companies return as dividends the excess of premium and investment income over the sum of incurred claims charges, expense charges (including amortization of acquisition expense charges), commissions, taxes, risk charges, and profit charges. Increases in actuarial reserves also enter the determination in the case of group life insurance with paid-up amounts and group permanent life insurance. Retrospective rate credits paid by stock companies are similar to dividends paid by mutual companies; in this section the term "dividends" will be used to cover both mutual life insurance company dividends and stock company retrospective rate credits.

It is important to emphasize that in determining dividends, the insurance company looks back over the preceding year, whereas in determining renewal premiums, it looks forward to the next year.

Company dividend formulas establish equity among policyholders and, together with the system of renewal rerating, are aimed at the development of surplus on each class of case in accordance with a general fiscal plan. The incurred claims charges used in dividends are based on the same concepts previously referred to in the discussion of renewal premium rates, but in many companies the credibility factor used is somewhat larger in dividends than in renewal rating. Determination of the expense charges is considerably more precise in dividends than in renewal premium rates.

Because of competition on premium rates on all coverages, and because of upward trends in medical care cost in particular, the premium rates on smaller cases (under 50 or 100 lives) are usually without dividend margins. Hence, dividends usually are paid only on larger cases.

In purchasing and continuing group insurance, the employer looks carefully at what is known technically as retention. Retention for the typical one-year term case is the excess of earned premiums over the sum of incurred claims and dividends. Retention, therefore, is very roughly a measure of the insurance company's charge for providing insurance and servicing the group case. It is somewhat misleading because it blankets in the investment income effects which can be positive or negative.

It is unfortunate that much group insurance is purchased by almost exclusive attention to retention. Some insurance companies pay a great deal more attention to the servicing of a group case than other companies; this is especially true in connection with assuring that the employees' health insurance claims are determined and settled on the most efficient basis. Some insurance companies provide a claims analysis and administration service known by various names, such as loss control engineering. This service involves sending skilled people from the home office to the various employer locations to work with providers of medical care and the employer's personnel administrators to assure the proper utilization of medical facilities, proper fees, and proper personnel attitudes. Unfortunately, many group cases have been awarded to companies which show lower retentions of 1 per cent of premiums at the expense of perhaps 5 per cent unnecessarily high claims costs.

Effect of Large Relative Amounts of Life Insurance on Dividends

Amounts of insurance under group life plans are usually related to amounts of salary in scheduled classifications. The ratio of amount of insurance to salary varies from about 50 per cent of annual salary to as much as 300 per cent of annual salary. The maximum amount under these schedules on sizable cases may be as much as $100,000 or more. Where the occurrence of claims for such maximum amounts could bring about a serious deficiency in the group's experience, special methods are used in determining the claims charges in the dividend formula. These methods fall into three general classifications:

1. ***Additional Risk-Averaging Method.*** Heavier emphasis on the average claims cost in the class of insurance may be used in claims charges. For instance, a one-thousand-life case, which normally would have full experience rating (i.e., no emphasis on the average level of claims) might have a 70 per cent weighting of actual claims together with a 30 per cent weighting of average claims in the class of case where the ratio of maximum amount of insurance to average amount of insurance is eight. The effect of additional averaging is to smooth out the charges between years of low claims and years of high claims. Dividend formulas usually also carry forward any deficiency resulting where the claims charge in a particular year, despite the averaging, is higher than the excess of premium over other charges. Such deficiency is then recovered gradually in following years as margins become available.

2. ***Extra Contingency Reserve Method.*** Contingency reserves may be built up out of dividend margins, and the high levels of claims, as they occur, are charged against the contingency reserve. The contingency reserves are then built up again to the desired level. Under this method the degree of experience rating in the claims charge itself is not adjusted.

3. ***Excess-Amounts Pooling Method.*** Nonmedical evidence, combined with any necessary medical evidence, may be obtained on the individuals with amounts of insurance in excess of the amount normally available with full experience rating. On the basis of this evidence of insurability, appropriate standard and substandard claims charge rates are determined for these individuals. These claims charge rates are then applied to the excess amounts. Some companies do not require nonmedical or medical evidence but rely entirely on the requirement of active work at inception of insurance; in this event the claims charge rates would reflect the average level of claims expected. No experience rating is used on these excess amounts except to the extent that the company can adjust the level of claims charges based upon experience in the pool of such excess amounts from all group life cases.

Dividends on Long-Term Disability Income Coverage

Special mention should be made of the dividend procedures in long-term disability income insurance. The size of a claim can be very high on a long-term disability policy providing five years of benefits, or benefits to age 65. The cost of claims on individual losses is subject to far more variations in this type of coverage than in group life insurance. Companies therefore determine their claims charges in this type of coverage with heavy emphasis on level of claims in the general class of cases and light emphasis on actual experience. The claims reserves (i.e., liabilities held for payment of incurred benefits not yet accrued) can run very high. In the long run, on a plan providing benefits to age 65, these claims reserves can run as high as seven to eight times the annual premium.

Claims Reserves

In the determination of the expected claims level for renewal rating and dividend determinations, the claims used as a starting point of the estimate are the so-called "incurred" claims of the year. Incurred claims include the full future financial liability of the insurance company for benefits. For instance, benefits which the company is committed to pay in the future may be for a disability occurring under short-term disability income coverage, for a hospital confinement arising under a hospital coverage, or for a whole series of medical care costs growing out of a particular illness included under major medical coverage. There are also lags in the reporting of claims to the insurance company. Many of these open and unreported claims are paid after the end of the policy year, and actuaries reflect this liability in what is known as a claims reserve.

Employers frequently confuse the incurred claims level with the paid claims level. The incurred claims of a particular policy are the claims paid during the policy year plus the claims reserve liability at the end of the policy year minus the claims reserve liability at the beginning of the policy year. In the first year of a case, there is no claims reserve at the beginning of the policy year, so that the incurred claims in the first policy year are the claims paid in the policy year plus the claims reserve at the end of the policy year.

The claims reserve is a substantial amount. In the case of life insurance, it is approximately 10 to 15 per cent of the yearly premium, reflecting unreported claims and the company's liability on reported but not yet paid claims (such as pending death claims and disability waiver-of-premium claims). In short-term disability income coverage the claims reserve is generally in the neighborhood of 15 per cent of premium; in basic medical expense coverage, including maternity benefits, it is about 25 to 30 per cent of premium; and in major medical coverage, it can run as high as 60 to 70 per cent of premium.

PREFUNDING OF MEDICAL EXPENSE INSURANCE AND LIFE INSURANCE FOR RETIRED EMPLOYEES

Medical Expense Insurance

Very little prefunding of medical care costs for future retired employees has been done, for two reasons. First, the absence of maternity and children costs offsets to a considerable degree the increase in the employee and wife costs. For an employer with a stable payroll and relatively constant average age of active and retired employees, the aggregate retired employee and wife premiums might run about 30 per cent of the aggregate active family premiums. This compares with a corresponding figure of about 200 per cent for a group life plan providing a flat amount of life insurance on active and retired employees.

The second and more important reason is that the rapid inflation of medical expense premium rates (4 to 8 per cent a year) presents such immediate cost problems to the employer that he rarely considers the prefunding of medical care.

Life Insurance

The cost of continuing life insurance on retired employees can become quite sizable relative to the cost of life insurance on active lives, especially where large amounts are continued for retired people. Occasionally, employers provide for prefunding of retired life costs during the active life service of each employee. There are three procedures in general use. The first procedure is very similar to that used on pension plans. Under this system an entry-age normal cost for providing the life insurance after retirement is determined, taking some age such as 45 as the entry age. At the time the prefunding is introduced, a past-service liability is determined and is funded over a period of ten years or more, as in pensions. The funds are used to pay one-year term premiums on the retired lives. For tax reasons, the funds must be dedicated to this use, so that the employer can never recover them. The income tax situation for these funds has never been publicly clarified.

The second procedure is to provide that the policy will not pay dividends. Dividends that would normally be paid are accumulated in a special reserve, which will be drawn upon later to level out premium costs as the number of retired lives increases. This procedure is used in two large group life plans: the Federal Employees Group Life Insurance Plan and the plan covering employees of the American Telephone and Telegraph Company.

The third procedure is the use of group paid-up life insurance or group permanent life insurance, as described in Chapter 30.

THE MINIMUM PREMIUM PLAN

State premium taxes on group life and group health premiums vary from 1.75 per cent to as much as 4 per cent, averaging somewhat over 2 per cent. On large cases, where retentions can be as low as 5 to 6 per cent, the net premium tax charge becomes as much as 35 per cent or more of retention. Under these circumstances, employers give serious consideration to self-insurance.

During 1962 a number of companies in the group insurance business introduced the minimum premium plan which does not change in any manner the risk of the life insurance company and reduces premium taxes to about 15 per cent of their level under a normal group insurance arrangement.

Where a large employer with retention of, say, 10 per cent has been handling claims payments himself on behalf of the insurance company by writing claims payment drafts on the insurance company, the insurance company can make an arrangement whereby it becomes liable for risk only after the claims payments during the policy year have risen to the level of, say, 85 per cent of the premium normally charged. The minimum premium arrangement provides that the employer, instead of writing drafts on the insurance company to pay claims, will write checks on the employer's own bank account. When the checks written during the policy year amount to 85 per cent of the normal premium for the case, the employer starts writing drafts on the insurance company or, alternatively, charges the insurance company for any further checks written on his own account.

In this example, in order to cover the risk, the insurance company need charge only 15 per cent of its normal premium. Out of this 15 per cent, the insurance company covers the drafts written; reimburses itself for its expenses, commissions, taxes, risk charge, and profit; and sets up whatever increase in normal claims reserves is needed. The insurance company remains liable for the manner in which the employer settles claims throughout the policy year and for the guarantee of continued claims payments to the employees as provided under the contract, even after the termination of the contract by the employer.

Whereas the only advantage to this arrangement is the premium tax saving, there appear to be numerous disadvantages. In the first place, only large employers can use this plan because it will operate properly only where there is full experience rating. Also, the employer needs a legal department to consider the joint legal commitments of the employer and the insurance company. He also needs a large insurance department to handle the processing of claims payments. He probably also ought to have an actuary to understand the very complicated contract language and to conduct the annual negotiations with the insurance company. Only for large, efficient employers will the increased cost of this organization be less than the savings in premium taxes.

Then, from a practical standpoint, the plan can be started only after at least one year of normal operation, during which claims reserves are set up by the insurance company.

Next, the employer loses the benefit of the administration and payment of claims by the insurance company. He therefore cannot avail himself effectively of loss control engineering. Although he saves in taxes, he may well lose much more in increased claims payments arising from uninvestigated medical activities in his various locations.

Another disadvantage is that the plan does not operate too well with group life insurance, especially where some employees have sizable amounts of life insurance. Claims on life insurance can vary considerably from year to year, and there does not appear to be any easy way of making settlement options available. Waiver-of-premium claims and conversions also add complications. Finally, the legal and premium tax status of this plan is not too well established.

The long-range solution to this problem does not appear to be the minimum premium plan approach but rather the equalization of premium taxes as between insured and uninsured plans.

SELECTED REFERENCES

Jackson, Paul H. "Experience Rating," *Transactions of the Society of Actuaries,* Vol. V (1953), p. 239.

Keffer, Ralph. "An Experience Rating Formula," *Transactions of the Actuarial Society of America,* Vol. XXX (1929), p. 130.

MacIntyre, Duncan M. *Voluntary Health Insurance and Rate Making.* Ithaca: Cornell University Press, 1962.

Pickrell, J. F. *Group Health Insurance.* Homewood, Ill.: Richard D. Irwin, Inc., 1961.

PART V

Pensions and Profit Sharing

Chapter 37

NATURE AND DEVELOPMENT OF PRIVATE PENSION PLANS

BY JOSEPH J. MELONE

Man is constantly seeking means by which to enhance his economic security. One cause of economic insecurity is the probable reduction of an individual's earning power at an advanced age. In this country, this risk is met through one or more of the following means: personal savings (including individual insurance and annuities), private pensions, and government-sponsored programs. The rather dramatic growth of private pensions in the past two decades has focused considerable interest on this form of income maintenance. The purpose of this chapter is to outline briefly the nature of the economic problem of old age, the rationale of the private pension movement, the reasons for the growth of these plans, and the broad characteristics of current private pension programs.

ECONOMIC PROBLEM OF OLD AGE

Increasing Longevity

The fact that life expectancy has been increasing is well recognized. However, that this increase in longevity is a recent and quite dramatic development is often not appreciated. Within the last 60 years the life expectancy at birth has increased from 47 years to approximately 70 years. This result has been achieved in spite of the limited gains in life expectancy in the last decade. The rates of mortality at the earlier ages are now so low that further improvements in mortality at these ages would have little impact on further extensions of the average length of life. If additional improvements in longevity are to be realized, reductions in mortality at the older ages are required. This impediment to further extensions in life expectancy may be overcome if medical advances result from the current concentration of research in the areas of the chronic and degenerative diseases.

One effect of the improvements in longevity in the twentieth century has been an absolute and relative increase in the population of persons aged 65 and over. In 1900, there were approximately three million persons aged 65 and over, whereas there were about 18 million aged persons in 1963. By 1980, persons aged 65 and over are expected to number about 24.5 million.[1] The proportion of the United States population aged 65 and over is currently about 9 per cent, whereas the proportion of the population in these age brackets in 1900 was about 4 per cent. It is estimated that aged persons will constitute about 10 per cent of the population by 1980. The problem of old-age economic security, therefore, is of concern to an increasing number and percentage of the United States population.

Nature of Risk of Excessive Longevity

It seems rather paradoxical to speak of the *risk* of excessive longevity. Good health and long life are considered by most people to be desirable rather than unfavorable contingencies. The concern in this discussion is, of course, restricted to the economic risk associated with longevity. Longevity is a source of economic insecurity in that an individual may outlive his financial capacity to maintain himself and his dependents.

The assumption is often made that the financial needs of an individual decrease after retirement. To some extent, this assumption is valid. The retired individual generally has no dependent children, and a home and its furnishings generally have been acquired by retirement age. However, the actual aggregate reduction in the financial needs of a person upon retirement has probably been overstated. Social pressures discourage any drastic change in one's standard of living. Furthermore, urbanization and its corollary, apartment living, minimize the prospect of retired parents moving in with their children. It is questionable, therefore, whether one should assume any significant decrease in basic financial needs upon retirement, at least for individuals in the low- and middle-income categories.

The extent to which an aged person will have the financial capacity to meet self-maintenance costs and those of dependents depends upon his employment opportunities and the prior provisions made to meet this contingency.

Employment Opportunities

It has been estimated that only 24 per cent of those 65 and over had some income from employment in June, 1961, and this percentage has been decreasing steadily in recent years.[2] To catalogue all of the many

---

[1] United States Department of Health, Education and Welfare, *Health, Education and Welfare Trends: 1962* (Washington, D.C.: U.S. Government Printing Office, 1962), p. 3.

[2] Lenore A. Epstein, "Sources and Size of Money Income of the Aged," *Social Security Bulletin*, Vol. XXV, No. 1 (January, 1962), p. 15.

factors which account for the reduction in the percentage of the aged in the labor force is an impossible task. A large number of older workers voluntarily retire from the labor force. If one has the necessary financial resources, he may wish to withdraw from active employment and live out his remaining years at a more leisurely pace. Others find it necessary for reasons of health to withdraw from the labor force at an advanced age. The aging process takes its toll, and many individuals are physically unable to operate at the level of efficiency attainable at the younger ages. Disabilities at the older ages tend to be more frequent and of longer duration.

Voluntary retirement and the physical inability to continue employment are undoubtedly important reasons for the decrease in the percentage of older persons participating in the labor force. However, these are probably not the most important factors affecting employment opportunities for the aged. The effects of industrialization and the development of the federal Old-Age, Survivors, and Disability Insurance program (OASDI), private pensions, and other employee benefit programs probably have had a more significant impact on this problem.

The rapid pace and dynamic evolution of industrial employments operate to the disadvantage of older persons. Automation and the mass-production assembly lines put a premium on physical dexterity and mental alertness. Employers generally are of the opinion, justifiable or not, that the younger workers are better suited to the demands of industrial employment. In an agricultural economy the able-bodied older person could continue to work, at least on a part-time basis.

The OASDI program and private pension plans, although created to alleviate the risk of excessive longevity, have aggravated the problem, in that these programs have tended to institutionalize age 65 as the normal retirement age. Also, some employers may hesitate to hire older workers on the assumption that these employees would increase pension and other employee benefit plan costs. It is difficult to generalize as to the impact of the older worker on employee benefit plan costs. Nevertheless, it must be recognized that an employer's attitude toward the hiring of older workers may be influenced by the assumption, justified or not, that fringe benefit costs will be adversely affected.

Capacity to Save

If employment opportunities for the aged are decreasing and financial needs are still substantial at advanced ages, the need for savings becomes quite apparent. Although data on the extent of savings among the aged are relatively sparse, some research studies have been performed in this area.[3] In a survey of the beneficiaries under OASDI conducted in 1957, it

[3] For a discussion of the results of these studies, see Mortimer Spiegelman, *Ensuring Medical Care for the Aged* (Homewood, Ill.: Richard D. Irwin, Inc., 1960), ch. ii.

was found that half of all aged beneficiaries had assets exceeding their liabilities by more than $4,920; half had a net worth of less than that amount. Almost one fourth had zero or minus net worth, and one fourth had a net worth of more than $13,700.[4] It was also found that homeownership constitutes the single most important asset of most aged persons. Assets other than the equity in a home of those aged 65 and over were relatively small. However, the value of homeownership for the economic security of the aged should not be underestimated. The studies indicate that a substantial proportion of the homes owned by the aged were clear of any mortgage. Homeownership reduces the income needs of the aged insofar as normal maintenance costs, and taxes are less than the amount of rent required for comparable housing accommodations. It has been estimated that the maintenance costs for an unencumbered home are about one third to 40 per cent less than the costs of renting comparable facilities.[5] Furthermore, there is the possibility that the home can be used in part as an income-producing asset.

It is difficult to generalize as to the economic status of the aged based on limited studies of the type described above. Mortimer Spiegelman, in his excellent book, *Ensuring Medical Care for the Aged,* points out that "the usual economic data relating to the aged are hardly sufficient for an adequate picture of the resources available to them in time of need."[6] He notes that the role of both the immediate and the extended family (i.e., children away from home, relatives, friends, and neighbors) is ignored in these studies. However, it does appear reasonable to conclude that the accumulated savings alone of many aged persons are not adequate to provide even a subsistence level of income for their remaining years.

There have been many forces at work which have restricted the growth of savings among the aged. Advertising, installment credit, and the media of mass communications encourage individuals to set their sights on a constantly increasing standard of living. This competition from consumption goods for current income dollars results in a lower priority being placed on the need for accumulating savings for old age. Also, the high levels of federal income tax rates reduce an income earner's capacity to save. In recent decades, inflation has presented one of the most important threats to the adequacy of savings programs. For employed persons, increases in the cost of living may be offset, in part or in whole, by increases in current earnings. That possibility does not exist for most aged persons. Therefore, these latter individuals are faced with the alternatives of accepting a lower standard of living or more rapidly liquidating their

[4] "Assets and Net Worth of Old-Age and Survivors Insurance Beneficiaries," *Social Security Bulletin,* Vol. XXII, No. 1 (January, 1959), p. 3.

[5] Mollie Orshansky, "Budget for an Elderly Couple," *Social Security Bulletin,* Vol. XXIII, No. 12 (December, 1960), p. 28.

[6] Spiegelman, *op. cit.,* p. 38.

accumulated savings. Fortunately, the rise in the cost of living has leveled off somewhat in the past five years and may not prove to be so critical a threat to savings in future years. Lastly, one must recognize that changing economic conditions may appreciably affect one's savings program. A severe depression may impair employment and earnings opportunities, and thereby necessitate the use of past savings to meet current living costs. The depression of the 1930's undoubtedly adversely affected the economic position of many of the current aged persons in our country. However, for those just entering upon their retirement years, the financial impact of the depression on their savings position was probably negligible. A substantial proportion of their working years covered the prosperous period beginning in the early 1940's. If this period of prosperity continues, the economic position of future aged persons may be considerably improved in comparison to the current group of individuals aged 65 and over.

RATIONALE OF PRIVATE PENSIONS

Early industrial pension plans were viewed as gratuities or rewards to employees for long and loyal service to the employer.[7] These plans were largely discretionary, and management made it quite clear that employees had no contractual rights to benefits under the plan. Continuation of the pension plan was dependent upon prevailing competitive conditions and management policy. Furthermore, management reserved the right to terminate benefit payments to pensioners for misconduct on the part of the beneficiary or for any other reasons justifying such action in the views of the employer.

Several reasons have been suggested as to why these early plans were established.[8] Some firms that had been established for a long period of years were increasingly faced with the problem of aged employees. These workers were often maintained on the payroll, and jobs suited to their capabilities had to be found. Also, in certain industries, notably railroads and utilities, the carelessness or inefficiencies of aged workers increased the probabilities of accidental injury to other employees and members of the public. Thus, pensions served as a logical method of removing superannuated employees from the payroll in a socially desirable manner. The adoption of a pension plan undoubtedly enhanced the reputation of the company in the community, as well as increasing the morale of the workers and the capacity of the employer to attract the more able em-

[7] For an excellent discussion of pension philosophies, see Jonas E. Mittelman, *The Vesting of Private Pensions* (Philadelphia: University of Pennsylvania, 1959), unpublished dissertation, ch. ii.

[8] Charles L. Dearing, *Industrial Pensions* (Washington, D.C.: Brookings Institution, 1954), pp. 38–39.

ployees. It has also been suggested that some employers established pension plans as a means of reducing strikes and to discourage the growth of unions. To the extent that benefit payments could be discontinued at the discretion of the employer, a pension plan could have been used as a weapon against union activity. This possibility, plus the paternalistic nature of early pension programs, largely accounts for the resistance of union leaders at the time to industrial pensions.

All of the above reasons explaining the growth of early pensions might be best categorized by a single concept, i.e., *business expediency*. Business expediency, by the very nature of the concept, implies that the establishment of a plan is a management prerogative and that the primary motivation for the creation of such plans was the economic benefit, direct or indirect, that accrued to the employer. But as the economy became more and more industrialized and pension plans became more prevalent, there was increasing interest in the view that employers had a moral obligation to provide for the economic security of retired workers. This point of view was expressed as early as 1912 by Lee Welling Squier, as follows: "From the standpoint of the whole system of social economy, no employer has a right to engage men in any occupation that exhausts the individual's industrial life in 10, 20 or 40 years; and then leave the remnant floating on society at large as a derelict at sea."[9] This rationale of private pensions has come to be known as the *human depreciation concept* and was the point of view taken by the United Mine Workers of America in their 1946 drive to establish a welfare fund:

> The United Mine Workers of America has assumed the position over the years that the cost of caring for the human equity in the coal industry is inherently as valid as the cost of the replacement of mining machinery, or the cost of paying taxes, or the cost of paying interest indebtedness, or any other factor incident to the production of a ton of coal for consumers' bins. . . . [The agreement establishing the Welfare Fund] recognized in principle the fact that the industry owed an obligation to those employees, and the coal miners could no longer be used up, crippled beyond repair and turned out to live or die subject to the charity of the community or the minimum contributions of the state.[10]

This analogy between human labor and industrial machines was also made in the report of the President's "fact-finding" board in the 1949 steelworkers' labor dispute in support of its conclusion that management had a responsibility to provide for the security of its workers: "We think that all industry, in the absence of adequate Government programs, owes an obligation to workers to provide for maintenance of the human body in

[9] Lee Welling Squier, *Old Age Dependency in the United States* (New York: Macmillan Co., 1912), p. 272.

[10] United Mine Workers of America Welfare and Retirement Fund, *Pensions for Coal Miners* (Washington, D.C., n.d.), p. 4.

the form of medical and similar benefits and full depreciation in the form of old-age retirement—in the same way as it does now for plant and machinery."[11] The report continues as follows: "What does that mean in terms of steelworkers? It should mean the use of earnings to insure against the full depreciation of the human body—say at age 65—in the form of a pension or retirement allowance."[12]

The validity of the human depreciation concept of private pensions has been challenged by many pension experts.[13] The process of aging is physiological and is not attributable to the employment relationship. Admittedly, the hazards of certain occupations undoubtedly shorten the life span of the employees involved. In those instances the employer can logically be held responsible only for the increase in the rate of aging due to the hazards of the occupation. More importantly, the analogy between men and machines is inherently unsound. A machine is an asset owned by the employer, and depreciation is merely an accounting technique for allocating the costs of equipment to various accounting periods. Employees, on the other hand, are free agents and sell their services to employers for a specified wage rate. An employee, unlike a machine, is free to move from one employer to another. The differences between men and machines are so great that one must question the value of the analogy as a basis for a rationale of private pensions. As Dearing notes: "Any economic or moral responsibility that is imposed on the employer for the welfare of workers after termination of the labor contract should be grounded on firmer reasoning than is supplied by the machine-worker analogy."[14]

In recent years a view of private pensions that has achieved broader acceptance is the *deferred wage concept*. This concept views a pension benefit as part of a wage package which is composed of cash wages and other employee fringe benefits. The deferred wage concept has particular appeal with reference to negotiated pension plans. The assumption is made that labor and management negotiators think in terms of total labor costs. Therefore, if labor negotiates a pension benefit, the amount of funds available for increases in cash wages are reduced accordingly. This theory of private pensions was expressed as early as 1913:

> In order to get a full understanding of old-age and service pensions, they should be considered as a part of the real wages of a workman. There is a tendency to speak of these pensions as being paid by the company, or, in cases

---

[11] Steel Industry Board, *Report to the President of the United States on the Labor Dispute in the Basic Steel Industry* (Washington, D.C.: U.S. Government Printing Office, September 10, 1949), p. 55.

[12] *Ibid.*, p. 65.

[13] For example, see Dan M. McGill, *Fundamentals of Private Pensions* (2d ed.; Homewood, Ill.: Richard D. Irwin, Inc., 1964), p. 16. See also Dearing, *op. cit.*, pp. 62–63 and 241–43; and Mittelman, *op. cit.*, pp. 28–34.

[14] Dearing, *op. cit.*, p. 243.

where the employee contributes a portion, as being paid partly by the employer and partly by the employee. In a certain sense, of course, this may be correct, but it leads to confusion. A pension system considered as part of the real wages of an employee is really paid by the employee, not perhaps in money, but in the foregoing of an increase in wages which he might obtain except for the establishment of a pension system.[15]

The deferred wage concept has also been challenged on several grounds. First, it is noted that some employers who pay the prevailing cash wage rate for the particular industry also provide a pension benefit. Thus, it can be argued that in these cases the pension benefit is offered in addition to, rather than in lieu of, a cash wage increase. Second, the deferred wage concept ignores the possible argument that the employer is willing to accept a lower profit margin in order to provide a pension plan for employees. Third, it is sometimes argued that if pension benefits are a form of wage, then terminating employees should be entitled to the part of the retirement benefit that has been earned to the date of termination. In practice, one finds that only a small proportion of the plans provide for the full and immediate vesting of all benefits. However, it can be argued that the deferred wage concept does not necessarily require the full and immediate vesting of benefits. Proponents of this concept view the pension benefit as a wage, the receipt of which is conditioned upon the employee remaining in the service of the employer for a specified number of years. This view of the pension benefit is similar, conceptually, to the pure endowment, the consideration of the employee being the reduction in cash wages accepted in lieu of the pension benefit.

In spite of the appeal of the deferred wage theory, it is questionable whether the private pension movement can be explained solely in terms of this concept. Indeed, there is probably no one rationale or theory that fully explains the "reason for being" of private pensions. This conclusion is not surprising in view of the fact that these plans are *private*, and the demands or reasons that gave rise to one plan may be quite different in the case of another plan.

DEVELOPMENT OF INDUSTRIAL PENSION PLANS

The beginnings of industrial pension plans in the United States date back to the establishment of the American Express Company plan in 1875.[16] The second formal plan was established in 1880 by the Baltimore & Ohio Railroad Company. During the next half century, approximately four hundred plans were established. These early pension plans were

[15] Albert deRoode, "Pensions as Wages," *American Economic Review*, Vol. III, No. 2 (June, 1913), p. 287.

[16] Murray Webb Latimer, *Industrial Pension Systems* (New York: Industrial Relations Counselors, Inc., 1932), p. 21.

generally found in the railroad, banking, and public utility fields. The development of pensions in the manufacturing industries was somewhat slower, due largely to the fact that most manufacturing companies were still relatively young and therefore not confronted with the superannuation problems of the railroads and public utilities.

Insurance companies entered the pension business with the issuance of the first group annuity contract by the Metropolitan Life Insurance Company on December 25, 1921.[17] The second contract was issued by the Metropolitan in 1924 to an employer who already had a retirement plan on a "pay as you go" basis.[18] In 1924 the Equitable Life Assurance Society announced its intention of offering a group pension service, thus becoming the second company to enter the field.[19]

The rate of growth of private pensions was retarded by the depression of the thirties. However, the data indicate that insured pension plans continued to grow during the decade of the thirties both as to number of plans and as to persons covered.[20]

The bulk of the growth in private pension plans has occurred since 1940. Two developments during the Second World War had a significant impact on the expansion of pension programs. First, the high rates (approximately 82 per cent) of normal and excess profits taxes imposed on corporations encouraged some firms to establish plans. Since the employer's contributions to a *qualified* pension plan are deductible for federal income tax purposes, a portion of the plan's liabilities could be funded with 18-cent dollars. Furthermore, the employer's contributions to a pension fund do not constitute taxable income to the employee in the year in which contributions are made. The pension benefits derived from employer contributions are taxed when received by the employee. However, the employee is expected to be in a lower tax bracket when retirement benefits are received.

The second wartime development which helped to stimulate the growth of pensions was the creation of a wage stabilization program as part of a general price control scheme. Employers, in competing for labor, therefore, could not offer the inducement of higher wages. Under these conditions, union leaders found it difficult to prove to their membership the merits of unionism. Therefore, the War Labor Board, in 1944–45, attempted to relieve the pressure from management and labor for higher wage rates by permitting the establishment of fringe benefit programs, including pensions. This policy further stimulated the growth of pension plans during this period.

---

[17] Kenneth Black, Jr., *Group Annuities* (Philadelphia: University of Pennsylvania Press, 1955), p. 9.

[18] *Ibid.*, p. 11.

[19] *Ibid.*

[20] Mittelman, *op. cit.*, p. 10.

From 1945 to 1949 the rate of growth of new plans fell off markedly. During this postwar period, employee interest centered upon cash wage increases in an attempt to recover the lost ground suffered during the period of wage stabilization. In the latter part of the decade of the forties, union leaders began once again expressing an interest in the negotiation of pension programs. The renewal of interest in pensions was probably due to two factors. First, there was increasing antagonism on the part of the public against what were viewed by many persons as excessive union demands for cash wage increases. The negotiation of fringe benefits was one way of possibly reducing pressures from this quarter. Second, some union leaders argued that social security benefits were inadequate, and a supplement in the form of private pension benefits was considered to be necessary. Also, certain labor officials believed that the negotiation of employer-supported pensions would weaken the resistance of the latter toward liberalizations of social security benefit levels. Thus, pension demands became a central issue in the labor negotiations in the coal, automobile, and steel industries in the late forties. Although unions had negotiated pension benefits prior to this period, it was not until the late forties that a major segment of labor made a concerted effort to bargain for private pensions.

Labor's drive for pension benefits was facilitated by a National Labor Relations Board ruling in 1948 that employers had a legal obligation to bargain over the terms of pension plans. Until that time, there was some question as to whether employee benefit programs fell within the traditional subject areas for collective bargaining, i.e., wages, hours, and other conditions of employment. The issue was resolved when the National Labor Relations Board held that pension benefits constitute wages, and the provisions of these plans affected conditions of employment.[21] Upon appeal, the court upheld the NLRB decision, although it questioned the assumption that such benefits are wages.[22] The result of these decisions was that an employer cannot install or terminate or alter the terms of a pension plan covering organized workers without the approval of the authorized bargaining agent for those employees. Furthermore, management has this obligation regardless of whether the plan is contributory or noncontributory, voluntary or compulsory, and regardless of whether the plan was established before or after the certification of the bargaining unit.

Labor was quick to respond to these decisions, and the 1950's were marked by union demands for the establishment of new pension plans,

[21] See McGill, *op. cit.*, pp. 29–30, for a more detailed discussion of this case (*Inland Steel Company* v. *United Steelworkers of America*, 77 NLRB 4 [1948]).

[22] *Inland Steel Company* v. *National Labor Relations Board*, 170 F.(2d) 247, 251 (1949).

liberalization of existing plans, and the supplanting of employer-sponsored programs with negotiated plans. Undoubtedly, labor's interest in private pensions has been an important factor in the tremendous growth in plans since 1949. The net number of pension and profit sharing plans in effect has increased from about 12,000 in 1949 to about 82,000 plans in 1962.

CURRENT SCOPE OF PRIVATE PENSIONS

Coverage of Plans

It was estimated that there were approximately 26 million employees, active and retired, covered under private pension plans as of the end of 1962. Therefore, approximately one third of the labor force is covered under private pension plans. Since plans have been established by most large employers, the future extension of private pension coverage depends largely on the extent to which programs are started by smaller employers. The fact that smaller employers generally do not have pension plans is understandable. The costs of a pension program are fairly substantial; and many small firms are unable, or at least hesitant, to assume a financial obligation of such magnitude. Also, there is probably less pressure on small employers to establish pension plans. The employees of these firms are often not represented by a union, and this source of pressure to establish plans is nonexistent. Even if the employees are organized, the high rates of turnover among employees or the economic condition of the employers or the industry may reduce the prospects for negotiating a retirement benefit. Furthermore, small employers do not seem to have the personnel problem of larger firms, that is, the need to match the employee benefit programs being offered by competing firms.

However, small employers must compete with the large firms for qualified employees; and as pensions become more common, it may be increasingly necessary for small firms to provide pension benefits. Also, the problem of establishing pension plans in industries characterized by small employers and high rates of employee turnover has been partially met by the recent growth of multiemployer pension plans. A multiemployer pension plan is a plan that covers the employees of two or more financially unrelated employers. Pension contributions are payable into one common fund, and benefits are payable to all employees from the pooled assets of the fund. Employees are free to transfer from one participating employer to another without loss of earned pension credits. These plans generally require uniform contribution rates and uniform benefit provisions. Although there are a few nonnegotiated multiemployer plans in operation, these plans have been established almost exclusively as a result of collective bargaining. These plans cover more than three million employees and account for one third of the employees covered under collectively bargained plans of all types and about one sixth of the total coverage of private plans.[23]

Another factor which probably to some extent discouraged the establishment of pension plans by small employers has been the unfavorable federal income tax treatment, prior to 1962, accorded plans established by sole proprietorships and partnerships. A sole proprietorship or a partnership can deduct for federal income tax purposes the contributions to a qualified pension plan made on behalf of employees. But no tax deduction was permitted for contributions under those plans made on behalf of the sole proprietors or partners. The Keogh Act, passed by Congress in 1962, amended the Internal Revenue Code to permit tax deductions for contributions made to pension plans on behalf of sole proprietors and partners. In order to be entitled to these deductions, the plan must meet the requirements set forth in the 1962 amendment. There are limitations on the amount of deductions for contributions made on behalf of the self-employed owners, and the Act requires that all employees who have a specified number of years' service with the firm must be included in the plan.[24]

It is difficult to determine to what extent these developments will encourage the growth of pension plans among smaller employers.

Benefit Levels

The amount of the retirement income benefit has an important bearing on the value of pension programs in meeting the risk of excessive longevity. There are, as one would expect, considerable variations in the level of retirement benefits provided by different plans. Pension benefit formulas are often related to an employee's compensation and/or years of service, although flat benefit amounts are also quite prevalent. For example, a plan may provide that an employee is entitled to a retirement benefit of 1 per cent of annual compensation for each year of service. If an employee was covered under this plan for thirty years and had an average annual salary of $10,000, his retirement benefit would be $3,000 a year. The early negotiated plans provided a flat benefit (e.g., $100 per month) less any social security benefits received by the retired worker. Therefore, any increase in social security benefits reduced the employer's cost of providing private pensions. The union leaders hoped that plans of this type would reduce employers' resistance to the liberalization of social security benefits. In recent years, labor has favored benefit formulas related to compensation or a monthly retirement benefit (e.g., $4.00) per

---

[23] See Chapter 43 for further analysis of multiemployer pension plans.

[24] See Chapter 45 for further analysis of pension and profit sharing plans for self-employed individuals.

year of service, without any offset of an employee's social security benefits.

What constitutes an ideal or adequate benefit level for private pensions is a subjective concept. It has been suggested that a reasonable objective would be to provide the employee, through private pensions and social security, a retirement income equal to about 50 per cent of his average annual earnings during his last five to ten years of employment. Although there are some plans which meet this objective, a sizable number of plans provide benefits at levels far short of this goal.

Pension plans often provide benefits in addition to a normal retirement benefit. For example, a plan may permit retirement at an age earlier than the normal retirement age. The early retirement benefit amount is almost always less than the normal pension. The benefit formula often defines the benefit as the actuarial equivalent of the normal pension benefit. Also, it may be necessary to terminate an employee's services before normal retirement age because he is permanently and totally disabled. A disabled employee may be eligible for early retirement if this benefit is available under the plan. Some plans provide a disability benefit separate and distinct from any provision for early retirement.

A pension plan may also provide either a preretirement or a post-retirement death benefit, or both. Pension plans generally do not provide a death benefit, with the exception of those plans funded by individual life insurance policies or group permanent insurance contracts.

Lastly, a withdrawal or vested benefit may be provided to employees under a pension plan. The nature of vested benefits is discussed more fully in the following section.

Security of Benefits

The possibility that employees currently covered under private pension plans may never receive any benefits under those plans is one of the most important issues involved in private pension planning. If the employee does not receive the benefits promised under the plan, then the pension program has added little to the old-age economic security of the employee. Indeed, under such circumstances, the pension plan has had a negative effect on the employee's economic security. If an employee assumed that this source of income would be available at retirement, he would have less incentive to make other provisions for his old age during his working years.

For what reasons might an employee not receive the retirement benefit promised under the plan? First, pension plans usually require that the employee be a certain age, usually 65, and perform a fairly long period of continuous service for the employer in order to be entitled to a pension. In many plans, if the employee leaves the firm before the eligibility requirements are met, all rights to pension benefits are forfeited. Therefore, many employees currently covered under pension plans may never receive retirement benefits under those plans.

Some plans do provide vested benefits. A vested benefit is that portion of a participant's benefit the entitlement to which is not contingent upon continuation of employment.[25] Since an employee is always entitled to the return of his own contributions upon termination of employment, the term "vesting" refers to benefits derived solely from employer contributions.

The absence of vesting provisions in many plans is of increasing concern to many management, labor, and governmental officials, and others interested in the private pension movement. Some interested parties have suggested that the favorable tax treatment currently accorded to pension programs should be available only to those plans that provide a vested benefit.

It can be argued that vesting should not be provided if a pension plan is viewed as a reward for long and loyal service to a particular employer. On the other hand, if one views pension benefits as a form of deferred compensation, the argument for a vesting provision becomes more sound. If vested benefits are provided, the cost of the pension plan will increase. Furthermore, rates of turnover vary greatly from industry to industry and among firms within an industry, and therefore the impact of a vesting provision on pension costs will vary significantly to match this diversity. There are implications other than cost adding to the complexity of the issue of vested benefits. The pension student should give some thought to the broad social and economic ramifications of vested pension benefits from the standpoint of management, labor, and society.

Another reason why employees may never realize the benefits promised under these plans is the fact that some pension plans are not adequately financed. If the plans are not properly financed, benefit payments may be reduced or terminated entirely at some future date, thereby impairing the old-age economic security programs of many participants. This problem is particularly significant in pension plans, since eligibility for benefit payments is earned over a considerable period of time. An employee may find that after many years of service for an employer, retirement benefits have been decreased or eliminated. It is difficult for that employee, at that point, to make adequate financial provision for his old age. The employer should be aware of the responsibility assumed in establishing a pension program, and provision should be made to finance the plan adequately. Fortunately, relatively few plans have run into financial difficulties in recent years. However, it remains to be seen how well these plans might fare under severe, adverse economic conditions.

---

[25] This definition has been tentatively approved by the Committee on Pension and Profit Sharing Terminology, which is sponsored jointly by the Commission on Insurance Terminology of the American Risk and Insurance Association and the Pension Research Council, University of Pennsylvania.

Funding Plan Benefits

The first financial decision to be made in pension planning is to determine whether benefits are to be funded or whether the plan is to be financed on a "pay as you go" basis. The tax advantages of funded plans that meet the requirements established by the Internal Revenue Service for *qualification* of pension plans have all but made the "pay as you go" plan obsolete. Having chosen one of these alternatives, the broad *financing policy* of the plan has been established. Assuming that agreement is reached on a financing policy of funding benefits, then several decisions under the general heading of *funding policy* must be made.

The first decision that must be made is the choice of a funding agency. A *funding agency*[26] is an organization or individual that provides facilities for the accumulation or administration of assets to be used for the payment of benefits under a pension plan. Funding agencies include life insurance companies, corporate fiduciaries, and individuals acting as trustees. These funding agencies have several different contracts or instruments through which pension benefits are funded. Insured pension plans, for example, may be funded through individual policies, deferred group annuities, deposit administration group annuities, and so forth. These various contracts are referred to as funding instruments. A *funding instrument* is an agreement or contract governing the conditions under which assets are accumulated or administered by a funding agency for the payment of benefits under a pension plan. Funding instruments include contracts with life insurance companies, and trust agreements with corporate fiduciaries or individuals acting as trustees.

An *insured plan,* then, is a pension plan for which the funding agency is a life insurance company; all contributions are paid directly or indirectly to the insurer, which pays all benefits to individual participants. A *trust fund plan* is a plan for which the funding agency is a corporate fiduciary or individual(s) acting as trustee(s); the responsibilities of the funding agency for investment of funds, and for any other functions, are generally provided for in a trust agreement. A *combination plan* is an arrangement under which two funding agencies are used, with a portion of the contributions placed in a trust fund and the balance paid to an insurance company as contributions under a group annuity contract or as premiums on individual annuity contracts and life insurance policies. The entire pension for each participant is generally paid by the insurance company, with transfers from the trust fund being made as required.

Of the nearly 26 million persons currently covered under private pension plans, about 20 million are covered under trust fund plans. These

[26] The definitions of funding terms used in this section reflect the thinking of members of the Committee on Pension and Profit Sharing Terminology. However, the definitions set forth herein have not yet been approved by the Committee and therefore should not be viewed as official adoptions by that body.

plans hold an estimated $39 billion of the total of $60 billion held in all private pension funds.

The trustee under a trust fund plan is usually a corporate trustee, although individuals often act as trustees of funds, particularly among multiemployer plans. The duties and functions of the trustees vary considerably among plans, i.e., from mere custodian of securities to full investment authority. In any case the responsibility of the trustee never extends beyond the prudent investment of trust assets. In other words, the trustee is never responsible for the adequacy or inadequacy of trust assets to meet the liabilities under the plan. The adequacy of the fund is the sole responsibility of the employer. Admittedly, the employer will usually seek advice from a consulting actuary in determining the amount of funds that should be set aside to meet the obligations arising under the plan. But the trustee is in no way responsible if these estimates prove to be erroneous or if the employer fails to make the necessary contributions.

Considerable variations in insurance company plans also exist because of the variety of pension products offered by insurers. Insurance companies offer a full spectrum of funding instruments varying from individual policies to an immediate participation contract and an associated separate account with equity investments. Thus, it can be seen that the pension client has a broad choice of insurance company pension products. The nature and the advantages and disadvantages of each funding instrument will be discussed at length in the following chapters. It will be seen that the spectrum of group annuity contracts offers varying degrees of flexibility to the employer. It should be recognized, however, that the increased flexibility to the employer is made possible only by the relinquishment of certain guarantees by the insurance company. In other words, the greater the flexibility of the plan, the greater the responsibility that rests with the employer as to the adequacy of the fund to provide the benefits promised under the plan.

PENSION PLAN DISCLOSURE LAWS

Federal Welfare and Pension Plans Disclosure Act

The Federal Welfare and Pension Plans Disclosure Act applies to private pension plans covering more than 25 persons. The law requires the administrator of the plan to file a description of the plan with the United States Department of Labor. The required information includes a description of the plan and the type of administration; the schedule of benefits; the names and addresses of any trustees; copies of the plan, bargaining agreement, trust agreement, or other instrument; financing arrangements; and procedures for processing claims for benefits.

Plans covering 100 or more participants are also required to file an annual financial report. This report requires information such as the amount of employer and employee contributions; the amount of benefits paid; a statement of the amount of specified types of assets; a statement of liabilities, receipts, and disbursements; and a detailed statement of the salaries, fees, and commissions charged to the plan, to whom paid, in what amount, and for what purposes. Specific data are required depending upon whether the plan is unfunded, insured, or trusteed, including, in the latter case, the type and basis of funding, actuarial assumptions used, and the amount of current and past service liabilities.

The plan administrator is required to make available to plan participants and beneficiaries copies of the plan description and the latest annual report in the principal office of the plan. This information must also be made available upon the written request of a plan participant or beneficiary by mailing such documents to the last known address of the person making such request. Also, two copies of the plan description and the annual report must be filed with the United States Department of Labor.

The Act requires that anyone handling funds or other property of an employee benefit plan must be bonded. The bonding requirement does not apply if benefits are payable solely from the general assets of a union or an employer. Penalties are imposed for any willful violation of any provision of the law or conviction for theft or embezzlement from an employee benefit plan.

State Disclosure Acts

Five states presently have welfare and pension plan disclosure laws. These states, and the years in which these laws were enacted, are Washington (1955), New York (1956), Connecticut (1957), Massachusetts (1957), and Wisconsin (1957).

The scope of coverage and the information required under the state statutes is generally less extensive than under the federal disclosure act. Regulation under the state statutes is more comprehensive than under the federal act to the extent that the state authorities in three states[27] must examine each plan at least once during a specified period—for example, three or five years. Under the federal law an investigation is permitted only upon complaint or if the Secretary of Labor suspects a violation of the Act.

SELECTED REFERENCES

Bronson, Dorrance C. "Pensions—1949," *Transactions of the Society of Actuaries*, Vol. I, No. 1 (1949), pp. 219–55. See also discussion on pages 256–94.

Harbrecht, Paul P. *Pension Funds and Economic Power*. New York: Twentieth Century Fund, 1959.

[27] New York, Washington, and Wisconsin.

McGill, Dan M. *Fulfilling Pension Expectations.* Homewood, Ill.: Richard D. Irwin, Inc., 1962.

McGill, Dan M. *Fundamentals of Private Pensions.* 2d ed. Homewood, Ill.: Richard D. Irwin, Inc., 1964.

Melone, Joseph J. *Collectively Bargained Multi-Employer Pension Plans.* Homewood, Ill.: Richard D. Irwin, Inc., 1963.

Patterson, Edwin W. *Legal Protection of Private Pension Expectations.* Homewood, Ill.: Richard D. Irwin, Inc., 1960.

Chapter 38

INDIVIDUAL POLICY PENSION PLANS

BY ADON N. SMITH, II

Pension plans financed through the use of individual policies account for about two thirds of all insured plans approved by the Internal Revenue Service. The principal reason for the popularity of the individual policy method is because it is a sound method of funding benefits for the small employer. This method is generally chosen by the smaller business firms, although many large concerns use individual policies to insure their executive, salaried, sales, and office personnel to provide them with the extra benefits inherent in such plans.

This chapter is concerned with an explanation of (1) the principal characteristics of the individual policies normally used to insure pension plans, particularly retirement annuity, retirement income, and whole life plus an auxiliary fund; (2) the specifications of plans and the additional benefits normally included, such as benefits upon death, both before and after retirement, disability, termination of service, and optional methods of settlement; (3) the adaptability of such contracts to finance a pension plan for the small business employer, with particular emphasis on the advantages to stockholder-employees; and (4) the simplicity of administration, the economy of operation, and the complete assumption of the major actuarial and investment risks by the insurance company.

Market

The market for individual policy pension plans has barely been tapped. Most of the larger corporations have already adopted and are financing programs through the use of deposit administration, deferred annuity and group permanent contracts, and self-administered trusts. There are thousands of small individual businesses, especially those with stockholder-employees, who have not yet had an opportunity to understand the extraordinary benefits and tax advantages that will accrue to them, their employees, and their families through the adoption of a well-designed and properly insured individual policy pension plan.

Although the number of individual policy plans being inaugurated from year to year is increasing, the average number of participants included in such plans is decreasing. For example, the 20,460 individual policy plans in effect at the end of 1960 covered an average of 30 participants each, whereas the plans adopted in the last two years covered an average of only 10. It is not unusual to find companies with less than five employees who have recently inaugurated a plan, and there are many plans covering only one or two employees.

Nature of Individual Policies

Individual retirement income, retirement annuity, and whole life policies used to fund pension trusts are generally the same types of policies an individual would purchase for himself. Some insurance companies issue a pension trust series of contracts with higher cash values in the early years and with special options for conversion to annuity incomes at retirement ages. Basically, all the policy rights and privileges available to an individual purchaser are contained in pension trust policies and are available for use by the owner—the trustee of the pension trust—for the benefit of the participants or their beneficiaries.

Premiums are based on assumptions made in the general areas of expected mortality of the insured persons, interest to be earned on invested policy reserves, and the cost of issuing and administering the policy contract. Both nonparticipating and participating policies can be used. Any dividends returned from the participating insurance are paid to the trustee and must, under most pension formulas, be used to reduce the employer's current contributions to the plan.

Individual policies have cash surrender and loan values. Subject to plan provisions and Treasury Department regulations, these values may be used to continue in force policies owned by the plan when an employer encounters temporary financial difficulties and cannot make the required annual contributions to the trust. Under these conditions, assuming the trust permits, the trustees may borrow the cash values on a pro rata basis to pay the current premiums due, or may use such cash values as collateral for a loan, the purpose of which is to pay the premiums due. Such loans must be subsequently repaid by the employer.

If an employer finds it necessary to terminate a pension plan, the trustee may transfer the individual policies to the respective employees. The employees may maintain policies on a premium-paying basis for their personal benefit and even change the type of coverage to a lower cost plan, subject to the insurer's rules. Or if the employee so desires, he may take paid-up insurance or surrender the policy for its cash value, to be paid in one sum or under one of the settlement options set forth in the policy contract.

Comparison of Contracts

To explain the difference between the three types of policies generally used to fund pension plans, assume a plan to provide a male employee, who is now aged 45, with a pension of $100 a month at age 65, payable for life with a minimum of at least 10 years' payments guaranteed. Because annuity rates vary from company to company due to different actuarial assumptions (mortality and assumed interest earnings), it will be assumed that $16,000 cash will be required at age 65 to guarantee this pension benefit.

Retirement Annuity Contracts. The retirement annuity contract provides for an annual level payment from the age of entry (45) to normal retirement date (age 65) in order to accumulate the fund required ($16,-000), which, in turn, is sufficient to guarantee the lifetime monthly income ($100 with 10 years certain). Figure 38–1 indicates the annual deposits

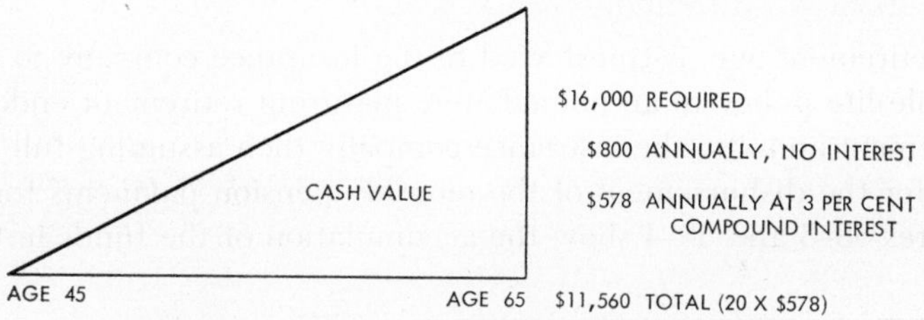

FIG. 38–1. Illustration of retirement annuity contract.

necessary without interest and assuming 3 per cent compound interest.

The insurance company will add an expense loading to cover the cost of all the services to be performed over the life of the employee, such as premium collection and disbursement of the funds either to a beneficiary or to the insured, perhaps covering a period of as much as 35 to 40 years, or longer.

Retirement Income Contracts. The retirement income contract is identical to the retirement annuity as far as the accumulation of the fund required at age 65 is concerned. Added to it is an insurance feature which provides an immediate death benefit, usually equal to $1,000 for each $10 of normal monthly retirement pension. Thus, in this illustration, the participant would have $10,000 of immediate coverage in the event of death until the accumulated cash value exceeds this sum; then the greater amount would be paid in the event of death prior to retirement. (See Figure 38–2.)

Whole Life and Auxiliary Fund. The whole life and auxiliary fund funding method requires deposits to two accounts during the accumulation period. First, an individual whole life contract is maintained by the payment of annual premiums which provide not only the death benefits prior to retirement, but also provide a portion (assume $4,000) of the cash required at the retirement age. Second, an auxiliary investment account is maintained to accumulate the balance of the $16,000 required. Thus, we must accumulate in the auxiliary fund a total of $12,000 which,

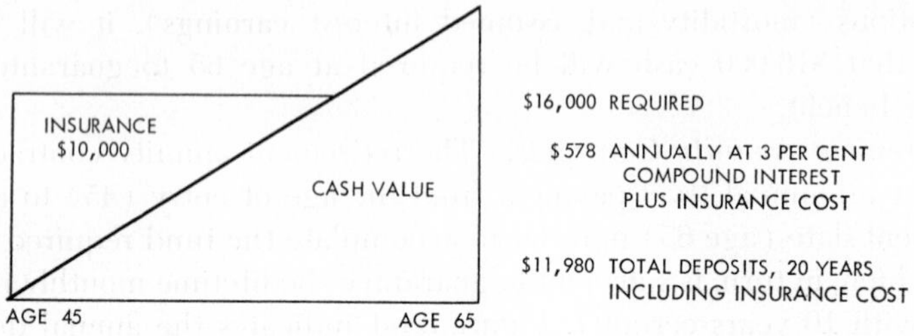

FIG. 38–2. Illustration of retirement income contract.

at the retirement age, is transferred to the insurance company to convert the whole life policy to an immediately maturing retirement endowment or retirement annuity, the insurance company then assuming full responsibility for the disbursement of the monthly pension payments for life.

Figures 38–3 and 38–4 show the accumulation of the funds in the two

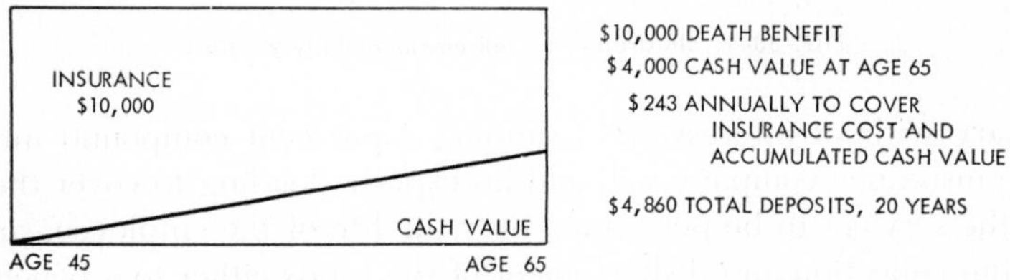

FIG. 38–3. Illustration of whole life contract.

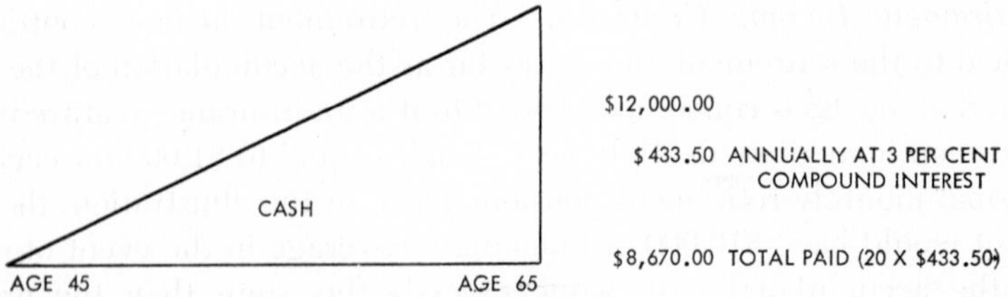

FIG. 38–4. Illustration of auxiliary fund accumulation.

accounts and the provision for the death benefit through the use of the whole life policy.

The $12,000 needed in the auxiliary fund may be invested directly by the plan trustees, by the trust department of a bank, or, in some instances, by the insurer under an auxiliary fund account or under a group deposit administration contract.

The investment and administrative expenses relative to the auxiliary fund are borne by the employer. If the insurance company agrees to hold the auxiliary fund, it will do so generally without charge, and will guarantee the principal and a minimum interest rate. Additional excess interest earnings will be credited to the fund when available.

The total estimated cost of the combination whole life and auxiliary fund is $676.50 annually, or a total in 20 years of $13,530.

The preceding illustrations indicate that the retirement annuity plan is the least costly, and this is due primarily to the fact that the death benefits under it are limited to the return of premiums paid or the cash value, whichever is larger. The retirement income policy costs slightly more than the retirement annuity because of the larger death benefit provided in the early years of the contract.

The whole life and auxiliary fund plan seems to cost more than either of the other two contracts. There are, however, two factors which will reduce the cost of the combination plan. First, prudent investment of the funds in the auxiliary fund might show an average net return of 5 or 6 per cent, including growth of equity investments. If 6 per cent compound interest were earned over a 20-year period, the annual deposit to the auxiliary fund would be reduced to $307.75. This would make the net annual deposit for both the whole life and the auxiliary fund $550.75 a year, or a total of $11,015 for the 20 years.

Second, it is very unlikely that all participants will live or remain with the company until retirement age. The trust may be written to make vesting in the auxiliary fund contingent upon survival to the normal retirement date. Amounts released through early termination of service are called forfeitures. These forfeitures must be used by the trustee to reduce the employer's future deposits. It is possible to discount in advance for assumed future mortality and employee turnover, thus reducing the employer's current outlay. Tables are available which incorporate these factors (including varying interest assumptions). Mortality discounts are generally used in connection with auxiliary fund deposits, but turnover discounts are rarely employed in the smaller plans because of the unlikelihood of achieving the results predicted.

Specifications

The design of any pension plan must first meet the requirements of the Internal Revenue Code and regulations. Within these limitations, it can be tailor-made to fit the purposes of the employer, the needs of the employees, and the budgets of both if employees contribute. Since individual policies not only insure death benefits but also, through the cash values, provide disability and retirement funds, it is possible for the small employer to have a fairly comprehensive over-all fringe benefit program through his pension trust. The specifications of the plan may be designed to provide substantial benefits before and after retirement for the principal stockholder-employees and a variety of settlement options at death or retirement age not usually included in other funding instruments.

Eligibility Requirements. Most individual policy pension plans base their eligibility requirements on *service, age,* or *salary,* or a combination of all three. Unless the corporation has been recently organized, there is usually a waiting period of three to five years before an employee becomes a participant. Some plans include a requirement such as the attainment of age 25 or perhaps 30, if female. Many plans provide benefits only for employees earning in excess of the social security base ($4,800).

The cash value of an individual policy in the first few years after it has been issued is less than the total premiums paid. Therefore, it is essential for the employer not to include in the plan employee-participants who are likely to terminate their services after only one or two years of coverage. If they do so, there is a loss to the trust, the employer, and the insurance company. Since the waiting period before eligibility usually does not affect the employee's ultimate pension benefit, but only delays his death and disability benefits, it is better for the employer to require a reasonable waiting period before enrolling employees in the plan.

If the whole life and auxiliary fund method is used, a shorter waiting period and age requirement may be adopted. Under this method, if an employee terminates, he usually forfeits any interest in the entire auxiliary fund; and unless he has had sufficient service, he may also forfeit any interest in the whole life policy. The amount recovered by the trustee will usually be greater than it would have been if retirement annuity or retirement income policies had been used.

Formulas for Retirement Benefits. Pension benefits are usually based on salary, service, or a combination of the two. Some of the major types of retirement benefit formulas are as follows:

1. Flat benefit formulas:
   a) Percentage: 30 per cent of salary as pension.
   b) Amount: $100 a month at retirement.
   c) Schedule:

Basic Annual Compensation		*Monthly*
From	*But Less than*	*Pension*
$ 0	$1,200	$10
1,200	2,400	20
2,400	3,600	30

An additional $10 monthly pension for each additional $1,200 annual compensation bracket.

2. Unit benefit formulas:
   a) Percentage: 1 per cent of salary per year of service.
   b) Amount: $2.50 a month per year of service.
3. Integrated formulas:
   a) Money purchase: 9.375 per cent of basic salary in excess of $4,800 as a deposit each year.
   b) Flat benefit: 30 per cent of salary over $4,800 as annual pension.
   c) Unit benefit: ¾ per cent of salary over $4,800 per year of service.
   d) Offset: 30 per cent of salary, less 100 per cent of basic social security as pension; $4.00 per year of service less social security; 2 per cent per year of service less social security.

Social security provides a basic monthly pension for all employees on their earnings up to $400 a month. The income from this source is often taken into account in determining the amount of pension to be provided by the employer's plan. The percentage of monthly income provided by social security is indicated in Table 38–1.

TABLE 38–1

PERCENTAGE OF MONTHLY INCOME PROVIDED BY SOCIAL SECURITY BENEFITS

Monthly Compensation	Monthly Benefit	Per Cent to Compensation
$ 200	$ 84	42%
250	95	38
350	116	33
400	127	32
500	127	25
600	127	21
800	127	16
1,200	127	11

Because social security benefits are calculated only on the first $400 a month of an employee's earnings, many employers feel that the first objective of any voluntary pension plan should be to equalize the effect social security will have on the employee's total retirement benefit. Such a procedure is called "integrating" with social security, and the ground rules, as set out in the regulations, are quite specific. A formula which takes full advantage of the integration rules is one which eliminates the first $4,800 of annual compensation as a basis for determining benefits and provides the maximum benefit on compensation in excess of that amount. If the plan provides a preretirement death benefit, and a retirement benefit based on the 10-year certain and continuous option, the maximum benefit which may be provided on excess compensation is 30 per cent of such excess.

If the employer feels that social security should be supplemented, then a formula can be designed which will provide a benefit based on the first $400 of compensation at one level (percentage) and a higher level (percentage) on compensation in excess of that which is covered by social security. The following are two examples of such formulas:

Ten per cent of compensation up to $400 a month and 40 per cent of comsation above that figure.

Twenty per cent of compensation up to $400 a month and 50 per cent of compensation above that figure.

Note that the maximum "spread" between the lower and upper level is 30 per cent, which is based on the assumption that a preretirement death benefit and a 10-year certain and continuous annuity will be included in the plan benefits.

Many employers feel that 50 per cent of compensation as a pension benefit is an ideal objective and adopt a formula which will produce such results. The 20–50 per cent formula mentioned above as an example would produce the benefits shown in Table 38–2.

TABLE 38–2

PENSION BENEFITS PROVIDED BY PLAN INTEGRATED WITH SOCIAL SECURITY ON 20–50 FORMULA BASIS

Monthly Compensation	Social Security	Plan Benefit	Total Pension	Per Cent to Compensation
$ 200	$ 84	$ 40	$124	62%
250	95	50	145	58
350	116	70	186	53
400	127	80	207	52
500	127	130	257	51
600	127	180	307	51
800	127	280	407	51
1,200	127	480	607	51

Salary and service formulas can be developed to take into account social security benefits, such as three fourths of 1 per cent of the first $400 monthly salary plus 1½ per cent of salary in excess of $400 a month times years of service. A maximum limitation on service may be employed, such as 25 or 30 years.

Compensation is usually defined as the basic annual rate exclusive of overtime and discretionary bonuses. However, many corporations provide for contractual bonuses based on profits, and these bonuses are often considered as part of the employee's compensation for purposes of determining pension benefits.

If retirement income or retirement annuity policies are used, the benefit formula should be worded to allow for increases in monthly benefits of $10 or more, since most insurers will not issue contracts in amounts of less than $1,000.

If a whole life and auxiliary fund plan is used, almost any formula can be applied and easily financed through the two accounts. The usual practice is to have $1,000 of insurance for each $10 of monthly pension, but it is possible to provide death benefits on one basis and pension benefits based on other criteria—the death benefit, therefore, not necessarily being in the usual ratio of 100 times the pension benefit. However, insurance benefits may not, according to IRS regulations, exceed the 100 times ratio.

Final pension benefits, where retirement annuity and retirement income policies are used, are normally determined on the basis of an employee's earnings at age 55, at age 60, or a five-year average prior to age 60. However, under the whole life and auxiliary fund plan the death benefit can be frozen at age 55 or 60 and the pension benefit determined by the employee's average pay either from age 60 to 65 or from age 55 to 65, or the highest consecutive five years in the 10-year period. This funding method, therefore, provides a more flexible determination of the final pension benefit, and it gives the participant a monthly income more nearly related to his final compensation.

Normal Retirement Age. The normal retirement age used in most plans is 65, mainly because this is when social security provides the full benefit. However, most plans provide early retirement options after age 60, and deferred retirement options with the consent of the company or its board of directors.

If employees over age 55 are eligible for the plan, their normal retirement age is usually after 10 years of plan participation, especially if the plan is funded through the use of retirement annuity or retirement income contracts. This gives the employer an opportunity to spread the costs of these participants' benefits over a 10-year period; otherwise the annual deposits to accumulate the pension fund could be too expensive.

Under the whole life and auxiliary fund method the normal retirement age of the older employees may also be deferred for 10 years. However, this is not necessary because under this method the retirement funds for the older employees can be withdrawn from the auxiliary fund account even after one or two years of participation of such older employees and the amounts repaid in the following 10 years or over the remaining future service of the other participants.

Contributions by Employees. Most individual policy pension plans do not require employee contributions because the cost of the plan, including death and disability benefits, is a deductible item as a corporate expense. Thus, assuming a federal income tax corporate rate of, say, 50 per cent, the corporation pays a net of 50 cents to contribute $1.00 to the plan. If an employee contributes, he must first receive at least $1.25 (at, say, a personal tax rate of 20 per cent) in order to retain $1.00 after taxes to contribute $1.00 to the plan.

Some employers pay the entire cost of a plan funded with retirement annuities (without insurance) and give each employee the option of contributing an additional amount so that the trustee can maintain for them a retirement income policy with the larger death benefit in the early years of the plan.

If retirement income or whole life policies are used to fund the pension plan, it is likely that some employees may not be insurable at standard rates. Many plans provide that if a policy is issued with an additional substandard rating, the employee may elect either to pay the cost of the rating or to request a retirement annuity contract based on the amount of the standard premium. Some insurance companies offer a graded death benefit contract instead of the annuity on substandard risks; and in this type of policy the death benefit is reduced, although the cash accumulated for retirement purposes is the same as under the standard risk contract.

Many plans allow the employee to purchase supplementary benefits which are added as riders either to the retirement income or to the whole life contracts. These may include the waiver of premium in the event of total disability, accidental death, or supplementary term or family income policy. This gives the employee several additional benefits which cannot be provided under most other funding instruments.

Employment Termination Benefits. Although the Internal Revenue Code and regulations do not require any vesting of funds accumulated in a pension plan until an early retirement age, except for contributions made by employees, most individual policy plans provide that an employee whose service is terminated, voluntarily or otherwise, will be entitled to some or all of the funds accumulated for him. Usually, the amount that will belong to the employee at termination of employment is determined either by his length of service with the employer or by his years of participation under the plan.

Under retirement annuity or retirement income contracts, vesting is usually at a fairly slow rate. For example, a typical plan might provide for vesting of 5 per cent of policy values for each year of service, with 100 per cent vesting after twenty years or attainment of age 60, whichever is the first to occur.

In the whole life and auxiliary fund plan, the general practice is to vest the whole life policy in the employee, with no vesting in the auxiliary account unless he has attained early retirement age. He may take over the individual policy at its original age and premium rate and either continue it, take paid-up insurance, or surrender it for its cash value. The auxiliary account is forfeited, and the amount recovered must be used to reduce the employer's subsequent deposits to the plan for the remaining participants.

Death Benefits. One of the advantages of the individual policy financing method is the automatic inclusion of death benefits in the plan. The illustrations of the three policies—retirement annuity, retirement income, and whole life and auxiliary fund—indicated that there is a difference in the amount of death benefits, but each contract provides a death benefit prior to the normal retirement date. Except for retirement annuities, the participant must be insurable in order to secure the insurance coverage. If a participant is not insurable at standard rates, he may elect to pay the extra rating required or to request the company to issue a retirement annuity contract or a graded death benefit contract, if such is available.

Many insurance companies will offer what is commonly called "guaranteed issue" to a trust covering ten or more participants. Under guaranteed issue, the insurer will waive medical evidence of insurability up to a certain maximum per life. The insurer typically will issue policies for $10,000, $15,000, $20,000, or even $30,000 of coverage, generally determined by the number of participants, the total volume, and the spread of risk.

The Treasury Department requires that the term cost for the net amount of insurance at risk be reported as taxable income to the employee in the year in which the premium is paid. The net amount of insurance at risk is determined by subtracting the cash value of the contract in the year from the face value and multiplying the remainder by the term rate at the employee's attained age. The government has provided a table of net term insurance rates (commonly known as "P.S. 58" rates), which may be used for this purpose.

Many times the reportable income attributable to the net amount of term insurance at risk will influence the employer as to the type of policy purchased. Retirement income policies rather than whole life may be selected because the amount of additional taxable income reportable is less under retirement income policies as compared with the whole life contracts.

For example, a typical employee, aged 45, may be entitled to a monthly pension of $1,000 and a $100,000 death benefit. Under the retirement income policy, the total amount of taxable income he will report between ages 45 and 59 (when the insurance coverage terminates) will be $5,658. Under the whole life plan, where there is a high element of insurance right up to the normal retirement date, the total amount of taxable income he would report for the twenty-year period would amount to $20,617.[1]

When, as previously discussed, the employer pays the entire cost of a

---

[1] The amount reportable for income tax under either the retirement income or the combination plan may be used as an offset under the Internal Revenue Code of 1954, Section 72(*f*)(1), in determining the employee's cost basis, in order to calculate the ratio of the nontaxable annuity income to be received by the participant.

retirement annuity policy and allows each employee to contribute a sufficient amount to cover the cost of the death benefit under the retirement income contract, the troublesome administrative detail of reporting the taxable income for each participant each year is eliminated.

Many employers prefer the retirement income method of financing their plans because the death benefit in the later years of participation, generally from ages 60 to 65, is substantially greater than under the whole life policy. The increasing death benefit at older ages is attractive to stockholder-employees, particularly because the amounts payable at death, if paid to a named beneficiary other than the estate of the insured, are currently exempt from federal estate tax.

Disability Benefits. If an employee becomes totally and permanently disabled, usually the total value accumulated in any one of the three types of policies, as well as the employee's share of the auxiliary fund, if any, becomes fully vested and belongs to the disabled employee. Waiver of premium in the event of total disability may be added to retirement income and retirement annuity contracts, so that if the employee becomes eligible for such benefits, the trust may transfer the contract to him, and it will continue to accumulate reserves and provide protection and full death benefits prior to retirement and the required pension funds at the normal retirement date with no further payment of premiums.

On the other hand, if the whole life and auxiliary fund method is used, the waiver of premium applies only to the whole life contract. This gives the employee full death benefits, but it will not accumulate the total pension fund, since no further deposits will be made to the auxiliary fund account unless the employer agrees to do so under the terms of the plan.

Some insurance companies provide not only for waiver of premiums, but also for the payment of a monthly income based on the face value of the policy. Therefore, it is possible under an individual policy plan—particularly retirement income contracts—to have the complete plan paid up if the employee is totally disabled and at the same time provide him with monthly income usually equal to 1 per cent of the face amount per month (i.e., $100 a month for each $10,000 of face amount).

Adaptability

To explain the use of individual policies in providing benefits for a small group of employees and to illustrate the substantial benefits available to a 90 per cent stockholder-employee—a typical plan covering all employees of a closely held corporation is outlined in Table 38–3.

To illustrate the financial situation of a corporation and employee-stockholder in a given tax year, with or without a plan, assume that the gross corporate income after all expenses, salaries, and depreciation, but before income taxes, amounts to $45,000. Without a plan, the corporation's

TABLE 38–3

ILLUSTRATION OF INDIVIDUAL POLICY PENSION PLAN PROVIDING 10 PER CENT OF COMPENSATION UP TO $400 A MONTH AND 40 PER CENT OF OVER $400 A MONTH TO SUPPLEMENT SOCIAL SECURITY—INCLUDING DEATH, DISABILITY, AND OPTIONAL METHODS OF SETTLEMENT FOR BENEFICIARY OR PARTICIPANT

Occupation	Age	Monthly Compensation	Monthly Social Security	Monthly Plan Pension	Total Monthly Benefit	Death Benefit	Insurance Investment*	Auxiliary Fund Investment†	Total Annual Investment	Taxable Insurance Cost‡
President (90% stockholder)	55	$2,000	$127	$ 690	$817	$ 69,000	$3,528.45	$ 6,375.60	$ 9,904.05	$934.26
Vice president	45	1,500	127	490	617	49,000	1,654.85	1,586.13	3,240.98	306.74
Treasurer	40	1,250	127	390	517	39,000	1,095.27	839.67	1,934.94	171.60
Sales manager	43	1,000	127	290	417	29,000	910.22	791.41	1,701.63	156.89
Salesman	40	866	127	230	357	23,000	648.39	495.19	1,143.58	101.20
Salesman	32	700	127	170	297	17,000	369.29	228.48	597.77	45.22
Office manager	38	600	127	130	257	13,000	344.39	251.42	595.81	50.18
Secretary	35	400	127	50	177	5,000	117.05	94.60	211.65	16.05
Secretary	32	350	116	40	156	4,000	91.76	64.80	156.56	10.64
Secretary	30	325	112	40	152	4,000	87.28	57.40	144.68	9.60
				$2,520		$252,000	$8,846.95	$10,784.70	$19,631.65	

* The insurance investment is based on gross annual premium of whole life policies covering death benefits and waiver of premium, and accumulating a portion of the retirement fund. Annual dividends will reduce premiums.

† Auxiliary fund investment is calculated on an annual level basis over the remaining future service of each participant, assuming 4 per cent compound interest and discounted on 1958 CSO Mortality Table. Annual adjustments in the amount to be deposited in this account will be determined by actual mortality, interest earnings, and turnover. Under this method the employer's risks are limited to auxiliary fund assumptions prior to retirement.

‡ Taxable insurance cost is adjusted annually according to Internal Revenue Service Ruling P.S. 58.

If retirement income policies were used to finance the plan, all the benefits would be insured by an individual policy issued for each participant. The annual outlay would be $21,688.73, reduced by dividends, terminations, and deaths. The adequacy of the mortality and interest assumptions and the guarantee of principal are all assumed by the insurance company.

If retirement annuities were used to fund the plan, all the benefits would be insured by an individual policy issued for each participant. The annual outlay would be $20,920.76, reduced by dividends, terminations, and deaths. The initial death benefit under the retirement annuity funding instrument is limited to the gross premiums paid until such time as the cash value accumulated exceeds this amount. The risks under this method are also all assumed by the insurance company.

net profit after taxes based on rates effective in 1965 would be calculated as follows:

Gross earnings before taxes		$45,000
Federal income tax: $25,000 at 22 per cent	$5,500	
20,000 at 48 per cent	9,600	15,100
Net profit added to corporate surplus		$29,900
Stockholder share of net profit, 90 per cent, which increases his taxable estate		$26,910

The adoption of the pension plan illustrated in Table 38–3 changes the corporation's net profit after taxes as follows:

Gross earnings before the plan	$45,000.00
Cost of the plan	19,631.65
Taxable income	$25,368.35
Federal income tax	5,676.81
Net profit to surplus	$19,691.54
Increase in stockholder's net worth (90 per cent of profit)	$17,722.39
Plus stockholder's share of pension cost	9,904.05
Total credit to stockholder	$27,626.44

From these figures, it is evident that the stockholder-employee's net worth has been increased; in addition, he is insured for the following benefits:

1. An immediate death benefit of $69,000 exempt from federal estate tax if payable to a named beneficiary other than his estate (Section 2039[*c*]).
2. Waiver-of-premium disability benefit to maintain insurance coverage in the event of total and permanent disability.
3. Total cash accumulated at age 65 of $111,754. This amount may be taken as a lump sum payment subject to long-term capital gains tax, or
4. The cash accumulated may be paid to him under any one of the five usual settlement options included in individual policies and taxed at ordinary rates as received, subject to annuity exceptions.
5. The stockholder-employee may defer his own retirement and take paid-up insurance of $45,402 plus the auxiliary account of $92,475 for a total benefit of $137,877. This amount will increase by annual dividends from the insurance policy plus earnings on the trust account until such time as the stockholder-employee dies or actually retires.

Thus, the stockholder and all of his employees are provided substantial death, disability, and retirement benefits plus severance pay.

Administration

After the final specifications of the plan have been decided upon, the attorney drafts the legal instruments covering the provisions of the plan and the trust. The insurance company and the life underwriter often supply the attorney with sample phrases and instruments as a guide. In addition, the insurer and underwriter will assist the attorney in gathering all information to be submitted to the Internal Revenue Service for plan approval.

Next, the board of directors of the corporation adopts the plan, and the company formally assumes two responsibilities: (1) to make the annual contributions required to maintain the plan, and (2) to explain and promote the plan in order to secure employee appreciation of the benefits provided. Employee understanding should lead to increased efficiency, loyalty, and devotion to the firm and its objectives.

The insurance company and the underwriter will not only handle many of the details necessary to install the plan, but they will also provide service from year to year. They provide the employer and the employees with:

1. A summary of the principal benefits of the plan in layman's language.
2. Specific information for each employee, which is explained to him in an individual interview in order to enroll him in the plan and to answer his questions.
3. A certificate of the employer's interest in the plan, outlining the death, disability, and retirement features, including the dovetailing of the pension coverage with his personal insurance, if desired.

Annually, the life underwriter and the insurer, with the assistance of the trustee, will determine any increases in benefits for present participants and will enroll new participants. They will also provide the employer with the annual net premiums due on old and new policies, as well as the amount required in the auxiliary fund if it is a combination plan.

The underwriter will assist the employer, the trustee, and the employee in all decisions regarding disbursement of benefits, either at the time of retirement, in the event of disability, or in the event of termination of service. If the employee dies and has not left specific instructions regarding any optional method of settlement, the employer, the trustee, the beneficiary, and the life underwriter will confer to arrange the best possible method of distribution to fit the current needs of the beneficiary.

To summarize, it is only necessary for the employer to make an annual contribution to the trustee; then the trustee, the insurance company, and the life underwriter perform all other services outside the employer's office. Annual reports are submitted to the employer, including schedules to justify his contribution as a deduction on his corporate income tax return.

A pension plan using insurance company services exclusively is an all-insured plan. It contains built-in guarantees as a basic part of each policy purchased by the trustee. The ceiling on premium cost is guaranteed for each unit as it is purchased. A floor on investment return is guaranteed. The safety of principal is guaranteed. The mortality and annuity assumptions are guaranteed. Only an all-insured pension plan can offer such guarantees, and only a life insurance company can offer an all-insured plan. For the small- and medium-sized firm, the individual policy pension plan is highly satisfactory. Many large companies which want pension benefits guaranteed and fully insured also use this method. The guarantees flowing from such policies cannot be overemphasized.

Some of the advantages of using individual policies as the sole investment medium for a pension trust are outlined below. They also apply to that portion of combination plans funded with individual whole life policies.

1. Administration is simplified for the trustee because the accumulations for each employee are automatically segregated in a personal account, the cash value of the policy. Values available to each employee are certain throughout the entire program.
2. The use of individual retirement annuity or retirement income policies eliminates all actuarial computations and the mortality risks normally assumed by the employer under other types of funding instruments.
3. Future values of policies as purchased are guaranteed in advance and are not subject to speculative hazards.
4. The hazards of market fluctuations are substantially eliminated.
5. When purchased, individual policies provide the employer with guaranteed maximum cost until their maturity date, insofar as the coverage already insured is concerned.
6. An individual policy is something most employees know about. They have personal insurance policies of their own, and know what they look like and quite often know what they say. This knowledge of the product funding the pension plan will enable more employees better to understand it.
7. All of the customary settlement options contained in individual policies are available to plan participants and their beneficiaries.
8. Use of individual policies with an auxiliary fund permits flexibility in funding through assumption adjustments in the auxiliary fund, while providing guarantees as to mortality assumptions and annuity costs.

Individual policy pension plans, as indicated at the beginning of this chapter, are the most popular form of providing benefits for small groups of employees. Corporations with many employees generally adopt some other method of funding their programs; and many of them provide pension benefits only through the pension program, and death and disability benefits through supplementary group coverages. Small, closely held corporations cannot usually secure maximum group life or disability coverage because of the minimum number of employees participating; therefore the use of individual policies provides these companies and their employees with an over-all fringe benefit program through the adoption of a well-conceived pension plan.

SELECTED REFERENCES

COMMERCE CLEARING HOUSE, INC. *Pension Plan Guide*. A loose-leaf service. Chicago, n.d.

Employee Benefit Plan Review. A monthly periodical.

McGILL, DAN M. *Fundamentals of Private Pensions*. 2d ed. Pension Research Council, Wharton School of Finance and Commerce, University of Pennsylvania. Homewood, Ill.: Richard D. Irwin, Inc., 1964.

McGILL, DAN M. (ed.). *Pensions: Problems and Trends*. S. S. Huebner Foundation for Insurance Education, University of Pennsylvania. Homewood, Ill.: Richard D. Irwin, Inc., 1955.

PRENTICE-HALL, INC. *Pension and Profit Sharing*. A loose-leaf service. Englewood Cliffs, N.J., n.d.

Chapter 39

GROUP DEFERRED ANNUITIES

BY RAY M. PETERSON

When an employer undertakes to provide pensions for some or all of his employees, he must make a number of important decisions. He may simply pay amounts based on the needs of each retired employee each month and charge such amounts as an operating expense in the month of payment; this arrangement is hardly likely to prove satisfactory. Generally, an employer will adopt a retirement plan under which pension benefits are determined in a systematic manner without regard to specific needs of individual employees, and he will make some provision for advance funding of these benefits.

Usually, the first step toward advance funding is to set aside and earmark enough money to continue each employee's pension for life when he retires. Most employers having a systematic retirement plan go much further than this. Where an employee's pension is based on his earnings during certain years of service, it is common to regard the portion of his pension based on a particular year of service as being earned during that year. In such a case an employer will usually aim to fund each year, that is, set aside in advance, an amount of money equal to the value of the portion of the pension earned during the year.

A funded plan will usually have its funds either with an insurance company or in a trust fund. If an employer decides to use an insurance company, the principal vehicles available are group deferred annuities, deposit administration group annuities, individual policy pension trusts, and group permanent contracts. At the end of 1962, pension plans using life insurance company contracts were distributed as shown in Table 39–1.[1]

The selection of a particular funding vehicle will in some instances be influenced by some of the desired plan provisions as well as the desired degree of advance funding. This chapter has to do primarily with the subject of group deferred annuities. Contracts of this type were first issued in the mid-twenties.

---

[1] Institute of Life Insurance, *Life Insurance Fact Book* (New York, 1963), p. 33.

TABLE 39–1

NUMBER OF PLANS AND PERSONS COVERED UNDER PENSION PLANS USING LIFE INSURANCE COMPANY CONTRACTS, 1962

	Number of Plans	Number of Persons Covered
Group deferred annuities	6,220	2,475,000
Deposit administration group annuities	4,310	2,135,000
Individual policy pension trusts	26,260	710,000
Others	4,020	450,000

PRINCIPAL CHARACTERISTICS

A typical group deferred annuity contract is issued by an insurance company to an employer without an intervening trustee. Probably every insurance company uses standardized forms and provisions for its group annuity contracts, but is is unlikely that any two contracts are ever identical. Two contracts might be the same initially; but inevitably, over the years, each one acquires a series of amendments peculiar to itself.

An employee for whom annuities are purchased under a group deferred annuity contract is given a certificate issued by the insurance company constituting a statement in substance of his rights and privileges. As a third-party beneficiary, his rights and privileges are determined by the contract.

Basic Feature

Under a group deferred annuity contract, the insurance company applies each premium (sometimes referred to as a consideration, purchase price installment, or purchase payment) as it is received to purchase a single-premium deferred annuity. This method of operation is the basic feature of group deferred annuities.

In his group annuity contract the employer usually makes provision both for benefits with respect to *past* service and for benefits with respect to *future* service, where past and future have reference to the effective date of the plan.

Future Service

The amount of future service annuity purchased for an employee in a particular year is usually based on his earnings during the year. This type of plan is commonly called a *defined benefit* plan. To illustrate, under a straight 1½ per cent defined benefit plan a deferred annuity of $75 per annum would be purchased for an employee who earned $5,000 during the year. If the same employee earned $5,400 the following year, his future service annuity for that year would be $81, and so on.

Most defined benefit plans involve two or more percentages in order to "integrate with social security." For example, the future service annuity might be 1 per cent of the first $4,800 of annual earnings and 2 per cent of the excess.

Some plans require employee contributions for future service benefits. Such contributions are generally fixed percentages of various portions of an employee's earnings. Thus, for the integrated plan just mentioned, employees might be required to contribute 2 per cent of the first $4,800 of annual earnings and 4 per cent of annual earnings in excess of $4,800, so that the ratio of employee contributions to benefits would be two to one. In a defined benefit plan the employer future service contributions are determined so as to cover the remainder of the cost. One consequence of this is that any change in the insurance company's group annuity premium rates is reflected entirely in the employer's contributions. Some group deferred annuity plans provide for the purchase for each eligible employee of a deferred annuity of a uniform amount for each year of service. Since the annuities are not directly related to the employee's earnings, such a plan is likely to be suitable only for a class of employees whose earnings do not vary widely—for example, the members of some unions.

In some group annuity plans, both the employee contributions and the employer contributions are based on the employee's earnings, and the amount of future service benefit purchased is the balancing item. This type of plan is called a *money purchase* plan. As an example, the employee and his employer might each contribute an amount equal to 5 per cent of the employee's earnings, so that the employee's benefit would be the annuity that 10 per cent of his earnings would buy under the group annuity contract. A serious disadvantage of the money purchase plan is that an increase in the insurance company's group annuity rates is reflected entirely in a decrease in the employee's benefit subsequently purchased. Another disadvantage is that the employer's total contribution is distributed in such a way as to buy a proportionately larger benefit for the employee who is young, and has little past service, than for the one who has put in many years of past service. Principally for these reasons, the money purchase plan is no longer as popular as it once was.

Past Service

It is the usual practice for the employer to pay the entire cost of past service benefits. In most cases, such benefits are purchased in installments over a period of years, particularly where the initial past service liability—that is, the amount required to purchase all past service benefits at the effective date of the plan—is relatively large. The amount of past service premium that an employer may deduct as an expense in calculating his federal income tax may be a controlling factor in determining the size of his annual past service installment. It is still fairly common to provide that past service premiums must be allocated so that each employee's past service annuity is fully purchased when he reaches retirement; but except for this possible limitation, past service premiums may be allocated in almost any orderly manner the employer desires for the contract provision.

Optional Employee Contributions

A few group deferred annuity plans give employees the option of making optional contributions to purchase supplementary annuities. Employers seldom share in paying the cost of such annuities, so that the ratio of the employee contributions to benefit is relatively unattractive, especially at the higher ages where employees are most interested and are able to budget part of their income for this purpose. Since contributing employees usually do not share in the distribution of surplus earnings of the insurer, a better result may be obtained by the purchase of an individual annuity contract. In practice, where this privilege is available, it is seldom exercised.

Benefits on Death or Withdrawal

An employee is assured that the amount payable upon his withdrawal or death prior to retirement will never be less than the sum of his contributions. Usually, the amount payable is the sum of his contributions with interest. The amount payable on death after retirement is usually the death benefit at retirement less the sum of all annuity payments actually made. An annuity with this type of death benefit is sometimes referred to as an annuity with guaranteed minimum return or a modified cash refund annuity. Instead of this, it is fairly common now for a group deferred annuity contract to provide for the purchase of life annuities with a five- or ten-year certain period.

The cost of an annuity with a death benefit is greater than that of one without. Therefore, the elimination of the death benefit would make it possible to provide a larger amount of annuity with a given level of premiums or, alternatively, the same amount of annuity with lower premiums. This could not be done, however, without imposing restrictions on the employee withdrawal benefit similar to the restrictions applicable to the employer withdrawal credit as described below under "Withdrawal Credits." Accordingly, it is generally regarded as impractical to eliminate the employee death benefit except in noncontributory plans.

Most contracts provide that a terminating employee who has satisfied certain age and/or service requirements will retain the right to the paid-up deferred annuity purchased by both his own and his employer's contributions, so long as he does not withdraw his own contributions. The requirements mentioned here are usually referred to as vesting requirements. Typical vesting requirements might be attainment of age 40 and completion of fifteen years of service, although the current trend is toward more liberal requirements. Lack of a vesting provision that is considered adequate by the Internal Revenue Service may raise questions of discrimination in the "qualification" of small group deferred annuity contracts.

Employee Annuity Options

All deferred annuities are purchased to begin at normal retirement date. Usually, however, an employee who is retiring early may elect a reduced annuity to begin on his early retirement date. The amount of his reduced annuity is computed as the actuarial equivalent of the annuity for service to date that he would otherwise receive commencing at normal retirement date. This simply means that on the basis of service to early retirement date, the value of his reduced annuity payments commencing on that date is the same on the average as the value of his normal annuity payments commencing on his normal retirement date.

In a typical group deferred annuity contract with normal retirement at age 65, the choice of early retirement at age 60 would result in reducing the accrued annuity by about 35 per cent for a male or 30 per cent for a female. It should be kept in mind that the employee who retires early must not only accept this substantial reduction in his accrued annuity, but he also must give up all of the annuity with which he would have been subsequently credited had he continued in employment to the normal retirement date. It is apparent, therefore, that retirement much in advance of the normal retirement date is not attractive financially to the average employee. For this reason, some employers provide at their own expense more attractive early retirement factors for employees who have completed substantial periods of service. This feature may be financed under the contract by a supplementary purchase at retirement.

A typical group deferred annuity contract also offers each employee the option of electing a reduced annuity with all or a specified fraction of such reduced annuity continued after his death to a specified joint annuitant. This is called the joint and survivor, or contingent annuity, option. Here again, the employee's reduced annuity and the joint annuitant's annuity are computed so that together they are actuarially equivalent to the basic annuity. Generally, this option must be elected several years prior to actual retirement unless satisfactory evidence of the employee's good health is submitted. Similarly, once this option has been elected to become effective at a specified retirement date, the election may be canceled only with the consent of the insurance company, which may be conditioned on satisfactory evidence of the good health of the joint annuitant. The election is canceled automatically, however, if either the annuitant or the joint annuitant dies before the annuitant's specified retirement date.

These conditions are imposed on the election and cancellation of the joint and survivor annuity option in order to minimize antiselection in mortality experience. Liberalization of the terms governing the election of this option can give rise to additional costs which must ultimately be borne by the employer unless the insurer sustains a net loss on the contract.

In a typical group deferred annuity, for a male employee retiring at age 65, with his wife who is two years younger designated as joint annuitant, the normal annuity is reduced by about 30 per cent when his wife's annuity, if she survives him, is for the same amount as his reduced annuity, and by about 17 per cent when his wife's annuity is for half the amount of his reduced annuity. To illustrate, if the employee in this case expects to be entitled to an annuity of $200 a month for life beginning at age 65, he could "exchange" $60 of his monthly income for an annuity of approximately $140 a month to his wife for life beginning at his death after age 65. Alternatively, he could "exchange" $34 of his normal annuity of $200 a month for an annuity of approximately $83 a month to his wife upon his death following retirement.

Two other options which may be included in a group annuity contract are (1) an option to defer commencement of annuity payments and (2) an option to convert a portion of the normal annuity into a temporary annuity. The first of these would generally be elected by an employee who was continuing in employment beyond his normal retirement date. In such a case the contract may provide for one of these arrangements: (*i*) the increase of his annuity to an "actuarially equivalent" amount, (*ii*) the accrual of additional annuity service credits, or (*iii*) no increase. As to the second, a temporary annuity would be elected by an employee retiring early; it would typically be for an amount equal to his estimated social security benefits and for the period from his retirement to the commencement of his social security benefits.

RATING PRACTICES

Premiums

Three basic factors enter into the calculation of every annuity premium: mortality, interest, and provision for expenses and contingencies (i.e., so-called "loading").

There has been a great improvement in mortality in the period during which group deferred annuities have been available, although this trend has been halted somewhat in the last few years. This increased longevity has made retirement more attractive to the average pensioner; but at the same time, it has made the cost progressively greater. For current purchases, most companies assume in their rates that mortality will follow some adaptation of the Group Annuity Table for 1951. This is usually called the *Ga* 1951 Table. The adaptation may take the form of introducing a projection scale allowing for future decreases in mortality, setting back the age, or some combination of the two.

While mortality has decreased, interest earnings at first decreased in the 1930's and 1940's, and then in recent years have increased. For a while, it was common for insurance companies to assume 2 or 2¼ per cent in their group annuity rates. Currently, however, the tendency is to assume 3¼ per cent or more; and this change, of course, has lowered the cost of annuities. Even 3¼ per cent may first appear to be overly conservative, since in 1962 the life insurance business in the United States earned, before federal income tax, 4.34 per cent on total invested funds[2] and probably made new investments at a rate in excess of 5¼ per cent per annum. It must be kept in mind, however, that these are average figures—many companies did not fare so well. Also, some companies, in their rate structures, may rely to some extent on interest margins to cover future mortality improvement. Most group annuity contracts are "qualified" under the Internal Revenue Code; therefore, these rates are significant, since they are subject to only a small residual federal income tax that varies among companies.

It must also be recognized that when premium dollars are invested today, the insurance company may be committed to earn the guaranteed interest rate on such dollars for as many as 50 or 60 years in the future. In a period of this length, it is certain that interest rates will not remain constant, but will move from time to time, down as well as up. In the long run, if the premiums charged prove to be greater than necessary, any margin will be reflected in the employer's cost in the form of dividends or rate adjustments.

Expenses under a group deferred annuity, including acquisition expenses, commissions, and state premium taxes, range from about 1½ or 2½ per cent of contributions on a very large case to 12½ or 15 per cent on a very small case. For group deferred annuity contracts covering 200 to 500 employees, such expenses may range from 5 to 3 per cent, respectively. The high rate of expense on very small cases is due in part to the fact that group annuity administration involves certain fixed expenses that are independent of size of case.

Acquisition expenses include the expenses of promotion and selling the business other than actual commissions.

Commission scales are graded downward with size of case, producing moderate-sized commissions on small cases and progressively smaller relative commissions on the larger cases. On a case with a total annual premium of $100,000, under a typical scale, the first-year commissions would be $3,300, or 3.3 per cent, and the renewal commissions would be

---

[2] *Ibid.*, p. 58.

$1,000, or 1 per cent each year. The same scale would produce first-year commissions of $9,300 and annual renewal commissions of $4,000 on a case with a total annual premium of $1 million. In the company with these commission scales a portion of the second-year and third-year commissions and all of the subsequent commissions are called "service fees," and are paid only if satisfactory service is rendered. Under this arrangement, service fees do not automatically terminate after ten years but may continue indefinitely.

Group annuity considerations are taxed in about half the states at rates ranging from 1 to 2½ per cent. An increasing number of states exempt from tax, in whole or in part, annuity considerations for "qualified" plans. Insurance companies generally recognize the actual tax rate of a state in surplus distribution or rerating practices rather than using an average rate.

A common loading for expenses and contingencies is 5 per cent of the gross premium. This loading obviously does not even cover all expenses, let alone provide a margin for contingencies on the very small cases; and it is not practical to have different premium scales with different loading percentages for cases of various sizes. Accordingly, most companies have adopted the practice of charging regular premiums on all cases and imposing an additional annual administrative, or contract, charge on smaller cases. This annual charge is generally between $500 and $750, and usually decreases as the premium increases. For example, the additional charge might be $750 less 1½ per cent of premiums in excess of $15,000. In this case the charge would be $225 for a $50,000 case, and zero for a case of $65,000 or more. It should be noted that when an employer pays an administrative or contract charge, no part of it is applied directly toward the purchase of annuities, and no part is included in any withdrawal credits.

The typical employer is much more interested in the premiums he must pay in dollars and cents than he is in the underlying mortality, interest, and expense factors. It is impossible to quote figures for a particular case without having all the necessary data; and even if the data are available, extensive calculations are required. It may be helpful, however, to compare some of the actual premium rates of various insurance companies. For this purpose, it is fairly common practice to look at the immediate life annuity rates for a male at age 65. Some typical rates in effect in 1963 are shown in Table 39–2.

Of course, if the total annual premium for a particular contract were calculated on each of the bases in Table 39–2, it would be highly unlikely that the results would be in direct proportion to the figures shown in the last column. Nevertheless, they would probably fall in order of size, as indicated there.

TABLE 39–2

GROUP ANNUITY RATE BASES

Mortality	Interest	Loading	Rate of Immediate Life Annuity of $1.00 per Month for Male Aged 65
Ga–1951, Projection Scale C, using rates for 1960 up to age 55 and generation of 1905 rates from there forward	3¼%	5%	$150.38
Ga–1951, Projection Scale C, for purchases in 1965	3½	4	143.43
Ga–1951, Projection Scale C, for purchases in 1960	3¼	5	145.36
Ga–1951, Projection Scale C (rates shown for purchases in 1963)	3½	5	143.97

Guarantees

Generally, in a group deferred annuity contract the initial rates and terms are guaranteed for all purchases during the first five years. The insurance company may change the rates and contract provisions annually thereafter on ninety days' notice, but such changes in rates more frequently than once every five years are rare, and such contract changes are usually limited to terms of the contract affected by a simultaneous rate change. Of course, the employer may request a contract change at any time, and in the event of such a request the insurance company may simultaneously modify any other terms of the contract which are affected. Such changes cannot penalize employees with respect to prior purchases.

It may be worth noting that, in effect, one of the guarantees which the insurance company gives is to keep the contract in force in accordance with its terms as long as the employer desires. As long as the employer carries out his responsibilities under the contract, the only basis for discontinuance on the part of the insurance company would be failure to maintain specified employee participation requirements, such as minimum number of lives and minimum percentage participation; and such a discontinuance would not alter the insurance company's guarantee to pay the annuities already purchased under the contract.

Withdrawal Credits

The employer's premiums under a group deferred annuity are discounted for mortality but not for withdrawals. Because of the mortality discount, no portion of the employer's premium is returned when an employee dies. Because of the absence of a withdrawal discount, however, the employer is usually entitled to a return of premiums when an employee's annuity is canceled. The procedure to be followed is perfectly clear when an employee dies while he is still employed, or if his annuity is canceled while he is in good health; it is not so clear when an employee withdraws in poor health. Generally, the employer is given a withdrawal credit upon cancellation of an employee annuity, provided the employee's health is not so seriously impaired as to make him ineligible for life insurance at moderately substandard rates. The credit is generally 100 per cent of the employer's premiums with interest where applied in payment of premiums for annuities for other employees. This is the standard practice for a continuing contract. If the purchase of annuities has been discontinued, a cash withdrawal value is allowed, usually equal to 95 per cent of accumulated premiums.

UNDERWRITING PRACTICES

When an employer decides to fund his pension plan through a group deferred annuity, he must choose the insurance company with which he will do business. In effect, he selects his insurer.

Underwriting at Issue

At the same time, every insurance company must determine which cases it will accept. In a sense, this is the first phase of what is called group annuity underwriting or selection. It corresponds to the underwriting that is done before a life insurance company issues an individual life insurance policy, but with this important difference: Individual policy underwriting is primarily concerned with mortality, while group annuity underwriting is primarily concerned with expenses.

Probably the most important underwriting requirement for a group deferred annuity contract is that there be reasonable assurance that the plan will be a permanent one. It is true that an insurance company would be interested in the continuance of its contracts in any event, and particularly in the case of a group deferred annuity because of the adverse employee reaction which might be created by early discontinuance. It is essential, however, that a group deferred annuity contract continue for several years at least, in order to cover the relatively high initial expenses that are incurred in placing the business on the company's books. In order to satisfy itself that a case will be permanent, the insurance company will usually look for evidence showing that the employer's business is stable and that he can pay his share of the cost under the plan.

Again, primarily because of the expense factor, groups below some minimum size and plans with meager benefit formulas are discouraged. The minimum may have reference to the number of eligible employees, the total annual premium, and/or the average premium per employee. A typical requirement is that there must be at least twenty-five eligible employees, and there must be at least 75 per cent participation if employees are required to contribute. A typical minimum annual premium might be $200 per life on the average, or at least $5,000 in total. Where an annual administrative or contract charge is imposed, it tends to discourage the very small cases and accordingly may be regarded as a substitute for the minium requirements as to number of lives and amount of premiums.

Finally, an insurance company will be able to use an appreciably higher interest rate in connection with a plan that qualifies under Section 401(*a*) of the Internal Revenue Code than for one that does not, and this is taken into account in establishing the initial rates. Therefore, it is important for the underwriter to determine at the outset whether or not a plan is likely to qualify. As a practical matter, this usually presents no underwriting problem, since the employer is generally anxious to have his plan qualify. Indeed, compliance with qualification requirements has some elements of automatic underwriting.

Underwriting Employee Elections

Although underwriting with respect to mortality is not important at the outset, it is important in connection with individual employee elections of certain alternative forms of annuity. If these elections are not underwritten carefully, on this account alone the insurance company may be obliged to pay out in benefits substantially more than the amount for which provision was made in its premiums.

Consider, for example, a noncontributory plan without any death benefit, and assume that an employee is permitted to elect the joint and survivor annuity option without restriction at any time up to his retirement date. Obviously, an employee in very bad health at retirement would elect the maximum amount for his joint annuitant. In this situation, his own annuity would be reduced, it is true. If he died a month or two later, however, the reduction in his own annuity payments would not begin to equal the value of the subsequent payments to his joint annuitant. Not all instances of individual antiselection are as obvious as this, but they all can contribute to produce an unfavorable mortality experience through the payment of benefits not contemplated in the basic annuity rates.

It is probable that not all antiselection with respect to the joint and survivor annuity option is eliminated by the typical requirement that the option be elected several years prior to retirement unless satisfactory evidence of the employee's good health is submitted. Most antiselection is eliminated by such a rule, however, and any remainder can presumably be covered by margins in the premiums charged.

Underwriting Amendments and Renewals

An employer may ask to have his group deferred annuity contract amended for many reasons: to change the future benefit formula, the employee contributions, or the eligibility requirements; to integrate with the latest social security benefits; to add a subsidiary; and others. In general, the underwriting considerations that are applicable at issue are equally applicable upon amendment, except, of course, that at amendment, they may be much more complicated. In any event, the insurance company which has entered into a group deferred annuity contract with an employer will make every possible effort to satisfy any reasonable request the employer may make for an amendment.

Finally, the insurance company must review each case to determine whether the rates should be changed each time the guarantees run out. The underwriting process is usually regarded as including both selection and pricing. At the time of issue, pricing is not important because the insurance company will usually have adopted a single standard rate basis that will be applicable to any case it is willing to accept. When a case is reviewed for possible rerating, however, the actual experience under the contract is taken into account, i.e., actual expenses, mortality, and investment results. In general, expenses as a percentage of total annual contributions vary inversely with size. Actual mortality experience is likely to fluctuate considerably for smaller cases and therefore may be smoothed or pooled to some extent. Until recently, it would have been substantially correct to say that all cases have the same investment experience. It is fairly common practice now, however, for insurance companies to distribute investment earnings so as to recognize the different earnings rates available on amounts invested in different years. Accordingly, a case with a proportionately large accumulation of funds invested years ago at low yields might currently show investment results differing considerably from those of a case with practically all its funds invested at present high yields. It remains true, of course, that the experience of all cases is influenced by major trends in investment experience and by the general mortality improvement which has been characteristic of the last thirty years. From time to time, these factors may become so significant that a company may decide to adopt new rates practically "across the board" on all its business as it is reviewed for rerating.

It will be evident that the underwriting of a group annuity contract is practically a continuous process.

COST

Since most group deferred annuity contracts provide for sharing in distributable surplus or retroactive rate credits, i.e., they are participating, this section, except for the final paragraph, concerns only contracts of this type.

It is occasionally pointed out that in the long run the amount an employer will have to pay for a pension plan for his employees will be simply:

1. Benefits paid to employees
plus actual expenses
minus interest earnings on funds
minus employee contributions

This might be described an an experience formula; it does not depend on the actuarial cost method used. It may be worthwhile to explain how it can be reconciled with the following more familiar formula for the amount the employer must pay for a group deferred annuity:

2. Employer's premiums
minus withdrawal credits
minus dividends declared by the insurance company

In the first place, formula 1 is true, strictly speaking, only in the case of a pension plan which has been wound up with all benefits paid and all expenses covered. Nevertheless, it is sometimes regarded as applicable at any given point of time. The difficulty with such a general application is that prior to the final winding-up of a plan, there will generally be advance funding for benefits. This is the case, for example, under a group deferred annuity contract. Most, if not all, of this advance funding will arise out of employer contributions or premiums. The employer may eventually obtain a withdrawal credit with respect to some of these contributions; but for the moment, at least, they are part of his cost; and under a plan which qualifies for special income tax treatment under the Internal Revenue Code, they are an irrevocable part of his cost.

Second, under a group deferred annuity contract, funds must be on hand not only to pay benefits in the future but also to cover the future expenses which will be incurred whether or not the employer continues to purchase annuities under the contract. Advance funding for future expenses on a guaranteed basis is one of the special advantages offered by an insured plan; if not fully understood, its effect on cost may be misinterpreted. Incidentally, the term "actual expenses" in formula 1 should not be taken too literally. Under a group annuity contract, every reasonable effort is made to allocate expenses as accurately as possible. Nevertheless, the nature of some expenses is such that the only practical way to charge them is on an averaging basis. The same, of course, is true of other funding instruments.

Third, an insurance company, as a matter of prudent business operation, charges group deferred annuity premiums which it is reasonably certain will be fully adequate. As the experience develops under the contract, funds not required to meet obligations are gradually returned in the form of dividends or rate adjustments. In the normal course, the nature of the guarantees is such that the insurance company must always attempt to maintain some margin to fulfill all obligations under the contract. Over a period of years, however, this margin in relation to total premiums should become smaller and smaller, and eventually insignificant.

Where a pension plan is completely terminated, as on the occasion of the dissolution of a company, a nonparticipating deferred and immediate annuity arrangement is available, i.e., a windup arrangement may be made that sets a final price for accrued benefits without waiting for the ultimate cost to emerge through the dividend or rate adjustment process. Such an arrangement is usually available only where the employer has gone out of business and there is no continuing entity to whom dividends may be paid.

COMPARISON WITH OTHER FUNDING INSTRUMENTS

There has been a good deal of discussion of the relative merits of the various agencies and instruments available for funding a pension plan. Each has its advantages and disadvantages, and needless to say, there is not complete agreement on every point. It is hoped that the following paragraphs may be regarded as a reasonably objective effort to outline briefly the position of group deferred annuities in such a comparison.

Principal Advantages

As an insured plan, a group deferred annuity contract shares in certain advantages which are common to all plans administered by insurance companies.

The position of a life insurance company in connection with a pension plan has often been compared with that of a general contractor in building a house. Just as the general contractor relieves a man of all the responsibilities and headaches that go with housebuilding, so the insurance company relieves the employer of all investment, all actuarial, and most administrative responsibilities and headaches involved in handling a pension plan. In general, a man—or an employer—can still devote his time and energies most productively in his own business.

A pension plan involves the skillful application of the science of life contingencies. Life insurance companies are staffed with actuaries who are experts in this field. In order to emphasize that the mortality risk in a pension plan is not a catastrophe risk, it is sometimes pointed out that "no one grows old suddenly."[3] Unfortunately, this fact is occasionally misinterpreted to justify doubtful mortality assumptions. It is true that if there are mortality losses under a pension plan, they will emerge gradually over a period of years and not all at once, but they will emerge nevertheless. Furthermore, inappropriate mortality assumptions in evaluating future benefits can conceal for many years ultimate mortality losses.

A pension plan involves the skillful investment of substantial sums of money. Life insurance companies are also staffed with experts in this

---

[3] Dan M. McGill, *Fundamentals of Private Pensions*, Pension Research Council, Wharton School of Finance and Commerce, University of Pennsylvania (2d ed.; Homewood, Ill.: Richard D. Irwin, Inc., 1964), footnote on p. 171.

field. Through pooling of assets, they provide greater diversification and security of investments than is otherwise possible. They are also in a favorable position to make advantageous investments in corporate securities through direct placement and in business and residential mortgages. Accordingly, an insurance company's net investment yield (gross yield less investment expenses) is high; this is particularly important for the relatively small employer for whom the investment yield on a small fund would be cut by relatively high investment expenses.

A life insurance company is the only type of organization that is prepared to offer guarantees with respect to mortality, investment, and expense, such as the guarantees available in a group deferred annuity contract. The provision of guarantees, of necessity, customarily involves a risk charge to cover the occasional loss which occurs and to set up safety margins—this is the essence of the insurance operation; but to the extent that it is practical to do so, the insurance company gives each participating group deferred annuity contract the benefit of its own experience. Unfortunately, this latter fact is sometimes twisted to "prove" that the guarantees are worthless. What is overlooked is that in some cases the experience is unfavorable so that the guarantees are called into play. Then annuities are paid even though the premiums originally charged have proved to be inadequate. The guarantees are important to the employer because they give him the assurance that, to the extent of prior purchases, his pension plan payments will do what they are intended to do; they are not just rough guesses but careful estimates backed up by an organization which promises to make good any losses if it is wrong. The guarantees are also important to the vested or retired employee because they give him the assurance that his accrued purchased pension will be paid no matter what happens; its payment will not depend upon the continued solvent existence of the employer.

In addition to the above advantages which are shared by all insured plans, the group deferred annuity method has the important advantage that each unit of annuity is fully purchased as it is earned.[4] This feature greatly simplifies matters if an employee terminates employment with all or part of his accrued annuity vested, or if it becomes necessary to terminate the plan. More than this, it means that even while the plan continues, no change of circumstances can alter the insurance company's promise to pay such annuities without further contributions from either the employer or the employee. In short, the group deferred annuity method satisfies the strictest tests of actuarial soundness.

The requirement of a yearly annuity purchase may constitute a real advantage to many employers, whether fully recognized or not, as a funding discipline that precludes unwise funding decisions that are pos-

[4] Strictly speaking, this is true only of future service benefits. If past service benefits are purchased in installments, then termination of employment with vesting of such benefits may involve further employer contributions.

sible under more flexible arrangements. For groups of small and moderate size that may be more vulnerable to the competitive risks of our free enterprise market economy than large groups, the guarantees of a group deferred annuity contract provide a service that enhances the security of the pensions for the employees of such groups.

In comparison with other insured plans, group deferred annuities are generally regarded as offering greater flexibility and lower cost than all other types except deposit administration group annuities. Group deferred annuities are generally not available, however, for plans covering fewer than 25 employees; and for groups near this minimum size, a group deferred annuity may offer little if any advantage, costwise, over insured plans such as those covered by individual policy pension trusts.

Principal Disadvantages

As just stated, the group deferred annuity method offers great flexibility. At the same time, it is inherently inflexible in some respects. For example, the purchase of specific amounts of annuity each year requires the payment of definite premiums at definite times.

A group deferred annuity contract is most suitable for a "career" or "average salary" plan and is not so readily adapted to a "final salary" type of plan in which an employee's pension is based on his average earnings during his last few years of employment. However, this is a disadvantage only in the case of an employer who wants such a plan. Many employers have preferred to avoid a final salary plan because it is regarded as involving a commitment to absorb the increases in retirement plan costs which occur as a result of increases in salary scales. Such increases in salary levels are usually, but not always, due to inflation. There has been a great preference for average salary plans, with adjustments—as they can be afforded—in the form of supplementary benefits when it is found that adjustments are necessary.

In calculating the amount the employer must contribute under a group deferred annuity contract each year, it is not practical to discount for withdrawals. This may make it appear that he has to pay more under a group deferred annuity contract than is necessary. In practice, it usually means simply that he has to pay a portion of his cost earlier; that is, he has to increase his provision for advance funding.

The fact that the investment of funds under group deferred annuities is restricted for all practical purposes to fixed-interest-bearing securities (e.g., high-grade bonds and mortgages) is regarded by many people as a serious disadvantage, particularly during a period of "economic expansion" or inflation when the effective yields on equities may be substantially higher than on fixed-interest investments. The variable annuity scheme overcomes this disadvantage, but also substitutes a variable annuity[5] for a

---

[5] See Chapter 42 on "Variable Annuities."

fixed-dollar annuity. The "segregated asset" or "separate account" arrangement, which in recent years has received legislative approval in Massachusetts, Connecticut, New York, and a number of other states, permits investment in equities, but the contract arrangement is essentially a type of deposit administration[6] group annuity rather than a group deferred annuity.

A few years ago, one of the greatest disadvantages of group deferred annuities, as well as other insurance company funding instruments, was the discriminatory taxes to which they were subject, especially the federal income tax on life insurance companies. In 1959, provision was made for substantially reducing the federal income tax on plans which "qualify" under Section 401(*a*) of the Internal Revenue Code; consequently, this discrimination is greatly minimized. Discriminatory premium taxes, however, still are levied in a number of states. If an employer's business is large enough, he may decide, with some justification, that the disadvantage of such taxes in the case of an insurance company plan is so great that it outweighs the advantages. The guarantees of an insured plan are particularly valuable to the smaller employer, and most small employer plans are insured. Consequently, these discriminatory taxes may fall most heavily on the small employer and, through him, upon his employees. This is a result that was certainly never intended and cannot be justified on any grounds.

SELECTED REFERENCES

ALVORD, MORGAN H. "Insured Pensions and Inflation," *Journal of the American Society of Chartered Life Underwriters.* Vol. XII, No. 4 (Fall, 1958), pp. 339–49.

BLACK, KENNETH, JR. *Group Annuities.* Philadelphia: University of Pennsylvania Press, 1955.

BRONSON, DORRANCE C. *Concepts of Actuarial Soundness in Pension Plans.* Pension Research Council, Wharton School of Finance and Commerce, University of Pennsylvania. Homewood, Ill.: Richard D. Irwin, Inc., 1957.

HAMILTON, JAMES A., and BRONSON, DORRANCE C. *Pensions.* New York: McGraw-Hill Book Co., Inc., 1958.

MCGILL, DAN M. *Fulfilling Pension Expectations.* Homewood, Ill.: Richard D. Irwin, Inc., 1962.

MCGILL, DAN M. *Fundamentals of Private Pensions.* 2d ed. Pension Research Council, Wharton School of Finance and Commerce, University of Pennsylvania. Homewood, Ill.: Richard D. Irwin, Inc., 1964.

PRENTICE-HALL, INC. *Pension and Profit Sharing.* A loose-leaf service. Englewood Cliffs, N.J., 1958.

WEISS, WILLARD A. "A Critical Analysis of Trustee and Insurance Company Administered Employee Retirement Plans," *Proceedings: Conference of Actuaries in Public Practice.* Vol. V, Book Section, 1955–56.

---

[6] See Chapter 40 on "Deposit Administration and Separate Accounts."

Chapter 40

DEPOSIT ADMINISTRATION AND SEPARATE ACCOUNTS

BY MORGAN H. ALVORD

Deposit administration pension plans are generally considered to have been originated about 1929. Significant interest in this type of plan did not develop, however, until the end of World War II. This interest was due largely to a growing desire on the part of larger employers for more flexibility in the funding of pensions, and to a need for a type of plan that was more suitable for the pension agreements negotiated with labor unions.

A group contract is usually issued directly to an employer in connection with deposit administration plans, although in some instances a trustee is the holder of the contract. Deposits are made periodically to a fund, or funds, established under the contract. This fund is maintained for active employees, and no part of it is allocated to a particular employee until an annuity is provided for him. This is usually done upon retirement by charging against the unallocated fund an amount sufficient to provide an immediate annuity for the retiring employee. It is not necessary for the insurance company to maintain any individual records until an annuity is provided.

The amount of the employer's periodic deposits is calculated by an actuary based on the actuarial cost method chosen by the employer. Either the insurance company or a consulting actuary acts in this capacity. The actuary's calculation of the deposits needed to provide the benefits of the plan, as well as his determination of the financial status of the plan, is based on assumptions as to future investment returns, mortality, expenses, retirement age, and, frequently, labor turnover and salary trends. The employer furnishes the actuary with statistical data with respect to his employees, approves the assumptions used, and assumes responsibility for the adequacy of the fund.

PLAN SPECIFICATIONS

Eligibility

All of the employees potentially eligible for benefits may be "covered" by the plan for cost determination purposes. Strict eligibility requirements are not needed, since no individual records have to be maintained and any additional administrative costs because of inclusion of all employees are negligible. The use of appropriate assumptions as to rates of termination makes it possible to discount in the cost calculations approximations to the savings which would arise from those who will not continue until retirement.

Employee Contributions

While the majority of plans are on an "employer pay all" basis, some plans require employees to pay part of the costs through their own contributions. Because of this employee participation, a plan of this kind differs from a noncontributory plan in certain important respects. Records of individual employee contributions are usually kept. Withdrawal and death benefits may be paid from the deposit administration fund. Restrictions as to eligibility similar to those under a group deferred annuity plan are usually imposed. A separate fund is often maintained for the employees' contributions, and deferred annuities are sometimes purchased with these contributions as made.

Retirement Age

A normal retirement age is established, but since no annuities need be purchased until actual retirement, there is significant flexibility in determining benefits for early and late retirements. To the extent permitted by the Internal Revenue Service, adjustment for early retirement may be more liberal than that produced by using actuarial equivalents. With respect to retirement after the normal retirement age, it is common to have benefits accrue for service to actual retirement, especially in union-negotiated plans.

Cost estimates may be based upon an assumption as to the expected average retirement age of the entire group of employees. It is common, for example, to assume a retirement age beyond normal retirement age when there is no compulsory retirement.

Pension Benefits

A flexible pension benefit provision may be adopted, since no annuities are purchased while the employees are in active employment. Rather than basing benefits upon average earnings, it is common to base them upon "final" earnings.[1] In estimating costs, an assumed salary scale is introduced, adding little to the complexities of valuations and calculation of normal costs, and improving accuracy of projections.

Other kinds of pension benefits which may be funded without difficulty under this type of contract include amounts based on earnings only, pensions depending solely upon years of service, minimum benefits which are independent of the basic formula, and pension benefits which are geared to social security benefits.

Withdrawal Benefits

Under a contributory pension plan an employee is permitted to withdraw his contributions under certain conditions, such as termination of employment. If cash refunds are paid to an employee from a deposit administration fund, there is usually a charge against the fund of 3 to 6 per cent. This charge may be avoided, however, in administering the plan if the administrator makes the payment from funds which otherwise would have been paid to the deposit administration fund. The insurance company then receives only the net amount.

Frequently, under a pension plan, there is a provision for vesting accrued pension benefits, in whole or in part, if an employee terminates employment after a certain age and number of years of service. Under a deposit administration plan the vested pension may remain as an obligation of the plan on a basis similar to that of the accrued benefits of the active employees, or the vested annuity may be purchased in full for the withdrawing employee.

Death Benefits

Death benefits before retirement arising from employee contributions are administered similarly to withdrawal benefits. An employer may desire, however, to include a modest death benefit in his pension plan which is not based upon employee contributions and which is incidental to the other benefits. When this is done, the actuary includes an allowance for this benefit in his cost estimates of the size of the annual deposit. If the death benefit payments exceed the expected amounts, the fund is correspondingly reduced, and future deposits have to be increased accordingly.

After retirement, various types of death benefits are usually available in the form of optional annuities, such as joint and survivor annuities, and annuities with payments guaranteed for a certain period and life thereafter. While similar options are available under group deferred annuity

[1] In order to avoid possible discrimination and difficulty with the Internal Revenue Service, it is usual to establish final earnings as the average of the last five or ten years' earnings prior to retirement age.

contracts, they may be provided under a deposit administration contract with less restrictions. For example, any requirements as to advance notice of an election of an option could be modified or eliminated if the purchase price of the annuity is appropriately increased to allow for antiselection.

Disability Benefits

When a disability retirement benefit is included in a pension program, the risk is generally assumed by the employer. The disability payments are usually made either directly by the employer or from a deposit administration fund. If such a fund is used, the insurance company or consulting actuary generally makes recommendations as to the amount of additional deposit which the employer should make. While the final determination of whether an employee qualifies for disability benefits is the responsibility of the employer or administrator of the plan, many employers find it of considerable value to use the facilities of the insurance company for advice.

Discontinuance Provisions

When deposits are discontinued, the retirement benefits already being paid are unaffected, since such benefits are provided by single-premium immediate annuities purchased from the fund at the time an employee retires. To the extent that vested deferred annuities have been purchased, the benefits provided by these annuities are similarly unaffected by a discontinuance of deposits.

If deposits are discontinued and the pension plan is continued under some other arrangement, the contract may usually be continued without further deposits. As employees retire, their annuities are purchased from the deposit administration fund until it is exhausted.

Most contracts provide that on discontinuance of deposits and of the pension plan, the deposit administration fund must be distributed among the active employees by the purchase of fully vested deferred annuities. This distribution may be made in several different ways, provided they are mutually satisfactory to the employer and the insurance company. The method is usually stipulated in the plan. Any appropriate method of allocating the fund to individual employees will be approved by the insurance company if it can be reasonably administered and does not involve selection against it by putting undue weight upon the healthy lives. One method, which is frequently made an automatic provision, is to apply the fund as far as it will go in the purchase of accrued benefits in full, starting with those nearest normal retirement age. Another method is to allocate the fund among active lives on some basis proportionate to accrued or prospective benefits. A variation is first to purchase accrued benefits in full for employees who qualify for vested benefits under the plan and then to use up any remaining portion of the fund in one of the two preceding ways. The requirement for distribution of the deposit administration fund stems, at least in part, from Internal Revenue Service requirements applicable to a qualified pension plan when terminated.

If a pension plan is continued in some other way, the employer may wish to transfer the deposit administration fund to the new funding agency. Almost all insurance companies will permit such a "cash-out" under some circumstances, although the conditions vary greatly between companies. This will be discussed in more detail in the next section of this chapter.

UNDERWRITING AND CONTRACTUAL PROVISIONS

Contract Holder

In offering to issue a contract, the insurance company considers various factors. The plan should presumably be permanent. The employer should be one whose earning power is sufficient to support his pension program, and his facilities to administer the plan should be adequate. Associations of employers and political subdivisions are carefully screened to see whether they have the legal right to enter into a contract of this nature and can meet the other important qualifications.

Minimums and Maximums

Originally, requirements as to minimum number of lives and deposits were quite high. During the last few years, however, competition and more experience with this type of contract have resulted in a sharp decrease in these minimums. The minimum number of lives permitted under a contract has been reduced during recent years to ten or even lower by some insurance companies. Minimum annual deposit requirements have also been decreased to $10,000 or even lower.

Insurance companies wish to avoid the possibility of receiving greatly increased deposits during periods when investment earnings are low and generally impose restrictions as to the size of the deposits they will accept in any one year. While these maximums vary considerably with different companies, most of them will usually accept much larger deposits on special request.

Inclusion of Plan Specifications

In most cases the specifications of the plan, such as eligibility, retirement age benefits, and the like, are included in the contract. In some instances, particularly where two funding instruments are used, the employer may wish to keep the specifications out of the contract and operate the plan under provisions in a formal document outside the contract. Subject to proper safeguards as to future changes in the provisions, a contract may be written in this manner. When this is done, the contract, of course, becomes a simpler document.

Contributory Plans

While the majority of deposit administration plans are on a noncontributory (i.e., "employer pay all") basis, there are some plans where the employees also make contributions. Under this type the insurance company requires that the fund always be sufficient to return the employees' contributions with whatever interest is guaranteed. A common provision is to require that the deposit administration fund always be at least 105 per cent of the employees' contributions with guaranteed interest. The additional 5 per cent provides a margin for any charges made upon cash payments from the fund.

When there are employee contributions, the contract usually has one of the three following provisions: (1) the contributions, when made, are applied to purchase deferred annuities; (2) the employee and employer contributions are applied to purchase deferred annuities at the time when the annuities vest, in accordance with the provisions of the plan; or (3) the employee contributions are maintained in a separate employee fund, or in the over-all fund, and are withdrawn from the active life fund at the time of retirement to provide immediate annuities.

Deposit Administration Fund

A deposit administration fund[2] is maintained under the contract on an unallocated basis for the active employees. This fund must always be kept in excess of the amount needed to purchase annuities as employees retire, in accordance with the requirements of the plan. Sufficient amounts are transferred from this fund when an employee retires and, sometimes, when his accrued pension becomes vested, to purchase the benefits to which he is entitled.

The principal of the fund is guaranteed, as well as a minimum interest rate. The annuity rates applicable to current contributions withdrawn in the future are also guaranteed. Since the interest and premium rates in effect when the contributions are made are guaranteed, it is necessary to require that withdrawals be made on a first-in, first-out basis, i.e., contributions are transferred in the order in which they are received.

Deposits

Great flexibility is permitted in the size of the deposits. Most insurance companies require that the amounts paid must be on a reasonably sound basis, although a considerable degree of business risk is permitted in the assumptions used in determining these amounts.

---

[2] Also referred to as "deposit fund," "deposit account," "active life fund," and "purchase payment fund."

Guarantees

These plans are similar in many ways to uninsured trusteed arrangements, but the insured plans contain important guarantees which are not available under wholly uninsured funding instruments. The most important are:

1. The principal of the fund is guaranteed, regardless of the investment experience of the insurance company.
2. When a contribution is made, a minimum interest rate is guaranteed, usually on a basis where the rates are graduated downward periodically, until the contribution is transferred from the deposit administration fund. In most contracts, this minimum guaranteed rate may be changed with respect to contributions made five years or more after the effective date of the contract. Investment earnings in excess of the minimum become available through the experience-rating procedures of the insurance company.
3. At the time a contribution is made, the annuity purchase rates which may be used when it is later withdrawn to purchase an annuity are guaranteed, usually on a basis where the rates are graduated upward periodically, until the contribution is withdrawn from the fund. Generally, these guaranteed annuity rates may be changed with respect to contributions made five years or more after the effective date of the contract.
4. Since annuities are purchased when employees retire or, in some cases, when the annuities become vested, the pensions, after purchase, are guaranteed for life, regardless of the future of the plan.

Discontinuance of Contributions

The principal ways in which contributions may be discontinued are:

1. By the employer upon appropriate notice.
2. By the insurance company under one of the following circumstances:
   a) If the number under the plan falls below some minimum, such as ten.
   b) If the insurance company desires to exercise its rights to modify certain terms of the contract and the employer does not agree.
   c) If any deposits are due and are not paid within the grace period.

When contributions are discontinued, the deposit administration fund may be distributed among the active employees by the purchase of paid-up deferred annuities on a basis where there is no selection because of health considerations (described in more detail in the plan specifications section).

If the pension plan is continued through some other funding agency, the employer may wish to transfer the fund to that new agency. Practices of insurance companies vary greatly in this respect, although none of them will permit the transfer of any annuities already being paid to retired employees. The practice of permitting a transfer of funds varies among insurance companies, although most of them are willing to make a decision at the time of discontinuance in the light of the circumstances of each individual case. Some insurers, however, include in their contracts a clause allowing the employer the option to transfer the deposit administration fund to another funding agency.

When a transfer of funds is permitted, the general practice is to allow a cash-out of the deposit administration fund, less a percentage which usually does not exceed 5 per cent. Such a cash-out may be spread equally over a period of ten years. Any unpaid balance in the fund will usually continue to be credited with interest at the guaranteed rate.

EXPERIENCE RATING

Whether a contract is issued by a stock or a mutual life insurance company, it is usually experience rated. Any rate credits or dividends resulting from this process are credited to the deposit administration fund and reduce the amount of deposits needed.

While there are differences in detail, the basic principles usually followed by insurance companies in experience rating are essentially the same. The experience fund of each case is credited with the deposits received and the interest rate allowed by the company to this class of contract. Since the assets arising from these contracts are commingled with the insurer's total assets, this interest rate represents the share of such contracts in the insurer's net interest earnings. The experience is then charged with the benefits paid and expenses incurred. The difference between the income and the charges is the experience rating fund.

Next, the "liabilities" of the deposit administration plan are determined. They consist of the actuarial and contingency reserves. The actuarial reserves are principally the liability of the insurance company because of the deposit administration fund and the reserves needed to pay any annuities already purchased for the employees. The contingency reserves are primarily a protection against possible, but not assumed, future developments which could result in larger payments on the part of the insurance company than anticipated. Any excess of the experience rating fund over the "liabilities" of the deposit administration plan is available as rate credits or dividends.

IMMEDIATE PARTICIPATION GUARANTEE

An immediate participation guarantee contract[3] is a form of deposit administration contract. As in the case of the latter, a fund is established, and deposits are made by the employer upon the advice of an actuary. The employer assumes responsibility for the adequacy of the fund to provide the benefits of the plan.

---

[3] Sometimes referred to as a "pension administration" or "direct-rated deposit administration" contract.

There are certain essential differences, however, between the normal type of deposit administration contract and an immediate participation one. Under the latter, there is no guarantee of a minimum rate of interest on the fund. Instead, interest at a rate on a basis described in the contract, generally closely related to the insurance company's net rate earned on its assets, is credited to the fund each year. Expenses incurred are similarly charged. When an employee retires, an annuity is normally not purchased.[4] Instead, the annuity payments are made directly out of the fund. In order to assure retired employees that their pensions will be paid as long as they live, these contracts contain a clause to the effect that if the fund should decrease to an amount just sufficient to purchase annuities at the rates specified in the contract for the retired employees, the fund shall immediately be applied for this purpose, and the "immediate participation" feature eliminated.

From the preceding, it is evident that there is no need to experience rate this type of contract in the usual manner, since the experience is immediately and automatically reflected each year through the procedures described. It is from this that the name "immediate participation guarantee" was derived.

It is general practice to offer this form of contract only to large-sized groups for which it is the insured counterpart of the self-insured plan. The insurance company guarantees, while of a qualitative nature, are nevertheless quite valuable and provide security of principal. It also has a known level of investment performance, and established standards of administrative and actuarial efficiency.

SUPPLEMENTARY DEPOSIT ADMINISTRATION

A deposit administration plan can be used very effectively in supplementing another pension plan. Under one arrangement, the basic plan provides for the current benefits and there is a deposit administration facility for past service benefits. Such an arrangement gives more flexibility in funding the past service benefits. The initial deposits can be based on anticipated labor turnover and less conservative interest and mortality assumptions, since the employer assumes responsibility for the adequacy of the fund. It is not necessary under this arrangement to allocate any of the deposits until an employee actually retires. In the event of discontinuance of contributions, the fund is available to be distributed on some pro rata basis among all the active employees. Under the normal group deferred annuity, all the premiums paid for past service usually have already been allocated on a "nearest to retirement age" basis.

---

[4] Some insurance companies do purchase annuities at the beginning of each year and then make adjustments at the end of the year, so that the effect is the same as if the annuities had not been purchased.

As an offset to these advantages, the use of a supplementary deposit administration plan for past service benefits with a basic group deferred annuity one for future service puts the plan on a hybrid basis, with only part of the benefits fully guaranteed. As in all pension planning, there is no one right way. The employer should select the funding basis which most nearly meets his individual requirements and desires.

Where there is a basic group deferred annuity plan with pensions based upon a definite formula, such as a certain percentage of each year's earnings during the employee's participation, a minimum pension benefit (which might be related to final pay, social security benefits, or other elements difficult to predict) may readily be supplied through a supplementary deposit administration plan. Since the need of providing for an additional pension to meet a minimum for any particular employee is difficult to predict, the flexibility of deposit administration funding is an excellent way of meeting this situation.

It is sometimes desired to provide a means of adjusting pension benefits to changes in cost of living. Here again, the flexibility of deposit administration funding provides an excellent way of accomplishing this through the establishment of a supplementary plan or minimum pension provision under which additional annuities would be provided in accordance with any increase in a recognized cost-of-living index.

A problem in most pension plans is to be able to retire some employees earlier than on the normal retirement date. Since an employee who retires early will not usually accrue his full benefits, a further actuarial reduction in his expected pension because of his early retirement often results in an inadequate income. A supplementary deposit administration plan provides a practical way of accumulating sufficient funds to allow larger pensions at early retirement than the actuarial equivalent.

It is desired under some pension plans to provide substantial death benefits through individual life insurance. This may be done by an arrangement so that when an employee retires, his ordinary life insurance under the individual policy pension trust or under a group permanent contract is converted to an annuity, with an additional annuity of sufficient amount being purchased from a supplementary deposit administration fund.

SEPARATE ACCOUNTS

A separate account[5] is a facility under which an employer may arrange with a life insurance company for the investment of pension funds arising from its own payments in an account operated separately from the general funds of the insurance company, on a basis which gives the employer the

[5] Also referred to as "segregated assets" and "flexible funding."

direct benefit of the investment experience of that account. Thus the income and gains or losses, realized or unrealized, from the assets in the account are credited to or charged against the account without regard to the other income, gains, or losses of the insurance company. The insurance company is not a trustee in such an arrangement. From a statutory standpoint the pension plan under which the employer makes his payments must be qualified under the Internal Revenue Code, and the annuities for retired employees must be fixed in amount.

The first separate account facilities underwritten by a United States life insurance company are generally considered to have been put into effect in 1961. This facility was the result of an increasing desire on the part of employers to invest a portion of their pension funds in equities. Before separate accounts could be offered generally, revisions in the federal tax laws were needed, permissive legislation had to be obtained from many states, and a decision from the Securities and Exchange Commission had to be secured exempting this medium of funding from its jurisdiction. Except for a few states, these barriers have been removed, and life insurance companies now have contracts available for almost every pension funding need.

A separate account facility is usually a part of a group deposit administration contract. The contract provides that the employer may allocate a portion of the pension plan contributions made under the contract to a separate investment account maintained by the insurance company with respect to this portion of its assets. The portion of the contributions which may be so allocated is usually subject to some maximum, such as one half or two thirds of total contributions. No employee contributions may be allocated to such account. The contributions not allocated to the separate account are usually allocated to a conventional deposit administration fund, with the principal and interest return guaranteed. At the time of retirement, sufficient amounts are withdrawn from this fund or the separate account to provide the annuity payments to which the employees are entitled under the pension plan. These annuities are fixed in amount and do not vary with investment experience, as is the case with variable annuities.

There are several types of separate accounts available. Under all of them the insurance company has the responsibility of deciding on the investments, and the only guarantee with respect to investment results is that the contributions allocated to the account will participate in its experience. An important type of this account is a pooled account. Each employer shares in the investment results in proportion to the size of its interest in the pooled account. The assets of this account are usually invested in equities, although the insurance company has some flexibility for other types of investment. Some companies offer several kinds of pooled accounts, so that an employer may select the type of investment he desires. Currently, these accounts are mainly for mortgages and bonds, in addition to equities. Where the annual payments into the account are large, some companies have individual separate accounts available in lieu of the pooled ones.

SPLIT FUNDING

Split funding is an arrangement under which one portion of the funding of a pension plan is on an insured basis and the other portion is on a trusteed basis. While the individual or group contracts which are generally issued for pension plans may be used for the insured portion, a great many of the pension plans on a split funding basis, particularly the larger ones, are funded through a combination deposit administration contract and a trust fund. The contract may be issued either directly to the employer or to the trust. In this latter event the contract becomes, in a sense, an asset of the trust.

Split funding is frequently used when an employer wishes to invest a portion of its pension funds in equities in a trust fund and still retain the other features of an insured plan. This may be accomplished in combination with a deposit administration plan. The balance of the deposits is paid to the deposit administration fund where it is commingled with the insurance company's assets for investment purposes. These investments are almost wholly of the fixed-dollar type. Insurance companies believe that in making investments of this kind, they are in a particularly advantageous position to obtain the highest returns. This is due to the fact that certain very favorable investment fields available to the insurance companies are not practical for trust funds. These include private placements with large corporations and the attendant savings in investment expenses, real estate, sale and lease-back arrangements, and mortgages on both city and farm property. Because of the magnitude of the investments made by an insurance company, it is able to maintain an experienced and competent investment department covering various fields for investments. This adds greatly to the flexibility of the insurance company, so that it can take full advantage of changes in the investment cycle. When investments in the mortgage field are more favorable than in the security markets, the bulk of its new investments can be made in that field, and vice versa.

Employers frequently desire to retain as many of the guarantees of an insured plan as possible, yet at the same time invest a portion of the pension funds through a trust. Split funding meets this need, since all the pension payments may be on a fully guaranteed basis through the purchase of single-premium annuities upon retirement. The principal of the funds invested in the deposit administration contract, as well as a minimum interest rate on these funds, is also guaranteed.

Insurance companies are well experienced in the administration of pension plans. They have offices in most of the fifty states, and this can be of considerable assistance in the payment of pensions to employees, who may be scattered widely after retirement. When employee contributions are involved, the guarantees of an insurance company are even more important. All of these advantages are available on a split funding basis.

SELECTED REFERENCES

ALVORD, MORGAN H. "Insured Pensions and Inflation," *Journal of the American Society of Chartered Life Underwriters,* Vol. XII, No. 4 (Fall, 1958).

BLACK, KENNETH, JR. *Group Annuities.* Philadelphia: University of Pennsylvania Press, 1955.

HAMILTON, JAMES A., and BRONSON, DORRANCE C. *Pensions.* New York: McGraw-Hill Book Co., Inc., 1958.

MCGILL, DAN M. *Fundamentals of Private Pensions.* 2d ed. Pension Research Council, Wharton School of Finance and Commerce, University of Pennsylvania. Homewood, Ill.: Richard D. Irwin, Inc., 1964.

Chapter 41

TRUST FUND PENSION PLANS

BY JAMES A. HAMILTON

A trust fund pension plan is an arrangement under which contributions to provide pension benefits are deposited with a trustee, normally a trust company, which invests the money, accumulates the earnings, and pays benefits directly to eligible employees. This chapter will deal with trust fund plans under which (1) the plan is definite, its specifications being set forth in a document adopted by the employer's board of directors, shareholders, or other responsible parties; (2) there is a definite trust agreement between the employer and a corporate trustee, or between the employer and individual trustees; (3) the plan and trust agreement are qualified under the appropriate sections of the Internal Revenue Code; and (4) there is substantial advance funding, and the trustee is responsible for investing and administering a growing corpus under the trust.[1]

Trust fund pension plans are widely used as private pension agencies. The trust fund antedates the insured fund in point of time. The number of participants covered by, and amount of assets implementing, trust fund pension plans considerably exceed their counterparts under insured pension plans. In point of number of plans, the insured plan is more frequently found because many small plans have been set up using the individual policy pension instrument.[2]

---

[1] See Chapter 38 for a treatment of individual policy pension plans, or what are often termed "pension trusts." Under such a plan the trustee normally acts solely as an intermediary between the employees (and the employer) covered under the plan and the insurer that issues the policies and contracts, and does not have responsibilities for investment of the contributions to the pension, nor necessarily for the payment of pension benefits. The student of pension matters will encounter the expressions "self-administered pension plan" and "self-administered trusteed plan," and will find them usually synonymous with the term "trust fund pension plan" as used here.

[2] See Chapter 38, "Individual Policy Pension Plans."

NATURE OF TRUST ARRANGEMENT

The Trust Agreement

The legal instrument which serves as the heart of the trust fund for pension plans is termed a trust agreement or trust indenture. In the trust agreement the duties and responsibilities of the trustees concerning the trust fund are spelled out. The trustee(s) may consist of one or more natural persons or (more frequently) a trust company or a bank having trust powers. Trustee responsibilities under a pension plan are varied; but in brief, they relate to the acceptance of the contributions to the pension plan, the investment and reinvestment of these contributions and other funds held in the trust, and the administration of the trust, including the disbursement of payments to beneficiaries.

The principal function of the trust agreement is to create the trust into which contributions flow and out of which benefits are disbursed. While the signing of the trust agreement by the interested parties—e.g., the employer and the trustee(s)—is an essential element, so also is the creation of a trust corpus by the contribution of an initial sum of money (perhaps a token amount).

The trust agreement usually includes provisions for amendments; for appointment of a successor trustee; for the keeping of necessary accounts; for irrevocability (insofar as contributions at hand are concerned); for payment of the trustee's expenses and fees; for distribution during the life of the trust, including the distribution of any funds allocated among participants upon termination of the plan; for protection of the trustee in case of loss to or diminution of the fund (in the absence of fault); and so forth.

A trust fund pension program, therefore, normally consists of two parts. One is the pension plan itself, which gives full information as to the type and magnitude of the benefits, conditions of eligibility for coverage under the pension plan, eligibility to receive benefit payments from the plan, and the many other provisions relating to the administration of the plan. The other is the trust agreement, which sets out the responsibilities of the trustee to whom the contributions under the pension plan are paid and by whom they are invested and the benefits disbursed. Sometimes, these two documents—the plan and the trust agreement—are combined into one; but in the majority of pension programs today, they are two separate instruments. An illustration of an advantage in having the instruments separate occurs in the event it becomes necessary to terminate the pension plan, since this step does not necessitate termination of the separate trust, which could continue to hold funds and pay them out in accordance with the provisions covering these payments.

Functions of the Trustee

Customarily, in a trust fund pension plan the trustee receives the money contributed by the employer or, if it is a contributory plan, by the employer and the employees jointly. The trustee then invests these funds according to the provisions of the trust agreement. Benefits are disbursed by the trustee when an employee retires, or when other payments are called for under the terms of the pension plan.

The trustee is constrained to operate the trust for the exclusive benefit of the employees participating in the pension plan.

In essence, these responsibilities are similar to the functions performed by a life insurance company under an insured funding instrument. Insurance company functions under pension plans have been detailed in other chapters of this *Handbook*.

Investment Powers of Trustee

The investment powers granted a trustee by the trust agreement are not the same in all instances. For example, the terms of the trust may be such as to restrict the trustee to certain types of investment, or they may grant complete freedom in the choice of investments (including investment in common trusts[3] administered by the trustee). Some trust agreements reserve to the employer (or his representatives, usually designated a "pension committee") the power to direct the investments to be purchased within such broad classes as may be specified in the trust; or the trustee may be given the authority to recommend investments to such committee, so that the committee may exercise its veto over any or all of such recommendations.

ESTABLISHMENT AND ADMINISTRATION OF A TRUST FUND PENSION PLAN

Early Considerations

In the actual operation of a trust fund plan, somewhat the same steps are taken as in the case of an insured plan. In considering the establishment of any pension plan (where an employer[4] is not obliged to set up a

[3] A "common trust" is a fund in which several trust funds have an interest. It results from the pooling of funds from the participating trusts, and thus extends the advantages of bulk purchasing of securities and the spreading of investment risk to a group of small pension trust funds.

[4] As used here, the term "employer" comprises management (which frequently initiates the action leading to consideration of a pension plan); the directors of the company, representing the stockholders, who sometimes initiate the action but in any event must approve of the action if initiated by management; and in a sense the stockholders, who have elected the directors and are represented by them. In some situations, depending on the bylaws of the company, the directors may authorize the

plan as, say, a result of negotiations with a union), the first consideration is logically to determine whether a pension plan is essential or desirable. In some situations, there may actually be a serious question as to whether the nature of the business is such as to justify the establishment of a pension plan. These early considerations concerning the economic position of the employer in relation to the fiscal requirements of a pension plan are fundamentally the responsibility of the employer, who calls on his accountants, legal counsel, and, frequently, a consulting actuary to evaluate his needs and capabilities in this direction. If the decision is to proceed, his next step is to acquaint himself with the benefits being offered by competitors in his industry and labor market. He must keep in mind the needs and wishes of his employees, and, through discussion with his directors, the attitude (and likelihood of approval) of his stockholders.

At this point, he needs to become familiar with rough cost indexes of various benefit possibilities. These his consulting actuary can provide. On the basis of these studies, he will decide on the type and level of benefits to include and on the actuarial cost method (contribution incidence) of his plan. The next major consideration is that of evaluating the relative merits of using the facilities of a life insurance company (in whole or in part) or of establishing a trust fund as the sole agency through which the plan will be funded.

Drafting of the Plan and Steps Related to Installation

Assume that the decision has been made to establish a trust fund for the funding of the pension plan. The next step is to draft the plan (the function of an attorney, either the employer's house counsel or outside counsel), with careful review by the consulting actuary to see that technical points are properly handled and equity is preserved among participants in the plan. The drafting of the trust agreement is also the responsibility of an attorney, with its final terms being subject to review and approval by the trustee (again, the trust agreement should be reviewed by the actuary for technicalities in his field). The communication of plan provisions to the participants (usually through a booklet describing the plan, conferences, and the distribution of other information of interest to employees) and the solicitation of those eligible (if the plan is contributory) are the next logical steps; these are the employer's proper functions. The clearance of the plan with the local district office of the Internal Revenue Service is also the function of the employer and his attorney; the actuary is responsible for the preparation of items required by the IRS which treat with actuarial liabilities under the plan and

establishment of a pension plan; but in others, specific approval of the stockholders is also required.

contribution levels. Forms required under the Federal Welfare and Pension Plans Disclosure Act, describing the plan and trust and operations under the program, must also be prepared by or for the employer.

The employer must set up administrative records and procedures, and obtain from the actuary appropriate reduction factors for early retirement, joint and survivor option factors, and other determinations relating to the substitution of one benefit for another actuarially equivalent one. Provision may be made for distributing, at annual intervals, announcements to participants showing the benefits accrued to date or benefits expected at retirement, amounts payable in the event of total and permanent disability or death, and other items of interest to participants.

Annual Valuations

The valuation of the plan for the purpose of determining the magnitude of the liabilities and the appropriate level of contributions is performed by the consulting actuary on the basis of actuarial assumptions he regards as appropriate, using the employee data assembled by the employer. The actuarial cost considerations relating to the intended incidence of contributions are recommended by the consulting actuary and approved or modified by the employer.

Determination of the current year's contribution to the trust is one of the main purposes of the valuation. The other main purpose of the valuation is to compare the liabilities of the plan with the assets held by the trust. Under a retrospective valuation the value of the benefits accrued to date is compared with the assets on hand, while under a prospective valuation the present value of all future benefits is measured against the assets on hand plus the present value of all contributions anticipated in the future. Under either type of actuarial valuation a variety of actuarial costing techniques may be considered for meeting the accruing liabilities under the plan. For example, these can vary from (1) the full payment at inception of the plan of all liability related to benefits credited in respect of service prior thereto (past service) with level contributions (in terms of dollars or per cent of covered payroll) annually thereafter; to (2) spreading (amortizing) over a period of years the past service cost, accompanied by annual contributions (level or otherwise) to fund each year's current service benefit; to (3) annual current service payments with no reduction in past service liability ("interest only"); to (4) payment only at retirement of the single-sum value of each participant's pension ("terminal funding"). Because of the differing effects on an employer's financial status (surplus and current earnings) and the need for preserving some reasonable degree of equity between present and future stockholders, it is essential that the employer be adequately informed as to the implications inherent in various costing approaches.

Actuarial Assumptions

In preparing his actuarial valuation, the actuary must select various assumptions: rates of mortality, both for active lives and for pensioners; rates of retirement, including disability; rates of termination of employment; assumed future salary scales; rate or rates of interest; and, sometimes, proportion of participants married, rates of remarriage, and such other actuarial assumptions as may be necessary, depending on the benefits and provisions contained in the plan. In a trust fund plan the selection of actuarial assumptions places a great degree of responsibility on the actuary, who draws upon his experience and professional judgment in selecting the factors he believes to be appropriate for the particular case. Usually, his selection is made with some degree of conservatism; but in certain circumstances, his function may be to select what he regards as realistic factors without any such margin. This flexibility to select from among various actuarial cost methods and to choose actuarial factors has long been present in the trust fund pension plan.

Expenses

The establishment and administration of any pension plan involves certain expenses. In the case of a trust fund pension plan, these expenses include:

1. The fees charged by the trustee for investment services, disbursement of benefits, and such other functions as the trustee may perform.
2. The fees of the attorney for drafting the plan and trust agreement, his assistance in obtaining approval of the plan from the Internal Revenue Service, and such other functions as he may perform.
3. The fees of the actuary, which initially cover his assistance with the development and design of the plan; his review of the plan and trust agreement as drafted; his determination of the actuarial liabilities under the plan and the appropriate levels of contributions; his assistance with IRS clearance; and his participation in assembling material required under the Federal Welfare and Pension Plans Disclosure Act, and preparation of announcements to employees.
4. Accounting fees where the employer has called upon outside accounting services for assistance (usually in connection with the matter of the effect of a pension plan on his profit status, and the treatment of pension plan contributions and liabilities in his annual statement and tax returns).

These services and the related expenses are not peculiar to trust fund plans but are found under any type of pension plan, whether they are paid separately from the contributions made to the plan (generally the situation with trust fund plans) or are included (as is the case of certain insured plans) as a part of the contribution level and, as to investment expenses, applied against the gross interest rate earned. The trustee customarily determines its expenses as a percentage of the assets held in trust, with the percentage rate declining as the assets increase. (There are other arrangements, too; for example, some trustees determine their fees as a percentage of the income of the trust.) Legal fees and accounting fees are determined according to the usual arrangements the employer may have with counsel and auditors. Actuarial fees are generally related to the amount of time spent, although in some instances they are based on the number of employees, with the charge per employee declining as the number of employees increases. No commissions are payable, nor are any federal or state taxes involved under trust fund pension plans.

In total, these various expenses normally represent but a small percentage of the contributions and investment income. Also, except for the trustee's fees (or investment expenses of the insurance company), which increase as the investment work increases with the pension fund growth, the other fees in years after the first tend to be lower than in the initial year. Of course, with smaller cases the fees tend to be a larger percentage of the contributions than with larger plans. Under any plan the employer must also be prepared to meet some modest additional cost in his own internal operation attributable to the added functions of keeping records, providing actuarial data, and furnishing assistance in the preparation of governmental filings.

Conversion to Trust Fund Financing

During the last decade or two, many employers have converted their pension plans, in whole or in part, to trust fund financing. In part, this was done because of various economies that could be effected thereby—in some cases, through a reduction in expense; and in most, through the possibility of capital gains or an increase in yield on invested funds. In many instances, it was believed that certain simplifications in the plan design and provisions would derive from trust fund financing.

TABLE 41-1

DISTRIBUTION OF INVESTMENTS BY TYPE IN TRUST FUND PENSION PLANS AND IN LIFE INSURANCE COMPANIES

	Trust Fund*	Insured†
United States government securities	7.7%	4.6%
Corporate bonds	43.6	38.7
Preferred and common stock	38.7	4.7
Mortgages	3.8	35.2
Other assets	6.2	16.8
	100.0%	100.0%

* Book value basis: Table 5 of Securities and Exchange Commission Release #S-1902.
† Commissioners' valuation basis: Total assets of United States life insurance companies (Institute of Life Insurance, *Life Insurance Fact Book* [New York, 1963]).

Investments

The distribution of investments of trust fund pension (and profit sharing) plans may be observed from Table 41–1. It will be noted that the distribution is quite different from that of life insurance companies, and the valuation bases differ as well.

The point of particular interest in Table 41–1 is the substantial percentage of assets implementing trust fund plans that are invested in equities. (If this table had been prepared with assets on the market value rather than the cost basis, the percentage would no doubt have been even higher.)

FURTHER FEATURES OF TRUST FUND PLANS[5]

Guarantees

By its very nature, the trust fund cannot make guarantees of any sort, excepting only that the trustee agrees to perform its duties to the best of its ability. If then, for some reason, contributions to the trust should be curtailed or discontinued, the trustee's function is to see that the available funds are applied to the intended purposes, in accordance with the provisions of the plan and the trust instrument.

As in most controversial topics, the question of whether a trust gains or loses by its inability to offer any guarantees over and beyond the capacity of the funds implementing a particular pension plan is a moot one. It would be difficult to dispute the fact that some form of guarantee of the principal of the trust fund, or some form of guarantee that a pension once commenced would be continued during a pensioner's lifetime, is desirable. Nevertheless, in any business transaction a guarantee is not without cost. If the asset values implementing a pension plan are to be guaranteed against diminution because of market vagaries, then any required supplementation of these assets must be made up from some source. If the guarantee is that pension payments will continue, and if the assets of the pension fund should not be adequate for this purpose, then they, too, must be augmented from another source.

Since each trust fund pension plan is completely independent of every

[5] Any objective presentation of the features of one particular form of pension funding is a most perplexing assignment. The textbook *Pensions* (New York: McGraw-Hill Book Co., Inc., 1958) was jointly authored by the writer of this chapter and his associate, Dorrance C. Bronson. When it was issued, the authors were taken to task by a number of insurance company executives because, it was claimed, we had favored trust funds in our presentation. Simultaneously, several representatives of trust companies stated we had favored the insured product. There is no known way of offering any presentation satisfactory to all groups.

other one, there is no way whereby one plan can be charged to subsidize another plan toward its obligations. In other words, if there should be an asset loss experienced by one plan, another plan or group of plans cannot be charged to make up that loss.[6] Similarly, if the mortality experience under one plan is in excess of what the actuary contemplated when he selected his mortality table(s) for the determination of contributions and reserves under the plan, all gains from this source belong wholly to that plan and cannot be diverted from that plan to pay for the poor experience under another plan where the mortality assumptions may have lacked conservatism in the light of hindsight.

It is the opinion of this writer that where larger pension plans are concerned, the trend—regardless of funding agency—is toward de-emphasizing guarantees in favor of greater recognition of the actual experience of each such individual plan.

Flexibility

Because each trust fund is completely independent of all other trust funds, a great deal of flexibility is possible in designing a pension plan to be so financed. Such flexibility applies to the basic benefit design, to the provision of supplementary benefits, to the costing method, and to the investment media (because what is done under one trust fund plan does not in any way affect any other). Furthermore, because there is no need to protect guarantees, the contributions deemed appropriate for a specified benefit structure sometimes may be relatively favorable. On the other hand, some students of this subject feel that the creation of a contingency fund as a part of the trust fund would have particular merit. Be this as it may, present IRS rules and regulations discourage this course of action.

The above features of the trust fund plan are no longer completely unique because insurance companies, having gradually come to recognize certain advantages of trust fund techniques, have adopted many of these principles insofar as they were permissible by state law, even though this meant some departure from the traditional insurance company guarantees.

History seems to lend support to the long-run advantages of equity investment in a pension fund portfolio. Since there is no way to remove all of the uncertainties in the funding of a pension plan, to place too much emphasis on guarantees at the expense of substantial potential asset growth could prove quite costly to the employer.

Variable Annuity Plans

Because of inflation and its effect on purchasing power of fixed pension dollars, there has been a movement of modest proportions toward what,

[6] An exception is where several plans are on a "pooled basis" for actuarial and investment experience, e.g., certain multiemployer union arrangements.

for convenience, may be termed "variable annuity" pension plans (see following chapter). In a variable annuity plan the funds implementing the plan are invested in equities, and the pensions paid will fluctuate in accordance with changes in the market value of these investments. Some insurance companies have displayed great interest in this line of activity, while others have strongly opposed variable annuities. Only a few small insurance companies have been established to provide variable annuities, and the laws in several "key" states militate, to date, against insurance companies in general offering this type of business. (There are some problems at the federal level as well.) There are no state or federal laws that operate to discourage the use of trust funds as the vehicle for a variable annuity, and, as a result, quite a number of "variable annuities" have been successfully established using trust fund financing.

Cost-of-Living Adjustments

Cost-of-living pensions provide, in essence, that the benefit received by a retired employee will be adjusted from time to time as the consumer price index changes. Here again, the amount of the pension is not fixed but varies with economic conditions. This type of benefit is only infrequently found[7] in private pension plans. It has been described as being, in effect, tantamount to having an employer "sign a blank check," because, regardless of what the consumer price index might be in the future, the employer would under such a plan undertake to provide benefits to all of his then pensioners in an amount determined according to a base year adjusted by the change in the consumer price index subsequent to that base year. On the other hand, if the pension fund is invested to a considerable degree in equities, long-range cost protection may be afforded the employer, and there could be a closer correspondence between pensions and living costs than exists under variable annuities. Although not widespread, this type of plan, again, is one that may be readily handled through trust fund financing.

Ancillary Benefits

There are many other features of pension plans frequently found in trust fund pension plans. One example is widows' and dependents' pension benefits (more popular in Europe than here, where so much group life insurance exists). Death benefits may also be included, which, although they must satisfy the condition imposed by the IRS that they be

---

[7] In 1962 the Civil Service Retirement Plan was amended to provide cost-of-living adjustments to pensioners under that plan, but without establishing the means to finance it.

incidental to the pension benefit, may be sizable.[8] Medical benefits to retired employees may be established as part of a pension plan (even though this benefit also must be of "incidental" value and the fund accumulated on its behalf must be accounted for separately from the regular pension benefit fund).

Spread Funding, Special Options, Flexibility of Contribution Levels

The funding of pension benefits for persons already retired on a quasi "pay as you go" basis may be easily handled under a trust fund plan through what is sometimes described as "spread funding." Special reduction factors that are not true actuarial equivalents may be used for early retirements, and for joint and survivor options in those instances where some special treatment (uniform for all employees) is desired. For example, under a trust fund plan, it is entirely feasible to permit an employee to elect a joint and survivor option within a year prior to retirement, or within one month of retirement, or even right up to retirement. Because of the opportunities for "antiselection" in such special arrangements, added costs will arise, and these can be easily recognized in the contribution levels under a trust fund pension plan. Variations in contribution levels from year to year to reflect changes in the profit position of the employer are readily handled within the limits of actuarial soundness.

Mergers

In the merger of two companies, each with a trust fund pension plan, it is comparatively simple to combine the two plans into one, while preserving the relative equities of the two groups of employees, by transferring funds from one trustee to another (or from both trustees to a third). The experience of the writer is that this step is facilitated if both funds are trusteed.

Utilization of Insurance Contracts

There are situations where it may be advantageous for a trust fund to utilize insured funding instruments. For example, when a plan is terminated and the available assets are allocated among the retired and applicable nonretired employees in accordance with the terms of the plan, then these funds may be used to purchase benefits from an insurance company, with the trust fund plan being then completely wound up.

Trust funds have been frequently used in direct association with in-

---

[8] The Revenue Act of 1964, by requiring that any group insurance in excess of $50,000 be either paid for by the employee or its cost be taxable to the employee, could result in the addition of death benefits to a greater degree than before to trust fund pension plans. Proceeds, payable on death, from a trust fund pension plan are taxed somewhat differently than if payable under a regular group life insurance policy. The tax treatment is more favorable in some instances and less favorable in others.

sured contracts in the financing of pension plans. For example, in many "pension trust" plans, individual life insurance policies are used to provide values at retirement age for a portion of the pension benefit then due, with separate contributions being made to an auxiliary trust fund designed so that as retirement age is reached, the two pieces of benefit will be precisely the amount provided under the pension plan's formula. In many instances, provision is made for sufficient assets to be transferred at retirement from the trust to the insurance company, so that the pension benefit is provided in its entirety through insured funding instruments.

In some instances, a trust fund has been used in association with a group annuity, usually of the deposit administration type. In such a case the employer splits his contributions into two parts, and assigns one part to one funding instrument and the balance to the other. Either this separation is performed according to a predetermined allocation, or it is varied according to the investment climate at the time the contributions are made. (Normally, certain prescribed minimum levels of funding are required under the deposit administration contract.)

A trust fund may utilize the services currently being offered by some insurers as an investment medium for a portion of the trust assets. For example, in a small- or medium-sized trust fund plan an insurance company may be prepared to offer investments in widely distributed mortgages or in certain large issues of privately placed bonds on a more favorable basis than could a trustee purchasing only for a single trust (although the development of common trusts for pooling pension plan investments tends to counter this consideration). Under these circumstances the employer may suggest that the trustee use an insurer's facilities for the investment of such portion of the assets as the insurance company could advantageously handle, relative to the portion advantageously invested by the trustee. These examples are merely illustrative of the great degree of flexibility possible where a trust fund is used in the funding of pension plan benefits.

Investment in Employer's Securities

While a qualified trust may not regularly carry on a trade or business if it is to preserve its tax-exempt status, it is possible for it to invest, if done at arm's length and within limits as to amount, in the securities of the employer creating the trust (including under certain conditions a corporate employer's unsecured debentures). To satisfy the restrictions imposed by the Internal Revenue Service with regard to "prohibited transactions," such investment must be made prudently on the basis of fair market value, offer a fair rate of return, and not affect the liquidity of the trust so as to impair the ability of the plan to meet its obligations. Any such investment in the employer's securities must be disclosed on a form designed by the Internal Revenue Service (Form 990–P).

Upon retirement an employee covered under a trust fund plan may obtain his full equity value in one sum if the plan so provides, and be taxed on the amount received (over and beyond his own contributions, if any) on a capital gains basis. If the employer's contributions have been partly invested in company stock and this stock is turned over to him, he is not taxable on any part of the gain in value of the stock until he sells it (and if he holds the stock until death occurs, it may be completely free of income tax).

A qualified trust may also loan funds directly to the employer, but only upon the receipt of adequate security and at a reasonable rate of interest. If properly written, it may make loans in a nondiscriminatory manner to participants in the plan who are not officers, shareholders, supervisors, or persons "highly compensated." Under certain conditions, and within reasonable limits, it may loan funds on a first trust deed to the employer to assist him in financing real estate needed in his business.

All of these transactions with the trust must be carefully handled in order to satisfy the rather strict requirements set up by the Internal Revenue Service, with the "prudent-man rule" being observed by trustees in the conduct of their business.

Use of Trust Funds for Small Plans

The trust fund has been used for many small plans (i.e., those covering relatively few employees). For many years, some consultants were reluctant to recommend trust funds for small groups of employees; but as time went on and the nature of the risk incidental to trust fund financing became better understood, this reluctance tended to disappear. In some measure, this may have been because of the knowledge that a trust fund plan may utilize insurance company funding instruments under situations where this is advantageous (e.g., in the event of the winding-up of a plan, or where there is a disproportionate amount of pension concentrated on one or more employees). In large measure, this probably has been because of (1) the flexibility possible in such a course; (2) a change in investment philosophy, making equity-type securities (growth potential) more popular, which until recently had been possible only through a trust fund plan; and (3) the availability, as noted earlier, of common trust funds in which equities are held and which admit of greater diversification than would be possible for a small fund investing on its own.

To some extent, this expansion in number of trust fund plans resulted from an appreciation that pensions are quite different from life insurance, under which there is always a chance of a heavy loss arising in a very short interval (such as would be related to a major catastrophe). In pensions, there are also opportunities for losses; but insofar as these are related to mortality, they generally arise very gradually over a period of years. The major risk in pensions lies in the asset side, where contributions made under a small pension plan could be subjected to serious and sudden loss if they were invested in a portfolio lacking diversification, with some of the investments turning out to be imprudent. Even here, though, it must be borne in mind that if a continuing plan is fairly well funded, any decline in assets because of unfavorable market conditions does not necessarily seriously affect the long-range financial position of the trust fund plan. Assets are usually carried at cost, or amortized cost. In relation to the fund the current disbursements to the pensioners are usually small and are substantially met from current contributions and/or from the interest earned on the fund accumulation. Accordingly, if the market ultimately recovers, no permanent harm need have been done. If, on the other hand, a plan must be terminated while the assets are still depressed in value, then pension benefits could be adversely affected.

During a period of inflation, employers seem to become less concerned with possible loss of capital than they are with the fact that their pension fund capital is not growing at least partly in step with the inflationary trend. If an employer's pension plan funding has not included some equity-type investments, he may have suffered in comparison with those that do in a period of inflation.

Finally, insurance companies may have influenced the trend toward trust fund plans for smaller cases by reducing the number of employees required under the deposit administration types of group annuity contract (which is primarily an investment medium without mortality guarantees until retirement). Originally, these deposit administration contracts were restricted to a minimum of 1,000 employees; but then, in succession, this requirement was reduced to 500, to 200, to 100; and now, in some companies, apparently no minimum number is required.

CONCLUSIONS

As a vehicle for funding private pension plans, the trust fund has been in use ever since it was first found desirable to separate pension funds from the liabilities, capital, or surplus of the employer's balance sheet. Trust funds are not in a position to offer guarantees either as to preservation of capital or as to continuation of benefits; but through sound actuarial planning, prudent programs of investment, and the fact that risks are spread over a considerable period of years, trust fund plans have prospered. If, for some reason, it appears advantageous for a particular trust fund to utilize insurance company funding instruments, it is, of course, always possible to do so.

Trust funds became increasingly popular as their attributes, of which the most important are flexibility and economy, became more generally understood. Partly because of the absence of federal and state income taxes where trust funds are held for qualified pension and profit sharing plans, and partly because of other economies resulting from their ability to invest in equities, they have provided benefits at relatively favorable cost.

Recently, some states have amended the insurance laws so that life insurance companies can purchase, within limits and subject to SEC rules, equity-type investments for insured pension plans. Also, in recent years, substantial reductions have been effected in the federal income tax on funds held by insurance companies for qualified pension plan purposes. The extent to which these recent changes will affect the relative popularity of trust funds in comparison with insurance company contracts as instruments for funding pension plans remains to be seen.

SELECTED REFERENCES

AMERICAN FEDERATION OF LABOR AND CONGRESS OF INDUSTRIAL ORGANIZATIONS. *Pension Plans under Collective Bargaining.* Publication # 132. Washington, D.C., 1964.

BRONSON, DORRANCE C. *Concepts of Actuarial Soundness in Pension Plans.* Pension Research Council, Wharton School of Finance and Commerce, University of Pennsylvania. Homewood, Ill.: Richard D. Irwin, Inc., 1957.

BUREAU OF NATIONAL AFFAIRS, INC. *Pensions and Profit Sharing.* Washington, D.C., 1953.

COUPER, WALTER J., and VAUGHAN, ROGER. *Pension Planning—Experience and Trends.* New York: Industrial Relations Counselors, Inc., 1954.

HAMILTON, JAMES A., and BRONSON, DORRANCE C. *Pensions.* New York: McGraw-Hill Book Co., Inc., 1958.

McGILL, DAN M. *Fundamentals of Private Pensions.* 2d ed. Pension Research Council, Wharton School of Finance and Commerce, University of Pennsylvania. Homewood, Ill.: Richard D. Irwin, Inc., 1964.

McGILL, DAN M. (ed.). *Pensions: Problems and Trends.* S. S. Huebner Foundation for Insurance Education, University of Pennsylvania. Homewood, Ill.: Richard D. Irwin, Inc., 1955.

WEISS, WILLARD A. "A Critical Analysis of Trustee and Insurance Company Administered Employee Retirement Plans," *Proceedings: Conference of Actuaries in Public Practice,* Vol. V (1955–56).

Chapter 42

VARIABLE ANNUITIES

BY WILLIAM C. GREENOUGH

Since its introduction in 1952, the variable annuity has become a much debated issue in insurance circles, reminiscent of the controversial appearance of the group concept a half century ago. The battle line is drawn between those who would like to see life insurance companies issue variable annuities to the general public and those who do not believe they should be issued at all, or at least not by life insurance companies. Subsequently, several new life insurance companies were established to do primarily a variable annuity business, and legislation was adopted in some states to authorize existing life insurance companies to offer variable annuities. As this chapter is written, in 1964, there are indications that major life insurance companies may soon be able to offer variable annuities, at least on a limited basis.

BACKGROUND

For decades—actually centuries—prior to the development of the variable annuity, the conventional approach in issuing annuities was that the insurer would guarantee the insured, for an agreed consideration, an income of a specified amount to begin at a convenient date and to continue for as long as the insured lived. The primary purpose was to assure the insured, through the principle of risk sharing, that he could have the largest income possible from his investments without any danger of outliving his income. The amount was specified in "the coin of the realm"—dollars, pounds, francs, rubles, marks. To accept the long-term risks of guaranteeing specified benefits, the insurer had to safeguard the reserves held against these risks by investing the funds "conservatively," that is, in a manner designed to protect the number of dollars assured, without concern as to the purchasing power of the dollars. Since capital values, interest, mortality, and expense—the actuarial ingredients of the annuity—were fixed obligations, the prudent insurer needed to maintain at least a minimum fixed return on his investments. In most cases the fixed return was provided by bonds and mortgages, with perhaps a small amount of stocks and real estate.

The suitability of the fixed-dollar annuity alone to provide retirement income assumes that the value of the dollar will remain relatively stable. On the other hand, the variable annuity rests on the assumption that the value of the dollar is likely to vary from time to time, probably both upward and downward. It shifts the emphasis from fixed-dollar guarantees to the need of retired individuals for more stable purchasing power. The variable annuity insurer provides the insured individual, for an agreed consideration, a dollar income based on the current value of a fixed number of *units* for as long as he lives. While the number of units is guaranteed, the current value of each unit is based on the performance of a fund generally composed of equity-type investments, rather than debt securities.

Definition

Thus a variable annuity is an annuity providing periodic payments, the dollar amount of each payment being determined from period to period primarily in accordance with the then current earnings and market value of a portfolio of equity assets, especially common stocks.

HOW A VARIABLE ANNUITY WORKS

The variable annuity principle can be applied in different ways. Its earliest and undoubtedly its most extensive use so far has been in the academic world, where the College Retirement Equities Fund (CREF) has been issuing variable annuities for faculty and staff members of institutions of higher education since 1952.

Although many provisions of the CREF variable annuity contract are designed specifically to meet the needs of educators, the basic principles of the CREF annuity are fairly similar to those of other variable annuities now being issued and in the proposal stages. Therefore, a description of how the CREF annuity works should provide some general idea of the techniques employed for variable annuities, as well as the underlying philosophy. However, actuarial and other technical aspects, as well as the terminology and the mechanics, can be quite different in other variable annuity plans.

CREF's part in the college professor's retirement program begins when he elects to have up to half of his future retirement savings (including his employer's contributions) placed in CREF. The rest goes to a fixed-dollar annuity provided by Teachers Insurance and Annuity Association. When the professor retires, he receives two lifetime annuities—one from TIAA, the other from CREF. The TIAA annuity provides a guaranteed, fixed-dollar retirement income that does not change in amount from year to year except as increased by dividends. The CREF annuity provides an income that varies year by year, reflecting the performance of the securities in CREF's portfolio.

The CREF annuity may best be understood by considering separately the premium payment, or accumulation stage, and the benefit payment, or annuity stage. There is one portfolio of assets, comprising the overall CREF fund. While accounting methods are used to divide this fund into two divisions, corresponding to the two stages and known as the accumulation fund and the annuity fund, there is no segregation of assets between these divisions. Largely for recording and reporting purposes, use is made in the CREF system of the terms "accumulation unit" and "annuity unit," but other methods can be used to account for the individual's interest in the fund.

Accumulation Stage

During this stage the participant and usually his employing college or university pay premiums to CREF month by month; and for each premium paid, the contract is credited with a number of accumulation units. The number of units credited varies from month to month. The accumulation fund is valued once each month, using closing stock market prices for the last day of the month. This total value is then divided by the number of outstanding accumulation units to determine the value of one accumulation unit. For a given premium, fewer units are credited when stock prices and consequently unit values are high; in a depressed market, unit values are lower, and more units are credited for the same premium. Additional accumulation units are credited to the individual's CREF certificate for investment income received by the fund.

Annuity Stage[1]

When an individual retires, his accumulation units are converted into annuity units. To determine the number of annuity units payable to the individual each month for the remainder of his life, the total current value of his accumulation units is divided by the product of the then current value of one annuity unit and an annuity factor that depends upon his age and the type of annuity selected. The number of annuity units, as then determined, remains constant for his lifetime; his retirement income at any one time will depend on the current value of the annuity unit multiplied by the number of annuity units to his credit.

Unlike the CREF accumulation unit, which is revalued once a month, the value of the CREF annuity unit is recomputed only once each year, so that the annuitant may budget his income closely for a year at a time.

---

[1] Robert M. Duncan, "A Retirement System Granting Unit Annuities and Investing in Equities," *Transactions of the Society of Actuaries,* Vol. IV, No. 9 (1952).

Valuation of the CREF annuity unit seems complex, but changes in the value of an annuity unit merely reflect changes in common stock prices and dividend payments, mortality experience, and expense items. Changes in the value of the CREF annuity unit result predominantly from changes in common stock performance, for CREF experience on the other factors, including mortality, is quite stable.

Other Variable Annuity Plans

The growth of CREF in the very special circumstances of college employment has been phenomenal, and this has been followed by adoption of variable annuities outside the college world. This growth has been diverse, as witness the four distinct headings under which such plans may be classified:

1. The CREF plan, limited to nonprofit educational institutions.
2. Trust-administered pension plans—most variable annuity plans in industry and in financial employments fall into this category.
3. Annuity contracts available from the few variable annuity life insurance companies selling to individuals and employers.
4. The variable annuity program offered state employees under the Wisconsin Retirement Fund.

In addition to the above, legislation has been adopted in some states under which variable annuities may be provided through the media of existing life insurance companies or through subsidiaries established by them. The Prudential Insurance Company of America took an early and prominent role in these efforts.

WHY THE VARIABLE ANNUITY?

Interest in the problem of inflation as it affects pensions arose after World War II. The inflationary situation brought home to many people for the first time what inflation is and how it can affect long-term, fixed-dollar savings. The spectacular growth of relatively new methods of saving, such as the mutual funds, and the expansion of credit may be due in some part to an effort by the public to "adjust" in some measure to inflation. Unfortunately, there was one segment of our society which found itself defenseless against the ravaging effect of inflation on money values. It was concern with this group—retired people with fixed incomes—that led to the development of the variable annuity by Teachers Insurance and Annuity Association of America.

TIAA had been established in 1918 by the Carnegie Foundation for the Advancement of Teaching and the Carnegie Corporation of New York to provide annuities and life insurance especially designed to meet the needs of educational organizations and their staff members. Inherent in its unique origin was the responsibility to provide college and university staff members with the greatest possible security available through insurance. To the college professor, with his low salary scale and lack of industry's profit sharing, stock option, and bonus plans, inflation posed a serious threat to retirement security. During the post-World War II period, TIAA undertook a comprehensive survey of the whole problem.

There was little question as to what the retired professor needed: It was an adequate income in terms of purchasing power. TIAA concluded that the most feasible approach to a solution of the problem would be to include equity investments along with fixed-dollar investments in a new

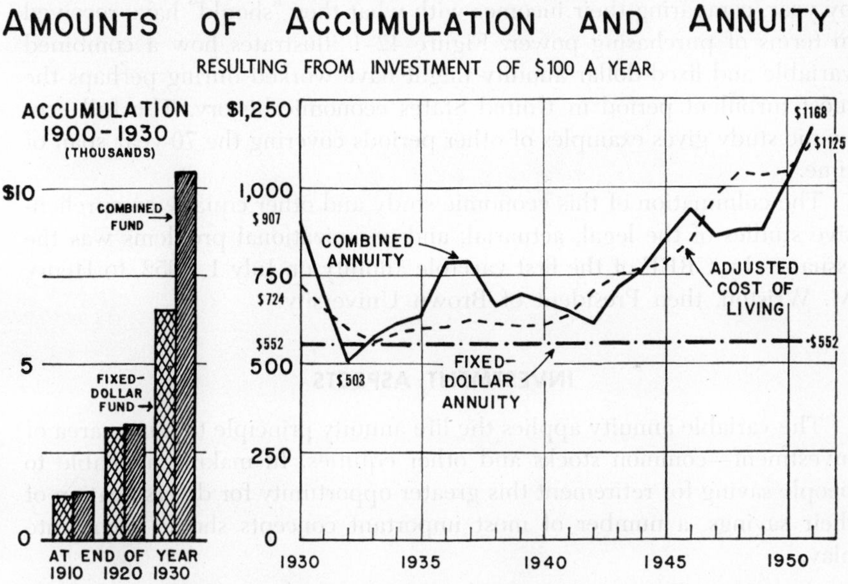

Fig. 42–1. Illustrative comparison of performance of fixed-dollar fund with combined fixed-dollar and common stock fund.

structure for retirement income. Substantial long-term correlation between a combined common stock and fixed-dollar fund, and the cost of living, was indicated through extensive research, including analysis of common stock indexes, comparison of stock indexes with cost-of-living indexes, comparison of various investment methods, and study of the performance of traditional methods of saving for old-age income. To test the hypothetical experience of variable annuities during different periods and economic conditions, illustrative "funds" were established beginning as early as 1880 and with annuities running through 1951.

Figure 42–1, derived from a comparison of performance of a fixed-dollar fund with that of a combined fixed-dollar and common stock fund, illustrates the retirement income picture for two individuals under the sample retirement plans.[2] In this case the two individuals "joined" their plans at age 35 in 1900, contributed premiums of $100 a year to their age 65 in 1930, and then retired, reaching age 85 in 1950. One contributed solely to a conventional fixed-dollar annuity; the other contributed half his premium to a fixed-dollar annuity, the other half to an equities fund annuity. At the end of the 30-year accumulation period in 1930, based on life insurance company net yields, the first individual would have accumulated a total of $6,499. Using indexes of common stock net yields and capital gains and losses for the equity fund portion, the combined fund would have accumulated $10,469 for the second individual. During retirement years, Figure 42–1 indicates the income for the two individuals year by year, comparing their incomes with what they "should" have received in terms of purchasing power. Figure 42–1 illustrates how a combined variable and fixed-dollar annuity might have worked during perhaps the most turbulent period in United States economic history. The full economic study gives examples of other periods covering the 70-year span of time.

The culmination of this economic study and other equally comprehensive studies of the legal, actuarial, and organizational problems was the issuance by CREF of the first variable annuity on July 1, 1952, to Henry M. Wriston, then President of Brown University.

INVESTMENT ASPECTS

The variable annuity applies the life annuity principle to a new area of investment—common stocks and other equities. In making available to people saving for retirement this greater opportunity for diversification of their savings, a number of most important concepts should come into play.

The Balancing Concept

Most students of the variable annuity are in agreement that an individual's retirement savings should be balanced between equity and fixed-dollar investments, i.e., balanced between the variable annuity and the conventional annuity. This was a major finding of the economic study of a 70-year period referred to in the previous section and was spelled out in the study's first three general conclusions:[3]

1. It is unwise to commit *all* of one's retirement savings to dollar obligations, since decreases in the purchasing power of the dollar can seriously reduce the value of a fixed-income annuity. Increases in the purchasing power of

---

[2] William C. Greenough, *A New Approach to Retirement Income* (New York: Teachers Insurance and Annuity Association of America, 1951), p. 23.

[3] *Ibid.*, p. 13.

the dollar, on the other hand, improve the status of the owner of a fixed-income annuity.

2. It is equally unwise to commit *all* of one's retirement savings to equity investments, since variations in prices of common stocks are much too pronounced to permit full reliance on them for the stable income needed during retirement. Changes in the value of common stocks and other equities are by no means perfectly correlated with cost-of-living changes, but they have provided a considerably better protection against inflation than have debt obligations.
3. Contributions to a retirement plan that are invested partly in debt obligations and partly in common stocks through an equities fund providing lifetime unit annuities offer promise of supplying retirement income that is at once reasonably free from violent fluctuations in amount and from serious depreciation through price level changes.

In trusteed variable annuity plans covering groups of employees, the concept of balance has generally been carried out by arranging that no more than half the pension contributions for each person can be placed on a variable basis, as is done in the TIAA–CREF system.

Especially in discussing variable annuities available to individuals, there are differences of opinion as to whether balance should be made compulsory by the insurer or by law, or merely stressed as desirable. If the insurer is to require the establishment and continuation of balanced savings, there are essentially two ways in which this may be done—through control of funds or through control of policies. Under the first method the annuitant would receive a single contract, but with supporting funds invested in both debt obligations and equities. The second method involves the issuance and continuance of two contracts, one a fixed-dollar annuity contract and the other a variable annuity contract.

Another approach to balancing would require individual programing only at the time of issuance of the variable annuity. The insurer would underwrite each applicant in order that provisions made for income on a variable basis would not exceed provisions made for income payable on a fixed-dollar basis, such as an individual's existing annuities, pension plan expectations, permanent life insurance, and other sources of anticipated fixed income at the time the variable annuity is issued.

Social security benefits are neutral in this connection. It is highly unlikely that OASDI benefits will ever be decreased. Hence, they provide a hedge against deflation and depression. In the event of inflation, it is highly likely that the benefits will be increased, so they provide a hedge against inflation. OASDI thus itself is a "balanced" plan for the level of benefits it provides and should not affect the "balance" of the supplementary retirement plan.

Investment Approach

From the standpoint of the individual annuity owner, probably the most vital decisions made by any issuer of variable annuities will be those prescribing and carrying out the investment policy. The investment of variable annuity pension funds involves some of the same questions involved in the formation of existing capital investment programs. The point to be emphasized, however, is that variable annuities comprise investment of funds to be used for retirement security, not short-term or speculative objectives.

A summary of some of the questions to be resolved should suggest the variations possible in the investment approach of different issuers of variable annuities.

Type of Investment. Probably because of the widespread utilization of common stocks in existing funds, the general impression is that investment for variable annuities automatically means investment in a common stock portfolio. However, most of the pension plans have a wide latitude, and could make use of preferred stocks, real estate, and other equity-type investments. Furthermore, should an annuity company carry out the balanced investment concept through a single contract, it would be essential that it have access to both debt and equity investments. Consequently, management must select the types which seem most suitable for its investment approach.

Diversification. Assuming that variable annuity plans will continue to be invested primarily in common stocks, proper diversification will be important. For example, to what extent will the company emphasize diversification among industries and individual companies? How many and what industries should be represented: oils, chemicals, utilities, retail trade, automobile, electrical equipment, and the like? How many different companies—30, 60, 150—will provide a list large enough for adequate diversification but small enough to permit continual portfolio review? Will the company encourage the individual to reap the benefits of "diversification over time" by encouraging consistent, periodic investment?

Yield versus Capital Gain. Another question that will be asked is whether capital gains or yield should be the major objective. The structure of the variable annuity is such that total gain, that is, the combined performance including both yield and capital items, is the important consideration. A high-yield, low-growth stock thus can be just as good an investment as its opposite. Tax considerations also enter in, but should not unduly influence the investment decisions in this connection.

To "Time" or Not to "Time." If a company is to follow the balanced investment concept, the method it selects for maintaining the balance will influence the method of investment. For a retirement plan such as TIAA–CREF, which maintains a balance through separate contracts, each with its own investments, dollar cost averaging is exceedingly effective. This method consists of investing approximately equal amounts (for each participant) in stocks at regular intervals of time so that the average cost of shares purchased is lower than the average price over the same period of time. On the other hand, a company which intends to maintain a balanced program utilizing one contract might select a "formula-timing" plan. These are plans in which ratios are maintained between stocks and bonds in an attempt to take advantage of broad market swings. The theory is that stocks will be sold and bonds purchased on a formula basis as stock prices advance, the reverse being true as stock prices decline. This ratio between equities and fixed investments might be set as a constant percentage or relative to the general stock price level. The theory sounds good, but formula-timing or selective-timing plans have not always worked out well in practice.

Quality. The greatest opportunity for mistakes lies, of course, in the grade or quality of equities purchased. No matter what basic philosophies are adopted, careful original selection of the equities chosen for the portfolio, and continual review of the companies and industries, is essential.

General Approach

As mentioned previously, the annuity principle is one of the really useful financial devices available to the average person to give him greater security in his old age. The life annuity provides that (1) the individual's income will continue as long as he lives, and (2) the income will be as large as possible by spreading capital as well as yield over his lifetime.

The source of support for the lifetime annuity payments can vary widely—

1. It can be based, as is the case with traditional annuities issued by life insurance companies, on a broadly diversified portfolio of government bonds, corporate bonds, mortgages, and a minor amount of equity investments, such as common stocks and real estate.
2. It can be based, as is frequent in public retirement systems, mostly on government bonds—federal, state, and municipal.
3. It can be based, as in trusteed plans, on a broadly diversified portfolio much like life insurance company investments, or a larger portion of equity investments can be added.
4. It can be based not on dollar values but on investments expressed in marks in Germany, francs in France, pounds in Britain. As an interesting side light, a fixed-dollar annuity received by a person now living abroad would be a variable annuity in terms of the foreign currency if there were exchange rate changes.
5. It can be based, as in the case of variable annuities, on common stocks and other equity investments, with the current value of the annuity income expressed in terms of "units." When a variable annuity based on equity investments is balanced in proper proportions with a traditional fixed-dollar annuity, the combination is likely to provide a much closer approach to a level annuity in terms of purchasing power.

Thus, neither the medium of exchange, the type of investments, nor the presence or absence of "guarantees" is the substance of life annuities. The significant and different aspect of a life annuity over other investment media is the assurance of payments to an individual throughout his remaining lifetime, no matter how long or short that may be, based on the spreading of both capital and earnings by use of actuarial mortality factors on a group basis.

Full-Participation Annuities

It has been said that with "guaranteed" fixed-dollar annuities the insurance company takes all the risks, and that with variable annuities the individual takes all the risks. Actually, with a fixed-dollar annuity the individual takes the risk of inflation; and with a variable annuity, he takes the risks of poor performance and receives the full advantage of good performance of equity investments.

Depending on the circumstances, long-term guarantees of mortality and expense items in the variable annuity portion may or may not be desirable. When mortality and expense factors are not guaranteed, adjustments are made year by year in the annuity unit value to reflect current experience. If guarantees are used, something must support the guarantees. This support is generally obtained by siphoning off some of the earnings to reserve funds and surplus, instead of paying it out to participants in current retirement income. This is appropriate, for instance, in group annuities covering heterogeneous groups, or where there otherwise would be no adequate control over the mortality and expense factors used in calculating benefits. If reasonable assumptions are made, and if the group to be covered is large, the variations in mortality and expense experience from year to year among a group of annuitants will only be an insignificant fraction of the variations resulting from changes in the performance of the common stock portfolio. A traditional fixed-dollar annuity guarantees the mortality, interest, and expense factors but leaves out the important item of purchasing power. In the variable annuity the important factor for the individual is his opportunity to participate fully in the growth and development of the American economy as reflected in his annuity payments.

So far, there has been too much effort expended in trying to push variable annuities into or out of pigeonholes carved long before variable annuities were invented. For example, the *essence* of a life annuity is the pooling and sharing of risks among annuitants, not its guarantees. There should be provision to issue variable annuities either on a fully participating basis or with noninvestment factors guaranteed. As indicated above, this would allow full and current participation, which should be available wherever desired and appropriate. A limit on expenses and a "reasonable" test on mortality assumptions would be an effective alternative to requiring guarantees.

Conclusion

It is generally agreed that variable annuities are an appropriate and significant development in protection during old age for college staff members, who comprise a highly literate clientele with stable employment served by a specialized insurance company dealing directly with the colleges and their staff members, and where the total size of the operation can never be large enough to exert economic power and control.

Many cogent reasons have been advanced to suggest that a program that works well in the particular framework of the colleges would also work well for the general public or for particular employers. A number of such plans are operating successfully. Many reasons have also been advanced against extension to the general public. Without taking sides in these debates, it is well to point out that the problem of inflation as it affects the retirement security of people in this country is at last receiving some share of the attention and discussion it deserves. Perhaps from these discussions will come improved protection against inflation for our retired people.

SELECTED REFERENCES

COLLEGE RETIREMENT EQUITIES FUND. *CREF—The First Ten Years' Experience: A Report to Participants* (available from CREF, 730 Third Avenue, New York 17, New York). 1962.

DOUGHERTY, CHARLES G. *Variable Annuities.* Statement before the Joint Insurance Committee, Massachusetts Legislature, Boston, September 29, 1958. New York: Metropolitan Life Insurance Co.

DUNCAN, ROBERT M. "A Retirement System Granting Unit Annuities and Investing in Equities," *Transactions of the Society of Actuaries,* Vol. IV, No. 9 (1952).

Dun's Review and Modern Industry, issues of September and October, 1956.

FREUND, WILLIAM. "The Status and Prospects of Variable Annuities," *Journal of Finance,* Vol. XVII, No. 2 (May, 1962), pp. 177–93.

GREENOUGH, WILLIAM C. *A New Approach to Retirement Income.* New York: Teachers Insurance and Annuity Association of America, 1951.

MACLEAN, JOSEPH B. "A New Retirement System with Provision for Variable Income," *Transactions of the Faculty of Actuaries,* Edinburgh, Vol. XVI (1956).

MORRISSEY, LEONARD E. "Dispute over the Variable Annuity," *Harvard Business Review,* Vol. XXXV, No. 1 (January-February, 1957), pp. 75–84.

SHANKS, CARROL M. "The Need for Variable Annuities." Statement before the Business Affairs Committee, House of Assembly, Trenton, New Jersey, May 13, 1955.

Chapter 43

MULTIEMPLOYER PENSION PLANS

BY MEYER MELNIKOFF

A multiemployer pension plan, in general, is any pension plan which covers the employees of two or more unrelated employers, on a basis providing for the pooling of experience on factors such as mortality and employee turnover. The pooling of funds solely for investment purposes is not considered to constitute a multiemployer plan if, in all other respects, the various employers continue to operate separate plans.

Pooling of Pensioner Mortality

The simplest type of multiemployer plan is one established by a trade association to cover the employees of participating employer members. Such a plan provides for all funds to be commingled for investment purposes, but for individual accounts to be maintained of the accumulated contributions made by each employer. When an employee retires, the amount estimated to be required for his pension is transferred from his employer's account to a combined pensioners account, from which his benefits, together with those of all other retired employees, are thereafter paid without reference to the assets or liabilities of the separate employers. The various employers may have different provisions, such as larger benefits or more liberal vesting, so long as the experience on such matters is not pooled. Plans of this type are generally administered entirely by the employers or their representatives. A plan of this general type is the National Health and Welfare Retirement Association, Inc., which offers pension coverage to many health and welfare agencies throughout the country.

Pooling of All Experience

Under another type of multiemployer plan, all contributions are immediately commingled and *all* experience is pooled (including even such factors as the rate of employee turnover). This type generally requires uniform provisions for all employees. Employer contributions for current benefit accruals are typically based on the application to each employer's roster of employees of a uniform set of cost factors. Each employer's costs of benefits for prior service, or accrued liability, are generally funded separately by him. State retirement plans for public employees, including teachers, are examples of this type. Such plans may, if desired, permit employees to retain pension credits when they transfer from one covered employer to another.

Pooling of Costs and Experience

Under a third type of multiemployer plan, each employer contributes on a uniform basis per employee, or per hour worked—without regard to the age or service composition of his employees. A pooled fund provides uniform benefits, with all elements of experience commingled. While not necessarily limited to plans established by collective bargaining, multiemployer plans have become prominent as a result of labor negotiations, and when reference is made to area-wide or multiemployer pension plans, this is the type of plan usually meant. The balance of this chapter will be devoted to negotiated multiemployer pension plans.

NEGOTIATED MULTIEMPLOYER PLANS

The International Ladies' Garment Workers' Union claims the first agreement for a multiemployer fund, negotiated in 1938 to provide vacation benefits, but it seems quite possible that a local union of the International Brotherhood of Electrical Workers had established a multiemployer pension plan in 1929. Developments were slow until after World War II. The 1949 report of the President's Steel Industry Fact-Finding Board was an important milestone—as it recommended a settlement in terms of a cents-per-hour contribution for pension and welfare plans, instead of a wage increase. In 1952, during the Korean War period of wage stabilization, the Construction Industry Stabilization Commission authorized a 7½-cent-per-hour contribution for health and welfare benefits by employers in the construction industry. The big spurt in multiemployer pension plans took place after 1954. By 1960, about eight hundred such plans were in effect, covering about 3.3 million workers. As of 1964, the number covered by such plans is undoubtedly much higher.

A great many different types of workers now have such plans, among them the construction trades, teamsters, longshoremen, bakery workers, lithographers, upholstery workers, hotel and restaurant trades, retail food clerks, seamen, coal miners, and men's and women's clothing workers. Most negotiated multiemployer pension plans developed in areas where there had already been established a tradition of multiemployer collective bargaining on other matters, such as wages and welfare benefits.

In some industries, especially those in which there are many small employers, effective private pension plans can be established only on a multiemployer basis, for the union is the primary cohesive factor in the individual's economic life. An advantage often cited by advocates of the multiemployer pension plan is that it permits (1) greater future mobility of labor, without impairing the accumulation of pension rights, and (2) more adequate recognition of prior service in the industry. Few other matters of employee relations involve similar concepts such as credits accumulated over long periods of service. It is also argued that the multiemployer plan, with uniform costs, permits the establishment of pension benefits in fields that are so highly competitive that differentials in pension costs would not be acceptable to the employers. The counter-argument, of course, is that the high-cost employer is thereby subsidized by the others. Generally, strong union interest and support are necessary to obtain the broad coverage required for a multiemployer pension plan.

THE DEVELOPMENT OF A JOINT, UNION-MANAGEMENT MULTIEMPLOYER PENSION PLAN

The basic collective bargaining agreement calls for contributions to a pension trust fund on the basis of a formula uniformly applicable to all employers who are parties to the agreement. Details are usually contained in a separate document, sometimes known as a pension agreement, which is executed at the same time as the collective bargaining agreement. Negotiations typically take place between one or more local unions and an association of employers; the pension agreement is signed by individuals authorized to act on behalf of these parties. Normally, the next step is for the principals, through their representatives, to adopt a trust instrument to govern the pension trust fund, and to select a board of trustees to establish the terms of the pension plan and to administer it. The pension plan is embodied in a separate instrument, which may be supplemented by rules and regulations on some details of plan interpretation.

Some Labor Law Aspects

If a multiemployer pension plan is to provide for union participation in the administration of the pension fund, it must conform with the Labor Management Relations Act of 1947. Under Section 302 of this Act, there must be:

1. A written agreement stating the basis on which contributions to the fund are to be made.
2. A trust fund to receive such contributions and to apply them for the sole and exclusive benefit of the employees and their families.
3. A board of trustees on which there is equal representation of employers and unions (sometimes supplemented by neutral representation).
4. Provision for arbitration of any deadlocks pertaining to administration of the fund.

5. Provision for an annual audit of the fund, to be available to all interested persons.
6. Separation of pension funds from other funds.

Other labor laws may also have application.

Some Tax Aspects

In addition, laws and regulations of the United States Treasury Department must be conformed to, in order to safeguard the tax deductibility by employers of their contributions, to insure the tax-free status of the fund, and to obtain certain tax advantages for the employees and their beneficiaries. Here, the great body of material which has developed in connection with single-employer pension plans is of limited application, but there are two special Treasury Department rulings for plans of this type. P.S. 64, dated November 9, 1950, and Revenue Ruling 55–681 deal with the fact that such plans generally provide for definite benefits, but are financed by a fixed rate of contribution made pursuant to a union contract, which may be terminated after a certain period, whereas qualified pension plans, under the law, are required to be of a more permanent nature. The Treasury Department has indicated that a plan will be held to be permanent and to provide for definitely determinable benefits if the trustees submit a certification that actuarial calculations have been prepared which indicate that the contributions expected during the term of the collective bargaining agreement will be not less than the greater of (1) the full costs of the prospective pensions for employees expected to retire under the plan during such term, and (2) the normal costs, plus interest on the unfunded liability, for all employees under the plan during the period. The trustees must also certify that the methods, assumptions, and results of such calculations are considered reasonable by them.

Any pension trust, including a negotiated multiemployer trust, must file with the United States Treasury Department, initially to obtain qualification, and annually thereafter, certain information called for by the Internal Revenue regulations, including a return on Treasury Form 990-P. The information required of the individual employers, to support deduction of their contributions, is generally relatively simple, in accordance with Revenue Ruling 55–204, as amended by Revenue Ruling 56–657, and may be limited on Treasury Form 2950 to: name of plan, date of most recent plan approval, amount of employer contribution, and amount of employee nondeferred compensation.

Section 401(*i*), added by the 1964 Revenue Act, may remove some of the pressure to qualify the terms of such pension plans by the end of the year in which contributions begin. It provides, only for certain union-negotiated multiemployer pension plans, for Treasury Department qualification to have retroactive effect.

THE DESIGN OF A NEGOTIATED MULTIEMPLOYER PENSION PLAN

Negotiated multiemployer pension plans represent a relatively new field of employee benefits. Many varieties of plan are being established to recognize differing situations. This section describes some of the major considerations.

The Covered Group

In the typical plan the covered group consists of the members of one or more collective bargaining units. Coverage is generally extended to all employees represented in collective bargaining by the union, whether or not they are members of the union.

Some plans cover the employees of the union in addition to the members of the collective bargaining unit. In such cases, it is normal for the union to contribute for its employees on the same basis as the other employers do, but without obtaining any of the rights which are given to other employers on such matters as the election of employer trustees. It should be noted that the propriety of including union employees has been questioned by the United States District Court for the Eastern District of Missouri in a recent case (*Kroger Company et al.* v. *Nicholas M. Blassie et al.*, January 8, 1964).

Contributions

Most plans of this type do not call for any contributions by the employees. The typical employer contribution is expressed in terms of a stated number of cents per hour worked or per hour compensated for (which would thereby include hours such as time off, vacation, and so forth). In some cases, this can be expressed in terms of contributions per week, per month, or even in terms of units of production, such as tons of coal. In a few cases the employer contribution for an employee is expressed in terms of a percentage of his pay. Care must be taken, of course, that the agreement with the employer on pension contributions precisely defines how the contribution should be determined.

Actuarial Aspects

The trustees, with technical guidance, have the task of establishing the schedule of benefits which they believe can be supported by the fixed contributions provided by negotiation. Difficult problems of judgment are involved. The ideal solution is a schedule of benefits which is precisely in equilibrium, over the long term, with the income that can be anticipated—starting with benefits that are high enough, but not too high. For example, assume that there is a group of 1,000 employees for whom contributions are to be paid at the rate of 10 cents an hour. Monthly, that would be about $15 per employee and $15,000 in total. Now, suppose that 50 employees retire in the first year. How much pension can they be paid? If $15,000 is divided among 50 men, each can receive $300 a month, provided no reserve is established for future payments. As the proportion of retired increases, the same total contributions would support smaller pensions. If employment should drop, the pensions would have to decrease; and if for some reason employment discontinued entirely, the pensions would have to discontinue also, even to all those who had already retired. This is hardly a prudent basis of operation.

To take the opposite extreme, the $180 paid each year on behalf of each person could be applied to purchase for him whatever amount of deferred pension it could buy. For a man aged 65, $180 might buy an immediate monthly pension of $1.25. For a man aged 45, $180 might buy a deferred monthly pension of $2.75; or for a man aged 30, a deferred monthly pension of $4.00. Clearly, however, it would not be feasible to retire a man at age 65 on a monthly pension of $1.25.

As neither of these extremes is acceptable, it is necessary to find an intermediate solution offering a schedule of benefits that is reasonably uniform for young and old. Further, in order that the plan can be maintained in good times and in bad times, regardless of the amount of employment, it is necessary to balance the benefits to be paid against the contributions expected. The problem recurs whenever there is a change in contribution rate. It is a delicate actuarial problem.

In the typical area-wide pension plan, the actuarial analysis requires assumptions for such elements as amount of work (and contributions), the rate of employee turnover (or the proportion who will retire), and the average age at which they will normally retire, in addition to the other, more customary pension cost factors, such as rate of interest and rates of mortality and perhaps disability. Furthermore, a very important, although implicit, assumption is needed with respect to the number of individuals who will be working in the covered group over the long-term future.

1. The estimate as to hours of employment may be very significant, particularly if benefits are only loosely linked to contributions. For example, if a full year of pension credit is given for 1,600 or more hours of work, then a reduction in the average work week from, say, 40 hours to 35 hours can seriously affect the financial structure of the plan if the pension contribution is reduced by one eighth without any reduction in the benefits to be provided.
2. In determining the anticipated rate of employee turnover, it must be realized that movement of employees within the covered group does not release any liabilities. Reliable statistics of the kind needed are rarely available, or necessarily indicative of the future, which may be affected by the very establishment of the plan—and tables used in other plans can be very inappropriate.
3. Since there is rarely a compulsory retirement age, it is reasonable to assume that employees will retire at an age somewhat higher than the

normal retirement age. An increase of one year in the average retirement age, say from 65 to 66, can increase the supportable dollar benefits by about 7½ per cent. However, this factor is subject to considerable influence by economic conditions; a reduction in employment can be expected to result in a reduction in the average age of retirement at the very time when the contributions to the fund are decreased.

The funding rate for past service benefits presents further questions which have heightened significance in multiemployer plans, because they affect the level of benefits. If it is assumed that only interest on the initial accrued liability need be paid, benefits are set at a higher level than under the more cautious approach of providing for the eventual liquidation of the past service liability over perhaps thirty years or less. The total size of the covered work force over the long-term future becomes very important in such considerations, as a declining work force would support a smaller benefit. Thinly funded plans sometimes contain clauses providing for the reduction of benefits when it becomes clear that the existing level cannot be continued, or the deferment of retirement until adequate funds are accumulated. Such provisions may affect the personnel policies of the employers.

Eligibility for Normal Retirement

Under most plans, normal retirement is permissive at age 65, but not compulsory. Minimum length of service within the groups covered by the plan is a customary requirement; sometimes, recognition is given to service in the trade but outside the geographical area covered by the plan. Some plans require a minimum period of employment during which contributions are made. A few plans have provided for normal retirement below the age of 65. Under some plans, women can retire at age 62. Plans in physically onerous or hazardous trades may provide for normal retirement at age 60.

The Benefit Formula

Benefit formulas differ greatly in existing plans. The simplest is to pay the same monthly pension, say $50, to each individual meeting the requirements for normal retirement. Because this formula provides scant relation between benefits and contributions, any financial equilibrium existing at the outset is readily upset by changed economic conditions and employment practices in the industry. From a strictly actuarial standpoint, it is better to provide for benefits related to length of service, such as $2.00 a month for each year of service. This requires an appropriate definition of a "year of service," taking account of the possible mobility and intermittent employment of the employees. This is sometimes done in terms of the number of hours worked in jobs covered by the plan; a specified number of hours (1,600–1,800) in a year can be considered as a full year, depending on the nature of the employment. Credit can be given for partial years of service, all of which may be added together to determine eligibility for pension as well as amount of pension.

In some cases an employee's benefits for service after the establishment of the plan may be determined as a percentage of the contributions made on his account. In this way the amount of covered employment of the individual is directly recognized. Such an approach is particularly helpful if the employer contribution rate is not the same for all employees.

A fundamental question is whether an employee's pension should be related to his earnings. If benefits *are* related to earnings, then contributions also should be related to earnings (although the converse need not be true). Earnings-related pensions may well be the trend of the future, especially in the skilled trades.

Where credit is given for service prior to the establishment of the plan, difficulties sometimes arise from the fact that complete records of employment of the individuals are seldom available. A few plans have, for this reason, limited prior service to the service with the last employer or with the employer with whom the employee has seniority. In some plans, this approach would not be practical. Various other methods have been used, including questionnaires to employees requesting employment histories, checking with social security records, or consulting records of union membership.

Under some plans, there is a limit to the total number of years for which credit may be given, such as, say, twenty-five, including both past and future service. The intention may be present to liberalize such provisions as and when experience warrants. Some plans shut off the accrual of credits at a specified age, such as 70, or even as low as 65—to encourage prompt retirement.

Continuity of Service

Under area-wide pension plans, it is necessary to find some way to define relatively continuous service in the area covered by the pension plan, while allowing for mobility of employees among the different employers covered as well as for some decrease in employment in the industry as a whole. Various types of so-called "grace" periods have been devised. For example, under some plans, it is possible for an employee to be considered as not having had a break in continuity of service as long as he works at least a minimum number of hours of covered employment in any period of two consecutive calendar years. It is customary to provide that a period of disability or military service should not serve to constitute a break in service. Some plans "excuse," without credit, employment represented by the union but outside the collective bargaining units covered by the plan, either outside the geographical area of the plan or otherwise working for an employer who is not a party to the plan.

Vesting

Despite the importance attached by unions generally to the question of transferability of benefits, few multiemployer pension plans contain any provision for the vesting of benefits when an individual severs his relationship with units covered by the plan. In some cases, recognition may be given to vesting of benefits for the individual who remains in the industry and area covered by the plan but is promoted to a supervisory job which is not covered by the plan. A few plans contain outright vesting, without regard to the position to which the employee transfers. Many plans make vested benefits payable only if the individual makes timely application.

Early Retirement

Many multiemployer pension plans provide only for retirement at or after the normal retirement age, such as age 65. This may be related to social security, under which, until recently, retirement benefits could not be drawn before age 65, except for disability. In some plans, this may reflect the very modest level of normal benefits, as well as concern as to the adequacy of the financing. Some plans permit voluntary early retirement for those who have satisfied certain conditions, at or after age 55, on accrued benefits, reduced for early commencement, on the basis of actuarial equivalence or an approximation. Liberal early retirement provisions may invite dangerous financial drains, especially in the early years, of plans that guarantee lifetime benefits to retiring employees by means of annuity purchases.

Disability Retirement

Some multiemployer pension plans contain provisions under which a pension is payable to individuals who become totally and permanently disabled while covered under the plan. In view of the coverage "grace" periods which most of these plans contain, there is generally no attempt to ascertain whether the disability was incurred while the individual was working in employment covered under the plan. A great many different formulas are used to determine the amount of the disability pension, and any disability income under workmen's compensation or accident and sickness plans may be deducted. The adjudication of disability can be a difficult problem. Under some plans a social security determination that disability exists will be considered as evidence of the eligibility for disability pension under the plan, but the right to discontinue this procedure is usually retained. In some plans, a procedure similar to arbitration may be used in resolving cases on which union and management cannot agree.

Death Benefits

Most multiemployer pension plans do not provide any death benefits before retirement other than return of any employee contributions, possibly with interest. Some contain modest benefits related in some way to the contributions made by employers on behalf of the individual. A few plans have provided for a death benefit after retirement in the form of a continuation of the pension for a period of perhaps two years after the employee's death. Other plans replace the life insurance discontinued at retirement by establishing under the pension plan a decreasing schedule of death benefits, or a subsidized contingent annuity option.

Some of the labor union pension plans established many years ago in the United States made provision for survivor pensions. There are current indications that multiemployer pension plans will in the future take more interest in survivor benefits, especially the types which serve to make the plans more attractive to younger employees for whom the retirement benefit may seem remote.

Retirement Test

Under a multiemployer pension plan, the test to determine if an employee has retired is not as routinely simple as in a single-employer plan. The basic objective is that benefits under the plan should not provide an income to those who continue to compete for work and may, by reason of the pension, even be able to work at lower rates than those who are not retired. Accordingly, it is quite common to find that the pension benefits are not paid in any month in which the retired employee engages in any employment covered by the pension plan or above a permitted maximum in such employment. In some cases, penalty clauses are added, so that an employee may lose, say, two months' pension for every month he works, or perhaps six months' pension plus one month for each month he works. In some cases the retirement test considers work not only in the area covered by the pension plan but work in a related craft or in the same craft but in a different geographical area. Some plans require pensioners to submit a form each year indicating the extent of their employment subject to the retirement test. In some cases, this provision may be integrated with the operation of the retirement test under social security, so that a month's pension is lost for every month for which a social security payment is lost. Many plans discontinue the retirement test completely above a stated age, such as 70.

Turnover of Employers

If an employer contributing under a multiemployer pension plan goes out of business and his employees are absorbed by the other employers covered under the plan, no unusual problems arise. However, in the design of a multiemployer pension plan, recognition must be given to the possibility that some employers may go out of business, or otherwise drop out of the plan, but leave large unfunded liabilities under the plan. The dangers may be particularly acute in the early years of a plan, and specific provision may, in some plans, be made only for a limited period. Under some plans, such a termination would bring about an analysis of the contributions made by the terminated employer and the liabilities of the plan for his employees, with adjustment of the amount of benefits to be paid for service with that employer to bring their value into line with the funds he had provided. Other plans provide that when an employer terminates coverage, the benefits thereafter payable to his employees may be reduced to a proportion of their accrued benefits, the proportion being determined as the proportion of accrued benefits that would be payable to all employees covered under the plan if the plan then terminated completely. Many different provisions are possible, of course. Under some plans, all benefits of an employee, for both past and future service, are determined by reference to the contributions made for him, and such plans tend to have greater protection against this risk.

A similar problem occurs in connection with the addition of new employers, who bring under the plan employees with past service which has not previously been credited. The design of the plan must recognize the possibility of this situation, and provide for it in some way which may be considered equitable and fair by all parties.

Reciprocal Agreements

There has been much discussion of the possibility of developing reciprocal agreements among multiemployer pension plans, as well as health and welfare plans, to cover the cases of employees who transfer employment from the jurisdiction of one fund to that of another. Under welfare plans, such agreements merely provide for facilitating the satisfaction of eligibility requirements for current benefits. Under pension plans, they may, in effect, provide for a special kind of vesting. There are several alternatives, all of them complex in their consequences. Thus far, relatively few reciprocal agreements have been made for pensions.

Multiunit Plans

Some multiemployer pension plans cover a larger group than the employees affected by one collective bargaining negotiation. Plans of this type include the nationwide plans for the bakery workers and upholstery workers, and the multistate plans for teamsters. Under such plans, there are additional problems not involved in the multiemployer plan which covers just one collective bargaining situation. Different negotiations may result in different rates of contribution, so that the plan may have some employers who contribute 5 cents an hour and others who contribute 10 cents an hour. In such cases, it is necessary to design the benefits under the plan to recognize not only different rates of contributions currently being made but also the possibility of transfer of employees among such employers, and of the change in the contribution rate of an employer in the course of time. A similar problem arises from the fact that different negotiations may result in pension contributions becoming effective at different dates. The employer who comes in late may be taking advantage of the others in a financial way if his employees receive the same benefits as other employees without the same contributions having been made for them. One answer may be to require retroactive coverage and deficiency contributions. Other possibilities are to limit the benefits for the group that comes in late.

ADMINISTRATION

A multiemployer pension plan is a large and complex financial structure, and deserves careful and competent administration, with effective controls on its financial operations to insure that contributions are made properly, employer delinquencies minimized, and adequate records maintained to insure that covered employees can know the amount of contributions made in their behalf.

There must be an "administrator" to control and manage the money received or contributed, and the board of trustees to whom he responds should maintain adequate records of its meetings and establish formal auditing control through independent certified accountants.

Under the Federal Welfare and Pension Plans Disclosure Act, for a plan of more than twenty-five individuals, reports must be made annually by the administrator containing complete descriptions of the plan, its financial statement, and certain additional information, including the nature of the assets and liabilities and the basis of funding. In addition to its filing with the United States Department of Labor, this information must be available to the participants in the plan upon proper request.

INVESTMENT OF NEGOTIATED MULTIEMPLOYER PENSION FUNDS

The investment of funds in a multiemployer plan carries with it, perhaps, an additional responsibility beyond that for a plan of a single employer. Where such an employer might stand behind his pension fund and accept responsibility for its ultimate solvency, it is doubtful that the many employers of a joint pension venture, where management and labor trustees stand between them and its results, will have any equivalent readiness to make up losses.

This implies a strict approach to financial prudence in the investment of funds. It also makes it at least dubious to recognize "social welfare" in investments at the expense of financial prudence. It suggests as a simple criterion that the nature of the assets should be such that full disclosure to the employees can be made at any time with little apprehension.

SUMMARY

There are several basic types of multiemployer pension plans. Most prominent currently are the negotiated multiemployer pension plans, which are of fairly recent origin but have grown very quickly in a few years. Their importance to the pension scene transcends even their large numerical stature, because they are the means by which private pension coverage can be extended to many individuals for whom such coverage would otherwise be most difficult. A healthy development of such plans, as part of the growth of pension plans generally, should help to preserve to the maximum extent possible the place of private pension plans in the United States.

SELECTED REFERENCES

ELKIN, JACK M. "Recent Developments in Multi-Employer Pension-Plan Specifications," *Proceedings: Conference of Actuaries in Public Practice,* Vol. IX (1959–60), p. 289.

MELONE, JOSEPH J. *Collectively Bargained Multi-Employer Pension Plans.* Homewood, Ill.: Richard D. Irwin, Inc., 1963.

MILJUS, ROBERT C., and JOHNSON, ALTON C. "Multi-Employer Pension Plans and Mobility." *Harvard Business Review,* Vol. 41, No. 5 (September-October, 1963), p. 147.

PRENTICE-HALL, INC. *Pension and Profit Sharing Report.* Paragraphs 2159, 6026, 6084, 6085, 6086, 7066, 7081, 19012. Englewood Cliffs, N.J., 1963.

UNITED STATES DEPARTMENT OF LABOR, BUREAU OF LABOR STATISTICS. *Multi-Employer Pension Plans under Collective Bargaining.* Bulletin No. 1326. Washington, D.C.: U.S. Government Printing Office, 1960.

Chapter 44

PROFIT SHARING PLANS

BY E. A. STARR

Profit sharing has been defined as an agreement freely entered into by which employees receive a share, fixed in advance, of the profits of a firm. More specifically, the Commissioner of Internal Revenue defines profit sharing as follows:

> A profit sharing plan is a plan established and maintained by an employer to provide for participation in his profits by his employees or their beneficiaries. The plan must provide a definite predetermined formula for allocating the contributions made to the plan among the participants and for distributing the funds accumulated under the plan after a fixed number of years, the attainment of a stated age, or upon prior occurrence of some event such as illness, disability, retirement, death, or severance of employment. . . .[1]

Profit sharing plans are of two principal types, namely, cash distribution plans and deferred distribution plans. The primary purpose of the cash distribution plan is to reward employees for their contribution to profits by sharing with them a portion of such profits, such shares being a supplement to the current compensation of each employee. None of the intended benefits of cash plans are deferred, nor is the income tax liability to the employees deferred on the shares which they receive.

On the other hand, deferred distribution plans defer the plan benefits as well as the employees' income tax liability on the amounts contributed for their benefit until some later time when distribution will be made in accordance with the plan's distribution provisions. The majority of such plans defer distribution until the participant attains a normal retirement date stipulated in the plan. Thus, while qualifying as profit sharing plans, they are primarily retirement plans; and their principal objectives are, in general, the same as pension plans.

Essential Differences between a Pension and a Profit Sharing Retirement Plan

Pension plans and profit sharing retirement plans differ in their basic concepts. Under a pension plan an employer undertakes either to provide

[1] Internal Revenue Code Regulations, Sec. 1.401–1(*b*)(1)(ii).

each participant with a definite guaranteed amount of pension benefit at his normal retirement date, or to contribute each year a definite amount, usually a percentage of an employee's compensation, which will accumulate and be used to provide pension income at the normal retirement date. Thus, the employer commits himself to a defined benefit and to contributions that must be made to provide such benefits. Theoretically, such contributions must be made each year, irrespective of business profits; but some flexibility in this regard is granted to employers, depending upon the type of plan and the actuarial cost method and funding instrument employed.

In contrast, under a profit sharing plan the employer guarantees nothing. He does not commit his business to providing fixed benefits or fixed contributions. The only commitment involved with a profit sharing plan, and then only if it employs a formula for determining the profits to be shared, is that contributions will be made in years in which the business has profits. In good profit years the contributions will be high and may equal or approach the maximum that would be tax-deductible by the employer. In modest profit years the contributions will be modest; and in no profit years, there will be no contributions. There would be no commitment, of course, in the case of the employer who adopts a profit sharing plan which includes no formula for determining the profits to be shared. Under such a plan the amount of the profits to be shared each year will be determined by the board of directors of the employer; and even in high profit years, there could be circumstances which would preclude sharing with the employees in such years any of the profits of the business.

Employees participating in a profit sharing retirement plan have no assurance, therefore, of what their benefits will be when they attain their normal retirement dates. It has been argued in some quarters that this is a disadvantage insofar as the employees are concerned and that the use of profit sharing for the purpose of providing retirement benefits should not, therefore, be encouraged. There may be some justification for this argument if only the viewpoint of the employee is being considered. It must be recognized, however, that when considering which plan may be best for his business, the privilege of making contributions to his plan only in those years in which his business has profits appeals to the employer, and this accounts—to some degree, at least—for the substantial increase in the number of profit sharing plans which have been adopted in recent years.

Qualification Requirements

For the employee participants to enjoy tax deferment of their profit sharing plan benefits, the plan must be qualified as tax-exempt under Section 501(*a*) of the Internal Revenue Code. To so qualify, it must meet the tests set forth in Section 401(*a*). The basic requirements for qualification of a profit sharing plan are, in general, the same as for a pension plan; e.g., (1) there must be a written plan and trust; (2) the plan must be permanent, not temporary, in nature; (3) the plan must benefit a broad classification of company employees, not just a few executives or highly compensated employees; (4) the plan must not discriminate in any manner in favor of employees who are officers, shareholders, supervisory employees, or highly compensated employees; and (5) the plan must be for the exclusive benefit of the employees and their beneficiaries, and no part of the funds contributed must revert directly or indirectly to the employer.

A profit sharing plan must meet certain additional requirements, the most important of which are: (1) Plan benefits must not be determined actuarially. This is in direct contrast to the actuarial soundness requirement for a pension plan. (2) The employer contributions must be allocated each year to the accounts of the individual employee participants but may not be allocated on a discretionary basis. The plan must contain a definite, predetermined formula for allocating contributions, interest, or other investment gains and forfeitures. (3) The amounts allocated to the accounts of the participants may not be distributed, except on death, disability, or severance of employment, until they have been accumulated for a "fixed period of years," which by Treasury Department ruling must be at least two years.[2] (4) If there is to be investment in life insurance for the benefit of the participants or their beneficiaries, such investment must be merely "incidental" (defined later) to the main purpose of the plan.

These requirements must be considered when designing a profit sharing plan that is intended to qualify as tax-exempt. Even so, each plan should be individually designed in order to meet the particular and perhaps unusual circumstances existing in a company. However, the basic framework of most deferred distribution profit sharing plans follows, in general, a similar pattern in respect to the important provisions.

THE PLAN PROVISIONS

The plan provisions usually found in most deferred distribution profit sharing plans are:

1. Purpose of the plan—the basic aims and objectives the plan is expected to accomplish.
2. Participating employees—who is to be included in the plan and the requirements which must be met before employees are eligible to become participants.
3. Contributions—the procedure to be followed by the company to determine the amount to be contributed each year (formula or otherwise) and the basis of employee contributions, if any.

---

[2] Revenue Ruling 54–231, 1954–1 Cumulative Bulletin 150; and Revenue Ruling 61–157, Part 2(*h*), 1961–2 Cumulative Bulletin 67.

4. Allocation to accounts of participants—the formula to be employed for determining the amount to be credited to the account of each participant.
5. Administrative committee—the manner of appointment or selection of the members, and their duties and powers.
6. The trustee—who will act, and the manner of appointment and the duties and powers.
7. Investment of trust funds—the type and kind of investments which will be permitted.
8. Distribution of trust funds to participants—the time and manner in which the trust funds will be paid to the participants or their beneficiaries.
9. Amendment or termination of plan—the conditions under which the company will have the right to alter, amend, or discontinue the plan.

Some plans may include additional provisions, but those listed are most important and should be included in every profit sharing retirement plan. Space precludes a detailed discussion of each of these provisions to illustrate the variations in their content which are possible from plan to plan. Comments concerning some of the provisions are essential, however, to an understanding of the subject.

Participating Employees

An employer adopting a profit sharing plan has some latitude in selecting the eligibility provisions which may best accomplish the intended objectives. Employees may be excluded as participants due to length of service, minimum or maximum age, sex, type of employment, type of pay, or amount of pay. Thus, some plans may include all full-time employees of a company, while others may include only such employees as have completed a service requirement of from one to five years and have attained a minimum age and are under a maximum age; or a plan may include only a class or classes of company employees, such as all salaried or clerical or all hourly rate employees, who have met a years-of-service and minimum and maximum age requirements; or only employees whose incomes exceed perhaps $4,800, the present wage base for social security taxes. Whatever restrictions are imposed must not result in the inclusion in the plan of only officers, shareholders, supervisory, or highly compensated employees. Section 401(*a*) of the Internal Revenue Code prohibits discrimination in favor of these four classes of employees, and each plan is carefully reviewed by the Internal Revenue Service before it is approved to determine whether the eligibility exclusions imposed may directly or indirectly result in such discrimination.

Generally, however, the eligibility provisions of a profit sharing plan are somewhat less restrictive than are those included in pension plans. This might be expected, since company contributions to a profit sharing plan, and therefore the plan costs, are not affected by the number of plan participants. Also, the termination from the plan of nonpermanent employees prior to the date benefits are fully vested simply increases the benefits of the remaining participants, due to the fact that any forfeitures are reallocated to the accounts of remaining participants.

Contributions

The formulas employed by companies in determining the profits to be shared are many and varied. In general, however, formulas will provide for a contribution of a percentage of the net profits of the company determined before payment of federal income taxes and state income taxes, if any, ranging from a low of about 5 per cent to a high of about 50 per cent. Formulas have been employed which vary the percentage of profits to be contributed in accordance with the amount of profits. For example, a scale of contributions such as that shown in Table 44–1 might be employed.

TABLE 44–1

ILLUSTRATIVE SCHEDULE OF PROFITS SHARED BY AMOUNT OF PROFITS

Company Net Profits before Taxes	Percentage of Profits to Be Contributed
$100,000 or less	0%
$100,000 to $200,000	20
$200,000 to $300,000	25
$300,000 to $400,000	30
$400,000 to $500,000	40
Over $500,000	50

Formulas of this type have also been adopted by some companies under which the percentage of profits to be contributed ranges downward in accordance with the increased profits rather than grading upward as in the case of the formula in Table 44–1.

It is no longer required that a profit sharing plan contain a definite, predetermined formula for determining the profits to be shared. Under such plans the amount of profits to be shared each year is determined annually by the board of directors of the employer. For such plans, there should be included in the contribution provision a simple statement to the effect that the amount to be contributed by the company will be determined by the board of directors on or before the year-end closing date of the business.

In any event, there is always included in the contribution provision a limitation that the maximum amount to be contributed by the company in any year will not exceed the amount that would be tax-deductible by the company in such year. Employer contributions to profit sharing plans which qualify under Section 401(*a*) are deductible within the limitations provided in Section 401(*a*)(3)(*A*) and (*B*) of the Internal Revenue Code. The primary limitation on the amount deductible in any year is "an amount not in excess of 15 per cent of the compensation otherwise paid or accrued during the taxable year to all employees of the . . . profit sharing plan." An employer who does not contribute in a year the maximum that would have been deductible in the year is permitted to carry forward to subsequent years such amounts and deduct them in a year when contributed, but to an extent not greater than twice the primary limitation or 30 per cent of the compensation otherwise paid or accrued in that year to the participants of the plan. In view of this, the contribution provision should not limit the employer's contribution to the 15 per cent primary limitation. Rather, it should simply limit such contributions to the maximum amount permitted the employer as a tax deduction for a year.

Allocation to Accounts of Participants

Allocation of the company's profit share to the accounts of participants must be made in accordance with a definite, predetermined formula applicable to all participants. Section 1.401–1(*b*)(ii) of the regulations provides: "A formula for distributing the accumulated funds among the participants is definite, for example, if it provides for a distribution in proportion to the basic compensation of each participant. . . ." In view of this, the great majority of profit sharing plans provide for the allocation of the profit sharing funds to the accounts of the participants in the ratio the compensation of the participant bears to the total compensation of all participants. In a year in which the company contributes the full 15 per cent of compensation permitted as a tax deduction, the account of each participant is credited with 15 per cent of the total compensation otherwise paid to him in that year. If the company contribution equals 10 per cent of the total compensation of participants, each participant's account is credited with 10 per cent of his total compensation, and so forth.

Some companies have employed allocation formulas which have the effect of providing somewhat larger benefits for employees with long service records than are provided for employees more recently employed. Such formulas require the setting-up of a point or unit system. Units are credited to each participant for completed years of service, and units are credited for compensation. To determine the amount of the company's contribution to be allocated to the account of each participant, the total units of all participants are added. The company's contribution is then divided by the total number of units to find the dollar value per unit. The number of units to the credit of each participant is then multiplied by the unit value, and the resulting product is the amount allocated to the account of each participant for the year.

Such formulas are satisfactory provided that, in actual operation, they do not result in the prohibited discrimination. If officers, shareholders, and highly compensated employees of a company have, in addition to greater compensation, longer service periods than do other employees, there is the possibility that the weighting of profit sharing allocations on the basis of service and compensation factors will result in discrimination. Allocation of the profit shares in proportion to the compensation alone is therefore the safest procedure to follow.

Under a contributory plan an allocation formula is sometimes employed which gives credit to each participant for three factors—service, compensation, and contributions. This arrangement is feasible when the amount to be contributed by the participants may vary at their election. For example, the plan may provide that each participant must contribute 2 per cent of his compensation, but that each participant will have the right to elect to contribute an additional amount up to but not exceeding 10 per cent of his compensation. The allocation provision may then provide that the company contribution to the plan will be allocated to the accounts of the participants somewhat as follows:

> For purposes of allocation, the total contributions of the company shall first be divided by three. Each part shall then be allocated to the individual accounts of participants on the following basis:
>
> One third in the ratio the participant's compensation bears to the total compensation of all participants, one third in the ratio which the participant's total years of service bear to the total years of service of all participants, and one third in the ratio the participant's contribution to the plan bears to the total contributions of all participants.

Allocation formulas of this type are satisfactory and will not have the effect of disqualifying a plan unless they produce the discriminatory results prohibited by Section 401(*a*)(4) of the Internal Revenue Code.

Distribution of Trust Funds to Participants

The amounts contributed to a profit sharing plan year by year must be allocated by the trustee to the individual accounts of the participants.[3] However, it is not essential to qualification that the plan fully vest in the participants the entire value of their accounts under all circumstances. Full vesting is required when a participant attains the normal retirement date stipulated in the plan, and benefits must fully vest if the plan is terminated or contributions are suspended.[4] Most plans fully vest also the participants' accounts at death or disability. However, the vesting conditions of various plans will differ in the amounts to be vested on a participant's severance of employment. An employer may establish any vesting conditions which will best accomplish the intended objectives of the plan, provided that the effect of the conditions does not, in the

[3] Revenue Ruling 61–157, Part 2(*t*).

[4] Revenue Ruling 61–157, Part 5(*c*)(1)(2) and (3).

operation of the plan, set up the discrimination that is prohibited. Vesting conditions will vary, therefore, from full and complete vesting at the outset, through graduating vesting upon completion of a stated service or age requirement, to no vesting until attainment of the normal or stated retirement age.

The majority of plans employ graduated vesting, with an increasing percentage of each participant's account vested for each year of completed service either as a plan participant or as an employee. Typically, such vesting arrangements will vest in the participants 5, 10, or 20 per cent of their account values for each year of plan participation with full vesting in 5, 10, or 20 years; or there may be no vesting for a period of years, such as five, with graduated vesting thereafter.

One of the attractive features of profit sharing for the full-time, permanent employees of a company is that the nonvested amounts remaining in the accounts of any terminating participants will be reallocated to their accounts by the trustee, usually in accordance with the same allocation formula that is employed in respect to employer contributions. Thus, their accounts can appreciate from this source as well as from company contributions and investment earnings. However, a plan's vesting conditions will be scrutinized carefully by the Internal Revenue Service to determine whether the rate of turnover of the employer may indicate the possibility that a substantial part of the total employer contributions may ultimately revert to the officers, shareholders, or highly compensated or supervisory employees. If this possibility exists, plan qualification may not be granted without some relaxation of the plan's vesting conditions.

Investment of Trust Funds

Some plans give wide latitude to the trustee (or the committee in directing the trustee) in the investment of the trust funds, while other plans restrict investment of the funds to certain types of investments. The decision as to which type of provision to employ in a plan rests with the employer.

There is one restriction in respect to investment of the profit sharing funds which must be complied with if approval is to be obtained under Section 401(*a*). Section 1.401(*b*)(5)(i) and (ii) of the regulations provides:

. . . no specific limitations are provided in Section 401(*a*) with respect to investments which may be made by the trustees of a trust qualifying under Section 401(*a*). Generally, the contributions may be used by the trustee to purchase any investments permitted by the trust agreement to the extent allowed by local law. However, such a trust will be subject to tax under Section 511 with respect to any "unrelated business taxable income" (as defined in Section 512) realized by it from its investments. Furthermore, the tax-exempt status of the trust will be forfeited if the investments made by the trustees constitute "prohibited transactions" within the meaning of Section 503. . . . Where the trust funds are invested in stock or securities of, or loaned to, the employer or other person described in Section 503(*c*), full disclosure must be made of the reasons for such arrangement and the conditions under which such investments are made in order that a determination may be made whether the trust serves any purpose other than constituting part of a plan for the exclusive benefit of employees. The trustee shall report any of such investment on the return which under Section 6033 it is required to file and shall with respect to any such investment furnish the information required by such return.

Revenue Ruling 61–157, Part 2(*r*), covers the requirements which must be met if investment in the securities of the employer is to be approved. Section 503(*c*), "Prohibited Transactions," is also pertinent. If, therefore, the investment provision of the plan makes it permissive for the trustee to purchase securities of the employer as an investment of the trust funds, it is important to secure the approval of the Commissioner prior to making such an investment. Failure to do so could have the effect of disqualifying the plan under Section 401(*a*) on the ground that the plan is not for the exclusive benefit of the employees or their beneficiaries, or that a prohibited transaction has occurred.

LIFE INSURANCE AND ANNUITIES

Many profit sharing plans contain a permissive provision at the outset for investment in insurance or annuity contracts. Many others have been amended or will be amended to permit such investments to be made. Some of the uses which may be made of life insurance and annuity contracts in connection with profit sharing plans are described in the following sections.

Key-Man Insurance

Many profit sharing trusts have purchased substantial amounts of life insurance on the principal officers of the employer in favor of the trust. The purpose of such insurance is to indemnify the trust and the employee participants against the loss in company contributions to the plan which may occur in the event of the death of the insureds, with the possible reduction in the profits of the business for a few years which so often occurs when the principal officer of a firm or the individual who has been largely responsible for the firm's profits dies.

Particularly in the smaller corporations, it is not unusual to find one or perhaps several key employees whose special skills, market knowledge, sales ability, or prestige with the firm's customers account in large measure for the firm's success and profits. Should this person or these persons die, not only would a serious replacement problem arise, but profits might fall off, at least temporarily.

A trust established by such a firm to permit the employees to share in the business profits has an insurable interest in the lives of the officers or key employees on whose continued activities in behalf of the firm the profits, or a major portion of them, depend. The purchase by the trust of an insurance policy on the life of such a person in favor of the trust will assure that in the event of his death the death proceeds of the policy will be received by the trustees, to be allocated to the accounts of the plan participants. The premiums on such a policy are payable by the trustee from trust funds. The policy ownership is in the trustee, and the trustee is the beneficiary. The policy is an asset of the trust, and each participant has a proportionate interest in it. When the insured dies, each account is credited with its proportionate share of the death benefit proceeds. The proceeds, when received by the trustee, constitute investment return on the trust funds. The proceeds will be allocated to the accounts, therefore, in the ratio of the account balances, rather than in accordance with the allocation formula employed for employer contributions.

Life Insurance on Stockholders

Another important use which has been made of life insurance under profit sharing trusts follows somewhat in principle the procedure just outlined, although the purpose of the insurance is entirely different. The great majority of corporations in the United States are close corporations, that is, the stock is closely held; it is not traded on the stock exchanges, and ownership is limited to a relatively few persons, who are usually officers of the corporation or family members or relatives of the principal officers. The participants of a profit sharing trust established by such a corporation have a great deal at stake in the continued existence of the principal stockowners who were responsible for setting up the trust and making it possible for the employees to share in company profits. What would happen if the principal stockholders should die and their stock pass by inheritance and then be sold to parties unfavorable to the trust participants' interests? Would the plan of sharing profits be continued, or would the succeeding ownership vote to discontinue the arrangement? Certainly, there would be no assurance in advance of what the outcome might be. In such situations, it is not unusual to find the trustees of the profit sharing plan entering into an arrangement, for the protection and benefit of the participants, with the principal stockholders of the company, whereby at their death the trust may become the purchaser of a deceased stockholder's shares. To assure that the purchase price of the stock will be available on the exact date when it is needed, the trustee will insure the lives of the stockholders in favor of the trust. The premiums for the policies will be charged to the accounts of the participants, who will be the ultimate beneficiaries.

This arrangement would entail investing in the stock of the employer, and approval of the Commissioner of Internal Revenue must be obtained for such an investment to be made. No binding agreement, therefore, should be entered into by the trustee with a stockholder in advance which will guarantee that such a purchase will be made from the stockholder's estate at death. An option agreement may, however, be executed, giving the trustee the right to purchase the shares from the deceased's estate subject to the approval of the Internal Revenue Service.

Carried to its final conclusion, this arrangement should certainly be considered as being for the benefit of the employee participants or their beneficiaries. Ultimately, the entire business might be owned by the trust and by the participants of the trust, who are also the employees of the business. Subsequently, however, the trust would be engaged in an "unrelated trade or business," and the income it receives from the business would be taxable to it on the basis provided in Section 512 of the Code. However, this would be preferable insofar as the participants are concerned to the problems they would face if, as the result of the stockholder-owner's death, the business might have to be sold by the heirs or liquidated.

Insurance on Participants

Life insurance policies are frequently purchased on the lives of some or all of the participants of a profit sharing trust. The amount invested in life insurance will usually vary from plan to plan, depending upon such factors as (1) the primary aims and objectives of the employer in respect to his plan; (2) the type of policies available from the insurance company selected to underwrite the benefits; (3) whether the plan is just being initiated, or whether it has been in effect for several years prior to investing in insurance company contracts; and (4) whether the employees are making a contribution to the plan.

In defining profit sharing plans in the Internal Revenue Code regulations, Section 1.401(*b*)(1)(ii), the Commissioner made life insurance a permissive investment of profit sharing funds by including this statement: ". . . but the amounts allocated to the account of a participant may be used to provide for him or his family incidental life or accident or health insurance." The term "incidental" is defined in Revenue Ruling 61–157 as:

> In the case of a profit sharing plan which provides for the use of trust funds to purchase or pay premiums on ordinary life insurance contracts, the insurance feature is deemed to be incidental if (1) the aggregate premiums for life insurance in the case of each participant are less than one half of the aggregate of the contributions allocated to him at any particular time and (2) the plan requires the trustee to convert the entire value of the life insurance contract at or before retirement into cash or to provide periodic income so that no portion of such value may be used to continue life insurance protection beyond retirement or to distribute the contract to the participant.

In view of this incidental life insurance death benefit test, not more than 49 per cent of the contributions to a participant's account should be invested in policies of the ordinary or whole life type; but for the sake of conservatism and flexibility, it is usually customary to limit such investment to not more than 25 or 33⅓ per cent of the average annual contribution. An even more conservative approach is to delay the purchase of life insurance on any employees until they have been participants for three or five years. At that time a modest percentage of their accumulated account balances would be used to purchase policies on their lives. To meet the second test, the whole life insurance contracts of most of the life insurance companies include a conversion feature permitting the policies to be converted or exchanged at or before the normal retirement date of the participant to an annuity contract for a stipulated conversion charge. The annuity rate factors included in the contract are guaranteed as of the issue date of the original policy. If this conversion option is not exercised to provide the employee with an annuity income at his retirement, the policy may be distributed to him by the trustee when he retires, to be continued in force, taken as paid up, or surrendered for its cash value at his discretion.

Policies of other than the ordinary or whole life type, or higher premium policies such as retirement income, endowment at 65, and the like, are sometimes used for insuring the participants of a profit sharing plan. However, one of the primary objectives in insuring a participant's life is to increase the amount of the death benefit that would be received by his beneficiary should he die before he has been a participant long enough to have a substantial accumulation in his account. Whole life policies are most frequently employed, therefore, in order to obtain the maximum amount of permanent insurance available for a given amount of premium.

It is not essential to plan qualification that all employee-participants be insured. If each employee is given the right to direct the trustee whether he should or should not be insured, the plan will continue as qualified, irrespective of the number who are insured. Revenue Ruling 61–157, Part 5(*t*), provides: "Where amounts to be distributed to participants under a profit sharing trust are measured by investments which have been earmarked for their respective accounts, the trustee is to invest each participant's interest proportionately unless all participants have the right to direct the trustee to select the type of investment with respect to their individual shares." Life insurance is considered to be an earmarked investment for the account of a participant; so, quite frequently, plans permit the participants to direct the trustee that such investment should be made for their accounts. Thus, it is immaterial whether only one, a few, or all of the participants elect to be insured. Those who need and want life insurance can obtain it under the plan on a most favorable basis. The premiums are paid by the trustee from dollars on which the income tax to the insured is deferred. The insurance policy, as a part of the profit sharing account of the participant, provides death benefit proceeds to the extent of the amount at risk (difference between policy face amount and its cash value), which will be free of income tax to the beneficiary. The entire proceeds, in addition to the participant's account balance, when paid to the beneficiary, if other than the participant's estate, will be free of estate tax. Thus, life insurance included as an investment of a part of the account of a profit sharing plan participant has many advantages for the participant and his beneficiary. This is the reason why so many profit sharing plans make it permissive for the trustee to make such an investment. Some of the important advantages are these:

1. Investment in insurance for the benefit of the participant entails no additional cost to the employer. The inclusion of life insurance in the plan does not increase the contribution requirements.
2. Greater death benefit protection is provided for the insured participant. If death occurs in the early years of participation, the life insurance proceeds received by the participant's beneficiary may equal a total of the profit sharing allocations which might otherwise have been made to the participant's account had he lived for as many as 10 or 20 years in the future.
3. Federal income tax advantages are created for the participant's beneficiaries. The net life insurance proceeds are free of income tax, in contrast to amounts distributed to the beneficiary that do not represent life insurance proceeds.
4. Federal estate tax advantages are increased. The insurance proceeds are excludable from the deceased participant's estate for estate tax purposes.
5. Such an investment stabilizes annuity rates against inflation. Life insurance in the plan provides a vehicle by means of which a monthly lifetime income at any time in the future may be payable to the participant at annuity rates guaranteed as of the date the policy is originally issued, even though annuity costs in the interim period may have increased substantially.
6. Such an investment permits wider diversification for investment of trust assets. Life insurance may represent the fixed dollar portion of the plan's investment portfolio, allowing a more liberal investment approach for other trust assets.
7. Life insurance gives immediate values to younger participants, creating a more complete employee benefit plan. Younger employees often find it difficult to appreciate the benefits that are deferred until retirement under a profit sharing plan, and will work harder for profits if there is some immediate value created for them or their beneficiaries by the plan.

Annuity Contracts on Participants

Some profit sharing plans permit the trustee to invest some part or all of each participant's account in single-premium or annual-premium deferred annuity contracts during the employee's years of active participation. Such contracts, depending upon the insurer selected and the provisions of the plan, may be issued on either a group or an individual contract basis. A group arrangement may have some advantages if all employees are to be covered and the required minimum participation, usually 75 per cent, can be maintained. However, where such investment is at the direction of the participants and there can be no assurance as to the number who will direct the trustee to invest in annuities, individual contracts are customarily employed.

Generally, the purchase of annuity contracts will be postponed until a participant attains his normal retirement date or severs his employment and is to receive a distribution prior to his normal retirement date. The purchase by the trustee of an annuity contract at the participant's normal retirement date is advantageous. This will guarantee that the funds accumulated in the account of the participant at his retirement will provide him with a monthly life income for the balance of his lifetime. The alternative is distribution to the participant by the trustee of his account balance in installments until the principal is exhausted. This gives no assurance that the retiring participant will not outlive the principal. Some trusts require the trustee to purchase an annuity contract on each participant at retirement. Others give the participants the option of directing the trustee either to purchase an annuity or to distribute the account balance in a single sum or in installments, usually over a fixed period of years, such as ten.

Distribution to a terminating participant of his vested benefit in the form of an annuity contract on severance of employment is also advantageous. This permits deferment for the employee of the immediate income tax liability on the amount he would otherwise receive. Section 1.402(*a*) (1) (*a*) (2) of the Internal Revenue Code Regulations provides: "If a trust distributes an annuity contract not containing a life insurance death benefit element, there is no tax to the distributee until such time as the contract is surrendered for its cash value or income benefits are received." Thus, by the simple procedure of making the distribution to a terminating participant in the form of an annuity contract, the income tax liability on the amount vested may be postponed, and may even be deferred until he subsequently attains age 65 and starts receiving income payments from the annuity contract.

SELECTED REFERENCES

BIEGEL, HERMAN C., and OTHERS. *Pensions and Profit-Sharing.* 2d ed. Washington, D.C.: Bureau of National Affairs, Inc., 1956.

COMMERCE CLEARING HOUSE, INC. *Pension Plan Guide.* A loose-leaf service. Chicago, n.d.

FLIPPO, EDWIN B. *Profit-Sharing in American Business.* Columbus: Ohio State University, 1954.

PRENTICE-HALL, INC. *Pension and Profit Sharing.* A loose-leaf service. Englewood Cliffs, N.J., n.d.

SPENCER, CHARLES D. & ASSOCIATES, INC. *Employee Benefit Plan Research Reports.* A loose-leaf service published weekly. Chicago.

Chapter 45

PENSION AND PROFIT SHARING PLANS FOR SELF-EMPLOYED INDIVIDUALS

BY R. W. BENDER AND C. H. WAIN

Eleven years of consideration by the Congress of retirement programs for self-employed persons culminated in the Self-Employed Individuals Tax Retirement Act of 1962 becoming law on October 10, 1962, effective for tax years starting in 1963.[1] Much planning has been done by the various funding agencies to prepare for greater future use of the opportunities afforded. The response of the self-employed, or changes in the law or regulations, may require further development work by the funding agencies. This chapter provides a general background in the law, regulations, and funding arrangements at the time of its writing. More detailed study of their then current status should be made at the time establishment of an actual plan covering self-employed persons is being considered.

Background

An employee of a United States corporation may become covered under the qualified pension and profit sharing plans of the corporation even though the employee is also a stockholder of the corporation. The tax deferment benefits flowing from such coverage are discussed in detail in other chapters. However, the general effect is that substantial amounts can be accumulated during a person's working lifetime with no income tax being incurred on the amounts set aside, or on the investment income generated by such amounts, until a distribution to the person is made. Until the 1962 Act became effective, a qualified plan could not cover the owner or partners of an unincorporated business. A qualified plan could be established for the other employees of such business.

Determined but unsuccessful efforts to create a federal tax-deferred basis for the self-employed to accumulate funds for retirement were made

[1] This chapter was written in February, 1964—a time when relatively few individuals had taken advantage of this law. However, extensive regulations have been adopted by the Internal Revenue Service to implement it.

in the United States during the 1950's. Bills to accomplish this, sponsored by Representative Eugene Keogh and numbered HR 10 in recent years, had been before Congress since 1951. They were supported by self-employed professional persons represented by their national and state associations. Opposition came from the Treasury because of the expected revenue loss. Also, there was some more general opposition, since the proposals might have resulted in placing the self-employed in a more advantageous position than other persons not covered under qualified plans, or covered under such plans for modest benefits.

Similar efforts in the United Kingdom resulted, in 1956, in an act permitting persons not covered by an employer-sponsored pension plan to purchase a special type of annuity contract and claim deductions for the contributions for such contracts. The deduction was limited to the smaller of 10 per cent of earnings or 750 pounds sterling (approximately $2,100 at the end of 1963).

Consideration of the same problem led, in 1957, to the Canadian Income Tax Act being amended to permit an individual to establish a Registered Retirement Savings Plan for himself. A Canadian not covered by what in the United States would be called a qualified pension plan may set up his own Savings Plan and contribute (and claim as a deduction) the smaller of $2,500 or 10 per cent of earned income. (A person covered by a qualified plan may also establish a Savings Plan, but the total of his own income tax deductions for both plans may not exceed the smaller of $1,500 or 10 per cent of earned income.) The Registered Retirement Savings Plan must be a contractual arrangement with provisions for a life income at retirement, which cannot begin later than age 71. A lump-sum payment is not available to the individual, but the accumulation can be paid to his beneficiary. Life insurance policies can be used, but only the savings element in the premium is deductible. There are substantial tax penalties if the plan is abandoned.

About the time the Canadian arrangement became effective, Congress was considering a bill permitting a self-employed individual to make contributions to a restricted retirement fund administered by a bank under a trust or custodial arrangement, or to purchase a restricted retirement policy. The amount deductible in any year would have excluded any cost of net insurance protection and could not have exceeded the smaller of 10 per cent of earnings or $5,000, with a lifetime limit of $100,000. Persons at higher ages at the time the bill became law would have been allowed greater annual deductions to permit, in effect, the funding of benefits for past service. There were no restrictions on withdrawal, but there were tax penalties if withdrawal occurred. A lump-sum payment was available at retirement, but capital gains tax treatment of the payment was not applicable. Instead, the tax was to be five times the increase in tax resulting from including 20 per cent of the lump sum in current taxable income. The insurance companies would have been required to do special source reporting to the Treasury with respect to these policies.

A version of HR 10 was passed by the House in 1959. When it reached the Senate, it was rewritten in its entirety, and many proposals by the Treasury were included. The Treasury took this opportunity to propose new restrictions on benefits for "owner-managers" covered under qualified plans of incorporated businesses. Substantial opposition developed to these new restrictions, and the revision never came to a vote in the Senate. The Act adopted in 1962 contained many of the Treasury proposals but, as a result of action in the House-Senate Conference, did not include any new restrictions on owner-managers covered under corporate plans.

The requirements for a qualified plan not covering a self-employed person are less onerous than those for one that does. This difference suggests the desirability of the self-employed person changing his status to that of a regular employee, if this is possible, and if other considerations do not make this unwise. In many states, persons in certain professions (for example, doctors or lawyers) cannot practice under a corporate arrangement. In recent years, some states have changed their laws to permit incorporation. Others now permit formation of associations with certain corporate characteristics, which may result in classification as a corporation for Internal Revenue Code purposes. An example of a situation of this type was the Kintner case. A group of physicians reorganized their partnership into an association and gave it certain corporate characteristics which permitted it to remain a partnership under Montana law but to be deemed a corporation by the courts for federal income tax purposes. A result of this was that the pension plan of the new entity, which covered the doctor-associates, was deemed qualified.

The courts in the Kintner case were interpreting what is now Section 7701(*a*) of the Internal Revenue Code, which defines the term "corporation" as including an association. The regulations initially established relating to this section describe the characteristics an organization must have to be classified as an association taxable as a corporation. Some of the changes in state laws have been patterned to aid in meeting these requirements. The procedures for obtaining a favorable ruling that a given organization is an association taxable as a corporation currently require the district director of internal revenue to refer the case to the national office. However, in December of 1963, proposed amended regulations were issued. They provided essentially that an organization established as a professional service corporation under local law will not normally be considered a corporation for Internal Revenue Code purposes. In any event, no rulings are to be issued by the Internal Revenue Service on specific professional service corporation plans until the final form of these regulations is adopted.

The above discussion does not pertain to the effect of an election, under Section 1361 of the Internal Revenue Code, of an unincorporated business enterprise to be taxed as a corporation. This section of the Code specifically provides that a proprietor or partner does not become an employee for qualified plan purposes, and can be covered under a qualified plan only as a self-employed person.

Self-Employed Individuals Tax Retirement Act of 1962

The Self-Employed Individuals Tax Retirement Act of 1962 permits a qualified plan to cover self-employed persons as employees if the plan:

1. Provides for the inclusion of certain full-time employees without ownership interests in the business if any self-employed person covered by the plan is an owner-employee (i.e., owns more than 10 per cent of the business);
2. Limits, for owner-employees, the employer contribution that can be made, and the times at which benefits can begin and the period over which they can be paid; and
3. Generally conforms to all requirements previously imposed on qualified plans not covering self-employed persons, as well as certain additional conditions.

The employees who must be included in the retirement plan are all full-time employees who have completed at least three years of service. "Full-time" is given the specific meaning of customarily working more than twenty hours weekly more than five months a year. Furthermore, all employees' rights in the plan must be fully vested, and either the benefits or the contributions must be provided on a nondiscriminatory basis.

The employer contributions to the plan that may be made for an owner-employee are currently limited to 10 per cent of his net earnings from self-employment, and are further limited to not more than $2,500 in any year. Amounts applied to provide life insurance protection are not considered as deductible contributions for this purpose. Earnings from self-employment include all earnings of a professional man derived from the practice of his profession, including that from assistants or technicians rendering service in his name. For other self-employed persons a drastic limitation is imposed if capital is a material income-producing factor in the business. If his share of the net profits of the business is $2,500 or more, this limitation is that not more than the greater of $2,500 or 30 per cent of his share may be considered as coming from personal services. If his share is less than $2,500, the entire share may be considered earnings. Furthermore, no definite standards are available to determine if capital is a material income-producing factor in any particular business.

The owner-employee is also limited as to the period in which his benefits can commence. A penalty tax is imposed if he receives benefits from the accumulated funds before he is age 59½ unless he is then totally and permanently disabled. His beneficiary, of course, can receive death benefits at his death without being subject to this age restriction. Furthermore, his benefits must commence before the end of his tax year in which he attains age 70½; and like the benefits for all other participants in the plan, his benefits must be paid over a period not greater than his lifetime or life expectancy, or the lifetime or joint life expectancy of himself and his spouse.

Another restriction discourages integration of plan benefits with social security benefits. Such integration is permitted only if the employer contributions to the plan for owner-employees are not more than one third of the total contributions. The integration takes the form of permitting employer contributions to the plan, plus employer-paid social security taxes, including self-employment taxes, to be a uniform per cent of earnings. Since social security taxes of self-employed persons are at one and a half times the rates applicable to other employees, employer contributions on earnings subject to social security taxes must be reduced for each self-employed person by $1.50 as compared to a $1.00 reduction for each other employee, even when all persons in the plan have earnings at least equal to the current social security wage base of $4,800.

The handling of voluntary contributions of participants gives an illustration of the application of general pension plan requirements to plans including the self-employed. Revenue Ruling 59–185 requires that voluntary employee contributions to any qualified retirement plan not exceed 10 per cent of earnings. The Internal Revenue Code, as amended by the Self-Employed Individuals Tax Retirement Act of 1962, contains a further limitation, in that it permits voluntary contributions by owner-employees only while other employees are covered by the plan and have the same privilege. Also, the annual amount of the additional contribution by an owner-employee is further limited to $2,500 per year.

If the contributions, including any additional voluntary contributions on behalf of owner-employees, should for any reason exceed the limits described above, the excess, plus interest attributable to them, less expenses of the funding agency, must be returned. If these excess contributions are not returned, tax penalties and exclusion from coverage may result.

As in other qualified plans, all employer contributions to a retirement plan on behalf of employees are, within broad limits, deductible from the income of the employer for federal income tax purposes. However, for a self-employed person (even one who is not an owner-employee), only the smallest of one half the employer contributions, 5 per cent of earnings from personal services, or $1,250 may be deducted.

Other limitations imposed by this law include the following:

1. Persons other than the self-employed may have the excess of a lump-sum distribution from a qualified plan over their contributions to it taxed as a capital gain. For the self-employed a special averaging provision is included. The amount of contributions (both employer and voluntary) on which the self-employed person previously paid income tax is deducted from the total distribution. Then the increase in the self-employed person's federal income tax in the year of distribution caused by adding one fifth of the balance of the distribution is determined. His federal income tax on the distribution is five times this increase.
2. The entire value of any distribution from the plan made at the death of a self-employed person is included in his gross estate for federal estate tax purposes. For other employees, only amounts arising from their own contributions are includable.
3. The beneficiary of a deceased self-employed person pays income tax on the entire amount of cash surrender value or other accumulation that is in excess of the nondeductible amounts that have been contributed to the plan. The difference between the total death benefit under a life insurance policy and its total cash value is not subject to income tax. For other employees, there is a $5,000 exclusion for employer-provided death benefits, and capital gains treatment for any balance.

A self-employed person who controls more than one business is subject to additional limitations. Generally speaking, if he wishes to establish a plan, he must do so for *all* his employees. The limits applicable to the self-employed person are not increased as a result of his activity being divided into several businesses.

Establishing a Plan

By establishing the dollar and percentage limits for the owner-employee on contributions, rather than on benefits, the law effectively encourages the establishment of money purchase plans providing whatever benefit is generated by contributions of a fixed percentage of earnings. This can be modified into a profit sharing arrangement by further limiting, in accordance with a definite formula which cannot be changed except for business necessity, the contributions for all participants other than owner-employees to a percentage of the profits of the business.

A plan providing a specified level of benefits is also possible. When the self-employed person is older than his employees, a smaller percentage of the salary of the employees would be contributed to the plan than would be contributed for the self-employed person. However, with the contribution limits for owner-employees restricted as drastically as they are, designing and operating a level-of-benefits plan is difficult, especially for partnerships. The self-employed person should consider the employee relations aspects of such a plan as well as the saving it permits over the money purchase basis.

Plans including the self-employed can be qualified using the regular procedures applicable to corporate plans. In addition, the Internal Revenue Service has developed a system for advance approval of master or prototype plans which can be submitted by an association of employers, a trustee, an insurance company, or other similar sponsors. Once approval is received for the master plan, the individual employer may use such a plan merely by adopting it as his own and making a few elections that may be permitted. Approval of the use of the plan by such employer may be requested by submitting a simple one-page statement (IRS Form 3673) to the Internal Revenue Service.

Use of Individual Insurance and Annuity Contracts

The plan may be funded in any of the ways available to a regular qualified plan. However, split-funded arrangements using individual life insurance policies and a supplementary fund may require substantial modification because the amounts in the supplementary fund are vested in the employee. Essentially, insurance benefits probably must disappear by the time the total of the policy values and the supplementary fund exceed $1,000 per $10 of retirement income. Plans, including those that do not cover self-employed individuals, can now be funded by individual life insurance and annuity contracts held by a bank custodian instead of a trustee. The object is to have a more economical way of accumulating the funds in these limited categories than normally occurs when a trusteeship is required. However, in practice the regulations appear to require such extensive services from custodians as to make the actual savings over a regular trusteeship quite limited.

The law also permits any qualified plan to be funded by nontransferable annuity contracts that do not have to be held by a trustee or custodian. This arrangement is practical from the standpoint of the Internal Revenue Service because the insurance companies can be subjected to strict requirements about reporting transactions involving the contracts. A nontransferable contract is one that cannot be sold or assigned to anyone but the issuer. Thus, conventional retirement annuity contracts can be made nontransferable by the addition of a simple endorsement. Furthermore, a policy that provides only incidental amounts of life insurance, as compared to its total retirement income benefits, may similarly be made a nontransferable annuity.

In using individual insurance and annuity contracts, a basic problem is whether to use level premium contracts or some special type that will permit flexible contributions. A level premium contract presents the advantages of insurance most clearly, since it can show the guaranteed amount of retirement and other benefits that will be provided. Since it tends to assure a definite level of premium income for the issuer, more adequate initial compensation can be provided for the agent than can be furnished under a flexible premium contract, while still producing sound results for the buyer. However, a level premium contract could not be used advantageously if contributions to the plan must always be closely related to actual current earnings. Fortunately, the law provides that the premium for a contract can be based on the average of the amounts that could have been contributed over the three-year period preceding issue, assuming the law had been in effect in those years. Any year in which the owner-employee had no earnings can be omitted. However, the allowable deduction for the premiums paid for a self-employed person is based on the lesser of the premium paid, excluding the cost of life insurance protection and other supplemental benefits, or the contribution that would have resulted if the plan were based on current earnings. An additional requirement is that if this provision is used for owner-employees, it must be used for other employees, at least whenever it would result in their receiving larger benefits. Also, in determining the amount to be contributed to a plan, the cost of any life insurance protection or other supplemental benefits must be included in the $2,500 contribution limit.

The advantages to the participant of a plan based on the three-year average provision of the law are the following.

1. An established benefit program can be maintained as long as premiums are continued, even though earnings may decline in some years.
2. Supplemental benefits, such as life insurance, can be easily provided by the plan.
3. No current income tax is payable on the earnings of the entire contributions to the plan, even though these exceed the amount that would be payable under a current earnings formula.

The advantages of a plan based on flexible premium contracts are the following:

1. The employer can keep costs close to earnings.
2. The maximum possible deductions from current income tax for contributions for self-employed persons will be obtained.

Whether a level premium or a flexible premium approach is selected, standard plans for carrying out either type will probably be prepared by many insurance companies. When funded by nontransferable contracts, they will provide an efficient way to establish a retirement plan under this complex law.

No reference has been made in any of the preceding to the use of existing policies. Present regulations prohibit the contribution of property, other than money, and this seems to prevent the use of existing policies. However, there have been some indications that the matter is still under consideration by the Internal Revenue Service.

Use of Group Contracts

As mentioned above, professional associations were strong advocates of HR 10 legislation. Now that such a law has become effective, many of these associations are at work establishing master plans and funding arrangements. The purpose of this activity is to strengthen the associations by rendering a valuable service to present members, and perhaps by attracting new members.

The association programs are apparently going to offer their members a choice among several instruments for funding their own individual plans, and the right to change from one funding instrument to another. This flexibility will probably be achieved at a lower rate of expense than would be incurred under other similar arrangements made on an individual basis. Master plans permitting these flexible arrangements will undoubtedly be filed with the Internal Revenue Service by many professional associations.

At the time this chapter was written, several national associations, including the American Bar Association and the American Medical Association, had announced their plans. Both of these associations had established pooled investment arrangements with a bank trustee, and had also arranged for group annuity contracts. Where a pooled investment trust is to be used for plans covering self-employed persons, the Securities and Exchange Commission requires registration under the Securities Act of 1933 on the basis that "securities" are being offered. (Security laws of some states may impose additional requirements.) As a result, each association has filed a comprehensive registration statement with the SEC which describes in detail the entire program, including the group annuity arrangement. A "prospectus" based on the filing has been distributed to the members of the association, along with other material needed to elect to participate in the arrangement.

Generally speaking, the participants are able to direct contributions to the plan, after deduction of an administrative charge, either entirely to the pooled trusts or to the group annuity contracts, or a portion to each. At retirement, funds can be transferred from the trusts to the group annuity contracts to purchase annuities.

Four deposit administration annuity contracts are used in the AMA program. Apparently, the basic preretirement record keeping for participants will be done by the AMA. The insurance companies will maintain unallocated deposit administration funds for the contributions directed to them, and will put annuities into effect or make lump-sum payments as directed by the administering agency.

The group annuity contract used in the ABA arrangement is a variation of the conventional group deferred annuity contract. Accounts are maintained for individuals, and all money received by the insurance company is allocated to individuals. The annuity purchase rate basis has a feature that, in effect, reflects the interest rates on new investments at the time contributions are made. Provision is also made for purchase of additional annuities at retirement by transfer of amounts from the pooled trusts.

The limited experience to date indicates that associations want to make available a facility for accumulating at least some portion of the contributions in equities. This can be done by the pooled trust device mentioned above, by the purchase of mutual fund shares from an investment company, or by the purchase of variable annuities. The SEC has decided it will not object to issue by insurance companies of a group variable annuity contract as a part of a qualified plan covering self-employed persons, provided the Securities Act of 1933 is complied with. As a result, insurance companies will be able, where state law permits, to issue two group annuity contracts—one conventional and one variable—to an association and thereby accommodate all the contributions made under the plan, including those going into equities.

Other Funding Facilities

Other funding agencies, including the United States government, are willing to accumulate funds for qualified plans covering the self-employed. Mutual fund shares may be used if the shares are held in a bank custodial account. Many mutual funds already use a bank in connection with their programs for gradual accumulation of shares. It is relatively easy to extend this arrangement with the bank to have it act as custodian under self-employed plans. Therefore, many mutual funds are proceeding to have master plans set up and will furnish the necessary documents to interested self-employed persons.

A somewhat similar arrangement is available from the trust departments of banks active in the pension business. These banks are willing to establish separately invested trusts but, because of the small amounts involved in most plans, will probably encourage the use of their collective trusts, which are similar in many respects to mutual funds. It may be that such collective trusts will have to comply with SEC registration requirements as well as those promulgated by the Comptroller of the Currency.

The new law provides that for qualified plan purposes an "annuity" includes a face amount certificate. A face amount certificate is a security issued by certain investment companies. It promises to pay a stated or determinable sum or sums at a fixed or determinable date or dates more than twenty-four months after issue. It can be purchased by periodic installments. Such a certificate must be nontransferable, unless it is to be held by a trustee or custodian.

Finally, the federal government has made available a special bond which can be purchased only in the name of an individual under a qualified plan. Interest, which is at the rate of 3¾ per cent per year, is paid only at redemption; and the bond can be redeemed only at death, on disability, or after the attainment of age 59½. It is nontransferable. As contributions are made, they are used to purchase these bonds. The bonds are usually distributed to the individual at retirement. No tax is payable until a bond is redeemed, and the tax then is at ordinary income rates and is based on the excess of the proceeds over the portion of the cost of the bond for which no tax deduction was taken.

Future

As mentioned in the opening sentences of this chapter, it is too early to tell how many persons will be covered under plans established as a result of the Self-Employed Individuals Tax Retirement Act of 1962. The experience under the somewhat less restrictive law in Canada may be of interest. There, many persons who could make deductible contributions do not do so because the amounts contributed become, in effect, inaccessible. In the United States the funds paid on behalf of self-employed persons are also inaccessible and are only partially deductible. Also, fully vested contributions must be made for certain employees of the self-employed person who is an owner-employee. These added features will require a careful appraisal by any self-employed person before setting up a plan, especially if he is not a professional person and therefore possibly subject to the severe limitations applicable when capital is a material factor in the earnings of the business. If he does decide to set up a plan, efficient means for establishing and funding it will be available.

Congress will probably consider proposals for liberalizations in the law. Possibly, also, there will be counterproposals for tightening requirements for other qualified plans to bring the self-employed requirements and those for other plans that include the owners of a business closer together. The resulting opposition and controversy may slow efforts to put a more liberal act into effect.

SELECTED REFERENCES

COX, ANDREW H. "H.R. 10 Final Regulations—General Review and Analysis," *Trusts and Estates,* Vol. 102 (November, 1963), pp. 1055–57, 1113–18.

HINCKLEY, CHARLES C. "The Keogh-Smathers Act—One Year Later," *Journal of the American Society of Chartered Life Underwriters,* Vol. XVIII, No. 1 (Winter, 1964), p. 49.

JOHNSON, GLENDON E. "Keogh Act: Past, Present and Future," *Journal of the American Society of Chartered Life Underwriters,* Vol. XVII, No. 2 (Spring, 1963), p. 101.

PRENTICE-HALL, INC. *Self-Employed Retirement Plans,* pp. 8001–23. A pension and profit sharing service. Englewood Cliffs, N.J., n.d.

"Report of Committee on Pension and Profit-Sharing Trusts," *Trusts and Estates,* Vol. 102 (October, 1963), pp. 967–78.

"20 Questions on Final Regulations under H.R. 10," *Trusts and Estates,* Vol. 102 (October, 1963), pp. 1035–37.

Chapter 46

DEFERRED COMPENSATION AND STOCK OPTION PLANS

BY CHARLES B. McCAFFREY

The impact of high individual income tax rates has resulted in a persistent search for a satisfactory means of increasing the true compensation of business executives. The tax factor, along with other forces, has brought about a variety of indirect compensation and incentive schemes, including a variety of deferred compensation and stock option plans.

Nature of Deferred Compensation

Broadly speaking, the term "deferred compensation" could encompass any postponed payment for services rendered. In that sense, practically all compensation is deferred, in that ordinarily the employee must perform his services before receiving his compensation, whether it be in the form of a semimonthly check or a year-end bonus.

Deferred compensation has a more specific meaning, however, in referring to plans in which compensation is received long after services are performed. Thus the term might properly include qualified pension and profit sharing plans, selective salary continuation plans, stock options, and the like. The distinguishing feature of these plans is that the lag between performance of services and receipt of payment for them, which usually exists under any method of compensation, is greatly exaggerated, often varying from several years to twenty years or more. Plans which defer a part of compensation and distribute currently the remainder are also classified as deferred compensation plans. The subject matter of this chapter will be limited to the selective type of plan, with particular emphasis on executive salary continuation and stock option arrangements.

Advantages of Deferred Compensation

The advantages of deferred compensation to both the executive and his employer are usually readily apparent. For the executive, there is an increase in his after-tax compensation resulting from deferring the receipt of part of his income until his retirement, death, or disability, when the need for it will grow and his income tax bracket presumably will be lower. For the employer, it provides an attractive lure, enabling him to obtain and retain outstanding management personnel in a competitive executive labor market.

A person who derives his income solely from personal services suffers serious tax disadvantages in comparison with one whose income stems from capital. The income of the executive, like that of the professional man, is likely to fluctuate widely during his working life span. Ordinarily, it takes years of education, training, and experience for him to reach his peak earnings position, with a large part of his lifetime earnings being concentrated in a relatively short period. Much of these earnings represents, to a considerable degree, a return of invested capital. Under well-recognized principles of thrift, a substantial portion of these peak earnings ought to be put aside to provide an adequate fund for the future.

Qualified pension and profit sharing plans alone are not the answer. The necessary limitations of these plans frequently render the benefits to top employees wholly inadequate.[1] What is needed is an above-average, over-all program, including deferred compensation, which will be acceptable to both the executive and his employer. The following factual situation is illustrative of the situation under discussion:

> Executive A of the Emanon Corporation is vice president in charge of sales. He is age 50 and plans to retire in 15 years. Last year, he was paid a salary of $25,000 and received a bonus, based on a percentage of sales, of $40,000. At no time during the past 10 years has his bonus fallen below $25,000. He is more than satisfied with the *amount* of his compensation, but he is deeply concerned about his inability to set aside enough, after taxes, to achieve his goal of retiring at age 65. For example, on his top $10,000 of earnings each year, A keeps less than $5,000.[2] If he were to defer it until retirement, he probably could keep $6,800 or more.

To anyone familiar with the technical aspects of formulating and establishing a qualified pension or profit sharing plan, the deferred compensation arrangement necessary to accomplish the desired result is refreshingly simple. In nonlegal terminology, the contractual arrangement could be summarized as follows: "For each year the executive performs services prior to termination of employment, the employer promises to pay him, or his designated beneficiary, in addition to any other current compensation for services rendered, $10,000 in annual installments, com-

---

[1] There are provisions prohibiting discrimination "in favor of employees who are officers, shareholders, persons whose principal duties consist in supervising the work of other employees, or highly compensated employees." Internal Revenue Code, Sec. 401(*a*)(4).

[2] Figure based on a joint return. It would be less than $4,000 on a separate return.

mencing on the first day of the year following his retirement, death, disability, or any other agreed-upon termination."

It is the current practice to include certain contingency provisions, depending on the desires and relative bargaining positions of the parties involved. There is no legal question as to the binding effect of such contracts. The question of most frequent concern to the executive who considers such an arrangement has to do with the future financial capacity of the employer to perform.

Funding

The importance of funding to the employee will vary depending on the nature, size, and financial status of the employer-firm. Where the employer is a relatively small corporation, the employee may be concerned about the firm's financial ability to pay when the time comes. He may be further concerned about the willingness of future management to meet the obligation out of future earnings, particularly when his services are not contributing to them. Of course, the firm is bound on the contract, but contracts have been known to be violated. Ordinarily, the employee will feel much more secure under the arrangement if some type of funding process is in effect. Also, most firms will prefer to fund their obligations over the period during which the employee is actually making his contribution to the firm.

The Funding Problem

Whether or not a plan of executive deferred compensation can be funded depends on what is meant by funding. A nonqualified plan cannot, from a practical point of view, be funded in the same sense that a qualified pension profit sharing plan is funded. It is not economically feasible under a nonqualified plan to separate the fund in such a way as to remove it from the future claims of creditors of the employer-firm and provide a current income tax advantage to the employee. For example, assuming a trusteed fund, if the employer is to get its deduction when the money is placed into the fund, the employee's rights in the fund must be nonforfeitable. But if his rights in the fund are nonforfeitable, he will be taxed in the year in which the money is deposited (under the economic-benefit or cash-equivalent theory). This latter result can be prevented by making the employee's rights to the fund contingent or forfeitable. But then the employer must forgo its deduction, not only currently, but forever.[3] Few employers would be interested in such an arrangement.

Nevertheless, some type of funding is desirable. The firm does have a liability to meet in the future. To ignore it for the present would be equivalent to overstating current profits. Sound business practice would

---

[3] Internal Revenue Code, Sec. 404(*a*)(*b*).

require a sinking fund into which annual deposits are made, sufficient to produce the sum necessary to meet the obligation when it becomes due. Such a fund would remain within the firm. The firm would own it. The employee would be given no rights in it whatsoever. Since the employee has no interest in the fund and cannot, at any time, compel a distribution from it, the fund should in no way alter or disturb the tax status of the proposed agreement. Of course, the employer-firm cannot deduct the annual deposits to the fund but, instead, will deduct the payments made from it to the employee at a later date. The employee will then be taxed as he receives the payments.

A Workable Solution Using Life Insurance

Funding can be in the form of cash, securities, annuities, or life insurance. Since, under many deferred compensation plans, the employer-firm will be assuming obligations that may be accelerated in the event of death or disability, insurance on the lives of the employees involved would appear to be the most appropriate funding instrument. The type of policy to be used would depend upon the individual circumstances in each case. A nonparticipating endowment or a participating endowment on a net basis usually can be made to fit in very well. A straight life policy may be used if the emphasis is to be on protection. For the average deferred compensation case, however, the paid-up-at-65 whole life contract on a gross basis seems to offer the greatest flexibility. The dividend each year can be used to purchase paid-up additions, thus increasing the build-up of cash values, so that the aggregate amounts available at age 65 will be sufficient to fund the entire pay-out.

Income Tax Considerations

The insurance contract on the life of the employee should be owned by the employer. The employer should apply for the policy, possess all incidents of ownership, pay the premiums, and collect all proceeds and avails. Any deviation from this procedure, particularly one which passes incidents of ownership to the insured employee, is likely to result in undesirable tax consequences.

For example, the Chrysler Corporation had a key employee too old to participate in the firm's regular pension plan. Prior to his retirement date, the Corporation purchased a single-premium annuity policy for the purpose of providing retirement benefits. The ownership and all rights under the policy were vested in the Chrysler Corporation. When the employee retired two years later, the Corporation transferred all rights in the policy to him. At the same time, the policy was endorsed with a provision making it nonassignable and prohibiting commutation, anticipation, or encumbrance. In other words, the employee had no right to any cash surrender value. He was only entitled to the annuity payment each year. Nevertheless, the court held that the entire value of the policy constituted income to the employee in the year in which it was delivered to him.[4]

The above case points up the importance of the employer retaining, *at all times,* all incidents of ownership in the policy. It is equally important that the employer be the beneficiary under the policy for both the living benefits (endowment proceeds, cash values, disability benefits, and the like) and the death benefits. Occasionally, the suggestion is made that the wife of the employee be made the beneficiary of the death proceeds. This may have a twofold purpose. It is desired that the amounts come to her as "insurance death proceeds," free of income tax.[5] Moreover, there is additional security in looking directly to the insurance company for the promised payments. Assuming the suggested designation to be revocable—and it ordinarily would be—it is to be *avoided* for two reasons:

1. In all probability, the employee would be taxed each year on the term cost of the net amount at risk under the theory of its being additional compensation. (The possibility of his being taxed on the full premium deposit seems rather remote, since the employer has complete ownership of the cash value portion and can take it at will.)
2. The ownership of the cash value would vest in the widow at her husband's death. The effect of this would be that either the employer would have made a gift of the cash value (unlikely) or the amount would be deemed additional compensation for past services rendered by her husband (most likely). If the latter is the result, then the entire cash value would be ordinary income to the widow in the year in which her right to it vests, viz., at the death of her husband.

The arrangement described above should not be confused with the conventional split-dollar plans, which do provide distinct tax advantages.

Cost Considerations

Where a deferred compensation plan is funded by life insurance, the following facts should be clearly understood. The required annual premium deposit consists of two things:

1. A capital transfer (cash into policy cash values). This part of the transaction can be likened to a transfer of corporate surplus funds into a savings account, government bonds, or some other type of fixed-dollar investment. It should be noted that the interest earnings on the fund are currently free of income tax.
2. An expense (the charge for the insurance element).

Neither segment of the premium deposit is a deductible item. Obviously, there could be no more expectation of deducting the capital transfer portion than of deducting a deposit to a bank account. As for the expense portion, it is not deductible because it is not considered a true expense of

---

[4] *Eliot C. Morse,* 17 TC 1244 (1952).

[5] Internal Revenue Code, Sec. 101(*a*).

operating the business. In fact, there is a specific provision in the Code prohibiting the deduction of premiums on business-owned life insurance.[6]

What It Costs the Corporation

Another question frequently arises in regard to deductibility and deferred compensation. Ordinarily couched in the form of an objection by the employer (apart from whether life insurance is considered or not), it runs somewhat as follows: "If we pay the executive $10,000 in cash this year, it only costs $5,000 (deductible expense).[7] If we set $10,000 aside for him, it takes $20,000 to do it (nondeductible item—$10,000 tax). Therefore, it costs us $15,000 more to defer it than to pay it."

A simple way to get a true picture of the situation is to isolate a segment of the firm's operating income before taxes, say, $100,000. Then, look at the effect on surplus under three separate sets of circumstances: (1) The $10,000 is not paid to the executive at all, (2) it is paid to him currently, (3) it is deferred until later.

Not Paid	*Paid Currently*	*Deferred*
$100,000 Gross income	$100,000 Gross income	$100,000 Gross income
50,000 Income tax	10,000 Bonus (deductible)	50,000 Income tax
	$ 90,000 Income before corporate tax	$ 50,000 Net after tax
	45,000 Income tax	10,000 Fund for deferred pay-out (nondeductible)
$ 50,000 Net for surplus	$ 45,000 Net for surplus	$ 40,000 Net for surplus

When the ultimate effect on corporate surplus is considered, the above figures clearly confirm the employer's initial statement, namely, that it costs the firm $5,000 to pay the executive $10,000 currently (a difference of $50,000 and $45,000 to surplus).

But what of the employer's conclusion that it costs $15,000 more to defer and set aside the $10,000? This is obviously false. The difference in effect on surplus between paying the executive and setting aside the deferred amount is only $5,000. Besides, the firm still has the use of the $10,000. If so desired, it could invest it in stocks, in bonds, in key-man life insurance, or in the business enterprise itself. In fact, the $10,000 could well be carried currently as a part of surplus, thus putting surplus in the same position, for the time being, as if the firm had not paid the executive.

[6] "No deduction shall be allowed for premiums paid on any life insurance policy covering the life of any officer or employee, or of any person financially interested in any trade or business carried on by the taxpayer, when the taxpayer is directly or indirectly a beneficiary under such policy." Internal Revenue Code, Sec. 264(*a*)(1).

[7] Assuming 50 per cent federal corporate income tax bracket.

If the annual deferred amount is invested in life insurance, the surplus account would be reduced by only the early-year cost of the protection element.

If the $10,000 is invested each year in life insurance, does that preclude the possibility of the aggregate deposits being used in the business if needed? Not at all. The cash value is available and readily acceptable at any time as collateral security for a nonrecourse loan. The issuing company itself will lend at 5 per cent, which constitutes an interest ceiling for borrowing purposes. It must also be remembered that if and when the cash values are being used in the business, the insurance company is crediting the borrowed amount with interest. Many companies, though guaranteeing 2 to 2½ per cent, are crediting in excess of 3 per cent currently. So, in determining the effective cost of borrowing the cash values for business purposes, the fact that the 5 per cent interest charge is deductible under present law (assuming a valid business purpose) and that the 3 per cent credited is currently free of income tax cannot be overlooked. Balancing each other, it is more like a 2½ per cent effective cost against a 3 per cent credit.

Employee Benefits

Assume that it has been agreed to make certain payments to the employee executive and/or his family commencing with his retirement, death, or disability. With multiple-purpose key-man life insurance as the funding instrument, the procedure, in brief, would be as follows:

Death Benefit. Though the executive is willing to defer certain amounts until retirement, he desires that his wife or other designated beneficiary collect every dollar he defers in the event he does not live to do so himself. In the type of case described, this is invariably a basic minimum demand.[8] Naturally, he will be pleased to accept a greater death benefit but ordinarily will not insist on it. This factor becomes of the greatest importance in gaining acceptance by the employer of the insured plan. A glance at Table 46–1 will reveal why.

This illustration compares the benefits, to a corporation in the 50 per cent bracket, of an unfunded plan with a plan funded by life insurance. The figures are based on a life fully paid at 65 participating policy issued on a male at age 50 with a gross annual premium of $10,000. The dividends are being used to purchase additional amounts of paid-up insur-

[8] It is of fundamental importance to distinguish between an employee deferring income that he could have agreed to take in cash currently, and an employer offering an additional retirement benefit in the nature of an informal, nonqualified pension plan to employees on a selective basis. There can be considerable difference between supplementary deferred income and deferring (in a sense) one's own income. There are many who will be pleased to accept the former so long as they are not asked to submit to the latter. Obviously, the forfeiture provisions can be made much stronger in the one case than in the other.

TABLE 46–1

FUNDED VERSUS UNFUNDED PLAN—A COST COMPARISON*

	If Death Occurs at Age 50	55	60	65	70	75	80	85
1. Net cost to corporation of payments to executive and/or beneficiary (50% tax bracket)	$ 5,000	$ 25,000	$ 50,000	$ 75,000	$ 75,000	$ 75,000	$ 75,000	$ 75,000
2. Reduced by tax-free offset of paid-up dividends under insured funded plan					8,742	17,902	27,419	37,198
3. Reduced net cost	$ 5,000	$ 25,000	$ 50,000	$ 75,000	$ 66,258	$ 57,098	$ 47,581	$ 37,802
4. Total insurance deposits	10,000	50,000	100,000	150,000 *C.V.(151,804)*†	150,000	150,000	150,000	150,000
5. Total net outlay under insured funded plan (line 3 + line 4)	15,000	75,000	150,000	225,000	216,258	207,098	197,581	187,802
6. Total recovery under insured funded plan	161,214	169,275	181,043	195,875	195,875 (209,095)	195,875 (222,959)	195,875 (237,791)	195,875 (250,234)
7. Excess or deficit of insurance proceeds over total outlay under insured funded plan	+146,214	+95,275	+31,043	−29,125	−20,383 (−15,905)	−11,223 (−2,041)	+1,706 (+12,791)	+8,073 (+25,234)
8. Advantages of insured plan over unfunded plan (compare line 1 with line 7)	151,214	119,275	81,043	45,875	54,617 (59,095)	63,777 (72,959)	73,294 (87,791)	83,073 (100,234)

* The illustrative dividend results shown herein are based on the dividend scale in use currently. They are not a guarantee, promise, or estimate of future results, which necessarily will depend on future experience.

† Total cash value at age 65 of $151,804 could be used to produce an income of approximately $800 a month for life with a full-refund feature.

ance. The figures, except for those which appear in parentheses and which will be referred to later, are self-explanatory. The advantages of the insured plan appear evident over the entire period of the deferred arrangement. The point to be noted and stressed is the tax-free benefit which will accrue to the corporation in the event of the employee's death prior to retirement. Line 7 shows the difference between the total net outlay under the insured plan (line 5) and the death proceeds (line 6), and may be considered free key-man indemnity. The term "free" is used in the sense that although this amount accrues to the benefit of the corporation, it was actually the insured's deferred income which paid for it. True, the benefit decreases each year until finally, as the employee approaches retirement, there is nothing left. But this is as it should be and is in keeping with the generally accepted principle of indemnity. There is no point in a firm being indemnified for the loss of a *retired* key man.

Observe that in the early years of the contract, this indemnity is quite substantial. The firm may agree to pay a portion of it, which, when added to the total amount deferred, would constitute a minimum death benefit. Such an amount might be measured by one or two years' base salary. To agree to pay the executive the full amount, however, particularly as it stands for the earlier years, might be objectionable on two grounds.

1. The amount, being quite large, could possibly be deemed an unreasonable payment for such relatively short service, and consequently not deductible.
2. Such an arrangement ties the policy itself too closely to the deferred contract. It might just possibly destroy the deferred tax treatment.

Retirement Benefit. When the executive reaches retirement age (herein assumed to be age 65), the corporation has several choices in regard to the use of the life insurance policy:

1. It may take the then cash value in cash or place it under one of the optional modes of settlement. In our example the estimated combined value at age 65 is $151,804, which is greater than the aggregate premium deposits of $150,000.

   The type of option selected will ordinarily depend upon the nature of the agreed-upon pay-out with the executive. It may be for 10 years or 15 years, as in the instant case. If a life income is desired, the particular policy used in the illustration will produce an income of approximately $800 per month, with a minimum guarantee of the return of the full cash value. Again, it should be stressed that it is the corporation which receives these monies from the insurance company, and it is the corporation which expenses them out to the executive. In effect, the corporation is the annuitant and will receive back its total deposits free of income tax, with only the interest element being taxable income under the annuity principle.[9]

   The executive, of course, will report the full amounts received by him. His net after taxes during the retirement pay-out should be compared

[9] Internal Revenue Code, Sec. 72(*a*).

with what he would retain currently on the same amount when added to his other income. In many cases the deferment will more than double the effectiveness of his savings for retirement.

2. Since at age 65 the suggested policy of insurance is fully paid up, the corporation may elect to keep it in force and ultimately collect the paid-up face value of $195,875 (see Table 46–1, line 6, ages 65 on). Meanwhile, the pay-out to the executive would be made out of current operating income. It should be noted that this particular policy continues to participate in dividends even though no further premium payments are required. The total paid-up dividends are shown in five-year intervals on line 2. These amounts are received free of income tax by the corporation and can be used each year to offset the pay-out to the executive. Observe that under this procedure the maximum cost or deficit to the corporation is $29,125 (line 7, age 65). This can only occur if the executive dies at age 65. If he dies earlier, the corporation's outlay is reduced by the saving in premium payments and by the greater excess of death proceeds over the total premium deposits; if he dies later, the outlay is reduced by the paid-up dividend.
3. The third choice is much the same as number two, with this difference: The corporation, instead of taking the paid-up dividends in cash, continues to use them to purchase paid-up additions. Under this arrangement the amount of the death benefit continues to increase, as indicated by the figures within the parentheses on line 6. Of course, the paid-up dividend setoff is postponed until the executive dies; so in determining the excess or deficit of insurance proceeds over the total corporate outlay (line 7), the total net outlay figure of $225,000, unreduced by the paid-up dividends, is the proper one. To use the reduced amounts of the later years for this purpose would be to count the paid-up dividend twice. Again, line 8 shows the over-all advantage to the corporation of the insured plan over an unfunded arrangement.

Disability Benefits. For a relatively small additional amount,[10] a waiver-of-premium provision can be inserted in the policy. Should the insured become disabled within the terms of this provision, the premium will be waived by the issuing company. The corporate owner then will be relieved of the necessity of making the annual premium deposit, and still the cash values in the policy will continue to grow and to enhance the surplus position. This amount comes into the corporation on a tax-free basis. Again assuming a 50 per cent tax bracket, the sum is equivalent to $20,000 of operating income. In fact, the corporation could expense out $20,000 per year to the disabled executive at no cost to it at all. Again isolating $100,000 of operating income and comparing the effect on surplus between no disability arrangement at all and the proposed insured plan utilizing the waiver-of-premium provision, the results would be as follows.

[10] The additional premium for the waiver provision would be $353.10 annually. Some companies write a waiver provision which extends to age 65 on a life paid-up-at-65 contract. This would fit in nicely with the proposed deferred compensation arrangement.

$100,000 Gross income	$10,000 Tax-free income
20,000 Disability pay-out (deductible)	↑
$ 80,000 Income before corporate tax	│
40,000 Income tax	↓
$ 40,000 +	$10,000 = $50,000 Net to surplus

Of course, it is not necessary for the corporation to go to the full extent of $20,000 a year. Very often the disability benefit agreement is limited to the amount the employee can receive tax free under a salary continuance plan.[11] The point to be kept in mind is that if the disability pay-out is less than twice the annual increase in the cash value, the corporation will realize a profit. In other words, the waiver-of-premium provision affords considerable flexibility.

STOCK OPTIONS

Stock options have become an important form of incentive compensation to executives. Typically, a stock option plan provides that the privilege of purchasing shares of the employer-company's stock shall become available to the executive at a future date, or series of future dates, at a specified price or prices. Very often the price selected is the one prevailing at the time the option is granted, but sometimes the option price is lower or higher than the price currently prevailing. Under the Revenue Act of 1964, qualified options must be issued at no lower than 100 per cent of the market price at the time the option is granted.

If the price of the company's stock rises—presumably through the management's good work for the corporation—the executive will find it profitable to exercise the option. Such a plan offers the apparent advantage of not requiring the expenditure of corporate funds. In fact, it brings some new money into the business. On the other side, if the option meets statutory requirements, it may offer major tax advantages to the executive.

The Qualified Stock Option

Briefly, a qualified stock option is an option granted to an individual, for any reason connected with his employment, by an employer-corporation to purchase stock in such corporation. In order to qualify the option for favorable tax treatment, the following conditions must be met:

1. The option price must conform with the statutory price structure prescribed in the Internal Revenue Code.[12] Generally speaking, the price must be fixed at 100 per cent or more of the fair market value of the stock at the date of grant.

---

[11] Internal Revenue Code, Sec. 105(*d*).

[12] Sec. 422(*a*)(*b*).

2. The optionee must be an employee of the corporation from the time of the granting of the option until three months prior to the date of exercising the option.
3. The option, by its terms, cannot be exercisable after the expiration of five years from the date of grant.
4. During the employee's lifetime, the option can only be exercised by him.
5. The option, by its terms, must not be transferable other than at death.
6. The disposition of stock acquired by exercise of an option must not occur within three years after the stock has been acquired.
7. The option must be to purchase stock of the employer-corporation or its parent or subsidiary (i.e., corporations linked by at least 50 per cent voting control).

Tax Status Favorable

The tax treatment of the qualified stock option is favorable to the executive-employee involved. In the first place, no taxable income results when the option right is granted.

Second, he has no taxable income when he exercises his right and purchases the shares, even though the option price is far below the then current market price. If, however, he desires the favorable treatment, he must not dispose of the shares within three years from the date he exercises the option.

Third, if the option price was at least 100 per cent of the fair market value of the stock at the time of the grant, the ultimate gain or loss on a subsequent sale will be capital gain or loss. The important point is that the taxable event does not occur until the stock is ultimately sold.

Purchase Price

In dealing with qualified stock options, the main problem to the executive is how to raise the cash to exercise the option.

In any estate planning, the possibility that holders of qualified stock options will die before exercising them should be considered. In many cases, these rights will be—or could be in the future—extremely valuable and should not be allowed to expire unexercised.

Then, too, there can be an out-of-pocket loss by failure to exercise the option. The value of the stock option (the difference between the option price and the fair market value of the stock at the date of death) will be included in the decedent's gross estate. This will result in an increased federal estate tax and a corresponding decrease in assets available for distribution to the heirs.

The Estate and Heirs

In the event the holder of an option dies before exercising his right, the privilege can pass to his estate or heirs with the same tax advantage that was available to him. Certain conditions imposed on the employee are waived for his estate or heirs, and this facilitates the use of the option. For example, the estate or heirs need not wait three years after the exercise of the option to dispose of the stock, although the stock must be held six months after it is purchased to receive capital gains rates. Also, the rule that the option must be exercised within three months after the employee leaves the corporation is not imposed on the estate or heirs, as long as the deceased was employed by the corporation within three months of his death.

The Use of Life Insurance

While the suspension of these conditions offers the estate or heirs somewhat more flexibility in planning the use of the option, two important reservations should be stressed. First, the Code requires that the option must be exercised within five years after it is granted. Thus, even though the value of the option is included in the decedent's gross estate, the inability of the estate or the heirs to exercise it may result in a considerable loss.

Also, the qualified stock option tax advantages are available only to the estate, heir, or anyone else who received the option by reason of the death of the employee. They are not available to anyone who received the option in any other manner, as, for instance, through a sale or a gift by the estate or heir. The latter condition, in effect, prohibits an estate or heir who lacks the funds to exercise the option partially to recoup the loss by a sale of the option. Also, it keeps an heir from making a gift of the option to a member of his family who has the funds to profit by its exercise.

This is a situation where life insurance can provide its services. Life insurance can provide the funds to secure the income tax advantages for the recipients of a qualified stock option. Without life insurance to protect the option, the executor or heir is faced with the problem of obtaining cash with which to purchase the stock. Other assets may be salable but only at a considerable loss. If the amount is large, adequate loans may not be available; and in any event, there is the problem of repayment and interest.

Life insurance can be made to fit nicely with the stock option arrangement. If the executive should die while an accompanying loan plan is outstanding, the insurance proceeds are available to pay off the debt. Should death occur before the executive has an opportunity to exercise the option at all, the life insurance proceeds can be used to purchase the stock.

SUMMARY

At present, two attractive means of providing substantial additional compensation for executives are deferred salary or bonus contracts and qualified stock option plans. In particular situations, one or the other may be more desirable, but there is no reason why both cannot be used by the one employer.

In addition to the substantial tax advantages to the employee, there usually will be sound business reasons for the use of such plans for the employer. Very often, in these arrangements, some type of funding is desirable. Life insurance and annuity contracts can appropriately be used for funding in a great many cases, especially in those situations requiring cash commitments at the time of death or disability.

SELECTED REFERENCES

BOMAR, FLEMING; MCANDREWS, J. E.; and KRAHMER, J. R. *Profit-Sharing and Other Forms of Deferred Compensation.* Rev. ed. Bryn Mawr, Pa.: American College of Life Underwriters, 1962.

BRYSON, BRADY O., and LEFEVRE, THOMAS V. *Tax Aspects of Executives' Compensation.* New York: Practicing Law Institute, 1955.

CASEY, WILLIAM J. *Executive Pay Plans.* New York: Institute for Business Planning, Inc., 1956.

CASEY, WILLIAM J. *Pay Plans.* A service in 2 vols. New York: Institute for Business Planning, Inc., n.d.

WASHINGTON, GEORGE THOMAS, and ROTHSCHILD, V. HENRY, 2D. *Compensating the Corporate Executive.* 2 vols. 3d ed. New York: Ronald Press Co., 1962.

PART VI

Business Uses of Life and Health Insurance

Chapter 47

KEY-MAN USES OF LIFE AND HEALTH INSURANCE

BY J. CARLTON SMITH

The Nature of Key-Man Life Insurance

A Form of Business Insurance. Key-man life insurance is insurance purchased by a business firm on the life of an owner or employee whose services contribute substantially to the success of the business. The key man may be thought of as a valuable asset that is insured by his firm—in the same way that a building is insured against physical damage.

The basic motive which prompts a business firm to purchase key-man life insurance is the desire to protect itself against the monetary loss which would result from the key man's premature death. All key-man insurance rests on this foundation of the value to the firm of the key man's services.

Because of the purpose for which it is owned, key-man life insurance is a type of business insurance. Business insurance, of course, also is used to fund buy-and-sell agreements in sole proprietorships, partnerships, and close corporations. Of these two, key-man insurance has the wider application. It is employed even by publicly owned corporations where a ready market for the stock may make a buy-and-sell agreement unnecessary.

The Human Factor in Business Success. The conclusion that the human factor is vitally important to success in business is inescapable. Studies have been made which indicate that incompetent management is the chief cause of business failure. Profits are to a large degree the result of the contributions of key men who possess the managerial skill and the experience to direct the efficient use of the material resources of the business.

Not only are human life values indispensable to the profitable utilization of property values, but life values are more vulnerable to loss. The danger of a business experiencing a serious loss by reason of the death of a key man is much greater than the danger of a serious fire loss. Moreover, the average fire will cause only partial destruction of the property, while the death of a key man produces a total loss for the firm. The plant destroyed by fire can be rebuilt, but the key man lost through death may have possessed skills and abilities which will be difficult, if not impossible, to find in a successor.

In the same manner that property values almost universally are protected by insurance from the many hazards to which they are exposed, so also should the business firm protect the human assets, which are often of even greater importance.

Factors That Make a Key Man. There are a number of factors that make a person a key man for life insurance purposes. Three of these factors deserve special emphasis.

1. *Skill and Knowledge.* In many business firms, there is one man whose technical knowledge, experience, or particular skill make him the most valuable asset of the firm and make him almost indispensable to the successful operation of the business. A key man may be a gifted executive, a research chemist who has developed new products for the firm, an extremely capable sales manager, or a highly efficient production man. In each case, the key man possesses skill and knowledge related to the firm's affairs which could be acquired by a successor only after considerable time.

2. *A Source of Business.* Often the key man of a firm is a valuable source of business. He has close personal contacts with substantial buyers of the goods or services produced by the firm. Business which comes to a firm because of personal ties with a key man can very quickly go elsewhere in the event of the key man's death. Such ties break easily, and cannot normally be kept intact by the key man's successor.

3. *A Source of Firm Credit.* In many businesses, some one man is the chief source and strength of the firm's credit. In some cases, he is a wealthy individual, either an active or an inactive part owner of the firm, who stands ready at all times to supply needed funds. Even more frequently, such a key man is indirectly an important source of credit from banks or others because of his integrity, the size of his personal fortune, or his managerial ability.

Services of Key-Man Life Insurance

Provides Indemnity in Case of Loss. The most effective method of offsetting the financial loss due to the death of a key man is to arrange for the payment of adequate life insurance proceeds to the business at the time of his death. The insurance proceeds will indemnify the business for the loss, at least in part, just as the firm would be indemnified by insurance in the case of property loss from fire, burglary, explosion, or robbery. When death strikes one of the leaders of a firm, the receipt by the business of a sizable amount of life insurance proceeds to compensate for at least a portion of the loss may be of the greatest importance to the profitable continuance of the business.

The indemnity provided by key-man insurance also places the firm in the position of being able to finance the replacement of the key man lost through death. In order to induce a man of equal experience to leave his present employer, it usually will be necessary to offer him either a substantial increase in salary or retirement benefits greater than those he now enjoys.

Accumulates a Business Emergency Fund. Permanent life insurance on the lives of active business owners and key executives provides a safe, convenient, and simple method for the gradual accumulation of a substantial emergency fund in the cash and loan values of the policies. Such insurance provides the business firm with considerable financial independence. Regardless of any stringency in general credit conditions, the firm may go to the life insurance policy and without publicity obtain the emergency funds needed by borrowing the required portion of the cash value. Furthermore, the rate of interest will never be higher than that fixed in the policy, regardless of conditions in the money market.

Many benefits are inherent in the use of permanent life insurance for purposes of accumulating a business emergency fund.

1. For the business firm, as for the individual, a plan is needed that will make the accumulation of a savings or emergency fund automatic and incidental. All business firms disburse funds on a regularly recurring basis to meet various expenses. The life insurance plan involves similar periodic payments, hardly distinguishable from those to meet expenses except that they flow into an accumulation fund to meet emergencies. Moreover, the life insurance plan adds some degree of compulsion to the accumulation of the business savings fund.

2. The savings fund accumulated under the life insurance plan is invested automatically with the other funds of the life insurance company, and represents a cross section of the assets of the entire country. Broad diversification is thus obtained. Furthermore, since the insurance plan of accumulation provides a highly specialized staff to invest the fund, the business managers are free to devote their undivided attention to the problems of operating their business.

3. The problem of "changing values" is a serious one in any plan for the accumulation of a business savings fund. Invested in normal channels, such a fund tends to reach its lowest value to the business just at the time it is needed most—in a period of financial stringency. But under the life insurance plan, values are *guaranteed in advance.* The firm is assured that the emergency fund will be larger in the year it is needed than ever before.

4. To make certain that the savings fund will not be invaded for current needs, the business savings plan should provide segregation of the

funds from the regular business assets. If the fund is accumulated in cash or in other liquid form, management may be tempted to use the fund in some current business project. Under the life insurance plan, the accumulations are held by the insurance company and kept entirely apart from the firm's other assets. Though available at any time, the insurance cash value is removed sufficiently from the normal business assets so that it is not looked upon as a fund available for routine business operations.

Strengthens the Credit of the Firm. Credit is the lifeblood of business. Companies whose credit is dependent upon the reputation, energy, and ability of a key man may suffer a tremendous shock upon his untimely death. In such circumstances, creditors normally press for payment, and debtors have a tendency to delay payment of their obligations. Many firms have been forced into dissolution or receivership because of their inability to obtain adequate operating capital during the critical months following the death of the key man. Whether or not a business will fail in these circumstances may well hinge on the presence or absence of insurance on the key man's life, payable to the firm.

Key-man insurance may have the effect of strengthening a firm's credit position, resulting in a greater volume of credit or better credit terms. There are three basic reasons why key-man insurance may provide this stronger credit position.

1. *Indemnity for the Loss of the Human Element.* The indemnity function of the insurance on the life of the key man strengthens the credit of the firm in case of the key man's death as well as during his lifetime. Lending institutions will usually renew and extend loans from time to time as long as the business is making money. But capital is timid and runs for safety at the first sign of trouble.

If the firm owns insurance on the life of the business owner or key man, at his death a large amount of cash automatically becomes available to the firm. The firm can liquidate the bank and other loans, and finance operations out of this cash fund until experience under the new management restores confidence in the business. Creditors are assured that their claims will be paid, and with this assurance are usually in no hurry for payment.

2. *Evidence of Character and Stability.* The maintenance of life insurance by the firm indicates character of management, and in the case of a permanent insurance policy, it indicates the willingness and ability to save. It also indicates that the firm recognizes its responsibilities to creditors, and is evidence of the good health of the key man. Key-man insurance adds stability to the business, since provisions for the insurance on the lives of the key personnel add a financial safety factor.

3. *Provides Supporting Collateral for Loans.* There are two basic types of loans. The first type, the collateral loan, is one secured by stocks or bonds or other evidences of wealth that are quickly marketable. The

lender places his chief reliance upon his ability to sell the pledged collateral if that should become necessary to protect the loan.

The second type, the unsecured loan, is one which requires the lender to depend primarily upon the capacity of the business to produce earnings with which to pay principal and interest. Creditors must be assured that the key men of the firm will live to produce the earnings with which to repay the loan, or that the firm will be indemnified in case of the death of any one of these key management men.

If fire insurance is necessary to safeguard property values used as security for collateral loans, life insurance should likewise be employed to safeguard the human values which justify the granting of loans secured only by the general credit of the firm. Through life insurance the firm is able to capitalize these human life values of the business upon which general creditors depend so largely.

Provides a Means of Funding a Deferred Compensation Arrangement for the Key Man. Still another service of key-man life insurance is that it may be combined with a deferred compensation plan for a key employee. The firm needs key-man life insurance to idemnify itself for loss in event of the key man's death during his working years. It also may need a deferred compensation plan as an added inducement to a valued key man who otherwise may be receptive to offers from competing concerns. A combination key-man deferred compensation plan may be adopted and funded with a single life insurance policy which performs the function both of indemnity to the firm in the event of death and of retirement income for the employee in the event of survival. Such a plan does not necessarily provide any benefits to the key man's family in the event of death during his working years, although such benefits can be provided through appropriate modifications of the plan.

Key-Man Life Insurance Arrangements

The Policy Provisions. Life insurance bought solely for key-man purposes is arranged more simply than other business insurance plans. No agreement between the key man and the firm is necessary, and no special contract is required. The key man is merely the subject of the insurance.

1. *The Applicant.* It is the practice of most companies to suggest that the firm apply for the insurance. The application is signed, for the firm as applicant, by an officer other than the insured. The key man will be asked to sign also to affirm the personal data appearing on the application and to acknowledge his willingness to be insured.

If a corporation is the applicant, most authorities suggest that a resolution be passed by the board of directors authorizing the purchase of the key-man insurance. It is advisable for the resolution to state the purpose of the life insurance, i.e., to indemnify the corporation partially for the loss it will suffer in the event of the key man's death. The adoption of a resolution may avoid complications and lawsuits, and some life companies require that a copy accompany the application for life insurance.

2. *Payment of Premiums.* The premiums for key-man life insurance are in all cases paid by the business firm. This appears to be the logical arrangement in view of the fact that the insurance is bought for the sole benefit of the firm.

3. *Ownership of the Policy.* The firm is always the owner of pure key-man life insurance. The insurance company will be informed that the firm is to be the owner of the policy either by notation in the application or by separate notification. The insurance company will include a clause in the policy providing that all incidents of ownership are vested in the firm.

4. *Beneficiary Designation.* Since key-man life insurance is bought primarily for the purpose of indemnifying the firm for at least a portion of the financial loss that will be sustained by the firm upon the key man's death, the firm in all cases should be named the beneficiary to receive the death proceeds.

5. *Type of Policy.* The type of policy used for key-man insurance purposes should be the best suited to the needs and premium-paying ability of the firm. Perhaps the best-suited policy in the typical case is straight life, with its ideal balance between the protection and investment elements. A higher premium policy can be used where there is need for a more rapidly accumulating business reserve fund than straight life will provide, as, for example, a policy that will be paid up at retirement age. In some cases, the premium outlay the firm can afford may dictate the use of term insurance.

6. *Waiver of Premium.* The key-man insurance policy may include a waiver-of-premium provision, which would relieve the firm of premium payments during the total and presumably permanent disability of a key man. If a key man should become disabled, it would be to the firm's advantage in most cases to retain the policy on his life. If the key man should recover, the firm would be assured of protection even if he had lost his insurability. If the key man's impaired health should dictate an early retirement, the firm could use the policy for the purpose of deferred compensation. If the disability should hasten the key man's death, the policy proceeds would indemnify the firm for the loss sustained.

Use of Existing Life Insurance. The transfer for value of an existing policy to the firm for the purpose of serving as key-man life insurance formerly entailed serious income tax disadvantages. The death proceeds were taxed as ordinary income after deducting the cost of the contract and premiums paid thereafter. Under the 1954 Internal Revenue Code,[1] however, such adverse tax treatment does not apply to a partnership if

[1] Internal Revenue Code, Sec. 101(*a*)(2)(*B*).

the key man is a partner, nor to a corporation if the key man is a shareholder or an officer.

Even in the absence of adverse tax treatment, perhaps in relatively few cases is it advisable to use existing life insurance. Only in rare instances will the key man be likely to own life insurance which he no longer needs as personal insurance. Typically, men tend to maintain the level of their life insurance at its highest peak and to buy additional amounts as they grow older. In most key-man cases, protection in favor of the firm will take the form of newly purchased life insurance.

Disposition of the Policy if the Key Man Leaves the Firm. When the key man leaves the firm, a question may arise as to whether the firm has the legal right to continue to pay premiums during his lifetime and to receive the proceeds upon his death. The majority of judicial decisions support the general rule that a policy which is valid when issued remains valid despite later termination of the beneficiary's insurable interest.

Although a firm may have the right to maintain insurance on the life of a former key man, there appears to be little justification for doing so. The basic need for the insurance for indemnification no longer exists. Therefore, it is best under most circumstances for the firm to sell the policy to the former key man, to be continued by him as personal insurance. If the key man does not wish to buy the policy, the firm may surrender it to the life insurance company. Whether sold to the former key man or surrendered to the insurance company, the cash value and the future premiums will be freed to buy key-man insurance on the former key man's successor, or on the lives of other key men.

Insurable Interest. It is important in key-man insurance to determine whether the business firm has an insurable interest in the key man's life. This is perhaps the primary legal question associated with key-man insurance.

The United States Supreme Court, in an important case,[2] upheld the validity of a policy purchased on the life of the president of a corporation for the purpose of indemnifying the corporation for the loss of earning power that would occur upon the president's death. Other court decisions have held that a business can have an insurable interest in (1) a substantial stockholder or director,[3] (2) an active manager,[4] and (3) a secretary or treasurer.[5] Although insurable interest rules vary among the states, most legal authorities agree that any firm (corporate or noncorporate) has an insurable interest in any person actively associated with the firm whose continued life would be of financial benefit to the business.

---

[2] *United States* v. *Supplee-Biddle Hardware Company*, 265 US 189.

[3] *Keckley* v. *Conshocton Glass Company*, 86 Ohio St. 213, 99 NE 299.

[4] *Wurzberg* v. *New York Life Insurance Company*, 140 Tenn. 59, 203 SW 332.

[5] *Reilly* v. *Penn Mutual Life Insurance Company*, 201 Iowa 555, 207 NW 583.

Valuation of a Key Man for Insurance Purposes. Because of the intangible nature of the human life value, many view the accurate evaluation of a key man's services to the firm as an almost unsolvable problem. It is true that there is no blanket formula for the appraisal of human life values, but it is equally true that no one formula exists in the field of property appraisals. As Dr. S. S. Huebner points out: "Expert appraisers of property values often are able to reach only fair approximations. . . . Many instances are on record where two or more groups of expert appraisers, working independently and at the same time on the appraisal of a given property, have reached conclusions that varied from 20 to 30 per cent."[6]

Many examples of the difficulty of accurately valuing property can be cited. Five expert appraisals of the value of the Empire State Building would almost certainly produce five different valuations. What could be more inexact than the valuation of a producing oil well, in the face of the impossibility of knowing how long it will produce and at what rate? The conclusion is forced upon us that the valuation of all property is at best an intelligent estimate. This truth is no more or less applicable to human life valuation than to the appraisal of tangible property.

In key-man insurance cases, valuation involves primarily the value of human services. Methods of appraising the life value for family insurance purposes are equally applicable to the appraisal of the value of a key man to his firm.[7] The value of a key man may be appraised by determining the principal sum which would be lost to the firm following his death. For example, assume that a key man, aged 50, has at least 10 years of active service ahead of him, and the firm estimates that its loss of earnings would be $20,000 annually after his death. Over the 10-year period, the firm would lose $200,000 if the key man should die tomorrow. We need to determine the amount of insurance which would produce an income to the firm of $1,667 a month ($20,000 annually) for 10 years. It is a simple matter to find the answer by consulting settlement option tables in a rate book or policy.

Estimating the share of the firm's annual earnings attributable to the key man involves a careful analysis of the value of his services. If the key man is engaged in some project for the firm, the loss resulting from the abandonment of the project upon his death may be a measure of his value to the firm. If the key man's death will result in the loss of the clientele he attracts to the firm, his value may be measured by the amount of the estimated loss of such trade.

Another measure of the value of a key man is the "replacement cost" either of training a successor or of inducing an experienced employee

---

[6] S. S. Huebner, *The Economics of Life Insurance* (3d ed.; New York: Appleton-Century-Crofts, Inc., 1959), p. 59.

[7] *Ibid.*, pp. 47–48.

engaged in the same work to leave his present firm. If a successor is to be trained, there will necessarily be a loss attributable to the less skillful performance of the duties involved. If a replacement is to be employed, it will be necessary to offer a higher salary or other costly inducement for him to leave his present employer.

From a practical standpoint, the factor of greatest importance is the acquisition without undue delay of a reasonable amount of insurance protection against the premature death of the key man. It is far better for a firm to hedge even partially against this potential loss than to delay indefinitely in search of an exact and scientific measure of the key man's value. In practice, the amount of coverage will usually be established by the owners in a more or less arbitrary fashion. In many cases, the amount of key-man insurance will be determined by the amount of premium outlay the firm feels it can afford on a permanent basis, even if the protection is admittedly only a fraction of the key man's value to the firm.

Whatever approach is employed in arriving at the valuation of the key man's services for life insurance purposes, it should be remembered that there is some maximum amount of coverage which the insurance company will issue on a given key man's life for the specific purpose of indemnifying the firm for the loss caused by his death. It is the duty of the home office underwriter to see that the amount of life insurance bears a reasonable relationship to the value of the key man to the firm. The typical limit for this purpose appears to be an amount equal to about five times the key man's annual earnings as a rule of thumb, with provision for issuing somewhat more in particular cases. The rationale of this limit appears to be that it is presumed that in most cases a replacement for the deceased key man can be found and completely trained within a five-year period.

Taxation of Key-Man Life Insurance

Federal Income Tax. *Deductibility of Premiums.* Key-man life insurance premiums are not deductible as a business expense. The Internal Revenue Code provides that no deduction is allowed for "premiums paid on any life insurance policy covering the life of any officer or employee, or any person financially interested in any trade or business carried on by the taxpayer, when the taxpayer is directly or indirectly a beneficiary under the policy.[8]

Increase in Cash Values. A large number of business firms are carrying substantial life insurance cash values on their balance sheets.[9] It is usual accounting practice to write up each year the increase during the current year in cash values of company-owned life insurance. Such increases in

[8] Internal Revenue Code, Sec. 264(*a*)(1).

[9] Todd Planning and Service Company, *Corporations Owning Substantial Amounts of Business Insurance* (Chicago: National Underwriter Co., 1964).

cash values, including those on key-man life insurance, are not subject to federal income taxation.

Suppose the key man leaves the firm, and the firm wishes to surrender the policy to the life insurance company for its cash value. There is a monetary gain if the cash surrender value received exceeds the aggregate net premiums and other consideration paid.[10] The gain is taxable as ordinary income.[11] However, the resulting tax may be limited by the five-year income averaging provisions of the Internal Revenue Code. If a loss results from the surrender of a policy, it is normally looked upon as the cost of insurance protection and is not deductible.

Taxability of Proceeds. Life insurance proceeds received by a firm upon the death of a key man are not subject to the federal income tax. The Internal Revenue Code provides that ". . . gross income does not include amounts received . . . under a life insurance contract, if such amounts are paid by reason of the death of the insured."[12] This rule applies to sole proprietors, partnerships, and corporations as beneficiaries.[13] An exception to the rule exists if the beneficiary is not an exempt transferee of a policy transferred for value as is indicated above in the discussion of "Use of Existing Life Insurance."

Accumulated Earnings Tax. The Internal Revenue Code provides for a penalty tax, called the accumulated earnings tax, on corporate income unreasonably accumulated.[14] In general, the tax is levied whenever the corporation allows earnings in excess of $100,000 to accumulate in reserves and corporate surplus beyond the reasonable needs of the business. Corporations may engage in this practice in order to avoid distribution of income and so reduce the individual income tax liability of stockholders.

The purchase of key-man life insurance by a corporation should not invite the accumulated earnings tax if there is a genuine need for the protection and if the type of policy and the amount of insurance are reasonable in light of the insured's value to the firm.

Before assessing an accumulated earnings tax, the Commissioner will examine the entire surplus account of the corporation. The size of the surplus account in relation to the apparent needs of the business, and the manner in which it is invested and employed, will be determinative factors. Where surplus is represented by physical plants, equipment, accounts receivable, inventories, and other assets essential to the conduct and anticipated expansion of the business, there is little chance of incurring the tax. In contrast, where there are large cash balances, loans to

---

[10] Internal Revenue Code, Sec. 72(*e*).

[11] *Avery* v. *Commissioner,* 111 F.(2d) 19.

[12] Internal Revenue Code, Sec. 101(*a*) (1).

[13] Regulation 1.101–1(*a*); *United States* v. *Supplee-Biddle Hardware Company,* 265 US 189.

[14] Internal Revenue Code, Secs. 531–37.

stockholders, and investments in securities and other properties unrelated to the conduct of the business, there is obvious danger that the tax will be imposed.

Federal Estate Tax. *Taxation of Key-Man Insurance Proceeds.* Life insurance proceeds are included in the estate of the insured for federal estate tax purposes (1) if they are payable to or for the benefit of his estate; or (2) if payable to others, he possessed any incidents of ownership in the policy on the date of his death.[15]

In key-man life insurance, the firm ordinarily possesses all incidents of ownership and is the beneficiary. The proceeds are not paid to the key man's estate, nor does he possess any incidents of ownership in the policy on the date of his death. The proceeds are therefore not includable in the key man's estate.

Effect of Insurance on Value of Key Man's Stock. A key man in a corporation is often a stockholder as well. A question arises as to whether the life insurance proceeds received by the corporation after the key man's death increase the value of his stock for purposes of determining his federal estate tax liability. The cases which have considered the problem seem uniform in holding that life insurance proceeds paid to a corporation under a key-man policy are corporation assets to be considered in valuing the corporation's stock in the insured key man's estate.[16] It may therefore be concluded that in the absence of offsetting factors, the receipt by the corporation of key-man life insurance proceeds will increase the value of the key man's stock for estate tax purposes.

A factor which may partially or wholly offset the effect of the life insurance proceeds on the value of the key man's stock is the loss the corporation sustains because of the key man's death. If, for example, the amount of key-man proceeds is $100,000 and it can be shown to the satisfaction of the tax authorities that the corporation sustained a loss of $100,000 as a result of the key man's death, the value of the key man's stock should not be increased by virtue of the existence of key-man insurance on his life. It has been held, however, that the loss sustained by the corporation must be adequately proved by the key man's estate in order to support a reduction in the value of the stock for estate tax purposes.[17] The adoption of a resolution by the board of directors authorizing the purchase and the payment of premiums, and stating the purposes for which the insurance is being purchased, is perhaps the most acceptable evidence in establishing the fact of loss to the firm upon the death of a key man.

---

[15] Internal Revenue Code, Sec. 2042.

[16] *Estate of W. A. Blair*, 4 BTA 959; *Estate of Edward Doerken*, 46 BTA 809; *In re Reed's Estate*, 243 NY 199, 153 NE 47; *In re Patton's Will*, 227 Wis. 407, 278 NW 866.

[17] *Estate of Scherer*, BTA Memo., 10–25–40.

Preoccupation with the effect of the life insurance proceeds on the value of the key man's stock for estate tax purposes should not be permitted to obscure the fact that the key man's estate will enjoy a gain through the possession of stock in a corporation which has received life insurance proceeds as a tax-free addition to surplus. If the tax authorities refuse to recognize the loss to the corporation of the key man's services as an offsetting factor, the gain is merely diminished, but not eliminated.

Key-Man Health Insurance

The Need. The total and permanent disability of a key man can result in as serious a loss to the business as that occasioned by the death of a key man. In either case, the services of the key man are permanently lost to the firm. Moreover, the incidence of the risk of total and permanent disability during the years of active employment is greater than that of death. The conclusion is inescapable that the need of business firms for this type of protection is great. Despite this fact, key-man health insurance has not been widely employed up to the present. This may be due in part to the fact that business uses of health insurance are a relatively recent development, and in part to the limitations which are presently inherent in the use of health insurance for key-man indemnification purposes.

Purpose of Key-Man Health Insurance. The purpose of pure key-man insurance, either life or health, is to indemnify the business for the loss caused by the premature cessation of the key man's services. This discussion will treat the use of health insurance as a means of indemnifying the firm for the loss occasioned by the total and permanent disability of a key man. The uses of health insurance to provide fringe benefits for key men and other employees will not be discussed, as they are treated elsewhere in this *Handbook*.

Indemnification for Loss through Life Insurance. Assuming that the key man's disability is destined to be truly total and permanent, the measure of the loss of his services to the firm is the same as that resulting from his death. Any life insurance which the firm owns on the key man's life may be retained for the purpose of ultimately reimbursing the business for a portion of this loss, but the recovery through that method may be long deferred because of the key man's continued life. If such life insurance bears the disability waiver-of-premium rider, the firm will enjoy some measure of immediate indemnity through being excused from paying further premiums. Other than this small indemnity, however, the recovery by the firm through life insurance of at least a substantial portion of the loss caused by the key man's disability may be long delayed.

Indemnity for Loss through Health Insurance. A more immediate and continuing indemnification for the loss caused by the total and permanent disability of a key man is available through the medium of health insurance, subject to the limitations which are discussed below. A business may arrange for the indemnification of at least a portion of that loss through the purchase of a disability income policy on the key man's life. The business will own, pay the premiums on, and be the beneficiary of the policy. The premiums are not deductible by the firm because it is the beneficiary.[18] It is the prevailing opinion that the disability income payments are received by the business free of income tax.[19]

Indemnity through Health Insurance—an Example. In the discussion earlier in this chapter of the valuation of a key man's services for life insurance purposes, an example was used in which it was assumed that the key man is aged 50 and that the loss to the firm will be $20,000 annually in the event of his premature death. Assuming further that the key man's salary is $15,000 annually, this example may be employed to illustrate the use of health insurance as a means of partially indemnifying the firm for the loss (equal to that caused by death) of the key man's services because of his total and permanent disability. It will not be possible to provide for total indemnification for the $20,000 annual loss, as health insurers commonly limit rather strictly the amount of disability income coverage which can be purchased. Such limitations are essential to protect the insurer, but they vary widely among companies. A typical limitation on coverage may be approximately 50 per cent of the monthly earnings from the insured's occupation. In our example, the key man earns $1,250 a month, and $625 a month in disability benefits will be the limit of purchase permitted by the 50 per cent limitation. The purchase by the firm of a disability income to age 60 or 65 policy on the key man's life will therefore provide for the indemnification of $7,500 of the $20,000 annual loss assumed. While not indemnifying the firm for the loss of the key man's services, the receipt of $7,500 a year will help cushion the effect upon the firm of the loss of the key man's services.

The Indemnity Motive—Practical Limitations. Provision by a business for indemnification in the event of the disability of a key man is not as feasible as is the provision for indemnification in the event of death. We have seen that key-man life insurance provides for indemnification only on a deferred basis, as the ultimate death of the key man must be awaited. Health insurance also has its limitations as a means of indemnification of the loss caused by disability.

1. *Limitation of Coverage.* We have seen in the example given above that the amount of disability income coverage obtainable will normally be somewhat less than the amount of the loss sustained each year by the firm. In any case where the annual loss to the firm because of the key man's disability is as high as or higher than the key man's salary, it usually will

---

[18] *Castner Garage,* 43 BTA 1; Regulation 1.162–1.

[19] *Castner Garage,* 43 BTA 1; *Peoples Finance & Thrift Company,* USCA–5, 184 F. (2d) 836. In both cases the corporate owners of the policies did not take business deductions for the premiums.

not be practicable to provide for more than 40 to 70 per cent indemnification of loss.

2. *Effect upon Key Man's Personal Coverage.* The purchase of disability income insurance by the firm on the key man's life may materially limit the key man's ability to obtain disability income protection for the benefit of himself and his family. There is a very real limit to the amount of disability income coverage which any given key man's salary income will sustain. If the firm owns the maximum limit for indemnity purposes, the key man may be unable to purchase any additional amount as personal coverage.

3. *Reluctance of Firm to Retain Benefits if Key Man Not Covered.* Perhaps a majority of business managers would be reluctant to receive disability income payments for the indemnification of the firm while at the same time the key man and his family were suffering extreme financial hardship as a result of the disability. If, under these circumstances, the firm pays over to the key man the payments it receives from the insurance company, there has been no indemnification of the firm for the loss of the key man's services.

4. *Refusal of Insurer to Permit Firm to Be Owner and Beneficiary.* The great majority of insurance companies will not issue a disability income policy with the business as owner and beneficiary, nor will they honor an assignment of the policy by the insured to the firm. Such companies take the position that only the key man has an insurable interest in replacing the loss arising from his disability.

The Indemnity Motive—Conclusions. The limitations of health insurance for key-man purposes seriously restrict its broad use, but do not prevent its feasibility in the proper sets of circumstances. As to the limitation on coverage, surely a 40 to 70 per cent indemnification goes a long way toward softening the blow to the firm of suddenly losing the services of a valued key man. The second and third limitations discussed above lose their effect in cases where the key man will have an adequate income in the event of disability provided by personal savings or a salary continuance plan, or both. There may be relatively few such cases, and this appears to be the area which most greatly restricts the use of health insurance for key-man indemnification purposes. The fourth limitation referred to above is of minor importance if the firm seeks out and purchases the coverage from one of the relatively few insurers which will issue it with the firm as owner and beneficiary, or which will permit an assignment by the insured to the firm. The limitations of key-man health insurance are real and vital, and they should be given careful consideration in planning for key-man indemnification purposes.

Key-Man Disability Indemnification—Conclusions. We have seen that neither key-man life insurance nor key-man health insurance provides for total and immediate indemnification to a firm for the loss caused by the total and permanent disability of a valued key man. The indemnification through life insurance must await the key man's death, while that through health insurance is only partial because of limits of coverage.

Perhaps the most ideal means available to a firm of providing for something approaching total indemnification for the loss of a key man's services because of disability is through the use of a combination of key-man life insurance and key-man health insurance. Key-man health insurance provides a means (subject to the limitations discussed above) of recovering from 40 to 70 per cent of the annual loss on a continuing basis until the key man dies or reaches retirement age. Key-man life insurance may be continued on the key man's life (without the necessity of paying premiums if the waiver-of-premium provision is included) so as ultimately to provide for the recovery of the remainder of the loss. Thus the combined use of key-man life insurance and key-man health insurance accomplishes an end which cannot be achieved by the use of either coverage standing alone.

SELECTED REFERENCES

Brown, Robert A., Jr., and O'Neill, Jack. "Appraising the Human Asset for Business Life Insurance Requirements," *Journal of the American Society of Chartered Life Underwriters,* Vol. XI, No. 4 (Fall, 1957), pp. 340–52.

Dickerson, O. D. *Health Insurance.* Rev. ed. Homewood, Ill.: Richard D. Irwin, Inc., 1963.

Dornfeld, Kivie. "Taxation Affecting Health Insurance," *Journal of the American Society of Chartered Life Underwriters,* Vol. XVII, No. 2 (Spring, 1963), pp. 116–30.

Gravengaard, H. P. *Key Men and Life Insurance.* Cincinnati: National Underwriter Co., 1953.

Harmelin, William, and Osler, Robert W. *Business Uses of Health Insurance.* Bryn Mawr, Pa.: American College of Life Underwriters, 1960.

Herring, Joseph D. "Key Man Insurance," *Journal of the American Society of Chartered Life Underwriters,* Vol. X, No. 1 (Winter, 1955), pp. 57–62.

Huebner, S. S. *The Economics of Life Insurance.* 3d ed. New York: Appleton-Century-Crofts, Inc., 1959.

Mehr, Robert I. "Key Man Life Insurance and the Business Enterprise," *Journal of the American Society of Chartered Life Underwriters,* Vol. IV, No. 2 (March, 1950), pp. 131–39.

Millett, Paul F. "Key-Man Life Insurance and Section 102," *Journal of the American Society of Chartered Life Underwriters,* Vol. I, No. 5 (September, 1947).

National Underwriter Company. *The Diamond Life Bulletins Service: Business Insurance Volume.* Cincinnati, 1963.

National Underwriter Company. *Selling Business Health Insurance.* Cincinnati, 1961.

Research and Review Service of America, Inc. *Advanced Underwriting and Estate Planning Service,* Vol. II. Indianapolis. Looseleaf Service.

RESEARCH AND REVIEW SERVICE OF AMERICA, INC. *The Role of Business Insurance in the Close Corporation.* Indianapolis, 1956.

SMITH, J. CARLTON. *Key Man Uses of Life Insurance.* Bryn Mawr, Pa.: American College of Life Underwriters, 1963.

WOLFE, DON M. "Business Uses of Health Insurance," *Weekly News Review Digest,* April 1, 1961, pp. 1–6.

Chapter 48

INSURANCE FOR BUSINESS CONTINUATION—PARTNERSHIPS

*BY EDWARD J. MINTZ**

The Internal Revenue Code of 1954 made major revisions in tax law and procedures. Included in the new Code is Section 1361, which permits a partner or proprietor of an unincorporated business to elect to be taxed as a corporation, provided certain prerequisites are met.

The passage of Section 64 of the Technical Amendments Act of 1958 (Sections 1371 through 1377 of the Internal Revenue Code) has introduced another new concept into the federal income tax laws. This section permits certain businesses to incorporate, or to remain incorporated, and enjoy all the advantages of incorporation and at the same time "elect" not to be taxed as a corporation. Certain conditions must be met before such an election is permitted. Briefly, the corporation must have but one class of stock, not more than ten stockholders, and the consent of all stockholders to the election. All of the stockholders must be citizens or residents of the United States, and none of the stock may be held by a trust. To be eligible for such an election, the corporation must derive no more than 20 per cent of its gross receipts from interest, dividends, rents, royalties, annuities, and gains from the sale or exchange of securities, and must derive no more than 80 per cent of its gross receipts from sources outside the United States.

Prior to the existence of these new concepts, businessmen were strongly swayed by tax considerations in deciding on the type of business enterprise best suited to the conduct of their business. While it appears to have been the intent of Congress to minimize the importance of such considerations, tax considerations continue to be a strong motive in

---

* The author wishes to express his sincere appreciation for the assistance given in the preparation of this chapter by Michael M. McKenny, Assistant Vice President, and John M. Smilgin, Advanced Underwriting Consultant, both of the home office staff of the New York Life Insurance Company; and to his associates, Virgil A. Frizzell and Morya N. Littlejohn.

selecting the type of business enterprise. In fact, the 1958 provisions have created entirely new tax concepts. However, traditional nontax concepts, such as limited liability and perpetual life, are now more carefully scrutinized by businessmen in making their decisions relative to the type of business organization best suited for them. Therefore, an understanding of the partnership form as contrasted with the corporate form is vital.

Nature of the Partnership

A partnership is an association of two or more persons who by express or implied agreement carry on a business for profit as co-owners. In the usual type of partnership, each partner devotes his entire time to the conduct of the firm's business. Each partner has authority to act for the partnership within the regular scope of partnership business, and each partner is personally liable for partnership obligations.

By statute in most states, limited partnerships are also permitted. A limited partnership consists of one or more general partners and one or more limited partners. Limited partners may not be active in the business, and most courts hold that a limited partner who is active in the conduct of partnership affairs will lose his status and be deemed a general partner. Unlike the liability of a general partner, which is unlimited, the ceiling on the liability of a limited partner is his capital contribution to the partnership.

A partnership differs from a corporation in the following important respects:

1. ***Control.*** A corporation is owned by its stockholders. Majority stockholders can alter corporate policy or change its program. The minority stockholders are subject to this majority rule. By contrast, each partner, in the absence of an agreement to the contrary, has full authority to act for the partnership within the scope of the partnership business.

2. ***Liability.*** A stockholder has limited liability. In the event that corporate assets are insufficient to meet corporate obligations, personal assets of stockholders cannot ordinarily be reached by creditors. On the other hand, a partner's liability is unlimited. Should partnership assets be insufficient to meet partnership obligations, creditors may reach the personal assets of the partners.

3. ***Formal Requirements.*** Since a corporation is a separate legal entity apart from its shareholders, its existence is controlled by statutes and case law in the state in which it is incorporated. The right to incorporate is a privilege granted by statute. By contrast, a partnership is created by an agreement between the partners. No formal writing is required; indeed, a great many partnerships are formed by oral agreement. However, most commentators agree that partnership agreements should be reduced to writing to avoid problems and misunderstandings. Such writings are usually called "articles of partnership."

4. ***Transferability.*** Unless there is a restrictive agreement between the stockholders to the contrary, stock in a corporation may be transferred without affecting the existence of the corporation. By contrast, the relationship between partners is personal. A partnership interest may not be sold or disposed of and business continuity persists unless all the remaining partners are willing to form a new partnership with the new owners.

5. ***Dissolution at Death.*** In the absence of an express agreement to the contrary, death dissolves a partnership; but corporate existence, as such, does not terminate on the passing of a stockholder.

6. ***Federal Income Taxation.*** Since the corporation is an entity apart from its stockholders, it, as such, is subject to pay a federal income tax. The partnership is required to file an information return with the federal government, but it does not pay an income tax. Instead, each partner is taxed on his share of the partnership earnings, whether distributed to the partners or retained in the business.

7. ***Employee Benefit Plans.*** Many corporate employers have instituted qualified pension and profit sharing plans for the benefit of their employees. In addition, many employers have also adopted group life and health insurance plans and other fringe benefits. A stockholder may or may not be an employee of the corporation in which he has an interest. If he is an employee, he may qualify for benefits under one or more of these fringe benefit plans. Since a partner is not an employee of his partnership, he cannot generally qualify for these fringe benefits. However, the Self-Employed Individuals Tax Retirement Act of 1962 (popularly known as the Keogh Act), permits a partnership to establish a qualified retirement plan for the partners and employees.[1]

Problems on the Death of a Partner

The common-law principle that death of a partner automatically dissolves the partnership has been incorporated into the Uniform Partnership Act. The Act has been adopted by at least three fourths of the states. Unless there is an agreement to the contrary, the surviving partners become liquidating trustees upon the death of a partner, and they are charged with the obligation of winding up the partnership business. If surviving partners continue to conduct the business and losses occur, they will be held personally liable. If there are profits, they must share them with the estate of the deceased partner. In other words, the surviving partners do all the work, have all the responsibility, and share any gains, but are solely liable for all losses.

A leading case that illustrates the danger of continuing a partnership business after a partner dies is *In re Ducker's Estate* (146 Misc. 899, 263 NYS 217 [1933]). In that case a father and son operated a hat business in

[1] See Chapter 45 for analysis of Self-Employed Individuals Tax Retirement Act of 1962.

New York as a partnership. On the father's death, the son and a friend of the deceased were named coexecutors. Rather than liquidate the business when the father died, the coexecutors decided to continue operating the business. They did so for about one year, and then they incorporated. Approximately seven years after the death of the father, the business became insolvent. Prior to insolvency, the business distributed to the other heirs, a brother and three sisters, about $65,000 in profits. The son, a coexecutor, who remained active in the business drew only $75 per week as compensation for his services. The court remarked that "the brothers and sisters . . . are in truth invoking the utmost rigor of the law against their brother." The court concluded that the continuance of the business was improper and that the organization of the corporation constituted a diversion of estate funds. The coexecutors were surcharged and obliged to pay over to the other four heirs the sum of $33,000 which the court found to be the value of their interest had the partnership been liquidated as required by law at the time of the father's death.

Occasionally, and for accounting purposes, some articles of partnership provide that upon the death of a partner, the surviving partners may carry on the partnership business to the end of the partnership's calendar or fiscal year. During this period, the surviving partners have all the responsibility and must share profits with the heirs of the deceased partner. If losses occur during this period, the heirs must assume their share of them. At the end of this period, a winding up of the partnership occurs.

Alternatives on the Death of a Partner

Upon the death of a partner, various alternatives with respect to the business may be followed, including the liquidation of the partnership, the formation of a new partnership, the sale of the business to outsiders, the sale of the business to surviving heirs, and the purchase of the deceased's interest by the surviving partner.

1. *Winding Up the Partnership—Liquidation.* Most partners are aware of the day-to-day problems that confront them in their business. Very few partners, however, understand or appreciate the almost insurmountable problems that occur when a partner dies. A surviving partner becomes a liquidating trustee charged with the primary duty of liquidating the business.

Liquidation is a thankless process. Accounts receivable become almost impossible to collect. The assets of the firm are disposed of through forced sale. At forced sale, valuable assets often are sacrificed for a fraction of their actual value. Customers go elsewhere. And most important is the fact that in liquidating the business, the surviving partner also liquidates his job.

2. *Formation of a New Partnership.* The surviving partner may attempt to form a new partnership with the widow or other heirs of the

deceased. Seldom are the heirs or the widow qualified to help carry on a business venture. If a partner's widow succeeds to his interest, she will have equal authority with the surviving partner. Business losses are not only possible; they are probable in such circumstances. Other problems occur. The surviving partner often thinks of expansion; a widow may be more interested in what she can get out of the business today. Differences of opinion are common. Disputes arise, and quite often these disputes result in expensive litigation.

Even assuming that a surviving partner is willing to enter into a new partnership with the widow of his deceased partner, there are other practical problems to consider. If the widow remarries, the surviving partner may be subject to harassment from both the widow and her new husband. The widow also assumes a burden she would not have if liquidation occurred. By becoming a partner, she subjects herself to unlimited liability in the event that partnership assets are insufficient to meet partnership obligations.

One further problem must be considered. If the interest of a deceased partner passes in whole or in part to a minor child or children, either by will or by operation of law, liquidation is virtually certain. The surviving partner will be unable to form a new partnership with minors, since they are not competent to enter into contracts and the partnership agreement is contractual in nature. Resort to the courts also will usually prove futile because few, if any, courts will permit the continuation of the business for the benefit of minors, no matter how profitable the venture may be.

3. ***Sale of the Business to Outsiders.*** One solution for the problems created on the death of a partner is a sale of the business to outsiders. On its face, this solution is illusory, since many problems face the parties in their effort to dispose of the business by sale.

The first problem, of course, is to find a buyer willing to pay a fair price for the business. Such a buyer must not only be willing to buy the business, but he must be financially able to pay the price. The search for a buyer can be a time-consuming process. The business is sure to suffer, since the surviving partner will be obliged to devote a great deal of his time to finding a buyer and then bargaining with him.

Once the decision to sell is announced, employees become apprehensive about their future. Resignations from the firm can be expected to follow. Customers refuse their patronage. Creditors press for payment. Business suffers.

Even if the survivor finds a satisfactory purchaser and can arrange for a sale, he must proceed with caution. In his role as liquidating trustee, he is charged with the care expected of a fiduciary. Absolute candor will be required of him in his dealings with the heirs of the deceased partner. In protecting the interests of the heirs, the court will scrutinize every action of the surviving partner to make certain he does not attempt to take advantage of his position for any personal gain. He will be required to give an accounting.

Finally, reasonable offers for the business may be refused because the widow in her wishful thinking has an exaggerated opinion of the worth of the firm, with the result that no alternative is available to the surviving partner other than to liquidate the business.

4. ***Heirs Buy Out the Surviving Partner.*** Theoretically, the heirs might be able to buy out the interest of the surviving partner. Such a plan is rarely practical. All the heirs must consent to such a purchase, and if any of them are minors, they cannot give such consent. Even if all the heirs are adults, it is doubtful that they will have sufficient capital on hand to pay cash for the surviving partner's interest. Any other financial arrangement which might depend on the continued successful operation of the business would probably prove unsatisfactory to him.

A sale to the heirs of the deceased partner is also a foolish course of action for the surviving partner. He is selling himself out of a job. This can be particularly vexing if the survivor is of advanced years.

Also, if the surviving partner sells his interest to the heirs, he may establish a new business enterprise essentially similar to the one he has sold to the heirs. With his prior experience, he can be expected to be a forceful competitor. Customers of the old firm may well choose to patronize the new firm. This may prove disastrous to the heirs, particularly if they are inexperienced in business and financial matters. To protect themselves from competition from the surviving partner, they may provide for safeguards in the contract of sale. Such provisions are usually called "covenants not to compete" and usually provide that the surviving partner may not engage in a similar business for a specified period of years.

5. ***Surviving Partner Purchases the Interest of the Deceased.*** Here, too, the problems that face the surviving partner are formidable. In his fiduciary capacity as a liquidating trustee, he must take every precaution to make certain he does not take advantage of his position. He owes a duty of full disclosure to the heirs of the deceased partner. As has been previously noted, the heirs probably have an exaggerated opinion as to the worth of the business. Bargaining with the heirs may prove to be a frustrating experience. Payments for the interest are a further problem. Unless the survivor has sufficient savings to meet the purchase price—a highly unlikely event—he will be forced to give promissory notes with definite due dates. Meeting these note payments may be a very difficult undertaking. Failure to make payment on a note when due may result in the liquidation the survivor tried so hard to avoid.

Of the various alternatives discussed, a purchase by the surviving partner is the most logical. Undoubtedly, he is the person best equipped to continue carrying on the business. Two major obstacles stand in his path: (1) What price shall he pay, and (2) where will he get the money to pay for it?

A Formal Lifetime Agreement as the Solution

Most of the problems that occur on the death of a partner can be avoided by careful planning on the part of the partners during their lifetime. The ideal solution is a written agreement, drawn by an attorney, governing the disposition of the partnership interest on the death of either partner.

A provision in a partner's will providing for continuity is generally inadequate, since it does not bind the survivor. A provision in the will granting the surviving partner an option to purchase the deceased's partnership interest will be of no value if the will is successfully contested or denied probate, and in any event it gives the heirs no protection.

A formal agreement, usually called a "buy-and-sell" agreement, whereby the partners agree that in the event of the death of either partner the survivor is obligated to buy and the estate is obligated to sell the partnership interest, is the most intelligent solution to the problem.

The reasons why a buy-and-sell arrangement is usually the most satisfactory approach are:

1. The survivor will carry on the business. He has the experience and can maintain continuity for the benefit of employees and customers. He may want to bring in a new partner, and he may feel free to do so. Sooner or later, he may want to sell the business, but he does so at a time of his choosing, when market conditions are best suited for such a sale.
2. The estate of the deceased partner will receive payment in dollars for the partnership interest. These dollars will be available at a time when cash is sorely needed to meet death taxes, other expenses, and the income requirements for the widow and her family. If the surviving partner is given a mere option to purchase the interest, he may not exercise his rights. In such event, liquidation will follow.

Of course, the buy-and-sell agreement will be drawn by the partners' attorney and should contain, among other provisions, the stipulation that (1) each partner agrees that he will not sell or otherwise dispose of his interest during his lifetime without first offering it to the other partner at the contract price; and (2) the partners agree that on the death of either, the surviving partner must purchase and the estate of the deceased partner must sell and transfer the partnership interest of the deceased partner.

Another vital stipulation has to do with valuation procedures in establishing the purchase price of a deceased partner's interest. Quite often, *book value* will be the agreed-upon valuation provision. A careful draftsman will be certain to indicate in the agreement who is to be charged with the responsibility of determining the book value, and how it is to be determined. Frequently, an accountant (or a means of selecting one) is designated. The book value method may not always be the most equitable valuation approach. If the firm owns real property, it is probably carried on the books at cost less depreciation. If there has been an appreciation in the value of such property, it will not be reflected in the book value. A further shortcoming of the book value method is that it does not take into consideration any good will the firm may have developed.

In lieu of book value, the parties can set a *fixed price* in the agreement, and such fixed price will govern at the death of a partner. Here, too, there is the danger that the fixed price will be inequitable unless provision is made for periodic review. By agreement of the parties, the fixed price may be periodically changed to reflect changes in the value of the partnership interest.

Quite often, partners will prefer to use a *formula* in determining the value of the partnership. Two popular formula approaches are the "earnings capitalization method" and the "years purchase method." Under the former, the partners may agree that the value of their interest is based on the amount of profits earned by the business. Then they conclude that the value of the business is five times average annual earnings. Of course, they may select ten years or any other period they feel is appropriate. The shortcoming in this method is that earnings may not adequately reflect the value of the business because factors such as growth, future business potential, and the nature of the business are not taken into account.

Under the years purchase method, a value is placed on the firm's tangible assets. Then the firm's earnings over a certain period are averaged. The partners then assume an appropriate return commensurate with the risks involved in conducting the business. The assumed return on assets is subtracted from the average net earnings, and the difference is attributed to good will. The good will is capitalized and added to the tangible assets. The sum represents the value of the business. An example will illustrate this approach more clearly. Ten per cent is assumed as a fair return on capital in this illustration.

Tangible assets		$300,000
Five-year average net annual earnings	$40,000	
Less: Return on tangible assets (10 per cent of $300,000)	30,000	
Amount attributable to good will	$10,000	
Capitalized at 20 per cent (five years)		50,000
Value of the business		$350,000

If the estate of a deceased partner is subject to federal estate taxes, the valuation provision in the buy-and-sell agreement assumes an even bigger importance. A long line of court decisions, beginning with *Wilson* v. *Bowers* (57 F.[2d] 682, CA[2d] [1932]), establish the principle that if certain conditions are met in the agreement, the value set forth will govern for purposes of the federal estate tax. The conditions ordinarily necessary before the value in the agreement will fix the price for federal estate tax purposes are as follows:

1. The agreement must be the result of an arm's length transaction.
2. The agreement must require the estate to sell.
3. The surviving partner has a legally binding contract or option to purchase.
4. The deceased partner could not have disposed of his interest during his lifetime without first offering it to the other partner at a price not higher than the price to be paid had the sale been made by his estate to the other partner.

The Funding of the Business Purchase Agreement

An agreement that binds the surviving partner to buy and the estate of the deceased partner to sell the partnership interest at a price previously stipulated is an ideal solution for both the survivor and the heirs of the deceased partner. By entering into such an agreement, the parties create a market for their partnership interest at a price they themselves helped to establish under the terms of the agreement.

But there is still one important link missing. The surviving partner must have money to fulfill his obligation to buy the deceased's interest from the estate. If the survivor has sufficient cash or liquid assets to meet his obligation, he will be able to perform his end of the bargain with no difficulty. Rarely will a partner have the necessary funds on hand when they are needed. Even if he should have sufficient funds at the time he enters into the buy-and-sell agreement, there is no assurance that he will be in the same liquid position when his partner dies and he is called upon for payment.

Of course, the partners could fund their buy-out agreement by establishing a sinking fund. They could set aside a certain percentage of earnings each year, until such time as they have accumulated a fund large enough to meet any purchase obligations they have under the buy-out agreement. The trouble here is obvious. One of them may die prior to the time that enough has been accumulated by this approach. As a practical matter, such a sinking fund, if created, may prove to be too much of a temptation to the partners while they are living. If an attractive opportunity presents itself, the sinking fund would probably be invaded. This would, of course, defeat its purpose.

Perhaps the cash needed to pay the estate of the deceased partner could be borrowed by the survivor. Here, too, the pitfalls are obvious. While both partners are alive, borrowing may not be too difficult a procedure. At the death of either partner, credit may well disappear, and borrowed money may not be easily available, if available at all. Even assuming that it is possible to borrow the needed cash at the death of a partner, the survivor will face a double burden: He must repay the loan at periodic intervals, and he must pay the salary of the replacement he finds to do the work of the deceased partner. And not to be overlooked is the additional cost due to the current high interest rate money commands on the market.

Whether the partners create a sinking fund, or whether the surviving partner borrows the needed purchase money, the impact of income taxes cannot be overlooked. In a 32 per cent personal income tax bracket, approximately $1.47 must be earned before taxes in order to net $1.00 of purchase money; in a 50 per cent bracket, $2.00 of earnings are required. The purchase money thus becomes burdened with taxes in addition to interest charges. With income taxes as they are today, it becomes practically impossible for a surviving partner to meet a capital obligation out of current income.

Life Insurance—The Ideal Solution

The ideal way to fund a business purchase agreement is through life insurance on the lives of the partners. Such insurance will provide the funds when they are required, no matter how soon the death of a partner may occur. When the buy-and-sell agreement is first put into effect, the purchase price called for in the agreement will govern the amount of insurance needed to fund fully the buy-out contract. As the agreement is periodically reviewed, additional amounts of insurance may be purchased as the sale price increases.

A simple example will help to illustrate the so-called "crisscross" (or "cross-purchase") method of funding. Assume Able and Baker are partners. Assume further that the value of the partnership is $50,000, and that Able and Baker each have a 50 per cent interest. Able insures Baker for $25,000. Able is the premium payor, owner, and beneficiary under the contract insuring Baker's life. Baker in turn insures Able. Baker is the premium payor, owner, and beneficiary under the contract insuring Able's life. Assume Able dies. Baker has an obligation under the buy-and-sell agreement to pay to Able's estate $25,000, the price called for in the contract. At the same time, he collects $25,000, free of income tax, from the insurance company as beneficiary under the policy of life insurance on Able's life.

The event that gave rise to Baker's obligation under the buy-and-sell agreement—Able's death—also triggered the payment of the money needed. Able's estate has a policy of insurance on Baker's life. A clause can be included in the buy-and-sell agreement giving Baker the right to purchase the policy on his life from Able's estate for the cash value or any other sum agreed to in the buy-out contract. If Baker does not choose to exercise this right, Able's executor can terminate the policy and receive any cash value payable under the nonforfeiture options in the policy.

The clause providing for the disposition of the insurance on Baker's life reimburses Able's estate, at least in part, for the very modest cost of his having participated in the plan.

If there are three partners—Able, Baker, and Charlie—each with a $25,000 interest, the plan would work in the following manner:

Able would own, pay premiums on, and be beneficiary of	*Baker would own, pay premiums on, and be beneficiary of*	*Charlie would own, pay premiums on, and be beneficiary of*
$12,500 of insurance on Baker's life and	$12,500 of insurance on Able's life and	$12,500 of insurance on Able's life and
$12,500 of insurance on Charlie's life	$12,500 of insurance on Charlie's life	$12,500 of insurance on Baker's life

Assume Able dies. Baker and Charlie would each collect $12,500 of insurance proceeds, which they would turn over to Able's executor in exchange for Able's partnership interest. Under the terms of their buy-out agreement, Baker and Charlie each have a right to purchase the policies on their respective lives from Able's estate. Ownership of the purchased policy on Baker's life could be transferred to Charlie; ownership of the policy on Charlie's life could be transferred to Baker. These policies, together with the policies owned under the original arrangement, can be used to fund partially a new agreement between Baker and Charlie.

Partnership Ownership of Insurance Used to Fund the Agreement

If there are only two or three partners, as in the previous examples, the crisscross procedure is relatively simple. The partners insure each other. Where there is a large number of partners, the crisscross plan may not be entirely satisfactory. In the example illustrating a three-man partnership, a total of six policies was required. If there are ten partners, each partner will own nine policies on the lives of the other partners. This would mean that ninety policies would be necessary to fund the agreement. It may also mean that each policy would be for a small amount, and the benefit of a reduced premium offered by many insurance companies for policies with a relatively high minimum face value would be lost.

To overcome these obstacles, the "entity plan" (or partnership ownership plan) is usually suggested. If the entity plan is appropriate, the partnership will apply for, own, and be the beneficiary of the policy on the life of each partner. Each partner enters into an agreement with the partnership for the disposition of his partnership interest at death. When a partner dies, the insurance proceeds will be used to buy the partnership interest of the deceased partner, and the interests of the surviving partners will be proportionately increased. The entity method has much appeal because of its simplicity, especially where a large number of partners is involved or where the ages of the partners may vary substantially.

There is by no means complete agreement among experts as to the relative merits of the entity and cross-purchase plans. They can sometimes give rise to substantially different tax results, depending upon the particular facts and the particular terms of the agreement.

One of the principal disadvantages of the entity approach under the law prior to the Internal Revenue Code of 1954 was that where the partnership purchased the interest of a deceased partner with partnership insurance, there was a real danger that the surviving partners' income tax cost bases would not be increased for subsequent sales. The theory here was that the partnership, and not the partners, had purchased the deceased partner's interest.

This particular disadvantage has been substantially reduced under the Internal Revenue Code of 1954. Section 705(*a*) provides that a partner's distributive share of tax-exempt income received by the partnership is to be included in arriving at the adjusted cost basis of his interest in the partnership. Life insurance received by the partnership on the death of a partner would be one form of such tax-exempt income.

To illustrate the entity plan, assume the partnership has three equal partners, Able, Baker, and Charlie. Assume further that each of the partners is insured under a partnership ownership arrangement for $25,000. Able dies. The partnership receives $25,000. There will be an increase in the income tax cost basis to Baker and Charlie equal to $8,333, which would represent their respective distributive shares of the life insurance proceeds. If Baker and Charlie had each owned $12,500 of insurance on the life of Able under the crisscross method, there would be an increase in their respective income tax cost bases of $12,500 instead of the $8,333 increase where the partnership owns the insurance. A partner's cost basis, of course, becomes an important tax consideration in the event of subsequent sale of his partnership interest during his lifetime.

Special Problems of Professional Partnerships

The usual commercial partnership has tangible assets such as machinery, fixtures, supplies, and merchandise. By contrast, the physical assets of a professional partnership are usually at a minimum. The earning power of the professional partnership is not predicated upon capital but on personal services, skill, and good will. Generally, the good will contributed by a partner dies with the partner. When a professional partner dies, his widow cannot become a member of the partnership, since she does not possess the requisite training and experience. For these reasons, the need for a business purchase agreement funded with life insurance is often overlooked.

Quite often the surviving partners in a professional partnership feel morally obligated to distribute a part of the partnership earnings to the widow of a deceased partner for a limited period. Ideally, such an income-continuation plan should also be funded with life insurance. Under Section 736(*a*) and Section 707(*c*) of the Internal Revenue Code of 1954, such payments will be treated as taxable income to the recipient and will be deductible by the surviving partners.

It is not unusual to find a professional partnership that has physical assets of substantial worth. A law firm may have an extensive and expensive library, office furniture and fixtures, and other tangible assets. A professional partnership of doctors may have X-ray and laboratory equipment. In such circumstances, the partners may approach the problems that face them at death by providing for a two-part agreement. One part provides for a buy-out covering the physical assets of the partnership, and another part provides for income continuation for a limited period to the widow of a deceased partner.

SELECTED REFERENCES

FORSTER, RICHARD H. "Legal, Tax and Practical Problems under Partnership Purchase and Sale Agreements, Coupled with Life Insurance," *Southern California Law Review*, Vol. XIX, No. 1 (September, 1945).

LAIKIN, GEORGE J. "Death, Taxes and Your Business," *Trusts and Estates*, Vol. 86 (Oct., 1947), p. 372.

MINTZ, EDWARD J. *Business Estate Planning*. Louisville, Ky.: Insurance Field Co., 1963.

MINTZ, EDWARD J. "Family Financial Planning," *Journal of the American Society of Chartered Life Underwriters*, Vol. X, No. 4 (Summer, 1956), p. 224.

MINTZ, EDWARD J. *Selling Business Insurance*. Englewood Cliffs, N.J.: Prentice-Hall, Inc., 1954.

SNYDER, BERNHART R. "Cross-Purchase vs. Entity Buyouts for Partnerships," *Journal of the American Society of Chartered Life Underwriters*, Vol. XVII, No. 3 (Summer, 1963), pp. 203–11.

WHITE, EDWIN H. *Business Insurance*. 3d ed. Englewood Cliffs, N.J.: Prentice-Hall, Inc., 1963.

Chapter 49

INSURANCE FOR BUSINESS CONTINUATION—CORPORATIONS

BY STUART A. MONROE

The corporation, a popular form of business organization, is faced with a great variety of real and continuing risks. Like any business, it is subjected to all of the vicissitudes of the business cycle. Its continuing health is subjected to the whims of consumer demand for its products and services and the effectiveness of its management. Its material assets are subjected to fire, flood, and earthquake. Not the least important of the risks it faces is the potential destruction by death or disability of its principal owners. It is this latter risk with which this chapter will be concerned.

Nature of the Corporation

A corporation is a separate, distinct, and legally recognized entity, created by law and usually existing for the purpose of engaging in business for profit. The original capital is normally furnished in the form of money (but occasionally consists of property or services). Those who make the capital contributions receive stock entitling them to share in the management and profits of the enterprise. The corporation is created by state law, generally through the filing of a "certificate of incorporation." This certificate will set forth the name of the corporation, the number and types of shares which can be issued, the number of directors, and the purpose for which organized, as well as the type of business in which it may engage.

If the stockholders are few in number, the corporation is usually referred to as a "close corporation," which means that the stock is closely held. In a close corporation, the stockholders generally are active in the management and operation of the business as officers or employees. The stock is not listed on an exchange and has no ready market. It is this kind of corporation which lends itself best to the use of insurance for business continuation purposes.

Unlike a partner in a partnership, a stockholder has limited liability; that is, he cannot lose more than he has invested in the corporation. A general partner, on the other hand, can be held liable for everything he owns (outside and inside the partnership). In a partnership, upon the death of a partner, there is a dissolution of the business. This is not the case in a corporation. Stockholders may die, but the corporation lives on. Thus, there is, in effect, perpetual life in the case of most business corporations. When a stockholder dies, the shares of stock he owns pass to his executor or administrator and then to the beneficiaries of his estate. During lifetime, they may be transferred by the owner to another by sale or by gift. The ease of transfer from one owner to another is a major reason why the corporate form of doing business is so popular. The owner of the stock may vote it; and if the interest represents a majority, then such owner may vote the stock so as to elect at least a majority of the board of directors and thereby, for all practical purposes, manage the business.

In a closely held corporation, and as long as the business prospers, the livelihoods of the stockholders who are active in management are assured by salaries, bonuses, and, in some cases, dividends. Any excess earnings, if not distributed as dividends, are reflected in the increased value of the stock. The utility value of the stockholder's interest in the corporation is great to him, but it may not be to his family or to others who share in his estate. If one or more of his associate stockholders should predecease him, the value to him of his shares may be greatly diminished by reason of the associate's peculiar talents and abilities which are lost.

The problem that death creates in a partnership can be seen rather easily. There is a dissolution at death, and the parties are faced with the liquidation imposed by law unless some alternative solution can be worked out. A buy-and-sell agreement seems such a logical solution. But a corporation does not "die" with the death of a stockholder—it has continuing life. However, there are very real problems caused by the death of a principal stockholder in a close corporation.

Problems Caused by Death of Principal Stockholder

Upon the death of a principal stockholder the *surviving stockholders* must either:

1. Continue the business with the decedent's family or his estate beneficiaries, who may not be familiar with the business nor be able to work in harmony with the surviving stockholders; or
2. Buy the decedent's stock, provided they can raise the necessary cash and are willing to outbid competitors; or
3. Continue the business with any outsiders to whom the decedent's estate may sell his stock; or
4. Sell their stock for whatever the decedent's estate or other purchasers will offer.

The situation is just as bad from the standpoint of the family or other estate beneficiaries of the deceased stockholder. They may:

1. Continue in business with the surviving stockholders; or
2. Buy the stock of the surviving stockholders, provided they have the necessary cash; or
3. Continue in the business with any outsiders to whom the stock of the survivors may be sold; or
4. Sell the decedent's stock for whatever the surviving stockholders or other purchasers will offer.

The problems extend even further, in that a basic conflict often exists between the surviving stockholders and the widow. The widow needs income to replace her husband's salary. There may not be sufficient other income-producing property. It may not be possible or desirable to pay dividends on the stock. What can she do? This phase of the problem can best be explored by analyzing the basic elements of a share of stock.

Basic Elements of a Share of Stock

With respect to a closely held corporation, a share of stock can be said to comprise four separate elements: (1) the right to work, (2) the right to receive dividends, (3) the right to vote, and (4) the right to sell. Generally, a share of stock carries with it no right to work and to receive a salary. But in the closely owned corporation, an owner frequently makes his investment in the business to secure the status of a salaried officer as well as to become a stockholder. His stock interest plus his ability, while alive, will usually give him the right to work. In regard to these basic elements, consider the situations of the minority stockholder, the majority stockholder, and the equal stockholder.

The Minority Stockholder Situation. First, a minority stockholder dies owning, for example, a one-third interest. What is the problem facing his widow? It is one of income. Her husband's salary terminates immediately upon death, and she seeks a source to replace that income. She asks the surviving stockholders to place her on the payroll, but is politely told there is no place for her. As time goes on, the need for income may become more pressing. She asks the survivors when they expect to pay a dividend. Their reply is that they have never paid one; furthermore, at present, there is the need to establish a better credit position and purchase new machinery. There is no surplus for a dividend distribution. She now consults the attorney handling the estate. He advises that the payment of a dividend in this instance is, for all practical purposes, within the discretion of the board of directors and apparently the board feels the needs of the business do not warrant the declaration of a dividend. They can, in some instances, be compelled to declare a dividend, but these instances are exceedingly rare, costly, and time-consuming. Legal proceedings may make it impossible, or at least difficult, for the widow to obtain dividend payments. Pursuit of the "right to receive dividends" is fruitless. Obviously, two of the rights of a share of stock are eliminated.

She attends a stockholders' meeting to vote her stock, but finds it is of no avail. She only has a minority interest. The third right of the shareholder gives no relief.

Now, being somewhat desperate for income, she seeks to sell her stock and is advised that the best market would be the surviving stockholders. In discussing it with them, they ask her what she feels is a fair price for the stock. She indicates that her husband told her it was worth about $160 a share. Their response leaves no doubt about where they stand. In their opinion, the husband's valuation was substantially out of line, and the best offer from them is $85 a share. The squeeze is now on. She is forced to sell on their terms.

The Majority Stockholder Situation. Now, consider the second situation—that involving a deceased majority stockholder. The widow has the same basic problem—loss of income. The husband's salary must be replaced. But in this case, through the right to vote and elect directors, the widow can, in effect, control the corporation. Through her voting control, members friendly and sympathetic to her view can be placed on the board of directors. Because the board controls the appointment of officers and payment of compensation, the squeeze can be given to the surviving stockholder-officers. Here, we see that the position of the widow is quite reversed, but the surviving stockholders are in jeopardy.

The Equal Stockholder Situation. A third situation develops when the surviving stockholder and the widow each own an equal interest (50 per cent each). Neither person would be in control of the corporation. The basic conflict of interest would persist, but could not be resolved. This can be an extremely troublesome situation. Not infrequently, a deadlock results, which hurts both parties as well as the business itself.

The Situations Reversed. The implications of these three situations can be reversed. In the first one, the surviving and controlling stockholders dominated the widow. She was forced into a very unsatisfactory sale because of her need for income. Suppose the widow had sufficient income from outside sources. With no need to sell hastily, she could become a considerable nuisance to the corporation as a minority stockholder. In time, the survivors might be very willing and anxious to buy her out and this time at a price more favorable to her than to them. Thus, in this kind of situation the surviving stockholders may be subjected to harassment.

In the second situation the widow was the controlling stockholder and, as such, could squeeze the surviving stockholder-officers. However, the business could be one that required extremely competent management which the surviving stockholder-officers provided. The success of the corporation is dependent upon them. By threats to leave or to set up a competing corporation, they can often force their views upon the widow.

Her position then becomes a weak one. Finally, we saw two equal stockholders battling. Sometimes the widow may occupy the dominant position and cause the most trouble. But it could be the surviving stockholder, who by manipulation forces the widow into a weak position, so that she is compelled to sell on his terms.

Importance of Situation Analysis

These situations are intended to suggest that each case should be analyzed to visualize the situation upon the death of the client, and particularly the effect his death could have upon the value of his interest in the business as a part of his estate and from his family's viewpoint. This is especially significant when the client is a primary motivating force in the business and when the business interest comprises the major portion of his wealth.

There must also be considered the effect that the death of one of the other principal stockholders could have upon the interest of the client during his lifetime, and the possible complications which may arise in conducting the affairs of the corporation due to dissatisfaction among the heirs of such stockholder. Unless adequate precautions are taken, it is almost impossible for a closely held corporation to escape serious pressures one way or another at the death of a major stockholder or key man.

It is always desirable to take the long-range view to determine ways in which the values of a business may be preserved.

It is axiomatic that the prosperity of any business is dependent upon its management, and this is particularly true of a close corporation. Management can be most efficient and effective in the closely held corporation where it possesses voting control. It is almost always embarrassing for the survivors to have the family of the deceased as continuing stockholders. Such stockholders are seldom satisfied with the benefits received from the corporation after the death of the stockholder-officer when compared with the benefits they received during his lifetime. If a lag in profits occurs, they are apt to blame the management rather than recognizing that it might be due to unavoidable conditions, perhaps due to the death of the stockholder.

Thus, it can be seen that in many cases the transmission of the stock interest to his family by a stockowner poses a problem not only to the family but to the surviving stockholders as well. A restrictive agreement or buy-and-sell arrangement is a frequent solution to prevent distribution of stock interests into the hands of inactive or possibly unsympathetic individuals. The buy-and-sell agreement also provides the stockholder with a market assuring a fair and fixed price for his stock upon his death, and removes his family from the hazards, risks, and harassments of the business.

Retention of Stock Interest by the Family

It should not be assumed that every situation calls for the sale of the stock interest in a closely held corporation upon the death of a stockholder. There will be situations where, because the business is a highly profitable one and the personal guidance of the stockholder is not completely vital, the stock interest may be retained for the family. In other cases, the retention of the stock interest will be desired because there are family members who work in the business or who eventually will come into the business.

The factors which will influence the decision to retain or sell the stock interest will usually be:

1. Are there sons or sons-in-law for whom it should be retained and preserved?
2. Is the stock interest a majority one? If the interest is a minority one, can the family get along with the surviving shareholders, or will it be at their mercy?
3. What are the future prospects of the industry and the particular business within that industry? In short, is it a good investment?
4. Is competent management available?

If the decision is to retain the stock interest within the family, certain problems of valuation and liquidity will be encountered.

Valuation of Stock Interest

A basic problem is that of determining at what value the stock will be included in the gross estate of the decedent stockholder for federal estate tax purposes. Because a close corporation is one with very few stockholders, normally there is no market for the stock. The federal estate tax regulations require that the "fair market value" be ascertained. This is defined as the price a willing buyer will pay a willing seller, both being familiar with the facts. But such definition does not help very much in practical situations. Artificial means must be employed to arrive at "fair market value." The federal regulations state that the fair market value of unlisted stock is to be determined by taking the following factors into consideration: "the company's net worth, prospective earning power, dividend paying capacity, and other relevant factors." Three basic approaches to valuing unlisted stock are:

1. *The Company's Net Worth.* Book value or net worth usually means assets minus liabilities as they appear on the books of the corporation. Properly, such values as shown on the books should be adjusted to reflect their market value as of the valuation date.
2. *Earning Power—Good Will.* The company's earnings are capitalized, usually by means of a formula. A formula frequently employed is that of Appeal and Review Memo 34 (2 CB 31[1920]). Under this formula, the present tangible or book value is ascertained. Then the average of the tangible assets or book value over the past five years is obtained, and a

fair rate of return (generally 8 or 10 per cent) is attributed to such assets. The income thus obtained is subtracted from the average earnings (after corporate taxes and salaries) over the past five years. The difference represents the amount of earnings attributable to the intangible asset of good will. It is capitalized at a rate of return considerably higher than the one used above (frequently 20 per cent). The capitalized value of the intangibles or good will is then added to the present tangible or book value.

3. *Comparable Companies.* This approach uses as a method of valuation the market prices of stock of corporations engaged in the same or similar lines of business which are listed on a stock exchange or quoted by established security firms. The greater the similarity between the companies to be compared, not only as to the business engaged in, but also as to their capital structure, volume of business, and so forth, the greater the weight given to this method of valuation.

An important Treasury Department ruling (Revenue Ruling 59–60, CB 1959–1, 237, superseding Revenue Ruling 54–77, CB 1954–1, 187) contains a discussion of the factors involved in valuing closely held stock. The ruling lists the following eight factors to be considered in making valuations: nature and history of the business, economic outlook, book value and financial condition, earning capacity, dividend-paying capacity, good will, sales of the stock, and market price of stocks of similar corporations.

Estate Liquidity

A decision to retain the stock creates not only the problem of valuation but also that of estate liquidity. The problem of valuation will remain uncertain, but the hardship of raising cash for estate costs has been somewhat alleviated by Section 303 of the Internal Revenue Code.

Section 303, in effect, provides that a corporation may purchase its stock from a stockholder without the stockholder running the risk of having the purchase price declared a taxable dividend. However, certain stated conditions must be met.

The major condition is that the stock must constitute at least 35 per cent of the gross estate of a deceased stockholder, or 50 per cent of the taxable estate. If the decedent owned more than 75 per cent each of the outstanding stock of more than one corporation, and these stock interests were included in the gross estate, they may be combined for the purposes of meeting the 35 or 50 per cent rule.

The provision that Section 303 may be used when the stock interest is at least 50 per cent of the taxable estate makes its use possible in almost all estates when there is a surviving spouse and the maximum marital deduction is to be used. Since the taxable estate is the amount remaining after the deductions, marital deduction, and specific exemption are subtracted from the gross estate, the 50 per cent of "taxable estate" test is met more readily than might first appear. It is a rare situation when a stock interest of any consequence would not meet this test.

The estate or other holder of the stock may take advantage of the provisions of Section 303 through a sale of stock to the corporation to the extent of the total of the federal and state death taxes, funeral expenses, and administration costs. Furthermore, the estate may redeem corporate stock under Section 303 even though it has other liquid assets to meet these costs. The estate need not be "tight" for cash.

Section 6166 of the Internal Revenue Code is also of interest in this connection. This law, subject to certain requirements and limits, permits the estate owning an interest in a closely held business to pay that portion of the federal estate tax allocable to the business interest in installments over a period not to exceed ten years. The major pertinent requirements of this section are as follows:

1. Similar to Section 303, the value of the business interest included in the estate must exceed either 35 per cent of the gross estate or 50 per cent of the taxable estate. Two or more businesses can be combined to meet these requirements if the decedent held more than a 50 per cent interest in each such business.
2. When the business interest in the estate is stock in a close corporation, there must have been ten or fewer stockholders, or the decedent's stock interest must represent 20 per cent or more of the voting stock.
3. The installment payment privilege is available only for the portion of the total federal estate tax attributable to the inclusion of the business interest in the estate. The balance of the tax must be paid within the usual fifteen-month period after death.
4. Four per cent interest is charged on the unpaid balances.

State death taxes, administration expenses, and funeral costs, even though substantial in amount, cannot be paid by installments but must be paid in full within the usual limits.

Disposing of Stock Interest through Formal Agreement

In many instances, the answers to the questions previously posed as influencing retention or sale will lead to a decision that the stock interest should not be retained for the family. When disposition of the stock is indicated, a market can be best established by use of a buy-and-sell agreement.

There are four basic kinds of buy-and-sell agreements:

1. The purchaser is obligated to buy the stock, and the estate of the deceased stockholder is obligated to sell. This is frequently referred to as a mandatory agreement of purchase and sale.
2. The purchaser has an option to purchase the stock of the deceased stockholder; and if exercised, the estate must sell.
3. The estate of the deceased stockholder has an option to sell; and if exercised, the other party must buy.
4. Neither of the parties is obligated to buy or to sell, but if a stockholder or the estate of a deceased stockholder desires to sell, the stock must first be offered to the other parties before it can be sold to a third party. This is sometimes referred to as a "first-offer" type of agreement.

The mandatory buy-and-sell agreement is the one most frequently used when stockholders desire to dispose of their holdings upon death. When the agreement is between the corporation and the stockholders, with the corporation as purchaser, it is usually referred to as a *stock retirement agreement.* If between the stockholders only, the buy-and-sell agreement is referred to as a *stock purchase agreement.*

Whether the buy-and-sell agreement is one of stock retirement or stock purchase, the mandatory type of agreement accomplishes the desired basic results: it provides a market for the stock interest in the event of death, it prevents outsiders from acquiring an interest in the business, it removes the family from the hazards and risks of the business, and it provides liquidity to pay estate costs and taxes.

Parties

Not all of the stockholders need be included, whether the plan be stock retirement or stock purchase. Perhaps only three out of five stockholders desire a buy-and-sell agreement for their stock interest. The three stockholders can be parties to a stock purchase agreement among themselves, or a stock retirement plan can be entered into between these three stockholders and the corporation. Those stockholders desiring to participate will be parties to the agreement. If the plan is to be one of stock retirement, then the corporation, of course, must be a party to the agreement. When a trustee is used, the trustee becomes a party to the agreement as well.

Stock Retirement versus Stock Purchase

The fundamental differences between a stock retirement plan and a stock purchase plan may be analyzed as to enforceability, funding, premium payment, transfer of policies, income tax status, beneficiary designation, and estate tax status.

Enforceability. The difference between stock retirement and stock purchase with respect to enforceability centers on the power of a corporation to purchase its own stock. When the plan is stock retirement, a corporation, in most states, can purchase its own stock, provided it is done out of surplus and the interests of creditors are not jeopardized. If such a purchase cannot be made, then the agreement may be unenforceable. Where the agreement is stock purchase, no such problem arises.

Funding the Agreement. The buy-and-sell agreement, by its very nature, creates an obligation in the corporation or the survivors to purchase the stock interest of the first stockholder to die. The manner in which this obligation is to be discharged becomes most important. Do they wish to discharge this obligation from accumulated cash reserves, which may not be available at the time needed? Do they wish to use promissory notes? Or do they want installment payments over a long period of time? Since the obligation may mature with unexpected suddenness, the problem of providing funds to purchase the interest of a deceased owner is most satisfactorily solved through the use of life insurance.

Impact of Premium Payments. Under a stock retirement plan, the corporation will own the life insurance as well as being the beneficiary and paying the premiums. The premiums paid by the corporation are not deductible for income tax purposes, and the policy proceeds payable upon death are not includable in the corporation's gross income. The payment of premiums by the corporation has the effect of allocating the total amount of premiums among the stockholders according to their shareholdings. The larger, and often older, stockholder "pays" the major portion of the premiums, whereas the younger, and smaller, stockholder would "pay" very little. In a stock purchase plan, these positions would be reversed. If the parties to a stock retirement plan feel that the impact of the premiums is inequitable, a solution might be worked out by including a portion of the proceeds of the life insurance policy on the deceased stockholder's life in the purchase price formula. This would, in effect, reimburse the estate for the premiums advanced.

Under a stock purchase plan, the stockholders take out insurance on each others' lives and pay the premiums. For example, assume that a corporation valued at $100,000 is owned 60 per cent by A, 25 per cent by B, and 15 per cent by C. The life insurance arrangement in this instance might be as shown in Table 49–1.

TABLE 49–1

ILLUSTRATIVE LIFE INSURANCE ARRANGEMENT IN A STOCK PURCHASE PLAN FOR CLOSE CORPORATION

Policy	Life	Amount of Insurance	Owner, Beneficiary, Premium Payor
1.	A	$37,500	B
2.	A	22,500	C
3.	B	20,000	A
4.	B	5,000	C
5.	C	10,588	A
6.	C	4,412	B

The age and stock interest will determine the impact of the premium payments. If B and C are appreciably younger than A, it will be seen that they will pay far more in premiums than A. It can be argued that this is as it should be because the younger and smaller stockholders will benefit substantially should A die. Thus, they should bear the impact of the premiums on the life insurance required to acquire that ownership.

Transfer of Insurance Policies. Under a stock retirement plan, the life insurance policies are purchased and owned by the corporation, and only one policy may be required for each life. Under a stock purchase plan, many policies can be required (if five stockholders, twenty policies would be needed).

Upon the death of a stockholder under a stock retirement plan, no transfer of a policy is necessary. The corporation owns the policies on the surviving stockholders' lives.

Under a stock purchase plan with the policies owned by the stockholders on a cross-purchase arrangement, upon the death of one of them a transfer of each policy owned by the deceased stockholder on the survivors' lives to the survivors is necessary if the life insurance coverage is to remain the same and the policies are to integrate with the agreement. Each such transfer would constitute a "transfer for value" within the meaning of Section 101(*a*)(2) of the Internal Revenue Code. Under this section, transfers of life insurance policies may be made between partners, to a partnership, and to a corporation of which the insured is a stockholder or officer, without adverse tax consequences, but this is not so of transfers between stockholders. In respect to Section 101(*a*)(2), the stock retirement plan has an advantage over stock purchase.

Income Tax Basis. Under a stock retirement plan, the purchase of stock of a deceased stockholder by the corporation generally has the effect of increasing the value of the stock of the surviving stockholders. The cost basis of the survivors' stock, for determining gain or loss upon a subsequent sale for income tax purposes, has not changed.

To illustrate, let us assume that A, B, and C each paid $10,000 for 100 shares of stock. Today the corporation has capital and surplus of $60,000 (capital $30,000 and surplus $30,000). Each of the 300 shares has its original cost basis of $100 and, if sold at today's book value, would bring a price of $200, or a long-term capital gain of $100 per share.

If this corporation, pursuant to a stock retirement plan, owns $20,000 of life insurance on A's life and he dies, the proceeds would be used by the corporation to acquire A's 100 shares at the agreement price of $200 per share. The capital and surplus would remain at $60,000. The insurance would increase the surplus to $50,000, but then $20,000 would be used to purchase A's stock. This would leave 200 shares of stock outstanding: 100 owned by B and 100 owned by C. But with the corporation still valued at $60,000, each share would be worth $300 book value. If B or C should then sell his stock at book value, he would have a long-term capital gain of $200 per share.

It is important to note that A's estate would have no income tax problem at all. Property sold subsequent to death takes as its income tax basis the value used for estate tax purposes. The agreement price, $200, would control for federal estate tax purposes, and the income tax basis would be $200. Therefore, there is no gain on the transaction and no taxable income to the estate, despite the fact that A paid only $100 per share and never paid income tax on the increment.

Under a stock purchase plan, the result is a different one for the survivors. They acquire an increased income tax basis for their stockholdings purchased from the deceased stockholder's estate. Using the same situation as above, B and C would each purchase 50 shares from A's estate at $200 per share (the agreement price). B and C now own 150 shares each. The newly acquired shares would have an income tax cost basis of $200 per share (the price they paid), and 100 shares (the original holdings) would have a basis of $100 per share. B and C have a total cost basis for their stock of $20,000 each. A subsequent sale of the stock at $200 per share (book value of $60,000 divided by 300 shares) would result in no gain on 50 shares and $100 capital gain per share on 100 shares, or a total gain of only $10,000.

Beneficiary Designation. The beneficiary of the life insurance policies under a stock retirement plan will be the corporation because it has the obligation to purchase the stock interest. When it is desired under a stock retirement plan to use the services of a trustee, then, of course, the trustee will be the beneficiary of the insurance proceeds.

Different beneficiary designations have been used on stock purchase plans, not always properly. In some instances the estate of the insured has been used. This designation is not frequently used. The stock passes to the estate of the deceased stockholder, and if the insurance proceeds are also received by the estate, it would seem that the executor or administrator of the estate has control over both the stock and the proceeds. Creditors of the estate can attack the insurance proceeds.

In other situations, the designation of the deceased stockholder's wife or other family member is frequently motivated by a desire to obtain the optional modes of settlement for the beneficiary. Such a designation must be carefully worded, so that the estate will not be by-passed. Unless this precaution is taken, the following problems can result:

1. *Objections of Other Estate Beneficiaries.* Assume that the beneficiary of the insurance is the wife and the stockholder leaves no will. If there are children and some or all of them are minors, there is a question as to the position of the minor children. They will take an interest in the estate the same as adult children, but they cannot consent to any transfers. It is most unlikely that the administrator will convey the stock to the surviving stockholders when payment for it goes directly to the widow —ignoring the interests of the children.
2. *Creditors of the Estate.* If the estate does not possess sufficient cash or liquid assets to pay creditors or death taxes, can the stock be transferred to the surviving stockholders when payment, pursuant to the agreement, goes directly to the widow?
3. *Income Tax Base.* The *Legallet* case (1 BTA 294) held that a surviving partner did not receive an increased cost basis when the proceeds of

the life insurance policy were payable directly to the beneficiary of the deceased partner and were not received actually or constructively by the surviving partner. It would seem that the same conclusion would be reached under a similar situation involving a stock interest in a corporation.

These problems can be avoided by providing that the proceeds payable to the named beneficiary be held at interest for a period of time during which the purchaser or trustee will have a right of withdrawal. In most cases, such right will not have to be exercised, but it is available if a problem arises.

Naming the surviving stockholders as beneficiary is the most logical plan when the optional modes of settlement are not desired because those obligated to purchase the stock interest of a deceased stockholder receive the insurance proceeds. The contingent beneficiary should be the estate of the surviving stockholder.

The use of a trustee is often desired to assure performance pursuant to the terms of the agreement. Payment of the life insurance proceeds will then be made to the trustee in a single sum. The trustee disposes of the proceeds as directed by the agreement. Some life insurance companies will permit the use of settlement options when a trustee is the primary beneficiary if family members are named as secondary beneficiaries, or will grant the trustee a right of withdrawal.

Estate Tax Status. When the agreement is negotiated in good faith and at arm's length, and is binding during the lifetime of the owner as well as at death, the price agreed upon will probably be controlling for estate tax purposes.

Special Family Situations

There are numerous closely held corporation situations where the stockholders are members of the immediate family. For example, a father, a son, and a son-in-law comprise the stockholders, and a buy-and-sell agreement is contemplated. The implications of Sections 302 and 318 of the Internal Revenue Code must be observed.

Should they adopt a stock retirement arrangement, then upon the father's death the corporation will purchase the shares from his estate. Section 302 tells us that if this purchase completely terminates the estate's stock interest in the corporation or is "substantially disproportionate" (after the purchase the estate must own less than 50 per cent of outstanding voting stock, and at least 20 per cent of its holdings must be redeemed), capital gains treatment will be given to the transaction. Thus, no income tax problems are encountered. However, if these tests are not met, then the purchase of the estate's stock may be considered a dividend distribution by the corporation and the full purchase price taxed as ordinary income. The latter would be a most serious income tax burden.

The requirements of Section 302 seem simple enough—redeem *all* of the father's shares. But it is not so easy, because Section 318 invokes certain rules of attribution. This means that in certain instances, shares of stock in a corporation owned by one person are assumed to be owned by other members in his family unit, or vice versa. Also, stock ownership of estates, partnerships, corporations, or trusts is attributed to the estate beneficiaries, partners, stockholders, and trust beneficiaries, respectively, or vice versa. Therefore, in the above situation, if the son is a beneficiary of his father's estate, the estate will be deemed constructively to own the son's shares. Likewise, the son-in-law's stock will be deemed owned by his wife (the daughter) through family attribution and this, in turn, attributed to the father's estate if the daughter is a beneficiary. Thus, compliance with Section 302 becomes impossible, and we may have a dividend distribution with disastrous income tax consequences.

If a stock purchase arrangement is used in this situation, the income tax problem will not be involved. Sections 302 and 318 apply only to the purchase of its stock by a corporation.

Advantages of the Buy-and-Sell Agreement

The advantages of a buy-and-sell agreement funded through life insurance might be summarized as follows:

1. To the surviving stockholders:
   a) They become the sole owners of the business.
   b) Outside stock interests cannot interfere.
   c) The terms of the sale, such as price and payment, are fixed in advance.
   d) The cash to finance the purchase is provided automatically at the death of a stockholder by the life insurance.
2. To the family of the deceased stockholder:
   a) The family has an assured market for the stock at a fair price.
   b) The widow is free from business responsibility.
   c) The cash received in full for the stock interest is free from the hazards and risks of the business.
   d) Settlement of the estate can be made with dispatch because the cash received provides a fund from which estate costs and taxes can be paid.
   e) The value of the stock is fixed for estate tax purposes.
   f) Family dependency upon the fortunes of the business and its management is removed.

SELECTED REFERENCES

APPLEMAN, JOHN ALAN (ed.). *Basic Estate Planning*, chs. iv and v. Indianapolis: Bobbs-Merrill Co., 1957.

MCCABE, THOMAS C.; MITCHELL, WILLIAM H.; and PLOWDEN-WARDLAW, THOMAS C. "Integrating Life Insurance with Business Planning," *Journal of the American Society of Chartered Life Underwriters,* Vol. XII, No. 2 (Spring, 1958), p. 176.

STEINBERG, B. WILLIAM, and MONROE, STUART A. *Practical Property Planning—A Workbook of Estate Planning for the Life Underwriter.* Chicago: Planning Associates, 1958.

TREMAYNE, BERTRAM W., JR. "Estate Planning for the Man with a Business," *Washington University Law Quarterly,* Vol. 1955, No. 1, p. 40.

"The Use of Life Insurance to Fund Agreements Providing for Disposition of a Business Interest at Death," *Harvard Law Review,* Vol. LXXI (1958), pp. 687–712.

WHITE, EDWIN H. *Business Insurance.* 3d ed. Englewood Cliffs, N.J.: Prentice-Hall, Inc., 1963.

Chapter 50

INSURANCE FOR BUSINESS CONTINUATION—PROPRIETORSHIPS

BY SAMUEL L. ZEIGEN

About 70 per cent of the business entities of the American economy are sole proprietorships. The owners of each of these businesses must face many problems and decisions, not the least of which are those related to disability and premature death. Basically, the owner is concerned that suitable arrangements be made during his life to assure continuity of income for his family without undue delay and at a minimum cost in expenses and taxes. At the same time, he is concerned with continuity of income to himself in the event of disability and upon retirement.

Nature of Sole Proprietorship

The key factor in any discussion of proprietorship problems is the simple fact that a sole proprietor is an individual engaged in business for himself. The phrase is so simple as to be deceptive. The proprietor is not only in business for himself, he *is* the business itself. There is not the distinction, economic or legal, between the business activity and the businessman in the proprietorship that there is in the corporation-stockholder-executive relationship.

It is this unity of the proprietary business and its owner that creates the special problems of the proprietorship. Neither the law nor the proprietor's creditors nor the taxing authorities distinguish between the sole proprietor's business assets and his so-called "personal" assets, just as there are no such differences between his so-called "personal" liabilities and the liabilities of his business. His creditors ordinarily will be permitted to satisfy their claims from any assets, any property, anything of value which the proprietor owns, including his home, his car, his savings account, his securities. They need not and will not stop at the business assets. Life insurance payable to or for the benefit of a named personal beneficiary normally is not subject to claims of creditors of the insured. On the other hand, unpaid personal creditors can attach business assets.

In summary, then, almost all of a sole proprietor's assets are subject to any liabilities, without distinction as to the nature of the asset or the source of the liability. One thing more: These liabilities continue notwithstanding his death. They must be satisfied from the assets of his estate, including his business, which is a part of his estate.

Problems of the Sole Proprietorship

The sole proprietorship begins and ends with the proprietor himself. Whatever stops the proprietor from engaging in business activities cuts off the existence of the proprietary business. The common causes of such stoppages are death, permanent disability, sale of the entire business or all of its assets, retirement, abandonment, or voluntary or involuntary bankruptcy. A proprietor may never be disabled, may never retire or go into bankruptcy; but he must die, and his business will die with him unless he takes the necessary steps during his life to prevent this.

Death without a Will

If the proprietor dies without a will, a court will appoint an administrator of his estate. The estate, for the purposes of probate and administration, consists of whatever assets the proprietor owned at the time of his death, including his business, his home, and his personal belongings.

The estate, for purposes of estate taxation (state and federal), normally includes all these assets with few exceptions.[1] The value of life insurance owned by the proprietor is includable in the estate for tax purposes, even though payable to a named personal beneficiary.

Normally, the court appoints the widow as administratrix of her husband's estate. In such capacity, she has the duty of collecting all the assets; paying all debts, expenses, and taxes of the estate; and thereafter distributing whatever remains according to the intestacy laws of the state of the deceased proprietor's domicile.

Estate distribution must be made not in accordance with the personal wishes of the deceased proprietor, but as prescribed by the laws of the particular jurisdiction. Normally, the widow and children, if any, share in the estate in proportions that vary from state to state. In many states, the widow receives only one third, and the children receive the remainder in equal shares. If there are minor children surviving him, the sole proprietor's wife, as administratrix, probably will be ordered by the probate court to sell the business because it is not a "prudent" investment for minors.

In addition to the chance that the property may be distributed contrary to the proprietor's wishes, as well as the disappointment of his hopes for any continuation of the business by his son or sons, his wife has such

---

[1] Estate Tax Regulations, Sec. 20.2031–1.

additional (and unnecessary) expenses as paying the costs of the administrator's bond and the bond as guardian of any children's property during their minority.

Death with a Will

If the proprietor dies with a will, most of the foregoing problems will not arise. However, the mere fact that a will is in existence does not of itself solve all problems. In most instances a proprietor names his wife as executrix of his will. The fact that she is executrix does not give her any special rights with regard to the business unless such rights are expressly provided for in the will. Without such specific authority, she continues the operation of the business at her own personal financial risk.[2]

Since the business is presumed to die with its owner, the fact that the executrix continues to operate it without express authority under the will makes her liable for all losses and expenses of the business. This liability is a personal one, so that anything that she may own in her own name, as well as what she inherits from her husband, is subject to the claims arising from any losses or expenses in connection with the unauthorized continuation of the business. This includes any life insurance proceeds she has received in a lump sum from policies on the life of the proprietor, since such proceeds are exempt from claims of creditors of the insured but ordinarily not from creditors of the beneficiary.

If the wife is the sole heir as well as the designated executrix under the will, then her risk is minimized. However, if there are minor children or others who are legatees under the will, then she may run a very real risk. For at any time that losses result, these persons can sue the executrix, even though for many years they have enjoyed the benefit of profitable operations.[3]

Still another bar to unauthorized continuation of a proprietorship exists in the creditors of the business and the creditors of the estate. They may prefer cash settlement of their accounts rather than run the risk of continued business operations. And if the executrix or administratrix of the estate is so ill advised as to continue the proprietorship business without the consent of creditors, as well as heirs and/or legatees, she is subjecting all the assets of the business, all other estate assets, and her own personal assets to liability for claims and losses arising out of the unauthorized continuation of the business.

Some states have expressly authorized executors and administrators to continue operation of a business for the purposes of an orderly liquidation. Helpful as this may be, there are certain inherent limitations. The proprietor may not be a resident of such a state, and even in those favored states the period of grace is for a limited time. Would-be buyers may wait out

[2] *In re Wolfe's Estate*, 87 NYS (2d) 327.

[3] *In re Ducker's Estate*, 263 NYS 217.

the period, and the forced sale is simply delayed until the end of the period.

This risk of continuation of the business without authority is one of the most compelling reasons why an executor—whether it is the surviving spouse, a friend, or a corporate executor—may feel obliged to sell the business as promptly as practicable, notwithstanding that a forced sale almost always results in a loss. All of the above applies even more strongly to an administrator, who ordinarily has no authority whatever to continue the business.

Only by specific authorization in the will to continue the operations of the business can an executor be free from the pressure to sell at the earliest possible moment.

Even though his will authorizes continuation of the business, the proprietor still faces the practical problem of continuity of management. A wife does not always have business managerial ability, nor does she generally have business experience in depth. Furthermore, an executor who is a capable business excutive does not have the time nor, for that matter, the willingness to manage another's business at the expense of his own.

Even if the business can "run itself" because of efficient employees, it is not reasonable to assume that the wife will always get along with these employees. Perhaps even more important, skillful employees may not be willing to go on working for the benefit of absentee owners when they might go into business for themselves.

Valuation and Taxes

Total worth is not just an academic computation of values. For if the proprietor's total worth exceeds $60,000 at the date of death, his estate must file a federal estate tax return, whether or not a tax is actually due.[4]

Estate values, to a large extent, depend upon which of the alternative courses of action is adopted as to disposition of the business, that is, liquidation, continuation, or sale.

Liquidation or the piecemeal sale of the different assets, if completed within a reasonable time, may establish values by the actual amounts of cash received for the different items. Liquidation, like any other forced sale, usually causes a loss. Therefore, it should be avoided if at all possible.

Orderly liquidation should, however, be distinguished from forced liquidation. Orderly liquidation is the sale of various assets of the business *but* at times and places chosen by the seller. As a practical matter, this can only be done where the executor is empowered to continue the business for this purpose and only when adequate cash for current expenses is available.

[4] Estate Tax Regulations, Sec. 20.6018–1.

If the business is continued for an indefinite period, the value for estate tax purposes is not so-called "book value" but rather "market value," an estimate of what the business would be worth if sold as a going concern, including good will (if any). It is the valuation of good will more than any other item that may bring about a difference in the total value of the estate as determined by the taxing authorities and the estimates by the executor or administrator of the estate.

If there is a difference of opinion as to value, then the estate must pay the higher tax or go to court for relief.[5] Litigation could easily extend over a lengthy period, five years or even longer, until final determination.[6] If the taxing authorities prevail, then the estate may not be able to pay the larger tax, much less support the proprietor's family.

Valuation

In any study or discussion of the problems of a proprietary business, a constant and recurring theme is that of "valuation." Records furnish the necessary "cost" information, but "value" cannot be determined so readily or accurately.

At the proprietor's death the business is frequently a large, if not the major, portion of his gross estate for federal estate and state inheritance or estate tax purposes. Federal estate tax regulations set up certain valuation standards. These are set forth in Regulations 20.2031–3. Value is the "fair market value" which the Regulations say is "the net amount which a willing purchaser . . . would pay . . . to a willing seller, neither being under any compulsion to buy or to sell and both having reasonable knowledge of relevant facts." This "net value" is determined on the basis of all relevant factors, including (1) a fair appraisal of all the assets of the business, tangible and intangible, including good will, and (2) the demonstrated earning capacity of the business.

This definition is an optimistic one. It assumes that the estate of the proprietor will face no compulsion to sell at any price and blindly ignores those situations where, for reasons already given, the estate of the proprietor is under an economic gun and must sell at prices dictated by buyers who are well aware of the need to convert assets into ready cash. It is this discrepancy between the estate as it is and the estate as it should be that causes the Treasury Department to impose valuations (and taxes that follow such valuations) which seem to bear no relationship to the estate as it then actually exists. But this difference, often a very considerable one, can be avoided by the proper integration of the estate (will, trusts, and the like) and life insurance planning, so that the estate is *in fact* a "seller" which is not "under any compulsion . . . to sell."

---

5 *Estate of A. Bluestein,* 15 Tax Court 770.

6 *Claire* v. *Hoffman,* 2 Tax Court 1160; *Worcester County Trust,* 134 F.(2d) 576; *Laird,* 38 Board of Tax Appeals 926.

Given such an estate, the fair market value of assets can usually be reasonably estimated by reference to sales in one market or another. Demonstrated earning capacity is again a matter of record, usually the federal income tax records. But good will is always a source of contention and means the difference between a comparatively low estate valuation (and estate tax) or a considerably higher valuation (and estate tax). Yet, even here the Treasury may be limited to a reasonable and realistic valuation in those situations where the sole proprietor has agreed "for an adequate and full consideration in money or money's worth, that his interest passes at his death to. . . ." Otherwise, say the Regulations: "Special attention should be given to determining *an adequate value* of the good will of the business. . . ."

Thus the buy-and-sell agreement so frequently stressed as a means of averting panic sales and losses is also the means of keeping estate taxes within the realistic capabilities of the estate.

It must be stressed, however, that a written agreement does not have this effect simply because it embodies a price and conditions of sale. The Treasury requires something more, and that something more is stated in Regulations 20.2031–2(*h*), to the effect that

> little weight will be accorded a price contained in a . . . contract under which the decedent is free to dispose of the [business] at any price he chooses during his lifetime. . . . Even if the decedent is not free to dispose of the . . . [business] at any other than the . . . contract price, such price will be disregarded . . . unless it is determined that the agreement represents a bona fide business arrangement and not a device to pass the decedent's [business] to the natural objects of his bounty, for less than the adequate and full consideration in money or money's worth.

Within this limitation, which is but another way of stating that the agreement must represent a genuine purchase and sale, and not a gift "paper" agreement, the buy-and-sell agreement is the most effective way of predetermining estate (and estate tax) valuation for a proprietary business. In the absence of such an arm's-length agreement, the Treasury takes very seriously its own directive to pay "special attention . . . to determining an adequate value of the good will of the business. . . ."

But whether valuation is determined by such an agreement or by "pull and tug" between Treasury and taxpayer (and often with the courts acting as referee), valuation means taxes, and taxes are usually paid in cash. The best of plans to free the estate from the legal threat of loss by an adequate and planned will, to keep estate valuation within reasonable bounds by a valid buy-and-sell agreement, may be knocked under the auctioneer's hammer if the cash to meet the estate tax demands is not available. Taxes are payable normally in cash, and cash must be forthcoming either from (1) savings and earnings (and so much less for the proprietor's family); (2) sales of assets (by forced sale, which is a last desperate resort); or (3) life insurance proceeds (bought and planned for this very purpose).

It is not only in estate and gift tax matters that the proprietor is made to realize he is a "special" case. If, as with so many others, high income tax rates make him acutely conscious of the benefits of long-term capital gains, it may come as a rude shock to him to discover that in the sale of his proprietary business, he is not on a par with the corporate stockholder. When a stockholder sells his stock, he is making a sale of a capital asset, but a proprietary business is not a capital asset in and of itself; it is a collection of assets, the sale of some of which will result in capital gains treatment, and the sale of others will not. Thus, the gain from the sale is partly ordinary income and only partly capital gain.[7]

Alternative Courses upon Discontinuance of Proprietorship

A proprietor must determine whether his business should be liquidated piecemeal, continued in one form or another, or sold as a going business.

To choose the proper course, certain basic information is necessary:

1. An estimate of total worth.
2. The amount of cash needed for final expenses and taxes.
3. The monthly income needed to support his wife and children in their accustomed standard of living.
4. The income desired at disability or personal retirement.
5. Plans as to the future of his business.

Life Insurance as an Aid to Choosing Alternatives

In the event of a liquidation of the proprietorship, whether orderly or not, the sales price must usually provide all or most of the cash necessary for final expenses and taxes, unless supplemented by the proceeds of life insurance. Even if there is a continuation of the business, the only sure source of cash for this purpose will be life insurance proceeds. The same situation exists as to monies needed for support of the family. Whatever money is derived from the liquidation of the business, it is very likely that it will not be enough to provide for adequate support of the family unless life insurance funds are also available.

In a continuation of the business, and particularly during the period of re-establishment of the business activities following the death of the proprietor, life insurance can make up the difference between earnings from the business and the minimum amounts necessary for family support and care.

Sale to Third Parties

There are times when a proprietorship can be advantageously sold as a going concern to third parties.

[7] *Williams* v. *McGowan,* 152 F. (2d) 570.

Provided the executor is given adequate powers in the will, he may shape the sale to the best advantage of the proprietor's surviving family. Given appropriate legal powers by a properly drafted will, and given economic freedom by life insurance adequate to support the proprietor's family during the period of negotiating the sale, the executor is enabled to drive the best possible bargain under the circumstances.

Such a sale has the added advantage of creating its own measuring yardstick for taxation purposes. Provided the sale is made within the statutory period for the payment of state and federal estate taxes, a sale made to unrelated third parties who are dealing at arm's length may be accepted by the taxing authorities as fixing the fair market value of the proprietorship.

Choice of Solutions

Experience and professional ingenuity have provided certain general solutions which can be adapted to the particular proprietary problem. Whichever of the general alternatives the proprietor selects, he should make or revise his present will so as to provide his executor and/or trustee with all necessary powers to accomplish the desired objectives. It is important to define what are business assets if a sale is to be made. An attorney can give the necessary advice and prepare the legal instruments. The services of a life underwriter, an accountant, and a trust officer are also valuable.

Preparation for Disposition

Where a realistic appraisal indicates that the proprietorship will be an economically desirable business even after the loss of its owner, then liquidation, even an orderly liquidation, should be and can be avoided. The executor should be given adequate powers by will so that he can follow the course of best advantage for the proprietor's family. The executor should be empowered to incorporate the business. Such incorporation can be accomplished tax-free after the death of the proprietor. If there is to be a later sale, the sale of corporate stock is the sale of a capital asset which results in a capital gain.[8] As previously stated, the sale of a proprietorship is treated as a sale of miscellaneous assets, and the profits from such a sale are treated as a capital gain or ordinary income, depending upon the nature of the asset sold.[9]

If the continuation of the proprietorship business by the family of the proprietor after his death is the objective, incorporation will make it more feasible to keep key employees by giving or selling them minority stock interests without any loss of control of the business by the family of the

---

[8] Internal Revenue Code, Sec. 1221.

[9] *Williams* v. *McGowan, supra.*

proprietor. A fringe benefit program can be installed, with benefits extended to stockholder-employees as well as to other employees.

Liquidation

Realistically, most sole proprietorships lose a good part or all of their value upon the death of the proprietor. At best, there is a "salvage" value of outstanding receivables, stock in trade or inventory, if any, fixtures, and customers' lists. The executor should have power to continue the business as long as it is advantageous, until he can make an orderly liquidation for the best possible price. Other than this salvage, there is often nothing more to be gained from the proprietorship. It is not the business in and of itself, but rather the life insurance that the operation of the business enabled the proprietor to purchase, that will provide the principal future income and security for his family. Lacking such insurance protection, orderly liquidation may not be possible, since demands of creditors, taxes, and like expenses must be paid.

Sale to Key Employees

A sole proprietorship may be sold to key employees. An agreement can be entered into between the proprietor and one or more key employees. The proprietor agrees to sell during his life or at his death, and the employees agree to buy the business at a price or by a formula stipulated in the agreement.

The funds which will be used for such purchase can be guaranteed by life insurance bought by the selected employees on the life of the proprietor. If the employees have no money of their own available, they can be given a raise sufficient to enable them to pay the premiums. This extra salary is, of course, deductible for tax purposes by the proprietor and taxable to the employees. If necessary, loans can be made to the employees in the amount of the premiums, which can be repaid to the estate out of the profits of the business after the employees become the owners. In this way, a guaranteed market for the sale of the proprietorship can be created at a predetermined price.

The mechanics are quite simple. The estate is bound by written agreement to sell, and the employees are bound to buy the proprietary business. A price or a formula for determining the price at the death of the proprietor is agreed upon. To underwrite this purchase, the employees apply for and are the owners of the life insurance policies on the life of the proprietor in an amount equal to or as nearly equal as practicable to the agreed-upon purchase price. Since their livelihood depends in a very real sense upon the continuance of the life of the business, which is to say the continuance of the life of the proprietor, it is well recognized that the employees have an insurable interest in the life of their employer. Upon the proprietor's death, it is agreed that these insurance proceeds will be paid to the proprietor's estate as the full or partial purchase price of the business.

Apart from assuring for himself and his family a "good" price for his business, the proprietor's "good bargain" includes additional benefits. There are, for example, the added incentive and efficiency of operations where employees think of a business as their own. Key employees who look forward to being "owners" some time in the future are not likely to work for a competing firm even for a higher salary, nor are they likely to go into competition with the business. Another advantage which results is that the Treasury Department normally regards such an agreement as establishing the fair market value of the business for estate tax purposes and is not likely to seek to enforce an exaggerated value upon the estate.

It is not a valid objection to say that the proprietor is buying his own business from himself. For one thing, compensation paid to employees is a deductible expense, and the government will contribute to the underwriting of the premium costs to the extent of the proprietor's tax bracket, which may be 32 to 50 per cent or more. Stated in another way, the proprietor is using 68- to 50-cent dollars (the dollar less the federal income tax if it were not paid out as deductible compensation) to buy 100-cent dollars for the benefit of his family.

There is also the element of uncertainty; the proprietor may live three years or thirty years. By using the employee salary increase plan, the employer is indirectly carrying additional life insurance, the cost of which he deducts from his income as a business expense (i.e., payment of premiums before income taxes) instead of, as he must do on his personal life insurance, paying from his after-tax income. In all probability, not all the premium costs will be paid from additional compensation. The employee who feels that a purchase of his employer's business is within his grasp can usually be persuaded to put in some of his own money.

In some instances, it may be worth the proprietor's while to make an interest-free loan to his employees for this purpose by using the "split-dollar" insurance plan. Each year, he deposits an amount equal to the annual increase in cash value, and the employees pay the balance of the premium. At the death of the proprietor, his estate receives the cash value, and the employees receive the balance of the insurance proceeds or the total proceeds, depending on the plan adopted. But care must be exercised with respect to the mechanics of this arrangement in order to avoid the possibility of the entire policy proceeds being included in the insured's estate for federal estate tax purposes.

A proprietor need not hesitate to adopt such a plan because he fears that the employees may not use the insurance funds for the designated purpose of purchasing the business, agreement or no agreement. He can arrange, at a slight additional cost, to have the policies of insurance made payable to and held by a trust company, which will collect the proceeds and then make payment in accordance with the terms of the agreement.

Disability of Proprietor

While death is the most common cause of proprietorship termination, disability also may force the owner to liquidate during his lifetime in order to meet his current needs.

Disability of a sole proprietor in some ways can be more difficult to cope with than death itself. Disability is really economic death, with the additional expense of executive replacement and costly medical bills. Fortunately, insurance contracts are available that reimburse for normal or abnormal medical expenses as well as providing for a monthly income for the period of disability. The disability income or payments for medical expense received from the insurance company are free of income tax where the proprietor has paid the premiums.[10]

If disability is characterized as a form of death in life, many of the solutions which have been previously discussed are also available to him. For example, the proprietor may prevent a "forced liquidation" by giving a power of attorney to managerial employees to run the business until his recovery or the best possible sale of the business as a going concern.

The proprietor may sell his business to his employees. Here the buy-and-sell agreement may take on a different form—the proprietor may sell on terms which amount to his being paid a percentage of profits over a period of years. This gives employees the incentive to continue the business and gives him an income over a period of years. Life insurance can serve a vital protective function here by having the lives of the purchasing employees insured to make certain that the balance of any sums due and owing will be paid at their death to the proprietor or his estate.

Retirement and Succession

It is not always death or disability that causes the termination of a sole proprietorship. Very often, it is a peaceful retirement. Then the proprietor may indeed do as he wishes—liquidate, sell, or give away his business, whichever is most to his advantage or liking. To fund his retirement plans, he has not only his social security payments but the cash values of the life insurance policies that were to cushion his family against the blow of his premature death. This cash can now give him a guaranteed monthly annuity income which can be made payable after his death to his surviving wife plus the earnings from the disposition of his business.

Beginning with 1963, the proprietor can now adopt a pension or profit sharing plan under the terms of the Self-Employed Individuals Tax Retirement Act. He can contribute each year for his own benefit the lesser of

---

[10] Internal Revenue Code, Sec. 104.

10 per cent of earned income or $2,500, but can deduct only one half, or a maximum of $1,250. If both capital and personal services are material income-producing factors, earned income is limited to 30 per cent of net profits, or $2,500, whichever is greater. He must include all full-time employees with more than three years' service.[11]

Very often a proprietor seeks to transfer his business to a member of his family who is actively associated in business with him. If this is done during the lifetime of the proprietor, there may be a taxable gift, and the principal problem will be the valuation of the gift for the purpose of the federal gift tax.

If a son or sons succeed to the proprietorship either by gift or upon the death of the sole proprietor by inheritance under the laws of intestacy or by bequest under a will, there is no major tax problem insofar as the beneficiaries are concerned. But as a matter of practical planning, it would be beneficial to the son if he had insured the proprietor's life, thereby providing himself with a source of working capital upon the proprietor's death.

Sometimes, however, there is no son to carry on a proprietary business, or the business as such is not to his liking. Then the proprietor would be well advised to do more than simply retire. His best course of action is to sell the business. Once again, a sale to the employees of the proprietorship should be considered. For the reasons given before, the employees are a group of buyers who are often ready and willing but not always able to pay for the proprietary business. One method of arranging to overcome this objection is through a buy-and-sell agreement where, in return for the proprietary business, its assets, and good will, the purchasing employees pay as large a down payment as they can afford and then pay the agreed-upon balance out of the earnings and profits of the business over a period of years. Admittedly, there is the risk that the employees may not be able to maintain these payments, but this risk may be minimized by the proprietor's own knowledge of the capabilities of both his business and his employees. Life insurance is a recommended precaution against the premature death of employees prior to completion of payment.

Subchapter S, Tax-Option Corporation

Since 1958, Subchapter S, Sections 1371–77 of the Internal Revenue Code, has provided for a sole proprietor incorporating his business with the option of being taxed essentially as though he were doing business as a sole proprietorship.

The prior main disadvantages of incorporation to a sole proprietor were the inability to take losses in full as an ordinary tax deduction and the double taxation of profits, first as corporate profits, and again when

[11] See Chapter 45 for analysis of Self-Employed Individuals Tax Retirement Act of 1962.

those profits were paid out as dividends. The changed law obviates both these shortcomings; losses can be deducted in full, and the stockholder-taxpayer (the sole proprietor in his new guise) is taxable on all the corporate earnings, while the corporation pays no separate, additional corporate tax.

The advantages of this form of corporation are apparent. The corporate form may be used to split income among members of a family unit. Gifts of stock can be made readily and easily without giving up control of the business. Corporate stock lends itself more readily to sale, whether to employees of a company or to outside parties. Moreover, the company's own resources can be used to buy as much of the stockholder's stock from his estate as is necessary to pay administration expenses and estate taxes without incurring tax liability.[12] In addition, key employees can be wedded to the service of the company through minority stock interests without any loss of one-man control.

Furthermore, the sole proprietor becomes an employee of his own corporate entity, and all the fringe benefits can now become his: participation in a pension or profit sharing plan, or both; group life insurance; and group major medical insurance or other hospital, surgical, and medical plans. The contributions and premiums for such plans are deductible by the corporation and are not taxable to the proprietor as an employee.[13]

No matter what disposition the owner of such a corporation wishes to make of his business entity, stock interests are more readily sold or otherwise disposed of than a proprietary interest either during his lifetime or at his death. Other benefits of incorporation are also gained, such as, for example, the limitation of liability.

At the same time, however, corporate operation imposes additional costs, such as record-keeping formalities, minute books, and books of account. Even the special tax advantages may boomerang if in any year profits and earnings are so large as to place the individual taxpayer-stockholder in a higher tax bracket than would prevail under corporate income tax.

SELECTED REFERENCES

CASNER, A. JAMES. *Estate Planning*. 3d ed. Boston: Little, Brown & Co., 1961.

J. K. LASSER INSTITUTE. *Estate Tax Techniques*, Vol. II. New York: Matthew Bender & Co., Inc. Looseleaf service.

LEWIS, JAMES B. *The Estate Tax*. New York: Practicing Law Institute, 1960.

NATIONAL UNDERWRITER COMPANY. *The Diamond Life Bulletins Service: Business Insurance Volume*. Cincinnati, 1964.

[12] Internal Revenue Code, Sec. 303.

[13] Internal Revenue Code, Sec. 105. Also see footnote 10.

RESEARCH AND REVIEW SERVICE OF AMERICA INC. *Advanced Underwriting and Estate Planning Service,* Vol. II. Indianapolis, 1964.

RESEARCH AND REVIEW SERVICE OF AMERICA, INC. *The Tax and Business Course.* Indianapolis, 1964.

RICE, RALPH S. *Family Tax Planning.* New York: Matthew Bender & Co., Inc., 1964.

SHATTUCK, MAYO ADAMS, and FARR, JAMES F. *An Estate Planner's Handbook.* 2d ed. Boston: Little, Brown & Co., 1953.

WHITE, EDWIN H. *Business Insurance.* 3d ed. Englewood Cliffs, N.J.: Prentice-Hall, Inc., 1963.

WORMSER, RENÉ A. *Personal Estate Planning in a Changing World.* New York: Simon & Schuster, Inc., 1952.

ZEIGEN, SAMUEL L. "The Business Continuation Agreement," *Journal of the American Society of Chartered Life Underwriters,* Vol. VIII, No. 1 (Winter, 1953), pp. 29–40.

ZEIGEN, SAMUEL L. *What Every Lawyer and Accountant Should Know about Business Life Insurance.* Indianapolis: Research and Review Service of America, Inc., 1955.

Chapter 51

INCOME PROTECTION FOR BUSINESS CONTINUATION

BY WILLIAM HARMELIN

The prolonged disability of sole proprietors, active partners, or close corporation stockholders without adequate income protection usually results in the "economic death" of their businesses. When disability lasts long enough to destroy earning capacity, personal and business reserves are soon dissipated. Under these conditions, the individuals involved and their businesses face very serious economic problems.

It is common practice for sole proprietorships, partnerships, and close corporations to buy life insurance for the purpose of reducing the financial loss to a business and the threat to its continuance which are caused by the death of an owner or key employees. There has been an increasing awareness, however, of the need for similar insurance coverage to protect against the staggering financial losses which occur when these business people become disabled for long periods of time. Recently, a Certified Public Accountant wrote:

> The death or poor health of one of the owners or key men may seriously affect the business and its continued profitable operation. Planning for these human factors is often overlooked by many otherwise astute businessmen who have inventory costs, sales, expenses, and cost profit margins under finger tip control.
>
> The completely planned business enterprise gives to the one the same full and exacting attention as it does to the other. Moreover, the necessary planning to protect the business enterprise against human mishaps is relatively simple and will demand but little time at the planning level.[1]

These thoughts pinpoint the fact that business advisers are beginning to understand the meaning of Dr. S. S. Huebner's third kind of economic death: the "living death." In this connection, Dr. Huebner has stated: "He who becomes a living death, totally and permanently, is just as dead

[1] N. R. Caine, "Health a Big Factor in Business," *New York World Telegram*, April 25, 1963.

economically as he who is actually dead. . . . The difference between the 'living death' under conditions of permanency and the 'actual death' is only six feet of sod. And if anything, the living death is the worst economically."[2]

Disabilities lasting at least 90 days and averaging over five years in duration are about two and a half times as frequent as death before age 65. Of 300 men aged 35, over 100 will be disabled for 90 days or more before reaching age 65, with an average disability period of 6½ years.[3]

This chapter will deal with the economic effect of serious disabilities of sole proprietors, active partners, and stockholder-employees on their businesses. Proposed solutions to the various problems created by such disabilities also will be discussed.

EFFECT OF DISABILITY ON A BUSINESS

Sole Proprietorship

Sole proprietorships represent about 70 per cent of all business establishments. The sole proprietor is a man of many talents. In effect, he is the president, treasurer, purchasing agent, sales manager, and board of directors of the business—all rolled into one person.

The sole proprietor and the business are one and the same.[4] He makes his own decisions. He does not have to consult anyone. The business will prosper and grow in direct proportion to his know-how, personality, experience, reputation, judgment, and ability to work. Thus, the success of the business depends almost entirely on the owner's ability. If the business profits, he profits. If the business loses, he loses. He is personally liable for business debts even to the extent of his personal assets.

When the sole proprietor in most businesses becomes seriously disabled, the business suffers. Businesses do not run by themselves. Sole proprietors recognize this fact, and while they are in good health, they rarely take vacations for extended periods of time. However, when a serious sickness or accident compels them to remain away from the business for an extended period of time, the economic effects on the sole proprietorship, as well as on their personal lives, are often disastrous.

The business may continue to function while the sole proprietor is disabled. However, unless it is a most unusual business, profits will drop because of the loss of the special skills and mature judgment of the sole proprietor. If the sole proprietor cannot work for a long enough period in a business which requires his personal services, the business will fail.

[2] Unpublished observation made in lecture and confirmed by Dr. S. S. Huebner, President Emeritus, American College of Life Underwriters, Bryn Mawr, Pennsylvania.

[3] "Report of the Committee on Disability and Double Indemnity," *Transactions of the Society of Actuaries*, Vol. 5, No. 2 (1953), p. 70.

[4] A large number of professional people are sole proprietors, including accountants, attorneys, dentists, doctors, veterinarians, architects, and the like.

Partnership

The general business partnership is a type of business organization that in part attempts to avoid the weaknesses of the sole proprietorship. Instead of one person carrying the full burden of risk of the business, two or more people pool their credit, labor, and skills to do a more effective job. Partners strengthen a business by complementing one another with added skills, ability, and capital.

When an active partner suffers a long-term disability, the business loses his services just as quickly and surely as if he were dead. The other partners are faced with a multitude of problems suggested by such questions as:

1. Can they make the business earn enough to continue the disabled partner's income?
2. Can they assume the disabled partner's former job responsibilities in addition to their own?
3. Can they continue to give the prompt service their customers demand?
4. Can they continue to meet production schedules?
5. Can they afford to hire a replacement for the disabled partner? If they can afford him, where can one be found?
6. If no replacement is found, how long can the other partner or partners continue to do the work of two men without the danger of becoming disabled themselves?

In the personal service or professional partnership, often used by accountants, architects, dentists, doctors, engineers, lawyers, and others, the physical assets of the partnership are usually very limited. The earnings of most professional partnerships depend primarily upon personal services, skill, and good will. In a professional partnership, the good will created by a partner will, to a large extent, diminish on that partner's total and permanent disability. But the other partners often feel morally obligated to distribute part of the partnership earnings to the disabled partner for a period of time. However, when it becomes apparent that the disability will be permanent, the normal reaction is to try to buy out the interest of the disabled partner. Typically, the other partner or partners will not continue to carry the burden of paying the disabled partner his salary for an unlimited period of time, with the resulting reduction in compensation for themselves. Accordingly, the need for a buy-and-sell agreement is obvious.

Close Corporation

Stockholder-employees are in a position which is similar to that of partners. The closely held corporation is frequently referred to as an "incorporated partnership." Unlike the partnership, however, the withdrawal or death of a stockholder does not terminate the corporation. The business will continue, but major problems may remain.

The serious disability of a close corporation stockholder-employee whose services are important to the success of the business often has a number of effects:

1. The ability, skill, and services of the stockholder are lost to the business. Sooner or later, the firm must face the question of discontinuing his salary or other compensation for his services. Yet the disabled stockholder and his family cannot understand the need to pay a replacement. To them, the fact that the firm cannot afford the burden of double salaries is secondary compared to their need for funds.
2. The financial structure of the firm may be weakened. Suppliers who furnished goods on credit may become wary about future credit, banks may shorten credit lines, and other creditors may begin to be concerned and demand payment. Customers also may lose faith in the corporation's ability to meet its commitments.
3. The disabled stockholder's desires cannot parallel those of the active stockholders. The latter think of expansion and growth. The disabled stockholder wants to conserve capital to guarantee his own compensation without risk.
4. Although the disabled stockholder is unable to contribute to the business, he is entitled to his share of the profits. Also, in some firms, extra compensation to stockholder-employees over a fixed basic amount is related to gross income. If such an agreement is in effect, the disabled stockholder might continue to share in this extra compensation. Normally, the other stockholder or stockholders do everything in their power to keep payments to the disabled stockholder at a minimum because of his inability to contribute his efforts to the success of the company.

SOLUTIONS TO DISABILITY PROBLEMS WITHOUT DISABILITY INCOME INSURANCE

The Sole Proprietorship

When a sole proprietor becomes disabled, a member of the proprietor's family often tries to take over and run the business. This is difficult in any sole proprietorship. It is impossible in a profession, unless the member of the family has been trained and is licensed in that profession.

Sometimes an effort is made to hire a competent employee to run the business. However, it is usually very difficult to find a suitable replacement for the sole proprietor. Even if this can be done, the salary payments to the replacement will reduce the income left for the sole proprietor and his family. Most sole proprietorships can earn only one good income, and if a large part of that money must go to pay a replacement, there is usually little left for the disabled sole proprietor and his family.

Sometimes the disability of a sole proprietor makes it necessary to sell the business or practice. Whenever any business is sold under pressure, the buyer has an advantage. Unless the sole proprietor has considerable reserves and/or a continuing income, he may be at the mercy of the purchaser and be forced to sell at a distress price.

The Partnership

When a partner becomes disabled, a member of his family sometimes tries to fill his place. This situation is even more difficult than in the case of the sole proprietorship. If the member of the disabled partner's family is not acceptable to the other partner or partners, they do not have to engage in a partnership with him. Only in rare instances is a family member both qualified to make a contribution to the business and acceptable to the other partner or partners.

It is sometimes possible for the partnership to hire a replacement for the disabled partner at a lower salary than he had been earning. This may be a temporary and partial solution to the problem, but it is almost never a permanent solution.

The partnership may continue the disabled partner's salary for a period of time, perhaps six months to one year. Then, if he is still disabled, the other partner or partners may wish to buy him out. The problems in this situation relate to whether the partnership can afford to pay the disabled partner for six months to a year with no services performed and whether the other partner or partners will have the money to buy him out. The other partner or partners might borrow the money, or they might pay for the disabled partner's interest in installments out of earnings and capital. Either approach presents problems, however. Then, too, there remains the basic question of the members of the firm agreeing on a fair price. Further, the disabled partner might refuse to sell his share of the business even though he has been disabled for six months to a year, because he hopes to recover.

Another possible solution would be to attempt to negotiate a change in the status of the disabled member from a general partner to a limited partner with no voice in the business affairs of the partnership.[5] Obviously, some financial consideration to the disabled partner would be involved in this approach.

However, without advance provision, liquidation of the partnership may be the only practical solution to the situation. Under such circumstances, it is unlikely that the partners will realize the full value of the business as a going concern. All partners usually sustain considerable financial loss in such a liquidation. Accounts receivable must be collected quickly, and some of the firm's debtors will not pay under these conditions. The firm's debts will have to be paid. It could become necessary to sell the firm's assets at sacrifice prices. Good will may be lost. If the other partner or partners go back into business, they probably must start all

[5] The danger that such a limited partnership may be considered as an association taxable as a corporation should not arise merely because of this step. See William Harmelin and Morris Friedman, *Disability Insurance in the Business Buy-out Agreement* (rev. ed.; Indianapolis: Rough Notes Co., Inc., 1963), p. 62.

over again. Most of the problems of starting a new business may be encountered.

The Close Corporation

Possible solutions to the problems which arise in the close corporation when an active stockholder becomes totally disabled somewhat parallel those solutions described above for the partnership. If a member of the stockholder's family tries to take the place of the disabled stockholder, the likelihood of that person adequately filling the gap left by the loss of the services of the formerly active stockholder is remote. If buying the interest of the disabled stockholder seems to be the logical solution, then the questions of price, availability of funds to purchase the interest, and other such matters usually complicate the picture. It is rare that either the corporation or the other shareholders will have sufficient capital of their own to buy out the interest of a disabled stockholder without advance provision. From the point of view of the disabled stockholder, even if the funds can be supplied by the corporation or the other shareholders, his position is a difficult one. Unless the disabled party is in a much better financial condition than the average small businessman, he would be compelled to accept a settlement after a period of time as a noncontributing stockholder-employee of the corporation. The disabled party would not have as much bargaining power after the disability occurs as he would have had under an agreement which had been executed while all parties were contributing their full share to the success of the business.

SOLUTIONS TO DISABILITY PROBLEMS WITH DISABILITY INCOME INSURANCE

The Sole Proprietorship

In most instances the disabled sole proprietor has two major financial problems, namely, to provide sufficient income to support his family and pay his medical expenses, and to provide for the cost of hiring and reimbursing a competent replacement who is capable of operating his business successfully. A disability income insurance policy will provide a guaranteed income to the disabled sole proprietor and his family. Individually owned major medical expense protection will enable him to meet the catastrophic medical expenses which are likely to accompany the disability. These insurance payments will enable him to use part or all of his normal income from the business to hire and reimburse the right replacement. With the business operating successfully under the direction of a competent replacement, there may be some income left over for the disabled sole proprietor.

When the disability is of long-term or permanent duration, the major medical and disability income protection will afford the sole proprietor the necessary time to dispose of his business if he so desires. This will help to avoid a forced sale with the usual resulting loss. On the other hand, if he wishes to pass the business on to his son or some other relative, the payments from the insurance will enable him to hire a manager to run the business until his son or relative is ready to take over.

Although premiums for disability income insurance normally are not deductible as a business expense to the extent that benefits are payable to the sole proprietor,[6] benefit payments received from the insurance company generally are free of income tax.[7]

However, while premiums for disability income policies normally are not deductible as a business expense, recent cases have held that such premiums are deductible for federal income tax purposes as medical expenses. In the *Drayton Heard* case[8] the taxpayer tried to take as a medical expense deduction for federal income tax purposes all premiums paid for policies providing indemnity for accidental loss of life, limb, sight, and time, and also for reimbursement of medical expenses. The Tax Court held that only the amount of premium which provided for reimbursement of medical expenses constituted a deductible medical expense. This decision was reversed by the Third Circuit Court of Appeals. However, the Commissioner of Internal Revenue did not follow the latter decision.[9] Based on this, the law for all circuits other than the third was presumed to be that premiums paid for accidental death, dismemberment, and loss-of-time insurance were not deductible as a medical expense. This position continued until the *Kilgore* case.[10] Here the taxpayer deducted as medical expenses premiums for policies covering death, dismemberment, loss of sight, principal sum, loss of time due to sickness or accident, hospital expense, surgical expenses, major medical expense, and special disease expense. The Tax Court sustained the taxpayer's position by stating: "We hold that, subject to the statutory limitation of 3 per cent of the adjusted gross income, amounts paid for health or accident insurance are deductible as expenses for medical care under Section 213 of the Internal Revenue Code of 1954. We will no longer fol-

[6] Revenue Ruling 59–90, CB 1958–1, 88, and Revenue Ruling 55–331, CB 1955–1, 271, except premiums for a business overhead expense policy (Revenue Ruling 58–480, CB 1958–2, 62) and except that premiums paid for medical expense and specific reimbursement may be included in medical expenses. (Regulation 1.213–1(*e*)(1); Revenue Rulings 19, CB 1953–1, 59, 55–261, CB 1955–1, 307, and 55–331, CB 1955–1, 271.)

[7] Internal Revenue Code, Sec. 104 (*a*)(3); Regulation 1.101–1(*d*) except for benefits from a business overhead expense policy. (Revenue Ruling 55–264, CB 1955–1, 11).

[8] 30 TC 1093, reversed by the Third Circuit Court, 269 F. (2d) 911 (1959), appeal dismissed on another issue (1961), 285 F. (2d) 352.

[9] CB 1959–2, 457.

[10] Docket No. 93509, 38 TC, No. 38 filed June 11, 1962.

low our opinion in *Drayton Heard.*" The Commissioner did not appeal this decision, which was followed by four other similar decisions.[11]

In the case of *Pretzman* v. *United States*[12] the court went so far as to decide that the amount paid for disability waiver of premium on life insurance was a health insurance premium and hence qualified as a medical expense.

In the light of these recent decisions, it would appear at this writing that a taxpayer can deduct premiums paid for disability income policies, as well as for other health or accident insurance, as medical expenses for federal income tax purposes.[13] It should be noted, however, that up to the present time the Commissioner has not issued acquiescences in the court decisions on this point. However, in the case of *Edelman* v. *United States,* 64–1 USTC, par. 9309, the United States Court of Claims stated:

> The question is whether the total premiums paid for health and accident insurance policies were properly deductible as expenses for medical care. Defendant [the Commissioner of Internal Revenue] conceded in open court that the total premiums paid are deductible as expenses for medical care. Subsequently, defendant confirmed its concession by letter to the court.

As a result, acquiescences may now be issued by the Commissioner.

An exception to the general rules pertaining to the taxation of disability income insurance exists where the insurance is intended to provide business overhead expense coverage. Premiums paid for such disability income policies are treated as a direct business expense for tax purposes, and the benefits received are considered as gross income.[14] Business overhead expense plans are designed to provide funds to pay rent, electricity, heat, water, laundry, repairs, depreciation, salaries for employees, and other fixed expenses which are normal and customary to the operation of a sole proprietorship or professional partnership. These plans do not permit the payment of an income to the disabled party. Most such plans pay benefits after thirty days of total disability. Monthly benefits can be purchased up to the average amount of monthly expense during the six

---

[11] *Breen,* 21 TCM 1228 (1962); *Edwards,* 39 TC 78 (1962); *Coburn,* 21 TCM 1447 (1962); *Wilson,* TCM 1963–188 (1963).

[12] U.S. District Court, Southern District, Ohio, March 30, 1963; 63–1 USTC, par. 9413.

[13] It may be that a portion of the disability income benefits received under such policies would be included in the taxpayer's gross income as attributable to medical expenses previously deducted. This taxable portion of the benefits probably would be limited, however, to the prior year's premium for the disability income coverage. See Kivie Dornfeld, "Taxation Affecting Health Insurance," *Journal of the American Society of Chartered Life Underwriters,* Vol. XVII, No. 2 (Spring, 1963), pp. 119–20, for a discussion of this point.

[14] Premiums a business expense: Revenue Ruling 58–480, CB 1958–2, 62. Benefits includable as gross income: Revenue Ruling 55–264, CB 1955–1, 11. However, it must be stressed that a standard disability income policy does not qualify for the premium deduction even if intended as payment of business overhead expense: Revenue Ruling 58–480, CB 1958–2, 62.

months immediately preceding the disability. Plans are offered with benefits for twelve to eighteen months.

The Partnership

Partnerships closely resemble sole proprietorships in the basic need for health insurance protection. The disabled partner needs income and funds with which to pay medical bills. The big difference is that when a partner is disabled, he becomes a financial drain on the business and his partner or partners. For this reason, a partnership buy-and-sell agreement, to be financed through disability income insurance, usually is needed.

Under the cross-purchase type of partnership buy-and-sell agreement, it has been well established that premiums paid by one partner for life insurance which he owns on the life of another partner do not constitute deductible business expenses for federal income tax purposes. Similarly, premiums paid by one partner for disability income insurance on another partner will not be deductible as business expenses.

If the partner paying the premiums is the owner and beneficiary of the disability income policy, he will receive tax-free funds with which to pay for part, if not all, of his obligation under a disability buy-out provision. This solution is not ideal because it does not provide a lump sum payment. However, it is one method of providing funds for the installment purchase of a business interest.

Under the entity type of partnership buy-and-sell agreement, the partnership would be the purchaser of a disabled partner's interest. The disability income benefits would be used to pay the disabled partner for his partnership interest.

To the extent that payments by a partnership to a partner are not attributable to the retiring partner's interest in the assets of the partnership (other than unrealized receivables), they will be considered "guaranteed payments" (if the payment is determined without regard to income of the partnership) and will be deductible by the partnership[15] and taxable to the partner as ordinary income.[16] The Internal Revenue Service has ruled that amounts paid by a partnership to a partner who is absent from work due to sickness or accident cannot be excluded from the disabled partner's gross income under Section 105(*d*) of the Internal Revenue Code.[17] This principle has been adopted in the Income Tax Regulations respecting so-called "guaranteed payments" taxable to a partner as ordinary income. If the partnership is the owner and beneficiary of the disability income insurance on the partners, benefits received by the partnership and paid over to a partner will be taxed in full to the partner

[15] See Sec. 1.736–1 of the Income Tax Regulations.

[16] If the payments are attributable to unrealized receivables or to good will not provided for in the partnership agreement, they will also be deductible by the partnership and taxable as ordinary income to the partner.

[17] See Revenue Ruling 56–326, CB 1956–2, p. 100.

as guaranteed payments. Yet, if benefits are paid directly to the partner, they will be completely excludable from his gross income.[18] Of course, when taxed to a partner as guaranteed payments, such benefits are deducted in computing the partnership's net income which reduces the taxable distributive shares of the other partners.

For the most advantageous tax treatment to the disabled party, however, disability income benefits should not flow through the partnership but should be paid directly to the disabled partner.

Premiums paid for disability income insurance, whether paid by the partnership or by the partners individually, are considered nondeductible expenses under Section 262 of the Internal Revenue Code,[19] subject to the *Kilgore, Breen, Edwards, Coburn, Wilson,* and *Pretzman* decisions previously mentioned.

Disability provisions in a partnership agreement may contemplate a specified period during which the disabled partner will receive disability income benefits. These will either be taxed to him (if paid by the partnership) or received tax-free (if received by him directly from the insurance company). Thereafter, payments would be made by the partnership in purchase of the disabled partner's interest.

If a shortage of funds makes it impractical to acquire the total interest of the disabled partner, the purchase of that part of his interest for which cash is available, combined with the suppression of the disabled partner's business voice to that of a limited partner, may satisfy the need.

The Close Corporation

The working stockholders of a close corporation are in a position which is very similar to that of partners. Their need for disability income and major medical expense insurance parallels the need of partners.

Where a corporate employer purchases health insurance on behalf of one or more employees, the premium cost is deductible by the corporation as a business expense under Section 162 of the Code if (1) the corporation is not a beneficiary under the policy; (2) the premiums are paid in consideration of personal services actually rendered by the employee; and (3) the total compensation paid to the employee, including the premiums, is not unreasonable compensation for the services rendered.[20]

The example given in the cited ruling stipulates that the employee is not a stockholder. In the opinion of many authorities,[21] however, if the foregoing tests are met, the premium cost is excludable from gross income of the covered employee, in accordance with the provisions of Section 106 of the Code.[22]

[18] Sec. 104(*a*)(3) of the Code.

[19] See Revenue Ruling 58–90, *IRB* 1958–11, p. 12, which so treats such premiums paid by a sole proprietor.

[20] See Revenue Ruling 58–90, *Internal Revenue Bulletin* 1958–11, p. 12.

[21] Dornfeld, *op. cit.*, pp. 120–22.

[22] See Sec. 1.106–1 of the Income Tax Regulations.

In the example described in Revenue Ruling 58–90, the employee had all the rights of ownership in the policy. Furthermore, the benefits under the policy comprised only income replacement payments. The benefits were found to be excludable from the employee's gross income to the extent permitted under the general rules relating to wage continuation plans.[23]

The Code, in both Section 106, relating to nontaxability to the employee of the employer's premium cost, and in Section 105, covering the limited nontaxability to the employee of his benefits, refers to "accident and health plans." The regulations make it clear that a plan may cover one or more employees, and that there may be different plans for different employees or classes of employees.

The cross-purchase arrangement in the close corporation is identical to that used in the partnership.

Under the entity arrangement, premiums paid by the corporation will not be deductible, since the benefits under the policy will be payable to the corporation, becoming part of its general assets, whether or not intended to fund a plan of disability payments.

The tax treatment to the corporation of the disability benefits it receives, as owner and beneficiary of the policy, on the disability of the insured employee has been the subject of much uncertainty. Following normal tax logic, it would appear that receipts flowing from nondeductible expenditures should be excludable from gross income.[24]

Amounts paid by the corporation to the disabled stockholder on account of the purchase price of his stock will be nondeductible to the corporation and, to the extent of any gain realized, treated as a capital gain to the individual. Disability, unlike death, does not result in a stepped-up basis for the stock and the escape from taxation of the appreciation in its value.

In this instance the corporation can apply the probably tax-free proceeds of the health insurance policy toward its obligation under the buy-out agreement.

If, in addition, the corporation were to make payments to the employee-stockholder under a wage continuation plan, the payments would be deductible by the corporation and tax-free to the employee to the extent permitted under such plans.

A CHECK LIST OF IMPORTANT POINTS TO BE COVERED IN THE DISABILITY BUY-AND-SELL PORTION OF A BUSINESS AGREEMENT

The following check list is intended to serve as a guide to important points to be covered in a disability buy-and-sell agreement.[25]

[23] Sec. 105(*d*) of the Code.

[24] See Dornfeld, *op. cit.*, p. 126, for a discussion on this point.

[25] See Appendix O for sample agreement. Also see Harmelin and Friedman, *op. cit.*

1. *Definition of Disability*

If the provisions of a specific insurance policy are used as a measure of disability, the acceptance within the terms of the buy-and-sell agreement of the insurance company's definition of what constitutes total disability will settle the matter.

2. *Amount of Salary during Disability before Buy-Out*

With respect to salary to be paid during disability, one agreement, for example, states: "Full salary plus bonuses for three months. Full salary less salary of replacement but not less than one-half salary, plus bonuses for additional nine months. After twelve months, 25 per cent of salary plus bonuses for one year."

3. *When Buy-Out Becomes Mandatory*

Provision as to when buy-out becomes mandatory will vary with the nature of the business and the thinking of the parties to the agreement. If the business does not require the personal services of the partners or stockholders, a disability buy-out is not very important. However, if the business requires the personal services of the partners or stockholders, a disability buy-out provision is needed. Here is the provision of one such agreement: "If the said period of disability shall extend for a period of more than two (2) years, then and in that event the nondisabled stockholder shall purchase, and the disabled stockholder shall sell, the interest of the disabled stockholder for the purchase price specified in Article Second of this agreement upon the following terms and conditions."

4. *Source of Funds for Buy-Out*

If there is no guarantee of funds when the disability occurs, it may be difficult to fulfill the conditions of the agreement. Noncancellable disability income insurance or disability income coverage written with life insurance is recommended to produce the funds on an installment basis when the disability occurs.

5. *Number of Installments to Effect the Buy-Out*

The number of installments to effect the buy-out will often depend upon the relationship between the value established for the interest of the disabled party and the earnings of the business without the services of the disabled party. This decision should be given serious consideration by the principals with the guidance of their accountant and attorney.

6. *Disposition of Business Life Insurance Policies on the Healthy and Disabled Partners When Disability Buy-Out Becomes Effective*

With reference to the disposition of business life insurance policies on the healthy and disabled partners when disability buy-out becomes effective, one agreement, for example, provides: "As soon as practicable, the disabled partner shall transfer his partnership interest to the partnership in exchange for any life insurance policies owned by the partnership on the disabled partner's life and a series of negotiable promissory notes made by the partnership and the nondisabled partner to the disabled partner with interest at 5 per cent per annum."

7. *Provision for Contingency of Death during Period Disability Buy-Out Payments Are Being Made*

With reference to the contingency of death during the period the disability buy-out payments are being made, one agreement, for example, covers this point as follows: "If selling partner dies before all notes are paid, purchasing partner receives insurance proceeds and pays balance due to legal representative of selling partner."

CONCLUSION

The weight of evidence is that the sole proprietorship, the partnership, the close corporation, and the active owners of such businesses add stability to their business and personal requirements by using an insured plan of disability income protection in the business continuation situation. Without insurance, the problems which result are often insurmountable.

While a number of favorable tax advantages have been outlined, the motivation for using insured income protection programs is not to take advantage of a tax situation but rather to guarantee that when the problem arises, the money will be there.

The future for disability income protection for business continuation purposes is very bright.

SELECTED REFERENCES

BROWN, ROBERT A., JR. "The Role of Disability Income Insurance in the Business Continuation Plan," *Journal of the American Society of Chartered Life Underwriters,* Vol. VIII, No. 1 (Winter, 1953), pp. 50–57.

DORNFELD, KIVIE. "Taxation Affecting Health Insurance," *Journal of the American Society of Chartered Life Underwriters,* Vol. XVII, No. 2 (Spring, 1963), pp. 116–30.

HARMELIN, WILLIAM, and FRIEDMAN, MORRIS. *Disability Insurance in the Business Buy-out Agreement.* Rev. ed. Indianapolis: Rough Notes Co., Inc., 1963.

HARMELIN, WILLIAM, and OSLER, ROBERT W. *Business Uses of Health Insurance.* Bryn Mawr, Pa.: American College of Life Underwriters, 1960.

MEHR, ROBERT I., and OSLER, ROBERT W. *Modern Life Insurance.* 3d ed. New York: Macmillan Co., 1961.

PART VII

Government Life and Health Benefits

Chapter 52

SOCIAL SECURITY BENEFITS

BY ROBERT J. MYERS

The social security program significantly affects the lives of the vast majority of the citizens of the United States. Although this program is commonly called "social security," a more accurate title is "old-age, survivors, and disability insurance"—or, in alphabet style, OASDI. It was inaugurated by the Social Security Act of 1935 and has been changed from time to time by amendatory legislation.

About 19 million persons received monthly benefits under the program in December, 1963. About 76 million persons paid contributions (or taxes) under it in 1963. Many millions of other persons are also directly affected by the program in that they are potential beneficiaries in the event of the retirement, death, or disability of the covered workers.

The financial impact of the program can be seen from the facts that total benefit disbursements in 1963 amounted to $15.4 billion, while total contribution income was about the same, $15.5 billion. The administrative expenses involved in collecting the contributions, maintaining the earnings records, and paying the benefits were about $350 million in 1963, or 2¼ per cent of the contribution income. The assets of the trust funds of the OASDI system amounted to $20.6 billion at the end of 1963 and had earned interest income of about $590 million in the year.[1]

---

[1] The Committee on Social Insurance Terminology of the Commission on Insurance Terminology of the American Risk and Insurance Association is currently concerned with a definition of "social insurance." The word "insurance" is formally included in the title of the OASDI program; similarly, much insurance terminology is utilized in describing the program. Broadly speaking, it may be said that the system is social insurance, which is a term widely used internationally. At times, the issue has been raised as to whether it is really proper to use the word "insurance" in connection with social security or social insurance. It would seem that this is justified because of the broad pooling mechanism utilized in social security systems, even though from a strictly legalistic standpoint, proper usage of this word might also require that a lawful and binding contract be present. It should be clearly recognized that social insurance and private insurance (including government insurance plans on a contractual basis) have certain elements in common and certain elements that are distinctly different. This is not to say that because of such differences, one form is good, and the other form is bad. Rather, both forms have important—and complementary—roles to play in our economic and social life.

COVERAGE PROVISIONS OF OASDI SYSTEM

Virtually all gainfully employed persons are covered under the program (or could be covered by election). The major exceptions are self-employed physicians, most policemen and firemen with their own retirement systems, federal government employees under the civil service retirement system, low-income self-employed persons, and farm and domestic workers with irregular employment. Railroad workers have their own separate system under the Railroad Retirement Act but are, in essence, covered under OASDI as a result of the provision for transfer of wage credits of employees with less than ten years of service and as a result of the financial interchange provisions between the two systems.

Nonfarm Self-Employed

All nonfarm self-employed persons except physicians are covered—both nonprofessional, such as store owners, and professional, such as lawyers and dentists. Earnings are reported annually on the income tax return, with no coverage when such earnings are less than $400.

Farm Operators

Farmers are covered on the same general basis as other self-employed persons, except for a special simplified reporting option based on gross income for those with low net incomes.

Ministers

Ministers may be covered by individual voluntary election. Their earnings are considered as self-employment income even if their compensation is in the form of a regular salary. Such election must, in general, be made within two years after coverage is first available. This method was adopted because of the principle of separation of church and state and because some ministers do not wish to be considered as "employees."

Employees of Nonfarm Private Employers

All employees in private industry and commerce are compulsorily covered, with no minimum restrictions as to amount of earnings or length of employment. Full-time life insurance agents are defined to be "employees" regardless of their common-law status.

Employees of Nonprofit Organizations

Coverage for employees of nonprofit organizations such as churches, private hospitals, and private schools is at the option of each employing unit but requires the concurring vote of the employee concerned. Once coverage is established, however, it is compulsory for new employees.

Employees of State and Local Governments

Employees of state and local governments can be covered at the option of the state and of the employing unit. Where there is an existing retirement system, a majority of the employees therein must vote in favor of coverage; however, policemen and firemen under an existing retirement system cannot be covered, except in a few specified states. There are also a number of special provisions for designated states in regard to coverage extension to employees under existing retirement systems. Such elective coverage, as to the employer, is necessary for constitutional reasons.

Employees of Federal Government

Virtually all federal civilian employees not under an existing retirement system and all members of the uniformed services are covered on a regular contributory basis.

Employees of Foreign Governments and International Agencies

American citizen employees of foreign governments and international governmental organizations who work in the United States are covered, on a compulsory basis, as self-employed persons. These persons must pay income tax, and the contributions can be collected in that way; at the same time, their employers cannot be compelled to pay the tax.

Farm Workers

Farm employment is covered if cash wages in a year from a particular employer amount to at least $150 or if there are twenty or more days of employment remunerated on a time basis.

Domestic Workers

Domestic servants are covered if cash wages are $50 or more in a quarter from a single employer.

Employment Abroad

The preceding coverage discussion relates to employment in the United States (including American Samoa, Guam, Puerto Rico, and the Virgin Islands) and on American vessels and airplanes. In addition, United States citizens working for American employers abroad are covered. Also, at the option of the American employer, United States citizens working for foreign subsidiaries of American companies may be included in the system.

Military Service Wage Credits

The "noncontributory" wage credits of $160 a month for military service after September 15, 1940, terminated at the end of 1956, since regular contributory coverage began then. The OASDI system is reimbursed for the additional benefits paid with respect to the "noncontributory" credits.

OASDI INSURED STATUS CONDITIONS

There are three kinds of insured status: full, current, and disability. Fully insured status provides eligibility for all types of old-age and survivor benefits (with certain minor exceptions, where the currently insured status must also be present). Currently insured status gives eligibility for certain survivor benefits. Disability insured status is a partial requirement for the disability "freeze" and for disability monthly benefits. Insured status is defined in terms of quarters of coverage—either \$50 of wages paid in a calendar quarter or \$100 of self-employment income credited to that quarter (except as noted hereafter). With certain minor exceptions, covered self-employed individuals are always credited with four quarters of coverage each year, as is also the case for persons with the maximum amount of taxable wages in a year. Special rules similar to those for self-employed individuals apply to farm workers.

Fully insured status is achieved if the individual has at least as many quarters of coverage (acquired at any time) as the number of years elapsing after 1950 (or age 21, if later) and before the year of attainment of age 65 for men and 62 for women, with minimum and maximum requirements of six to 40 quarters of coverage, respectively. For example, men who attain age 65 in 1964 (and women who attain age 62 then) are fully insured by obtaining 13 quarters of coverage at any time (1963 minus 1950).

Currently insured status is achieved by having six quarters of coverage in the 13-quarter period ending with the quarter of death, attainment of minimum retirement age, or actual retirement.

Disability insured status is achieved by having 20 quarters of coverage in the 40-quarter period ending with the quarter of disablement. Periods of permanent and total disability for individuals who have both fully insured status and disability insured status do not "count against" the individual in measuring the elapsed period for any of the insured status categories (the "disability freeze" provision).

OASDI BENEFICIARY CATEGORIES

Old-Age Beneficiaries

Fully insured individuals are eligible for a full old-age benefit at age 65. The amount of this benefit is 100 per cent of the primary insurance amount (defined later). The old-age benefit can be claimed between ages 62 and 65, but then there is reduction in the benefit of 5/9 per cent for each month below age 65 at time of retirement. Thus a person retiring at exact age 62 receives a 20 per cent lifetime reduction (5/9 per cent times thirty-six months equals 20 per cent), which closely approximates an "actuarial equivalent" basis.

Disability Benefits

An individual is eligible for disability benefits if he is permanently and totally disabled and has been so disabled for at least six months, and has fully and disability insured statuses. By total and permanent disability is meant inability to engage in any substantial gainful activity by reason of a medically determinable impairment that can be expected to be of long-continued and indefinite duration. The waiting period of six consecutive months of disability is not a presumptive period which, if satisfied, would "prove" the existence of a qualifying permanent disability. The determinations of disability are to be made by state agencies (generally the vocational rehabilitation unit) with review by the Social Security Administration (which may reverse the finding of disability but may not reverse a denial of the existence of disability except on a direct appeal of the individual).

The determination of continuance of disability is to be made by the Social Security Administration. Individuals must, in general, undertake vocational rehabilitation training, during the first year of which benefits will be paid regardless of earnings. With this exception, there is no permitted amount of earnings as there is for retired workers and for dependent and survivor beneficiaries (retirement test). Rather, a disability beneficiary might have small earnings and still continue to receive benefits as long as he is considered not able to engage in any substantial gainful activity. The disability benefits terminate at age 65, and the beneficiary then goes on the old-age benefit roll.

Supplementary Benefits

If the retired or disabled individual has a wife aged 62 or over (or regardless of her age, if she has a child under age 18 in her care, or a child of any age who has been permanently and totally disabled since before age 18), an additional benefit of 50 per cent is payable, with a similar addition for each eligible child (subject to the family maximum provisions). A wife between age 62 and age 65 without an eligible child can elect to receive reduced benefits, which are based on a reduction factor of $^{25}/_{36}$ per cent for each month under age 65 at time of claiming benefit, such reduction to continue during the joint lifetime of the couple. Thus a wife claiming benefits at exact age 62 has a 25 per cent reduction—somewhat less than the approximately 30 per cent needed on an "actuarial equivalent" basis. A larger reduction than for the women workers is required because it applies only while both are alive, rather than during the entire lifetime of the woman worker. Husband's benefits are payable in respect to a retired or disabled female worker if he is aged 62 or over and has been chiefly dependent on her and if she was currently insured at the time of retirement or disability.

Survivor Benefits

Widow's benefits are payable at age 62 if the deceased husband was fully insured (including deaths after retirement). Parallel benefits are also payable with respect to dependent widowers aged 62 or over. This benefit is 82½ per cent of the primary insurance amount.

When a fully insured worker dies, parents' benefits are payable (upon attainment of age 62) to parents who have been dependent upon such individual. The benefit is 82½ per cent the primary insurance amount if there is one parent and 75 per cent each if there are two parents.

When a fully or currently insured individual dies leaving a child under age 18 (or regardless of age if permanently and totally disabled since before age 18), benefits are payable to such child and to the widowed mother while having care of an eligible child. These child survivor benefits are also payable in respect to the death of an insured female worker where dependency of a child is provable and, in any event, in all cases where such woman was currently insured. The benefits are 75 per cent of the primary insurance amount for the widowed mother and 75 per cent for each child, subject to the family maximum provision.

Lump-Sum Death Payments

In all cases of death of a fully or currently insured individual, a lump-sum death payment of three times the primary insurance amount is payable. This payment, however, may not exceed $255, the maximum amount available under the 1952 Act (which has not been increased by the subsequent amendments). The lump sum is payable in full to a surviving spouse but in other cases may not exceed the actual burial costs.

General Provisions

No individual can receive the full amount of more than one type of monthly benefit. For instance, if a woman has an old-age benefit in her own right and a wife's or widow's benefit from her husband's earnings, then, in effect, only the larger of the two benefits may be received. Payments are made only after an individual files a claim. Retroactive payments of monthly benefits for as long as twelve months before filing of claim may be made. Certain restrictions on payment of benefits apply to persons convicted of crimes affecting the security of the nation.

OASDI BENEFIT AMOUNTS

The *primary insurance amount* (PIA), from which all benefits are determined, is based on the average wage of the insured individual.

Average Monthly Wage

The concept of *average monthly wage* (AMW) used in OASDI is, in essence, that computed over the entire potential period of coverage, but with certain periods of low earnings being disregarded. In general, the average is computed from the beginning of 1951 (or age 22, if later) to the beginning of the year of death, attainment of age 65 for men and age 62 for women, or disability, whichever is applicable. In computing this average, five calendar years may be dropped from consideration (whichever years' omission will produce the highest average wage); further, years with high earnings beginning with the year of attainment of age 65 for men and age 62 for women may be substituted for previous years with lower earnings.

For example, consider a man who attains age 65 in 1964 and who has had maximum covered wages in all years since 1950 ($3,600 in 1951–54, $4,200 in 1955–58, and $4,800 thereafter). Suppose that he retires at the end of 1965. His AMW is based on his eight "best" years (1964 minus 1951, minus 5). These "best" years include seven at $4,800 and one at $4,200.

In addition, under the "disability freeze" provision, periods of disability may be eliminated; such disability must be of at least six months' duration, and the disabled worker must have both fully insured status and disability insured status. Also, the AMW may be computed back to the beginning of 1937 on the same basis as when computed back to 1951, if a larger benefit will result.

Benefit Formula

In all previous laws before the 1958 amendments, definite benefit formulas were prescribed. Thus, for example, the 1954 Act benefit formula applicable to earnings after 1950 was 55 per cent of the first $110 of AMW, plus 20 per cent of the next $240 of AMW (reflecting the $4,200 earnings base). Under the 1958 amendments a considerably different procedure was prescribed, with a benefit table giving the PIA (in integral dollars) for various ranges of AMW (e.g., where the AMW is $114–18, the PIA is $66). The benefit table also provides for conversion of benefits for those on the roll before January, 1959, so as to result in an increase of about 7 per cent in the PIA (or $3.00, if larger). The benefit table also shows the maximum family benefit applicable for each PIA (e.g., $99 where the AMW is $114–18).

Actually, the benefit table is based on a definite formula and on definite minimum and maximum benefit provisions, so that in reality, these are built into the table. Certain approximations have been made because of the grouping involved in rounding the benefits to the nearest dollar.

The benefit formula underlying the benefit table is 58.85 per cent of the first $110 of AMW, plus 21.40 per cent of the next $290 of AMW (except that in some cases, for AMW under $85, a slightly higher amount is payable so as to fit in with the increased minimum benefit). The minimum PIA, before reduction for early retirement of those workers claiming benefits before age 65, is $40 a month (increased from $33 by the 1961 amendments).

The benefit table also provides for the determination of the PIA when it is more advantageous for the beneficiary to compute the AMW back to 1937 and to use the benefit computation method of the 1939 Act. Under these circumstances, Table 52–1 shows illustrative results.

TABLE 52–1

PRIMARY INSURANCE AMOUNTS COMPUTED UNDER METHOD OF 1939 ACT

Benefit Computed under Method of 1939 Act	Primary Insurance Amount
$10	$40
15	43
20	50
25	61
30	71
35	79
40	87
45*	95

* Maximum possible is $45.60 (which produces same PIA as $45.00).

Minimum and Maximum Family Benefits

The minimum family benefit for survivors (applicable only when there is one such survivor) is $40. The maximum family benefit is the smaller of $254 (twice the maximum possible PIA) or 80 per cent of AMW (the upper end of the range in the table). For example, where the AMW is $200, the maximum family benefit is $161.60—80 per cent of $202, which is the upper end of the AMW group in which $200 falls. The 80 per cent maximum, however, may not reduce benefits below 150 per cent of the PIA. Table 52–2 shows the maximums applicable for various average wages.

TABLE 52–2

MAXIMUM FAMILY BENEFITS BY AVERAGE MONTHLY WAGE

Average Monthly Wage	Primary Insurance Amount	Maximum Family Benefit
$ 67 or under	$ 40	$60
68–127	41– 68	1½ times PIA
128–319	69–109	80% of AMW
320–400	110–127	$254

Table 52–3 shows illustrative monthly benefits for various categories, giving consideration to the applicable benefit proportions, the minimum and maximum benefit provisions, and the reductions for workers and wives claiming benefits before age 65.

OASDI RETIREMENT TEST

Benefits for retired workers and their eligible dependents, for eligible dependents of disability beneficiaries, and for survivors are, in general, not paid when the beneficiary is engaged in substantial employment, nor are benefits paid to the eligible dependents of a retired worker who is engaged in substantial employment. This provision is termed the "retirement test"—to some extent, a misnomer in regard to young beneficiaries.

Benefits are payable for all months in a year if the annual earnings from all types of employment (whether or not covered) are $1,200 or less. If earnings exceed $1,200, then $1.00 of benefits may be withheld for each $2.00 of the first $500 of such "excess earnings," and thereafter the withholding is on a "dollar-for-dollar" basis. In no event are benefits withheld for a month in which the individual has wages of $100 or less and does not render substantial self-employment services. Moreover, the retirement test is not applicable at all after the individual reaches age 72.

As an example of how the retirement test operates, consider a retired worker under age 72 with an eligible wife, whose monthly family benefit is $180. If he works only from March through December at $200 per month, then he will without question receive benefits for January and February. His benefits of $1,800 for the other ten months will be reduced by $550, since the excess of his earnings over $1,200 is $800, and there is a reduction in benefits of $250 for the first $500 and of $300 for the remaining $300. In actual practice, this individual might receive his benefits through September and then have them suspended, with a final accounting and adjustment after the end of the year.

PAYMENTS OF OASDI BENEFITS ABROAD

Benefits are not payable in the case of deported persons, whose rights are terminated until they are subsequently lawfully admitted. In the case of persons residing in certain countries where there is no reasonable assurance that checks can be delivered or cashed at full value, the benefits are withheld but can subsequently be paid if conditions change.

For aliens residing outside the United States who came on the roll after 1956, benefits are payable only if the insured worker has forty or more quarters of coverage or resided in the United States for ten or more years, or if the country of which he is a citizen has a reciprocity treaty with the United States or has a general social insurance or pension system that will

TABLE 52–3

ILLUSTRATIVE MONTHLY BENEFITS UNDER OASDI SYSTEM FOR VARIOUS FAMILY CATEGORIES, BASED ON EARNINGS AFTER 1950
(All Figures Rounded to Nearest Dollar)

Average Monthly Wage	Aged 65 or Over at Retirement*	Worker Retiring at Age 62	Worker Aged 65 or Over with			Widow Aged 62 or Over§	Widow and One Child#	Widow and Two Children‖	Widow and Three or More Children**	One Child Alone
			Wife Aged 65 or Over at Retirement†	Wife Aged 62 at Retirement	Wife and One Child*‡					
$ 50	$ 40	$ 32	$ 60	$ 55	$ 60	$ 40	$ 60	$ 60	$ 60	$40
100	59	47	89	81	89	49	89	89	89	44
150	73	58	110	100	120	60	110	120	120	55
200	84	67	126	116	162	69	126	162	162	63
250	95	76	143	131	190	78	143	190	203	71
300	105	84	158	144	210	87	158	210	240	79
350	116	93	174	160	232	96	174	232	254	87
400	127	102	191	175	254	105	191	254	254	95

* Also applies to disability beneficiary.
† Also applies to worker and dependent husband aged 65 or over, and to worker and one child.
‡ Also applies to worker and two children; or to worker, dependent husband aged 65 or over, and one child.
§ Also applies to aged dependent parent (62 or over).
# Also applies to two aged dependent parents or two children alone.
‖ Also applies to three children alone.
** Also applies to four or more children alone.

continue full benefits to United States citizens while outside of that foreign country.

OASDI FINANCING PROVISIONS

The benefits and administrative expenses are paid out of two separate trust funds. The old-age and survivor benefits come from the Old-Age and Survivor Insurance Trust Fund, while the monthly benefits for disabled workers and their dependents come from the Disability Insurance Trust Fund. A separate trust fund was established for the disability program when it was inaugurated so that any unfavorable experience of this program would not endanger the OASI portion of the system.

The income to these trust funds is derived from contributions (taxes) on covered workers and employers, and from interest earnings on investments. The total contribution income is divided so that an amount based on a combined employer-employee rate of ½ per cent (and ⅜ per cent for the self-employed) is allocated to the DI Trust Fund and the remainder goes to the OASI Trust Fund.

Other than for a relatively small cash working balance, the trust funds are invested in interest-bearing debt obligations of the United States. These can be either marketable issues or special issues bearing an interest rate approximating the average market yield rate on all government obligations having at least four years to run until earliest maturity as of the issuance date of the special issue. In actual practice, most of the invested assets are in special issues.

The contribution rates—past, present, and scheduled in the law for the future for the OASDI system—are shown in Table 52–4, along

TABLE 52–4

PAST AND FUTURE FINANCING PROVISIONS OF OASDI SYSTEM

Period	Maximum Earnings Base	Combined Employer-Employee Tax Rate	Self-Employed Tax Rate
1937–49	$3,000	2.00%	*
1950	3,000	3.00	*
1951–53	3,600	3.00	2.25 %
1954	3,600	4.00	3.00
1955–56	4,200	4.00	3.00
1957–58	4,200	4.50	3.375
1959	4,800	5.00	3.75
1960–61	4,800	6.00	4.50
1962	4,800	6.25	4.70
1963–65	4,800	7.25	5.40
1966–67	4,800	8.25	6.20
1968 and after	4,800	9.25	6.90

* Self-employed not covered in this period.

with the applicable maximum taxable and creditable earnings base.

Congress, in connection with the 1950 Act and subsequent amendments, has consistently enunciated the principle that the program should be self-supporting from the contributions of the covered workers and their employers, according to the intermediate cost estimates. Of course, it would be only by coincidence that an exact balance would be shown. Generally, there has been a small deficiency, under the intermediate cost estimate, as between the level contribution rate needed to finance the benefits and the level contribution rate that is equivalent to the graded contribution rates in the law. This is indicated in Table 52–5 for the system as it was following the 1961 amendments (in percentage of taxable payroll).

TABLE 52–5

ACTUARIAL BALANCE OF BENEFIT COSTS AND CONTRIBUTIONS UNDER OASDI FOR 1961 AND 1963 ESTIMATES

LEVEL EQUIVALENT	1961 ESTIMATES		1963 ESTIMATES	
	OASI	DI	OASI	DI
Benefit costs*	8.79%	0.56%	8.71%	0.64%
Contributions	8.55	0.50	8.61	0.50
Actuarial balance†	−0.24	−0.06	−0.10	−0.14

* Including adjustments (1) to reflect lower contribution rate for self-employed as compared with employer-employee rate, (2) for existing trust fund, and (3) for administrative expenses.

† A negative figure indicates the extent of lack of actuarial balance.

Although the financing of OASDI differs in certain respects from that of private pension plans, these differences are more of degree than type, except that the OASDI financing is based on the "open-group" concept (i.e., assuming that new entrants will always come into the plan—as the law generally requires) rather than the "closed-group" basis properly applicable to private plans. The graded contribution schedule is intended to finance fully the system without any need for government subsidy.

Although benefit payments and contribution income in the immediate future will be quite closely in balance, this will not always be the case if the contributions rise according to the schedule in the law. Accordingly, quite sizable trust funds will develop, the interest on which will help to finance the system.

Finally, one of the most important points in connection with the sound financing of the OASDI system is that, over the years, there has been a strong cost-consciousness on the part of Congress and all others who have been concerned with the program.

BASIC PRINCIPLES OF OASDI SYSTEM

There are a number of what might be termed "basic principles" of OASDI and, even more broadly, basic principles of many social insurance systems. Among these are the following: (1) The benefits are based on presumptive need, (2) the benefits provide a floor of protection, (3) the benefits are related to earnings, (4) a balance between social adequacy and individual equity is present, and (5) the financing is on a self-supporting contributory basis.

Benefits Based on Presumptive Need

Certain categories of social risk are established by the law, and benefits are, in general, paid when these eventuate. Thus, for example, old-age benefits are not payable automatically upon attainment of a given age, such as 62, but rather only upon retirement. Likewise, benefits for surviving widows are not payable for their full lifetime, but rather only while they have eligible children present or are aged 62 or over, and only so long as they are not remarried (and also subject to their not being substantially gainfully employed).

The retirement requirement is frequently misunderstood as being a kind of means or needs test (that is, a test of the individual's situation to make certain he needs the income to meet subsistence-level economic requirements). When considered in that light, some critics believe that the retirement test is unfair, in that only earned income is used as a criterion for paying benefits, while investment income is disregarded. This procedure, however, is essential if there is to be a system paying retirement benefits, and not a charity program based on individual needs as determined by social workers. The latter would be an inimical basis insofar as insurance companies and other savings organizations are concerned because individual and group thrift would be discouraged thereby. Furthermore, the elimination of the retirement test would be very costly, requiring an increase of about 1 per cent in the combined employer-employee contribution rate. It would be questionable whether to pay "retirement" benefits to fully employed persons would be the best use of this money (over $2 billion annually).

Floor-of-Protection Concept

It is generally agreed that OASDI benefits should provide only a minimum floor of protection against the various risks. There is however, a great diversity of opinion as to how far apart the floor and the ceiling should be. At one extreme, there are those who believe that the floor should be very low. At the other extreme, some believe that the floor should be high enough to provide a comfortable standard of living by itself, disregarding any economic security that individual or group methods might provide. The middle ground, perhaps, is that the OASDI benefits should, along with other income and assets, be sufficient to yield a reasonably satisfactory minimum standard of living for the great majority of individuals. Then, any small residual group still in need should be taken care of by supplementary public assistance.

Earnings-Related Benefits

Because of the floor-of-protection concept, it seems desirable from a social standpoint that benefits should be relatively larger for those with low earnings than for those with high earnings. Accordingly, the benefit formula under the OASDI system has always been heavily "weighted," so that a higher benefit rate applies to the lower portion of earnings than to the higher portion. Thus the higher income groups receive greater benefits, but there is the weighting in favor of low-income groups. Since contributions (or taxes) are likewise related to earnings—directly proportional, up to the maximum earnings base—there is some appeal to the public in the fact that the higher an individual's earnings are (and likewise his taxes), the higher his benefits will be.

Individual Equity and Social Adequacy

Whenever a social security system involves contributions from the potential beneficiaries, the question of individual equity versus social adequacy arises. Individual equity means that the contributor receives benefit protection directly related to the amount of his contributions or, in other words, actuarially equivalent thereto. Social adequacy means that the benefits paid will provide for all contributors a certain standard of living. The two concepts are thus generally in direct conflict, and social security systems usually have a benefit basis falling somewhere between complete individual equity and complete social adequacy. The tendency is generally more toward social adequacy than individual equity, and this is the case with the OASDI system.

Individual private insurance policies are, of course, necessarily based on the individual equity concept. This does not mean that each individual will necessarily always get his money back plus interest (as in the case of a savings bank account or some government bonds). Rather, insurance company contracts have premium rates actuarially determined for the benefits provided, so that policyholders in the same risk class pay the same amount for the same benefits.

The concept of social adequacy must, of necessity, play a large part in group plans and in social security systems. If too much individual equity were to prevail when a system is started, the benefits paid would be relatively small, since they might be related solely to contributions paid or to service rendered after the effective date. Thus, many years would elapse before the system would begin to meet the purposes for which it was established.

Self-Supporting Contributory Financing

In brief, the principle of self-supporting contributory financing means that no general revenue appropriations will be needed to pay the benefits (and the administrative expenses). Available for such purposes under OASDI will be the contributions (taxes) from workers and employers and the interest earned on the trust funds resulting from the excess of income over outgo of the system (which, by law, must be invested only in United States government securities). Such interest does not represent "contributions" or "financial support" from either the general treasury or the general taxpayer, since the interest on these investments has to be paid, regardless of whether they are held by the trust funds or by private investors.

The basic financing principle for OASDI—adopted by Congress in 1950—is that the program should be completely self-supporting from contributions of workers and employers. Self-support can be achieved by any number of different contribution schedules—ranging, at one extreme, from a schedule higher in the early years than in the later ones (possibly sufficiently so as to produce a "fully funded reserve") to, at the other extreme, a schedule so slowly graded up that "pay as you go" financing would, in effect, result. The actual basis adopted for OASDI has been between "pay as you go" and "fully funded," but much nearer the former.

In carrying out this principle, the employer and employee share the cost equally. Self-employed individuals pay a tax rate equal to 75 per cent of the combined employer-employee rate—a "political" and "practical" compromise between paying only the employee rate and paying the combined employer-employee rate.

DEVELOPMENT OF OASDI SYSTEM

The original 1935 Act (effective in 1937) provided only for retirement benefits (with no supplements for dependents) and lump-sum death payments (in the nature of refunds of accumulated contributions) for workers in commerce and industry. The 1939 amendments broadened the program by including monthly survivor benefits and supplementary monthly benefits for retired workers with certain kinds of dependents. In addition, the size of the benefits payable in the early years of operation was increased, while benefits in the long-distant future for workers without dependents were decreased.

During the 1940's the legislative enactments related primarily to financing. Several times, the scheduled increase in the contribution rates was postponed, and the initial rate of 1 per cent each from employer and employee was continued until 1950.

The 1950 amendments modified the system by a sizable extension of coverage to employments previously not included, by roughly doubling the size of the benefits, and by liberalizing the retirement test. The principal effects of the 1952 amendments were to raise the benefit level slightly and to liberalize further the retirement test. The 1954 amendments extended coverage even further (to virtually all types of employment), again increased the benefit level, further liberalized the retirement test, introduced the "disability freeze" provision (similar to disability waiver-of-premium coverage in private insurance), and increased the ultimate contribution rates.

The 1956 amendments extended coverage on a regular contributory basis to the armed forces, enlarged some beneficiary categories (by providing child's benefits beyond age 18 if disabled), lowered the minimum eligibility age for benefits for women from age 65 to age 62 (but with "actuarial" reductions for all except widows), added monthly disability benefits beginning at age 50, and provided an immediate increase in the tax rates (to support the disability benefits). The 1958 amendments increased benefits slightly, liberalized the disability benefits by adding dependents' benefits, and strengthened the financing basis.

The 1960 amendments made disability benefits available regardless of age (i.e., eliminated the age 50 requirement) and improved the retirement test by making it more flexible (so that an individual could gradually ease off from full employment to retirement without losing money by working). The 1961 amendments lowered the minimum eligibility age for benefits for men from age 65 to age 62 (but with "actuarial" reductions as for women), raised the benefit rate for widows aged 62 or over, and increased the contribution schedule to meet these costs.

SELECTED REFERENCES

BURNS, EVELINE M. *Social Security and Public Policy.* New York: McGraw-Hill Book Co., Inc., 1956.

COHEN, WILBUR J. *Retirement Policies under Social Security.* Berkeley: University of California Press, 1957.

CORSON, JOHN J., and MCCONNELL, JOHN W. *Economic Needs of Older People.* New York: Twentieth Century Fund, 1956.

MYERS, ROBERT J. *Actuarial Cost Estimates for Hospital Insurance Bill.* Actuarial Study No. 57. Washington, D.C.: Social Security Administration, 1963.

MYERS, ROBERT J. *Long-Range Cost Estimates for OASDI System,* 1963. Actuarial Study No. 58. Washington, D.C.: Social Security Administration, 1963.

MYERS, ROBERT J. *Methodology Involved in Developing Long-Range Cost Estimates for the OASDI System.* Actuarial Study No. 49. Washington, D.C.: Social Security Administration, 1959.

MYERS, ROBERT J. "OASDI Cost Estimates and Valuations," *Proceedings of the Casualty Actuarial Society,* Vol. XLVI (1959).

MYERS, ROBERT J. *OASDI Provisions: Legislative History, 1935–61.* Washington, D.C.: Social Security Administration, 1962.

MYERS, ROBERT J. *Social Insurance and Allied Government Programs.* Homewood, Ill.: Richard D. Irwin, Inc., 1964.

Spiegelman, Mortimer. *Ensuring Medical Care for the Aged.* Homewood, Ill.: Richard D. Irwin, Inc., 1960.

United States Social Security Board. *Social Security in America.* Washington, D.C.: U.S. Government Printing Office, 1937.

Witte, Edwin E. *The Development of the Social Security Act.* Madison: University of Wisconsin Press, 1962.

Chapter 53

GOVERNMENT LIFE INSURANCE AND VETERANS' BENEFITS

BY DAVID A. IVRY

A great opportunity for service exists for the life and health underwriter who is familiar with the fundamentals of government life insurance and veterans' benefits. It is estimated that veterans and their dependents comprise half of the population of the United States. It is unfortunate that many veterans are not sufficiently aware of the benefits to which they are entitled. The purpose of this chapter is to present the salient features of these benefits, with special emphasis on those features important to the work of the underwriter.

Government life insurance first came into existence during World War I. War risk insurance became available in 1917; in 1919 a program was instituted known as United States Government Life Insurance (USGLI).

A more significant program was launched in 1940 known as National Service Life Insurance (NSLI). At the height of this program the insurance in force exceeded $140 billion. This figure closely approximated commercial life insurance ownership in the United States in 1945. A high percentage of NSLI coverage was terminated when servicemen returned to civilian life.

The NSLI program caused much controversy, and a number of investigations were made of its operation, cost, and justification. These investigations culminated in the passing of Public Law 23 by the Eighty-second Congress in April, 1951 (the Servicemen's Indemnity and Insurance Acts). By the terms of the law, the sale of *new* NSLI and USGLI was terminated. A new system was instituted which provided for a gratuitous indemnity of $10,000 for all members of the armed forces serving on or after June 27, 1950. The coverage which could be continued after return to civilian life was greatly restricted. The gratuitous indemnity program was terminated as of January 1, 1957, by Public Law 881 of the Eighty-fourth Congress. This law made a number of major changes in the benefit program for servicemen and veterans, effective on January 1, 1957.

Again, in 1958, Congress amended the government insurance programs in a few areas. These new changes will be discussed in appropriate sections of this chapter.

On August 29, 1959, Congress passed Public Law 211. This act significantly amended certain features in the area of veterans' benefits. The changes center around two programs—(1) disability pension for nonservice-connected disability, and (2) pension for nonservice-connected death of a wartime veteran.

UNITED STATES GOVERNMENT LIFE INSURANCE

Only about $2 billion of USGLI is outstanding at the present time. Inasmuch as a life underwriter will rarely encounter a client who owns insurance issued under this program, this subject warrants little discussion.

In 1917 an amendment to the War Risk Insurance Act provided life and disability insurance for members of the armed forces. This war risk insurance was on the yearly renewable term plan. In May, 1919, the introduction of United States Government Life Insurance provided for conversion of war risk policies to permanent plans. A subsequent act made USGLI available to all members of the armed forces, and this privilege continued until the appearance of National Service Life Insurance. Discharged veterans of World War I who performed active service between October 6, 1917, and July 2, 1921, and who had not previously carried the insurance, or who had allowed it to lapse, became eligible to apply for USGLI from 1928 until its sale was terminated on April 25, 1951. In 1928, earlier beneficiary restrictions were removed, and a special disability income rider was offered for the first time. USGLI has not been issued since April 25, 1951.

United States Government Life Insurance is written on six permanent plans: straight (ordinary) life, 20-payment life, 30-payment life, 20-year endowment, 30-year endowment, and endowment at age 62. It is also written on a five-year term plan, renewable indefinitely. The maximum amount of insurance available under USGLI is $10,000.

NATIONAL SERVICE LIFE INSURANCE

General Provisions

National Service Life Insurance was available to all persons on active duty between October 8, 1940, and April 25, 1951. It was also available to discharged veterans who served between October 8, 1940, and September 2, 1945, inclusive. It has not been issued since April 25, 1951.

Premiums charged for NSLI are on a net basis, with no loading for expenses. Administrative expenses and the excess cost of death and disability claims which can be traced to the extra hazards of military service are paid by separate appropriations and not from the NSLI trust fund. The actuarial assumptions used for premium and reserve calculations are the American Experience Table of Mortality and 3 per cent interest. Surrender values under NSLI are equal to the full legal reserve. Life income settlement options are likewise based on the American Experience Table and 3 per cent, with no differentiation between males and females. Waiver of premium is included in all policies at no extra premium charge.

The face amount of the insurance issued ranges from a minimum of $1,000 to a maximum of $10,000, in multiples of $500. It should be noted that the maximum obtainable under government insurance programs, separately or combined, is $10,000.

Originally, NSLI could be paid only to a restricted list of beneficiaries; but since 1946, there have been no limitations. The final contingent beneficiary is the estate of the insured, unless otherwise specified, even where a settlement option has been chosen by the insured. Changes of beneficiaries may be made freely.

Types of Policies

National Service Life Insurance is available on seven plans: five-year term (renewable indefinitely, convertible at any time), straight (ordinary) life, 30-payment life, 20-payment life, endowment at 65, endowment at 60, and 20-year endowment.

The policy, if on a term basis, may be converted as of attained age, as of original age, or at any point in between. When dated back, the difference in reserves must be paid. The term policy can be converted, while the insured is totally disabled, to any permanent plan other than an endowment plan.

A permanent plan may be exchanged for one with a higher reserve upon the payment of the difference in reserves. This may not be done if the insured is totally disabled. If the exchange is to a permanent plan with a lower reserve, evidence of good health must be submitted. The difference in reserves is paid to the insured, or it may be applied to future premiums.

Nonforfeiture Options and Policy Loans

The nonforfeiture options parallel in nature those of private insurance. A policyholder may surrender his policy for cash, accept a reduced paid-up policy, or choose extended term insurance. Extended term is the automatic option. Insurance surrendered for cash or for paid-up insurance cannot be reinstated.

A policyowner may borrow up to 94 per cent of the cash value; the rate of interest applicable to such loans is 4 per cent. NSLI cannot be assigned by the insured.

Reinstatement Provisions

NSLI policies are very liberal with regard to reinstatement. A policy may be reinstated within three months of lapse if a statement of comparative health is furnished. After three months, medical evidence of good health must be submitted, except when a permanent policy on extended term has at least five years to run, or if an endowment policy on extended term will run to the maturity date.

The financial obligation to reinstate a lapsed permanent policy is payment of all back premiums, plus interest. Reinstatement can be made at any time within the extended term period. A lapsed term policy must be reinstated prior to the expiration of the current term period. The financial obligation is payment of two monthly premiums—one for the month of lapse and one for the current month.

Settlement Options

There are four settlement options available under NSLI policies:

Option 1—Lump Sum. Can be elected only by the insured.

Option 2—Fixed-Period Option. Payable in monthly installments ranging from 36 months to 240 months in multiples of 12 (3 per cent interest guaranteed).

Option 3—Life Income with Ten Years Certain. Payable in monthly installments.

Option 4—Refund Life Income. Face amount guaranteed, payable in monthly installments. (Where payments under this option will involve a guarantee of less than 120 months, Option 3 becomes applicable.)

Lump sum may be considered a settlement option under NSLI policies. It is not the automatic mode of settlement, and it can be elected only by the insured. The automatic option, where no choice is made by the insured or the beneficiary, is the fixed-period option for the minimum period (36 months). There is no interest option permitting proceeds to be left on deposit with the government at interest.

A beneficiary may elect a different settlement option from the one selected by the insured, provided that the guaranteed installment period is not shortened. Thus a beneficiary may choose to receive payments under Option 2 for 240 months, where the insured has chosen Option 2 for 120 months. The reverse, however, cannot be effected.

It has been mentioned previously that the life income options are based on the American Experience Table of Mortality and a 3 per cent interest assumption. Furthermore, there is no differentiation between males and females. These factors make the life income options especially attractive in NSLI policies. A female beneficiary of a NSLI policy will receive a significantly larger life income than would be available from the same amount of proceeds administered under a comparable life income option of a private insurance company.

A feature of NSLI that is not as liberal as in private insurance is the inability to have cash values paid under income arrangements. Furthermore, the life income options are not available to the insured upon the maturity of an endowment policy. The proceeds at maturity may only be applied under Options 1 or 2.

Dividends

National Service Life Insurance is written on a participating basis. Dividends may be taken in cash, used to prepay premiums, left on deposit with 3 per cent interest guaranteed, or left on deposit at interest subject to automatic use to prevent a policy from lapsing. Dividends payable have been extremely liberal, particularly for the policyholder who has retained his NSLI on a term basis. The use of the American Experience Table and the government subsidy for claims traceable to the extra hazards of service help explain the substantial dividends which have been paid.

Disability Benefits

All NSLI policies include, at no extra premium charge, a waiver-of-premium feature. Total disability must commence prior to age 60, and there is a six-month waiting period.

For an extra premium, a total disability income rider is available on NSLI policies. Originally, the disability income was $5.00 per month per $1,000 of insurance. Congress, in 1958, approved a $10.00-a-month benefit per $1,000 of insurance, which became effective on November 1, 1958. Those desiring to add the new income must qualify physically. The disability must commence prior to age 60, and there is a six-month waiting period.

SERVICEMEN'S INDEMNITY AND INSURANCE ACTS OF 1951 (PUBLIC LAW 23, EIGHTY-SECOND CONGRESS)

Public Law 23 attempted to provide a more equitable and economical life insurance program for members of the armed forces. It also made provision for the gradual withdrawal of the government from insuring discharged veterans, except in a limited way and on a more modern actuarial basis. Some of the provisions of Public Law 23, it will be noted, were altered by Congress in 1958.

The over-all limit of $10,000 was retained as the maximum amount of government life insurance permitted to be in force on any basis at any one time for any person. New NSLI and USGLI policies could no longer be issued as of April 25, 1951.

Gratuitous Indemnity

Under this program, persons on active duty were automatically insured for $10,000, less the amount of any NSLI or USGLI maintained in force.

The commencement of this program was June 27, 1950. It was terminated as of January 1, 1957, by the Servicemen's and Veterans' Survivor Benefit Act of 1956. Thus the "free insurance" program was applicable from June 27, 1950, to January 1, 1957. Beneficiary designations were restricted. In cases of death, only one settlement plan was available—monthly installments for ten years ($92.90 a month). This settlement arrangement assumed a 2¼ per cent interest basis.

Postservice Insurance (Modernized NSLI)

Public Law 23 limited the postservice insurance rights of veterans who had been protected by the gratuitous indemnity while in service.

For most veterans, Public Law 23 restricted the postservice coverage to five-year renewable term insurance, nonconvertible and nonparticipating. The actuarial assumptions used were modernized—the 1941 CSO Table and 2¼ per cent interest. The life income payments were to be based on the Annuity Table of 1949, with differentiation made between males and females. This term insurance was to be available upon application within 120 days after separation, without evidence of insurability.

For the disabled veteran the program was not so restrictive. If a veteran was found to be uninsurable by Veterans Administration standards of good health as a result of a service-connected disability of a "compensable" type, he could secure insurance on any of the seven NSLI plans (but with modern actuarial assumptions). The insurance is on a nonparticipating basis only. The disability must be of a compensable type even though the extent of the disability may be rated less than the 10 per cent required for compensation. Application for coverage had to be made within one year after the determination of such disability by the Veterans Administration.

In 1958, Congress liberalized certain aspects of this program. Commencing on January 1, 1959, the former nonconvertible term insurance could be converted to any of the six permanent plans previously discussed under NSLI. However, the modernized actuarial assumptions were utilized, and the insurance was to be nonparticipating. In addition, the so-called "RS" term insurance could be exchanged for a new type of convertible policy called "limited convertible five-year level premium term." The limited convertible term plan has much lower premium rates but cannot be issued or renewed after age 50.

RELATED VETERANS' BENEFITS

A large number of related programs involving veterans' benefits exist in addition to the aforementioned insurance programs. All of these programs cannot be discussed in this chapter. Attention will be given to those programs that have the most relevance to the work of the life underwriter. They are replete with technical details. The following presentation will be, for the sake of clarity, fairly general. Eligibility for any particular benefit involves final determination by the proper government agency.

The expression "wartime service" appears in the following pages. This term refers to service during the following periods:

1. For veterans of World War I—service between April 6, 1917, and November 18, 1918 (April 2, 1920, if service was in Russia).
2. For veterans of World War II—service between September 16, 1940, and July 25, 1947.
3. For veterans of the Korean conflict—service between June 27, 1950, and January 31, 1955.

Compensation for Service-Connected Disability

The Veterans Administration pays compensation for a service-connected disability to a veteran or serviceman. This disability is paid, without regard to other income of the veteran, on the basis of average impairment of earning capacity.

The basic monthly rates are as shown in Table 53–1 (peacetime service rates are 80 per cent of wartime service rates).

TABLE 53–1

SCHEDULE OF SERVICE-CONNECTED DISABILITY BENEFITS

Rating	Wartime Service	Peacetime Service
10%	$ 20.00	$ 16.00
20	38.00	30.40
30	58.00	46.40
40	77.00	61.60
50	107.00	85.60
60	128.00	102.40
70	149.00	119.20
80	170.00	136.00
90	191.00	152.80
100	250.00	200.00

Under this program, special allowances for specific conditions may increase these amounts to a total of $725 for wartime service and $580 for peacetime service. Additional allowances may be made for dependents of a disabled veteran with at least a 50 per cent rating.

Pension for Nonservice-Connected Disability

This program is available only for veterans of wartime service, not for veterans of peacetime service. The veteran must be totally and permanently disabled, as determined by the Veterans Administration.

The law, as amended in 1959, provides for a sliding scale of pensions, as indicated in Table 53–2.

The rates are increased by $70 when the veteran needs regular aid and attendance. There is generally no reduction of pension because of hospitalization or maintenance by the Veterans Administration in cases of veterans who have a wife or child. The pension of a veteran without a wife or child is reduced to $30 a month after two full calendar months of care.

TABLE 53–2

SCHEDULE OF NONSERVICE-CONNECTED DISABILITY BENEFITS

VETERAN, NO DEPENDENTS

Annual Income: More than	Annual Income: But Equal to or Less than	Monthly Pension
	$ 600	$85
$ 600	1,200	70
1,200	1,800	40

VETERAN WITH DEPENDENTS

Annual Income		Monthly Pension		
More than	But Equal to or Less than	Veteran and One Dependent	Veteran and Two Dependents	Veteran and Three or More Dependents
	$1,000	$90	$95	$100
$1,000	2,000	75	75	75
2,000	3,000	45	45	45

If the veteran's wife has a separate income, generally all such income over $1,200 will be counted as the veteran's income. The law provides for discretionary authority for measuring the net worth of a veteran. A determination may be made that the applicant is not eligible for a pension because of his net worth.

All veterans who come on the pension rolls on or after July 1, 1960, will receive pensions under the above-described system. A different system prevailed for some years. For those veterans who were on the pension rolls on June 30, 1960, a choice was permitted between the old system and the new system. A decision, once made, cannot be revoked.

Dependency and Indemnity Compensation for Service-Connected Death Occurring on or after January 1, 1957

Under this program, no distinction is made between wartime and peacetime service. Benefits are payable to widows, and children, with no outside-income limitations.

Compensation is payable upon the death of a veteran or serviceman resulting from injury or disease incurred or aggravated in line of duty while on active duty or inactive duty training. Such compensation is also payable upon the death of a veteran resulting from a disability compensable under the laws of the Veterans Administration.

The monthly benefit payable to the widow is $120 plus 12 per cent of the monthly basic pay now being received by a serviceman whose rank and years of service are the same as those of the deceased veteran. Minimum payment is $122. The benefit to the widow is payable until death or remarriage. An additional benefit of $39 a month is payable for a child between the ages of 18 and 21, while attending an approved educational institution.[1] A monthly benefit of $77 is payable for an unmarried child over the age of 18 who before this age becomes permanently incapable of self-support. The payments continue as long as total disability lasts.

Where there is no eligible widow, compensation is payable to the children until age 18, or until age 21 if attending an approved educational institution. Again, there is special provision for the disabled child.

The basic monthly payments are:

One child	$ 77
Two children	110
Three children	143
Each additional child	28

In addition to benefits payable to a widow or children, this program provides benefits for parents of the veteran. The benefits for parents, however, are subject to limitations on other income.

Pension for Nonservice-Connected Death of Wartime Veteran

This program is of concern only to veterans of wartime service and their families. Public Law 211, passed in 1959, drastically revised this program. There are now two systems under which this pension is paid—the prior system and the current pension system which went into effect on July 1, 1960. All of those widows or children who were on the rolls on June 30, 1960, are given a choice of continuing to draw pensions under the prior system or of coming under the current system. Once the choice is made to come under the current system, it is final and unalterable. Widows and children coming on the rolls on or after July 1, 1960, come under the current pension system.

The new law removes the requirement of a service-incurred disability at the time of death for a World War II or Korean conflict veteran. This requirement exists under the old law for pensions payable to widows and

[1] Substantially larger educational benefits are payable if there is qualification under the War Orphans Education Assistance Program.

children for nonservice-connected death. With this significant change, widows and children of World War II and Korean conflict veterans are placed on the same basis as widows and children of World War I veterans.

The conditions of a veteran's service are as follows: The veteran must have had 90 days' service, unless discharged sooner for service-connected disability; *or* he must have been receiving or have been entitled to receive compensation or retirement pay for a service-connected disability incurred during the war; *and* he must have been discharged under conditions other than dishonorable.

The new law provides for a sliding scale of pensions, as indicated in Table 53–3.

TABLE 53–3

SCALE OF PENSION BENEFITS FOR WIDOWS AND CHILDREN UPON NONSERVICE-CONNECTED DEATH OF WARTIME VETERAN

	Annual Income		Monthly Pension
	More than	But Equal to or Less than	
Widow, no child		$ 600	$60
	$ 600	1,200	45
	1,200	1,800	25
Widow, one child*		$1,000	$75
	$1,000	2,000	60
	2,000	3,000	40
No widow, one or more children†		$1,800	$35 for one child and $15 for each additional child

* Plus $15 for each additional child.
† Earned income excluded.

Public Law 211 changes the "outside-income" definitions of past laws. Especially important is a reversal in the treatment of life insurance proceeds. Payments from life insurance are to be counted as income as received. This is true if income is received in a lump sum or under settlement options.

In addition, the law provides for discretionary authority for measuring the net worth of a widow or child. A determination may be made that the applicant is not eligible for a pension because of his net worth.

It is apparent that while many widows will not receive pensions because of the above stipulations, a very high percentage of children will qualify. However, reports from some of the offices of the Veterans Administration indicate that in certain cases, these monthly benefits may not be used as family support income during a child's minority. In these cases the funds may have to be accumulated for his later use. The funds may be expended for the child's college education if the parent has no other adequate means for such education.

It is well to note that at this time, there appears to be no standard procedure with regard to this question.

The pensions payable under this program are in general subject to the same remarriage and age limitations found in the previously discussed "compensation for service-connected death" program.

Burial Benefit for Veterans

A cash allowance of $250 is available to defray the burial expenses of a veteran of wartime service discharged other than dishonorably. Such allowance also exists with regard to the burial expense of a veteran of peacetime service who has been discharged for a disability incurred in the line of duty, or who is receiving disability compensation.

There are some miscellaneous benefits available, including burial in a national or Veterans Administration cemetery, provision of a headstone, an American flag, and the like.

Social Security

Beginning with January 1, 1957, members of the armed forces have been covered under the federal Old Age, Survivors, and Disability Insurance system on a contributory basis. The status of the serviceman now is identical to that of his counterpart in civilian life who is in covered employment. Free military wage credits, formerly granted for social security, were discontinued after December 31, 1956. These military wage credits were at the rate of $160 for each month in which there was uniformed service. A veteran who was in service before January 1, 1957, may, of course, utilize these free wage credits in computing the average monthly wage for social security purposes. In this connection, he may apply the "dropout" provision.

An eligible service member dying after December 31, 1956, without being fully and currently insured, is deemed to be fully and currently insured for the purpose of paying survivor benefits.

CONCLUSION

Government life insurance and related benefits are often the subject of legislative action. A professional underwriter must keep up to date in this dynamic field. He can do this by obtaining the latest pamphlets issued by the Veterans Administration and by studying the trade press, company bulletins, and other sources of information.

The life insurance programs made available by the United States government and the related benefits for veterans afford a genuine opportunity for the alert underwriter to render service to a large segment of our population. At the same time, these programs develop clients for the sale of private life and health insurance in much the same manner as does the social security system. Government life insurance and veterans' benefits combine with private life and health insurance in helping to build economic security for the veteran and his family.

SELECTED REFERENCES

LIFE INSURANCE AGENCY MANAGEMENT ASSOCIATION. *Veterans' Benefits.* 9th ed. Hartford, February, 1964.

McGILL, DAN M. *An Analysis of Government Life Insurance.* Philadelphia: S. S. Huebner Foundation for Insurance Education, University of Pennsylvania Press, 1949.

REID, CHARLES K., II. *Fundamentals of Government Life Insurance and Related Benefits.* Rev. ed. Bryn Mawr, Pa.: American College of Life Underwriters, 1958.

VETERANS ADMINISTRATION. *National Service Life Insurance and Servicemen's Indemnity.* VA Pamphlet 9–3. Rev. ed. Washington, D.C.: U.S. Government Printing Office, May, 1955.

VETERANS ADMINISTRATION. *National Service Life Insurance: Information and Premium Rates.* VA Pamphlet 90–3. Rev. ed. Washington, D.C.: U.S. Government Printing Office, March, 1959.

VETERANS ADMINISTRATION. *United States Government Life Insurance.* VA Pamphlet 9–1. Rev. ed. Washington, D.C.: U.S. Government Printing Office, May, 1955.

VETERANS ADMINISTRATION, INFORMATION SERVICE. *Federal Benefits for Veterans and Dependents.* VA Fact Sheet IS–1. Washington, D.C.: U.S. Government Printing Office, February, 1963.

Chapter 54

GOVERNMENT HEALTH BENEFITS

BY JOHN F. ADAMS

Public interest in the problems associated with ill health has increased markedly in recent years. Chiefly, this interest has centered in the areas of medical care cost and loss of income associated with lost time due to illness. Special problems, such as those of the retired worker and long-term invalidism, have also received considerable attention. Also of interest have been the great strides in preventive and curative medicine, and their great potential for saving and extending lives and maintaining productivity.

Government Programs

Government programs dealing with income loss and medical care costs during periods of disability are of various types. They include federal programs aimed at providing medical care through publicly financed health programs and facilities designed to provide essential medical care for certain groups of the population. In addition, federal grant-in-aid programs exist to assist in financing joint federal-state programs of the same type. At the state level, departments of public health as well as specialized agencies, including rehabilitation facilities related to the workmen's compensation programs, have been organized to deal with other aspects of the problem. In addition, a number of local government agencies, particularly in the large cities, have begun increasingly to develop unified programs for dealing with the problems of ill health, including provision of financial aid in some cases.

At the same time that programs providing for medical care were developing, others designed to replace some part of the lost personal income were being established. One of the oldest and broadest of these programs is workmen's compensation, which provides coverage against medical care costs and lost income due to industrial injury and, in many cases, occupational disease. Coverage against wage losses resulting from accidents or disease is provided by the disability income coverage under the Old Age, Survivors, and Disability Income program in cases of "total and permanent disability" and, in four states, through temporary disability insurance programs. In addition, limited medical benefits are provided to older (age 65 and over) people by the states and federal government under the public assistance programs,[1] and hospital care grants are provided to participating states under the Kerr-Mills medical expense grant program.

Special programs also have been developed by the federal government. For example, disability income and, in some cases, medical care costs have been provided for some years for federal civilian employees under the terms of the Civil Service Retirement Act and the Federal Employees Compensation Act, and for railroad employees under the Railroad Retirement Act. Marine hospitals have long provided medical care for merchant marine employees at no cost to the patients.

DISABILITY INCOME COVERAGES PROVIDED BY THE FEDERAL GOVERNMENT

Disability Benefits under the Social Security Act

Several provisions benefiting the disabled are contained in the Social Security Act. The provisions relating to income include (1) freezing benefit rights during a period of disability, and (2) a disability income benefit. Other provisions relate to vendor medical services including professional fees, hospital care, pharmaceuticals, and the like. These are described in detail in Chapter 52.

Other Benefits for Disability Provided at the Federal Level

The Railroad Retirement Act provides a disability income program somewhat similar to that provided by the Social Security Act except that it applies only to employees of railroads and their affiliates. Broadly, the program provides for annuities for employees permanently disabled on the job who have 20 or more years of service and who are currently working in the railroad industry. A similar annuity will be paid to a worker aged 60 or above, but less than age 65, if he has 10 or more years of service and is currently covered, provided he is permanently disabled for work in his regular railroad occupation. Furthermore, on medical certification that a worker is permanently disabled for all regular work, if he has 10 years of service and a current connection in the railroad industry, regardless of his age, he may qualify for a disability annuity. In all cases, these annuities are computed in the same manner as age annuities and are paid as if the subject employee were aged 65. All of these annuities also are related substantially to permanent rather than to temporary disability, and all are financed as a part of the regular railroad retirement benefit program.

[1] See Chapter 52, "Social Security Benefits."

Under the 1946 amendment to the Railroad Unemployment Insurance Act, a temporary nonoccupational disability income program was established. By its terms a qualified worker who is injured or ill and unable to work is entitled to receive income benefits during the period of such disability after the seventh day and thereafter for up to 130 days,[2] the maximum number of days of benefits payable in any benefit year. To qualify for benefits, the worker must have $750 or more of credited wages in his base year and a medical certificate of his inability to work. The benefit rates are related to base-year earnings, ranging from $5.00 to $10.20 per day, related to base-year earnings of from $750 to $5,400. No provision is made for medical care expense. The worker may be required to take a medical examination to continue the income benefits. The receipt of these benefits does not affect or reduce in any way the worker's rights to proceed against the railroad under the employer liability laws where injury was due to a work-connected accident.

These benefits are paid for periods of temporary disability only and are separate from those paid for "permanent" disability, discussed above. This program for temporary disability is financed by a payroll tax levied exclusively on employers which ranges from 0.5 per cent to 3 per cent of covered payroll.

Under the civil service retirement system, substantial numbers of federal employees are entitled to disability benefits. Disability retirement benefits are payable to any federal employee who has been covered in civilian service for five or more years by the Civil Service Retirement Act and who is classified as totally and permanently disabled. This benefit is computed in exactly the same manner as a civil service retirement annuity, but may not be less than 40 per cent of the average monthly pay during the worker's five highest years.[3] These benefits are financed by joint contribution of employee and employer.

Federal employees are also covered by the Federal Employees Compensation Act, which was originally passed in 1916. The last substantial amendments were passed in 1949. This program, in essence, is workmen's compensation for federal employees. When a federal civilian employee is injured on the job, he is entitled to receive full medical care from designated doctors and hospital facilities and, if single, two thirds, or if he has

[2] Benefits are paid on the basis of registration periods. In the first 14-day registration period, the worker is eligible for benefits for all days over seven in which he was disabled; in each subsequent registration period (14 days) in which the worker is disabled, he is eligible for all days over four up to a maximum of 130 days in a benefit year. It may be noted that such benefits are payable for maternity under certain circumstances.

[3] Special disability retirement benefits are payable to federal employees dealing with criminals (such as FBI and Secret Service) and to members of Congress, the foreign service, and military personnel. These programs differ in many respects but, generally, they provide larger benefits than are payable under the regular civil service program.

dependents, three fourths, of his regular compensation up to $121 per week during the period of such disability. Where the injury results in disability and lost time of less than 21 days, a three-day waiting period is required; if the disability extends for more than 21 days, there is no waiting period. Such compensation will be paid as long as the disability continues. If constant care is required, an additional benefit of up to $75 per month may be allowed.

In addition to other benefits, the worker may receive a scheduled benefit for the loss of a member or its use. Loss of two members is presumptively total and permanent disability. The Act also provides a program for vocational rehabilitation. Additional benefits (up to $50 monthly for life) may be provided to make up for reduced earning power after completion of such program.

Survivors' benefits are also available to widows and children under this Act. In the event of death due to injury or disease, burial benefits of up to $400 are payable. A benefit of 45 per cent of the deceased's monthly salary, not to exceed $525 per month, is payable to a widow so long as she does not remarry. If there are dependent children, the widow's benefit will be reduced to 40 per cent of the deceased's monthly wage (at the time of injury), and an additional 15 per cent will be allowed for each child under age 18, up to a maximum of 75 per cent of the employee's wage.

It should be noted that this program for federal civilian employees provides income during periods of disability due to work-connected injury. Such benefits may not be paid if the employee elects to collect annual and/or sick leave benefits, or to take a permanent disability retirement benefit. He may elect either, but he may not collect both.[4]

In summary, the federal government provides some benefits when selected groups in the population sustain income loss due to disability through the provisions of the Social Security Act, the Railroad Retirement Act, the Civil Service Retirement Act, the Federal Employees Compensation Act, and the Longshoremen's and Harbor Workers' Compensation Act, which together make the protection available to nearly 95 per cent of

[4] In addition, the federal government provides temporary disability benefits for longshoremen, harbor workers, and maritime workers. No attempt is made to spell out the details of these programs here, but benefits for periods of temporary disability are payable to these workers, if they are otherwise qualified. The reader may obtain details on these programs from "Unemployment Compensation for Maritime Workers," *Laws Relating to Social Security and Unemployment Compensation* (Washington, D.C.: U.S. Government Printing Office, 1960), p. 83; and *U.S. Code Annotated, Navigation and Navigable Waters,* Title 33, Secs. 901–50 (St. Paul: West Publishing Co., 1959; as amended, through 1962); or Bureau of Labor Standards, United States Department of Labor, *State Workmen's Compensation Laws,* Preliminary Table (Washington, D.C.: U.S. Government Printing Office, 1963); and Bureau of Labor Standards, United States Department of Labor, *Medical Care under Workmen's Compensation,* Bulletin 244 (Washington, D.C.: U.S. Government Printing Office, 1962).

the American civilian labor force and their dependents. While available to 95 per cent, the proportion actually covered is much smaller. Age limits and time elapsed in covered employment and financial qualifications reduce this substantially.

Other programs covering selected employees in other activities, such as the military, also seek to deal with the disability hazard. These coverages seek to replace a portion of income and, in some cases, include provision for medical expense or medical care. In general, the income benefits are related to the covered earnings of the individual, though the benefit amounts may vary considerably for similar situations under the different programs.

It may be noted in this connection that the programs differ somewhat in aim. In effect, the nonsocial security federal coverages are more nearly similar to industrial fringe benefits than to the broadly based social security type of program.[5]

DISABILITY INCOME PROGRAMS PROVIDED AT THE STATE LEVEL

Income security against the hazard of disability, at the state government level, is provided through temporary disability insurance (in four states) and through workmen's compensation laws.

Temporary Disability Insurance[6]

Four states now provide programs to help provide for income losses due to disability not related to one's work. Three of these programs, those of California, New Jersey, and Rhode Island, are administered by the employment security agencies in the respective states and are geared to provide benefits on bases somewhat similar to those used in the unemployment insurance programs. The other state, New York, administers the program through the workmen's compensation agency. In each of these

---

[5] Disability income benefits also are paid by the federal government to disabled veterans (injured in the course of duty and/or who have service-connected permanent disabilities). Details concerning qualifications and benefits payable to this group may be found in Chapter 53.

[6] Summary and tabular materials on state temporary disability insurance plans are well presented in Bureau of Employment Security, United States Department of Labor, *Significant Disability Insurance Data, 1959* (Washington, D.C.: U.S. Government Printing Office, March, 1961); *Comparison of State Unemployment Insurance Laws as of January 1, 1962* (Washington, D.C.: U.S. Government Printing Office, 1962), pp. 129–41; and *Comparison of Temporary Disability Insurance Laws,* September, 1963, which is reproduced in Appendix P. The following material has been based, in large part, on these references. Forrest L. Miller, Deputy Director, Unemployment Insurance Service, United States Department of Labor, has both supplied the writer with revised materials, including the table presented in Appendix P, and reviewed the text in this section.

cases, cash benefits are paid to qualified individuals to replace a portion of wages lost due to disability.

The provisions of these four laws as of September, 1963, are summarized in Appendix P. The reader should refer to the laws in each of the states for specific current information. The text hereafter highlights some of the principal provisions governing these coverages, but it is not a complete description of any one law nor of the exceptions to these laws.

In general, coverage is extended to workers employed by a firm covered under the unemployment insurance acts in California, New Jersey, and Rhode Island. This would include all employers of one or more paying quarterly wages of $100 or more, including agricultural workers together with such self-employeds as may elect coverage in California, employers of one or more at any time in Rhode Island, and employers of four or more for twenty weeks in New Jersey, subject to certain exclusions. In New York the coverage provisions differ somewhat from those of both the unemployment insurance and the workmen's compensation programs. Broadly, employees of firms having one or more employees for thirty days are covered.[7]

These programs aim to provide some portion of income lost due to disability. However, in both California and Rhode Island, provided that the worker has sufficient covered base-period wages to qualify, benefits are paid whether workers are employed in a covered or noncovered industry, or are unemployed when the disability begins. Two separate benefit systems are provided in New Jersey and New York under these circumstances.[8]

Benefits are payable under these programs for disabilities which are defined as compensable. Generally, this means nonwork-connected sicknesses or injuries which are not otherwise covered by workmen's compensation laws. By definition, this restricts eligibility to workers who are unable to perform their regular work because of accident or illness, mental or physical.[9] There are some differences in the laws, however. In all cases except Rhode Island and California, persons eligible for workmen's compensation are excluded. In Rhode Island, no deduction is made for workmen's compensation benefits unless they are received simultane-

---

[7] Maritime workers and state employees, though covered under unemployment insurance, are excluded from this program. In addition, workers who are receiving or who are entitled to receive old-age and survivors' insurance benefits may elect not to be covered by this program. In all four states, workers may elect not to be covered for religious reasons. See Appendix P.

[8] In New York, responsibility for paying benefits to workers who are unemployed when a disability begins is placed on the last employer if disability occurs within four weeks of his separation. If such disability occurs after the fourth week and up to the twenty-sixth week of unemployment, benefits will be paid by the Special State Fund, provided the worker is otherwise eligible. See Appendix P.

[9] See Appendix P for details.

ously, in which case total benefits cannot exceed the smaller of $62, excluding dependents' benefits, or 85 per cent of average weekly wages on the last job prior to disability. Moreover, there is no deduction for workmen's compensation received after the period to which it relates or as a lump-sum payment. In California, benefits are paid the permanently disabled, despite the fact that workmen's compensation benefits are received. Moreover, in that state, if the disability benefit is larger than the compensation benefit, the difference may be paid from the former fund. In both New Jersey and New York, permanent partial benefits under workmen's compensation and disability benefits may also be received.[10] In addition to workmen's compensation, sick benefits paid by an employer in New York may be offset against or otherwise used to reduce the benefit amounts. Since each of the laws differs on these points, the reader is urged to check the law if he is in one of these four states.

Benefits are payable to qualified individuals in all four states when unable to work because of illness. Qualification and eligibility determinations as well as benefit amount determinations for temporary disability insurance, although similar to those used in unemployment insurance, differ in a number of respects.

Broadly, the benefit formula for disabled unemployed and employed workers in New Jersey is the same as for unemployment insurance, ranging from $10 to $50 weekly for from 13 to 26 weeks.[11] In Rhode Island also, the benefit formula applicable for all covered workers is the same as for unemployment insurance, ranging from $12 to 50 per cent of the average weekly wages of all covered workers (55 per cent of average weekly wages plus $3.00 per dependent up to $12) for from 12 to 26 weeks. In California the weekly benefit amount varies from $10 to $70 on the basis of a high-quarter wage schedule, payable for a uniform potential of 26 weeks per disability. This produces a somewhat higher benefit during periods of disability than during periods of covered unemployment. In addition to the weekly benefit, hospital benefits of $12 a day for 20 days are payable in any one benefit period. No waiting period is required for these benefits or for regular benefits for the hospitalized claimants, by comparison with the seven-consecutive-day waiting period for others. The duration is separate from that for unemployment insurance.

New York, on the other hand, provides a schedule of benefits ranging from $20 to $50 per week for a uniform potential duration period of 26

[10] In New York, disability insurance is not payable for a work-connected injury, even though no workmen's compensation is payable.

[11] Separate benefit years are provided for unemployment and disability insurance in Rhode Island. In New Jersey, for employed workers, there are separate benefit periods; for unemployed workers, however, the maximum combined duration period for benefits may not exceed 150 per cent of the maximum duration for either program separately.

weeks, the amount being based upon one half the average weekly wage during the last eight weeks of covered employment prior to the commencement of the disability. If the average is less than $20, the weekly benefit is equal to the average pay. For specific benefit amounts in each of the four states, the law in each state should be consulted.

It is notable that in California, New Jersey, and New York, employers may insure this hazard with the state fund or provide comparable coverage through use of private insurance contracts. To qualify for a private contract (or self-insurance) in California, the benefits must be as good in all respects as those payable under the state law, and better in at least one respect. New Jersey requires that the benefits must be at least as favorable as under the state plan, while New York does not require adherence to a statutory formula, whether workers are insured with the state fund or with a private carrier. However, in New York, benefits must be the actuarial equivalent of the statutory formula. Cash benefits may be reduced, for example, if the plan of insurance provides a shorter waiting period than that set by law or other benefits, such as hospitalization costs.

Temporary disability benefits are financed by various means. In Rhode Island and California, employees are taxed at the rate of 1 per cent of wages up to $3,600 and $5,100, respectively.[12] In New Jersey, both employers and employees are taxed, though the employee percentage is larger than the employer's in most cases (New Jersey employee, 0.5 per cent; employer from 0.1 to 0.75 per cent on the first $3,000 of covered wages). In New York, employees may be taxed up to 0.5 per cent of wages up to $60 per week. Employers are required to pay any additional amounts required.

In summary, it may be indicated that provision of temporary disability insurance has not become general or uniform as to pattern in the United States. Four states provide it, essentially through employee contributions, although in some cases where it is provided privately the employer has paid the entire premium. However, since private coverage is offered in three of the states, the provisions differ considerably, even within some of the states. Generally, the systems operate in a manner somewhat similar to unemployment insurance and are supervised closely by the state. Maintenance of minimum income during periods of disability is the principal aim of these systems.

Workmen's Compensation

During the latter part of the nineteenth century, with the growth of industrialization in the United States, the problem of providing for indus-

[12] In 1964, $5,100; in 1965 and thereafter, $5,600.

trial accident and disease had become so significant in numbers and so difficult of satisfactory solution under the historical common-law doctrine of employer liability that various groups began to try to evolve a more efficacious and equitable technique for dealing with them. Investigating committees were established at both federal and state levels, and by many interested groups, to review and to study the effects of developments in Europe and to draft proposals for legislation for possible use in the United States. Following adoption of the federal statute covering on-the-job accidents, revisions were begun, and state action was initiated slowly in this field.

The first attempts to deal with the problem uniformly at the state level were made between 1900 and 1910. By 1920, all but six of the states in the United States had adopted employer liability or workmen's compensation legislation of some variety. At the present time, all of the states and the federal government have workmen's compensation statutes covering some portion of the industrial and, in some cases, other types of employees within their respective jurisdictions.

In general, the workmen's compensation statutes establish the principle that injury in the course of employment—and in some cases, this includes industrial disease—is compensable without regard to the question of fault. In effect, the doctrine holds that injuries under certain conditions and some occupational diseases (in some states) are compensable by the employer, not because he is assumed to have basic responsibility for them, but because social policy has determined that industry, as one of its costs of operation, must assume such responsibility. Work-connected injury and disease thus become labor costs of operation, and such expense is justified on this basis.

The basic theory underlying the law holds that in return for assumption of responsibility for social or individual costs resulting from damage in the performance of assigned tasks in employment, the employer's liability for such costs should be limited. Thus, in effect, all workmen's compensation laws provide that while compensation for injury shall be paid without regard to fault, the amount of the compensation so payable is fixed by law. Such compensation includes medical care costs, to a greater or lesser extent, depending upon the state; disability income for such period as may be required, up to some limit; and for certain specific injuries, such as dismemberment, specific lump-sum benefits. In most cases the statutes contain specific exclusions for self-inflicted injury and injury while intoxicated and, in some cases, provide for supplementary or elective liability coverage.

Typically, disabilities are classified into groups: total and partial, temporary and permanent. In most cases the benefits payable for all types of total disability are the same, as far as weekly benefits are concerned, but the maximum number of weeks over which payments can be made differs.

The amounts payable in both cases are usually determined as some portion of weekly wages. Where disability is permanent and total, the procedure normally involves payment of a weekly indemnity for some specific period of weeks up to a maximum of some given amount. For example, in Pennsylvania, payments for total and permanent disability will extend for the period of the disability. The maximum weekly indemnity is $47.50, the minimum is $27.50 per week, or 90 per cent of the actual wage, if less, but in no event less than $20.00.

In the event of disability due to dismemberment or loss of sight, specific schedules of benefits are provided. These benefits may be paid either weekly or in a lump sum. Partial disabilities may be temporary, for a short or long period of time, and may or may not begin as a total disability. In these cases the payments usually take two forms: first, replacement of the scheduled proportion of wages during the period of total disability; thereafter a scheduled payment equal to some part of the full weekly indemnity for some given period of time—as, for example, 50 weeks. The theory here is that these payments will serve to make up some portion of the future wage loss resulting from the injury causing the disability.

The objective of workmen's compensation is to assist the injured workman in recovering so that he can return to work. There are two broad philosophies evident in the program as it exists in the several states. In all jurisdictions the objective of workmen's compensation is to relieve the injured of some of the burden of medical expense and to replace some portion of the wage loss resulting from the disability while he continues unable to work. In some jurisdictions an additional effort is made to restore the individual, in the sense of rehabilitating him for work after injury, albeit at a different job, in the industrial system. In a few cases, this attitude has developed to the point where rehabilitation, in fact, has become the chief purpose of the statute from the social viewpoint.

Because workmen's compensation is a state program, except for federal employees and certain others, one must look to state laws for any description of the coverage and benefits available. There are wide variations in the program in the various states. The provisions of the several state acts are summarized in broad terms as of 1963 in Appendix Q.[13] The reader is urged to use the summary as an indication of scope and treatment, but to refer to the law in his state for specific current information.

With regard to coverage, the typical workmen's compensation law excludes many of the nonhazardous occupations and, even among the

[13] The workmen's compensation laws are summarized in some detail in Bureau of Labor Standards, United States Department of Labor, *State Workmen's Compensation Laws,* Bulletin 161 (rev.; Washington, D.C.: U.S. Government Printing Office, May, 1964). See also Bureau of Labor Standards, United States Department of Labor, *Medical Care under Workmen's Compensation,* Bulletin 244. Much of this summary was based upon these reference sources.

covered industrial groups, requires participation only by employers of more than some given number of regular employees. The exemptions on the basis of number of employees range from none to fifteen employees. There are no numerical exemptions in twenty-five jurisdictions; the remainder all have some.

The coverage, though required by law, is provided by a monopoly state fund in only a few (eight) of the states. In others (33), it may be provided by private carriers; while in still others (11), it may be provided competitively by either the state fund or a private carrier. In many of these latter jurisdictions, self-insurance is also permitted. The program for federal employees, described earlier, is provided by direct appropriations of Congress.

There are wide variations in benefits available under the law. In some cases, medical care costs are paid without limit. In other states, only limited amounts are available for medical care costs. In all states, covered workmen are provided with a disability income usually amounting to a proportion of weekly earnings, the most usual being 50–66⅔ per cent of the covered earnings up to some limit.

Although the program is broad in scope and coverage, there are considerable numbers of workers in American industry who have no coverage under workmen's compensation. As indicated earlier, only workers in "covered employment" are specifically protected by the law. This results from exclusions of some employments specifically, excluding workers in firms having less than some given number of employees, and, in addition, results from the fact that in certain states the law is elective, i.e., the employer has the right to determine whether to proceed under the conditions of employer liability or workmen's compensation statutes.

There are certain other limitations upon the function of workmen's compensation laws. The accident or injury must have resulted directly from some work performed under the constructive direction of an employer. This means that only those accidents which occur in the course of employment, as defined by the law, are covered. In many cases, occupational disease is not covered at all, despite the fact that there is a direct correlation between the occurrence of the disease and the performance of a specific job.

Benefits are payable in the form of weekly compensation in cash in all jurisdictions; there is a waiting period of from two to seven days in all but one state.[14]

In addition to disability payments for weeks of work lost, most jurisdictions also make rather detailed provisions for medical expense. These are paid without limit in some 40 jurisdictions. In other cases the maximum amounts are set.

---

[14] Oregon is the only jurisdiction within the United States in which an injured worker may receive a benefit immediately following the incidence of injury.

In addition to these medical cost benefits which are payable, rehabilitation allowances also are provided in some cases. Five jurisdictions, for example, in connection with workmen's compensation, provide for rehabilitation centers. Some other states also provide for added weekly indemnities or retraining allowances for varying periods of time to permit victims of industrial accidents to utilize public programs or facilities which are available to provide rehabilitation services. (See Appendix Q.)

In addition to paying some or all of the medical care costs and replacing some part of lost wages, death benefits are payable to survivors of fatal-accident victims in most states. The amounts payable in weekly benefits vary widely, ranging from a maximum total of $10,000 to $25,000, except that 11 jurisdictions pay a specified benefit to widows for the period of their widowhood, and these and a few others impose no overall limit on these benefits.

In analyzing the workmen's compensation program from the standpoint of coverages and in relation to a basic program of protection, it is clear that there are extremely wide variations as to both coverage and benefits among the states. There are also considerable differences in the treatment an individual may receive, given a similar accident, between two jurisdictions or, in some cases, even within the same jurisdiction. There are many practical considerations—as, for example, questions concerning the liability of the insurer in particular cases, and concerning the actual extent of the injury and the medical requirements for treating it properly. Careful analysis of the law and the practices in each state is therefore essential to making a reasonable judgment as to the extent and value of this coverage.

Other Industrial Accident Coverages

It should be noted that the Railroad Retirement Act, the Federal Employer's Liability Act, the Federal Employees Compensation Act, and the Longshoremen's and Harbor Workers' Compensation Act all provide for compensation for injury in the course of employment. These programs were discussed earlier in this chapter, along with other federal programs. The railroad program differs from the others in that compensation for occupational industry, as such, requires that the injured employee proceed through the courts, proving negligence in order to establish liability. While the railroad worker may be able to collect disability benefits if injured on the job, the program is not designed primarily to provide for occupational injuries. The extent of the railroad temporary disability is limited to wage loss, no medical care being provided.

A form of cash disability income is provided in the form ot sick leave by the federal and many state and local governments. This is not strictly a disability coverage in the sense that it is used in this chapter, but it does provide some financial aid for short-term illness. In a small minority of state and local governments, total and permanent disability may be covered under the terms of the pension plan, with no provision for temporary disability other than sick leave. State and local governments have not provided for disability in this sense in a large proportion of the cases.

SELECTED REFERENCES

COHEN, WILBUR J. *Retirement Policies under Social Security.* Berkeley: University of California Press, 1957.

MYERS, ROBERT J. *Social Insurance and Allied Government Programs.* Homewood, Ill.: Richard D. Irwin, Inc., 1964.

OSBORN, GRANT M. *Compulsory Temporary Disability Insurance in the United States.* Homewood, Ill.: Richard D. Irwin, Inc., 1958.

TURNBULL, JOHN G.; WILLIAMS, C. ARTHUR, JR.; and CHEIT, EARL F. *Economic and Social Security.* 2d ed. New York: Ronald Press Co., 1962.

PART VIII

Programing and Estate Planning

Chapter 55

DETERMINING NEEDS

BY PAUL S. MILLS

"How much insurance do I need?"

Perhaps no other question about insurance is more frequently asked. Most persons at one time or another have at least pondered this question in their own minds.

With respect to the "human life value," this question, in its broadest sense, is asked in recognition of the three hazards which threaten the flow of a person's earned income—premature death, disability, and old age.

There is no simple answer. Appraising the economic worth of a human life is a complicated and inexact process because so much prophecy and projection are involved.

One approach to the determination of the amount of life insurance the head of a family should carry is to estimate the family head's human life value. The first step in this process is the estimation of the portion of the individual's average earnings which is devoted to his family by eliminating the cost of his own maintenance, income taxes, and life insurance premiums from his average earnings. The second step is to ascertain the remaining productive lifetime of the individual, presumably to normal retirement age. The individual's human life value then becomes the present value of the amount of his earnings devoted to the family for his remaining productive lifetime, discounted at a reasonable rate of interest. According to this approach, the human life value represents the amount of insurance the individual should carry to protect his family against the loss of his human life value in the event of his death.

Another approach, which is perhaps the most practical one in determining how much life and health insurance is needed, is to analyze the various needs of the family in the event of the immediate death or disability of the breadwinner. In analyzing these needs, the life underwriter assumes the role of a diagnostician. The physician who, without carefully examining his patients, prescribed uniformly for all would violate the precepts of his profession. The same would be true of the life underwriter who recommended the same type and amount of insurance for every individual, ignoring the importance of diagnostic analysis in each individual case.

BASIC FAMILY NEEDS

Immediate Cash Fund

The immediate cash or cleanup fund is the sum of money necessary to meet the immediate cash requirements of the deceased's estate. Whether the family is of modest, moderate, or substantial means, the need for an immediate cash fund is almost universal. In addition to the usual obligations which are a part of the family's economic picture, the event of death itself creates new obligations. Among the items to be considered in arriving at the amount of this immediate cash fund are the following:

Expenses of last illness (doctor, hospital, nurses' fees)
Burial expense (cemetery lot, marker, funeral)
Current household bills
Installment debts
Personal loans and unpaid notes
Estate administration costs
Estate and inheritance taxes
Federal income taxes not withheld
Property taxes
Unsatisfied judgments

It is necessary to make "educated estimates" in order to determine the amount of funds needed for cleanup purposes. For example, last illness expenses may be large or small, depending upon the circumstances surrounding death. Prolonged medical and hospital care often precedes death. In the absence of adequate medical expense insurance,[1] the obligation for the estate may be substantial.

Burial costs are subject to rather close approximation, with variations subject to the personal wishes of the family.

A family may have relatively heavy obligations due to recent installment purchases, such as for a car or appliances. Also, an examination of buying habits over a period of years may reveal an average outstanding installment debt, excluding any mortgage on the home, of $1,000 or more. Circumstances may be altered, however, by the existence of credit life insurance.

The immediate cash fund also should include an amount to pay the estimated costs of estate administration. These will vary, of course, but

---

[1] Some authorities have argued that last illness expenses should be covered by health insurance rather than life insurance because the amount of these expenses is very uncertain prior to death. If this approach is followed, the problem of estimating last illness expenses will be substantially eliminated.

allowance should be made for costs approximating 5 to 7 per cent of the value of property subject to probate.

The man of substantial means may have created an estate which will be subjected to heavy death taxes. Unless cash funds are readily available, his administrator or executor may be forced to liquidate securities or other property at a disadvantageous time, resulting in unnecessary losses to the family. Careful planning will serve to minimize such death costs and also to make the necessary funds readily available at the time of death. Life insurance is particularly appropriate for this purpose because death, the event which creates the need for cash to pay death costs, creates the fund. Furthermore, because of the annual-premium payment method, these life insurance dollars will be available at a cost of only a few cents each if death comes early.

It should be obvious that the determination of the need for a cleanup fund and the amount of such a fund should be based on a careful study of each particular case. A summation of the amounts needed for each item in the above list may result in a sum much larger than that arrived at by applying some "average" figure. Any error should be on the conservative side to provide for the unforeseen. If extra funds are available, they will most likely be needed for the readjustment period, which is described below.

It is possible for the cleanup fund to consist of cash or nonfluctuating assets readily convertible into cash. Few families, however, accumulate such a fund or keep it intact for cleanup purposes. The ideal plan consists of using life insurance for this purpose. When death occurs and the fund is needed, the life insurance proceeds are immediately available.

Readjustment Income

The term "readjustment income" is used here to describe that income which is made available to the family for a limited period of time immediately following the death of the breadwinner. The purpose of the readjustment income is to give the widow and children a chance to readjust to their new financial situation, normally a much less satisfactory one. It is a time for adjusting to the new way of life, for marshalling assets, for determining future sources and amounts of income, and for contemplating a new (usually lower) standard of living. Questions of moving, retraining for employment, hiring a housekeeper, and the like must be resolved. Time is needed to make sound decisions, and the readjustment income is intended to provide this time without undue financial pressures.

The readjustment period may be from a few months to perhaps two or three years, depending on the circumstances. In the event of death, the amount of the readjustment income, generally speaking, should approximately equal the husband's "take-home" pay less the amount required for his personal maintenance and other noncontinuing outlays. Where the ultimate adjustment to be made is a substantial one, or where unusual circumstances exist, the stepdown in standard of living may be made in successive stages, thus lessening the impact.

Someone has said that "a widow lives in a woman's world but with a man's problems." It is during the readjustment period particularly that the widow should be given all possible financial help in making the transition from housewife to head of the household.

Just as dependents often need a readjustment income during a period following the breadwinner's death, the entire family needs a readjustment income in the event of the disability of the breadwinner. In this situation, practically all former living expenses continue, and to them is added the further financial burden of medical care expenses for the disabled breadwinner. Provision should be made for a continuing flow of income approximately equal to the previous income of the family. This readjustment income probably should be available for a minimum of one or two years.

Family Income Period

The "family income period" also is frequently referred to as the "dependency period." These terms are used to describe those years during which the children are dependent upon the breadwinner or his widow for care and support. This may be considered as extending to age 18 of the youngest child. On the other hand, it may be considered by many families as extending to the end of the period of formal education, including college.

It has been frequently said that in the event of his death, "the most valuable gift a man can leave his children is their mother's time." Ideally, and particularly when children are young, the dependency period income should be sufficient for the widow to devote her full time to the family and maintain a standard of living comparable to that provided by the husband's earnings. Practically, it may be impossible to provide so adequately. In such cases, the dependency period income will be lower than that during the readjustment period just described.

In every case, however, the income figure established for the dependency period should include allowances for the basic necessities: food, clothing, shelter, and medical care. The problem of shelter may be minimized through the existence of a special mortgage redemption fund, to be discussed later. But even then, the cost of home maintenance, repairs, insurance, and taxes must be considered. There also should be due recognition of the rising costs to be reckoned with as children become teenagers.

The costs of owning and operating a family car also are substantial. While the availability of public transportation may eliminate this expense for the family, in most instances a car is considered a necessity today. If such is the case, the dependency period income should include the costs involved.

In addition to providing the basic necessities, the dependency period income should reflect recognition of the need for a reasonable amount of recreation and entertainment essential to emotional health.

Determination of the amount of dependency period income should be arrived at on the basis of a thorough analysis of the family budget. Care should be exercised to prevent underestimation of those items which are of a continuing nature. Since the dependency period may be of long duration, it is best to assume that rising costs are likely to be faced, not just in terms of the general price level, but also in terms of increasing home maintenance costs and increased financial requirements of the children with the passing of the years. Allowances, of course, should be made for those expenditures which will be reduced or eliminated because of the breadwinner's removal from the family circle.

Life insurance, properly co-ordinated with income from other assets and expected social security benefits, plays a most important role in the financial planning for the dependency period. In recognition of this particular need, the life insurance industry has developed a special policy or rider, the family income policy or rider, which has become widely used.

The necessity of providing adequate income to the family during the crucial child-rearing years in the event of the death of the breadwinner points up the need for making similar provision for the family, including the breadwinner, in the event of his disability. In the event of long-term disability, however, the problem is further aggravated by the fact that the breadwinner remains as a nonproducing consumer. Also, in addition to the regular family expenses referred to earlier, there may be continuing medical expenses for the disabled breadwinner. It makes economic sense, then, to determine as accurately as possible the amount of income needed to cover the family's needs and to provide sufficient health insurance to enable the family to weather this particularly critical period—the formative years for the children.

In the event of total and permanent disability, of course, the need for income to the husband and wife extends beyond this dependency period and may continue for the duration of their lives, even though in lesser amount.

Emergency Fund

Even the most carefully planned income may be insufficient to meet the costs of unforeseen events, such as accidents, serious illnesses, or unusual expenses resulting from homeownership. Although the impact of such events may be minimized through carrying appropriate types of insurance, the establishment of an emergency fund is considered wise by financial advisers.

From a practical as well as a psychological point of view, the establishment of an emergency fund makes sense. It is the kind of fund which financial counselors recommend even while the breadwinner is living. It is often recommended that this fund be equivalent to at least three months' income. Its purpose is to meet the unexpected financial problems which invariably arise from time to time. The existence of such a fund permits the family to meet these emergencies without having to make serious inroads on basic income over a prolonged period. Also, such a fund helps avoid the necessity of cashing in relatively nonliquid assets at a financial disadvantage.

It would appear that an increasing number of families are creating emergency funds, using various savings media. Where the required savings accumulation has not been completed, the head of the family can arrange for a life insurance emergency fund. The growing cash value of the insurance can be borrowed if emergencies arise during his lifetime. The total fund required for his family will be created automatically upon his death. This fund can be left with the insurance company, and withdrawals can be provided for at the discretion of the widow. If these funds are not exhausted during the dependency period, they will undoubtedly be a welcome source of cash or additional income to the widow after her child-rearing responsibilities have ended, or perhaps they can serve as an educational fund for the children.

Life Income for the Widow

The end of the dependency period marks the beginning of a new and often more trying period for the widow. The fact that she has devoted her full attention to her children during their formative years results in a serious problem for her when the children are grown and independent. Long absence from the labor market, in addition to her age, puts her in an unenviable position. The marketable skills which may once have been at her command have rusted with disuse. She finds herself suddenly thrust into competition with younger, more competent women. Many doors of employment are closed to her because of pension plan limitations. Furthermore, her need for a job may come at a time when prevailing economic conditions are unfavorable.

After the children become self-supporting, the income needs of the widow are substantially reduced. She no longer needs the housing space required when the children were at home. Therefore, her shelter costs may be reduced. She may find that a smaller home or an apartment will be better suited to her circumstances.

In some instances, the widow may find gainful employment and provide at least a part of her own support. However, survivor benefits under social security may be reduced or lost if her earnings exceed given amounts. Then, too, disability may make her completely dependent upon provisions her husband made for her during his lifetime.

Ideally, the husband should arrange for a life income to his wife in an amount sufficient to provide adequately for her basic needs and, to the extent possible, for the comforts to which she has been accustomed. Such an arrangement will protect the children as well as the widow, in that it will prevent the burden of her support from falling on the children at the very time they are struggling to make their own start in life. Even a modest income will enable her to be a guest in her children's homes rather than a financial burden. Financial independence for the widow also helps her to avoid the humiliation of having to ask her children for money or shelter. One has but to imagine the humiliation which comes from asking for money to grasp the importance of arranging a life income for the widow.

All available assets must be used to the greatest advantage in meeting this need. Social security benefits, if available, must be taken into consideration. Additional income requirements can be met through the purchase of insurance on the life of the husband. The proceeds of this insurance, payable on a life income basis, provide the most practical means of meeting the additional income needs of the widow.

Retirement Income

Ultimately, most men retire from active work, and at this point their income is cut off or greatly reduced. In our society, age 65 generally has been selected as the arbitrary line of demarcation between active employment and retirement. Statistically, the average man can anticipate 12.9 years of life beyond this age, according to a widely used mortality table.

In financial planning by the individual, failure to appreciate the significance of all the expenses which must be met after age 65 perhaps constitutes the greatest weakness. For example, the 12.9 years of life expectancy mentioned above can be translated in terms of 14,125 meals alone. Even if the home is paid for, it must be maintained. It is true that living costs may have decreased because the children are grown and educated. But all too often, these decreases are partially offset by increased medical costs due to the infirmities of old age.

From a practical point of view, many expenses can be reduced when a man retires from active employment. For example, his personal maintenance expenses related to his employment, such as transportation, meals, and clothing, will be eliminated or decreased. After retirement, the cost of shelter also may be minimized by moving into smaller and more suitable housing. There is an increasing trend toward moving to an area where climatic conditions are better for the aged, and where clothing and heating costs are cut to a minimum. On the other hand, the desirable standard of living after retirement will include some activities, such as travel, which the new freedom from work makes possible.

While the amount of retirement income needed will obviously vary among individuals, there clearly is an irreducible minimum. A rule-of-thumb estimate of the needed retirement income might be approximately 50 to 60 per cent of the preretirement income.

Private pension plans and social security benefits are becoming increasingly significant in meeting the income needs of the aged. Also, many affluent people accumulate capital in the form of stocks and bonds, with the thought of living off the income which these produce. While stocks and bonds have a definite place in the financial planning of many people, there are three inherent problems in their use for providing a basic retirement income: (1) the ability to accumulate the amount of capital required to produce an adequate income from the dividends or interest, (2) the uncertainty of investment values at retirement age, and (3) the hazard of trying to spread the principal over the individual's remaining lifetime if dividend and interest income is insufficient.

When permanent forms of life insurance are used in a family's financial planning, the same contracts which guarantee the security of the family in the event of the breadwinner's premature death also will provide retirement income for him and his wife. The annuity option is unique for this purpose. It provides for the scientific distribution of the principal and interest over the remaining lifetime of the insured, either with or without a refund feature, thus assuring an income which he cannot outlive.

Mortgage Redemption or Continuation of Mortgage Payments

Liberalization of mortgage terms and increased emphasis on the benefits of homeownership have led to a vast increase in such ownership since World War II. For example, it has been reported that 57 per cent of all nonfarm families live in their own homes; 70 per cent of families with incomes over $7,500 own their own homes; and homeowners with mortgages pay an average of over $500 yearly—principal and interest.[2]

The existing mortgage gives rise to this question: What will happen if the head of the family dies before the debt is paid? Interestingly, the risk of the mortgagor's dying before the mortgage is repaid is considerably greater than the chance that his home will burn. In fact, it is estimated that there are 16.3 deaths of mortgagors for every one fire in mortgaged homes.[3] Nevertheless, fire insurance is considered essential by homeowners and is made a contractual requirement by mortgagees.

Unless provision is made for a special lump-sum payment, the dependency period income must be sufficient to meet the mortgage payments. Otherwise, the family probably will be forced to sell the home.

Long-term mortgages, which have become quite common, involve sub-

[2] Life Insurance Agency Management Association, *The New Single Needs Sales*, File 660 (Hartford, 1958), p. 49.

[3] *Ibid.*, p. 50.

stantial interest payments which add several thousand dollars to the cost of a home. For example, in meeting the regular payments under an $18,000, twenty-year amortizing mortgage at 5 per cent interest, the interest charges will total $10,508.77. The total interest payments under a $10,000 mortgage with the same terms will amount to $5,840 in round figures.

These interest dollars become increasingly important to a family which must adjust to a reduced income. By arranging for a lump-sum payment of life insurance, the breadwinner can guarantee that funds will be on hand to liquidate the mortgage at his death, thus eliminating the remaining interest dollars from the family budget.

If income is interrupted by the disability of the breadwinner, even for a few months, the family may be hard pressed to continue mortgage payments. The amount of such payments should be considered in calculating the amount of disability income needed.

Education Fund

The value of a college education is readily acknowledged by modern parents. As a larger and larger percentage of young people go to college, the competition for the better jobs is becoming increasingly sharpened. The untrained or poorly trained man or woman is finding fewer opportunities for advantageous employment or advancement. Other benefits of a college education which are very important are the cultural and social advantages, which lead to a fuller enjoyment of life.

Many will argue that the boy who really wants a college education will find a way to get it. Thousands of young people earn a substantial part of the costs of their education while on the campus. But the parent who relies on this possibility overlooks a growing problem. As the facilities of the colleges become overtaxed, the competition for entrance and the scholastic requirements for remaining in school will weed out more and more marginal students. A student whose scholarship is marginal because he must devote many hours to outside employment will be at a distinct disadvantage. The entire future of such a boy or girl may hang in the balance because financial help is not available during these critical years. Most educators discourage efforts to earn a substantial portion of college costs during the school year because the scholastic attainments and the health of the student may suffer.

The costs of higher education have continued to climb, and the sharp rise of recent years is almost certain to continue. With college costs already running from $1,400 to $3,000 annually, the family with just three children to educate faces a total cost that could run to $35,000.

The most satisfactory solution to this problem is to arrange life insurance which will deliver the necessary dollars when they are needed, whether the father lives or not.

Some fathers use endowments on the lives of their children to provide these funds. In such instances, inclusion of the payor clause is a must if the funds are to be there at college age if the father dies prematurely. Other parents use insurance on their own lives, recognizing that the cash values can be utilized as educational funds. Where the insurance is so arranged, for example, the father might select a whole life policy of such face amount as to provide the necessary cash value at the college age of the child. If the father dies before the child enters college, the amount of the death proceeds in this case is a multiple of the college funds required, and the excess usually can be well used for other purposes. It is the role of the life underwriter to recommend the kind and amount of insurance needed to fit each situation.

MISCELLANEOUS NEEDS

There are certain needs which, though not present in every situation, are sufficiently prevalent to warrant consideration by the professional life underwriter. The ability to point out these needs and demonstrate the effectiveness of life and health insurance to meet them should be a part of the underwriter's service to his clientele.

The Dependent Parent

Many men and women are the sole support of aged parents, or at least make a substantial contribution to their support. In such cases, the untimely death of the son or daughter providing support will create a real hardship. Life insurance can be used to guarantee the continuation of payments to the parent for life. By means of a survivorship annuity, the cost of making such an arrangement for an aged parent can be reduced to a minimum.

There is increasing recognition of the need to provide for medical care of dependent parents. One method of accomplishing this is through the purchase of appropriate health insurance coverage for the parents. Substantial strides have been made in the health insurance coverages which are available for aged persons, and more will certainly be forthcoming in the future. The family faced with this need should not overlook the problem and the coverages currently available.

The Handicapped Child

Nothing causes greater concern to a parent than the thought of a handicapped child being left without means of support. Here again, the necessary maintenance requirements can be determined and translated in terms of life insurance proceeds to be paid on a life income basis. In certain circumstances, the need for a trusteed arrangement may be indicated.

Special Occasion Funds

Some husbands like to add a special touch to their financial planning. There is a certain sentiment attached to the possibility of using life insurance to continue special remembrances beyond death. By a special settlement arrangement the life insurance company can contract to deliver a check of a specified amount on special occasions such as Christmas, a birthday, or a wedding anniversary.

Special Bequests

Those who make substantial contributions to a church, to a college, or to a similar worthy purpose may desire to provide for the continuation of such donations after death. Even those who have not made substantial annual contributions to a given cause during life may find appeal in the idea of having such a memorial contribution made at death. Life insurance again provides the ideal medium.

BASIC BUSINESS NEEDS[4]

Key-Man Insurance

The family is the most important business in existence, with the husband as the "key man." The earning power of the husband is subject to cancellation by death or total disability. Unless these earnings are replaced from other sources, the family, considered as a business unit, becomes insolvent.

Just as in the case of the family, a business organization also may need funds to tide it over a period of lost or reduced earnings resulting from the death of a key member of the management, sales, or research team. Key-man insurance is a universally recognized business life insurance need. The death of a key man may result in reduced sales, interruption of a vital research project, lower production, or an impaired credit standing. Life insurance owned by the firm on the life of the key man will, in the event of his death, offset a loss in earnings and provide the funds necessary to find, hire, and develop a replacement.

Disability of a key man presents a dual problem. Not only are his services lost to the firm temporarily or permanently, but management may feel the moral obligation to continue his income at least for a reasonable period and possibly until he is eligible for retirement benefits. Adequate key-man disability income insurance preserves the assets of the firm while also discharging this moral obligation. Under present federal income tax provisions, such insurance is made attractive to the firm as well as to the recipient of the benefits.

---

[4] See Chapters 47 through 51 for a development of these basic business needs.

Business Continuation Insurance

The vast majority of business firms in the United States are small, employing fewer than ten people. The ownership and operation of a small firm, whether it be a proprietorship, a partnership, or a close corporation, is vested in the hands of one or a very few individuals. The owners are usually entirely dependent upon the business as a source of income; and the destiny of the firm, in turn, lies in the continued active participation of the owner or owners.

It is estimated that 80 per cent of the sole proprietorships are liquidated within six months after the death of the owner. The partnership, being a personal relationship, is dissolved at the death of one of the partners. When a stockholder in a close corporation dies, his stock passes into the hands of his heirs through his estate. These circumstances have led to a rapid growth of business life insurance purchased to fund business continuation or buy-and-sell agreements.

In the case of the proprietorship, it may be desirable for a key employee to have an agreement with the proprietor whereby the employee will purchase the business from the estate of the deceased owner. Life insurance owned by the employee on the life of the proprietor provides the necessary purchase funds when death occurs. Thus, the estate of the deceased has a ready-made market for the business.

Partners also may enter into a buy-and-sell agreement. These agreements provide for the purchase of a deceased partner's interest from his estate by the surviving partners or by the partnership, depending on the type of agreement used. Here again, life insurance is ideal for funding the arrangement. Through a cross-purchase or entity type of agreement, life insurance can be used to fund the agreement in whole or in part. Thus, instead of facing the problems of liquidation, the survivors are enabled to continue the business as their own. The family of the deceased partner can be assured of a fair price for his interest.

A binding buy-and-sell agreement arranged by the stockholders of a close corporation may provide for the purchase of the stock of a deceased stockholder by the surviving stockholders, or it may provide for retirement of his stock through its purchase by the corporation. In the absence of such arrangements, the deceased's stock goes through his estate and may end up in the hands of his heirs or may be sold to an outsider. In either event, numerous problems may arise to plague the interested parties. Life insurance, purchased by the stockholders or by the corporation, depending on the disposition to be made of the deceased's stock, will guarantee the availability of the necessary funds to carry out the buy-and-sell agreement.

The need for disability insurance in buy-and-sell agreements is becoming increasingly apparent. This subject is discussed at length in Chapter 51.

SELECTED REFERENCES

HUEBNER, S. S., and BLACK, KENNETH, JR. *Life Insurance*. 6th ed. New York: Appleton-Century-Crofts, Inc., 1964.

LIFE INSURANCE AGENCY MANAGEMENT ASSOCIATION. *The New Single Needs Sales*, File 660. Hartford, 1958.

MEHR, ROBERT I., and OSLER, ROBERT W. *Modern Life Insurance*. 3d ed. New York: Macmillan Co., 1961.

SULLIVAN, HAROLD L. *Needs and the Life Underwriter*. Bryn Mawr, Pa.: American College of Life Underwriters, 1957.

Chapter 56

BENEFICIARY DESIGNATIONS AND ASSIGNMENTS

BY HARRY S. REDEKER

BENEFICIARY DESIGNATIONS

Life insurance policies issued today uniformly contain provisions permitting the designation of a beneficiary to receive the proceeds payable at the insured's death. There are additional provisions that the beneficiary may be changed and successively changed. All these provisions will usually be found under a heading such as "Beneficiary" or "Change of Beneficiary." Too frequently, just one beneficiary is named when a policy is issued, and the designation is not reviewed again for many years. This chapter will discuss some of the important points that should be considered when a beneficiary designation is contemplated, and why the beneficiary designation must be reviewed with reasonable frequency.

Who May Designate and Change Beneficiaries

The right to name a beneficiary, and to change a beneficiary from time to time, is vested in the "policyowner." The insured is usually the owner of the policy, but there are many policies outstanding which have been applied for and are owned by someone other than the insured, or in which ownership has been transferred by the insured after the policy is in force. Throughout this chapter the discussion will assume that the insured is the owner, except where the context clearly indicates otherwise.

Revocable and Irrevocable Beneficiaries

An insured normally reserves the right, on his sole signature, to designate and change the beneficiary. Such a beneficiary is said to be designated "revocably," and the modern rule prevailing in all but a few states is that the beneficiary's interest is a mere expectancy. Further, this rule allows the insured to exercise every right under the policy without the beneficiary's consent.

Where the right to change the beneficiary is not reserved to the insured, the designation of beneficiary is said to be "irrevocable." Here the beneficiary acquires a vested interest which the insured cannot change or defeat, except with the beneficiary's consent. There may be uncertainty as to the effect of an irrevocable beneficiary designation, in that, at one extreme, such beneficiary's interest may be limited merely to a requirement that his or her consent be obtained to effect a change of beneficiary. At the other extreme, the beneficiary may be regarded as actually possessing incidents of ownership jointly with the insured so as to require the beneficiary's consent before the insured may exercise any rights under the policy. This uncertainty may arise either because of the failure of a company to specify the rights that flow from an irrevocable beneficiary designation or because of different interpretations made by the courts. As a protection to the company, as well as to the other parties in interest, many companies specify the precise rights created by an irrevocable designation. Such a beneficiary clause may read as follows:

> The insured hereunder having so requested, it is agreed and understood that the insured may not revoke and change the beneficiary designated under this policy during the beneficiary's lifetime without the written consent of the beneficiary so designated. While said policy remains payable to such beneficiary during the beneficiary's lifetime, the insured, without the written consent of such beneficiary, may not make loans on this policy, except for the sole purpose of paying a premium or premiums on this policy, or interest on any indebtedness on this policy, or both, and the insured may not exercise, without the written consent of such beneficiary, any other option, right, or privilege provided therein, including but not limited to the right to elect any of the nonforfeiture provisions thereof or the right to assign this policy. The insured and not the said beneficiary shall have the right to receive all amounts payable hereunder if this policy matures as an endowment.

Today the irrevocable beneficiary designation is in limited use. It is seen most frequently in agreements relating to separation and divorce, where provision for the maintenance of an insurance policy is included in the agreement, and where it is desired specifically to restrain the insured in the exercise of the various policy rights without actually transferring ownership to the beneficiary. If the irrevocable beneficiary predeceases the insured, the insured regains full control over the policy.

Instead of merely restraining the insured in the exercise of rights, the beneficiary clause may divest him of all incidents of ownership. This would constitute a transfer of ownership by the insured. Usually, such transfer is accomplished by means of an absolute assignment, as is discussed later.

Primary and Contingent Beneficiaries

Consider this beneficiary designation: "Mary Doe, wife of the insured, if living at the death of the insured, otherwise to such of the lawful children of the insured as may be living at the death of the insured." Mary

Doe is known as the "primary beneficiary"; the children, as "contingent beneficiaries." Two or more primary beneficiaries may be named to share the proceeds equally, and second contingent beneficiaries may be designated in the event that no one of the primary or contingent beneficiaries survives the insured. Normally, it is considered good practice to designate more than one beneficiary.

Most policies currently being issued provide that if all named beneficiaries die before the insured, the proceeds of the policy, at the insured's death, will then be paid to the insured's estate. Where the owner of the policy is someone other than the insured, however, it is usual to provide that if all named beneficiaries predecease the insured, the policy proceeds, at the insured's death, will be paid to the owner, or to the owner's estate.

Insurable Interest

For many years, there was doubt whether a policy, valid at its inception, could be payable to a beneficiary or an assignee who, at the death of the insured, had no "insurable interest" in the life of the insured. Broadly speaking, "insurable interest" arises either out of close family relationships or from substantial economic interest in the continued life of the person insured. In other words, there must be a reasonable ground to expect some benefit or advantage from the continuance of the insured's life. In more recent years, either by judicial decision or by statute, a person has been regarded as having an insurable interest in his own life. He may, therefore, contract for insurance of which he is the owner and may name a beneficiary who has no insurable interest in his life. However, if the policy is applied for and owned by someone other than the insured, the applicant-owner must have an insurable interest in the life of the insured.

Identity of the Beneficiary

The following are several of the more popular types of beneficiary designation:

The Insured's Estate. The proceeds may be made payable to the executors or administrators of the insured and thereby added to the other probate assets of the estate. This arrangement is useful if the proceeds are intended to cover debts, funeral expenses, taxes, and expenses of administering the estate. Such a designation, however, will incur state inheritance taxes, probate costs, and claims of the insured's creditors—results normally avoided where others, such as the insured's wife, are designated.

Specifically Named Persons. The most commonly used designation is that which names the wife of the insured as primary beneficiary, with the children as contingent beneficiaries. The designation may read: "Mary Doe, wife of the insured, if living at the death of the insured, otherwise to such of John Doe and Susan Doe, children of the insured, equally, or to the survivor of them, as may be living at the death of the insured."

It is customary to describe the beneficiary by his family relationship to the insured, or as a "friend," "business associate," "fiancee," or the like.

Class Designations. It is sometimes desired to designate a group of persons without identifying the individual members of the group. This is known as a class designation. The designation of "lawful children of the insured" is a common example of such a class designation. The beneficiaries actually entitled to receive the proceeds at the death of the insured will be determined by the members of the class in existence at that time. Such a designation automatically includes members of the class who may be born after the date of the beneficiary designation and before the insured's death. Companies tend to limit the designation of this type of beneficiary to classes of people closely related to the insured, and in which the members of the class are easily identified. It is unusual for company practices to permit class beneficiary designations for other than children, grandchildren, brothers, and sisters; and some companies have limitations even in those groups.

When it is desired to name children as beneficiaries, the simplest and usually the safest way is to designate "children of the insured" as a class. If the children are designated by name as "John Doe and Susan Doe, children of the insured," then unnamed children or children born after the date of the beneficiary designation will be excluded. If this result is not desired, "children of the insured," or "children of the insured, including John Doe and Susan Doe," should be designated.

A class designation sometimes observed, but with much less frequency than formerly, is "children born of the marriage of the insured and his said wife." Such designation will exclude as beneficiaries the insured's own children born of an earlier or later marriage, and all children born to his wife by a former marriage. All adopted children will also be excluded under such limited designation. The request for payment to children born of the marriage seemingly stems from a desire to eliminate alleged illegitimate children as beneficiaries. Such children, however, are generally eliminated by the routine provisions of beneficiary agreements prepared by companies today, which provide, for example, that " 'child' or 'children' as used herein shall include only lawful and legally adopted sons and daughters." An alleged illegitimate child of the husband-insured probably would have no valid claim as beneficiary even without such an express provision. Of course, provision may be made for an illegitimate child acknowledged by the insured by simply designating him as beneficiary by name.

The safer procedure, again, is to use "children of the insured," or "children of the insured, including John Doe and Susan Doe." If there are children by a former marriage of the insured's wife, they must be specifically named to be included under the beneficiary designation. Usually, this is done by some phraseology such as "children of the insured, and John Smith and Margaret Smith, children of the insured's wife."

One final word concerning adopted children: Adoption proceedings may require months or even years in some states. Until the proceedings are completed, such children would not be included in a class designation of "children of the insured." To share in the proceeds, their names would have to be included specifically in the beneficiary designation.

"Per Stirpes" or "Per Capita"?

These are formidable, legalistic phrases. They arise mostly in the construction of wills, and the lawbooks are filled with decisions that attempt to determine which type of distribution was intended.

To illustrate the problem, let us assume that an insured has provided that the proceeds of his policy shall be paid to his children, John, William, and Mary, and to surviving children of a deceased child. Suppose John and Mary die before the insured. John leaves four children surviving him. Mary has no children. How shall the proceeds of the policy be divided at the insured's death?

"Per stirpes" means "by branches" of the family. A per stirpes distribution gives the share of the deceased child to his children. Accordingly, under a per stirpes distribution, William would take one half the proceeds, and John's surviving children would divide the other half among them.

"Per capita," on the other hand, means "by heads." A per capita distribution will give one share of the proceeds to each beneficiary. On a per capita basis, William and each of John's four children would receive one fifth of the proceeds.

Per stirpes distributions are more popular. It is most important that the written request for the agreement accurately reflect the distribution desired by the insured, and that such distribution be clearly set forth in the beneficiary designation.

Business Organizations

An insured may name a corporation or a partnership as beneficiary in the same manner as he would an individual. The problems here are essentially the same as with the individually designated beneficiary. However, with the partnership, better practice dictates that the partnership be named as an entity instead of naming the individual partners, unless under the particular state law there is some doubt that a partnership will be recognized as a legal entity. If the partnership is designated as an entity, additions or withdrawals of partners should present no question as to the proper payee of the proceeds at the death of the insured. Such a designation might read: "Brown and Company, a partnership, or its assigns."

As for naming a corporation, the customary form is: "The XYZ Company, a Pennsylvania corporation, its successors or assigns." The use of the phrase "its successors or assigns" will cover a possible change in the corporate structure, such as a merger or consolidation occurring after the date of the beneficiary designation and before the death of the insured.

When naming a corporation as beneficiary, it is wise to check the exact corporate title. A corporation may be popularly known by one name, but its correct corporate title may be quite different. Moreover, several corporations may have similar names. This is particularly true in the case of charitable organizations, such as hospitals, churches, or homes for the ill or aged. In some instances, these charitable organizations may not even be incorporated. Difficulty might be encountered in having payment made to the organization if it is merely designated by name, for there may be trustees or some group of individuals responsible for the receipt and payment of monies by the organization. The proper designation in such instances would be the trustees or other group of individuals. The administrative officer of the organization can give the proper information.

Trustees

The insured may wish to have the death proceeds paid to a trustee who will administer the fund for the beneficiaries of a trust. The trust may be established either under an agreement signed by the insured and the trustee or under the insured's will.

Where the life insurance trust agreement created during lifetime is used, a typical trustee beneficiary designation would read: "Henry Black and the XYZ Trust Company, trustees, their successor or successors in trust, under trust agreement dated ____________ . . . ." The insured's wife is often named as an individual cotrustee. Additional provisions are frequently incorporated by companies preparing the designation to relieve them of responsibility for proper administration of the trust.

Some insureds name the wife as primary beneficiary and the trustee as contingent beneficiary. The proceeds may be paid to the wife in one sum, or they may be retained or distributed for the wife's benefit under one or more of the optional modes of settlement discussed in the following chapter. Proceeds payable to the trustee as contingent beneficiary upon the death of the last to die of the insured and his wife are usually paid in one sum. Company rules often prohibit use of the settlement options by a trustee, but some companies will permit a trustee to use these options if the one for whose benefit the arrangement is made is a minor.

The designation of trustees under the insured's will as beneficiary introduces complications which are avoided by a signed agreement executed during the lifetime of the insured. A trust created under a will can take no effect if the will fails to qualify for probate or if it should be declared invalid for any reason. There may be a question of the validity of such an arrangement under some state laws. There is a danger that the insured may change his will and forget to change the beneficiary designation that ties into the will. A new will may name no trustee. Even if one is named, the insured may no longer desire the proceeds of the particular life insurance policy to be payable to the trustees under the will.

The will may create two or more trusts with different trustees, and a problem would be presented as to which trustee should receive the proceeds. In spite of these potential complications, the practice of the designation of testamentary trustees as beneficiaries has increased during recent years. Several states have passed laws which encourage the practice by specifically providing that proceeds payable to a testamentary trustee will not attract state inheritance taxes and will not be subject to the claims of creditors. An example of this type of law may be found in Section 47(*f*) of the New York Decedents' Estate Law. Prior to these special laws, it was felt that proceeds payable to a testamentary trustee would be subject to claims of creditors and subject to state inheritance tax in the same manner as if the proceeds were payable to the insured's estate. The designation of trustees under the insured's will as beneficiaries should not be attempted without careful study by the insured's lawyer. The following is a typical designation:

> The proceeds should be paid to the trustees designated under the insured's will or their successor or successors in trust; but if the company receives written evidence satisfactory to it that:
>
> 1. The trustees for any reason fail to serve and no successor trustee was appointed; or
> 2. A will of the insured, which was admitted to probate, made no provision for trustees; or
> 3. A personal representative of the insured has been appointed in intestacy;
>
> then, in any such event, the proceeds shall be paid to the executors or administrators of the insured; provided, however, that the company shall be fully discharged for any payment made to said trustees before receipt of written evidence satisfactory to it that said trustees are not entitled to payment under the provisions of this designation.

Minor Beneficiaries

Under the common law, a minor under the age of 21 cannot give a valid release for receipt of life insurance proceeds. Many states have lowered the age at which a minor attains majority. Many other states have adopted enabling statutes, specifically applicable to insurance. Some of these enabling statutes authorize minors of a designated age, such as 15 or 18, to contract for insurance, give a valid discharge for benefits accruing or money payable, and otherwise exercise all rights in the policies as though the minor had attained majority. Other state statutes permit payment of a modest amount, such as $2,000 or $3,000, directly to a minor. If one of these special statutes does not apply, it is necessary to have a guardian appointed to receive payment on behalf of the minor, with the attendant formality, expense, legal steps, and numerous restrictions as to who may be guardian and what he may do without specific court approval.

The problem is simplified by permitting the proceeds to be retained at interest by the company with the full right reserved for the minor's benefit to withdraw or to elect any other settlement option in the policy. The minor is named as beneficiary, but it is provided that if he is still a minor at the time for payment to him, a trustee, rather than a guardian, will receive the payments on behalf of the minor and may exercise the specified withdrawal privileges. The trustee is also empowered to select one or more of the installment options in the policy in lieu of the interest option. The trustee may be appointed under a separate formal trust agreement or, under the practice followed by some companies, may be named in the settlement agreement or beneficiary clause. There may also be provision for a successor trustee if the one first named fails to serve or ceases to serve. The settlement agreement itself may contain a simple provision to the effect that the trustee shall hold and expend the monies received from the life insurance company for the benefit of the minor until age 21 and shall then pay him any unexpended funds. The extent to which these various procedures may be utilized will depend on company practice in each case.

A specimen "informal" trustee arrangement may read as follows:

> Any sum payable as herein provided to any of said beneficiaries during such beneficiary's minority shall be paid to Jane Doe, sister of the insured, as trustee for such beneficiary. In the event said sister shall for any reason fail to serve or cease to serve as trustee for such beneficiary, any sum payable as herein provided to such beneficiary during his minority shall be paid to Mary Smith, aunt of the insured, as successor trustee. If the right to withdraw proceeds or elect other options is granted a beneficiary during his minority, such right or election shall be exercisable by said trustee(s). All sums payable to said trustee(s) shall be held and expended for the maintenance, support, and education of such minor beneficiary in the discretion of the trustee(s), except as may be otherwise provided in a separate trust instrument, and when such beneficiary shall attain the age of 21 years, the trustee(s) shall pay over any unexpended funds. As respects any payment made to said trustee(s), the company shall be under no liability to see or be responsible for the proper discharge of the trust or any part thereof, and any such payment to said trustee(s) shall fully discharge the company for the amount so paid. If the trustee(s) designated above shall for any reason fail to serve or cease to serve as trustee(s), a successor or substitute trustee shall be appointed by a court of competent jurisdiction. The company shall not be charged with notice of a separate trust instrument, a change of trustee(s), the death of such beneficiary, the termination of the trust, or of rights under the trust, until written evidence thereof is received at the home office.

How to Designate and Change Beneficiaries

The first beneficiary designation usually appears in the application for the policy. Requirements for subsequent change are given in the policy, and these requirements are ordinarily simple. Typically, the policy provides that the request for change shall be made in writing on a form satisfactory to the company, and each company supplies forms for this purpose. A typical form is shown in Figure 56–1. Most of the older policies require endorsement of the policy to effect a change of beneficiary, but the modern trend is to make the change effective after approval or recording of a form filed with the company without physically endorsing the policy.

There are instances where an insured desires to change the beneficiary but for some reason is unable to comply with all the prescribed formalities. For example, the policy may require its submission for endorsement of the change, but the present beneficiary may be wrongfully withholding possession from the insured. As another example, the insured may execute the forms, mail them to the insurance company, and then die before the company has completed its formalities. In such case, a majority of courts will rule that if the insured does all that he could be reasonably expected to do to indicate his intention to make the change, the change will be deemed to have been accomplished. However, courts generally do not permit the change to be made by a will or a codicil to a will.

Ordinarily, a change in the relationship of the parties will not of itself affect an existing beneficiary designation. Suppose "Jane Doe, wife of the insured," is designated as beneficiary under her husband's policy and that Jane and her husband are divorced. Further suppose that the husband does not change the beneficiary. Unless the divorce decree or a specific statute in the particular state terminates a divorced wife's interest in the policy, Jane would be entitled to receive the proceeds upon the death of her ex-husband. Courts rule that the words "wife of the insured" are merely descriptive of the relationship and that the insured intends that the proceeds shall be paid to the named individual.

Common Accident or Common Disaster Clauses

An insured and his wife rarely die in a common accident or common disaster. However, where they travel together frequently, the contingency should be considered. As mentioned previously, a popular beneficiary arrangement may provide, in substance: "Jane Smith, wife of the insured, if living at the death of the insured, otherwise equally to such of the children of the insured as may be living at the death of the insured." Under such a designation, if the wife survives the insured for only a few moments, her estate will be entitled to payment of the proceeds. Accordingly, the proceeds will be exposed to probate costs and possible claims of her creditors, and will pass in accordance either with the terms of her will or to those entitled as her heirs under the intestate laws if she left no will. This result can be avoided by making all or a portion of the proceeds payable to the wife under the interest option (explained in the following chapter), subject to her full right of withdrawal, and naming children or

THE LIFE INSURANCE COMPANY
PHILADELPHIA 1, PA.

Policy Number(s) 000000

Life of JOHN DOE

BENEFICIARY DESIGNATION
(Use Only for One Sum Settlements)

ARTICLE 1—This Designation cancels all prior beneficiary and mode of settlement designations under each policy. At the death of the insured, proceeds will be paid in one sum to living beneficiaries in the order of Classes designated below. Proceeds shall not include amounts payable upon the death of a wife or child under a Family Plan policy or under a Family Benefit. The owner of the policy may change this Designation.

Please type or print each beneficiary's full given name and relationship to insured

CLASS A PRIMARY BENEFICIARY

MARY DOE, wife

(If Contingent Beneficiaries are to be designated, they should either be listed by name or designated as a class in Class B. Second Contingent Beneficiaries should be designated in Class C.)

CLASS B FIRST CONTINGENT BENEFICIARY

Children of the insured

For "per stirpes" distribution check here ☐ Pay to children of each deceased Class B beneficiary as provided in Article 3.

CLASS C SECOND CONTINGENT BENEFICIARY

NONE

For "per stirpes" distribution check here ☐ Pay to children of each deceased Class C beneficiary as provided in Article 3.

CLASS D FINAL BENEFICIARY The owner of the policy, if living, otherwise the executors or administrators of the owner of the policy.

ARTICLE 2—The provisions appearing on the other side of this form are incorporated in this Designation.

Dated____________19____ ONLY THE ORIGINAL COPY SHOULD BE SIGNED ____________ Policy Owner

DO NOT WRITE BELOW THIS LINE

Original signed copy dated__________is filed with The Life Insurance Company.

____________Registrar ____________ Date

205 No. 2-1-62

FIG. 56–1. Typical beneficiary designation change form.

ARTICLE 3—PAYMENT TO CHILDREN OF A DECEASED BENEFICIARY: If this Article has been elected under Article 1 on the other side by placing an "X" or a check mark in the proper box ☐ in Class B or Class C, and if a beneficiary in a Class is deceased at the death of the insured, the share that would have been paid to such beneficiary had he been then living shall be paid in one sum equally to his then living children.

ARTICLE 4—BENEFICIARY: Each class of beneficiary will receive payment in the order designated in Article 1. No payment will be made to any class of beneficiary unless all beneficiaries in all preceding classes have died before the insured. Unless otherwise specified, two or more beneficiaries in any one class will share equally. If more than one beneficiary is designated in a class, the share of a beneficiary of that class who dies before the insured will be paid to the beneficiaries of that class who survive the insured, (subject to the provisions of Article 3, if elected), in the proportion that their shares as set forth in Article 1 bear to each other.

ARTICLE 5—ASSIGNMENT: The rights of every beneficiary of each policy are subordinate to the rights of any assignee who has filed a written assignment at the Home Office of the Company, whether the assignment was made before or after the date of this Designation. If such assignment is in effect at the insured's death, the Company may, at its option, pay the entire proceeds to the assignee or may deduct from the proceeds and pay to the assignee the amount owed to the assignee, as certified in writing by the assignee or any officer or partner of the assignee, and pay only the remaining proceeds to the beneficiary.

ARTICLE 6—MINOR BENEFICIARIES: Any payment to a minor beneficiary will be made only to his legally appointed guardian, unless a statute provides for payment directly to the minor.

ARTICLE 7—RELIANCE ON AFFIDAVIT AS TO BENEFICIARIES: The Company may rely on an affidavit by any beneficiary relating to the dates of birth, death, marriage or remarriage, names and addresses and other facts concerning all beneficiaries, and the Company is hereby released from all liability in relying and acting upon the statements contained in such affidavit.

ARTICLE 8—EFFECT OF CHANGE OF BENEFICIARY UNDER ANY POLICY: A future change of beneficiary of any policy in this Designation shall terminate the Designation with regard to that policy.

ARTICLE 9—CANCELLATION OF POLICY ENDORSEMENT REQUIREMENT: The Company is requested to waive all provisions of any policy under this Designation requiring endorsement of beneficiary changes, and to endorse any such policy as follows:

> "The beneficiary of this policy has been changed according to written request filed with the Company.
>
> "Every request for change of beneficiary shall be in writing on a form satisfactory to the Company. No change of beneficiary will take effect until the request has been filed at the Home Office of the Company, but when filed will take effect as of the date of the request, whether or not the insured is living at the time the request is filed, but without prejudice to the Company because of any payment made by it before receipt of the request at its Home Office. All provisions of the policy requiring endorsement of change of beneficiary are canceled."

ARTICLE 10—"PROCEEDS" DEFINED: The proceeds of a policy will be all amounts payable by reason of the insured's death under the provisions of the policy (including the commuted value of any guaranteed deferred payments). Proceeds shall not include surrender values, amounts payable at maturity of the policy during the insured's lifetime, or any refund payable under a Receipt for Advanced Premiums.

ARTICLE 11—DEFINITIONS AND CONSTRUCTION OF TERMS: "Child" and "Children" as used herein shall include both lawful and legally adopted sons and daughters, but not grandchildren or other descendants. "Brothers" and "Sisters" shall include half-brothers and half-sisters. Masculine terms shall apply to either sex and the singular shall include the plural. "Insured" shall mean "annuitant" when such meaning applies.

ARTICLE 12—MISCELLANEOUS: The furnishing by the Company or the filing with the Company of this form shall not constitute an admission that any policy under this Designation is in full force or is in effect under a Non-Forfeiture Option. If, in the opinion of the Company, this form is not properly completed, the Company may declare it of no binding effect.

FIG. 56–1 (*Continued*). Reverse side.

other persons as contingent beneficiaries to receive any proceeds remaining with the company whether the wife dies before or after the insured. If the wife survives the insured, the proceeds are subject to her complete control. If, in a common accident, the wife dies either before or shortly after the insured, the proceeds will be paid to the contingent beneficiaries rather than be tied up in the estate of the insured or his wife.

A second popular procedure for handling the common disaster situation is to provide a cash payment to the wife only if she is living on, say, the thirtieth day after the insured's death. This second procedure has potential disadvantages that are avoided by using the interest option with the proceeds subject to withdrawal. If the wife survives the specified period and then dies, the proceeds will become part of her estate, as in the case of the designation first described in the preceding paragraph. The wife is not protected against possible claims of her creditors, as she would be under the standard clauses incorporated in agreements using the interest option or other settlement options. Further, this second procedure invites a "tax trap" which is avoided by use of the interest option procedure—in larger estates where qualification for the marital deduction will minimize federal estate taxes, the deduction is lost if the common disaster actually occurs, and if the wife dies after the insured's death and within the period specified.

It has been suggested that when proceeds are payable in one sum, the Uniform Simultaneous Death Act, which is in force in a great majority of states, takes care of the contingency of common accident or common disaster. This is not the case. That Act merely provides that if it cannot be determined whether the insured or the beneficiary died first, the insured will be presumed to have survived. Where proved that the wife survived the insured by as little as one second, the Uniform Simultaneous Death Act obviously does not apply. Also, statutes are ambiguous as concerns parties dying "as a result of a common disaster," since one may live for some time and still die as a result of a common disaster.

State Exemption Statutes and Their Effect

Practically all states, by statute, place life insurance beyond the reach of creditors of the insured under some circumstances. These statutes are known as "exemption statutes," and their provisions vary greatly. Under the most common type of statute the exemption applies if the policies are payable to or for the benefit of the wife, children, or other relatives dependent on the insured, even though the insured retains the right to change the beneficiary. Some statutes apply the exemption if the policy is payable to any beneficiary other than the insured's estate. In a few states the exemption is limited to some stated amount of proceeds or to proceeds purchased by a stated amount of annual premium.

Spendthrift Clauses and Their Use

Spendthrift clauses are concerned with creditors of the beneficiary, not creditors of the insured. There are a few states whose statutes automatically exempt life insurance proceeds from claims of the beneficiary's creditors. In a substantial number of states, though, by statute or by court decisions, the policyowner may use a so-called "spendthrift clause" if settlement options are specified for the beneficiary. Life insurance companies customarily include spendthrift clauses in agreements by which optional modes of settlement are elected. A typical clause reads as follows:

> Unless otherwise provided in this settlement option agreement, no beneficiary may commute, anticipate, encumber, alienate, withdraw, or assign any portion of his share of the proceeds. To the extent permitted by law, no payments to a beneficiary will be subject to his debts, contracts, or engagements, nor may they be levied upon or attached.

In a very few states, such spendthrift clauses are apparently considered to be against the public policy of the state and will not be upheld.

Federal Tax Liens

State exemption statutes do not give full protection against creditors if the creditor is the United States government under a federal tax lien. In such instances, the government may reach the lifetime values, even though the taxpayer-insured may have designated his wife, child, or dependent relative as beneficiary. If a lien arises against the insured during his lifetime, and the insured then dies, the government can reach the proceeds to the extent of the cash value just prior to the day of death. If the beneficiary owes taxes, the government, after the insured's death, could reach the proceeds payable to the beneficiary under a lien arising against the beneficiary.

ASSIGNMENTS

Life insurance contracts are freely assignable by the insured unless some limitation is placed in the policy. Life insurance companies routinely furnish assignment forms. By an assignment the insured transfers his rights in the policy to the assignee. The extent to which these rights are transferred depends upon the provisions of the policy concerning assignments, the intention of the parties as expressed in the assignment form, and the circumstances surrounding the actual assignment.

Types of Assignments

Assignments are conventionally of two types: absolute and collateral. The absolute assignment normally is intended to make the assignee the owner of every right in the policy that the insured possessed before the assignment. When the transaction is completed, the insured will have no further interest in the policy. Phraseology of absolute assignments differs. In essence, it is stated that the insured transfers to the assignee all the insured's right, title, and interest in the policy. Some companies suggest the use of an "ownership clause" to accomplish the assignment or transfer of ownership rights.

The collateral assignment, on the other hand, is a more limited type of transfer. It contemplates a security arrangement to protect the assignee who has lent money to the insured. After the indebtedness is repaid, it is contemplated that the assignee will release his interest to the insured, i.e., that he will transfer back the rights transferred by the assignment. If the collateral assignment is still in force at the death of the insured, under usual procedure the assignee certifies to the insurance company the amount of indebtedness, including interest at that time, and receives that amount in a lump sum. Any excess proceeds are then payable to the named beneficiary in accordance with the beneficiary designation.

"Collateral" or "Absolute" Assignment for Security Transactions?

Even though the arrangement is one merely of security calling for a collateral assignment, many lenders insist on receiving a form called an "absolute assignment." This insistence probably stems from the practice of some life insurance companies of demanding joint signatures of the insured and the assignee if the latter wishes to deal with the policy. Even the use of the absolute assignment form may not assure the assignee in every case that the company will deal with him alone. Despite the sweeping language, it may not spell out clearly the prematurity rights the assignee is intended to have. Too often the parties to the assignment fail to make their intentions plain in this respect.

Problems such as these led to the creation of a middle-ground form of assignment by the joint efforts of the Bank Management Commission of the American Bankers Association and representatives of the Association of Life Insurance Counsel. This form is shown as Figure 56–2. It states clearly five specific rights that pass to the assignee and that may be exercised by the assignee alone. Included is the sole right to collect the proceeds at the death of the insured on the date of the maturity of the policy, and the sole right to surrender the policy for its cash surrender value. Without impairing the right of the assignee to surrender the policy, certain rights are reserved to the insured. Included are the right to receive disability benefits that do not reduce the amount of insurance, and the right to designate and change the beneficiary. Also, the assignee promises not to surrender the policy without giving the insured notice of his intention to surrender. This so-called "ABA assignment form" is now in use by many banks, and is recommended by a substantial number of insurance companies. In fact, many companies have adopted it as their own standard form.

Notice of Assignment to the Insurance Company

To protect the assignee fully, notice must be given the life insurance company that the assignment has been made. If a company with no notice of assignment makes payment of the proceeds to a later assignee or to a named beneficiary, it cannot be made to pay a second time. A typical policy provision concerning assignments is: "No assignment shall be binding upon the company until the original or a duplicate thereof is filed at its home office. The company assumes no obligation as to the effect, sufficiency, or validity of any assignment. All assignments shall be subject to any indebtedness to the company on this policy.

Need the Beneficiary Be Changed before Assignment of the Policy?

Some modern policies and some beneficiary forms provide, in effect, that "the rights of any revocable beneficiary will be subordinate to the rights of any assignee of record with the company, whether the assignment was made before or after the date of the beneficiary designation." When this provision appears, most banks will accept the assignment, and most life insurance companies will record the assignment without change of beneficiary. Unless there is clear-cut language in the policy that the beneficiary's interest is diminished by an assignment, or unless the assignment is to be made to the beneficiary named in the policy, the best practice is to change the beneficiary to the insured's estate prior to making the assignment. Frequently, a second change of beneficiary is made, to be recorded immediately following the assignment, to reinstate the beneficiary designation. At least one company follows the procedure of incorporating requests for both changes of beneficiary in the assignment form itself.

If someone other than the assignee is designated as beneficiary at the time the assignment is made, and if this possibility and its effect are not covered in the policy or the beneficiary designation form, there is a question whether the assignee or the named beneficiary will be entitled to payment of the proceeds when the insured dies. A different answer may be given in the case of an absolute assignment than in the case of a collateral assignment transaction.

As respects absolute assignments, one view interprets the assignment either as a change of beneficiary or as the destruction of the interest of the beneficiary. Under this view, the assignee is entitled to receive the proceeds of the policy when the insured dies. Under the opposite view, the policy specifies a definite procedure for changing the beneficiary, and this procedure must be followed. The theory in support of this view is that the named beneficiary would have received the proceeds at the insured's death had there been no assignment, and a mere change in ownership rights should not change this concept or this result.

FORM APPROVED BY
BANK MANAGEMENT COMMISSION
AMERICAN BANKERS ASSOCIATION

FORM No. 10—LIFE INSURANCE ASSIGNMENT

ASSIGNMENT OF LIFE INSURANCE POLICY AS COLLATERAL

A. **For Value Received** the undersigned hereby assign, transfer and set over to XYZ BANK AND TRUST COMPANY of Philadelphia, Pa. its successors and assigns, (herein called the "Assignee") Policy No. 000000 issued by

The Life Insurance Company of Philadelphia, Pa.

(herein called the "Insurer") and any supplementary contracts issued in connection therewith (said policy and contracts being herein called the "Policy"), upon the life of JOHN DOE of Philadelphia, Pa. and all claims, options, privileges, rights, title and interest therein and thereunder (except as provided in Paragraph C hereof), subject to all the terms and conditions of the Policy and to all superior liens, if any, which the Insurer may have against the Policy. The undersigned by this instrument jointly and severally agree and the Assignee by the acceptance of this assignment agrees to the conditions and provisions herein set forth.

B. It is expressly agreed that, without detracting from the generality of the foregoing, the following specific rights are included in this assignment and pass by virtue hereof:
1. The sole right to collect from the Insurer the net proceeds of the Policy when it becomes a claim by death or maturity;
2. The sole right to surrender the Policy and receive the surrender value thereof at any time provided by the terms of the Policy and at such other times as the Insurer may allow;
3. The sole right to obtain one or more loans or advances on the Policy, either from the Insurer or, at any time, from other persons, and to pledge or assign the Policy as security for such loans or advances;
4. The sole right to collect and receive all distributions or shares of surplus, dividend deposits or additions to the Policy now or hereafter made or apportioned thereto, and to exercise any and all options contained in the Policy with respect thereto; provided, that unless and until the Assignee shall notify the Insurer in writing to the contrary, the distributions or shares of surplus, dividend deposits and additions shall continue on the plan in force at the time of this assignment; and
5. The sole right to exercise all nonforfeiture rights permitted by the terms of the Policy or allowed by the Insurer and to receive all benefits and advantages derived therefrom.

C. It is expressly agreed that the following specific rights, so long as the Policy has not been surrendered, are reserved and excluded from this assignment and do not pass by virtue hereof:
1. The right to collect from the Insurer any disability benefit payable in cash that does not reduce the amount of insurance;
2. The right to designate and change the beneficiary;
3. The right to elect any optional mode of settlement permitted by the Policy or allowed by the Insurer;

but the reservation of these rights shall in no way impair the right of the Assignee to surrender the Policy completely with all its incidents or impair any other right of the Assignee hereunder, and any designation or change of beneficiary or election of a mode of settlement shall be made subject to this assignment and to the rights of the Assignee hereunder.

D. This assignment is made and the Policy is to be held as collateral security for any and all liabilities of the undersigned, or any of them, to the Assignee, either now existing or that may hereafter arise in the ordinary course of business between any of the undersigned and the Assignee (all of which liabilities secured or to become secured are herein called "Liabilities").

E. The Assignee covenants and agrees with the undersigned as follows:
1. That any balance of sums received hereunder from the Insurer remaining after payment of the then existing Liabilities, matured or unmatured, shall be paid by the Assignee to the persons entitled thereto under the terms of the Policy had this assignment not been executed;
2. That the Assignee will not exercise either the right to surrender the Policy or (except for the purpose of paying premiums) the right to obtain policy loans from the Insurer, until there has been default in any of the Liabilities or a failure to pay any premium when due, nor until twenty days after the Assignee shall have mailed, by first-class mail, to the undersigned at the addresses last supplied in writing to the Assignee specifically referring to this assignment, notice of intention to exercise such right; and
3. That the Assignee will upon request forward without unreasonable delay to the Insurer the Policy for endorsement of any designation or change of beneficiary or any election of an optional mode of settlement.

F. The Insurer is hereby authorized to recognize the Assignee's claims to rights hereunder without investigating the reason for any action taken by the Assignee, or the validity or the amount of the Liabilities or the existence of any default therein, or the giving of any notice under Paragraph E (2) above or otherwise, or the application to be made by the Assignee of any amounts to be paid to the Assignee. The sole signature of the Assignee shall be sufficient for the exercise of any rights under the Policy assigned hereby and the sole receipt of the Assignee for any sums received shall be a full discharge and release therefor to the Insurer. Checks for all or any part of the sums payable under the Policy and assigned herein, shall be drawn to the exclusive order of the Assignee if, when, and in such amounts as may be, requested by the Assignee.

G. The Assignee shall be under no obligation to pay any premium, or the principal of or interest on any loans or advances on the Policy whether or not obtained by the Assignee, or any other charges on the Policy, but any such amounts so paid by the Assignee from its own funds, shall become a part of the Liabilities hereby secured, shall be due immediately, and shall draw interest at a rate fixed by the Assignee from time to time not exceeding 6% per annum.

H. The exercise of any right, option, privilege or power given herein to the Assignee shall be at the option of the Assignee, but (except as restricted by Paragraph E (2) above) the Assignee may exercise any such right, option, privilege or power without notice to, or assent by, or affecting the liability of, or releasing any interest hereby assigned by the undersigned, or any of them.

I. The Assignee may take or release other security, may release any party primarily or secondarily liable for any of the Liabilities, may grant extensions, renewals or indulgences with respect to the Liabilities, or may apply to the Liabilities in such order as the Assignee shall determine, the proceeds of the Policy hereby assigned or any amount received on account of the Policy by the exercise of any right permitted under this assignment, without resorting or regard to other security.

J. In the event of any conflict between the provisions of this assignment and provisions of the note or other evidence of any Liability, with respect to the Policy or rights of collateral security therein, the provisions of this assignment shall prevail.

K. Each of the undersigned declares that no proceedings in bankruptcy are pending against him and that his property is not subject to any assignment for the benefit of creditors.

Signed and sealed this ________ day of ____________, 19____.

____________________ *Witness*	____________________ (L.S.) *Insured or Owner*
____________________	____________________ *Address*
____________________ *Witness*	____________________ (L.S.) *Beneficiary*
____________________	____________________ *Address*

751 No. 2—10-45 .Co

FIG. 56–2. ABA–10 collateral assignment form.

When the question has been litigated under a transaction in which an assignment was given as collateral security for money loaned, most courts have ruled that the rights of the assignee are superior to those of the beneficiary. Since assignments are used so frequently in collateral security transactions, there are compelling business reasons for a rule of law that will give maximum protection to those who lend money with policy values as security. However, some few courts have ruled that the beneficiary cannot be deprived of his interest without his consent, unless a change of beneficiary is made exactly as provided in the policy.

Obviously, troublesome questions such as those just described can be avoided by a change of beneficiary prior to making the assignment when that procedure is indicated.

CONCLUSION

A sufficient number of problems has been discussed in this chapter to indicate the need for careful study of all the facts when an insured considers the designation of a beneficiary or the making of an assignment of his policy. Beneficiary designations become outmoded with the passage of time. Countless beneficiary designations and assignments now in existence may one day pose problems ranging from delay in payment of proceeds to exclusion of those whom the insured had intended should share as beneficiaries. Lawyers, life underwriters, trust officers, accountants, and people in home offices and field offices of life insurance companies can render a significant service by being on the alert to discover these problem areas and then calling them to the insured's attention either for correction of an existing transaction or, if the transaction is not yet concluded, so that the necessary steps may be taken to avoid the problem.

SELECTED REFERENCES

FLITCRAFT, INC. *Settlement Options: The Programming Manual.* New York, annual editions.

KRUEGER, HARRY, and WAGGONER, LELAND T. (eds.). *The Life Insurance Policy Contract.* Boston: Little, Brown & Co., 1953.

MACLEAN, JOSEPH B. *Life Insurance.* 9th ed. New York: McGraw-Hill Book Co., Inc., 1962.

MCGILL, DAN M. (ed.). *The Beneficiary in Life Insurance.* Rev. ed. Homewood, Ill.: Richard D. Irwin, Inc., 1956.

REDEKER, HARRY S., and REID, CHARLES K., II. Rev. ed. *Life Insurance Settlement Options.* Homewood, Ill.: Richard D. Irwin, Inc., 1964.

Chapter 57

SETTLEMENT OPTIONS

BY CHARLES K. REID, II

The idea of measuring wealth in terms of income instead of capital is of comparatively recent origin in the United States and Canada, though of long standing in some older European economies. However, as early as 1867, American companies allowed payment of proceeds in installments over a period of years. Life insurance programing based on income needs began to take shape after World War I; since then, there has been rapid growth in the use of settlement options.

THE IMPORTANCE OF SETTLEMENT OPTIONS

The demand for settlement options, particularly installment options, arose mainly from the needs for safety and for amounts of income beyond what could be provided for the beneficiary by interest yield alone. Rarely could a family build an estate large enough to provide adequate income without using principal, even through the creative power of life insurance. The depression of the 1930's, the Social Security Act, and government and private insurance and pension programs have all contributed to public interest in security of income, and thus to a growing interest in life insurance settlement options.

Settlement options provide unconditional guarantees, while affording the policyowner a simple and practical income arrangement for himself or his beneficiaries. They enable the life underwriter and his client to translate meaningless capital amounts into terms of periodic income, thus helping both parties to pinpoint family needs and understand the solution.

SETTLEMENT OPTIONS DEFINED[1]

Most individual life insurance policies offer five methods for settling proceeds. Subject to individual company rules, these methods or options

[1] A definitive treatment of life insurance settlement options may be found in the volume *Life Insurance Settlement Options,* by Harry S. Redeker and Charles K. Reid, II (rev. ed.; Homewood, Ill.: Richard D. Irwin, Inc., 1964).

may be used singly or in combination. Additional options can often be secured upon request, and some or all of them may be available in forms of policies other than individual life insurance contracts, such as group insurance and certain annuity contracts.

Cash or Lump Sum

Cash settlement is not usually listed as an "option" because most policies provide for lump-sum settlement in the absence of some other direction by the policyowner or beneficiary. However, some policies specifically provide for death or retirement benefits to be paid in installments unless otherwise directed, and if a lump-sum settlement is desired, it must be elected before the policy matures.

Normally, if proceeds are payable in cash, the beneficiary may elect to receive payment under one of the income settlement options instead of taking the cash sum. Notwithstanding this right, there are several disadvantages to a lump-sum settlement, even where the insured intends to make proceeds available in cash:

1. It does not protect against the possibility that the insured and the beneficiary may die in a "common disaster" or that the beneficiary may survive the insured by only a short time, and then die. The standard "common disaster" or "delayed payment" clauses generally offered cannot protect adequately against either contingency, under a cash settlement arrangement, and these clauses may have undesirable tax results. (This problem is covered more fully in Chapter 56.)
2. It does not protect against creditors of the beneficiary. Such protection can usually be obtained by inserting a creditor-protection or "spendthrift" clause in income settlement agreements executed before the insured's death. Usually, such a clause provides that the beneficiary cannot withdraw or assign proceeds unless otherwise stipulated in the agreement, and that proceeds shall be free of attachment by creditors to the extent permitted by law.
3. It may result in proceeds passing unnecessarily through the beneficiary's estate, even where the beneficiary elects an income plan in lieu of the cash settlement. Depending on company rules and applicable state laws, such a beneficiary may or may not be permitted to designate contingent beneficiaries, or even to redesignate any who may have been named originally by the insured.
4. It may result in imposing unnecessary restrictions on election of an income settlement plan by the beneficiary. Most companies will allow the policyowner to elect arrangements not specifically granted by the letter of the contract. Usually, such company practices are more liberal with regard to plans requested by the policyowner than for those requested by a beneficiary named to receive a cash settlement.
5. It may cause the beneficiary to lose interest on the proceeds between the date of the insured's death and the date on which payment is made or an income settlement plan elected. Many policies do not provide for such interest, and company practices vary widely on this point.

Mainly for these reasons, a cash settlement is not generally recommended for personal life insurance, except for small policies or for payments to an estate or trust. Even in the latter situations, there are often good reasons for use of an income option, where permitted by company practice.

Interest Option

Proceeds are retained by the company, and interest at a minimum guaranteed rate is paid to the beneficiary monthly, quarterly, semiannually, or annually. Many companies pay surplus, or excess, interest if any is earned above the minimum rate, either at the end of each year or in the same periodic manner as the basic guaranteed payments. Any surplus, or excess, earnings above the minimum rate are usually paid at the end of each year. An unlimited withdrawal right may be given the beneficiary, or withdrawals may be limited to a specified annual sum, or to a total cumulative amount. The beneficiary may also be given the right to elect another settlement option or combination of options; or it may be directed that such a change occur automatically at some stated age or date, or on the happening of a specified event.

Fixed-Period Option

Proceeds are payable in equal monthly (or less frequent) installments liquidating principal with interest over a specified period of years, from one to as many as 25 or 30 years. The specified rate of payment per $1,000 of proceeds is based on a guaranteed interest factor, and any surplus interest declared may be paid at the end of each year or used to increase the next year's installments. Usually, the payee may be given the right to commute all remaining unpaid installments and withdraw in a lump sum; but because of the nature of this option, partial withdrawals are not generally permitted.

Fixed-Amount Option

Proceeds are payable in regular installments of specified amount until principal and interest are exhausted. Basically similar to the fixed-period option, and usually based on the same guaranteed interest factor in a given policy, the fixed-amount option is much more flexible. Generally, the beneficiary may be given the right to withdraw principal or to elect other options as outlined above for the interest option. In addition, the level of installment payments may be varied to meet certain needs. For example, payments might be specified at the rate of $100 per month for two years, $75 per month for the next year, and $50 per month thereafter until proceeds and interest are exhausted. The effects of increases or decreases in total proceeds arising from surplus interest, dividends, or loans are quite different from those applying to the fixed-period option.

Such factors will affect the length of time over which fixed-amount installments are payable, but not the amount of each installment.

Life Income Options

Sometimes called "life insurance in reverse," the life income or annuity options provide orderly liquidation of proceeds with interest over the payee's entire lifetime. These options spread the risk of "living too long," just as life insurance spreads the risk of "dying too soon." They are peculiar to life insurance companies, as no other financial institution provides a guarantee of income for life.

The amount of each periodic installment per $1,000 of proceeds is determined by the type of annuity selected, the rate of interest, the age of the payee when the income commences, and the sex of the payee. The four principal forms of life income option are outlined below. Not all policies contain these four options or all their variations; however, those not provided in the policy often may be secured by special request.

Life Income Option. Installments are payable as long as the payee lives, with no guarantee that total payments will equal the principal sum. Because there is no guarantee to return principal, this option provides the highest rate of life income. However, most people wish to avoid the risk of capital loss through early death of the life annuity payee because they have other relatives whom they wish to protect. For example, this form of pure life annuity income normally would not be used for a widow with young children, because it affords the children no protection in case of their mother's early death.

Refund Life Income Option. Payments are guaranteed as long as the payee lives, but if his or her death occurs before receiving an amount equal to the principal sum, the difference between total payments and the principal sum is paid to a second payee.

Life Income Option with Period Certain. Payments are guaranteed for as long as the payee lives, but should death occur before payments have been made for a specified number of "years (or months) certain," installments may be continued to successive payees until the end of the certain period, or the commuted value of unpaid certain installments may be paid in cash or in some other specified manner. Usually, the certain period runs for five, 10, 15, or 20 years, the most popular periods being 10 and 20 years.

Joint and Survivorship Life Income Option. This variation of the life income option provides an income for two lives, usually for the lifetime of the insured and his wife when the insured retires. Often the option also can be used for two beneficiaries, such as parents, upon the death of the insured. Under some plans, payments are continued in the same amount to the second payee. In others, at the death of one payee, installments are reduced to three fourths, two thirds, or one half of the original amount for the second payee's remaining lifetime.

SPECIAL ARRANGEMENTS OR POLICIES

A wide variety of income patterns may be arranged by using the various options outlined above. However, some companies have set up special options to meet specific needs, based on one or more of the standard options. For example, special educational settlement plans and family income or family maintenance options are sometimes offered. Many companies offer special policies payable directly in income, the construction of which is based on one or more of the standard options. Finally, most policies provide a "catchall" clause such as "proceeds may be payable in any other manner mutually agreeable to the policyowner or beneficiary and the company."

USE OF SETTLEMENT OPTIONS TO COVER NEEDS

Basic family needs are outlined below in the order normally considered in a life insurance program, along with suggestions on the use of settlement options to meet the needs. Sometimes the entire insurance estate is set up on a basis tantamount to payment in cash, as when proceeds are settled under the interest option with an unlimited right to withdraw proceeds and the further right to elect other options in the policy, subject to company rules. On the other hand, there are many situations in which an attempt is made to tie up all or most of the proceeds under rigid settlement plans that are apt to become out of date with the passage of time and may come to work real hardship on the beneficiaries. A better approach may be to develop a pattern of cash and income payments that meets basic family requirements, with appropriate flexibility provided through intelligent withdrawal privileges. Various uses of the settlement options are discussed below from the standpoint of meeting major family needs encountered at the death of the breadwinner.

Cash Funds

There are at least three principal needs for cash funds: the immediate cash or cleanup fund, the mortgage cancellation fund, and the emergency fund. Though these needs are often regarded as requiring a lump-sum settlement, such is not generally recommended for the reasons given earlier, except where the amount is small (perhaps under $2,000) or where the beneficiary is an estate or a trust.

With these exceptions, proceeds intended to be made available in cash should normally be retained under one of the settlement options, and three general principles may be found helpful in setting up such cash funds.

First, a settlement option, normally the interest option with an unlimited right of withdrawal, should be used, to avoid the disadvantages of a cash payment.

Second, whenever the interest (or other) option is used with an unlimited withdrawal right, the right to elect any other option in the policy at any time should be requested, to the extent that company rules permit. This right may preserve favorable income rates in the policy. Without it, a change of option requested by the beneficiary after the insured's death may be granted only on the basis of income rates in new policies being issued at that time. Such "then current" rates are often less favorable than those in older policies. There may also be an income tax disadvantage if the beneficiary elects to change to an installment option, unless the right to make such a change is specified in the settlement agreement.

Third, beneficiaries for each fund should be chosen on the basis of the purpose of the particular fund. The first and second principles indicate the basic design of a settlement option plan for cash funds. The third principle is discussed below as it applies to each of the three major types of cash need.

Immediate Cash or Cleanup Fund. Most estates are modest and are composed largely of life insurance. Usually, the wife is the sole heir, and the cleanup fund can logically be settled under the interest option for the wife, subject to unlimited right of withdrawal and the right to elect other options. However, it is important that the insured's estate be named contingent beneficiary rather than minor children, because generally funds payable to minors may not be used for any other purpose than their exclusive benefit. Failure to provide ready cash for estate obligations in case of the death of both husband and wife could result in the forced sale of estate assets at a fraction of their value. If the estate is small, even family silver and heirlooms intended for the children might have to be sacrificed.

However, simply naming the estate contingent beneficiary under the above plan is not enough, because the wife could die many years after the insured, leaving unused proceeds on deposit which would then require the insured's estate to be reopened. This can be a costly process. A settlement plan based on the following form of request to a company will cover this situation and meet most cleanup needs satisfactorily:

> Hold proceeds under the interest option with interest payable monthly (or less frequently if required by company rules) to my wife, if living, otherwise in equal shares to my surviving children, subject to the right to withdraw all or any part of the proceeds at any time, and to the further right to elect any other option in the policy at any time (in accordance with company rules), provided that if my said wife predeceases me, or survives me and dies within six months (or one year, or some other desired period) after my death, pay the proceeds or any remainder thereof to my estate, instead of to the contingent beneficiaries named above.

Alternatively, payment of the immediate cash fund may be made directly to the insured's estate as primary beneficiary. This is entirely logical because the estate has primary responsibility for debts and expenses. It may be especially appealing where the insured desires to relieve his widow of administrative details, where the widow is to receive only a portion of the estate rather than being the sole heir, or where taxes and other estate settlement costs will be large and the insured does not wish to rely on his widow to pay them. However, one disadvantage of this method is that any exemption from state death taxes that might apply to life insurance proceeds would be lost.

Though settlement options are not always available to an estate, a number of companies permit retention of proceeds under the interest option, with interest payable to the estate of the insured for a limited period of time during which the executor has the right to withdraw principal as needed. Any balance remaining at the end of the specified period may be made payable to the widow or other named beneficiaries, in cash or under an income option.

Another alternative is to make the immediate cash or cleanup fund payable to the trustees under a life insurance trust, which may be especially attractive where the amount required is large. Such an arrangement may result in saving state death taxes and administration expenses, and it has the added advantage of affording protection against claims of creditors.

Mortgage Cancellation or Permanent Home Fund. For most families home ownership is preferable to renting on a long-term basis. Therefore, a fund is often provided to cancel an existing mortgage or, alternatively, to help the widow buy a home for which the family has planned, even though the plan has not been carried out prior to the insured's death.

Where the insured holds title to the home in his own name, the mortgage cancellation fund may be paid to his estate. However, if the home is owned jointly, or if the wife is expected to purchase the home, such payment should normally be made to her under the interest option with the right to withdraw proceeds or elect other options. In most such cases, children would be logical contingent beneficiaries. However, there may be special situations where the estate of the last survivor of the husband and wife might be a more logical choice, such as in the unusual case where even though the children are orphaned, it is desired to clear the mortgage and maintain the home for their use.

Emergency Funds. Emergency funds can be provided in a number of ways. If a separate policy or a portion of the proceeds from a large policy is set up for this purpose, the interest option with the right to withdraw or elect other options will normally prove satisfactory. Beneficiaries would be the wife, if living, otherwise the children.

In some cases, emergency funds can be provided by allowing withdrawal rights under a plan for providing family income which has been set up on the fixed-amount option. In such cases, the beneficiary should be warned that excessive use of the withdrawal privilege may sharply reduce or eliminate future income for her support in later life.

If desired, the right to withdraw can be limited under either plan, thus preventing premature dissipation of proceeds.

Regular Income for the Family

While income needs can be classified generally as readjustment, dependency period, social security gap, and the widow's life income, relating to separate periods in the economic life of a family, they also overlap in some respects. Thus, while discussed separately, they must be considered in relation to each other.

Readjustment Income. Often, it is deemed necessary or desirable to provide a larger amount of income to the widow during the first year or two after the insured's death than is possible to provide on a permanent basis. The fixed-period option may be used to provide this extra income, but the fixed-amount option may be a better choice because it is more flexible. The latter will be found especially helpful where a step-down income is desired, or where the extra readjustment income is to come from a large policy allocated primarily to other income needs. Obviously, the interest option with right to withdraw proceeds or elect other options may also be used to provide readjustment income.

Dependency Period Income. The period of dependency for minor children commences at the insured's death, extends through the readjustment period, and continues until the children become self-supporting. Often, social security payments will cover a large part of this need until the children reach age 18. For families in the middle or upper income brackets, however, this source may represent only a small portion of the total income required. Some of the need for dependency period income may be met by interest payable on life insurance proceeds retained for later use, such as educational funds or funds to be settled later under a life income option for the widow.

Generally, the fixed-amount option will provide the best arrangement because the income can be specified definitely and because this option is flexible. Provision can be made for partial withdrawal rights and settlement of proceeds remaining at the end of the dependency period under another option, such as one of the life income options.

Social Security Gap Fund. Since no social security benefits are payable between the youngest child's eighteenth birthday and the widow's age 62, the need for increased income from insurance during this period is obvious, even though total income needs may be less than during the dependency years. Sufficient proceeds to fill this gap under the fixed-amount or fixed-period option may be retained at interest until the youngest child is 18. Or proceeds held at interest until that time may be settled on one of the life income options with an appropriate period certain, depending on the age of the widow and other factors in the situation. Often the face amount of a family income or family maintenance policy will become payable at or after the time the gap begins, and can logically be settled on one of the installment or life income options at that time.

Widow's Life Income. While the need for an income which the widow cannot possibly outlive is recognized as basic, this does not necessarily mean that the life income option should be used for payments commencing at the death of the insured. Nor does the fact that the widow's life income is considered chronologically as following the end of the dependency period indicate that this is the proper time for commencement of life income option payments. The determining factor will normally be the extent to which the policyowner wishes to preserve guaranteed values for children or other contingent beneficiaries. The age of the widow as primary beneficiary may also be an important factor, because, generally speaking, life income rates will not be found attractive, as compared to income from the interest option, until age 50 or 55. Her health may also have a bearing. If it is poor, some other option may be used to preserve policy values for contingent beneficiaries. Obviously, other factors in choosing the life annuity option, and in choosing the certain period to be used in connection with it, are the characteristics and ages of the contingent beneficiaries to be protected.

Accordingly, it is common practice to hold sufficient proceeds under the interest option until the widow reaches age 50, 55, or later, or at least until the end of the dependency period, to provide the income she will need in later life. Additional proceeds are then settled on the fixed-period or fixed-amount option to supplement interest earned on the amount held for such later life income and thus to bring the dependency and gap period incomes up to the required levels.

There are exceptional cases where there may be no children or other members of the family the insured desires to protect, or where everyone except the widow has been adequately cared for from other funds. In such cases, the shortest possible certain period may be indicated, to give the widow the largest possible annuity income. Here, settlement under the straight life annuity—without refund or guarantee of principal return—may be entirely logical, if such a plan is available from the company. However, such cases are rare, and most situations are better solved by the approach suggested in the preceding paragraph.

Income for Children

Normally, while the widow is living, all income is payable to her for the support of herself and the children, except in some large estates where it may be desirable to allocate some income directly to children as a means of reducing the over-all income tax burden. In most cases, children become direct beneficiaries of life insurance only after both parents have died.

The income needs of minor children are not easily projected, and often settlement agreements that endeavor to carry out specific income patterns for them are very complicated. A more practical approach is to retain each child's share under the interest option, with the right to withdraw all or any part of that share or to elect any settlement option in the policy. While the minor is named as beneficiary, his guardian or trustee during minority may elect the type of settlement best suited for the child as needs arise. This plan is simple and flexible, but it does not of itself provide the ideal solution, because life insurance companies cannot usually make payments directly to a minor. If the minor is named directly, payments will be administered by a court-appointed guardian, which can prove very costly.

A popular procedure in larger estates is to use a formal trust agreement, often naming a corporate trustee. Some companies permit naming an individual trustee in the policy to administer payments for specified minor beneficiaries, but merely naming the trustee without specifying powers and duties may give rise to certain legal problems.

A better approach, and one which seems to overcome the usual difficulties associated with payment of insurance proceeds or income to minor beneficiaries, is to spell out general trust powers in an income settlement agreement which names a trustee. Such an arrangement is discussed more fully in Chapter 56, as well as other methods of providing income for children.

Obviously, it is important for the client to consult his attorney regarding the use of trust provisions in a life insurance income settlement agreement, as well as the various other methods of settling proceeds for minor beneficiaries.

Educational Funds

It is generally recognized that life insurance is an excellent vehicle for accumulating funds to provide higher education for young people. Sometimes an endowment policy on the child's life is used for this purpose, but it is usually preferable to have the insurance issued on a parent's life. Normally, the father is insured, but sometimes the circumstances indicate insurance on the mother's life.

Assuming the life insured is the father's, educational funds are usually payable to the wife as primary beneficiary. Most men prefer to allow their wives full discretion in handling these funds, often by settling proceeds under the interest option with right to withdraw principal and to elect other options. Special educational income provisions are not required in case the wife also dies before the child or children finish college, if each child's share is also retained at interest with right to withdraw or change options. The child's guardian or a named trustee may act on his behalf to withdraw funds as needed or to set up an appropriate income when he is ready for college.

Some parents, however, prefer to set up definite monthly income patterns for the child, both before and during college. These may be arranged in a variety of ways under the standard settlement options, or under the special educational settlement plans offered by most companies. For example, payments for college expenses can be set to commence at a definite time, or when requested by the child's mother—or his guardian or trustee if she is not living—or when evidence is furnished that the child has enrolled in a school of higher learning. Maintenance income may be made payable on a twelve-month basis, or perhaps for nine or ten months in each college year if the child is expected to work during summer vacations. Tuition and other expenses falling due by semesters can be covered by special extra payments at the beginning of each semester and, if desired, a final "graduation gift" check can be arranged.

Whatever the general pattern, it is important to keep educational settlement provisions as simple and flexible as possible, and particularly to consider the channels through which such funds should be paid if both parents die before the child finishes college.

Special Purpose Funds

In addition to providing for basic family requirements, life insurance proceeds are often used to meet various special situations or secondary needs. For example, one might wish to provide for one or more aged relatives. Frequently, it may be necessary to make such provision, as where a son is the sole or chief support of his parents.

If the older person lives with the insured, his or her requirements may be considered as part of the total family income that should be paid to the widow, but a direct provision may be more desirable. If total life insurance is adequate, it is easy to allocate a portion of the proceeds to the older person. This portion might be settled on the interest option, with a limited or unlimited withdrawal privilege and, of course, the right to change to other options. Or it might be settled on the fixed-amount option or, depending upon age and condition of health, on the life income option with an appropriate period certain.

In any case, the widow and children normally should be named contingent beneficiaries. Insofar as permitted by company practice, proceeds coming to them at the death of the older relative should be added to the other insurance payable to them and dovetailed into the overall pattern of family income.

Another special purpose fund might provide for Christmas, birthday, or anniversary gifts. Proceeds can be held on deposit, with interest payable annually at Christmas or at some other specified time. The fixed-amount option is often used to pay a stated sum each year on some such particular date, or the interest option with a right to withdraw a limited sum of principal annually at the specified time.

Many people are interested in religious, charitable, or educational institutions and would like to make some provision for them through life insurance. Such bequests to qualified organizations are exempt from death taxes, and where the organization is the owner of the life insurance policy, premiums thereon are considered as contributions for income tax purposes. Generally, any payment of proceeds to such an organization should be made in a lump sum, but it is most important that the organization be clearly named and identified.

Settlement options enter the charitable bequest picture primarily where it is desired to name a religious, charitable, or educational institution to receive whatever may remain after the death of all members of the insured's immediate family. Whether or not it is possible to make any direct bequests, many policyowners would like to name such organizations as final contingent beneficiaries of policies allocated to family needs. This can readily be arranged by incorporating appropriate provisions into the income settlement agreements covering distribution of policy proceeds.

SOME GENERAL RULES

Election of Settlement Options

Usually, the owner of a life insurance policy may specify that proceeds be payable under one of the income options. In most cases the owner is the insured, but sometimes the owner is a person or corporation other than the insured. Generally, where the insured owns the policy, he may elect settlement options for beneficiaries or for payments to himself. In the latter case, the options may usually be applied either to the proceeds of a matured endowment policy or to the cash value of some other permanent contract. Company practices vary as to the extent to which an owner who is not the insured may utilize the settlement options.

After the insured's death the beneficiary of a lump-sum settlement may normally elect an income plan instead of taking the cash. Also, a beneficiary may be able to change an income plan set up before the death of the insured, to the extent that the income plan permits such changes to be made.

The extent to which trustees or business entities, as owners or beneficiaries of life insurance policies, can use the settlement options varies with the company and the circumstances. For example, the proceeds of business life insurance purchased to fund a buy-and-sell agreement can often be set up under settlement options, while at the same time giving the corporation or other purchaser of the deceased's business interest, as well as his estate, access to the proceeds until the buy-and-sell transaction is completed. Settlement options are frequently used in connection with life insurance purchased to support pension and deferred compensation plans for employees.

Basic Company Rules for Using Options

As a rule, not less than $1,000 may be placed under a settlement option. A number of companies have raised this minimum to $2,000 in recent years. Often a minimum installment is also specified in the policy, such as a periodic installment of not less than $10 or $20 to each beneficiary. In addition to these limitations, the fixed-amount option usually contains an additional requirement that installments be not less than a specified minimum rate per $1,000 of initial proceeds, perhaps $5.00 or $6.00 per month per $1,000. This is to insure that all proceeds and interest will be paid out in a reasonable period of time.

Company rules also limit the length of time that proceeds will be retained under a settlement option. These apply primarily to the interest option, as liquidation of proceeds is generally automatic within a reasonable time under the installment and life income options. Most companies will retain proceeds at interest for the lifetime of the primary beneficiary or until the death of the survivor of joint primary beneficiaries. Some companies will also hold proceeds for the lifetime of a contingent beneficiary, but the majority will not. Frequently, a time limit of thirty years after the death of the insured is specified for proceeds held at interest for a contingent beneficiary. In a few cases, the time limit for a contingent beneficiary is expressed in terms of his or her age, usually between age 21 and age 35. Normally, interest payments cannot be continued to a third beneficiary.

Requesting Settlement Agreements[2]

Income settlement agreements may be requested in the application for a new policy. However, in most cases, space is inadequate to describe properly what is wanted, and a separate memorandum is better. Obviously, in the case of a policy already in force, some kind of letter or memorandum is indicated.

Many companies have simplified this procedure by furnishing check lists or form letters for use by agents of their own or of other companies. An increasing number of companies have carried this one step further in furnishing settlement agreements themselves in check list form. One copy of such a check list is returned to the insured for attachment to his policy,

---

[2] Appendix R illustrates a specimen settlement agreement. Appendixes S and T show a typical settlement option request form and a typical "block" settlement agreement.

after being recorded and certified by the home office. Some companies still handle settlement option elections by means of individually drafted agreements and by physically endorsing the arrangement on the policy itself.

PROPER USE OF SETTLEMENT OPTIONS

It is relatively easy to use settlement option income rates to help measure needs for life insurance in terms of income. Not so easy is the job of designing an income settlement plan that will actually distribute the life insurance proceeds, once they have been created, for the maximum benefit of those whom the insurance is to protect. Often, there is a temptation to make the plan too flexible, actually little more than a lump-sum settlement. On the other hand, there is the opposite temptation to tie proceeds up too tightly, without reasonable provision for unforeseen changes in needs. All cases, whether simple or complex, also require frequent and conscientious review to keep them up to date with changing family circumstances.

The practitioner will find available many sources of the detailed additional knowledge necessary to help him do an adequate job in this area.

SELECTED REFERENCES

FLITCRAFT, INC. *Settlement Options.* New York, published annually.

LIFE INSURANCE AGENCY MANAGEMENT ASSOCIATION. *The How of Settlement Options.* Hartford, 1959.

REDEKER, HARRY S., and REID, CHARLES K., II. Rev. ed. *Life Insurance Settlement Options.* Homewood, Ill.: Richard D. Irwin, Inc., 1964.

Chapter 58

TRUSTS AND THEIR USES

BY FREDERICK C. ROZELLE, JR.

The trust device has an ancient history. It has been traced back through the English common law of the fifteenth century to the Germanic institution of the Salman, and similarities can be found in the old Roman and Hindu laws. The modern history of trusts in America, however, especially as to their widespread use, covers only recent decades.

The wealth of our nation, in terms of dollars, is now held by a much larger group of people than at the beginning of the twentieth century. Individuals and families have sought the use of competent management for this wealth, frequently during their lifetime, but especially for the time after their death. A logical development of this need for financial management has been the growth of the trusts and the development of a large number of institutions intended to provide this financial management.

Since the subject of trusts is immensely broad and complex, a brief treatment of the subject must necessarily omit many major areas and treat in an elemental manner the subjects included. This chapter deals only with the principal trusts used in the estate planning process.

Nature of a Trust

A trust may be defined as a method or instrument under which one person (the *donor* or *settlor*) transfers property to another person (the *trustee*) for administration and distribution in a certain manner for the benefit of a third person (the trust *beneficiary*). Hence the distinguishing feature of a trust is found in the fact that the legal title to property is in one person while the beneficial interest in that property is in another person. The common denominator of all true trusts is the separation of the legal and beneficial interests in property.

Purposes of a Trust

The purposes of estate planning trusts may be summarized as follows:

1. To provide competent management of the property in an estate for the benefit of those in whom the donor is most interested, thereby relieving

the family of the burden of financial management and losses from poor management.

2. To obviate the need for a guardian of property for those for whom such an arrangement would otherwise be necessary, such as minor children or legally incompetent adults. An able trustee can provide for the use of trust assets in the best possible way for such beneficiaries, with great flexibility and with the opportunity for individual judgment, and without the attendant restrictions and expenses of a legal guardianship. At the same time, one type of care or control can be provided for one beneficiary for whom such control is desirable, while quite different provisions can be made for another—all within a single trust instrument.
3. To provide for the splitting of trust income among several beneficiaries in order to shift income from those in higher income tax brackets in favor of those with lower incomes. In this way, each trust beneficiary normally is taxed only for the income he receives and in his own income tax bracket, thus providing more purchasing power for the individual beneficiaries. This kind of objective is accomplished, for example, by giving the trustee the discretion to pay out the income among "the members of the group consisting of my wife, my issue, and my father and mother." Although income tax benefits are frequently obtained by a trust with such "spray" or "sprinkling" powers, this kind of trust is more usually used where the donor realizes that his beneficiaries' needs vary and is anxious to make it possible for the trustee to meet these requirements—as in the case where both spouses have died leaving children. Since the children are going to have different clothing, medical, and educational needs at different times, the spray powers enable a trustee to direct the income and/or principal of the trust to those whose needs are temporarily most critical, leaving the final "equal" distribution to the time when the youngest living child is through college.[1]
4. To resolve the dilemma of the average donor of a trust, who is torn between giving his beneficiaries full access to the assets of his estate and protecting them from the dangers of their own weaknesses. To protect against the latter, the donor may well include a "spendthrift trust" clause to preclude the reaching of assets of the trust by the creditors of the beneficiary or by one to whom a beneficiary might sell or assign his interest for the dubious benefit of obtaining spendable "cash."[2]
5. To eliminate successive transfer costs. Trusts have not only the ability to assure qualification of a full marital deduction share of an estate, but also the ability to create a separate share which gives adequate benefit to a spouse, for example, while remaining "nonmarital" in tax character. This latter share, while includable in the donor's estate for federal estate tax purposes, will not normally be included again in the spouse's estate. Since it need not necessarily be taxed again for several generations, this can save a considerable amount of federal estate taxes. The number of generations through which such trusts can be perpetuated is limited by the law of the state controlling the operation of the trusts; this law is usually referred to as "the rule against perpetuities."
6. To make it easily possible to co-ordinate income-producing assets of divergent natures into a single, easily managed instrumentality.

---

[1] An excellent example of this type of trust is the one which Anderson Bridge established in the specimen trust included in Appendix U.

[2] See Article Ten in the specimen trust in Appendix U.

The Basic Types of Trust

The two basic types of trusts are the living (or *inter vivos*) trust and the testamentary trust. A *living trust* is one that is definitely and expressly created by the donor during his lifetime and becomes operative during his lifetime. It may be revocable or irrevocable and, as a matter of fact, may be revocable for a certain period and then irrevocable, or vice versa. While it may be relatively inactive during the donor's life, because it limits the duties of the trustee, it necessarily has a separate legal existence and is affected by the donor's will only insofar as the provisions of the two may relate to each other.

The *testamentary trust* is one created in the will of the donor (who is then the testator), and its terms and provisions are all contained in the will. This type of trust comes into being at the time when the will is finally probated and the estate settled.

Uses of Testamentary Trusts

Historically, the testamentary trust is the more important type of trust, but in current estate planning it is used far less frequently than the living trust. It seems to offer very few advantages over the living trust. Perhaps the most significant of these are:

1. Because the carrying-out of the terms of the will is a matter of concern to the probate courts, the operation of the trust is supervised by these courts, and it is the obligation of the trustee to file regular and accurate accounts with the courts. Thus the testamentary trust provides a watchdog function, which can be especially important where there are individuals, and not necessarily able ones, serving as trustees.
2. In some jurisdictions a testamentary trust offers the only opportunity to co-ordinate all income-producing property under the terms of one trust, since the living trust technique is not usable for this purpose.

Uses of Living Trusts

The living trust is especially suitable as a primary estate planning vehicle.

Frequently, an individual reaches the point where he becomes aware that he does not have the time, the inclination, the talent, nor the health to maintain supervision of his investments. The living trust is an ideal solution to this problem, for, in addition to giving him the investment management services he wishes, it offers a way to continue the payment of income and principal without any interruption at the time of his death or in the event of his incapacity. At the same time, it gives him an opportunity to measure the effectiveness of his trustee during his lifetime while any appropriate change still can be made. The principal reason for the establishment of the living trust may be, for example, encroaching age or poor health. If the donor gives adequate powers to the trustee in the living trust, the trustee can then assume the entire burden of maintaining all the donor's financial affairs in a proper state of order, including the payment of bills, filing of income tax returns, seeing to the adequacy of medical care and living accommodations, and the important and often overlooked function of providing for the donor's entire family.

Usually, on the death of the donor, the living trust will either continue for the benefit of or provide for the distribution of its assets to other beneficiaries. Since this process normally takes place outside the jurisdiction of the probate courts, the assets of the trust are generally not subject to the usual executors' fees, legal and other expenses, delays, or involvements of probating the will (if there is one) of the donor. Furthermore, the living trust is rarely subject to the kind of challenge to which a will may be subjected; even more rarely is such a challenge successful.

Because a living trust is in the nature of a private agreement between the various parties concerned, it is not a matter of public record, and its size and terms are not public knowledge. This greatly lessens the beneficiaries' attractiveness to all those whose self-dealing interests might otherwise cause them to pay a visit.

The laws of many states limit the kinds of trustees which can be selected to serve in a testamentary trust. Not infrequently, for example, a state will forbid an out-of-state corporate fiduciary from serving as trustee. A living trust greatly increases the donor's freedom in selecting a trustee of the property which he is willing to include in his trust—though in some areas, where competent local management abounds, this is of less concern that in others.

When used as the primary estate planning vehicle with a co-ordinated will, the living trust seems to be the simplest way to combine all the income-producing property into one easily managed, efficient, and effective fund. This is accomplished, in most cases, by the use of a so-called "pour-over" will, which simply directs the executor to pay all the debts and expenses of the estate, to fulfill whatever specific bequests the testator wishes to make (such as leaving all the tangible personal effects to his wife), and then to take any remaining property—the "rest and residue" of the estate—and pay it to the then trustees of the previously established living trust. This pour-over technique is certainly the preferred technique in many jurisdictions—particularly where the assets of the estate include substantial life insurance—and has led to the development of the life insurance trust, a particular kind of living trust.

Life Insurance Trust

The term "life insurance trust" is a generic one used here to describe an arrangement whereby a donor creates an inactive, or "unfunded," living trust (as opposed to the previously described "funded" living trust) and designates the trustees of the trust as the beneficiary of his life insurance.

Often the donor deposits the policies with the trustees. By the terms of the trust and the policies, the donor carefully reserves to himself all the rights of ownership in the policies, including the right to cash them in, to change the beneficiary, and to borrow on them. He has the obligation to pay the premiums. The trustee's only responsibility, then, is to be able to return the policies to the donor when he wants them. Effectively, the donor has simply said to the trustee: "If I die before I change my mind, this is what I want you to do with the money you're going to receive. *But* I reserve the right to change my mind either by changing the policies or amending the trust instrument, or by revoking the whole arrangement." The trustee has, then, little or nothing to do during the donor's lifetime and, accordingly, generally makes no charge for his services until the trust becomes active.

Obviously, a life insurance trust becomes active at the instant of the death of the donor; but a thoughtfully drafted one will allow for the possibility that the donor will, for one or more of the reasons mentioned above, wish to activate the trust during his lifetime by delivering cash, securities, or other property to the trustees for them to manage. Such provisions are particularly valuable for the donor who suddenly must leave on an extended business trip and wants his property effectively managed while he is gone, or for the donor who expects shortly to undergo a major operation, the prognosis of which is uncertain or unfavorable. Thus, a life insurance trust may simply become a normal, active, funded living trust for temporary or extended periods of time.

Out of the concept of the life insurance trust has grown the idea of other types of inactive trusts which exist largely to be the recipient of the pour-over from the probate estate. Some of these include merely a nominal amount of cash, while others have a Series "E" bond as the corpus. But they all have in common the fact that little or nothing in the way of duties on the part of the trustees is called for; therefore, there is little or no attendant expense.

Mention has been made of the "inactive trust-pour-over will" technique as being the basis for the preferred approach to the estate plan, and there are a number of reasons for this. In the first place, a testamentary trust is uncertain—it may never be established and, in any case, is usually not established until the administration of the estate is complete, which could involve many years. Wills are always subject to the challenge of interested parties, which adds to the delay, and they are occasionally disallowed for one or more reasons.

Not infrequently, it is desirable or necessary to keep an estate open for as many years as possible. Among the things which make this necessary are those mentioned above, as well as the claims of normal creditors; suits against the estate for imagined or real injuries from automobile accidents, malpractice, and the like; and the settlement or compromise of differences between the taxing authorities and the executor on such points as the qualification for the marital deduction, the value of future interests, or the valuation of a business interest. If the executor has elected under Section 6166 of the Internal Revenue Code to pay the estate tax in installments, then the estate may be open for as many as ten years, and sometimes the executor will *want* to keep the estate open to take advantage of the leverage provided by the fact that the estate is a separate income-tax-paying entity. In any estate of material size, it is highly unlikely that the estate will be settled within a year because the executor will wish to analyze the wisdom of electing the optional valuation date a year from the date of death; and usually, he will wait the allowable fifteen months from the date of death before he pays the federal estate tax.

In addition to the element of uncertainty, however, other factors make the testamentary trust approach less desirable, especially where the estate planner wants to include life insurance proceeds as a part of the trust assets. In the first place, life insurance companies in general are unwilling to designate trustees of a testamentary trust as the beneficiary of the policies (for a variety of reasons) and prefer to make the policies payable simply to the estate. But if the proceeds are paid to the estate, many of the unique aspects of life insurance are lost, for the proceeds then become subject to the claims of the creditors of the insured, subject to estate-settling expenses, including executors' fees, and subject in many jurisdictions to state estate or inheritance taxes which normally would not be levied. Furthermore, in the case of those relatively few insurance companies which are willing that trustees of a testamentary trust be designated, most will only wait a limited period of time (such as two years after death) for the trust to be established before they will insist that outright payment be made to the executors instead. Lastly, if all the life insurance is payable to the estate or testamentary trust, the family is left with the problem of how to obtain sufficient money to cover living expenses while the estate is being settled; widow's allowances from an estate frequently have a way of being inadequate.

Much life insurance is purchased and owned for the purpose of meeting the liquidity needs of an estate, and a life insurance trust is almost essential if this purpose is to be assured and to be fulfilled economically. What are the alternatives to the use of such a trust? Life insurance can be made payable to the estate, but this is often undesirable and expensive. The insured's wife may simply be designated as beneficiary, but there is little or no assurance that she will be alive or able to use the insurance proceeds. Even if she is alive and well, it may be very undesirable from the point of view of her own self-interest for her to give money to the executor to meet the debts and expenses of the estate. If she dies with the insured and the proceeds go into her estate or to minor children, there is a virtual guarantee that the proceeds *cannot* be used to meet the insured's liquidity needs.

Thus the life insurance trust is the most satisfactory way that life insurance can be wisely and discriminatingly used for liquidity purposes. The trustee can be authorized to use his discretion in making the funds available to the executor—can do so in the best interests of the family, and can withhold the funds when it is not.[3]

In a few jurisdictions, it may be undesirable to make use of the pour-over procedure because of unique local conditions, but even in these jurisdictions the life insurance trust can be very valuable for the management and disbursement of the insurance proceeds during the time the estate is being settled. Then, when the testamentary trust is established, the life insurance trust can terminate and pour over to the trustees of the testamentary trust.

A Special Type of Inactive Trust

Frequently, a special type of inactive trust is established by the owner of a closely held corporation who wants his business continued after his death. Let us assume that this corporation pays no dividends (and this is a factor only insofar as trustees' fees are concerned). The owner merely transfers his stock from himself to his living trust, makes himself a co-trustee of the trust, and reserves to himself as trustee all the voting power and control and responsibility for the close corporation stock. Thus the other trustees have nothing to do, unless the stock is dividend-paying, and consequently make no charge.

This arrangement is a highly desirable one from a number of points of view—the most important being that it assures uninterrupted management of the corporation either in the event of the owner's death or in the event of his incapacity. Continuity is provided by the owner's own selection of successor management through his choice of the cotrustee, who, by the terms of the trust, will assume active responsibility either the instant the owner dies or as soon as the other trustee can determine the extent to which an accident or illness has affected his competency. Otherwise, upon the occurrence of any of these events, a delay—a hiatus—is bound to occur in the estate. It is a matter of weeks before the executor can be appointed and given the authority to act; and in the case of disability, very likely a much longer time will pass before the donor's incompetence can be legally established and a conservator or guardian appointed. This delay could be, and has been, fatal to a number of businesses. Also, because the stock in the corporation would pass to the heirs according to the terms of the trust rather than by the terms of the will, effective management of the

---

[3] See Article Fourteen in the Anderson Bridge trust in Appendix U.

business would not be deferred by the delays, red tape, and expenses of settling the donor's estate. Further economies thus would be effected. The efficacy of this arrangement depends most of all upon a well-drafted trust with adequate powers for the trustees to act. Quality draftsmanship is the key to any effective trust—as well as the thoughtful selection of trustees who will always act only in the interest of the donor rather than in their own interest.

The Irrevocable Living Trust

Heavy emphasis has been given in this analysis to the use of revocable living trusts—ones which can be terminated at any time by a simple act of the donor. There is also the irrevocable type of living trust not subject to termination by the donor. Irrevocable trusts are generally useful only for highly specialized purposes, and one cannot be too cautious in approaching the establishment of such a trust with deliberate care.

Irrevocable trusts can be separated into at least four different categories: (1) short-term trusts, (2) trusts which are established to conform with Section 2503(*c*) of the Internal Revenue Code, (3) long-term trusts, and (4) trusts which are irrevocable for the duration of a special need. One final caveat: Almost inevitably, irrevocable trusts involve one or more areas of the gift tax law, and one should be careful to be sure he knows whether his gift is of a present interest for gift tax purposes and therefore qualifies for the annual exclusion, or whether it is of a future interest for gift tax purposes and does not qualify for the annual exclusion, or both. The importance of this distinction is borne out by the fact that under the terms of the annual exclusion a single donor may give up to $3,000 per year to as many donees as he wishes without having to pay a gift tax on the gift and without having to file a gift tax return for the gift. One must also take care to be aware of any estate tax considerations which might result from the donor's having retained some interest in the property of the trust or power over the trust itself. Obviously, the counsel of an able tax lawyer should be sought before any move is irretrievable.

The expression "short-term trust," when used in its most popular sense, refers to that type of trust with a minimum life of more than 10 years, or for a beneficiary's lifetime which is expected not to be significantly greater and could be somewhat shorter. An illustration is the case of a man (or woman) who supports his spouse's parent. He can, perhaps, afford with reasonable ease to do this out of his own income after income taxes; but if he is in a high tax bracket, it takes considerable gross income to give an adequate net-after-tax amount to his wife's parent. If he has, on the other hand, income-producing property, the use of which and the income from which he feels he can forgo, he can put that property in a trust lasting for the life of the parent, or 10 years and a day, whichever is shorter, with the result that the income can be paid to the parent and taxed to the parent (presumably at lower tax rates) rather than to himself. The property itself may revert to the donor when the trust terminates.

This illustration has been selected to avoid the complicating factor of a state law which obligates the donor to support the beneficiary. There are many areas where the obligation to support does not exist, and the short-term trust will normally be successful in splitting the income away from the donor's personal income tax picture when used in these areas. However, most states recognize that a man is obligated to support his children until they are 21 and to support his wife, and there is reason to believe that in some states he has the obligation to provide some support for his parents. Where a short-term trust is set up to fulfill such an obligation, or any other legal obligation of the donor, it seems that the income from the trust inevitably will be taxed to the donor.

On the other hand, if it is intended that the trust accumulate the income for 10 years and then terminate, with the accumulated income going to a wife or child and the principal reverting to the donor, then it currently seems clear that the income will not be taxed to the donor, nor will it be taxed to the donee except for the last year's income when the trust terminates. It will, of course, be taxed to the trust.

The general purpose of a short-term trust is, then, to give away the income from property for any of a variety of reasons and to separate that income from the donor's own taxable income, but still to retain the ultimate use of the principal by having it revert to the donor at some future time which, if measured by the calendar, is more than 10 years from the time the trust is established or later additions to it are made.

It is sometimes intended, however, that the trust principal not revert to the donor but rather that it be distributed to the income beneficiary, or even a third beneficiary, when the trust is partially or completely terminated. If such a trust is for a minor and is distributed to the minor at age 21, then the trust falls within the area of Section 2503(*c*) of the current tax code and takes its name from that section. If the trust conforms to the provisions of Section 2503(*c*), the gifts made to the trust are of a present interest, for gift tax purposes, even though enjoyment of the gift by the child may be deferred until that time in the future when he reaches the age of 21. Otherwise, such a trust would fall into the category of long-term trusts.

The third group of irrevocable trusts may be referred to as "long-term trusts" to distinguish the purposes of such trusts from those of the short-term trusts. In the case of short-term trusts, as the expression is used by sophisticated practitioners, the gift of the donor is only of the income from the trust, while in the case of long-term trusts, the gift is of both the income and the trust property itself, though not necessarily to the same parties. The Section 2503(*c*) trusts would all be of the long-term variety but for their specific treatment by the Internal Revenue Code.

Long-term irrevocable trusts are most frequently used where it is the desire of the donor to have a modicum of control and investment management provided for a beneficiary who is, perhaps, either immature or otherwise unable adequately to handle the property himself. It is also used where none of the just-mentioned considerations are involved but where the trust is, for tax reasons, to run through more than one generation before its assets are to be distributed. The trusts may contain almost any provisions which the donor wishes, as long as they are legal and practical, with income and principal being made available only under certain conditions, or under any conditions, or in the trustees' discretion, as with the spray trust mentioned earlier. However, it should be remembered that long-term irrevocable trusts usually involve gifts of a future interest as well as gifts of a present interest.

Occasionally, irrevocable trusts are set up by a donor to protect himself from his own weaknesses. Perhaps he is subject to cyclical mental illness and wants his funds protected during periods of temporary aberration. Perhaps he wishes protection against his own judgment in a proposed business undertaking or during unusually high earning years (as with a movie star, a baseball player, or a prize fighter.) Such trusts normally involve no income or gift tax considerations and exist only for the duration of the particular need, and are irrevocable only to keep the donor from changing his mind at an inopportune time.

Business Insurance Trust

Business continuation agreements are frequently made subject to the terms of business insurance trusts. Such trusts are designed to put the trustee in the position of being the stakeholder, and the parties to the trust generally rely on the trustee to be an impartial referee who sees to it that the terms of the agreement are faithfully carried out. As the holder of both the corporate stock (where appropriate) and the insurance policies (if they are the funding medium), the trustee sees to it that the business does not suffer, sometimes disastrously, through unnecessary delay in the purchase of the deceased's interest. Also, the trustee may help the deceased's family in negotiating with an associate who recognizes the strength of the position from which he bargains and decides to renege or otherwise fail to keep his end of the bargain.

With a trustee who usually gets as his fee only a small percentage of the funds which pass through his hands, all parties are assured of a policeman whose sole motivation and responsibility are that the purchase-and-sale agreement is the cause of an orderly transition in the life of the business rather than a disorderly, heartbreaking, and expensive series of court battles.

SELECTED REFERENCES

CASNER, A. JAMES. *Estate Planning*. 3d ed. Boston: Little, Brown & Co., 1961. Supplement, 1963.

SCOTT, AUSTIN WAKEMAN. *Abridgment of the Law of Trusts*. Boston: Little, Brown & Co., 1960.

SHATTUCK, MAYO ADAMS, and FARR, JAMES F. *An Estate Planner's Handbook*. 2d ed. Boston: Little, Brown & Co., 1953.

STEPHENSON, GILBERT T. *Drafting Wills and Trust Agreements*. 2 Vols. Boston: Little, Brown & Co., 1952 and 1955.

TRACHTMAN, JOSEPH. *Estate Planning*. New York: Practicing Law Institute, 1964.

Chapter 59

TAXATION OF LIFE AND HEALTH INSURANCE

BY WILLIAM J. BOWE

Income, gift, and estate taxation of life and health insurance policies and their proceeds will be treated in this chapter. The discussion will be almost exclusively restricted to the federal tax laws. State laws vary widely in detail, though in general they tend to follow the main principles of the federal statute. Frequently, substantial differences result from the fact that while a state has adopted the federal pattern as of a particular date, it has failed to amend its law to conform to more recent federal changes.

INCOME TAXATION OF LIFE INSURANCE

Proceeds Received by Reason of Death

The federal law treats the proceeds of life insurance paid by reason of the death of an insured quite differently from gains on policies that mature during the lifetime of an insured. This major distinction should be kept in mind in reading the material that follows. Speaking very generally, death proceeds escape income tax; proceeds from policies that mature during life are treated the same as most other receipts.

Lump-Sum Payments. Where the insured's beneficiary on his death receives the proceeds in a lump sum, the entire gain is exempt from income tax.[1] This is frequently thought of as according special tax favoritism to life insurance contracts, but this is true only with respect to a limited group of cases. If a husband pays $10,000 of premiums during his life on a $25,000 policy owned by him and payable to his wife, and the wife on his death receives the face amount in a lump sum, the entire gain of $15,000 escapes income tax. But the same would be true if the husband had purchased General Motors stock for $10,000 and left it by will to his

[1] Internal Revenue Code, Sec. 101.

wife at a time when it was worth $25,000. However, if the wife had purchased a policy on her husband's life, the insurance exemption would still apply, whereas his death would not eliminate any profit she might have on any other asset owned by her.[2] Hence, to this extent, insurance is favored by our federal income tax laws.

The insurance exemption applies to business insurance as well as individual insurance. It is immaterial whether the beneficiary is an individual, a partnership, a trust, or a corporation, or whether the insurance was taken out for family or business reasons. There are some important exceptions to this rule of tax exemption. While they are of limited application, they have occasionally caused substantial hardships that might have been avoided. Thus the transfer-for-value rule frequently has been a pitfall for the uninformed. Occasionally, the full amount of the proceeds may be taxed as a dividend or as compensation or as alimony.[3] These exceptions are treated later in this chapter.

Interest Option. Where the proceeds are left at interest on the death of the insured, the annual interest payments are taxable as ordinary income to the primary beneficiary. The principal amount, when later paid, is exempt. Thus, if a husband designates his wife to receive the interest for her life, the face amount to be paid to the children on her death, the interest payments to the wife constitute taxable income; the principal payments to the children are tax-exempt.

Installment Options. Prior to the 1954 Code, the entire amount received under any installment option was included within the exemption, whether the installments were to be received over a fixed number of years, or for life, or for life with a stated number of years guaranteed. This rule was criticized as being unduly favorable. Obviously, part of every payment under an installment option is made up of earnings on the principal amount held by the company. Thus, if the face amount were $50,000 and the option selected guaranteed installments for ten years, the annual installments, for purposes of illustration, may be assumed to be $5,500. The extra $500 would represent not the proceeds of the insurance, but rather the interest received as a result of the investment of the proceeds by the company. Congress determined in 1954 to tax this "interest element." First, it should be noted that the change applies only to insureds dying after August 16, 1954. For this reason, many beneficiaries are today receiving, and will continue to receive for many years, installment payments that are fully exempt, since they are governed by the old

---

[2] This statement is subject to the exception that in a community property state the surviving spouse's interest in the community property receives a new cost basis on the death of the other spouse.

[3] Where the policy represents a pure gamble, i.e., where the policy is taken out by one who has no insurable interest in the life of the insured, the proceeds may be taxed for what they really are—gambling profits.

law. Second, Congress felt that the tax advantage inherent in the old law might properly be retained, at least partially, in the case of widows in order to discourage the selection of lump-sum payments with the consequent temptation to squander the proceeds. Hence, the 1954 Code provides a special "interest element exclusion" of $1,000 in the case of a surviving spouse (widow or widower) with respect to all policies on an insured's life.

Assume that a husband died after August 16, 1954. He left a $50,000 policy, the proceeds to be paid in installments of $5,500 a year to his daughter for 10 years. To determine the amount to be excluded from income each year as principal, the face amount may be divided by the number of years of anticipated payments. In this case the portion to be excluded from gross income each year is $5,000. Over the 10-year period the full face amount will be received tax-free. All amounts received each year in excess of $5,000 will be taxable as ordinary income.

Suppose the installments are for the beneficiary's (other than the insured's spouse) life rather than for a fixed number of years. In this case the face amount may be divided by the beneficiary's present life expectancy. Assume this to be 20 years and the face amount to be $50,000. All amounts received in excess of $2,500 per year would be taxable. Of course, in this case, it is quite possible that the beneficiary may not live for his exact expectancy. Hence the assurance of receiving exactly the face amount tax-free is uncertain. Because the $2,500 yearly exclusion continues for his life, he may receive more or less than the face amount tax-free, depending on how long he lives. Congress felt, however, that it would be preferable to fix the amount of the exclusion definitely at the start, in the interest of simplicity of administration.

Where, as is most frequently the case, the installment option selected will be for life with a fixed number of years guaranteed, the problem becomes somewhat more complicated.[4] Assume that the option in the above case was for the wife for life with 20 years certain, any remaining installments (in the event of her death before the expiration of the 20-year period) to go to the daughter. Here the value of the refund feature, the contingent rights of the daughter, must first be subtracted from the face amount before the wife's yearly exclusion may be determined. For purposes of illustration, let us assume the refund feature to have a value of $5,000. Assume further that the wife has a 20-year expectancy. Thus, the amount she is entitled to receive tax-free is $45,000, and the amount to be excluded under the general rule each year from her income would be $2,250. In addition, as the wife of the insured, she may,

[4] The Regulations set forth in detail examples and tables that may be referred to for the solution of particular cases. In this connection, it should be noted that the Regulations provide that the life expectancy of a beneficiary is to be determined by the insurance company's mortality tables.

of course, exclude an additional $1,000 because of the special interest element exclusion noted above.

This change in the law has to some extent removed the tax advantage formerly available through use of an installment option. However, the special $1,000 exception in favor of a spouse means that in most cases the current law is as favorable as the old rule where a husband or wife is the primary beneficiary.

Transfer-for-Value Rule. Unfortunately, the Code has long contained a provision that the rules as to tax exemption do not apply where the policy has been sold or transferred for value. Assume that A takes out a policy on his own life for $50,000, pays two $1,000 premiums, and sells the policy to B for $1,500. B subsequently pays three $1,000 premiums, and A dies. On receipt of the $50,000 proceeds, B becomes taxable on his entire profit, $45,500 ($50,000 less his cost, i.e., $1,500 purchase price plus $3,000 premiums). Congress was apparently afraid that people might speculate in policies as they do in stocks or real estate. To the extent that this is true, of course, the same tax consequences should apply to profits made on insurance contracts as on other investments. But it is extremely doubtful that the few cases where such speculations are entered into are sufficiently significant to offset the cases of extreme hardship that have arisen from the application of these rules to typical family situations.

The rule had such undesirable effects on business transactions, particularly buy-and-sell agreements, that Congress was persuaded to make an exception to the exception. The rule does not apply under the 1954 Code to transfers of policies for value to the insured, to a partner of the insured, to a partnership of which the insured is a member, or to a corporation of which the insured is a stockholder officer.[5] Thus, it is possible for a corporation to buy an existing policy on the life of a stockholder or for one partner to buy an existing policy on the life of another partner and not run afoul of the rule. This has greatly eased the problems that were encountered in buy-and-sell and stock redemption agreements, but it is unfortunate that Congress did not go all the way and abolish the exception entirely.

A and B are brothers. A has $20,000 of insurance. Personal financial problems prevent his continuing to pay the premiums. He plans to let the policy lapse or to surrender it for its cash value. B, realizing that if this happens, he will most likely have to bear the burden of A's death expense and also help his family, arranges with A to buy the policy from him for its cash value. The policy immediately loses its tax-exempt status. Illustrations might be multiplied. Even in close families, fairness will dictate payment for policies where emergencies arise that require them to be

[5] But note that one stockholder may not buy a policy on the life of another stockholder within this exception.

transferred to other family members who are better able to continue the premium burden. Where children need or think they need immediate funds, parents may hesitate to stand by and see them sacrifice valuable insurance contracts and yet be unwilling to make gifts of the funds needed. Parental discipline frequently dictates that they buy rather than give. Here the motivation for the purchase of an insurance contract will be as remote as can be imagined from the speculation at which the rule was aimed.

About all that can be said is that this unfortunate exception must be constantly kept in mind if disastrous and unnecessary tax consequences are to be avoided.[6] A bill introduced in the 1962 Congress would have exempted from the transfer-for-value rule all cases where the transferee had an insurable interest in the life of the insured at the date of transfer. While it failed of passage, it is hoped that this eminently sensible solution of the problem will ultimately become law.

Proceeds as Compensation. Suppose a corporation takes out key-man insurance on the life of its president. He reaches retirement. The key-man need ceases. However, under a deferred compensation contract the insured is to receive monthly amounts for his life, with a lump payment to his wife at his death. To satisfy this latter obligation, the directors change the beneficiary designation to his wife, retaining, however, all the incidents of ownership in the policy. On receipt of the proceeds, the wife will have compensation income. It is as though the proceeds had been paid to the corporation and then used by it to discharge the postdeath obligation. The corporation will ordinarily be entitled to a deduction for salary paid. But the taxation of the lump sum all in one year may greatly nullify the expected benefit. Further, it is not clear that this income will in all or most cases qualify for the new averaging provisions introduced into the Code in 1964. Hence, it may be preferable in cases like these for the corporation to receive the proceeds and spread the payments to the widow over a period of years in order to keep them within lower brackets.

Proceeds as Dividends. Occasionally, in a family corporation the company will purchase, own, and pay the premiums on insurance on the life of the principal executive stockholder but name his wife and children as beneficiaries. Over the years the wife and children may receive substantial stock interests through gifts. On the death of the insured and the payment of the proceeds to the beneficiaries, they may be treated as having received dividend income. Up to the moment of death the corporation was the owner of a valuable asset, the insurance contract. With the death,

---

[6] Where policies are transferred within the family by absolute assignment to reduce estate taxes, care should be taken to eliminate any possibility that the transferor could be regarded as receiving any value in exchange for the assignment. It must be a pure gift if the transfer-for-value rule is to be avoided.

these rights shifted irrevocably to the stockholders. Whenever a corporate asset passes without a *quid pro quo* from a corporation to a stockholder, there is a dividend to the extent of the corporation's earnings and profits.[7]

In the recent *Doran* case,[8] this rule came into sharp focus. The corporation was considering a buy-and-sell agreement among its stockholders. It was first proposed that the corporation purchase and pay for insurance on the lives of its six stockholders. There was to be a contract among the stockholders that on the death of any one of them the proceeds would be paid to the corporation and disbursed as a special dividend to the surviving stockholders, who would use the money to purchase the stock of the deceased. Obviously, under this arrangement, each survivor would have dividend income. The same result would follow if, instead of naming the corporation beneficiary, the individuals had been designated. The company first applied for a policy on the life of its president, requesting that his estate be named beneficiary. Similar applications were made on the lives of the others. The insurer declined to issue the policies in this form but issued policies with the corporation as beneficiary. These were rejected, and new applications were made for policies to be paid to the president and treasurer of the company as trustees. Unfortunately, it was never made clear who really owned the policies that were issued—the corporation or the stockholders. The trustees were only the nominal owners. The application stated, in the case of the president, "that he was president of the applicant." It stated that the interest which the beneficiary had in the life of the insured was that of "employer." The corporation paid the premiums. All these facts would tend to show the corporation as the real owner. However, the corporation did not carry the policies as assets on its books, an indication that the stockholders were the real owners.

The rules of law are clear. If a corporation pays premiums on insurance owned by a stockholder, the amount of the premium is dividend income to the stockholder. If the corporation owns the policy, it is obviously not income to the stockholder, since he derives no immediate realized benefit from the payment. But if the proceeds are subsequently payable to him, he has dividend income at that time in the amount then received, the face of the policy. What troubled the courts in the Doran case was not the application of these rules but the question of who really owned the policies. The Tax Court thought the corporation was the owner. Hence, it held the proceeds taxable as dividends. The Circuit Court of Appeals held that the stockholders were the real owners. Hence the proceeds were not taxable dividends. While not called upon to decide the question, it

[7] The recent *Ducros* case (246 F.[2d] 49 [1959]) is contra to the statement in the text, but it seems wrong on principle and is generally recognized as of doubtful authority.

[8] *Doran* v. *Commissioner,* 246 F.(2d) 934.

seems clear that on this interpretation of the facts, each premium payment would have been a dividend.

Proceeds as Alimony. Not infrequently, insurance policies are transferred in connection with the settlement of marital rights on divorce. These transfers have raised tax problems. Where the insurance is assigned absolutely to the wife as part of the divorce settlement, she would seem to be a transferee for value. If the husband continues to pay the premiums, each premium payment represents additional alimony income to the wife and is a deductible alimony payment by the husband. On his death and receipt of the proceeds by her, the transferee rules apply. On the other hand, the husband may retain ownership of the policy but promise that it will be used to insure the continuance of postdeath payments to the wife. In this case the premium payments are not alimony (since he owns the contract), but every dollar of every installment payment made to the wife after his death will presumably be taxable as alimony income. Occasionally, the policy is transferred to the wife with a provision that ownership will revert to the husband-insured if his wife predeceases him. Here, no deduction is allowed for the premium payments, since there is no certainty that they will not ultimately be for the benefit of the husband rather than the wife.

Proceeds Received Other Than by Reason of Death

Lump Sum. Where the proceeds become payable during the life of the insured, the profit is subject to income tax. Assume that A purchases an endowment policy in the face amount of $30,000, to mature at age 65. Annual premiums are $600. If he dies before 65, the full amount will be received tax-free by his beneficiary, since the proceeds will become payable by reason of his death. If he lives to be 65 and receives the proceeds in a lump sum, he computes his profit by subtracting from the maturity value his investment in the contract. If we assume he paid net premiums of $500 a year ($600 less dividend reductions averaging $100) for forty years, his cost would amount to $20,000; his taxable gain would be $10,000. Under a liberalized provision of the 1954 Code, the tax on this gain could not be greater than would have been payable had the amount been received ratably over a three-year period. The 1964 Revenue Act repealed this spreading device since all like hardship cases due to "income bunching" in a single year will for the future be taken care of by the new averaging provisions of the Code.

Interest Option. If, prior to maturity, the insured elects the interest option without any immediate right to withdraw the principal, he will delay the recognition of any gain. The gain will be taxed when the face amount becomes available. If this does not occur until his death, the gain will be taxed to the second beneficiary. It will not fall within the insurance exemption, since the proceeds will have lost their "insurance character" on the earlier maturity of the contract.

The interest, of course, will be taxable each year as received.

Installment Options. The rules prior to 1954 were unsatisfactory. In the case of installments to be paid over a fixed number of years, the full amount of each payment was received tax-free until the insured had recovered his investment. Thereafter, every dollar was taxable as ordinary income. Thus, if the investment were $25,000 and the payments were $3,000 a year for 20 years, the first eight payments and one third of the ninth payment were received tax-free. However, where the installments were payable for life, the old 3 per cent rule applied. Under this rule a portion of each payment equal to 3 per cent of the cost was taxed as income; the balance was treated as return of capital. As the rate was unrealistic, in practically no cases did an insured live long enough to recover his investment. The unfairness of this rule tended to encourage the selection of a fixed number of years' option in many cases where, absent tax considerations, the annuity for life (with a minimum number of years certain) would have been preferable.

Under the 1954 Code, these two options are taxed in much the same way. The gain is spread over the years of the anticipated payments.

Assume, by varying slightly the above facts, a $50,000 policy: net cost, $36,000; annual payments from maturity proceeds, $3,000; fixed period, 20 years. The first step is to determine an exclusion ratio. This is done by taking the investment in the contract, $36,000, and dividing it by the expected recovery, $60,000 (20 times $3,000). Sixty thousand dollars divided into $36,000 gives six tenths. Therefore, six tenths of each $3,000 payment, or $1,800, represents return of cost; the excess is taxable income. Over the 20-year period the full amount of the investment will be recovered tax-free. If a life annuity is selected, the expected recovery is based on the annuitant's life expectancy.[9] If the annuity has a minimum number of years guaranteed, then the value of the refund feature is first subtracted from the investment in the contract.

If a policy matured prior to 1954, the taxpayer, before computing his exclusion ratio under the 1954 Code, must first reduce his investment in the contract by the amount received tax-free under the rules of the 1939 Code. If we assume an original cost of $20,000 and that under the old 3 per cent rule the taxpayer had recovered $5,000 tax-free prior to 1954, then his investment for purposes of the new rule will be $15,000. If his expected recovery for all future years is $30,000, then his exclusion ratio for years after 1953 will be 50 per cent.

Prior to 1954, if an insured elected *after* maturity to receive the pro-

---

[9] See footnote 4.

ceeds under one of these options, he was nevertheless taxed as though he had received the proceeds in a lump sum under the doctrine of constructive receipt, since, for a short period, the funds were unqualifiedly available for withdrawal. This obviously was a pitfall, because in many cases, no thought was given to the matter until maturity. The 1954 Code happily corrected this trap by providing a sixty-day grace period after maturity within which an installment option may be selected and the tax spread over the years of actual receipt according to the rules discussed above.

Proceeds as Alimony, Dividend, or Compensation. Just as the proceeds of policies paid by reason of death may be taxable in full because under the circumstances of the particular cases, they are properly classifiable as alimony, or dividend, or compensation, so may the proceeds of policies that mature during life. Assume that A owes B $10,000 for services rendered. To secure the payment, he names B the beneficiary of his endowment policy, retaining, however, the incidents of ownership in the policy (the usual type of collateral assignment). The policy matures, and B receives the proceeds. A will be taxed on the actual gain. B will be taxed on the receipt of $10,000 of compensation income. For illustrations of possible alimony or dividend income, see the earlier discussion.

Gain on Sale of a Policy. Earlier cases appeared to hold that any gain on the sale of a policy received capital gain treatment, on the theory that the policy was a capital asset.[10] The more recent cases hold such gain taxable as ordinary income.

Loss on Sale or Surrender of a Policy. No loss is recognized on the sale or surrender of a policy. The result is justified by the fact that the taxpayer has had the benefit of the protection over the years; hence, in a true economic sense, no loss has been sustained.

Exchange of Policies. Generally speaking, under the 1939 Code, if a policy was exchanged for a different policy, gain was recognized to the extent of the excess in value of the new policy over the net premiums paid for the old policy. To avoid the recognition of this gain, the 1954 Code provided that no gain was to be recognized on the exchange of the following:

1. A whole life contract for another whole life contract, an endowment insurance contract, or an annuity contract.
2. An endowment insurance contract for another endowment insurance contract, if the contract received provides for payments beginning at a date not later than the date payments would have begun under the old contract, or for an annuity contract.
3. An annuity contract for another annuity contract.

---

[10] *Phillips* v. *Commissioner,* 30 TC No. 87 (reversed on appeal, 275 F.[2d] 33).

Note that the exchange of an annuity contract or of an endowment contract for a whole life or limited life contract continues to be a taxable exchange. The reason is to prevent avoidance of tax due on maturity of endowments and annuities by conversions to whole life contracts.

Deductibility of Premiums

Life insurance premiums, with some few exceptions, are not deductible for income tax purposes.[11] Usually, the premium deduction is disallowed as a family or living expense. But even if classifiable as an expense in connection with a business transaction, it will be disallowed under a specific provision which forbids deduction of "premiums paid on any life insurance policy covering the life of any officer or employee or of any other person financially interested in any trade or business carried on by the taxpayer where the taxpayer is directly or indirectly a beneficiary under the policy." Further, the premium payment is to some extent a capital expenditure. In addition, the disallowance is offset by the general rule that the proceeds received by reason of death are tax-free.

Occasionally, the premiums may be deductible not as premiums but as some other type of expense. We have seen that under some circumstances, premiums paid may constitute alimony and hence be deductible. Where an employer pays premiums on policies owned by an employee, the amount of the premium may be deducted as additional compensation. If a policy has been irrevocably assigned to a charity, premium payments thereafter may be deducted under and subject to the limitations of the charitable deduction section. Unless the premium may be characterized as a payment under one of the traditional deduction sections, no deduction is allowed, since none is allowable for premiums as such.

Under the 1954 Code, no interest deduction is allowed in the case of indebtedness incurred or continued to purchase or carry a single premium life insurance, endowment, or annuity contract. In addition, if substantially all the premiums are paid within four years of the date on which the contract was purchased, the contract is treated as if it were a single premium contract. Similarly, where a purchaser borrows an amount equal to a substantial portion of the premiums and, instead of purchasing the policy outright, deposits the funds with the insurer for future premiums, this also is treated as if it were a single premium contract. These rules denying any deduction for interest were made even more rigid by the 1964 amendments, which deny any interest deduction for amounts borrowed under a systematic plan to borrow amounts equal to the increase

[11] Premiums paid by employers under group policies had long been deductible as a fringe benefit and at the same time excluded from the incomes of the employee-insureds. The 1964 Revenue Act limits the employee exclusion for group term insurance furnished by the employer to the amount of the premiums paid for the first $50,000 of coverage.

in the cash values to pay part or all of the premiums. This amendment applies to contracts purchased after August 6, 1963. However, if any four of the first seven premiums are not paid with borrowed funds in connection with the plan, the interest deduction will not be denied.

ESTATE TAXATION OF LIFE INSURANCE

Tests of Inclusion of Proceeds in Gross Estate

Although many state inheritance tax laws exempt life insurance proceeds, there is no insurance exemption under the federal estate tax law. This was not always true. Prior to 1942, in addition to the general exemption of $40,000, insurance proceeds paid to named beneficiaries up to $40,000 were specifically exempted. In that year, Congress eliminated the insurance exemption and increased the general exemption to $60,000.

The Code now requires the inclusion in the estate of a decedent of all insurance on his life (1) if the proceeds are payable to or for the benefit of his estate or (2) if, at the time of his death, he possessed any incidents of ownership in the policy.[12] A third test, payment of premiums, was happily discarded by the 1954 Code.

Payable to the Insured's Estate

It is generally unwise to name the estate of an insured person as beneficiary. This may result in subjecting the proceeds to state death taxes.[13] It frequently makes the proceeds available to creditors and increases the fees of executors and administrators. It should be noted that in some states, even though the estate is specifically designated beneficiary, the proceeds are payable by statute directly to the widow and children, free of the claims of creditors. Such insurance in these jurisdictions escapes this test of inclusion. On the other hand, if the proceeds are payable for the benefit of the estate, even though to a third-party beneficiary, they will be caught by the test. The Regulations have long provided that the proceeds are receivable for the "benefit of the estate, wherever there is an obligation legally binding on the recipients to use such proceeds for the payment of taxes, debts, or charges which are enforceable against the estate."

Ownership Test

Since 1954, it has been possible to free the proceeds of life insurance from the federal estate tax by transfer of the policy and all incidents of ownership in it to a donee during the life of the insured. Incidents of

[12] Policies on the lives of others owned by a decedent are included in his estate. The problem of valuation is the same as for gift tax purposes.

[13] Where state laws exempt insurance proceeds from inheritance tax, the exemption generally applies only when the proceeds are payable to named beneficiaries.

ownership include the right to change the beneficiary, the right to surrender the policy for its cash value, the right to elect the various options, and the like. All must be transferred, by absolute assignment or other legal means, to the donee to avoid the inclusion of the insured's policy in *his* estate.

Such an assignment may fail to accomplish the intended result if the courts later determine that it was made in contemplation of death. Fortunately, the federal statute now provides that transfers made more than three years before death are not subject to the contemplation-of-death rules. However, if the insured, after such an assignment, continues to pay the premiums, there is always the risk that the last three premium payments may be held to have been made in contemplation of death.[14] Where this happens, a portion of the proceeds may be subject to estate tax—what portion is not yet definitely settled by case law. It is possible that only the dollar amount of the last three premiums would be included in the gross estate, but it seems much more likely that the rule of the Lieberman case[15] will be applied. In that case the policy was found to have been transferred in contemplation of death, but for the two years the insured survived after the transfer, the premiums had been paid by his donee. The court held that the proportionate part of the insurance purchased by the last two premiums should be excluded from the gross estate and that this amount was to be arrived at by taking the proportion of the proceeds which the last two premiums bore to the total premiums paid. Applying the philosophy of this case, if the insured paid all the premiums—five before the gift and five after the gift—and if the last three were held to have been paid in contemplation of death, three tenths of the proceeds may be taxed at his death.

Marital Deduction

The marital deduction allowed in computing the federal estate tax permits up to one half of the adjusted gross estate to escape tax on the death of a spouse to the extent that estate value is left to the surviving spouse either outright or more or less outright, e.g., for life with a general power of appointment.

The proceeds of insurance included in the estate of the insured may qualify for this marital deduction if they are payable (1) in a lump sum to the surviving spouse, (2) to a trust which itself qualifies, or (3) under

[14] Where an insured, instead of directly paying the premiums, furnishes funds to his donee that are used to pay the premiums, it is possible that he will be held to have paid the premiums indirectly. The question of whether premium payments were made in contemplation of death will depend on all the facts and circumstances of each particular case.

[15] *Lieberman* v. *Hassett*, 50 F. Supp. 527; appealed on this issue, 148 F.(2d) 247.

any one of the optional modes of settlement if (*a*) the principal or any remaining unpaid installments are payable to the spouse's estate on her death or (*b*) the surviving spouse is given a general power to designate the beneficiary of the principal remaining at her death. Under this last method (3[*b*]) the Regulations state that all of the following requirements must be met:

1. The proceeds or a specific portion thereof must be held by the insurer subject to an agreement either to pay the proceeds or the specific portion thereof in installments, or to pay the interest thereon, with all such amounts payable during the life of the surviving spouse payable only to her.
2. Such installments or interest must be payable annually, or more frequently, commencing not later than thirteen months after the decedent's death.
3. The surviving spouse must have the power, exercisable in favor of herself or her estate, to appoint all such amounts so held by the insurer.
4. Such power in the surviving spouse must be exercisable by such spouse alone and in all events, whether by will or during life.
5. Such amounts must not be subject to a power in any other person to appoint any part thereof to any person other than the surviving spouse.

GIFT TAXATION OF LIFE INSURANCE

Advantages of Gifts of Life Insurance Policies

Gifts of life insurance, especially since the elimination of the premium payment test, offer attractive estate tax savings in many cases. The donor does not feel poorer in any real sense. The value of what is given away, for gift tax purposes, is frequently nominal, and always substantially less than what is removed from the taxable estate. The donee's "dependence" on his donor as *pater familias* is not lessened to any appreciable extent, as it would be if the gift were of General Motors stock, for example, or of almost any type of property other than insurance.

Valuation

The gift tax value of a single premium or fully paid-up policy is its replacement cost. Annual-premium policies are valued at the interpolated terminal reserve (slightly more than the cash surrender value in most cases) plus premiums paid beyond the date of gift, except that a newly issued policy will be valued at its cost. The Regulations give the following illustration:

A gift is made four months after the last premium date of an ordinary life insurance policy issued nine years and four months prior to the gift thereof by the insured, who was 35 years of age at date of issue. The gross annual premium is $2,811. The computation follows:

Terminal reserve at end of tenth year	$14,601.00
Terminal reserve at end of ninth year	12,965.00
Increase	$ 1,636.00
One third of such increase (the gift having been made four months following the last preceding premium due date) is	$ 545.33
Terminal reserve at end of ninth year	12,965.00
Interpolated terminal reserve at date of gift	$13,510.33
Two thirds of gross premium ($2,811)	1,874.00
Value of gift	$15,384.33

The reason for the more favorable rule in the cases of policies on which further premiums remain to be paid is that replacement cost figures are not available because of the absence of any market for comparable contracts.

Exemption and Exclusions

Gifts of policies qualify for the $30,000 lifetime exemption. They also qualify for the $3,000 annual gift tax exclusion, provided the form of the gift does not make it a future interest. Any transfer of a policy outright to a single individual will constitute a gift of a present interest. If the donor continues to pay the premiums, each premium payment will constitute a gift of a present interest. Difficulties arise where the policy is transferred jointly to two or more donees. If the rights in the policy can be exercised only by joint action of the donees, then the gift is a future interest, since no one donee has any present right immediately to possess and enjoy any part of the gift. His enjoyment is conditioned on the will of his co-donee.

Where the policy is assigned to a trust, the terms of the trust will determine whether the exclusion is available. Generally, the original assignment and the payment of any future premiums by the donor will constitute gifts of future interest. The only way to assure the full exclusion for the value of the policy and the premium payments is to give the donee beneficiary an unrestricted power to withdraw the corpus in full at any time and thus terminate the trust.[16] This power gives the donee a present interest in the policy but has the disadvantage that the full value of the trust will be included in the gross estate of the donee. Hence the question is always a choice between obtaining the annual exclusions for the donor (who plans to continue to pay the premiums) or sheltering the proceeds from estate tax on the death of the donee.

---

[16] Gifts in trust for the benefit of minors are by special statutory provision entitled to the exclusion without the withdrawal privilege if the trustee may use both income and principal for the support of the minor and if any unexpended principal and accumulated income must be distributed to the minor at 21 or, if he be dead, to his estate, or as he may appoint by will under a general power of appointment.

Marital Privileges

Where the assignee is a person other than a spouse, the gift-splitting privilege is available. This is true whether the transfer be outright or to a trust, so long as the spouse is not given any contingent interest.

The gift tax marital deduction will generally be available if the assignment is to a spouse, provided the rights given to the spouse meet certain requirements. These are substantially the same as the estate tax requirements noted above.

Inadvertent Gift of Policy Proceeds

A pitfall to watch in policies owned by one other than the insured is the inadvertent gift of the proceeds which occurs on the maturity of a policy by reason of death or otherwise if a person other than the owner is named beneficiary. In these cases, it is a good general rule that the owner should always name himself beneficiary. If the insured, even where he is the owner, designates another as beneficiary of an endowment contract, a taxable gift will occur when the policy matures by reason of the insured's attaining the stated age. Thus, if A takes out a $20,000 policy to mature at age 65, naming B as revocable beneficiary, B will receive the face amount of the policy on A's sixty-fifth birthday. On these facts, A made a gift to B of $20,000 on the maturity date.

The same rule applies where the proceeds are received by reason of death. Assume that the father purchases and assigns to the mother a policy on the father's life. The children are named revocable beneficiaries. On the father's death, the mother will be held to have made a taxable gift to the children. The reason for this is that up to the very moment of the father's death, the mother had all the incidents of ownership in this policy. With the father's death and at the mother's direction the valuable rights under the contract shifted from the mother to the children. She lost her contract rights; the children gained them. The courts have held that the taxable gift is the face amount of the contract rather than the cash surrender value. An even less obvious pitfall occurs where the mother, owning a policy on the father's life, elects the interest option without withdrawal privileges, in favor of herself, the proceeds to be paid to the children on her death. Here, she not only makes a taxable gift of the remainder interest in the policy on the father's death, but the proceeds on her later death will be included in her taxable estate, on the theory that she made a transfer with a reserved life estate.

HEALTH INSURANCE

Deduction of Premiums

Premiums paid on health insurance policies are deductible as medical expenses within the limitations of the medical expenses section of the

Code. The Commissioner has consistently taken the position that the deduction may be taken only for the portion of the premium attributable to hospitalization, surgical, and medical expense coverage. The courts, however, in general have held the entire premium on policies providing for indemnity for accidental loss of life, limb, sight, or time, and also providing reimbursement of medical expenses, to be deductible.

Where the premiums are paid by an employer, he may deduct them as business expenses. Further, the 1954 Code specifically provides that with respect to employee plans, "gross income shall not include contributions by an employer to accident or health plans for compensation (through insurance or otherwise) to his employees for personal injuries or sickness."

Exclusion from Taxable Income of Most Benefits Received

Individual Policies. Since 1918, amounts received "through accident and health insurance for personal injuries or sickness" have been exempt from income tax. Accident and health insurance includes medical, hospital, and surgical expense, as well as indemnity for loss of earnings. Under the 1939 Code, this exemption applied irrespective of who paid the premiums or who received the proceeds.[17] However, any amounts received for medical expenses, to the extent that such expenses were deducted in a prior year on the insured's income tax return, must be reported as income. This is simply one aspect of the general income tax principle that where an amount is deducted in one year and is recovered in another, the latter recovery (though otherwise exempt) is taxable as income to offset the benefit derived from the earlier deduction.

Under the 1954 Code, these rules were continued with respect to individual policies. All amounts received under such policies are excluded from income. The area of change deals with employee health plans where the employer pays all or part of the premiums.

Employee Policies. Where the employer pays the entire premium pursuant to a plan, and it is therefore not includable in the employee's income as noted above, the law states that all amounts received under such policies shall be included in the employee's income, but subject to the following very important exceptions. Under these exceptions, there are excluded, and hence not taxable, (1) all amounts which reimburse the employee for medical, surgical, and hospital costs for himself, his spouse, or any dependent, without limitation as to amount;[18] (2) amounts paid, without regard to absence from work, for permanent loss or loss of use of a member or function of the body, or for permanent disfigurement of the employee, his spouse, or his dependents; and (3) amounts in lieu of wages for a period during which the employee is absent from work on

[17] A transferee of the policy for value was, however, denied the exemption.

[18] Unless previously deducted on his income tax return for a prior year.

account of personal injury or sickness, but not exceeding $100 a week. Prior to 1964 there was a seven-day waiting period in the event of sickness unless the employee was hospitalized for at least one "hospital" day during that period. Under the 1964 Act, no sick pay exclusion will be allowed for wage continuation payments for the first thirty consecutive days of a period of absence if such payments are over 75 per cent of the regular weekly rate of wages. But sick pay received after the thirty-day waiting period may be excluded up to $100 a week. If the weekly rate of sick pay does not exceed 75 per cent of the employee's regular weekly rate of wages, and if the employee is hospitalized for one day during the period, he can exclude such payments received during the first thirty days up to a rate of $75 a week. But if he is not hospitalized, no exclusion is allowed for the first seven days and the $75 maximum will apply to the remainder of the first thirty days.

Thus the effect of the 1954 Code changes is to limit the exemption for loss-of-earning payments to a maximum of $100 a week under employment plans where the cost is borne by the employer. Where, under a contributing plan, a portion only of the premiums is paid by the employer, the percentage of the loss-of-earnings payments attributable to the employee's share of the premiums is not subject to the $100 maximum limitation.

SELECTED REFERENCES

APPLEMAN, JOHN ALAN (ed.). *Basic Estate Planning.* Indianapolis: Bobbs-Merrill Co., 1957.

BOWE, WILLIAM J. *Estate Planning and Taxation.* Buffalo: Dennis & Co., 1957.

FOOSANER, S. J. *Tax Uses of Life Insurance.* Chicago: Callaghan & Co., 1957.

HARRIS, HOMER. *Family Estate Planning Guide.* Mt. Kisco, N.Y.: Baker, Voorhis & Co., Inc., 1957.

J. K. LASSER INSTITUTE. *Estate Tax Techniques.* Albany: Mathew Bender & Co., Inc. Looseleaf service.

LOUNDES, C. L. B., and KRAMER, R. *Federal Estate and Gift Taxes.* 2d ed. St. Paul: West Publishing Co., 1962.

STATE FARM LIFE INSURANCE COMPANY. *Advanced Underwriting and Taxation Handbook,* Vol. II. Bloomington, Ill., 1963.

TULANE TAX INSTITUTE. *Income, Estate and Gift Taxation of Life, Accident and Sickness Insurance and Annuities under the 1954 Code,* p. 467. New Orleans, 1956.

Chapter 60

SPLIT-DOLLAR AND RELATED PLANS

BY WILLIAM B. LYNCH

Split-dollar insurance is a form of insurance co-ownership and is used primarily as a means for one person to help another carry the life insurance protection he needs. The policy must be for permanent insurance because the "split" occurs along the line dividing the cash value from the pure protection. Usually, one person pays the portion of each premium equal to the annual increase in cash value, and the insured pays the balance. The result is that the insured obtains insurance protection at very little cost to himself, as will become evident in the course of this discussion, with the principal cost being borne by the one helping him.

Split-dollar insurance has been in use for a considerable time, at least since the 1930's. Now considered primarily an employee benefit plan, it probably began as a simple arrangement between a father and his son. For many years, it was hampered by its uncertain tax status, but all that changed in late 1955 with Revenue Ruling 55–713.[1] This ruling pointed out that split-dollar plans resemble loans without interest; held that the forbearance of interest is not a taxable event; and concluded that the proceeds, on death, would be tax-free to all parties receiving them. In other words, the plans faced no readily evident tax problems. This gave great impetus to the promotion of the plans and today they stand as one of the common forms of insurance ownership.

Typically, the split-dollar plan exists between an insured and his employer; therefore the rest of this discussion refers to the party providing the premium assistance as the "employer." Bear in mind, however, that *anyone* can share premiums with another. The plan is not limited to the employment relationship.

How It Works

Basic Patterns. With the usual level premium insurance plans the insured's protection is level. At any given point in time, this protection consists of two parts—the cash value or reserve and the amount at risk.

[1] 1955–2 C.B. 23 (1955). The full text of the ruling appears in footnote 3, below.

With split-dollar plans, however, the employer is entitled to the cash value—or to at least enough of it to equal its own premiums. As a direct result, the insured's protection tends to decline as the cash value goes up. This is clearly shown in Table 60–1. In the tenth year of the plan, for example, the insured's protection has fallen to $79,954. At that point, the employer's share would be $20,046, so that the *total* death benefit remains level at $100,000. By age 65, the insured's protection would have fallen to $55,312.

TABLE 60–1

SPLIT-DOLLAR INSURANCE LEDGER ILLUSTRATION USING DIVIDENDS TO REDUCE PREMIUMS*
Age 40, $100,000 Straight Life, Gross Annual Premium $2,783

Start of Policy Year	Net Premium Deposit*	Premium Division		Death Benefit	
		By Employer	By Insured	To Employer	To Family
1	$2,783	$1,126	$1,657	$ 1,126	$98,874
2	2,563	2,346	217	3,472	96,528
3	2,492	2,367	125	5,839	94,161
4	2,423	1,985	438	7,824	92,176
5	2,357	2,002	355	9,826	90,174
6	2,294	2,019	275	11,845	88,155
7	2,233	2,033	200	13,878	86,122
8	2,176	2,045	131	15,923	84,077
9	2,122	2,057	65	17,980	82,020
10	2,072	2,066	6	20,046	79,954
11	2,024	2,024		22,070	77,930
12	1,961	1,961		24,031	75,969
13	1,901	1,901		25,932	74,068
14	1,845	1,845		27,777	72,223
15	1,791	1,791		29,568	70,432
16	1,738	1,738		31,306	68,694
17	1,686	1,686		32,992	67,008
18	1,634	1,634		34,626	65,374
19	1,583	1,583		36,209	63,791
20	1,531	1,531		37,740	62,260
Age 65	1,298	1,298		44,688	55,312

* The dividends, and consequent net premium deposit shown, are not guaranteed.

To counteract this, many participating policies permit dividends to be used to purchase one-year term insurance. This term insurance increases in amount each year, keeping exact pace with the cash value of the basic policy. As a result, the employee's protection for the family is kept level from the second premium on. This is shown in Table 60–2. Sooner or later, of course, the piper must be paid. One cannot go on indefinitely buying larger and larger amounts of term insurance at older and older ages without finally running out of dividends enough to meet the price. One major company projects that this point would be reached when the insured attains age 65, for a male aged 40 at issuance of his policy, using early dividend balances to reduce premiums. That would be the last year in which the protection for the insured would be level. From then on, it would decline at an ever steeper rate. Had early dividend balances been accumulated for later use, the same company would project a final level year at age 68. Many nonparticipating policies achieve much the same leveling result by building the cost of the increasing term feature into the basic premium.

TABLE 60–2

SPLIT-DOLLAR INSURANCE LEDGER ILLUSTRATION
USING DIVIDENDS TO PURCHASE ONE-YEAR TERM INSURANCE AND REDUCE PREMIUMS*
Age 40, $100,000 Straight Life, Gross Annual Premium $2,783

Start of Policy Year	Net Premium Deposit*	Premium Division		Death Benefit*	
		By Employer	By Insured	To Employer	To Family
1.	$2,783	$1,126	$1,657	$ 1,126	$ 98,874
2.	2,577	2,346	231	3,472	100,000
3.	2,517	2,367	150	5,839	100,000
4.	2,459	1,985	474	7,824	100,000
5.	2 407	2,002	405	9,826	100,000
6.	2,359	2,019	340	11,845	100,000
7.	2,315	2,033	282	13,878	100,000
8.	2,279	2,045	234	15,923	100,000
9.	2,249	2,057	192	17,980	100,000
10.	2,226	2,066	160	20,046	100,000
11.	2,210	2,073	137	22,119	100,000
12.	2,183	2,079	104	24,198	100,000
13.	2,164	2,083	81	26,281	100,000
14.	2,155	2,083	72	28,364	100,000
15.	2,154	2,083	71	30,447	100,000
16.	2,161	2,079	82	32,526	100,000
17.	2,177	2,075	102	34,601	100,000
18.	2,203	2,066	137	36,667	100,000
19.	2,239	2,057	182	38,724	100,000
20.	2,286	2,045	241	40,769	100,000
Age 65.	2,760	1,949	811	50,727	100,000

* The dividends are not guaranteed, and there is consequently no guarantee of the net premium shown nor of the one-year term insurance reflected in the death benefits shown. The one-year term rates illustrated are not guaranteed.

Notice, in Table 60–1, that in the first year the employer pays $1,126 toward the premium. The second year the employer pays $2,346, then $2,367 the third year, and so on. These amounts paid by the employer are equal to each year's increase in the cash surrender value of the policy. The insured pays any balance of the premium each year. By the eleventh year, the annual cash value increase is *greater* than the net premium, so the insured pays no more, yet his protection continues. His annual cost to age 65 would average about $1.80 per $1,000 of protection. It should be borne in mind, however, that the policy dividends are not guaranteed. Were they to change from those illustrated, the insured's costs would correspondingly change.

In Table 60–2, some of the dividends are used to buy the annual term insurance, with the result that the net premium stays relatively high and always exceeds the cash value increases. The insured never quite gets away from the payments. Nevertheless, he would obtain his $100,000 of level protection at an average annual cost to age 65 of less than $3.25 per $1,000.

Pattern Variations. The plans illustrated in Tables 60–1 and 60–2 use straight life, probably the most commonly used policy form but certainly not the only one available. Any permanent policy can be used, and the parties should use a type suited to their purposes. For example, split dollar for employee benefit plans is often best funded with a policy paid up by age 65. This corresponds with the usual retirement date for the insured and, in addition, grants the insured nonterminating level protection for the rest of his life after retirement. That would be true even without the one-year term option because, once the policy becomes paid up, the employer would make no further premium deposits and so not increase its own interest in the proceeds past age 65. If the policy is participating, any dividends that are paid may compensate the employer for this continued use of its funds. Endowment policies are ideally suited to plans combining split-dollar and deferred compensation, it being thereby possible to present an attractive system assuring the executive of the same cash benefits, live or die. Various kinds of term insurance riders may be attached to the basic policy, either to give some key-man protection to the employer (in which case the employer pays the extra cost of the rider) or to give the insured some optional additional protection (in which case he pays the extra cost). The advantage is, of course, that term insurance purchased as a rider is usually much less expensive than term insurance purchased alone.

Aside from variations in the policies themselves, there are many ways to split the premiums and even the proceeds. Again, Tables 60–1 and 60–2 follow the most common pattern. The contracts used in those tables are high early cash value policies. When the earliest split-dollar plans were written, there were no such policies available. Often the policies showed no cash values at all in the first year or so, requiring the insured alone to bear the full early premiums. The high early cash value policies were invented to correct this, and Table 60–1 shows the result: The insured would pay but $1,657 out of a total first-year premium of $2,783. Despite this, however, and despite the low over-all cost to the insured, he often has difficulty with that still-heavy first premium. Consequently, many plans permit the insured to average his share of the premiums over some selected number of years. For example, the insured in Table 60–1 might pay a level premium of $347 each year for ten years. The employer, in that case, would have to pay a larger portion of the first premium. Going a major step further, the insured might skip the first premium payment altogether. In fact, that was the very case in Revenue Ruling 55–713, mentioned earlier. The employer would simply hold the policy as key-man insurance for the first year, with premium splitting beginning the second year. If, nevertheless, it is desirable to give the insured some benefit during the first year, a one-year salary continuation plan could be provided out of the proceeds in the event of his death.

It is often contended that because the employer in split-dollar plans always gets its share of the premiums back, the plan costs it nothing. This is obviously untrue if any value is placed on the use of money. *The employer's cost for supplying its share of the premium is the cost of its lost use of the money.* Since nearly all of the employer's share of the premiums can be obtained through policy loans and nearly all policies have a guaranteed maximum loan rate of 5 per cent, it is obvious that the maximum cost to an employer is 5 per cent per annum on its share of the premiums. If, under the circumstances, an employer is allowed to deduct the interest, then its cost would be even lower. Still, why not make the plan truly costless to the employer? This can be done by so dividing the proceeds at the time of the insured's death that the employer receives back not only its premium deposits as such, but a portion equal to its interest costs as well.

As previously indicated, many plans are designed to ease the insured's initial premium burden. Suppose, instead, that the insured is required to pay the *entire* first premium. By so doing, he would acquire an interest in the first-year cash value, against which his subsequent premiums can be drawn. Some policies are so designed that after the insured pays the first premium, he never again pays another. This can have a gratifying effect, since many persons fail to provide themselves with the protection they need through an unwillingness to commit themselves to long premium payment programs.

Major Systems

Having decided on the plan pattern he wishes to apply, the underwriter must then choose one of the two major split-dollar systems. The basic mechanics of these systems are compared in Figure 60–1, and each possesses its own special advantages.

Collateral Assignment System. The collateral assignment system has the undoubted advantage that it is easy to explain. The insured owns his own policy and puts it up as security for loans, just as he would at the bank. The only difference is that the loans carry no interest. This corresponds with everyone's conception of insurance in general and loans in particular. If the insured's employment terminates, and the plan with it, no policy repurchase is required—the insured simply pays off the loans.

The direct benefit of participating policy dividends goes to the insured as owner of the policy under the collateral assignment system. The insured's ownership of the policy has other effects. For one, it is mechanically easier to remove the policy from his taxable estate by an absolute assignment (subject to the collateral assignment) to his wife or to someone else. For another, the insured's ownership may permit him to use an old policy, virtually impossible when the employer owns an old policy and wants to apply the endorsement system. That impossibility stems

Item	Collateral Assignment System	Endorsement System
Policy applicant	Insured	Employer
Policy owner	Insured	Employer
Premium division	All paid by insured, subject to receipt of loan from employer equal to year's cash value increase	All paid by employer, subject to reimbursement from insured for excess of premiums over year's cash value increase
Death benefits	All to insured's designee, subject to repayment of loan to employer	Split: Portion equal to employer's share of total premiums to employer; balance to insured's designee

FIG. 60–1. Comparison of collateral assignment and endorsement split-dollar systems.

from the fact that after the first few years the insured's share of the premium virtually stops—stops altogether, in Table 60–1, with the eleventh year. When the insured pays too little for his protection, it may well be held that part of the employer's premiums are taxable income to him or, worse, that the proceeds on death are taxable income to his beneficiary. If an old employer-owned policy must be used, it should first be sold to the insured and the collateral assignment system followed.

Because the collateral assignment system involves loans as a part of its basic mechanism, it lends itself well to an insured's averaging his share of the premiums, itself calling for a series of loans. The part of the loan attributable to the averaging should, however, be repaid in a reasonably short time, e.g., during the first ten policy years.

Endorsement System. The endorsement system has the better historical position, since it is the specific system described in Revenue Ruling 55–713. This fact, together with the employer's retention of policy ownership and control, may be more appealing to stockholders—and stockholder reaction can be important in many cases. The absence of any actual loan to the employee may appeal to the stockholders, too, and some states have laws prohibiting or restricting loans by corporations to their officers.

Split-dollar plans are often combined with other uses, such as selective deferred compensation or stock redemption plans. These combinations are much more easily carried out when the corporation, and not the insured, is the owner of the policy. A combination, in fact, may be one with a purely business purpose, e.g., plant expansion or equipment acquisitions. As owner, the company would have direct access to the policy cash values for these purposes. Apart from convenience, this might help the corporation avoid assessment of the accumulated earnings tax under Internal Revenue Code Section 531. One test, incidentally, of whether that section applies to a corporation is the existence of outstanding loans to stockholding employees. A plan which skips the first premium can, as a practical matter, better use the endorsement system.

Putting the Plan Together

With the pattern and the system tailored to their own facts, the parties are ready to put the package together. One component will usually be a written agreement. Drafting this is the attorney's province, and many insurance companies have prepared sample forms to assist him, covering a wide range of plans.

Under the collateral assignment system, the life insurance policy is applied for and owned by the insured. Premium notices are sent to him, and he designates the beneficiaries of his choice. Upon issuance of the policy the insured assigns it to his employer as collateral security for loans to be advanced. The assignment form most often used is the ABA–10 form adopted by the American Bankers Association.[2] Many banks and insurance companies have supplies of these available.

The second step is the execution of the written plan agreement, describing the policy by number, amount, insurer, and ownership. The parties are the insured and the employer. They typically agree that as long as the insured remains employed, the employer will lend him each year without interest an amount equal to the lesser of the year's net premium or the cash value increase. These loans are normally repayable only at death, out of the policy proceeds, or on the earlier termination of employment. Unless gross premiums or nonparticipating policies are used, the future premiums will not be known when the plan is installed, nor will the insured or the employer be readily able to compute the loans to be made each year. Here the parties can prepare an open-end note and work sheet like that in Figure 60–2, with the underwriter providing the cash value information in column *B*. With such a form, the parties can fill in their own information each year.

The agreement usually has provisions for termination of the plan—for example, if the insured leaves his employment. In this event, the insured may be required within a fixed time to pay off the loan in full, and the agreement should make it possible for him to do this through a policy loan. That may require either a release of the policy by the employer to

[2] See Chapter 56 for analysis and illustration of ABA–10 form.

the insured or the employer's securing such a loan on his behalf before releasing the policy.

Under the endorsement system the policy is applied for and owned by the employer, who receives the premium notices. In many plans, the primary beneficiary endorsement is a simple split, with the portion of the proceeds equal to the cash value at any time going to the employer and the balance to the insured's own beneficiary. In other plans, such as

The undersigned promises to pay to the order of ______(Employer)______, on demand and without interest, the cumulative total of the amount shown in column *C*, below, opposite which he has placed his initials in column *D*, below. Such amounts so owed are secured by collateral assignment to said payee of Policy Number ____________ issued by ______(Insurance Company)______ on the life of the undersigned.

In Year	*(A) Net Premium per Premium Notice*	*(B) Guaranteed Cash Value Increase*	*(C) Enter Lesser of (A) or (B)*	*(D) Initials of Undersigned*
1964	$2,783	$1,126	$1,126	______
65	______	2,346	______	______
66	______	2,367	______	______
67	______	1,985	______	______
68	______	2,002	______	______
1969	______	2,019	______	______
70	______	2,033	______	______
71	______	2,045	______	______
72	______	2,057	______	______
73	______	2,066	______	______
etc.	etc.	etc.	etc.	etc.

Dated ____________, 19___ ______________________

(Insured)

FIG. 60–2. Open-end note and work sheet for collateral assignment split-dollar system (age 40, $100,000 straight life, gross annual premium $2,783).

that in Table 60–1, the employer's portion is the lesser of the cash value or its share of total premiums. It is this beneficiary endorsement which gives the system its name. While it is common for the employer itself to make the entire endorsement, including the part for the insured's benefit, some insurance companies permit the insured to make his own designation directly. In that sense, he has a direct ownership in a piece of the policy, and this kind of system is sometimes called a "split-ownership" plan.

The second step is the execution of the written plan agreement. The parties typically agree that as long as the insured remains employed, the employer will pay all premiums as they become due, and the insured will pay over to the employer each year any excess of the premium over the year's cash value increase. In exchange for the insured's making these payments, the employer permits him to name his own beneficiaries for the part of the death benefits which exceeds the cash value at any time, or which exceeds the lesser of the cash value or the employer's total share of the premiums. Just as with the collateral assignment system, future participating premiums will be unknown. The premium division is easy for the parties to compute, however, if they use a work sheet like that in Figure 60–3.

The amount computed each year for column *C*, below, is the amount payable by the insured to the employer each year, on or before the due date in such year, for the annual premium on the policy, all in accordance with the provisions of Section ________ of that certain split-dollar agreement dated ________ ______, 19____, to which this work sheet is annexed.

In Year	(*A*) *Net Premium per Premium Notice*	(*B*) *Guaranteed Cash Value Increase*	(*C*) *Enter Excess, if Any, of (A) over (B)*
1964	$2,783	$1,126	$1,657
65	________	2,346	________
66	________	2,367	________
67	________	1,985	________
68	________	2,002	________
1969	________	2,019	________
70	________	2,033	________
71	________	2,045	________
72	________	2,057	________
73	________	2,066	________
etc.	etc.	etc.	etc.

FIG. 60–3. Work sheet for endorsement split-dollar system (age 40, $100,000 straight life, gross annual premium $2,783).

Provisions in the agreement for termination of the plan should include procedures for transferring ownership of the policy from the employer to the insured. This transfer is a sale and requires that the employer execute an absolute assignment form. The purchase price is usually the employer's share of total premiums. The insured may find it necessary to borrow against the policy to meet this price, and provision should be made in the agreement for that contingency.

Taxation

Income Taxation. Reference already has been made to Revenue Ruling 55–713, the basic tax authority for split-dollar plans.[3] The ruling

[3] The full text of the ruling is as follows:

"Advice has been requested as to whether the portion of insurance premiums paid by an employer, to the extent of the cash surrender value under an insurance policy covering the life of an employee constitutes additional income to the employee.

"In the instant case *Y* corporation entered into a contract with *B* to render services as its president for a period of 5 years in consideration of an annual salary together first pointed out that premiums paid by an employer on a policy of insurance on the life of an employee who is permitted to designate his beneficiaries are ordinarily taxable income to the employee. It distinguished a split-dollar plan from that type of arrangement principally on the grounds that "in all essential respects" a split-dollar plan resembles annual loans without interest, presumably more than it resembles an insurance plan. The ruling took the then novel position, without citation of authority of any kind, that "the mere making available of money does not result in realized income to the payee." Thereupon, it held that the premium payments were neither income to the employee nor deductions

---

with stipulations for the payment of certain specified amounts in the event of his disability and upon his death to his designated beneficiaries. In order to protect itself against contingent liabilities resulting from the above agreement, *Y* corporation purchased as sole owner and beneficiary several policies of ordinary life insurance on the life of *B* in the amount of its total liability under the contract. Pursuant to a supplemental agreement it was provided that *B* had the option to assist in the payment of premiums on one or more of the policies in return for a partial control over the distribution of death benefits thereunder. Under the agreement the gross premium less the amount of any dividends would be paid in part by *Y* corporation to the extent of the increase in cash surrender value for any taxable year and the balance would be paid by *B*. Both the *Y* corporation and *B* would each have separate ownership rights during his lifetime with the right of *B* to designate the beneficiary under the policies for that part of the proceeds equal to the excess of the face amount payable under each policy over the cash surrender value. The *Y* corporation would continue to be the beneficiary under the policies to the extent of the cash surrender value which would be available for general corporate purposes. Upon termination of *B*'s employment *Y* corporation agrees, upon *B*'s election, to (1) sell its ownership interest in the life insurance contracts to *B* for an amount equal to the larger of the gross premiums it has paid or the guaranteed cash values in its portion of the policies; or (2) assign to *B* all of its ownership interest in such policies except an amount equal to the guaranteed cash surrender value at the date of the assignment, provided, however, if *B* defaults on any future premiums the corporation may reassert its rights to ownership. *B* elected to share the cost of the life insurance policies.

"Generally, for tax purposes premiums paid by an employer on the ordinary type of life insurance policy on the life of its employee who is permitted to designate the beneficiary under the policy constitutes taxable income to the employee. O.D. 627, C.B. 3, 104 (1920); G.C.M. 8432, C.B. IX–2, 114 (1930). Likewise, it has been held that it makes no difference whether the insured employee is entitled to designate the beneficiary under the policy the proceeds of which inure directly to the benefit of the employee's beneficiary or his estate. G.C.M. 16069, C.B. XV–1, 84 (1936).

"In the instant case the substance of the insurance arrangement between the parties is in all essential respects the same as if *Y* corporation makes annual loans without interest, of a sum of money equal to the annual increases in the cash surrender value of the policies of insurance taken out on the life of *B*. The mere making available of money does not result in realized income to the payee or a deduction to the payor.

"In view of the foregoing, it is held that:

"(1) No realization of taxable income by *B* will result upon the payment of the portion of the premiums by *Y*, and *Y* will receive no deduction for such payment.

"(2) The portion of the proceeds of the policies payable upon the death of *B* to the *Y* corporation and to the designated beneficiary of *B* would not be included in the gross income of the *Y* corporation or of *B*'s beneficiary under the provisions of Section 101(*a*) of the Internal Revenue Code of 1954 or Section 22(*b*)(1) of the Internal Revenue Code of 1939."

to the employer and that the proceeds on the employee's death would be tax-tree to each group receiving them.

Certain nagging problems remain, the chief one concerning stockholding employees, especially those who control their closely held companies. Several private rulings have held that Revenue Ruling 55–713 was not intended to apply to stockholders, without stating what does apply. There seems to be one serious possibility: the penalty tax under Internal Revenue Code Section 531. This tax is levied on close corporations which accumulate rather than distribute their incomes in order to shelter those incomes from the high personal brackets of their stockholders. A good defense against this tax is a showing that the accumulations are for the reasonable needs of the business. In the matter of a stockholder's split dollar, however, just the contrary would be easier to prove. The reasonable needs of the business, however, are likely to include obtaining and keeping skilled employees, so a plan with an "employee" label is likely safer than one with a "stockholder" label. To give the label substance, the plan should be extended to cover nonstockholding employees on a substantial basis. If broadening the base proves unpalatable, the corporation might effect maximum loans against the policies and invest the proceeds in the business, so using the accumulations for its needs.

Estate Taxation. Life insurance proceeds will be included in the gross estate of the insured if payable to his estate, or if he possesses any incidents of ownership in the policy at the time of his death, either alone or in conjunction with any other person. It is easy enough to avoid these provisions if proper care is taken, but it is equally easy to assume that they have been avoided when they have not. The typical split-dollar plan terminates, for example, upon termination of the insured's employment. If the plan is under the collateral assignment system, little danger exists for the reason that termination of the plan means only termination of the borrowing rights. Under the endorsement system, on the other hand, the right to designate beneficiaries ceases. This is an insurance right, an "incident of ownership." When the plan hopes to avoid the estate tax, of course, the person having the beneficiary designation right would be someone other than the insured, perhaps his wife. But *her* right would terminate on the insured's termination of employment. That is, despite appearances, he may well have a power to affect the policy which is an incident of ownership. Therefore, if the estate tax is to be avoided, and if the endorsement system is to be used, the plan should not terminate with the end of the insured's employment nor on any other event within his control.

Case Examples of Split-Dollar Plans

Example 1. The Harbor Shipyard is a small company with seven full-time employees. It wishes to install an employee life insurance program and is impressed with the fact that the company's premiums would be tax-deductible under group insurance. At the insurance agent's suggestion, however, a split-dollar plan is installed wherein each insured pays the full first premium on his own policy through payroll withholding. The company is to pay the balance of the premiums. Each insured appreciates more what the company is doing for having himself paid the first premium, and the plan is arranged so that Harbor Shipyard will not only receive a return of its premiums but interest as well. As a result, the company can provide its program at a zero cost and not a merely deductible one.

Example 2. John Garmor and Henry Philips are the equal stockholders of Garmor-Philips, Inc. They are studying the possibility of a stock purchase agreement and conclude that, but for one thing, a cross-purchase plan would be better suited to their purposes than a redemption plan. That one thing is that Garmor-Philips, Inc., in a lower tax bracket than the individuals, could fund more efficiently than they. But they now have a cross-purchase plan, with the funding borne by the company through split-dollar insurance. Each stockholder owns a policy on the other's life, collaterally assigned to the company.

Example 3. Coast Girder Corporation is a sizable company with the usual pension plan and group benefits. Some years ago, it created a selective deferred compensation plan for certain officers. The plan has been funded by annual deposits to individual securities investment accounts owned by the company for the benefit of each participating officer. These investments have been profitable, and the accounts have grown. The absence, nevertheless, of protection for an officer's account—future deposits and growth—in the event of his death leads Coast Girder to adopt a split-dollar plan wherein the company's portion of each premium is fully financed by policy loans, with the interest costs taken from the insured's investment account.

Example 4. Seven of the officers of Granite Rubber Company, Inc., have qualified stock options. These options run for five years. In the event of an officer's death, his estate may exercise his option to the same extent as he, for three months after his death. Recognizing that in the event of the death of any officer during the option period, his family would have to produce cash to exercise his option, the company provides split-dollar insurance for each officer in an amount related to his own option program.

Example 5. Ernie Hamilton's father has amassed a considerable estate through astute investments and enjoys a large annual income, including $50,000 from securities and real estate. He places 10 per cent of these holdings in a reversionary trust, the net income of which is invested in a split-dollar program for Ernie. The trust will terminate on Ernie's death, with the cash value share of insurance being distributed to Ernie's mother and the balance to Ernie's family.

RELATED PLANS

So-called "minimum deposit" and "bank loan" plans are related to the collateral assignment system of split-dollar insurance. They involve actual loans, secured by the borrower's insurance policy but bearing interest. While the usual policy or bank loans may be obtained at any time, in varying amounts and for a variety of reasons, these special plans usually follow a systematic borrowing program which keeps the loans at or near their maximums at all times.

Under a minimum deposit plan, the insurance company lends the money. Under a bank loan plan, of course, a bank lends the money. The earliest plans appear to have been on a bank loan basis, but a great shift has taken place, and today nearly all seem to be on the minimum deposit basis. The reason for this shift doubtless has been the sharp rise in bank interest rates while most insurance companies guarantee a flat 5 per cent. Another point may be that a policy loan never has a repayment schedule—indeed, need not be repaid at all until death. Then, too, a policy loan carries with it no personal liability, and that sometimes brings a sense of relief to the borrower.

The characteristic feature of a minimum deposit or bank loan plan is the small early outlay and the large later one. For example, if the policy illustrated in Figure 60–1 were being carried under a minimum deposit plan, with actual dividends as there assumed and with interest at 5 per cent, the insured's second-year outlay would be $273.30 ($217.00 premium and $56.30 interest), and his outlay for the twentieth year would be $1,810.45 (all interest). Interestingly, that twentieth-year outlay would actually exceed the year's normal net premium on the policy by $279.45. Why, then, should anyone wish to get into such a program? Most insureds are optimistic, certain that, 10 or 20 years from now, they will be better able to pay premiums and will not have to borrow.

In the past, the tax deductibility of interest was an added inducement. Consider the extreme case of the man in a 91 per cent income tax bracket. For him, in the policy illustrated and before the law on the deductibility of interest was changed, the second year's cost would have been $222.07 ($217.00 premium and $5.07 net interest), and that for the twentieth year would have been $162.94 (all net interest). For all insurance policies purchased on or after August 7, 1963, no interest deduction will be allowed under the usual mimimum deposit or bank loan arrangement unless the full premiums are carried without financing of any kind for at least four of the first seven policy years. Interest may still be deducted for insurance loans incurred to meet emergencies or for business purposes, even during early policy years, but not for early systematic loans intended merely to pay premiums.

SELECTED REFERENCES

BARTON, ROBERT M. and VOEGELIN, HAROLD S. "Interest Deduction in Tax Planning," *Eleventh Tax Institute, University of Southern California School of Law* (1959), pp. 774–87.

LYNCH, WILLIAM B. "Trio from the Institutes," *Journal of the American Society of Life Underwriters,* Vol. XVI, No. 4 (Fall, 1962), p. 323.

TESKE, MELVIN C. "Bank Loan Insurance and Minimum Deposit Plans," *New York University Eighteenth Annual Institute on Federal Taxation* (1960), p. 479.

Chapter 61

PROGRAMING LIFE INSURANCE

BY HAROLD W. GARDINER

The Meaning of Programing

Life insurance programing is an organized planning procedure through which a competent life underwriter brings to bear his accumulated experience and intellectual resources to guide his client toward the ownership of a balanced pattern of life insurance policies fitted to the needs of the client. Programing includes the determination of all the pertinent facts about the client's situation, his goals, and his purposes. It involves the correlation of his life insurance, expected social security benefits, and other assets in the client's estate to produce a balanced combination that will best serve the needs of the client in the light of all the circumstances surrounding his situation.

The philosophy of programing also involves the "human life value" concept, which holds that the head of a family represents an important economic value to the members of his family. Thus, in the event of the untimely death or disability of that family head, advance arrangements can be and should have been made through a carefully planned life insurance program that will replace, insofar as is practicable, the economic benefits for the family that he would have supplied had he lived.

Programing is the professional approach to the use of life insurance. It parallels the work of the attorney, who, in his practice, must first obtain and analyze the facts, then determine what principles of law are involved, and, finally, plan his presentation to the court. Similarly, it can be likened to the work of the family doctor, who first determines the symptoms of the patient's illness through careful examination and questioning, makes a diagnosis which establishes the condition to be treated, and then sets up a regime of treatment designed to cure the illness. Programing provides the same sound professional approach to the life insurance needs of the client.

The quality which distinguishes programing from other methods of approaching the sale of life insurance is the emphasis that is given to the particular situation of the client and the identification of the needs that are present in his situation, rather than stressing the features of the policy or policies that may be employed to satisfy those needs which characterize the single-needs or "package" approach to selling life insurance.

The typical life insurance buyer seems much to prefer the programing approach to his life insurance purchases. This conclusion was indicated in a recent study conducted jointly by the Life Insurance Agency Management Association and the Life Underwriter Training Council.[1] Their survey concluded that the programing approach was associated with high life insurance ownership goals, a greater understanding of life insurance, and a belief on the part of the buyers that agents sell on a needs basis.[2] In one fashion or another, most well-qualified life underwriters prefer to employ this type of technique.

The Scope of Programing

Programing and its procedures can range from the relatively simple to the fairly complex. Programing tends to be simple when the client's situation is uncomplicated and the family has few potential sources of income other than social security benefits and life insurance. Programing tends to become complex as business interests and other forms of property assume increasingly important proportions in the total situation. Generally speaking, when other property considerations begin to loom larger than the life insurance in a client's affairs, and estate conservation becomes more important than estate creation, the procedures change significantly, and the case will go out of the realm of even advanced programing and should be treated as an estate planning case. The boundary between these two approaches is not exactly defined and is based primarily on the exercise of judgment by the life underwriter.

Programing service is particularly appropriate for people whose situations suggest probable growth. Professional people, self-employed persons, business executives, other people in managerial work, and engineers are typical candidates for programing. People in the professions, such as accountants, attorneys, and physicians, will be especially receptive to programing because of the obvious parallels between the programing technique and their own professional methods.

The Benefits of the Programing Approach

The benefits to the client inherent in the programing approach are obvious. The life insurance he owns and the life insurance he purchases are fitted together in such fashion as to give him the maximum appropriate

---

[1] Life Insurance Agency Management Association, *Life Insurance in Focus,* Vol. I (Hartford, 1961), pp. 70–77.

[2] *Ibid.,* pp. 2 and 76.

benefits in return for the minimum dollar investment. Not only are his affairs put in good order at the time the programing is done, but inherent in the programing procedure is a systematic follow-through which periodically will bring the program up to date to take care of changing circumstances.

The benefits of the programing approach to the life underwriter are equally evident. The client is better satisfied with the insurance he buys within the framework of programing, so that business persists better and is of greater value. The client is better pleased with his purchase and therefore is a good center of influence for the life underwriter. Perhaps most important of all, programing brings the underwriter the personal satisfaction of having done a good, professionally approached job. As in any profession, this personal satisfaction is an important factor.

Life insurance companies like the programing approach because they are able to do a better job for their policyowners in this way. They also are able to do this job at a more favorable cost because those policyowners who have been sold on a programing basis tend to keep their policies in force over longer periods of time.

Thus, in those situations where it is appropriate, the programing method of applying the services of life insurance to the needs of the client is better for all parties concerned.

Over-all Programing Objectives

The prime objective of programing is to provide security arrangements for the family involved—security both in terms of an adequate amount of income in the event of the death of the income producer and in terms of cash to take care of the family's collateral needs, such as cash for estate administration purposes, education of children, and other special demands. An almost equally important benefit of programing is the built-in accumulation of substantial savings that can be very meaningful to the insured at the time of his retirement or in the event of emergencies during his lifetime.

The individual needs of various members of the family can be catalogued and provision made for them. The settlement arrangements can be flexible or inflexible, depending upon the characteristics and degree of independence of the individuals involved. If it is not possible to provide adequately for all who might be concerned, then priorities can be established until such time as the ownership of an adequate amount of life insurance to take care of all needs can be accomplished.

Summing up, programing can be simple or comprehensive; it can be flexible or inflexible; it can be all encompassing or over only some of the needs that exist, depending upon the situation and the resources of the person whose affairs are being programed.

Programing Steps

The programing process consists of four principal steps. They are as follows:

1. Fact finding.
2. Fixing financial goals and objectives.
3. Identifying the problem or problems that grow out of the situation as it exists when compared with the goals and objectives.
4. Developing the solution or solutions to the problems that are uncovered.

Fact Finding

The goal of fact finding is for the underwriter and the client jointly to bring out and explore all the essential information relating to the client's situation. In fact finding, the first point to be emphasized is the necessity for following a pattern, a form, or a check list. A procedure of this sort is an essential precaution to make certain that no significant consideration is omitted. Some programers have memorized a pattern of information which they meticulously follow in asking questions, but the procedure is the same as though a form had been used. (Figure 61–1 is a sample of a fairly typical check list in questionnaire form.)

It is always dangerous for a fact-finding interview to follow the fashion of census taking, with the underwriter merely seeking statistical answers to questions on the blank. Getting to know and understand the thinking behind the answers given by the client is of the greatest importance. The goal is to become acquainted with the inner man. What motivates this client? What are his real objectives? What stands between him and their realization? A proper fact-finding interview will often serve to clarify the answers to these questions in the mind of the client himself. Actually, in the great majority of cases, identifying the problem to be solved and developing the solution to that problem will follow almost as a matter of course where the fact finding has been thorough and adequate.

The initial area of interest will be securing identifying information relating to the client and the immediate members of his family. If there are any special family relationships that create unusual interests or obligations, these should be brought out. Familiar examples are the dependent father or mother, or a child suffering from either a physical or a mental disability. Not infrequently, there will be an aunt, an uncle, or a cousin in the picture who ordinarily would not have a close claim on the client, but who, because of special relationships developing through the years, has a very firm hold upon the affections and interests of the head of the family. This may extend on occasion to trusted servants or special friends of long standing who have no legal claim on the client at all, but who are remembered in bequests and other displays of interest by their benefactor.

CONFIDENTIAL SURVEY

for

Name Robert K. Park, DDS

Date of Birth May 18, 1930 Place of Birth Morgan, Utah

Residence Address 4038 W. State Phone 939-3662

Business Address 6211 N. 35th Ave. Phone 939-6251

Occupation Dentist Employer Self

and family

Wife's Name Delores Jean Date of Birth June 5, 1932

Wife's Maiden Name Westenfelder Place of Birth Grace, Idaho

Children	Date of Birth	Children	Date of Birth
Pamela	March 2, 1953		
Jeffrey	Nov. 29, 1962		

Date

The purpose of this service is to help crystallize your financial objectives and those of your family, and to make recommendations for their attainment. The value of the recommendations will depend on the completeness of the information on which they are based. All data will be held in strictest confidence.

—1—

FIG. 61–1. Illustrative programing survey form used in fact-finding interview.

Another area to be explored has to do with the client's will. If any doubts are suggested by the answers to questions in this area, an examination of the will by the client's attorney is to be recommended. If the client has no will, the underwriter will certainly recommend that the client consult his own attorney with regard to drafting a will.

A third area of fact finding has to do with the client's ownership of real estate. Many problems are uncovered in this field. The key question may

Your family situation

1. Partial Dependents None Relationship
 Possible Dependents None Relationship
 Charitable and Educational Bequests None
2. Will — Place and Date Executed July 1, 1960 Where Kept? Home
 Executors Dr. D. R. Park Witnesses ?

 Guardians Dr. D. R. Park Will — Members of Family Jean
3. Real Estate Home Owned by Jointly Current Value $16,000 Mortgage Balance $14,500
 Interest 4 3/4 % Monthly Payments $136.00 PITI Term of Mortgage 30 Expires 1992
 Rented — Lease Obligation None Other Real Estate — Location, Value, and Ownership None
 Purchase Money Provided by From Savings
 Where would your family reside in the event of your death? in this home
4. Veteran of World War I? No World War II? No Korea? Yes
 Date Inducted 9-1-50 Date Discharged 9-1-51 Months of Active Duty See Note
 Branch Navy Rank Serial No. Reserve Status Inactive
 Amount of Retirement or Disability Pension $ None Why?
 Aviation Activities — Complete Details, Past, Present, and Future None

5. What is your family longevity? 70 + What is your own health record? Good
 Parents' Ages: Fa. — Mo. 76 Health/Cause of Death: Fa. 73-Coronary Mo.
 Wife's Parents' Ages: Fa. 50 Mo. 54 Health/Cause of Death: Fa. Mo.
6. Do you have any systematic method of saving other than Life Insurance; if so, purpose: No regular plan— Does put some away monthly
7. Income — Approximate total, including salary, bonus, investments, etc. 19,500 Gross - ± 12,000 net

 Other members of family None Source
8. What is your yearly investing surplus? Approx $500
9. Probable inheritances (Self and Each Member of Family): None

10. Amount and Kind of General Estate Personal property
11. Eligible for Social Security Yes S.S. Number 529-34-3824
12. Does your Company provide: Group Insurance No Pension Plan No Profit-Sharing Plan No H. & A. No
 Benefits and Premiums None

—2—

FIG. 61–1 (*Continued*).

concern the disposition of the real estate when the owner dies. The most prevalent application of life insurance in connection with real estate is to provide funds to retire an outstanding mortgage in the event of the client's premature death.

Attention should be directed to the significance of veteran status for clients who have served in the armed forces. The death and disability

Details of present life insurance and annuity policies (self and family):

Company	Policy Number	Amount	Plan	Date of Issue	Premium	Assignment or Loan — Date	Use of Dividend
N.S.L.I.	1907-44-67	10,000	WL	7-29-53	155.10 A	None	P.R.
Group	104 GT 35023	20,000	Term	10-1-58	± 100 A	—	—
S.W. Life	1051206	17,000	D-Term	8-10-61	± 120 A	—	—
N.W.M.	5558377	10,000	Fam. Inc.	11-21-63	316.70 A	None	P.R.

Disability Income Policies $600 Mo. Non-Can? Yes

Where do you keep your policies? Home

Proof of Age: Self Birth Certificate All Beneficiaries Same

Your requirements

In planning your program of financial security, these are the major needs that occur in sequence of time.

IMMEDIATE CASH FUNDS

How much will be needed at your death to pay bills, funeral expenses, notes at the bank, unexpired contracts, Income, Inheritance, and Estate Taxes?

$3,000? | $5,000? | $10,000? | $20,000? | *Your requirements* 10,000

Will you desire to have the mortgage paid off? If so, how much will be required?

$5,000? | $10,000? | $15,000? | $20,000? | *Your requirements* 14,755

How much will be needed to provide a reserve fund for emergencies?

$2,000? | $4,000? | $6,000? | $10,000? | *Your requirements* 6,000

INCOME FOR YOUR FAMILY FOR 16 **YEARS**

How much income per month will your family need to furnish the ordinary comforts until your children are grown?

$300? | $400? | $500? | $600? | *Your requiremen* See Chart

PERMANENT INCOME FOR YOUR WIFE

How much income per month will your wife need, after the children are grown, to provide her with the ordinary comforts of life?

$100? | $200? | $300? | $400? | *Your requirements* 300

EDUCATIONAL FUND

How much money would be required to furnish each of your children with the necessary funds for a college education?

$2,000? | $4,000? | $6,000? | $8,000? | *Your requirements* 12,000

RETIREMENT FUND

How much income per month do you want to provide for yourself and your wife, commencing at age 55, 60, or 65?

$200? | $300? | $400? | $500? | *Your requirements* 600 @ 65

—3—

FIG. 61–1 (*Continued*).

benefits are often substantial and can carry considerable weight in shaping the ultimate program.

One area of importance that can have considerable influence on the program is the probable insurability of the client. Family longevity and other questions of this sort having to do with the client's insurability can give advance warning of a problem in this area. In cases where the client

Your estate situation

13. Attorney: Henry Langendorf Accountant: Lillian Templeton
Trust Officer: None Bank: Valley National

14. Details of any trust, revocable or irrevocable, created by you or any member of your family: None

15. Details of any Gift Tax Exemptions, annual and lifetime, exercised by you or other members of your family: None

Your business situation

16. Business Interest: Stockholder: No Partner: No Proprietor: No Employee: No
Have you other business interests? No
Do you have a buy and sell, or retirement agreement in your own, or any other business? No

Do you own Business Life Insurance on any person? no
Does anyone own Business Life Insurance on your life? No
Does your company own Keyman Insurance on your life? no Others?

Question #4 - Public Health Service 6-1-57 to 11-1-60
Lt. Commander Inactive Reserve

—4—

FIG. 61–1 (*Continued*).

is completely uninsurable, insurance on his wife often provides the best available alternative method of accumulating and distributing the required funds, as well as protecting the children from the economic loss involved in the mother's death.

The client will be well advised to give the life underwriter a complete picture of his income, as well as the financial situation of all members of his family. This is essential to any sound evaluation of his problems; the

Determination of gross estate, death taxes, net estate and estate liquidity

To determine gross estate

Items of Gross Estate:		
Cash — In Savings Banks	$ 2,000	
Cash — In Checking Accounts	$ 1,000	
Household Furnishings	$ 5,000	
Personal Property	$ 10,000	
Home — Current Value (Less Mortgage)	$ 2,000	
Real Estate (Other Than Home)	$	
Stocks and Bonds (Liquid)	$ 1,000	
Stocks and Bonds (Non-Liquid)	$	
Life Insurance (less loans) allocated for payment of Estate Taxes	$	
Life Insurance (less loans) payable to named beneficiaries	$ 75,210	
Proceeds from Employee Benefit Plans	$	
Notes and Accounts Receivable	$ 6,000	
Close Corporation or Partnership Interest (consider as liquid asset only if under agreement to sell — purchase price guaranteed)	$	
Any other items Value of practice	$ 36,000	
Any other items	$	
1. TOTAL GROSS ESTATE		$ 138,210

To determine death taxes

Debts and expenses:		
Debts (current bills, notes, deferred payment plans — etc.)	$ 7,000	
Funeral and last expenses	$ 2,500	
*Administration Expenses (average for estate of similar size)	$ 10,100	
2. TOTAL DEBTS AND EXPENSES		$ 19,600
3. ADJUSTED GROSS ESTATE (Subtract Item 2 from Item 1)		$ 118,610
Deductions and Exemptions		
Marital deduction	$ 59,305	
Charitable and educational bequests	$ 0	
Exemption	$ 60,000	
4. TOTAL DEDUCTIONS AND EXEMPTIONS		$ 119,305
5. TAXABLE ESTATE (Subtract Item 4 from Item 3)		$ 0
Death Taxes:		
Federal Estate Tax	$	
State death tax	$	
6. TOTAL DEATH TAXES		$

To determine net distributable estate

7. TOTAL GROSS ESTATE (Item 1)		$ 138,210
Debts, expenses and death taxes		
Total debts and expenses (Item 2)	$ 19,600	
Total death taxes (Item 6)	$	
8. TOTAL DEBTS, EXPENSES AND DEATH TAXES		$
9. NET DISTRIBUTABLE ESTATE (Subtract Item 8 from Item 7)		$

To determine estate liquidity

10. TOTAL DEBTS, EXPENSES AND DEATH TAXES (Item 8)		$
11. GENERAL (CASH) BEQUESTS		$
12. TOTAL CASH REQUIREMENTS (Item 10 plus Item 11)		$
13. LIQUID ASSETS IN ESTATE		$
14. CASH Excess / Deficit FOR ESTATE REQUIREMENTS (Item 12 minus Item 13)		$

*Life insurance payable to named beneficiaries is not subject to administration expenses as it is not a part of the legal estate; this is true whether or not it is includible in the taxable estate. Jointly owned property which passes directly to the survivor (e.g., some savings accounts, real estate, war bonds, etc.) likewise is not subject to administration expenses, although it is includible in the taxable estate of the person whose funds created it.

—5—

FIG. 61–1 (*Continued*).

life underwriter cannot do a proper job unless he has full and correct information.

Another area that needs to be explored involves the facts relating to the client's expected social security benefits, together with a full set of facts regarding the fringe benefits growing out of his employment. These benefits may be rather substantial; frequently, they are not well understood by the client and should be carefully explored.

The importance of accurate information about the client's present insurance is obvious. There is a tendency to mention the amount and not much more than that. Experience has proven that the only safe procedure in this respect is for the life underwriter to examine personally all policies involved to make certain that he has full and correct data.

Good programing frequently will involve the client's attorney, accountant, trust officer, and banker. For this reason, the life underwriter needs to know the names of these professional advisors and, as far as practicable, the recommendations they have made to the client with regard to the organization of his affairs.

An impressive proportion of candidates for programing will be the beneficiaries, in one form or another, of a trust, or will be otherwise involved with a trust. Therefore, this type of property interest needs to be carefully explored.

Not directly related to trusts, but in the same area of general property status, will be the gift tax exemptions. If a gift tax exemption has been exercised, the life underwriter will need to know about it, so that he will not count on suggesting the use of that exemption again in planning the program.

The type of client to whom programing has a special appeal may well have business interests of one sort or another. In preparing to develop a program, therefore, it is of the greatest importance that the underwriter know about all such business interests and be familiar with the client's thinking regarding them. Does the client plan to dispose of the business interest in the event of his death, or does he intend that a member of his family will succeed him to that interest? Guaranteeing the client's sons the necessary resources to succeed to their father's interest in the business, for example, demands careful forethought and planning. This is an area that needs to be explored thoroughly, and the underwriter should be careful to avoid taking for granted any conventional conclusions.

In the simpler programing situations, determination of the gross estate for tax purposes will not ordinarily be necessary. In complex situations, or in cases involving estates of substantial amounts, measurement of the gross estate can become very important. In the fact-finding form used in the illustration above, a survey has been set up to assist in appropriate cases in the determination of the gross estate, death taxes, net estate, and estate liquidity of the client. This involves a very complete, detailed, and important inquiry. It includes reference to available deductions and exemptions, including the marital deduction. The measurement of the client's gross estate, death taxes, and net estate will determine how much cash should be provided at death for estate liquidity purposes. The liquidity of the general estate will determine what proportion of this cash at death must come from life insurance sources. In many instances, it will be better for all of the money to come from life insurance, even though some of it could be raised through other avenues. In any event, this is an area that needs to be thoroughly surveyed.

Fixing Financial Goals and Objectives

In determining the goals and objectives of the client, the initial effort should be directed to learning what the client already has in mind. If he has formulated some goals that are clear-cut and firm, and which prove to be adequate when tested in the fact-finding interview, these goals can be accepted as the basis for the programing.

In most cases, however, the client will not have sufficient background upon which to base a well-thought-out pattern of specific objectives, and will need helpful guidance in arriving at appropriate figures for the several phases of the family cycle. In such cases, by trying for size various sums for cash, mortgage, readjustment, income for the family, life income for the wife, education for the children, and retirement, a satisfactory series of financial objectives can be negotiated and agreed upon.[3]

For those who like a formula approach, the "C–E–E–½–¼–½" formula has proven helpful. Translated, this formula proposes that a person who owns his own home can set up a reasonably satisfactory program if: "C"—he provides cash at death equal to the amount of any mortgage and the usual provisions for other debts and death expenses; "E"—he provides an emergency fund normally equal to a half year's income; "E"—he provides funds for the college education of his children based upon the current amounts recommended by appropriate colleges or universities; "½"—he provides income during the dependency of his children equal to one half of his current gross income; "¼"—he provides an income for the remainder of his wife's life equal to one fourth of his present gross income; and "½"—he sets as his goal for retirement income a figure equal to one half of the income he is earning at the time of his retirement. This is, of course, but one example of several such formula methods.

Summing up, it can be said that a major purpose of fact finding is to determine accurately the real goals and motivations of the client and to measure his present resources available for their fulfillment. The best fact finding is that in which the client does most of the talking, and in which the underwriter is primarily an interested and helpful listener. If these two qualities are present in the fact-finding interview, the client's objectives are likely to be clearly defined, and the facts will fall neatly into place to provide a complete picture from which a program can be developed that will fulfill his goals.

---

[3] For a detailed discussion of these basic family needs, see Chapter 55, "Determining Needs."

Identifying the Problem or Problems to Be Solved

Where the fact finding has been thorough, the problem or problems to be solved will generally be quite evident. A mistake sometimes made in programing is to rush off to a solution of the first problem that is revealed. This mistake should be resisted firmly. If an objective job of programing is to be done, the underwriter must be aware of all the problems in the case and must balance them one against the other until he has arranged them in their proper perspective and given each its appropriate weight. Sometimes, all of the problems identified can be solved. More often, only the most important can be dealt with in a single programing procedure. Which problem or problems does the client consider to be the most important? Is there a particular problem or series of problems that may return to trouble both the client and the underwriter if they are not dealt with at this time? These are questions which must be asked in assigning priorities among problems when all the client's existing problems cannot be solved at once. Then, as the client's income and resources increase, the remaining problems can be met in the future.

Through a process of thinking through and talking out the situation as revealed by the fact finding and bringing to bear the life underwriter's intellectual resources together with the client's intimate knowledge of his situation, colored by his motives, it will be clear just what the true problem or problems are in each case. It would be fair to say that once the problem has been identified, that problem is half solved.

The Solution

In most instances of simple programing, the solution to the problems posed by the situation will be both clear-cut and obvious to the experienced life underwriter. In more complex situations, the life underwriter frequently will want to work out two or three alternate solutions to the problem, and then go through a process of fitting and trying to determine the one to recommend to the client. Very often, in this process of trying several different solutions, a further solution, different from any of those originally considered and employing the best qualities of each, will be evolved. Almost invariably, there is more than one good solution to a given situation.

The starting point in developing a solution in a programing situation is a proper marshaling of the objectives of the client. Setting up these objectives in chronological order in terms of the way in which these needs will occur with the passage of time is a very helpful procedure. There are various mechanical aids which assist in this process; Figure 61–2 is illustrative of the kind of programing work sheet which may be used.

The key to this particular form is the line marked "WANTS," which is related to the several phases of the life situation set up in successive columns identified in terms of periods of years.

Spending the Present Insurance

With the objectives of the client marshaled in some organized fashion, the next step is to determine how far the client's present assets, including his life insurance, expected social security benefits, and employee benefits, go toward meeting these objectives. Social security, being relatively inflexible, should be applied to the pattern first, since the employment of other assets will have to be shaped around the income provided by social security.

In determining the way in which the present policies are to be employed, it should be recognized that group insurance usually lends itself more satisfactorily to cash needs than for other purposes. On the other hand, National Service Life Insurance, United States Government Life Insurance, and older policies of life insurance companies normally should be allocated to the provision of life income, because the settlement benefits under the life income options of these policies often are considerably more liberal than those found in newer policies, which reflect improved mortality.

Determining the Amount and Kind of New Insurance Required

When the present life insurance and the expected social security benefits have been applied to the objectives in the situation, the areas still to be taken care of normally will be evident. The key questions to be answered in arriving at a solution to the needs still to be covered are generally these:

1. How much new property needs to be created through the medium of life insurance in order to solve the problems in this particular program?
2. What plan or plans of life insurance are best suited to the solution of these problems?
3. Whose lives should be insured?
4. Who should own the life insurance?
5. Who should be the beneficiary or beneficiaries?
6. Should settlement options be set up immediately, or should they be recommended as a pattern of procedure to be followed by the beneficiary?
7. Should settlement under the options be flexible or restrictive?
8. What supplementary agreements or other documents are required to fulfill the program?

The answers to most of these questions will grow out of the information that was developed in the fact-finding interview. The particular life situation of the client, when properly revealed in the fact-finding proce-

WORK SHEET FOR DETERMINING CAPITAL REQUIRED

Note to Agent and Stenographer: This work sheet is not to be reproduced in the finished booklet. When your calculations have been completed, simply fold it back out of the way so that is will be available if you need it for future reference. - - - The initials C, E, E, stand for "Cash Funds," "Emergency Funds," and "Educational Funds." The total of the three is inserted in the "WANTS" line.

	Amt.	Description	C. 24755 E. 6,000 E. 12,000	Income Yrs. 1	Income Yrs. 1	Income Yrs. 1	Income Yrs. 4	Income Yrs. 9	Income Yrs. 14	Income Yrs. Life	R.I. Age 65 Self	And Wife
		WANTS →	42755	1000	750	600	500	500	300	300	500	500
		SOCIAL SECURITY	255	254	254	254	254	191	-0-	105	127	191
A	10000	National Service Life		39	39	39	39	39	39	39	42	42
B	28710	N.W. Mutual 3,000 Cash, 3710 B-16 22,000 Int: the I/R	3000	68	68	68	68	68	78	78	32	32
C	20000	Group	20000									
D	16,500	S.W. Life	16500									
E	75,210	Total Present Insurance	39755	361	361	361	361	298	117	222	201	265
F		Needs	3000	639	389	239	139	202	183	78	399	335
G	13636	New		28	28	28	28	28	28	78		
H	22048			45	45	45	45	45	155	X		
I	12500			26	26	26	26	129	X			
J	1830			4	4	4	40	X				
K	1614			3	3	136	X					
L	3357			7	283	X						
M	6241			526	X							
N	3000		3000	X							215	215
O	64226	Totals	42755	1000	750	600	500	500	300	300	416	480
P												
Q												
R												

dures, usually will detail the specifications of the solution in similar fashion.

The life underwriter will fit appropriate amounts of new insurance into each of the shortage areas by a process of measuring the incomes still to be provided and converting these figures into the face amount of life insurance required to provide those incomes. The total of these new insurance entries is the amount of new insurance required to meet the objectives set forth in the program.

The plan of insurance to be recommended is determined largely by the retirement income goal. If straight life policies in the face amount needed for the protection of the family in the event of the insured's premature death will provide sufficient cash values at age 65 to fulfill the retirement needs, straight life normally would be the suggested plan. On the other hand, if the retirement income needs are greater than would be provided by the straight life values, a higher premium plan is indicated. Depending upon the arithmetic in particular situations, the plan of insurance recommended might thus vary from a family income policy to a high-premium retirement income contract. However, retirement income policies frequently involve unrealistically large premium payments for the client's budget and thus usually will not be a practicable solution.

In arriving at the amount of insurance needed, some life underwriters prefer the so-called "discount" method of calculation to the work sheet illustration employed in this chapter. The resulting figures will be similar. It is solely a matter of personal preference as to methods. Both procedures have strong proponents.[4]

Compromises That May Be Employed Where the Client's Financial Resources Do Not Permit His Immediate Purchase of the Full Program

Quite often, when a program has been laid out with reasonably developed objectives, it nevertheless will represent a new premium outlay beyond the ability of the client to pay the increased premiums. This must lead inevitably to a compromise decision. There are two normal alternatives in this situation. The first is to reduce the client's objectives. However, if they have been soundly established in the beginning, this is generally undesirable. The second alternative is to provide an interim solution through the employment of some form of term insurance for a part of the program. The term insurance then can be converted to a permanent plan as the financial situation of the client improves. This normally is considered the better approach.

The form of term insurance most frequently used for this purpose is the so-called "family income benefit," where a term insurance addition to the basic policy is available to provide increased protection until the client

[4] Basic tables of values used in programing are included in Appendix V.

can afford conversion to a permanent plan. Other forms of term insurance can be used in similar fashion.

If there is no likelihood that the client's income will increase, then there probably is no alternative to reducing the objectives. The use of term insurance over prolonged periods is almost invariably unsatisfactory.

Planning for Distribution of Proceeds

In determining the solution to the client's problems, it was necessary for the underwriter to make certain assumptions as to the fashion in which the present insurance, as well as the new insurance, would be employed to provide the required incomes during the successive phases of the growth and development of the client's family. When a decision has been reached as to the acceptance or modification of the plan, and the new insurance that is to be put in force has been provided, the next step is to prepare a plan for implementing the distribution of the proceeds. The first decision that must be made in this area is whether the settlement plan will be made on a flexible or an inflexible basis. Ordinarily, the flexible approach is the preferred one; but under certain circumstances, particularly involving those not competent to act for themselves or to act judiciously for themselves, an inflexible arrangement will be indicated.

If a flexible procedure is selected, the most important step will be the designation of proper beneficiaries for each element of the program. Money to be used for cash needs and estate costs, for example, normally will be payable to the wife of the insured or the executor of the estate, to make certain that these obligations are recognized and paid.

On the other hand, unless a trust arrangement is to be employed, the policies that are to be used to provide income for members of the family normally will be made payable to the wife or, in the event that she does not survive the insured, to the children who are designated as contingent beneficiaries. A letter filed with the policies, or with the audit record of the program that has been set, suggesting appropriate settlement options to be arranged by the beneficiary with the company often is preferred to having the settlement endorsed on the policy. This approach recognizes that changed conditions may make a different settlement arrangement desirable at the time of settlement than was contemplated at the time the program was set up.

An alternative arrangement that is frequently recommended where flexible settlement has been agreed upon is to arrange for the policy proceeds to be left with the company under the interest option with the right reserved to the beneficiary and the contingent beneficiaries in turn either to withdraw proceeds or to have them settled under other options or a combination of options to the extent that company rules will permit. This plan enables the contingent beneficiaries to take advantage of the settlement options in the event that the primary beneficiary has not disposed of the proceeds, and it offers other advantages as well.

Where rigid settlement arrangements are desired, however, these should be selected and approved by the client and endorsed on the policies during his lifetime. In this regard, it will be helpful for the reader to refer to the chapters on beneficiary designations and settlement options for further information.[5] It is very important that inflexible settlement agreements be kept up to date at all times.

Whatever is done in the way of endorsing or merely recommending settlement arrangements under the various policies should take into account the points made earlier, particularly with respect to using older policies, USGLI, and NSLI for life income purposes. The difference between the rates of return in these policies when employed in this fashion and the life income rates contained in policies currently being issued is a very significant one. The client will certainly want his beneficiaries to gain this advantage.

Illustrative Programing

Perhaps a better way to visualize the programing process is to go through a simple program, step by step. The objectives illustrated are obviously more modest than would be appropriate for most professional men and business executives, but they demonstrate the procedure.

In the fact finding which was illustrated, the client indicated a need for $14,700 for mortgage redemption, $10,000 for other cash funds, $6,000 in emergency funds, $12,000 for educational purposes, an income requirement scaling down from his present net income of $1,000 per month to a figure of $500 a month in the fourth year and thereafter during the period in which the children are growing up, and, finally, $300 per month life income to the widow for the remainder of her life. This particular client indicated that he would like to have a retirement income for himself and his wife of at least $500 per month.

The illustrative work sheet (Figure 61–2) indicates that present insurance would take care of the cash funds needed, would provide for the emergency funds desired, and would furnish all but $3,000 of the educational funds desired. Employing present life insurance and social security in the most effective combination would help provide the income needed during the years in which the children were growing up; but even after the three-year stepdown covered by the readjustment provisions, there was still a shortage ranging from $139 per month up to $202 per month during the remainder of the first sixteen years of the program. When the youngest child reached age 18, social security benefits would cease and would not be available again until the widow reached age 62. The present

[5] See Chapter 56, "Beneficiary Designations and Assignments," and Chapter 57, "Settlement Options."

life insurance would provide $117 per month during this period, leaving a shortage of $183 per month between the widow's age 48 and her age 62, when social security would re-enter the picture. New life insurance would be required to make up this shortage. New life insurance would also be needed to supply the $78-per-month shortage during the remainder of her lifetime. In terms of retirement, the present life insurance and social security would furnish $201 per month to the insured if his wife did not survive to age 65, or the combination of present life insurance and social security would furnish $265 a month to husband and wife, if both survived. This situation, compared with the objective of $500 per month in each instance, indicates a need for additional retirement income of $235 to $299 per month.

On the simplified chart shown in Figure 61–3, these arrangements are illustrated graphically. Benefits provided by present life insurance are shown in crosshatched form. Expected benefits from social security are indicated by the herringbone area. The remaining white area illustrates the difference between the client's objectives and the benefits provided by his present insurance and social security. This difference must be covered by the purchase of new policies.

Future Programing Services

At the moment it is completed, a life insurance program should represent the best arrangement of resources with respect to the client's objectives that a competent life underwriter can recommend in the light of the situation. In the ordinary course of events, this program should be appropriate and sound until some change takes place in the client's situation.

Change, however, is characteristic of our way of life. The underwriter can build in certain provisions in the program that will accommodate a measure of change, but the only safe procedure to follow is to review the program periodically and regularly to make certain that it does properly meet the objectives of the client in the light of his present circumstances.

As the client's earned income increases and his family's standard of living improves, there will be a need for greater amounts of income in the program. As additional children are born, there will need to be provisions for these newcomers. The client's indebtedness picture also may change substantially, and this is almost certain to happen in the course of the acquisition of a new and larger home.

All of these considerations highlight the fact that an insurance program, just like a will, needs to be reviewed perhaps once a year, and certainly every second or third year. The changes that take place can be readily accommodated in a program which is kept up to date, and sound business judgment dictates the regular review of the program with the life underwriter on such a continuing basis.

The use of audits and charts, dated to indicate the time of the most

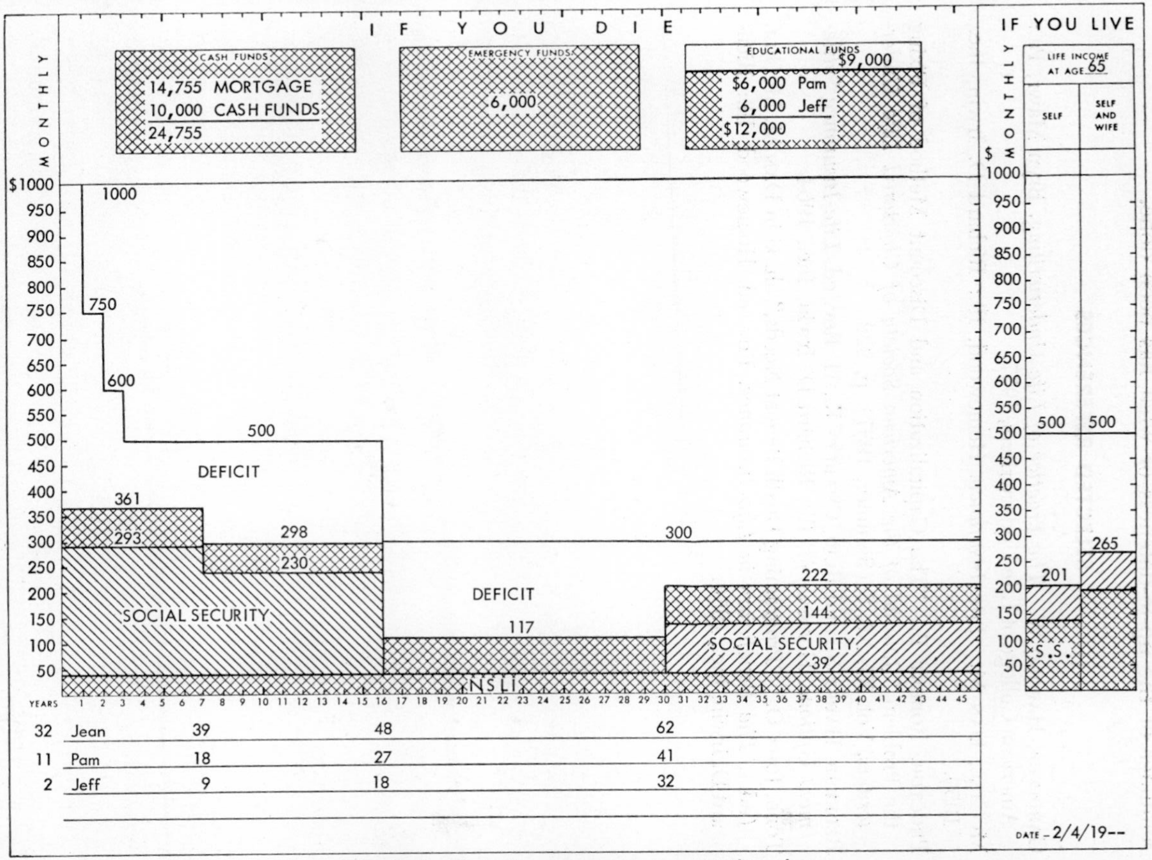

FIG. 61–3. Illustrative programing presentation plan.

recent revision, will be helpful to the client, will be invaluable to his beneficiaries in the event of his death, and will constitute a continuing reminder of the up-to-dateness of what has been done.

SELECTED REFERENCES

GARDINER, HAROLD W. *The Practice of Life Underwriting.* Bryn Mawr, Pa.: American College of Life Underwriters, 1957.

McGILL, DAN M. *Life Insurance.* Homewood, Ill.: Richard D. Irwin, Inc., 1959.

PROCTOR, ROBERT B. "The Capitalization and Discount Method of Fixing the Problem," *Journal of the American Society of Chartered Life Underwriters,* Vol. XI, No. 3 (Summer, 1957), p. 222.

REDEKER, HARRY S., and REID, CHARLES K., II. Rev. ed. *Life Insurance Settlement Options.* Homewood, Ill.: Richard D. Irwin, Inc., 1964.

TODD, JOHN O. "Programing Death Benefit Needs," ch. xi in DAN M. McGILL (ed.), *The Beneficiary in Life Insurance.* Rev. ed. Homewood, Ill.: Richard D. Irwin, Inc., 1956.

Chapter 62

PROGRAMING HEALTH INSURANCE

BY ROBERT W. OSLER

The great bulk of health insurance is being sold on a policy or single need basis. True programing, as it is known in the field of life insurance, is as yet an undeveloped procedure in health insurance. It cannot be called unknown. Here and there, some few health (and fewer life) insurance men are operating on a programing basis in the health insurance field, but they are in a minority.

Inasmuch as insurance is an individual prescription rather than a panacea, it cannot be said that true professional service is being rendered in any line until program selling develops. Further, from a pure production standpoint, real health insurance volume—so badly needed to offset the pressures for socialized coverage—will not come until programing is the general practice instead of the rarity it is today.

Actually, for the life underwriter, programing health insurance calls for little new knowledge and almost no new techniques. The primary purpose of this discussion of programing health insurance benefits is to demonstrate that fact.

Background to Programing

Necessary to intelligent programing of health insurance is an awareness of three basic facts:

1. *Death, old age, and disability are NOT economic problems.* They are merely perils that give rise to a basic economic problem. The basic economic problem is *loss of income.* Which of the three perils causes the loss makes no difference in the result. A family without income by reason of the disability of its wage earner is in no better economic position for the duration of that disability than is one without income by reason of his death. Disability even poses a graver problem than death: There is one more mouth to feed. A widow with two children has two dependents; the economic widow of a disabled man has three.

To plan income insurance benefits to take care of the basic economic problem in case of death alone, old age alone, or disability alone—or any combination of two without the third—is to treat a cardio-renal-vascular case in any one or two of the areas of his disturbance without treating him in all three.

2. *"Policy selling" and "policy buying" are as poor practices in the field of health insurance as they are in the field of life insurance.* The income insurance needs of any given person are as individual as his needs for medication. A man's needs for income protection can be adequately cared for only by careful diagnosis of his individual needs.

3. *Insurance costs money.* Insurance involves clerical and administrative work. That work must be paid for, and the person or persons who must pay for it are the person or persons who ask for the service—the insureds. To the rate for insurance must be added the costs of administration of the insurance fund. Therefore, to insure anything that can be paid for out of pocket or budgeted is to cost oneself money.

It is not the first dollar of loss that causes economic distress; it is the last. The first step in programing health insurance is to determine how much of any loss or cost can be paid for *direct*, and then insure from that point on, not merely insure up to it.

How much can be paid direct should not be decided on the basis of mere convenience. The fact that any given amount paid direct may cause such inconvenience as delaying the purchase of a new car, postponing a vacation, or making some purchase not essential to preservation of the family unit is not sufficient reason for insuring.

It is uneconomic and a clear waste of money to insure any loss that merely "hurts." Insurance should be purchased only against losses that can be truly ruinous.

Few are the individuals (or families) who, from the standpoint of economics, need first-dollar coverage. Even fewer are those who do not need coverages of depth.

Awareness of these three basic facts is essential to the proper programing of health insurance benefits.

A lesson in programing health insurance benefits can be learned also by drawing an analogy between an industrial plant and a wage earner.

The owner of an industrial plant knows that his property is subject to certain physical perils such as fire, windstorm, explosion, and the like. If one of these perils strikes, it will cost money to repair the damage. Therefore, he takes property insurance to indemnify him for such damage.

Just so, a wage earner is subject to perils that can cause him physical damage that it will cost money to "repair." Good business practice calls for him to take health insurance coverage that will help reimburse him for the cost of such repairs to his body or health.

The owner of the industrial plant also realizes that one of the physical perils could cause damage so extensive that the plant would have to be shut down while repairs are being made. If it shuts down, the income it earns will be cut off. Therefore, he takes business interruption insurance in order to have some income while the plant cannot operate.

Just so, any of the perils a wage earner faces could cause damage to his body or health so extensive that he would have to "shut down" his earning operations while "repairs" are being made. Good business practice calls for him to have insurance that will give him at least some income while he cannot "operate," i.e., get out and work.

Some indication of the importance of this need for personal "business interruption" insurance is indicated by a comparison of the frequency of disabilities lasting three months with those of death on an age-specific basis as shown in Table 62–1. The death rate is taken from the 1958 CSO table. The rate of disablement is based on the D Table contained in the report of the Industry Advisory Committee on Reserves for Individual Health Insurance Policies, accepted by the Accident and Health Committee of the National Association of Insurance Commissioners in 1963.

TABLE 62–1

Comparison of Chances of Long-Term Disability with Chances of Death at Quinquennial Central Ages

Age at Time of Disablement	Number per 1,000 Still Disabled at End of 3 Months	Number per 1,000 Dying at the Given Age	Chances of Disability Compared with Death
22	6.64	1.86	3.56 to 1
27	6.57	1.99	3.30 to 1
32	7.78	2.25	3.45 to 1
37	9.81	2.80	3.50 to 1
42	12.57	4.17	3.01 to 1
47	16.76	6.36	2.63 to 1
52	22.72	9.96	2.28 to 1
57	32.38	15.54	2.08 to 1
62	46.66	24.31	1.91 to 1
67	67.16	38.04	1.76 to 1
72	103.01	58.65	1.75 to 1

In the field of health insurance, there are two basic types of coverage: medical expense and disability income. Programing health insurance benefits begins with a survey or analysis of the individual and family needs for each type of coverage.

MEDICAL EXPENSE COVERAGE

Needs for medical expense coverage can be analyzed in three categories: (1) the needs of the wage earner himself, (2) the needs of individual family members, and (3) the needs of survivors in the event the "damage" to any family member is extensive enough to cause death.

Needs of the Wage Earner

Any type of disability is almost certain to create some medical expense (using the term here and throughout the chapter in a broad sense that covers hospital, surgical, nursing, medicinal, and all such related expenses). Therefore, a wage earner needs medical expense coverage—not for the $5.00 X ray or the overnight hospital stay for a routine test, but for the type of expenses that impose a burden that endangers the economic status of the family.

Loss of limb or eyesight results in a permanent impairment that can reduce the ability to earn. Therefore, there is justification for lump-sum benefits in the event of dismemberment.

Needs of Family Members

Each member of the family is subject to medical expense loss. Therefore, each should be adequately covered with medical expense insurance.

Any member of the family may also suffer permanent impairment from loss of limb or eyesight. Such impairment may create extra costs and cause present or future reduction in either direct or indirect earning ability.

Dismemberment in the case of a married woman who is not employed outside the home will cause no direct loss but will cause an indirect loss of income to her or the family. Her impairment may be such that it will be necessary to hire household help, the cost of which must be deducted from the family income and hence constitutes a "loss" that it is economically legitimate to insure.

Dismemberment in the case of a child may create both initial and continuing extra expense for the family, and the child's future earning power may be impaired.

Needs of Survivors

Accident or sickness can result in death. If either does, two needs arise: (1) replacement for the survivors of some part of the earning power lost (direct in the case of a wage earner, indirect in the case of a nonwage-earning member of the family whose services in the home will have to be replaced with paid help), and (2) reimbursement for some part of medical expenses.

Benefits for accidental death are available. There is no coverage for death from sickness ("natural death") in the field of health insurance benefits. As stated, programing is a matter of compounding an individual prescription in each case. It is impossible to make categorical statements about types of coverages that should be used. However, it would appear valid to say that inasmuch as there must be life insurance for death from sickness, and inasmuch as such life insurance will also pay in case of accidental death, it is probable that the area of insurance for death should be left entirely in the life field in most programs.

Death will almost always leave medical bills for the survivors to pay. They should, therefore, be provided with coverage to pay the amount of those bills over and above what can be paid out of pocket. The medical expense insurance provided in case of nonfatal accident or sickness will automatically pay the survivors.

Each family member should have an immediate cash fund for final expenses. Some final expenses can be estimated fairly closely: outstanding bills and accrued taxes (in the case of a wage earner), funeral, cemetery lot, marker, and the like. When the amount of a future obligation is known in advance, it can be handled with a fixed fund. The most practical way for the majority of people to set up a fixed fund for known final expenses is through life insurance.

Some final expenses cannot be estimated with any degree of accuracy. They are, in the main, the expenses of final illness. Where the amount of a future obligation is unknown, it cannot be handled with a fixed fund. It must be insured—and *it cannot be insured through life insurance.* Life insurance can provide only a fixed fund. Only health insurance can provide an economically valid, immediate cash fund for the unknown final medical expenses.

The immediate cash fund of each member of the family should consist of adequate life insurance to cover those final expenses that can be estimated with some degree of accuracy, *plus medical expense insurance to cover those final expenses the amount of which cannot be estimated with any degree of accuracy.*

In many income insurance programs (using the term to include both life and health coverages), there also is usually a need for an "emergency" fund for survivors. This need arises from the fact that the guaranteed income the family will have in the event of the death of the wage earner is, in the vast majority of programs, marginal. The family can get by *if* there are no heavy, unbudgeted expenses. Such expenses may be of either one of two types.

They May Be Expenses Arising from Obsolescence. Simple examples are a roof that wears out or a furnace that breaks down. Obsolescence is not insurable. In theory, it is budgetable; but under the marginal income on which a family without a wage earner may be operating, there may be no funds to set aside in an obsolescence account. Therefore, it is sometimes deemed advisable to use life insurance to set up a fixed fund on which the survivors may draw in the event obsolescence expenses are beyond their income.

They May Be Expenses Arising from a Fortuitous Event. Fire, wind storm, or other physical peril may strike—or accident or illness may create medical expense. Undoubtedly, in calculating the minimum income needs of the family in case of the death of the wage earner, the budget has been set up to pay the premiums on property insurance to take care of fortuitous property losses. In contrast, however, it is almost universal practice to seek to provide for fortuitous losses arising by reason of accident or illness through a fixed fund.

It is quite common to say in programing: "We'll set up an emergency fund on which your widow can draw in case one of the children has an expensive illness or your wife has to have an operation."

This is unsound programing. *Emergency medical expenses of surviving members of a family cannot be insured with life insurance* because life insurance can provide survivors with a fixed fund only.

Fortuitous medical expenses for survivors must be *insured.* Such insurance can be provided in either one of two ways:

1. Its cost should be considered when determining the minimum income on which a family without a wage earner can get along, and the premium for it should be paid just as the premium for property insurance is paid.
2. If the cost of medical expense insurance is not included in the minimum budget, then sufficient life insurance proceeds should be left on the interest-only option to pay the premium. If the amount of proceeds that can be so set aside is not sufficient to earn enough interest to pay the premium, the proceeds can be paid out in equal installments of an amount sufficient to meet the premium, with the attempt being to keep the insurance in force at least during the critical years before the children are self-supporting.[1]

DISABILITY INCOME COVERAGE

The needs for income coverage do not lend themselves to discussion by family members, inasmuch as disability income (loss-of-time) insurance is available only to a direct wage earner.[2] Therefore, the treatment of disability income coverage needs will be by type of need.

The basic needs for disability income coverage parallel closely those for life insurance because, as pointed out, the problem involved is loss of income. What causes the loss does not change the nature of the need.

The basic income coverage needs are:

Mortgage insurance
Readjustment income
Dependency period income
Educational fund
Continuing income

As in life insurance programing, the over-all objective is to provide sufficient income for the family to maintain a reasonable standard of living. The purpose of breaking the over-all objective down into need "packages" is threefold: (1) to determine what the over-all income need

[1] Obviously, this method of handling the premium is simply one of increasing the minimum family income by the amount of the premium, and is, therefore, one and the same with the first suggested method. It does, however, have a psychological value: If the money for the premium is segregated, as this method segregates it, there is less likelihood that the survivors will lapse the coverage to make their basic income go further. Moreover, if the money comes in from the emergency fund once a year at premium-paying time, it is surer to be there than if it is up to the family to budget it out of monthly income.

[2] Limited amounts of disability income are to be found available for unemployed women or students.

is (just as it is necessary to know what the various items for which money will be needed are before a family budget can be set up); (2) to dramatize the needs to the client; and (3) to help get some part of the program in force if the client will not or cannot buy all of it.

There seem to be two basic philosophies in the application of disability income insurance. One holds that the number of disabilities running beyond two years is so small statistically that there is little point in writing benefit durations for longer than such length of time. This same school of thought also usually holds that waiting periods should be short: seven days or not more than 14 days.

In support of the argument that few disabilities run over two years is the fact that the Conference Modification of the Class III Disability Table (the current standard for valuation of the active lives reserve in guaranteed renewable forms) shows the following at age 35:

Out of those disabled seven days, 6.5 per cent will be disabled at the end of 24 months.

Out of those disabled 14 days, 10.25 per cent will be disabled at the end of 24 months.

Out of those disabled 30 days, 2.6 per cent will still be disabled at the end of 24 months.

The argument of advocates of short waiting periods is that frequent claims are not only good public and policyholder relations and an excellent prospecting tool, but also a conservation measure. Many people, they point out, have group disability income, which almost always has very short waiting periods. If the group plan delivers them several checks (however small) while the individual plan delivers nothing, these people will become convinced that the group plan is "better" and lapse their individual coverage.

The short-duration, short-waiting-period philosophy might well be called that of the practical salesman. On the other hand, however, is the philosophy of the technician. The technician will point out that severity of loss, not frequency, should be the deciding factor in insuring, and that although short-term disabilities are the most frequent, long-term disabilities cause the major portion of the economic loss from disability. Well over one third of the people disabled at any given time have been disabled over eighteen months, and 13.6 per cent of them have been disabled over ten years.[3]

It means little to the man who is disabled over two years that he is a statistical fragment, the technician will point out. As for short waiting periods, they point out that it is economically wasteful to insure any loss that can be paid direct.

It is not the province of this chapter to analyze the arguments of the two schools of thought, except to say that inasmuch as the author adheres

[3] O. D. Dickerson, *Health Insurance* (rev. ed.; Homewood, Ill.: Richard D. Irwin, Inc., 1963), Table 8, p. 28.

to what we have called the "technician's school," the following example of programing is based on the principles of that school. The adherent to the "practical salesman's school" can still learn from the example because in his programing, he will concentrate on the short-duration needs.

Mortgage Insurance

The biggest single investment and the biggest single debt of the average family is a home with a mortgage on it. Mortgage payments often pinch the budget when the family has full earning power. If that earning power is cut off for any extended period, the mortgage debt piles up. The result can be a forced and disadvantageous sale of the equity, if not foreclosure.

If the house is lost because of disability, the effect on the family is no different than if it had been lost by reason of the death of the breadwinner. It is illogical, therefore, to use mortgage life insurance while ignoring mortgage disability coverage.

Mortgage disability insurance can consist of a loss-of-time policy paying a monthly amount equivalent to the mortgage installment and of a benefit duration as nearly equal as possible to the number of years the mortgage yet has to run.[4] Consideration should also be given to having the amount of benefits exceed the mortgage installment somewhat in order to provide help with taxes and maintenance.

In the case of a family that does not own its home but is renting, a "rent insurance" policy may be suggested—a monthly benefit equal to the monthly rental figure.

The reason for suggesting rent insurance as a separate package goes back to the threefold purpose in breaking the over-all family income need down into packages in the first place. If the client buys the whole program (i.e., sufficient disability income to maintain a reasonable standard of living), rent insurance need not be a separate policy but simply an item in the budget developed in the process of determining the total income needed.

In selecting a policy to use for mortgage insurance, it should be remembered that the first mortgage installment will not be due for a time after a man's income stops. Therefore, a 15- to 30-day waiting period should be used. A longer waiting period is indicated (1) if the client's employer has a plan for salary continuance in case of disability (in which instance the waiting period should coincide with the ending of the employer benefits),[5] and (2) if the family has cash reserves to pay the installments for some months. Paying the installments out of cash reserves follows the principle set forth earlier in this chapter: elimination of first-dollar cover-

[4] Monthly decreasing term policies are beginning to appear for mortgage insurance use.

[5] This assumes that the plan continues a high percentage of earned income. If it provides too low a percentage, there may not be enough money to pay living costs and the mortgage, too. In this case, mortgage insurance benefits will be needed sooner.

ages wherever possible in order to free premium money to take care of other needs—and particularly for the purchase of coverages of sufficient depth.

Readjustment Income

The principle of disability readjustment income is exactly the same as that for such income in case of death (because, again, the problem is loss of income, not which peril caused it). That principle is the fact that it is almost always a big jump down from the level of earned income to the level of the income that will continue after earning power is gone. It will reduce the shock of the drop and make panic liquidation of possessions less likely if the family has a year or so to organize itself and its budget before it starts living on the greatly reduced income.

The readjustment income plan may be intended to come as close as possible to continuing a family's net income for a few months to a year after loss of earning power, or it may be a stepdown plan for reducing income over a period of several years.

If, in any given case, there is an indication of need for a readjustment plan in the event of the death of the wage earner, the indication is equally for one in case of disability.

In fact, disability readjustment income may be psychologically more important than death readjustment. When a man dies, the family knows immediately that his earning power is irretrievably lost and that it has to adjust to a lower budget. Therefore, it sets about at once to conserve assets.

However, when a man is disabled, it is psychological self-defense for the family to think he may recover (even if medical evidence is against it). Therefore, the family is more likely to go on living at its earned income level by drawing on assets it should be conserving: savings accounts and life insurance cash values, for prime examples. When it finally becomes convinced that the wage earner will not recover his earning power or that the disability will be of such duration that the living scale will have to be reduced, it may have exhausted all reserve funds (and, in the case of life insurance, so impaired its value that it will eventually lapse).

Setting up the readjustment income plan is merely a matter of using a disability income policy with relatively short-duration benefits to pay an added amount of monthly income—added to the basic, continuing disability income provided.

First-dollar coverage should be avoided by use of a waiting period, the length of which is determined by the employer's salary continuation plan or practices and by the family reserves.

Dependency Period Income

This need is, again, identical with the same need for life insurance. There must be income during the growing-up years of the family if it is to be kept together and if the mother is to be kept in the home. However, whereas in the case of the death of the father it is considered *desirable* to keep the mother in the home in contrast to working, in the case of his disability, it may be *essential* that she not work. If he cannot take care of himself, either she will have to be there all day, or she will have to spend a high proportion of her earnings (after taxes) to hire care for him.

Setting the amount of the dependency period income is a matter of determining the minimum income on which the family could get along without any earnings and then using a policy that will pay that minimum. If the minimum desired requires too much premium money, then either adjustments will have to be made elsewhere in the program, or the desired minimum will have to be reduced. Since a sound program of income insurance calls for co-ordinating life and health coverages, any adjustments should be program-wide, not simply in the health benefits.

If the need is for $400 a month in case earned income is cut off (whether by death or disability) and there is insufficient premium money to provide $400, then the figure may have to be adjusted downward throughout the program. It is invalid programing to reduce either health insurance alone or life insurance alone. To reduce one and not the other is tantamount to trying to predict the future.

An imbalance between income in case of death and income in case of disability may be forced in instances in which the minimum income set by the family in a given case is too high for the health insurance underwriting limits. Short of the complication of underwriting limits, however, whatever is the minimum needed in the event of death, the same amount is needed in case of disability. Lack of income is lack of income, regardless of cause.

In determining the policy to use for the dependency period, the principle of coverage in depth rather than of first-dollar loss should be observed. The waiting period should be selected in view of the facts in the case. Often, disability income riders on life insurance will make a good basis for building the dependency period income. Usually, however, the income from them will have to be supplemented with straight loss-of-time policies. The minimum disability income needed may be more than the amount of life insurance with disability rider in the program. Further, the life policy disability income rider commonly has a waiting period that will strain the reserves of the average family—another reason for supplemental loss-of-time policies if life riders form part of the basic disability income in the program.

Educational Fund

The disability educational fund is difficult to handle (especially in the smaller program) with coverages now on the market.

Needed is a deferred benefit policy providing that in the event the insured is disabled at any time and the disability continues to a named beneficiary's eighteenth birthday, income will be paid for the ensuing four years or until the end of the disability, whichever might come first.[6]

At the present time, the only exact way to set up a disability educational fund is by the use of a life insurance educational endowment policy with waiver of premium in the event of the disability of the payor. However, the high rate for the short-term educational endowment policy often uses up premium money needed for more primary coverages—dependency period income, for example.

Various devices for handling the educational fund need in case of disability can be worked out in a program. For instance, a disability income policy can be used to pay benefits to be banked for future college costs. Or a whole life insurance policy can be set up for the college fund in the event of death, with waiver of premium to preserve the cash values to help with college costs in the event of disability. However, all of these devices for handling the educational fund in the event of disability are makeshift; and in this area, health insurance programing is inadequate with the policy portfolio the business offers today.

Continuing Income

After the children are grown, the parents will still need income. True, first things must be put first in programing. Getting the children to an age of self-support comes ahead of providing income after they are grown. If absolutely necessary, they can contribute the income their parents have to have. It is also theoretically possible for the wife to go out and work. However, in the first place, even in the best of times, jobs for older women who have not worked in business or industry for years are less than plentiful; in the second place, there is the aforementioned problem of caring for the disabled husband. Therefore, continuing income should be provided until such time as retirement benefits (if any) start.

In setting up the health insurance program, as in setting up the life program, the best procedure is usually to work "from the bottom up." Minimum needs after the children are grown should be decided first. Then the basic disability income protection should be provided by a policy of benefit duration to the date any guaranteed retirement benefit will start. The areas of greater income need should then be "filled in" with shorter duration policies. Imposed on this floor of income will be one policy to pay the *additional* income needed during the years the mortgage

[6] It may be argued that no such policy is on the market because there is no "demand" for it. However, it is not the history of policy development that many policies originate from public demand. The demand usually arises only after the policy is offered for sale.

has to run; another to provide the *additional* income needed for whatever period readjustment income is desired; another to provide the *additional* income needed during the dependency years; and still others for any special additional income needs appearing in a given case.

An adequate program of health insurance should include medical expense coverages at all stages and on into retirement. Lifetime medical expense coverages are available even on a guaranteed renewable basis, as are coverages at issue ages over 65.

In determining the disability incomes to be provided at each stage of the program (and in setting the minimum retirement income needed when integrating the life and health insurance programs), the premium necessary for medical expense coverage on family members should be added into the budget on which the amounts of income provided are predicated.

Other Aspects

A health insurance program embracing the health insurance needs of the individual only may not be complete. Where an individual is involved in business ownership, there may be other needs of paramount importance related to this ownership. However, a discussion of business disability insurance will be found elsewhere in this volume (see Chapters 47 and 51), and the underwriter interested in rendering real income insurance service should hold in mind that there is an area of widespread use and need for health insurance in all business continuation areas.[7]

Finally, little is being done as yet in the area of true programing of *income insurance needs*—which calls for integration of life and health coverages to develop a program valid in principles and effective in benefits. It is to be hoped that developments in this field will come quickly, for they are badly needed by literally millions of people.

---

[7] A few other treatments of this area are in Robert I. Mehr and Robert W. Osler, *Modern Life Insurance* (3d ed.; New York: Macmillan Co., 1961); in a chapter by this author in Robert I. Mehr and E. E. Cammack, *Principles of Insurance* (3d ed.; Homewood, Ill.: Richird D. Irwin, Inc., 1961), pp. 617 ff.; in Robert W. Osler, *Guide to Health Insurance* (Indianapolis: Rough Notes Co., Inc., 1960); in William Harmelin and Morris Friedman, *Disability Insurance in the Buy-out Agreement* (Indianapolis: Rough Notes Co., Inc., 1959); in Robert W. Osler, "Buy-and-Sell in Business Disability Cases," *Insurance Salesman,* Vol. XCIX, No. 2 (1956), p. 57; in Robert A. Brown, Jr., "The Role of Disability Income Insurance in the Business Continuation Plan," *Journal of the American Society of Chartered Life Underwriters,* Vol. VIII, No. 1 (Winter, 1953), p. 50; in Hugh M. MacKay, "Disability, Retirement or Death of a Partner," *Journal of the American Society of Chartered Life Underwriters,* Vol. XIII, No. 1 (Winter, 1958), p. 53; in William Harmelin and Robert W. Osler, *Business Uses of Health Insurance* (Bryn Mawr, Pa.: American College of Life Underwriters, 1960); and in Robert W. Osler, *Nine Business Uses of Health Insurance* (Indianapolis: Research and Review Service of America, Inc., 1961).

A CASE EXAMPLE IN PROGRAMING HEALTH INSURANCE BENEFITS

The following example of programing health insurance benefits is synthetic. The assumptions are not an attempt at realism but merely to illustrate the process. Further, in any programing situation, there will be almost as many different ideas of how to handle any given situation as there are agents looking at the facts in the case. This example is not offered as the "ideal" program but merely as one that attempts to illustrate the principles this chapter has set forth.

Further, the case example will not quote rates. To do so would risk plunging the whole illustration into the never-ending discussion of optionably renewable versus noncancellable contracts. The result would be attention diverted from programing principles, the illustration of which is the sole purpose of the example. The concentration will be on programing; the type of policy used is up to the individual programer.

Finally, it must be recognized that some of the principles set forth in this chapter may be beyond the policy portfolio of any given company. The result is that it may be necessary to use the policies of more than one company to set up a program.

It could be argued that in view of the inadequacy of policy portfolios, the principles set forth in this chapter are impractical. However, it is the aforementioned observation that throughout the history of the insurance business, policies have been developed to meet demands from the field more often than vice versa. Therefore, the author believes that the development of the practice of programing health insurance benefits will lead directly to the development of policy forms needed for adequate programing.

Viewed in this light, there is nothing impractical about the principles set forth.

Assumptions

For the purposes of this completely synthetic case example, the following assumptions are made:

The family consists of a father, aged 35; a mother, aged 32; a son, aged 10; and a daughter, aged 8.

The father's occupation is the best classification by whatever occupational classification system is used.

Annual earnings of the father, net after income taxes, are $10,000. There is no significant investment income.

The only health insurance protection the family now has is (1) a $10-a-day hospitalization policy for 100 days, $200 surgical schedule, twenty times daily hospital benefit for miscellaneous; and (2) an employer disability salary continuance plan paying $300 a month for 90 days.

The family agrees that it could, if forced to, get along on $400 a month, if most of the amount were tax-free, until the children are grown—$250 after they are grown.

The family is buying a house on a mortgage. Mortgage payments (including principal, interest, and reserves for taxes and insurance) are $100 a month, and the mortgage has ten years yet to run.

The family has a life insurance program providing the $400-a-month minimum it says it must have; a readjustment income to bring it down in more than one jump from the approximately $833 a month it now has net after taxes; mortgage insurance to clear the house in case of the death of the father; and an immediate cash fund of more than $2,500—which is $1,500 for final expenses that can be estimated fairly accurately in advance, plus $1,000 for final illness expenses.

Let it be stated once again (but for the last time) that whether or not these assumptions are "typical," certain assumptions are a *sine qua non* of a case example. Those here have been chosen to illustrate the principles set forth in the chapter. The purpose of this example is to illustrate a process, not to report an actual case.

Immediate Cash Fund

A cardinal principle of programing is "first needs first." It would appear that in this example the first need is the immediate cash situation.

The example assumes that the final-bill situation has been thoroughly explored. This family happens to be a paragon of financial conservatism. It operates as nearly on a true cash basis as possible. All its charge accounts are on a 30-day basis. It is buying nothing on time except a car, and it agrees that in the event of the destruction of earned income, it should dispose of the car as unnecessary to family life.[8] Having no investment income to speak of (merely interest on a minor savings account), and having a reserve for real property taxes included in its mortgage payments, it has virtually no problem of accrued taxes. Therefore, in the event of the death of the father, calculable final expenses would be largely funeral, cemetery lot, and marker, which $1,500 would cover.

However, while $1,500 would cover calculable final expenses, the amount assumes that the wage earner will die instantaneously. There is no way to guarantee this assumption. Therefore, programing on the basis of life insurance alone, the "solution" is to put "something extra" in the immediate cash fund to take care of the final medical bills. As stated, it is assumed that the life insurance program is so "tight" that only $1,000 can be allotted for that use. This is what has been described as invalid

[8] There *must* be some family, somewhere, that would agree that a car is not vital to health, safety, or morality.

programing because it is an attempt to prepare for a bill of unknown amount with a fixed fund. Medical expenses being what they are today, $1,000 is pocket money.

The first move in this program should be, in the opinion of the author, strengthening the immediate cash situation with true medical expense insurance. Note that the present hospitalization policy owned by his family will pay a maximum of $1,400 ($10 DBR × 100 days, plus top surgical of $200, plus 20 × DBR of $10 a day = $1,400). Further, this maximum benefit would be possible only under the "top" combination of circumstances (such as most expensive surgical procedure and so forth).

Medical insurance of $1,400 is inadequate. Therefore, the first program recommendation here is replacement of the present hospital policy with a major medical expense policy having at least a $5,000 maximum. Such a policy will cost little, if any, more than the first-dollar policy now owned.

Therefore, the major medical expense can be added to the program with no additional premium outlay; and when it is, the following things result:

1. There is a true, *insured* immediate cash fund. Instead of hoping that $1,000 will cover the bills, there is up to $5,000 available.

2. There are freed for other uses $1,000 of the $2,500 previously allotted to the immediate cash fund.

3. Further, assuming that the major medical expense policy covers the family, we now have true medical expense insurance on everyone in that family.

Emergency Fund

It would seem that the emergency fund is the next order of business—taking first things first. Under the life-only program, we had nothing to spare for the emergency fund—except anything that might have been left over after final bills. Now, we have $1,000 freed for emergency use. This will cover the deductible under the major medical expense. If a policy with percentage participation is used, it will also cover part of this liability.

If any part of the $1,000 of life insurance proceeds originally assigned to the immediate cash fund is left, it should be paid out in installments that will continue the major medical expense policy in force on the survivors as long as possible, in order to give true emergency fund protection for at least that length of time.

Mortgage Insurance

Considering the immediate cash and emergency fund needs the most pressing, in that order, the next most pressing is probably the mortgage situation.

The obvious solution is a $100-a-month disability income policy that will cover disability from either accident or sickness for ten years—the length of time the mortgage payments have to run. The policy should probably have a thirty-day waiting period, for reasons set forth in the foregoing discussion of the mortgage need. For the purposes of this case example, assume the mortgage situation is so handled.[9]

The Role of Social Security

In planning health insurance incomes, as in planning those from life insurance, it is necessary to take into account the payments available from federal Old-Age, Survivors, and Disability Insurance. There are two philosophies for handling such benefits. One is to use them as a base line. This is the most common practice in life insurance programing. The other is to set the base line of income with private insurance and let the social security benefits "come in on top."

While the "base-line" philosophy may be well adapted to life insurance planning, it is not as well adapted to health insurance. Social security pays only for permanent and total disability. As long as there is any residual earning power, OASDI does not consider the disability "total." It is possible, therefore, to incur a disability that is economically disastrous to a family for which social security does not pay benefits. If social security has been used as the base line of income, the family is in serious trouble.

For this reason (and recognizing fully that there are strong arguments for the base-line philosophy), this case example follows the "in on top" handling of social security.

Base-Line Income

The family has agreed it can get along on $400 a month until the children are grown and $250 a month thereafter. In other words, $250 a month is the base line of income. Since the need for this amount of income runs from the date of disability to the date retirement income begins, a policy is needed with benefits that run to age 65 for both sickness and accident.

What waiting or elimination period should be used in this policy depends on the family situation viewed from the standpoint of its liquid

---

[9] Mortgage installments usually include what amounts to installments on annual property taxes and insurance. How much of the installment on any given mortgage is payment to principal and interest only depends entirely on that particular mortgage. Let us assume here that $70 of the $100 is principal and interest, and the rest is for the reserve funds for taxes and insurance. Thus, even after the mortgage is paid off, the family will continue to have to put out $30 a month for insurance and taxes. Therefore, exact programing would call for one of two things: (*a*) 10-year disability income policy for $70 a month to meet the payments to principal and interest, and a $30-a-month policy with lifetime accident and sickness benefits (or sickness benefits to age 65) to take care of the continuing need for money to meet the insurance and taxes; or (*b*) inclusion of the $30 a month in the base income of the family plus a $70-a-month, 10-year mortgage policy.

reserves, the salary continuation plan offered by the employer, and other such considerations. Certainly, in the case of a $10,000-a-year net income family, at least a thirty-day waiting period should be considered.

Dependency Period Income

A base line of $250 a month of income has been established. However, during the years when the children are wholly dependent on the father's earned income, the family says it must have $400. Making the common assumption that the dependency ends at each child's age 18, this family needs $150 a month on top of the base line of income for the next 10 years. Fortunately, policies with 10-year benefit durations are widely available.[10] Considerations regarding the elimination period to select are the same as in the case of the base-line policy.[11]

Readjustment Income

A readjustment income is not indicated in every case, and whether or not it is depends on individual case considerations. In this example, the family is dropping from $833 a month after taxes to $400 a month. The drop is a sharp one. It would seem economically sound to give the family a little while to prepare for the drop—say, a year of income as close to the net they had before disability as it is possible to come under underwriting limitations.

Assume that the man in the example has a $14,000-a-year gross income before taxes. This income ought to support an application for a total of $600 a month even under very conservative underwriting rules. Therefore, the readjustment income could consist of a policy for $200 a month for one year.

The readjustment fund will serve also in cases of short-term disability. making retrenchment during such disabilities less necessary. This factor is more important than it may seem at first glance. When a man acquires a disability from which recovery in several months, at most, is indicated, the family will tend to go on spending at the same rate as before the disability. The result may be that it dips seriously into cash reserves and,

---

[10] Common benefit durations in today's disability income policies are one, one and a half, two, three, five, and ten years, and to age 65 (sometimes for life, especially in case of disability from accident). If a benefit duration other than one of these is needed, a choice must be made between underinsuring (using a benefit period shorter than required) or overinsuring (using one longer than required). The choice will depend on the individual case and the philosophy of the individual programer. As this is written, reducing term policies from any issue age to any attained age are beginning to appear. They will greatly improve this aspect of programing.

[11] It should be held in mind in setting elimination periods that where the present employer supplies long-term salary continuation or group benefits (say, ninety days or more), it is not altogether safe to set the elimination period equally as long. A new employer might not be as liberal, leaving a gap between the termination of employer benefits and the beginning of personal benefits.

perhaps, impairs the cash values of its life insurance. It would appear to be sound programing to provide higher income for short-term disabilities in which the need for financial retrenchment is not so obvious to the family as it is in the case of the long-term disability.

Educational Fund

As has been said, an exact solution for the educational fund is a juvenile endowment with payor benefit. However, as has also been noted, the high premium of such forms often pinches the more primary elements of a program.

A cash value policy on the life of the father with waiver of premium will provide some funds for college in case of disability prior to or during the college years. It will not provide enough, however, to pay all college expenses—that is, unless the amount of premium put into it is roughly equivalent to that put into a juvenile endowment.

Further money for college may be obtained from social security benefits. This case example has adopted the principle of setting up the base line of income through insurance and allowing the social security benefits to come in as extra money. If this extra money is saved during the years prior to college, it will accumulate to a substantial college fund.

For instance, assume that the head of the example family acquires a total and permanent disability (as defined by social security) today, and assume that he is eligible for the maximum benefit six months from now. Assume further that he saves all payments from social security and invests them as received at 3 per cent net after income tax. By the time the boy is 18 and ready for college, invested social security funds will amount to around $25,000, enough money to send both children through college even if college costs increase as fast as predicted by those promoting taxes and endowments for colleges.

It is true, of course, that the likelihood that the family will *not* save all the money or even any substantial portion of it is great, but it has already been pointed out that the ideal solution to the problem of money for college in case of disability does not now exist.

Completed in chart form, the disability program appears as shown in Figure 62–1.

This is not a case example of a *perfect* health insurance program. It is, rather, a synthetic case designed to illustrate the foregoing principles. If readers will consider it in that light, the author will concede any objections they may have to his specific recommendations.

Finally, the author would like to enter this plea in his defense:

He does not profess to be an expert in the area of programing health insurance benefits. Almost all he knows on the subject he has worked out himself. That statement is not a brag but an apology. He feels certain that within as short a time as a decade, those who run across this chapter

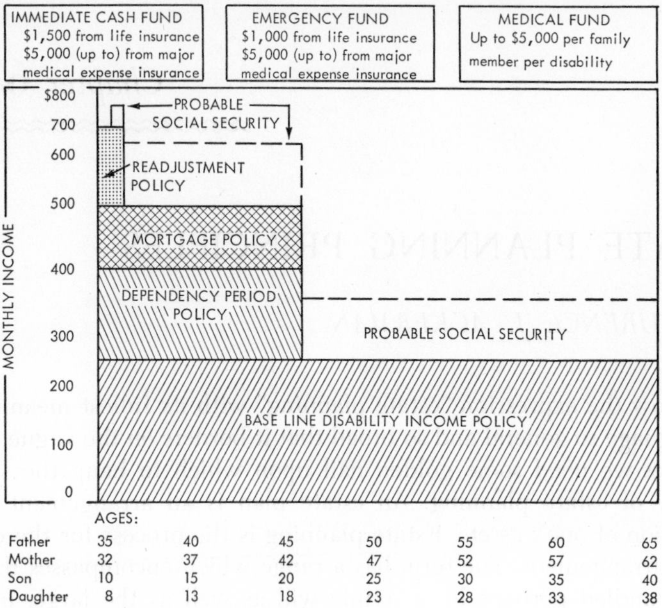

FIG. 62–1. Illustrative health insurance program.

in its original form will remark: "He surely didn't know much about programing health insurance, did he?"

He doesn't. His one hope is that what he has had to say in this chapter will inspire field men to go out and start programing health insurance (particularly integrating the programing of health and life insurance). If they do, they will move beyond the stumbling, pioneer suggestions of this chapter *fast*.

SELECTED REFERENCES

HIGHFIELD, WILLIAM. *Why You Should Program Your Sickness & Accident Insurance*. Indianapolis: Research and Review Service of America, Inc., 1957.

MEHR, ROBERT I., and CAMMACK, E. E. *Principles of Insurance*. 3d ed. Homewood, Ill.: Richard D. Irwin, Inc., 1961.

MEHR, ROBERT, and OSLER, ROBERT W. *Modern Life Insurance*. 3d ed. New York: Macmillan Co., 1961.

OSLER, ROBERT W. *Guide to Health Insurance*. Rev. ed. Indianapolis: Rough Notes Co., Inc., 1961.

OSLER, ROBERT W. "Programming A & S," *Insurance Salesman*, Vol. XCVIII, No. 12 (1955), p. 23; and Vol. XCIX, No. 1 (1956), p. 56.

OSLER, ROBERT W. "Programing Health Insurance Benefits," *Journal of the American Society of Chartered Life Underwriters*, Vol. XIII, No. 1 (Winter, 1958), p. 27.

Chapter 63

ESTATE PLANNING PRINCIPLES

BY LAURENCE J. ACKERMAN

To endow the expression "estate planning" with its fullest meaning calls for language so general and so broad that it borders on the vague and the trite. Yet we need some golden nail upon which to hang the seamless tapestry of estate planning. An estate plan is an arrangement for the devolution of one's assets. Estate planning is the process for the creation of this arrangement. The term has a range which encompasses the small estate handled perhaps by a simple will as well as the large, intricate, complex estate with its army of vehicles of estate transfer.

Cautions regarding Estate Planning

Three caveats are important at this point. Estate planning and tax planning are not synonymous terms. The latter is only a facet of the former. Its function is to minimize the tax burden involved in the disposition of the estate. Too often, the estate owner seems motivated more by hate than by love. His hatred for taxes outstrips his love for his family; he may permit tax considerations to dictate the disposition of his estate. To elevate tax savings to the supreme role—to display indifference to family needs—is, in essence, saying: "My money won't do my family much good when I die, but look how little tax I'll have to pay."

The second caution is to criticize the term "estate planning" as not the aptest of expressions. There is too much connotation in it of a singular devotion to a plan for the estate when the owner dies. But the estate planner is concerned usually with the wisest and most prudent use of his client's assets during his lifetime as well as after his death. Estate planning is a two-phase undertaking. It seeks to maximize, for the estate owner and his family, the security and enjoyment flowing from property ownership, both during lifetime and after death.

The third alert is the erroneous yet widespread belief that estate planning is the special privilege of the large estates. Both in lifetime and in testamentary planning, many common problems are found in the large and in the small estate. Frequently, the differences are only in degree and not in kind. It is the small estate owner who can least afford to neglect estate planning or to make an estate planning mistake. The failure or waste of a single asset in his estate could bring hardship both to him and to his family.

Estate Planning Not New

Estate planning is not a new art. It is one of the oldest of the arts, although it may be one of the newest of the professions. The privilege of disposing of one's property at time of death was permitted by the early Egyptians. The Code of Hammurabi made provision for both testate and intestate succession. Turning to one of our direct legal ancestors, the English legal complex, we see the modern trust evolving out of the "use" found in feudal times. The Statute of Wills came into being in 1540 in the time of Henry VIII. The rule against perpetuities appeared in 1685. The law against accumulations emerged in 1800. Forces were building up which called for counsel and advice in the disposition of one's property interests.

In America, it was the tax statutes of the nineteenth and twentieth centuries which acted as the catalysts for the tremendous interest in estate planning. In the latter part of the nineteenth century, states enacted inheritance taxes. In 1913 the United States income tax law was passed. The United States estate tax statute came on the scene in 1915. The United States gift tax followed in 1932. In predictable manner, the rates of taxes accelerated rapidly over the intervening years. The net result was a rapid quickening of the interest in and need for estate planning.

Forces of Estate Impairment

Viewing the vistas of today, we see many obstacles of impairment which tend to shrink estates, decrease their efficiency, and frustrate estate owners' objectives. A few of these forces of estate erosion might be mentioned. First, there are the costs associated with the death itself, such as last illness and funeral expenses. Then there are the current unpaid bills and the more substantial, longer range debts, such as the mortgage, installment contracts, and business obligations with claims against the personal assets. Probably there will be unpaid income and property taxes. There are the costs of estate transfer which include the administration expenses, state inheritance taxes, United States estate tax, and, in Canada, Canadian succession duties. These are obvious obstacles of impairment.

But there are more subtle elements of estate impairment. Our economic climate influences estates in a most profound and pervasive manner. The erosion in value of the dollar because of inflation compels constant reappraisal and rearrangement of the family estate. To ignore the direction of economic change is to impose a continual levy on one's capital. The failure of one's assets to provide persistent and expected income can destroy the most praiseworthy estate plan.

Instability of values can be another thief of estate assets. It might occur through improper management of a business asset, through the impact of changes in consumer preferences or obsolescence, or through improper management of the general estate assets after death.

An important obstacle of impairment is lack of liquidity to pay the financial costs associated with death and to honor cash bequests. These may compel sacrifice of assets which have substantial income-producing power for the family.

Sometimes the improper use of vehicles of transfer can produce an estate impairment. Lawyers and other estate planning advisers occasionally find that estate assets, under the legal documents in force, will pass to unintended beneficiaries. This may be accounted for by an old will which was not kept current with family change.

It is not unusual to find life insurance improperly arranged. A major function of the life insurance in the estate is to bridge the gap between the income potential of the other estate assets and the needs of the beneficiaries. The life insurance may have been programed with little or no consideration of the adequacy of the other estate income. The lack of co-ordination between the attorney planning the general estate and the life underwriter planning the life insurance estate is all too frequent, and may have disastrous results.

Sometimes the most ambitious and airtight estate plan is destroyed by prolonged and expensive disabilities. Not only is a person faced with loss of income, but his problem is compounded by the financial involvements of the illness itself. Health insurance will be a guarantor of the completion of estate plans in the same manner as life insurance.

By no means to complete the full array of obstacles of estate impairment, but merely to offer one more illustration, the legal documents associated with the estate plan may have considerable impact. They may have a rigidity which materially penalizes the objects of the estate owner's bounty. Management "from the grave" has led to weird and tragic consequences.

Estate Planning Process

Designing and fabricating an estate plan is almost always a custom-tailored effort. People differ so in their temperaments, in their sets of values, in their asset and liability statements, in their family responsibilities and relationships, that even though the material may be the same in many cases, the pattern and cut of the plan should probably always be different. The estate planner must have a viewpoint the opposite of Procrustes and not stretch or shorten his client's objectives to fit some preconceived arrangement.

The estate planning process, for purpose of analysis, can be broken up into six component parts. First, an adequate fact base must be fashioned. Once this is done, the obstacles of impairment which threaten the estate might be identified as a second step. Third, an estate plan can be formulated. Fourth, the proposed plan should be tested in a hypothetical framework. Fifth, the final plan should be implemented by the execution of the appropriate legal documents. Sixth, the plan should be subject to periodic review to test its adequacy in the crucible of time.

1. ***Getting the Facts.*** Facts are the lifeblood of any effective estate plan. Professionals in the field have struggled with this problem at length. As a result, there are numbers of lists, questionnaires, factfinders, and the like to aid in the fact-gathering operation.

No one doubts the value of adequate and exact facts. The real mark of the professional estate planner, however, is the ability to extract these facts from the estate owner. Simple and complex psychological theories have been concocted to explain the bashful silence of many estate owners when confronted with questions about their personal and financial lives. But the sad truth remains: Questionnaires are easy to assemble; full and accurate answers from the client, not so simple a task. The facts sought can be divided into five categories: (*a*) domicile, (*b*) family, (*c*) property, (*d*) current estate plans, (*e*) estate owner's objectives.

Domicile is significant in the estate plan. It identifies the law which will govern the validity of the will and most of its provisions. With our nomadic civilization, tracking down domicile is not a mild task at times. There has been at least one reported case in which each of four states attempted to collect death taxes. Each claimed to be the domicile of the decedent.

Family facts are equally important. Needed is such elementary information as the full names and dates of birth of the estate owner, his wife, his children, his grandchildren, and any other intended beneficiaries. One must unearth such personal information as the character of the wife and her business acumen, the state of health of the testator and his beneficiaries, the amount of wealth now available to the wife and children, and the attitudes of individual family members toward each other.

Next comes the *property* profile of the estate owner. This must be exhaustive and detailed. A complete rundown of the person's assets and liabilities is essential. Some of the details which are required are cash in individual accounts and in various types of joint accounts, real estate owned separately and jointly, tangible personal property owned individually and jointly, securities owned individually and jointly, business interests, personal life insurance, employee benefits, social security rights, claims under wills and trusts, and rights in future interests. Shifting to the other side of the balance sheet, full information must be procured about the estate owner's obligations. Such items as debts, accrued taxes, mortgages, leases, installment contracts, and so forth must be explored. All of this sounds dreary, unromantic, and dull. To the experienced estate planner, this is often one of the most exciting and illuminating parts of the process. Few estate owners ever go through such a procedure with themselves. When they do it under the guidance of the estate planner, the estate owners are often surprised, amazed, chagrined, even angered, and sometimes delighted by what they see. It is during this phase of the estate planning activity that the seeds of sound planning ideas can be sown in the owner's mind.

What is the *current estate plan* of the owner? Every estate owner has a plan, whether developed consciously or accidentally. What vehicles of transfer is he currently utilizing? The planner will obtain copies of all instruments impinging on the owner's current plan, including the will and any trusts. He will probe for any reversionary interests possessed by the property owner. The question of gifts will be investigated. If the estate owner has made gifts, then questions will be asked as to when the gifts were made, to whom, the nature of the assets, how made, and whether they were reported for gift tax purposes.

Finally, in the fact category, there is the very important *objectives* portion. One must ascertain the estate owner's philosophy about the financial maintenance and security of his family. Some estate owners have a mortal fear of entrusting substantial sums of money in a lump amount to their widows and children. Others feel that such an experience is the only way to sound money management. Some heads of families feel that their children should receive comparatively little and should fight their way through life, as their fathers did. In some estate owners, there is a keen and deep sensitivity to societal obligations and a desire to return the bulk of their wealth to the community in the form of charitable bequests. Very frequently, the estate owner has not thought through these all-important questions. The estate planner then has to don the mantle of the devil's advocate and help to evoke a concrete, definitive philosophy from the estate owner.

In the traditional situation, the objectives may not be serious. The typical individual will probably prefer to give specific items of property to certain persons or institutions, with the remainder to his wife and children.

Business interests almost always involve extended discussion between the estate planner and the estate owner. One reason is that business interests often comprise a substantial part of the estate. The estate owner may be the sole proprietor of the business, or the asset may be a share in a partnership, or stock ownership in a close corporation, or a combination of these three types of legal interest. Many vital decisions must be made. A basic exploration revolves about the question: Will the estate owner's objective be served best through retention of the business interest in the family, or should it be sold? This often produces a crisis in the relationship between the estate owner and the estate planner. So many times, the coldly logical, analytical businessman becomes an impractical dreamer when it comes to the disposition of his business interest. The path to the decision may be a hard and rocky one. To the time of the testator's death, the business may be the mainspring of his economic and personal development. Once he dies, it becomes an investment of an estate, valuable only if it can produce a predicted level of income.

A stream of queries flows from the estate planner if the estate owner indicates a strong desire to retain the business interest. How dependent will the family be on the business for its support? Are there family members who can manage the enterprise? If not, are there key employees available for the managerial role? What potential rifts might develop between these key employees and the family after the estate owner's death? How stable have the business earnings been in the past, and what does the future look like? What capital contributions will be necessary to keep the profit stream running in its accustomed manner?

If the decision is to sell, will it be for cash? If so, where will the funds to buy come from? Discussion must take place about the valuation question.

Only a few of the areas of objectives have been mentioned. They portray some of the dimensions in this area of the estate planning procedure.

To obtain the facts, the estate planner must talk with the estate owner and probably with members of his family. It may be unwise to do this on a mass basis. Individual consultations may be preferable. Business advisors, such as the life underwriter, the estate owner's accountant, his attorney, and his local banker, can all furnish important data. The planner should examine such instruments as income and gift tax returns, wills and trusts, life insurance policies, deeds, mortgages, business interest agreements, and any other legal documents pertinent to the facts for estate planning. Even if no new illumination is cast on the problem, an examination of these documents should aid the estate planner in confirming the accuracy of the data furnished by the estate owner in their discussions.

2. *Evaluating Estate Impairment Items.* Once the facts have been amassed and arranged, the obstacles of estate impairment can be appraised and estimated dollarwise. What guess can be made as to last illness and burial expenses? What measure can be placed on the debt structure of the decedent? What are the probable transfer costs, such as executor's commissions, attorney's fees, miscellaneous probate fees, state inheritance taxes, and estate taxes? What unpaid real estate and personal property taxes will there be? What unpaid federal income tax will remain at time of death? One might include in this estimate possible income tax deficiencies for prior years. Can the widow's and children's allowances be roughly computed? Aside from the information furnished by the estate owner, the planner will be aided by his experience and the various insurance and tax "services" in making his rough "guestimates" of these costs. These estimates will furnish the cash requirements needed at time of death and will create additional background material for the preparation of the estate plan.

3. ***Designing the Plan.*** Step three is the design of the plan. As a fact gatherer, the estate planner played the role of an investigator. In appraising the obstacles of impairment, he displayed his knowledge of the probate process and the complexities of taxes. Now, new characteristics are called into play. The planner must show that he has creative skill and the ability to weld together the estate owner's variegated assets into a smooth, acceptable house of security. He must help the testator produce the liquidity necessary to discharge the estate obligations. He must produce a plan which can take the rest of the assets and move them in the direction of his client's wishes. The planner has a variety of vehicles of transfer to accomplish these objectives. Through trial and error and experimentation, he will finally bring forth the ultimate plan. Probably the estate owner has a current plan, and the new one may well be a rearrangement of the old plan.

It is not possible within the confines of this conceptual approach to estate planning to mention all or to dig deeply into any of the available vehicles of transfer. As in the previous steps, a few will be mentioned for illustrative purposes.

The *will* is a key vehicle of transfer. A useful device attached to this vehicle is the marital deduction. It spawned the two-trust approach in the will to replace the pre-1948 single trust. In one trust, all income will be paid to the wife during her lifetime. She is given full power of appointment, by the will, over the trust property. In default of the exercise of the power by the wife, the trust property will be paid to the children of the testator and the wife. This trust is drawn to qualify for the marital deduction. Thus, it is not taxed in the husband's estate for federal estate tax purposes. In the other trust, the income is payable to the wife for life. On her death the property would be paid to the children. The assets in this trust do not qualify for the marital deduction and are, therefore, taxable in the husband's estate. But they would not be a part of the wife's gross estate for federal estate tax purposes.

The use of the marital deduction has as its basic consideration the saving of taxes. But every tax saving has its price, be it in the form of loss of control of an asset (e.g., a gift), the compromise of one's objectives (e.g., the desire to cut the wife's income if she remarries), or possible deferred increase in transfer costs (e.g., in the wife's estate if the marital deduction is employed). Therefore, even in the marital deduction the estate planner will weigh the tax saving against the price paid to obtain it.

The estate planner will also evaluate the property which goes into the marital deduction trust. He may consider it wise for the husband to avoid using assets with strong potential for appreciation in value. A substantial increase in the value of the assets which are qualified for the marital deduction will produce a proportionate increase in taxes on the subsequent death of the wife. If the assets are liquid, this is not a serious problem. But if the assets are not easily marketable, the wife's estate faces not only an increased transfer tax liability, but also an increased cash deficit to pay the tax. Contrariwise, it may be appropriate to use assets which will depreciate in value. These will have an opposite effect to the use of the appreciating assets in the estate of the wife. For example, insurance proceeds may be qualified for the marital deduction under some type of fixed or life income arrangement.

Another important vehicle of transfer is *life insurance*. It is the only practical plan which can guarantee that cash will be available at death to meet the financial costs of death. The use of life insurance to meet estate liabilities may prevent the forced sale of prime assets. This, in turn, will reduce the ultimate shrinkage in estate values and perhaps keep alive a source of income for the beneficiary of the decedent. The presence of life insurance with a named beneficiary will in some states bring savings in state taxes. Probate and administration costs also will be saved. For these reasons, many planners point out that a dollar of insurance is far more valuable at death than a dollar in cash—as in a bank. It is difficult to conceive of an estate plan today which does not employ life insurance as a significant catalyst to its accomplishment. In the final analysis, insurance in the estate plan will be determined by the needs for liquidity, flexibility, tax minimization, investment, and the requirements of family income.

Trusts, both *inter vivos* and testamentary, are used as vehicles of transfer.[1] Sometimes, when there is the possibility of heavy cash requirements at death, or perhaps a need for broad discretion over income and principal, an *inter vivos* life insurance trust might be created.

When there is both an *inter vivos* trust and a testamentary trust, the planner may suggest that both be combined and administered as one. One way to do this is through a "pour-over" trust. Both trusts may well have the same distributive provisions, the same beneficiaries, the same trustee(s). The trustee of the testamentary trust will be authorized to turn over the assets, when received from the executor, to the trustee of the *inter vivos* trust. Local law governs the availability of this technique, and its use has increased substantially during the past few years.

The *gift* is another effective tool for estate planning. It has significance beyond transfer tax savings. It can be utilized to buy life insurance for liquidity purposes without increasing the estate tax liability. It can be used to serve specific desires the estate owner may have for his children. It might serve as a medium to continue control of a business interest within

---

[1] See Chapter 58 on "Trusts and Their Uses."

the family. In its use, there must always be a consideration of the price paid for the advantage—namely, loss of control of this asset.

Joint ownership is often suggested as an effective vehicle of transfer. It has the advantage that upon the death of a co-owner, the share of the deceased automatically passes to the survivor and is no longer part of the deceased's estate for administration purposes. But for federal estate tax purposes the estate of the decedent is subject to tax for the full value of the entire property if the deceased furnished all of the money for the purchase. The survivor has to prove the extent of her contributions, if any. In addition to this fact, joint ownership can have adverse results which may negate any positive value it has. Jointly owned property may be taxed in the husband's estate and later in the wife's estate. Joint ownership may result in an unwanted distribution of property. Assume that the wife survives, along with some children. The property passes to her as surviving joint tenant. She remarries. Husband No. 2 may then receive a substantial portion of the property left by the first husband. The latter would probably have preferred that his children receive the property. Instead, much of it could go to an "outsider."

Other examples of tools utilized in estate planning are *sprinkling trusts, private annuities, powers of appointment,* and *charitable foundations.*

4. *Testing the Plan.* Once a complete plan has been agreed upon, step four is in order. This is to test the proposal. A few of the criteria employed can be mentioned. Does the plan seem to accomplish its objective? One way to assay this is to put the plan through a hypothetical administration and to test the resulting net income and its distribution. Have all of the assets been meshed together into a single workable plan? Finally, is the plan flexible enough to meet the test of today and the probable tests of tomorrow?

5. *Executing Legal Documents.* Step five introduces a new skill for one member of the estate planning team—draftsmanship by the attorney. Here the planner must worship at the shrine of concise and unambiguous draftsmanship. He must prepare, or have prepared, all of the legal instruments necessary to carry out the plan.

6. *Periodic Review.* Finally, it must be remembered that family situations change, laws change, the tax structure goes through a periodic revolution, and economic forces run through cycles. This risk and this uncertainty produce a need for constant attention and perhaps occasional revision. Many estate planners review their clients' situation on an annual basis.

Advantages of Planned Estate

There are many advantages to the planned estate. It enables an estate owner to preadminister his estate and gain an insight into its probable costs and its potential for the achievement of his objectives. A planned estate should ordinarily minimize transfer taxes. A planned estate should be superior to an unplanned one in the achievement of the estate owner's objectives for his family. A planned estate should bring greater peace of mind to the estate owner. A planned estate should give the estate owner greater freedom of financial action.

The Estate Planning Team

The field of estate planning has led such a dynamic life during the past twenty-five years that it has engendered at least one major status conflict. This revolves about the question: Who should do estate planning? Some five groups claim this privilege but fortunately not to the exclusion of each other. These are the lawyers, the life underwriters, the trust officers, the accountants, and the investment counselors.

The lawyer may claim that the estate plan is essentially a legal transaction and therefore falls essentially within his jurisdiction. The life underwriter may contend that life insurance today is so vital a part of the estate plan that without his active participation, estate planning has little meaning for the typical estate owner. The trust officer may state that his vast practical experience in such matters stamps him as the person best fitted to serve the estate owner. The accountant may point to his intimate knowledge of his client's affairs and to his exhaustive experience and know-how in the field of taxation. The investment adviser offers his knowledge of investment media as a badge entitling him to participate in the estate planning process.

Estate planning today is so complex and subtle a process that it calls for team play. Each of these professional groups can play a role in the accomplishment of the estate owner's objectives without any necessary conflict. The life underwriter is frequently the initiator of the idea because, unlike the lawyer and accountant, his is a license to solicit business. He can supply a vehicle of transfer through life insurance. He is in a position to recommend the most effective settlement options. The lawyer will draft the legal instruments which will furnish the motive power for the execution of the estate plan. The accountant can be of help in supplying the intimate financial data necessary to the formulation of the estate plan. He is also the appropriate person to resolve the vital question of *value* for the closely held business interest. The trust officer can lend advice on the practicalities of the estate plan and can play a major role in the estate administration. If the estate is large enough, the investment adviser can be a vital person on the team.

In 1953 an article[2] was published, under the sponsorship of the National Conference of Lawyers and Life Insurance Companies, entitled

[2] Harry S. Redeker, "Some Guideposts for Cooperation between Lawyers and Life Insurance Representatives," *Journal of the American Society of Chartered Life Underwriters,* Vol. VIII, No. 1 (Winter, 1953), pp. 86–99.

"Some Guideposts for Cooperation between Lawyers and Life Insurance Representatives." This Conference was organized in 1951. Its membership comprised the membership of the Joint Committee on Practice of Law of the American Life Convention and the Life Insurance Association of America along with the American Bar Association's Standing Committee on Unauthorized Practice of the Law. The article, which was circulated widely, attempted to outline areas of activity in which lawyers, life underwriters, and home office counsel could co-operate in the complexity of estate planning. The Conference has handled complaints, has issued informative bulletins, and, most important of all, has served to keep the lines of communication and mutual discussion open between the life insurance industry and the organized Bar.

In the "Guideposts" article, it was agreed that the life underwriter may prepare a thorough analysis of the client's life insurance estate. He may advise on beneficiary changes; the use of optional modes of settlement; whether policies should be converted or paid up; the appropriate plan under which new insurance should be written; and the use of supplementary features, such as disability riders, accidental death benefits, term riders, and the like. Forms dealing with the disposition of insurance proceeds by the company, approved by home office counsel, may be provided by the life underwriter.

A life underwriter may, in discussing an insurance program with a prospect, refer to general subjects which it would be pertinent for the prospect's lawyer to consider in his advice to his client. Further, the life underwriter may develop for his prospect an over-all estate plan, solely for the purpose of demonstrating the compelling necessity of putting his affairs in order and inducing the client to consult his lawyer.

The "Guideposts" article was most helpful in clarifying the role of the life underwriter in the estate planning process. It did not alter certain propositions found in the 1948 "National Statement of Principles of Cooperation between Life Underwriters and Lawyers." In substance, the unaltered principles are that a life underwriter may *not:*

1. Practice law; give legal advice; and prepare legal documents, such as wills, trust agreements, and business insurance agreements.
2. Dissuade a client from seeking the advice of legal counsel or attempt to divert legal business from one attorney to another.
3. Act as intermediary and furnish attorneys who will give cost-free legal advice to the underwriter's clients or prospects.
4. Share the attorney's fee or pay any part of his life insurance commission to an attorney or other person not a life underwriter.
5. Obtain legal opinions from an attorney and circularize them as selling documents.

Estate planning is a flourishing area of service to the American public. If reasonable freedom in the acquisition, conservation, and distribution of property can be maintained, then estate planning should always be a great challenge to superior minds engaged in the professions concerned.

SELECTED REFERENCES

CASEY, WILLIAM J. *New Estate Planning Ideas.* New York: Institute for Business Planning, Inc., 1958.

Estate Planners Quarterly. New York: Farnsworth Publishing Co.

MACNEILL, EARL S. *Making the Most of Your Estate.* New York: Harper & Bros., 1957.

SHATTUCK, MAYO ADAMS, and FARR, JAMES F. *An Estate Planner's Handbook.* 2d ed. Boston: Little, Brown & Co., 1953.

TRACHTMAN, JOSEPH. *Estate Planning.* New York: Practicing Law Institute, 1964.

WORMSER, RENÉ A. *Guide to Estate Planning.* Englewood Cliffs, N.J.: Prentice-Hall, Inc., 1958.

Chapter 64

ESTATE PLANNING—AN ILLUSTRATION

BY LAWRENCE G. KNECHT

The previous chapter has set forth the basic theory and principles which are involved in any and all estate planning cases. However, as so often happens in all technical fields, when the principles are applied in actual practice, somehow things go wrong because of a lack of ability to work them out in a live problem.

What this chapter will attempt, therefore, is to take a specific case and show, in step-by-step fashion, how the case proceeds in applying the principles from the very beginning until the close. The emphasis all the way through will be on *procedure* and *technique* rather than the specific facts of the particular case.

Many estate planners have found that the procedure of estate planning, which is commonly thought of as a single operation, is far more easily understood and handled if considered as being in *three* distinct steps, which are:

1. An analysis of the entire estate as it presently exists.
2. A simple enumeration of the problems, that is, those specific points in which the present estate plan fails to accomplish the owner's objectives.
3. The actual planning stage, where corrective procedures to eliminate or reduce these problems are studied, implemented, and tested.

ANALYSIS OF THE CASE (ESTABLISHING THE FACTS)

General Observations

Before planning can start, a base point must first be established. Therefore, the estate owner's exact present situation must be ascertained. This includes all his present assets, his liabilities, his will (or no will, as the case may be), his life insurance under its present settlement provisions, his income and its specific sources and outgo, shown by definite categories, and all the rest of the picture. Obviously, not only the nature of the assets themselves must be ascertained, but also whether those assets are in the sole name of the estate owner or in the names of himself and any other person or persons. If they are in more than one name, is the title joint and survivorship, or something else?

In addition to a complete statement of all assets and liabilities, including the precise way in which titles are held, there must also be available copies of any wills of the estate owner and his wife, trusts of which they are either donors or beneficiaries, expectancies, all insurance policies, and, if the client owns an interest in a closely held business, copies of financial statements of the business for the last five years (including both balance sheets and operating statements). Last, but not least, specific authority should be obtained to consult with the estate owner's attorney and insurance companies.

Data of the Illustrative Case

Family and Wills. The estate owner, Mr. White, is an active, equal partner in a successful two-man firm; he is 38 years old; his wife is 35 years of age; and they have three children—two daughters aged 12 and 10, and a boy aged 7, all in good health. They are residents of Ohio. Both the estate owner and his wife have wills but no trusts. His will, after providing for the payment of debts and funeral expenses, leaves his home and personal effects to his wife outright and provides that the balance of his estate is to go to his wife for life only and at her death to the children. The wife is also named as executrix and, as such, is given specific power to continue his interest in the partnership; thereafter, she is given power as life tenant to continue to operate the partnership without liability for depreciation.

The wife's will is simple, leaving all her assets to her husband if he survives, but if not, then to her children. In both wills the estate owner's sister is designated as guardian of minor children.

Inventory of Assets. Mr. White's assets and those of his wife are as follows:

Item	Mr. White's Assets	Wife's Assets	Joint and Survivor
Cash on hand and in bank	$ 2,000	$ 1,000	
Series "E" bonds (payable on death to wife)	1,000		
Series "E" bonds (joint with wife)			$2,500
Series "E" bonds (joint with children)			1,500
Mutual fund shares	3,750		
Home (tenancy in common)	10,000	10,000	
Real estate (parking lot in Erie, Pennsylvania)	10,000		
Personal effects	3,000	4,500	
Partnership interest (book value)	44,350		
Life insurance	33,000		
$5,000 policy on wife's life, owned by husband (cash value)	400		

His present liabilities consist of the following:

Current bills and accounts (personal)	$ 700
Accrued taxes on home	400
Accrued taxes on parking lot	300
Mortgage on home	2,000
Income tax (based upon one quarter of last year's return)	2,200

Of the "E" bonds held jointly with his wife, she contributed 20 per cent of the purchase price.

Neither the estate owner nor his wife has made any gifts in the past in excess of the current statutory exclusion.

Life Insurance. With regard to Mr. White's life insurance, it consists of three policies, the first being his National Service Life Insurance of $10,000, on which his wife is the primary beneficiary and his parents are secondary beneficiaries. This is payable in a lump sum. The second policy for $5,000 was taken out in 1948. It, too, is payable in a lump sum to his wife but, alternatively, to his children. The third policy, which he purchased in 1951, is a family income policy, having a present commuted value of $18,000. His wife is the primary beneficiary, and the children are the secondary beneficiaries. The policy is payable on income installment provisions of about $100 per month, and his wife has no right to commute or withdraw or change the secondary beneficiary; payment to the children is to be in a lump sum. He has maximum coverage under social security.

Income and Expenses. From the standpoint of his income, he draws $1,000 per month out of the partnership (plus extra amounts at times to pay income taxes). In addition to this, his parking lot pays annual rents of $1,500. From this, he must pay the real estate taxes of $300, but he has no maintenance expense, since the tenant under the lease is required to pay all such items. He receives around $150 per year as dividends on his mutual fund shares.

The wife will need $8,000 for the first year after his death, and then an income of $7,200 at least until the children are through college. He wants a $4,000 emergency fund and $6,000 for each child's education.

The Partnership. The partnership is in the plastics business, manufacturing various items of toys and sundry gadgets used in the premium business. The business started about six years ago, with the two present partners each contributing a nominal amount of capital. It has proved to be a very successful operation. The estate owner is the production "brain" and knows how to figure costs, design dies, schedule production, and get the maximum efficiency out of the plant. The partner is the sales genius of the organization, who has proved his ability to go into a competitive situation and walk away with orders in spite of competition.

The company has a reputation in the business of turning out good jobs in a short time and at a low price. By and large, the relationship of the two partners is excellent, although the other partner is a free spender on his expense account. The two partners have an oral understanding that when one of them dies, the survivor will carry on the business with the family of the decedent. Both appreciate, however, that the survivor will have quite a load because neither of the partners' wives has any business experience.

The other partner, Mr. Lewis, is 42 years of age and in good health; he also draws $1,000 a month (plus) out of the business.

The firm, on an accrual basis for income tax, has earned over the past five years an average net of $60,000 per year. The accountant has advised the partners that if the company were incorporated, around $12,000 for each of them would be considered a reasonable allowance for salary. Their balance sheets also show that over the last five years the average invested capital was about $28,000.

The present balance sheet indicates that their total assets are $111,500, with liabilities of $22,800, leaving a net worth of $88,700. However, if the business were liquidated, the net realizable value from the assets, after paying all liabilities, is estimated at $65,200. They lease the property in which they operate, but the rental is so favorable that the property could be sublet to other tenants for at least as much as they are paying.

Running the Hypothetical Probate

The Theory. With this factual background to start with, the next job is the analysis, i.e., to find out what would happen with reference to the total estate picture if Mr. White, the estate owner, were to die today without having made any changes of any kind. To do this, the procedure is that of a hypothetical probate following exactly the same steps that would be taken in running the estate through the process of administration. The factual summary plus the hypothetical probate combine to form the first step of the total procedure set out in the previous chapter on estate planning principles.

There is a division of opinion as to how specific or general the analysis should be. In actual practice, some estate reports are very meticulous and detailed, whereas others are the roughest approximations of tax and other factors. The persons who favor the latter method usually argue that there is no real point in making the figures exact because the amount involved in the present estate will never actually be the exact amount when the estate becomes a reality, and that therefore spending time on details is wasteful. The argument on the other side is that if one follows the broad estimate theory, he will in most instances overlook some of the extremely important details, and in almost every instance will be unable to present to the estate owner any sort of accurate picture of the postprobate estate and the family income.

As between these two extremes, it would seem that the average analyst will be better off to do a thorough and meticulous job than to do the very rough estimate sort. Those who take the pains to do the job completely find that it is far more effective.

This chapter presents the form of detailed analysis on the theory that if one understands how it is done this way, he can readily shift over to a shorter form.

Inventory and Classification of Assets. The first step in analysis is to make an inventory and classification of the assets, listing all the items which will be involved in this estate and at the same time separating those which will pass to the executor and those which will either pass by survivorship or pass by contract or devise directly to the beneficiaries without going through the probate estate. Following that procedure in the present case, the schedule will be as follows:

SCHEDULE I

Assets	*Estate Owner's Value*
Solely owned assets:	
Cash	$ 2,000
Mutual fund	3,750
Parking lot (Erie, Pennsylvania)	10,000
Personal effects	3,000
Partnership interest	44,350
Policy on wife (cash value)	400
Probate estate	$ 63,500
Property passing by survivorship:	
Government "E" bonds (to wife)	2,500
Government "E" bonds (to children)	1,500
Property passing by trust, contract, or devise:	
Government "E" bonds (to wife)	1,000
Home (half interest)	10,000
Life insurance	33,000
Total of all assets	$111,500

Retention or Conversion (Tentative). The next step will be a tentative determination as to whether the executor will convert the assets coming into his possession into cash or whether he will attempt to retain them. In this case, because the estate owner expressed a desire that his family retain all the assets he has except the cash, the schedule will look like this:

SCHEDULE II

Probate Assets	*Cash*	*Retention*
Cash	$2,000	
Mutual fund		$ 3,750
Parking lot (Erie, Pennsylvania)		10,000
Personal effects		3,000
Partnership interest		44,350
Policy on wife (cash value)		400

Valuation for Taxes. 1. *The Partnership.* A subject which is of concern to the executor early in the administration is the position of the estate with reference to death taxes; accordingly, very early, he will attempt to arrive at an estimate of the value of the property which will be included in the gross estate. It is obvious that the major problem here will relate to the valuation of the partnership interest for tax purposes. It may be assumed that the Treasury Department will look closely at this retained partnership interest to determine whether there may be an element of good will which should be added into the valuation figure. Arriving at a value which might reasonably result from negotiations between Internal Revenue agents and counsel for the estate is a difficult problem, but if the analyst takes an average of the value arrived at through the use of the book value, capitalizing the earnings, and applying the ARM (Appeal and Review Memo #34) formula, he should come reasonably close to what will probably happen.

In this case, he might use the average earnings of $60,000, subtract therefrom the sum of $24,000 (as representing what would be an allowance for salaries, as though this were a corporation), and multiply the difference of $36,000 by a factor of 9, which gives a potential value of the partnership of $324,000. In applying the ARM formula, he again uses the earnings (adjusted by deducting salary allowance), subtracts $2,800 as representing a 10 per cent return on the average invested capital of $28,000, and multiplies the difference by 5, which gives a figure of $166,-000. This is probably what the Treasury will claim is the present capitalized value of the good will alone. If he then adds this capitalized good will value to the present book value of $88,700, he comes up with a possible valuation of the partnership of $254,700. If one adds the capitalized earnings value ($324,000) plus the ARM value ($254,700) plus the present book value ($88,700) and divides the total by three, he finds that the average figure for the partnership as a whole would be roughly $222,470, so that the estate owner's one half would thus carry a tax value of $111,235.

2. *The Gross Estate.* The gross estate for the United States estate tax is as shown in Schedule III. The figures are self-explanatory, with the possible exception that only $2,000 of the $2,500 jointly held "E" bonds

SCHEDULE III

Cash on hand and in bank	$ 2,000
Mutual fund shares	3,750
Parking lot in Erie, Pennsylvania	10,000
Personal effects	3,000
Partnership interest	111,235
Policy on wife (cash value)	400
Government "E" bonds (to wife)	2,000
Government "E" bonds (to children)	1,500
Government "E" bonds (to wife)	1,000
Home (half interest)	10,000
Life insurance	33,000
	$177,885

passing to the wife have been included because the wife contributed 20 per cent to the total purchase price of these bonds, using funds which had come to her from her mother.

3. *Deductions.* The next step will be to determine the taxable estate, and the schedule will be as shown in Schedule IV. It will be observed that the marital deduction is less than the maximum allowable, which is attributable to the fact that the residuary probate estate will not qualify because it goes to the wife for life only and without any power of appointment. The only assets qualifying for the marital deduction will be personal effects, $3,000; equity in home, $9,000; widow's allowance, $8,000; Series "E" bonds, $2,000; National Service Life Insurance, $10,000; second policy of insurance, $5,000; and government bonds, payable at death, $1,000.

SCHEDULE IV

Total gross estate (from Schedule III)		$177,885
Costs of administration (5 per cent of $63,500)	$3,175	
Current bills	700	
One half of accrued taxes on home	200	
Accrued taxes on Pennsylvania property	300	
Income tax	2,200	
Funeral and last expense (estimated)	2,500	
One half of mortgage on home	1,000	
Total deductions under Revenue Code Section 2053		10,075
Adjusted gross estate		$167,810
Marital deduction		38,000
		$129,810
Exemption		60,000
Taxable estate		$ 69,810

Cash Requirements. Having ascertained that the United States estate tax will come to $12,060, the total cash requirements in the estate are as follows:

SCHEDULE V

Liabilities

Current bills payable	$ 700
Accrued taxes:	
Realty—Ohio (one half)	200
Realty—Pennsylvania	300
United States income tax (one quarter of last year's estimate)	2,200
Funeral and last expenses	2,500
Widow's allowance	8,000
Administration costs (5 per cent on $63,500)	3,175
State inheritance tax (Ohio)	1,500
Minimum United States estate tax	12,060
Total cash requirements	$30,515

(The mortgage is not included here on the theory that the wife will simply continue to make the monthly payments.)

Liquidating the Cash Requirements. From what source will this cash come? To begin with, reference back to Schedule II shows that there is $2,000 in the bank, which the executor will have toward these costs. That schedule tentatively marked all the other assets for retention (following the estate owner's preference). It is clear by this time, however, that the actual retention of all those assets will be impossible. What can be done about the deficit? There are a number of alternatives, but for purposes of illustration, it may be assumed that the widow's allowance, instead of being paid in cash, will be satisfied by distributing to her a fractional part of the partnership interest; that the mutual fund shares will have to be sold; that the parking lot will have to be sold; and that the balance of the cash will have to come from the wife, who will cash in her "E" bonds, utilize her personal bank account, and take some of the lump-sum insurance proceeds. Outside of selling the personal effects and the partnership interest, there is no other answer.

The Family Income. In any event, after the funds are paid to the executor, who in turn pays the bills, the estate will be closed, and then the question arises of how the family will fare on the basis of the actual assets which are left and the income which can be expected from them. For the moment, in considering this income expectancy, assume that the partnership will continue to earn money and that the widow will be able to withdraw from those earnings the same amount as her husband is currently withdrawing, namely, $1,000 or so per month. On this basis, the wife's position will shape up along the line shown in Schedule VI.

SCHEDULE VI

	Principal	*Income*
Personal effects (of husband)	$ 3,000	
Policy on wife (cash value)	400	
Business interest	111,235	$12,000
Reinvested lump-sum insurance proceeds	12,173	360
Proceeds under policy options (estimated)	18,000	1,200
Realty—home	20,000	
Personal effects (of wife)	4,500	
Social security		3,049
Total from all sources		$16,609
Fixed charges		1,560
Net income		$15,049
Income tax		10,000
Spendable income		$ 5,049
Income requirement		$ 7,200

In the category of fixed charges in this income schedule, there are included three items: the monthly payment on the mortgage, the annual taxes, and the maintenance costs on the home.

This picture, however, is not complete. It shows only what will happen if everything works out *successfully* in the business and the wife is able to withdraw $1,000 per month. It will be noted that even under those conditions the spendable income is considerably lower than the income requirement, which is attributed primarily to the very large income tax. The reason this income tax figure is so large is that although the wife is actually *drawing* only $12,000 per year, she is taxed on $31,500, which is her one-half share of the current partnership profits.

If a second step is taken in the analysis of the income picture and it is assumed that the worst were to happen to the business, namely, that it would be unable to pay anything to her, then her spendable income would amount to a little over $2,000 per year.

The Wife's Estate at Her Subsequent Death. At this stage of the analysis, then, the analyst has established what will happen in the husband's estate if he dies first and if the present arrangements are unaltered. Next, he will ascertain what will happen in the wife's estate at her subsequent death under the present program. He finds that her taxable estate will be very small, that the total cash requirements will amount to about $9,600, and that there will be adequate cash by virtue of the fact that in her estate there will be the remainder of the lump-sum insurance proceeds from her husband. After her estate is through probate, the children will then have (from both parents) the home, the personal effects, the remainder of the family income policy, the $1,500 of Series "E" bonds, and the partnership interest.

With regard to the partnership interest, however, it will be impossible to carry any further the fiction of retention by the family. At this stage, with both husband and wife being gone, there would be no adult member of the family with whom the survivor could make a contract, even if he were willing to do so. Certainly, no businessman in his right mind would carry on a partnership with three minors as partners, and it is very dubious whether the probate court would allow the guardian to do so. As a result, the partnership would have to be liquidated, at its liquidating value of $65,200, with a total of $32,600 going to the estate owner's family. This over-all picture will leave the children with something around $80,000 in total assets, including the house, the personal effects, the family income policy, and the liquidated partnership, all producing an income of a little over $1,500, plus social security.

Reversing the Order of Death. Even now the analysis is not complete because it does not show what would happen if the orders of death were reversed. If the wife dies first, her estate will be immaterial, since its sole assets will be her personal effects and half the home. Now the husband's estate must be run through on another set of schedules, but with the assets owned jointly with the wife now becoming a part of his probate estate and the partnership appearing in the estate at its liquidated value rather than at either its book value or its inflated tax value. Without running through the actual schedules again, because of limitations of space, the picture shows that the husband will have a gross estate of $118,850, with deductions of $11,318, leaving an adjusted gross estate of $107,532 and a taxable estate of $47,532, on which the United States estate tax will be $6,496 and the Ohio inheritance tax will come to $480. The total cash requirements in his estate will amount to $18,300. There will, however, be ample cash to take care of these from the cash on hand, the $5,000 of insurance on the wife's life, and cash from the liquidation of the partnership.

The children, after conclusion of the administration, will then have an asset and income picture as follows:

	Principal	*Income*
Cash	$24,806	$ 744
Mutual fund shares	3,750	150
Realty:		
Parking lot—Pennsylvania	10,000	1,500
Home	20,000	0
Personal effects	7,500	0
Insurance proceeds:		
Family income policy	18,000	540
Policy on wife	5,000	150
Government "E" bonds	1,500	45
Social security		2,400
Total from all sources		$5,529
Less: Fixed expenses on home and lot		1,200
Net income		$4,329
Income tax		100
Spendable income		$4,239

In addition to this, under the present arrangements, the $10,000 NSLI will go to Mr. White's parents.

FINDING THE OBSTACLES OR PROBLEMS

General Observations

Now the analysis is complete. The estate owner knows precisely what will happen in the event that both he and his wife die without making any change in their present arrangements, regardless of the order of deaths. This then concludes the *first step* in the over-all estate-planning procedure.

The next step, as mentioned at the outset of this chapter, consists of enumerating the particular problems which the analysis has disclosed or, as stated in the previous chapter, in determining the obstacles. In other words, in what respects does the present estate plan fail to accomplish the estate owner's objectives? Before considering the actual problems in this case, it will be helpful to appreciate that the problems which will be found in *any* case will always fall in one of four different categories:

1. ***Transfer Costs.*** The first major problem area relates to the fact that transfer costs at some place or places in the over-all picture are unnecessarily high. When the term "transfer costs" is used, it refers to the total of taxes and costs of administration. Note that the transfer costs are a problem not because they are large but because they are *unnecessarily* high and could be reduced to a more reasonable figure by using ideas that are consistent with the estate owner's objectives.

2. ***Liquidation.*** In a great many estates, even after the transfer costs are reduced to a reasonable minimum, there still are not sufficient liquid assets to meet all the cash requirements. This arises most frequently in the case of an owner of an interest in a closely held business where the objective is to retain that interest.

3. ***Disposition of Assets.*** Here the problem area deals with those basic questions of "who gets what, and when, and how?" Control of a closely held business is often found going to persons who are not qualified to enter into management, or other forms of property pass to individuals who are quite incapable of administering it. Similarly, there are many cases of real injustices being done to various beneficiaries who are inadequately provided for.

4. ***Family Income Problems.*** This is an old and familiar field, but when encountered in estate planning, it has many new phases. While it is most common to find situations of the family income being insufficient, sometimes the income going to a given beneficiary is more than that beneficiary will need, giving rise to unnecessary income taxes. The analysis will show the relative dependence of the family upon the income from the business in order to help the estate owner ascertain the degree of risk entailed in his decision to retain that interest. Here also are the problems of how the family funds will be managed, and the source of education and emergency funds.

One of the primary advantages in simply enumerating the problems, after completing the analysis and before going into the planning, is that the analyst can thereby get the agreement of the estate owner, the attorney, the trust officer, and whoever else may be involved in the actual planning phase on what things in this picture need to have attention. Then, as the various estate planning ideas are considered, they can be related back to the agreed problems to ascertain how far any given proposal will go in solving each problem. As a result of this procedure, a lot of disagreements that might otherwise develop can be eliminated. For example, the attorney or the trust officer will in most cases immediately suggest the use of a trust in order to avoid the common error of overqualification for the marital deduction. This is usually a very wise suggestion, but the point of the matter is that it relates only to the reduction of transfer costs and possibly, incidentally, to the liquidation or management problem, and does not necessarily have any bearing upon the income problem, where the only answer may be more life insurance.

The Specific Problems

1. ***As to Transfer Costs.*** If these problem areas are now applied to the partnership case, they indicate: First of all, as to transfer costs, the only place where taxes are unreasonably high is in the estate of the husband where he dies first. This is occasioned by the fact that he is utilizing only $38,000 of the marital deduction against a possible maximum deduction of almost $84,000. This results in his estate paying an unnecessary federal estate tax of something over $11,000, which, if saved, would help to reduce the liquidation problem and would also help on the family income. In the transfer cost area, one notes also that part of these taxes is attributable to the fact that the partnership interest, which carries a book value of about $44,000, has a tax value of almost three times that amount.

2. ***As to Liquidation.*** Next, in looking at the liquidation picture, it is apparent that if the husband dies first, there is a substantial deficit in the estate, resulting in a forced sale of assets which the estate owner has indicated he would like his family to have. Of course, to the extent that transfer costs are reduced, as mentioned above, the liquidation problem can be alleviated. However, that will not completely solve it, because even with the taxes reduced, there will still be a deficit. The liquidation problem arises primarily because of the retention of the partnership interest.

3. ***As to Disposition of Assets.*** Passing now to the third category of possible problems, the question is whether the present arrangement for division of assets is in good shape, taking into consideration the ages and business experience of the people involved and considering particularly the attendant risk. Here, several negative factors are apparent: First, under the present arrangement, if both husband and wife are gone, property will pass outright to minors, involving the necessity of a guardianship, with its obvious disadvantages.

Second, there is the admitted fact that the wife has no business experience and that in foisting upon her the responsibility of participating in the management of a business of which she knows nothing, the will places upon her, and also upon the surviving partner, a tremendous responsibility. The degree of that risk is even greater than the estate owner appreciates because, from a legal standpoint, both partners are jointly and severally liable. Thus, if the surviving partner were to make some unfortunate business decision involving substantial liabilities, the wife as a partner would be *personally* liable to the full extent of those liabilities. Furthermore, her personal liability would not be limited to business assets but would also subject all her own personal holdings, including even her home, to the claims of business creditors. A third although minor point under this same heading is that the policy of life insurance (NSLI) goes to the estate owner's parents rather than his children, if his wife predeceases him.

4. ***As to the Family Income.*** Finally, as to the family income situation, the analysis demonstrates that the income will not be sufficient to give the family the spendable income it will require. This is true whether the partnership does or does not continue its present earning scale. Coupled with this is the fact that if the business should fail, the family would lose the capital tied up in the business, and the income would be even further reduced. As one further factor, under the present arrangements there is no adequate provision for education and emergency funds.

So much for enumerating the problems. Considering all of them, anyone can readily see that the decision with reference to the partnership is actually the key to the whole situation. Of course, the various documents, including the wills and the insurance policies, need further consideration, but the starting point will necessarily have to be the problem of the partnership.

Up to this point, therefore, all the facts have been established, as well as all the obstacles or problems in the setup as it now stands. The case is now ready to proceed to the third step.

DESIGNING A PLAN

In this particular case, when the whole matter was presented to the estate owner, his accountant, and his counsel, it resulted in a long and serious discussion about the advisability of retaining the partnership. At the conclusion, all the parties were in accord that at least as of the present time, retention of the partnership would not be advisable. It was felt that the risk to the family was simply not justified.

The first planning procedure agreed upon, therefore, was that there should be a buy-and-sell agreement between the two partners, the price tentatively to be set at $100,000 for each partner's interest. It was agreed that the agreement would be funded by $200,000 of life insurance—$100,000 owned by each partner on the other's life.

Next, it was decided that the estate owner would need management of the estate funds both for his wife and for his children. Because of the age of the wife, it was also decided that the family would be better off if the insurance policies became a part of a trust arrangement, and that the estate owner should set up an insurance trust, which in turn would be split into marital (with full marital deduction) and nonmarital trusts. It was agreed that the nonmarital part would provide for income to the wife; that the trustee might advance principal as needed; that the trustee could use funds from the nonmarital portion for education and family emergencies; and finally, that after both husband and wife were gone, distribution of one half of each child's share should be made at age 28, with the balance being distributed to each at age 35.

As a companion to this insurance trust, the husband's will would provide that his interest in the home and his personal effects should go to his wife and that the balance of his estate (including the remainder of the cash received from the buy-and-sell agreement) should "pour over" into the insurance trust.

It was also agreed that the wife's will should leave everything to the husband, if he survived; but if he should not, then the wife's estate should also be left to the insurance trust. The result of this program would be that all the assets from both husband and wife, including all insurance proceeds, would wind up in a single trust for the benefit of the children, regardless of the order of death.

TESTING THE PLAN

With a tentative program thus agreed upon, the next question was whether its operation would really improve the picture, and, if so, by how much. Therefore, the analyst made a "test run" to prove the economic results. This analysis showed that if the husband died first and the wife second, the new program would save approximately $6,000 in transfer costs. It was also found, however, that if the wife died first and the husband second, the transfer costs would be increased by about $20,000. The reason for this increase was that in this order of death, in the husband's estate at present there was no alternative except the liquidation of the partnership at $32,000; whereas under the new plan the children would have available the $100,000 proceeds from the buy-and-sell agreement, or an increase of almost $70,000.

The second significant thing which the revised analysis brought out was that the family income picture under the new plan showed spendable income of almost $6,300—completely independent of business income. This, admittedly, was about $1,000 less than the minimum needed. However, both the lawyer and the estate owner felt that since there would be over $140,000 in liquid assets in trust, this deficiency of income would not be too important because, to that extent of the deficiency, principal could be used.

Finally, it was observed that the new plan would completely eliminate all the liquidation problems in both the husband's estate and that of the wife, regardless of the order of death.

IMPLEMENTING THE PLAN

With the tentative plan thus proved out and consequently accepted by all concerned, the next step was that of putting it into effect. The lawyer, of course, had the greatest amount of work to do in drafting the insurance trust and the wills. The drafts were checked out with the client and reviewed by the trust officer.

In the meantime, both of the partners were examined, and each partner applied for and purchased a $100,000 straight life policy on the life of the other partner. In addition to the trust agreement and the wills, the attorney also prepared a buy-and-sell agreement between the partners; and with the signing of all of these documents and the delivery of the policies, the entire job was completed.

PERIODIC REVIEWS

Although the client expressed complete satisfaction with the results of the estate planning job, he was cautioned, particularly by the lawyer, that the lapse of time, with its attendant changes in the family situation, in the valuation of the business, and in the nature and extent of his assets, could easily make this plan as obsolete as was his old one. It was consequently agreed that the plan should be reviewed at least every three years, and preferably every two years; and to that end the trust officer agreed that as these review times came around, he would see to it that the matter was called to the attention of the lawyer, the life underwriter, and the client so that an adequate follow-up was assured.

SELECTED REFERENCES

See citations at end of previous chapter.

PART IX

Marketing Life and Health Insurance

Chapter 65

LIFE UNDERWRITING AS A CAREER

BY CHARLES J. ZIMMERMAN

Other chapters of this book discuss the many and varied aspects of life and health insurance. From them the reader will gain a deep appreciation of the unique ability of insurance to solve problems for individuals, for groups of individuals, and for businesses.

Life and health insurance could never accomplish its great purpose if it were not for the life underwriter[1] who demonstrates to the individual buyer how this insurance can help *him* solve *his* individual problems. The growth of life and health insurance in the United States and Canada, as contrasted to other countries, is primarily the result of the aggressive efforts of the thousands of life and health underwriters the companies have inducted and trained to a degree of competence unmatched anywhere else in the world.

The life underwriter, then, is the lifeblood of this business. He is the force through which it has grown and prospered in the past and through which it will grow and prosper in the future.

This chapter will attempt to portray the selling and servicing of life and health insurance as a career—its responsibilities, its rewards, its opportunities, its challenges, and its difficulties.

The Life Underwriter's Role in Our Economy

The business of personal insurance is essentially the business of life and living under conditions of freedom. Personal insurance is inextricably intertwined with the ambitions and aspirations of people, with their triumphs and tragedies, with their motives and motivations, and with their attitudes and actions. Ownership of personal insurance is a measure of the character of people. For the overwhelming majority of men, it represents an efficient and effective method—and one within their means—through which they can respond to their financial responsibilities as heads of families or businesses.

[1] "Life underwriter," as used in this chapter, carries the broad connotation of a person associated with the marketing of life *and* health insurance, and also the connotation of a career of selling life and health insurance in a professional manner.

Life insurance cannot insure against death any more than health insurance can insure against disability. Together, they can and do insure against economic loss resulting from death, from disability, and from old-age dependency. Insurance can and does insure a better life, provided that free men who have the right of choice act on their responsibility by making the right choice.

Often, it is not easy to make the right choice. Sometimes the choice to provide for oneself and one's loved ones, through a potentially long-term commitment to pay insurance premiums, must be balanced against the ego recognition, pleasure in use, and pride in display of some tangible possession. In a broader sense the choice is between whether a man will rightly assume his responsibility to provide for himself and his family or whether he will unfairly place this burden on others.

It is in helping men to make the right choice that the service of a well-selected, well-trained, well-educated, and conscientious life underwriter plays a key role. He helps the individual to recognize his need for personal and family security; and by pointing out how much and what kind of insurance is required to fulfill those needs, the life underwriter helps his client to change insecurity to security, fear to faith, dependency to independence.

Thus, the life underwriter bears a great and wonderful responsibility to the people he serves and, in fact, to the world in which we live. As he helps each individual to do all within his power to assure a better, more certain life for himself and his family, this will be reflected in a better community, a better nation, and, ultimately, a better world.

Getting Started

Depending upon the company and agency he joins, the underwriter usually specializes in one of the three basic forms of life insurance—ordinary, group, or industrial. On the health insurance side, he may sell policies or policy riders to provide the insured with income in the event of disability, and/or hospitalization and surgical insurance to take care of medical expense.

Whatever his specialty, much of the underwriter's time, especially at first, is spent developing a list of prospective buyers. These are gathered from the people he knows and does business with, from his observation of people with whom he regularly comes in contact, referred leads from the people who become his clients, newspaper accounts of things happening to people (marriages, births, promotions, changes in business firms), lists of people whom he circularizes with direct-mail letters, and so forth. This phase of the job is crucial; and it is easiest for the type of man who meets people easily, is alert to things going on around him, and whose sincere interest in the welfare of other people motivates him to seek out those who have need of his services.

Calling on his prospects, the underwriter determines what problems they have that can best be solved by personal insurance. These can vary from the simple need for a final expense fund to the need for a complete program of protection for a family or for a business and its employees. He then shows how insurance can solve the problem and attempts to persuade the prospect to adopt his recommendation.

His responsibility does not end with the sale of a policy. The life underwriter has an obligation to keep in touch with his clients to see that their insurance is kept up to date to meet changing conditions and situations, and that it continues to accomplish the objectives for which it is carried. His job is an unusual combination of counselor and salesman.

As a counselor, he must win the confidence of his prospect, so that the prospect will freely discuss his situation and problems. As a counselor, he must be able to advise wisely on proper solutions to those problems. As a salesman, he must possess the persuasive ability to get the prospect to take action on his recommendations. To play a professional role in both instances, he must at all times place his client's interests above his own.

"Success breeds success" in underwriting as well as in other vocations. As the underwriter establishes a reputation for competence and reliability among a growing group of clients, those clients more readily refer him to others. His job of prospecting becomes easier. He discovers that new clients more readily act on his recommendations because of the confidence built up by his broadening professional reputation. Thus, the building of a personal insurance clientele is similar to what a doctor or a lawyer or an architect must do, except that the underwriter has the advantage that he can go out and seek people whom he wants as clients.

Training and Education

Time was, many decades ago, when a new recruit, figuratively, was given a rate book and a pat on the back and told to go out and sell. Fortunately for the public, the business, and the new underwriter himself, those days are gone forever. Today the practical and professional education and training available to the underwriter new to insurance are possibly without equal in the business world.

Most companies start with intensive product and sales training from the minute he signs his contract. In some cases, this training starts even prior to the time the contract is signed. This training may be at either the home office or the agency. Often, it involves some training at both places.

The now prevalent concept of continuous education and training exposes the new underwriter to three training cycles lasting over a period of years: fundamental, intermediate, and advanced. Most of this training involves personal supervision by an experienced insurance man skilled in training procedures. Usually, it will include joint field work on actual cases.

Many men without prior sales experience have become successful insurance salesmen because of the fine sales training programs of the companies. They are taught what to say in all types of interviews and how to say it. Therefore, a lack of sales experience should not deter a person from considering this work.

In addition to company training, there are institutional programs available to men in all companies. One of these is a two-year course sponsored by the Life Underwriter Training Council. Thousands of men are taking these intermediate sales training courses each year in weekly classes conducted from coast to coast. The improvement in the professional competence of men participating in this program has been remarkable; and year after year, students completing the LUTC life and health courses report substantial increases in personal production.

Men aspiring to the professional designation of Chartered Life Underwriter (C.L.U.) may enroll in an advanced educational program leading to five college-level examinations. Subjects include life and health insurance, economics, social problems, law, trusts, taxes, finance, and others deemed essential to the well-rounded education of a professional life underwriter. The C.L.U. program is administered by the American College of Life Underwriters, whose high standards are evident from the fact that after thirty-seven years, only 11,622 men have been granted the C.L.U. designation. Continuing studies of the performance of those C.L.U.s engaged in field underwriting indicate that their education is highly valuable. About 95 per cent make a lifetime career in insurance. They produce about 60 per cent more and earn about 60 per cent more than non-C.L.U.s of comparable background and experience. The public is coming more and more to recognize C.L.U.s as men who serve their clients in a truly professional manner.

C.L.U.s are eligible for membership in the American Society of Chartered Life Underwriters, a professional society with nearly 150 chapters throughout the United States. The Society provides a variety of services for its members, including the *C.L.U. Journal* and many types of continuing education.

Beyond these programs, successful men in life and health insurance constantly pursue a self-study program. For example, there are many books published on estate planning, business insurance, health insurance, group insurance, and pension planning, which the underwriter can study on his own to further his knowledge and ability to operate in such fields. Numerous professional and trade journals constantly publish articles by experts in various fields. There are monthly services, to which a man may subscribe, which give sales ideas, describe sales techniques, and offer up-to-the-minute information on the constantly changing factors which influence the purchase of life insurance.

Indeed, there is no end to the process of learning about the ways in which insurance can be applied to the problems of individuals and businesses. This ever-widening horizon is one of many aspects of this career which attracts men to it and holds their interest after they get started.

Opportunity for Personal Development and Growth

The life underwriter has an unlimited opportunity to develop and grow in a very broad sense. New ways in which insurance can solve personal and business problems are being discovered constantly. This provides an ever-renewing challenge to the alert and ambitious life underwriter to keep up with the parade. As he does so, he becomes a broader man, a more interesting man.

It is fascinating to see men with records of modest achievement in other fields enter the life and health insurance business and develop almost miraculously. Their imaginations become fired with the dynamics and the vitality of their work, and they find resources within themselves of which they never before had been aware. They apply these newfound talents with industry and energy, and become men who would stand out in any group as leaders possessed of great creative capacity, as men proud and happy in their work and eager to reach the ever-broadening horizon they see ahead of them. A career in the selling of life and health insurance gives a man full opportunity for self-development and self-expression.

Financial Compensation

One of the great advantages of a career as an underwriter is that there is no theoretical ceiling on how much money can be made. The individual life underwriter is paid what he *earns*, not what someone else thinks a particular job may be worth.

Most companies have financing plans—either salary, drawing account, or commission, or a combination of these—to help a man get started until such time as he can make his own way on a commission basis.

Getting started in this career requires little or no capital, as compared to most other businesses with similar opportunities for independence and ultimate earnings. But it does require a big investment of time and effort, especially at the beginning, just as is necessary in starting any business or professional undertaking.

As in every vocation, there are varying levels of ultimate earnings among life underwriters, but the following illustration of some averages may be helpful.

In one of the larger companies writing only individual life insurance, the average earnings in 1963 of the men who had been with that company five years or longer were over $11,600, with one in five of that group earning over $20,000. The average earnings of the company's top 100 men were $29,493, and the average amount sold in 1963 by these 100 men was $1,643,620 (face amount of protection). About one third of the entire sales force (367 men) qualified for the company's Leaders Club and had average earnings of more than $17,000.

A recent survey of field underwriters holding the Chartered Life Underwriter designation revealed that the median income of that group from life insurance alone was more than $17,500.

A recent survey of members of the industry-wide Million Dollar Round Table showed that average annual income of this group was a little over $35,000. There are individual MDRT members whose incomes are three or more times that figure.

It is true that these income figures are for groups above the average of all life underwriters. But no man should enter a new career unless he feels, and others qualified to advise him also feel, that he has the potential to be better than average. Indeed, the average man in this or in any other calling tends to be a mediocre man. Therefore, figures which indicate the income of above-average men have been used purposely, so that those who consider themselves above average will have a truer picture of their own possible earning capacity.

It should be kept in mind that life and health insurance selling has one income advantage over most other sales jobs: the advantage of recurring income from the same sale. The man who sells an automobile receives but one commission. The man who sells an insurance policy receives, in addition to a first-year commission, a renewal or service commission each year as subsequent premiums are paid. These renewals last for a specified period of years, usually nine, and many companies pay a service fee beyond that period.

The question of compulsory retirement never bothers the life underwriter. Even though most companies provide pension plans for their representatives, men can continue to write new business, and many persons over 60 are enjoying the best incomes of their careers. Even after 65 or 70, these men can continue to lead active and productive lives if they choose to do so.

Although there is ample opportunity for top earnings, no one should be misled into thinking this career provides any overnight, "get rich quick" scheme. Some few men do reach income levels of $15,000 or better in their second or third year, some even earlier. Most, however, climb to substantial levels over a longer period. And, of course, there are some, because of lesser ability or lack of initiative, who remain at lower levels throughout their careers. But the opportunity is there for all, and it is entirely up to the individual as to how far he will go.

Other Rewards and Satisfactions

In addition to the opportunity to earn a good income, the underwriter enjoys many other rewards and satisfactions.

High among these is certainly the satisfaction of knowing that he is serving the best interests of his fellow men, that they will be better off because of his efforts. Those who have seen insurance in action may have seen a widow and her children able to retain not only a roof over their heads and food on the table, but also their customary standard of living, because of insurance. They may have seen a family spared a serious drain on its finances because of disability income and medical expense insurance. They may have seen a young man able to attend college only because a father provided life insurance for that purpose. They may have seen an elderly couple enjoying their retirement years only because of income from an insurance program. They may have seen a business continued for the benefit of valued employees following the death of the owner because the proceeds of life insurance enabled these employees to pay the heirs of the deceased owner a fair price for the business. These situations and many others are the end result of the efforts of some underwriter, from which he can surely take well-deserved pride and satisfaction.

Today, many jobs look attractive on the surface because the starting pay is high. Experience shows, however, that in most cases, real job satisfaction comes only from that rarer situation where both income and personal pride are in balance. The underwriter enjoys that rare combination in his job and has the opportunity to serve often beyond his own most far-reaching expectations.

Another factor of job satisfaction is the independence enjoyed by the underwriter. Although he receives initial training and guidance, he soon finds he is enjoying an opportunity to operate on his own rarely equaled in other businesses or professions. He can usually, for example, select his own market, develop his own techniques, and plan his own time so that he can get maximum pleasure from both work and recreation.

Prestige of the Underwriter

Even though they themselves take pride and satisfaction in their occupation, most men also want others to respect the work they do. To an ever-increasing degree the public respects the life underwriter and his service.

This prestige has been built over a long period of years by the thousands of underwriters who have performed their jobs well, who have become leaders in their communities, and who have conducted their business and personal affairs in such a way as to reflect credit on all of insurance.

The prestige of underwriters is being constantly reinforced by the broad public relations programs carried on by such organizations as the Institute of Life Insurance and the National Association of Life Underwriters, as well as by individual companies.

Opportunities in Management for the Successful Life Underwriter

Most successful life underwriters would not change places with men in any other phase of our business. However, for those who have an interest in management work or who eventually develop such an interest, there are ample opportunities.

Almost every company selects men for sales management work from among its own underwriters. Usually, such men will first serve as supervisors or assistant managers and then be appointed managers or general agents. In this capacity, they will be primarily sales managers for the company in their assigned territories and will represent their company in all phases of sales and service. They are responsible for the selection, training, supervision, and development of new salesmen, as well as for the continued education, training, and development of established men.

Such men must possess broad executive judgment and be outstanding leaders. Individual initiative is important because they have considerable leeway in the operation of their branch offices. Since the income of a general agent or manager is geared to the volume and quality of business produced and the number and quality of the underwriters in the office he supervises, there is full opportunity for liberal financial rewards. Men who enjoy working with other men and helping them to succeed will find this work especially attractive. The demand for young men of proven capacity and qualities of leadership is growing constantly. In addition, age, or length of service, is important but not the primary qualification, as is the case in many large commercial corporations.

All companies have sales departments in their home offices. These are staffed primarily with men who have had sales and sales management experience. These men play key roles in the over-all operation and growth of their companies.

As far as the opportunity to get to top management levels is concerned, many men who started their careers as life underwriters have become senior officers of their companies. The presidents of a number of companies started their careers as underwriters. Many other top officials of companies started out the same way. First-hand knowledge of selling operations is extremely helpful to any home office executive.

When a man embarks on a career as an underwriter, he has a great deal of flexibility in the path he may ultimately follow. He may decide that he prefers the independence and the other advantages of remaining an underwriter, and most decide that way. If he likes field sales management and demonstrates capacity for such work, he will find companies eager for his services. Or he may like work at the home office level; and here again, his field experience will be extremely helpful.

Is This a Career for You?

The man who is thinking about launching a career in the selling of life and health insurance should conduct a careful self-analysis on certain basic points. He should ask himself, in substance:

First, do I have a genuine interest in other people and their problems? Second, have I in my past work, in school, college, or military service, been able to sell myself effectively and successfully to others? Third, do I have initiative; am I a "self-starter"; do I like to think creatively? Fourth, do I have determination; have I seen tasks through to their ultimate conclusion; can I persevere in the face of discouragement? Finally, am I intrigued by an opportunity in which the potential financial reward is great but which will require plenty of hard work; do I possess above-average physical energy?

If the results of this self-analysis are favorable, then he will want to talk to the representatives of various companies. They will have aptitude tests that will further assist in determining whether he is suited to this type of work.

Choice of company is not so important as the choice of the particular office or agency in which a man will begin his career. Investigate that office or agency on the following points: First, who will be my trainer and supervisor, and how will I respond to that person? Second, with what kind of men will I be associated in the agency? A man's career will be happier and probably more successful if these are men he instinctively likes. Third, what has been the record in this agency of developing good underwriters, especially men of my own age?

The Future and Its Opportunity for the Life Underwriter

Early in this chapter the statement was made that the underwriter is the lifeblood of the life and health insurance business, and the force through which it has grown and prospered in the past and through which it will grow and prosper in the future.

The future holds great promise for the business. The entire economy is constantly expanding, and the market for life and health insurance will keep pace with and may well exceed the rate of growth of the economy.

The projected rapid growth of the United States population, accompanied by higher rates of productivity, holds out the promise of expanded markets for products and services, including life and health insurance.

Of equal long-range significance is the fact that our future citizens will be better educated. With better education will come an increased understanding of the need for exercising personal responsibility in providing personal security, and of the part which ownership of adequate life and health insurance can play in meeting this need.

Increased productivity, speeded by technological advances, will give the individual a higher standard of living to protect, as well as more real disposable income with which to protect it. Life and health insurance will play a major part in providing this protection.

People are still deplorably underinsured in relation to their needs and in relation to their ability to satisfy those needs for personal security. The market for individually purchased security programs will be one of dynamic expansion. New markets will be developed, and underdeveloped markets will be more adequately exploited.

There will be an even greater acceptance of life and health insurance in the future. Among other factors bringing this about is the tremendous increase in benefit payments, which will result in greater understanding and appreciation of the importance of personal insurance.

Improved standards of living and giant strides in medical science have resulted in a greatly increased span of life. The pathway from the cradle to the grave has indeed been lengthened. But it is important to note that only that part of the pathway which we tread as consumers has been lengthened. Our younger people enter the labor force at a more advanced age than in the past, spending many more years and many more dollars to prepare themselves for life as producers through increased education and training. And more and more of our people are leaving the labor force at an earlier age to spend more years as consumers at the other end of the path. This means that our people must provide greater personal security during their productive years for their children as they start on the pathway of life and for themselves as they walk into the sunset of life. Obviously, there will be increasing need for more life and health insurance to protect this lengthened period of dependency.

Insurance is fulfilling an ever more important service in American business life. Partnership and stock purchase insurance, as well as insurance to fund profit sharing and deferred compensation plans, are becoming an accepted part of sound financial planning. Pension plans and a myriad of other welfare coverages, such as group life, group hospitalization, group health, and major medical benefits are being provided by business for its employees. Such benefits are today the rule, rather than the exception, in forward-looking business organizations.

These, then, are some of the factors which will bring about the tremendous future market for insurance. This expanding market means that there will be an even greater need and opportunity for the well-selected and well-trained career life underwriter.

Not only is the future bright for the career life underwriter, but he will continue to provide a better future for the people he serves. Because of the security programs he arranges for his clients, he will make it possible for them to pass on to succeeding generations not only property, but the opportunity to lead a better life because of that property. He will help them pass on love, decency, and dignity. Life underwriters, in their everyday work, speak effectively and persuasively for a better future for man and mankind.

SELECTED REFERENCES

ADVISORY COUNCIL ON LIFE UNDERWRITER EDUCATION AND TRAINING. *Educational and Training Resources for Development of Career Life and Health Insurance Agents.* New York: Institute of Life Insurance, 1963.

ANDERSON, KENNETH L. *Invitation to a Career.* Rev. ed. Indianapolis: Research and Review Service of America, Inc., 1962.

HUEBNER, S. S. *The Professional Concept in Life Underwriting.* Rev. ed. Bryn Mawr, Pa.: American College of Life Underwriters, 1963.

INSTITUTE OF LIFE INSURANCE. *Where Will You Be Seven Years from Now?* New York, 1962.

LAMB, CURTIS. *Life Opportunities.* Rev. ed. Cincinnati: National Underwriter Co., 1961.

LIFE INSURANCE AGENCY MANAGEMENT ASSOCIATION. *Career Underwriting —A Life Work.* Hartford, 1960.

Chapter 66

THE SALES PROCESS

BY BENJAMIN N. WOODSON

The objective of the salesman is to lead his prospect to affirmative action.

But before we can expect our prospect to *buy* our product, and buy it now, we must lead him to *want* it. And before we can expect him to want it, we must lead him to realize that our product will *benefit* him. And this in its turn will frequently require that we help him realize a *need* for the benefit, a *sense of lack* in his affairs, which can be satisfied by the benefits we have for sale.

And before we show him his need for the benefits we have to offer, we must hold his *interested attention.*

This inventory of the steps which the mind of our prospect must take before he becomes our buyer serves to tell the story of the sales process. It suggests that the full process is comprised of four separate, interdependent, equally important steps, as follows:

First, we must gain the *attention* of our buyer-to-be, and quickly convert mere attention into *interest.*

Second, we must help him to sense his *need for,* or present *lack of,* the benefits our product offers him.

Third, we must dramatize those benefits so effectively, and identify them with the prospect so intimately, that we convert his sense of *need* into a sense of *want.*

Fourth, we must then sharpen his wants and lead him to *act now* by helping him overcome his doubts, by answering his last-minute questions, by encouraging him to overcome that natural human inertia which is an obstacle to every sale, and by making an affirmative decision the easiest decision.

The WANT Is the Key to the Sale

First, it should be noted that the full process may be condensed, and, as a matter of fact, frequently is automatically condensed, in proportion to the degree to which a *want* already exists. For example, assuming all surrounding circumstances to be favorable, we can sell a steak dinner to a hungry man in a flash, just by giving him a whiff or a glimpse of a sirloin hot off the broiler, or even by the merest word of suggestion. Such a prospect is "easy" and is ready for decision and action because his urgent *need* is well known to him, and his resultant want is acute and sharply defined.

This simple illustration emphasizes the obvious but important truth that the central component of the sales process is *the want.* The earlier steps in the sales process are merely preliminaries to the creation of a sense of want; the subsequent steps are principally those of intensifying the want until affirmative action becomes the inevitable outcome. *The want, then, is always the key to the sale.* The fact is that a man usually buys that which he wants—even, regrettably, that which he cannot always reasonably or wisely afford. Within any reasonable limits, he buys what he wants, if he wants it and wants it enough, even if the decision bends or breaks his budget.

Parenthetically, let it be noted that while the consequences of this truism about human nature may sometimes bring pangs of conscience to the salesman of nonessentials and luxuries, the life underwriter is spared any such discomfort. He is instead uplifted in his daily work by the realization that he sells *thrift:* that while virtually every other salesman who crosses a prospect's threshold is there to help him *spend* his money, the underwriter is there to help him *save* a larger share of his income.

STEP I: GAIN ATTENTION, AROUSE INTEREST

The salesman's purpose at the outset is to gain promptly his listener's concentrated attention, and convert it quickly into *interested* attention.

We may pass by without further comment the obvious importance of good grooming, good manners, and a pleasant smile, and concern ourselves only with the ideas we shall employ in our quest of attention and interest.

Here the key to effectiveness is simple: The ideas which will serve best are those which are *about* the listener, and which pertain to *his* interests, not those which relate to ourselves or our own interests.

Our prospect is precisely like all the rest of us—he is occupied and largely preoccupied with the pursuit of happiness for himself and his family, and with concern for the welfare of himself and his family. The sales process begins, then, with our concern for the prospect's comfort, success, and welfare; with references to *his* job, his home, his family; with consideration to his children, his house, his pocketbook, his car, his dog, and his cat—and with such relationships as we can quickly establish between our product or service and his interests or possessions. And if we would convert his *attention* into lively *interest,* we shall be wise to talk about the things which interest *him;* we shall do well to talk in terms of *his* interests, not ours.

This is illustrated by almost any well-written advertisement. Pick up a magazine or newspaper, and observe how the steamship line or railway, the air line or the bus company, undertakes to interest you in the purchase of its ticket. Notice that while the interest of the advertiser is in the operation of his own organization and in selling you the transportation which he is in business to provide, he (the advertiser) nevertheless undertakes to speak to you in terms of *your* interests. He is much too wise and clever to say: "You should buy our ticket because we would like to have your business." Instead, the caption says: "Picture YOURSELF in Honolulu" (or Bali, or London, or Sun Valley). He talks *to* you, *about* you—and you like it! We all do, always.

Yes, those who pay hundreds and thousands of dollars for a page of advertising have learned by hard experience how to gain the attention of the reader in the first few seconds, and quickly convert that attention into interest. They have learned that if they are to hold his attention and interest long enough to describe to him at proper length the benefits they have to offer, long enough to make his wants for their product sufficiently urgent to produce action, they must speak to him about himself and his interests, not about their product.

A successful life underwriter who specializes in mortgage coverage sales has employed this principle by using his hobby of photography in his work. He brings to the prospect a good picture of his (the prospect's) home! It is a gift calculated to arouse a measure of interest and appreciation in even the most uninterested and unappreciative man—because it is *his* home. And obviously, a discussion of the photograph, and of the home which it pictures, leads naturally to a discussion of mortgage cancellation insurance.

If we hope to gain attention and convert it into interest, let us speak to our listener about *himself* and *his* welfare and *his* interests.

STEP II: IDENTIFY THE NEED

Our ultimate purpose is to lead our prospect to affirmative action, by helping him to discover his *want* for our product. This we shall accomplish by *dramatizing* the benefits we can offer the buyer and *identifying* those benefits closely with him in his own mind.

Sometimes the need for the benefit we have to offer is so obvious and so clearly defined that the want already exists, strong and urgent, so that only a touch of motivation is needed to lead to a sale. Our hungry man, ready to buy our steak, is an example.

But on other occasions the want is not so well developed and urgent, and in those circumstances the salesman must build the foundation for the wants which he realizes must be identified and intensified. This he will do by emphasis upon the need which usually must underlie the want: by uncovering a need which has not yet been recognized or by making more acute and pressing a need of which its owner is already aware.

Needs Lead to Wants

Let us illustrate this by considering a typical automobile owner. Since we have presumed him to be typical, we may reasonably assume that he *wants* a new car; that he will *always* want a new car, except from time to time during the first few months of his ownership of a brand-new car! But we know also that this want of his will be latent much of the time; specifically, it will be inactive until he reaches a certain point in the deterioration of his present automobile, after which his desire for a new car will begin to be acute.

If he is highly conscious of automobile styles and keenly interested in motor cars, as many men are, he may begin to want a new car as soon as he first sees this year's models on the street, or even as soon as he hears they are on the way. If, more typically, he is comparatively indifferent to automobile styles, his sense of lack may not be aroused until he reaches a fairly advanced point in the depreciation of his present car.

Suppose he brings his car into your motor agency for a repair job shortly before his sense of lack has been aroused—at that exact point where you, an automobile salesman, feel it would be to his advantage to trade in his old car for a new one, but where he has not yet realized any pressing sense of lack or need. Now, even though his desire for a new car is latent at this moment, you may find that the merest suggestion will create in his consciousness a sudden *sense of need* for a new car—the suggestion that the old car's need for repairs gives evidence that it can no longer deliver the dependable and trouble-free transportation he wants, or the suggestion that the old car is of a style which is obsolescent and not worthy of him, or his position, or his neighborhood.

The sudden change of viewpoint which can result from such a suggestion—a familiar story to all of us and one which is repeated hundreds of times each day, no doubt—illustrates dramatically a fundamental principle and an essential step in the sales process: the creation of a sense of desire, a want, by uncovering a need or by putting new urgency into a need which has been recognized but not regarded as acute and pressing.

In general, salesmen of consumer goods which satisfy wants already well established by habit or social custom have less need to develop a sense of lack than does the salesman of such a solid and conservative product as that sold by the life underwriter. The man who sells insurance, unlike the salesman who offers consumer goods, does not often find an adequate sense of want for his product ready-made and waiting for him. He offers benefits which are tangible to the utmost, but delivered in the "intangible" form of an insurance policy; he offers benefits long deferred, but requiring an immediate sacrifice. *It is therefore necessary for him to identify a need for his product and make it so clear to his prospect that it becomes a want, and then dramatize the benefits of the product vividly in the eyes of the prospect, making the want so acute that it cries out for satisfaction.*

Problem—and Opportunity

The frequent obscuring of the need for life and health insurance is at once the underwriter's great problem and his great opportunity.

It is a problem because all too often the underwriter too quickly assumes that his prospect fully understands his need for insurance. The underwriter's problem is really himself, for by nature he is highly sensitive to human needs, especially those for which life and health insurance are designed. By his very nature, he equates too readily his sensitivity of need with that of his prospect. It is a problem because apparently it is an underwriter's natural tendency to talk about the satisfaction of the need rather than about the need itself, to talk about a policy rather than about the satisfactions and the benefits it offers. It is a problem because apparently it is difficult for us to learn the basic truths that few men have any adequate awareness of the need for life and health insurance until it is uncovered by the underwriter, and that men will not want life and health insurance until they first sense fully a need for it.

This is well illustrated in the words of a successful life insurance man who tells how the turn for the better came in his affairs when finally he learned this lesson. He relates that he achieved only indifferent success, during his early months and years in the business, when he followed his natural inclinations and devoted (so he estimates) 5 per cent of his typical interview to a discussion of the *need* and 95 per cent to a discussion of the *policy* which might satisfy the need and solve the prospect's financial problems.

Then, he says, he learned by hard experience to reverse the proportions, and came instead to devote 95 per cent of the interview to the need—to uncovering the need, to making it crystal-clear, effectively converting it into a want, and then dramatically making the want irresistible—*then* giving 5 per cent of his attention to finding the policy or policies required to satisfy the need. His sales increased enormously, his ratio of sales to interviews improved dramatically, and his personal financial rewards improved in proportion.

But if the obscurity of the need is a problem to the underwriter, it is his great *opportunity* as well. This is true because the need for life and health insurance is usually so pressing, so acute, that we need only to make that need abundantly clear in order to create a want so urgent that it will demand—yes, demand!—prompt satisfaction.

The Sales Insistence of the Need

It is the life underwriter's great advantage that the *sales resistance* which all salesmen must encounter in all walks of selling is, in life and health underwriting, outweighed by the *sales insistence* of the many and pressing needs for insurance, once those needs are made sufficiently clear.

Sales resistance, of course, is only natural. Every salesman of every commodity must meet it, even the man who sells those durable consumer goods we all desire in endless quantity and infinite variety. The consumer has schooled himself to present a protective armor of sales resistance to every salesman every day. He has learned that his desires are limitless but that his dollars are not; and of necessity, he has cultivated the habit of buying carefully and deliberately. He has learned to hesitate even when he ardently desires that which is offered him.

And so sales resistance is natural. *But it is also natural that sales resistance diminishes as the urgency of the need increases.* If a salesman were on hand to offer you a fire extinguisher just as you saw a tiny flame in your kitchen threatening to spread into blazing disaster, your sales resistance would be *nil.* If a salesman were to drive along the highway and offer you a new tire while you were looking at a flat rear wheel ten miles from town and ruefully remembering that you left your spare at the service station yesterday, you would make little point of the fact that you have a brother-in-law in the tire business.

Thus, urgent and pressing needs create sales insistence which overbalances sales resistance. This is a happy and fortunate fact for the life underwriter. It tells him that once he persuades a man to take 30 minutes out of his busy life to look seriously at the needs for life and health insurance which he has been building up across his entire thirty years, their urgency will outweigh the prospect's natural sales resistance, and will press him onward toward decision and action.

For example:

Two or three partners, duly encouraged by their life underwriter, have decided to create a buy-and-sell agreement so that the heirs of the first to die may sell their interest quickly and surely and profitably, and so that the survivors may own the business in its entirety. But once the buy-and-sell problem has been solved, a new problem arises, for at this point the young partners first recognize the survivors' problem of finding the needed funds. When that problem becomes sufficiently clear, the *need* for life insurance is suddenly so pressing and so urgent that sales insistence takes over, and the sale is ready for completion.

A young family man, with no assets of consequence save his earning power, suddenly comes face to face for the first time with the certainty that his *needs for income*—either his family's needs in the event of his untimely death or his own needs in retirement—will outlive his earning power. He then begins to realize that when earning power is gone, there will be no income save property or investment income. And as the next step, he must inevitably recognize that life insurance is the *only* property he can buy in sufficient amounts to do the job, and on terms that he can meet. When thus he sees through his *needs,* sales insistence will outweigh sales resistance, and his decision will be all but automatic.

A man of substantial means becomes aware for the first time of the extent to which federal and state taxes will bite into his estate. Then he realizes that his executor may be forced to sacrifice business interests for a fraction of what they are worth *now* during the owner's lifetime, or to sell securities or property on an unfavorable market, or both. Next, he learns that by means of single-premium life insurance, he can prepay his taxes at a significant discount and also gain the advantage of deciding for himself what assets shall be sold for the purpose, rather than leaving that decision to his executor. *Then* he learns that by means of annual-premium life insurance, he can do the same job on easy terms, and perhaps sell *no* assets! At that point the sales insistence of his urgent need drives all sales resistance out of his consciousness, and a purchase follows naturally.

It is indeed the life underwriter's great good fortune that the sales insistence of the several needs for life and health insurance is so great, so urgent, so irresistible. It is his good luck—it is his compensation for the difficulties and problems of selling a so-called "intangible"—that when he has uncovered the need and made it sufficiently clear, its urgency will create a want sufficiently powerful to brush aside all sales resistance.

It is his good fortune that irresistible sales insistence lies inherent in the simple fact that in our modern complex economy, *there must be dollars for tomorrow as well as dollars for today.*

And it is his good fortune, too, that *sales resistance* comes naturally to almost every man. For without it, the average man might so unbalance his budget with the purchase of things he can eat or drink, wear or drive, sit and look at or show to his neighbors, that he would be left with no single penny of today's income for the purchase of dollars tomorrow!

STEP III: TRANSLATE *NEEDS* INTO *WANTS*

If the sale hinges on recognizing a need and intensifying the want, then in turn the process of intensifying the want hinges upon *dramatizing* the benefits we have to offer and *identifying* those benefits with our listener in his own mind.

It is an obvious fact—but one so obvious that we are prone to overlook it—*that our prospect is interested in the benefits our product can give him, and not in our product itself.*

This is a truth we can easily fail to recognize, but it is no less important on that account. We may assume, for example, that we are interested in that broiler-hot steak of which we have previously spoken, but what we *really* are willing to pay for is the satisfaction of our hunger which the steak will provide, and the pleasing stimulation of our taste buds which it offers. We may assume that the lady wants a new hat, but what she *really* wants and is willing to pay for is the admiring glances of men, the appreciative or envious glances of other women, and the confidence in herself which these things engender.

Indeed, men always buy the benefit, never the commodity. And the man who would achieve mastery of the sales process and skill in accentuating wants until they create their own irresistible pressures must learn to sell the *benefit,* not the *commodity,* and to identify the benefit intimately with his prospect in his own mind.

Sell Benefits, Not Commodities

Let us examine, as an extreme instance, a man's purchase of a home. This is for most men the largest purchase of a lifetime. It is assuredly the purchase of a "tangible." It might seem at first blush that this is the exception to prove the rule, and that in this instance it is truly the commodity itself which a man buys, not the benefit.

But consider. Even though this is the purchase of property in its most tangible form (so much so that the law speaks of it as *real* estate or *real* property!), it, too, is purchased for the benefits it offers, and not for its own sake. Let it be acknowledged at once that the home is bought, first of all, because it affords shelter, because it offers a base of operations, a place for its owner to hang his hat, eat his meals, and sleep his night's sleep. But if these things were all he wanted, he could acquire them by renting, or he could buy them for a much smaller outlay than he is contemplating.

What he also seeks—indeed, what he really wants for his dollars, and what he is about to buy at very considerable cost—are such benefits as the sense of security and peace of mind which go with ownership rather than tenancy, the personal satisfaction and family prestige which derive from the neighborhood and the home in which he and his family live, the social and school advantages the home can offer his children, the physical comfort and pride of possession which it offers to him, and most of all, the touch of immortality which he senses in the confidence that his children will carry with them happy memories of their childhood home when they are parents and he is a grandparent, and long thereafter when they are grandparents and he is gone.

It would seem, then, that even the biggest and most tangible purchase of a lifetime is made in quest of *benefit* rather than for the *product* or commodity itself.

And at the other extreme of the price range, we know if we but stop to consider for a moment that a man who buys a 98-cent package of razor blades doesn't want *blades:* He wants a quick, clean shave; he wants freedom from nicks and cuts and scratches; he wants freedom from five-o'clock shadow; he wants the social approval which all these things beget.

The man who spends several thousand dollars for central air conditioning in his home, or several hundred dollars for a single window unit, has no interest in the commodity as such. Indeed, he resents its intrusion upon the limited space in his basement or garage, or its interference with the symmetrical appearance of his home! But he is willing to pay heavily for cool, clean, filtered air and its contributions to quiet, calm, and peaceful home life; for deep and restful sleep on a hot summer night; and for the luxury of creating his own private, personal climate by touching a dial in his downstairs hall.

To the life underwriter, this means (in sharp distinction from a mere discussion of the policy), *first,* uncovering the need, *then* describing and dramatizing the benefits which life and health insurance offers both to the owner himself and to his family. It means painting word pictures of life and health insurance in action. It means the constant use of the two words which are the salesman's two best friends in forcing himself to discuss benefits instead of commodities—the words "for example." It means emphasis upon guaranteed borrowing power as a direct and positive benefit to the insured himself, available in the immediate future rather than in the long years to come. It means emphasis upon freedom from investment cares and worries. It means emphasis upon the proposition that the man whose life and health insurance program is adequate is the happy possessor of a lifetime financial program which assures him that he has made adequate provision for tomorrow and entitles him therefore to spend all the rest of his income for the needs and luxuries of today. And perhaps above all else, it means emphasis upon the peace of mind which is the most direct and immediate benefit the life underwriter has for sale.

We say "perhaps above all else," for surely the most *immediate* and most devoutly to be desired benefit the life underwriter can offer is peace of mind: the tranquillity which rests upon a balanced budget, upon the awareness of financial security, upon the consciousness that at least a few dollars are readily available in the event of true emergency, upon a sense of financial progress from year to year, and upon freedom from worry about the safety of those dollars which have been accumulated so slowly and so painfully.

Let us conclude this consideration of benefit versus commodity by turning for a moment to the hardware business for an illustration which should forever stand in our memory.

Let us reflect upon the fact that every year in America a million or more quarter-inch drills are purchased by a million or more men—*no one of whom wants a quarter-inch drill!*

No, no man who buys a quarter-inch drill wants a quarter-inch drill. He wants a quarter-inch hole in a piece of wood or a piece of metal.

STEP IV: SECURING ACTION NOW

We have gained our listener's attention and converted attention into active interest by talking in terms of *his* problems and by indicating a relationship between his interests and our product which offers possible advantage to him. We have uncovered his *need* for our product or service as systematically as a doctor reading a blood pressure uncovers the urgent need for a loss in weight. Having uncovered the need, isolated it, viewed it from every angle, made it crystal-clear, and eliminated possible alternative solutions, we have introduced our product as the ideal solution to his problem. And *then* we have dramatized, emphasized, and maximized the benefits he will enjoy by using our product to satisfy the need, and thus have intensified to the utmost his *want* for what we have for sale.

Now, he may be ready to say: "I'll take it. Wrap it up!" And sometimes, he does say so. But more often not.

If he does not, let us not be discouraged. Let us recognize, instead, that hesitation at this point is natural and is to be expected. Let us recognize that we must be prepared to meet his hesitation and to help him arrive at a decision. Let us recognize that this is merely a part of the sales process, albeit an extremely important part.

For his hesitation is only natural and normal. He may hesitate because he doesn't understand. He may hesitate because, though he wants what we have for sale, he may not want it *enough* to outweigh his desire for other commodities or services he might purchase instead, and because he has only so many dollars to spend and can spend them only once. He may hesitate because of doubt, because of lack of confidence. And if for none of these reasons, he may still hesitate because of *inertia*—natural, everyday, human inertia.

If he hesitates because his wants are not sufficiently acute, obviously our course of action is to sharpen those wants still further. We must make them keen enough to compete successfully with other wants for other things he could buy instead, many of which would give immediate sensory or social satisfaction instead of long-term personal satisfaction. We must review his needs and rule out alternative solutions to his problem until it is clear that his problem *must* be solved and that no other solution will serve.

Then we must dramatize to the utmost the personal benefits to the prospect himself—the fact that most of the money he proposes to set aside for life insurance will be saved, not spent; the fact that within a few short years, he will have made available to himself always thereafter the guaranteed borrowing power we throw in as an added benefit with every policy we deliver; the enormous value of the peace of mind we have to offer; the tremendous sense of personal satisfaction which will be adequate reward for the sacrifice entailed.

If it appears that he hesitates because of doubt, we may reassure him with third-party endorsements concerning the wisdom of the action we have proposed, and also the integrity of the institution of life and health insurance itself and of our company. We may introduce documentary evidence, logic, borrowed prestige, until his questions are answered and his doubts resolved.

We may also help him sense his needs and wants more clearly, and help him overcome his doubts and reservations, by citing the experiences of other men with similar problems who have used successfully the solution he is now considering. This is to say, we use examples and illustrations, because they serve to dramatize the benefit, and because men tend to follow the example of others. All of which is to say that we help along the sales process whenever we introduce again our two best friends: the two words "for example."

Overcoming Inertia

Almost every salesman (unless he be that fortunate fellow who sells piping-hot sirloin steaks to prospects who are both hungry and prosperous) must encounter that natural human indisposition to make a decision, that natural inertia which counsels against taking action *now.*

Most of us tend to postpone a decision as long as we can, and postpone it even longer when it involves spending money, and even longer yet when the product or service to be purchased does not offer immediate sensory satisfaction! And so it is only human nature to hesitate, to postpone, to delay a decision "until the first of the month or the first of the year"—which is to say that it is only human nature to yield to the promptings of inertia, that law of human nature and of physics which dictates that a body at rest tends to remain at rest until acted upon by some outside force.

Let us make no mistake about it, we must deal with inertia one way or another. It is ever present. In the few instances where we seem to have no problem with inertia, it must be that we have succeeded in making the want so acute as to cause the prospect to arouse himself, to take the initiative, to overcome inertia on his own account, and to say to himself: "*I'll do it!*"

Basically, there are two things we can do with inertia. First, we can employ enough pure muscle to overcome it. We can make the need so abundantly clear, the want so urgent and consuming, that we *overcome* inertia.

Or second, we can use inertia as a *help* instead of a *hindrance.* We can let the prospect's natural reluctance to make a decision or to take action help him make a decision by default: to take action by his very inaction.

We can do this with propriety and confidence, knowing that he will welcome this assistance if he is truly ready to make an affirmative decision, and that conversely he will arouse himself, overcome inertia, and take positive action to avoid or postpone his decision if indeed that be his desire.

Let us see how simply we can use inertia as a help instead of a hindrance, by watching a prospective buyer as he listens to a salesman of a household appliance such as a refrigerator or a washing machine. Let us assume that the prospect has spent the entire afternoon with his wife looking at competing products and is ready to buy, but is confused by conflicting claims and the general similarity of the many different makes he has seen today.

The salesman is summarizing his case and reviewing his list of advantages, and then he says: "Why don't you let me send it out?"

Now inertia does its work. Inertia, whispering into the prospect's ear, says to his subconscious mind: "Now, you know you dislike making decisions, and you dislike spending money, so why don't you just sit tight and do nothing for a while?" And the salesman has lost his sale. He so handled the situation that if his prospect yielded to the urging of inertia and did nothing, *he refrained from buying.*

But watch now while the salesman, summarizing his case, ends with the words: ". . . and I can have this wonderful new machine in your home this very afternoon—*I'll call the shipping room now.*" As he reaches for the phone to the shipping room, inertia again whispers into the prospect's ear: "Now, you know you dislike making decisions, and this kind fellow, realizing this, has helped you make your decision! You know you must have a new machine soon, and this is a good one, so why don't you just sit tight and do nothing?" And if the prospect heeds the counsel of inertia and does nothing, *he has bought!*

Moreover, he will be glad of it. And he bought of his own free will, be it noted, for if he is not ready to make a decision, it will be easy enough for him to lean forward in his chair and say: "No, don't call that shipping room just yet; I have some more shopping to do first."

The basic point is that if we meet inertia head on, we must summon enough strength to overcome it, for in the usual and natural state of affairs, if the buyer takes no action (that is, if he heeds the advice of inertia and does nothing), he *refrains* from buying. But it is usually entirely possible, perhaps even easy, for the salesman to reverse the situation 180 degrees, so that if the prospective buyer heeds the promptings of inertia and does nothing, *he makes a favorable decision by refraining from action!*

This is nothing more or less than the use of implied consent, a closing device familiar to every salesman of every commodity and employed by all of us in our everyday lives. (Watch any youngster asking his parents' permission to go to the movies!) It is a principle which takes on new significance and which we see in new perspective, however, when we come face to face with the meaning of inertia and its influence upon every sale, and indeed upon every human action.

The life underwriter uses the equivalent of "I'll call the shipping room now" when he reaches for the telephone and says: "I'll call the doctor now," or when he starts to fill out the application and asks: "Were you born right here in Houston?" or—better yet—when he says, with pen poised over an application blank: "To whom do you usually make your life insurance payable?"

If we would secure action, we must make the decision to buy easier than the decision not to buy. Even the prospective buyer who needs life insurance, knows that he needs it, can pay for it, and intends to buy it soon hesitates to buy it *now*. And so, as he stands poised upon the fence, we must make it easier for him to jump to our side of the fence than to the other side, and for this purpose the use of implied consent is time-tested and proven. Thus, instead of saying "Do you want it?" or "When would you like to start?" we say: "You will have to be examined, of course—will it be more convenient for you to go with me to the doctor's office during business hours or in the evening?"

Challenging to Decision and Action

We can sometimes overcome inertia, intensify desire, and secure action by introducing a challenge. This is often done successfully by a frank recognition of the fact that not every man sees his responsibilities to his wife and children, and to his own future, clearly enough to make the sacrifices necessary to meet those responsibilities. We say: "Of course, it must be realized that a great deal of courage is needed to make the very real sacrifices which this program entails. Not every man has that kind of courage. But those who do, realize a sense of achievement and an inner glow of satisfaction which constitute a rich reward, etc. . . ."

We may challenge also by raising the question of availability. It is profoundly true that life and health insurance is one of the few commodities or services which money alone cannot buy. The man who is to buy life and health insurance must have money, of course. But in addition, he must have good health, mental and physical, and a good personal record, moral and financial. Thus, we may properly and unhesitatingly raise the issue of whether or not our prospective buyer will be able to secure our product, once he decides that he wants it.

We therefore say to our listener: "Sir, life insurance is bought with *three* mediums of exchange, not just one. The price of insurance is money, plus good health, plus good character. I know you have the necessary money, and I know you have the necessary character, for I can readily inform myself on both of those subjects by inquiry; and if you did not qualify on both counts, I would not be here. But I do not know whether you have the necessary health, *and neither do you.* No, not even if you were examined last week! So before we become too greatly attached to the benefits and conveniences this policy could bring into your life, let us determine whether you can get it. I'll call the doctor now, to see what choice of dates and hours he can give us."

It has been wisely and well said that "refusal to sell is an incentive to buy." Ponder upon this principle, and learn to use the hint of unavailability as an incentive to buy, a *challenge* to decision and action.

Summary

Our goal is to lead the prospect from a starting point of "no need, no want, no interest" easily and comfortably and smoothly, a step at a time, to a favorable decision and action now.

The key to success is to lead him to *want* our product. But if we try to make him want it merely by describing it in glowing terms, we shall be building a structure without a foundation. Our course, then, is to establish conclusively a *need* for our product and service, a need so well defined, so incapable of solution except by means of our product, that the prospect's awareness of need creates its own irresistible pressure and grows into a *want* so urgent, so demanding, that he is ready to buy. Then we dramatize the *benefits* of our policy; and finally, we help him arrive at an affirmative decision by making the favorable decision easier for him than the unfavorable one.

The sales process may be likened to that of taking the prospective buyer by the hand and leading him, a step at a time, up a stairway.

First, we must gain his attention and interest sufficiently to cause him to be willing to give us his hand for the moment. Then we must lead him a step or two up the stairs, to the point where he can stand on tiptoe and glimpse the benefits awaiting him at the top of the flight. His interest thus aroused, we lead him several further steps upward by showing him his need for those benefits, and several more by dramatizing the benefits and applying them to his own affairs.

Finally, when we have led him to a point near the upper landing, we go a step ahead of him and—still holding him by the hand—gently help him upward so that it becomes easier for him to decide to go on up to the landing than to turn back downward.

Step by step, we lead him, guide him, and motivate him from the first step at the bottom of the stairs to the place of decision and action at the top.

SELECTED REFERENCES

LIFE INSURANCE AGENCY MANAGEMENT ASSOCIATION. *The Approach as a Sale in Itself.* File 663.1. Hartford, 1953.

Life Insurance Agency Management Association. *The Close.* File 663.4. Hartford, 1960.

Life Insurance Agency Management Association. *The New Single Needs Sales.* File 660. Hartford, 1958.

Speicher, Paul. *154 Messages from Paul Speicher.* Indianapolis: Research & Review Service of America.

Woodson, Benjamin N. *More Power to You.* Indianapolis: Research & Review Service of America, Inc., 1951.

Woodson, Benjamin N. *The Set of the Sail.* Indianapolis: Research & Review Service of America, Inc., 1963.

Chapter 67

LEGAL RESPONSIBILITIES OF THE LIFE UNDERWRITER

BY JOHN BARKER, JR.

Public confidence is the foundation upon which the structure of the life and health insurance industry is built. This is forcibly demonstrated when a policyholder entrusts his dollars to the safekeeping of an insurance company in return for a promise. At first blush, it might seem that the policyholder ought to demand more security in exchange for those dollars than a mere undertaking to pay at some future date when a certain contingency occurs. Yet not one policyholder in a million makes such a request. Why? Because he has confidence in the character, the competence, and the integrity of the underwriter and the company that he represents. This public confidence has been built up over the years in large part by the efforts of countless life underwriters, who have been motivated not by fear of legal penalties for any dereliction, but by loyalty to the company they represent, by a mutual respect for each other, and primarily by a desire to be of assistance to their clients in an area where only they are truly expert.[1]

These factors should be kept in mind as this chapter is read. What the law requires the agent to do or refrain from doing will be discussed; but in the last analysis, these legal directives should constitute only the minimum standard governing his actions. His ultimate success will be determined in proportion to the respect and good will of his policyholders and clients. These attributes may be attained and preserved not merely by walking within the periphery of what is considered legal, but also bv following the dictates of his own conscience as to what is fair and square.

[1] The terms "life underwriter" and "agent" are used interchangeably in this chapter and are intended broadly to include health insurance underwriters and agents, inasmuch as the legal responsibilities of the former are virtually indistinguishable from the latter. The most significant area of contrast is that of countersignature requirements where, by reason of the historical relationship between the casualty and health insurance fields, the countersignature requirements for health insurance are often more onerous than those applicable to life insurance.

Responsibility of Agent to Prospect and Policyholder

The agent should be thoroughly conversant with the terms and conditions and benefits of all of the contracts offered by his company, so as to fulfill his responsibility of describing these accurately to his prospect. It is his duty to see that the applicant knows exactly what he is to receive in exchange for his premiums. If he is selling participating insurance, he should always make it clear that dividends which are projected for the future are not guaranteed but are merely illustrative in nature. The need for a clear and accurate statement by the agent is graphically illustrated by the following true case.

In 1934 an applicant purchased an endowment policy which guaranteed him an income of $25 per month upon reaching age 65. The agent who sold the policy explained that dividends earned over the years could be left on deposit to increase the ultimate monthly income. Using the 1934 scale as an illustration, the agent informed the insured that he might expect to receive as much as $40 per month upon reaching age 65. The agent also presented a prospectus in which these dividend illustrations were set forth, as was also a legend to the effect that the dividends shown were merely illustrative in nature and were not to be construed either as estimates or as guarantees for future years. Twenty years later the policyholder checked the status of his contract with the company and was astonished when informed that he could expect to receive only $32 per month. This lesser amount reflected the result of a lowering of interest rates on investments during the period in question. The insured communicated his astonishment to the insurance commissioner of his state, to his two United States senators, to his congressman, and also to the chairman of the Federal Trade Commission. While the company had neither violated any statute nor engaged in any misrepresentation or concealment, nevertheless its reputation was damaged by the agent's failure to fix in the policyholder's mind the fact that the dividend projection was merely an illustration which could not be guaranteed.

For some time the New York insurance laws have forbidden companies transacting business in that state to "make any estimate as to the dividends or share of surplus to be received in the future" on any policy or contract. There are similar statutes in other states, and most of the leading companies have insisted on the use of a prominently displayed precautionary legend on sales promotional material where dividend projections are employed. The following is typical of these clauses: "These results include dividends which are illustrative only and are neither estimates nor guarantees of any dividend. Illustrations are based on the 1963 dividend scale of the company."

A recent federal court decision involving a so-called "minimum deposit" plan bears directly on the life underwriter's responsibility to a policyowner. An insured with an annual income of $9,600 was persuaded to take a $100,000 ten-payment life policy with an annual premium of $7,265. The agent urged the insured to convert his existing policies to limited-pay life and to take out policy loans to pay for the cost of conversion as well as the first premium of the $100,000 policy. He also advised the insured to obtain a bank loan to pay future premiums. In addition to being extremely complicated, the agent's presentation was based upon a 40 per cent tax bracket rather than the insured's actual 26 per cent. Before a year had expired, the agent persuaded the insured to take out a $50,000 life policy on his wife, again using an illustration based on a 40 per cent tax bracket to demonstrate the advantages of the minimum deposit plan. Several months later the insured consulted an investment broker and another insurance agent, who told him he could not afford the existing program and advised him to terminate the insurance. When the insured informed the original writing agent of his desire to cancel the plan, the agent refused to co-operate. The insured then cancelled the policies and sued the agent in the federal district court. The court found for the policyholder, awarding him actual damages of $13,309.98 plus interest, $2,500 for mental suffering, and $10,000 as exemplary and punitive damages (*Knox* v. *Anderson,* USDC Hawaii [1958], 159 F. Supp. 795).

While some life insurance lawyers have disagreed with this decision, the fact remains that it was upheld on appeal; further, the United States Supreme Court, on June 11, 1962, declined to review it. We must regard this result as a warning to the life underwriter that, in the words of the Court, "he should be held responsible for the intelligent fulfillment of the duties he has assumed by his actions." The agent should make certain that any illustrations submitted to a prospective policyholder are accurate, do not mislead, and are based upon the prospect's actual financial status, rather than upon a hypothetical situation which, although it may advertise the advantages of a particular plan, has no relation to the actual facts.

Responsibility of Agent to Company

Another important consideration is the rule that the company is presumed to know whatever facts are communicated to the agent in the course of his activity in the marketing of the company's policies, whether or not such facts are actually communicated to the company by the agent. The positive aspect of this legal principle should be obvious to the agent: He should communicate to his home office whatever material facts he learns in the course of his activities as agent. He should remember that the company will probably be liable irrespective of his communication or lack of it, and he should therefore demonstrate his loyalty by apprising the company of any material information regarding the proposed insured.

Occasionally, the companies will attempt to limit the effect of this rule of law by an exculpatory clause, either in the application or in the policy, stating that no information given to the agent shall be binding on the insurer unless that information is included in writing in the application. In *New York Life* v. *Fletcher,* 117 US 519, the Supreme Court of the United States held such a clause effective to relieve the company of liability, where the agent, without the knowledge of the insured, falsified the answers to several material questions in the application. Other courts, however, have held such clauses ineffective to relieve the company of liability and have distinguished the Fletcher case on the ground that in that case the insured himself was presumed to have had knowledge of the fraud, as he signed the falsified application, though he claimed he had not read the answers written thereon by the agent. In general, therefore, while an exculpatory clause may offer partial protection to the company, its value is uncertain at best, as in other instances in which a unilateral effort is made to vitiate the effect of a rule of law.

The agent who receives premiums is under a duty to transmit them with dispatch either to the general agent, to the manager, or to the home office, depending upon the procedures in effect in the particular company. He may only collect up to the amount of the premium due, except in a situation where an official receipt for discounted premiums is to be issued.

The authority of the agent may be expressly limited by the terms of the application or the policy. Where such limitation is set forth in the application, it is generally binding on the applicant subject to the limitations set forth above. Thus, where an agent exceeds his authority by the terms of the application, as, for example, by waiving a condition appearing therein, the applicant is held to be put on notice regarding the limits on the agent's authority, and cannot successfully contend that the agent has waived the condition in question.

The "conditional receipt" is a common device in situations where premiums are paid in advance and the applicant is desirous of protection from time of payment. Unfortunately, the interpretation of these receipts has led to frequent litigation. Many applicants, accustomed to so-called "binders" in the purchase of fire insurance on their homes or casualty insurance on their automobiles, mistakenly believe they are receiving binding coverage under their life policies; but obviously, this must depend on their insurability, which is a factor that can only be determined subsequently.

In this situation the applicant is in fact receiving an acknowledgment of payment of the first premium, together with an agreement that the insurance applied for is effective as of the date of the receipt, assuming that the applicant is insurable at the later of two times: when the premium is paid or when the required medical examination is completed. The courts, in considering the language of these conditional receipts, have used the sales presentation of the agent as a factor pointing to ambiguity of the document, despite the lack of authority on the agent's part to alter the language of the receipt. The public relations effect of these cases should be taken into account by the agent and weighed against his zeal in closing the case.

The same principle applies to a limitation of an agent's authority contained in the policy. As long as the limitation is unequivocally expressed, the insured cannot be heard to say that he thought the agent had authority to vary the terms of the policy. In most jurisdictions, however, this exculpatory clause will not be effective when the policy has not yet been delivered. Let us assume, for example, that the agent agrees with the prospect to waive a condition contained in the application. If the only limitation on the agent's authority is contained in the policy, then the prospect is not on notice of the limitation at the time the condition was waived, and therefore the company cannot take advantage of the limitation.

Some companies have sought to protect themselves from liability in the event of a misappropriation of the premiums by the agent, and have inserted a clause in the application which has the effect of making the agent, in the case of an attempted payment prior to delivery of the policy, the agent of the proposed insured rather than of the company. In the absence of this exculpatory clause, however, if the agent fails either through fraud or through negligence to transmit the premium to the company, then it is generally recognized that he has the power to bind his principal, the company, and that the latter will be liable for whatever consequences result. This type of provision is less prevalent today, because insurance companies have recognized the desirability of placing the contract in force by prompt collection of the first premium.

Scope of Authority—Power to Bind Company

In resolving the important question of when the agent is acting "within the scope of his authority," the two basic types of authority, "actual" and "apparent," should be examined. The *actual* authority of the agent is created and defined by the written documents which are the basis of his professional existence, namely, his own contract with the general agent or the company, the application, the policy contract, and any other document which may fix the limits of his authority.

The *apparent* authority of the agent is evidenced by the reasonable belief of the prospect regarding the power of the agent to bind the company. This apparent authority must be created by the acts or omissions of the company itself—it cannot be created by the agent. Custom or usage in the insurance industry also plays an important role in determining the apparent authority of the agent. Though the precedents in law are not always uniform in this area, the test is whether the client had reasonable ground to rely upon the acts or representations of the agent.

Assuming that the foregoing elements regarding authority are present, the agent may bind his company regardless of whether the company profited by the act of the agent. The only question is whether he acted within the scope of authority, actual or apparent. This liability has been extended even to cases of slander and libel by some courts.

There are surprisingly few cases where a company or general agent has been held responsible for the negligent driving of an agent in an automobile. This is doubtless due to the fact that the average life underwriter is an "independent contractor" in the true sense. He directs his own activities and in general determines for himself when and how he shall pursue his calling. In companies where agents actually have contracts of employment which establish their status as employees, however, and in the case of agents who are financed under some form of compensation that is tantamount to salary, the hazard of liability for the employer is increased, particularly where it can be shown that the automobile was operated on company business. The basic test is the extent to which the activities of the agent are in fact supervised and directed by the general agent or the company.

Relations with Attorneys and Other Professions

The evolution and progress of the life underwriter during the past four decades has been from trade to profession. Companies have realized that education, training, and competence are of greater significance than a golf score in the low eighties. Sometimes, in supplying expert advice and service in this complex economy of ours, the life underwriter has invaded the territory of the lawyer. Obviously, he cannot be expected to have a lawyer available every time he interviews a prospect, but if he presumes to give legal advice or to practice law, then he may be subject to serious penalties. The unauthorized practice of law is a crime in most states, and this is not so much for the protection of the lawyer as the public, which has a right to be counseled by those who have studied law and qualified for the legal profession.

The friction between these two professions has been reduced to a minimum by two co-operative enterprises, both of which have been conducted at the national level. In 1948 the "National Statement of Principles of Cooperation between Life Underwriters and Lawyers" was issued by the National Conference of Lawyers and Life Underwriters, and received the full approval of the House of Delegates of the American Bar Association and the National Council and the Board of Trustees of the National Association of Life Underwriters.[2] In this Statement, it is recognized that

---

[2] Several passages from the Statement are:

In recent years, much of the actual negotiation of the sale of life insurance contracts involves estate planning. The acquisition of life insurance has become a complex problem by its ever increasing relation to plans of testamentary disposition, wills and living trusts, to partnerships and close corporation contracts, and to problems of taxation. The solution of such problems requires a man to make

both expert insurance service and skilled legal guidance may be required in the course of life insurance negotiations and estate planning. In this event "the simultaneous and harmonious attention of a representative of each profession in solving the problems of the same client will provide the safest and most efficient service."

This Statement is perhaps even more lucid in restricting the scope of the lawyer's activities than it is for the life underwriter. The lawyer who reviews a transaction involving insurance is not permitted to share in the agent's commission. He may not enter into a fee-splitting arrangement with the agent. He should not attempt to divert business from one life underwriter to another. He is not allowed to share his legal fees with the life underwriter as a consideration for the referral of legal business; and finally, he may not allow a legal opinion to be utilized as a selling document for insurance.

The life underwriter is also subjected to certain sanctions by the Statement. It is made clear that he has no right to prepare legal documents or otherwise to practice law. It is improper for him to dissuade a client from seeking the advice of legal counsel. While he is precluded from furnishing attorneys as part of his service to clients, it is generally believed that he may recommend a qualified lawyer when so requested. The life underwriter must not participate in the attorney's fee; and of course, he may not share his own commission with any person who is not a licensed agent. There is nothing to prevent him, however, from obtaining legal advice or

---

far-reaching decisions. These decisions often are, or, upon the happening of death, become, irrevocable. The American public should therefore receive not only expert insurance service and disinterested advice but also skilled and disinterested legal guidance and advice when necessary; both are often required in problems arising out of negotiation for and use of life insurance, and when this is the case, the simultaneous and harmonious attention of a representative of each profession in solving the problems of the same client will provide the safest and most efficient service.

Fair dealing with the public and an observance of laws which have been enacted throughout the United States require that all legal service and advice should at all times be given by an individual trained in the law and duly licensed to practice; anyone who gives legal advice should be solely devoted to the interest of his client and permit no personal consideration whatsoever to weaken his exclusive loyalty to his client.

. . . .

(1) A life underwriter has no right to practice law or to give legal advice or to hold himself out as having such rights. He should not attempt to do so directly or indirectly. Therefore, he must never prepare for execution by his client legal documents of any kind, such as wills or codicils thereto, trust agreements, corporation charters, minutes, by-laws or business insurance agreements. When submitting an involved mode of settlement, or one which may affect a client's prior disposition of property by his Last Will and Testament, the life underwriter should suggest that the same be submitted to the client's attorney for approval.

In estate planning, all transfers of property, except simple modes of settlement under life insurance policies or changes of beneficiary thereof, should be recommended subject to the approval of the client's attorney. Since these decisions should in the final analysis be subject to the approval of the client's attorney, it is important for the life underwriter to collaborate with his client's attorney as early as possible in the negotiations so as to afford his client the safest and most effective service.

It is improper for a life underwriter, in submitting to his client an estate planning report, to attach thereto or insert therein any forms of legal instruments or of specific legal clauses.

. . . .

Nothing herein contained is intended to restrict or limit the life underwriter's legitimate activities in measuring the client's need for life insurance, determining the amount and type needed, developing a comprehensive life insurance program in relation to the client's other plans and affairs, and selling such insurance; the ethics of his profession require him not to recommend the purchase of additional insurance unless needed. Such activities are for the benefit of those insured and their dependents only insofar as they are consistent with the foregoing statement of principles.

a written legal opinion from an attorney for his *own* guidance in the conduct of his business.

The second important co-operative enterprise between the two professions was the formation in 1951 of the National Conference of Lawyers and Life Insurance Companies. The membership of this Conference is composed of life insurance officials and members of the Standing Committee on Unauthorized Practice of Law of the American Bar Association. One of the primary functions of this Conference is "to review from time to time any practices by life insurance companies or their field representatives which are alleged to constitute an unauthorized practice of law or practices by lawyers which are alleged to violate the Statement of Principles, and to give consideration to the proper spheres of activity of the two groups in discharging their respective responsibilities to the public." In 1953 the Conference issued a tract entitled "Some Guideposts for Cooperation between Lawyers and Life Insurance Representatives," which has been widely circulated, and which contains a more comprehensive delineation of the Statement of Principles and the rules of conduct to be followed by the two groups.

This matter has received continued study since the original "Guideposts" article was published, and in 1963 the Conference revised its work under the subtitle "Guideposts Revisited," appearing in the Winter, 1963, issue of the *Journal of the American Society of Chartered Life Underwriters* (Volume XVII, No. 1). This article should be studied by every conscientious agent.[3]

The primary objective of both the life insurance industry and the Bar should always be to give the best possible advice and service to the public in a free society. This high-minded purpose requires harmony and understanding. As a competent salesman, the life underwriter can stimulate the interest of his prospect in estate planning and motivate him to discuss his problems with his own counsel. If he allows himself to become enmeshed in the legal technicalities that the law schools attempt to train their students to solve, then he will not only expose himself to charges of unauthorized law practice but will also lose valuable time at the expense of his principal vocation, which is to supply life insurance protection to the public.

---

[3] Worthy of particular attention is the recent decision of the Oregon Supreme Court in *Oregon State Bar* v. *John M. Miller and Company, Inc.*, Supreme Court of Oregon, September 18, 1963, stating in part: "An insurance salesman can explain to his prospective customer alternative methods of disposing of assets, including life insurance, which are available to taxpayers *generally*. He may inform his prospect in general terms that life insurance may be an effective means of minimizing his taxes. He cannot properly advise a prospective purchaser with respect to his *specific* need for life insurance as against some other form of disposition of his estate, unless the advice can be given without drawing upon the law to explain the basis for making the choice of alternatives."

Advertising—Fair Trade Practice Laws

The McCarran Act of 1945, which resulted from the 1944 SEUA decision of the United States Supreme Court that insurance was involved in interstate commerce and hence subject to federal control and regulation, provided that, generally speaking, the federal antitrust laws should not be applicable to the business of insurance until June 30, 1948, and then only to the extent that such business was not regulated by state law.[4] During this interval and in subsequent years, all states have enacted fair trade practice acts designed to render life insurance activities more effectively and completely subject to investigation and regulation by the various state insurance commissioners, rather than to have such activities dealt with by the Federal Trade Commission at Washington. The Federal Trade Commission Acts created a bureau with power to deal with unfair methods of competition and unfair or deceptive practices in commerce. These might conceivably include misrepresentations, false advertising, discrimination, rebates, and other unlawful and unethical practices in the life and health insurance fields. Recent holdings of the United States Supreme Court, however, have confirmed the opinion widely held in the insurance industry that the states are adequately covering this regulatory field by their fair trade practice acts.

These acts include among their prohibitions any misrepresentation or false advertising of policy contracts, and false information and advertising generally. While most advertising copy originates in the home office, the statutory prohibitions are equally applicable to the agent. Some guides which provide a basis for legitimate advertising may be found in the "model" rules adopted by the National Association of Insurance Commissioners, and also in the rules of the Federal Trade Commission.

The term "advertisement" is not restricted to items found in trade journals, newspapers, and magazines. It is more broadly defined as any item, regardless of source or medium used, which the company or its agents and brokers employ to solicit sales. Specifically included are prepared sales talks, presentations, and material of all kinds for use by agents or brokers, and representations made by the agents and brokers in accordance therewith. Intracompany and house-organ material would not be included unless used by the agent as a sales device. If this material should be found to be deceptive or misleading, perhaps the company might escape responsibility where it had not condoned and approved the use, but obviously the agent would be responsible. The crux of the situation is whether the material is used as a sales piece; and a person so using it must accept responsibility if it has reason to mislead, and does in fact mislead, the recipient.

---

[4] See discussion of SEUA decision in Chapter 77.

The success of a life underwriter is based upon his reputation and prestige, which in turn depend upon the degree of trust and confidence in which he is held by his clients. Without attempting to turn this tract into a sermon, it may still be said that the truth is a most effective weapon in the eternal struggle of man.

Rebate Laws

Most states prohibit an agent or broker from granting a rebate as an inducement to purchase a policy of life insurance. These antirebate statutes are closely related to the antidiscrimination laws. The latter, however, are more properly directed against the company in order to prevent any discrimination in establishing the rates charged for the insurance protection, and the discussion in this chapter will be limited to the antirebate statutes.

The power of the state to control this aspect of the premiums charged for life insurance has been held constitutional on the ground that a state legislature has the right to regulate the conduct of the insurance profession within its borders and that prohibiting rebates is a valid exercise of that right. Furthermore, it has been held that the constitutionally guaranteed rights of the individual agent are not unjustly abridged by the penalties imposed in these rebate laws.

There are many ways in which the agent may violate the antirebate statutes aside from the obvious method of remitting part of the premium to the insured. For example, certain contractual agreements between the agent and the insured, under which the latter derives a benefit which is a direct result of his purchase of the policy from the agent, have been held to be a violation. Also, it has been recognized that an agreement by an agent to obtain a loan for a prospective policyholder from the agent's company in return for the purchase of a policy through the agent constitutes a violation of the antirebate statutes.

There are also precedents holding that no violation has occurred. One reason for some leniency on the part of the courts is that most of these statutes are criminal in nature and therefore they are sometimes construed in favor of the defendant. One court ruled that the purchasing of drinks for a prospective applicant did not constitute rebating where the proposed insured was proved to be sober and in sound mental condition. It was also held that the antirebate statute had not been violated where the agent took in payment a note for 50 per cent of the first premium and permitted the insured to retain the other 50 per cent, which happened to coincide with the agent's commission, in consideration for the promise of the insured to furnish the agent with names of prospective clients.

Most states permit a qualified life underwriter to insure his own life and receive the commission. This practice is ordinarily permitted by a statute which establishes it as an exception to the antirebate laws.

The effect of these antirebate statutes is ordinarily restricted to penalizing the agent involved. If the company had no knowledge of the agent's misconduct, it cannot be held to have violated the law. Since the statutes are designed to protect the policyholder, it has been held that the company cannot avoid a contract entered into as a result of an unlawful rebate. However, some states have passed statutes making the receiving of a rebate, as well as its granting, a criminal offense.

A few of the court decisions involving the criminal prosecution of the agent have been described. The more usual method of enforcing these laws which are so important to the preservation of the standards of our business is by complaint to the insurance commissioner or to the local life underwriters association. In most states the commissioner is empowered to suspend or revoke the license of an offending agent. Furthermore, his underwriters organization may vote to suspend him from membership. While this would not necessarily prevent him from continuing in business, it might do such damage to his prestige and reputation as to discourage him from this particular career.

Twisting Prohibitions

"Twisting" is defined as persuading a policyholder by misrepresentation to discontinue or lapse a policy in order that the agent may sell him a new policy. The word itself affords an apt and graphic description of the offense. The life insurance program of the client is wrenched out of its natural shape so that the policyholder gets a distorted view, questions his previous judgment, and is led to tear down his old plan and to start a new one, usually on less favorable terms.

Life insurance is the most widely practiced form of thrift in America today, and its conservation is important to most of our families. Twisting laws are designed to protect the public against the unscrupulous, smooth-talking salesman whose concern is not with the best interest of the policyholder but rather with the commissions that may be produced by the sale of new insurance. There are, of course, cases where replacement of existing insurance may be of advantage to the insured, and this is the reason why the twisting laws are founded on misrepresentation or deceit.

It is obviously not a crime merely to persuade a man to change from one kind of policy to another or from one company to another, or from old insurance to new; but it is a crime to lead the policyholder to take this step without knowledge of all of the pertinent facts. In order to sell a new policy, the twister misrepresents and distorts the truth.

The fair trade practices acts, referred to earlier, contain prohibitions against twisting. Despite these enactments, however, the replacement problem has grown alarmingly in recent years. Policyholders have been persuaded to drop existing policies and to take out new policies by agents who were motivated more by a desire for commissions than the needs of the insured. To counter this trend, over twenty states have issued regulations designed to protect the policyholder who is advised to exchange his existing coverage for new. Most of these regulations require a complete disclosure in writing of the comparative cost of the old and new policies, as well as a comparison of the provisions of both policies. Also, the comparison must be presented to the original insurer to allow that company to study the proposal and present its advice to its insured. The regulations thus complement the antitwisting statutes by curing the evidentiary problem of not having written material on which to base a prosecution.

It is important to note that the insured retains his constitutionally guaranteed freedom to contract as he chooses. The agent must present his facts completely and accurately; the result is up to the insured. This concerns the underwriter in his most vital role—that of providing the client with the best insurance program available. Our business is often criticized because of the technical terminology used in its policy contracts, and considerable progress has been made in overcoming this complaint; but in the last analysis the client is entitled to be served by an agent who will explain the benefits in a straightforward and honest fashion.

The twisting statutes lead quite naturally to a consideration of the attitude to be taken by the life underwriter toward other underwriters and other companies. A life insurance company is a fiduciary organization, and the salesman is offering its services for the creation and preservation of funds to meet contingencies that are generally certain to occur. Thus the confidence of the buyer in the ability of the company to carry out its promises is a matter of prime importance. Since all of our principal legal reserve life insurance companies operate on the same general principles, any attempt to disturb the client's confidence in one company may destroy his confidence in the soundness of the business as a whole. Most states have statutes prohibiting the defamation of the character of any company doing business in that state. This type of law should pose no problem to the ethical life underwriter. Its observance will benefit the agent far more than any temporary advantage he might gain by its violation.

Licensing of Agents and Brokers under State Laws

The licensing of insurance agents and brokers is governed by statutes passed by the legislatures of the several states. The rules of the state in the licensing of insurance agents and brokers may be manifested in several ways. For example, the state may require prospective agents to take and pass an examination before it will issue a license allowing them to solicit life insurance within its borders. The state may extract a license fee or privilege tax from the insurance agent. It may deny a license to a minor or to a corporation. It may require that the company which the agent represents be licensed to do business within the state. These rules and requirements have been held to lie within the power of the state and not to conflict with any provision of the federal Constitution.

Generally, a person may be licensed as a broker without having any connection with a life company. He is regarded as an independent agent who may place business with any company which will accept it. The significant legal difference between an agent and a broker is that the former represents the company and the latter represents the insured. There are some states, however, where the broker must be licensed for the company with which he places the insurance.

Many states have reciprocal licensing statutes. Under these statutes an individual who is licensed in one state may obtain a license in the state having such a statute without taking an examination to determine his qualifications. These statutes usually extend this privilege only to those agents who are licensed by a state which grants a similar privilege to residents of the other state and which has qualification requirements substantially equivalent to the latter's.

Nonresident Agents and Interstate Brokers

Most states permit nonresidents to be licensed as agents and brokers. Those which do not generally require applications submitted on the lives of their residents to be signed by a resident agent. While it would be fortunate if the laws of all states were uniform in this area, the agent should realize that they are not and that any violation of these laws can reflect discredit on himself and his company. All responsible companies are aware of this problem and have established procedures to insure compliance with such statutes. The agent should not hesitate to ask the assistance of the home office when he encounters this problem area.

Territorial Limits of Agency

The territorial limits of an agency may be defined by the contract between the agent and the company, or they may be left unspecified. In either event the rules are inclined to be flexible in this area, as it is naturally difficult to restrict the moves of a life underwriter. Frequently, this will be controlled by an intracompany agreement or by an oral understanding that any activity outside a particular agent's territory will be conducted only after clearance with the general agent or manager in the other locality. This is sometimes a source of rancor within a company, but at least it seems that an agent who is given a free rein should not be heard to complain when his own home territory is invaded by others.

Termination of Agency

One of the essential characteristics of an agency is that it may be revoked at will by either party, in the absence of limitations imposed by the terms of the agency contract itself or unless it is coupled with an interest. However, there are court decisions upholding the right of the company to terminate the contract whether or not the contract provides for such termination by either party. For example, if the agent is guilty of conduct which is incompatible with his status as an agent, such as failing to devote his full time to the company's business where full-time activity is specified in the contract, the contract may be terminated by the company; and of course, it may always be terminated in the event of the misconduct of the agent.

Normally, under accepted rules of agency, an agency coupled with an interest may not be terminated at will without giving rise to an action for damages. Under most agency contracts the agent acquires a right to renewal commissions based on business he has written. It has been held that the right to these renewal commissions does not create such an interest as would prevent the termination of the agency. The right to the renewal commissions is determined by the wording of the contract. If no penalty is imposed under the terms of the contract for a voluntary termination by the agent, then the commissions would continue to be paid to the agent. Some agents' contracts contain a penalty clause which diminishes the amount of renewals by a stated per cent if the agent, subsequent to his termination, is employed by a competitor. Most courts have held these penalty clauses to be effective, though at least one case (*Carson* v. *Sun Life*, 56 Ga. App. 164) holds that a penalty clause of this nature is void as contrary to public policy.

As in the case of all contracts for personal service, the death of the agent terminates the contract automatically. Whatever renewals are payable to the agent under his contract are normally paid to his executor. The agent should designate the ultimate recipient of these commissions in his will, though some companies will allow a recipient to be named in the agent's contract. This arrangement runs the risk of being attacked as an invalid testamentary disposition not conforming to the applicable statute on wills. The safer course is to route the commissions through the estate via the will to the ultimate taker. In passing, it should be noted that it has been held that the estate of the deceased agent may not recover commissions on premiums paid after the death of the agent unless the commissions were fully earned before death.

Another important area to be considered regarding termination is the effect such termination has upon the policyholder or client. If the policyholder has no notice of the termination of the agency relationship, the agent retains the power to bind his former principal. The policyholder is entitled to assume that the agency is still in effect until he is notified of its termination. This is of particular importance where the policyholder is accustomed to paying his premiums to the agent rather than directly to the home office of the company. The company cannot lapse the policy for nonpayment of premiums in the absence of notice to the policyholder that he is to pay his premiums to another agent, or directly to the home office. The burden is therefore on the company if it wishes to protect itself in this area.

SELECTED REFERENCES

ASCHEMEYER, FRANK P. "Cooperation between Life Insurance Representatives and Lawyers—Guideposts Revisited," *Journal of the American Society of Chartered Life Underwriters*, Vol. XVII, No. 1 (Winter, 1963).

CAMPBELL, HUGH S. "The Agency Contract and Its Variations—Part II," *Association of Life Insurance Counsel Proceedings*, Vol. X (1950), p. 273.

CAVANAUGH, DANIEL P. "The Agency Contract and Its Variations—Part III," *Association of Life Insurance Counsel Proceedings*, Vol. X (1950), p. 289.

COUCH, GEORGE J. *Cyclopedia of Insurance Law*, Secs. 486–578. Rochester, N.Y.: Lawyers Co-operative Publishing Co., 1951.

COXWORTH, G. EDGAR. "Handling of Funds by Agents," *Association of Life Insurance Counsel Proceedings*, Vol. X (1950), p. 337.

DUCKWORTH, J. LON. "Knowledge of Representatives—Notice to Company," *Association of Life Insurance Counsel Proceedings*, Vol. XV (1960), p. 71.

GREIDER, JANICE E., and BEADLES, WILLIAM T. *Law and the Life Insurance Contract*. Homewood, Ill.: Richard D. Irwin, Inc., 1960.

MAGOVERN, JOHN J. "The Agency Contract and Its Variations—Part I," *Association of Life Insurance Counsel Proceedings*, Vol. X (1950), p. 253.

OAKES, BARRY; HOLT, JOHN FOX; and NASH, THOMAS G., JR. *Agency Law Handbook*, p. 48. Chicago: American Life Convention Legal Section, 1960.

O'NEILL, EUGENE T. "Conditional Receipt v. Binding Receipt," *Association of Life Insurance Counsel Proceedings*, Vol. XIII (1956), p. 219.

STEELE, ALLEN M. "Legal Duties and Liabilities of the Life Insurance Agent," *Association of Life Insurance Counsel Proceedings*, Vol. XIV (1959), p. 423.

VANCE, WILLIAM R. *Handbook on the Law of Insurance*. 3d ed. by BUIST M. ANDERSON. St. Paul: West Publishing Co., 1951.

Chapter 68

SALES MANAGEMENT

BY FREDERIC M. PEIRCE

The sales management function in a life insurance company is the responsibility of the agency department (sometimes called the sales or marketing department). Within the framework of company policy and its financial goals, the agency department will determine the geographical territory in which its sales efforts will be concentrated, the market or markets it will attempt to reach, the types of policy forms it will offer in those markets, the kind and quality of sales organization it will build and maintain, and, in conjunction with the actuarial department of the company, often will agree upon the rates with which it feels it can be competitive within those markets.

In mature companies, these decisions must be made within the framework of long-established marketing patterns. The company may sell life insurance only, or it may sell life and health insurance. It may offer these coverages to individuals only, or it may offer them to both individuals and groups. It may operate with full-time career agents compensated on a commission basis under the direction of a commission-compensated general agent, or that of a salaried branch manager; or it may utilize the debit system, under which its agents receive a service salary to collect premiums on and service existing business within specifically assigned territories, plus a commission on new sales. It may concentrate on brokerage business, not maintaining a sales organization of its own, but securing its business by soliciting excess business from the agents of other companies or by inviting the life and health business written by general property and casualty agents. The company pattern may be one or many combinations of these philosophies.

The greater the financial responsibility the company assumes for the costs of agent and field office development, the more control it tends to exercise over the methods to be followed to achieve satisfactory results. In the purely general agency company, the general agent is given the franchise to represent his company in a specified territory, is expected to provide all the capital necessary to develop a successful sales organization, and is given wide latitude in the procedures he follows to do so. His compensation is obtained from commissions, both immediate and deferred, on his own personally produced business, and on that produced by his agents. In a branch office company the manager is a salaried employee of the company and invests no capital of his own. The entire financial risk is assumed by the company, and a great deal of control normally is exercised by the agency department over the methods used to develop men and business. In practice today, the general agency company finds few men able to make the sizable investment required to develop a successful agency; it therefore subsidizes them to greater or lesser degree and, in exchange, requires them to follow company procedures in agency development.

The degree of control and supervision provided by the home office agency department will determine its composition. In a general agency company where methods and procedures are left largely to the individual

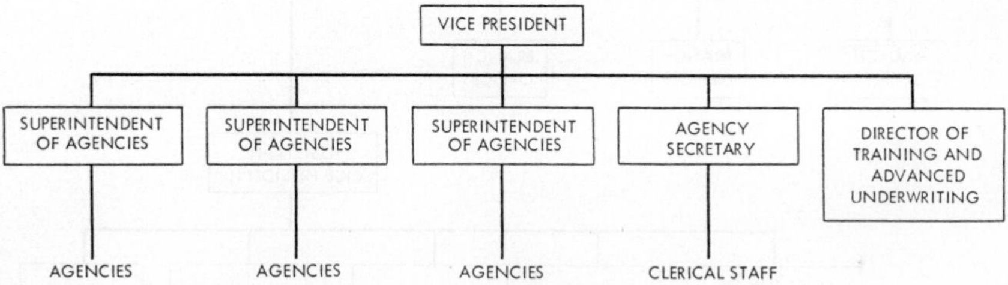

FIG. 68–1. Agency department organization chart—general agency company.

general agents, department staffing may be minimal. Typically, it will be headed by a vice president who is also a general officer of the company. He will have several line assistants (frequently called superintendents of agencies) who will be responsible for the actual supervision of the general agencies. There will be staff assistants for the administrative activities of the department, such as record keeping, field services, and conservation of business. Frequently, one of these staff assistants is designated as agency secretary and supervises the clerical staff of the department. The organizational chart of such a department might appear as in Figure 68–1.

By contrast, the agency department operating on the branch office plan, because it determines and directs the specific procedures to be followed by the field manager, will be staffed with many more specialists. There may be a director of manpower development, with the responsibility for the recruiting and selection of new agents; a director of training concerned with the administration of the company's standard training program; a director of advanced underwriting; a director of health insurance sales; a director of brokerage sales—each a specialist in his particular area and charged with the responsibility of promoting his specialty among the field offices. The organization chart of the department might appear as in Figure 68–2.

The agency department, then, is the fountainhead for the sales management process. It must be held accountable for developing the field sales offices and the managers who direct them, must supply them, supervise them, and motivate them. Through them must be obtained the salesmen—

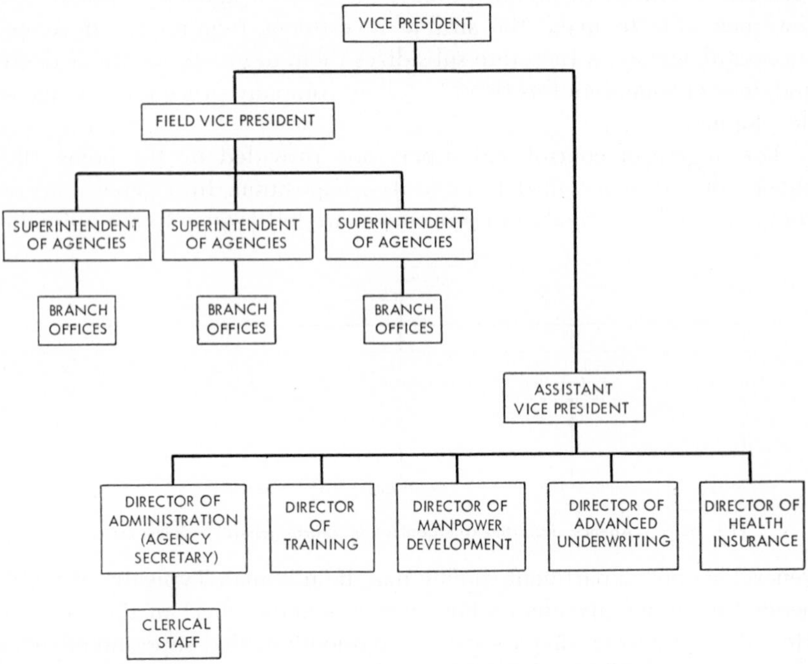

FIG. 68–2. Agency organization chart—branch office company.

the life insurance agents who will actually produce the business the company needs. Regardless of title or financial or working arrangement with the home office—great latitude or little—the functions and duties of the agency head remain the same: to build a sales organization which will produce adequate amounts of new life and health insurance for the company. For the purposes of this chapter, the agency head will be titled "manager."

Duties of the Manager

As executive head of a field office, the agency manager's responsibilities are diverse. He represents his company in a territory which may encompass a whole state, a series of counties, or a city; or he may be a member of but one of several agencies for his company in a large metropolitan area. He is authorized to secure applications for life and health insurance, to appoint field underwriters, to accept premium payments for transmission to the company home office. His office will handle the details of requests for payment of policy proceeds and policy changes. In short, in his community, he *is* his company.

In the process of producing men and business and representing his company in his territory, the sales manager must play many roles. Equally important to his production responsibilities is his function as a business manager. No consideration of sales management would be complete without recognizing the interrelationship between the two areas of activity.

Each of his sales management activities incurs a cost. Securing, housing, financing, and training a new man involve a substantial investment of time and money. Housing and supervising the established life underwriter carries a price tag. But the results secured determine the profit. The degree of success which the manager achieves in retaining the maximum number out of the total men recruited, the rate of production per man, and the quality and persistency of the sales they make, all have a major bearing on financial results. The essence of the sales manager's job, then, is the obtention and retention of men in sufficient quantity and quality to produce a sufficient amount of new life and health insurance sales of good quality to enable the sales agency to operate profitably.

Plan of Organization of the Agency

In the small or newly established agency the manager's staff will usually be limited to a cashier, who handles the details of new applications, premium payments, commission accounting, and home office correspondence; and a secretary. As the agency expands, the cashier's department will add other clerical staff. Today, many companies are collecting premiums directly in the home office, thus relieving materially the amount of work necessary at the agency level to maintain current premium payment records.

As production increases, the sales manager may add a supervisor or assistant manager to aid him in recruiting and training. If the agency is interested in securing business from general insurance agents, a brokerage supervisor may be added to the staff. Further development may bring the appointment of supervisors to build production units of their own, either in the agency city or in nearby suburban areas. Should the agency specialize in pension work, estate planning, or group insurance, the manager's staff will include specialists in these areas. Frequently, also, large producers in the agency will have secretarial help of their own. Thus a fully developed, substantial agency, consisting of both line and staff personnel, might appear as indicated in Figure 68–3.

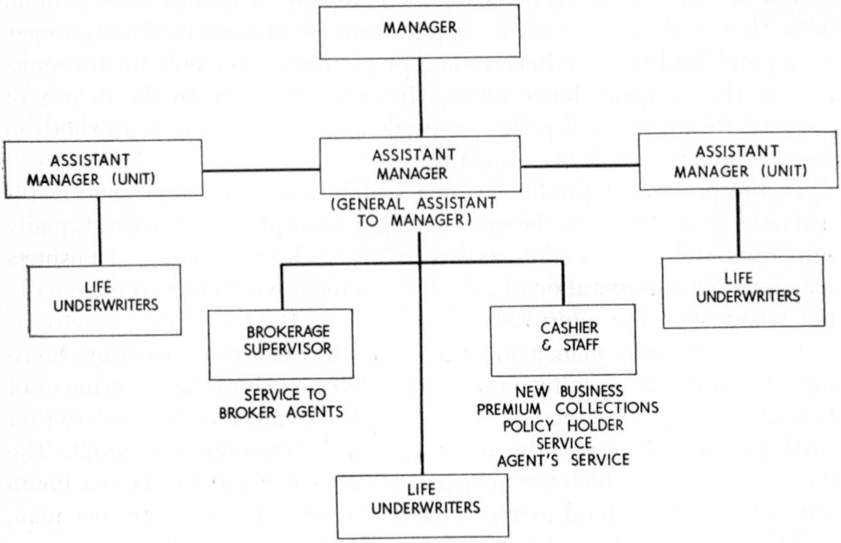

FIG. 68–3. Agency organization chart.

Plan of Development

The foundation of every successful agency is a clear concept on the part of the manager of the kind of agency he wants to develop, the methods he will follow to reach his objective, and the timetable he expects to follow to obtain it. Whether he is starting a new agency or taking charge of an existing one, sound executive operation indicates that he take inventory of his resources, familiarize himself with the potential of the market in which he plans to operate, decide the philosophy or principles upon which his agency will be conducted, and plan his objectives and the manner by which he hopes to reach them.

His resources will consist of the present organization which he may inherit, the business in force which his company has in the territory, the financial support which his company is willing to give him, and his own knowledge and experience. His decision as to the type of agency he wants to build will be colored by his own background, by his belief in how life insurance should be sold, and by the type of market available to him. His company's marketing philosophies will also have a bearing. He may believe that his agency should be composed of a limited number of quality men with high average production, concentrating their efforts on prospects in the middle and upper income brackets. If the territory in which he plans to operate will support it, if his company's facilities include the materials he needs, if he has the technical knowledge and qualifications required, and if his financial resources are adequate to finance agents over a longer period, he will plan his agency development toward the middle and upper income market. On the other hand, his analysis may suggest that the territory would best support an agency concentrating on single-need sales, or simple programing; and he would design his agency development plan to produce an organization best suited to that type of selling.

Each decision will have a bearing on the others to be made. For example, most agencies will reflect the manager's own background and selling style. The type of agency which the manager determines he wants will suggest the kind of recruits he wants to seek and the kind of training they will require. The age and income status of the men he wants will determine what his financing investment will be. The type of agency he decides upon will, in turn, influence its location. Should he decide, for example, to concentrate in the beginning on a brokerage agency, it is most probable that its location should be downtown near the financial district. Conversely, an agency of full-time men making the majority of their sales calls out of the downtown area, or in the evening hours, could well be located in a suburban area.

It is not possible to explore in detail all of the variations in situations which might exist, nor to suggest all of the steps which should be taken in the development of a blueprint for the operation of an agency. Interested readers will find suggested texts at the end of the chapter covering the subject in greater detail. It cannot be overemphasized, however, that the development of a plan involving careful objective analysis of the manager's resources and situation, of the results he hopes to achieve, and of the methods by which he proposes to achieve them will be the most productive effort he will make. As a result, the sales manager will build his agency by a known, logical, and orderly process, each step of which he has planned.

Developing Manpower

The first step in developing manpower is to look for men. Every means at the manager's command will be used to come in contact with the type of salesman he wants for his agency. He will be alert to possible candidates in every contact he makes. He will enlist the aid of those who are interested in his success and ask them to recommend to him people they know who meet the qualifications he has established for his agency. He may advertise in the local press. He may invite the assistance of policyowners and local employment services. His associates in the agency will be asked to recommend individuals. Just as an agent develops a "sixth sense" enabling him to identify situations to which life insurance might be the answer, similarly the manager sharpens his sensibilities to be alert to men who might be candidates for his sales organization.

The manager's search is for a person who meets specific standards. Usually, he is between 25 and 40 years of age, is married, has a college education, has a history of success in his past business connections, is dissatisfied with the opportunities offered by his present occupation, and has demonstrated by his life to date that he has a liking for people and the ability to move among them with reasonable ease.

These are basic qualifications which the man must meet. Having obtained the name, the manager will contact him and attempt to interest him in considering a career in life insurance selling. At this stage, both are exploring the possibility—the manager that the man may be a candidate he wants, and the man that this may be a career he wants.

Several mechanical facilities are available to the manager to help him obtain a complete record of the man he is considering. His company will have an application form on which the past personal and business history of the man is recorded. An inspection report will be obtained reporting objectively the man's status and habits. References will be checked. He will be asked to complete an Aptitude Index, a selection device perfected especially for life underwriters which indicates those out of a group whose chances for success in life insurance selling are at a minimum, enabling the manager to eliminate quickly the obvious misfits.

These mechanical devices are helpful in adding to the manager's knowledge of the candidate, but are not sufficient evidence upon which to base his decision. In addition, he will spend many hours in exploratory interviews with his prospect (and with the prospect and his wife), delving into his interests, his ambitions, his relations with people, his willingness to work to achieve his ambition. The more thorough the manager's knowledge of the man he is considering, the better his judgment as to the prospect's chances for success.

During the period of investigation the manager will increase the candidate's understanding of the opportunities in life and health insurance selling in order that he may be in a position to evaluate his real interest. This process is not always a step-by-step, orderly one. It is difficult to structure the recruiting process by some artificial recitation of events and timing.

Presenting the Career

As soon as the manager decides his candidate measures up to the desired qualifications and appears to have the necessary potential, he begins actively to discuss with him the possibilities of a career in life and health insurance selling in his agency and in his company. Usually, this step is identified as presenting the career. Its purpose is to acquaint the prospect fully with all of the opportunities in the career, as well as the difficulties he might encounter, in order that he will be able to make an intelligent decision. The manager will describe in specific terms the opportunities, both in income and in prestige. He will emphasize the socially beneficial aspects of life underwriting. He will ask successful men in the agency to add the motivating influence of their own experience and, by contact with the candidate, add their own judgment as to his potential. In turn, they are valuable exhibits of what the new candidate might anticipate for himself, and may sharpen his desire to become a part of the agency and the company. The manager may take his candidate with him on field calls to help the prospect visualize himself writing life and health insurance. The manager will thoroughly explain the training which the agency and the company make available, so that the candidate will understand exactly how he will be made ready to sell insurance successfully. He will try to convince the agent-prospect that the company and the agency offer the best available opportunity for such a career.

Being salesmen by training, the tendency of many managers during the "presenting of the career" phase in the induction process is to sell the career and to paint a very rosy picture of the opportunities the candidate will have. Sometimes, in their enthusiasm, they fail to point out with equal clarity the difficulties also inherent in the career. A study by the Life Insurance Agency Management Association indicates that the prospective agent who understood thoroughly before embarking upon the career its disadvantages as well as its advantages survived better and produced more than the candidate who understood only the favorable aspects. It is for this reason that the more able manager, in this stage of the negotiations, tries to serve as a well-informed consultant, helping the candidate to see all sides of the opportunity and to reach a sound decision. It is a skillful process, whereby the prospect will feel the magic of the opportunity for service and for self-development and, at the same time, understand the price which must be paid for that opportunity.

Precontract Training

In recent years a process called precontract training has been used increasingly for a dual purpose: (1) to help the prospect salesman gain an understanding of the work he will be required to perform and (2) to enable the manager to determine how the man likes life and health insurance and how well he responds to training. Precontract training makes it possible for the man to obtain basic training while still continuing in his previous occupation. He will learn the fundamentals about the purpose and uses of life and health insurance, policy forms, premiums, and the like. He may learn a simple sales presentation and may even accompany the manager or trainer on a few sales interviews. Precontract training is, in effect, a sort of "trial marriage" where the manager and the candidate have an opportunity to decide before final commitments are made if they like each other and if the candidate will enjoy the kind of work involved in selling life and health insurance.

Compensation

Of major interest to the potential life underwriter is the amount of compensation he will earn. Traditionally, life insurance selling is a commission business. Originally, most companies paid a commission on the premiums for the first policy year as they were paid to the company, such commission usually being at least half of such premium. In addition, renewal premiums on life insurance were paid, usually for nine policy years. Thus, approximately half of the commission was received immediately, and the balance was spread to build a renewal income.

In recent years, several changes have taken place in the commission system. Following the renewal period, a "service fee" has been added, usually 2 per cent of the premium, to compensate the underwriter for maintaining contact with and taking an interest in the insurance welfare of the policyowner. This fee is normally contingent on the underwriter continuing his services to the company prior to retirement. In addition, most companies have added a welfare benefit plan which provides group life and health insurance, together with a retirement plan, the amounts of which are in proportion to the production results secured by the underwriter. Commercial health insurance traditionally has a level annual commission continuing as long as the policy is renewed. Noncancellable health insurance usually has commission scales shaped somewhat like life insurance, with first-year commissions higher than renewal commissions, and with perhaps continuing service fees.

Thus the modern-day compensation plan provides the incentive which comes from current payments in direct proportion to results. At the same time, it builds a continuing income from renewals and provides the security offered by group life and health coverage, with adequate provision for retirement years. It is, in effect, a plan that combines current income, deferred compensation, and retirement income in attractive proportions to achieve lifelong financial security.

Financing the New Man

In most cases the new man comes into the life and health insurance calling from a salary job and with fixed personal expenses usually greater than the cash income his early sales efforts can produce. To meet this situation, many companies today make available to their managers a financing plan which enables them to offer new underwriters what is in essence a salary during their first several months—in many cases, for the first two or three years. The amount will be determined by a carefully considered budget realistically reflecting the established expenses of the new man and his family. Typically, these plans continue for 24, 30, or 36 months, which should be sufficient time for the new recruit to develop adequate skills in selling.

The financing plan usually also contains a validation schedule which requires him to earn cash commissions sufficient to justify his continuance under the plan. Because of the deferred nature of his compensation, the validation schedule requires modest amounts of cash commissions to be earned during the first few months but increases the requirement on an ascending curve. Today the majority of such plans contain a company contribution, substantial in the early months and decreasing to zero at the end of the period of financing, the contribution being equal to the difference between the monthly income and the amount of cash commissions required. This contribution is a training allowance or subsidy not chargeable to the agent but instead considered to be a company investment made in the expectation of developing a successful agent. See Table 68–1 for an illustrative financing plan.

TABLE 68–1

ILLUSTRATIVE FINANCING PLAN BASED ON $100 MONTHLY ADVANCE

End of Months	Training Allowance (Cumulative)	Required Commission (Cumulative)	Total
3	$ 245	$ 55	$ 300
6	450	150	600
9	615	285	900
12	740	460	1,200
15	847	653	1,500
18	928	872	1,800
21	992	1,108	2,100
24	1,024	1,376	2,400
27	1,020	1,680	2,700
30	998	2,002	3,000

Under the plans of many companies, during the continuance of the financing plan the agent gives up the vesting of his renewal commissions. Thus, in order to start his career in life insurance selling, he postpones the traditional building up of renewal commissions.

All men will not survive the financing period, nor will they be able to meet the somewhat rigorous demands of successful life underwriting. In such instances the manager may be asked to share some part of the loss sustained as the result of the man's inability to perform satisfactorily.

The knowledge that he must make a personal financial investment in new men is an added incentive for the manager to select the men with care and to exert every possible effort to assure their success. The validation schedule provides a self-operating yardstick and postselection device which helps the manager to make his decision promptly. If the new underwriter cannot succeed, it is better for all concerned that he be eliminated quickly.

Training the New Man

The training step is one of the most important of all the phases in manpower development. Its objective is, first, to develop in the new underwriter the skills of salesmanship. Without skillful and persuasive sales ability, he will not make a living. Second, he must have technical knowledge of the life insurance business, even though at the start it may be limited only to a basic understanding of policy forms and benefits. Third, he needs to acquire a clear concept of what a competent life underwriter is and does—a mental image of how he is expected to perform. Finally, he needs an understanding of the philosophy of life insurance—the basic human needs it is designed to indemnify.

One of the most important and exacting requirements of a manager is the ability to build skill in selling. With reasonable intelligence, it is not difficult for the new man to acquire knowledge of the various forms of insurance, of company underwriting rules, and of the mathematical basis of premiums. But persuading people to invest dollars today to purchase benefits which may not be needed until some indefinite future day requires a high order of selling skill. That skill must be developed through patient coaching by the sales manager, both in the office and in the field.

The usual method followed is to adopt a tested and proven sales presentation which follows a logical pattern of progression through the approach to the prospect, the sales presentation itself, the close, and the answering of objections. The new recruit is required to learn the presentation verbatim and is drilled in its use until it becomes a natural story for him to tell. Practice in the office is followed by coaching in the field through joint calls with the trainer until the new man develops the ability to tell a sales story persuasively and well.

There are many mechanical and technical matters which he must learn. He needs thorough grounding in the mechanics of life and health insurance—the types of policy coverages and the uses for each, the premium rate book and how to determine premium rates, the company's rules for acceptance of risks, and how to complete the various forms required. Most companies have excellent courses to cover these areas, and material is also available on a commercial or an institutional basis.

The new recruit must also acquire a whole new set of habits of work. Rather than having work prescribed to him automatically, as was perhaps the case in his previous occupation, he must now create his own work by finding for himself people to whom he can talk about life and health insurance. Many men are unable to make this transition without careful training and supervision by the sales manager. Vital to the new man's success will be the kind of training and supervision that will result in his filling each day with a proper balance of prospecting, service, and sales calls.

He will have little chance for success unless early in his career he gains a clear concept of *what life and health insurance is* and *what it will do.* Without a full understanding of the needs for income which arise when the family head dies—money for final expenses, for the adjustment period, for the education of minor children, for the widow during the balance of her life, for the mortgage on the home; or when illness or accident wipes out his earning capacity, either temporarily or permanently—the new man cannot possibly be an effective life and health insurance salesman. To the sales manager falls the responsibility of instilling this understanding as a part of the initial training. Then, as the underwriter matures, the manager will enlarge his understanding, and train him in the needs and uses of life and health insurance for other than family purposes—to indemnify a company for the loss of a key executive by death or by illness, to buy out a deceased partner's share of a business, or to provide funds for retirement of personnel. Although most training programs cover the needs, uses, and functions of life insurance, a skillful trainer will make certain that the new man's understanding of them is not academic. Every sale of life and health insurance occurs only because a human need exists. The salesman must become adept in applying his knowledge to human situations.

Training men is not an easy task. It requires many hours of drill in sales presentations. It requires patient explanation. It requires the ability to transfer skill. It requires the ability to instill enthusiasm as well as understanding. It is an arduous and sometimes tedious part of the manager's responsibilities. Yet it is one of the most essential of all of his tasks. Sales managers cannot exist for long without successfully trained salesmen.

Supervision

The manager's responsibility for developing his men into career salesmen does not end with their initial training. As they mature in experience, he will observe more clearly their individual potentialities and will determine the action needed to help them reach that potential. The process of measuring each man's abilities and of using managerial skill to help him develop those abilities should be the most fascinating and challenging part of the sales manager's job. It is, perhaps, the finest example of the art of management.

Motivation is one of the prime skills of leadership. Each individual has his own set of hopes and ambitions, and people whose good opinion he values. The manager who studies each of his men so that he understands that person's motivations and then builds upon them truly becomes a builder of men. Motivation is an art, not a science. The understanding and use of motivation will reward the manager manyfold.

Sales management calls for the highest qualities of leadership in the agency head. The salesmen will pattern their conduct on the manager's conduct. Their personal image of what a career life underwriter is and does will directly reflect the teachings and examples of their manager. Their basic belief in the value of life and health insurance as a way of financial living will mirror their manager's belief. This imposes a great responsibility on the manager to act and talk in such a manner that he will serve as a worthy model for his men.

Inevitably, as he lives in close association with each of his men, the manager becomes involved in their personal lives as well as in their business lives. Some life insurance sales managers will not agree that the personal lives of the members of their sales staffs are their concern. However, no man can give his best to his job if he is worried and distraught about a family problem. Personal, financial, marital, or health problems invariably affect business efficiency. Assistance in solving these problems—sincerely and objectively given—will help eliminate this block to business effectiveness and increase the bond of personal loyalty.

Sound working relationships with all of the people whose good opinion is important to the success of the sales agency are necessary. Many members of the community will be valuable centers of influence for the manager—if they become convinced that his is a sales office staffed with able men.

A Career in Life Insurance Sales Management

Throughout this chapter, there are recurring references to the qualities of leadership that must be exercised, and therefore possessed, by those engaged in life insurance sales management. There are other qualifications. The manager must possess vocational competence. Generally, a record of several years of successful life and health insurance selling is considered an essential prerequisite for sales management. A top-flight salesman will not necessarily make a top-flight manager. The sales manager without a reasonable record of sales to his credit, however, will find it difficult to train other men to sell.

Finally, the successful manager must be endowed with a deep interest in helping others. His interest in training, motivating, and supervising his men should have its roots not only in the objective realization that they are essential to his success as a manager but in an abiding and genuine desire to help them grow as individuals and as underwriters.

Many companies now have management development programs designed to uncover men with management potential and to provide them with a special opportunity for training in management. Several companies also have college recruiting programs and each year bring college graduates into their companies for a program designed to develop the graduates into trained managers by the end of their fifth year. During the first few years, the recruit will concentrate on selling. Usually, during the third year, he will devote a portion of his time to management activities as a supervisor or assistant manager, gradually working into full management at the end of the fifth year.

Several valuable institutional facilities are also available for the interested prospective manager. The Life Insurance Agency Management Association, an organization devoted to research in sales management, maintained by the life insurance companies, publishes a study course in agency management for the prospective manager of an ordinary agency, and a similar course in district management for the prospective manager of a weekly premium or combination agency office. These courses may be studied individually but are more effective if they are administered by a mature manager. Under the auspices of the General Agents and Managers Conference of the National Association of Life Underwriters, study classes led by experienced managers are conducted in cities in selected areas in the United States each year.

The LIAMA also conducts two-week schools in field management at strategic regional locations. During the two weeks the responsibilities of life insurance sales management are explored in detail. An added benefit is the close association with 50 to 60 men, also concerned with life insurance sales management, with whom opinions and experience can be exchanged.

The American College of Life Underwriters makes available a study program leading to a Certificate in Agency Management which encompasses a broad field of professional and management subjects, including sales management. The College, through local Chartered Life Underwriter chapters, arranges study groups in major cities in the United States each year. All or any of these are available to the individual whose company or personal situation might not provide the opportunity for developing the management education he seeks.

The rewards of successful sales management are substantial. The man who creates and maintains an organization of career life underwriters, producing substantial amounts of new business for his company, receives an income far better than average. Furthermore, he has created a continuing estate. It has been said that the life insurance sales manager can have no better annuity than a group of successful life underwriters who yearly produce substantial amounts of new business for him.

There are satisfactions beyond the monetary reward. Directing the destinies of other people always carries great responsibility. It also offers the opportunity for the deep personal pleasure which comes from seeing men the manager has brought into life insurance from occupations where their future was limited grow in ability and stature under his guidance.

Sales management involves many skills; but perhaps the most important of them all, and the one producing the most lasting satisfaction, is the ability to help men develop and capitalize on their own capacities, and thus grow in success and career satisfaction under the guidance of a successful manager.

SELECTED REFERENCES

BELL, HUGH S. *Hugh Bell's Book of Management Methods.* Indianapolis: Research & Review Service of America, Inc., 1955.

BOILEAU, WALLIS; STALNAKER, ARMAND C.; and LUCK, THOMAS J. *Life Insurance Agency Financial Management.* Homewood, Ill.: Richard D. Irwin, Inc., 1958.

CUMMINGS, O. S. *How to Build a Successful Life Insurance Agency.* Indianapolis: Research & Review Service of America, Inc., 1950.

DRUCKER, PETER F. *The Practice of Management.* New York: Harper & Bros., 1954.

LIFE INSURANCE AGENCY MANAGEMENT ASSOCIATION. *Keeping Agency Operations Profitable.* Hartford, 1960.

LIFE INSURANCE AGENCY MANAGEMENT ASSOCIATION. *Management Planning.* Hartford, 1960.

LIFE INSURANCE AGENCY MANAGEMENT ASSOCIATION. *Managing an Agency.* Hartford, 1958.

MCGILL, DAN M. (ed.). *Life Insurance Sales Management.* Homewood, Ill.: Richard D. Irwin, Inc., 1957.

Chapter 69

PUBLIC RELATIONS FOR THE UNDERWRITER AND AGENCY

BY JOHN L. LOBINGIER, JR.

At all levels of the life and health insurance business, there has for many years been evidence of an increasing effort and desire (1) to bring business practices in tune with the public interest and (2) to inform the public about these practices. Since these points take into account the power of public opinion, there is nothing soft-headed about them. They are today accepted as sound business tactics.

Some people call such an approach the building of "good public relations."

Other things being equal, the public's opinion of any insurance company depends largely on the conduct of its underwriters, the men and women who come face to face with the public every day. For example, Bill Smith, the company's representative in Maintown, is likely to be "the company" in the minds of Maintown citizens; he may even be "the insurance business."

Quite apart from these considerations, most field underwriters today realize that their own personal sales success depends upon how well they can interpret public needs and desires—and then upon how well they are able to serve these needs and desires.

In short, the underwriter who would build good public relations for himself, as well as for his company and business, must perform in the public interest. And one thing more: He must also take reasonable steps to inform people about his good performance, so that he may build his "prestige" and gain what a public relations man might call "earned recognition." This involves ability to communicate effectively with people, and some recommended techniques are suggested later in the chapter. The starting place is to try to determine what people who are buyers or potential buyers of personal insurance want from their underwriter.

People Want Knowledge

Millions of people own their own homes. Millions of people have savings bank accounts. But in either instance, more own some form of life or health insurance. The largest single financial investment for many of these persons is in their life insurance. No wonder they want an underwriter who knows what he is doing and who is able to advise them correctly on this investment.

Through opinion surveys, John Public is heard to say to his underwriter: "I bank on your knowledge to help me make the right decision on life and health insurance, to save me from costly mistakes!"

But sheer knowledge isn't enough. John Public demands that his underwriter "be able to translate knowledge into nontechnical terms I can readily understand."

Experience shows that this last point, like any public relations principle, ties right into sales. Few people have ever bought insurance because they admired the technical brilliance with which their underwriter discussed his subject. People buy insurance, and always will, because it meets their personal and family needs. They buy for human, heartfelt reasons—not because of the actuarial, legal, or technical aspects of the matter. Business history shows that as sales talks increase in complexity, sales decline.

Perhaps this is why one underwriter, a man who specializes in the most complicated form of estate planning, underscores the point: "I always try to talk and write in terms familiar to the prospect. I try to stay away from jawbreakers such as 'nonforfeiture provisions, optional modes of settlement, supplementary contracts with no life contingency.' I try to find easy ways to say the same things in the language of my prospect."

The underwriter who would win the confidence and respect of his clients needs (1) knowledge of his subject and (2) the ability to translate that knowledge into terms the prospect can comprehend. Moreover, it is obvious that no successful underwriter can afford to let his knowledge remain static. John Public expects him to keep abreast of new developments that may affect the financial security of John and his family.

How do underwriters gain the knowledge they need? Through sound agency and company training; also through self-study. The picture is measurably enhanced in those agencies where underwriters are encouraged to enroll in institutional courses such as those offered by the Life Underwriter Training Council (covering both life and health insurance) and the American College of Life Underwriters. The American College program leads to the only professional designation in life and health insurance with wide public recognition—that of Chartered Life Underwriter (C.L.U.).

People Want Integrity

"A reputation for undeviating honesty," said an advertising executive recently, "can open more doors and sell more business than any other single asset." The same could have been said by an underwriter, for it holds true in any business.

When people are asked what they like or do not like about the actions of their underwriter, they seldom mention integrity as such. Yet it is implicit in comments like these:

I want to know what the policy will *not* do, as well as what it will do. I want the full story before misfortune strikes, not after.

Keep your word. Show up when you say you will. Send me that information you promised.

Didn't your company write me a letter offering a free gift? How come I never got it?

Many other observations could be cited as evidence of public dislike for (1) unfair tricks to gain a hearing or make a sale, (2) misstatements of fact, and (3) unhealthy competitive practices. But perhaps they all boil down to one key point: "Ask me to buy life and health insurance, Mr. Underwriter, only when you sincerely believe your recommendation is the best solution to my problem!"

This seems to be the cornerstone on which more and more underwriters are basing their sales philosophy. One man explains: "I try always to put myself in the prospect's shoes and advise him to buy the plan I would like to have recommended to me." Chartered Life Underwriters will recognize this as the philosophy behind their own Charge. It is the professional way to sell. It is also practical—for it builds long-term good will and long-term sales success.

Sell John Jones juvenile insurance on the life of his young son? If John is a young man with low income and little other insurance, the underwriter with integrity will do his best to persuade John to take care of basic family protection needs first.

Sell Bill Brown a family plan? The underwriter with integrity will be glad to sell it to Bill. But he will not present it as "the absolute cure for all of Bill's protection problems. And he will do everything he can to dissuade Bill from surrendering other valuable policies that should, in Bill's best interests, be retained.

No matter what kind of plan is under consideration—health or life—the consensus of leading underwriters across the country suggests that two simple tests be applied to each sales attempt:

1. Am I reasonably certain my prospect has a definite need for the plan I am recommending?

2. Have I tried to help him understand clearly just how the plan will work in all aspects, pointing out limitations as well as benefits?

People Want Personal Interest

Many years ago a prominent businessman said: "I look with favor on the agent who comes to solve my insurance problems, not his commission problems. I also want a man who doesn't neglect me after he has my name on the dotted line."

Public opinion polls reveal that the great majority of buyers feel the same way today. This indicates that the underwriter who can convey a feeling of real interest in his client—and mean it—is likely to make the sale and, at the same time, build excellent public relations for himself, his company, and all of insurance.

Here are representative comments from the public:

Mr. Underwriter, before you make your recommendations, find out something about me, my family, and my needs.

If I buy, deliver the policy yourself. Go over it with me, and impress me again with the important parts.

Don't let your interest in me degenerate into overfamiliarity or insincere flattery. Your trump cards will always be normal courtesy and respect.

Don't sell me and forget me. Keep in touch with my situation. How about contacting me about once a year to be sure my insurance is still doing what I bought it to do?

When the time comes for my life or health policy to pay off, will you (or someone reliable) be on hand to render prompt, efficient service?

Not long ago a well-known company asked its policyowners: "How long has it been since you saw an agent from this company?" For three out of five repliers, it had been five years or more! Here is evidence of a vulnerable spot in life insurance public relations—the failure of so many underwriters to render service after the sale.

The situation is not to be taken lightly when we see some life companies with over half of their business tied up in agreements that are predicated on family conditions at the time of sale. When these agreements are not changed as family conditions change, there is danger that programs will mature and *not* do the job they were originally intended to do. When and if this happens on a large scale, the groundwork is laid for some of the most serious public relations problems we could possibly anticipate.

One underwriter advances this theory: "I feel that the buyer pays me to keep his insurance up to date. He does this when he pays my renewal commissions. And so I attempt to see each of my buyers, or contact them by phone, at least once a year. In doing this, my first purpose is to be sure the insurance I sold is still in tune with the buyer's situation."

Service is no chore to a growing group of underwriters who find profit in it. Listen to a nationally known woman underwriter who regularly allocates a portion of each week to policyowner calls: "These people accept me; they're much easier to see than strangers. I know them. I know their problems, their dreams, their financial situations, and many other intimate details that help me make the right recommendations. Why disregard such advantages to seek out people about whom I know nothing?"

A company president who is a former general agent sums up the problem when he says: "If service is something the policyowner finds he can, or does, do without, he'll eventually refuse to pay for it. Someone else will give him a free choice: sales and service at a price, or cash and carry at a lower price."

A Possible Pitfall

Many underwriters concentrate solely on selling life insurance, which is understandable. Yet what happens when one of their clients becomes sick or otherwise disabled, suddenly realizing that he does not own adequate health insurance? May he not lay the blame on his "life only" man?

One insurance editor thinks so. He says: "Too many agents are preparing their policyowners to die while not preparing them to live." He even suggests that "failure to tell a prospect about health insurance is failure to render complete service."

This section is not intended to be an incitement to total "one-stop selling." Nor is it intended as a judgment on where any underwriter's accountability begins and ends. It is merely intended to point out a possible public relations pitfall, so that each underwriter may examine his own conscience in such matters and act accordingly.

Special Care When Selling Health Insurance

"But the agent didn't tell me about that."

Here is one of the most frequently heard public complaints on disputes over health insurance claims. When these complaints occur, they can be detrimental to sales, devastating to public relations!

Underwriters who sell both life and health insurance know that on sales of the latter, they are going to see their product in action with some frequency. Firsthand, they are going to see case after case where the insurance they sold is either paying off the way the buyer expected it to—or failing to do so.

Recognizing this, one general agent tersely instructs his associates to "tell the full story—and tell it straight!" He goes on to emphasize that a prime aim in all health insurance sales must be to avoid misunderstandings, now or later. He urges each underwriter to try to bring out all facts of interest to the prospect—once in the sales interview, again on policy delivery.

"While the buyer may not like some of the exclusions," he notes, "that buyer cannot help but feel you really have his interests uppermost in giving him all the facts."

Unfortunately, the average health insurance buyer may tend to be confused, since there are so many health hazards (and degrees of hazard) and so many different ways of writing policies to meet these hazards. It makes the underwriter's task of explanation doubly difficult but, at the same time, doubly important.

Client Building

Analyzing John Public's testimony in the preceding sections, we arrive at two inescapable conclusions:

1. People today place a high value on the services of their underwriter, and they expect a lot from him.
2. People indicate strongly that they want to be treated as clients, not as casual customers.

What is a client? According to Webster, a client is "one who employs the services of any professional man." Does not this suggest that the public is casting a ballot for the underwriter who will approach them professionally, serve their needs as counselor, and do it on a continuing, rather than one-shot, basis?

How to develop clients? "It starts with the initial approach," says one manager whose branch includes several million-dollar producers. He explains: "Our underwriters try to approach each prospect professionally, knowing that they may not ever talk about buying life insurance unless—

Underwriter and prospect can agree together that a problem exists that can best be solved by some form of personal insurance.

The prospect also agrees to the problem and to do something about it.

The underwriter can bring the prospect to the point where he is willing to consider taking action *now*.

"Then, and only then, we feel, should the purchase of insurance be brought into the discussion."

Implicit in client building is the concept of helping people to appreciate the need for *adequate* life and health insurance. A study by the Life Insurance Agency Management Association and the Life Underwriter Training Council reveals that "the ownership objectives of many household heads are low . . . even at the upper income level where the ability to carry out an adequate program is not limited by economic considerations."

LIAMA-LUTC researchers do not attribute this situation to "disbelief in life insurance as such" or to "major sins of commission" on the part of underwriters or companies. Rather, they say, it appears to be due to the failure of many people to understand and realistically plan for the economic impact that the death of the family head would have on his survivors.

It would seem that helping the family head to reach a realistic appraisal of his family's needs is one of the most useful and profitable services the underwriter can render.

What about programing versus package selling? Which way is more likely to build clients? Apparently, clients can be built under either system, for every day we see successful underwriters doing it both ways. The important point seems not to be whether it is a program or a package, but whether the sale is made strictly on the basis of a need.

Is it profitable to make the professional approach inherent in client building? Let us listen to one million-dollar producer:

> With this professional approach, I'm able to develop satisfied clients who buy—from me—all the insurance they need at the moment. *Sales!*
>
> Because I keep in touch with them, they continue to buy from me. *Repeat sales!*
>
> Because I help them to appreciate what they have bought, they keep it in force. *Persistency!*
>
> And because they like what I've done for them, they send other good prospects to me. *Referred leads!*

Prestige Building

What is prestige? It is the reason John Johnson was asked to direct the United Fund campaign. It is the deference people give to the editor of the newspaper, whether they agree with today's editorial or not. It is what prompts any one of us to consult a particular doctor, or lawyer, or insurance man.

Prestige is what the underwriter hopes he has in the mind of the man he is going to see tomorrow at 10:00 A.M. It is what he hopes he has in the minds of all his clients, as well as neighbors in the community, competitors, and associates in the agency and at the home office.

Strip prestige of all trappings, and the real reason why any underwriter needs it and wants it is *to lower sales resistance.* At the same time, it helps him to build the public good will that is so necessary to his success.

When an individual consistently does a good job of selling, along the lines suggested above, he may develop a vast amount of personal prestige. Yet the very best insurance men sense that sound performance alone is not enough. They do one thing more. They employ reasonable and systematic steps to get earned recognition and additional prestige for the good job they are doing in selling insurance.

Another way to put it is that the public-relations-minded underwriter endeavors (with good taste) to become well known. He thereby enhances his prestige, and he is able to be an even more successful salesman than he was before!

An underwriter, who will be called Jack Smith, has been selling for nearly 20 years in a medium-sized city in Illinois. An excellent salesman, Jack makes a comfortable living and has developed a large clientele who think of him as their "insurance man." Jack attributes a substantial part of his success to the following five-point program for building prestige:

1. ***He Serves the Business.*** Jack not only is a member of his local life underwriters association; he has been active on committees and last year was a delegate to the national convention. He believes it is important to get along with competitors—and he does.

2. ***He Serves the Community.*** Being both able and willing, Jack is frequently in demand for community posts. In 20 years, he has had many responsibilities, from running the Heart Fund campaign to serving on the city council. But he never breaks a rule he made early in his career: Take on only one major job each year. This keeps Jack from spreading himself too thin. It also reserves the major portion of his time for his main job, which is—and he never forgets it—*selling personal insurance!*

3. ***He Does Some Speaking and Writing.*** Jack is always glad to talk to local groups on his favorite subject of family financial planning. Beyond this, he has developed several talks on phases of his favorite hobby—photography. On occasion, the local financial editor has asked him to write for the paper. He also tries to write at least one article a year for some insurance magazine.

4. ***He Uses Publicity and Advertising.*** With help from his general agent, Jack finds his business accomplishments publicized from time to time in the local news columns. Jack also contributes his share to a co-operative newspaper advertising program offered by his home office. He finds both of these methods excellent ways to keep his name in front of his insuring public.

5. ***He Cultivates Policyowners, Prospects, and Centers of Influence.*** In addition to personal calls on policyowners, Jack uses his company-provided mailer. Thus, each month his name is imprinted on an attractive appointment calendar which goes into the homes and offices of a selected group of policyowners, as well as some key prospects and centers of influence. He also sends news clippings to people whose names or pictures appear in the paper. Time might be a problem if his wife did not clip the items, insert them in company folders, and handle the mailing—after Jack has added brief penned notes. His wife also maintains a birthday list. At one sitting, Jack will write brief notes on a group of cards covering several months, and his "better half" oversees the mailing operation.

While this is one man's plan for prestige building, it is not necessarily transferable to another underwriter in another town. "What is important," and Jack says this himself, "is that each individual decide what activities are reasonable and worth while for him to engage in; then follow through according to plan."

Activities for the Agency

A man may do much prestige building on his own; witness Jack Smith. Results are enhanced, however, when an influential third party is able to say some complimentary things about Jack Smith that Jack would not say about himself. This is where the agency head comes in: He can be of inestimable help in building prestige for the underwriters in his agency.

Consider the one time in particular when the underwriter needs all the prestige he can muster—when first appointed. At this critical time, it is important to have a news story in the paper. It is also important to have a dignified announcement sent to people upon whom the new underwriter may call, and have it sent *before* calls are made. These become routine matters for managers interested in top-notch public relations for their agencies.

Occasional mailings from a manager on behalf of his underwriters can be effective. For example, one manager in a large California city each year writes a personal letter to a selected list of clients submitted by each National Quality Award winner in his agency. The opening lines of last year's letter illustrate the tack:

> DEAR MR. LEAVITT:
> Since we all like to share good news, I think you'll be especially glad to hear something about your life insurance man he might not tell you himself. For the ninth consecutive year, Mortimer Macintosh has won the recognition of the life insurance business by earning the National Quality Award. . . .

The power of publicizing this particular award lies in the emphasis on quality of service, rather than volume of sales. Some insurance leaders today question the wisdom of publicly proclaiming the fact that John Underwriter "last year sold $1 million of life insurance"—or any other amount. Publicity on production figures would seem to convey to the public an impression at odds with the concept of professional underwriting, which members of the public say they prefer, and which the business in other ways tries to foster.

As a practical help in reminding underwriters to call on their policyowners, one agency manager operates a master reminder file. Each man is urged to use it by notifying the girl in charge as to when he wants policyowner names called up. When a call-up date arrives, the underwriter finds a note on his desk to the effect that: "According to our record, your last date of contact with Joseph J. Jacobson was October 14, 1963." The note provides the cue for action on the part of the underwriter.

In a small New England town, one agency holds an annual conference for policyowners. Each underwriter is allowed to invite two clients. The program normally includes discussion, in lay terms, about some important coverage, in addition to an open forum where policyowners may contribute ideas for improvement of service, new insurance plans, or anything at all. In a recent report on these conferences the manager said: "Sometimes we get an idea we can use right in the agency; other times, we pass along suggestions to the home office. Whether workable ideas emerge or not, however, we are delighted to see our guests go out with enthusiasm for the job our agency is doing!"

A Texas manager writes a welcoming letter to each new policyowner. Although the wording is standard, each letter is individually typed and signed. Do his underwriters like the idea? He says: "Several times I've tried to reduce our secretarial work, but my men flatly refuse to let me cut out this welcome-letter plan." One obvious danger in such a plan is that a second-time buyer may get a second letter. The manager solves this with a central card file, which is consulted before new letters are typed.

An unusual public relations plan is described by another agency head:

> Once a month or so, we invite a man from a different line of business to speak to our agency meeting. We tell him frankly that we want to know more about the problems of his business. Last month, we had an architect; next time, it may be a florist, banker, or advertising man. The guest is complimented to be asked, and he passes the word around that ours is a "live wire" agency. It's obvious that such meetings are also helpful in prospecting, since our underwriters obtain valuable information about many different lines of business.

One Agency's Plan

"We aim systematically to lay a groundwork of good public relations for each member of our agency," says a general agent whose base of operations is in a southern city of about 90,000. Here, he outlines his four-point plan:

> 1. *Publicity.* Our home office isn't big enough to offer a press release service, so we do our own stories on the appointment of new agents, on the naming of agency leaders, on interesting cases of life insurance in action, and special achievements. Our cashier's assistant does the actual write-ups, but I handle all personal contacts with the city editor.
>
> 2. *Advertising.* We run agency ads every other week, each featuring one member of the agency force. We've tried them both ways, but find that ads without pictures aren't worth much to us. We also feel that our advertising must run over a long period of time. In each ad, we try to get across just one powerful idea.
>
> 3. *Building Prestige—in the Eyes of Policyowners.* I try to send one personal letter a year to policyowners of each agent. Sometimes, I refer to a company or institutional honor the man has won. Sometimes, I enclose a reprint of an article the man has written for our company magazine. This takes ingenuity and work, but we find it well worth the effort.
>
> 4. *Building Prestige—with the Community.* Our men are encouraged to join the underwriters association and work on projects. I also encourage them to take LUTC, and when they're ready, C.L.U. study. I want my men in a reasonable number of community activities, so we run a modest training

program (usually night sessions) where we groom ourselves to assume leadership in community life. We help each other develop ability to speak, run a meeting, organize and carry out a project. We want our men unafraid to assume leading roles around town.

Office Check List

Agency office services, particularly those touching the public, can be vital in good public relations. Potentially sensitive points may often be overlooked, and so one company public relations department has developed a check list for its managers across the nation. Here are excerpts:

Do visitors to the agency gain an impression of efficiency and good taste?

Is a competent, courteous person assigned to counter service?

Do visitors find interesting information in the rack—about insurance and about the company?

Does the manager require that all serious complaints be referred to him personally?

Are staff members trained in meeting the public?

Are incoming telephone calls handled in friendly fashion to the complete satisfaction of the caller?

Does the person who answers the phone have a facility with names? Is she reliable in taking messages? Does she bluntly ask: "Who's calling?" Or does she tactfully inquire: "May I tell Mr. Producer who is calling?"

When someone writes to the agency, is each letter acknowledged promptly, even if the full answer must wait?

Are agency letters neat in appearance? Are they human and friendly? Is there an absence of cumbersome, technical phrases?

Communicating Effectively

By now, it must be apparent that every contact and every communication with the public has its effect upon public relations. What do people think of Mr. Underwriter and his agency? Often, their opinions may be based upon something seemingly as simple as the way the operator answers the phone, the impact of a letter, the inference from a remark, the impression gained from an advertisement or news story. Since "communicating effectively" is one of the indispensable planks in any public relations platform, it is hoped that the reader may find some help and guidance in the following all-too-brief discussion of techniques.

Better Letters

It need not take special skill to write the kind of letters that can build good will for an underwriter or an agency—not if the writer has the ability to think clearly and talk to people in a friendly, interesting way. It may help to think of each letter as a substitute for what you would say if you were there in person. So be yourself—and keep in mind five basic principles:

1. *Get to the Point.* Your reader is a busy man. He may be willing to read what you have to say about him and his problems—but beyond that,

he's not much interested. So move quickly to the main point. If you ask for specific action, do so clearly and courteously in the last paragraph.

2. ***Personalize Your Letters.*** Even when writing from a standard form, try to inject some personal touches. Right at the start, establish a warm, personal feeling. When you can, turn ideas around to make maximum use of "you" and minimum use of "I." Compliment the reader when you can do it sincerely.

3. ***Avoid Technical Language.*** A sure way to kill a sale is to confuse the prospect. Make your letters as simple as you aim to make your sales presentations. For example, instead of saying: "One of your options is to take the paid-up value of your contract . . . ," why not: "One possibility is to change your policy to a smaller amount of insurance on which you'll have no more premiums to pay."

4. ***Make Your Letters Friendly.*** Perhaps the reader has never seen you. A friendly letter can create a good first impression and pave the way for future contracts. A bad letter, on the other hand, can create a devastating impression which you may never be able to overcome. Implicit in friendliness is courtesy. Even though irritated, you can be courteous, and this is particularly important in answering complaints.

5. ***Arouse the Reader's Interest.*** Get your letters off to a fast start by avoiding stilted openings. Where appropriate, relate the point of your letter to something you are reasonably sure is of great interest to the reader—such as his children, his home, his desire to save money.

Better Telephone Conversations

Face to face, the underwriter may rely on his redeeming smile, his neat dress, his friendly manner—all the personality at his command—to put himself across. Over the phone, his voice alone must do the job. What he says and the way he says it become all-important. Poor telephone technique creates ill will and loses business for underwriter and agency. Below are ten tips to telephone success. They apply generally to all kinds of conversations—from the office operator who may take a message, to the underwriter calling for an appointment, to the agency head in his discussion with an irate policyholder.

1. Treat every phone call as if it were from the most important policyowner.
2. Be sincere in what you say and cheerful as you say it. The person at the other end thinks of you as "the agency," or "the company," or even "the insurance business."
3. Speak distinctly and directly into the transmitter, with your mouth about one-half inch away.
4. When answering the phone, identify yourself, the agency, the company —according to circumstances. Never just say "Hello," which tells the caller only that he has reached someone, somewhere.
5. When making a call, it is just as important to identify yourself and your organization at the outset.

6. Answer promptly. Your quick response implies an alert organization.
7. Have paper and pencil close to your phone.
8. Long conversations, dragged out to the point of diminishing returns, are a frequent cause of annoyance.
9. If your conversation is cut off, telephone etiquette says the original caller puts through a new call.
10. When there is doubt about who should move first to end a conversation, etiquette again says it is up to the original caller.

Better Advertising

Underwriters and agencies choosing to advertise locally may do so in any of a number of media—for example, newspapers, radio, television, outdoor signs, car cards, exhibits, local magazines, farm papers, short films or slides for use in local movie houses, book matches. In just a day's time, one of these advertisements can take a message to many more prospects than a whole group of underwriters could possibly ferret out and see in weeks of hard work. However, the ad by itself will not close any sales.

One leading underwriter who advertises regularly in local newspapers has this to say: "I find advertising is a good way to place my message before a large group of prospects. For me, it's a good way to prospect, to preapproach, and to build my prestige and make myself well known. To make actual sales, however, I still have to *see people*."

He might have added that he finds it much easier to see the people who have seen his advertising.

While some underwriters and agencies find media advertising highly profitable, others do no advertising. Some of the determining factors have to be individual objectives, size of town, and media available, as well as ability to follow up and take advantage of advertising that is done. Professional counsel from specialists in the home office or from a local advertising agency can be helpful. In addition, careful consideration of the following questions is recommended:

1. *Why will we advertise?* Will our purpose be direct leads? To make ourselves better known? To keep people reminded that we are in business? Have we a definite, worth-while purpose?
2. *How much will we spend?* Will we look upon advertising as an expense or an investment? Are we prepared to spend enough money to gain the results we want?
3. *Where will we advertise?* This depends upon whom we want to reach. Is there a medium in our town that fairly well pinpoints our market? Or is our town so big that the messages we can afford may either be lost or be spread over too much waste circulation?
4. *What will we say?* What is especially desirable about our product or service? What ideas will appeal strongly to the prospects who read, see, or hear our messages?
5. *How long will we advertise?* Are we prepared to give our advertising plan a fair trial over a reasonable period of time?

6. *Do we expect miracles?* Are we prepared to work extra hard at prospecting and seeing people, to be sure we gain maximum value from our advertising?
7. *How will we go about it?* Does the company offer a co-operative plan to help with the cost—and ideas? If not, where can we get qualified help locally?

Better Newspaper Publicity

"If you want your news releases printed locally," a general agent advises, "first find out what the local papers consider to be news." This is sound. For while news is universally defined as new and timely information of interest to readers, the ways in which different newspapers treat the same news event vary widely. Newspapers have their own personalities, policies, and particular reader groups to which they cater. When the underwriter or agency head knows the characteristics of his local papers, especially how financial news is handled, he is able to plan his publicity accordingly.

Before sending a story, consider these check points:

1. Will the story interest readers of the paper?
2. Have we got our facts straight?
3. Will the news be current by the time we get it to the paper?
4. Is the story written factually and without propagandizing?

What makes news? The following are just a few of the events that in a recent year provided the basis for local news stories (often with pictures) about agencies and agency activities in papers across the country:

Appointment of a new underwriter.

Qualification of underwriters for attendance at a business conference.

Life insurance in action. As an example: placing pension trust plan on employees of local manufacturing plant.

Agency leader for the year.

Year-end story on agency performance, including comparison of benefits paid and sales with previous year, and standing of agency in relation to others in company.

Interview with president of company on visit to agency.

Opening of new agency office.

Significant anniversary of agency or individual.

Statement or prediction by agency manager on timely subject.

Forum for policyowners.

Agency participation in training workers for United Fund campaign.

How to Plan Your Public Relations

Whether an individual underwriter or an agency organization is planning public relations action, consideration of the following four questions can point the way to a practical course:

1. ***Which Groups Are Important?*** At the outset, it helps to set apart each group that seems important to your business success. This is because

it is always better to direct one's public relations at a specific somebody, rather than a general everybody. If an underwriter were taking this first step, he might list active prospects, policyowners, and influential citizens in the community. He would first concentrate his public relations efforts on these, giving each group individual attention. Later, he might try to develop better relations with other groups, such as his agency associates, home office staff, and competitors; or subgroups, such as educators, editors, and trust officers.

2. *What Does Each Group Think of You Now?* Before taking any public relations action, it is wise to determine just how one stands with each target group. The underwriter might take his policyowner group, for example, asking himself:

Do my policyowners seem to like me as a person?

Have any of my clients bought from other underwriters since I sold them last?

How many would proudly name me as their "insurance man"?

Do many of my clients voluntarily give me names?

Would they go to bat for me and for private enterprise as represented by the insurance business?

This process takes frank, honest appraisal. The individual can do some; his agency head can help. In some cases, policyowners may be asked for their candid opinions.

3. *What Do You Want Each Group to Think of You?* In this step, specific goals are set for building good relations with each target group. Using as an example the underwriter and his desire to cultivate his policyowners, the following may be some of his aims:

That policyowners think of him as an "insurance counselor."

That they believe him to be a man of character, a man who knows everything that needs to be known about personal insurance, a man in whose recommendations they may have confidence.

That they believe he gives them personal attention, "something a little extra" in the way of service.

That they voluntarily recommend his service to others.

That they like him as a person.

4. *How Can You Best Achieve Your Goals?* Now the individual is ready to plan the action that is likely to bring about the specific favorable opinions desired with each target group. Earlier, it was noted that this action must begin with sound performance in selling and service. It was also seen that it must include reasonable methods for getting credit for that sound performance with each target group.

This chapter has aimed to illustrate and suggest workable activities on both counts. Hopefully, the reader will go on to develop his own plan of activities to fit his own particular situation. The result of all this—for the underwriter, the agency, or both—can be public relations of the highest order, which, far from being soft-headed, offers the most practical course to sales success!

SELECTED REFERENCES

INSTITUTE OF LIFE INSURANCE. *Setting Up a Public Service Program.* New York.

INSTITUTE OF LIFE INSURANCE. *The Most Respected Man In Town.* New York.

LIFE INSURANCE AGENCY MANAGEMENT ASSOCIATION. *Breaking the Ice.* Hartford, 1956.

LIFE INSURANCE AGENCY MANAGEMENT ASSOCIATION. *How to Make Your Agency Well Known.* Hartford, 1957.

LIFE INSURANCE AGENCY MANAGEMENT ASSOCIATION. *Life Insurance in Focus,* Vols. I–IV. Hartford, 1960. Results of a joint study with the Life Underwriter Training Council.

LIFE INSURANCE AGENCY MANAGEMENT ASSOCIATION. *Public Relations to Help you Sell.* Hartford, 1957.

STONE, MILDRED. *Better Life Insurance Letters.* Cincinnati: National Underwriter Co., 1949.

PART X

The Institution of Life and Health Insurance

Chapter 70

STRUCTURE OF THE LIFE AND HEALTH INSURANCE BUSINESS

BY BLAKE T. NEWTON, JR.

IMPACT OF PERSONAL INSURANCE

Life and health insurance exercises a profound influence on the financial stability and the health of individuals and families, and on the availability to the economy of the capital it needs for growth.

Six out of every seven families in the United States own life insurance; four out of five have health insurance. In the single year of 1963, Americans received a total of $17.8 billion[1] in benefits from life and health insurance.

Use of Life and Health Insurance

Ownership of life insurance in the United States at the beginning of 1964 reached an average of more than $12,000 for each family in the nation. This figure had more than doubled in a decade, while the average family's disposable income had risen only about 40 per cent. Despite this increase in the ratio of protection to income, the average amount of life insurance equaled only about twenty-two months' disposable income as 1964 began.

Total life insurance in force with legal reserve companies was about $730 billion at the start of 1964. All other forms of insurance, including veterans' insurance issued by the federal government, and fraternal, assessment, and savings bank life insurance, provided another $55 billion of coverage.

Health insurance at the beginning of 1964 provided protection for an estimated 145 million Americans, or 77 per cent of the civilian population of the United States. Two decades earlier, only about 19 per cent of the population had any form of health insurance protection.

[1] Figures for 1963 are preliminary.

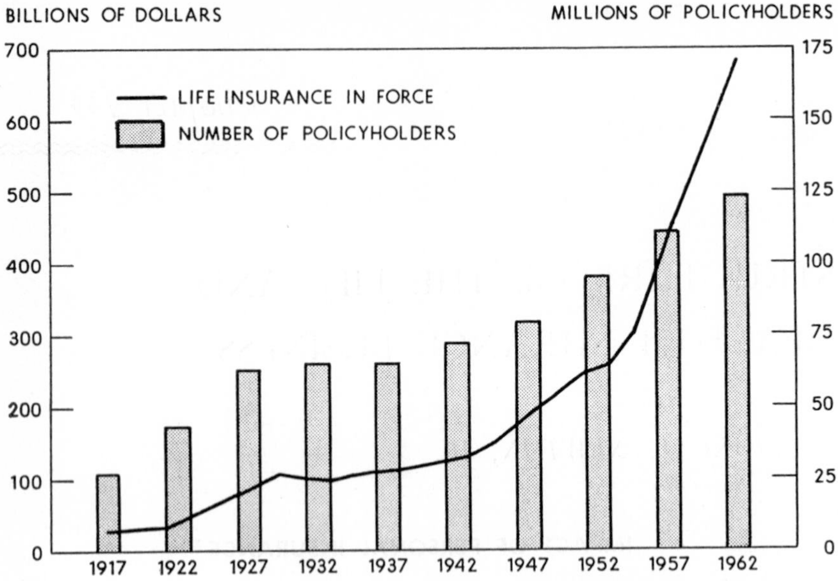

SOURCE: Institute of Life Insurance.

FIG. 70–1. Life insurance ownership in the United States.

Life Insurance Growth

Life insurance in force with legal reserve companies has grown markedly since the end of World War II. At the start of 1946 the total was $151.8 billion, just over a fifth of the figure at the beginning of 1964. Yet all types of coverage have not shared equally in this postwar growth. Industrial coverage, for example, has remained at about the level it reached in 1955. Group insurance increased tenfold during the postwar period, and credit insurance multiplied more than a hundredfold. Ordinary insurance, the backbone of most families' protection, grew at a rate close to that for the average of all types.

The variations in growth patterns among these four types of coverage have important implications for company development. Group life and credit life, which usually require relatively small policy reserves, produce a relatively small ratio of assets to insurance in force. Industrial life requires large sales forces in relation to the amount of insurance serviced. Ordinary insurance often fosters development of brokerage outlets in metropolitan areas, in addition to maintenance of the company's own sales force.

Operating costs of a company vary with the types of coverage offered and several other factors. The average amount of policies, which depends in part on type of coverage, affects company costs and development. Another factor is geographic distribution. Smaller companies operate

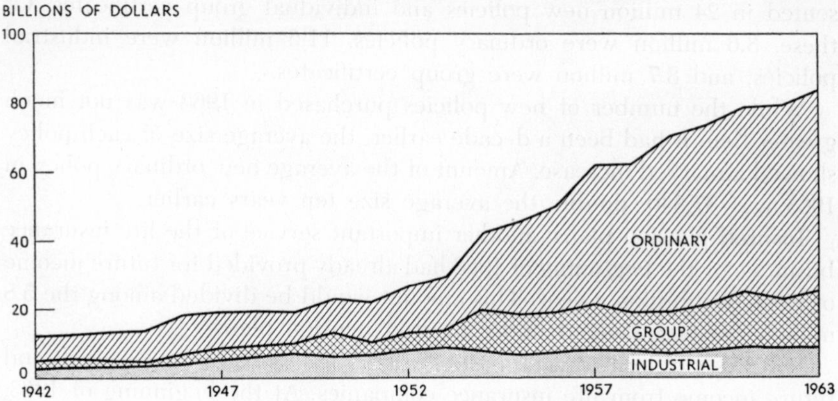

SOURCE: Life Insurance Agency Management Association and Institute of Life Insurance.

FIG. 70–2. Growth of life insurance by types.

within a single state or a region; the very largest companies operate in all fifty states.

Health Insurance Growth

Differing patterns of growth have also been evident in health insurance. In the decade ended in 1963, the number of persons with loss-of-income insurance rose 15 per cent; with hospital expense insurance, 49 per cent; with surgical expense, 67 per cent; with regular medical expense, 137 per cent; and with major medical expense, 3,300 per cent.

As in life insurance, these variations have profound effects on company development. For example, rising costs and increasing use of medical care have had greater effect on companies offering regular medical, hospital, and surgical coverages than on those offering high-limit major medical insurance, though the latter coverage has also been profoundly affected by these changes.

Claims and other costs vary not only with the types of coverage a company offers, but with geographic area. As in the case of life insurance, costs vary with the number of states served. Another factor is also important in health insurance: Costs of medical care vary considerably from area to area, and even from locality to locality.

Life Insurance Purchases

American families bought $87.5 billion of new life insurance in 1963. Ten years earlier, purchases totaled $36.2 billion, or about two fifths of the recent rate. About four fifths of recent purchases have been of individual insurance (ordinary and industrial).

In 1963, Americans bought $63.3 billion of ordinary insurance, $7 billion of industrial, and $17.3 billion of group. These totals were represented in 24 million new policies and individual group certificates. Of these, 8.6 million were ordinary policies, 11.6 million were industrial policies, and 3.7 million were group certificates.

While the number of new policies purchased in 1963 was not much greater than it had been a decade earlier, the average size of each policy showed a marked increase. Amount of the average new ordinary policy in 1963 was $7,340, double the average size ten years earlier.

Insured pension plans, another important service of the life insurance business, by the beginning of 1963 had already provided for future income of early $3.2 billion a year. This amount would be divided among the 5.8 million persons covered under insured pension plans.

Purchases of individual annuities also added to Americans' present and future income from life insurance companies. At the beginning of 1963, families and individuals were receiving nearly $175 million a year from purchased annuities. Another $115 million a year in future benefits was fully paid for, and $280 million a year in future benefits was partially paid for under deferred annuities.

Another major addition to Americans' income from life insurance companies was provided through supplementary contracts, issued to distribute death payments or accumulated cash values. These contracts totaled $990 million in current annual income in 1962.

Health Insurance Purchases

A primary measure of progress in the health insurance business is the total number of persons insured. In this the business continues to make satisfactory progress.

During 1963 alone, an additional 3.6 million Americans came under the protection of health insurance. Some 3.6 million more people were covered under hospital expense plans during the course of the year, bringing the total number protected to an estimated 145 million.

An additional 3.8 million persons had surgical expense insurance by the end of the year, for a total of 135 million covered. Regular medical expense insurance was extended to 2.8 million more persons, for a total of 101 million. More than 3.2 million more persons came under insurance companies' major medical expense plans, bringing the total number covered to 41.5 million. Some 600,000 more wage earners were covered under loss-of-income plans, for a total of 45.5 million persons covered by the end of 1963.

Measured by premium payments, health insurance purchases have been increasing markedly. In 1963, premiums totaled $10.4 billion, an increase of $1.1 billion over the 1962 figure. Over the course of 10 years the increase in annual premiums amounted to $7 billion.

During the same decade the average family doubled the share of its disposable income devoted to health insurance. In 1963, American families spent 2.6 cents out of every after-tax dollar for health insurance, compared with 1.3 cents 10 years earlier. Higher family incomes, permitting more adequate health coverage, are one reason for the increase. Another is the increasing demand for insurance offering more comprehensive protection and more liberal benefits, to keep pace with increasing use and rising costs of medical services.

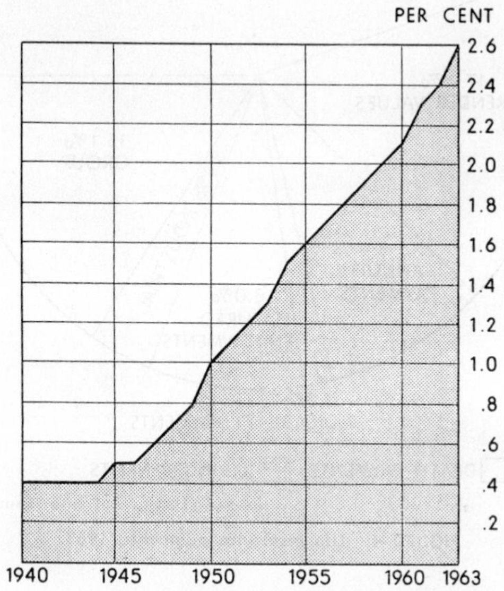

SOURCE: Institute of Life Insurance.

FIG. 70–3. Total health insurance premiums as a percentage of disposable income.

Personal Insurance Benefits

Life insurance companies have long paid more to living policyholders than to the survivors of those who have died. More than half of total payments continue to be in the form of these living benefits to policyholders, despite the dramatic dollar increase in death payments as ownership of life insurance increases.

These living benefits come from a variety of sources. In 1963, they were, in order of decreasing size, policy dividends, surrender values, annuity payments, matured endowments, and disability payments.

Health insurance benefits have grown markedly since World War II, especially with the great growth in group plans. Starting in 1947 with roughly equal benefit totals of less than $200 million each, insurance companies' group and individual plans diverged widely in their growth. By 1963, group insurance benefits had grown to about $3.2 billion for the year, while individual policy benefits exceeded $920 million. Of the $3.7

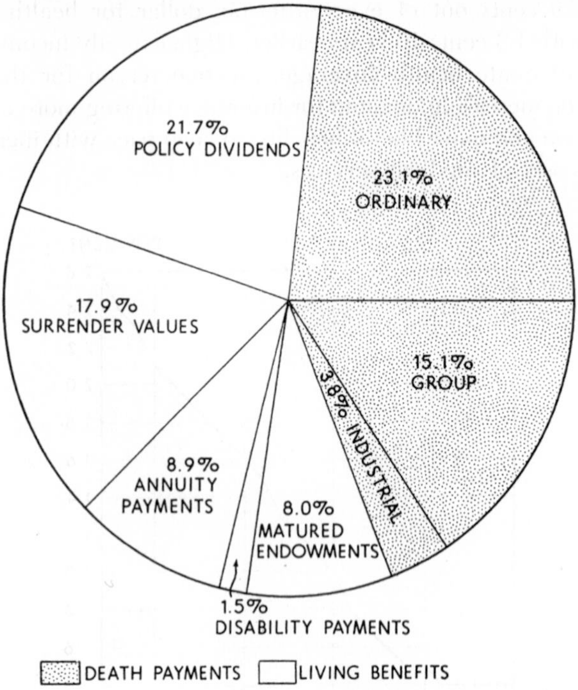

Source: Institute of Life Insurance.

FIG. 70–4. Life insurance payments, 1963.

billion in benefits paid in 1963 by organizations other than insurance companies, about three quarters was paid under group plans.

INSURING COMPANIES AND CARRIERS

The company structures of the life insurance and health insurance business are quite different. Most life insurance is issued by legal reserve companies of two basic types: mutual companies owned by their policyholders, and stock companies owned by stockholders. Health insurance, by contrast, is issued by several different types of carriers: life, casualty, and health-only insurance companies; hospital and medical service plans such as Blue Cross and Blue Shield; prepaid group medical plans; and others.

Life Insurance Companies

The first American life insurance company was founded in 1759 under a somewhat unwieldy name: "The Corporation for Relief of Poor and Distressed Presbyterian Ministers and of the Poor and Distressed Widows and Children of Presbyterian Ministers." Still in business today, under the more economical title "Presbyterian Ministers' Fund," the company was one of more than 1,500 in business in 1963. Much of this growth has come recently; at the beginning of 1946, there were only 473 United States life companies.

As the increasing number of companies might suggest, the life insurance business today is highly competitive, and shows every sign of becoming more so.

Many newer and smaller firms specialize in providing coverage in a single state, or in a limited few. One result has been a spread of company home offices across the nation. By 1963, there were at least two companies' home offices in every state, and at least one in each of more than 360 communities. This wide dispersal of companies has in turn aided the distribution of life insurance to families everywhere.

The great majority of United States life companies, including nearly all the newer ones, are stock companies. About 1,350 of the more than 1,500 companies in business in 1964 were stockholder-owned. Even though only about 10 per cent of all companies were mutual, they accounted together for about 60 per cent of the life insurance in force. The typical mutual company is older as well as a great deal larger than the typical stock company.

A mutual company's funds are held for the exclusive benefit of policyholders, who own the company. Mutual companies issue participating policies which pay annual dividends to policyholders. These dividends reduce the cost of the policy from the amount of the original premium.

A stock company's financing is provided by its stockholders, who assume management responsibility and receive a return on their investment. Stock companies issue nonparticipating policies. The premiums for nonparticipating policies are lower than for comparable policies paying dividends, and costs are fixed for the life of the policy. Some stock companies issue both participating and nonparticipating policies.

Aside from the legal reserve companies, other life insurers together accounted in 1963 for less than 8 per cent of all insurance in force. Chief among these other insurers are fraternals, which issue policies to members of fraternal organizations under special laws; assessment companies, issuing policies on which premiums are set and can be varied according to the companies' experience; savings banks, which, in three states, issue policies under special laws; and the federal government, which operates the veterans' insurance program.

Health Insurance Carriers

More than 1,800 insuring organizations were offering health insurance protection to the American public in 1962. Nearly half of these organizations were insurance companies; the rest were of a wide variety of types.

When health insurance coverage in this country originated over a century ago, casualty insurance companies were the only insurers. The majority of health business written by insurance companies is now written by life companies. There are now more than twice as many life companies in the field as casualty companies.

As 1963 began, 593 life companies were writing health policies, compared with 244 casualty companies. Another 42 companies were monoline carriers, offering health insurance only. The number of life insurance companies entering the health field continues to exceed the number of casualty insurers. Slowest numerical growth has been among monoline insurers. All three types may be operated either as mutual or as stock companies, and health insurance may be either a dominant or a small part of their total business.

Of the total of 879 life, casualty, and monoline insurance companies in the health field at the start of 1963, more than 90 per cent offered individual and family coverages, and 63 per cent offered group insurance. Most companies offering group insurance also offer individual insurance.

Aside from insurance companies, the most widely known health insurers are Blue Cross, Blue Shield, and other plans sponsored by hospitals or medical societies. These plans are usually organized on a state or regional basis. At the start of 1963, there were 77 Blue Cross plans offering hospital-medical coverages and 71 Blue Shield plans offering surgical coverages.

In several communities, group practice plans have been set up on a prepayment basis. Under these plans a group of physicians, surgeons, dentists, or optometrists contracts to provide health care as required for a monthly or annual fee. Perhaps the best known among these plans are the Health Insurance Plan of Greater New York and the Kaiser Foundation Health Plan, based in California.

Other independent plans, such as those sponsored by unions, employers, or fraternal societies, often provide care on a medical group practice basis. Some independent plans have members throughout the nation.

ORGANIZATIONS IN THE BUSINESS

The many organizations in the life and health insurance business, or related to it, have been an important source of its strength. They have contributed to constructive growth, have served as a common ground for exchange of ideas and information, have helped find solutions to common problems, and have stimulated that competition which serves the public interest.

Because of the considerable interrelationships between life and health insurance, some of these organizations serve both areas. At least sixteen organizations warrant specific listing.

American Life Convention

An organization of life insurance companies dedicated to the advancement of the social and economic purposes of personal insurance and to the consideration of management problems in the business. It also supports constructive legislative and administrative measures.

American Society of Chartered Life Underwriters

The national professional organization whose membership is limited to those in life and health insurance who have earned the Chartered Life Underwriter diploma. It publishes the *Journal of the American Society of Chartered Life Underwriters,* provides a continuing education program for its members, and functions co-operatively through approximately 145 local chapters.

Health Insurance Association of America

An organization of insurance companies of all types that write health coverages. It represents company views, provides forums for discussion, promotes high ethical standards, undertakes research, and represents member companies in legislative matters.

Health Insurance Council

Composed of eight organizations of health insurance carriers. It provides liaison between the health insurance business and medical, hospital, and other groups concerned with health services.

Health Insurance Institute

A central source of health insurance information for the public, and for such special audiences as the press, educators, labor unions, and employer groups. It represents insurance companies in the health field.

Home Office Life Underwriters Association

An organization to advance the sound underwriting of life insurance risks, and to seek out the most effective and most liberal standards for risk acceptance.

Institute of Life Insurance

A public relations and research organization. It provides a central source of life insurance information for the general public and for a variety of special sectors of the public, including the press, educators, and women's organizations. It also performs or sponsors research in the statistical and basic social aspects of the business.

International Association of Health Underwriters

An organization devoted to advancing the professional status of accident and health insurance agents.

Life Insurance Agency Management Association

An organization of agency department executives of life insurance companies. It engages in continuous research and training in marketing and life insurance.

Life Insurance Association of America

An organization of management-level life insurance executives. It is concerned with advancing the interests of policyholders and of the business. It also closely follows legislation of interest to its membership and to policyholders.

Life Insurance Medical Research Fund

A fund supported by life insurance companies. It makes grants totaling over $1 million each year to finance medical research and education, especially in the fields of heart and circulatory disease.

Life Office Management Association

An organization devoted to the continuing improvement of life insurance management through the exchange of experience and research findings of member companies, and through development of education programs for office employees.

Life Underwriter Training Council

Sponsor of locally administered courses in sales techniques for life and health insurance agents. Agents must qualify for LUTC training.

Million Dollar Round Table

An international organization of life insurance agents that seeks to set high standards for life agents through establishment of exacting membership standards, in terms of both sales volume and ethics. It also provides a forum for the exchange of sales and technical information.

National Association of Life Underwriters

An organization of life insurance agents, dedicated to support of legal reserve life insurance and to the advancement of agents' professional status through the quality of their service.

Society of Actuaries

The national professional organization of life and health insurance actuaries. It qualifies an actuary for professional status, and studies problems in the technical and management aspects of the business.

Many other organizations in the life and health insurance business make continuing contributions to its effectiveness and public service. Notable among these are the organizations of companies' specialists in legal, medical, investment, public relations, and accounting and statistical areas.

An independent educational institution which serves life and health insurance is the American College of Life Underwriters. This nonprofit organization provides a variety of collegiate-level courses in life and health insurance, acts as a national examining board for those aspiring to the Chartered Life Underwriter (C.L.U.) designation, and carries out research activities in life and health insurance.

The American Risk and Insurance Association is a learned society devoted to furthering the science of risk and insurance through education, research, literature, and communications. Its members include university teachers of insurance and many other persons with a scientific interest in insurance.

The National Association of Insurance Commissioners is an organization of state supervisory officials in insurance. It operates as an exchange medium for ideas and trends, and seeks to effect the greatest possible standardization of the regulatory practices of the states.

In sum total, these organizations have made an important contribution to the advancement of life and health insurance in the interest of the policyholders. Their contribution is extraordinary in the business world. On the one hand, they serve to intensify competition among individual companies in the business; on the other, they provide the framework for extensive co-operation in research and methods. Both these functions operate to improve the service the business provides the public.

ECONOMIC AND SOCIAL CONTRIBUTIONS

The importance of life and health insurance to the nation's economy is not due solely to the size of the companies' financial operations. It is also due to the unique manner in which insurance funds are channeled toward certain specific social ends. As investors and as employers, insurance companies make vital contributions to the health and stability of the nation's economy. Specifically, in their role as insurers, providing money when the family most needs it, they make a direct contribution to the health and stability of society's basic unit.

Guaranteeing Family Plans

The sum of benefit payments which life and health insurers paid in 1963 is impressive: $17.8 billion. To the individual or family receiving a small share of this total, insurance benefits may be more than impressive; they may be a life line.

Life insurance payments are the principal assets available to most families on the death of the income producer, and cash values are a major repository of family funds for emergencies. Health insurance payments are helping Americans meet an increasing share of their health costs,

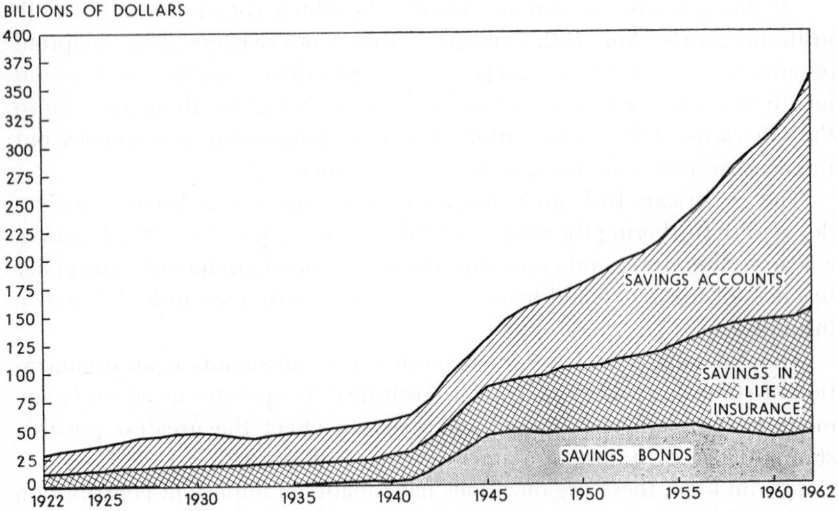

SOURCE: Compiled by Federal Loan Bank Board.

FIG. 70–5. Selected long-term savings media, 1932–62.

permitting a rising standard of health maintenance. Health insurance is also channeling an increasing share of total benefits to families stricken with unusually costly accidents or illnesses.

The special function of cash value life insurance as a medium of savings is worth mention. At the beginning of 1964, life insurance was one of the most important long-term savings media, providing about $110 billion of financial resources for American families. (See Figure 70–5.)

Financing National Growth

The interrelationship between the economic health of the nation and that of its people seems obvious, yet it is not widely appreciated. In supporting the growth of the national economy through carefully selected investments, the insurance business contributes to individual financial security as well.

Because of the nature of its investments, the insurance business frequently contributes directly to the welfare of individuals and families. Consider life insurance companies' investments in housing, for example. During a period of swift population growth from 1945 through 1963, life companies made more than $50 billion of residential mortgage loans. Assuming an average loan of $10,000 during that period, the business made it possible for over five million American families to improve their living standards by purchasing homes.

Sometimes the contribution to individual welfare is not so obviously direct. For example, insurers' investments in business and industry promote a vital economic growth, increasing both the national product and total employment.

From 1948 through 1961, American business and industry borrowed a total of $63 billion in net new money. More than half of that total, $32.3 billion, came from the life insurance companies of the nation.

Life insurance investments of all kinds totaled $141 billion at the beginning of 1964. Substantially all these assets were held to meet future obligations to policyholders. Because of the long-term nature of these obligations as compared with those of health and other types of insurance, life insurance investments play a much more important part in the national economy.

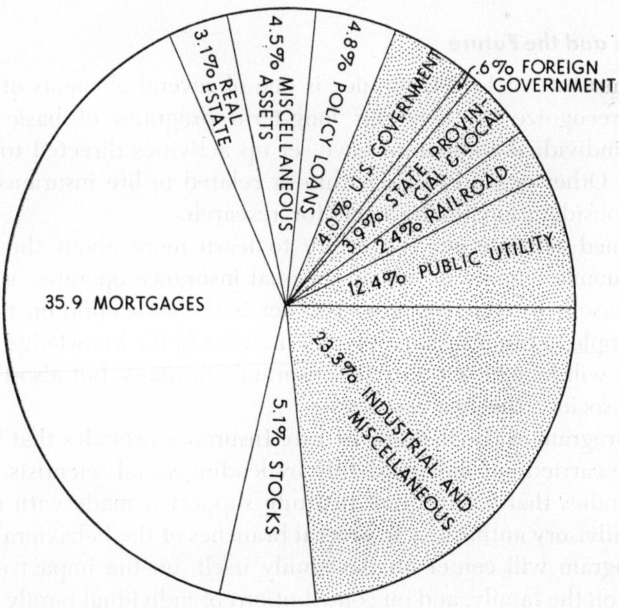

SOURCE: Institute of Life Insurance.

FIG. 70–6. Distribution of assets of U.S. life insurance companies, January 1, 1964.

Mortgages accounted for 35.9 per cent of all company investments as 1964 began. Industrial and miscellaneous bonds comprised 23.3 per cent of company portfolios; utility and railroad bonds, 14.8 per cent; and bonds of governments (federal, state, local, and foreign), 8.5 per cent. Stocks accounted for 5.1 per cent of the total; policy loans, for 4.8 per cent; real estate, for 3.1 per cent; and miscellaneous assets, for 4.5 per cent. (See Figure 70–6.)

Insurers as Employers

All branches of the insurance business employed more than 1.1 million persons in 1963, according to a survey by the Bureau of the Census sponsored by the Institute of Life Insurance.

Some division was possible between those employed in life insurance and those in other lines. No dividing lines can be drawn between those in health and nonhealth lines, primarily because of the overlapping among health carriers between life and various nonlife insurers. Some persons employed largely in health insurance undoubtedly appear in the life insurance totals; others, in the nonlife totals.

The survey indicates that 675,000 of the total insurance employees had some connection with life insurance. Of 406,000 agents, 49 per cent sold life coverages primarily, and 65 per cent sold enough life insurance to derive at least 10 per cent of their income from that source.

Research and the Future

The Institute of Life Insurance is one of several elements of the business to recognize the need for long-term programs of basic research. Several individual companies have set up activities directed toward this purpose. Other organizations within or related to life insurance are also giving consideration to the need for research.

Informed self-interest, the desire to learn more about the changing socioeconomic climate in which personal insurance operates, is only one of the reasons for this concern. Another is the conviction on the part of many people in life insurance that an increase in the knowledge of human behavior will benefit not only the insurance business, but also the people and the society the business serves.

The program of the Institute of Life Insurance provides that its studies are to be carried out independently by leading social scientists. Selection of the studies that will receive Institute support is made with the assistance of advisory authorities in several branches of the behavioral sciences. This program will center on the family itself, on the impact of societal changes on the family, and on contributions of individual family members' attitudes to its behavior as a unit.

These programs cannot help but aid the business in its primary task: to respond quickly to the changing needs of American families.

SELECTED REFERENCES

HEALTH INSURANCE INSTITUTE. *Source Book of Health Insurance Data, 1962.* New York, 1963.

INSTITUTE OF LIFE INSURANCE. *Life Insurance Fact Book.* New York, 1963.

Chapter 71

COMPANY ORGANIZATION AND MANAGEMENT

BY EDMUND L. ZALINSKI

Life and health insurance are written by a great variety of carriers, including stock companies, mutual companies, fraternal associations, savings banks, state funds, and the United States government. Further, the size of insurance companies varies from the new and tiny company with but few employees to the mature giant companies with thousands of employees.

Regardless of legal status, operational philosophy, or size, certain aspects of organization and management are common to all life and health insurance carriers. While this analysis of company organization and management is primarily concerned with the private, corporate form of insurance carrier of medium size, most of what is presented is also applicable to other types of carriers.

Almost all of this analysis is equally applicable to companies writing solely life insurance or solely health insurance. The reader should find discrimination between the two relatively easy. The analysis found here concentrates upon the typical management situation in both life and health companies, especially since the integration of management for both lines has increasingly become the modern practice.

Form of Organization

Companies engaged in life and health insurance for the most part apply the same basic principles of organization used by other forms of business enterprise, the exact combination depending upon the circumstances surrounding the formation and growth of each concern. The simplest form, more likely to be dominant in smaller companies, is line organization, where all authority comes from a single individual, usually the president. More common is line and staff, where executive officers rely upon advisory officers and departments, or where some line officers also have staff duties. The latter situation is sometimes referred to as a functional organization, particularly where officers whose duties primarily are advisory or staff also have the "line" authority to place their recommendations into operation.

Levels of Authority

In all forms of organized human activity, whether they be military, religious, co-operative, charitable, or for profit, there are various levels of authority. The individual or group possessing final authority delegates specific authority to others in subordinate positions to make decisions and take certain action. Levels of authority are usually kept at a minimum to shorten lines of communication and to facilitate the making and execution of decisions. It is also important that both the authority and the responsibility for a given project or function be placed in one individual located as closely as possible to the actual point of execution. The failure to support responsibility with authority results in inefficiency and delay.

In the typical company, there are at least four major levels of authority: the directorial level, the executive level, the managerial level, and the supervisory level. It is therefore essential that there be a clear statement of functions for each level of authority, as well as a definite fixing of responsibility, in order to minimize the possibility of overlapping, tension, friction, or neglect of important functions.

Departmentalization

Companies also make extensive use of the plan of departmentalization on a functional, product, and geographical basis. Functional departmentalization is exemplified, for example, by the actuarial department, which has the responsibility for a variety of related functions all the way from mortality studies to annual statement preparation. Product departmentalization is illustrated by the establishment of an individual insurance department, a group insurance department, and a health insurance department within the same company. Geographical departmentalization is typified by the allocation of responsibility for insurance sales and service in a certain group of states or territories to a superintendent of agencies or a regional vice president.

Board of Directors

A stock company is owned and primarily controlled by its stockholders; in a mutual company the owners and primary source of control are the policyholders. The owners delegate their authority to a board of directors, which has the responsibility for both long-range planning and the evaluation of results.

The board of directors is often composed of people in banking, commerce, and industry who have been selected either for their prestige or for their specialized knowledge or background experience. The authority of the board of directors and the numerous designations and duties of officers are spelled out in the company charter and bylaws. The board of directors usually holds monthly or quarterly meetings, and in the intervals between these meetings the board's affairs are handled by committees of the board and corporate officers.

Officers

The board of directors elects the executive officer of the company, who plans and directs all business activities. Usually, the chief executive officer of the company proposes policy, which the board either accepts, modifies, or rejects. He also appoints, with board approval, such other officers and department heads as are necessary to carry on the business of the company; and these, in turn, delegate a portion of their authority to unit supervisors, who are responsible for the daily operating results of a small group of people performing similar or related functions.

Large companies frequently have a board chairman who is the chief executive officer and a president who is the chief administrative officer. However, in smaller companies, there is often no board chairman, and the president is both chief executive and administrative officer. In addition, there are usually several vice presidents, and other principal department heads such as actuary, controller, secretary, and treasurer. The particular duties or activities of top-ranking officers in different companies and departments depend on company size, types of insurance offered for sale, methods of distribution, the pattern of organization which has been established, and the qualifications of the officers themselves. For example, the issuing of a new policy may be the duty of the secretary's department in one company and the underwriting department in another. The drafting of a policy may be the responsibility of the actuarial or the legal department. Policyholder service may be handled by the agency department, by the secretary, or by an independent policyholder service department.

Committees

Considerable work in companies is done by committees which are found at board level and also at interdepartmental and intradepartmental levels.

The committees appointed by the board meet more frequently than the board and not only report to the board but also are on occasion empowered to act when the board is not in session. They usually include an *executive* committee, which is the principal policy-making committee of the board; a *finance* committee, which concerns itself with investment policy and authorizes specific investment commitments; an *auditing* committee, which audits the accounts of the company periodically, normally through a professional auditing firm; and a *nominating* committee, which is concerned with the recommendation of replacements on the board of directors. In many instances the executive committee has the responsibility for making recommendations to the board on all financial and administrative matters, as well as those relating to the insurance business. Other board committees are sometimes appointed, such as a public relations committee, and others to deal with mortgages, real estate, and claims.

Interdepartmental committees are particularly useful in co-ordinating the efforts of interested departments toward the attainment of company objectives. They normally report their findings to the officer responsible for their appointment, who then decides upon a course of action. Standing interdepartmental committees with representation from all interested departments may include an *insurance* committee, which advises on rates, products, benefits, and related items; an *administrative* committee, which considers questions of operating policy; a *public relations* or *advertising* committee, concerned with policy in these areas; an *agency* committee, dealing with field problems; and a *manpower and employee benefits* committee to handle employee relations and other home office matters.

While the types of committees referred to above are generally indicative of subjects usually treated by board committees and committees appointed by chief executive officers, there is some variation in different companies. Public relations, for example, is handled by a board committee in some companies and by a management committee in others.

Intradepartmental committees, as their name implies, are appointed by department heads for the purpose of co-ordinating the activities of departmental divisions or units for greater effectiveness. The exact number of committees and their functions will vary according to the needs of each company and the desires of its directors and officers.

Organization Chart

It is a relatively simple matter to prepare an organization chart, showing the levels of authority represented by horizontal lines and departmentalization represented by vertical lines, which appears to be logical, well balanced, and effective. Just as a balance sheet presents a photograph of corporate finances at a particular moment, so an organization chart presents a structural picture of a company at a given time. Organization charts should be designed to take maximum advantage of the abilities of each key individual; the right people are far more essential than any particular form of organization and management. The organization chart must be constantly kept up to date as changes occur in personnel and duties, and as the organization grows and develops. The organization chart presented in Figure 71–1 illustrates the organization pattern of a

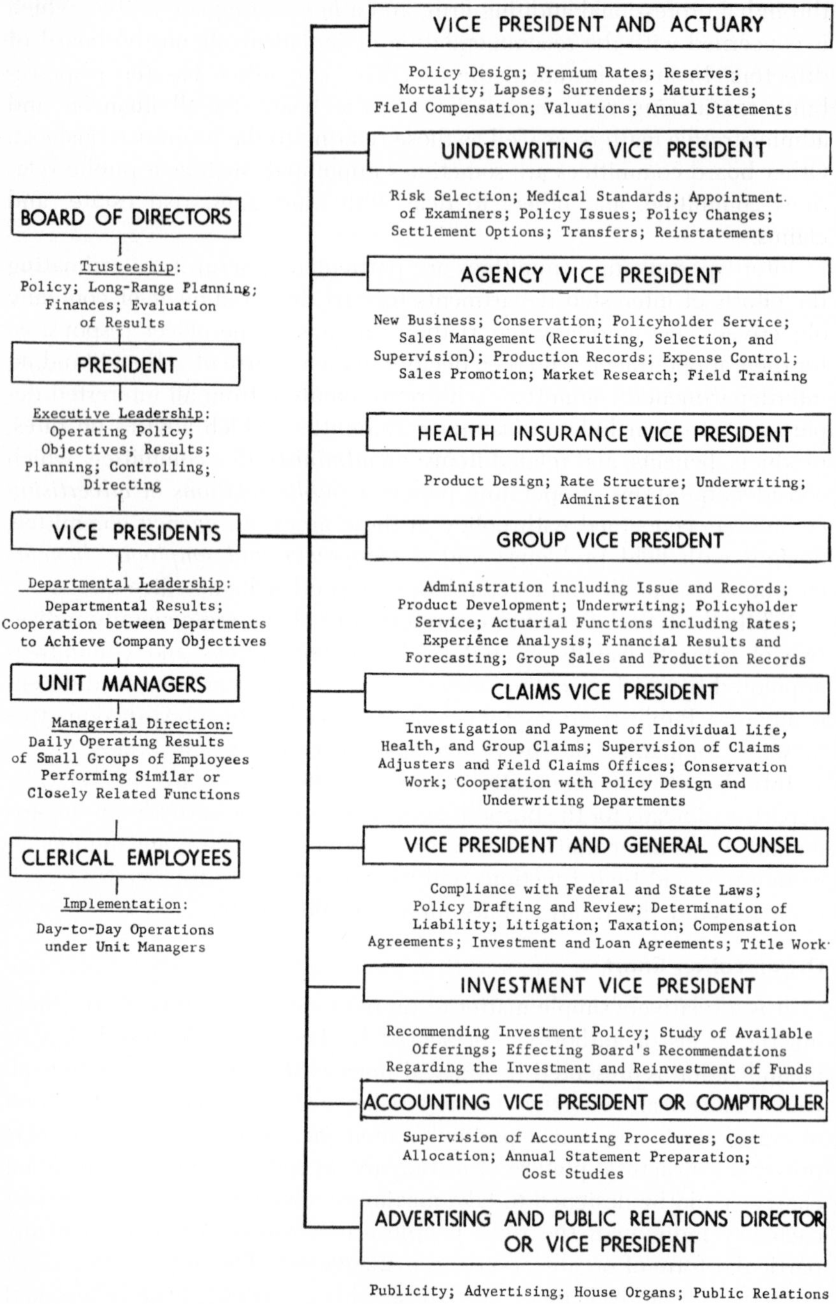
BOARD OF DIRECTORS
Trusteeship: Policy; Long-Range Planning; Finances; Evaluation of Results
PRESIDENT
Executive Leadership: Operating Policy; Objectives; Results; Planning; Controlling; Directing
VICE PRESIDENTS
Departmental Leadership: Departmental Results; Cooperation between Departments to Achieve Company Objectives
UNIT MANAGERS
Managerial Direction: Daily Operating Results of Small Groups of Employees Performing Similar or Closely Related Functions
CLERICAL EMPLOYEES
Implementation: Day-to-Day Operations under Unit Managers
VICE PRESIDENT AND ACTUARY
Policy Design; Premium Rates; Reserves; Mortality; Lapses; Surrenders; Maturities; Field Compensation; Valuations; Annual Statements
UNDERWRITING VICE PRESIDENT
Risk Selection; Medical Standards; Appointment of Examiners; Policy Issues; Policy Changes; Settlement Options; Transfers; Reinstatements
AGENCY VICE PRESIDENT
New Business; Conservation; Policyholder Service; Sales Management (Recruiting, Selection, and Supervision); Production Records; Expense Control; Sales Promotion; Market Research; Field Training
HEALTH INSURANCE VICE PRESIDENT
Product Design; Rate Structure; Underwriting; Administration
GROUP VICE PRESIDENT
Administration including Issue and Records; Product Development; Underwriting; Policyholder Service; Actuarial Functions including Rates; Experience Analysis; Financial Results and Forecasting; Group Sales and Production Records
CLAIMS VICE PRESIDENT
Investigation and Payment of Individual Life, Health, and Group Claims; Supervision of Claims Adjusters and Field Claims Offices; Conservation Work; Cooperation with Policy Design and Underwriting Departments
VICE PRESIDENT AND GENERAL COUNSEL
Compliance with Federal and State Laws; Policy Drafting and Review; Determination of Liability; Litigation; Taxation; Compensation Agreements; Investment and Loan Agreements; Title Work
INVESTMENT VICE PRESIDENT
Recommending Investment Policy; Study of Available Offerings; Effecting Board's Recommendations Regarding the Investment and Reinvestment of Funds
ACCOUNTING VICE PRESIDENT OR COMPTROLLER
Supervision of Accounting Procedures; Cost Allocation; Annual Statement Preparation; Cost Studies
ADVERTISING AND PUBLIC RELATIONS DIRECTOR OR VICE PRESIDENT
Publicity; Advertising; House Organs; Public Relations

FIG. 71–1. Functional organization chart of a medium-sized life and health insurance company.

typical company writing individual and group life and health insurance but not debit insurance, and shows in brief form the functions of each department.

The exact number of departments and their functions vary from company to company, depending upon the company's needs. However, the major departments of an insurance company usually include actuarial, underwriting, agency, individual health, group, claims, legal, investment and finance, accounting and auditing, and advertising and public relations.

Actuarial Department

The actuarial department sees that the company's insurance operations are conducted on a sound basis. Periodic duties include policy design, the calculation of premium rates and reserves, the drafting of new policies, securing policy approval from state insurance departments, mortality and lapse studies, and aiding in the establishment of commission scales and compensation plans for field management personnel. Routine duties embrace the maintenance of complete records of insurance in force and terminations, including lapses, surrenders, maturities, and changes; the calculation of dividends and loan values; and the like. The actuarial department also prepares the gain and loss exhibit and, with other departments, is responsible for the correctness of the annual financial statements required by state insurance departments.

Underwriting Department

The underwriting, medical, issue, and policy service (or change) functions may be handled by one department in a small company or be divided into three or more units in a very large organization.

The underwriting department's job is to select and classify individual risks. The lay underwriter reviews the application, the agent's statement, the physical examination, and the inspection report in order to determine the applicant's insurability. He is aided by the medical director (or in large companies the medical department), who establishes medical standards of insurability and appoints local examiners from among the practicing physicians in each locality. The medical director also reviews the medical reports of local examiners and helps the lay underwriters to decide whether the applicant is acceptable from the standpoint of health and physical condition. The final underwriting decision weighs the various factors affecting insurability—age, occupation, environment, finances, insurable interest, medical history, and physical findings.

The issue and policyholder service departments handle the issuance of new policies, policy changes, settlement options, reinstatements, transfers, and other similar transactions.

Agency Department

The agency department is responsible for the sale of new business, conservation of old business, and field service to policyholders. Its line functions include the recruitment and supervision of the company's agents and all other field personnel. Staff functions include planning the number and location of field offices, the preparation of cost and expense control information, the development of sales training and sales promotion programs, and the maintenance of detailed production records which are used to determine field management compensation.

The agency vice president maintains close co-operation between the line and staff officers of the agency department. He must at the same time make certain that the views of the agency department are considered by other company vice presidents in arriving at decisions which may affect the agency force and the products the company offers for sale, its underwriting policy, and service to policyholders. This is accomplished by individual conferences and also by membership of the agency vice president or his representative on important interdepartmental standing committees, such as the insurance committee. The latter contains representatives from both the underwriting and the actuarial departments, as well as the agency department.

The responsibility for production activities is usually divided by territory among a number of superintendents of agencies, who spend most of their time in the field directing the activities of managers or general agents and their agents under the over-all supervision of the agency vice president. The administrative work, which is usually performed by these superintendents in connection with the operation of field offices, includes the rental of space, replacement of personnel, salary administration, and the procurement of necessary supplies and equipment.

At the head of each field office is a manager or general agent, responsible for the selection and direction of agents and the supervision of the assistant manager and all other agency employees. The manager is a company employee, whereas the general agent, as the name implies, is an independent contractor with a franchise to appoint field underwriters and promote company business in an assigned territory. As companies have assumed closer control over their sales operations, the differences between the status of general agents and managers have become less and less distinct. In the case of smaller or newer companies with limited resources for financing sales development, the less costly (general agency) system is used at the outset and is oftentimes continued indefinitely. The Life Insurance Agency Management Association lists over two hundred separate functions which fall under the direction of the field office head. Briefly, he needs to be a skilled practitioner of the principles and psychology of management, human relations, and leadership; he needs to be well versed in sales management, market research, and financial management, and to be active in the insurance business and in the community in which he lives. The field office head is responsible for the leadership which field underwriters receive, the quality and quantity of business secured, and the kind of service provided to the public.

Managers or general agents are assisted in their work by assistant managers or supervisors, who may perform all of the functions of the field office head in a secondary capacity or be specialists in recruiting, training, supervision, or some other phase of agency operation. Because they are often responsible for the training and day-to-day supervision of field underwriters, assistant managers are in a position to exert great influence on the performance of the field underwriters, and hence on the success of the agency and company.

The office supervisor or cashier is usually responsible for field office records, the direction of clerical work, and the handling of all monies which clear through the field office. In general agency companies the cashier is frequently an employee of the general agent, whereas in many managerial companies the cashier is not directly responsible to the manager but reports to a home office vice president in charge of agency administration, thus freeing the manager's time entirely for the recruiting, training, and supervision of field underwriters.

Insurance is offered to the public by three types of agents: the ordinary company agent, the combination company agent, and the independent agent or broker. The ordinary company agent sells life and health insurance and group insurance, if they are offered by the company he represents. However, many ordinary company agents concentrate their efforts in a particular market or in a particular income or business group. They may be general practitioners, or specialists in pensions, business insurance, or estate planning. The ordinary company agent usually collects only the first premium, renewal premiums being remitted directly to the company. The combination company agent, while selling most of the same products as his counterpart, receives a part of his compensation for conservation work and for collecting premiums from those of his policyholders who pay on a weekly or monthly basis. The independent agent or broker typically places his business with several companies and represents the client in dealing with the company; he frequently sells property, individual health, and group insurance in addition to individual life coverages.

Individual Health Insurance Department

One approach to the sale of individual health insurance is to regard it simply as another form of life insurance product. Where this view is taken, the responsibility for product design, premium rates, reserves, sales, and training is merely shared by existing departments, and integration is complete. Another approach is for a company to establish a completely separate health insurance department with its own underwriting, claims, and administrative units. Actually, most companies fall somewhere between the two extremes, the exact position being determined by the degree of emphasis the company wishes to place upon health business, the competence of personnel within existing departments in health matters, the size of the company, and the character of the investment it wishes to make in this line of business.

Group Department

Group insurance is a dynamic, rapidly changing, highly competitive field which puts great emphasis on service. Procedures required for both administration and sales differ substantially from those used for individual insurance and require specially trained technicians in both the home office and the field.

Because of these considerations, most major group insurance companies have established separate divisions or units to handle the major group functions of administration, underwriting, actuarial services, field sales, and field services. Research and planning are sometimes carried on in an integrated actuarial department, and the individual lines sales force is frequently given some responsibility for assisting in group sales. Both a substantial investment of money and a separate group department headed by a capable group executive with a properly balanced perspective on sales and underwriting problems are a requirement for companies which expect to compete successfully for group business.

Claims Department

Claims handling in companies selling only individual life insurance is a relatively simple matter. It is usually not difficult to determine whether a policy has matured as a death claim or as an endowment, has lapsed, or has been surrendered if proper records have been maintained. Claims functions in monoline companies are usually handled by other departments, such as policyholder service or actuarial. However, in the health or group insurance fields the claims-handling problems become much more complex, and the establishment of a separate claims department with a regional claims organization throughout the territory in which the company operates frequently is desirable. Field claims offices are responsible for securing claims information, seeing that the necessary forms are obtained and forwarded to the home office for approval, and making certain that settlement release procedures are taken care of once claims have been approved. The home office claims department works closely with the contracts and law departments in the designing of policy contract language.

Law Department

The law department of a company has the responsibility of making certain that the company's insurance operations comply with federal and state laws and insurance departments' regulations. Usually, it assists in the preparation of policies and other forms, and aids in the determination of the company's liability for payment, as well as handling any litigation which may result. The law department co-operates with the accounting and auditing departments in determining company liability for taxes. It also handles the legal phases of investing policyholders' funds, including the preparation of loan agreements and title work for mortgage loan and real estate investments.

Investment and Finance Department

The duties of the investment and finance department include both studying available offerings and carrying out the recommendations of the finance committee and the board of directors. Normally, annual cash income exceeds the amount of death or health claims and all other classes of payment, and these funds must be invested. In addition, there is a considerable reinvestment of funds due to turnover of existing investments, including bond maturities, repayments of mortgage loans, and sales.

Accounting and Auditing Department

The accounting and auditing department, under the direction of the controller, is responsible for establishing and supervising the company's accounting procedures. Accounting in an insurance company is frequently more complicated than in many other types of business because of the long-range nature of the product, the large variety of transactions, and the huge number of individual items which must be recorded.

Public Relations and Advertising Department

This department is concerned not only with the advertising of company products but in seeing to it that good communications are maintained between the company and the various sectors of the public which it serves.

One of the most serious problems facing American business today is in the area of communications. Insurance companies utilizing several levels of authority and several types of departmentalization usually take active steps to see that all communications skills are used effectively and continuously. Often the business is conducted on a far-flung, nationwide basis involving hundreds and even thousands of people many miles distant from one another. In addition, the company may be dealing with millions of policyholders and beneficiaries, and with contracts which will not mature for many years in the future. Every action and every statement of significance may have some effect upon the general public, the company's policyholders, its employees, its agents, its stockholders, and the insurance business. All of the various communications channels may be utilized at one time or another, including individual contacts, meetings, conferences, conventions, house organs, correspondence, manuals, advisory councils, reports, and advertising. The skill and effectiveness with which each of these media is used play an important role in determing the company's success.

Other Departments

Large life insurance companies usually have a number of other departments. The most important of these are personnel and real estate. The personnel department plays a significant role in large life insurance companies because they employ thousands of people. It handles such matters as implementation of the company's personnel policy, procurement and termination of employees, the training of office employees, wage and salary administration, job evaluation, insurance and pension benefits, and so on. Since large life insurance companies have substantial home office buildings and operate nationally, the real estate department also plays a significant role, including building maintenance, layout and remodeling, the negotiation of leases, the care of furniture and equipment, and related matters.

Also important in such companies are the secretary's and the treasurer's departments (often these are combined into one department). In connection with meetings of the board, the executive committee, or the stockholders, the secretary's department sends notices, prepares agenda, and keeps the minutes. With regard to stockholders meetings, it also sends and tabulates the proxies, and arranges for judges of election and related matters. The treasurer's department is frequently responsible for such duties as the collection and disbursement of funds, and the custodianship of securities and other valuable property. Purchasing is sometimes a division of the treasurer's department; in the very largest companies, it occupies departmental status.

Most insurance companies of any size also have a planning, or methods and procedures, department. This unit is responsible for studying the operations of other departments with a view to work simplification and economies of operation. It may report to the controller or to the president, or to an administrative vice president if the company has one.

Additional departments which are common to most large companies, regardless of the nature of their business, include addressograph, cafeteria or service dining rooms, expense control, mailing, payroll, statistical, supply, tax, telegraph and teletype, transcribing, and transportation.

Home office departments need to be kept continuously informed on changing conditions in the field and new developments within the business. Both home office and field personnel must be kept advised regarding company policies, products, and plans, particularly as they may affect each individual in his job.

Influence of State Regulation

Company policy and management are profoundly influenced by state regulation, but state regulation itself has been greatly influenced by company management practices. State laws and regulations have, on the one hand, been adopted to prevent unsatisfactory management practices. On the other hand, the management practices followed by some companies were found to serve the public interest so well that they were made mandatory for all companies. Generally speaking, state regulation is aimed at the protection of policyholders and the public, but is not especially concerned with the welfare of the stockholder. Specifically, the statutes of a typical insurance code affecting life and health insurance can be fitted into one of the following five categories:

1. Safeguarding the funds which are guaranteed to fulfill the obligations of of the insurance contracts.
2. Preventing undertakings that are hazardous or contrary to the public interest.
3. Preventing deception or misunderstanding.
4. Assuring equity and preventing unfair discrimination among policyholders.
5. Obtaining tax revenue.

Company Formation

Insight into the organization and management of companies may be gained by tracing briefly the steps involved in organizing such a company. It is necessary to incorporate, secure a charter, draft bylaws, and obtain licenses from those jurisdictions in which the company intends to operate. Equally important is the availability of sufficient funds not only to launch the company but also to keep it going over a substantial number of years. In the formation of a new life and health insurance company, there is a continuous strain on the surplus caused by the large initial expense of placing business on the books. Over 100 per cent of the first premium is spent in this way. In addition, reserves must be set up for future liabilities—to a lesser extent for health insurance than for life insurance. This reserve and the excess initial expense must come from the company's surplus.

New companies often rely on consulting firms and part-time assistance in order to save money and because the volume of business they expect to do initially does not appear to justify the employment of full-time technicians. In addition, the executive staff may serve in several capacities. For example, the chief executive might also double as sales manager, actuary, accountant, or lawyer, depending on the nature of his past experience.

A new company's organization chart typically would be a very simple one, with few levels of authority and a minimum of departmentalization. Continued growth would lead to a larger number of officers and employees, greater specialization, more levels of authority, and increased departmentalization. Growth of the company would lead to more concentration on co-ordination of effort through effective policies, procedures, and communications.

New companies usually find it desirable to decide on the geographical area in which they intend to operate, the types of policies they intend to sell, and the segment of the market they desire to develop, based upon their resources in money and manpower. Some companies, for example, have decided to concentrate in certain states, or even cities; others have specialized in the credit life or mortgage protection market; and still others, in selling insurance to college seniors, graduate students, and medical interns.

Unique Characteristics

Insurance companies, while similar in many respects to other businesses, are unlike many other forms of business, in that they require a combination of technical specialists in such fields as investments, law, actuarial science, selection of risks, and salesmanship. A hard-driving and aggressive agency force is necessary to sell a product which has been conservatively designed by actuaries to a policyholder who will be objectively appraised by underwriters. The top management of a company has the responsibility for preserving a balance between sound operation and the desire for a product which can be sold with a minimum of difficulty and with the greatest possibility for success. Life and health insurance is a service type of business employing large numbers of people and differs from manufacturing concerns in that there is no raw material to be bought, inventoried, or processed. There is never any scarcity of supply or problem of manufacture, nor is a large investment in capital goods required.

Both banks and insurance companies handle other people's money. Banks operate on a relatively short-term basis, whereas insurance companies make contracts the fulfillment of which may depend upon the rate of interest earned, expenses incurred, and mortality and morbidity experience over 10, 20, or even 50 years in the future. Insurance companies accumulate billions of dollars in assets due to the long-term nature of their business. Because of this, their investment activities are not only greater than those of most other types of business enterprise but are vital to safeguarding the interests of policyholders.

The importance of decisions by insurance company management is magnified by the long-term nature of the business. It may be many years before it is possible to tell whether company management is wise or incompetent, or whether its decisions have been good or bad, whereas the quality of management in most businesses can be determined by their profits from year to year. This places a premium on the selection of capable insurance company management.

SELECTED REFERENCES

GLOVER, JOHN DESMOND, and HOWER, RALPH M. *The Administrator.* 4th ed. Homewood, Ill.: Richard D. Irwin, Inc., 1963.

GULICK, LUTHER, and URWICK, L. F. (eds.) *Papers on the Science of Administration.* New York: Institute of Public Administration, 1937.

HUEBNER, S. S., and BLACK, KENNETH, JR. *Life Insurance.* 6th ed. New York: Appleton-Century-Crofts, Inc., 1964.

MACLEAN, JOSEPH B. *Life Insurance.* 9th ed. New York: McGraw-Hill Book Co., Inc., 1962.

MCGILL, DAN M. *Life Insurance.* Homewood, Ill.: Richard D. Irwin, Inc., 1959.

MEHR, ROBERT I., and OSLER, ROBERT W. *Modern Life Insurance.* 3d ed. New York: Macmillan Co., 1961.

NEUSCHEL, RICHARD F. "An Outsider Looks at the Major Management Problems of the Life Insurance Industry," *Proceedings of the Fifty-Seventh Annual Meeting, American Life Convention,* 1962, pp. 196–217.

VOLK, H. J., and ALLSOPP, THOMAS. *Life Insurance Company Organization.* Bryn Mawr, Pa.: American College of Life Underwriters, 1955.

Chapter 72

COMPANY INVESTMENTS

BY J. HARRY WOOD

Life insurance companies are major financial institutions with over $140 billion invested in our economy. Thus, in addition to their vital purpose of making available the "magic of averages" through insurance, they also play a large economic role in our society.

This chapter will deal with the source of these funds; why they have attained their size and yet will continue to grow; investment policy; the determination of the character of the investments; liquidity; valuation of assets; other guiding principles; legal requirements; the actual distribution of investments by category; changes in the area of "private placements"; interest earnings; and finally, why life insurance is such a safe investment for the individual policyholder.

SOURCES OF FUNDS

The assets of the companies totaled $127 billion at the beginning of 1962 and $133 billion at the end of the year. This sum increased to $141 billion by the beginning of 1964 and will probably increase to about $156 billion by the end of 1965. This increase is at the rate of about $7.5 billion per year. What are the sources of such large sums?

These assets (both past and current) are being accumulated as the result of:

1. The level premium plan, which results in the creation of policy reserves.
2. Policy settlement proceeds left with the companies.
3. Policy dividend accumulations and dividends payable.
4. Capital stock.
5. Contingency funds and other surplus funds.
6. Miscellaneous, including cash, accounts receivable, and premiums due.
7. Earnings on investments.

The Level Premium Plan

A larger proportion of persons who are aged 50 will die during the next twelve months than those aged 25. In brief, the higher the age, the higher the rate of death.

If "pure protection" only was sold, a company would charge each person at the beginning of the year just enough to pay his proportionate cost of the death claims of insured people his own age, plus the cost, or overhead, of doing business. The premium rate would be quite low at young ages, becoming progressively higher year by year until the annual rate per thousand dollars of pure protection would become impossibly high at the older ages. This plan, known as one-year renewable term, has been proved by experience to be impractical, so a level premium plan was devised.

If the premium is to remain level even though mortality costs increase with age, then obviously the amount collected in the early years of the policy must be substantially in excess of the cost of "pure protection" and overhead. This excess is invested, and the obligation is recorded in a liability account known as the "reserve"—an amount carefully calculated to be sufficient, together with interest on the reserve and future premiums, to meet all future claims.

Thus, the premium paid for a permanent plan of life insurance is composed of three elements: loading, or the expense of conducting the business; a mortality charge, or one's proportionate share of the current year's death claims; and largest of all, the savings element. This savings element will, if one lives, eventually equal the face amount of the policy. These yearly increasing values are the required policy reserves—hence the phrase "legal reserve" life insurance. In addition to the reserves of life insurance policies, there are also reserves behind annuity policies.

These insurance and annuity reserves accounted for about 77 per cent of the $133 billion, or approximately $103 billion.

Policy Settlement Proceeds

When a policy becomes payable by reason of death or maturity as an endowment, the proceeds may be left with the company under a supplemental agreement. More than $4.8 billion were held at the end of 1962, under agreements not involving a survivorship element.

Dividends Held

Surplus distributions on participating policies, known as dividends, may be used in several ways, one of which is to leave them on deposit with the company. Almost $4 billion were on deposit at year-end 1962; in addition, approximately $2.1 billion had been apportioned for distribution during the coming year—or a total amount under this heading of approximately $6.1 billion.

Capital Stock

(Stock companies only.) This is a relatively small item of $978 million, and its nature is indicated by its name.

Surplus Funds

These are funds for the further protection of policyholders. The unassigned surplus amounted to $7.9 billion and other special surplus funds to $2.4 billion, or a total of $10.3 billion. Surplus funds are a "source," since they were originally earnings, and instead of being "paid out" were "paid into" a surplus account and, as such, invested.

Miscellaneous

This is a catchall classification of "all other" items not included above. The accumulated total held as of the end of 1962 was $7.5 billion.

The sum total of all the foregoing liabilities and surplus funds amounted to $133.3 billion at the beginning of 1963. Figure 72–1 is a graphic presentation of these facts.

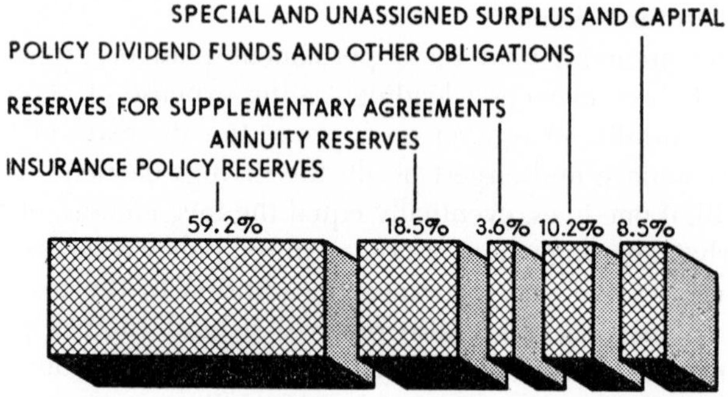

Source: Institute of Life Insurance.

FIG. 72–1. Obligations and surplus funds of United States life insurance companies, 1962 ($133,300,000,000).

Earnings on Investments

As all of the previously mentioned items were invested, they earned interest, rents, or dividends. Some of these earnings were paid out, but the greater part was required to be used to increase the assets offsetting the reserves under life and annuity policies. Such investment earnings were $5 billion during 1962.

Asset Increases

The assets should continue to increase in amount by about $6.5 billion per year as the sources continue to provide additional income to be invested. During 1962 the income from all sources amounted to $26 billion: premiums from life, annuity, and health policies amounted to $19.4 billion; investment income, to $5 billion; and all other income, such as the proceeds of policies and dividends left with the companies, to $1.6 billion. Benefits, dividends to policyholders, expenses, and taxes actually paid out amounted to some $19.8 billion, leaving about $6.2 billion to increase the assets during the year without counting valuation and other changes, which in 1962 brought the total asset increase to about $6.5 billion.

The life insurance companies are making investments on every business day. The total invested during any one year, however, will exceed the amount of the increase in assets, because some investments are maturing and others are being sold. This cash flow—the amount to be invested during the period of twelve months—is currently about $15 billion per year, rather than merely the $6.5 billion increase.

GROWTH OF LIFE INSURANCE ASSETS

With assets already exceeding $140 billion and the likelihood that the total will exceed $200 billion by the end of 1973, two rather basic questions might be asked: Why are such large amounts accumulated, and to whom do they belong?

The why? Eventually, we shall all be dead; eventually, then, all life insurance policies which remain in force must be paid either as death claims or as matured endowments. A $1,000 policy must eventually pay $1,000 to someone; the company must have the funds to pay this amount when it becomes due.

At the end of 1942, life insurance in force in United States life companies amounted to $130 billion, about the same as the amount of assets held by the companies at the end of 1962.

Total assets at the end of 1942 were $35 billion, or about one fourth the face amount of insurance in force. During the next twenty years, while the assets were increasing to $133 billion, insurance in force was increasing to $715 billion.[1] Assets in 1962 totaled about one fifth of insurance in force.

Again, why? It has already been explained that under the level premium plan, an excess is collected during the earlier years of the policy. This excess builds up a reserve in each such policy; these reserves under all life insurance policies amounted to $77.9 billion at the end of 1962.

These reserves are not a matter of company choice, but are required by law; hence the descriptive phrase "legal reserve life insurance."

Two things about these reserves should be mentioned: First, the companies are required by the terms of each policy contract to credit interest on the amount of the reserve at a guaranteed rate for the life of the contract; and second, the reserve under each policy, popularly known as

[1] To be technically accurate in this type of comparison, we should use only life insurance (ordinary and industrial) which has cash or reserve values, and exclude from assets all other reserves, especially annuities.

the cash value, belongs to the owner of the policy.[2] Furthermore, the company must pay a definite, contractually fixed number of dollars upon the death of the insured, or upon maturity of the policy as an endowment, or must pay the cash value upon demand if the policyowner so requests.

Thus the large growth in assets is required both by the very nature of level premium insurance and by law.

More than 90 per cent of the total assets of the companies are held for the account of or are subject to the claims of the individual policyholder. Even the remaining 10 per cent are held for the ultimate protection of the policyholders' interests.

INVESTMENT POLICY

Objectives

It should now be apparent that both the logical and the legal requirements of the level premium plan of life insurance determine the primary objectives of the financial managers of the companies as they invest their assets.

To review the requirements:

1. The amount "owed" to any policyholder under his contract at any given time is a definite number of dollars; in the event of death the amount to be paid to the beneficiary is a definite number of dollars.
2. The time when payment will be required of the company is unknown. The company must be able to pay at any and all times.
3. The companies guarantee a definite rate of interest to be applied to increase the reserves under the policies.

If a company could not meet the above requirements, it would be insolvent. Laws pertaining to insurance companies are designed primarily to avoid conditions or actions leading to insolvency.

The primary objective of the investment managers is to make investments such that the company will always be able to meet its requirements both as to interest rate on the reserves and as to payments under the policies. In short, the primary objective is to make investments which will enable it to meet all of its liabilities at the required times.

What Determines the Character of the Investments

The nature of the liabilities of any financial institution will determine the character of the investments which should be made. The financial liabilities of a life insurance company are quite different from those of a commercial bank, a college endowment, or a fire insurance company.

[2] During the early years the cash value, which the policyholder can withdraw, seldom equals the reserve. A technical discussion of this point is outside the scope of this chapter. Purists would maintain that it is stretching a point to say that the reserve belongs to anyone, as it is a liability item. A realist, however, will not object to the statement as made.

Hence the proper investments for one of these institutions will be quite different from those which would be required by the others.

The nature of the liabilities of a life insurance company might be summarized as follows:

First, the liabilities are in "fixed" dollars, i.e., neither inflation nor deflation will affect the number of dollars required. The life insurance company must know that when an investment comes due, the amount of dollars promised will be forthcoming. The only investments which fulfill this requirement are bonds and mortgages. Equity investments, i.e., real estate and common stocks, do not assure a given number of dollars at a definite time, so the percentage of assets in them is both small and limited.

Second, about 85 per cent of the total assets belong directly to policyholders and beneficiaries through reserves and other policy obligations, and on these the companies have guaranteed a rate of interest. This guarantee is not just for one year but, with minor exceptions, for the period the money is held. The guarantee on policies written prior to the adoption of the CSO Table in 1947–48 was usually 3 per cent or 3½ per cent; since that time, new policies have carried guarantees ranging from 2½ per cent to 3½ per cent. The guarantees under the new 1958 CSO Table will continue at about the same rate. The companies must have sufficient net interest earnings on their investments to support the guarantees; they strive for higher interest earnings for competitive reasons.

The search for the best interest return on sound investments results in shifts of emphasis from mortgages to bonds, or to different kinds of mortgages or bonds on new investments, depending upon the relative attractiveness of the respective interest rates. For example, in 1945, nearly 46 per cent of the total assets were in United States government bonds (although in part this was for patriotic reasons), 14.8 per cent were in mortgages, and 22.5 per cent were in corporate bonds. Seventeen years later, in 1962, these ratios had changed to the following: United States government bonds, less than 5 per cent; mortgages, 35 per cent; and corporate bonds, over 38 per cent.

Third, the assets of the life insurance companies increase every year; there has been an increase in each of the past 75 years, including the period of the Great Depression. This phenomenon will continue for the indefinite future. Even if a typical company ceased writing all new business, it would be 20 years before it would have to liquidate any substantial number of investments for reasons of liquidity; for a period of 10 to 15 years, its assets would continue to grow.

Liquidity

The result of the constant growth in assets is that the life insurance companies, unlike most other financial institutions, do not give much weight to the qualities of liquidity or marketability when making their investments.

True, life insurance companies need money every day to pay off maturing obligations, which are of two kinds: (1) death claims, maturing endowments, payments under annuities, health insurance policies, and supplementary agreements; and (2) demands of policyholders for cash by borrowing against the value of the policy or its outright surrender, both of which are guaranteed as to right and as to amount.

Yet, large as these demands are, they do not affect investment policy because the income of the companies from their investments and premiums exceeds the outgoing payments. This has been so for each year since life insurance really began to grow and develop.

Even the statement often made that the maturity date of investments is spaced so that funds will always be available to meet future demands is mostly an erroneous one. Spacing arises from two other considerations: first, the bonds and mortgages purchased from year to year will have different dates of issue and hence different maturity dates; and second, no one knows what the interest rate will be in any future year, so it is sound policy to plan so that a disproportionate amount will not have to be reinvested in any one future year at an unknown interest rate.

A life insurance company has little need for liquidity; it has great need for the safety of principal of its investments, and for as high a yield as it is possible to have consistent with the first requirement—safety. Higher yields are normally found in longer-term investments; liquidity normally demands short-term investments.

In short, liquidity and marketability are of little importance in life insurance investments.

Valuation of Assets

Liquidity is of little importance because income has been and will continue to exceed outgo, as indicated by the $6.5 billion annual increase in assets. When one considers the safety of life insurance funds, the question is whether the assets will always be sufficient to meet maturing obligations, rather than the purely hypothetical question as to whether, if all policyholders should ask for their funds on a given day, the companies could liquidate all assets immediately and for book value.

This leads to the concept of valuation. In the preceding section, it was mentioned that life insurance companies generally should make long-term investments in order to obtain the highest yields.

Yields, or the going interest rates, are constantly changing as a result of supply-demand factors. The market price of an old bond or mortgage depends upon its coupon yield compared to the current or going rate, and the years to maturity. For example, a 30-year $1,000 bond was issued 10 years ago at a 3 per cent coupon, or interest rate. Today the bond has a maturity of 20 years. If the current, or going, market rate of interest is 4 per cent for comparable 20-year bonds of new issues, this old bond will sell for only about $863; conversely, if the current interest rate has declined to 2½ per cent, then our 3 per cent bond will bring about $1,078 on the market.

It would be both unnecessary and unwise for a life insurance company to mark the book value of its investment up or down with the market, whether daily or annually. It would be a meaningless activity.

The sound method, both in theory and in practice, for valuation of high-quality bonds is the "amortized book value." If a bond is purchased below par, its book value is written up proportionately each year as it approaches maturity; conversely, if the purchase price was above par, it is written down in the same manner.

Mortgages are carried at the book value of their unpaid balances so long as there is no default in payments. Real estate owned for investment purposes is usually carried at its depreciated book value.

"Private placements" have posed new questions; but generally, book value is a satisfactory criterion and, in truth, about the only practical one.

Common stocks are valued at the market on the annual date when the valuation is made.

Preferred stocks, beginning with 1957, are carried at an "adjusted value." This value is arrived at initially by reducing the closing market price for the preceding year by one fifth of the amount of market decline during the current year; in a rising market the adjusted value would be increased by one fifth of the market rise.[3]

Other Guiding Principles

To recapitulate, several guiding principles of investment policy have been discussed, namely:

1. That the security of principal be always in mind.
2. That the yield or return be certain both as to amount and to time.
3. That the yield be high enough to satisfy the guarantees under the company's contracts.
4. That liquidity, maturity date, and marketability factors are relatively less important to life insurance companies than to other financial institutions.

There are, of course, other principles which are followed by all companies, particularly those pertaining to diversification, to commingling, and to trusteeship.

[3] For a detailed explanation see *Final Report to Insurance Companies, Societies and Associations re: Annual Statements as of December 31, 1957*, published on June 17, 1957, by the National Association of Insurance Commissioners Committee on Valuation of Securities, Chicago. This report also states in detail the loss and fluctuation reserve requirements to be held against the adjusted value.

Diversification. No investment is absolutely safe either as to payment of principal or as to interest. Some are safer than others, but unforeseen developments may affect those which seemed at the time of purchase to be among the best. Therefore, the principle of diversification is followed to be more certain that the primary objectives are realized. Diversification requires that investment be made in several industries, not just one, and in several companies within any one industry; and also that the investments be spread out geographically, not concentrated in one city, state, or area.

Commingling. Each dollar received from any source is, when invested, spread pro rata through all the separate investments of the company. If a company had one hundred investments of equal size, then one cent of each dollar would be invested in each investment. This principle is of particular value to the individual policyholder, as he gets the benefit and the security of a vast diversification. By way of contrast, a trust would normally legally be required not to commingle the funds of one individual with those of another.

Trusteeship. While the commingling of life insurance funds is contrary to the strict separation of trust funds, nonetheless the traditions of the trusteeship have become a part of the management philosophy of the companies. Every action must have the ultimate benefit of the policyholder in mind; company officers may not profit from any financial dealings, and certainly the "prudent man theory" which guides the trust officer is ever present. Members of the boards of directors are more likely to think and act as trustees for the policyholder than as representatives for any other groups, either employees or stockholders (if any).

Legal Requirements of Investments

Most states have laws regulating the investments which life insurance companies may make. It may be said that in a broad sense, these laws attempt to make mandatory the principles outlined in the preceding sections.

Specifically, the laws usually mention the allowable fields of investments, and exclude or limit others. For example, for a bond to qualify, the issuing corporation must have earned more than the amount of the required interest payments for a specified period of years; common stocks may be prohibited or, as in New York, limited to 5 per cent of assets or 50 per cent of surplus, whichever is the smaller.

Furthermore, the laws frequently limit the accumulation of surplus. New York State, for example, sets the maximum amount of surplus as 10 per cent of reserves and policy liabilities. A limited surplus in turn restricts the investment risks which a life insurance company is warranted in taking.

For example, if investments in common stocks were unlimited while surplus was limited to 10 per cent of liabilities, it is clear that financial emergencies could arise. If a portfolio in this illustration were invested 50 per cent in common stocks, then a decline of 20 per cent in the market price of the stocks would wipe out the surplus, and the company would be technically insolvent.

Thus, it is readily seen that the principles of the laws designed to determine investment policy are those which should be followed anyway. (This is a general statement; often the laws prohibit or limit new developments, or at least defer permissibility for years.)

DISTRIBUTION OF INVESTMENTS

Table 72–1 gives the amount in billions of dollars of each of the broad categories of investments of life insurance companies as of January 1, 1963, as well as the percentage that each bears to the whole. Figure 72–2 is a graphic display of similar data.

TABLE 72–1

INVESTMENTS OF UNITED STATES LIFE INSURANCE COMPANIES, JANUARY 1, 1963
(000,000 Omitted)

Investment	Amount	Percentage
United States government securities	$ 6,170	4.6%
All other government bonds	6,008	4.5
Railroad bonds	3,496	2.6
Public utility bonds	17,330	13.0
Industrial and miscellaneous bonds	30,718	23.1
Stocks	6,302	4.7
Mortgages	46,902	35.2
Real estate	4,107	3.1
Policy loans	6,234	4.7
Miscellaneous assets	6,024	4.5
Total	$133,291	100.0%

Source: Institute of Life Insurance.

United States Government Bonds

This is the premier security of all; but there is a price to be paid for such security, namely, a lower interest return than for other bonds of the same maturity. Life insurance companies desire the best possible yield and, therefore, tend to hold United States government bonds (which offer supreme security but comparatively lower yields) only when there are shortages in supply of other types of bonds—during war periods, for example. High-grade corporate bonds will normally yield 0.2 to 0.6 of 1 per cent more; or stated another way, United States government bonds will yield 5 per cent to 15 per cent less. Table 72–2 indicates how the amounts

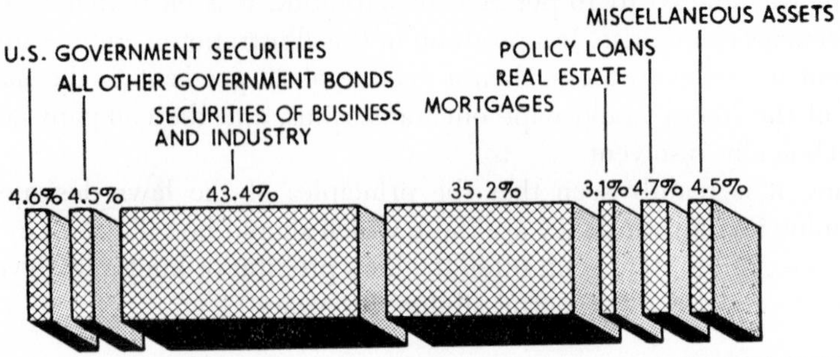

FIG. 72–2. Assets of United States life insurance companies, 1962 ($133,300,000,000).

and percentages of government bonds as well as other investments have varied over the years.

All Other Government Securities

This category may be divided into foreign government bonds, mostly Canadian, amounting to $659 million, and state, provincial, and local bonds, totaling $5,349 million. Because of a difference in the method of income taxation, life insurance companies do not find "municipal" bonds as attractive relatively as do some other financial institutions.

Railroad Bonds

While railroad bond holdings are currently $3.5 billion, they are at the low for this century, percentagewise: 2.6 per cent compared to the 30.5 per cent of 45 years earlier.

Public Utility Bonds

These are the bonds issued primarily by telephone, electric, and natural gas corporations. These corporations have grown rapidly, have needed huge amounts of capital, have had stable earnings, and pay an attractive rate. No wonder, then, that the life insurance companies have constantly increased the amount held; the $17.3 billion total is 153 times that of 45 years ago.

Industrial and Miscellaneous Bonds

The largest growth in investments during the past 25 years has occurred in this classification. In 1937, less than $1 billion of these bonds were held, or 3.7 per cent of the total assets; 25 years later the volume had increased 30 times to $30.7 billion and to 23.1 per cent of total assets. Only mortgages exceeded this category in total size.

Mortgages

Mortgages have always bulked large as the favorite investment of the life insurance companies. Because mortgages do not have the marketabil-

TABLE 42-2

DISTRIBUTION OF ASSETS OF UNITED STATES LIFE INSURANCE COMPANIES IN SELECTED YEARS (1917–62)

Year	United States Government Securities	Foreign Government Bonds	State, Provincial, and Local Bonds	Railroad Bonds	Public Utility Bonds	Industrial and Miscellaneous Bonds	Stocks	Mortgages	Real Estate	Policy Loans	Miscellaneous Assets	Total
	Amount (000,000 Omitted)											
1917	$ 70	$ 163	$ 329	$1,813	$ 113	$ 49	$ 83	$ 2,021	$ 179	$ 810	$ 311	$ 5,941
1920	830	169	350	1,775	125	49	75	2,442	172	859	474	7,320
1925	627	154	530	2,238	687	97	81	4,808	266	1,446	604	11,538
1930	319	160	1,023	2,931	1,631	367	519	7,598	548	2,807	977	18,880
1935	2,853	189	1,685	2,625	2,114	575	583	5,357	1,990	3,540	1,705	23,216
1940	5,767	288	2,392	2,830	4,273	1,542	605	5,972	2,065	3,091	1,977	30,802
1945	20,583	915	1,047	2,948	5,212	1,900	999	6,636	857	1,962	1,738	44,797
1950	13,459	1,060	1,547	3,187	10,587	9,526	2,103	16,102	1,445	2,413	2,591	64,020
1954	9,070	481	2,549	3,757	13,511	16,926	3,268	25,976	2,298	3,127	3,523	84,486
1955	8,576	410	2,696	3,912	13,968	18,179	3,633	29,445	2,581	3,290	3,742	90,432
1958	7,183	320	3,510	3,843	15,938	23,439	4,109	37,062	3,364	4,188	4,624	107,580
1959	6,868	349	4,135	3,774	16,455	25,105	4,561	39,197	3,651	4,618	4,937	113,650
1960	6,427	437	4,576	3,668	16,719	26,728	4,981	41,771	3,765	5,231	5,273	119,576
1961	6,134	476	5,039	3,594	16,999	28,690	6,258	44,203	4,007	5,733	5,683	126,816
1962	6,170	659	5,349	3,496	17,300	30,718	6,302	46,902	4,107	6,234	6,024	133,291
	Percentage											
1917	1.2%	2.8%	5.6%	30.5%	1.9%	0.8%	1.4%	34.0%	3.0%	13.6%	5.2%	100.0%
1920	11.3	2.3	4.8	24.3	1.7	0.7	1.0	33.4	2.3	11.7	6.5	100.0
1925	5.4	1.3	4.6	19.4	6.0	0.8	0.7	41.7	2.3	12.5	5.3	100.0
1930	1.7	0.9	5.4	15.5	8.6	1.9	2.8	40.2	2.9	14.9	5.2	100.0
1935	12.3	0.8	7.3	11.3	9.1	2.5	2.5	23.1	8.6	15.2	7.3	100.0
1940	18.7	1.0	7.8	9.2	13.9	5.0	2.0	19.4	6.7	10.0	6.3	100.0
1945	45.9	2.1	2.3	6.6	11.6	4.3	2.2	14.8	1.9	4.4	3.9	100.0
1950	21.0	1.7	2.4	5.0	16.5	14.9	3.3	25.1	2.2	3.8	4.1	100.0
1954	10.7	0.5	3.1	4.5	16.0	20.0	3.9	30.7	2.7	3.7	4.2	100.0
1955	9.5	0.4	3.0	4.3	15.5	20.1	4.0	32.6	2.9	3.6	4.1	100.0
1958	6.7	0.3	3.3	3.6	14.8	21.8	3.8	34.4	3.1	3.9	4.3	100.0
1959	6.0	0.3	3.7	3.3	14.5	22.1	4.0	34.5	3.2	4.1	4.3	100.0
1960	5.4	0.3	3.8	3.1	14.0	22.4	4.2	34.9	3.1	4.4	4.4	100.0
1961	4.9	0.3	4.0	2.8	13.4	22.6	4.9	34.9	3.2	4.5	4.5	100.0
1962	4.6	0.5	4.0	2.6	13.0	23.1	4.7	35.2	3.1	4.7	4.5	100.0

Sources: *Spectator Year Book* and Institute of Life Insurance.

ity of bonds, and because of the requirement of some specialized knowledge, the yield has been higher usually—so they have fitted the investment policy requirements very well. The percentage of total assets in mortgages, currently 35.2 per cent, is almost the same as that of 45 years ago, although in between the percentage has varied from 40.2 per cent in 1930 to 14.8 per cent in 1945 and 1946.

Stocks

Investments in stocks are limited by law and by the nature of the liabilities already discussed. The present percentage is 4.7 per cent and has always been relatively small. The total amount of $6,302 million in stocks at the end of 1962 was 65 per cent common and 35 per cent preferred. Except for the last eight years, preferreds always exceeded common by a considerable amount.

Real Estate

Real estate, an equity investment, as are common stocks, has likewise been limited both by law and by policy. Until the 1940's, these holdings were limited to home office property and (temporarily) to property acquired through mortgage foreclosure. More recently, there have been investments in housing developments and in so-called "purchase and leaseback" arrangements. Even so, real estate continues to be one of the smallest categories, 3.1 per cent.

Policy Loans

When a company lends money to a policyholder, the loan is no different in essence than if the money had been lent to a large corporation—both are investments to the life insurance company. In recent years, about 4 per cent of the assets have been so employed; currently, the percentage is 4.7 per cent.

Miscellaneous Assets

Percentagewise, this category in the past two decades accounted for between 3 and 7 per cent of assets; currently, the figure is 4.5. This group of remaining assets is composed chiefly of due and deferred premiums, collateral loans, accounts receivable, and cash.

PRIVATE PLACEMENTS

One of the greatest changes in the area of investments by many life insurance companies—particularly those of moderate to larger size—is in the area known as "private placements."

Normally, a bond issue is registered with the SEC (Securities and Exchange Commission) and is sold publicly, usually to many different buyers. A private placement, on the other hand, is negotiated directly with the issuer, usually with an investment banking firm acting as agent, with a limited number of purchasers, and often involving only one purchaser.

The chief reason for mentioning private placements in this chapter, however, is to call attention to the change this procedure requires in the investment departments of the lending institutions.

In buying publicly issued bonds, companies may—and many do—depend on the ratings of the issue by Moody's or Standard & Poor's. To lend on a negotiated deal, or private placement, an investment department must have able analysts and people knowledgeable about business—manufacturing, finance companies, and so forth. The ability required is a combination of that of a bank loan officer and/or stock analyst.

Private placements have grown to such popularity that some life insurance companies today seldom purchase a publicly issued bond. During each of the years 1956 through 1961, private placements accounted for over 85 per cent of the purchases of corporate obligations by life companies.

The reasons for private placement of corporate debt issues as opposed to offering them up for bidding are many—and often subject to argument. Those favoring private placements stress their speed and flexibility, feeling that these advantages offset the possibility of a higher interest rate. For example, if the outlook is for a sharp rise in interest rates, the borrower and lender can quickly arrange a private sale under market conditions known to both parties. This advantage is lost, according to the advocates of private deals, when a registration statement is filed with the Securities and Exchange Commission, since this often takes as long as a month to clear.

Many corporations like the "custom fit" of private placements, particularly with repayment and other terms of the contract. This flexibility on the part of the agent is often possible because he can line up the eventual buyers by presenting them with a price. In a competitive sale, customers are usually reluctant to commit themselves because they do not know what the price tag will show.

In addition, in a private sale the borrower can save on advertising and various other fees. As for the placement costs, the *Bond Buyer* has estimated that the compensation paid in a competitive sale is about $7.00 per $1,000 bond. This compares with an agent's fee for a private placement of between $2.50 and $5.00. The expenses were based on a typical prime utility issue of about $20 million. Many private placements, of course, are far smaller than this, running perhaps from $500,000 to $5 million. There are no effective minimum or maximum limits on the size of private placements, and examples may be found of larger amounts.

Finally, should the necessity for changes in terms or other contingencies arise, the borrower in a private placement not only has relatively few bondholders to contact, but benefits from a closer relationship which facilitates such negotiations. In a widespread public distribution the investors are numerous, many of them unknown and sometimes completely inaccessible.

Opponents of private corporate financing, that is, those who favor public competitive offerings, say that except for refunding previous issues sold at higher interest cost, the benefits of a private transaction are few.

Proponents of public sales point out that the borrower is in the driver's seat when he sets the terms instead of having to bend the indenture to suit the potential buyer. Another point they make is that the use of private placements often enables smaller issuers to obtain financing which, because of the limited marketability of their securities and lack of readily available information, might not otherwise be obtainable.

Opposition to private placements stems primarily from the belief that each issue should be registered and examined by the SEC; but those holding this view should bear in mind that SEC registration is designed to protect the general public, not the life insurance companies who are the principal users of the private placement mechanism.

INTEREST EARNINGS

Life insurance companies make investments in order to earn a return. They must earn a return, since they guarantee interest to policyholders on their policy reserves. However, the net rate of interest earned on invested funds will vary by company and will vary for all companies over a period of time. Several factors are pertinent.

First, of course, is the fact that the interest rate achieved on new investments will be determined to a large degree by the "going rate," which in turn is dependent upon supply-demand factors. Secondly, with $133.3 billion in assets and about $15 billion (or approximately 10 per cent of total assets) to be invested each year, changes in interest rates have only a slow effect on over-all earnings. This results in relative stability of earnings from investments. Finally, the investment policy of any particular company plus its investment department effectiveness inevitably will bring about results different from the over-all average.

Table 72–3 indicates the rate of interest earned on invested funds, yearly, from 1915 through 1962.

From 1915 through 1932, net interest rates varied between 4.66 per cent and 5.18 per cent; then a long decline followed to a low of 2.88 per cent in 1947. Since the latter date, there has been a small increase each year to reach 4.34 per cent in 1962, before federal income taxes. If we use the 10 years 1921–30 as a bench mark, when the rate uniformly exceeded 5 per cent, averaging 5.09 per cent, then we shall see that investment earnings per dollar of assets declined by 43 per cent by 1947 and that even in 1962, they were back to only about 85 per cent of the decade of the twenties. Investment income on a percentage basis is approximately five sixths of the average of the twenties.

This results in a higher cost of life insurance per thousand than would otherwise be the case. This natural result is obscured by the fact that improving mortality or lower death rates have acted to lower costs.

As interest rates declined during the 25 years from 1923 through 1947, companies lowered the interest guarantees used in new policies. In the last few years, there has been a tendency to raise the interest guarantees.

TABLE 72–3

NET RATE OF INTEREST EARNED ON INVESTED FUNDS (1915–62)
United States Life Insurance Companies

Year	Rate	Year	Rate	Year	Rate	Year	Rate
1915	4.77%	1927	5.05%	1939	3.54%	1951	3.18%
1916	4.80	1928	5.05	1940	3.45	1952	3.28
1917	4.81	1929	5.05	1941	3.42	1953	3.36
1918	4.72	1930	5.05	1942	3.44	1954	3.46
1919	4.66	1931	4.93	1943	3.33	1955	3.51
1920	4.83	1932	4.65	1944	3.23	1956	3.63
1921	5.02	1933	4.25	1945	3.11	1957	3.75
1922	5.12	1934	3.92	1946	2.93	1958	3.85
1923	5.18	1935	3.70	1947	2.88	1959	3.96
1924	5.17	1936	3.71	1948	2.96	1960	4.11
1925	5.11	1937	3.69	1949	3.06	1961	4.22
1926	5.09	1938	3.59	1950	3.13	1962	4.34

Source: Institute of Life Insurance. The net interest rate is the ratio of the net investment income for the year to the mean invested assets (including cash) decreased by one half the net investment income. Before 1940 the rates were calculated after deducting only such federal income taxes as were deducted by the individual companies in arriving at their net investment income. Beginning with 1940, the rates are calculated before deducting any federal income taxes.

Another result, as we have previously observed, is that the investment departments are constantly searching for sound investments which will yield the highest investment return commensurate with the all-important requirement of absolute safety of principal.

THE SAFETY OF LIFE INSURANCE AS AN INVESTMENT FOR THE INDIVIDUAL POLICYHOLDER

Persons owning life insurance may have abiding faith in the safety of their life insurance investment. The most important reason is that the assets of each individual company will continue to increase in amount for the foreseeable future. The implication of this fact, as far as safety of investment is concerned, is that life insurance companies, almost alone of all financial institutions, do not have to liquidate investments during times of poor economic conditions. They are never forced to sell when prices are low; rather, they continue to buy. As a corollary, buying at low as well as at high prices results in investments being made at average prices.

The ability of life insurance companies to avoid capital losses resulting from forced liquidation of investments during times of poor economic conditions has been a major factor in the companies' outstanding record of preservation of principal. The ability to avoid losses from such forced liquidation will continue as long as the assets of the companies continue to increase, which will be for at least 15 or 20 years after insurance in force has stopped increasing—and that time will not come so long as population continues to increase, our standard of living either remains steady or continues to increase, and our country continues to follow the principle of private, competitive enterprise.

The investment principles and objectives have proven sound because they were adopted to meet the requirements of the life insurance business. The policies followed to reach or attain the objectives have proven sound because they are the result of logic, the "prudent man theory," experience, and law.

For the individual, there is nothing safer or more necessary than life insurance. For the country, this financial institution is of vital importance because it collects the small savings of 122 million people and pools them so that they become of great aid to the total economy.

SELECTED REFERENCES

CONKLIN, GEORGE T. JR. "Factors Determining the Investment Policies of Life Insurance Companies," *Journal of the American Society of Chartered Life Underwriters,* Vol. XI, No. 1 (Winter, 1956).

CONKLIN, GEORGE T., JR. "The Investments of Life Insurance Companies," *Journal of the American Society of Chartered Life Underwriters,* Vol. XI, No. 2 (Spring, 1957).

FRAINE, HAROLD G. *Valuation of Securities Holdings of Life Insurance Companies.* Homewood, Ill.: Richard D. Irwin, Inc., 1962.

HUEBNER, S. S., and BLACK, KENNETH, JR. *Life Insurance.* 6th ed. New York: Appleton-Century-Crofts, Inc., 1964.

INSTITUTE OF LIFE INSURANCE. *Life Insurance Fact Book.* New York, published annually.

MACLEAN, JOSEPH B. *Life Insurance.* 9th ed. New York: McGraw-Hill Book Co., Inc., 1962.

MCCAHAN, DAVID (ed.). *Investment of Life Insurance Funds.* Philadelphia: University of Pennsylvania Press, 1953.

MCGILL, DAN M. *Life Insurance.* Homewood, Ill.: Richard D. Irwin, Inc., 1959.

Chapter 73

COMPANY ANNUAL STATEMENT

BY B. FRANKLIN BLAIR

Because life and health insurance companies differ fundamentally from most other forms of business enterprise, the annual financial reports of such insurance companies differ considerably from those of most other corporations. The purpose of this chapter is to describe the significant information contained in a typical report of such a company. For obvious reasons, this chapter does not cover the details of such a broad subject or mention unusual situations which pertain only to small segments of the insurance business.

ANNUAL STATEMENT FILED WITH INSURANCE DEPARTMENT

Each company must file an annual statement (on a calendar-year basis) with the insurance department of its home state and that of every other state in which it is licensed to do business. These annual statements must be on a standard form, called "convention blank" or "association blank," which (with a few relatively minor exceptions) is the same in every state and is prescribed by the National Association of Insurance Commissioners.[1] The NAIC has also set forth detailed instructions for completing this blank, so that all companies use as nearly identical methods as are practicable in making the various entries.

The convention blank form of annual statement measures about 12 inches by 18 inches and, for a large company, may contain well over one hundred pages of detailed tables. As a result, its circulation is limited, so that policyowners, stockholders, or field underwriters (agents) rarely see this form. However, anyone who is sufficiently interested may go to a state insurance department and examine the form for any company doing business in that state, since these convention blanks are public documents.

[1] See Chapters 77 and 78 for further information on the regulation of life and health insurance.

Using the convention blank as a source of basic data, most (if not all) companies prepare an annual report to their policyowners and/or stockholders. Throughout this chapter the term "annual report" refers to such reports. Because the term "annual statement" is confusingly similar to "annual report," the official annual statement will be referred to throughout as the "convention blank."

In addition to filing the convention blank, each company is subject to regular audits, or "examinations," usually at triennial intervals. The examinations are under the supervision of the insurance department of the home state, but representatives of other states participate in the examination on a "zone basis." During these comprehensive examinations the state examiners not only check the correctness of the company's convention blank but also investigate such matters as claims practices and other dealings with policyowners. Reports on these examinations are available to the public in the insurance departments of many states.

TECHNICAL TERMS

Explanations of a few technical terms which appear in the convention blank may make it easier to understand annual statements. These include the following:

Ledger Assets

Ledger assets are assets which have actually been entered on the books (ledgers) of the company because the transaction by which each of these assets was acquired has actually been completed. Cash and investments (including policy loans) are the main ledger assets.

Nonledger Assets

Nonledger assets are those assets which have not yet been entered on the books of the company. The more important ones are:

1. *Overdue Investment Income (Interest, Rents, Dividends).* This is usually small except in severe depressions.
2. *Accrued Investment Income.* This is income which has "accrued" on each investment since the last interest due date preceding the date of the report. For example, on a bond with interest payable semiannually on May 1 and November 1, there would be two months' accrued interest on December 31.
3. *Net Premiums Overdue or Deferred on Insurance and Annuities.* Net premium as used in the convention blank means the *tabular* net premium, which is the gross premium less the loading added for expenses. The net premiums overdue or deferred for the balance of the current policy year may be counted as assets when the reserves are calculated on the assumption that premiums are paid annually. This is traditional in connection with ordinary insurance and annuities, and is recognized in the convention blank. Because the reserve liability set up

is the same as though premiums for the full year had already been paid, the nonledger asset of net overdue and deferred premiums is needed as an offset.[2]

Admitted Assets

Admitted assets are those recognized as sound assets by the various state regulatory authorities and hence "admitted" to the balance sheet in the convention blank. The assets shown in an annual report are all admitted assets.

Nonadmitted Assets

Nonadmitted assets are those not recognized as sound or admitted assets. The common types of nonadmitted assets are:

1. *Furniture and Equipment.* The value after depreciation of furniture and equipment is treated as an asset in many other types of businesses but is not counted as a good asset by an insurance company because of the difficulty of realizing this value if the company is liquidated.[3]
2. *Agents' Balances.* Advances to agents, even though secured by commission equities, are nonadmitted assets.
3. *Overdue and Accrued Interest on Certain Overdue Mortgages.*[4] Companies are allowed a certain amount of choice in determining the length of the period after which overdue and accrued interest on mortgages should be treated as a nonadmitted asset. This item has been negligible in recent years.

Some nonadmitted assets are ledger assets (e.g., agents' balances), and some are nonledger assets (e.g., overdue interest).

Amortized Basis

The amortized basis is used to determine the admitted asset value of most bonds which are not in default and have a good investment rating.[5] On this basis, which is independent of current market values, the values of a bond at the end of successive years proceed by regular adjustments up or down (as the case may be) from the purchase price to the maturity value. The adjustments are so calculated that the interest received plus

---

[2] Overdue or deferred premiums are not assets in the usual sense, since they are not recoverable by law. Moreover, if and when they are collected, certain expenses such as commissions and premium taxes become payable by the company. It is therefore appropriate that they should be set up as an asset on a "net" basis, as specified by the NAIC.

[3] A number of states make an exception for large-scale electronic data-processing equipment, allowing its value after depreciation to be counted as a good asset.

[4] No item of overdue interest is carried as an asset on bonds in default, because the market value of such bonds reflects any interest in default.

[5] The term "bonds" is used throughout this chapter in a broad sense, including such investments as debentures, notes, trust certificates, and Treasury bills.

upward adjustments (or minus downward adjustments) represents the same percentage yield every year on the amortized value for that year.

Nonamortizable Securities

Nonamortizable securities are those which cannot be valued on the amortized basis.[6] This category includes:

1. All stocks
2. Income bonds and perpetual bonds
3. Bonds in default
4. Certain bonds with low investment ratings

The admitted asset value of a nonamortizable security is its market value as published by the NAIC, except that the "adjusted value" is used for preferred stocks "in good standing." The adjusted value is essentially the previous year's adjusted value plus (or minus) one fifth of the difference between the current year's market value and the previous year's adjusted value.

Accrued or Revenue Basis; Cash Basis

If income or disbursements reported include only items which have been actually received or disbursed and put through the books, the income or disbursements are said to be on a "cash basis." If, however, items are included which have not been actually received or disbursed, but which will be attributable to the current accounting period, the income or disbursements are said to be on an "accrued basis" or "revenue basis."

Examples of income items which have not actually been received are accrued interest and overdue premiums. Examples of disbursement items which have not actually been disbursed are claims in course of settlement and taxes payable in the following year on the current year's operations.

Supplementary Contracts

Supplementary contracts arise when policy proceeds are left under optional methods of settlement.

BALANCE SHEET

The most essential feature of a convention blank or an annual report is probably the statement of financial condition, or balance sheet. This consists of a statement of the assets of the company and a statement of the liabilities (or obligations) and the capital and surplus.

The excess of the assets over the liabilities consists of capital (in a

[6] The term "securities" has a specialized meaning in insurance company parlance. It covers bonds and stocks, but not mortgages.

stock company) and surplus funds (both special and unassigned). As will be discussed in more detail later, the relation of the capital and surplus to the liabilities is often used as a very rough indication of the financial stability of the company.

Assets

In a typical company, investments (including policy loans) and cash represent 95 per cent or more of the assets.[7] The other kinds of admitted assets usually represent only small percentages of the total admitted assets and include the three types of nonledger assets mentioned above and also large-scale electronic data-processing equipment.

Liabilities

Reserves. By far the largest part of the liabilities of a life or health insurance company is represented by the single category "reserves."[8] Minimum standards for the calculation of most reserves are prescribed by the regulatory authorities. Where minimum standards are not prescribed, a company must satisfy the authorities that the reserve basis used is adequate. The details of the basis of the reserves are reported in the convention blank. In a number of states the insurance department makes an independent calculation of the reserves of domestic companies. Therefore, the adequacy of the reserve item can ordinarily be taken for granted.

In general, the lower the interest rate used for valuation, the larger is the reserve. Therefore, a low valuation interest rate is usually regarded as conservative and indicative of a strong basis of valuation. Also, the reserves are larger on a net level premium basis than on a preliminary term basis, so that the net level premium basis is the more conservative. However, there are a number of other factors—such as the margins in the gross premiums and the size of the nonforfeiture benefits guaranteed—which should be taken into consideration in appraising the conservatism of a valuation basis.

In this chapter, reserves are regarded as including amounts held by the company under supplementary contracts, both with and without life contingencies.

Other Liabilities. The "other liability" items may be grouped into the following broad categories:

1. *Dividends Left to Accumulate at Interest.* The liability shown will include accrued interest to the date of the statement.
2. *Premiums Received in Advance and Premium Deposit Funds.* On premiums received in advance, the liability is the then discounted value, at the rate of discount allowed, of the premiums received but not yet due.

---

[7] See Chapter 72 for analysis of company investments.

[8] See Chapter 12 for analysis of reserves.

3. *Policyowner Dividends for the Following Year.* In respect to participating business, the generally accepted practice (except on group insurance) is to set up as a liability the estimated amount of dividends to policyowners for the entire following calendar year. This is on the theory that dividends in a given calendar year should be paid out of surplus earned in the preceding calendar year.
4. *Claims in Course of Settlement.* This or some similar heading embraces the following liabilities:

   a) Claims due but unpaid. This liability should be very small or nonexistent, since claims are usually paid as soon as the completed papers are received.
   b) Resisted claims. This is also usually a small item.
   c) Other claims in course of settlement. This includes claims which are still under investigation or for which complete papers have not been received.
   d) Estimated liability for claims incurred on or before December 31 but not reported by that date.
5. *Taxes Accrued, Payable in Following Year.* Much of the premium tax and federal income tax incurred in any year is not due until the following year, so that the liability for accrued taxes is usually substantial.
6. *Miscellaneous Liabilities.* The following are typical examples of miscellaneous liabilities:

   a) Expenses (including commissions) due or accrued but not yet paid.
   b) Dividends due to policyowners but not yet paid because they are to be applied to reduce premiums which have not been paid.
   c) Investment income paid in advance. Any interest (usually on mortgages and policy loans) or rents due after December 31 but paid to the company on or before December 31 must be set up as a liability, so that the surplus is just the same as though the interest is not received until the year it is due.
   d) Liability for funded retirement plans for employees or agents. This liability may be included in the regular reserves mentioned above or as a miscellaneous liability.
7. *Mandatory Securities Valuation Reserve.* Beginning in 1951, the convention blank for life and health companies has included as a liability a "mandatory securities valuation reserve." The amount of this reserve is determined by rather complex rules established by the NAIC.[9] The purpose is to accumulate a reserve over a period of years to protect against adverse fluctuations in the values of securities (bonds and stocks) and against losses on their sale. The reserve is built up by annual increments until it reaches a specified maximum. The amount of the increment for any one year depends on the values of the bonds and stocks held, and on the net capital gains on bonds and stocks during the year. Companies have been permitted, within limits, to add to the reserve more than the required increment.

   It was anticipated originally that it might take nearly twenty years for most companies to build the mandatory securities valuation reserve up

[9] Revision of these rules and of the rules for the valuation of securities is under consideration in 1964 by committees representing the NAIC and the life insurance business.

to the maximum. However, because of large capital gains (both realized and unrealized) since 1951, many companies with common stock holdings reached the maximum as early as 1955.

This reserve relates only to bonds and stocks. It is not intended to protect against depreciation in the values of other types of investments, such as mortgages and real estate; such investments have no effect on the size of this reserve.

8. *Special Liabilities.* Companies occasionally set up liability items of various kinds to cover special situations where there is greater uncertainty than usual as to whether there actually will be any additional liability, or where it is too difficult to determine exactly the amount of the extra liability to warrant including it in the regular items. Such items would be shown separately in the convention blank. In the annual report, however, these special items would probably be included under "miscellaneous liabilities" unless they were unusually large.

Capital and Surplus

As indicated earlier, the excess of assets over liabilities consists of capital and surplus.[10] Capital, of course, appears only on the balance sheets of stock companies. Although it represents the interest of the stockholders in the company, it nevertheless is available for the protection of the policyowners. Their interests come before those of the stockholders if the company runs into any difficulties.

Surplus appears in the convention blank (and also in the annual report) in one of two forms:

1. *Special Surplus Funds.* In some companies, part or all of the surplus is allocated to cover special contingencies. The types of contingencies which might be covered are illustrated by the following actual examples: "Voluntary Reserve for Strengthening of Policy Reserves," "Group Life Insurance Reserve for Epidemics," and "Special Reserve for Possible Loss or Fluctuation in the Value of Investments." A company may even carry its entire surplus in one special surplus fund to cover all unforeseen contingencies.
2. *Unassigned Surplus.* This represents either the entire surplus or the part not assigned to cover specific or general contingencies.

The earmarking of surplus to cover special contingencies can be changed from year to year. For example, a special reserve for investment fluctuation set up at the end of one year could be used during the following year to take care of mortality fluctuations.

---

[10] There is some tendency in the annual reports of companies (in other types of business as well as in insurance) to replace the word "surplus" by some term such as "contingency reserve" or "margin for contingencies." This tendency stems from the possible unfavorable connotation of "surplus," which implies an excess, or more than is needed. Thus, surplus might imply to policyowners that a life company was retaining larger funds than necessary and paying smaller dividends to them than it could.

SUMMARY OF OPERATIONS

The "summary of operations" in the convention blank presents an analysis on an *accrued* basis of the operating income of the company for the year and of the disposition of the income, excluding in both cases certain types of nonrecurring items, such as capital gains and losses. These nonrecurring items are included in the "surplus account," described later.

Income

Income ordinarily consists of the following items:

1. *Premiums from Policyowners.* This is usually by far the largest income item.
2. *Considerations for Supplementary Contracts (Settlement Options) and Dividends Left to Accumulate at Interest.* Death claims, maturities, and surrenders are included in the benefits paid, even when the proceeds are placed under a settlement option. Therefore the amount of such proceeds must also be included in income if the books are to balance. A similar situation exists with respect to dividends left to accumulate, because such dividends are included in dividends paid.
3. *Investment Income (Interest, Dividends, Rents, and Other Income Arising from Investments).* The convention blank calls for reporting investment income on a "net" basis, that is, *after* deducting investment expenses and taxes. (Federal income tax is not regarded as an investment tax.[11])
4. *Miscellaneous Income.* This is usually quite small in relation to total income; it includes minor items which do not fit clearly into one of the first three categories mentioned.

Deductions from Income

It might be expected that "income" would be followed by "outgo" in the summary of operations. However, the term "outgo" should not, strictly speaking, be used as the counterpart of "income." Much of the income of a life insurance company does not actually "go out" in the same year it is received but instead is retained for the benefit of policyowners and beneficiaries in the form of increased reserves and increased surplus (if the company is growing satisfactorily). Therefore, a more accurate term, such as "disposition of income" or "how the income was applied," is often used in annual reports to refer to the various items deducted from income to obtain the net gain from operations.

Many of the "deductions from income" are self-explanatory. The items may be grouped into the following major categories:

---

[11] The method of handling federal income tax was radically changed in the convention blank for 1963. The new method is used throughout this chapter.

1. *Contractual Benefits to Policyowners and Beneficiaries.* These benefits include:

   a) Death benefits (including accidental death benefits).
   b) Matured endowments.
   c) Disability and health insurance benefits.
   d) Annuity payments (including annuity surrender values).
   e) Cash surrender values of insurance.
   f) Payments under supplementary contracts.
   g) Withdrawals of accumulated dividends.

   As mentioned earlier, the figures for benefits paid include policy proceeds left with the company under supplementary contracts as well as proceeds paid out in cash.
2. *Increase in Required Reserves Held for the Benefit of Policyowners and Beneficiaries.* This represents the increase in these reserves from the beginning of the year to the end of the year.
3. *Operating Expenses and Taxes.* This category excludes investment expenses and taxes (which are deducted from gross investment income) and also excludes federal income taxes. The principal types of disbursements included here are:

   a) Compensation of employees.
   b) Compensation of agents. A substantial part of the total expenses usually consists of commissions and other forms of compensation to agents (including brokers).
   c) General operating expense. This includes such expenses as rent, furniture, equipment, supplies, printing, postage, telephone, and advertising. In order to keep expenses on a comparable basis whether the home office is owned or rented, a company which owns a home office building is required to charge itself rent on a reasonable basis. As a result, home office rent is counted both as an expense and as an offsetting income item when the home office is owned. Except among the smaller companies, most companies own their home offices.
   d) Taxes, such as state taxes on premiums (which are a substantial amount), miscellaneous license fees, and social security taxes.

Net Gain from Operations and Dividends to Policyowners

In the last part of the summary of operations in the convention blank, the net gain from operations, dividends to policyowners, and federal income tax (excluding the tax on capital gains) are taken into consideration. Capital gains and losses are excluded in this last part, which is essentially as follows:

1. Net gain from operations before dividends to policyowners and federal income taxes—this net gain is equal to the income less the above deductions from income.
2. Dividends to policyowners.
3. Net gain from operations after dividends to policyowners and before federal income taxes (item 1 minus item 2).
4. Federal income taxes incurred.
5. Net gain from operations after dividends to policyowners and federal income taxes (item 3 minus item 4).

Treatment of Federal Income Tax

The federal income tax on an accrued basis is divided into the following three parts, each of which is treated differently in the convention blank:

1. Tax on current year's operations (excluding tax on capital gains)—this part is the same as item 4, mentioned in the preceding paragraph.
2. Tax on capital gains realized during the year—this part is deducted from the year's capital gains before the capital gains are brought into the surplus account, as described below.
3. Extraordinary amounts of taxes relating to prior years, including extraordinary refunds of taxes relating to prior years.

SURPLUS ACCOUNT

In the convention blank the summary of operations is followed by an analysis of the surplus account, which reconciles the surplus at the beginning and end of the year. The method of reconciliation is as follows:

To the unassigned surplus at the beginning of the year, add any additions during the year, such as:

1. Net gain from operations *after* dividends to policyowners and federal income taxes (excluding tax on capital gains) and excluding capital gains and losses.
2. Net capital gains (realized and unrealized), less any federal income tax on realized gains.
3. Decrease in mandatory securities valuation reserve.
4. Decreases in special surplus funds.
5. Increase in surplus of "separate account business" (this term is explained later).

From the sum, subtract any deductions from unassigned surplus during the year, such as:

1. Dividends to stockholders.
2. Net capital losses (realized and unrealized).
3. Extraordinary taxes relating to prior years.
4. Increase in reserves on account of change in valuation basis (reserve strengthening).
5. Increase in mandatory securities valuation reserve.
6. Increases in special surplus funds.
7. Decrease in surplus of separate account business.

The balance is equal to the unassigned surplus at the end of the year.

The surplus account is very helpful in giving an over-all view of all factors affecting the company's surplus.

SEPARATE ACCOUNT BLANK

A number of states have recently passed legislation granting to domestic life insurance companies the right, subject to certain prescribed conditions, to establish "separate accounts" for the handling of funds paid to a company in connection with pension or profit sharing plans.[12] Any investment income and any capital gains or losses on a separate account are credited or charged to the separate account. The insurance company in general makes no guarantees under a separate account and has no liability other than for proper handling of the funds.

At the present time, all detailed entries in respect to separate accounts are recorded in a special "separate account blank" to be completed by each insurance company which is doing any separate account business. Certain items and totals from the separate account blank are then included in the regular convention blank in order that the latter may show the financial picture for the entire company.

This method of handling separate accounts is a temporary expedient, first adopted for the year 1962. Changes in this method are under study by committees representing the NAIC and the life insurance business.

DIFFERENCES BETWEEN LIFE INSURANCE ACCOUNTING AND GENERALLY ACCEPTED ACCOUNTING PRACTICES

Financial reports of life and health insurance companies differ considerably from those of most other corporations largely because such insurance companies have unique accounting problems, arising from the long-term nature of their insurance policies and from the assumptions which must be made with respect to mortality, morbidity, and investment return.[13] Major differences between the accounting practices of such insurance companies and generally accepted accounting practices include the following points:

1. Commissions and other costs of acquiring premium income are charged to operations as they are incurred, rather than being deferred and charged to operations as the related income is produced. As a result, there is usually a substantial drain on surplus for each new policy sold (par-

---

[12] See Chapter 40 for analysis of separate accounts pension funding.

[13] "The results in any given year, as shown by a life insurance company's annual statement, are so much the product of estimates of future liabilities based on probabilities that the results themselves are essentially estimates instead of actualities" (statement by American Life Convention, Life Insurance Association of America, and Life Insurance Conference, submitted on June 24, 1963, to Subcommittee on Securities of the Senate Banking and Currency Committee).

ticularly if reserves are set up on the net level premium basis). Consequently, an increase in the amount of new insurance sold may produce the anomalous result of a decrease in the net gain from operations, and a decrease in the new insurance sold may result in an increase in the net gain from operations.

2. The asset values used for bonds and for preferred stocks are amortized values and "adjusted" values, respectively, rather than current market values.
3. The "nonadmitted assets," described earlier, are arbitrarily excluded from the assets as shown in the convention blank and in annual reports.
4. The asset values used for any stocks owned of insurance company affiliates are the latter's book value without any recognition of market value or of any excess of cost over related book value.
5. The mandatory securities valuation reserve is set up as a liability, rather than being subtracted from the assets, which is a more generally accepted method of handling reserves set up against decreases in the values of assets. Moreover, the amount of the mandatory securities valuation reserve is not directly related to the quality and current value of the securities.
6. No liability is set up for future income tax liability on any accrued but unrealized net capital gains.

EXHIBITS AND SCHEDULES IN THE CONVENTION BLANK

Exhibits

Following the summary of operations and the surplus account in the convention blank is what is called the "gain and loss exhibit." The first part of this exhibit consists of a breakdown of each item in the summary of operations by *line of business,* as follows: (1) industrial, (2) ordinary, (3) group life insurance, (4) group annuities, (5) group health insurance, and (6) individual health insurance. The *ordinary* line is further subdivided into (1) life insurance, (2) disability, (3) accidental death benefits, (4) annuities, and (5) supplementary contracts.

The second part of the gain and loss exhibit is an analysis (by line of business, excluding health insurance) of the increase (or decrease) in the policy reserves from the beginning of the year to the end of the year.

There are many other exhibits and schedules in the convention blank which provide analyses of or further details in regard to items which appear only in total in the balance sheet or the summary of operations. The numbered exhibits cover the following subjects:

Exhibit 1. Premium income and commissions.
Exhibits 2 and 3. Investment income.
Exhibit 4. Capital gains and losses.
Exhibit 5. General expenses.
Exhibit 6. Taxes, licenses, and fees (excluding federal income taxes).
Exhibit 7. Dividends to policyowners.
Exhibits 8, 9, and 10. Policy and supplementary contract reserves.
Exhibit 11. Policy claims.

Exhibit 12. Reconciliation of ledger assets from the end of the previous year to the end of the current year.

Exhibits 13 and 14. Ledger, nonledger, nonadmitted, and admitted assets.

There is also a "policy exhibit" analyzing the life insurance issued, terminated, and in force, and a corresponding "annuity exhibit." Following the exhibits, there is a page of "general interrogatories" about the company's history and operations.

Schedules

In general, the lettered schedules show even more detail than the numbered exhibits. Among the more important schedules are those dealing with invested assets: Schedule A, real estate; Schedule B, mortgages; Schedule C, collateral loans; Schedule D, bonds and stocks; and Schedule BA, other invested assets, such as transportation equipment, mineral rights, and oil royalties. These schedules show, in various classifications, the amounts owned at the end of the year and purchases and sales during the year. In Schedules C, D, and BA, each holding is listed individually.

Other important lettered schedules give detailed information on the following subjects:

Schedule E. Bank balances.

Schedule F. Resisted and compromised claims.

Schedule G. Salaries of ten highest paid persons and of all others receiving more than $20,000 a year.

Schedule J. Legal fees.

Schedule K. Expenses in connection with appearances before legislative bodies.

Schedule L. Proceedings at the last annual election of directors.

Schedule M. Dividends per $1,000 of insurance paid to policyowners in the current year on certain plans of life insurance.

Schedule T. Premiums received, analyzed by state—this schedule is helpful to the state taxing authorities in checking the payment of premium taxes.

ANNUAL REPORTS TO POLICYOWNERS AND STOCKHOLDERS

The scope and the amount of detail included in annual reports to policyowners and/or stockholders vary considerably from company to company (and even from year to year in many companies). In general, the annual reports present in condensed form the balance sheet, the summary of operations, and the surplus account. Frequently, a number of other items are presented. Also, there is often considerable explanatory text, frequently of a sales promotion nature. The information given in the report serves its purpose only when it is read and understood, so companies try to make their reports readable and useful in promoting good public relations.

Differences between Annual Reports and Convention Blank

In addition to the fact that the information in an annual report is condensed, there are often other differences between the presentation of information in an annual report and the presentation in the convention blank, particularly in the summary of operations. The more common important areas of difference include the following:

1. In the convention blank, considerations for supplementary contracts are shown separately from premiums. In annual reports, considerations for supplementary contracts are often included in premiums.
2. In the convention blank, investment income is reported on a *net* basis, that is, *after* deducting investment expenses and taxes. Many companies, in their annual reports, follow the precedent of the convention blank and show net investment income; but a number of companies show investment income on a *gross* basis, that is, *before* deducting investment expenses and taxes (in which case these investment expenses and taxes are included with other expenses and taxes in the "deductions from income"). Or a company may use some intermediate basis, deducting certain parts (but not all) of investment expenses and taxes to determine the investment income shown in its annual report.
3. In the convention blank, the "dividends to policyowners" item is the next to the last deduction in the summary of operations. However, many companies, in their annual reports, include dividends to policyowners with other benefit payments to policyowners and beneficiaries, so that such dividends appear instead as one of the first deductions from income. By following this procedure, these companies avoid showing the "net gain from operations before dividends to policyowners." The term "net gain" may carry an incorrect connotation, implying that the company, as distinguished from the policyowners, is profiting from the gain. Therefore, there is some feeling that using the term "net gain" is inadvisable. This applies particularly to "net gain before dividends," which is almost always a comparatively large figure in companies issuing participating insurance. The use in annual reports of the term "net gain after dividends" may also be avoided by using some title such as "transfer to surplus account" for what would otherwise be "net gain from operations after dividends to policyholders and federal income tax."
4. In the convention blank, all capital gains and losses are included in the surplus account. However, some companies, in their annual reports, instead include some or all of their net capital gains in regular income.

"ADJUSTED" FIGURES FOR STOCK INSURANCE COMPANIES

A buyer or seller of capital stock in a life or health insurance company wants to have as good an idea as possible of what is a fair price. The book value of the stock may not necessarily be a good indicator of its fair market value, partly because there is usually a drain on surplus when new business is sold, and partly because in many companies (particularly the older ones) there is probably some understatement of surplus as a result of valuing assets low and liabilities high.

To attempt to arrive at a better indicator of reasonable prices for insurance company stocks, many stock analysts and some insurance trade publications calculate "adjusted book values" and "adjusted earnings" for each company, taking into consideration by rough rules of thumb the value of (1) the insurance in force and (2) the increase during the year in the insurance in force.

The values assigned vary by the type of insurance. Typical schedules used for nonparticipating insurance might be somewhat as follows:

Individual life and endowment. . .	$15 to $25 per $1,000 insurance
Individual term.	$5.00 to $7.50 per $1,000 insurance
Group life.	$2.00 to $5.00 per $1,000 insurance
Individual health.	25 to 35 per cent of premiums
Group health.	0 to 10 per cent of premiums

The value assigned to participating business would depend in part on any statute or charter limitations on the earnings that stockholders may derive from participating business.

"Conditional reserves" and their increase during the year may also be treated as equivalent to surplus in calculating "adjusted book values" and "adjusted earnings." These conditional reserves include the mandatory securities valuation reserve and amounts voluntarily set aside by management as reserves for possible future contingencies.

It should be strongly emphasized that these rough rules of thumb for determining "adjusted book values" and "adjusted earnings" overlook many factors which have a marked effect on the proper value of the insurance in force. Among the more important of these factors are (1) the level of the gross premiums, (2) the interest rates assumed and earned, (3) the recent mortality experience, (4) the recent lapse rates, (5) the level of expenses, (6) the bases for valuing the insurance and annuity reserves, and (7) the quality of the assets.

The use of empirical schedules of the value of insurance as described above is by no means the only method used by analysts. Unfortunately, few of these methods take into consideration the characteristics of a particular company. Moreover, these methods generally involve the implicit assumption of the continuance of past trends for the life of the company. Hence the analyst is merely substituting different assumptions for those used by the company itself either by choice or by requirement of regulatory authorities.

While calculations of "adjusted" figures are within the authority of a security analyst, they are not within the authority of the company itself. In a number of states a company cannot publish the amount of its surplus on any basis other than that in the convention blank filed with the insurance department. Therefore, these adjustments necessarily have the weakness that they are made by persons outside rather than inside the company.

THE STRENGTH OF A COMPANY AS REVEALED BY ITS ANNUAL STATEMENT

How Realistic Are Balance Sheets?

"Value the assets low and the liabilities high." This epigram probably represents the basic policy of the great majority of the life companies which have been established long enough to have the margins required for such a corporate policy. This does not mean that management arbitrarily fixes a low value on assets and a high value on liabilities, but simply that management generally tends, where a choice is presented, to choose the low value for an asset item and the high value for a liability item. State regulatory authorities often have encouraged this attitude in order to provide additional protection for the policyowners. Some examples of the application of such a policy will be presented.

Assets. Because of the definite rules of the NAIC on the valuation of securities and mortgages, conservatism in the valuation of specific assets is largely limited to two minor categories. These are:

1. *Real Estate, Particularly the Home Office and Real Estate Acquired by Foreclosure.* Real estate is supposed to be carried at its market value, but there is almost always leeway for judgment as to what is a fair market value at any time. Life companies usually tend to choose a conservative value; this tendency is furthered by the fact that it is common to write values down in deflationary periods but unusual to write them up in inflationary periods.
2. *Nonadmitted Assets.* Furniture and equipment are valuable assets in a going company (although they would probably have little value in the unlikely circumstance that the company had to be liquidated). The balances of most agents will eventually be collected. Therefore, treating furniture and equipment and agents' balances as nonadmitted assets tends to understate the true value of the assets.

The fact that no value is assigned to good will, to the agency force, or to future earnings on the insurance in force, is, of course, another instance of conservatism in determining the assets.

Liabilities. There is much more room for judgment in valuing the liabilities than in valuing the assets because the contingent nature of the major liabilities makes it necessary to assume interest rates for the calculation of present values as well as mortality and morbidity tables to measure any contingencies involved.

Unlike the convention blank, an annual report almost never gives any indication of the mortality and interest bases used in the calculation of reserves or of whether the life insurance reserves are calculated by the net level premium method or by a modified preliminary term method. As a result, it is almost impossible to tell from an annual report whether the reserve basis is at or near the prescribed minimum or whether the basis involves substantial margins of conservatism. Some trade publications, however, give information on the interest rates used in reserve calculations and also on the extent to which the net level premium method or other methods are used to determine the life insurance reserves.

Conservatism also may be introduced by the methods used in the valuation of some of the minor liabilities. An area in which companies differ considerably in setting up liabilities is the funding of retirement plans for employees and agents. With formal pension plans steadily becoming more nearly a *sine qua non* for good employee relations, it is probable that sooner or later all life companies will set up formal funded plans. Viewed in this light, companies which have not set up reserves for past service credits could be regarded as having undervalued their future liability for this item.

The mandatory securities valuation reserve is designed to involve a definite overstatement of liabilities. It introduces some inconsistencies between companies, since the relative size of the reserve is affected by all capital gains and losses on securities from 1951 on as well as by the current investment portfolio.

Measures of the Strength of a Company

Although the entire picture—assets, liabilities, insurance in force, level of premiums, mortality experience, and so forth—is necessary in appraising the strength of a life company, nevertheless the single item which is of greatest significance as an indicator of the strength of a company is total surplus (including capital stock and special surplus funds as well as unassigned surplus). This figure is compared in most annual reports with the corresponding figure for the previous year, and the significant factors affecting the change from one year to the next are usually explained. It is particularly important that a suitable explanation be given if there is a decrease in surplus.

As an absolute figure, the amount of the surplus has little meaning. The surplus can only be evaluated in relation to some measuring rod. The two most commonly used relationships are (1) surplus as a percentage of liabilities and (2) surplus per $1,000 of insurance in force.

Surplus as a Percentage of Liabilities. Use of the ratio of surplus to liabilities has received the quasi approval of regulatory authorities, as evidenced by the fact that one large state limits surplus in life companies writing participating policies to $850,000 or 10 per cent of "policy reserves and policy liabilities," if greater.[14] Nevertheless, this ratio is not completely satisfactory, because the surplus needed in relation to particular liabilities varies by type of business.

For example, the reserves on both group and health insurance are

[14] The general purpose of this law is to prevent an undue accumulation of surplus at the expense of policyowners and to insure *annual* distribution of dividends.

usually quite small in relation to the amounts at risk. Therefore, a surplus of 10 per cent of the reserves might be inadequate on group or health insurance. On the other hand, on types of business which do not involve mortality or morbidity contingencies—such types as supplementary contracts without life contingencies or dividends left to accumulate—surplus is needed only to protect against investment contingencies, so that a comparatively small surplus in relation to the liability would be satisfactory. Moreover, business with reserves on a minimum basis should probably have more surplus in relation to its liabilities than business with reserves on a very conservative basis.

When surplus is expressed as a percentage of liabilities, no allowance is made for the proportions of the various types of liabilities. Therefore, this ratio is not entirely satisfactory for comparing companies which differ significantly in the composition of their business or in the basis of their reserves. Despite this drawback, this ratio is probably the most nearly satisfactory simple criterion for measuring the financial strength of a company.

Because the mandatory securities valuation reserve is not a true liability, it can be argued that it should be subtracted from liabilities before calculating the ratio of surplus to liabilities. This refinement is theoretically justifiable but is probably unnecessary from a practical viewpoint.

Surplus per $1,000 of Insurance. Surplus per $1,000 of insurance in force has the advantage of giving greater weight to group insurance than does the ratio of surplus to liabilities. But surplus per $1,000 of insurance in force also has some disadvantages. This figure probably gives too great weight to group insurance. Also, it does not give any weight to annuities, supplementary contracts, health insurance, and the minor types of liabilities; all of these categories certainly need some surplus held for them. A minor disadvantage is the problem of how to handle reinsurance in calculating this figure. Business ceded to another company as reinsurance is usually included in the amount of insurance in force; but clearly, not much surplus is needed on business ceded to another company on the coinsurance basis.[15]

To a certain extent, the ratio of surplus to liabilities and the surplus per $1,000 of insurance are figures which complement each other. Probably a truer picture of a company can generally be obtained by looking at both figures than by looking at either figure alone.

Effect of Mandatory Securities Valuation Reserve. The mandatory securities valuation reserve, when it reaches its permitted maximum (as it has in a number of companies), may represent 3 or even 4 per cent of the assets. Reserves of this size may be expected to have some long-term influence on the amounts retained as surplus, because a company with a

---

[15] See Chapter 74 for analysis of reinsurance.

large mandatory securities valuation reserve would be likely to hold a smaller surplus than an equally prudent company with a small reserve (all other things being equal). Therefore, it seems reasonable to speculate that both the ratio of surplus to liabilities and the amount of surplus per $1,000 of insurance in force may tend in general to decrease very gradually over a period of years.

Other Measures of Strength. Two ratios which are sometimes used as measures of the strength of a company involve "assets" instead of surplus. These ratios are (1) assets as a percentage of the liabilities and (2) assets per $1,000 of insurance in force.

Because the assets are equal to the liabilities plus the surplus, the figure for assets as a percentage of liabilities is simply 100 per cent more than the figure for surplus as a percentage of liabilities. Therefore, similar results will be obtained whether comparisons are based on the ratio of surplus to liabilities or on the ratio of assets to liabilities.

On the other hand, the amount of assets per $1,000 of insurance in force is almost completely meaningless as a measure of the strength of a company. This figure does not reflect the strength of a company as much as it does the age and composition of the company's business.

SELECTED REFERENCES

BLAIR, B. FRANKLIN. *Interpreting Life Insurance Company Annual Reports.* Bryn Mawr, Pa.: American College of Life Underwriters, 1960.

GOLD, M. L. "Valuing a Life Insurance Company," *Transactions of the Society of Actuaries,* Vol. XIV, No. 3 (1962), pp. 139–57.

MACLEAN, JOSEPH B. *Life Insurance.* 9th ed. New York: McGraw-Hill Book Co., Inc., 1962.

WIGHTMAN, E. C. *Life Insurance Statements and Accounts. New York:* Life Office Management Association, 1952.

Chapter 74

LIFE AND HEALTH REINSURANCE

BY WALTER W. STEFFEN

Reinsurance Defined

Reinsurance can be defined as an insurance agreement or contract under which one insurer, often called the *ceding company,* is indemnified against loss by another insurer, called the *reinsurer,* arising out of an insurance policy written by the original insurer. Thus a reinsurance contract is a separate insurance agreement and presupposes the existence of an original policy. This is emphasized by the terms of the usual reinsurance agreement, which state that it is an agreement solely between the insurer and the reinsurer, and creates no right or legal relationship whatever between the reinsurer and any insured or beneficiary of a policy issued by the insurer.

There are two exceptions to the application of this indemnity principle. Reinsurance agreements specifically provide that reinsurance shall be paid without diminution because of the insolvency of the original insurer (in such an event the original insurer might pay less than the full amount of claims). It is also specifically provided in reinsurance agreements that both the insurer and the reinsurer share in any reduction in the amount of compromised claims or adjustment in the amount of claims involving a misstatement of age.

The reinsurance agreement is the master contract under which individual policies of reinsurance, called *cessions,* are placed in effect and administered. The agreement is unlimited in duration but may be terminated with respect to new business on proper notice by either party. It is customary to say that in placing reinsurance, in effect, the original insurer is ceding reinsurance to the reinsurer.

Values of Reinsurance

Through the use of reinsurance, an insurer will be able to issue policies for amounts in excess of its retention limit. It is in the best interest of the insuring public that this be true. It is also in the best interests of the insurer and the reinsurer. It is an obvious convenience if an applicant can purchase insurance in the required amount from one company rather than being forced to purchase a number of policies with varying conditions from a number of companies. Also, insurance protection will be distributed to a greater proportion of those needing protection if the life underwriters of many companies are in a position to supply insurance protection to applicants requiring large amounts and to applicants who are not eligible for insurance at standard rates. Life underwriters benefit through the placing of additional insurance in an expanded market. The insurance industry benefits by reducing the waste arising out of policies which are applied for but not issued.

Further, the knowledge of the industry regarding classification of impaired risks is increased in the most economical manner, since reinsuring companies serve as a focal point for the collection of such risks where statistically significant volumes of consistently underwritten and coded business are accumulated and subjected to extensive analysis by an experienced staff. Improved underwriting standards are promulgated as a result of such analyses. This process is more efficient than if each insuring company found it necessary to attempt to perform its own underwriting research—even, as is unlikely to be the case except for a very few of the largest companies, if statistically significant volumes of such business were available for study. Finally, the reinsurer benefits through the acquisition of business which is expected to prove profitable in the long run.

Retention Limit

The maximum amount of insurance which an insurer will carry on one life at its own risk without reinsurance protection is called the *retention limit* of the insurer. Fundamentally, the retention limit is set so as to avoid inconvenient fluctuations in earnings because of claims involving large amounts. Although determination of a retention limit is in part an actuarial problem, it also involves considerations not subject to precise quantitative analysis. The factors of significance in setting the retention are the amount of the insurer's surplus, the expected mortality, the distribution of insurance in force per life, the distribution of new issues by size, the distribution of in-force and new issues by age at issue and underwriting classification, underwriting skill, the degree of earnings stability desired, and the cost of the reinsurance ceded.

The statistical aspect of the problem is handled most conveniently, although incompletely, by a branch of actuarial mathematics known as the collective theory of risk. As a practical matter, however, the limit is usually set conservatively by studying the impact of retentions of different levels on the volumes of business which would be ceded at those levels, the retention limit being established at a level which will keep the volume of business ceded, and therefore the cost of reinsurance, at a reasonable level. After an appropriate retention limit for standard business issued at the central ages has been determined, the limit typically is graded down at the higher issue ages and for substandard risks. This is done primarily because classification of risks at extreme ages and those which do not qualify for standard insurance is less certain than the classification of standard risks at the more common issue ages.

Reinsurance agreements provide that the ceding company may increase its limit of retention on new business and specify the conditions under which amounts of existing reinsurance may be reduced because of the increased limit of retention. Amounts of reinsurance so reduced are said to be recaptured.

Relationship of Insurer and Reinsurer

The outstanding characteristic of the relationship between insurer and reinsurer is that of utmost good faith. The frequently used description "gentlemen's agreement" is appropriate. The obligation of the insuring company to disclose information about the risk to the reinsurer even exceeds the obligation of the insured to disclose such information in his dealings with the original insurer. In return, the reinsurer follows in every respect the fortunes of the insuring company on policies reinsured. Since it is impractical to attempt to cover all situations which may arise, the reinsurance agreement is drafted along broad and general lines. Binding arbitration of differences of opinion or interpretation is provided for by the reinsurance treaty. The arbitrators are not bound by any rules of law and are required to regard the treaty from the standpoints of practical business and equity rather than of strict law. Insurers and reinsurers generally take great pride in the fact that almost all differences of opinion are resolved by the parties to the agreement. Arbitration is extremely rare in the field of life insurance.

Life Reinsurance Plans

Ordinary life reinsurance is usually accomplished on one of three plans: (1) risk premium reinsurance (RPR), sometimes referred to as yearly renewable term (YRT) or annual renewable term (ART); (2) coinsurance; and (3) modified coinsurance.

Risk Premium Reinsurance. The RPR plan is the one used by the largest number of companies in this country. Under the RPR plan the insurer buys reinsurance for the net amount at risk allocable to amounts of insurance in excess of its retention limit. The net amount at risk is the face amount of the policy payable upon the insured's death less the terminal reserve. This reflects the fact that the reserve will be released at death, thereby diminishing the insurer's net surplus loss. The relatively small terminal reserves involved on level term insurance of twenty years' or less duration and on decreasing term insurance of all durations are ignored as an administrative convenience.

The RPR premium is as specified in the reinsurance agreement. Customarily, the first-year reinsurance premium is one half the renewal premium for the same attained age, in recognition of the fact that the original insurer's first-year expenses are higher than its renewal expenses. Table 74–1 illustrates the calculation. This example is based on reinsurance of $10,000 of whole life insurance with reserves according to the 1958 CSO Table, 3 per cent interest, Commissioners Reserve Valuation Method, and assuming that premiums are paid annually and claims are paid at the end of the policy year of death. The insured is a male aged 35 at issue.

Customarily, further distinctions are made in reinsurance premium rates by sex, by underwriting classification, and according to whether or

TABLE 74–1

ILLUSTRATIVE PREMIUM COMPUTATIONS FOR RISK PREMIUM REINSURANCE PLAN

Attained Age	Gross Amount of Reinsurance	Terminal Reserve Thereon	Net Amount at Risk	Life Reinsurance Premium per Thousand	Total Life Reinsurance Premium
35.	$10,000	$ 0	$10,000	$2.07*	$20.70
36.	10,000	149	9,851	4.35	42.85
37.	10,000	300	9,700	4.59	44.52
38.	10,000	455	9,545	4.85	46.29
39.	10,000	613	9,387	5.14	48.25

* Renewal premium is $4.13 per $1,000 at age 35.

not the insurer is to receive experience refunds from the reinsurer in the event of favorable reinsurance experience. Naturally, nonrefund rates are lower than experience refund rates. It is also usually provided that the amount of insurance to be placed in the experience refund account on an individual life be limited to stabilize the insuring company's net reinsurance cost. Amounts in excess of this prescribed maximum are most frequently reinsured on the basis of lower nonrefund reinsurance premium rates—although certain other methods of net reinsurance cost stabilization are used by various reinsurers. In life reinsurance the experience refund typically depends solely on the experience in the reinsurance account of the individual original insurer, although a system of pooled refunds based on the over-all experience of the reinsurer is sometimes used for special categories of risks.

Because the RPR premiums contain no investment element, the premiums for risks subject to percentage extra mortality would be multiples of the standard reinsurance premiums were it not for the expense element. Although premiums for substandard risks must reflect the higher expenses associated with substandard business, the total expense is less than a multiple of the standard expense. Thus, substandard premiums are somewhat less than multiples of standard premiums. Table 74–2, showing renewal RPR rates per $1,000 for a risk aged 35, will illustrate differences between male, female, refund, nonrefund, and standard and substandard premiums.

When the insured is assessed a flat extra premium, such as $5.00 per thousand per year, the extra premium allocable to reinsured amounts, less a commission and expense allowance, is paid to the reinsurer. Customarily, standard reserves are used to determine the net amount at risk on all substandard business. Reinsurance premiums are paid annually with a refund on termination other than the policy anniversary. Of course, RPR premiums are payable during the continuance of the risk, even though the original policy may become paid up. It is customary for reinsurance claims to be payable in one sum, regardless of the mode of settlement selected under the provisions of the original policy. Typically, an insurance company pays premium tax on its premium income before deduction of premiums paid for reinsurance ceded and before addition of premiums received on reinsurance accepted. Therefore a reinsurer reimburses the original insurer for the premium taxes allocable to the insurer's ceded premiums.

TABLE 74–2

ILLUSTRATIVE RISK PREMIUM REINSURANCE PREMIUM RATES

	Standard Mortality	200 Per Cent of Standard Mortality	300 Per Cent of Standard Mortality	400 Per Cent of Standard Mortality	500 Per Cent of Standard Mortality
Male refund	$4.13	$7.39	$10.65	$13.91	$17.17
Male nonrefund	3.24	5.80	8.36	10.92	13.48
Female refund	3.54	6.41	9.28	12.15	15.02
Female nonrefund	2.92	5.31	7.70	10.09	12.48

The RPR plan is widely used because of its many advantages. These advantages include the following:

1. The original insurer retains the investment element of the premium necessary to accumulate the policy reserve. Therefore, excess interest earning thereon will accrue to the insuring company, although there is the associated risk of investment losses. Also, to a young company the increased assets resulting from the retention of this investment element of the premium may be important as a measure of prestige.
2. Administratively, the plan is simple and easily understood. There are no dividends, commissions, or cash surrender values with which one need be concerned.
3. Since the reinsurance is all on the term plan, the computation of experience refunds also is simple and easily understood.

4. The reinsurer's investment in the business is modest so that, typically, business is eligible for recapture after it has been in force for five years and meets the other applicable recapture provisions of the reinsurance agreement. This five-year period gives the reinsurer an opportunity to recover its initial expense.
5. The expense of installing the reinsurance plan is minimal, since no extensive analysis of the insurer's price, commission, and benefit structure is required.

Accidental death benefits are reinsured either with life coverages or alone. Because of the small premium involved, it is important that the expense of administration of accidental death reinsurance without life be kept at a minimum. This is accomplished by simplified procedures which utilize a cession card and avoid the forwarding of any other papers to the reinsurer except in unusual circumstances. Typically, a scale of rates varying by occupational class but constant by attained age is used. As is true in the case of life reinsurance, a reduced first-year premium rate applies. The use of a flat rate is a great administrative convenience, but it may mean that at certain points in the original insurer's accidental death price structure the reinsurance premium may exceed the insurer's net premium income. This generally will be offset at other points of the insurer's accidental death price structure by reinsurance premiums substantially below the insurer's net premium income. Thus, this method works satisfactorily unless the insurer's distribution of business is unusual. It also should be remembered that antiselection by amount is a continuing feature of the studies of accidental death experience; therefore, the reinsurer's claim cost can be expected to be higher than the average claim cost of the original insurer. Because of the volatility of the accidental death coverage, experience refunds typically are a function of the reinsurer's over-all experience rather than being based solely on the experience of the individual reinsurance account.

It is customary to reinsure waiver-of-premium and disability income benefits in proportion to the amount of life insurance reinsured.

Coinsurance Plan. Confusion sometimes exists regarding the coinsurance plan as used in life reinsurance. In life reinsurance the term "coinsurance" is used to denote a plan of indemnity reinsurance.[1] The coinsurance plan involves reinsurance on the basis of the plan issued by the original insurer to the insured, and the reinsurance premium is the premium charged by the original insurer. Where the original insurer grades its premiums by size of policy, the reinsurance premium is that for the highest amount band or that excluding any policy fee, depending upon the method of grading used by the original insurer. The reinsurer pays

[1] This can be contrasted with an arrangement where two insurers are liable jointly to an insured. The term "coinsurance" is used in different ways in health insurance and in property insurance.

commissions and service fees according to the scale paid by the insurer. Service fees are frequently replaced by fully vested commissions of reduced amount, but with equivalent value, as an administrative convenience. An additional expense allowance, generally expressed as a percentage of the premium, is also paid by the reinsurer. The reinsurer thus accumulates the investment element of the premium and sets up the full reserve on the reinsured portion according to the valuation basis of the original insurer. The reinsurer grants cash surrender and other nonforfeiture values according to the provisions of the insurer's policy and follows the dividend scale of the insurer if the insurance is participating. As is true in the case of RPR, premiums are paid annually, and the reinsurer customarily reimburses the insurer for premium taxes. When dividends are graded by size, the reinsurer typically reimburses the insurer on the assumption that all dividends on reinsured policies are at the highest amount band rate. The reinsurer does not participate in policy loans, thus making the coinsurance method inappropriate for business under which it is expected that full policy loans will be maintained.

The advantages of the coinsurance plan are as follows:

1. When applied to participating business, the insurer has the guarantee that the reinsurer will follow the changes in its dividend scale and that the reinsurance net cost will follow the insurer's net cost.
2. Where the original insurer establishes reserves on the net level premium basis, the additional surplus loss (a frequently quoted average figure for this loss being $21 per thousand) necessitated by establishing the higher first-year reserve is absorbed by the reinsurer on the reinsured portion of the business.
3. Coupon policies sometimes sold by younger companies may involve a substantial surplus drain. Reinsurance on the coinsurance plan provides a means of passing on to the reinsurer a portion of this drain on reinsured business.
4. It might also be said that the coinsurance plan passes on to the reinsurer the investment risk on reinsured policies. It is doubtful, however, that this would often be considered as an advantage. However, in the case of very large policies which will ultimately represent "demand deposits" of unusually large magnitude in relation to the financial position of the insuring company, the coinsurance plan may be quite desirable for this reason.

The disadvantages of the coinsurance plan are as follows:

1. The assets of the original insurer are diminished.
2. Administration is somewhat more complex, particularly for participating business.
3. The time limit on recapture is longer because of the reinsurer's greater investment in the business. If the initial investment is substantial and the return is to be delayed for a long period of time, recapture may not be granted at all.
4. The determination of profits and, therefore, the experience refund formula must be more complex because many more items contributing to a

profit or loss on the business must be properly accounted for. In the computation of experience refunds, interest income is credited at the reinsurer's net earned rate less an allowance for capital losses in excess of capital gains.

5. An extensive analysis of the insurer's price structure is required in order to determine an appropriate expense allowance.

Modified Coinsurance Plan. The modified coinsurance plan is the same as the coinsurance plan, except that each year the current year's mean reserve on the reinsured portion, less the preceding year's mean reserve on the reinsured portion, plus interest thereon, is returned to the insurer. To avoid substantial transfers of funds at year end, this mean reserve adjustment is frequently made in periodic installments throughout the year. The interest rate referred to is the insurer's net earned rate less an adjustment for capital losses in excess of capital gains. This modification of the coinsurance plan removes one of the major disadvantages of this plan, in that the original insurer's assets are not diminished. In fact, since the reserve returned usually exceeds the reinsurer's net income at early policy durations, the insurer's assets are increased in these cases.

Automatic and Facultative Methods of Ceding Reinsurance

Reinsurance may be placed in effect either automatically or facultatively. When the facultative method is used, the insurer sends to the reinsurer copies of the application and all other evidence of insurability it has acquired. The reinsurer then classifies the risk (either immediately or upon receipt of such further evidence as it may require) and notifies the insurer by telegram of the basis on which it will accept the risk. When the automatic method is used, the insurer classifies the risk and notifies the reinsurer of the amount that has been ceded at the insurer's classification. Automatic reinsurance agreements specify the conditions under which the insurer may use the automatic method. The typical automatic reinsurance agreement provides that the insurer may cede automatically a percentage, say 400 per cent, of the amount of its retention on standard business and 400 per cent of the amount actually retained on the current application on substandard business. It is customary to provide that the insurer must retain its retention limit for the age and underwriting classification assigned the risk to avail itself of the automatic facility. All reinsurance which does not fall within the category eligible for automatic binding must be handled on a facultative basis. It is also usual for the reinsurance agreement to provide that reinsurance shall be by the facultative method when the total amount of insurance in force and applied for in all companies on a life exceeds, say, $1 million.

As might be expected, most reinsurance agreements that extend automatic facilities are obligatory, and most that provide for reinsurance by the facultative method only are nonobligatory. Under an obligatory treaty the insurer is required, in accordance with the provisions of the agreement, to cede its excess business to the reinsurer.

Much reinsurance that could be placed by the automatic method is, in practice, placed by the facultative method due to the preference of the insurer. The main advantage to the insurer of the automatic method is avoidance of any delay. The advantage to the insurer of the facultative method is that it receives the reinsurer's underwriting opinion before the policy is released. On occasion, the reinsurer may have had previous applications or may receive concurrent applications for reinsurance on the same life from different companies; and for this reason, it may have more complete underwriting information than any single insurer.

By agreeing to accept all business ceded automatically, the reinsurer is relying on the underwriting judgment of the insurer and is bound to accept a case even though it may not agree with the underwriting decision. The reinsurer is protected by the requirement that the original insurer retain its full retention limit, which assures a measure of self-interest. In actual practice, when any question of proper underwriting classification exists, the insurer usually does not use its automatic facility but instead secures an independent underwriting opinion by submitting the case facultatively.

Individual Health Reinsurance

In the individual health insurance field, principal sum benefits for accidental death and dismemberment and disability income benefits, particularly where there is a long maximum period of indemnity, frequently involve a substantial risk on an individual insured. Medical expense benefits rarely involve potential liabilities great enough to require reinsurance. A possible exception might be major medical benefits written by a young company with a modest surplus; most frequently, however, such a young company would restrict itself to basic hospitalization coverages if it entered the health insurance field at all. Principal sum benefits are reinsured in the same manner as accidental death benefits issued with life insurance. The reinsurer's premium structure, as is true of the premium structure of the original insurer, will take into account differences in the two coverages. The most important of these differences is the different degree of selection exercised by the insured. Higher accidental death claim costs will, for example, be characteristic of policies providing accidental death coverage only. Reinsurance of such benefits is usually on the coinsurance plan.

Reinsurance of disability income benefits also is most frequently on the coinsurance plan. This is because of the great variety of benefits offered by the different companies and because of the influence of a particular company's underwriting and claims administration philosophy on loss ratios. Typically, the insurer's retention might vary by occupational class and indemnity limit. If the insurer issues substandard disability income business, reduced limits of retention typically would apply to the business. The rationale behind reduced retentions for more hazardous occupations and otherwise substandard lives is the same as in life insurance. Gradation of retention limits by indemnity limit is, of course, a direct reflection of the lesser risk on policies with shorter indemnity limits.

A second plan of disability income reinsurance, which has been used with increasing frequency in recent years, is a form of excess-of-loss coverage commonly referred to as extended waiting period reinsurance. Under this plan of reinsurance the original insurer pays the entire claim for the first 12, 24, 36, or 60 months of disability. Thereafter the reinsurer indemnifies the original insurer for a portion, usually not to exceed 75 per cent, of the continuing claim payments. As an example of the operation of this type of reinsurance, consider a policy providing 24 months' sickness and lifetime accident benefits issued in the amount of $500 per month. Assume that the insurer purchases reinsurance on the extended waiting period plan and retains $500 per month for the first two years of claims and 25 per cent of the monthly benefit thereafter. In the event of an accident claim under which the insurer pays a monthly benefit for more than 24 months, the reinsurer would make no indemnification for the first 24 monthly payments and would indemnify the original insurer for 75 per cent of the claim payments beyond the twenty-fourth month. The insurer's retention would therefore be $500 per month for 24 months and $125 per month thereafter. Combinations of the coinsurance and extended waiting period plans can be used to tailor the protection to the needs of the insurer.

Nonproportional Reinsurance

With the exception of extended waiting period reinsurance of disability income benefits, the plans of reinsurance which have been discussed up to this point can be called proportional plans. The term "proportional" is appropriate, since the proportion of a claim for which the reinsurer will reimburse the insurer is known prior to the happening of the event insured against. Plans of reinsurance which do not meet this proportional definition can be called nonproportional plans. Almost all life reinsurance is on proportional plans.

It is apparent that extended waiting period disability income reinsurance is nonproportional—the reinsurer will have no liability if the claim terminates before the end of the extended waiting period. Thereafter the proportion of the total claim reimbursed by the reinsurer varies according to the length of the claim.

The most complete form of nonproportional reinsurance is commonly called *stop loss reinsurance*. Under this plan the reinsurer might indemnify the original insurer for, say, 90 per cent of aggregate net claims in a calendar year in excess of, say, 120 per cent of net expected claims for that year; the reinsurer's liability also is subject to a maximum amount. The attractiveness of this direct approach to the problem of mortality fluctuations is apparent. However, formidable practical and theoretical problems would prevent the reinsurer from covering war claims and would likely prevent the reinsurer from guaranteeing the price structure or the continuation of the reinsurance coverage. Insurers who have issued guaranteed renewable coverage without a war exclusion provision at guaranteed premium rates may find such incomplete reinsurance protection to be unsatisfactory. For this reason, stop loss reinsurance may never have wide application to life insurance, where the basic coverage is guaranteed renewable at a guaranteed premium.

Another form of nonproportional reinsurance, which has found considerable favor with life companies as a form of supplementary reinsurance protection, is known as catastrophe or disaster reinsurance. Under this plan the reinsurer pays losses in excess of a pre-established deductible or disaster retention when, say, three or more claims result from a single accidental occurrence, such as, for example, an airplane crash. The reinsurer's liability is subject to a maximum amount per accident.

Group Reinsurance

Group underwriting controls, most particularly that control which relates the maximum amount of insurance on one life to the size of the group, serve to stabilize the financial experience of the insurer. The operation of any experience refund arrangement also stabilizes the insurer's experience, as an unfavorable claims experience is offset—partially, at least—by a reduction in experience refunds or dividends. Most group-writing companies are therefore willing to retain amounts of group coverage in addition to their individual ordinary limit of retention on the life. Amounts of group coverage in excess of that provided by the group schedule issued on the basis of individual evidence of insurability can, where required, be reinsured according to individual ordinary reinsurance methods.

Most commonly, reinsurance of group-underwritten business is transacted on a quota-share basis. Thereby the group underwriting controls automatically protect the interests of both the insurer and the reinsurer, and administration of the reinsurance is kept simple. Alternatively, when amounts of group coverage in excess of a specified limit themselves form a group which conforms to the underwriting rules of the reinsurer, such excess amounts may be reinsured as a group.

SELECTED REFERENCES

DOUGHERTY, EDWARD A. "Ordinary Life Insurance Limits," *Transactions of the Society of Actuaries,* Vol. V (1953), p. 125.

FEAY, HERBERT L. "Introduction to Nonproportional Reinsurance," *Transactions of the Society of Actuaries,* Vol. XII, No. 32 (1960), p. 22.

KALMBACH, L. J. "Life Reinsurance," in LIFE OFFICE MANAGEMENT ASSOCIATION, *Life Office Management Readings in Life Insurance,* Vol. V, p. 251. New York, 1946.

MCGILL, DAN M. "Reinsurance of Life Risks," *Journal of the American Society of Chartered Life Underwriters,* Vol. XII, No. 2 (1958), p. 163.

MENGE, WALTER O. "The Life Reinsurance Market Today," *World Insurance Trends* (eds. DAVIS W. GREGG and DAN M. MCGILL). Philadelphia: University of Pennsylvania Press, 1959.

ORMSBY, CHARLES A. "The Cost to Reinsure Individual Life Insurance Policies," *Transactions of the Society of Actuaries,* Vol. IV, No. 10 (1952), p. 448.

ROHM, JOHN T. "Life Reinsurance," in *Proceedings: Conference of Actuaries in Public Practice,* Vol. V (1955), p. 100.

Chapter 75

CLAIMS ADMINISTRATION IN LIFE AND HEALTH INSURANCE

BY LAWRENCE B. GILMAN

In one form or another, every life insurance policy contains a promise to pay. The payment of benefits—the final product of operations which may have extended over many decades—fulfills the primary purpose of insurance, namely, to provide protection against the hazards of untimely death, disability, or dependent old age. Claims administration is the process by which an insurance company meets its final obligations under the insurance policy.

CLAIMS PHILOSOPHY

A claims philosophy is necessary for consistent claims administration. Because the administration of claims is more of an art than an exact science, and because there are many gray areas of indeterminate meaning and intent, an insurance company must develop and communicate a claims philosophy that will give its claims personnel broad direction and guidance.

Claims administration in modern life and health insurance is not a static process. New policy wording, new types of benefits, and new coverages constantly reflect new underwriting approaches; and the experience gained under each, where favorable, creates pressure for liberal interpretations in claims administration. Competition is also a potent force in creating pressures for liberal claims policies.

In addition, marketing programs and policies change from time to time; and these changes eventually involve the claims man with new and different groups of claimants, such as, for example, substandard risks, the elderly, and members of associations newly eligible for group insurance. The almost constant advances in underwriting standards to provide coverage for greater numbers of applicants result in ever-different claims problems. Further, the growing understanding that the insurance industry must play an increasing role in the financing of medical care has brought new responsibilities to claims people. In this dynamic climate of change, competition, and constant improvement, it is now more necessary than ever that a company evolve a claims philosophy; and as a result of all of the forces working on the claims administrator, today's philosophy will probably be different from that developed in prior years.

One company has developed a model claims philosophy along the following lines:

To endeavor to provide prompt, efficient, and courteous service.

To endeavor at all times to perform faithfully the company's obligations, and to reflect an impression of the company as a fair, sound, and reputable organization.

To endeavor to protect the company against fraud and misrepresentation, and to safeguard the policyowners' funds.

To resolve the issue, in cases of reasonable doubt, in favor of the policyowner or beneficiary; and in cases of technical policy provisions, to look to the intent rather than the technical language of the provision.

To endeavor to treat all policyowners with fairness, and to give all policyowners equal treatment in accordance with the provisions of their policies.

To settle cases involving life insurance for no less than the amount of the company's liability, except in unusual cases where the company is approached with an offer of settlement and there is a substantial question of fact in issue.

To endeavor to develop the abilities of the company's employees, and to keep them knowledgeable concerning progressive developments in the industry.

To endeavor at all times to maintain a high level of communication and understanding with other departments of the company and with other elements of the insurance industry.

ROLE OF THE CLAIMS ADMINISTRATOR

The claims administrator serves many sectors of the public. Principally, he deals with policyowners and policy beneficiaries. Beyond these, however, he has increasingly greater contacts with doctors, hospitals, lawyers, social workers, life underwriters, brokers, trust officers, and many others, such as state medical examiners, state insurance departments, and rehabilitation experts.

Because of his unique position—that of fulfilling the obligations guaranteed by the contract—and because of his many public contacts, the claims man probably is one of the greatest single forces available to a company for promoting good public relations. The residual impression left by a claims man extends far beyond his own company—it probably is a prime source for the creation of public opinion of the insurance business as a whole.

The claims administrator is a moving force within the company. Since he is close to the public, and since he carries out the provisions of the policy, he has the best available information as to whether or not the policies being sold are really meeting the needs of the insuring public who have purchased the coverages. He also is in an excellent position to observe the operation of contract provisions, including exceptions or exclusions, that may be more expensive to administer and cause more adverse public reaction than they are worth. In addition, he may identify contract wording which does not seem to permit the carrying-out of the intent of the company.

Since the claims administrator has firsthand information about the insureds and the product, he is a part of the company team engaged in regular creative development of improved products.

The typical insurance organization is composed of a number of distinct operations, each performing a specialized function. Claims operations usually are structured in one of two ways. There may be a separate department which handles all claims; or there may be several separate claims groups, each of which takes complete charge of only a given line of business—for example, group, ordinary life, industrial life, and individual health insurance.

The claims department itself normally keeps no individual policy records. Instead, it relies on other departments to maintain the necessary records and to provide funds for benefit payments. The claims department is usually responsible for approving or denying claims, paying benefits, accounting for benefit dollars disbursed, and recording claims statistics necessary for company operations.

In performing its several functions, the claims department generally is expected to be progressive, to fulfill the company's obligations promptly, to promote good public relations, and to be economical in its operations. Modern business systems have helped meet these obligations and have increasingly become a part of sound claims administration.

GENERAL CLAIMS PROCEDURES

Up to this point, the general nature and functions of claims administration in life and health insurance have been examined. Now, the "how" of claims administration will be explored. The core of claims administration is the evaluation of proofs and the final approval or denial of the benefits claimed. Before this process can occur, however, there must have been a loss or liability on the part of the insurer, and the claimant must have notified the insurer of his desire to assert the rights covering such event given him in the contract. To best facilitate this process, and to permit some uniformity of operations, insurers customarily provide forms for making claims.

Claim Proofs

In recent years, there has been much good work done through industry-wide co-operative efforts to promote uniform claim forms. Working with the American Medical Association and the American Hospital Association, industry committees have taken the best of many forms, standardized their language, provided for a logical sequence of questions, and then promoted them for general use. Continued progress in this important field should be actively supported.

In addition to claim forms, a company may require other evidence of loss to clarify a factual situation and to come to a proper decision. Such additional proofs may include death certificates, medical statements by attending physicians, hospital bills, and autopsy reports. The good claims administrator seeks constantly to reduce, simplify, and clarify the data which he requires from claimants and others.

The purpose of the claim form is to elicit the facts concerning the particular loss claimed in an easily usable form. Since there are many kinds of claims, it follows that there are forms used with questions that are pertinent to the particular classes of policies or claims involved.

Claims Examination

Claims examination and evaluation is the principal job of the claims administrator. Methods of claims examination vary with the type of claim and with the claims philosophy of the company. However, there are certain basic procedures common to all claims. These procedures are briefly described below before the specific aspects of the administration of life and health insurance claims are considered.

Identification of the Insured. This first step is necessary so that the claims man can make use of the basic policy records. The factors involved usually are the policy number, the insured's name, and perhaps his age. On group insurance claims the claims administrator must go one step further. After identifying the policyholder—the employer—the claims administrator must identify the insured person under the group policy. Such identification is usually established through name and certificate number, or perhaps through the social security or employee number of the insured person.

Determination of Benefits Claimed. This is usually evident if the appropriate claim statement or forms have been submitted. Within the broad categories of death, disability, or medical expense claims, the claims administrator must then determine what specific benefits apply.

Determination of Policy Status. This usually involves an examination of the company records concerning the policy, such as the application, the record of premium payment, and any record of policy loans and surrenders. In addition, if it is a group case, and if the policy is in force, it is necessary to determine that the certificate holder is currently insured. Where insurance does not appear to be in force, the claims examiner must be careful to look for any policy provision that might have extended the coverage. He must also determine whether or not the initial loss actually occurred at some earlier date when the insurance coverage was in effect.

Determination of the Extent, if Any, of Total Liability. In making this determination for individual policies the examiner must be careful to note any additional amounts which might be due under the policy, such as, for example, policy dividends, interest, and paid-up additions. He also must recognize any necessary deductions from the proceeds, such as existing policy loans, loan interest due, or unpaid premiums. All coverages must be carefully checked at this stage, particularly amendments to group policies.

LIFE INSURANCE CLAIMS ADMINISTRATION

Life insurance policies generally provide fixed benefits for certain specific losses. These benefits, which may be multiple benefits under some circumstances, are all spelled out in the policy. On group life policies the benefits may vary for certain classes or salary grades of employees.

Claims for Death Benefits

Proofs of death which are acceptable to the company may consist of the claimant's statement on the claim form and a certificate of death or a statement by the physician attending the deceased at the time of death. On group policies the employer also provides information about the coverage for the employee, such as the date last worked, reason for leaving work, and salary grade.

There is one prime qualifying situation on death claims arising out of the incontestable provision in individual or family life insurance contracts. If death has occurred within a specified period after the issuance of the policy (usually two years), the company may contest payment of the claim if there is proof of material misrepresentation by the policyowner in the application for the policy. Even though the policy itself may have passed the period of contestablility, the claims administrator must be careful that there were no additional benefit riders added after the issuance of the policy which still may be within their own contestable period. Reinstatements also may give rise to new contestable periods. Should a claim be contestable, the claims man must examine the case thoroughly, and often must make a detailed investigation of past medical records through interview with the family physician or review of hospital records. Such an investigation is to determine whether or not the statements made in the application were true and complete, and, if not, whether the application would have been accepted and the risk assumed if the true facts had been stated initially.

Accidental Death Claims. These claims require special handling. In these cases, it is probably necessary for the claims administrator to investigate beyond the initial claim proofs, although sometimes a simple newspaper clipping describing the accident might suffice. In analyzing the claim facts, the examiner must determine whether or not the death was "accidental" within the terms of the specific policy involved. Over the years, there have been differences of interpretation and a variety of court decisions over the distinction between "accidental" and "accidental means."[1] Some companies have eliminated the consideration of "means" in accidental death claims either by contract language or by claims administration policy. Where the distinction is still maintained, the examiner must be aware of the differences in court decisions and interpretations in the various states applying to the term "accidental means."

Multiple indemnity benefits for accidental death have further qualifying limitations as part of the policy. The claims administrator must be certain that all of these limiting conditions are met because the potential liability on such cases can be sizable. An example of these limitations is the requirement that accidental death must have occurred while the insured was a passenger on a public conveyance operated by a common carrier for passenger service.

Suicide. Death by suicide requires careful consideration by the claims administrator because most individual and family policies contain a suicide clause which limits the benefit amount payable when death is the result of suicide within a specified period (usually two years) after the issuance of the policy.

Hazardous Occupations. Hazardous occupations or avocations, such as aviation, no longer generally prohibit one from purchasing life insurance. However, if policies have such an exclusion, the claims man must check this carefully and look into the cause and circumstances of the insured's death. Should death be found to fall within such an exclusion, the company usually only pays either an amount equal to the premiums paid for the policy, plus interest, or the cash surrender value of the policy. Such exclusions apply only to individual policies.

War. Deaths resulting from war, either declared or undeclared, normally are covered except under accidental death coverage. An exclusion may be included in policies issued during time of war.

Termination of Coverage. Death after termination of the insurance poses problems for the claims administrator in that he must make certain, under both individual and group policies, that there are no extensions of coverage set forth in the policy. For example, total disability may have occurred while the policy was in force, and thus the coverage of the basic policy may have been extended under the terms of the waiver-of-premium provision.

Apparent Errors in Age. Such errors should be checked by the claims administrator. In these cases the statement of the insured's age in the claim proofs may be different than that shown on the original application.

---

[1] See Chapter 22 for a discussion of the distinction between "accidental death" and "death by accidental means."

Although the company probably would have issued a policy had the insured's correct age been known when the policy was applied for, the premium rate would have been different. When discrepancies in age appear to exist, the claims examiner should attempt to determine the correct age and then should have the policy recalculated on the basis of the true age. This action may result either in a higher policy amount to be paid or in a reduced policy amount. However, modern claims practice is to waive minor discrepancies in age. Age also has a bearing on accidental death coverage, since these benefits are generally restricted to those persons between the ages of five and 70.

HEALTH INSURANCE CLAIMS ADMINISTRATION

Claims for Total and Permanent Disability Benefits

Life insurance policies often provide either for waiver of premiums or for both waiver of premiums and monthly income payments in the event of total and permanent disability. Disability income coverage also may be provided under separate individual or group contracts and either for "long-term" or for "short-term" durations. The source of most problems with disability claims lies in the construction to be placed on the words "total" and "permanent."

Historically, this coverage was originally intended to provide benefits only if the insured had become totally and permanently disabled for life. However, the original concept has been modified over the years. The policies typically define "total" disability as the inability of the insured to engage in any occupation for remuneration or profit. Because of court interpretations and changes in insurance operational philosophy, this definition of total disability generally is interpreted to mean the inability of the insured to carry on for profit his own occupation or some other occupation for which he is reasonably fitted by experience or training. Also, total disability need not be of a permanent nature or for life. Usually, the policies provide that total disability for a prescribed period, such as four or six months, is presumed to be permanent.

Group life contracts require that the disability must be total and permanent. This means that, to all appearances, total disability will continue for life or for an indefinite future period. Evidence of continuance of total disability is required annually under most group life contracts.

As in death claims, proof that the claimant is disabled is furnished to the claims administrator through claim forms. These forms contain statements by the claimant as to the nature and cause of his disability, its history, the type of work he did, when he last worked, and whether or not the accident or sickness resulted from his employment. A physician's statement indicating his diagnosis, the degree of disability, its history, and its progress and prognosis also is necessary. On group claims the employer also completes a statement indicating the reason for termination of active work and the employee's insurance status.

From these records and any reports of investigation or medical examination deemed necessary by the insurer, the examiner must determine, on the basis of judgment and experience, whether or not the insured is totally and permanently disabled within the wording of the policy provision, applicable court decisions, and the company's prevailing claims philosophy.

Under individual policies, contestability is one of the prime qualifying situations in disabilty claims. There are several possible categories into which a disability claim may fall with respect to contestability. One is where both the life insurance policy and the disability provision are contestable and there is a material misrepresentation (in the application) concerning a prior physical impairment or medical treatment which could result in the rescission of the policy. In another situation the life insurance policy is incontestable, but the disability provision remains contestable. Thus a material misrepresentation would make possible the rescission of only the disability provision. Where both the policy and the disability provision are incontestable, neither coverage can be rescinded by the insurer. However, if disability results from bodily injury or disease sustained or contracted prior to the payment of the first premium on the policy, the claim may be denied under a pre-existing exclusion clause of the disability provision and is not a matter of contestability but rather of the nonexistence of coverage.

Age limitations also affect the claimant's eligibility for benefits under disability claims. Generally, the policies stipulate that total disability must commence prior to a stated age of the insured, such as age 55 or 60.

Also, it is usually provided that the disability must commence while the person is insured, and that if the insurance has terminated, proof of the disability must be furnished within a definite period of time after the date of termination. Thus, if proofs are received by the insurer within the prescribed time after the insurance coverage has terminated, it is necessary to ascertain exactly when total disability commenced. If disability commenced prior to the time coverage ceased, the claim can, of course, be considered.

The right to require proof of continuing disability annually is generally provided for in most policies. However, this right is not always exercised when it is obvious from the nature of the injury or disease that the insured will continue to be totally and permanently disabled. When additional information indicates that the insured has recovered, the examiner terminates benefits and restores the policy to a premium-paying basis.

Under most individual policies, if death occurs during the continuance of disability, all disability benefits terminate, and the face amount of the policy is payable. Under group policies the disability benefits also cease, and the face amount—or the difference between the face amount and the benefits already paid as installments under the disability coverage—is due.

Claims for Short-Term Disability Benefits

Loss-of-income claims present different problems. The benefits provided under this coverage may vary with the cause of the disability—that is, whether the prime cause was disease or accidental injury. Also, there is usually a waiting or elimination period described in the policy during which no benefits are payable; and this, too, may vary with the cause of disability.

Group health policies generally limit benefits to claims arising from conditions which were not occupational in origin, and individual health policies usually exclude conditions for which workmen's compensation benefits are payable. The policies generally provide certain benefits while the claimant is totally disabled. To make sure that total disability has in fact continued, periodic additional medical proofs may be required. These additional proofs take the form of supplementary statements from the attending physician or examinations by a company physician.

Claims for Dismemberment Benefits

Dismemberment benefits are provided under some individual and group insurance policies for specific losses, such as the total and irrecoverable loss of the sight of both eyes, loss of both hands or both feet, or one hand and one foot, or the loss of either one hand or one foot. Proofs of loss are similar to those required for other benefits, except that special questions appear on the claim form to make the claim examination easier. Examples of these include: "Give date and exact point of severance," "State amount of vision in each eye," and "Is corrective operation contemplated?"

Unlike individual policies, group contracts generally require that the loss must occur within ninety days of the accident which caused the loss. On the other hand, individual policies normally require that the loss be sustained prior to the policy anniversary nearest the insured's sixtieth birthday. There is generally no such age limitation in a group policy.

Claims for Medical Expense Benefits

Health insurance policies, both group and individual, also may provide reimbursement for medical expenses incurred because of accidental bodily injury or disease. Some policies also cover dependents of the insured for medical expense benefits. One feature of medical expense policies is the variety of coverages involved. The most frequently sold coverages seem to be hospitalization and surgical coverage, and major medical expense insurance—although there are many others available, such as diagnostic, dread disease, and dental coverages.

Individual health insurance policies generally are similar to group policies in the coverages provided; however, they are different in that they are individually underwritten, they sometimes exclude payment for losses arising from specific physical conditions, and they may be contested for a specified period of time. Individual policies also sometimes exclude losses that arise from hazardous occupations or avocations, or pre-existing conditions. In addition, some include age limitations. Under both individual and group policies, benefits for maternity are usually provided on a reduced basis or are not provided at all.

Variability characterizes both group and individual health insurance policies. Combinations of benefits, benefit maximums, covered medical expenses, and qualifying language all vary from contract to contract. In group insurance, benefits and benefit limitations may be tailored to meet the specific needs of a particular customer. Each day sees innovations in health insurance, such as special group contracts, individual plans for the elderly, and the pooled-risk plans which characterize the several "sixty-five" offerings for older citizens. All of this means that the health insurance claims administrator must be flexible in his approach and creative in his method of handling these complicated claims—all the while adhering to the basic claims philosophy favored by his company.

For health insurance policies providing medical expense benefits, the claims administrator must determine what services were performed, which of these services were covered by the specific policy at hand, how much in the way of benefits is provided for those services, and to whom the policy calls for payment.

Claim Proofs. Claim proofs for medical expense policies often consist of the claimant's statement, an attending physician's report, and, for group insurance, a policyholder's statement. In addition, the insurer requires itemized statements of services performed and the charges rendered for such services.

Unlike claims for most other types of policies, medical expense claims require that the claims man determine whether the proofs in question apply to a new claim or to some prior claim. This determination involves such questions as: "Has there been an intervening recovery between claims?" or "Has there been a return to work?" or "Is the current condition different from previous conditions?" Claim proofs are used to make this determination, although the claims administrator often must get additional information through his investigation in order to evaluate the claim properly. Once this decision has been made, the claims administrator then makes an examination of the claim and a determination of what benefits are due. During this examination of the claim the claims man should keep in mind the following typical conditions which generally are included in health insurance policies:

1. The attending physician in the case must be qualified according to the policy terms. Most policies state what types of physicians are acceptable under the particular policy. It may even be necessary for the claims man to check the applicable state law pertaining to licensing to make this determination.
2. The status of any hospital involved must be checked, since most policies are very specific as to what institutions qualify under the contract.
3. The status of the hospital patient is usually important in claims for hospitalization benefits. Since most policies provide benefits when there is in-patient care, the claims man must be careful to determine if the claimant is an in-patient. In examining the claim, however, he must remember that some policies also provide hospital benefits for out-patient care under special conditions, such as, for example, emergency treatment following an accident or minor surgery.
4. Where hospital care has been furnished at federal government expense, the policy language must be studied thoroughly, since benefits are generally excluded in such cases.

Major Medical Expense Claims

Major medical expense benefits are becoming increasingly popular because these plans provide a broad coverage desired by the public. Major medical claims occur under both individual and group policies.

The rapid growth of this broad coverage, the growing demand of the public for better medical treatment, and the ever-increasing cost of that care have challenged the claims man's ingenuity in dealing with the special problems of major medical coverage.

While the older forms of hospital, surgical, and medical coverages contained schedules listing fixed payments for surgical operations, laboratory tests, and other benefits, in major medical expense insurance the phrases "customary," "reasonable," and "necessary" have been substituted in the policy for many of the schedules previously used.[2] Although these give the claims man some opportunity for control, they also place upon him the obligation to make subjective judgments as to whether or not a given fee meets the imprecise tests imposed by the policy. In effect, responsibility for the cost of the product has been shared by the underwriter with the claims man. To help meet that responsibility, the claims man uses, to varying degrees, "schedules of relative values" and "normal cost guides."[3] There are such schedules for surgical procedures, diag-

---

[2] It should be noted, however, that major medical policies still contain certain inside dollar limits.

[3] These are studies of medical services, with each service assigned a measure of value in relation to others in the same medical practice field to which appropriate dollar-conversion factors can be applied. Examples: *California Medical Association 1960 Relative Value Studies;* and *Hospital Drug Reference: A Guide to Better Pharmaceutical and Drug Buying.*

nostic services, anesthesia, radiology, psychiatry, and pharmacy. In addition to medical complications, the claims man must temper his judgment with regard to the age and income of the insured, the geographic area in which the claim arose, and the physician's professional standing. In more difficult cases, he may have to resort to review committees set up by medical societies.

Duplicate Coverage

The insurance industry is concerned with duplicate coverage under health insurance policies because it is felt that overinsurance is not in the public interest. Overinsurance distorts the purpose of insurance, tends to encourage overutilization of service, and tends to increase the cost of medical care. Because of this concern, the insurance industry is actively promoting amendment of the Uniform Individual Accident and Sickness Policy Provisions Law. For the same reason, the industry has also proposed model antiduplication policy provisions for group health insurance. The claims man must be alert to detect situations where such duplicate coverage might exist, such as in the case of working wives, for example.

Duration of Claims

Excessive duration of hospital claims is checked through the use of statistical "norms" which define the average or customary length of stay for common conditions. Claims for periods of hospitalization which exceed the "normal" stay may cause the claims man to call for further confirming evidence of the need for continued hospital confinement.

Disability claims for loss-of-income benefits may pose a problem similar to that presented by hospital confinements for an excessive duration. The claims man frequently uses the same kind of statistical norms to evaluate the proofs for such disability claims. Where longer than normal disablement is claimed, the claims man must look for further facts to help him come to an equitable decision on the claim. In his search for evidence, he may make use of investigations, additional medical proof, and interviews with the claimant or his employer.

CLAIMS PAYMENT

The process of paying benefits involves several steps. The payee or payees must be determined. In life insurance contracts the insured has named a beneficiary or beneficiaries to receive the death proceeds, and this designation usually is a part of the policy. The claims administrator should be particularly careful to note any change of beneficiary or any assignment of the policy to someone other than the beneficiary. In group policies the beneficiary designation is on file with the employer or with the insurer. Health insurance policies generally provide for benefit payments to the insured; however, some policies specify that benefits will be paid to the physician or hospital, or to any other person named by the insured. The claims man must be certain to determine the correct payee because erroneous payments may force the insurer into duplicating the payments at a later date.

The amount payable is calculated as a part of the claim examination; however, the claims examiner must be aware of whether or not interest is payable on the proceeds of a death claim. This determination may already have been made by a policy provision. If not, company practice must be followed. Interest may be payable at the legal rate in the beneficiary's state, or at an arbitrary voted rate. Interest may be payable, for example, either from the date of death or from thirty days after the receipt of proof of death. The period during which interest is paid may be limited to six months or a year, and may depend on whether the delay was or was not caused by the claimant.

There are many methods of making actual benefits payments. Each of them must, however, encompass some means of accounting for the disbursement and of meeting the income-reporting requirements of the federal and state governments. The claims administrator must remember that many states require the insurer, on claims for death benefits, to notify the state when payment has been made or, in some instances, to obtain the state's consent to payment prior to the time payment is effected. Depending upon the state involved, the circumstances, and the amount of the benefit payment, the state may sometimes waive this requirement.

Not all claims are payable. On health insurance policies, where benefits are not payable because the loss is not covered, the insurer denies the claim, but the policy remains in force. On individual health and life insurance policies, where a material misrepresentation is proved and the policy is still contestable, the policy may be rescinded and a return of premiums offered. Sometimes the individual health policy may be kept in force but revised through a rider or waiver excluding benefits for loss from a certain condition or excluding coverage for an uninsurable family member.

Where the claimant is dissatisfied with the decision of the company and resorts to legal action against the insurer, the claim is usually turned over to the insurer's law department.

OTHER PAYMENTS

The claims administrator also handles benefit payments that do not arise as claims. Matured endowments, for example, do not require the submission of claim proofs. Benefits are due on a given date, and it is the responsibility of the insurer to see that payment is made. The same is true of group annuities which become due as pensions at a certain time and of individual annuities which mature at a certain date. The claims man's job here is to make certain that all is in order, that the correct payee receives the payments when due, and that the payments continue through the period specified in the policy. He also may be responsible for making periodic payments under optional methods of settlement—where the owner or the beneficiary under a life insurance policy elects not to have the payment made in one lump sum.

AIDS IN CLAIMS ADMINISTRATION

There are many sources of aid available to the claims administrator. Certainly, the insurer's own law and medical departments furnish valuable technical support. In addition, the Health Insurance Council—with its many grass-roots state committees—is very helpful to the individual claims administrator and to the insurance industry in providing information, arranging conferences on common problems, and interpreting and reporting the needs and attitudes of the many health care professions. Also, the Health Insurance Association of America and the Life Insurance Association of America are particularly helpful. The International Claim Association, another member organization of the Health Insurance Council, has as its objective "to promote good will, harmony, confidence, and cooperation generally among companies, and to devise and give effect to measures for the benefit of their policyholders, especially in matters relating to claims; and the observance of the amenities that should exist among companies and associations."

SELECTED REFERENCES

CLENDENING, LOGAN. *The Human Body.* New York: Alfred A. Knopf, Inc., 1945.

COX, BERKELEY. *Study Notes on Law.* Chicago: Society of Actuaries.

DICKERSON, O. D. *Health Insurance.* Rev. ed. Homewood, Ill.: Richard D. Irwin, Inc., 1963.

FAULKNER, EDWIN J. *Health Insurance.* New York: McGraw-Hill Book Co., Inc., 1960.

GREIDER, JANICE E., and BEADLES, WILLIAM T. *Law and the Life Insurance Contract.* Homewood, Ill.: Richard D. Irwin, Inc., 1960.

HARBAUGH, CHARLES H. *Adjuster's Manual.* 6th ed. by P. V. Reinartz. Philadelphia: Chilton Co., 1958.

INSURANCE ACCOUNTING AND STATISTICAL ASSOCIATION. *Proceedings.* Kansas City, Mo.: various years.

INTERNATIONAL CLAIM ASSOCIATION. *Law Committee Reports.* Omaha.

KRUEGER, HARRY, and WAGGONER, LELAND T. (ed.) *The Life Insurance Policy Contract.* Boston: Little, Brown & Co., 1953.

McCahan, David (ed.). *Accident and Sickness Insurance.* S. S. Huebner Foundation Lecture Series. Homewood, Ill.: Richard D. Irwin, Inc., 1954.

Rothenberg, R. E. (ed.). *Understanding Surgery.* New York: McGraw-Hill Book Co., Inc., 1955.

Society of Actuaries. *Accident and Sickness Insurance Provided through Individual Policies.* Chicago, 1963.

Vance, William R. *Handbook on the Law of Insurance.* 3d ed. by Buist M. Anderson. St. Paul: West Publishing Co., 1951.

Chapter 76

THE DEBIT SYSTEM AND INDUSTRIAL LIFE INSURANCE

BY FRANK B. MAHER

This chapter is concerned with two basic subjects rather than one. The debit system described is not limited to the sale and service of industrial life insurance. Far more so-called "ordinary" life insurance is sold and serviced through the debit system than industrial. On the other hand, practically all so-called "industrial" life insurance is sold and serviced through what might be called the debit system. The first part of the chapter is a description of a system; the second part is a brief analysis of a type of life insurance.[1]

THE DEBIT SYSTEM OF OPERATION

The debit system is a method of marketing life insurance. The product sold by the debit agent is not different from that sold by any other life underwriter, with the exception of certain provisions in weekly premium contracts or monthly premium debit contracts that may not appear in the ordinary contracts, and vice versa. The system is, in effect, a house-to-house marketing enterprise for the sale and servicing of life insurance and allied coverages.

The debit system had its origin in England in 1854. It was instituted primarily to meet the elementary life insurance needs of those working for a modest weekly wage. Policies were designated as "industrial" and were sold in small amounts; premiums were due and payable weekly to agent-collectors. Initially, the term "industrial insurance" implied that such policies were sold to the "industrial classes"; however, as will be seen later

[1] Terminology in this area is under study at the present time by the Commission on Insurance Terminology of the American Risk and Insurance Association. This Commission already has recommended that life insurance be classified as "individual" or "group," and that "ordinary" and "industrial" be dropped as terms used with the public. Recommendations subsequently will be made regarding appropriate terminology for the various forms of individual life insurance.

in this chapter, this is no longer an accepted definition. Some twenty years later the system was introduced in America essentially for the same reason, namely, to provide a modest amount of insurance for weekly wage earners.

Debit Defined

Originally, the term "debit" referred to the total amount of weekly premiums to be collected by the agent-collector on industrial insurance in force in a territory assigned to him. He was charged, or debited, with the total amount of premiums to be collected during the week. Then, as they were collected, he was credited with the actual payment received. Over the years the term has come to connote something entirely different. Now the debit is thought of as consisting of a certain number of policyowners, a certain amount of life insurance, a given geographical area, or a system of prospecting, canvassing, selling, and servicing.

It is important to note that the term "debit" no longer implies only the collection of premiums weekly, nor is it limited solely to industrial insurance. Many companies which originally sold only weekly premium industrial insurance now sell ordinary life as well as health insurance through the debit system.

A few companies have established premium notice ordinary debits. The words "premium notice" imply that the policyowner is notified of a premium due by a billing process and is expected to remit his premium to the company without benefit of a collection service. The word "ordinary" in this instance is used to distinguish such insurance from industrial; and it is applied to that class of insurance written, usually, for a minimum of $1,000, with premiums payable on a monthly, quarterly, semiannual, or annual basis. The term "premium notice ordinary debit," therefore, refers to policies which normally do not provide for a collection service. However, such policies are segregated by some companies according to given debit areas and assigned to debit agents for service and occasionally for collection of premiums in order to conserve the policy. The purpose of such assignment is to provide additional contacts for debit agents, resulting in opportunities for additional sales, as well as more effective conservation.

A few companies have experimented with small group insurance cases on a debit plan of operation. Finally, a few others, essentially life insurance companies, are selling property insurance (for the most part fire insurance) in small amounts, and collecting the premiums by means of a debit system.

Debit Agent Defined

The term "debit agent" refers to an employee of a life insurance company who has the responsibility of operating a debit. In addition to servicing established insurance accounts, he is engaged in selling all forms of insurance offered by his company. The term now is used interchangeably with "combination agent," for companies engaged in a debit operation have more and more become known as "combination companies." Originally, the debit agent sold, collected, and serviced only weekly premium insurance. Around the turn of the present century, however, companies began to direct the activities of their debit agents toward the sale of ordinary life insurance. The movement accelerated in the late twenties. Currently, the debit agent has the opportunity to sell any policy or any line of policies, i.e., life, health, or property, offered by his company, including group and pension plans. As a consequence, the one-time widespread difference between the activities of a debit agent and those of an agent selling ordinary life insurance for other than debit or combination companies has now narrowed considerably. By and large, any such difference is found in two essential areas: (1) In addition to selling all lines of insurance available in his company, the debit agent performs a collection function, a service function, and an accounting function among and for the debit policyowners, for which he receives specific compensation. (2) The debit agent, while licensed by the authority of his particular state, as is any other life insurance agent, has long been classified by certain government agencies as an employee of his company, contrasted to the independent contractor status generally accorded the ordinary agent.

Collection and Accounting Functions

Actual procedures of collection and accounting will vary by company, but the following is illustrative. In the first place, it should be noted that the agent collects on weekly premium and monthly premium debit accounts; he does not issue an individual receipt for each policy. Debit policies are entered in a *premium receipt book* (Figure 76–1); and usually, one book suffices for all weekly premium and monthly premium policies in each family account. The premium receipt book lists policies by number and name and premium individually, but provides for a single entry for the total family weekly premium or monthly premium due each time it is paid.

For his own records the agent maintains a *collection book* (Figures 76–2 and 76–3), wherein are listed the family accounts as they appear in the family premium receipt book. From his collection book, he transcribes periodically on an *account form* (Figure 76–4) the weekly premiums and monthly premiums collected, and processes such account through his local office, which in turn transmits final accounting records to the head office. While most companies require that the weekly premium account be prepared and submitted weekly, some companies require its submission monthly with the monthly premium account. This system obviates

†	MONTHLY POLICY NUMBER	NAME OF INSURED (ENTER FIRST AND LAST NAME)	POL *	MONTHLY PREMIUM	DATE OF POLICY MO. – DAY – YR.	TOTAL FAMILY PREMIUM
M	3803483	Michael Policyowner	A	10 68	11 26 57	30.14
M	4230461	Joseph "	B	6 20	3 12 59	
M	4879306	Michael "	C	13 26	3 17 61	
			D			
			E			
			F			

WEEKLY POLICY NUMBER	NAME OF INSURED (ENTER FIRST AND LAST NAME)	WEEKLY PREMIUM
39901347	Alice Policyowner	32
42572936	Alice "	43
45599521	Ernest "	30
45304219	Beatrice "	33
42753729	Joseph "	18

† Enter "M" If Monthly Debit Ord.
Enter "H" If Personal Health
Enter "P" If Monthly Premium Ind.

***POLICY IDENTIFICATION CODE**

The spaces on the pages for the record of premium payments are similarly lettered to identify the policy to which a premium payment is to be credited if premiums on all policies are not paid at one time. The "Family" space is for the entry of the total premium for all policies when paid at one time.

TOTAL	WEEKLY	PREMIUM	
1.56			

MONTHLY PREMIUMS

Mo. Due	Pol *	Date Paid Mo-Day-Yr.	Paid By Div'd	Paid By Cash	‡ Received By
MAY	A	5-7-63		10 68	A. N. Agent
	B	5-14-63		6 20	A. N. Agent
	C	5-21-63		13 26	A. N. Agent
	D				
	E				
	F				
FAMILY					
JUN	A	6-4-63		10 68	A. N. A.
	B	6-11-63		6 20	A. N. A.
	C	6-18-63		13 26	A. N. A.
	D				
	E				
	F				
FAMILY					
JUL	A	7-2-63		10 68	R. W. Agent
	B	7-9-63		6 20	R. W. Agent
	C	7-16-63		13 26	R. W. Agent
	D				
	E				
	F				
FAMILY					
AUG	A	8-6-63		10 68	R. W. A.
	B	8-13-63		6 20	R. W. A.
	C	8-20-63		13 26	R. W. A.
	D				
	E				
	F				
FAMILY					

WEEKLY PREMIUMS

Due Date of Premium		Date Paid Month	Date Paid Day	Paid By Div'd	Paid By Cash	‡ Received By	
MAY	1	May	7		1.56	A. N. Agent	18
	8	May	14		1.56		19
	15				1.56	A. N. Agent	20
	22	May	21		1.56		21
	29				1.56	A. N. Agent	22

BE SAFE — PAY PREMIUMS PROMPTLY

Due Date of Premium		Date Paid Month	Date Paid Day	Paid By Div'd	Paid By Cash	‡ Received By	
JUN	5	June	4		1.56	A. N. A.	23
	12	June	11		1.56		24
	19				1.56	A. N. A.	25
	26	June	18		1.56	A. N. A.	26

MAY WE HELP PROVIDE MONEY DURING DISABILITY AND FOR HOSPITAL AND MEDICAL EXPENSES?

Due Date of Premium		Date Paid Month	Date Paid Day	Paid By Div'd	Paid By Cash	‡ Received By	
JUL	3	July	2		1.56	R. W. Agent	
	10	July	9		1.56		28
	17				1.56	R. W. Agent	
	24	July	16		1.56		30
	31				1.56	R. W. Agent	

CONSULT YOUR AGENT if you have any question or desire any information about your insurance

Due Date of Premium		Date Paid Month	Date Paid Day	Paid By Div'd	Paid By Cash	‡ Received By	
AUG	7	Aug	6		1.56	R. W. A.	32
	14	Aug	13		1.56		33
	21				1.56	R. W. A.	34
	28	Aug	20		1.56	R. W. A.	35

‡ AGENT SHOULD SIGN FULL NAME FOR FIRST PAYMENT ON EACH PAGE OR WHEN HE FIRST SIGNS . . . AFTERWARDS INITIALS.

FIG. 76–1. Illustration of premium receipt book.

STREET	NO.	FLR.-APT.	FAMILY NAME	PAGE NUMBER
X	106	1	Policyowner	322

WEEKLY PREM.	DUE DATE	DATE PAID	AMOUNT PAID		WEEKLY PREM.	DUE DATE	DATE PAID	AMOUNT PAID		WEEKLY PREM.	DUE DATE	DATE PAID	AMOUNT PAID		WEEKLY PREM.	DUE DATE	DATE PAID	AMOUNT PAID		WEEKLY PREM.	DUE DATE	DATE PAID	AMOUNT PAID		M. P.
	JUL. 62 4			27		JAN. 63 2			1	1 56	JUL. 63 3	7-2	1 56	27		JAN. 64 1			1		JUL. 64 1			27	
	11			28		9		63	2	1 56	10			28		8			2		8			28	
	18			29		16			3	1 56	17	7-9	3 12	29		15		64	3		15			29	
	25			30		23			4	1 56	24			30		22			4		22			30	
	AUG. 62 1			31		30			5	1 56	31	7-16	3 12	31		29			5		29			31	
	8			32		FEB. 63 6			6	1 56	AUG. 63 7	8-6	1 56	32		FEB. 64 5			6		AUG. 64 5			32	
	15			33		13			7	1 56	14			33		12			7		12			33	
	22			34		20			8	1 56	21	8-13	3 12	34		19			8		19			34	
	29			35		27			9	1 56	28	8-20	1 56	35		26			9		26			35	
	SEP. 62 5			36		MAR. 63 6			10		SEP. 63 4			36		MAR. 64 4			10		SEP. 64 2			36	
	12		62	37		13			11		11		63	37		11			11		9		64	37	
	19			38		20			12		18			38		18			12		16			38	
	26			39		27			13		25			39		25			13		23			39	
	OCT. 62 3			40		APR. 63 3			14		OCT. 63 2			40		APR. 64 1			14		30			40	
	10			41		10			15		9			41		8			15	D. L. P. BEYOND SEPTEMBER 30, 1964					
	17			42		17			16		16			42		15			16						
	24			43		24			17		23			43		22			17						
	31			44		MAY 63 1			18		30			44		29			18						
	NOV. 62 7			45		8			19		NOV. 63 6			45		MAY 64 6			19						
	14			46		15			20		13			46		13			20						
	21			47		22			21		20			47		20			21						
	28			48		29			22		27			48		27			22						
	DEC. 62 5			49		JUN. 63 5			23		DEC. 63 4			49		JUN. 64 3			23						
	12			50		12			24		11			50		10			24						
	19			51		19			25		18			51		17			25						
	26			52		26			26		25			52		24			26						

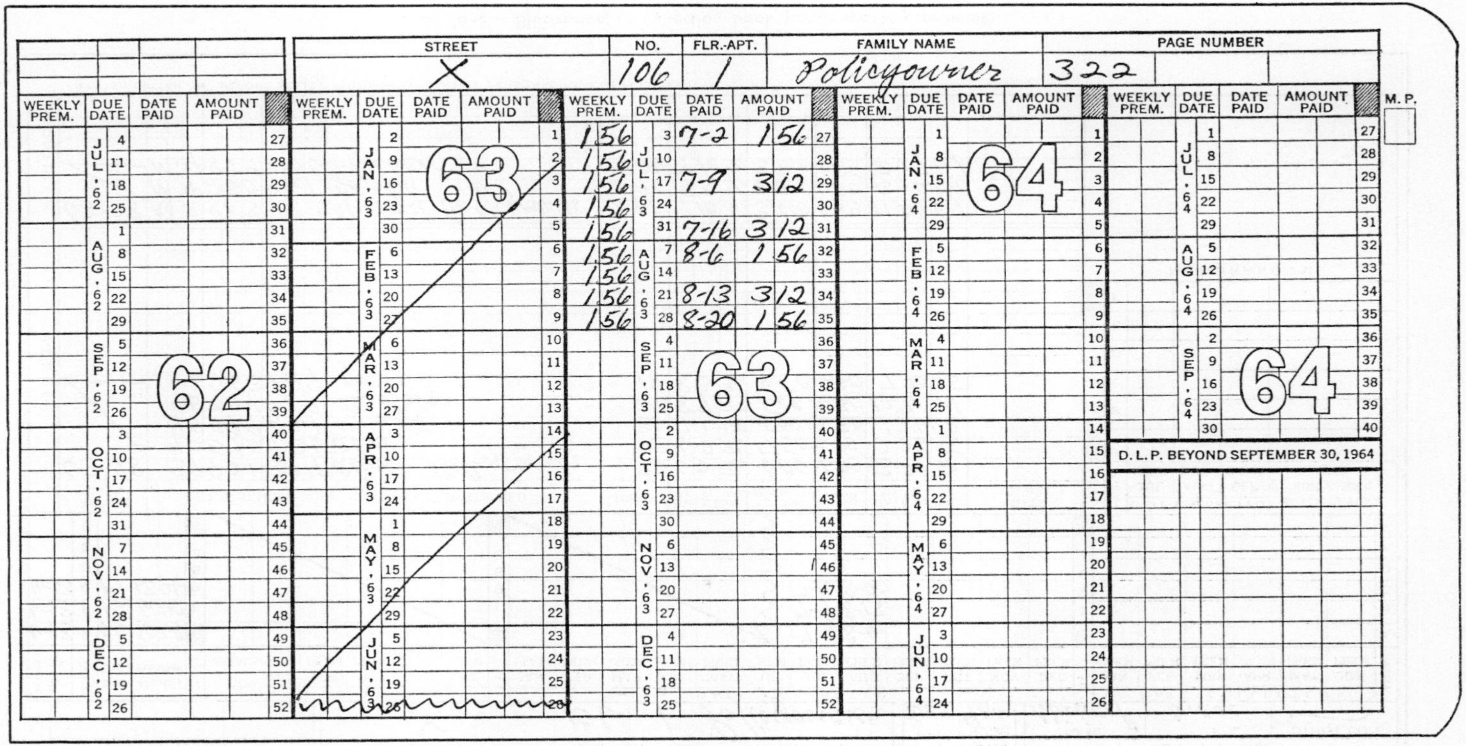

FIG. 76–2. Illustration of collection book page—weekly premium.

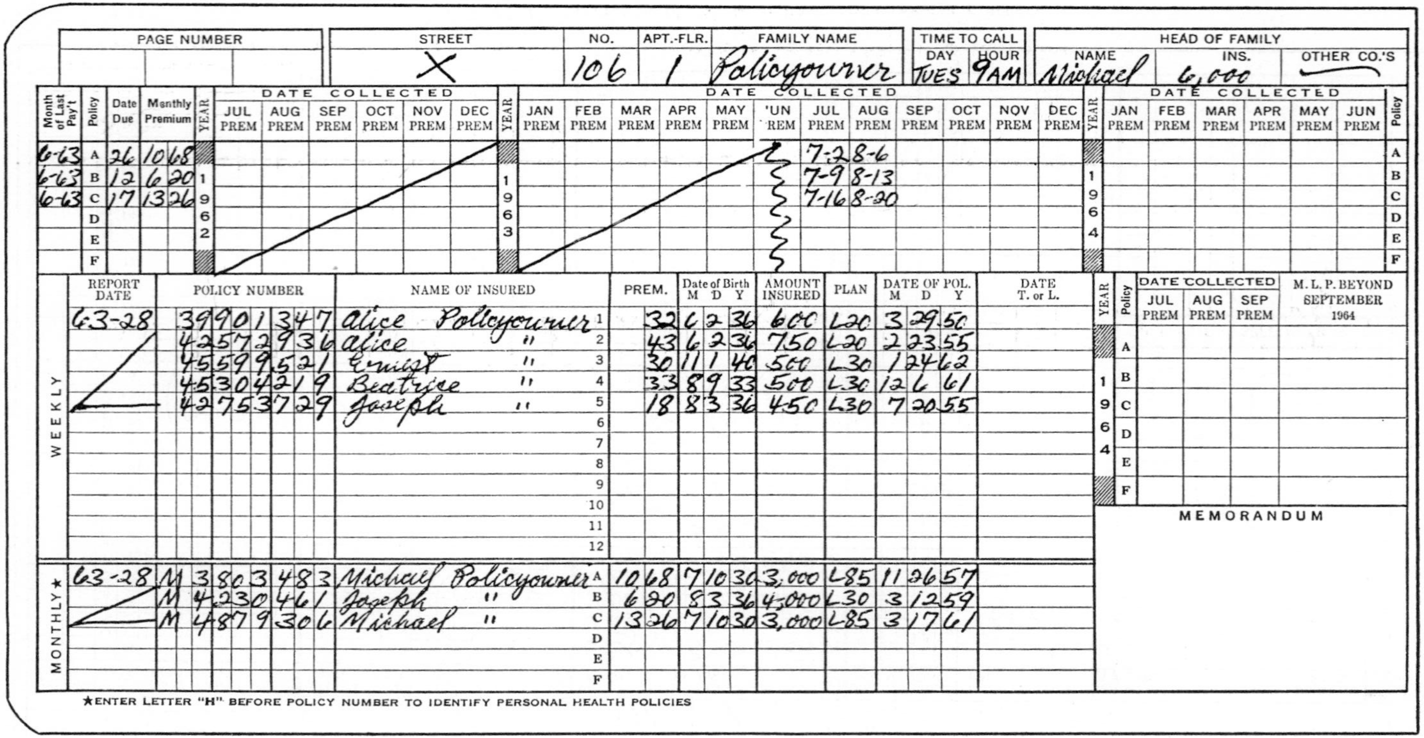

PAGE NUMBER | STREET: X | NO.: 106 | APT.-FLR.: 1 | FAMILY NAME: Policyowner | TIME TO CALL — DAY: TUES, HOUR: 9AM | HEAD OF FAMILY — NAME: Michael, INS.: 6,000, OTHER CO.'S: —

Month of Last Pay't	Policy	Date Due	Monthly Premium	Year 1962 (JUL–DEC PREM)	Year 1963 (JAN–JUN PREM)	1963 JUL PREM	1963 AUG PREM	Year 1964 (JAN–JUN PREM)	Policy
6-63	A	26	10 68			7-2	8-6		A
6-63	B	12	6 20			7-9	8-13		B
6-63	C	17	13 26			7-16	8-20		C
	D								D
	E								E
	F								F

	Report Date	Policy Number	Name of Insured		Prem.	Date of Birth M D Y	Amount Insured	Plan	Date of Pol. M D Y	Date T. or L.
WEEKLY	63-28	39901347	Alice Policyowner	1	32	6 2 36	600	L20	3 29 50	
		42572936	Alice "	2	43	6 2 36	750	L20	2 23 55	
		45599521	Ernest "	3	30	11 1 40	500	L30	1 24 62	
		45304219	Beatrice "	4	33	8 9 33	500	L30	12 6 61	
		42753729	Joseph "	5	18	8 3 36	450	L30	7 20 55	
				6						
				7						
				8						
				9						
				10						
				11						
				12						
MONTHLY★	63-28	M 3803483	Michael Policyowner	A	10 68	7 10 30	3,000	L85	11 26 57	
		M 4230461	Joseph "	B	6 20	8 3 36	4,000	L30	3 12 59	
		M 4879306	Michael "	C	13 26	7 10 30	3,000	L85	3 17 61	
				D						
				E						
				F						

YEAR 1964 — Policy A–F — DATE COLLECTED: JUL PREM, AUG PREM, SEP PREM — M. L. P. BEYOND SEPTEMBER 1964

MEMORANDUM

★ENTER LETTER "H" BEFORE POLICY NUMBER TO IDENTIFY PERSONAL HEALTH POLICIES

FIG. 76–3. Illustration of collection book page—monthly premium.

AGENT'S WEEKLY PREMIUM AND MONTHLY PREMIUM ACCOUNTS

CHECK ONE: Active X | Dis-ability | Vacant

Debit Number 12345

Report Date 63 (Year) 26 (Week)

Agent's Name R. W. Agent

District Northeast

Weekly Premium Dividend Settlements: C.B. Page	Amount	M.D.O. Credit Memos: Policy Number	Amount	Office Payments: Number	Amount
				234	24.00
				218	3.80
				217	6.26
				231	1.85
				255	2.24
		TOTAL			
		M.P.I. Dividend Settlements: Policy Number	Amount		
TOTAL		TOTAL			
Net Adj. (1779)		Net Adj. (1779)			
To Item 13		To Item 32		TOTAL	38.15

DEBIT PREMIUMS		WEEKLY PREMIUM		MONTHLY PREMIUM
Debit this account	1	243.28	18	1098.64
Advances this account	2	379.50	19	1883.52
Arrears last account	3		20	
Current Premiums	4	4.25	21	16.20
TOTAL	5	627.03	22	2998.36
CREDIT PREMIUMS				
Debit last account			23	1081.40
Arrears this account	6	121.76	24	538.33
Advances last account	7	261.46	25	1105.67
Current Premiums	8	6.36	26	14.75
TOTAL	9	389.58	27	2740.15
DEBIT SETTLEMENT				
Collections (5-9) (22-27)	10	237.45	28	258.21
Misc. Charges (*Code)	11		29	
TOTAL	12	237.45	30	258.21
CREDIT SETTLEMENT				
Dividends: Ind.	13			
Dividends: M.P.I.			32	
	14			
Misc. Credits (*Code)	15		33	
TOTAL	16	—	34	—
Bal. Due Co. (12-16) (30-34)	17	237.45	35	258.21

*Code for Miscellaneous Charges and Credits

M1. W.P. Shortage — M2. M.P. Shortage — M3. Int. on Lien Rein. — M4. Int. on Overdue Prem. — M5. W.P. Bal. Error — M6. M.P. Bal. Error

ACCOUNT SETTLEMENT ITEMS

Checks Name of Maker	AMOUNT	Checks Name of Maker	AMOUNT	Checks Name of Maker	AMOUNT			AMOUNT
						TOTAL CHECKS	89.28	
						TOTAL BILLS	51.00	
						TOTAL COIN	1.83	
						TOTAL CHECKS, BILLS & COIN		142.11
						MID-WEEK DEPOSITS		315.40
						OFFICE PAYMENTS		38.15
						M. D. O. CREDIT MEMOS		—
				TOTAL CHECKS		TOTAL (Equals Item 17 plus 35)		495.66

I certify that the foregoing is a full and true report of all collections made by me for the Company since my last previously rendered account; that I have not collected any money due to the Company except such as is included in the foregoing report; that the premiums specified in "Advances this Account" and in "Arrears this Account", were taken in full from the Collection Book of the debit, unless they represent balancing items established in accordance with the rules of the Company; that the entries of premium payments in the Collection Book correspond to the entries in the Premium Receipt books; that the amount of dividends for which credit is taken in this account has been properly credited in the policyholders premium receipt books and my collection book; that the amounts of office payments for which credit is taken in this account have been properly credited in my collection book; and that all Policies on the Weekly Premium Debit which are more than four weeks in arrears and all Policies on the Monthly Premium Debit which are more than thirty-one days in arrears have been placed on the Lapse Schedules.

____________________ AGENT

The amounts shown in Items 17 and 35 have been received ____________________ DISTRICT MANAGER or OFFICE SUPERVISOR

The account should be completed in triplicate by the Agent or Assistant District Manager and submitted to the District Office Supervisor with settlement on report day. One Copy will be returned to the Agent and the original will be forwarded to the Industrial Accounts Division.

FIG. 76–4. Illustration of debit agent's account form.

the need for the head office to maintain detailed accounting records for each small policy. The agent reports on his collections to the head office, therefore, in bulk on all policies in force on his debit, the only exception being a change in the status of an individual policy.

Service Function

The debit system, among other things, implies that all services normally required by policyowners will usually be performed in the home by the debit agent, obviating the necessity for policyowners to correspond with the company or call at the company's local office. Contractual changes, such as beneficial interest, name designations, and so forth, as well as the payment of dividends and cash surrender values and death claims, are all attended to by the agent at the home of the policyowner.

Evolution of the Job of Debit Agent

The debit agent's job has progressed through the years from servicing, selling, and collecting weekly premium insurance to the point where he now is capable of selling the entire line of his company. Furthermore, what was once known as a weekly premium debit has become a debit composed of weekly premium; monthly debit ordinary; health insurance; in some instances, premium notice ordinary and, in a few, certain classes of small group insurance; and limited forms of property insurance.

This evolution has come about through orderly processes and, quite naturally, has required, among other things, more rigid standards of recruitment and selection, as well as improved sales training and sales methods. In another generation the hiring of a debit agent was dictated largely by the need of the moment. Standards for recruitment and selection were practically nonexistent. Today, it will be found that most companies have set certain minimum standards with respect to formal education and will in most instances require of the recruit evidence of completion of at least the high school curriculum. The combination or debit companies have participated extensively in formal selection tests, particularly those developed by the Life Insurance Agency Management Association. In the early stages of development of the Aptitude Index, a product of the LIAMA, such companies sought to determine its applicability to selection in the field of debit employment. More recently, these companies have been experimenting with the Combination Inventory, another instrument of the LIAMA prepared for the use of combination companies. Others among the combination companies have availed themselves of testing instruments developed by themselves or by private organizations.

More and more, the use of such aids to judgment is becoming standard practice in the employment process. Employment applications for the position of agent in the combination companies are now designed to elicit from the applicant as much pertinent information about himself as possible. Statements in the application are subject to verification through personal investigation by supervisory officials. In addition, many companies insist upon outside credit reports. Finally, those responsible for the hiring process have been coached extensively in the exercise of sound judgment, so necessary in the final evaluation of the candidate's qualifications.

Sales training has found widespread acceptance among the companies employing debit agents. In the first instance, these agents have the benefit of their own company training programs, which usually combine theory and practice with stress on the DOC (Demonstration, Observation, Correction) method of training. Then it will be found that debit agents are encouraged to participate in industry-wide training programs such as offered by the Life Underwriter Training Council. This highly successful training venture, incidentally, has found a substantial number of its students among agents of combination companies. Furthermore, in ever-increasing numbers, debit agents are taking advantage of the Chartered Life Underwriter program. By itself, such extensive interest in training and self-improvement programs indicates that the job of the debit agent has gone far beyond the original assignment of collecting weekly premiums.

Agency Organization of Debit or Combination Company

The organization chart of the agency department of a combination company usually will reflect an organization built on a line-and-staff basis. (See Figure 76–5.) The line indicates the steps in field management supervision. In many companies, it will be found that the field organization is divided into broad geographic territories, each the responsibility of an executive called, in accordance with company practice, a regional manager, regional director of agencies, field vice president, or assistant vice president. The territory of one such supervisory official will include a number of district offices, each with a defined area of operation, and each in charge of a district manager. The district office serves a particular locale. It might, for example, encompass a city or a town. In the great metropolitan areas, one company might have several offices. However, each office would be assigned a clearly defined territory.

The district office is subdivided into smaller geographical units under the immediate supervision of an assistant district manager or staff manager. Depending upon the individual policy of the company, such units may be comprised of any number of debits, with the minimum usually four and the maximum usually ten.

The final refinement of the debit operation is the debit itself. Depending upon density of population and the extent of a company's progress in a particular area, debit lines are clearly defined for the operation of each

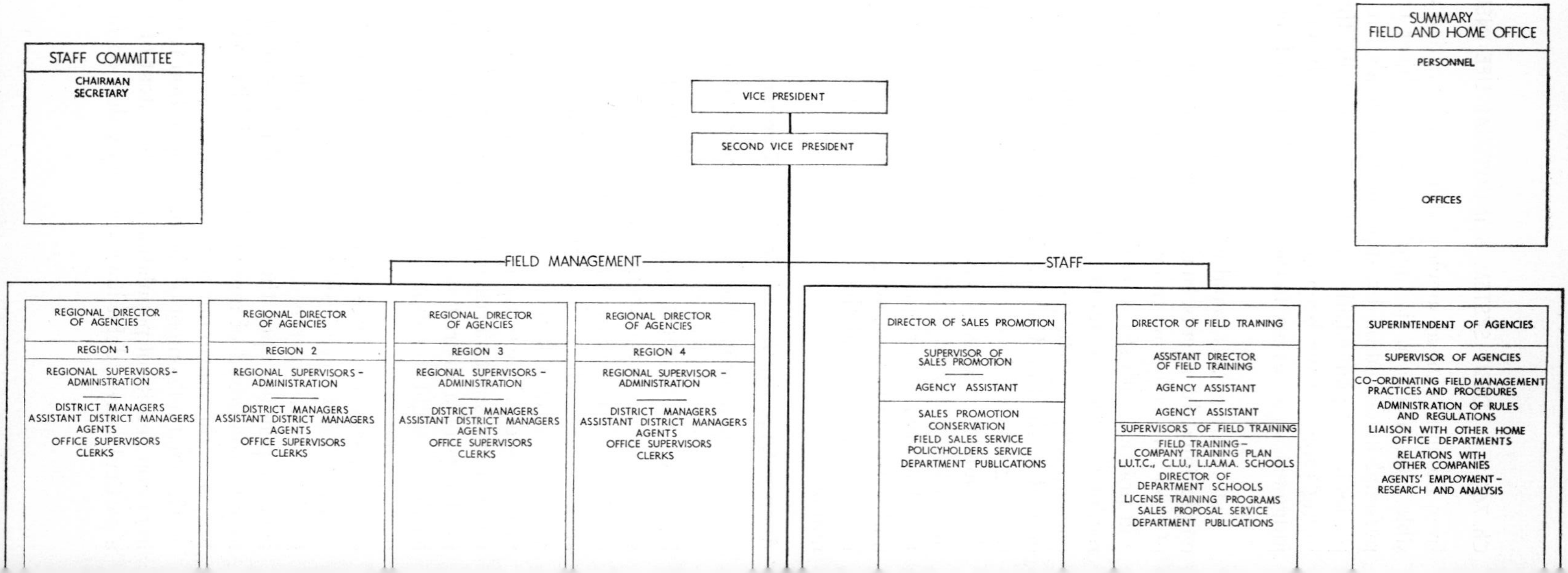
STAFF COMMITTEE
CHAIRMAN
SECRETARY
VICE PRESIDENT
SECOND VICE PRESIDENT
SUMMARY
FIELD AND HOME OFFICE
PERSONNEL
OFFICES
FIELD MANAGEMENT
STAFF
REGIONAL DIRECTOR OF AGENCIES
REGION 1
REGIONAL SUPERVISORS – ADMINISTRATION
DISTRICT MANAGERS
ASSISTANT DISTRICT MANAGERS
AGENTS
OFFICE SUPERVISORS
CLERKS
REGIONAL DIRECTOR OF AGENCIES
REGION 2
REGIONAL SUPERVISORS – ADMINISTRATION
DISTRICT MANAGERS
ASSISTANT DISTRICT MANAGERS
AGENTS
OFFICE SUPERVISORS
CLERKS
REGIONAL DIRECTOR OF AGENCIES
REGION 3
REGIONAL SUPERVISORS – ADMINISTRATION
DISTRICT MANAGERS
ASSISTANT DISTRICT MANAGERS
AGENTS
OFFICE SUPERVISORS
CLERKS
REGIONAL DIRECTOR OF AGENCIES
REGION 4
REGIONAL SUPERVISOR – ADMINISTRATION
DISTRICT MANAGERS
ASSISTANT DISTRICT MANAGERS
AGENTS
OFFICE SUPERVISORS
CLERKS
DIRECTOR OF SALES PROMOTION
SUPERVISOR OF SALES PROMOTION
AGENCY ASSISTANT
SALES PROMOTION
CONSERVATION
FIELD SALES SERVICE
POLICYHOLDERS SERVICE
DEPARTMENT PUBLICATIONS
DIRECTOR OF FIELD TRAINING
ASSISTANT DIRECTOR OF FIELD TRAINING
AGENCY ASSISTANT
AGENCY ASSISTANT
SUPERVISORS OF FIELD TRAINING
FIELD TRAINING –
COMPANY TRAINING PLAN
L.U.T.C., C.L.U., L.I.A.M.A. SCHOOLS
DIRECTOR OF DEPARTMENT SCHOOLS
LICENSE TRAINING PROGRAMS
SALES PROPOSAL SERVICE
DEPARTMENT PUBLICATIONS
SUPERINTENDENT OF AGENCIES
SUPERVISOR OF AGENCIES
CO-ORDINATING FIELD MANAGEMENT PRACTICES AND PROCEDURES
ADMINISTRATION OF RULES AND REGULATIONS
LIAISON WITH OTHER HOME OFFICE DEPARTMENTS
RELATIONS WITH OTHER COMPANIES
AGENTS' EMPLOYMENT – RESEARCH AND ANALYSIS

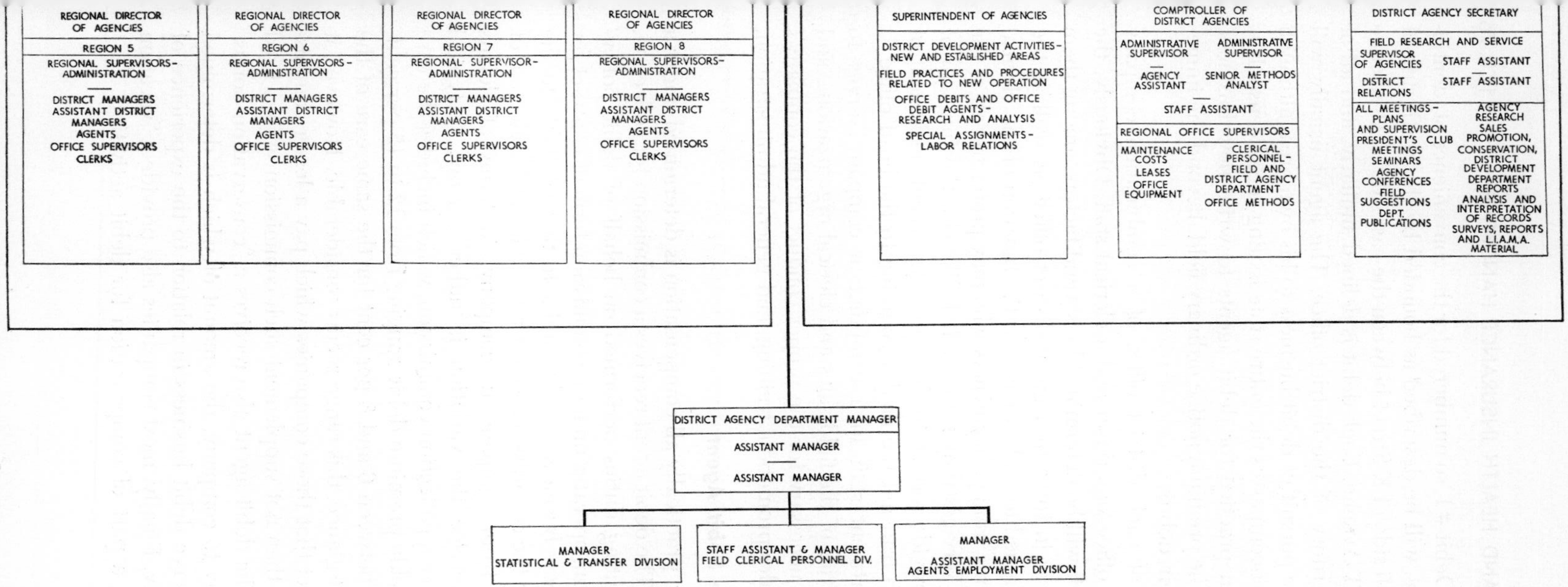

FIG. 76–5. District agency department organization chart.

agent. For example, Debit #1, so numbered for the convenience of identification, in a given city, will be described as bounded by the north side of D Street and the south side of K Street between the east side of M Avenue and the west side of T Avenue. Each debit is defined similarly, and all of them include the territory of the district office. The agent usually will confine the aggressive pursuit of debit business to his own area, although his license authority encompasses the entire state issuing such license. It is more or less common practice for debit agents to write new business, more particularly in the premium notice ordinary field, beyond the immediate confines of their debits.

The complement of each district office of a combination company includes a cashier or office supervisor and a clerical staff. Obviously, the size of the clerical staff will be determined by several factors, among them the amount of business in force in a given district office, as well as the number of agents assigned to such office. It is the function of the clerical staff to accept payments from policyowners who may prefer to call at the office and to provide services they require. It is likewise the function of the clerical staff to provide service to the agents, to accept settlement of their accounts, and to transmit the final accounting to the head office.

The agency department staff in a combination company serves to co-ordinate the activities of the field sales and clerical organizations, and provides the services necessary for the proper conduct of the company's business, including sales promotion, training, and general administration.

Compensation of the Debit Agent

In most companies, practically all compensation is determined under a commission formula. The debit agent receives a commission for collection, servicing, and accounting duties performed on behalf of debit policyowners and, in addition, operates under a commission form of contract for the procurement of new business largely similar to that available to the ordinary agent. While the commission fee for the service and collection of the debit will vary from company to company, in terms of dollars available for such service the variation is rather narrow. A typical debit agent will receive a collection commission, which includes the care and servicing of a weekly premium debit, ranging from 12 to 15 per cent, and a commission of between 6 and 8 per cent for the same care of the monthly debit. At first glance, this range seems considerable. However, it is narrowed by the fact that those companies which pay a lesser commission more frequently than not supplement such commission with a fixed expense allowance. The debit agent also receives a "conservation bonus" varying from company to company, the amount of which is determined by his ability to conserve debit business in relation to the experience of the company generally. Finally, most companies also provide a "vacation pay" which becomes a part of compensation for debit activities.

As has been said, commissions for the procurement of new business in the premium notice ordinary branch are, in the aggregate, much the same as those paid to the ordinary agent. In spendable dollars, more times than not, they will be less; but the debit agent, almost without variation, is the beneficiary of a company pension plan and participates in extensive security benefits. A major portion of the contribution for all such benefits is usually assumed by the company. New business commissions for monthly debit ordinary will in most instances be found to be slightly less than those paid for premium notice ordinary. In turn, new business commissions for weekly premium business have a lower scale than monthly debit ordinary commissions.

Advantages of the Debit System

To the Buying Public. Evidence is abundant that life insurance is a product which must be sold and is not, in most instances, bought. The debit agent has almost unlimited access to the homes of America, and more particularly to the homes of wage earners. Thus does he effect a wide distribution of life insurance among the American people which might not be possible if there were no debit system. The experienced debit agent enjoys a personal relationship with the families on his debit. This enables him to advise and counsel them on their life insurance needs with a better understanding of family situations than one would have in a less intimate relationship.

To the Agent. The debit agent has a continuing relationship with an ever-growing number of families and a relationship which in many respects is unique. The alert agent is aware of changing situations and changing needs in the family and can relate them to all other family circumstances, aiding him immeasurably in his selling activities. He has the advantage of a specific place to go week in and week out and the further advantage of a built-in, endless chain system of prospecting because of his continuing personal contacts with so many people.

To the Company. Perhaps nothing influenced more the decision of certain companies to adopt the debit system than the then existing need for a broader base on which to build at a time when life insurance in this country was in its infancy. The system accomplished the objective of those who introduced it. Among other things, it has afforded an unusual spread of risk, as well as the opportunity to do business in a mass market, resulting in sound and extensive growth. It is of interest to note that the two largest, and three of the six largest, life insurance companies in America operate a debit system.

Finally, the debit system has been a highly significant factor in the progress of the life insurance business in America. Through this system, generations of wage earners came to know the benefits of life insurance; and over the years of its existence, it has touched the lives of countless millions of persons. One might logically conclude, therefore, that the influence of the agent operating under the debit system and thereby bringing the services and protection of life insurance into the homes of the great mass of the people has done much to establish public confidence in the institution of life insurance generally. It is extremely doubtful that such widespread acceptance of life insurance could have been achieved in other circumstances.

INDUSTRIAL LIFE INSURANCE

To define precisely the term "industrial life insurance" is difficult. Originally, it implied policies of small amounts with premiums due and payable weekly to agent-collectors, and it further implied that such policies were sold to the "industrial classes." This is no longer so. Furthermore, industrial life insurance now means different things to different companies. By and large, however, it is insurance issued in small amounts, usually less than $1,000 in face, with premiums collected at frequent intervals. The most common premium interval is weekly, although monthly premium industrial insurance is also written by some companies.

Section 201 of the Insurance Law of New York sets forth the following in defining industrial life insurance: "That form of life insurance either (*a*) under which premiums are payable weekly, or (*b*) under which premiums are payable monthly or oftener, but less often than weekly, if the face amount of insurance provided in any such policy is less than $1,000 and if the words 'industrial policy' are printed upon the policy as part of the descriptive matter." Obviously, this definition binds companies operating in New York State, but it does not apply to companies in many other states where a precise definition may not be contained in the statutes.

The Industrial Life Insurance Contract

At the time industrial life insurance was introduced in this country, contracts differed widely from those designated as ordinary life insurance. Through the years, such differences have largely disappeared. Fundamentally, today the industrial life insurance contract is not different from other forms of individual life insurance. It is level premium insurance based on accepted mortality tables, with specified nonforfeiture values, including the right to take paid-up insurance for a reduced amount, to have the policy continued for its face amount for a limited period of time, or to cancel the contract and accept the cash surrender value thereof. More frequently than not, the industrial contract is sold in units of premiums, the face amount of the policy being determined by the amount of weekly or monthly premium the purchaser elects to pay. In the early beginnings of the business, the minimum unit was as little as three cents per week. While the three-cent policy has long since disappeared, many companies will sell an industrial weekly premium policy for a minimum premium of 10 cents per week.

Differences in Industrial and Ordinary Contracts

The major differences in industrial life insurance contracts as compared to ordinary life insurance contracts may be summarized as follows:

Dividends and Cash Surrender Values. Normally, dividends and cash surrender values do not become available until the policy has been in effect for three years.

Loan Values and Assignments. Because of the small amounts of industrial policies, it is not considered desirable to make loan values available. In addition, industrial life insurance contracts cannot be assigned although, in most instances, exceptions will be made when the assignee is a duly qualified bank.

Settlement Options. As a rule, settlement options are not available because of the small amount of the average policy.

Mortality Table. A mortality table suitable to the experience among industrial policyowners is generally used rather than the standard mortality table for ordinary life insurance.

Variety of Contracts. In most companies, types of contracts are limited in number in contrast to the wide variety of contracts issued as ordinary life insurance.

Facility of Payment Clause. Most industrial life insurance contracts contain a facility of payment clause which recognizes the need for prompt payment of death claims among the owners of small policies. If the named beneficiary were deceased or incompetent at the time the policy became a claim, it would be necessary to await the appointment of an executor or guardian before payment of proceeds, a situation not particularly desirable among people who for the most part have no need for such appointment. Therefore the facility of payment clause provides that the company may, under specified conditions, pay the benefit to any relative of the deceased by blood or by marriage who appears to the company to be unqualifiedly entitled to payment—for example, a person so described who would be responsible for the burial of the deceased. Such a clause usually specifies that the provision will be invoked only if the named beneficiary fails to make proper claim within a reasonable time after the death of the insured, or if the beneficiary is the estate of the insured or predeceases the insured.

Accidental Death and Dismemberment Provision. Industrial life insurance contracts usually include accidental death and dismemberment benefits as standard features of the contracts, without additional premium.

Cost of Industrial Life Insurance

A life insurance policy paid for by the week, or with the privilege of paying weekly, must of necessity call for a premium higher than policies paid less frequently. This would be true of any other product one might purchase, for it follows that the more liberal the installment plan, the higher the cost to the purchaser. It holds true with respect to ordinary life insurance. In that branch of the business a policy paid monthly, quarterly, or semiannually results in a higher yearly premium than the premium for the same policy paid once each year. Carried to the extreme, the cheapest form of individual life insurance is the single premium policy.

In the main, industrial life insurance is purchased largely by those working for a weekly wage. The family budget more frequently than not is sensitive to and affected by fluctuations caused by somewhat less stable employment of these wage earners. As a consequence, it is to be expected that the lapse ratio will be higher than the lapse ratio of ordinary life insurance policies.

Another factor of cost is mortality. Although mortality among industrial policyowners has improved tremendously over the years, the death rate continues appreciably higher than the death rate among ordinary policyowners.

As the business has progressed, companies have been working effectively to improve the industrial life insurance policy and, in the face of rising costs generally, have taken all possible measures to reduce the expense charge. As a result, over the years the difference in cost between the industrial life insurance policy and the ordinary policy has narrowed considerably. Furthermore, industrial policyowners in many companies receive a discount if they elect to pay premiums at the company office and not avail themselves of the services of an agent. It remains evident, however, that most of these policyowners prefer the services of an agent when paying premiums, for in the companies where the discount is available, the majority of industrial insurance accounts continue to be collected at the home.

Industrial Life Insurance in Relation to Other Forms of Individual Life Insurance

A rapidly expanding economy in recent years and a widespread improvement in the economic status of the wage earner, as well as his acceptance of life insurance as a vehicle for personal independence and security, have slowed the rate of growth of industrial life insurance when compared to the growth of life insurance generally. It is wholly evident that the wage earner is participating extensively in the purchase of more life insurance protection of increasingly higher amounts. At the end of 1932, there were 79 million industrial life insurance policies in force in the

United States for a total of $16,669,000,000 or, in volume, about 18 per cent of all individual life insurance then owned by the American people. According to the 1963 *Life Insurance Fact Book* of the Institute of Life Insurance, at the end of 1962 there were in force 95 million industrial life insurance policies for a face amount of $39,638,000,000. This represented approximately 9.3 per cent of all of the individual life insurance in force in that year. Obviously, the rate of growth has slowed considerably; yet, at the same time, it is evident that industrial life insurance remains a substantial part of the individual life insurance business in this country.

SELECTED REFERENCES

DAVIS, MALVIN E. *Industrial Life Insurance in the United States.* New York: McGraw-Hill Book Co., Inc., 1944.

HUEBNER, S. S., and BLACK, KENNETH, JR. *Life Insurance.* 6th ed. New York: Appleton-Century-Crofts, Inc., 1964.

INSTITUTE OF LIFE INSURANCE. *Life Insurance Fact Book.* New York, 1963.

MACLEAN, JOSEPH B. *Life Insurance.* 9th ed. New York: McGraw-Hill Book Co., Inc., 1962.

MCGILL, DAN M. *Life Insurance.* Homewood, Ill.: Richard D. Irwin, Inc., 1959.

MEHR, ROBERT I., and OSLER, ROBERT W. *Modern Life Insurance.* 3d ed. New York: Macmillan Co., 1961.

Chapter 77

REGULATION OF LIFE INSURANCE

BY EUGENE M. THORÉ

It has long been held that life insurance is a business affected with a public interest. As such, it is subject to close governmental regulation. In the case of life insurance, this regulation is provided primarily by the states rather than the federal government. The purpose of this chapter is to point out why life insurance is a closely supervised business, to outline the areas of state regulation, and to give some idea of the effectiveness of this supervision.

Why Life Insurance Is a Closely Supervised Business

There were in the United States at the end of 1963 approximately 134 million life insurance policyholders. If the individual beneficiaries named under their policies were taken into account, around 85 per cent of the total population could be said to have a direct interest in the life insurance in force in the nation.

The number of persons who choose life insurance as a means of obtaining financial protection has steadily increased over the years, and there is every indication that it will continue to do so. For many of them, it is the only voluntary financial resource to make provision for their dependents, old age, or economic emergencies.

Thus the remarkable growth and extremely wide distribution of life insurance coverage in the United States clearly identifies it as a business closely associated with the public welfare. Sound management and financial stability of the companies are obviously matters of great importance to a multitude of people. This is the chief basis for governmental supervision.

Another reason is the intrinsic nature of the life insurance business. Life insurance policies and contracts are usually written on a long-term basis. It is often many years between the time a policy is taken out and the time when it becomes a claim. Meanwhile, in order to meet its obligations as they fall due, the company must build up adequate reserves, with appropriate assumptions for interest rates and mortality. An important part of governmental supervision, therefore, has to do with the establishment of reserve standards. Regulation of minimum cash surrender values and other nonforfeiture values is another significant supervisory area.

The life insurance policy itself is somewhat technical. It is necessarily long in order to be specific on each point covered, and the average policyholder may not be familiar with some of the terms that must be used. Furthermore, it is a contract which the policyholder has no part in preparing. Statutory requirements for the inclusion in policies of certain standard provisions and insurance department approval of new policy forms are therefore designed to protect the policyholder against provisions which would limit benefits unduly, or the omission of others such as those which cover nonforfeiture or reinstatement.

In larger aspect, it must be borne in mind that the chief element of life insurance protection is stewardship—that the provisions of the policy purchased in good faith, with the expectancy that it will accomplish certain objectives, will be scrupulously carried out. This is the consideration underlying all insurance supervisory responsibility.

State Insurance Supervision

The life insurance business historically has been regulated by the several states through insurance departments which apply and enforce a large body of laws specifically designed for this business. These departments vary in size from modest units of the state's governmental structure to very large departments with a number of subordinate officials. The growth of the departments in the various states has tended to follow their insurance needs and has been responsive to such factors as the number and size of companies and the state's population and wealth.

State insurance supervision is almost as old as the life insurance business itself. Until the middle of the nineteenth century, few life insurance companies existed; and these, it was felt, were sufficiently regulated if they made the same reports to the state as were required of other types of financial corporations. In 1851 the State of New York, where most of the large companies were located, began to require a deposit of securities, which was not large. About this time, too, it introduced a special questionnaire in connection with life insurance company reports.

New Hampshire (in 1851) and Massachusetts (in 1852) were the first states to create state supervisory agencies through the creation of boards of insurance commissioners. Perhaps this historical development was of a more formal nature in Massachusetts, since those specified for the board were the secretary, treasurer, and auditor of the commonwealth. Additionally, three years later, Massachusetts appointed an independent board and created a separate insurance department. It discharged its duties vigorously—sometimes in the face of insurance company opposition—and numbered among its early achievements the establishment of a standard of solvency for life insurance companies and the enactment of a compulsory nonforfeiture law.

New York established the next insurance department in 1859; and one by one, other states followed suit. Special departments or specified officals were charged by 35 states with the supervision of insurance during the decade that followed. Today, every state, as well as the District of Columbia, has so provided.

The National Association of Insurance Commissioners

Great impetus was given to state insurance supervision by the formation in 1871 of the National Association of Insurance Commissioners, originally called the National Convention of Insurance Commissioners.

Its founding and continuing purpose, as set forth in the present form of its constitution, is "to promote uniformity in legislation affecting insurance; to encourage uniformity in departmental rulings under the insurance laws of the several states; to disseminate information of value to insurance supervisory officials in the performance of their duties; to establish ways and means of fully protecting the interests of insurance policyholders of the various states, territories, and insular possessions of the United States; and to preserve to the several states the regulation of the business of insurance."

Meeting twice each year, with interim meetings of the Commissioners located within the several zones, the National Association of Insurance Commissioners has kept abreast of the changing patterns and growing complexities of the insurance business. Through its endeavors, much beneficial legislation to implement proper supervisory needs has come onto the state statute books. It has assisted also in the development of the vast body of state insurance regulatory controls which are reviewed later in this chapter. A considerable degree of uniformity in state requirements has been achieved, although the attainment of more complete uniformity is still a goal of the business. Additionally, a host of problems not susceptible to legislative solutions have been resolved. Among its more recent achievements the Commissioners' Association numbers the following:

1. Uniform rules have been adopted for the valuation of securities in the annual statement blank.
2. A standard mortality table for ordinary and industrial insurance has been developed.
3. New standard valuation and nonforfeiture laws have been drafted, and their enactment has produced a uniform pattern in these areas in virtually all the states.
4. The so-called "zone system" for the triennial examination of life insurance companies has been developed. Under this system, examiner teams from several state insurance departments examine companies under the general direction of the insurance department of a company's home state.

Development of Life Insurance Laws

Perhaps the most important landmark in the history of state supervision of insurance, the repercussions of which were felt throughout the United States, was the famous Armstrong Investigation in 1905–06. This investigation, under a committee empowered by the New York legislature to "examine into the business and affairs of life insurance companies doing business in the State of New York," conducted a sweeping survey of the current practices of these companies, many of which had become the subject of public criticism. The program of remedial legislation recommended by the committee included proposals:[1]

1. Relating to the organization of companies, election of directors, and conversion of stock into mutual companies.
2. Limiting the right to hold real estate, prohibiting investment in stocks, and forbidding syndicate participations in security transactions.
3. Limiting the amount of new business, expenses of operation, and amount of surplus and contingency funds that may be accumulated.
4. Forbidding tontine dividend plans by requiring that mutual life insurance companies must distribute surplus annually and not otherwise.
5. Dealing with the contents of policy forms and the rights of policyholders.
6. Prescribing the detail to be reported in annual statements.

These proposals were adopted with minor modifications; and many were copied in other states, providing an encouraging degree of uniformity. While most of the laws have proved to be beneficial, others reflected excessive zeal for reform and have since been modified.

Most states now have satisfactory and comprehensive insurance regulatory statutes. In the postwar period, many states have enacted complete insurance code revisions, while others which already possessed comprehensive statutes have modernized their provisions where necessary. These codes and laws have developed in the states over the years, sometimes swiftly, and again at a more leisurely pace. No less than six new code revisions were in progress in 1964.

The Laws at the Present Time

The tremendous growth of the life insurance business and its broad social and economic implications have brought to the state insurance departments a wide range of duties. Among the responsibilities of the present-day chief state insurance department official are the approval and control of all types of insurance companies, both old and new; periodic examination of the affairs of companies doing business in the state; licens-

[1] *Report of the Joint Committee of the Senate and Assembly of the State of New York, Appointed to Investigate the Affairs of Life Insurance Companies, in Exhibits, Reports and Index of Legislative Insurance Investigating Committee* (Albany, 1906), Vol. VII.

ing of agents; and compelling compliance with agents' qualification laws. In all states the companies are required to file annual statements with the insurance department, giving the information as to their operations called for in the "convention blank." In many states an important insurance department function is the examination and approval of policy forms, application blanks, and similar documents. In some states the department annually checks the calculation of the policy reserve. In all jurisdictions the departments have certain responsibilities in connection with the taxes, licenses, and fees both of companies and of agents.

The insurance laws now in effect in the United States fall roughly into five principal categories.

In the first category are the laws governing the organization, powers, and duties of the insurance department. These laws exist in all states and usually are part of the insurance law itself. They set forth the qualifications, powers, and duties of the insurance commissioner and his office. The commissioner has the power under the statutes to license companies and their agents. He has the authority to revoke those licenses and to impose other penalties for violations of the law. He is required to make detailed examinations periodically of all insurers of his own state, usually not less frequently than every three years, and is empowered to examine the affairs of all insurers authorized to do business in his state as often as he deems advisable. The commissioner also has some quasi-judicial powers. He may conduct hearings, compel the attendance of witnesses, and require the production of relevant evidence. Woven throughout the insurance laws are the various rules he has to follow in order to administer properly the many responsibilities and obligations he has as supervisor of an extremely complex business. Although the commissioner is granted many express powers by statute, the courts are inclined to augment them with a rather extensive amount of additional powers which may be reasonably implied from the statutes.

In the second category are the laws relating to the powers, limitations, and requirements of insurance companies, both those domiciled in the state and those chartered elsewhere but doing business in the state. As to domestic companies, all states prescribe the manner in which companies may be formed; establish minimum financial requirements (which have shown an upward trend in recent years); define the classes of insurance business a company may conduct (which are usually limited to certain classes or kinds, e.g., life, health, and annuities); frequently cover the dissolution or merger of companies; and sometimes prescribe how insurance obligations of companies ceasing to do business may be reinsured. The laws with respect to companies of other states generally cover requirements for admission to do business in the state and customarily provide for admission standards equivalent to the standards required for domestic companies.

Standards for the investment of funds held by insurance companies are spelled out in detail in the statutes of most states. Local conditions and economic factors produce some variation in these lists of authorized investments, but they are consistently strict, with the avowed intention of guaranteeing soundness and security as well as the opportunity for earning income. Standards of valuation of such investments are also prescribed, and the efforts of the National Association of Insurance Commissioners in applying these standards have resulted in a pattern of uniformity in all of the states.

Insurance companies are required to file with the insurance department an annual statement as to their financial condition. This is a compilation in great detail of the various aspects of the company's operations. It follows a prescribed form, developed by the National Association of Insurance Commissioners. In some instances, it is supplemented by special schedules required by a particular state. Its contents are the subject also of periodic examinations by personnel of the various insurance departments. These examinations constitute a complete audit of the company's financial status and its operations. If, despite these precautions, a company becomes insolvent, additional statutes spell out in detail the procedures to be followed for reinsurance, rehabilitation, or liquidation of the company and its obligations. The statutes of all states contain numerous provisions proscribing unfair or otherwise improper trade practices in the insurance business, including such matters as false advertising, defamation, coercion, boycott, discrimination, and rebating.

In the third classification are the laws with respect to the qualifications and licensing of agents. These have always been a matter of concern in the regulation of insurance, since the company does business with the insuring public through the agent. It is essential to both that he is competent and trustworthy. While much of the regulation of agents is contained in department rulings and instructions which implement the statutes, the statutes themselves are written in sufficient detail to set forth clearly the standards by which the insurance departments are to be guided in determining the qualifications of the applicant agent to begin or continue his calling. After defining precisely what an agent is, these statutes require that before he can act as an agent, an applicant must possess a license. Varying methods are used to determine his competence, character, and background, including comprehensive examinations designed to demonstrate the applicant's knowledge of the insurance laws of the state and evidence of completion of company training courses which teach the prospective applicant the substance of his business and how to apply it properly.

The statutes also prescribe in some detail the grounds for revocation, suspension, or denial of license for an agent and the procedures necessary before arriving at such a conclusion. The agent, of course, has the right to review and appeal to the courts.

A considerable portion of the laws regulating agents is devoted to the spelling-out of specific practices which are considered improper. These include such things as rebating, misrepresentation, twisting, inducements, and coercion. Since revoking or suspending the license of an agent may be too severe for a relatively minor infraction of the insurance laws, many states have provided in their statutes for a system of limited fines.

In the fourth category are the laws bearing on the insurance contract and the rights of policyholders and beneficiaries which arise from those contracts. While there is no standard insurance policy form in the life insurance business such as may be found in the field of fire insurance, the statutes prescribe certain basic required policy provisions. While the provisions of these laws are not exactly the same in all states, they establish a pattern which is found in life insurance contracts wherever they may be issued.

For example, ordinary life insurance policies must contain (1) a provision for a grace period, usually thirty days, for the payment of the premium then due, during which time the policy stays in force; (2) a provision that the validity of the policy will not be contested after a specified period, usually after it has been in force during the lifetime of the insured for a period of two years from its date of issue; (3) a provision making the policy and application the entire contract between the policyholder and the company, and providing that all statements in the application shall be considered as representations and not warranties; (4) a provision that in the event of misstatement of age, any amount payable or benefits accruing shall be such as the premium would have purchased if the age had been stated correctly; (5) a provision in participating policies for annual ascertaining and apportioning of divisible surplus after the third policy year; (6) a provision for nonforfeiture benefits and cash surrender values; (7) a provision for policy loans after the third policy year; (8) a provision requiring that if the policy proceeds may be payable in installments which are determinable at the time the policy is issued, a table showing the amounts of the guaranteed installments must be included; (9) a provision that unless the policy has been surrendered or the paid-up term insurance has expired, the policy can be reinstated within a specified period, usually three years from the date of premium default, upon proper application, evidence of insurability satisfactory to the company, and payment of premiums in arrears.

In addition, the statutes of some states list certain provisions or clauses which are forbidden. These include a prohibition against requiring the commencement of any action of law or in equity against the company within any period shorter than that provided by the law of the state. Some states also have statutes which prohibit the exclusion or limitation of liability in general for deaths caused in a specific manner or while the insured has a specific status. However, these laws do not prohibit the exclusion of risks of war, air travel, specified hazardous occupations, foreign residency, or suicide during the first two policy years. Where any of these exclusions or limitations exist, the policy must provide that in the event of death falling within the permitted exclusion, the company shall pay an amount not less than the current reserve attributable to the policy. While these required and prohibited policy provision statutes apply only to policies of ordinary insurance, industrial insurance and group life insurance policies are also subject to statutes in many states requiring certain standard provisions which are appropriate to them.

In brief, the regulating law itself builds into contracts of life insurance certain basic contractual provisions designed to safeguard the interests of the insuring public.

While certain standard policy provisions are prescribed, the law permits a salutary degree of flexibility by allowing companies to issue policies containing provisions which are more liberal for the policyholder than those prescribed. This makes possible the exercise of individual company initiative and facilitates modernization of new contracts as warranted by new developments and the needs of our society. The public is benefited thereby but at the same time is protected against any possible unwholesome effects, since all new policy forms must be submitted to insurance departments for their approval. The statutes set forth in general terms the procedure for this approval and spell out for the guidance of the insurance department a variety of grounds upon which it may base its disapproval of a new policy or provision submitted to it.

Brief mention might also be made of a number of miscellaneous statutes enacted in many of the states which deal with such matters as rights of minors to contract for insurance, exemption of proceeds from claims of creditors, simultaneous death of the insured and the beneficiary, insurable interest, investment by guardians of minors' funds in life insurance, and assignment of policies. In addition to these and the main categories of statutes which have evolved over the years, as reviewed above, new types of statutes dealing with current demands for new insurance services are being enacted in the various states. For example, to meet the growing interest in the equity funding of employee pension plans, laws are currently being enacted to permit and to regulate the establishment by life insurance companies of separate equity investment accounts for funding pension plans, and providing that amounts allocated to such accounts need not be subject to the severe limitations otherwise applicable with respect to investments in common stocks.

Finally, there are the tax laws. Life insurance companies pay substantial taxes, both to the federal government and to the states. It is the purpose of this chapter to consider tax matters only as they relate to the states. The most important of these is the state premium tax. All states impose these taxes on life insurance companies at rates which average about 2 per cent of the premiums paid by policyholders for their life insurance protection. While a majority of the states tax all companies alike, some apply the tax only to out-of-state companies or favor their domestic companies with a preferential rate. In 1962 the total taxes, licenses, and fees paid to the states by the life insurance business was $442 million.[2] In the case of every state the tax receipts far exceed the cost of regulation and in large part represent revenue for general governmental purposes.

Insurance Supervision a Function of the States

Insurance supervision is traditionally a function of the state insurance departments. State supervision was not perfect in its formative years, and the question of whether federal supervision was preferable was considered from time to time by Congressional committees and within the life insurance business itself, where, particularly around the turn of the century, federal supervision had some advocates. To date, however, each time the issue has come to the fore, it has been decided in favor of state regulation over federal regulation.

In the decade that followed the establishment of the first state insurance departments, conditions in the business had become chaotic as a result of conflicts which arose out of discriminatory state legislation designed primarily for home state companies. The National Banking Act which was passed in 1864 suggested a solution, namely, controlling the business, which was becoming national in scope, from Washington. Accordingly, first in 1866 and again in 1868, bills for the federal incorporation of insurance companies were introduced in Congress. Neither bill was enacted.

The scene next shifted to the courts. The concept that the states should supervise insurance was based upon the Tenth Amendment to the Constitution of the United States, which provides: "The powers not delegated to the United States by the Constitution, nor prohibited by it to the States, are reserved to the States respectively, or to the people." On the other hand, Section 8 of Article I of the Constitution delegates to the federal government the power "to regulate Commerce with foreign Nations, and among the several States, and with the Indian Tribes." In the late 1860's, one Samuel B. Paul, an agent representing New York fire insurance companies in the state of Virginia, refused to comply with the state's Deposit and Licensing Law, contending that insurance was commerce and hence beyond the power of the state to regulate. The issue went to the United States Supreme Court, which, in 1869, handed down a momentous decision in the case of *Paul* v. *Virginia.*[3] Affirming the conviction of Paul by the lower court, the Supreme Court said: "Issuing a policy of

[2] Institute of Life Insurance, *Life Insurance Fact Book* (New York, 1963), p. 55.

[3] 8 Wall, 75 US 168 (1869).

insurance is not a transaction of commerce. The policies are simple contracts of indemnity against loss by fire. . . . Such contracts are not interstate transactions. . . ."

While only fire insurance companies were involved in the case, it was clear that the decision in *Paul* v. *Virginia* applied to all lines of insurance, including life. This decision, coming in the early years of insurance supervision, was therefore the foundation of that body of state law intended to provide for the supervision of all branches of the insurance business. The critics of state supervision, nevertheless, were undaunted. Bills for federal supervision of insurance were considered by Congress on a number of occasions; but in each case, they were not enacted. Then, in 1913 the Supreme Court, in the case of *New York Life Insurance Company* v. *Deer Lodge County*,[4] reiterated its earlier position that insurance was not commerce.

The SEUA Decision and Its Aftermath

On June 5, 1944, the entire business and state supervision received its greatest challenge as a result of the decision of the United States Supreme Court in the case of *United States* v. *South-Eastern Underwriters Association*.[5] It held that the fire insurance business—and by analogy, all other lines of insurance—was commerce and thus, when conducted across state lines, was subject to the regulatory power of the federal government. On the same day the Court, in the case of *Polish National Alliance* v. *National Labor Relations Board*, held that a fraternal benefit society was subject to the National Labor Relations Act, since it was an insurance company and its operations "affect" commerce within the meaning of that Act.[6]

This reversal of the doctrine of *Paul* v. *Virginia* immediately confronted the states, the Congress, and the insurance business with a number of serious problems. In the first place, it cast doubt on many state regulatory and tax laws which had been enacted without consideration of the Commerce Clause as a possible limitation on state authority. In the second place, it raised questions concerning the application to insurance of various federal statutes which had been passed without having insurance in mind and which had previously been inapplicable to insurance, but which might now become applicable because the statutes by their terms pertained to commerce generally. Accordingly, there arose a multitude of questions as to what laws were to govern, whether there was to be duplicative federal and state regulation, and what was to be done in the case of inconsistent federal and state laws.

Early in 1945, Congress enacted Public Law 15, also known as the

---

[4] 231 US 495 (1913).

[5] 322 US 533 (1944).

[6] 322 US 643 (1944).

McCarran Act, providing that continued regulation and taxation of insurance by the states is in the public interest, and that the business of insurance shall be subject to such state laws. Congress further declared that Congressional silence shall not be construed as a barrier to state regulation or taxation of insurance, and that no federal act shall supersede any state law on this subject unless the federal statute expressly mentions insurance. Taking up specifically the Sherman Act, the Clayton Act, and the Federal Trade Commission Act, Congress granted a moratorium until 1948 to give the states time to enact additional legislation in these areas, and provided that thereafter those three federal statutes shall apply to the business of insurance to the extent that such business is not regulated by state law.

The states were quick to accept this Congressional invitation to assume continued responsibility for the regulation of the insurance business. One of the immediate consequences of Public Law 15 was the formation of an all-industry committee composed of representatives of practically all branches of the insurance business to work in conjunction with the National Association of Insurance Commissioners in developing additional state laws. This joint endeavor produced significant results. For example, at the end of 1957, virtually all jurisdictions had enacted fair trade practices laws, patterned somewhat after the Federal Trade Commission Act, prohibiting unfair methods of competition and unfair practices in the insurance business. Almost as many states have adopted service-of-process laws designed to enable claimants under insurance policies to bring actions in their home states against insurers not licensed to do business there. Other such uniform state laws were similarly developed and adopted by a number of the states.

Of special significance in the fire, casualty, and surety fields, all of the states also have enacted rate regulatory laws to provide supervision for the rating bureaus, which have long been considered necessary in those areas for the pooling of information and the determination of rates which are neither too low nor too high. Laws of this type are unnecessary in the case of the life insurance business, however, since each company is able to establish its own premium rates on the basis of mortality tables plus individual experience, and the characteristics of the business are such that competitive forces can be relied on to prevent either ruinously low or excessively high rates.

Supreme Court decisions have also served to clarify the extent of state responsibility for insurance regulation. In one case the Court, without reliance on Public Law 15, upheld a state regulatory law designed to protect its citizens, even though interstate commerce was involved.[7] In another case the Court relied on Public Law 15 to sustain a state premium

---

[7] *Robertson* v. *California,* 328 US 440 (1946).

tax applying exclusively to out-of-state companies, the Court assuming that in the absence of that Act the tax would be unconstitutionally discriminatory as against interstate commerce.[8] More recently, the Court has held that the imposition of a premium tax on policies written outside the state by a nonadmitted insurer on property within the state violates the due process clause of the Fourteenth Amendment and is not saved by Public Law 15.[9] In the field of insurance advertising the Court has held that under Public Law 15 the Federal Trade Commission does not have jurisdiction over insurance advertising of companies licensed in states which have enacted their own laws regulating such advertising.[10] This case involved the provision of Public Law 15, previously mentioned, stipulating that the Sherman Act, the Clayton Act, and the Federal Trade Commission Act shall apply to insurance to the extent that such business is not regulated by state law. The Court rejected the contention of the Federal Trade Commission that this provision should be construed to permit concurrent state and federal regulation. In a later case a mail-order insurer contested the regulatory authority of the Federal Trade Commission on the ground that the law of its domicile regulated the advertising it disseminated in states in which it was not licensed. The Court rejected this contention, holding that Public Law 15 meant regulation by the states in which the insurer's advertising activities were directed and had impact.[11]

It thus appears that—in general, at least—the states, by virtue of Public Law 15, continue to have about the same authority and responsibility for the regulation of the business of insurance as they had prior to the SEUA decision.

Some Federal Laws Are Applicable

It should not be assumed, however, that the business of insurance is completely free from all federal regulatory laws, or that the cases reviewed have settled all questions of state versus federal jurisdiction. Under Public Law 15 the National Labor Relations Act and the Fair Labor Standards Act, as well as the boycott and coercion prohibitions of the Sherman Act, are fully applicable to the business of insurance. Very recently, the Supreme Court has ruled that certain variable annuities sold by life insurance companies are not "insurance" as that term is used in the exemption provisions of the Securities Act of 1933 and the Investment Company Act of 1940, and therefore are subject to those federal statutes, leaving untouched the question of the status of such contracts under state

[8] *Prudential Insurance Company* v. *Benjamin,* 328 US 408 (1946).

[9] *State Board of Insurance (Texas)* v. *Todd Shipyards Corporation,* 370 US 451 (1962).

[10] *Federal Trade Commission* v. *National Casualty Company,* 357 US 560 (1958).

[11] *Federal Trade Commission* v. *Travelers Health Association,* 362 US 293 (1960).

insurance laws. Additionally, the provision in Public Law 15 that the Sherman Act, the Clayton Act, and the Federal Trade Commission Act shall be applicable to insurance to the extent that the business is not regulated by state law offers a basis for the assertion of some federal regulatory power in areas where federal agencies may consider state legislation to be incomplete or not of the type contemplated by the McCarran Act.

The Effectiveness of State Regulation

In contrast with the many who feel that the business of insurance is better regulated at the state level, where such regulation is close to the people it serves, it must be assumed that a few advocates of federal regulation will continue to contend that any business of such magnitude should be regulated, at least in part, at the federal level. Accordingly, it may be expected that from time to time in the future, there will be suggestions that the determination made by Congress in Public Law 15—that the public interest will best be served by the continued regulation of insurance by the states—should be reviewed.

One thing is clear: The power of the states to regulate the interstate aspects of the insurance business is subject to the will of Congress. The Congress is free to withdraw or limit this power at any time it desires to do so. The effectiveness of state supervision, and its capacity to meet developments within the insurance business that raise issues of national concern, will undoubtedly be the determining factors in any future decisions reached by Congress in this regard.

Since the Armstrong Investigation of 1905–06, the record of state regulation is good. The statutory pattern reviewed earlier in this chapter is a sound demonstration of a comprehensive state regulatory system. There are many other evidences of the efficacy of state regulation. Financial failures in the life insurance business have been conspicuously low. Abusive practices have been comparatively few and have been promptly attacked by the state regulatory authorities. As the business has matured, most of the companies have acquired a deep sense of public responsibility and thus have voluntarily established a high degree of integrity and performance which in a major way has set a standard for both those who are engaged in and those who regulate the life insurance business. At the same time, there can be no doubt that the constant scrutiny and close supervision provided by the insurance departments of the several states played an important role in the development of the high standards of conduct which characterize the business of life insurance.

SELECTED REFERENCES

Cowee, John W. *Federal Regulation of Insurance.* Madison: University of Wisconsin Press, 1948.

MACLEAN, JOSEPH B. *Life Insurance.* 9th ed. New York: McGraw-Hill Book Co., Inc., 1962.

PATTERSON, EDWIN W. *The Insurance Commissioner in the United States.* Cambridge: Harvard University Press, 1927.

ROHRER, MARGARET. *State Regulation of Insurance.* Berkeley: Bureau of Public Administration, University of California, 1951.

Chapter 78

REGULATION OF HEALTH INSURANCE

*BY ROBERT R. NEAL**

The historical and legal bases for the state regulatory system have been covered adequately in the preceding chapter. The material therein as to incorporation and regulation of insurance companies, powers and duties of the insurance supervisory officials, qualifications and licensing of agents,[1] much of the statutory pattern applicable to insurance contracts, and the mechanics of policy form approval applies to health insurance. Accordingly, this chapter is restricted to some of the unique applications of state regulation to health insurance.

CHARACTERISTICS OF HEALTH INSURANCE INFLUENCING REGULATION

At the outset, it should be recognized that health insurance has at least eight distinctive characteristics which have in varying degrees influenced the manner in which it is regulated.

First, health insurance is written by prepayment plans (the regulation of which is outside the scope of this chapter) and by nearly all major types of insurance companies: life and casualty, stock and mutual, monoline and multiline, domestic, foreign, and alien. The regulatory implication of this fact may be expressed in the nature of a dilemma for legislatures and state insurance departments. Regulation must be accomplished in such a manner as to achieve its objective, protecting the public interest, without unnecessarily creating artificial competitive disadvantages for any of the several types of carriers involved.

Second, health insurance provides coverage for losses[2] which are often

---

* The author expresses deep appreciation to his colleagues on the staff of the Health Insurance Association of America, and especially to Richard A. Edwards, for invaluable assistance in the preparation of this chapter.

[1] The regulation of health insurance underwriters is virtually identical with that of life underwriters, and therefore the analysis of such subject is included in Chapter 67, "Legal Responsibilities of the Life Underwriter."

[2] The rapid growth of voluntary health insurance has been accompanied by usage of certain terms within the business (e.g., loss, hazard, risk, etc.) in such a way as to differ to some extent from the standard dictionary definitions thereof. The Commission

repetitive or recurrent. In contrast to life insurance, where the loss is on a "one-to-a-customer" basis, an insured may have any number of injuries or illnesses. Regulatory consequences of this fact include, for example, the necessity for determinations as to whether any given loss is attributable to an earlier or a new illness or disability for such purposes as the reapplication of a deductible or the initiation of a new benefit period.

Third, health insurance provides coverage for losses the occurrence of which is often difficult to determine. The very existence and severity of an injury or illness are frequently matters upon which competent medical opinion may differ, in contrast to such objectively determinable certainties as the death of a person, destruction of a building by fire, or damage to an automobile by collision. Regulatory consequences of this fact include, for example, the review of policy provisions which provide criteria to determine whether a disability is "total" or "partial."

Fourth, health insurance provides coverage for a whole spectrum of risks, with a corresponding range of liability on the part of the insurer. The benefits payable by the insurer usually differ according to the extent of the covered expenses incurred by the insured, as distinguished from a fixed-sum liability. Regulatory consequences of this fact include, for example, the need to prevent the marketing of trivial and misleading benefits.

Fifth, health insurance nearly always involves parties other than the insured and the insurer—i.e., the physician, the hospital, and the other providers of medical care. Regulatory consequences of this fact include, for example, the review of policy provisions which define the providers whose services are covered, as well as the services which are or are not within the scope of the policy, and provisions to guarantee preservation of the insured's free choice of his physician.

Sixth, health insurance provides coverage for risks which are significantly affected by economic cycles and by substantial geographical differentials in the costs of medical care. Regulatory consequences of these facts include, as to the former, the control of excessive loss-of-time insurance to prevent malingering and, as to the latter, deterrents to the misutilization of medical care facilities.

Seventh, health insurance must keep pace with the incredible dynamics of medical technology. Regulatory consequences of this fact include, for example, legislative and administrative recognition of the necessity for experimentation as to new forms of coverage and for flexibility in the preparation of policy forms.

---

on Insurance Terminology of the American Risk and Insurance Association has undertaken the development of a glossary designed to provide the public, the commissioners, and the insurance business with definitions which accurately reflect modern usage. At the time of this writing, the Commission's work has not yet progressed to the point of providing authoritative definitions of several terms used in this chapter.

Eighth, the maximum extension of health insurance coverage compatible with preservation of the voluntary system under state supervision is clearly in the public interest. But there is also a great diversity among individuals as to the types of coverage they need and their respective financial resources. Regulatory consequences of these facts include, for example, legislative and administrative recognition of the need for a wide variety of coverages, and the correlative impracticality of a standard or uniform policy, as well as continual efforts by insurers to enlarge the number of insureds by designing new insurance mechanisms.

REGULATION OF INDIVIDUAL HEALTH INSURANCE FORMS

The interaction of the foregoing characteristics of health insurance, and some factors extraneous to this chapter, have significantly influenced the pattern of state regulation.

Legislation affecting the content of health insurance forms (policies, riders, and endorsements) may be classified as permissive, mandatory, or prohibitory. Each such category may be further classified as either substantive law or policy provisions law.

If substantive law, the statute simply describes the end to be achieved, and the insurance department determines whether the language drafted by the insurer does in fact achieve such end.

If policy provisions law, the statute either compels the use of specific provisions in the words of the statute (or a not less favorable substitute) or provides that if the insurer elects to use any provision on a designated subject, the provision must be that contained in the statute or one which the commissioner finds to be not less favorable to the policyholder or beneficiary. The former are called required provisions; the latter, optional provisions.

On June 15, 1950, the National Association of Insurance Commissioners approved and adopted the Uniform Individual Accident and Sickness Policy Provisions Law to "permit the use of uniform standard policy provisions in all policy forms in every state. . . ." Subsequently, every state enacted or accepted the Uniform Law, although with occasional variations in the text. The 1950 Uniform Law displaced an earlier effort toward the same end, namely, the Standard Provisions Law of 1912, which had proved unsatisfactory (only twenty-nine states adopted it) largely by reason of its inflexibility. Under the 1912 law, provisions differing from the text of the statute could not be used even if they were not less favorable to the policyholder; this was corrected in the 1950 law.

Enactment by a state of the Uniform Individual Accident and Sickness Policy Provisions Law is only a first step in regulation of individual health insurance forms. It is followed by administrative implementation and supervision. As an aid to insurers in the preparation of individual health insurance policies, and as a stimulus to uniformity by the several insurance departments in their administrative implementation and supervision, the NAIC adopted *The Official Guide,* the third edition of which became effective on January 1, 1947. The *Guide* outlines the procedure for filing forms, and provides a check list for the examiners' review of contracts. Although much of the *Guide* has been superseded by the text of the 1950 law, it is still applicable in part. In December, 1948, the NAIC approved a *Statement of Principles* for individual health insurance policies, which statement contains standards or criteria for construction of policy forms, interpretation of certain types of policy provisions, and the preparation of advertising and solicitation material.

The NAIC adopted model advertising rules in December, 1955, and developed an interpretive guide for such rules in 1956. They have been relied upon by most insurance commissioners as particularizations of general statutory prohibitions against deceptive or misleading health insurance advertising.

Administrative implementation has taken the form of regulations, rules, circular letters, and bulletins. Analogous to the evolution of the common law, a considerable body of "precedent" has been formed by the decisions of each state insurance department as to the compatibility of a particular policy provision with the Uniform Law. The New York State Insurance Department, after consultation with the business, has recently distributed its "precedents" or policy approval standards to policy examiners and insurance companies doing business in New York State.

Administrative supervision of insurer compliance with the Uniform Law is made effective primarily in the review of policy forms required by statute to be filed with and approved by the insurance department prior to sale. Nearly all important forms—policies, riders, endorsements, and applications—must be filed with the commissioner. But not all such forms are filed for approval in all states; some are filed merely for the information of the department. Some states require that forms delivered therein must also be approved by the insurer's domiciliary state prior to such delivery.

Each form filed for approval is assigned by the commissioner or one of his deputies to an examiner, who reviews the form for compliance with the Uniform Law as enacted in his state and with the applicable administrative interpretation thereof. The insurer is then advised either that the form is approved or that it cannot be approved until specified changes are made, assurances are given by the insurer as to its underwriting and claims practices on a given subject, or additional information is provided. Inasmuch as signficant and indefensible competitive disadvantages may be created by an excessive interval of time between receipt of a form by a department and its review, some states have enacted so-called "deemer" laws, which provide that a form filed with the insurance department is "deemed" approved unless the department advises the insurer to the contrary within a specified number of days after the filing.

If an examiner disapproves a form and, after exhausting informal procedures, the insurer is of the opinion that such disapproval is contrary to law, the usual procedure for review is to request a hearing, formal or informal, before the insurance commissioner. If the examiner's decision is affirmed after such a hearing, judicial review is available. The scope of such review is, of course, narrow.

REGULATION OF INDIVIDUAL HEALTH INSURANCE RATES

Rate regulation of the type used in casualty insurance has been found not to be in the public interest with respect to health insurance. Casualty-type rate regulation would be inappropriate in health insurance for the following reasons: (1) the multiplicity of health insurance policy forms, coverages, and benefits; (2) the keen rate competition among insurers as distinguished from formation of rates in concert; (3) the fact that rate regulation impedes continued experimentation with better forms of coverage needed to keep pace with improving medical technology; and (4) a series of administrative and political problems for which no acceptable solution is apparent.

The typical individual health insurance statutory provision on premiums requires that they be filed with the commissioner and prohibits benefits which are unreasonable in relation to the premium charged. Satisfaction of this standard is one of the requirements for securing approval of the policy form or avoiding withdrawal of approval. The original purpose of this standard was to provide insurance departments with a means to prevent the sale of contracts whose benefits were so limited or restricted as to make the protection of the contract illusory.

To the general rule that individual health insurance premiums are not prescribed, but need only be reasonable in relation to the benefits, there are a limited number of exceptions. Three illustrations suffice.

First, credit insurance has been subjected in many states to a degree of rate control more akin to the casualty type.

Second, several states have required prior approval by the commissioner of the premiums charged for individual health insurance policies issued under the so-called "state sixty-five" plans, which are designed to provide health insurance to the aged by a form of pooling and without individual underwriting.

Third, Section 162–6 of the New York Insurance Law has established rate regulation for certain individual policies issued at age 60 or above by exercise of conversion rights required to be contained in group health insurance policies.

REGULATION OF GROUP HEALTH INSURANCE FORMS

The eight characteristics of health insurance influencing regulation, enumerated earlier in this chapter, are applicable to group as well as individual coverage. But there are at least four additional characteristics of group contracts which have significantly influenced the pattern of state regulation of such contracts.

First, although the distinction between substantive law and policy provisions law is applicable to group as well as individual health insurance, there is, for the reasons enumerated below, no necessity for a uniform policy provisions law for group contracts. Several states have enacted standard provisions for group health insurance policies, but such standard provisions are usually expressed as substantive law and are usually much less comprehensive than those applicable to individual policies.

Second, the phenomenal growth in the number of persons protected by group health insurance has been stimulated at least in part by the recognition by state legislators and state insurance commissioners of the need for flexibility in the preparation and administration of group contracts. Many group contracts are, in the jargon of the business, "tailor-made" to provide the particular combination of benefits and other program details requested by the group policyholder, such as the employer or the union.

Third, the need for flexibility, and thus the undesirability of a uniform policy provisions law in group contracts, is buttressed by the effect of collective bargaining upon the content of many group contracts. Because the employer is required by federal labor laws to bargain with the union as to health insurance benefits, state insurance commissioners are properly reluctant to frustrate such bargaining by requiring an insurer to use policy provisions that might be inconsistent with the desired results. This does not mean, of course, that the employer and the union may use collective bargaining to override a well-defined public policy of the state, but it does mean that an insurer should be permitted to issue the group coverage requested by the employer and union unless to do so would clearly contravene public policy.

Fourth, the need for detailed regulation of what the group purchaser can buy is considerably less than the need for such regulation of individual policies. Any deceptive advertising or other unethical conduct by a group insurer would be immediately thwarted by the experienced staff or consultants of the employer or union, or by the sheer intensity of the competition in the group health field. In point of fact, unethical or misleading activity by health insurers is minimal because of state regulation and the insurers' own self-regulation.

None of the foregoing is intended to suggest that group health insurance is inadequately regulated; quite the contrary is true. Such regulation is expressed with lesser emphasis upon policy provision control and greater emphasis upon substantive law. For example, group health insurance statutes typically define eligible groups and the types of coverage which may be issued to such groups.

REGULATION OF GROUP INSURANCE RATES

The degree of insurance rate regulation is usually inversely proportional to the variety of benefit patterns and contract provisions offered to the public. Standard policies, such as those used in individual fire and casualty insurance, tend to be subject to full-scale rate regulation. Individual health insurance policies, only part of the content of which is controlled by the Uniform Individual Accident and Sickness Policy Provisions Law, are typically subject to the "not unreasonable in relation to the benefits provided" standard just discussed. Although a few states have a statutory minimum first-year rate structure, or apply the "not unreasonable in relation to the benefits provided" standard, in general, group health insurance contracts are not subject to rate control. Such regulation is unnecessary by reason of the extraordinarily vigorous competition among insurers in this field and by the widespread use of experience-rating formulas. Under the latter a first-year premium is established by actuarial estimates of the probable morbidity, and the premium is thereafter adjusted downward or upward to reflect differentials between actual and anticipated experience. One of the public benefits of experience rating is that each employer or union is provided with a substantial monetary incentive for encouragement of individual safety and health conservation programs.

REGULATION OF FRANCHISE HEALTH INSURANCE

On June 12, 1946, the NAIC adopted the following definition of franchise insurance:

> Accident and health insurance on a franchise plan is hereby declared to be that form of accident and health insurance issued to
>
> (1) Five or more employees of any corporation, copartnership or individual employer or any governmental corporation, agency or department thereof, or
>
> (2) Ten or more members of any trade or professional association or of a labor union or of any other association having had an active existence for at least two years where such association or union has a constitution or by-laws and is formed in good faith for purposes other than that of obtaining insurance;
>
> Where such persons, with or without their dependents, are issued the same form of an individual policy varying only as to amounts and kinds of coverage applied for by such persons, under an arrangement whereby the premiums on such policies may be paid to the Insurer periodically by the employer, with or without payroll deductions, or by the association for its members, or by some designated person acting on behalf of such employer or association.

This definition has been adopted officially by less than a majority of the states. In some states, there is no statutory recognition of this form of coverage, but virtually all states permit the issuance of franchise policies and regulate them in the same manner as individual policies. The characteristics of franchise insurance are enumerated in the above definition. It should be noted that such an arrangement provides an additional means for extending the economies of mass selling to a large number of people, many of whom would not qualify for "true group" coverage.

REGULATION OF BLANKET HEALTH INSURANCE

Blanket health insurance is similar to group insurance in that it is typically issued to an employer, a union, a common carrier, an educational institution, or a subdivision of government as a means of providing defined coverage for anyone having a specified relationship with such a policyholder. For example, an insurer may issue a blanket policy to cover all employees who are on a particular hazardous job or all who attend a specified union picnic. Similarly, blanket policies are frequently issued to educational institutions to protect their students, to associations to protect their members, and to governmental subdivisions to protect certain of their employees, such as firemen. When such contracts are issued to employers, the coverage is normally defined by reference to exceptional hazards incident to such employment. The regulation of blanket health insurance is similar in most respects to the regulation of group health insurance.

CURRENT OR RECENT REGULATORY PROBLEMS

Despite the convenience of classifying the major forms of health insurance and their respective regulatory patterns, major regulatory issues usually involve more than one such form of coverage. Indeed, major regulatory issues frequently arise from or affect a combination of lines of insurance, such as life and health or casualty and health. The following enumeration of some of the current or recent major regulatory issues illustrates the complexity of modern health insurance regulation.

First, the NAIC and the industry have recently expressed concern over the trend toward noninsured employee benefit plans. Indeed, in December, 1962, the NAIC formally adopted a resolution urging each commissioner "to give immediate consideration to the need of legislation within his State placing employee benefit plans under appropriate State supervision to the end that public interest in such matters is adequately protected and that any existing inequities in regulation, taxation, or otherwise, which induce the adoption of non-insured plans in the employee benefit field, be removed."

Second, for the past several years the NAIC and the business have made intensive studies of overinsurance and duplication of benefits. The basic concept is that medical care insurance benefits in excess of the expenses of an illness or disability provide a profit to the insured, an incentive for malingering and thus misutilization of medical care facilities, a source of irritation to the providers of medical care who see their patients profiting financially from their services, and a stimulus to rising costs of medical care. A similar misuse of the insurance mechanism occurs when disability income benefits, which are tax-exempt, exceed the "take-home" pay of the insured. The present overinsurance provisions of the Uniform Individual Accident and Sickness Policy Provisions Law are so inadequate that they are used in very few policies. The principal reason for the inadequacy of the hospital-surgical-medical overinsurance provisions is that they were drafted, prior to the expansive growth of guaranteed renewable and noncancellable forms of coverage, on the assumption that the insurer could refuse renewal of a policy upon learning of the existence of overinsurance on that particular risk. Under guaranteed renewable or noncancellable coverage, however, such an assumption is invalid. Appropriate amendments to the overinsurance provisions of the Uniform Law were recommended by the NAIC in December, 1963.

Third, the nature and extent of extraterritorial regulation and taxation provide a persistent and complex regulatory problem. Primary responsibility and authority for regulation rest, of course, upon the chartering or domiciliary state of the insurer. But the state wherein the insured employee, union member, or beneficiary resides also has an interest in protecting those of its citizens who purchase coverage from foreign and alien insurers. These two factors, coupled with the growth of group health insurance across state lines, as well as direct-mail health insurance, have given recent emphasis to the constitutional limitations upon extraterritoriality. A significant case upon this point is *State Board of Insurance* v. *Todd Shipyards Corporation,*[3] wherein the Supreme Court of the United States invalidated a Texas statute which imposed a 5 per cent gross premium tax on every person who purchased from an insurer not licensed in Texas a policy covering risks situated in that state. The importance of the *Todd* case lies not in the invalidation of the Texas statute, but in the fact that the Court used the occasion to point out that even though the Congress had, by the enactment of Public Law 15, granted the states immunity from the regulatory and taxing limitations of the commerce clause of the United States Constitution, this fact did not affect the continued force of the due process clause of the Fourteenth Amendment in limiting extraterritorial taxation under the doctrine of *Allgeyer* v. *Louisiana,*[4] *St. Louis Cotton Compress Company* v. *Arkansas,*[5] and *Connecticut General Life Insurance Company* v. *Johnson.*[6]

Fourth, individual health insurance may be classified by permanency

[3] 370 US 451 (1962).

[4] 165 US 78 (1897).

[5] 260 US 346 (1922).

[6] 303 US 77 (1938).

of coverage into four general categories: noncancellable and guaranteed renewable, which assures renewal at the same premium rate for a specified number of years or to an attained age of the insured; guaranteed renewable, which assures renewal for a specified number of years or to an attained age of the insured, but with the insurer reserving the right to change the premium on the basis of a class of policies; optionally renewable, which is subject to termination by the insurer; and single-premium nonrenewable, which assures coverage for the life of the contract, without renewal thereafter. These four classes, given in descending order of permanency and cost, all have a useful role to play in protecting the public against the risks of illness or disability. But each year usually sees the introduction in various state legislatures of bills which would either forbid the issuance of optionally renewable policies or in some manner limit the right of the insurer to refuse renewal of such policies. By the insurers' own volition, the modern trend is clearly toward greater permanency of coverage and minimal exercise of the reserved right to refuse renewal. Furthermore, the fact that optionally renewable contracts have a lower cost than those containing guaranteed options for renewal leads people to purchase coverage or supplemental coverage in many instances where they are not ready to pay the higher cost for the same benefits on a more permanent basis. Finally, such contracts permit an insurer to experiment with new forms of coverage until such time as the experience thus acquired dictates whether it is feasible to offer the coverage in noncancellable and guaranteed renewable, or guaranteed renewable plans. Despite these important attributes of optionally renewable contracts, "mandatory noncan" legislative proposals will doubtless continue to be offered.

Fifth, a related and equally persistent regulatory issue, this time affecting both group and individual coverages, arises from the frequent contention that the continuance or renewal of health insurance policies constitutes the issuance of a new contract. The importance of this issue is the avenue which it opens for circumvention of constitutional limitations upon retroactive application of legislation. That is to say, the protection afforded insurance contracts by the contract clause and the Fourteenth Amendment due process clause of the United States Constitution, as well as state constitutional counterparts of both, would mean little indeed if each renewal had the effect of requiring compliance with all statutes enacted or regulations promulgated after the issuance of the policy. Fortunately, most courts have held that a renewal does not have such effect when the contract provides for renewal, but a minority of courts have ruled to the contrary.

Sixth, New York State has enacted mandatory conversion legislation for both family and group contracts. Under such legislation, most persons whose coverage under the family or group policy is terminated are entitled, without evidence of insurability and upon seasonable application, to an individual policy providing benefits at least the equivalent of those specified in the statute. Although many insurers offered conversion privileges to group customers prior to the enactment of the New York legislation, and continue to do so country-wide, the insurance business was and is of the opinion that employers should not be compelled to purchase the more expensive coverage which contains guaranteed conversion privileges. Mandatory conversion requirements tend to discourage continuance of coverage under group contracts for retired employees or union members, and the latter method usually provides greater benefits for less premium than is possible by the use of individual conversion policies. Nevertheless, there are frequently legislative proposals in other states which would create mandatory conversion obligations.

These examples of current regulatory problems are not an exhaustive enumeration of even the major issues, but it is hoped that their description—read in the light of the regulatory characteristics and patterns offered earlier in the chapter—will provide an introduction to the nature of health insurance regulation.

SELECTED REFERENCES

DICKERSON, O. D. *Health Insurance.* Rev. ed. Homewood, Ill.: Richard D. Irwin, Inc., 1963.

FAULKNER, EDWIN J. *Health Insurance.* New York: McGraw-Hill Book Co., Inc., 1960.

FOLLMANN, J. F., JR. "Regulation of Accident and Sickness Insurance," *Accident and Sickness Insurance* (ed. David McCahan). S. S. Huebner Foundation Series. Homewood, Ill.: Richard D. Irwin, Inc., 1954.

MCALEVEY, JOHN F. "Present Status of State Regulation of the Accident and Health Business," *Insurance Law Journal*, 1956.

STRAUB, ADELBERT G., JR. (ed.). *Examination of Insurance Companies.* 7 vols. New York: New York State Insurance Department, 1955.

Chapter 79

IMPORTANT VARIATIONS IN CANADIAN LIFE INSURANCE

BY D. E. KILGOUR

The development of the institution of life insurance in Canada has, to a large extent, paralleled that in the United States. The result is a marked similarity between plans of insurance and policy forms, investment practices, company organization and management, methods and techniques of selection and training of agents, and other agency operations. Nevertheless, there are important variations in practice between the life insurance companies of these two great nations. Some of these stem from certain fundamental legislative differences; others may be attributed to economic and geographic considerations.

Canadian life insurance companies have been aggressively managed and have gone far afield. Many companies do business in the United States and the United Kingdom, and a number do business in other countries. More than two million people in fifty different countries own policies in Canadian companies in an amount in excess of $15.6 billion, so that life insurance constitutes one of Canada's most important "exports." On the other hand, Canadians own life insurance to the extent of 179 per cent of their national income, which is the highest percentage in the world.

Canadian life insurance companies are subject to several corporate restrictions not generally applicable in other countries. Chief among these are the following: (1) They may not acquire more than 30 per cent of the common stock, nor more than 30 per cent of the total issue of stock, of a corporation; moreover, they may not invest their life insurance funds in the stock of another life insurance company. This automatically prevents the acquisiton of one life insurance company by another, or the acquisition of a casualty company by a life insurance company. This is in marked contrast to many British and United States insurers doing business in Canada who have these wider corporate powers. (2) If securities are shown in the balance sheets at book values, the current practice which is encouraged by the Canadian Department of Insurance is to provide in the liabilities for any excess of book values over maximum statutory values. Maximum statutory values mean amortized values in the case of securities issued or guaranteed by the government of Canada, any province of Canada, the United Kingdom, or the United States, and market values for all other securities. This is in contrast to the situation in the United States, where companies must use amortized values for virtually all bonds and market values in the case of other securities. Companies in the United States, however, maintain a mandatory security valuation reserve in their liabilities.

Life insurance in Canada developed principally through stock companies. A high degree of policyholder participation in earnings has been traditional, because stock companies have for many years made use of their statutory powers to sell participating as well as nonparticipating insurance. Companies are required to keep separate accounts for participating and nonparticipating insurance. Shareholders in small companies are limited by statute to a maximum of 10 per cent of the earnings on participating business. A sliding scale further reduces the shareholders' interest as the company becomes larger, so that shareholders are limited to 2½ per cent of earnings on participating insurance when the mean participating fund exceeds $1 billion. Many companies have voluntarily limited shareholder interest in participating earnings to 5 per cent, even when the sliding scale in the statute would allow them to take more. In recent years, five Canadian stock life insurance companies have adopted plans to convert from a stock basis to a mutual basis. Two of these companies completed conversion in 1962.

Also worthy of note is the fact that interest rates have been consistently higher in Canada than in the United States, and this is frequently reflected in premium rates and dividend scales.

Government Regulation of Life Insurance

Government supervision of life insurance is much the same in Canada as it is in the United States, but it has developed along somewhat different lines. The significant feature in Canada is the dual control exercised by the federal and provincial (equivalent to state) governments.

Insurance legislation was historically the subject of long and involved constitutional conflict between the federal and provincial authorities.[1] This conflict has been resolved practically, if not strictly constitutionally; and it may be said that the primary responsibility of the federal government is the solvency of the Canadian, British, and foreign insurance

[1] *In re Insurance Act* (1932), A.C. 45.

companies licensed or registered by it, for the protection of the insuring public. This responsibility is authorized by and administered under the Department of Insurance Act, the Foreign Insurance Companies Act (1932), and the Canadian and British Insurance Companies Act (1932),[2] which, when read together, represent the codified insurance laws of Canada as distinguished from the provincial laws. They are the only general acts of the Parliament of Canada relating directly to insurance.

With regard to all companies licensed or registered by it, whether domestic or foreign, the federal government is concerned with such matters as the maintenance in Canada of adequate assets, the proper accounting, and the conditions under which an insurance company may be declared insolvent and prevented from further transaction of business. With regard to domestic companies, it is also concerned with more specific matters, such as the methods of incorporation, the powers of directors and officers, the manner in which they may be elected or appointed, and the types of investments which may be made. That the Canadian Insurance Department, through which the federal government operates, has always functioned efficiently is evidenced by the fact that no Canadian legal reserve life insurance company licensed by the federal government has ever occasioned the loss of a dollar to any policyholder through failure to carry out its obligations under its policy contracts. The same is true for more than the past eighty years with respect to Canadian policyholders insured with companies from other countries doing business in Canada.

The sphere of the provincial departments of insurance extends to the supervision of insurers licensed by them, whether or not they hold federal certificates of registry, and to the supervision of provincial companies operating under provincial charter exclusively. In addition, the provincial governments are concerned with the regulation of the terms, conditions, and incidents of the contracts of all insurers, and with the licensing and regulation of agents, brokers, and adjusters.

The so-called Uniform Life Insurance Act of the Provinces of Canada[3] (applicable in all provinces except Quebec) contains provisions relating to the rights and status of beneficiaries, their designation by the insured, the destination of the insurance money, and, generally, all provisions respecting life insurance contracts other than those relating to the incorporation, licensing, and regulation of insurers. In all provinces except Newfoundland, the Uniform Act is contained in a separate part of a general insurance act; in Newfoundland, it is a separate enactment. Revisions and amendments have been substantially uniform in all provinces on the recommendation of the Association of Superintendents of Insurance for

[2] *Revised Statutes of Canada,* 1952, C. 70, C. 125, C. 31.

[3] References herein will be made to Ontario legislation, *Revised Statutes of Ontario,* 1960, C. 190, as revised by 1961–62, C. 63.

the provinces of Canada. A comprehensive revision was adopted in final form by the Superintendents in 1959; after enactment by all provinces (except Quebec), it came into force on July 1, 1962. It applies not only to contracts made after this date but also to those made at an earlier date.

The only exception to this pattern of uniformity is the Province of Quebec, where the law relating to life insurance contracts is to be found mainly in the *Quebec Civil Code,* the Husbands' and Parents' Life Insurance Act,[4] and the Quebec Insurance Act.[5] Quebec is largely a French-speaking province which, under the Canadian Constitution, is guaranteed the right to its own law, which stems from that of France.

Policy Contract

Canadian policies, in form and substance, are essentially comparable to American policies. But whereas the latter are subject to strict legislative control regarding required provisions and their wording, Canadian policies are governed by statute law only as to the substance of some of their provisions. The result is that some provisions of Canadian policies are different from corresponding provisions of American ones.

Every individual policy[6] subject to the Uniform Act must set forth the name or a sufficient description of the insured (i.e., the applicant) and of the person whose life is insured; the amount, or the method of determining the amount, of the insurance money payable and the conditions under which it becomes payable; and the amount, or the method of determining the amount, of the premium and the period of grace within which it may be paid. Quebec law requires essentially the same policy contents, including a declaration of the commencement and duration of the risk and the signing and dating by the insurer.[7]

In addition, the Uniform Act requires every policy to include the conditions upon which the policy may, if it lapses, be reinstated. The policy must show whether the insurance is participating or nonparticipating; if it provides surrender, loan, paid-up, or extended options, they must be set forth in the policy.

Legally, a policy need contain no further provisions, and even these mandatory terms and conditions are not required to be in the form of standard provisions. This also applies to other subject matter dealt with in the Uniform Act, such as incontestability and suicide. Life insurance companies are therefore permitted complete freedom of expression in drafting policy contracts, provided the intent of the statutory provisions of the law is not changed except in a manner more favorable to the insured.

---

[4] *Revised Statutes of Quebec,* 1941, C. 301.

[5] *Ibid.,* C. 299.

[6] For contents of group life insurance policy, see Uniform Act, S. 142.

[7] *Quebec Civil Code,* Art. 2587.

It should be noted that while the Uniform Act is not as confining as the various state insurance codes with respect to required provisions and their wording, it does provide that the provisions in the application, the policy, any document attached to the policy when issued, and any amendment to the contract agreed upon in writing after the policy is issued constitute the entire contract.[8] Thus, for instance, while the written application or a copy thereof need not be attached to the policy, it is made a part of the policy whether or not it is attached.

Beneficiaries. Prior to the 1962 revision of the Uniform Act, there were three classes of beneficiaries: beneficiaries for value, preferred beneficiaries, and ordinary beneficiaries. A "beneficiary for value" acquired a vested interest in the policy. If the insured named a "preferred beneficiary," a trust was created in favor of that beneficiary, and the insurance money was therefore beyond the insured's control, subject to certain exceptions. The insured could change the beneficiary to another member of the preferred class, but he could not go outside that class without the consent of a named preferred beneficiary. The preferred class was defined as the spouse, child, grandchild, or parent of the life insured. All others were "ordinary beneficiaries," who were similar to revocable beneficiaries in the United States.

The most significant change in the 1962 revision was the elimination of the beneficiary for value, the preferred beneficiary and the trust in his favor, and the ordinary beneficiary, and the substitution therefor of beneficiaries who may be appointed revocably or irrevocably. Any beneficiary for value or preferred beneficiary, designated as such prior to July 1, 1962, does, however, retain his rights as they then existed. These rights will continue to be governed by the previous law unless and until a beneficiary for value ceases to be a beneficiary of that class, or until a preferred beneficiary by death or by a release of interest has ceased to retain the rights which the previous law gave to that class of beneficiary.[9] In the case of a preferred beneficiary, this means that if he consents to a change to a beneficiary outside the "preferred" class, the new law will apply to the policy. Also, if a preferred beneficiary releases his interest to the insured and the insured reappoints him as beneficiary, the provisions of the new law will apply.

The designation of an irrevocable beneficiary must be effected in the contract or by a declaration in writing (other than a declaration in a will), which declaration must be filed with the company during the lifetime of the person whose life is insured.[10] If, however, an irrevocable designation is contained in a will or in a declaration that is not so filed, the

---

[8] Uniform Act, S. 140(2).

[9] *Ibid.*, S. 138(2), (3).

[10] *Ibid.*, S. 157(1).

beneficiary will be deemed to have been designated revocably.[11] Once a beneficiary has been designated irrevocably, the insured may not, while the beneficiary is living, alter or revoke the designation or deal with the policy in any way without the consent of the beneficiary, but the insured remains entitled to dividends.

It is important to note that the result of the provisions just mentioned is that an irrevocable designation must be a conscious and positive act. This differs from the situation in the United States, where a designation is deemed to be irrevocable unless the power to revoke the designation is expressly enunciated.

If any beneficiary is named in a contract, the insurance money is free from the claims of the insured's creditors from the time it becomes payable. If, on the other hand, the beneficiary is a spouse, child, grandchild, or parent of the person whose life is insured, or if any beneficiary is designated irrevocably, the insurance money is free from the claims of the insured's creditors, both before and after the time it becomes payable.[12]

The Province of Nova Scotia deviated somewhat from the uniform provision regarding irrevocable beneficiaries. The significance of this deviation is that where an insured makes an irrevocable designation of beneficiary, the insured must sign a statement acknowledging that he understands the effect of the irrevocable designation, and the agent must also sign a statement certifying that he has fully explained to the insured (not in the presence of the beneficiary) the nature and effect of the irrevocable designation.[13]

In contrast to the purely contractual practice in the United States of including a "spendthrift" provision in settlement agreements elected by an insured, this matter is specifically dealt with by statute in the common-law provinces of Canada.[14]

There are only two classes of beneficiaries in Quebec: those who obtain their rights from Article 1029 of the *Civil Code,* and those, corresponding to preferred beneficiaries, who are nominated under the Husbands' and Parents' Life Insurance Act, and who consist of the wife, their children, his children, or her children.[15] An implied trust is created in favor of these so-called "preferred" beneficiaries by virtue of which the insurance money does not go into the insured's estate and is not subject to his debts or those of the persons benefited. Once a preferred beneficiary has been named, changes may be made within the class, but consent of the beneficiary is required to a change outside the class. The validity of this consent, however, must be viewed in light of the provisions of the *Civil Code*

[11] *Ibid.,* S. 157(2).

[12] *Ibid.,* S. 162.

[13] *Statutes of Nova Scotia,* 1962, C. 9, S. 148(3).

[14] Uniform Act, S. 183.

[15] *Revised Statutes of Quebec,* 1941, C. 301, S. 3.

which prohibit the conferring by husband and wife of benefits *inter vivos* upon each other.[16]

Other beneficiaries in Quebec who have accepted the benefit obtain by law a vested interest. Some authorities are inclined to the view that this interest may be made subject to divestment by reserving in the appointment of beneficiary the right to make subsequent changes.[17] The law on this matter, however, is not settled.

Incontestability. It is only the statements made by the insured (applicant) and the person whose life is insured in the application and on the medical examination, and written statements or answers furnished as evidence of insurability (e.g., statements respecting airplane travel) that are incontestable, and not the policy itself. Consequently, the question of what constitutes a "contest" of the policy, over which there has been considerable controversy in the United States, does not arise. War and aviation exclusion clauses and other provisions relating to coverage can be enforced without question even after the contestable period has expired.

If the insured or the person whose life is insured fails to disclose or misrepresents any material fact within his knowledge, the contract is voidable by the insurer.[18]

Quebec law does not place any limit on the period during which a statement may be contested. In practice, a two-year incontestability clause is generally used in policies subject to Quebec law.

The provision regarding incontestability does not apply to the disability benefit or to a misstatement of age. Insurers usually take advantage of this exception, and concealment or misstatement of a material fact renders this benefit liable to forfeiture on discovery. The provision regarding incontestability does apply, however, to the accidental means death benefit.

Reinstatement. The reinstatement provision in the Uniform Act is similar to the corresponding provision in United States policies. This statutory provision has no counterpart in the laws governing a Quebec contract, the rights in this regard being covered entirely by agreement between the parties.

There are two additional provisions in the Uniform Act respecting reinstatement which are of particular interest, since they establish the law on questions which have caused some difficulty in the United States. The first provides that in the case of reinstated policies, the two-year incontestability period, insofar as it affects the rights of the insurer, runs from the date of reinstatement. In a similar manner, the period of time fixed by

[16] *Quebec Civil Code,* Art. 1265.

[17] *Adam* v. *Ouellette* (1947), S.C.R. 283. There is still some controversy on this point.

[18] Uniform Act, S. 149.

the policy contract, during which the contract shall be void in the event of suicide, also commences with the date of reinstatement instead of the original date of the policy.[19]

There is no comparable law in Quebec. The *Civil Code* provides that insurance effected by a person on his own life is void if he dies by suicide;[20] but in practice, companies pay suicide claims if the policy has been in force for two years or more.

Cash Values and Nonforfeiture Provisions. Insurers in Canada are not compelled by law to include in their policies cash values and the various loan and nonforfeiture benefits. Nevertheless, it is the invariable practice of most companies to show tables of cash values, paid-up insurance values, and, usually, extended insurance values, which are for the most part comparable to those required by law in the United States. If there is default in the payment of premiums under a policy that has acquired a cash value, the automatic nonforfeiture benefit is usually a premium loan.

Juvenile Insurance. The revision of the Uniform Act increased from 15 to 16 the age at which a minor may apply for a policy, but broadened the powers of the minor to give him the right to apply for insurance on the life of any person, and to deal other than as beneficiary with any policy in which he has an interest, e.g., a policy assigned to him by someone else.[21] A new provision gives a minor beneficiary of the age of 18 years the capacity to receive insurance money and give a good discharge therefor.[22] This will overcome problems that have arisen where policy proceeds have been payable to a minor child or a minor wife.

Quebec law provides that a minor of 15 or over may insure his own life. He may not, however, on his own deal with such policy.[23] Moreover, there is no procedure in the case of third-party contracts for the naming of successor owners.

Both the Uniform Act and the law of Quebec have removed the limits on the benefits payable on policies on children. Any limitations now become a matter of underwriting and of contract.

Miscellaneous Provisions. The Uniform Act also contains important procedural provisions which contribute to the efficient handling and payment of claims. For instance, where the insurer admits the validity of the contract but is not satisfied with the sufficiency of the proof furnished by the claimant of his right to the proceeds, or of the maturity of the contract, or of the age of the life insured, or of the name and age of the beneficiary, either the insurer or the claimant may ask the court to decide

---

[19] *Ibid.*, S. 155(2), (3), (4).

[20] *Civil Code*, Art. 2593.

[21] Uniform Act, S. 168.

[22] *Ibid.*, S. 169.

[23] *Revised Statutes of Quebec*, 1951, C. 299, S. 219.

the issue.[24] The court may either declare the proof sufficient, or direct that further proof be furnished. In any event, payment by the insurer in accordance with the court's order operates as a complete discharge. A similar procedure is available where the person whose life is insured has not been heard of for seven years, in which case either the insurer or the claimant may seek a declaration from the court as to presumption of death.[25]

In cases where the claim has been properly proved and the insurer admits liability but is unable to make payment because there are adverse claimants, or the person entitled to the money cannot be located, or there is no person capable of giving and authorized to give a valid discharge who is willing to do so, the insurer may apply for an order to pay the money into court.[26] If the beneficiary is a minor, the insurer may, after one month from the maturity of the contract, pay the money directly into court without applying for an order.[27] Somewhat similar relief is granted to an insurer in Quebec where there are contending claimants.[28] A declaration of presumption of death may also be obtained in Quebec.[29]

The revision of the Uniform Act has effected two other significant changes. In addition to setting out who is deemed to have an insurable interest in the life insured, a provision has been added declaring that a policy is not void for lack of insurable interest if the person whose life is insured has consented in writing to the insurance being placed on his life.[30] In the case of a child under age 16, a parent can give this consent.

The Uniform Act continues to provide that unless the application or policy provides otherwise, the policy does not take effect until it is delivered and the first premium is paid.[31] A provision has been added, however, whereby a policy is deemed to have been delivered when the company has delivered it to an agent for unconditional delivery to the insured.[32] This, of course, does not preclude the company from attaching conditions to the delivery of the policy, such as a condition that the agent deliver it only if the life insured is in good health. In such a case the provision would not apply.

Taxation of Life Insurance

The taxing powers of the Canadian federal government are constitutionally unlimited, whereas those of the provincial governments are re-

24 Uniform Act, S. 175.

25 *Ibid.*, S. 176.

26 *Ibid.*, S. 181.

27 *Ibid.*, S. 187(1).

28 *Revised Statutes of Quebec*, 1941, C. 71, S. 58.

29 *Quebec Civil Code*, Art. 2593(*a*).

30 Uniform Act, S. 144.

31 *Ibid.*, S. 146(1).

32 *Ibid.*, S. 146(2).

stricted to direct taxation, which has been interpreted by the courts to be that "which is demanded from the very person who it is intended or desired should pay it." This constitutional tax structure has been modified in recent years by the introduction of federal-provincial tax-sharing agreements which are renegotiated every five years, whereby all provinces, with the exception of Quebec, Ontario, and British Columbia, have agreed, among other things, to withdraw from the succession duty field. In return, the federal government has agreed to make annual payments to compensate for the loss of revenue.

In the past, the field of income tax was included in the tax-sharing agreements; however, in 1962, income tax was removed from such tax-sharing agreements, and the various provinces levy such taxes individually. The tax is collected by the federal agency (except in Quebec) through the administrative machinery previously developed, and the money is remitted to the individual provinces.

Only Ontario, Quebec, and British Columbia have retained their right to impose succession duties. In the succession duty legislation of each of these provinces, life insurance proceeds are specifically assessable to duty.

Federal Income Tax.[33] Life insurance premiums are normally not deductible expenses for income tax purposes in Canada, nor are the so-called "dividends" paid to participating policyholders by life insurance companies taxed as income to the policyowner. This is similar to the United States tax law. The Canadian income tax treatment of life insurance, however, is significantly different in some aspects from the treatment afforded by the United States tax law. The following might be considered representative.

For instance, where policy proceeds are payable in a lump sum, the amount received is clearly a capital receipt and not subject to income tax. This applies in the case of settlement on death, or at maturity of an endowment policy, or earlier surrender. Where the proceeds of a policy are left on deposit or are payable under some other settlement option, however, the full interest portion of such payments will be subject to income tax. The $1,000 interest exclusion granted by Section 101(*d*)(1) of the United States Internal Revenue Code of 1954 to a surviving spouse under an agreement to pay the proceeds as a life income or in installments has no counterpart in Canadian income tax laws.

There is no transfer-for-value rule applicable to insurance proceeds in Canada. If a policy or any interest in a policy has been transferred for a valuable consideration, the transferee receives the whole of the proceeds free of income tax.

Policy proceeds are frequently used by a Canadian business to con-

[33] References herein will be made to the Canadian Income Tax Act, *Revised Statutes of Canada,* 1952, C. 148, described as in the Income Tax Act.

tinue, either on a contractual or on a voluntary basis, all or part of an employee's salary to his dependents for a reasonable period of time. Such payments, when paid voluntarily, are not strictly deductible, since they do not constitute a legitimate business expense.[34] It is understood, however, that a voluntary lump-sum payment to the widow of an officer of a company following death for less than a year's salary is deductible, according to current departmental practice.

These death benefit payments, whether voluntary or contractual, are taxable as income in the hands of the recipient where such payment is made to the widow of the officer or employee. The amount of the death benefit included in income is reduced by an amount equal to the deceased employee's remuneration for the last year of employment, or $10,000, whichever is the lesser. If the amount actually received as a death benefit is less than either of these amounts, the exemption will be limited to the amount so received.[35]

As in the United States, the split-dollar plan is regarded, for Canadian income tax purposes, as though interest-free loans are actually made by the employer to the employee in amounts equal to the annual increase in the cash surrender value of the policy. The Canadian Income Tax Act, however, introduces a variation with respect to a shareholder-employee. If the corporation makes a loan to him, the amount thereof is deemed to have been received as a taxable dividend, unless the loan is repaid within a year from the end of the taxation year of the corporation in which the loan was made.[36] This means, of course, that the split-dollar plan has little attraction for a shareholder-employee, even though he may, on repaying the loan to his company, deduct the amount repaid in the year of repayment.[37]

Group insurance in Canada enjoys a position similar to that in the United States. The premiums paid by an employer are deductible as a business expense and are not taxable in the hands of the employee, except to a limited extent.[38] Since 1960 the portion of the premium paid by an employer for any group life insurance which is applicable to insurance on a taxpayer's life in excess of $25,000 is required to be included in the income of the taxpayer, if such insurance was effected in respect of, in the course of, or by virtue of his office or employment, or former office or employment.[39] In addition, the government has introduced legislation that would have the effect of excluding from an employee's income the benefits received from his employer's contributions only in respect of group term life insurance.

---

[34] Income Tax Act, S. 12(1)(*a*).

[35] *Ibid.*, S. 139(1) (*j*) (i).

[36] *Ibid.*, S. 8(2).

[37] *Ibid.*, S. 11(1)(*da*).

[38] *Ibid.*, S. 5(1)(*a*).

[39] *Ibid.*, S. 6(1)(*db*).

Annuities. The general rule is that whereas a taxpayer, in computing his income, is not entitled to deduct the expenses, premiums, or other costs of an annuity contract, only the interest portion of annuity payments is taxable.[40] There are two exceptions to this principle, namely, when annuity payments constitute benefits under a registered superannuation or pension plan, or under a registered retirement savings plan, under which premium contributions have been exempt from income tax.

In addition, the government has amended the law to provide that with respect to any annuity contract entered into after June 13, 1963, and not registered as a registered retirement savings plan, that part of the proceeds of the contract that consists of interest accumulated prior to the date on which the annuity commences is to be included in computing income of the recipient unless such proceeds are received as a life annuity or as a refund of premiums upon the death of the holder of the annuity contract.

Contributions by an employer and employee to a registered pension plan are deductible from their respective taxable incomes within certain defined limits.[41]

Payments may be received from such a plan on three occasions, namely, retirement, termination of service, or death. In the case of retirement, the pension benefits are fully taxable as received.[42]

On termination of service the employee has the option, depending upon the terms and provisions of the plan, of taking a lump-sum settlement or a paid-up deferred annuity, or continuing the contract on a premium-paying basis, or a combination of the foregoing. If he elects to take the benefits in a lump sum, he may either add the amount received to his income in that year and pay tax at the applicable rate, or pay a special tax based on an "average" rate over the past three years.[43] Alternatively, he may transfer the amount received to another registered retirement savings plan or a deferred profit sharing plan or a registered pension plan, and the amount so transferred may be deducted in computing his income if transferred within the same taxation year or within sixty days thereafter.[44]

If the employee elects to receive a paid-up deferred annuity on termination of service, he has two alternatives. He may pay the income tax on the present value of the deferred annuity, in which case the company may amend or rewrite the policy, which is treated thereafter as an ordinary annuity contract. Or the employee may continue the paid-up deferred

---

[40] *Ibid.*, S. 6(1)(*a*)(iii) and S. 11(1)(*k*).

[41] *Ibid.*, S. 11(1)(*g*) and S. 11(1)(*i*).

[42] *Ibid.*, S. 6(1)(*a*)(iv).

[43] Income Tax Act, S. 36.

[44] *Ibid.*, S. 11(1)(*u*).

annuity subject to the tax liability, and eventually pay tax on the total monthly income or on the single sum at maturity or on the death benefit when he dies, or on the surrender value if he subsequently surrenders the policy.

Finally, if the employee, upon withdrawal from a registered pension plan, continues his original individual policy on a premium-paying basis, he pays income tax on the present value of the deferred annuity. The policy, which is thereafter considered for tax purposes as though it had never been in the plan, may be rewritten by the company on its usual type of policy form.

A lump-sum payment out of a pension plan upon the death of an employee is ordinarily income in the year received, but the recipient taxpayer (whether the employee's estate or a named beneficiary) may exclude such payment from his income for that year and instead pay tax based on an "average" rate over the past three years.[45] If the payments on death are made in the form of an annuity to the widow,[46] it appears that she pays income tax each year only on the amounts received.

The other exception to the general principle concerning the taxation of annuity payments is when they constitute benefits under a registered retirement savings plan. These plans were authorized by amendment to the federal Income Tax Act in 1957[47] and are intended to achieve greater equality of tax treatment, by allowing professional and other self-employed persons who are not eligible to participate in a registered pension plan to obtain similar tax advantages.

The principal features of a registered retirement savings plan are:

1. No benefits are payable prior to maturity other than refund of premiums and payment of interest if the annuitant fails to survive to retirement age.
2. The taxpayer may elect an annuity for his life, with no guaranteed period or a guaranteed period not exceeding 15 years.
3. The taxpayer may elect a joint life and last survivor annuity for the benefit of the taxpayer and his or her spouse, with or without a guaranteed period, not exceeding 15 years, and under which provision may also be made for payments to be reduced on the first death.
4. Premiums are deductible, within certain defined limits, in computing earned income only.
5. The contract matures not later than the annuitant's seventy-first birthday.
6. Annuity payments are fully taxable as and when received.
7. If the contract is part of a life insurance policy, only the portion of the premium considered to be the cost of the annuity (which is determined through the use of a somewhat complicated formula) is deductible.
8. Once annuity payments commence, no further premiums may be deducted.

---

45 *Ibid.*, S. 36.

46 Optional methods of settlement on death are allowed, but on a restricted basis.

47 Income Tax Act, S. 79(*B*).

9. The plan includes a provision stipulating that no annuity payable thereunder is capable, either in whole or in part, of surrender, commutation, or assignment.
10. If a policyholder dies during the lifetime of the plan and before annuity payments have commenced, income tax of 15 per cent is levied at the time of death on the greater of either the cash value plus accumulated dividends or the total of tax-exempt premiums paid.
11. The plan may be revised or amended to provide for the payment or transfer of any funds, on behalf of an annuitant, to another registered retirement savings plan or to a pension fund.
12. If a plan is deregistered by means of the surrendering of the policy, the cash value becomes fully taxable in the hands of the individual in the year in which he receives it. This cash received is added to all his other income for the year and raises the rate of tax accordingly. In no event can the rate of income tax on the money received be less than 25 per cent, and in this regard an amount equal to 25 per cent of any amount paid to the policyholder at the time of deregistration or later must be deducted at the source and remitted to the Department of National Revenue.
13. A plan may be co-ordinated with benefits under the Old Age Security Act; the value must be sufficient to furnish a reasonable lifetime income after deducting an amount required to fund a period certain income to age 70, at which time the old-age security income starts. A plan can thus be used to bridge the gap between, say, age 65, the normal retirement age, and age 70, enabling the annuitant to receive a constant lifetime income from the date of his retirement.
14. Contracts in existence prior to 1957 may also qualify.

While life insurance in Canada is provided solely by private life insurance companies and fraternal benefit societies, annuities, both individual and group, have been sold not only by those institutions but also by the federal government since the Government Annuities Act was passed in 1908.[48] Any person resident or domiciled in Canada may purchase an immediate or deferred annuity through the Annuities Branch of the Department of Labour. The annuities are payable for life in monthly installments (unless otherwise provided) and may be guaranteed up to twenty years in any event. The maximum amount of annuity purchasable by any annuitant or by joint annuitants is now $1,200 a year.

Federal Estate Tax. A new Estate Tax Act was passed in 1958 by the Parliament of Canada.[49] It became effective on January 1, 1959, and applies to the estates of persons dying after that date. The Dominion Succession Duty Act, which had been in effect since 1941, continues on the statute books and applies to the estates of all persons who died before the new Estate Tax Act came into force.

One of the major changes introduced by the Estate Tax Act concerns life insurance. The "keeping-up" or "premium-paying" test found in the

---

[48] *Revised Statutes of Canada*, 1952, C. 132.

[49] *Statutes of Canada*, 1958, C. 29, herein referred to as the Estate Tax Act.

Dominion Succession Duty Act has been replaced by the concept of "owning."[50] This is similar to the United States estate tax law. However, the United States Internal Revenue Code provision that a 5 per cent reversionary interest is an incident of ownership which will subject the proceeds of insurance to taxation in the insured's estate has no counterpart in the new Act.

There is another important variation concerning third-party insurance. Where a policy, immediately prior to the death of the deceased, is owned either alone or in common with any other person (except the deceased or his "controlled" trustee), by a corporation controlled by the deceased, and the proceeds are payable to the corporation (with no part of the proceeds payable to the deceased or to his wife or children), the amount of the proceeds of the policy that exceeds the net income of the corporation during the five complete fiscal years preceding the date of death is taxable in the deceased's estate.[51] There is no double taxation, however, since any such excess amount is excluded in valuing the deceased's shares.[52]

Neither the Estate Tax Act nor the Dominion Succession Duty Act provides for a marital deduction similar to that contained in the United States tax law.[53] The Estate Tax Act allows a deduction of $60,000 for a widow and $10,000 for each child under 21, or over 21 and dependent on the deceased; these deductions are not specific to the persons concerned and are applicable whether or not they receive a benefit from the estate.

Estate tax is imposed on any superannuation or pension benefit payable on or after the death of the deceased.[54] Also, in determining the value of such benefit, no allowance or deduction may be made for income tax.[55] It appears, therefore, that pension plan payments are subject to two separate taxes which overlap. The Income Tax Act makes provision for some relief from the impact of the two taxes on pensions and death benefits by providing that where a taxpayer inherits a pension, he may, in computing his income for income tax purposes, deduct from pension monies he receives in any given taxation year a proportion of the amount so received, the proportion being:

> (Canadian estate tax applicable to pension plus provincial succession duty attributable to pension) divided by (value of pension for purposes of Estate Tax Act).[56]

---

[50] Estate Tax Act, SS. 3(1)(*m*), 3(5).

[51] *Ibid.*, SS. 3(1)(*m*)(ii), 58(1)(*c*).

[52] *Ibid.*, S. 32.

[53] See United States Internal Revenue Code, 1954, Sec. 2056.

[54] Estate Tax Act, S. 3(1)(*k*).

[55] *Ibid.*, S. 26.

[56] Income Tax Act, S. 11(1)(*v*).

In contrast to the situation in the United States, where the value of a business interest may be "pegged" for estate tax purposes under a proper buy-and-sell agreement, in Canada the true or fair market value of a deceased's business interest, and not necessarily that at which his surviving associates have power to take it over, is its value for estate tax purposes. It is interesting to see how liability for payment of the estate tax attributable to such a business interest is handled by the Estate Tax Act.

Where a person, according to the terms of a buy-and-sell agreement made by him at any time, commits himself to transfer his interest on or before his death at a certain price, and the property increases in value so that at his death it is worth more than the stipulated price, the excess would be considered property passing directly to the purchaser as successor, and he would bear the primary responsibility for payment of tax on such amount. The stipulated contract price (minus any monetary consideration paid to the deceased during his lifetime) is taxable in the deceased's general estate. If, however, the interest decreased in value, the full price bargained for is nevertheless taxable in the deceased's estate, since the estate can legally enforce payment of such contract price against the purchaser (assuming that he is solvent).[57]

The use of a method of valuation which always accurately reflects the fair market value of the business is therefore in the best interests of all concerned.

Federal Gift Tax.[58] A gift of a life insurance policy occurs when an individual applies for a new policy payable to a beneficiary other than his estate and retains no rights of ownership in it. Likewise, there is a gift when a policyowner absolutely assigns a policy for inadequate consideration and retains no ownership rights in it. The gift may be made directly or in trust, and the policy may be on the life of the donor or another. If certain ownership rights are retained, the gift occurs when they are relinquished.

Gifts of life insurance to charities and in contemplation of death are exempt from gift tax, as are gifts of life insurance taking effect upon the death of the donor or so given that the donee would not obtain the benefit thereof until the death of the donor.

The Canadian gift tax law does not provide for a gift tax marital deduction, nor does it contain a split-gift advantage. There is no lifetime exclusion applicable to life insurance, nor is any specific differentiation made between "present" and "future" interests.

Premiums paid by the insured after the policy has been assigned are subject to gift tax. Gifts to any one person, however, which in the aggre-

---

[57] Estate Tax Act, S. 3(1)(*i*).

[58] Gift tax provisions found in Part IV, Income Tax Act, SS. 111 to 115, inclusive.

gate do not exceed $1,000 in the taxation year are exempt. An individual may also deduct from the aggregate value of gifts which he has made during the taxation year $4,000, or one half of the difference between his taxable income for the preceding year and the amount of his income tax thereon, whichever is greater.

Social Security

Responsibility for social welfare in Canada originally rested in the main on the provinces, which in turn delegated an important share of that responsibility to the municipalities. The welfare needs of Canadians in an increasingly industrialized society, however, have led to a greater emphasis on social security programs, which could be developed only at the higher levels of government. Thus, this concept of constitutional responsibility has changed markedly over the last decade and a half. During that period, new permanent programs have been introduced at the federal level: unemployment insurance in 1943, family allowances for all children under 16 years of age in 1945, health grants in 1948, social security payments to all persons over 70 years in 1952, disabled persons' allowances in 1954, and hospital insurance in 1958.

Old Age Security Act.[59] The Old Age Security Act of 1952, as amended, provides a universal pension of $75 a month (increased from $65 effective from October 1, 1963), payable by the federal government to all persons aged 70 or over, subject to a residence qualification. To qualify for pension, a person must have resided in Canada for 10 years immediately preceding its commencement or, if absent during that period, must have been actually present in Canada prior to it for double any period of absence and must have resided in Canada at least one year immediately preceding commencement of pension. Payment of pension may be continued for any period of residence outside Canada if the pensioner has resided in Canada for at least 25 years after attaining the age of 21; or if he has not, it may be continued for six consecutive months exclusive of the month of departure from Canada.

The pension is financed on a "pay as you go" method through a 3 per cent sales tax, a 3 per cent tax on corporation income, and, subject to a limit of $90 a year, a 3 per cent tax on taxable personal income. Effective on January 1, 1964, the rate on taxable personal income has been raised to 4 per cent, with a maximum of $120 a year. Taxes are paid into the Old Age Security Fund. If they are insufficient to meet the pension payments, temporary loans or grants are made from the Consolidated Revenue Fund. The pension is paid from the Consolidated Revenue Fund and charged to the Old Age Security Fund. The program is administered by the Department of National Health and Welfare through regional offices located in each provincial capital.

[59] *Revised Statutes of Canada*, 1952, C. 200.

Persons in receipt of old-age assistance, payable to persons aged 65 to 69 who pass a specified means test, on reaching age 70 are automatically transferred to old-age security. Others make application to the regional office. Recipients of old-age security who are in need may receive supplementary aid under general assistance programs in the provinces. Aid is also provided under the Unemployment Assistance Act, administered by the provinces and municipalities on an individual assessment of need; and the cost of this program is shared with the federal government.

In addition to the foregoing, the federal government has signified its intention of establishing a contributory pension system related to the individual's wage scale. Implementation of the proposed scheme is tentatively scheduled to commence in 1965.

Taxation of Life Insurance Companies

Federal income tax is levied under the Income Tax Act and is paid by stock companies only. The tax is imposed on the net income credited to the shareholder's account minus certain deductions.[60] In addition, the Corporation Income Tax Acts of Quebec and Ontario require life insurance companies to pay income tax. The net income credited to the shareholder's account is divided to show the portion attributable to each of these provinces on the basis of premium income, and a tax is payable on the portion applicable to each. However, an offset against the federal income tax otherwise payable is allowed in respect of income tax paid to each of these two provinces, which serves virtually to eliminate the incidence of double taxation.

Premium tax statutes were enacted by all provinces in 1957. Prior to that time, life insurance companies paid premium taxes to the federal government in accordance with the provisions of the federal-provincial tax-sharing agreements in effect between the government of Canada and the provinces (except Quebec). The rate under the provincial statutes is 2 per cent on insurance premiums less insurance dividends. Annuity considerations are not taxed. The tax returns in each province are not identical in form but produce taxable income on a uniform basis.

There are, in addition to the above, various miscellaneous taxes and fees imposed by the federal, provincial, and municipal authorities which affect the operation of a life insurance company doing business in Canada. These include transfer fees on the sale of securities and various business and property taxes, all of which appear to have their counterparts in the United States.

Conclusion

This chapter has been a study of differences in Canadian life insurance. It might be reiterated that the similarities are much greater than the

---

[60] Income Tax Act, S. 30.

differences and that life insurance personnel move back and forth between Canada and the United States with perhaps no greater adjustment than moving from one company to another.

SELECTED REFERENCES

Canadian and British Insurance Companies Act, 1932. Ottawa, Can.: The Queen's Printer, 1932.

The Life Insurance Laws of Quebec. Toronto: Stone & Cox, Ltd.

McVitty, E. H. *A Commentary on the Life Insurance Laws of Canada.* Toronto: Life Insurance Institute of Canada.

The Revised Uniform Life Insurance Act of the Provinces of Canada except Quebec. Toronto: Stone & Cox, Ltd.

Chapter 80

FRATERNAL LIFE AND HEALTH INSURANCE

*BY CHARLES C. CENTER**

Fraternal insurance in the United States dates from 1868, when the Ancient Order of United Workmen at Meadville, Pennsylvania, was founded by John Jordan Upchurch. While evidence suggests there were earlier fraternal societies in the United States, it is impossible to verify as a fact that the earlier ones undertook to cover the lives of their members with insurance. During the years since its inception, fraternal life and health insurance has evidenced many changes both in theory and in practice. To understand more fully this unique institution, it is necessary to trace its development and changes, and to examine the social environment which brought about these changes.

Historical Background

During the era immediately following the Civil War, the United States was largely an agrarian society. The rural population was proportionally high, and a majority of the people who moved from the farms to the cities became members of the laboring class. Today's middle-income group of salaried employees, "blue-collar" workers, and businessmen was proportionally smaller. The two groups—agrarian and labor—included a substantial percentage of the total population of the United States and, in the main, were not protected by life insurance.

The explanation for lack of life insurance protection seems fairly simple. The persons in the agrarian and labor groups, for the most part,

---

* The author wishes to express his appreciation for the assistance he received in the preparation of this chapter in the first edition from Henry Aronson, Research Assistant, University of Wisconsin; R. L. Blodgett, President, National Mutual Benefit Society; W. Cable Jackson, President, National Fraternal Congress of America; and Walter Rugland, President, Aid Association for Lutherans. Henry Scheig, Vice President and Actuary, Aid Association for Lutherans, assisted in the revision.

were in lower income brackets. They were less able to afford ordinary life insurance, the only private company protection offered at that time. With a minimum size policy of $1,000 and premiums payable annually, semiannually, and quarterly, ordinary life insurance was beyond the reach of most of the country's population.

Distrust of Private Companies

An explanation of greater import concerns the nature of the private insurance business in the post-Civil War period. The problem of offering nonforfeiture values and the difficulties involved with understanding level premiums and reserve accumulations invoked the distrust of many people toward the industry. This situation, coupled with the then inherent distrust and apprehension of the farm and labor segments toward large corporations, saw commercial insurers confronted with suspicion and skepticism. Lending support to these attitudes were the failures of some private insurance companies in the depression of 1873.

These factors, together with the need for protection for the lower income groups, produced an environment ripe for the introduction of other forms of life insurance protection. One, industrial life insurance, has been discussed in another chapter. Another successful vehicle for this protection was fraternal life insurance. This new type of insurance and insurer should be viewed from two points of view—protective and social.

Purposes of Fraternals

Fraternal insurance, as it was offered through the fraternal lodge, differed from private insurance. In the late nineteenth century the social activities available to lower income groups were few as compared to those of today. The movies, radio, television, and phonograph had not yet been produced. Social visits were limited, as the automobile was still a thing of the future. The idea of offering life insurance through an organization in which all participants were socially connected was the thought of Upchurch when he founded the Ancient Order of United Workmen. Members of the Ancient Order of United Workmen, being mechanics and artisans, had a trade in common. Below are listed the objectives found within the framework of the constitution of the Ancient Order of United Workmen, which is representative of fraternals of that time.

1. To unite into one common brotherhood all persons employed in the mechanical arts.
2. To create a means of prompt and effective co-operation in matters of common interest.
3. To oppose inimical legislation and to foster favorable legislation.
4. To establish libraries and provide for lectures and other means of education.
5. To employ all legitimate means to establish and to maintain harmony and equity between employers and employees.

6. To ameliorate the conditions of unfortunate, afflicted, and oppressed members.
7. To establish an insurance fund out of which not less than $500 should be paid to the legal heirs of a deceased member.

It is obvious from the above-stated objectives that much more was intended than merely to provide insurance benefits. The social organization was very important in the growth of the fraternal concept. The membership of the social group or lodge was organized on a restricted basis. The typical basis was either, or a combination of, race, occupation, sex, or religion. The names of a few of the societies will indicate the lines along which they were organized; the Modern Woodmen of America, the Order of Railway Conductors of America, the Free Sons of Israel, and the Daughters of America.

An important aspect of lodge organization was the ritualistic ceremony. To further the ties between the members, to attract new members, and to attain an air of individuality, rituals, costumes, and initiations were very complex and colorful. The frequency of meetings ranged from weekly to monthly; and group co-operative dinners, picnics, Christmas parties, athletic activities, dances, and the like were held. These types of activities are fostered to varying degrees by fraternal lodges today.

A third feature of the fraternal idea was the practice of incorporating welfare, benevolent, and/or charitable works into their programs. The welfare of the fraternal member and his family became a responsibility accepted by the organization. Hospitals, visiting committees, sanitariums, and financial help were provided for the less fortunate members. These services were made possible through periodic contributions by members into extra funds, aside from insurance assessments. Because of the lodge organization, geographical proximity of the members, and the fraternal bond, members willingly helped one another in time of need. Even today, an important aspect of the fraternal life insurance organization is the benevolent activities in which it engages.

The Lodge System

The lodge or other local group is stated to be the foundation stone of the fraternal society. Most fraternal societies also have supreme lodges, the organizations varying with size, location, and objectives of the particular group; and some have lodges on the state level. Where state lodges are operative, delegates from the lower lodges comprise their membership. A supreme lodge is the governing body and sets policies for the fraternal organization as a whole.

Delegates to the state and supreme lodges are elected from the members of the local lodges. From the beginning of the fraternal movement a representative form of government has been a distinguishing factor between fraternal life societies and private life companies. All state statutes require fraternals to maintain a representative type of government. Voting by proxy is usually not permitted.[1] Further, by statutory requirement, supreme lodges usually meet at least once every four years to elect officers and determine policy.[2]

Those societies which do not have either state or supreme (grand) lodges maintain a ruling board of directors or trustees. These ruling groups are elected by the member lodges, or by direct vote of membership utilizing a representative form of government.

Early Insurance Plans

The initial method of providing death benefits for members of fraternal societies was the uniform post-mortem assessment plan. Again, the Ancient Order of United Workmen provides a typical example. When a member first joined, he contributed a $1.00 initiation fee. Upon the death of a member, each surviving member was to contribute $1.00. The benefit to the beneficiaries of the deceased member totaled $1.00 per active member, with an upper limit of $2,000. If the membership totaled more than two thousand, the contribution was the member's pro rata share of $2,000. This idea of assessment insurance was most appealing. As previously mentioned, large elements in the population were distrustful of reserves maintained by private insurers, and an insurance system not requiring payment of a reserve to the insurer was very attractive. The theory of fraternalism was further carried out in a uniform assessment, with each member contributing the same amount. This appeared to eliminate the discrimination that fraternalists thought occurred in private insurance.

The defects inherent in the assessment idea soon became obvious from both the financial and the marketing standpoints. When many deaths occurred during a year, a society operating on a post-mortem uniform assessment basis was burdened with collections. Expenses were developing into a significant portion of the premium. The most important defect in pure assessment insurance, however, was a lack of reserve to offset the high mortality cost found in a society with an increasing average age. Theoretically, if young members joined at a rate capable of maintaining a constant age distribution, an assessment type of operation could continue to function successfully.

Experience indicated, however, that new members were not attracted by a uniform rate of assessment. As the average age of the group tended to increase, assessments became more frequent, thus raising the cost per year for protection. When younger members realized they were paying an amount out of proportion to the degree of their risk, they started to drop

[1] New York Sec. 452(*f*); Wisconsin Sec. 208.02.

[2] New York Sec. 452 (*c*).

out. This loss plus the difficulty in securing new, younger members compounded the problem; the society either disbanded, merged, or was forced to a scientific method of computing premiums.

Because of member dissatisfaction with the uniform assessment plan, the concept of graded assessment contributions was developed. This principle of graded assessments was an attempt to rectify the inherently discriminatory feature of the uniform assessment method. Members' assessments on the graded assessment plan were based on the age of each member when entering the society. The premium was determined by age at entry into the society; once determined, the premium was presumed to remain level for the duration of the member's life. For example, assume the following to be a scale of graded assessments:

Age of Entry	*Assessment per Month*
21–25	$1.00
26–30	1.25
31–35	1.50
36–40	1.75

If the age of entry was 23 years, the member would have a monthly assessment of $1.00 for the rest of his life. Similarly, if the age of entry was 40 years, the assessment per month would be $1.75.

The problems that plagued uniform assessment operations soon affected the graded assessment plans. With the introduction of the latter plan, membership increased rapidly for a time, providing a younger age distribution and thus a lower mortality rate. As the average age of members in societies adopting the new plan increased again, mortality costs rose, and financial problems appeared. By the turn of the century, it was apparent that to maintain financial solvency, the fraternals had to adopt scientific methods both in settling rates and in providing reserves.

The National Fraternal Congress, an association of twelve fraternal benefit societies, recognized the above problems in 1895 and for the first time, statistics of 25 commercial companies and 27 fraternal benefit societies were given in tabulated form and compared. Out of these statistics grew the National Fraternal Congress Table of Mortality. Problems of insolvency were further discussed in meetings at Mobile, Alabama, with the National Convention of Insurance Commissioners, and later at a meeting in New York City in 1912. The effect of these meetings and the legislation which grew out of them was to bring fraternals onto a sound actuarial basis. They had "cleaned their own house" and started another chapter in their long history.

Statutory Enactments

Through the years, statutes have been enacted by the various states to define and regulate fraternal societies. Proposed uniform legislation has finally been attained through the co-operation of the National Association of Insurance Commissioners and the National Fraternal Congress of America. A completed model code known as the Uniform Fraternal Code was approved by both organizations in 1955, and an updated revision of this Code was approved by both organizations in 1962. This Code has been adopted by a number of the states in its entirety; and in other states, it has been adopted in part. The Uniform Fraternal Code defines a fraternal benefit society as follows:

> Any incorporated society, order or supreme lodge, without capital stock, conducted solely for the benefit of its members and their beneficiaries and not for profit, operated on a lodge system with ritualistic form of work, having a representative form of government, and which makes provision for the payment of benefits in accordance with this Article, is hereby declared to be a fraternal benefit society.

This definition is much the same as that previously found in the statutes of the various states. These statutory definitions of fraternal benefit societies indicate significant differences between a commercial and a fraternal insurance organization.

Earlier in this chapter the lodge organization was discussed. Statutory definitions of a fraternal benefit society include a requirement that such societies must "operate on a lodge system." The Uniform Fraternal Code defines the lodge system as follows:

> A society having a supreme legislative or governing body and subordinate lodges or branches by whatever name known, into which members are elected, initiated or admitted in accordance with its constitution, laws, ritual and rules, which subordinate lodges or branches shall be required by the laws of the society to hold regular meetings at least once in each month, shall be deemed to be operating on the lodge system.

While all members of fraternal benefit societies, by statute, must be members of some local lodge of the society, the importance of the social aspects of the local lodge has greatly diminished. This is easily understandable in the light of modern developments in communication and travel. In many societies, altruistic and educational activities which are carried on today are of greater importance than the ritualistic ceremonies which were of great significance in earlier years.

A fraternal benefit society must have a representative form of government. The Uniform Fraternal Code defines a representative form of government as follows:

> A society shall be deemed to have a representative form of government when:
>
> (*a*) it provides in its constitution or laws for a supreme legislative or governing body, composed of representatives elected either by the members or by delegates elected directly or indirectly by the members, together with such other members of such body as may be prescribed by the society's constitution and laws;

(*b*) the representatives elected constitute a majority in number and have not less than two thirds of the votes nor less than the votes required to amend its constitution and laws;

(*c*) the meetings of the supreme legislative or governing body and the election of officers, representatives or delegates are held as often as once in four calendar years;

(*d*) each insured member shall be eligible for election to act or serve as a delegate to such meeting;

(*e*) the society has a board of directors charged with the responsibility for managing its affairs in the interim between meetings of its supreme legislative or governing body, subject to control by such body and having powers and duties delegated to it in the constitution or laws of the society;

(*f*) such board of directors is elected by the supreme legislative or governing body, except in case of filling a vacancy in the interim between meetings of such body;

(*g*) the officers are elected either by the supreme legislative or governing body or by the board of directors; and

(*h*) the members, officers, representatives or delegates shall not vote by proxy.

The fact that proxies are not allowed is an indication that legislators are still interested in maintaining a more personal type of organization than is found in private insurance companies.

The nonprofit requirement is emphasized in statutory definitions. A fraternal society is "without capital stock, formed, organized and carried on solely for the benefit of its members, and of their beneficiaries and not for profit." It may be noted that this quotation also literally applies to a mutual life insurance company. Any surplus generated from the operation of a society belongs to the membership, and is usually distributed to the membership as a surplus refund in much the same manner as dividends are distributed to policyholders of mutual life companies.

The "Open" Contract

Perhaps the most significant difference between fraternal insurance and private company insurance is the so-called "open-contract" provision of the insurance contracts of fraternals as compared with the so-called "closed-contract" provisions of company contracts. The insurance policy forms used by companies specify that the policy, together with the application for insurance, including declaration of insurability signed by the applicant, constitutes the entire contract. In contrast, the laws governing fraternal societies require that the contract consist not only of the certificate of insurance and the application for membership, including declaration of insurability made by the applicant, but also that the charter or articles of incorporation, the constitution and bylaws of the society, and all amendments thereto constitute the contract. The fraternal laws further require that the society's constitution or bylaws shall contain a provision that, should the society's reserves become impaired by loss of assets, excessive mortality, or any other reason, the governing body of the society may require an extra payment from the members to restore solvency. (Some state laws require that this provision appear in the certificate form.) If a member elects not to make this extra payment, it will remain as a lien against the reserve of his certificate.

The Uniform Fraternal Code contains the following with respect to the "open-contract" provisions of fraternal insurance societies:

> The certificate, together with any riders or endorsements attached thereto, the charter or articles of incorporation, the constitution and laws of the society, the application for membership, and declaration of insurability, if any, signed by the applicant, and all amendments to each thereof, shall constitute the agreement, as of the date of issuance, between the society and the member, and the certificate shall so state. A copy of the application for membership and of the declaration of insurability, if any, shall be endorsed upon or attached to the certificate.
>
> Any changes, additions or amendments to the charter or articles of incorporation, constitution or laws duly made or enacted subsequent to the issuance of the certificate, shall bind the member and the beneficiaries, and shall govern and control the agreement in all respects the same as though such changes, additions or amendments had been made prior to and were in force at the time of the application for membership, except that no change, addition, or amendment shall destroy or diminish benefits which the society contracted to give the member as of the date of issuance.
>
> A society shall provide in its constitution or laws that if its reserves as to all or any class of certificates become impaired, its board of directors or corresponding body may require that there shall be paid by the member of the society the amount of the member's equitable proportion of such deficiency as ascertained by its board, and that if the payment be not made it shall stand as an indebtedness against the certificate and draw interest not to exceed five per cent per annum compounded annually.

The open contract has been criticized by private company insurers, who claim it is an indefinite agreement rendering a member of a fraternal benefit society vulnerable to rate increases. While, technically, there may be validity in this charge, it is rejoined that no fraternal as a result of the open contract can or will levy so-called "assessments" except under conditions which would in all likelihood result in receivership for a commercial company. For a fraternal to follow such procedures would require sanction of the insurance department of the state in which the society is domiciled. Financial difficulties endangering solvency present the only occasion when differences between the open and the closed contract become apparent. A commercial company in such circumstances would be required by the state to reorganize through reinsurance, merger, or receivership. In the same situation a fraternal would restore solvency through a policy lien approved by the members and authorized by the insurance commissioner of the state. In no case would the lien exceed the cash value contained in the policy. In case the member failed to pay his pro rata share of the reserve impairment, the lien would stand until the impairment had been remedied, at which time it would be removed. Costs of reorganization would thus be avoided by this procedure.

Exemption from Taxes

A further difference between the companies and the fraternal benefit societies is that the latter are exempt from federal income taxes, and from state, local, and municipal taxes, with the exception of taxes and special assessments on real estate and office equipment. This exemption is justified on the basis of the benevolent activities carried on by the societies, a philosophy analogous to that of nontaxation of churches, charitable institutions, and mutual savings banks. Fraternalists state that their expenditures for sanitariums, hospitals, homes for the aged, juvenile activities, heart, cancer, and polio benefits, and the like, amount to more than would have been paid in premium taxes if they were imposed. Few states have created minimum standards relating to such expenditures.

Field Organization

The field organization of many of the larger fraternals today does not differ from that of private company insurers. This was not always the case. When the first fraternals were organized, new members were obtained through the lodge. Each lodge had a deputy, sometimes referred to as an organizer or field worker, whose job it was to obtain applicants to start new lodges wherever possible. These field men were usually remunerated by a flat sum per member obtained. Members were also encouraged to solicit new members. The marketing plan of fraternals today has grown to resemble that of their company counterparts. Many fraternals have a vice president or other officer in charge of sales, a field force of full-time agents, and extensive training programs. Recognition of these similarities has led to membership privileges for fraternal agents in many local associations of the National Association of Life Underwriters. The Uniform Code provides for licensing of all full-time fraternal agents.

Reserve Funds

A noted difference between the fraternals and private companies is in the maintenance of separate reserve funds by the former. The original level assessment societies maintained separate funds for expenses, for mortality, and for benevolent projects. This practice became a firmly entrenched tradition through the years. Today, however, less than one half of the states require maintenance of separate funds by fraternal societies. There is a marked trend on the part of state requirements to eliminate the multifund provision. Section 32 of the Uniform Code allows the maintenance of a single fund, or multiple if desired, and reads in part as follows:

A society may create, maintain, invest, disburse, and apply any special fund or funds necessary to carry out any purpose permitted by the law of such society.

Every society, the admitted assets of which are less than the sum of its accrued liabilities and reserves under all of its certificates when valued according to standards required for certificates issued after one year from the effective date of this Article, shall, in every provision of the laws of the society for payments by members of such society, in whatever form made, distinctly state the purpose of the same and the proportion thereof which may be used for expenses, and no part of the money collected for mortuary or disability purposes or the net accretions thereto shall be used for expenses.

Provisions of Insurance Certificates

The rights, benefits, conditions, and privileges accruing to the parties to a fraternal certificate are defined by the certificate itself, the bylaws and constitution of the society, the statutes of the states applying to fraternal societies, and, where none of these apply, by the common law. Any lack of uniformity within fraternal contract provisions can be explained by these diverse influences working upon the fraternal insurance certificate.

The fraternal society, in being family-oriented, historically restricted the classes of people which could be named beneficiaries in the insurance certificate. Today the contract provisions provide for beneficiary designations which are much more liberal. The member retains the right to change beneficiaries at will, provided that the substitute beneficiary falls into the approved class as defined by statute or the society.

A feature found in some fraternal certificates is the facility of payment clause. This clause is common to industrial insurance contracts, but not in ordinary life insurance contracts. The facility of payment provision defines instances where the fraternal society or the insurance company may disburse death benefits to others than the named beneficiaries or where there is no named beneficiary.

Settlement options are available to beneficiaries of fraternal insurance contracts but generally not to as great an extent as those available to holders of company contracts. Kip[3] states that the difference can probably be explained by the smaller size of the average fraternal contract as compared to the average company contract. He further states that the majority of settlements are made in a lump-sum payment. However, the use of income options is constantly increasing.

The transition of fraternal societies from an assessment to a legal reserve basis was necessarily accompanied by reserve accumulation in which the insured developed equities. The nonforfeiture values offered by fraternals are the same as those offered by private insurers, differing

[3] Richard deRaismes Kip, *Fraternal Life Insurance in America* (Philadelphia: College Offset Press, 1953), p. 122.

only as to which option will be utilized in the event of a lapse of premium payment without an election by the insured. Whereas private insurers usually utilize extended term or automatic premium loan in the event of a lapse, there seems to be no generally used option among fraternal societies. Section 16 of the Uniform Code provides for nonforfeiture values and states that "as to certificates issued on or after the effective date of this Article, a society shall grant at least one paid-up nonforfeiture benefit."

Two features found in the fraternal insurance certificate which closely resemble provisions in the private contract are the granting of a grace period and an incontestable clause.[4] The former is provided for in some statutes and/or in the bylaws of the society. The period is usually thirty days, similar to that provided for in commercial contracts. The incontestable clause varies with societies, but is included in all fraternal certificates.

Growth and Current Status—Life Insurance

Total fraternal life insurance in force as of January 1, 1963, amounted to $12,897,857,649, while total assets amounted to $3,368,386,477.[5] Total fraternal life insurance in force decreased during the early part of this century until 1940, by which time practically all fraternal societies had completely changed from the original assessment plan to the legal reserve basis. Since 1940 a substantial growth has occurred. The in-force volume has more than doubled in the last twenty-three years. This suggests strongly that the period of adjustment from inadequate rates to the reserve basis plan has been successfully bridged. Other factors bearing on the growth pattern shown in Table 80–1 are the development of group life insurance on a very large scale, and the conversion to private mutual companies of some of the fraternal societies.

Health Insurance

Fraternal societies have made a most important contribution to the life insurance industry of this country by pioneering in the development of total and permanent disability coverages attached to life insurance contracts. The first disability tables used in this country were constructed by Franklin B. Mead and Arthur Hunter from the disability experience of certain fraternal societies.

Fraternal societies have been hesitant to enter the health insurance field, apart from incidental benefits attached to life insurance certificates. Because of the closer relationship between the societies and their members than exists in the commercial field, societies would probably be

---

[4] Uniform Fraternal Code, Sec. 20(1)(*c*) and Sec. 20(1)(*i*).

[5] "Combined Statistics and Consolidated Chart of Fraternal Societies," *Fraternal Monitor* (Indianapolis), 1963.

forced to conduct this business on a more liberal underwriting and claim basis. Many societies do not offer separate health insurance at all; and among those which do, there are only a few that have written such plans for many years and which have any significant premium volume at the present time.

Prior to 1935 a number of societies wrote a limited "sick benefit" coverage which was always attached to a life insurance certificate. The provisions for this benefit were generally contained in the society's bylaws. Most societies discontinued this weekly indemnity benefit in the early 1930's.

TABLE 80–1

FRATERNAL LIFE INSURANCE IN FORCE IN UNITED STATES AND CANADIAN SOCIETIES

(000,000 Omitted)

Year	Amount
1915	$ 8,675
1920	9,466
1925	9,060
1930	8,245
1935	5,995
1940	5,867
1945	6,425
1950	7,394
1955	8,612
1960	11,880
1961	12,134
1962	12,898

Source: "Combined Statistics and Consolidated Chart of Fraternal Societies," *Fraternal Monitor* (Indianapolis), 1963.

Some limited interest in separate health insurance by fraternal societies has developed in the last few years. These benefits generally follow standard provisions applicable to commercial companies.

Fraternal societies have continued to attach disability and accidental death benefits to life insurance certificates. Three societies presently write only an accident indemnity benefit, with no regular life insurance being sold. The total in force for these three societies as of January 1, 1963, is $2,493,000,000 (not included in Table 80–1).

Summary

The history of fraternal insurance during the twentieth century has been one of evolution from the assessment to the legal reserve plan of operation. Because of changes in the social and cultural environment, the lodge system and its original sphere of activity at the local level have declined in importance. Thus, one of fraternalism's strongest attractions in a largely agricultural, immobile society has greatly diminished. Leaders in the fraternal system maintain strongly, however, that the local lodge continues to be an integral part of that system. The other advantage of earlier days—a form of insurance which was the antithesis of that offered by the distrusted private company—has all but disappeared. The differences today between *the insurance operations* of a good fraternal benefit society and a good private company have declined to a point where they hardly seem significant; whether the difference between the open and closed contract is significant would depend upon the financial strengths of the organizations in question.

Those differences which serve to contrast the two types of organization are most largely found in the noninsurance activities of the fraternal benefit societies. The lodge system, a representative form of government, and programs of charitable or eleemosynary nature comprise these remaining differences. The fraternal benefit societies will continue to be a separate and significant part of the total system of insurance protection available to the American people as long as these differences are maintained.

SELECTED REFERENCES

BAYSE, WALTER. *History and Operation of Fraternal Insurance.* Rochester, N.Y.: Fraternal Monitor, 1919.

Correspondence and briefs between W. CABLE JACKSON, Director, Modern Woodmen of America, and JACK NUSSBAUM, Secretary, National Association of Life Underwriters, 1955. Unpublished.

HAMILTON, ARTHUR S. (compiler). *Statistics of Fraternal Benefit Societies.* Rochester, N.Y.: Fraternal Monitor, 1900 to 1957. Succeeding issues published by *Fraternal Monitor*, Indianapolis.

HUEBNER, S. S., and BLACK, KENNETH, JR. *Life Insurance.* 6th ed. New York: Appleton-Century-Crofts, Inc., 1964.

KIP, RICHARD DERAISMES. *Fraternal Life Insurance in America.* Philadelphia: College Offset Press, 1953.

LANDIS, ABB. *Fraternal Societies and Fraternal Orders.* Rochester, N.Y.: Fraternal Monitor, 1900.

NEW YORK STATE INSURANCE DEPARTMENT. *Examination of Insurance Companies,* Vol. IV, ch. v. Albany, 1954.

O'DONNELL, TERENCE. *History of Life Insurance in Its Formative Years.* Chicago: American Conservation Co., 1936.

RESEARCH AND REVIEW SERVICE OF AMERICA, INC. *Fraternal Life Insurance.* Indianapolis, 1938.

STALSON, J. OWEN. *Marketing Life Insurance: Its History in America.* Cambridge: Harvard University Press, 1942.

Wisconsin Insurance Laws, chs. 200, 204, 208. Madison, 1961.

Chapter 81

SAVINGS BANK LIFE INSURANCE

BY DONALD R. JOHNSON

Savings bank life insurance was originated in 1905 by Louis D. Brandeis, a lawyer who later became an Associate Justice of the United States Supreme Court. Justice Brandeis sought with this experiment a lower cost distribution of private life insurance, especially to wage earners, than was available through the industrial life policies.

HISTORY OF SAVINGS BANK LIFE INSURANCE

Massachusetts

Just prior to the Armstrong Investigation of life insurance early in this century, a group of New England policyholders of one of the life insurance companies formed a Policyholders Protective Committee and retained Brandeis as counsel to undertake an intensive investigation of the life insurance situation.

As a result of his work with this committee, Brandeis conceived the idea of extending by legislative action the mutual savings bank business to include the issuing of life insurance policies. He was of the opinion that the mutual savings banks had adequately demonstrated their record of safety and economy of operations, and that without much added expense, inasmuch as they were already going concerns, these banks could offer life insurance over the counter to the thrifty poor at rates less than those charged by the life companies. In addition, the banks would further lower acquisition costs by substituting unpaid agencies, through which applications for insurance and annuities might be made and at which premiums might be paid, for the usual soliciting company agent.

In late 1906, Brandeis formed the Massachusetts League for Savings Bank Insurance, a group composed of prominent citizens whose job it was to publicize the plan to permit savings banks to issue life insurance. Brandeis himself was extremely active on behalf of "the cause"; he addressed audiences almost nightly during the campaign. In addition, many newspapers and labor unions joined in the movement to secure passage of a savings bank life insurance act.

On the other hand, opposed to the Brandeis proposal were a number of sources, including the life insurance companies, public officials, and many of the savings bankers themselves.

By May, 1907, the Brandeis proposal had received the approval of both the Insurance Committee of the Massachusetts legislature and the banking commissioner. It then received the necessary majority in the House and in the upper chamber; and on June 26, 1907, the final step—the signing of the act by Governor Guild—took place. Thus, Massachusetts became the first state in the union to inaugurate a program of savings bank life insurance.

The new law permitted any mutual savings bank within the state to establish a life insurance department if it had complied with all of the provisions of the act. This meant that a bank had to raise, from outside sources, two funds: a special expense guaranty fund of $5,000 to meet the expenses of the life insurance department if premium loadings should be insufficient, and a special insurance guaranty fund of $20,000 to assure the satisfaction of all policy obligations. In addition, the savings bank had to secure a joint certificate from the commissioner of banks and the commissioner of insurance stating that a savings bank life insurance department had been established. The new department was then empowered to issue life insurance policies to residents of the commonwealth in amounts not to exceed $500 per insured, and annuity contracts that did not exceed $200 of annual income per annuitant. Inasmuch as there were 189 mutual savings banks in Massachusetts at the time the act was passed, this meant that it was theoretically possible, at least, for an individual to purchase $94,500 of savings bank life insurance if all of the banks were to join the system. In 1938 the authorities of the system placed into effect an arbitrary limit of $25,000 of savings bank life insurance that could be purchased by any one individual. The individual limit is now $36,000.

Progress was slow during the early years. By the end of the first year of operations the lone issuing bank and all agency outlets that had joined the system had a total of 282 policies in force, amounting to approximately $115,000 of insurance.

Beginning with the decade of the 1920's, the movement began to gain momentum as the result of a state-wide promotional campaign conducted by Brandeis and his followers, coupled with the support given the program by interested manufacturers and mercantilists, who established agencies at their places of business.

As of October 31, 1963, the system had approximately $934,384,000 of life insurance in force. This amount has been produced by a state-wide insurance organization composed of 36 issuing banks and 134 agency banks, in addition to approximately 90 other agencies consisting of credit unions, co-operative banks, national banks, and trust companies.

New York

New York State, the second state to join the savings bank life insurance program, became seriously interested in the movement in the late 1930's. As far back as 1909, bills had been introduced before the Assembly and Senate of New York, advocating the establishment of a savings bank life insurance system, but in each instance, they had died in the committee rooms.

In 1937, Justice Brandeis entered the campaign to extend savings bank life insurance to the Empire State. Together with several other advocates of the system, Brandeis organized the Savings Bank Life Insurance League of New York. The League waged an intensive educational campaign and sought, in general, newspaper support, and, in particular, the support of Governor Lehman. Gubernatorial support was forthcoming in the Governor's annual message to the Senate and Assembly when, on January 5, 1938, he urged the passage of an enabling act that would authorize mutual savings banks in New York to establish life insurance departments.

Immediately following Governor Lehman's message, a bill was introduced into the Senate and a companion measure into the Assembly for the enactment of savings bank life insurance legislation.

Opposed to the passage of such a law were the New York Savings Bank Association, the New York State Chamber of Commerce, and the Superintendent of Insurance. After a great deal of debate, the bill was finally passed on March 16, and it was signed by Governor Lehman on April 6, 1938. The bill was patterned very closely after the Massachusetts plan, with the exception that the state-wide maximum amount of savings bank life insurance permitted a New York resident was set at $3,000, in contrast to the $25,000 maximum in effect in Massachusetts at that time.

In its first year of production, the New York system had in force nearly $6 million of life insurance. As of December 31, 1963, the system, composed of 57 issuing banks and 43 agency banks, had approximately $693,213,000 of life insurance in force.

Connecticut

Serious interest in savings bank life insurance was not forthcoming in Connecticut until early 1941, when Governor-elect Robert A. Hurley, backed by a Bridgeport newspaper, urged the adoption of a savings bank life insurance act in his inaugural address to the General Assembly. Prior to this, savings bank life insurance bills had been presented before the legislature but had never been brought to a vote.

Shortly after the Governor's address, four separate savings bank life insurance bills were introduced in the House and Senate, and a public hearing on the proposals was scheduled for early March. After there had been much debate, and after at least two compromise bills had been offered, the proposal met with the approval of both chambers of the Connecticut legislature and was signed by Governor Hurley in June, 1941. Thus, Connecticut became the third state and, to date, the last state to foster a program of savings bank life insurance.

On January 2, 1942, the Connecticut system became a reality with the issuance of the first policy to Governor Hurley by the Bridgeport People's Savings Bank. The system, the smallest in the three states, both in amount of life insurance in force and in number of member banks, has progressed at a slow but steady pace. By the end of 1942, it had $1,171,000 of individual insurance in force. As of December 31, 1963, there was approximately $78,146,000 of individual and group life insurance in force, produced by 13 issuing and 32 agency banks out of a total of 71 Connecticut mutual savings banks.

Thus, these three savings bank life insurance systems that function in three heavily populated states, totaling approximately 21.5 million people, and that have nearly 400 of the nation's 528 mutual savings banks, have in force after a composite period of 101 years of underwriting nearly $1,706,000,000 of life insurance.[1]

Expansion to Other States

Other states have evidenced some interest in establishing a savings bank life insurance system. Pennsylvania, Rhode Island, Maryland, Maine, New Jersey, New Hampshire, Delaware, Missouri, and one or two others have given consideration to the movement.

Although no new state-wide systems have come into the savings bank life insurance fold, legislation was enacted in Connecticut in 1962 that created a central or national facility through which savings banks in the several states mentioned above can participate in the program without having to establish individual state systems.

This new company, the Savings Bank Life Insurance Company, is located in Hartford, Connecticut, and is owned by the participating mutual savings banks. It conducts business only with member banks; it does not deal directly with the public.

Despite this recent development, it still remains true that the mortgage business, not life insurance, is the dominating business of these mutual savings banks, and apathy on the part of many savings bankers is one of the chief deterrents to the growth of this program.

ORGANIZATION OF THE PROGRAM

The system of savings bank life insurance in the three states concerned is composed of (1) a central administrative body; (2) savings and insur-

[1] Since 1905, life insurance in force in the United States in legal reserve life insurance companies has grown from approximately $12 billion to nearly $750 billion.

ance banks, also called issuing banks, i.e., savings banks which have established life insurance departments; and (3) savings banks which serve in the capacity of agency banks. In addition, as previously indicated, the Massachusetts system numbers a sizable group of other agencies that have been formed by credit unions, co-operative banks, commercial banks and trust companies, and by employers.

The Central Administrative Bodies

Organization. In general, the operation of a savings bank life insurance system is governed by the laws of the state in which it functions. In Massachusetts the law, in effect, establishes a trichotomy of administration, inasmuch as it creates a General Insurance Guaranty Fund, a Division of Savings Bank Life Insurance, and a Savings Bank Life Insurance Council. The over-all supervision of the system is vested in the trustees of the General Insurance Guaranty Fund. This body consists of seven unpaid trustees, who are appointed by the governor for a term of seven years. Each appointee must be a trustee of a mutual savings bank.

The trustees appoint, with the approval of the governor, a deputy commissioner of savings bank life insurance, who administers the work of the Division of Savings Bank Life Insurance.

The Division of Savings Bank Life Insurance is one of the three divisions of the commonwealth's Department of Banking and Insurance, the other two divisions being the Division of Banks and the Division of Insurance, and consists of a deputy commissioner, the state actuary, and the state medical director, together with their respective staffs, and two instructors whose duty it is to make known the savings bank life insurance program among industrial employees. All personnel in this Division are salaried by the state, although the issuing banks now reimburse the state in full for its expenditures on behalf of the system.

The third administrative body is the Savings Bank Life Insurance Council. This body formulates and executes general policies affecting the system as a whole, in addition to its other duties of advertising and promotion, general public relations, and "home office" functions of photostating applications, preparing and maintaining records, serving as a clearinghouse for premiums collected and policies serviced by agencies, preparing reports, and conducting various research projects.

In contrast to the Massachusetts pattern, the administration and operation of the New York and Connecticut systems is made the responsibility of the respective savings bank's life insurance fund. In each state the fund consists of seven trustees appointed by the superintendent of banks in the case of the New York system, and by the governor in the Connecticut system. New York requires that each appointee be a trustee of a savings bank, whereas the Connecticut law requires that only five trustees be trustees of savings banks; the remaining two trustees, in an attempt to gain a broader viewpoint and give recognition to the general public, may come from fields outside the mutual savings banks.

Purpose and Duties. The primary purpose of the central administrative body in each case is to serve as guarantor of all policy and contract obligations of the issuing banks in its system of operations. In addition, the governing body provides the actuarial and underwriting services, including the services of a medical director for all of the savings and insurance banks.

One of the most important functions of the central body is that of unifying, on a state-wide basis, the mortality experience of each life insurance department within its system. As a result of such unification, the gains and losses from mortality of any one member bank's life insurance department are not determined solely by its own experience, but take into consideration the mortality experience of all the life insurance departments. This gives each life insurance department a mortality experience identical with the others in that state.

Expense Allocation. The law in each of the savings bank life insurance states makes provision for the reimbursement, either monthly or annually, by the savings and insurance banks to the central administrative body for the expenses incurred by this body in its operations. All expenses of the governing body, with the exception of investment expenses and expenses of administration of these investments, are allocated among savings and insurance banks on such basis as the trustees of the central body deem to be equitable and proper.

Investments. In each of the three systems the law declares that assets of the supervisory body, that is, the sum initially deposited by the savings and issuing banks with the governing body, plus the monthly contributions from the banks, which are based on premium income, shall be invested in the same classes of securities and in the same manner in which the deposits of the savings departments are invested. This means that the life insurance departments of the savings banks may invest, with certain limitations, in real estate mortgages; United States Treasury bonds and bonds of the several states; municipal, railway, public utility, and corporate bonds; obligations of savings and loan banks, federal land banks, federal intermediate credit banks, and federal home loan banks; and Canadian government bonds. In addition, Massachusetts and Connecticut banks may invest, within certain limits, in preferred and common stocks.

Issuing Banks

In each of the three states, for a savings bank to join the savings bank life insurance system, it is required that the board of trustees must have voted by a two-thirds majority to establish a life insurance department. This report is filed with either the commissioner of banks, the commissioner of insurance, or both. If the state official is assured that the vote was in conformity with the law, that the required surplus funds are on hand, that the investment in the guaranty fund of the central administrative body has been made, and that the condition of the bank permits the establishment of a life insurance department, then a certificate may be issued declaring such a department to be established.

Only the New York system provides for the state licensing of savings bank life insurance personnel who deal directly with the public. All three systems require the filing of annual reports with the appropriate state office, and all three states now tax the premium income of the life insurance departments of the savings banks in the same manner as they tax the premium income of the life insurance companies. In addition, the life insurance departments of the banks now pay federal income taxes on the same basis as do the private life companies.

Agency Banks

Although an issuing bank may not employ insurance solicitors or persons to make house-to-house collections of premiums, the law in each of the three states provides that the trustees of a savings and insurance bank may establish such agencies for the receipt of applications for life insurance and premium payments as the state officials approve. For their services rendered to issuing banks, agencies generally receive 2 or 3 per cent of the premium income they collect.

OPERATION OF THE PROGRAM

Once the certificate of authorization has been issued, the savings and insurance bank may conduct the business of life insurance, including the sale of annuities, with all the rights, powers, and privileges, and subject to all the duties, liabilities, and restrictions relating to domestic legal reserve life insurance companies. However, the savings bank life insurance program is exempted from the organizational provisions regarding the minimum deposit required of mutual life insurance companies, and the minimum number and amount of life insurance applications.

Issuing Bank Operations

The issuing bank is charged with the responsibility of accepting the application, arranging for the medical examination, issuing the policy, maintaining necessary records, collecting premiums, investing policyholders' funds, servicing the policy, and, finally, paying the claim upon death or maturity of the policy. In addition, the bank actively promotes new business on its own or in conjunction with its systemwide Savings Bank Life Insurance Council's advertising program.

In the usual course of operations the insurance department of the issuing bank alone deals with the applicants and with its policyholders. In general, the three systems write life insurance on approved applicants from age one month to age 70. Women are accepted on the same basis as men except for more stringent restrictions on term insurance and the waiver-of-premium rider.

All three systems do a limited amount of nonmedical underwriting. New York issues up to $5,000 of life insurance on a nonmedical basis to applicants aged five years to 35 years. Connecticut, likewise, writes up to $5,000 of nonmedical business, subject to certain limitations; Massachusetts issues a maximum of $2,000 of nonmedical insurance up to age 35.

In addition, all three systems write coverage on substandard lives. The Massachusetts system employs either an age rating or a flat extra premium for handling its substandard risks. The New York system makes use of either a percentage extra mortality table or a flat extra premium. Connecticut uses only a flat extra premium for its substandard issues. A study of the underwriting action taken by the three systems in recent years shows a declination rate of about 4 per cent.

Once the policy has been issued, it is the contention of the savings bank life insurance officials that the insurance "stays sold," that is, it remains in force. During the past few years the ratio of lapses and surrenders of ordinary policies to the mean number of ordinary policies in force has ranged from a low of 1.3 per cent to a high of 2.8 per cent. To account for this low lapse ratio, these same officials declare that the individual insured "sells himself" on his need for protection and acts accordingly.

Three restrictions peculiar to savings bank life insurance are placed on the operations of the savings and insurance banks. In the first place, there is a limit placed on the amount of savings bank life insurance that any one individual may carry. In Massachusetts, the limit is $36,000; in New York, it is $10,000; and in Connecticut, it is $5,000. Secondly, no application may be accepted by an issuing bank from a person who is not a resident of the state concerned or who is not regularly employed therein. The third restriction prohibits the issuing banks from employing either agents for solicitation of business or persons to make house-to-house premium collections.

Each life insurance department is responsible for its own direct expenses, and joint expenses of the savings department and the life insurance department are apportioned between the two departments in an equitable manner. Funds of the life insurance department may be invested in the same manner and in the same types of investments as savings department funds and funds of the central administrative bodies are invested. In addition to these investments, a life insurance department in any of the three systems is authorized to grant policy loans. Generally speaking, the issuing banks invest more heavily in real estate mortgages than do the life insurance companies.[2]

Agency Operations

Mutual savings banks not interested in becoming issuing banks because of limited quarters, personnel, or area may become agency banks for the system. As such, they serve the system by advertising and promoting savings bank life insurance, answering inquiries, assisting in the completion of applications, and arranging for medical examinations.

After the medical director of the state system has approved the application, the issuing bank writes the policy and forwards it to the agency for delivery to the insured. Likewise, premium notices and dividend checks are sent to the agency by the issuing bank to be delivered to the policyholder. The agency bank collects the premium and provides all services, including the handling of policy loans and claim settlements. In return, the agency bank is paid a small percentage of premiums collected, currently 3 per cent in each of the three systems, with the exception of single-premium policies, for which the agencies are paid 2 per cent of the premium.

POLICIES AND POLICY PROVISIONS

The three savings bank life insurance systems offer a well-rounded and rather complete line of life insurance coverages, including whole life, term, endowment insurance, and group insurance. In addition, Massachusetts banks offer two types of annuities, deferred and single-premium annuities. Special, or combination, policies are offered by all three systems. These include a family income policy in Massachusetts and, in each of the three systems, a family plan policy providing coverage on each parent and on each child.

Other policies offered by the savings banks include a savings-insurance plan, group life insurance, group credit life insurance, and, in Connecticut, a combination of life and disability coverage known as the home mortgage security plan.

The savings-insurance plan, offered in each of the three systems, combines a savings account with a permanent type of life insurance policy. From the savings account, built up by weekly or monthly deposits, are deducted periodically the premiums on the life insurance policy as they become due.

---

[2] In recent years the three savings bank life insurance systems have invested from 50 to 70 per cent of admitted assets in mortgages. In contrast to this, the life insurance companies have averaged about 35 per cent of assets in mortgage investments.

Group insurance likewise is written by all three systems. Although there is no limitation in the statutes of any of the three savings bank life insurance states as to the maximum amount of coverage that may be written on an employee of a group, the central administrative body of each system has established an arbitrary limit. This individual limit per group employee is, in Massachusetts, $30,000; in New York, $15,000; and in Connecticut, $10,000. Thus, because of the right of conversion that is given in the group contract, it is possible for an employee leaving the group to convert his group coverage to an individual policy and carry, in Massachusetts, a maximum of $66,000 of savings bank life insurance, $25,000 in New York, and $15,000 in Connecticut.

Group credit life insurance, found only in the Connecticut system, was begun in March, 1955, by the People's Savings Bank of Bridgeport, for the purpose of insuring home improvement borrowers up to the amount of their loans. Generally, such loans do not exceed $2,500 and are usually written for less than $1,000.

One of the unique combination savings bank life insurance policies is the home mortgage security plan introduced by the Connecticut system. It is designed to meet the monthly mortgage payments of the insured mortgagor in case of his disability or premature death. If disability occurs before age 61, monthly mortgage payments may be made by the insurer for as long a period as five years. If, on the other hand, the insured should die, the plan provides for the continuation, by the insurer, of the monthly mortgage payments to the mortgagee, a mutual savings bank, for up to two years' time. Inasmuch as the savings banks are not authorized to write any health insurance coverage, the disability part of the home mortgage security plan is underwritten by a casualty insurer.

Most of the policy provisions are comparable to those found in policies issued by the life insurance companies, but a few of the savings bank life insurance provisions are more favorable to the insured than are the company provisions. Conversely, in at least one of the systems, one or more provisions are less favorable.

On the favorable side are the nonforfeiture values found in the permanent types of savings bank life insurance policies. The savings bank life insurance law in each instance states that these values, based on the full net level premium reserve method according to the Commissioners 1958 Standard Ordinary Mortality Table with interest at 2½ per cent, shall begin in the first policy year. In some instances, nonparticipating extended term insurance is available after the policy has been in effect for as short a time as one month. Some life company actuaries, however, are of the opinion that this legal requirement is more liberal to discontinuing policyholders than is justified.

Also favorable to the insured is the granting of a first-year dividend, payment of which is not dependent upon the payment of the subsequent year's premium. It may be difficult to justify the granting of a first-year dividend in view of the fact that even in the savings bank life insurance program—a nonagency program—the first-year premium is not sufficient to meet expenses and the full level premium reserve requirement. Such a dividend is granted, according to an official of one of the systems, to meet competition and to please the public in an attempt to interest them in becoming policyholders of the system. Furthermore, according to the same official, the payment of a first-year dividend enables the policyholder to pay about the same amount of net premium each year instead of a larger amount in the first few years and a smaller amount thereafter.

On the other hand, the settlement options available vary by states in accordance with the individual maximum amount of insurance permitted within each of the systems. Thus, Massachusetts and New York offer the four usual settlement options, namely, an installment amount option, an installment time option, a life income option, and an interest option. Connecticut, with a $5,000 maximum, offers only two settlement options—the interest option and the installment amount option.

To add flexibility to the settlement options, the right of commutation and withdrawal is available to the beneficiary, except in the life income option, unless such right has been denied the beneficiary by the insured.

Each of the three systems now offers the waiver-of-premium disability benefit, but in none of the systems is the accidental death benefit available.

NET COST

Much, if not all, of the savings bank life insurance program's advertising stresses "low cost" as an important characteristic of its product. This stems, of course, from lower acquisition costs on behalf of the savings banks, inasmuch as they operate on a nonagency basis and have no agents' commissions to pay. They have, however, other merchandising costs. Moreover, it should be pointed out that a dollar-and-cents basis of comparison fails to give any recognition to the value of the services performed by the life insurance company agent, such as motivating an applicant to purchase the right kinds of life and health insurance in adequate amounts, and the programing of this insurance to fit the insured's circumstances.

The emphasis placed on low cost is no idle claim. Generally speaking, the savings banks have been able to write life insurance at a net cost lower than that of most of the life insurance companies. However, several of the life insurance companies compare favorably in this respect with the savings banks, and in certain instances the net cost position of the life insurance companies has been less than that of one or more of the savings bank life insurance systems.

Whether the net cost position, generally favoring the savings banks, will continue indefinitely into the future is difficult to determine. The use of special policies, sold in relatively high minimum amounts by the life companies, has tended to reduce the savings bank cost advantage for such policyholders. In addition, increased emphasis on the part of many life insurance companies on reducing premiums by size of policy (or increasing dividends) will tend to have an equalizing effect.

SELECTED REFERENCES

BERMAN, EDWARD. *Operation of Savings Bank Life Insurance in Massachusetts and New York.* Bulletin No. 688. Washington, D.C.: U.S. Department of Labor, 1941.

JOHNSON, DONALD R. *Savings Bank Life Insurance.* Homewood, Ill.: Richard D. Irwin, Inc., 1963.

MASON, A. T. *The Brandeis Way.* Princeton: Princeton University Press, 1938.

Chapter 82

A BRIEF HISTORY*

BY PAUL A. NORTON

Insurance is as old as man's quest for financial security. The germ of the idea traces back four thousand years, to the time when the cargoes of Babylonian caravans and Phoenician ships were pledged as security for loans. Later, we know that during the period of the Roman Empire, religious and fraternal societies paid out benefits upon the death of their members. But despite this ancient lineage, life insurance as we know it today is a relatively new development. It evolved from a great transformation in Western life which began in the nineteenth century: the decline of an agrarian society and the rise of an industrial one. Industrialization—with its cities, factories, cash economy, and an urban "saving" class—set the stage for life insurance as a large-scale, national institution. Life insurance, it can truly be said, is a product of modern industrial democracy.

The growth of the insurance business in America well illustrates this point. Up to the nineteenth century, only a handful of life insurance policies had been written in this country. Some were granted by the Presbyterian Ministers' Fund, which was formed in 1759 as the first life insurance company in America, and a few others by the Insurance Company of North America, originally chartered in 1794. (A chronology of historic dates in the development of life and health insurance in the United States is found in Appendix A.) The remainder were issued by individual insurers. Working out of coffeehouses where colonial merchants congregated, these individual underwriters (the term "underwriter" arose when a person willing to take a portion of the risk wrote his name beneath the contract, and was thus said to have underwritten, or guaranteed, the insurance) at first underwrote marine insurance only. Occasionally, however, they wrote policies covering the risk of capture by pirates and eventually added policies covering death during a voy-

* This historical review will be devoted chiefly to the long steady development of life insurance, with a brief section at the end on the history of health insurance. The principal developments and important growth of health insurance did not occur until recent decades, when it became more closely allied with life insurance.

age. Yet such policies were small in number; and by the end of the eighteenth century, few Americans had ever been protected, at any stage of their lives, by life insurance.

Actually, early America had little need for such protection. In 1800 the United States was overwhelmingly a land of farmers. Only six cities—Philadelphia, New York, Boston, Charleston, Baltimore, and Salem—numbered populations above 8,000. Of the total population—a scant five million persons—fully nine tenths were chiefly engaged in agriculture. In this agrarian society the farm itself afforded family protection. The crops and herds provided food; the woodlot, fuel; the nearby wilderness, game animals; and the home stood as an enduring shelter for the aged and the infirm. The security of every individual was the concern of family and friends. Small wonder, then, that in this society, life insurance made little progress.

Industrialization Sets the Stage

But in the early nineteenth century, America, like western Europe before it, began to undergo a fundamental change. Stimulated by the War of 1812, which shut off European imports, the nation began to industrialize. As factories sprang up throughout New England and the Middle states, the sons and daughters of farmers rushed to man them, and towns and cities began an explosive growth. Within a few short years, while the population of the entire United States increased 334 per cent, that of towns and cities—attracting farmers from far and wide—shot up over 1,000 per cent (from 525,000 in 1810 to 6.2 million by 1860).[1] This migration profoundly altered the structure of American social life and set in motion an urban society urgently in need of life insurance.

In transplanting himself from farm to city, the new urban dweller left his traditional security behind. Gone was the certainty of food and shelter and the surety that relatives—now often days' distance away—would offer assistance in time of need. In these circumstances, many of the new urbanites became receptive to the idea of "outside" insurance. Fortunately, they now had the means to buy such protection. Unlike the agrarian society from which they came, where the barter system had prevailed, city workers were paid in coin. They lived in a cash society, and the more frugal and self-reliant among them were now able to *buy* security and financial protection for their families.

The Early Years

Responding to this need for a new kind of security, scores of new life insurance companies were organized in the early decades of the 1800's.

[1] Figures include population of cities and towns of 2,500 and over. See Bureau of the Census, U.S. Department of Commerce, *Historical Statistics of the United States, 1789–1945* (Washington, D.C.: U.S. Government Printing Office, 1949).

Many of these were unsoundly financed and soon dropped out of existence; others, however, met with considerable success. The great advantage of these companies over the earlier individual underwriters was that policyholders could generally rely upon them to meet their obligations. Too often the coffeehouse underwriters not only disputed claims but were unable to pay even those they freely acknowledged. With the organization of the stock companies in the early 1800's, life insurance at last began to be organized on a systematic, businesslike basis.

In spite of substantial progress, life insurance was not yet out of its infancy. As late as 1840, there was only $4,690,000 worth of life insurance in force throughout the United States. The business, however, was on the brink of its first great forward stride. Its immense growth truly began in what for insurance companies could be called the "golden forties."

For the nation as a whole the 1840's represented a period of great ferment and growth. It saw the first inrush of German, Irish, and Scandinavian immigrants; the building of a vast network of turnpikes and canals linking the eastern seaboard with the fast-growing trans-Appalachian states; the Mexican War; the acquisition of Oregon, Texas, New Mexico, and California; and, most important for the future of life insurance, a tremendous acceleration of the process of urbanization and industrialization which had commenced such a short time before. As the industrial system took hold, life insurance became more essential—and more popular—than ever before. Greatly contributing to this growth were two important changes within the life insurance business itself: the start of mutual companies and the development of more aggressive sales techniques, particularly the rise of the agency system.

The Rise of Mutuals

The idea of mutuality—whereby policyholders share in the divisible surplus of the business—was not new. For years, there had been mutual life insurance companies in England; and in America, mutuals in the fire insurance field were not uncommon. But it was not until 1843 that the first life mutual began business in this country—the Mutual Life Insurance Company of New York. Formed in 1842 by Morris Robinson, a former Canadian and ex-banker, its first policies were issued in February of 1843. It was soon followed by the New England Mutual Life Insurance Company, which began issuing policies later in 1843 (although it was chartered in 1835); State Mutual (1844); Mutual Benefit and New York Life (1845); Connecticut Mutual (1846); Penn Mutual (1847); and many more.

New Sales Techniques

By this time, too, insurance was being sold more aggressively than ever before. Unlike earlier firms, which often waited for customers to come to them, the new mutuals, along with their competitors, the stock companies, now began employing new sales techniques. Promotion circulars were sent out; advertisements extolling the virtues of life insurance were placed in magazines and newspapers; and above all, scores of new agents were hired to seek out prospects.

By today's standards, relations between these early agents and their companies were casual indeed. The agent received no formal contract, his appointment being made verbally or by letter; and he was given no training whatever. Armed with little more than a form sheet listing his duties and a rate and commission schedule (the commission was usually 5 per cent or 10 per cent on first-year premiums and 5 per cent for a limited period on renewals), the agent set out to market insurance. In the 1840's, this was no easy task. The product he was selling was still unfamiliar to most people and, compared to today, enormously high in cost ($25 to $30 per $1,000 on a participating policy at age 30—at a time when the average factory worker was earning $1.50 a day). The agent, moreover, was prevented from selling large policies even to those able to afford them, since most companies had policy limits between $5,000 and $10,000.

Mid-Century Growth

Despite its high cost and limited coverage, life insurance was being sold. By 1850, insurance in force had reached $97.1 million; and by the outbreak of the Civil War, this figure had leaped to $173.3 million, a spectacular rise of over 3,000 per cent within two decades.

Not even the war seriously interrupted the progress of the business. Before the war's end, insurance in force was increasing at a faster rate than ever, and in the immediate postwar period the increase reached a fabulous 50 per cent a year. Every year saw the formation of new companies—24 began business within the two-year period 1866–67, and in New York State alone, the number reporting to the State Insurance Department rose from 17 to 71 between 1862 and 1870.

This period also saw a number of other notable changes: the widespread application of nonforfeiture provisions (first recognized as a policyholder's right by New York Life in 1860); the beginnings of fraternal insurance (imported from England along with its friendly societies—the Odd Fellows, Foresters, and others); the growth of the general agency system, which came into use in the early 1860's and by 1865 was the "generally accepted method for the organization of the selling of life insurance";[2] the decline of term insurance (which predominated up to the 1840's) and the ascendancy of the level premium, whole life type; and an outstanding actuarial accomplishment, the construction of a new mortality table by Sheppard Homans of Mutual Life. Homans' achievement lay in

[2] R. Carlyle Buley, *The American Life Convention: 1906–1952* (New York: Appleton-Century-Crofts, Inc., 1953), Vol. I, p. 80.

his discovery that mortality rates in America were higher at the younger and older ages and much lower at the middle ages than in England. His table, the first American Experience Mortality Table, was widely used for three quarters of a century. By the close of the 1860's the insurance business had witnessed its first great period of growth. Insurance in force stood at what was then the colossal figure of $2 billion.

The Business in Crisis

Yet the situation was not as bright as it seemed. Much of this growth had not been as healthy as it might have been, a reflection of a basic change in the tone of American business and political life which began in the postwar era.

America's post-bellum period was a raw and lusty age. Encouraged by the Civil War, with its unprecedented demand for manufactured goods of every description, Americans feverishly set out to turn their nation into an industrial colossus overnight. Hastily, railroads were flung across mountains; the earth was opened for its wealth of iron ore, copper, and coal; cables were strung from continent to continent; and new industries sprang up overnight. But in the process—in an excess of raw, creative energy—the rules of the game were often forgotten. During the Grant administrations the ethics of business and political life reached a low ebb. Politicians figured in "salary grabs," brazen tax frauds, and land steals. Corruption reached almost to the doors of the White House itself, for in the Credit Mobilier scandal, Vice President Schuyler Colfax was a leading figure. And in business, "defalcations, stock-watering, wildcat investment schemes, railway wrecking were accepted parts of commercial life."[3]

Quite naturally, the life insurance business—which by now had begun to play a leading role in American social and economic life—was not immune to these influences. In the competitive race to sell insurance, the policyholder was often forgotten, and the "earlier emphasis upon . . . life insurance as a great cooperative scheme, an eleemosynary principle with unlimited liberating possibilities which would alleviate, even eliminate, human distress,"[4] was largely overlooked. Instead, many life insurance practitioners came to look upon the business chiefly as a means of accumulating power and prestige. With this philosophy, sound business practices were frequently forgotten. Commissions were recklessly raised, advertising claims were grotesquely inflated, agencies raided one another to lure away star salesmen, showy offices were erected which sometimes cost more than the total assets of the company, dividends were declared that had not been earned, risks were accepted carelessly, scant concern was shown for proper methods of premium and reserve calculations, and

[3] Samuel Eliot Morison and Henry Steele Commager, *The Growth of the American Republic* (New York: Oxford University Press, 1940), Vol. I, pp. 74–75.

[4] Buley, *op. cit.*, p. 91.

a few shakily financed companies even went so far as to frighten "enough policyholders into forfeiting so that liabilities could be scaled down to somewhere near the assets on hand."[5]

By the 1870's, life insurance companies were paying heavily for their sins. Public disclosure of abuses caused numerous Americans to take a searching look at the business; and because of their concern at what they saw, new business fell off alarmingly. Before long, company after company began to fail. Thirty-three life insurance firms went to the wall between 1870 and 1872. Another 48 followed during the 1873–77 period—a time of general depression which contributed to the industry's decline—and by 1882, only 55 companies remained of the 129 which had been doing business in 1870. Without a doubt, the seventies, as an authority in the field once observed, "must be accounted the most trying period in the history of American life insurance."[6]

To some extent, the downfall of many firms was occasioned not only by extravagance, inefficiency, or dishonesty, but by the strict enforcement of state insurance laws, particularly those relating to reserves and the admittance of assets. These laws—indeed, the state insurance departments themselves—were relatively new, the outcome of a long campaign waged a few years earlier by Elizur Wright, "the father of life insurance in America."

Beginnings of State Regulation

In the early years of the nineteenth century, state regulation of life insurance in America had been almost totally unknown. What few rules existed were set forth in the charters of individual companies. But in the 1840's, Wright, a schoolteacher, newspaper editor, and fiery abolitionist, became concerned with the hit-or-miss methods used by most insurance companies in calculating their reserves. With prodigious effort, he compiled a series of net valuation tables (involving in all nearly 200,000 calculations), which showed what reserve should be held at the end of each year during the life of various policies. Wright thought that life insurance companies should be legally obligated to maintain adequate reserves, and in 1858 almost singlehandedly lobbied a version of his legal reserve principle through the Massachusetts legislature. This, plus Wright's appointment in that same year as head of the Massachusetts state insurance department,[7] marks the beginning of effective state regulation of life insurance in this country. Other states soon passed similar

[5] *Ibid.*, p. 92.

[6] John A. McCall, President, New York Life Insurance Company, quoted in *ibid.*, p. 90.

[7] In 1852, Massachusetts set up a board of insurance commissioners composed of the secretary, treasurer, and auditor of the state. They were replaced in 1855 by a formally organized insurance department, generally regarded as the first in the United States.

regulatory laws; and within a decade, thirty-five states had established special insurance departments or delegated the supervision of insurance to an official specifically appointed for that purpose.

New Policies, New Methods, New Growth

This closer state supervision, combined with the pruning-out of weaker companies during the depressed seventies, had, by the 1880's, restored much of the industry's vigor. Meanwhile, the economy in general had recovered as well. Industrial expansion had gained new momentum; money in circulation had greatly increased; the population had risen to 50 million (up from 17 million in 1840); the West was being rapidly peopled; and more important still, the population of cities—where the need for life insurance was greatest and most clearly recognized—had risen to 22½ per cent of the total population, compared with 8½ per cent two decades earlier. In this atmosphere of confidence and growth the life insurance business resumed its forward surge.

Increasingly, after 1880, life insurance was liberalized, and its benefits were shared more broadly throughout the nation. As the West grew, older companies expanded, and new ones sprang up to provide protection for the mounting number of cattlemen, miners, and farmers who were turning this region into a settled part of the nation. In the East, and in other parts of the country as well, industrial insurance, first introduced in America by the Prudential in 1875 to meet the insurance needs of low-income groups, began to be much more widely sold. Simultaneously, older types of insurance were greatly improved. As Americans began to travel more, travel restrictions were removed (this had started with the policies of the Home Life of New York in 1886). Cash and surrender values were written into ordinary life policies. Thirty days' grace on premium payments became more common. Policies were beginning to appear containing statements of incontestability. The insuring of substandard risks became more widespread (this had been pioneered by Connecticut General in 1865), and in 1896 the first policies providing waiver of premiums if the insured should become totally disabled were issued. Along with these changes, insurance in force steadily mounted. It rose from $1,522,000,000 in 1880 to $3,522,000,000 in 1890 and by the end of the century had leaped to $7.5 billion. At this point the life insurance business in America had reached a size unequaled in any other country in the world.

The Armstrong Investigation

Its size, in fact, soon proved a momentary disadvantage. At the turn of the century, with the nation in an era of "frenzied finance," and with the "muckrakers" exposing questionable business practices—some real and some imagined—the power and influence, as well as the operating methods, of the life insurance business were subjected to careful scrutiny.

Were life insurance companies, many wondered, fit custodians for so much of the nation's wealth? Despite the many reputable firms, there were reasons for thinking that some, at least, were not. More than a few, it appeared, had engaged in shady practices. As the public became aware of these evils, there arose outraged cries for an investigation of the entire business, and in 1905 a part of this difficult task was handed to a group of carefully chosen men, the Armstrong Investigating Committee, which was charged with investigating the life insurance business in New York.

It is to the credit of the committee that the business as a whole was not victimized. From the outset, Charles Evans Hughes, Chief Counsel for the committee, made it clear that the purpose of the investigation was not to condemn, but to protect and strengthen the business by ridding it of undesirable practices.

The New York Insurance Code, adopted in 1906, included nearly all of the committee's recommendations. The Code called for closer regulation by the state insurance department of the election of company officers; the prohibition of investments in common stocks, subsequently modified; a limitation on the amount that could be spent in securing new business; and the outlawing of the deferred dividend system. All in all, the Armstrong Investigation amounted to a sober, responsible housecleaning of the industry—a boon not only to the public but to the business as well. In fact, the stoutest defenders of the committee's regulations were responsible insurance companies themselves, which quite naturally wished to allay the suspicion that the business was peopled wholly by self-seekers.

For a time following the Armstrong Investigation, new insurance fell off sharply, but this slackening was of short duration. Soon, public confidence was restored; and throughout the next quarter of a century, encouraged partly by Americans' favorable experience with government life insurance during World War I, new business, insurance in force, and assets steadily climbed. In 1929 alone, a record $20 billion of new insurance was written; and in that year, insurance in force passed the $100-billion mark.

As with other periods of progress, this one had been accompanied by numerous beneficial advances within the business. Among them were the introduction of group insurance (just prior to World War I), the inclusion in policies of disability clauses and double indemnity benefits, and the development of optional settlements of policy proceeds. The business also prospered because of the steadily growing use of life insurance for business purposes and because of the reduced cost of insurance—owing to favorable mortality experience, high interest rates, and relative freedom from capital losses.

Depression Decade

It was from this position of strength that the insurance business entered the depression decade of the 1930's. When the stock market crashed in the autumn of 1929, it brought on the worst economic setback in United States history. By 1932, stocks were worth little more than a tenth of their 1929 values, about 13 million people were unemployed, and the national income had been cut in half.

For a time the effect on the life insurance business was severe. Sharp decreases in the amount of new insurance written were seen in 1931 and 1932; and in the latter year, for the first time in a generation, total insurance in force declined. Meanwhile, owing chiefly to suicides, the business suffered high mortality experience (suicides rose to 30 per cent above normal during the early years of the thirties), and disability claims and losses enormously increased. Lapses and surrenders were also high; and owing to defaults in mortgage payments and to lower interest rates, earnings fell off sharply.

Nevertheless, compared with most American businesses, life insurance fared exceedingly well. Of a total of about 350 companies, only 20 went into the hands of receivers. Of these, not one was of major size. The actual insurance involved in these failures amounted to only a little more than 1 per cent of the total insurance in force in all companies. But even this was reinsured by solvent companies, so that the actual loss to policyholders was practically nil. This unequaled record of strength and stability, under the harshest economic conditions, is one of which the business may well be proud.

The Modern Quest for Security

Curiously enough, in one way the depression probably proved a boon to the life insurance business. So deep and long-lasting were its effects that Americans, more earnestly than ever before, began a determined search for financial security, a quest which persists to the present day. The Social Security Act, signed by the President in August, 1935, is a part of this trend. Amended in 1939 to provide survivors' benefits, the Act, in effect, provides a large volume of government life insurance. Yet, far from satisfying Americans' insurance needs and cutting into private insurance sales, it in fact re-emphasized the value of financial protection and helped whet the nation's appetite for more. The result of this search for security has been a spectacular increase in life insurance in force, particularly in the years since World War II.

In their efforts to build themselves a more or less "insured society," Americans in recent years have increasingly used life insurance as one of the major tools. Today, the skilled, full-time practitioners of the life insurance art transact the far greater portion of the life insurance business. Over the years, life insurance companies have placed increasing emphasis on the education and training of their agents. This training is now conducted on three levels: the training courses, running from six months to two years, offered by individual companies; the courses offered by the Life Underwriter Training Council; and the rigorous advanced training program conducted in colleges, study groups, and insurance company classrooms under the auspices of the American College of Life Underwriters. The latter organization was formed in 1927 to raise the standards of insurance education and has been a notable success. Its graduates, designated as Chartered Life Underwriters (C.L.U.), are generally the industry's most deeply informed, thoroughly professional underwriters.

The introduction of new policies in recent years, most notably the family plan; the enormous growth of low-cost group insurance, which tripled in the decade 1953–63; the great rise of annuities since the war, together with the mounting use of insured pension plans and credit life insurance—all demonstrate the wide-ranging usefulness of life insurance to a broadening range of people. Today, with six out of seven American families carrying at least some protection, and with $785 billion of life insurance in force, Americans, it is clear, are recognizing the urgent need for insurance in our modern industrial society—a society, it is important to note, that life insurance itself has helped create.

Premium Payments and National Progress

Along with its protection side, America's life insurance business traditionally has played another—and highly important—role: investing in the nation's economy. For a century or more, life insurance funds, the savings of millions of frugal Americans, have been poured back into the economy. During the early national period, when Americans were vigorously tying their land together through a network of turnpikes and canals, an ally was found in the life insurance business, which helped buy the bonds to pay for these improvements. Again, when the Civil War threatened to sunder the nation, the industry responded by making huge purchases of government bonds, helping to bolster the Union's credit and thereby stimulating industry. In the same century, when research and ingenuity made possible new conveniences, life insurance companies gave freely of their support to a succession of vital public utilities undertakings: gas, light, water, telephone, telegraph, and electric power.

There has been scarcely a field in which life insurance funds have not prominently figured. Through mortgage loans, particularly during the housing crises following the Civil War and World Wars I and II, life insurance money has provided homes for millions of Americans. On occasion, insurance funds have even helped feed the world. Money lent farmers during World War I permitted farm mechanization, which in turn ameliorated the food shortage that accompanied the war. Municipalities have received life insurance assistance, too. As populations increased, the demand for municipal services—roads, hospitals, and schools—grew apace, and insurance companies helped provide the capital for them.

But increasingly, the biggest beneficiary of the life insurance dollar has been American industry. Where once, as we have seen, life insurance had to wait upon industrial development, the life insurance business has since become a great storehouse of investment capital feeding our industrial growth. Through the purchase of industrial bonds, through the use of the "sale and lease-back" device, which frees corporate capital for other purposes, and by the investment of funds in preferred and common stocks, life insurance companies have energized American business and quickened our national growth.

Today, life insurance plays an indispensable role in modern industrial life. With its systematic means of funneling funds into the economy, plus its protection side—an ingenious means of guarding millions of Americans against financial hazard—life insurance has earned an honored place at the center of the American scene. In sum, life insurance, the product of man's eternal quest for security, has proved itself one of the most useful institutions ever devised by man.

HEALTH INSURANCE

The history of health insurance in the United States, though reaching back more than one hundred years, is one of halting early developments and experiments and rapidly accelerating later developments and growth, particularly since the mid-1930's.

The companies that first began issuing accident insurance, and later such coverages as employers' liability and workmen's compensation, were chiefly multiple-line casualty insurance companies. In the decades of the 1930's and 1940's, many life insurance companies entered the health insurance field; and by 1950, they were providing slightly over one half of all individual health insurance coverage. By 1961 the life insurance companies were writing over 86 per cent of the individual health insurance.

The first company to offer health insurance against the cost of medical care was the Massachusetts Health Insurance Company of Boston, organized in 1847. Three years later, the Franklin Health Assurance Company of Massachusetts was organized to issue the first accident insurance.

One of the most hazardous activities of the latter half of the nineteenth century was travel, especially by rail and steamboat, and the early growth of health insurance was mainly in coverage against such travel accidents. The first company formed to offer accident insurance on a basis resembling its modern form was the Travelers Insurance Company of Hartford, organized in 1863, which first provided insurance against railway mishaps, and later against all types of accidents.

The success of accident insurance paved the way for the first ventures into sickness and disability income insurance, and the first individual policies offering disability insurance appeared in 1890. The first decade of the new century saw the introduction of surgical benefits and hospital expense benefits (in some individual disability income policies); and in

1907 the first noncancellable, guaranteed renewable disability income policy was issued.

During the 1920's, many liberalizations were made under pressure of competition and without adequate experience or statistical data. The combination of overliberal benefits, excessive amounts of indemnity on individual risks, and the adverse economic conditions of the depression following 1929 brought about a retrenchment at that time.[8] With the beginning of economic recovery, however, this trend was reversed. The late forties saw the beginning of a truly surging growth, still continuing, in health insurance coverage and in the extension of its benefits.

One reason for this rapid advance in health insurance, in addition to the entrance of more life insurance companies into the field, was the establishment of Blue Cross/Blue Shield and other independent hospital-medical expense plans. These latter are on a group insurance basis; and where, prior to the 1930's, most health insurance was under individual plans, the greater amount of coverage today is under group policies. Group health insurance now figures prominently among employee benefits offered by industry.

The first city-wide Blue Cross plan was inaugurated by a group of hospitals in Sacramento, California, in 1932. The first of the Blue-Shield-type plans was begun in 1939.

By 1962, total premium payments from health insurance policies had risen to $9.3 billion. Of this total, $3.7 billion represented subscription income of Blue Cross/Blue Shield organizations and other hospital-medical plans. As an indication of the acceleration in coverage that has occurred in recent years, the growth in premium income received by voluntary insurers between 1957 and 1962 was 68 per cent.

Significant developments in health insurance coverage during the past fifteen years have included major medical expense policies, guaranteed renewable lifetime hospital-surgical expense coverages, the mass enrollment and state plans for senior citizens, and a continuing interest on the part of the federal government in some kind of government-financed medical expense protection for elderly people.

The first major medical expense type policy was issued in 1949 by the Liberty Mutual Insurance Company. Under this type of plan a person or member of his family can be protected against so-called "catastrophic" illnesses that involve prolonged medical costs that could otherwise be crippling to a family budget. Such plans, covering medical costs up to, for example, $15,000, are usually issued with a deductible clause. Often the deductible amount is met by some basic health insurance plan.

Accompanying the recent growth in health insurance, and affecting both its need by the general public and its premium costs, have been the

[8] E. L. Bartleson *et al.*, *Health Insurance Provided through Individual Policies* (Chicago: Society of Actuaries, 1963).

great advances made in recent decades in medical science and continued rising costs of medical care of all kinds. Many formerly incurable or crippling diseases have been brought under control by the medical profession; more medical care in and out of hospitals is available; but also, the cost of medical care continues to rise rapidly.

These factors have awakened more people to the need for health insurance protection, and the future of health insurance would appear to be one of continued rapid growth.

SELECTED REFERENCES

BARTLESON, E. L., *et al.* *Health Insurance Provided through Individual Policies.* Chicago: Society of Actuaries, 1963.

BULEY, R. CARLYLE. *The American Life Convention: 1906–1952.* 2 vols. New York: Appleton-Century-Crofts, Inc., 1953.

EILERS, R. D. *Regulation of Blue Cross and Blue Shield Plans.* Homewood, Ill.: Richard D. Irwin, Inc., 1963.

HEALTH INSURANCE COUNCIL. *The Health Insurance Story.* New York, n.d.

HEALTH INSURANCE INSTITUTE. *Source Book of Health Insurance Data, 1962.* New York, 1963.

MACLEAN, JOSEPH B. *Life Insurance.* 9th ed. New York: McGraw-Hill Book Co., Inc., 1962.

O'DONNELL, TERENCE. *History of Life Insurance in Its Formative Years.* Chicago: American Conservation Co., 1936.

STALSON, J. OWEN. *Marketing Life Insurance: Its History in America.* Cambridge: Harvard University Press, 1942.

Appendixes

A. Historic Dates in the Development of Life and Health Insurance in the United States

LIFE INSURANCE*

1759 The first life insurance company in the United States, "The Corporation for Relief of Poor and Distressed Presbyterian Ministers and of the Poor and Distressed Widows and Children of Presbyterian Ministers," was established in Philadelphia by the Synod of the Presbyterian Church. This company, now Presbyterian Ministers' Fund, is the oldest life insurance company in continued existence in the world.

1794 The Insurance Company of North America chartered; was the first general insurance company to sell life insurance in America. In five years only six policies were issued and the company discontinued its life insurance business in 1804.

1807 Israel Whelen of Philadelphia appointed agent for the Pelican Life Insurance Company of London. Probably first agent for level premium life insurance in America.

1812 Pennsylvania Company for Insurance on Lives and Granting Annuities incorporated; first corporation to be organized in America for the sole purpose of issuing life insurance policies and annuities. First policy issued 1813. It discontinued issuing life policies in 1872.

1830 New York Life Insurance and Trust Company started, notable as first American life company to employ agents. This company later discontinued its life insurance business and was subsequently merged with the Bank of New York.

1835 Charter granted New England Mutual Life Insurance Company of Boston. First mutual company to be chartered in America. Did not actually begin business until 1843.

1836 The Girard Life Insurance, Annuity and Trust Company of Philadelphia established upon a new principle, that of granting policyholders participation in profits, although it was a stock company. The first dividends were allotted in 1844 as additions of insurance to policies in force three or more years. This company later became a trust company only.

1840 The legislature of the state of New York enacted a law which provided that the proceeds of a policy made out to a widow as beneficiary would be paid to her and were exempt from claims of creditors. This strengthened immeasurably the protective power of a life insurance policy.

1842 The Mutual Life Insurance Company of New York was chartered, marking the beginning of mutual life insurance as it is known today. First policy issued February 1, 1843.

1848 First policy loans granted about this time.

---

* Reprinted with permission from the *Fact Book*, 1964, Institute of Life Insurance, 488 Madison Avenue, New York, N.Y.

1849 New York's first general insurance law passed.

1851 New Hampshire established the first regulatory body to examine the affairs of insurance companies.

1853 Policy valuation tables, which had been worked on by Elizur Wright for nine years, published.

1859 New York State established an insurance department.

1861 Massachusetts first state to require nonforfeiture values as part of life policies.

1861 First war risk insurance written by life companies in Civil War.

1864 Incontestable clause first written into policies by any American company.

1868 American Experience Table of Mortality first published as a part of New York law. Covered experience 1843–1858.

1869 Earliest organization of life insurance agents recorded in Chicago.

1871 First convention of State Insurance Commissioners, in New York City, in May.

1873 First weekly premium policy issued in the United States.

1875 Industrial insurance agency system introduced in the United States.

1880 Cash surrender values first established by law in Massachusetts.

1897 Series of lectures given on life insurance at Harvard University.

1905 Armstrong investigation of life insurance by New York State Legislature, resulting in many changes in insurance laws.

1906 New York insurance laws revised.

1909 Standard provisions for life insurance policies adopted in New York State.

1911 First group life insurance for employees of an employer.

1917 Life insurance for servicemen of World War I offered by Government under War Risk Insurance Act; such insurance is now known as U.S. Government Life Insurance.

1918 American Men Ultimate Mortality Table published. Covered experience 1900–1915.

1928 First examinations held for Chartered Life Underwriters, resulting in awards of CLU degrees to qualified agents.

1938 The 1937 Standard Annuity Mortality Table published. Based primarily on experience 1932–1936.

1939 Temporary National Economic Committee investigation of life insurance.

1940 National Service Life Insurance Act, providing insurance for men and women in service in World War II, adopted by Congress.

1941 Commissioners 1941 Standard Ordinary Table of Mortality based on experience 1930–1940 published.

1944 U.S. Supreme Court held insurance to be commerce.

1948 Legislation permitting "Standard Nonforfeiture and Valuation" methods of computation effective in nearly all states.

1951 New York insurance laws revised to permit limited investment in qualified common stocks.

1951 Servicemen's Indemnity Act adopted by Congress. Provides automatic indemnity of $10,000 for death in the Armed Forces after June 26, 1950, and permits issuance of insurance under certain conditions after separation from service.

1954 Federal Employees' Group Life Insurance Act providing group life insurance and accidental death and dismemberment insurance to civilian offices and employees of the United States Government through private insurance companies.

1958 Commissioners 1958 Standard Ordinary Table of Mortality based on experience 1950–1954 published.

HEALTH INSURANCE*

1798 U.S. Marine Hospital Service established by U.S. Congress. Compulsory deductions for hospital service were made from seamen's wages.

1847 Organization of Massachusetts Health Insurance Company of Boston. First U.S. company organized to issue insurance against the costs of medical care.

1850 Franklin Health Assurance Company of Massachusetts organized; first insurance company authorized to issue accident insurance in the United States.

1863 Founding of Travelers Insurance Company of Hartford. The company offered accident insurance for railway mishaps; then all forms of accident protection. It was the first company to issue accident insurance on a basis resembling its present form.

1890 Introduction of individual insurance policies offering disability income protection from certain specified diseases.

1903 Limited surgical benefits included in some individual disability income policies.

1905 Hospital expense benefits first offered in some individual disability income policies in the form of a benefit increase while the disabled insured person was hospitalized.

1907 First noncancellable and guaranteed renewable disability income policy offered in the U.S.

1912 Uniform Standard Provisions Law promulgated by the National Association of Insurance Commissioners.

1921 First noncancellable and guaranteed renewable disability policy issued to contain a stated maximum indemnity period for total disability due to sickness with no aggregate limit.

1932 First city-wide Blue Cross plan tried out with a group of hospitals in Sacramento, Calif.

1937 Organization of Health Service Plan Commission (Blue Cross Commission).

1939 Establishment of the California Physicians' Service, the first Blue Shield-type plan formed.

* Reprinted with permission from *Source Book of Health Insurance Data*, 1963, Health Insurance Institute, 488 Madison Avenue, New York, N.Y.

1946 Organization of Blue Shield Medical Care Plans, Inc. (Blue Shield Commission).

1946 Formation of the Health Insurance Council, a federation of eight insurance associations organized to give technical and practical assistance on health insurance to the providers of medical care.

1948 First noncancellable and guaranteed renewable hospital-surgical-medical policy issued providing protection to age 65.

1949 First major medical group insurance contract issued. Liberty Mutual Insurance Company issued this contract to the Elfun Society—management personnel of General Electric Company.

1952 First noncancellable and guaranteed renewable hospital-surgical-medical policy issued providing protection for the lifetime of the policyholder.

1955 First guaranteed renewable lifetime hospital-surgical policy designed for older age people.

1958 First comprehensive major medical individual insurance policy issued.

B. Application for Life Insurance Policy, Including Medical Examiner's Report

Application for Insurance—Life
Part I

THE ____________ LIFE INSURANCE COMPANY

(for Company use only) Policy No. ....

1. Proposed Insured. (Please print full name.) ☐ Male ☐ Female

2. (a) Place of birth. (b) Date of birth. Month | Day | Year (c) Age nearest birthday.

3. Address of Proposed Insured.
(a) Residence: Street City County State
(b) Business:
(c) Send premium notices to ☐ Residence ☐ Business
If neither indicated, send to residence.

4. (a) Principal occupation. (Give exact duties.)
(b) Other occupation, if any. (c) Any change contemplated? (Give details.)
(d) Any hazardous sports or hobbies? (Give details.)

5. (a) Do you intend to change your residence, or travel outside the U.S.A.? (Give details.)
(b) Are you now a member of, or do you intend to join the armed forces or the armed forces reserve of any nation? (If "Yes," give exact status.)

6. Is the policy applied for to replace insurance now in force in this or any other company? (If "Yes," give details.)

7. Have you ever taken or do you intend to take instruction in the operation of an aircraft either as a pilot or as a crew member?
☐ Yes (Complete Aviation Supplement.) ☐ No

8. Have you ever applied for or been examined for any insurance without a policy of the exact kind and amount applied for being issued or have you been refused renewal or reinstatement of any policy? (Give details.)

9. (a) Sum to be insured $ (b) Plan
(c) Premiums payable: ☐ Annually ☐ Semiannually ☐ Quarterly ☐ Monthly ☐ Penn Check
(d) Automatic Premium Loan option operative? ☐ Yes ☐ No
(e) Additional benefits desired: ☐ Accidental Death Benefit ☐ Disability Waiver Prem. ☐ Dis. Waiver Prem. & Mo. Inc. ☐ Option to Purchase Additional Ins. (Amount $)
(f) Dividends: ☐ Paid-up additional insurance (not available on term) ☐ Reduce premiums ☐ Cash ☐ Accumulate at interest

10. Owner and beneficiary (If a separate Owner and Beneficiary Designation will be made, do not complete this Question 10):
(a) Owner: ☐ Proposed Insured; ☐ .... while living, thereafter............
(b) Death benefit beneficiary: Surviving beneficiary (equally if more than one) in lowest numbered class in which a beneficiary survives Proposed Insured, as follows:

	Name	Relationship	Date of Birth
Class 1			
Class 2			

If no beneficiary in the above classes survives, executors or administrators of ☐ Proposed Insured; ☐ ....
(c) Endowment or monthly income beneficiary (if on endowment plan): Proposed Insured or as otherwise requested under "Remarks."

11. Total insurance on your life, including Health and Accident?

Company	Life Insurance	Disability Mo. Inc.	Accidental Death Ben.	Issue Date

12. Are any applications for insurance now pending or contemplated? (State companies and amounts.)

13. Has full payment for the first premium on the insurance applied for been made? ☐ Yes (Amount $) ☐ No

Remarks (Enter here any special instructions.)

Amendments and Corrections (For Home Office use only.)

I, the Proposed Insured, to whom the above statements and answers relate, represent that they are written as made by me and are full, complete and true to the best of my knowledge and belief. I, the Proposed Insured or the applicant if other than the Proposed Insured, agree that they and the statements of the Proposed Insured in Part II shall be a part of the contract of insurance if issued; that I shall be bound by such statements and answers; and that the Company, believing them to be true, shall rely and act upon them; and I also understand and agree that:

1. Part II of this application shall consist of statements made by the Proposed Insured to a medical examiner or, if the policy is issued without a medical examination, to the agent and which are considered by the Company in acting on this application for insurance.
2. No insurance shall be in force until the first premium is paid in full and the policy is delivered while the health, habits, occupation and other facts relating to the Proposed Insured are the same as described in Part I and Part II and any amendments or supplements thereto, except that insurance shall be in force from the date of Part I or Part II of this application, whichever is the later, as provided in and subject to the conditions of the receipt attached to Part I if (when Part I is signed and in exchange for such receipt signed by the Company's agent) payment of the first premium is made in full.
3. Notice to or knowledge of an agent or a medical examiner is not notice to or knowledge of the Company, and no agent or medical examiner is authorized to accept risks, to pass upon acceptability for insurance, or to modify, alter or enlarge any contract of insurance.
4. Acceptance of any policy issued on this application shall be a ratification of any amendments or corrections noted by the Company in the space in Part I marked "Amendments and Corrections."

Signed at ...., State of .... Signature of Proposed Insured

on the .... day of ...., 19............

Witness: .... Signature of Applicant if not Proposed Insured

5800-5

PREMIUM RECEIPT

This receipt is to be given by the agent to the applicant only if payment of the first premium in full is received when Part I of the application is signed. **Otherwise this receipt must not be detached. The receipt is void if altered or modified.**

Received from............the first............premium of $............ on proposed Life Insurance in the amount of $............on the life of............ for which an application bearing the number of this receipt has been made to The ________ Life Insurance Company. Insurance as applied for in such application (subject to the terms of the policy applied for) shall be in force from the date of Part I or Part II of the application, whichever is the later, if (1) the amount paid in exchange for this receipt is the amount of the full first premium for the policy applied for and this receipt is signed by the Company's agent and delivered at the time Part I of the application is signed and (2) on the date of Part I or Part II, whichever is the later, the Proposed Insured is acceptable, as later determined by the Company, under the Company's rules for insurance on the plan, at the premium rate and for the amount applied for. Such determination shall be made without regard to any change occurring after such date in health or other facts relating to the Proposed Insured. If the Company shall determine that the Proposed Insured was not so acceptable or if the above conditions are not otherwise met, the payment received shall be returned upon surrender of this receipt.

Signed the............day of............, 19............ .... Agent

Application for Life Insurance Policy (Continued)

AGENT'S CERTIFICATE

1. How long and how intimately have you known the Proposed Insured?

2. What knowledge or information have you as to Proposed Insured's habits, particularly the use of intoxicants?

3. Marital status? ☐ Married ☐ Single ☐ Widowed ☐ Divorced

4. Previous addresses during past two years
   (a) Residence: Street City County State
   ....
   ....
   (b) Business:..............................
   ....

Give below names and addresses of three references.
....
....
....
....
....
....
....

5. What is Proposed Insured's
   (a) Approximate worth? $..........
   (b) Income? Earned—$..........
   Unearned—$..........
   (c) Employer's name?..........
   (d) Occupation during past five years?..........

6. If this application was taken on a nonmedical basis, did you personally obtain the answers on Part I and Part II from the Proposed Insured?

7. Was this Proposed Insured referred to you by a broker or agent of this or another Insurance Company?

8. Do you unqualifiedly recommend the Proposed Insured for acceptance?

.............., 19........ ....
Signature of Soliciting Agent

The General Agent is to complete and sign the following form:

(a) Soliciting Agent is..............................
(Please Print)

(b) I hereby endorse the above certificate

....
General Agent

IF PROPOSED INSURED IS A WOMAN—MARRIED, WIDOWED OR DIVORCED—COMPLETE THE FOLLOWING:

Full Maiden Name..............................

1. (a) Will the premium be paid with her personal funds?
   (b) If not, by whom will premiums be paid?
   (c) If she has an income other than that derived from her given occupation, state source and amount annually.

2. If married, state:
   (a) Husband's name..............................
   (b) Amount of insurance husband carries in Wife's favor. (If not insured, explain reason.)

3. If a divorcee, state:
   (a) By whom divorce was obtained..............Date..............
   (b) On what grounds?

Application for Life Insurance Policy (Medical Examiner's Report)

Application for Insurance—Part II THE ____________ LIFE INSURANCE COMPANY

Full Name of Proposed Insured...Date of Birth..........................

(for Company use only)

Policy No.................

1. (a) Family History	Age if Living	State of Health	Age at Death	Cause of Death
Father				
Mother				
Full Brothers No. Living				
Full Brothers No. Dead				
Full Sisters No. Living				
Full Sisters No. Dead				

(b) Has either parent or any brother or sister had diabetes, or heart disease?

2. (a) How often and to what extent during the past 5 years have you used alcoholic beverages?

(b) Have you ever taken treatment or a cure for alcoholism or drug addiction? (If "Yes," give details.)

3. (a) Are you in good health?

(b) Do you have any deformity?

4. (a) When did you last consult or receive treatment from any physician or practitioner?

(b) For what reason?

(c) Give name and address.

(d) State name of every other physician or practitioner whom you have consulted for any reason within the past 5 years. (Give all dates and details.)

5. Have you ever had a health or physical examination? (If "Yes," under "Details" give reasons, dates, names and addresses of persons who made examinations.)

6. Answer "Yes" or "No." Under "Details" give reasons, dates and names of physicians or practitioners consulted.

(a) Have you lost any time from your work during the past 5 years due to illness or injury? a........

(b) Have you ever been x-rayed for diagnosis or treatment? b........

(c) Have you ever had an elecfrocardiogram? c........

(d) Have you ever been in a clinic, hospital, or institution for surgery, diagnosis or treatment? d........

(e) Has future surgery been recommended or is any contemplated? e........

(f) Have you ever applied for or received sickness or disability benefits from the Veteran's Administration, any insurance company or other source? f........

(g) Were you ever rejected or medically discharged from military service? g........

7. Have you been aware of any suspicion of, or have you ever had or been treated for any of the following disorders or ailments? (Give details.)

(a) Convulsions, dizzy spells, fainting spells, epilepsy, nervous breakdown or other disorder of the brain or nervous system? a........

(b) Asthma, pleurisy, tuberculosis or any other respiratory disorder? b........

(c) Rectal, stomach, intestinal, liver or gall bladder disorder or hernia? c........

(d) Any disorder of reproductive or urinary systems including kidneys? d........

(e) Heart palpitation, abnormal pulse, shortness of breath, chest pain, high blood pressure, varicose veins or any disorder of heart or blood? e........

(f) Arthritis, rheumatic fever, injury or disorder of bones, joints, or muscles? f........

(g) Any impairment, defect or disorder of the eye, ear, nose or throat? g........

(h) Diabetes, albumin or sugar in urine, or ever been on prescribed diet? h........

(i) Cancer, other growths or any disorder of the glands or skin? i........

8. During the past 5 years have you had any illness, disease or injury other than as stated above?

9. (Omit if statements are made to medical examiner.)

(a) Height.............. ft. .... in.; weight .... lbs.

(b) Any weight change in past 2 years. Gain ....lbs. Loss ....lbs. Reasons.

DETAILS: Give information required to complete answers to previous questions. Identify by question number.

I represent that the statements and answers in this Part II are written as made by me, and are full, complete and true to the best of my knowledge and belief, and agree that they shall be a part of the contract of insurance if issued.

To the extent permitted by law I, on behalf of myself and of any person who shall have or claim any interest in any policy issued hereunder, waive all provisions of law forbidding any physician or other person who has attended or examined me, or who may hereafter attend or examine me, from disclosing any knowledge or information thereby acquired, and hereby authorize such physicians or other persons to make such disclosure to the Company or its authorized representative.

Signed at..............................State of..............................on the..................day of..............................., 19.......

Witness: ....

5802-6 Medical Examiner (Agent if Non-Medical) Signature of Proposed Insured

...., 19........

Dr...

....

In connection with an application to The ________ Life Insurance Company, detailed information is desired concerning the conditions for which I have consulted you. I will appreciate your courtesy in supplying that company with all data it may request.

....

...., 19........

Dr...

....

In connection with an application to The ________ Life Insurance Company, detailed information is desired concerning the conditions for which I have consulted you. I will appreciate your courtesy in supplying that company with all data it may request.

....

Application for Life Insurance Policy (Medical Examiner's Report) (Continued)

MEDICAL FEE VOUCHER—DETACH THIS VOUCHER AND MAIL IMMEDIATELY TO MEDICAL DIRECTOR

The ________ Life Insurance Company, ____________________.

Forward completed examination report to General Agent. Under no circumstances deliver to any one else.

Examination fees are paid the 15th of the following month. Fee for this examination must not be accepted from agents, applicants or examinees.

Name of person examined...Date Examined..................

Examination for.................. ☐ Life.................. ☐ Health..................

Name of agent..................

Please detail confidential information of any nature..................

....

....

....

Signature of Examiner..................M.D. Address..................

PRINT OR WRITE PLAINLY

REPORT OF EXAMINING PHYSICIAN

1. (a) Are you alone with the examinee?..................
(b) Do you believe examinee older than stated?..................
(c) How long and intimately have you known examinee?..................
(d) Does examinee appear frail, anemic, unhealthy? (Details.)..................

2. Is there any deformity, loss of member, impaired sight or hearing? (Describe fully under Remarks. If any defect in vision or hearing, give degree. Is other eye or ear normal?)

3. (a) Height (in shoes)..........ft..........in. Did you measure?..................
(b) Weight (without coat and vest)..........lbs. Did you weigh?..................
(If 20% over or under standard weight—Scale weight required.)
(c) How long has present weight been maintained?..................
(d) What is the most examinee ever weighed?..........When?..........
(Give full details under Remarks regarding gain or loss in past two years.)
(e) Measurement of chest, nipple level: Inspiration..................
Expiration..................
(f) Measurement of abdomen at level of umbilicus..................

4. Is there a history of, or on examination do you find any abnormality of the: (Give full details under Remarks.)
(a) Brain or Nervous System?..................
(b) Reflexes: Pupillary?..................Knee?..................
(c) Respiratory System?..................
(d) Gastro-intestinal System?..................
(e) Genito-urinary System?..................
(f) Endocrine System?..................

5. Blood Pressure:
(a) Systolic..................Diastolic (cessation of sound)..................
(b) Time of day..................A.M..................P.M..................

6. Heart rate and rhythm:

	Pulse Rate	Regular?	If Irregular No. per Min.
(a) Examinee seated at rest	....	....	....
(b) Immediately after exercise (25 hops each foot)	....	....	....
(c) Two minutes after exercise	....	....	....

(d) Is hypertrophy present?..................
(e) Murmur present?..........Systolic..........Diastolic..........
(f) Is the murmur transmitted?..................
(g) What is the location of the murmur?..................
(h) Diagnosis of the heart condition..................
(i) Is there a history of precordial or thoracic pain, shortness of breath or acute indigestion? (Full details under Remarks.)..........
(j) Any history of rheumatic fever or other infectious disease? (Full details under Remarks.)

7. Urine: (a) Sp. gr...........(b) Albumin..........(c) Sugar..........
(d) Do you know specimen examined was voided by examinee?..........
(If albumin or sugar present or a genito-urinary history in past five years, send a portion of specimen examined to Home Office.)
(e) Have you sent specimen to Home Office?..................
(f) Have you reported all specimens examined?..................

8. Are there any other factors to your knowledge or observation which might influence health or longevity?

9. Females
(a) Is she pregnant?..........(b) How far advanced?..........
(c) Has she had any gynecological disorder?..................

Remarks

Where was this examination made?

Name of Agent.................. Your office..........Examinee's office..........Examinee's residence..........

Signature of Examiner..................M.D. Address..................Date..........

C. Specimen Inspection Report Form—Life Form and Health Form

RETAIL CREDIT COMPANY
LIFE REPORT

District, Agcy., or Branch

CONFIDENTIAL

Acct. No.

OFFICE

INSURANCE HISTORY

Date	Acct. No.	Amt.	Fam. or Indiv.

Date:

NAME:

Address:
Occupation on Inq.
& Employer:

Date of Birth A Health App'd for $ Per . ☐ Hospitalization ☐ Major Medical Exp.

SPECIMEN REPORT

			NO	YES	
	1.	ANY REASON FOR NOT RECOMMENDING APPLICANT?	☐	☐	Feature(s)
	2.	On what date was this inspection made?			
IDENTITY	3—A.	How many years has each of your informants known him?	A.		
	B.	How many days since you or your informants have seen him? *(If not within two weeks, explain fully.)*	B.		
RACE—AGE	4—A.	What is racial descent or nationality? (Greek, Anglo-Saxon, Negro, Italian, etc.)	A.		
	B.	Is there any reason to doubt accuracy of birth date given?	B.		
FINANCES	5—A.	What would you estimate his net worth?	A. $		
	B.	What is his annual earned income from his work or business?	B. $		
	C.	Has he any income from investments, rentals, pension, etc.? *(If so, state source, amount.)*	C.		

				NO	YES	
OCCUPATION	6—A.	Does the occupation or job differ in name from that given in heading of this report?	A.			
	B.	Has he any part-time or off-season occupation? Does he plan work or travel in foreign countries?	B.			
	C.	Does he or his employer sell or manufacture beer, wine or liquor?	C.			
DRIVING RECORD	7.	Is he a fast, reckless, or careless driver?				**IF YES,** See Questions on Back.
AVIATION—SPORTS	8—A.	Has he taken flying lessons, either as member of armed forces or as civilian, owned or piloted a plane, or flown in planes not operated by scheduled airlines?	A.			
	B.	Does he engage in hazardous sports? (Racing, skin-diving, sky diving, skiing, etc.)	B.			
HEALTH	9—A.	Is there anything unhealthy about his appearance, such as being very thin or having excess weight?				**IF YES,** See Questions on Back.

	12.	Do you learn of any member of his family (blood relation) having had heart trouble, cancer, diabetes or mental trouble? (If so, who and which disease.)		
HABITS	13—A.	Is he a steady, frequent drinker (daily, almost daily, several times a week)?	A.	
IF SO,		B. How often?	B.	
		C. How many drinks does he take on these occasions?	C.	
		D. What does he usually drink (beer, wine or whiskey)?	D.	
	14.	Does he now or has he in the past used beer, wine or whiskey to noticeable excess or intoxication?		IF YES, See Questions on Back.
REPUTATION	15.	Do any of following apply to this applicant: Heavy debts? Domestic trouble? Drug habit? Connection with illegal liquor? Irregular beneficiary?		
	16.	Is there any criticism of character or morals?		

REMARKS: 17. COMMENT BELOW ON TOPICS LISTED AT LEFT; GIVE DETAILS OF "YES" OR INCOMPLETE ANSWERS.

A. BUSINESS:
Employer's name, line and size of business? Name of applicant's job? How long so employed? If less than 1 year, previous occupation?

B. ANSWER HANDY GUIDE QUESTIONS, IF APPLICABLE.

C. PERSONAL—HOME ENVIRONMENT: Married, single, or divorced? Any children? Type of associates. Comment on home environment, manner of living, standing in community.

RETAIL CREDIT COMPANY

Form 1—2-62

PRINTED IN U.S.A.

Signature of person making report__________

OVER—SEE ADDITIONAL QUESTIONS ON BACK

LIFE REPORT

Specimen Inspection Report Form—Life Form and Health Form (Continued)

#17 Continued

DETAILS OF APPEARANCE:

If answer to Question 9—A is "Yes," answer following:

18—A. How does he appear unhealthy (complexion, weight, or what)?________ B. Describe. (If overweight or underweight, give details.)

DETAILS OF HEALTH HISTORY:

If answer to Question 10 is "Yes," answer following:

19. Nature of illness, operation or injury?________
20. Approximate date it occurred?________

21—A. How long confined or "laid up"?________

B. Completely recovered? ________

SPECIMEN REPORT

22—A. Attended by Dr. (Name)________

Address ________

B. Confined to hospital?________ If so, name and address:

Name ________

Address ________

23. Any effect on present health?________ Details:

DETAILS OF DRIVING RECORD:

If answer to Question 7 is "Yes," answer following:

24. When, where, and under what circumstances does applicant drive in a fast or reckless manner? (Open highway, congested areas, etc.—if known to drive considerably in excess of speed limit, cover.)
25. Any evidence of unsupervised racing?________ Give details:
26. Any arrests? (Approximate dates)________
27. Charges? ________

If convicted, approximate dates ________

28. Any accidents?________ If so, approximate dates and details:
29. License ever suspended or revoked?________ If so, cause, date and whether he drove without a license?

THE FOLLOWING QUESTIONS APPLY TO EITHER PAST OR PRESENT EXCESSIVE DRINKING
(as indicated in answers to Questions Nos. 30 and 31).

		How often? (Once a week, once a month, etc.)
32. Classify drinking on these occasions and state how often:		
A. Getting "drunk," stupefied, entirely out of control of usual faculties?	A.	A.
B. Loud, boisterous, or obviously under influence, although still in possession of most of faculties?	B.	B.
C. Mild excess, just getting "feeling good"; exhilaration or stimulation?	C.	C.
33. Do (did) these occasions last for an evening, a day, two days, a week, or for how long?		
34. How long has (had) he been drinking to this extent?		
35. WHEN WAS THE LAST OCCASION OF THIS SORT?		
36. If applicant is an excessive drinker at present, does he drive a car during periods of intoxication?		
37. Has applicant ever taken any "cure" for liquor habit? (If so, when? Any subsequent lapse?)		

38. Tell how applicant drinks, if social or solitary, or if because of domestic or other trouble, how it affects him, whether ever arrested, and details to give clear picture of drinking habits; if habits have changed, tell how and how long since change; if reformed, what led to reformation (ill health, domestic trouble or what)?

INSPECTOR: Do not write in this space.

(Use Continuation of Report, Form 5166, for additional remarks.)

1 R—11-61

Specimen Inspection Report Form—Life Form and Health Form (Continued)

RETAIL CREDIT COMPANY
HEALTH REPORT

CONFIDENTIAL

District or Pol. No.

Acct. No.

OFFICE

INSURANCE HISTORY

Date	Acct. No.	Indem. $	Wk. or Mo.	Fam. or Indiv.

Date:

NAME:

Address:
Duties on Inq., & Employer:

Date of Birth | Indem. App'd $ | Per | Carried $ | Per | Life App'd $ | ☐ Hosp. | ☐ M. M. Ex.

1. ANY REASON FOR NOT RECOMMENDING APPLICANT?	NO ☐ YES ☐	Feature(s)
2. On what date was this inspection made?		
3—A. How many years has each of your informants known him? B. How many days since you or your informants have seen him? (If not within two weeks, explain fully.)	A. B.	IDENTITY
4—A. What is racial descent or nationality? (Greek, Anglo-Saxon, Negro, Italian, etc.) B. Is there any reason to doubt accuracy of birth date given?	A. B.	RACE—AGE
5—A. What is his annual earned income from work or business? (If professional man or self-employed, give net and gross.) B. In addition to above, what amount (if any) does he also receive from commissions, year-end bonus, etc. (If none, so state.) C. Are your answers to two preceding questions exact figures or estimates? (State which.) D. If exact figures, who gave them (employer, banker, or who)? E. If not exact figures, who gave estimates reported above? F. Is there any reason to question sufficiency of earned income for amount of insurance applied and carried? (If so, explain in Remarks.)	A. $ B. $ C. D. E. F.	EARNED INCOME
6—A. How much annual income does he have from investments, rentals, pensions, etc.? B. What would you estimate his net worth?	A. $ B. $	UNEARNED INCOME—WORTH
	NO | YES	
7—A. Do duties or job differ in name from that given in heading of this report? B. Has he any part-time or off-season occupation? Does he plan work or travel in foreign countries?	A. B.	DUTIES

SPECIMEN REPORT

11. Do you learn of any illness, operation, or injury, past or present?

12. Do you learn of any impairment which caused rejection for military service, or, if he served in armed forces, do you learn he was discharged for medical reasons?

13. Do you learn of any member of his family (blood relation) having had heart trouble, cancer, diabetes or mental trouble? (If so, who and which disease.)

HABITS

14—A. Is he a steady, frequent drinker (daily, almost daily, several times a week)? A.

IF SO,
- B. How often? B.
- C. How many drinks does he take on these occasions? C.
- D. What does he usually drink (beer, wine or whiskey)? D.

15. Does he now or has he in the past used beer, wine or whiskey to noticeable excess or intoxication?

IF YES, see Questions on Back.

REPUTATION

16. Do any of the following apply to this applicant: Unfair business practices or dealings? Heavy debts? Domestic trouble? Drug habit? Connection with illegal liquor?

17. Is there any criticism of character, morals, or general reputation?

REMARKS: 18. COMMENT BELOW ON TOPICS LISTED AT LEFT: GIVE DETAILS OF "YES" OR INCOMPLETE ANSWERS.

A. **BUSINESS:** Employer's name, line of business? Number of employees? Name of applicant's job? How long so employed? If less than 1 year, previous occupation? If self-employed, is business operated from home?

B. **DUTIES:** Tell exactly what he does. What articles or materials sold or handled? Any outside duties, such as travel, selling, or driving delivery vehicle? How much of time so spent?

C. **PERSONAL— HOME ENVIRONMENT:** Married, single, or divorced? Any children? Type of associates. Comment on home environment, manner of living, standing in community. If woman, name of father or husband; his occupation, worth and income.

RETAIL CREDIT COMPANY

Signature of person making report

Form 32—3-63 PRINTED IN U.S.A.

OVER—SEE ADDITIONAL QUESTIONS ON BACK

HEALTH REPORT

Specimen Inspection Report Form—Life Form and Health Form (Continued)

#18 Continued

DETAILS OF APPEARANCE:

If answer to Question 10—A is "Yes," answer following:

19—A. How does he appear unhealthy (complexion, weight, or what?) ________ B. Describe. (If overweight or underweight, give details.)

DETAILS OF HEALTH HISTORY:

If answer to Question 11 is "Yes," answer following:

20. Nature of illness, operation or injury? ________

21. Approximate date it occurred? ________

22—A. How long confined or "laid up"? ________

B. Completely recovered? ________

23—A. Attended by Dr. (Name) ________

Address ________

B. Confined to hospital? ________ If so, name and address:

Name ________

Address ________

24. Any effect on present health? ________ Details:

SPECIMEN REPORT

DETAILS OF DRIVING RECORD:

If answer to Question 8 is "Yes," answer following:

25. When, where, and under what circumstances does applicant drive in a fast or reckless manner? (Open highway, congested areas, etc.—if known to drive considerably in excess of speed limit, cover.)

26. Any evidence of unsupervised racing? ________ Give details:

27. Any arrests? (Approximate dates) ________

28. Charges? ________

If convicted, approximate dates ________

29. Any accidents? ________ If so, approximate dates and details:

If answer to Question 15 is "Yes," please give these additional details to show drinking habits as definitely as possible:

31. Does applicant ever drink to noticeable excess or intoxication?

32. If not now, did he formerly indulge to this extent?

THE FOLLOWING QUESTIONS APPLY TO EITHER PAST OR PRESENT EXCESSIVE DRINKING
(as indicated in answers to Questions Nos. 31 and 32).

		How often? (Once a week, once a month, etc.)
33. Classify drinking on these occasions and state how often:		
A. Getting "drunk," stupefied, entirely out of control of usual faculties?	A.	A.
B. Loud, boisterous, or obviously under influence, although still in possession of most of faculties?	B.	B.
C. Mild excess, just getting "feeling good"; exhilaration or stimulation?	C.	C.

34. Do (did) these occasions last for an evening, a day, two days, a week, or for how long?

35. How long has (had) he been drinking to this extent?

36. WHEN WAS THE LAST OCCASION OF THIS SORT?

37. If applicant is an excessive drinker at present, does he drive a car during periods of intoxication?

38. Has applicant ever taken any "cure" for liquor habit? (If so, when? Any subsequent lapse?)

39. Tell how applicant drinks, if social or solitary, or if because of domestic or other trouble, how it affects him, whether ever arrested, and details to give clear picture of drinking habits; if habits have changed, tell how and how long since change; if reformed, what led to reformation (ill health, domestic trouble or what)?

INSPECTOR: Do not write in this space.

(Use Continuation of Report, Form 5166, for additional remarks.)

32-R—1-63

D. Specimen Individual Life Insurance Contract (Straight Life)

THE ______________ LIFE INSURANCE COMPANY

INSURED WILLIAM PENN

$25,000 SUM INSURED

POLICY NUMBER 0 000 000

March 1, 1964 POLICY DATE

THE ______________ LIFE INSURANCE COMPANY agrees, subject to the provisions of this policy, to pay the Sum Insured to the beneficiary upon receipt of due proof of the Insured's death and to provide all other benefits stated in this policy.

The benefits, provisions and conditions on the following pages are part of this policy.

Executed by The ______________ Life Insurance Company at ______________ on the date of issue.

SECRETARY

PRESIDENT

DEPUTY REGISTRAR

WHOLE LIFE POLICY

Sum Insured Payable at Death—Premiums Payable for Life—Annual Dividends—Supplemental Benefits, if any, Listed in Schedule of Benefits on Page 3

Specimen Individual Life Insurance Contract (Continued)

THIS POLICY is a valuable asset. Your Company urges you to consult it directly or through its Agent for analysis and explanation of any proposal you may receive for discontinuance and replacement of this policy since the proposal may be against your interest.

TO COLLECT THE INSURANCE under this policy, or to obtain any of its benefits, write to the Company at its Home Office or to its nearest Agent. Service will be prompt and without charge.

Please notify the Company promptly of any change in your address.

ANNUAL MEETING AND ELECTION

This company is a mutual life insurance company. It has no stockholders. Members are entitled to vote in person or by proxy at the annual meeting and election of Trustees held at the Home Office, ______________________ on the third Monday of February. The owner of this policy is a member while it is in force before maturity and before proceeds are applied under a settlement option. Further information may be obtained from the Secretary.

GUIDE TO POLICY PROVISIONS

Any additional provisions and a copy of the application follow page 12.

WHOLE LIFE POLICY

Sum Insured Payable at Death—Premiums Payable for Life—
Annual Dividends—Supplemental Benefits, if any,
Listed in Schedule of Benefits on Page 3

THE ______________ LIFE INSURANCE COMPANY

Specimen Individual Life Insurance Contract (Continued)

9001

POLICY SPECIFICATIONS

INSURED	WILLIAM PENN	$25,000	SUM INSURED
POLICY NUMBER	0 000 000	MARCH 1, 1964	POLICY DATE
AGE	35	STANDARD	PREMIUM CLASS

THE DATE OF ISSUE IS THE POLICY DATE

OWNER AND BENEFICIARY AS PROVIDED IN APPLICATION

Schedule of Benefits

Description	Amount	
WHOLE LIFE INSURANCE	$25,000	SUM INSURED
OPTION TO PURCHASE ADDITIONAL INSURANCE (OPAI)--$10,000 OPTION AMOUNT	-	

Schedule of Premiums

PREMIUMS PAYABLE ANNUALLY, AS FOLLOWS

BEGINNING AS OF	TOTAL PREMIUM	SPECIFIC AMOUNTS INCLUDED IN PREMIUM FOR STATED SUPPLEMENTARY BENEFITS OPAI
MAR 1, 1964	$596.00	$20.00
MAR 1, 1969	$576.00	

FIRST PREMIUM IF PREMIUMS ARE PAID

ANNUALLY	SEMIANNUALLY	QUARTERLY	MONTHLY
$596.00	$301.15	$152.55	$51.25

(Page 3)

Specimen Individual Life Insurance Contract (Continued)

PREMIUM PAYMENT

Payment of Premiums—This contract is made in consideration of payment of premiums as provided herein.

Premiums are due during the lifetime of the Insured in the amount and at the interval stated in the Schedule of Premiums on page 3 (unless changed as provided below), determined from the beginning date indicated in the schedule, provided that the first premium shall be due on or before delivery of the policy. Each premium is payable at the Home Office or to an authorized representative of the Company in exchange for a receipt signed by the President, Vice President or Secretary and duly countersigned or for a receipt given as provided in the application for this policy.

Upon request by the owner, the method of premium payment may be changed to annual, semiannual, quarterly or monthly based on the Company's premium rates in effect at the date of issue. Consent of the Company is required for a change to a monthly basis. No change in method of payment which would result in a premium of less than $10.00 shall be made. Acceptance by the Company of payment of a premium, including payment by policy loan, which is not under the method currently in effect shall constitute a change in method of premium payment.

Failure to pay any premium when due shall constitute a default in premium payment. The due date of such premium shall be the date of default.

Grace Period—A grace period of 31 days shall be granted for the payment of a premium in default other than the first during which the policy shall remain in force. If a premium in default is not paid during the grace period, this policy shall lapse and cease to be in force except as provided in the Benefits on Lapse provision.

Reinstatement—This policy may be reinstated within five years after lapse for nonpayment of premiums unless it has been surrendered. Reinstatement is subject to (i) receipt of evidence of insurability satisfactory to the Company, (ii) payment of all overdue premiums with compound interest at the rate of 5% per year and (iii) payment of the excess of any indebtedness existing at the end of the grace period increased by compound interest from such date at the rate of 5% per year, plus any indebtedness incurred after the end of the grace period, over the Loan Value on the date of reinstatement. Any indebtedness or interest under (iii) which is not repaid on reinstatement shall constitute a policy loan.

DIVIDENDS

This policy shall participate in divisible surplus while it is in force except as provided in the Benefits on Lapse provision and the Settlement Options section. Dividends of such surplus, if any, to be apportioned to this policy shall be determined annually by the Board of Trustees. Each dividend shall be payable at the end of the policy year, unless this policy is in force under the Settlement Options section, except that any dividend for the first policy year shall not be payable until the premium for the second policy year has been paid.

The owner may elect to have dividends applied under one of the following dividend options:

(1) **Paid-up Additions**—Applied to purchase participating paid-up additional life insurance.

(2) **Premium Payment**—Applied in reduction of any premium due if the remainder of such premium is paid.

(3) **Cash**—Paid in cash.

(4) **Dividend Accumulations**—Left to accumulate at compound interest at the rate awarded annually by the Board of Trustees which shall not be less than 2½% per year.

If no option is elected, dividend option (1) shall apply. If dividend option (2) has been elected but is not applicable because the policy is fully paid or paid-up, dividend option (1) shall apply unless another option is elected.

The owner may surrender any paid-up additions and may withdraw any dividend credits unless they are required as security for a loan on the policy.

Paid-up additions and dividend credits shall be paid to the beneficiary upon maturity of this policy by death of the Insured.

Post-mortem Dividend—If this policy matures by death of the Insured after the first policy year, the Company shall pay such post-mortem dividend of surplus as may be awarded by the Board of Trustees.

Dividend Credits—As used in this policy "dividend credits" means (i) accumulations under dividend option (4), including accrued interest thereon, (ii) any dividend as to which dividend option (2) has been elected but is not applicable because of maturity, lapse or surrender and (iii) any post-mortem dividend.

LOAN PROVISIONS

Policy Loans—The owner may before surrender or maturity of this policy obtain a loan for an amount not exceeding the Loan Value except while this policy is in force as extended term insurance. Any loan under this section shall be made on the sole security of this policy and upon proper assignment of the policy to the Company.

The Loan Value on a premium due date or at the end of a policy year shall be the Tabular Cash Value on such date plus any dividend credits and the value of any paid-up additions. The Loan Value at any other time shall be the amount which with interest at the rate of 5% per year to the next premium due date or, if this policy is in force as a fully paid or paid-up policy, to the end of the current policy year, will equal the sum of (i) the Tabular Cash Value on the next premium due date or, if this policy is in force as a fully paid or paid-up policy, at the end of the current policy year plus (ii) any dividend credits and the value of any paid-up additions as of the date the determination is made.

Specimen Individual Life Insurance Contract (Continued)

Any indebtedness and any due and unpaid premiums shall be deducted from the amount advanced under the loan.

Loans shall bear interest at the rate of 5% per year payable at the end of each policy year. Interest not paid when due shall be added to the loan and shall bear interest at the same rate.

"Indebtedness" as used in this policy means outstanding policy loans made under this policy, including automatic premium loans, together with any interest due or accrued. Indebtedness may be repaid in full or in part at any time before maturity or surrender of the policy, provided that if a premium is in default beyond the grace period indebtedness may be repaid only upon reinstatement of the policy. Indebtedness shall be deducted from any amount payable under this policy upon maturity by death of the Insured.

If at the end of a policy year indebtedness exceeds the Loan Value, this policy shall terminate 31 days after notice of termination has been mailed to the owner and any assignee of record at the Home Office, and that portion of any premium paid which is applicable to a period beyond the end of such policy year shall be paid to the owner.

The Company may defer making any loan, except to pay premiums on policies of the Company, for not more than six months after application therefor.

Automatic Premium Loan Option—While the automatic premium loan option is in effect, any premium remaining unpaid at the end of the grace period shall be paid by a policy loan on the last day of such period unless the resulting indebtedness would exceed the Loan Value, provided that not more than two consecutive premiums, or six consecutive premiums if premiums are payable monthly, shall be paid by automatic premium loans. If the Loan Value is insufficient for payment of an overdue premium, payment by policy loan shall be made of the next smaller premium, semiannual or quarterly (but not monthly), for which the Loan Value is sufficient.

This option shall be in effect if requested in the application for this policy or in a written request received by the Company before expiration of the grace period for payment of a premium in default. Upon written request by the owner this option may be terminated and shall not apply to any premium due and unpaid at the time such request is received by the Company or to any subsequent premium.

OWNERSHIP AND BENEFICIARY

Ownership—All privileges of ownership under this policy are vested in the owner designated in the application for this policy unless otherwise provided by an owner designation attached at issue or changed by a subsequent owner designation or assignment.

The owner may exercise all privileges of ownership without the consent of any other person. "Privileges of ownership" means the right before maturity to change the beneficiary one or more times, to receive any benefits under the policy, to exercise all rights and privileges provided under the policy, to assign or transfer the policy or any rights thereunder and to agree to modify the policy terms.

Beneficiary—The beneficiary of this policy at time of issue is designated in the application for this policy unless otherwise provided by a beneficiary designation attached at issue. Such designation is subject to change as provided below.

The interest of any beneficiary who dies before the Insured shall vest in the owner unless otherwise provided. The rights of any beneficiary shall be subject to the rights of an assignee under an assignment by the owner. Joinder by a beneficiary with the owner in an assignment made before maturity shall transfer to the assignee, to the extent of his interest under the assignment, any interest which such beneficiary might otherwise acquire in proceeds payable at maturity.

Change of Owner and Beneficiary—The owner or beneficiary may be changed by filing a written designation at the Home Office in form acceptable to the Company. No owner or beneficiary designation shall be effective until so filed but when so filed shall take effect as of the date it was made, subject to any action taken by the Company before its receipt at the Home Office.

Unless otherwise specifically provided the terms "children," "grandchildren," "brothers" and "sisters" when used in an owner or beneficiary designation shall include legally adopted children and those of the half blood.

Assignment—This policy may be assigned before maturity, but no assignment or transfer of any interest under it shall bind the Company until the original thereof has been filed at the Home Office. The Company assumes no obligation as to the effect or validity of any assignment or transfer.

GENERAL PROVISIONS

The Contract—This policy and the application therefor, a copy of which is attached to and made a part of this policy, constitute the entire contract.

All statements in the application shall be deemed representations and not warranties. No statement shall void this policy or be used as a defense against any claim hereunder unless contained in the application and a copy of such application is attached to the policy when issued.

Modification of Contract—Only the President, a Vice President, the Actuary, the Secretary, an Associate or Assistant Actuary or an Assistant Secretary may modify this policy or waive any of its conditions. No agent is authorized to modify, alter or enlarge this contract, or to bind the Company by any promise or undertaking as to distribution of surplus or future award of interest.

Policy Payments—All payments by the Company under this policy are payable at the Home Office. The Company may require surrender of the policy upon settlement at maturity or under the Cash Surrender provision.

Specimen Individual Life Insurance Contract (Continued)

Premium Adjustment—The amount payable upon maturity of this policy by death of the Insured shall be:

(a) increased by the portion of any premium paid which is applicable to the period, if any, beyond the end of the policy month in which the Insured's death occurs, provided that no such adjustment will be made with respect to any premium waived under an agreement for waiver of premiums;

(b) decreased, if a premium is due and unpaid on the date of the Insured's death, by any portion of such premium applicable to the period ending on the last day of the policy month in which the Insured's death occurs.

Interest on Policy Proceeds—If upon maturity the policy proceeds are paid in one sum, the Company shall pay interest on such proceeds from the date of maturity to the date of payment, but not for a period of more than one year, at the rate awarded annually by the Board of Trustees which shall not be less than 2½% per year.

Maturity—As used in this policy "maturity" means maturity of this policy by death of the Insured or by exercise of the Endowment Privilege.

Policy Date—Policy years, months and anniversaries shall be determined from the policy date.

Age—The age stated in the Policy Specifications on page 3 is the age of the Insured on the birthday nearest the policy date and as used in this policy "attained age" means such age increased by the number of completed years and months after the policy date.

Incontestability—This policy shall be incontestable after it has been in force during the lifetime of the Insured for two years from the date of issue except for nonpayment of premiums.

Suicide—If the Insured commits suicide, while sane or insane, within two years from the date of issue, the liability of the Company shall be limited to the payment to the beneficiary of an amount equal to the premiums paid less any indebtedness.

Misstatement of Age or Sex—If the age or sex of the Insured has been misstated, the amount payable shall be such as the premium paid would have purchased on the basis of the correct age and sex and any date in the Schedule of Premiums based on the assumption that the Insured will be a specified age on such date shall be adjusted, if necessary, for the Insured's correct age.

SETTLEMENT OPTIONS

An optional income settlement may be substituted for a one sum payment of all or part of the proceeds payable under this policy upon maturity or surrender by election of one of the following settlement options. The right to elect and payment under a settlement option are subject to the limitations stated in this section.

Option A—Income for Fixed Period—Equal monthly payments for a fixed period of years not exceeding 30.

Option B—Income for 20 Years Certain and Life—Equal monthly payments for 20 years certain and thereafter during the lifetime of the option annuitant, terminating with the last payment preceding death.

Option C—Income for 10 Years Certain and Life—Equal monthly payments for 10 years certain and thereafter during the lifetime of the option annuitant, terminating with the last payment preceding death.

Option D—Interest Income—Interest on the proceeds at an effective rate of 2½% per year ($25.00 annually, $12.42 semiannually, $6.19 quarterly or $2.06 monthly for each $1,000 of proceeds applied under this option), increased by any additions as provided below.

Option E—Income of Fixed Amount—Monthly, quarterly, semiannual or annual payments of a fixed amount until the proceeds applied under this option together with interest credited on the balance at an effective rate of 2½% per year, increased by any additions as provided below, have been paid, provided the total of such payments each year must be at least $60.00 for each $1,000 applied under this option.

The final payment shall consist of any balance of proceeds plus accrued interest equal to or less than the fixed amount.

Option FR—Income for Life with Refund Period—Equal monthly payments during the lifetime of the option annuitant terminating with the last payment preceding death, provided that such payments shall continue, unless commuted as provided below, after death of the option annuitant until the total of such payments and a final payment in a lesser amount, if required, equal the amount applied under this option.

Option G—Joint and Survivor Income—Level Amount—Equal monthly payments during the joint lifetime of two option annuitants and the lifetime of the survivor, terminating with the last payment preceding the death of the survivor.

Option G-1—Joint and Survivor Income—Reducing to Two-thirds—Equal monthly payments during the joint lifetime of two option annuitants and continuing during the lifetime of the survivor in an amount equal to two-thirds of the monthly payment during the joint lifetime, terminating with the last payment preceding the death of the survivor.

Option J—Income for 5 Years Certain and Life—Equal monthly payments for 5 years certain and thereafter during the lifetime of the option annuitant, terminating with the last payment preceding death.

Option K—Income for Life—Equal monthly payments during the lifetime of the option annuitant (without refund or certain period), terminating with the last payment preceding death.

The amounts payable under Options A, B, C, FR, G, G-1, J and K are shown in the Settlement Option Tables below.

Alternative Nonparticipating Life Income—The payee, before commencement of payments under Option B, C, FR, G, G-1, J or K and in the absence of provision otherwise in the election of the option, may elect to receive in place of the income payable in accordance with the Settlement Option

Specimen Individual Life Insurance Contract (Continued)

Tables a nonparticipating monthly income equal to 103% of the monthly income under a comparable annuity based on the Company's rates in use for single premium nonparticipating immediate annuities at the time the option payments are to commence, adjusted to make the first payment immediate, provided the Company is then issuing annuities comparable to the option elected.

Income Period—The income period under an option shall commence as of the date of maturity or surrender. Monthly income payments under Option A, B, C, FR, G, G-1, J or K shall be payable in advance. Income payments under Option D or E shall be payable at the end of the payment interval elected, unless otherwise provided in an election consented to by the Company.

Election of Income Option—Limitations on Use—The owner may before maturity elect an option or change or revoke a previous election of option. If no election by the owner is in effect at maturity, the beneficiary entitled to payment of the policy proceeds may, before payment at maturity has been made and within one year after maturity, elect an option. Provision in a beneficiary designation, an assignment or other instrument filed with the Company directing payment under an option shall constitute an election.

"Option annuitant" as used in this section means a natural person on whose life the payments under Option B, C, FR, G, G-1, J or K are based. An option annuitant (or at least one of the option annuitants under Option G or G-1) shall, unless otherwise consented to by the Company, be (i) the beneficiary in the case of an election which takes effect at maturity or which is made by the beneficiary after maturity and (ii) either the owner of the policy at issue or the Insured in the case of an election upon surrender.

"Payee" as used in this section means the person entitled to receive payments under an option. The payee (or at least one of the payees under Option G or G-1) shall, unless otherwise consented to by the Company, be (i) the beneficiary in the case of an election which takes effect at maturity or which is made by the beneficiary after maturity and (ii) either the owner or the Insured in the case of an election upon surrender. Consent of the Company is required to the designation of a payee who is not a natural person named individually in his own right, provided that a fiduciary may be designated payee if payments will terminate within 21 years.

A corporation or other business entity which is the owner of this policy at issue may, if the Insured is an employee or stockholder, elect a life income option with the Insured or his spouse as option annuitant and with the corporation or other business entity, the Insured or his spouse as payee.

Consent of the Company shall be required to an election which provides for the use of more than one option or designation of successive or contingent beneficiaries.

Unconditional acceptance by the Company of an election shall constitute consent.

Any portion of the proceeds payable to a collateral assignee shall be paid in one sum and the balance may be applied under an option in accordance with the provisions of this section.

Minimum Amounts—The minimum amount which may be applied under an option for any payee is $1,000 and no election may provide for income payments to any payee of less than $10.00 each unless otherwise provided in an election consented to by the Company.

If, because of the above limitation, payment may not be made under an option which has been elected, the amount directed to be applied under the option shall be paid in one sum to the payee to whom the first income payment would have been made.

Participation—The income under Option A, interest under Options D and E and the income during the certain or refund period under Options B, C, FR and J (unless the Alternative Nonparticipating Life Income provision has been elected) shall be increased by such additions as may be awarded from divisible surplus by the Board of Trustees. The income under Options B, C, FR and J after the certain or refund period and the income under Options G, G-1 and K shall not participate in divisible surplus.

Withdrawal Privilege—The payee, unless the election provides otherwise, (i) may, before any payment has been made under an option, withdraw proceeds payable thereunder, (ii) may withdraw the commuted value of income payments to become due under Options A, B, C, FR or J during the fixed, certain or refund period, or (iii) may withdraw the principal held under Option D or E. There shall be no right to withdraw the commuted value of income payments falling due after the certain or refund periods under Options B, C, FR and J or any income payments under Options G, G-1 and K.

The Company may defer payment upon exercise of the withdrawal privilege for a period not exceeding six months from the date of request for payment.

The commuted value of income payments for purposes of this provision shall be calculated on the basis of compound interest at the rate of 2½% per year provided that if payment under the Alternative Nonparticipating Life Income provision has been elected the commutation rate shall be the rate specified by the Company at the time such election becomes effective.

Death of Option Annuitant or Payee—Upon the death of the option annuitant under Option B, C, FR or J the commuted value of remaining payments certain or refund payments under the option, or upon the death of the payee under Option A, D or E the commuted value of remaining payments in the case of Option A or the balance of the principal held under the option with accrued interest in the case of Option D or E, shall be paid in one sum to the payee or the payee's executors or administrators unless otherwise provided in an election consented to by the Company. Upon the death of the payee under Option B, C, FR or J before the option annuitant, income payments shall continue to the payee's executors or administrators unless otherwise provided in an election consented to by the Company.

Assignment—Creditors—The amount applied under an option and any payment thereunder may not be assigned or encumbered and, to the extent permitted by law, shall not be subject to levy, attachment or other judicial process for the payment of the payee's debts or obligations.

Proof of Age and Continued Life of Option Annuitant—The Company may require proof of age and continued life of an option annuitant. If the age or sex of an option annuitant is misstated, appropriate adjustment shall be made in the payments.

Specimen Individual Life Insurance Contract (Continued)

SETTLEMENT OPTION TABLES

Monthly Income for each $1,000 of Proceeds Applied under a Settlement Option

Option A—Income for Fixed Period of Years

Number of Years	1	2	3	4	5	6	7	8	9	10	11	12	13	14	15
Monthly Income	$84.30	42.67	28.80	21.86	17.70	14.93	12.95	11.47	10.32	9.40	8.64	8.02	7.49	7.03	6.64
Number of Years	16	17	18	19	20	21	22	23	24	25	26	27	28	29	30
Monthly Income	$6.30	6.00	5.73	5.49	5.28	5.08	4.91	4.75	4.60	4.46	4.34	4.23	4.12	4.02	3.93

Options B, C, FR, J and K—Monthly Life Income

The amount of income will be based on the age of the option annuitant on the birthday nearest the date of the first payment.

Age of Option Annuitant	Option B 20 Years Certain Male	Option B Female	Option C 10 Years Certain Male	Option C Female	Option J 5 Years Certain Male	Option J Female	Option FR With Refund Period Male	Option FR Female	Option K Without Refund or Certain Period Male	Option K Female
15 and under	$2.97	$2.87	$2.98	$2.88	$2.99	$2.89	$2.96	$2.86	$3.00	$2.90
16	2.98	2.88	2.99	2.89	3.00	2.90	2.97	2.87	3.01	2.91
17	3.00	2.89	3.01	2.90	3.02	2.91	2.99	2.88	3.03	2.92
18	3.02	2.91	3.03	2.92	3.04	2.93	3.01	2.90	3.05	2.94
19	3.04	2.93	3.05	2.94	3.06	2.95	3.03	2.92	3.07	2.96
20	3.06	2.94	3.07	2.95	3.08	2.96	3.05	2.93	3.09	2.97
21	3.09	2.96	3.10	2.97	3.11	2.98	3.08	2.95	3.12	2.99
22	3.11	2.98	3.12	2.99	3.13	3.00	3.10	2.97	3.14	3.01
23	3.13	3.00	3.14	3.01	3.15	3.02	3.12	2.99	3.16	3.03
24	3.16	3.02	3.17	3.03	3.18	3.04	3.15	3.01	3.19	3.05
25	3.18	3.04	3.19	3.05	3.20	3.06	3.17	3.03	3.21	3.07
26	3.21	3.06	3.22	3.07	3.23	3.08	3.20	3.05	3.24	3.09
27	3.24	3.08	3.25	3.09	3.26	3.10	3.23	3.07	3.27	3.11
28	3.27	3.11	3.28	3.12	3.29	3.13	3.25	3.10	3.30	3.14
29	3.30	3.13	3.31	3.14	3.32	3.15	3.28	3.12	3.33	3.16
30	3.33	3.15	3.34	3.16	3.35	3.17	3.31	3.14	3.36	3.18
31	3.36	3.18	3.38	3.19	3.39	3.20	3.34	3.17	3.40	3.21
32	3.39	3.21	3.41	3.22	3.42	3.23	3.37	3.20	3.43	3.24
33	3.43	3.24	3.45	3.25	3.46	3.26	3.41	3.23	3.47	3.27
34	3.46	3.27	3.49	3.28	3.50	3.29	3.44	3.26	3.51	3.30
35	3.50	3.30	3.53	3.31	3.54	3.32	3.48	3.29	3.55	3.33
36	3.54	3.33	3.57	3.34	3.58	3.35	3.52	3.32	3.59	3.36
37	3.58	3.36	3.62	3.38	3.63	3.39	3.56	3.35	3.64	3.40
38	3.62	3.40	3.66	3.41	3.67	3.42	3.60	3.38	3.68	3.43
39	3.66	3.43	3.71	3.45	3.72	3.46	3.64	3.42	3.73	3.47
40	3.71	3.47	3.76	3.49	3.77	3.50	3.68	3.45	3.78	3.51
41	3.75	3.51	3.82	3.53	3.83	3.54	3.73	3.49	3.84	3.55
42	3.80	3.55	3.87	3.57	3.89	3.58	3.78	3.53	3.90	3.59
43	3.85	3.59	3.93	3.62	3.95	3.63	3.83	3.57	3.96	3.64
44	3.90	3.63	3.99	3.67	4.01	3.68	3.88	3.61	4.02	3.69
45	3.96	3.68	4.05	3.72	4.08	3.73	3.94	3.66	4.09	3.74
46	4.01	3.72	4.12	3.77	4.15	3.78	4.00	3.70	4.16	3.79
47	4.07	3.77	4.19	3.83	4.22	3.84	4.06	3.75	4.23	3.85
48	4.12	3.82	4.27	3.88	4.30	3.90	4.11	3.80	4.31	3.91
49	4.18	3.88	4.34	3.94	4.38	3.96	4.19	3.86	4.39	3.97

Age of Option Annuitant	Option B 20 Years Certain Male	Option B Female	Option C 10 Years Certain Male	Option C Female	Option J 5 Years Certain Male	Option J Female	Option FR With Refund Period Male	Option FR Female	Option K Without Refund or Certain Period Male	Option K Female
50	$4.24	$3.93	$4.43	$4.01	$4.47	$4.02	$4.25	$3.91	$4.48	$4.03
51	4.30	3.99	4.51	4.08	4.56	4.09	4.33	3.97	4.57	4.11
52	4.37	4.05	4.60	4.15	4.65	4.17	4.40	4.04	4.67	4.19
53	4.43	4.11	4.70	4.22	4.76	4.24	4.48	4.10	4.78	4.27
54	4.49	4.17	4.80	4.30	4.87	4.33	4.56	4.17	4.89	4.35
55	4.56	4.23	4.90	4.38	4.98	4.41	4.65	4.24	5.01	4.44
56	4.62	4.30	5.01	4.47	5.10	4.50	4.74	4.31	5.14	4.53
57	4.69	4.36	5.13	4.56	5.23	4.60	4.84	4.39	5.28	4.63
58	4.75	4.43	5.25	4.66	5.37	4.71	4.94	4.48	5.42	4.74
59	4.81	4.50	5.37	4.76	5.51	4.82	5.04	4.56	5.57	4.86
60	4.88	4.57	5.50	4.87	5.67	4.93	5.15	4.66	5.73	4.98
61	4.94	4.64	5.64	4.98	5.83	5.06	5.26	4.75	5.90	5.11
62	4.99	4.72	5.78	5.10	6.00	5.19	5.38	4.85	6.07	5.25
63	5.05	4.79	5.93	5.23	6.18	5.33	5.51	4.96	6.26	5.39
64	5.10	4.86	6.09	5.36	6.37	5.48	5.64	5.08	6.45	5.55
65	5.15	4.92	6.25	5.50	6.56	5.64	5.78	5.20	6.65	5.71
66	5.20	4.99	6.41	5.65	6.77	5.81	5.92	5.32	6.86	5.89
67	5.24	5.05	6.56	5.80	6.99	6.00	6.07	5.46	7.09	6.08
68	5.25	5.11	6.71	5.96	7.22	6.19	6.23	5.60	7.32	6.27
69	5.25	5.17	6.87	6.13	7.46	6.40	6.40	5.75	7.57	6.49
70	5.25	5.22	7.03	6.30	7.72	6.62	6.57	5.91	7.83	6.71
71	5.25	5.25	7.20	6.48	7.98	6.85	6.76	6.07	8.14	6.95
72	5.25	5.25	7.37	6.66	8.26	7.10	6.95	6.25	8.47	7.20
73	5.25	5.25	7.54	6.85	8.56	7.36	7.16	6.44	8.83	7.47
74	5.25	5.25	7.71	7.05	8.86	7.65	7.37	6.64	9.20	7.76
75	5.25	5.25	7.87	7.25	9.18	7.95	7.60	6.87	9.61	8.06
76	5.25	5.25	8.03	7.44	9.51	8.27	7.83	7.08	10.03	8.43
77	5.25	5.25	8.19	7.64	9.85	8.61	8.08	7.32	10.49	8.84
78	5.25	5.25	8.34	7.84	10.21	8.97	8.35	7.58	10.98	9.28
79	5.25	5.25	8.49	8.04	10.58	9.35	8.62	7.85	11.51	9.75
80	5.25	5.25	8.62	8.23	10.95	9.75	8.92	8.15	12.07	10.27
81	5.25	5.25	8.75	8.41	11.34	10.18	9.23	8.46	12.67	10.83
82	5.25	5.25	8.87	8.58	11.73	10.62	9.55	8.79	13.31	11.44
83	5.25	5.25	8.98	8.74	12.13	11.07	9.89	9.16	14.00	12.11
84	5.25	5.25	9.08	8.89	12.54	11.55	10.26	9.53	14.74	12.84
85 and over	5.25	5.25	9.17	9.02	12.94	12.03	10.65	9.94	15.53	13.63

Options G and G-1—Joint and Survivor Monthly Life Income

The amount of income will be based on the ages of the option annuitants on their respective birthdays nearest the date of the first payment. The tables show income for certain ages for one male and one female option annuitant. The amount is shown under the age of the male and opposite the age of the female. Amounts of income for other combinations of ages or for option annuitants of the same sex will be furnished upon request.

Option G—Same Income Continued to Survivor — Age of Male Option Annuitant: 50	55	60	62	65	68	70	75	Age of Female Option Annuitant	Option G-1—Two-Thirds of Income Continued to Survivor — Age of Male Option Annuitant: 50	55	60	62	65	68	70	75
$3.64	$3.74	$3.82	$3.85	$3.89	$3.92	$3.94	$3.97	50	$4.02	$4.19	$4.38	$4.46	$4.57	$4.69	$4.76	$4.97
3.80	3.95	4.08	4.13	4.19	4.24	4.27	4.33	55	4.22	4.43	4.65	4.75	4.88	5.02	5.11	5.36
3.84	4.00	4.14	4.19	4.26	4.31	4.35	4.41	56	4.26	4.47	4.71	4.81	4.95	5.09	5.19	5.44
3.87	4.04	4.20	4.25	4.32	4.39	4.42	4.50	57	4.30	4.52	4.77	4.87	5.02	5.17	5.27	5.53
3.90	4.08	4.25	4.31	4.39	4.46	4.51	4.59	58	4.34	4.58	4.83	4.94	5.09	5.25	5.35	5.63
3.93	4.13	4.31	4.38	4.47	4.55	4.59	4.69	59	4.39	4.63	4.90	5.01	5.17	5.33	5.44	5.73
3.96	4.17	4.37	4.44	4.54	4.63	4.68	4.79	60	4.44	4.69	4.97	5.08	5.25	5.42	5.53	5.84
3.99	4.22	4.43	4.51	4.62	4.71	4.77	4.89	61	4.48	4.74	5.03	5.15	5.33	5.51	5.63	5.95
4.02	4.26	4.49	4.57	4.69	4.80	4.86	5.00	62	4.53	4.80	5.10	5.23	5.42	5.60	5.73	6.06
4.05	4.30	4.55	4.64	4.77	4.89	4.95	5.11	63	4.58	4.86	5.17	5.30	5.50	5.69	5.82	6.18
4.08	4.34	4.61	4.71	4.85	4.98	5.05	5.22	64	4.63	4.92	5.25	5.38	5.59	5.79	5.93	6.31
4.11	4.38	4.67	4.77	4.93	5.07	5.15	5.34	65	4.67	4.98	5.32	5.46	5.68	5.89	6.04	6.43
4.13	4.42	4.72	4.84	5.01	5.16	5.26	5.47	66	4.72	5.04	5.40	5.54	5.77	6.00	6.15	6.57
4.16	4.46	4.78	4.91	5.09	5.26	5.36	5.60	67	4.77	5.10	5.47	5.63	5.87	6.11	6.27	6.71
4.18	4.50	4.84	4.97	5.16	5.35	5.46	5.72	68	4.82	5.16	5.55	5.71	5.96	6.21	6.38	6.84
4.20	4.53	4.89	5.04	5.25	5.45	5.57	5.86	69	4.88	5.22	5.63	5.80	6.06	6.32	6.50	7.00
4.22	4.57	4.95	5.10	5.32	5.54	5.68	6.00	70	4.93	5.29	5.71	5.88	6.16	6.44	6.62	7.15
4.31	4.72	5.19	5.39	5.70	6.01	6.21	6.74	75	5.18	5.60	6.11	6.32	6.67	7.02	7.27	7.97

Specimen Individual Life Insurance Contract (Continued)

(Page 10)

TABLE OF VALUES

THE FOLLOWING TABLE SHOWS TABULAR CASH VALUES AND OTHER VALUES APPLICABLE AT THE END OF THE INDICATED POLICY YEARS PROVIDED ALL PREMIUMS DUE HAVE BEEN PAID. THESE VALUES ARE COMPUTED IN ACCORDANCE WITH THE CASH SURRENDER AND BENEFITS ON LAPSE SECTION AND ARE BEFORE ADJUSTMENT FOR ANY DIVIDEND CREDITS, PAID-UP ADDITIONS OR INDEBTEDNESS. VALUES NOT SHOWN IN THE TABLE WILL BE FURNISHED UPON REQUEST.

END OF POLICY YEAR	ATTAINED AGE OF INSURED	TABULAR CASH OR LOAN VALUE	EXTENDED TERM INSURANCE		PAID-UP LIFE INSURANCE
			YEARS	DAYS	
1	36	$ 25	0	108	$ 75
2	37	525	5	91	1,200
3	38	1,025	8	224	2,275
4	39	1,550	11	55	3,350
5	40	2,075	12	363	4,400
6	41	2,525	14	30	5,250
7	42	2,950	14	301	6,000
8	43	3,400	15	168	6,775
9	44	3,850	15	342	7,500
10	45	4,300	16	100	8,225
11	46	4,750	16	184	8,900
12	47	5,225	16	257	9,600
13	48	5,700	16	301	10,275
14	49	6,150	16	300	10,875
15	50	6,625	16	297	11,475
16	51	7,100	16	275	12,075
17	52	7,575	16	236	12,650
18	53	8,050	16	184	13,200
19	54	8,550	16	134	13,775
20	55	9,025	16	60	14,275
25	60	11,400	14	337	16,600
27	62	12,325	14	130	17,400
30	65	13,700	13	175	18,525

NONFORFEITURE FACTORS FOR $1,000 SUM INSURED
FIRST 5 YEARS $22.410 THEREAFTER $18.278

TABULAR CASH VALUE EQUALS FULL NET LEVEL PREMIUM RESERVE AT END OF 5 YEARS AND THEREAFTER

WHOLE LIFE INSURANCE
AGE 35 - MALE
$25,000 SUM INSURED

Specimen Individual Life Insurance Contract (Continued)

CASH SURRENDER AND BENEFITS ON LAPSE

Cash Surrender—The owner may surrender this policy for its Net Cash Value by filing with the Company a written request in form satisfactory to the Company.

"Net Cash Value" as used in this policy means the Tabular Cash Value plus any dividend credits and the value of any paid-up additions and less any indebtedness. Tabular Cash Values at the end of certain policy years are shown in the Table of Values.

The Company may defer payment of the Net Cash Value upon surrender for a period not exceeding six months. If payment is so deferred for a period of 30 days or more, interest at the rate of 2½% per year shall be paid for the period of deferment.

Benefits on Lapse—In the event of default in premium payment, the owner may elect one of the following benefits or may surrender the policy for its Net Cash Value as provided under the Cash Surrender provision:

(1) **Extended Term Insurance**—The policy may be continued as nonparticipating paid-up extended term insurance payable to the beneficiary in an amount equal to the Sum Insured increased by the amount of any paid-up additions and dividend credits and decreased by any indebtedness. The term of such insurance shall commence as of the date of default and shall be for such period as the Net Cash Value will provide when applied as a net single premium at the Insured's attained age. If the Net Cash Value is more than sufficient to provide paid-up life insurance for the amount of extended term insurance, the paid-up life insurance benefit shall apply in place of such extended term insurance.

This benefit shall not be available if this policy is in a special premium class.

(2) **Paid-up Life Insurance**—The policy may be continued as participating paid-up life insurance payable to the beneficiary in such amount as the Net Cash Value will provide when applied as a net single premium at the Insured's attained age.

The extended term insurance benefit shall be automatically effective upon expiration of the grace period in the absence of election of the paid-up life insurance benefit except that if this policy is in a special premium class the paid-up life insurance benefit shall automatically apply. The owner may elect the paid-up life insurance benefit in place of the extended term insurance benefit by filing a written election with the Company within 60 days after the date of default.

Periods of extended term insurance and amounts of paid-up insurance at the end of certain policy years (before adjustment for any dividend credits, paid-up additions or indebtedness) are shown in the Table of Values.

Basis of Computation—The Tabular Cash Value at the end of a policy year for which a full premium has been paid is an amount equal to the excess, if any, of the present value on that date of the future guaranteed life insurance benefits provided by this policy (excluding any paid-up additions) over the then present value of the applicable nonforfeiture factors shown in the Table of Values for each subsequent policy year. At or after the end of the policy year indicated in the Table of Values, the Tabular Cash Value is equal to the full net level premium reserve. When determined as of a date during a policy year, except while this policy is in force as extended term insurance or paid-up life insurance, the Tabular Cash Value shall be computed as provided above with due allowance for the time elapsed in that year and the portion of such year for which premiums have been paid. During the 60 day period after default in premium payment, the Tabular Cash Value shall be the Tabular Cash Value as of the date of default.

The Tabular Cash Value shall be computed on the basis of $1,000 Sum Insured and adjusted in the proportion of the Sum Insured to $1,000.

If this policy is in force as extended term or paid-up life insurance, the Tabular Cash Value shall be equal to the reserve on such insurance, provided that during the 30 day period after a policy anniversary it shall be equal to the reserve as of such anniversary.

The value of paid-up additions shall be equal to the reserve on such additions but not less than the reserve as of the immediately preceding policy anniversary nor less than the amount of dividends used to provide such additions.

The reserves for this policy shall be computed by the net level premium method. All reserves, present values and net single premiums referred to herein are based on the Commissioners 1958 Standard Ordinary Mortality Table if the Insured is a male or the Commissioners 1958 Female Standard Ordinary Mortality Table if the Insured is a female, except that the reserves and net single premiums for any extended term insurance are based on the Commissioners 1958 Extended Term Insurance Table or the Commissioners 1958 Female Extended Term Insurance Table, in all cases using continuous functions and compound interest at 2½% per year.

Benefits provided by any supplemental agreement made a part of this policy shall be excluded from the computation of any policy value unless otherwise provided in such agreement.

All policy values and benefits are equal to or greater than those required by law.

FULL PAID AND ENDOWMENT PRIVILEGES

Full Paid Privilege—The Company shall endorse this policy as fully paid for the Sum Insured upon written election by the owner received at or within 31 days after the end of a policy year if (i) at the end of such policy year the Tabular Cash Value plus any dividend credits and the value of any paid-up additions equals or exceeds the net single premium required to make the policy fully paid and (ii) dividend credits and paid-up additions equal in value to the excess of such net single premium over the Tabular Cash Value as of the end of such policy year are surrendered to the Company. Supplemental agreements which do not terminate as a result of such election shall also be made fully paid. The net single premium shall be calculated at the attained age of the Insured on the basis of computation stated in the Cash Surrender and

Specimen Individual Life Insurance Contract (Continued)

(Page 12)

Benefits on Lapse section except that in the case of any supplemental agreement the basis of computation shall be as determined by the Company. The policy after endorsement as fully paid shall be subject to any indebtedness which is not repaid.

Endowment Privilege—Upon written election by the owner received by the Company at or within 31 days after the end of a policy year when the Tabular Cash Value plus any dividend credits and the value of any paid-up additions equals or exceeds the Sum Insured, this policy shall mature as an endowment payable to the owner in the amount of the Net Cash Value at the end of such year.

CHANGE OF PLAN

If no premium is in default and before lapse or maturity, the owner may, upon written request, exchange this policy without evidence of insurability for a new policy on the life of the Insured for the same Sum Insured on another plan of insurance with a higher premium rate, subject to the following conditions:

(1) The new policy shall be on a life or endowment plan which was available on the date of application for this policy, provided that Company consent shall be required if the new plan requires payment of premiums for less than five years after the date of exchange.

(2) The new policy shall be issued on the policy form and at the premium rate which would have been used if this policy had originally been issued on the new plan and shall have the same policy date as this policy.

(3) The following amount shall be paid to the Company at the time of exchange:

(a) if exchange is made within five years after the policy date—an amount equal to the difference in premiums (adjusted for dividends, if any) for the two plans of insurance for the period before the exchange, plus compound interest at the rate of 5% per year;

(b) if exchange is made five or more years after the policy date—an amount equal to the difference between the Tabular Casn Values (or, if greater, the difference in reserves) for the two plans of insurance on the date of exchange, plus an amount not in excess of 5% of such difference;

provided that in determining the amount of such payment the premium and any reserve or value for any supplemental agreement shall be excluded.

(4) If this policy is in a special premium class, the new policy shall be in the same class and the payment at the time of exchange shall be subject to adjustment as determined by the Company.

(5) Addition or continuance of any supplemental agreement in the new policy shall be subject to consent of the Company and such additional payment as the Company may require.

(6) If any paid-up additions are outstanding at the date of exchange, the value of such additions shall be applied to purchase paid-up additions conforming to the provisions of the new policy. Any dividend credits at the date of exchange shall be transferred to the new policy.

(7) The new policy shall be subject to any indebtedness outstanding against this policy and to any assignment of this policy.

Any change of plan other than as provided in this section shall be subject to the Company's consent.

Specimen Individual Life Insurance Contract (Continued)

OPTION TO PURCHASE ADDITIONAL INSURANCE

THE ____ MUTUAL LIFE INSURANCE COMPANY agrees, subject to the provisions of this supplemental agreement, that the owner of this policy shall have the option to purchase additional insurance on the Insured's life in the Option Amount stated in the Schedule of Benefits on page 3:

(a) as of each Regular Option Date stated in the following schedule, unless cancelled by exercise of the option as of a Special Option Date, and

(b) as of each available Special Option Date,

provided that there shall be no option to purchase additional insurance after the option has been exercised the maximum number of times stated in the following schedule.

Age of Insured*	REGULAR OPTION DATES Policy Anniversaries on Which the Insured's Age Nearest Birthday is:	Maximum Number of Times Option May be Exercised
24 or Younger	25, 28, 31, 34, 37, 40	6
25, 26 or 27	28, 31, 34, 37, 40	5
28, 29 or 30	31, 34, 37, 40	4
31, 32 or 33	34, 37, 40	3
34, 35 or 36	37, 40	2
37 or 38	40	1

* Age shown is the age on the birthday nearest the policy date or the date of issue of this agreement, if later.

The Company also agrees to provide automatic term insurance during Special Term Periods as provided below.

Special Option Dates—The 90th day after each of the following events shall be a Special Option Date, provided the Insured is a male and provided such date occurs before termination of this agreement:

(1) marriage of the Insured

(2) live birth of a child of the Insured's marriage

(3) legal adoption by the Insured of a child less than 18 years of age.

In the event of a multiple birth or adoption, each birth or adoption shall be considered to be a separate event giving rise to a separate Special Option Date.

Special Option Dates are alternatives to Regular Option Dates and the exercise of the option as of a Special Option Date shall cancel the next succeeding uncancelled Regular Option Date, or if it coincides with an uncancelled Regular Option Date, shall cancel such Option Date. The exercise of the option on more than one Special Option Date arising from a multiple birth shall be considered as the exercise of the option one time in determining the number of times the option may be exercised.

Additional Policy—Any policy of additional insurance purchased under this agreement shall

(1) be on a life or endowment plan which at the Option Date as of which the option is exercised is available under the Company's rules as to minimum amount, plan of insurance and age of the Insured and shall be issued at the premium rate and on the policy form then in use by the Company for the age of the Insured on the birthday nearest such date;

(2) be in the same premium class and subject to the same limitations of risk as this policy;

(3) insure only the life of the Insured, except that an additional policy purchased as of a Special Option Date resulting from the marriage of the Insured may be a Family Policy if such plan is then issued by the Company;

(4) become effective on the Option Date as of which the option is exercised provided the Insured is then living, which date shall be the policy date for the new policy. If the Insured dies before such Option Date any premium paid for such policy shall be refunded.

A supplemental disability or accidental death benefit agreement may be included in the additional policy only with the consent of the Company and subject to such requirements as it may make except that such consent shall not be required for inclusion of a supplemental disability waiver of premium agreement if a disability benefit is included in this policy on the date the option is elected. Such disability waiver of premium benefit shall apply only to disability commencing after all conditions for exercise of the option have been met.

Option Credit—The premium for the first policy year for each policy purchased under this agreement shall be reduced by an option credit of $1.00 for each $1,000 of Option Amount.

Exercise of Option—Exercise of the option shall be subject to the following conditions:

(1) Premiums shall have been paid to the date as of which the option is exercised or, in the event it is exercised as of a Special Option Date, no premium shall then be in default beyond the grace period for payment.

(2) The option shall be exercised by filing written application for the additional insurance and payment of the full first premium at the Home Office or to an agent of the Company on the Option Date or during the 90 days preceding. If exercised as of a Special Option Date the application shall be accompanied by proof of the event which gives rise to the Special Option Date.

(3) Exercise of the option shall be subject to compliance with requirements of law as to insurable interest in the Insured's life, and if the owner of this policy is other than the Insured the option may be exercised only with the written consent of the Insured.

(4) If the owner is not the Insured and does not exercise the option as of an Option Date, the Insured with the written consent of the owner may exercise the option as of such date.

(5) The right to purchase additional insurance on an Option Date, if not exercised, shall expire on such date but failure to exercise the option as of one date shall not affect the right to exercise the option as of a later date or dates.

(6) In issuing the additional insurance, the Company shall rely solely upon any evidence of insurability required in connection with the issue of this policy and any reinstatement thereof and shall not require any additional evidence of insurability as a condition to the exercise of the option.

OPAI-70

Specimen Individual Life Insurance Contract (Concluded)

Automatic Term Insurance—If the Insured is a male the Company agrees, upon receipt of due proof that the death of the Insured has occurred during one or more of the Special Term Periods defined below and upon proof of the event which gives rise to such period, to pay as an additional death benefit an amount equal to the additional insurance which could have been purchased as a result of such event whether or not the option has been exercised at the time of the Insured's death. Such additional death benefit shall be paid in accordance with the beneficiary designation under the policy in the same manner as if such benefit and any other death benefit payable under the policy upon the Insured's death formed a single amount.

A Special Term Period shall commence on the date of each event which gives rise to a Special Option Date, provided the Insured is living at the time of occurrence of the event, and shall terminate with the day preceding the Special Option Date which results from such event.

Premiums—Premiums for this agreement are included in the premiums in the Schedule of Premiums on page 3. After termination of this agreement premiums shown in the Schedule of Premiums shall be reduced by any amount which has been included in such premiums for this agreement.

Termination—This agreement shall terminate:

(a) on the policy anniversary nearest the Insured's 40th birthday or upon cancellation of the last Regular Option Date by exercise of the option as of a Special Option Date;

(b) upon maturity, expiry or surrender of the policy;

(c) upon lapse of the policy, whether or not it remains in force as extended term or paid-up insurance;

(d) upon election of the Life Option if the policy is on the endowment or retirement income plan; or

(e) on the premium due date next following receipt by the Company at the Home Office of a request for discontinuance of this agreement and presentation of the policy for appropriate endorsement.

Reinstatement—Reinstatement of this policy after lapse shall reinstate this agreement only as to Option Dates occurring after the date of reinstatement, except that reinstatement shall be effective to reinstate this agreement as to any Special Option Date which occurs after reinstatement as the result of an event which occurred before reinstatement.

Policy and Agreement—This agreement is part of the policy to which it is attached and is subject to the provisions of such policy except as otherwise provided in this agreement. The date of issue of this agreement is the date of issue of the policy unless another date is specified below.

PRESIDENT

E. Death Rates and Expectation of Life under Various Mortality and Annuity Tables*

	American Experience (1843–1858)		Commissioners 1941 Standard Ordinary (1930–1940)		Commissioners 1958 Standard Ordinary (1950–1954)		Annuity Table for 1949—Male (1939–1949)		United States Total Population (1949–1951)	
Age	Deaths Per 1000	Expectation of Life-Years	Deaths Per 1000	Expectation of Life-Years	Deaths Per 1000	Expectation of Life-Years	Deaths Per 1000	Expectation of Life-Years	Deaths Per 1000	Expectation of Life-Years
0	154.70	41.45	22.58	62.33	7.08	68.30	4.04	73.18	29.76	68.07
1	63.49	47.94	5.77	62.76	1.76	67.78	1.58	72.48	2.30	69.16
2	35.50	50.16	4.14	62.12	1.52	66.90	.89	71.59	1.39	68.31
3	23.91	50.98	3.38	61.37	1.46	66.00	.72	70.65	1.05	67.41
4	17.70	51.22	2.99	60.58	1.40	65.10	.63	69.70	.86	66.48
5	13.60	51.13	2.76	59.76	1.35	64.19	.57	68.75	.76	65.54
6	11.37	50.83	2.61	58.92	1.30	63.27	.53	67.78	.68	64.59
7	9.75	50.41	2.47	58.08	1.26	62.35	.50	66.82	.61	63.63
8	8.63	49.90	2.31	57.22	1.23	61.43	.49	65.85	.56	62.67
9	7.90	49.33	2.12	56.35	1.21	60.51	.48	64.89	.54	61.70
10	7.49	48.72	1.97	55.47	1.21	59.58	.48	63.92	.53	60.74
11	7.52	48.08	1.91	54.58	1.23	58.65	.49	62.95	.54	59.77
12	7.54	47.45	1.92	53.68	1.26	57.72	.50	61.98	.58	58.80
13	7.57	46.80	1.98	52.78	1.32	56.80	.51	61.01	.65	57.83
14	7.60	46.16	2.07	51.89	1.39	55.87	.52	60.04	.75	56.87
15	7.63	45.50	2.15	50.99	1.46	54.95	.54	59.07	.87	55.91
16	7.66	44.85	2.19	50.10	1.54	54.03	.55	58.10	1.00	54.96
17	7.69	44.19	2.25	49.21	1.62	53.11	.57	57.13	1.10	54.02
18	7.73	43.53	2.30	48.32	1.69	52.19	.58	56.17	1.19	53.07
19	7.77	42.87	2.37	47.43	1.74	51.28	.60	55.20	1.27	52.14
20	7.80	42.20	2.43	46.54	1.79	50.37	.62	54.23	1.35	51.20
21	7.86	41.53	2.51	45.66	1.83	49.46	.65	53.27	1.41	50.27
22	7.91	40.85	2.59	44.77	1.86	48.55	.67	52.30	1.47	49.34
23	7.96	40.17	2.68	43.88	1.89	47.64	.70	51.33	1.50	48.41
24	8.01	39.49	2.77	43.00	1.91	46.73	.73	50.37	1.52	47.49
25	8.06	38.81	2.88	42.12	1.93	45.82	.77	49.41	1.53	46.56
26	8.13	38.12	2.99	41.24	1.96	44.90	.81	48.44	1.55	45.63
27	8.20	37.43	3.11	40.36	1.99	43.99	.85	47.48	1.59	44.70
28	8.26	36.73	3.25	39.49	2.03	43.08	.90	46.52	1.64	43.77
29	8.34	36.03	3.40	38.61	2.08	42.16	.95	45.56	1.71	42.84
30	8.43	35.33	3.56	37.74	2.13	41.25	1.00	44.61	1.79	41.91
31	8.51	34.63	3.73	36.88	2.19	40.34	1.07	43.65	1.88	40.99
32	8.61	33.92	3.92	36.01	2.25	39.43	1.14	42.70	2.00	40.06
33	8.72	33.21	4.12	35.15	2.32	38.51	1.21	41.75	2.13	39.14
34	8.83	32.50	4.35	34.29	2.40	37.60	1.30	40.80	2.27	38.22
35	8.95	31.78	4.59	33.44	2.51	36.69	1.39	39.85	2.43	37.31
36	9.09	31.07	4.86	32.59	2.64	35.78	1.49	38.90	2.62	36.40
37	9.23	30.35	5.15	31.75	2.80	34.88	1.61	37.96	2.84	35.49
38	9.41	29.62	5.46	30.91	3.01	33.97	1.73	37.02	3.09	34.59
39	9.59	28.90	5.81	30.08	3.25	33.07	1.87	36.08	3.37	33.70
40	9.79	28.18	6.18	29.25	3.53	32.18	2.03	35.15	3.68	32.81
41	10.01	27.45	6.59	28.43	3.84	31.29	2.22	34.22	4.02	31.93
42	10.25	26.72	7.03	27.62	4.17	30.41	2.48	33.30	4.40	31.06
43	10.52	26.00	7.51	26.81	4.53	29.54	2.80	32.38	4.81	30.19
44	10.83	25.27	8.04	26.01	4.92	28.67	3.19	31.47	5.27	29.34
45	11.16	24.54	8.61	25.21	5.35	27.81	3.63	30.57	5.75	28.49
46	11.56	23.81	9.23	24.43	5.83	26.95	4.12	29.68	6.28	27.65
47	12.00	23.08	9.91	23.65	6.36	26.11	4.66	28.80	6.85	26.82
48	12.51	22.36	10.64	22.88	6.95	25.27	5.25	27.93	7.45	26.00
49	13.11	21.63	11.45	22.12	7.60	24.45	5.88	27.07	8.08	25.20
50	13.78	20.91	12.32	21.37	8.32	23.63	6.56	26.23	8.76	24.40
51	14.54	20.20	13.27	20.64	9.11	22.82	7.28	25.40	9.50	23.61
52	15.39	19.49	14.30	19.91	9.96	22.03	8.04	24.58	10.33	22.83
53	16.33	18.79	15.43	19.19	10.89	21.25	8.84	23.78	11.24	22.06

* Reprinted with permission from the *Fact Book*, 1963, Institute of Life Insurance, 488 Madison Avenue, New York, N.Y.

Death Rates and Expectation of Life under Various Mortality and Annuity Tables (Concluded)

	American Experience (1843–1858)		Commissioners 1941 Standard Ordinary (1930–1940)		Commissioners 1958 Standard Ordinary (1950–1954)		Annuity Table for 1949—Male (1939–1949)		United States Total Population (1949–1951)	
Age	Deaths Per 1000	Expectation of Life-Years	Deaths Per 1000	Expectation of Life-Years	Deaths Per 1000	Expectation of Life-Years	Deaths Per 1000	Expectation of Life-Years	Deaths Per 1000	Expectation of Life-Years
54	17.40	18.09	16.65	18.48	11.90	20.47	9.68	22.99	12.22	21.31
55	18.57	17.40	17.98	17.78	13.00	19.71	10.56	22.20	13.27	20.57
56	19.89	16.72	19.43	17.10	14.21	18.97	11.49	21.44	14.41	19.84
57	21.34	16.05	21.00	16.43	15.54	18.23	12.46	20.68	15.63	19.12
58	22.94	15.39	22.71	15.77	17.00	17.51	13.48	19.93	16.93	18.41
59	24.72	14.74	24.57	15.13	18.59	16.81	14.54	19.20	18.30	17.72
60	26.69	14.10	26.59	14.50	20.34	16.12	15.66	18.48	19.77	17.04
61	28.88	13.47	28.78	13.88	22.24	15.44	16.87	17.76	21.33	16.38
62	31.29	12.86	31.18	13.27	24.31	14.78	18.20	17.06	23.02	15.72
63	33.94	12.26	33.76	12.69	26.57	14.14	19.67	16.37	24.75	15.08
64	36.87	11.67	36.58	12.11	29.04	13.51	21.28	15.68	26.52	14.45
65	40.13	11.10	39.64	11.55	31.75	12.90	23.07	15.01	28.43	13.83
66	43.71	10.54	42.96	11.01	34.74	12.31	25.03	14.36	30.60	13.22
67	47.65	10.00	46.56	10.48	38.04	11.73	27.19	13.71	33.13	12.62
68	52.00	9.47	50.46	9.97	41.68	11.17	29.58	13.08	35.98	12.04
69	56.76	8.97	54.70	9.47	45.61	10.64	32.20	12.46	39.08	11.47
70	61.99	8.48	59.30	8.99	49.79	10.12	35.09	11.86	42.49	10.92
71	67.67	8.00	64.27	8.52	54.15	9.63	38.27	11.28	46.26	10.38
72	73.73	7.55	69.66	8.08	58.65	9.15	41.77	10.71	50.44	9.86
73	80.18	7.11	75.50	7.64	63.26	8.69	45.62	10.15	54.99	9.35
74	87.03	6.68	81.81	7.23	68.12	8.24	49.85	9.61	59.88	8.87
75	94.37	6.27	88.64	6.82	73.37	7.81	54.50	9.09	65.16	8.40
76	102.31	5.88	96.02	6.44	79.18	7.39	59.61	8.58	70.89	7.95
77	111.06	5.49	103.99	6.07	85.70	6.98	65.22	8.10	77.13	7.52
78	120.83	5.11	112.59	5.72	93.06	6.59	71.37	7.63	83.80	7.11
79	131.73	4.74	121.86	5.38	101.19	6.21	78.11	7.17	90.85	6.71
80	144.47	4.39	131.85	5.06	109.98	5.85	85.50	6.74	98.41	6.34
81	158.60	4.05	142.60	4.75	119.35	5.51	93.59	6.32	106.61	5.97
82	174.30	3.71	154.16	4.46	129.17	5.19	102.44	5.92	115.58	5.63
83	191.56	3.39	166.57	4.18	139.38	4.89	112.11	5.54	125.33	5.29
84	211.36	3.08	179.88	3.91	150.01	4.60	122.67	5.18	135.76	4.98
85	235.55	2.77	194.13	3.66	161.14	4.32	134.18	4.84	146.88	4.69
86	265.68	2.47	209.37	3.42	172.82	4.06	146.71	4.51	158.67	4.41
87	303.02	2.18	225.63	3.19	185.13	3.80	160.33	4.20	171.12	4.14
88	346.69	1.91	243.00	2.98	198.25	3.55	175.12	3.90	184.24	3.90
89	395.86	1.66	261.44	2.77	212.46	3.31	191.15	3.62	198.03	3.66
90	454.55	1.42	280.99	2.58	228.14	3.06	208.49	3.36	212.49	3.44
91	532.47	1.19	301.73	2.39	245.77	2.82	227.19	3.12	227.62	3.24
92	634.26	.98	323.64	2.21	265.93	2.58	247.33	2.88	243.43	3.04
93	734.18	.80	346.66	2.03	289.30	2.33	268.96	2.67	260.12	2.86
94	857.14	.64	371.00	1.84	316.66	2.07	292.12	2.47	277.68	2.69
95	1,000.00	.50	396.21	1.63	351.24	1.80	316.83	2.28	295.82	2.54
96			447.19	1.37	400.56	1.51	343.12	2.10	314.23	2.39
97			548.26	1.08	488.42	1.18	370.97	1.94	332.60	2.26
98			724.67	.78	668.15	.83	400.35	1.79	351.15	2.14
99			1,000.00	.50	1,000.00	.50	431.20	1.65	370.06	2.03
100							463.41	1.52	389.04	1.92
101							496.87	1.40	407.79	1.83
102							531.39	1.29	426.00	1.74
103							566.76	1.20	443.54	1.66
104							602.71	1.10	460.60	1.59
105							638.96	1.02	477.40	1.53
106							675.14	.94	494.13	1.46
107							710.90	.86	511.00	1.40
108							745.82	.75	528.10	1.34
109							1,000.00	.50	545.29	1.29

F. Selected Compound Interest and Discount Functions

2 Per Cent

	Amount of 1 How $1 Left at Compound Interest Will Grow	Amount of 1 Per Annum How $1 Deposited Periodically Will Grow	Present Value of 1 What $1 Due in the Future Is Worth Today	Present Value of 1 Per Annum What $1 Payable Periodically Is Worth Today
1	1.020 000	1.000 000	.980 392	.980 392
2	1.040 400	2.020 000	.961 169	1.941 561
3	1.061 208	3.060 400	.942 322	2.883 883
4	1.082 432	4.121 608	.923 845	3.807 729
5	1.104 081	5.204 040	.905 731	4.713 460
6	1.126 162	6.308 121	.887 971	5.601 431
7	1.148 686	7.434 283	.870 560	6.471 991
8	1.171 659	8.582 969	.853 490	7.325 481
9	1.195 093	9.754 628	.836 755	8.162 237
10	1.218 994	10.949 721	.820 348	8.982 585
11	1.243 374	12.168 715	.804 263	9.786 848
12	1.268 242	13.412 090	.788 493	10.575 341
13	1.293 607	14.680 332	.773 033	11.348 374
14	1.319 479	15.973 938	.757 875	12.106 249
15	1.345 868	17.293 417	.743 015	12.849 264
16	1.372 786	18.639 285	.728 446	13.577 709
17	1.400 241	20.012 071	.714 163	14.291 872
18	1.428 246	21.412 312	.700 159	14.992 031
19	1.456 811	22.840 559	.686 431	15.678 462
20	1.485 947	24.297 370	.672 971	16.351 433
21	1.515 666	25.783 317	.659 776	17.011 209
22	1.545 980	27.298 984	.646 839	17.658 048
23	1.576 899	28.844 963	.634 156	18.292 204
24	1.608 437	30.421 862	.621 721	18.913 926
25	1.640 606	32.030 300	.609 531	19.523 456
26	1.673 418	33.670 906	.597 579	20.121 036
27	1.706 886	35.344 324	.585 862	20.706 898
28	1.741 024	37.051 210	.574 375	21.281 272
29	1.775 845	38.792 235	.563 112	21.844 385
30	1.811 362	40.568 079	.552 071	22.396 456
31	1.847 589	42.379 441	.541 246	22.937 702
32	1.884 541	44.227 030	.530 633	23.468 335
33	1.922 231	46.111 570	.520 229	23.988 564
34	1.960 676	48.033 802	.510 028	24.498 592
35	1.999 890	49.994 478	.500 028	24.998 619
36	2.039 887	51.994 367	.490 223	25.488 842
37	2.080 685	54.034 255	.480 611	25.969 453
38	2.122 299	56.114 940	.471 187	26.440 641
39	2.164 745	58.237 238	.461 948	26.902 589
40	2.208 040	60.401 983	.452 890	27.355 479
41	2.252 200	62.610 023	.444 010	27.799 489
42	2.297 244	64.862 223	.435 304	28.234 794

Selected Compound Interest and Discount Functions (Continued)

2 Per Cent

	Amount of 1 How $1 Left at Compound Interest Will Grow	Amount of 1 Per Annum How $1 Deposited Periodically Will Grow	Present Value of 1 What $1 Due in the Future Is Worth Today	Present Value of 1 Per Annum What $1 Payable Periodically Is Worth Today
43	2.343 189	67.159 468	.426 769	28.661 562
44	2.390 053	69.502 657	.418 401	29.079 963
45	2.437 854	71.892 710	.410 197	29.490 160
46	2.486 611	74.330 564	.402 154	29.892 314
47	2.536 344	76.817 176	.394 268	30.286 582
48	2.587 070	79.353 519	.386 538	30.673 120
49	2.638 812	81.940 590	.378 958	31.052 078
50	2.691 588	84.579 401	.371 528	31.423 606
51	2.745 420	87.270 989	.364 243	31.787 849
52	2.800 328	90.016 409	.357 101	32.144 950
53	2.856 335	92.816 737	.350 099	32.495 049
54	2.913 461	95.673 072	.343 234	32.838 283
55	2.971 731	98.586 534	.336 504	33.174 788
56	3.031 165	101.558 264	.329 906	33.504 694
57	3.091 789	104.589 430	.323 437	33.828 131
58	3.153 624	107.681 218	.317 095	34.145 226
59	3.216 697	110.834 843	.310 878	34.456 104
60	3.281 031	114.051 539	.304 782	34.760 887
61	3.346 651	117.332 570	.298 806	35.059 693
62	3.413 584	120.679 222	.292 947	35.352 640
63	3.481 856	124.092 806	.287 203	35.639 843
64	3.551 493	127.574 662	.281 572	35.921 415
65	3.622 523	131.126 155	.276 051	36.197 466
66	3.694 974	134.748 679	.270 638	36.468 103
67	3.768 873	138.443 652	.265 331	36.733 435
68	3.844 251	142.212 525	.260 129	36.993 564
69	3.921 136	146.056 776	.255 028	37.248 592
70	3.999 558	149.977 911	.250 028	37.498 619
71	4.079 549	153.977 469	.245 125	37.743 744
72	4.161 140	158.057 019	.240 319	37.984 063
73	4.244 363	162.218 159	.235 607	38.219 670
74	4.329 250	166.462 522	.230 987	38.450 657
75	4.415 835	170.791 773	.226 458	38.677 114
76	4.504 152	175.207 608	.222 017	38.899 132
77	4.594 235	179.711 760	.217 664	39.116 796
78	4.686 120	184.305 996	.213 396	39.330 192
79	4.779 842	188.992 115	.209 212	39.539 404
80	4.875 439	193.771 958	.205 110	39.744 514
81	4.972 948	198.647 397	.201 088	39.945 602
82	5.072 407	203.620 345	.197 145	40.142 747
83	5.173 855	208.692 752	.193 279	40.336 026
84	5.277 332	213.866 607	.189 490	40.525 516
85	5.382 879	219.143 939	.185 774	40.711 290

Selected Compound Interest and Discount Functions (Continued)

2 Per Cent

	Amount of 1 How $1 Left at Compound Interest Will Grow	Amount of 1 Per Annum How $1 Deposited Periodically Will Grow	Present Value of 1 What $1 Due in the Future Is Worth Today	Present Value of 1 Per Annum What $1 Payable Periodically Is Worth Today
86	5.490 536	224.526 818	.182 132	40.893 422
87	5.600 347	230.017 354	.178 560	41.071 982
88	5.712 354	235.617 701	.175 059	41.247 041
89	5.826 601	241.330 055	.171 627	41.418 668
90	5.943 133	247.156 656	.168 261	41.586 929
91	6.061 996	253.099 789	.164 962	41.751 891
92	6.183 236	259.161 785	.161 728	41.913 619
93	6.306 900	265.345 021	.158 556	42.072 175
94	6.433 038	271.651 921	.155 448	42.227 623
95	6.561 699	278.084 960	.152 400	42.380 023
96	6.692 933	284.646 659	.149 411	42.529 434
97	6.826 792	291.339 592	.146 482	42.675 916
98	6.963 328	298.166 384	.143 609	42.819 525
99	7.102 594	305.129 712	.140 794	42.960 319
100	7.244 646	312.232 306	.138 033	43.098 352

2¼ Per Cent

1	1.022 500	1.000 000	.977 995	.977 995
2	1.045 506	2.022 500	.956 474	1.934 470
3	1.069 030	3.068 006	.935 427	2.869 897
4	1.093 083	4.137 036	.914 843	3.784 740
5	1.117 678	5.230 120	.894 712	4.679 453
6	1.142 825	6.347 797	.875 024	5.554 477
7	1.168 539	7.490 623	.855 769	6.410 246
8	1.194 831	8.659 162	.836 938	7.247 185
9	1.221 715	9.853 993	.818 522	8.065 706
10	1.249 203	11.075 708	.800 510	8.866 216
11	1.277 311	12.324 911	.782 895	9.649 111
12	1.306 050	13.602 222	.765 667	10.414 779
13	1.335 436	14.908 272	.748 819	11.163 598
14	1.365 483	16.243 708	.732 341	11.895 939
15	1.396 207	17.609 191	.716 226	12.612 166
16	1.427 621	19.005 398	.700 466	13.312 631
17	1.459 743	20.433 020	.685 052	13.997 683
18	1.492 587	21.892 763	.669 978	14.667 661
19	1.526 170	23.385 350	.655 235	15.322 896
20	1.560 509	24.911 520	.640 816	15.963 712
21	1.595 621	26.472 029	.626 715	16.590 428
22	1.631 522	28.067 650	.612 925	17.203 352
23	1.668 231	29.699 172	.599 437	17.802 790

Selected Compound Interest and Discount Functions (Continued)

2¼ Per Cent

	Amount of 1 How $1 Left at Compound Interest Will Grow	Amount of 1 Per Annum How $1 Deposited Periodically Will Grow	Present Value of 1 What $1 Due in the Future Is Worth Today	Present Value of 1 Per Annum What $1 Payable Periodically Is Worth Today
24	1.705 767	31.367 403	.586 247	18.389 036
25	1.744 146	33.073 170	.573 346	18.962 383
26	1.783 390	34.817 316	.560 730	19.523 113
27	1.823 516	36.600 706	.548 391	20.071 504
28	1.864 545	38.424 222	.536 324	20.607 828
29	1.906 497	40.288 767	.524 522	21.132 350
30	1.949 393	42.195 264	.512 980	21.645 330
31	1.993 255	44.144 657	.501 692	22.147 022
32	2.038 103	46.137 912	.490 652	22.637 674
33	2.083 960	48.176 015	.479 856	23.117 530
34	2.130 849	50.259 976	.469 296	23.586 826
35	2.178 794	52.390 825	.458 970	24.045 796
36	2.227 816	54.569 619	.448 870	24.494 666
37	2.277 942	56.797 435	.438 993	24.933 658
38	2.329 196	59.075 377	.429 333	25.362 991
39	2.381 603	61.404 573	.419 885	25.782 876
40	2.435 189	63.786 176	.410 646	26.193 522
41	2.489 981	66.221 365	.401 610	26.595 132
42	2.546 005	68.711 346	.392 772	26.987 904
43	2.603 290	71.257 351	.384 130	27.372 033
44	2.661 864	73.860 642	.375 677	27.747 710
45	2.721 756	76.522 506	.367 410	28.115 120
46	2.782 996	79.244 262	.359 325	28.474 444
47	2.845 613	82.027 258	.351 418	28.825 863
48	2.909 640	84.872 872	.343 685	29.169 548
49	2.975 107	87.782 511	.336 122	29.505 670
50	3.042 046	90.757 618	.328 726	29.834 396
51	3.110 492	93.799 664	.321 493	30.155 889
52	3.180 479	96.910 157	.314 418	30.470 307
53	3.252 039	100.090 635	.307 499	30.777 806
54	3.325 210	103.342 674	.300 733	31.078 539
55	3.400 027	106.667 885	.294 115	31.372 654
56	3.476 528	110.067 912	.287 643	31.660 298
57	3.554 750	113.544 440	.281 314	31.941 611
58	3.634 732	117.099 190	.275 123	32.216 735
59	3.716 513	120.733 922	.269 069	32.485 804
60	3.800 135	124.450 435	.263 149	32.748 953
61	3.885 638	128.250 570	.257 358	33.006 311
62	3.973 065	132.136 208	.251 695	33.258 006

Selected Compound Interest and Discount Functions (Continued)

2¼ Per Cent

	Amount of 1 How $1 Left at Compound Interest Will Grow	Amount of 1 Per Annum How $1 Deposited Periodically Will Grow	Present Value of 1 What $1 Due in the Future Is Worth Today	Present Value of 1 Per Annum What $1 Payable Periodically Is Worth Today
63	4.062 459	136.109 272	.246 156	33.504 162
64	4.153 864	140.171 731	.240 740	33.744 902
65	4.247 326	144.325 595	.235 442	33.980 344
66	4.342 891	148.572 921	.230 261	34.210 605
67	4.440 606	152.915 811	.225 195	34.435 800
68	4.540 519	157.536 417	.220 239	34.656 039
69	4.642 681	161.896 937	.215 393	34.871 432
70	4.747 141	166.539 618	.210 653	35.082 085
71	4.853 952	171.286 759	.206 018	35.288 103
72	4.963 166	176.140 711	.201 484	35.489 587
73	5.074 837	181.103 877	.197 051	35.686 638
74	5.189 021	186.178 714	.192 715	35.879 352
75	5.305 774	191.367 735	.188 474	36.067 826
76	5.425 154	196.673 509	.184 327	36.252 153
77	5.547 220	202.098 663	.180 270	36.432 423
78	5.672 032	207.645 883	.176 304	36.608 727
79	5.799 653	213.317 916	.172 424	36.781 151
80	5.930 145	219.117 569	.168 630	36.949 781
81	6.063 574	225.047 714	.164 919	37.114 700
82	6.200 004	231.111 288	.161 290	37.275 990
83	6.339 504	237.311 292	.157 741	37.433 731
84	6.482 143	243.650 796	.154 270	37.588 001
85	6.627 991	250.132 939	.150 875	37.738 877
86	6.777 121	256.760 930	.147 555	37.886 432
87	6.929 606	263.538 051	.144 308	38.030 740
88	7.085 522	270.467 657	.141 133	38.171 873
89	7.244 947	277.553 179	.138 027	38.309 900
90	7.407 958	284.798 126	.134 990	38.444 890
91	7.574 637	292.206 083	.132 020	38.576 910
92	7.745 066	299.780 720	.129 114	38.706 024
93	7.919 330	307.525 786	.126 273	38.832 298
94	8.097 515	315.445 117	.123 495	38.955 792
95	8.279 709	323.542 632	.120 777	39.076 569
96	8.466 003	331.822 341	.118 119	39.194 689
97	8.656 488	340.288 344	.115 520	39.310 209
98	8.851 259	348.944 831	.112 978	39.423 187
99	9.050 412	357.796 090	.110 492	39.533 680
100	9.254 046	366.846 502	.108 061	39.641 741

Selected Compound Interest and Discount Functions (Continued)

2½ Per Cent

	Amount of 1 How $1 Left at Compound Interest Will Grow	Amount of 1 Per Annum How $1 Deposited Periodically Will Grow	Present Value of 1 What $1 Due in the Future Is Worth Today	Present Value of 1 Per Annum What $1 Payable Periodically Is Worth Today
1	1.025 000	1.000 000	.975 610	.975 610
2	1.050 625	2.025 000	.951 814	1.927 424
3	1.076 891	3.075 625	.928 599	2.856 024
4	1.103 813	4.152 516	.905 951	3.761 974
5	1.131 408	5.256 329	.883 854	4.645 828
6	1.159 693	6.387 737	.862 297	5.508 125
7	1.188 686	7.547 430	.841 265	6.349 391
8	1.218 403	8.736 116	.820 747	7.170 137
9	1.248 863	9.954 519	.800 728	7.970 866
10	1.280 085	11.203 382	.781 198	8.752 064
11	1.312 087	12.483 466	.762 145	9.514 209
12	1.344 889	13.795 553	.743 556	10.257 765
13	1.378 511	15.140 442	.725 420	10.983 185
14	1.412 974	16.518 953	.707 727	11.690 912
15	1.448 298	17.931 927	.690 466	12.381 378
16	1.484 506	19.380 225	.673 625	13.055 003
17	1.521 618	20.864 730	.657 195	13.712 198
18	1.559 659	22.386 349	.641 166	14.353 364
19	1.598 650	23.946 007	.625 528	14.978 891
20	1.638 616	25.544 658	.610 271	15.589 162
21	1.679 582	27.183 274	.595 386	16.184 549
22	1.721 571	28.862 856	.580 865	16.765 413
23	1.764 611	30.584 427	.566 697	17.332 110
24	1.808 726	32.349 038	.552 875	17.884 986
25	1.853 944	34.157 764	.539 391	18.424 376
26	1.900 293	36.011 708	.526 235	18.950 611
27	1.947 800	37.912 001	.513 400	19.464 011
28	1.996 495	39.859 801	.500 878	19.964 889
29	2.046 407	41.856 296	.488 661	20.453 550
30	2.097 568	43.902 703	.476 743	20.930 293
31	2.150 007	46.000 271	.465 115	21.395 407
32	2.203 757	48.150 278	.453 771	21.849 178
33	2.258 851	50.354 034	.442 703	22.291 881
34	2.315 322	52.612 885	.431 905	22.723 786
35	2.373 205	54.928 207	.421 371	23.145 157
36	2.432 535	57.301 413	.411 094	23.556 251
37	2.493 349	59.733 948	.401 067	23.957 318
38	2.555 682	62.227 297	.391 285	24.348 603

Selected Compound Interest and Discount Functions (Continued)

2½ Per Cent

	Amount of 1 How $1 Left at Compound Interest Will Grow	Amount of 1 Per Annum How $1 Deposited Periodically Will Grow	Present Value of 1 What $1 Due in the Future Is Worth Today	Present Value of 1 Per Annum What $1 Payable Periodically Is Worth Today
39	2.619 574	64.782 979	.381 741	24.730 344
40	2.685 064	67.402 554	.372 431	25.102 775
41	2.752 190	70.087 617	.363 347	25.466 122
42	2.820 995	72.839 808	.354 485	25.820 607
43	2.891 520	75.660 803	.345 839	26.166 446
44	2.963 808	78.552 323	.337 404	26.503 849
45	3.037 903	81.516 131	.329 174	26.833 024
46	3.113 851	84.554 034	.321 146	27.154 170
47	3.191 697	87.667 885	.313 313	27.467 483
48	3.271 490	90.859 582	.305 671	27.773 154
49	3.353 277	94.131 072	.298 216	28.071 369
50	3.437 109	97.484 349	.290 942	28.362 312
51	3.523 036	100.921 458	.283 846	28.646 158
52	3.611 112	104.444 494	.276 923	28.923 081
53	3.701 390	108.055 606	.270 169	29.193 249
54	3.793 925	111.756 996	.263 579	29.456 829
55	3.888 773	115.550 921	.257 151	29.713 979
56	3.985 992	119.439 694	.250 879	29.964 858
57	4.085 642	123.425 687	.244 760	30.209 617
58	4.187 783	127.511 329	.238 790	30.448 407
59	4.292 478	131.699 112	.232 966	30.681 373
60	4.399 790	135.991 590	.227 284	30.908 656
61	4.509 784	140.391 380	.221 740	31.130 397
62	4.622 529	144.901 164	.216 332	31.346 728
63	4.738 092	149.523 693	.211 055	31.557 784
64	4.856 545	154.261 786	.205 908	31.763 691
65	4.977 958	159.118 330	.200 886	31.964 577
66	5.102 407	164.096 289	.195 986	32.160 563
67	5.229 967	169.198 696	.191 206	32.351 769
68	5.360 717	174.428 663	.186 542	32.538 311
69	5.494 734	179.789 380	.181 992	32.720 303
70	5.632 103	185.284 114	.177 554	32.897 857
71	5.772 905	190.916 217	.173 223	33.071 080
72	5.917 228	196.689 122	.168 998	33.240 078
73	6.065 159	202.606 351	.164 876	33.404 954
74	6.216 788	208.671 509	.160 855	33.565 809
75	6.372 207	214.888 297	.156 931	33.722 740
76	6.531 513	221.260 504	.153 104	33.875 844
77	6.694 800	227.792 017	.149 370	34.025 214

Selected Compound Interest and Discount Functions (Continued)

2½ Per Cent

	Amount of 1 How $1 Left at Compound Interest Will Grow	Amount of 1 Per Annum How $1 Deposited Periodically Will Grow	Present Value of 1 What $1 Due in the Future Is Worth Today	Present Value of 1 Per Annum What $1 Payable Periodically Is Worth Today
78	6.862 170	234.486 818	.145 726	34.170 940
79	7.033 725	241.348 988	.142 172	34.313 113
80	7.209 568	248.382 713	.138 705	34.451 817
81	7.389 807	255.592 280	.135 322	34.587 139
82	7.574 552	262.982 087	.132 021	34.719 160
83	7.763 916	270.556 640	.128 801	34.847 961
84	7.958 014	278.320 556	.125 659	34.973 620
85	8.156 964	286.278 570	.122 595	35.096 215
86	8.360 888	294.435 534	.119 605	35.215 819
87	8.569 911	302.796 422	.116 687	35.332 507
88	8.784 158	311.366 333	.113 841	35.446 348
89	9.003 762	320.150 491	.111 065	35.557 413
90	9.228 856	329.154 253	.108 356	35.665 768
91	9.459 578	338.383 110	.105 713	35.771 481
92	9.696 067	347.842 687	.103 135	35.874 616
93	9.938 469	357.538 755	.100 619	35.975 235
94	10.186 931	367.477 223	.098 165	36.073 400
95	10.441 604	377.664 154	.095 771	36.169 171
96	10.702 644	388.105 758	.093 435	36.262 606
97	10.970 210	398.808 402	.091 156	36.353 762
98	11.244 465	409.778 612	.088 933	36.442 694
99	11.525 577	421.023 077	.086 764	36.529 458
100	11.813 716	432.548 654	.084 647	36.614 105

2¾ Per Cent

1	1.027 500	1.000 000	.973 236	.973 236
2	1.055 756	2.027 500	.947 188	1.920 424
3	1.084 790	3.083 256	.921 838	2.842 262
4	1.114 621	4.168 046	.897 166	3.739 428
5	1.145 273	5.282 667	.873 154	4.612 582
6	1.176 768	6.427 940	.849 785	5.462 367
7	1.209 129	7.604 709	.827 041	6.289 408
8	1.242 381	8.813 838	.804 906	7.094 314
9	1.276 546	10.056 219	.783 364	7.877 678
10	1.311 651	11.332 765	.762 398	8.640 076
11	1.347 721	12.644 416	.741 993	9.382 069
12	1.384 784	13.992 137	.722 134	10.104 204
13	1.422 865	15.376 921	.702 807	10.807 011
14	1.461 994	16.799 786	.683 997	11.491 008
15	1.502 199	18.261 781	.665 691	12.156 699

Selected Compound Interest and Discount Functions (Continued)

2¾ Per Cent

	Amount of 1 How $1 Left at Compound Interest Will Grow	Amount of 1 Per Annum How $1 Deposited Periodically Will Grow	Present Value of 1 What $1 Due in the Future Is Worth Today	Present Value of 1 Per Annum What $1 Payable Periodically Is Worth Today
16	1.543 509	19.763 979	.647 874	12.804 573
17	1.585 956	21.307 489	.630 535	13.435 108
18	1.629 570	22.893 445	.613 659	14.048 767
19	1.674 383	24.523 015	.597 235	14.646 002
20	1.720 428	26.197 398	.581 251	15.227 252
21	1.767 740	27.917 826	.565 694	15.792 946
22	1.816 353	29.685 566	.550 554	16.343 500
23	1.866 303	31.501 919	.535 819	16.879 319
24	1.917 626	33.368 222	.521 478	17.400 797
25	1.970 361	35.285 848	.507 521	17.908 318
26	2.024 546	37.256 209	.497 938	18.402 256
27	2.080 221	39.280 755	.480 718	18.882 974
28	2.137 427	41.360 975	.467 852	19.350 826
29	2.196 206	43.498 402	.455 331	19.806 157
30	2.256 602	45.694 608	.443 144	20.249 301
31	2.318 658	47.951 210	.431 284	20.680 585
32	2.382 421	50.269 868	.419 741	21.100 326
33	2.447 938	52.652 290	.408 507	21.508 833
34	2.215 256	55.100 228	.397 574	21.906 407
35	2.584 426	57.615 484	.386 933	22.293 340
36	2.655 498	60.199 910	.376 577	22.669 918
37	2.728 524	62.855 407	.366 499	23.036 416
38	2.803 558	65.583 931	.356 690	23.393 106
39	2.880 656	68.387 489	.347 143	23.740 249
40	2.959 874	71.268 145	.337 852	24.078 101
41	3.041 271	74.228 019	.328 810	24.406 911
42	3.124 905	77.269 289	.320 010	24.726 921
43	3.210 840	80.394 195	.311 445	25.038 366
44	3.299 138	83.605 035	.303 109	25.341 475
45	3.389 865	86.904 174	.294 997	25.636 472
46	3.483 086	90.294 039	.287 102	25.923 574
47	3.578 871	93.777 125	.279 418	26.202 992
48	3.677 290	97.355 996	.271 939	26.474 931
49	3.778 415	101.033 285	.264 661	26.739 592
50	3.882 322	104.811 701	.257 578	26.997 170
51	3.989 086	108.694 023	.250 684	27.247 854
52	4.098 785	112.683 108	.243 975	27.491 829
53	4.211 502	116.781 894	.237 445	27.729 274
54	4.327 318	120.993 396	.231 090	27.960 364
55	4.446 320	125.320 714	.224 905	28.185 269

Selected Compound Interest and Discount Functions (Continued)

2¾ Per Cent

	Amount of 1 How $1 Left at Compound Interest Will Grow	Amount of 1 Per Annum How $1 Deposited Periodically Will Grow	Present Value of 1 What $1 Due in the Future Is Worth Today	Present Value of 1 Per Annum What $1 Payable Periodically Is Worth Today
56	4.568 593	129.767 034	.218 886	28.404 155
57	4.694 230	134.335 627	.213 027	28.617 182
58	4.823 321	139.029 857	.207 326	28.824 508
59	4.955 962	143.853 178	.201 777	29.026 285
60	5.092 251	148.809 140	.196 377	29.222 662
61	5.232 288	153.901 392	.191 121	29.413 783
62	5.376 176	159.133 680	.186 006	29.599 789
63	5.524 021	164.509 856	.181 028	29.780 816
64	5.675 932	170.033 877	.176 183	29.956 999
65	5.832 020	175.708 809	.171 467	30.128 466
66	5.992 400	181.541 829	.166 878	30.295 344
67	6.157 191	187.534 229	.162 412	30.457 756
68	6.326 514	193.691 420	.158 065	30.615 821
69	6.500 493	200.017 934	.153 834	30.769 655
70	6.679 257	206.518 427	.149 717	30.919 372
71	6.862 936	213.197 684	.145 710	31.065 083
72	7.051 667	220.060 621	.141 810	31.206 893
73	7.245 588	227.112 288	.138 015	31.344 908
74	7.444 842	234.357 876	.134 321	31.479 229
75	7.649 575	241.802 717	.130 726	31.609 956
76	7.859 938	249.452 292	.127 227	31.737 183
77	8.076 086	257.312 230	.123 882	31.861 005
78	8.298 179	265.388 316	.120 508	31.981 514
79	8.526 379	273.686 495	.117 283	32.098 797
80	8.760 854	282.212 873	.114 144	32.212 941
81	9.001 778	290.973 727	.111 089	32.324 030
82	9.249 326	299.975 505	.108 116	32.432 146
83	9.503 683	309.224 831	.105 222	32.537 368
84	9.765 034	318.728 514	.102 406	32.639 775
85	10.033 573	328.493 548	.099 665	32.739 440
86	10.309 496	338.527 121	.096 998	32.836 438
87	10.593 007	348.836 617	.094 402	32.930 840
88	10.884 315	359.429 624	.091 875	33.022 715
89	11.183 633	370.313 938	.089 416	33.112 132
90	11.491 183	381.497 572	.087 023	33.199 155
91	11.807 191	392.988 755	.084 694	33.283 849
92	12.131 889	404.795 946	.082 427	33.366 276
93	12.465 515	416.927 834	.080 221	33.446 498
94	12.808 317	429.393 350	.078 074	33.524 572
95	13.160 546	442.201 667	.075 985	33.600 557

Selected Compound Interest and Discount Functions (Continued)

2¾ Per Cent

	Amount of 1 How $1 Left at Compound Interest Will Grow	Amount of 1 Per Annum How $1 Deposited Periodically Will Grow	Present Value of 1 What $1 Due in the Future Is Worth Today	Present Value of 1 Per Annum What $1 Payable Periodically Is Worth Today
96	13.522 461	455.362 213	.073 951	33.674 508
97	13.894 329	468.884 673	.071 972	33.746 480
98	14.276 423	482.779 002	.070 046	33.816 525
99	14.669 024	497.055 424	.068 171	33.884 696
100	15.072 422	511.724 449	.066 346	33.951 042

3 Per Cent

	Amount of 1 How $1 Left at Compound Interest Will Grow	Amount of 1 Per Annum How $1 Deposited Periodically Will Grow	Present Value of 1 What $1 Due in the Future Is Worth Today	Present Value of 1 Per Annum What $1 Payable Periodically Is Worth Today
1	1.030 000	1.000 000	.970 874	.970 874
2	1.060 900	2.030 000	.942 596	1.913 470
3	1.092 727	3.090 900	.915 142	2.828 611
4	1.125 509	4.183 627	.888 487	3.717 098
5	1.159 274	5.309 136	.862 609	4.579 707
6	1.194 052	6.468 410	.837 484	5.417 191
7	1.229 874	7.662 462	.813 092	6.230 283
8	1.266 770	8.892 336	.789 409	7.019 692
9	1.304 773	10.159 106	.766 417	7.786 109
10	1.343 916	11.463 879	.744 094	8.530 203
11	1.384 234	12.807 796	.722 421	9.252 624
12	1.425 761	14.192 030	.701 380	9.954 004
13	1.468 534	15.617 790	.680 951	10.634 955
14	1.512 590	17.086 324	.661 118	11.296 073
15	1.557 967	18.598 914	.641 862	11.937 935
16	1.604 706	20.156 881	.623 167	12.561 102
17	1.652 848	21.761 588	.605 016	13.166 118
18	1.702 433	23.414 435	.587 395	13.753 513
19	1.753 506	25.116 868	.570 286	14.323 799
20	1.806 111	26.870 374	.553 676	14.877 475
21	1.860 295	28.676 486	.537 549	15.415 024
22	1.916 103	30.536 780	.521 893	15.936 917
23	1.973 587	32.452 884	.506 692	16.443 608
24	2.032 794	34.426 470	.491 934	16.935 542
25	2.093 778	36.459 264	.477 606	17.413 148
26	2.156 591	38.553 042	.463 695	17.876 842
27	2.221 289	40.709 634	.450 189	18.327 031
28	2.287 928	42.930 923	.437 077	18.764 108
29	2.356 566	45.218 850	.424 346	19.188 455
30	2.427 262	47.575 416	.411 987	19.600 441
31	2.500 080	50.002 678	.399 987	20.000 428
32	2.575 083	52.502 759	.388 337	20.388 766
33	2.652 335	55.077 841	.377 026	20.765 792

Selected Compound Interest and Discount Functions (Continued)

3 Per Cent

	Amount of 1 How $1 Left at Compound Interest Will Grow	Amount of 1 Per Annum How $1 Deposited Periodically Will Grow	Present Value of 1 What $1 Due in the Future Is Worth Today	Present Value of 1 Per Annum What $1 Payable Periodically Is Worth Today
34	2.731 905	57.730 177	.366 045	21.131 837
35	2.813 862	60.462 082	.355 383	21.487 220
36	2.898 278	63.275 944	.345 032	21.832 252
37	2.985 227	66.174 223	.334 983	22.167 235
38	3.074 783	69.159 449	.325 226	22.492 462
39	3.167 027	72.234 233	.315 754	22.808 215
40	3.262 038	75.401 260	.306 557	23.114 772
41	3.359 899	78.663 298	.297 628	23.412 400
42	3.460 696	82.023 196	.288 959	23.701 359
43	3.564 517	85.483 892	.280 543	23.981 902
44	3.671 452	89.048 409	.272 372	24.254 274
45	3.781 596	92.719 861	.264 439	24.518 713
46	3.895 044	96.501 457	.256 737	24.775 449
47	4.011 895	100.396 501	.249 259	25.024 708
48	4.132 252	104.408 396	.241 999	25.266 707
49	4.256 219	108.540 648	.234 950	25.501 657
50	4.383 906	112.796 867	.228 107	25.729 764
51	4.515 423	117.180 773	.221 463	25.941 227
52	4.650 886	121.696 197	.215 013	26.166 240
53	4.790 412	126.347 082	.208 750	26.374 990
54	4.934 125	131.137 495	.202 670	26.577 660
55	5.082 149	136.071 620	.196 767	26.774 428
56	5.234 613	141.153 768	.191 036	26.965 464
57	5.391 651	146.388 381	.185 472	27.150 936
58	5.553 401	151.780 033	.180 070	27.331 005
59	5.720 003	157.333 434	.174 825	27.505 831
60	5.891 603	163.053 437	.169 733	27.675 564
61	6.068 351	168.945 040	.164 789	27.840 353
62	6.250 402	175.013 391	.159 990	28.000 343
63	6.437 914	181.263 793	.155 330	28.155 673
64	6.631 051	187.701 707	.150 806	28.306 478
65	6.829 983	194.332 758	.146 413	28.452 892
66	7.034 882	201.162 741	.142 149	28.595 040
67	7.245 929	208.197 623	.138 009	28.733 049
68	7.463 307	215.443 551	.133 989	28.867 038
69	7.687 206	222.906 858	.130 086	28.997 124
70	7.917 822	230.594 064	.126 297	29.123 421
71	8.155 537	238.511 886	.122 619	29.246 040
72	8.400 017	246.667 242	.119 047	29.365 088

Selected Compound Interest and Discount Functions (Concluded)

3 Per Cent

	Amount of 1 How $1 Left at Compound Interest Will Grow	Amount of 1 Per Annum How $1 Deposited Periodically Will Grow	Present Value of 1 What $1 Due in the Future Is Worth Today	Present Value of 1 Per Annum What $1 Payable Periodically Is Worth Today
73	8.652 018	255.067 259	.115 580	29.480 667
74	8.911 578	263.719 277	.112 214	29.592 881
75	9.178 926	272.630 856	.108 945	29.701 826
76	9.454 293	281.809 781	.105 772	29.807 598
77	9.737 922	291.264 075	.102 691	29.910 290
78	10.030 060	301.001 997	.099 700	30.009 990
79	10.330 962	311.032 057	.096 796	30.106 786
80	10.640 891	321.363 019	.093 977	30.200 763
81	10.960 117	332.003 909	.091 240	30.292 003
82	11.288 921	342.964 026	.088 582	30.380 586
83	11.627 588	354.252 947	.086 002	30.466 588
84	11.976 416	365.880 536	.083 497	30.550 086
85	12.335 709	377.856 952	.081 065	30.631 151
86	12.705 780	390.192 660	.078 704	30.709 855
87	13.086 953	402.898 440	.076 412	30.786 267
88	13.479 562	415.985 393	.074 186	30.860 454
89	13.883 949	429.464 955	.072 026	30.932 479
90	14.300 467	443.348 904	.069 928	31.002 407
91	14.729 481	457.649 371	.067 891	31.070 298
92	15.171 366	472.378 852	.065 914	31.136 212
93	15.626 507	487.550 217	.063 994	31.200 206
94	16.095 302	503.176 724	.062 130	31.262 336
95	16.578 161	519.272 026	.060 320	31.322 656
96	17.075 506	535.850 186	.058 563	31.381 219
97	17.587 771	552.925 692	.056 858	31.438 077
98	18.115 404	570.513 463	.055 202	31.493 279
99	18.658 866	588.628 867	.053 594	31.546 872
100	19.218 632	607.287 733	.052 033	31.598 905

G. Net Level Premiums at 2½% under the 1941 CSO Table and 1958 CSO Table at Quinquennial Ages for Various Plans of Insurance

Issue Age	Ordinary Life		20-Payment Life		20-Year Endowment		20-Year Term	
	1941	1958	1941	1958	1941	1958	1941	1958
0	$ 8.21	$ 6.39	$16.49	$13.23	$41.07	$39.29	$ 3.92	$ 1.73
5	8.28	7.03	16.18	14.17	39.44	38.93	2.25	1.43
10	9.36	8.05	17.69	15.73	39.40	39.01	2.36	1.60
15	10.77	9.29	19.60	17.52	39.59	39.16	2.81	1.85
20	12.49	10.75	21.76	19.48	39.87	39.28	3.46	2.13
25	14.60	12.55	24.23	21.68	40.30	39.44	4.47	2.63
30	17.22	14.80	27.04	24.23	40.96	39.78	5.99	3.58
35	20.50	17.67	30.30	27.24	41.98	40.44	8.28	5.27
40	24.65	21.38	34.14	30.84	43.54	41.62	11.73	8.06
45	29.98	26.16	38.78	35.15	45.95	43.54	16.85	12.38
50	36.90	32.38	44.58	40.50	49.67	46.61	24.33	18.96
55	46.01	40.57	52.16	47.39	55.42	51.49	35.01	28.53
60	58.18	51.50	62.49	56.66	64.30	59.10	49.78	41.72
65	74.65	66.21	77.12	69.54	77.92	70.76	69.47	59.57
70	97.20	85.94	98.22	87.62	98.48	88.09	94.92	82.34

H. The 1950 Uniform Individual Accident and Sickness Policy Provisions Law—N.A.I.C.

Section 1. DEFINITION OF ACCIDENT AND SICKNESS INSURANCE POLICY. The term "policy of accident and sickness insurance" as used herein includes any policy or contract covering the kind or kinds of insurance described in .... (*insert here the section of law authorizing accident and sickness insurance*).

(*Note: If the insurance law of the state in which this draft is proposed for enactment does not have a section specifically authorizing the various types of insurance which may be written, this section should be modified to define accident and sickness insurance as "insurance against loss resulting from sickness or from bodily injury or death by accident, or both."*)

Section 2. FORM OF POLICY.

(A) No policy of accident and sickness insurance shall be delivered or issued for delivery to any person in this state unless:

(1) the entire money and other considerations therefor are expressed therein; and

(2) the time at which the insurance takes effect and terminates is expressed therein; and

(3) it purports to insure only one person, except that a policy may insure, originally or by subsequent amendment, upon the application of an adult member of a family who shall be deemed the policyholder, any two or more eligible members of that family, including husband, wife, dependent children or any children under a specified age which shall not exceed nineteen years and any other person dependent upon the policyholder; and

(*Note: In states having community property systems derived from the civil law it is suggested that in the foregoing subparagraph the words "an adult member" be replaced with "the head."*)

(4) the style, arrangement and over-all appearance of the policy give no undue prominence to any portion of the text, and unless every printed portion of the text of the policy and of any endorsements or attached papers is plainly printed in light-faced type of a style in general use, the size of which shall be uniform and not less than ten-point with a lower-case unspaced alphabet length not less than one hundred and twenty-point (the "text" shall include all printed matter except the name and address of the insurer, name or title of the policy, the brief description if any, and captions and subcaptions); and

(5) the exceptions and reductions of indemnity are set forth in the

policy and, except those which are set forth in section 3 of this act, are printed, at the insurer's option, either included with the benefit provision to which they apply, or under an appropriate caption such as "EXCEPTIONS," or "EXCEPTIONS AND REDUCTIONS," provided that if an exception or reduction specifically applies only to a particular benefit of the policy, a statement of such exception or reduction shall be included with the benefit provision to which it applies; and

(6) each such form, including riders and endorsements, shall be identified by a form number in the lower left-hand corner of the first page thereof; and

(7) it contains no provision purporting to make any portion of the charter, rules, constitution, or by-laws of the insurer a part of the policy unless such portion is set forth in full in the policy, except in the case of the incorporation of, or reference to, a statement of rates or classification of risks, or short-rate table filed with the (*Commissioner*).

(B) If any policy is issued by an insurer domiciled in this state for delivery to a person residing in another state, and if the official having responsibility for the administration of the insurance laws of such other state shall have advised the (*Commissioner*) that any such policy is not subject to approval or disapproval by such official, the (*Commissioner*) may by ruling require that such policy meet the standards set forth in subsection (A) of this section and in section 3.

Section 3. ACCIDENT AND SICKNESS POLICY PROVISIONS.

(*A*) ***Required Provisions***

Except as provided in paragraph (C) of this section each such policy delivered or issued for delivery to any person in this state shall contain the provisions specified in this subsection in the words in which the same appear in this section; provided, however, that the insurer may, at its option, substitute for one or more of such provisions corresponding provisions of different wording approved by the (*Commissioner*) which are in each instance not less favorable in any respect to the insured or the beneficiary. Such provisions shall be preceded individually by the caption appearing in this subsection or, at the option of the insurer, by such appropriate individual or group captions or subcaptions as the (*Commissioner*) may approve.

(1) A provision as follows:

Entire Contract; Changes: This policy, including the endorsements and the attached papers, if any, constitutes the entire contract of insurance. No change in this policy shall be valid until approved by an executive officer of the insurer and unless such approval be endorsed hereon or attached hereto. No agent has authority to change this policy or to waive any of its provisions.

(*Note: When enacted in states which prohibit amendment of a policy form by means other than attached printed rider upon a separate piece of paper the new law should contain (but not as a required policy pro-*

vision) an added section defining "endorsement" in such a manner as to make the new law consistent with current statutes.)

(2) A provision as follows:

Time Limit on Certain Defenses: (a) After three years from the date of issue of this policy no misstatements, except fraudulent misstatements, made by the applicant in the application for such policy shall be used to void the policy or to deny a claim for loss incurred or disability (as defined in the policy) commencing after the expiration of such three year period.

(The foregoing policy provision shall not be so construed as to affect any legal requirement for avoidance of a policy or denial of a claim during such initial three year period, nor to limit the application of section 3 (B), (1), (2), (3), (4) and (5) in the event of misstatement with respect to age or occupation or other insurance.)

(A policy which the insured has the right to continue in force subject to its terms by the timely payment of premium (1) until at least age 50 or, (2) in the case of a policy issued after age 44, for at least five years from its date of issue, may contain in lieu of the foregoing the following provision (from which the clause in parentheses may be omitted at the insurer's option) under the caption "INCONTESTABLE":

After this policy has been in force for a period of three years during the lifetime of the insured (excluding any period during which the insured is disabled), it shall become incontestable as to the statements contained in the application.)

(b) No claim for loss incurred or disability (as defined in the policy) commencing after three years from the date of issue of this policy shall be reduced or denied on the ground that a disease or physical condition not excluded from coverage by name or specific description effective on the date of loss had existed prior to the effective date of coverage of this policy.

(3) A provision as follows:

Grace Period: A grace period of .... (*insert a number not less than "7" for weekly premium policies, "10" for monthly premium policies and "31" for all other policies*) days will be granted for the payment of each premium falling due after the first premium, during which grace period the policy shall continue in force.

(A policy which contains a cancellation provision may add, at the end of the above provision,

subject to the right of the insurer to cancel in accordance with the cancellation provision hereof.

A policy in which the insurer reserves the right to refuse any renewal shall have, at the beginning of the above provision,

Unless not less than five days prior to the premium due date the insurer has delivered to the insured or has mailed to his last address as shown by the records of the insurer written notice of its intention not to renew this policy beyond the period for which the premium has been accepted,).

(4) A provision as follows:

Reinstatement: If any renewal premium be not paid within the time granted the insured for payment, a subsequent acceptance of premium by the insurer or by any agent duly authorized by the insurer to accept such premium, without requiring in connection therewith an application for reinstatement, shall reinstate the policy; provided, however, that if the insurer or such agent requires an application for reinstatement and issues a conditional receipt for the premium tendered, the policy will be reinstated upon approval of such application by the insurer or, lacking such approval, upon the forty-fifth day following the date of such conditional receipt unless the insurer has previously notified the insured in writing of its disapproval of such application. The reinstated policy shall cover only loss resulting from such accidental injury as may be sustained after the date of reinstatement and loss due to such sickness as may begin more than ten days after such date. In all other respects the insured and insurer shall have the same rights thereunder as they had under the policy immediately before the due date of the defaulted premium, subject to any provisions endorsed hereon or attached hereto in connection with the reinstatement. Any premium accepted in connection with a reinstatement shall be applied to a period for which premium has not been previously paid, but not to any period more than sixty days prior to the date of reinstatement.

(The last sentence of the above provision may be omitted from any policy which the insured has the right to continue in force subject to its terms by the timely payment of premiums (1) until at least age 50 or, (2) in the case of a policy issued after age 44, for at least five years from its date of issue.)

(5) A provision as follows:

Notice of Claim: Written notice of claim must be given to the insurer within twenty days after the occurrence or commencement of any loss covered by the policy, or as soon thereafter as is reasonably possible. Notice given by or on behalf of the insured or the beneficiary to the insurer at .... (*insert the location of such office as the insurer may designate for the purpose*), or to any authorized agent of the insurer, with information sufficient to identify the insured, shall be deemed notice to the insurer.

(In a policy providing a loss-of-time benefit which may be payable for at least two years, an insurer may at its option insert the following between the first and second sentences of the above provision:

Subject to the qualifications set forth below, if the insured suffers loss of time on account of disability for which indemnity may be payable for at least two years, he shall, at least once in every six months after having given notice of claim, give to the insurer notice of continuance of said disability, except in the event of legal incapacity. The period of six months following any filing of proof by the insured or any payment by the insurer on account of such claim or any denial of liability in whole or in part by the insurer shall be excluded in applying this provision. Delay in the giving of such notice shall not impair the insured's right to any indemnity which would otherwise have accrued during the period of six months preceding the date on which such notice is actually given.)

(6) A provision as follows:

Claim Forms: The insurer, upon receipt of a notice of claim, will furnish to the claimant such forms as are usually furnished by it for filing proofs of loss. If such forms are not furnished within fifteen days after the giving of such notice the claimant shall be deemed to have complied with the requirements of this policy as to proof of loss upon submitting, within the time fixed in the policy for filing proofs of loss, written proof covering the occurrence, the character and the extent of the loss for which claim is made.

(7) A provision as follows:

Proofs of Loss: Written proof of loss must be furnished to the insurer at its said office in case of claim for loss for which this policy provides any periodic payment contingent upon continuing loss within ninety days after the termination of the period for which the insurer is liable and in case of claim for any other loss within ninety days after the date of such loss. Failure to furnish such proof within the time required shall not invalidate nor reduce any claim if it was not reasonably possible to give proof within such time, provided such proof is furnished as soon as reasonably possible and in no event, except in the absence of legal capacity, later than one year from the time proof is otherwise required.

(8) A provision as follows:

Time of Payment of Claims: Indemnities payable under this policy for any loss other than loss for which this policy provides any periodic payment will be paid immediately upon receipt of due written proof of such loss. Subject to due written proof of loss, all accrued indemnities for loss for which this policy provides periodic payment will be paid .... (*insert period for payment which must not be less frequently than monthly*) and any balance remaining unpaid upon the termination of liability will be paid immediately upon receipt of due written proof.

(9) A provision as follows:

Payment of Claims: Indemnity for loss of life will be payable in accordance with the beneficiary designation and the provisions respecting such payment which may be prescribed herein and effective at the time of payment. If no such designation or provision is then effective, such indemnity shall be payable to the estate of the insured. Any other accrued indemnities unpaid at the insured's death may, at the option of the insurer, be paid either to such beneficiary or to such estate. All other indemnities will be payable to the insured.

(The following provisions, or either of them, may be included with the foregoing provision at the option of the insurer:

If any indemnity of this policy shall be payable to the estate of the insured, or to an insured or beneficiary who is a minor or otherwise not competent to give a valid release, the insurer may pay such indemnity, up to an amount not exceeding $............ (*insert an amount which shall not exceed $1000*), to any relative by blood or connection by marriage of the insured or beneficiary who is deemed by the insurer to be equitably entitled thereto. Any payment made by the insurer in good faith pursuant to this provision shall fully discharge the insurer to the extent of such payment.

Subject to any written direction of the insured in the application or otherwise all or a portion of any indemnities provided by this policy on account of hospital, nursing, medical, or surgical services may, at the insurer's option and unless the insured requests otherwise in writing not later than the time of filing proofs of such loss, be paid directly to the hospital or person rendering such services; but it is not required that the service be rendered by a particular hospital or person.)

(10) A provision as follows:

Physical Examinations and Autopsy: The insurer at its own expense shall have the right and opportunity to examine the person of the insured when and as often as it may reasonably require during the pendency of a claim hereunder and to make an autopsy in case of death where it is not forbidden by law.

(11) A provision as follows:

Legal Actions: No action at law or in equity shall be brought to recover on this policy prior to the expiration of sixty days after written proof of loss has been furnished in accordance with the requirements of this policy. No such action shall be brought after the expiration of three years after the time written proof of loss is required to be furnished.

(12) A provision as follows:

Change of Beneficiary: Unless the insured makes an irrevocable designation of beneficiary, the right to change of beneficiary is reserved to the insured and the consent of the beneficiary or beneficiaries shall not be requisite to surrender or assignment of this policy or to any change of beneficiary or beneficiaries, or to any other changes in this policy.

(The first clause of this provision, relating to the irrevocable designation of beneficiary, may be omitted at the insurer's option.)

(*B*) *Other Provisions*

Except as provided in paragraph (C) of this section, no such policy delivered or issued for delivery to any person in this state shall contain provisions respecting the matters set forth below unless such provisions are in the words in which the same appear in this section; provided, however, that the insurer may, at its option, use in lieu of any such provision a corresponding provision of different wording approved by the (*Commissioner*) which is not less favorable in any respect to the insured or the beneficiary. Any such provision contained in the policy shall be preceded individually by the appropriate caption appearing in this subsection or, at the option of the insurer, by such appropriate individual or group captions or subcaptions as the (*Commissioner*) may approve.

(1) A provision as follows:

Change of Occupation: If the insured be injured or contract sickness after having changed his occupation to one classified by the insurer as more hazardous than that stated in this policy or while doing for compensation anything pertaining to an occupation so classified, the insurer will pay only such portion of the indemnities provided in this policy as the premium paid would have purchased at the rates and within the limits fixed by the insurer for such more hazardous occupation. If the insured changes his occupation to one classified by the insurer as less hazardous than that stated in this policy, the insurer, upon receipt of proof of such change of occupation, will reduce the premium rate accordingly, and will return the excess pro-rata unearned premium from the date of change of occupation or from the policy anniversary date immediately preceding receipt of such proof, whichever is the more recent. In applying this provision, the classification of occupational risk and the premium rates shall be such as have been last filed by the insurer prior to the occurrence of the loss for which the insurer is liable or prior to date of proof of change in occupation with the state official having supervision of insurance in the state where the insured resided at the time this policy was issued; but if such filing was not required, then the classification of occupational risk and the premium rates shall be those last made effective by the insurer in such state prior to the occurrence of the loss or prior to the date of proof of change in occupation.

(2) A provision as follows:

Misstatement of Age: If the age of the insured has been misstated, all amounts payable under this policy shall be such as the premium paid would have purchased at the correct age.

(3) A provision as follows:

Other Insurance in This Insurer: If an accident or sickness or accident and sickness policy or policies previously issued by the insurer to the insured be in force concurrently herewith, making the aggregate indemnity for .... (*insert type of coverage or coverages*) in excess of $................(*insert maximum limit of indemnity or indemnities*) the excess insurance shall be void and all premiums paid for such excess shall be returned to the insured or to his estate.

Or, in lieu thereof:

Insurance effective at any one time on the insured under a like policy or policies in this insurer is limited to the one such policy elected by the insured, his beneficiary or his estate, as the case may be, and the insurer will return all premiums paid for all other such policies.

(4) A provision as follows:

Insurance with Other Insurers: If there be other valid coverage, not with this insurer, providing benefits for the same loss on a provision of service basis or on an expense incurred basis and of which this insurer has not been given written notice prior to the occurrence or commencement of loss, the only liability under any expense incurred coverage of this policy shall be for such proportion of the loss as the amount which would otherwise have been payable hereunder plus the total of the like amounts under all such other valid coverages for the same loss of which this insurer had notice bears to the total like amounts under all valid coverages for such loss, and for the return of such portion of the premiums paid as shall exceed the pro-rata portion for the amount so determined. For the purpose of applying this provision when other coverage is on a provision of service basis, the "like amount" of such other coverage shall be taken as the amount which the services rendered would have cost in the absence of such coverage.

(If the foregoing policy provision is included in a policy which also contains the next following policy provision there shall be added to the caption of the foregoing provision the phrase "—EXPENSE INCURRED BENEFITS." The insurer may, at its option, include in this provision a definition of "other valid coverage," approved as to form by the (*Commissioner*), which definition shall be limited in subject matter to coverage provided by organizations subject to regulation by insurance law or by insurance authorities of this or any other state of the United States or any province of Canada, and by hospital or medical service organizations, and to any other coverage the inclusion of which may be approved by the (*Commissioner*). In the absence of such definition such term shall not include group insurance, automobile medical payments insurance, or coverage provided by hospital or medical service organizations or by union welfare plans or employer or employee benefit organizations. For the purpose of applying the foregoing policy provision with respect to any insured, any amount of benefit provided for such insured pursuant to any compulsory benefit statute (including any workmen's compensation or employer's liability statute) whether provided by a governmental agency or otherwise shall in all cases be deemed to be "other valid coverage" of which the insurer has had notice. In applying the foregoing policy provision no third party liability coverage shall be included as "other valid coverage.")

(5) A provision as follows:

Insurance with Other Insurers: If there be other valid coverage, not with this insurer, providing benefits for the same loss on other than an expense incurred basis and of which this insurer has not been given written notice prior to the occurrence or commencement of loss, the only liability for such benefits under this policy shall be for such proportion of the indemnities otherwise provided hereunder for such loss as the like indemnities of which the insurer had notice (including the indemnities under this policy) bear to the total amount of all like indemnities for such loss, and for the return of such portion of the premium paid as shall exceed the pro-rata portion for the indemnities thus determined.

(If the foregoing policy provision is included in a policy which also contains the next preceding policy provision there shall be added to the caption of the foregoing provision the phrase "—OTHER BENEFITS." The insurer may, at its option, include in this provision a definition of "other valid coverage," approved as to form by the (*Commissioner*), which definition shall be limited in subject matter to coverage provided by organizations subject to regulation by insurance law or by insurance authorities of this or any other state of the United States or any province of Canada, and to any other coverage the inclusion of which may be approved by the (*Commissioner*). In the absence of such definition such term shall not include group insurance, or benefits provided by union welfare plans or by employer or employee benefit organizations. For the purpose of applying the foregoing policy provision with respect to any insured, any amount of benefit provided for such insured pursuant to any compulsory benefit statute (including any workmen's compensation or employer's liability statute) whether provided by a governmental agency or otherwise shall in all cases be deemed to be "other valid coverage" of which the insurer has had notice. In applying the foregoing policy provision no third party liability coverage shall be included as "other valid coverage.")

(6) A provision as follows:

Relation of Earnings to Insurance: If the total monthly amount of loss of time benefits promised for the same loss under all valid loss of time coverage upon the insured, whether payable on a weekly or monthly basis, shall exceed the monthly earnings of the insured at the time disability commenced or his average monthly earnings for the period of two years immediately preceding a disability for which claim is made, whichever is the greater, the insurer will be liable only for such proportionate amount of such benefits under this policy as the amount of such monthly earnings or such average monthly earnings of the insured bears to the total amount of monthly benefits for the same loss under all such coverage upon the insured at the time such disability commences and for the return of such part of the premiums paid during such two years as shall exceed the pro-rata amount of the premiums for the benefits actually paid hereunder; but this shall not operate to reduce the total monthly amount of benefits payable under all such coverage upon the insured below the sum of two hundred dollars or the sum of the monthly benefits specified in such coverages, whichever is the lesser, nor shall it operate to reduce benefits other than those payable for loss of time.

(The foregoing policy provision may be inserted only in a policy which the insured has the right to continue in force subject to its terms by the timely payment of premiums (1) until at least age 50 or, (2) in the case of a policy issued after age 44, for at least five years from its date of issue. The insurer may, at its option, include in this provision a definition of "valid loss of time coverage," approved as to form by the (*Commissioner*), which definition shall be limited in subject matter to coverage provided by governmental agencies or by organizations subject to regulation by insurance law or by insurance authorities of this or any other state of the United States or any province of Canada, or to any other coverage the inclusion of which may be approved by the (*Commissioner*) or any combination of such coverages. In the absence of such definition such term shall not include any coverage provided for such insured pursuant to any compulsory benefit statute (including any workmen's compensation or employer's liability statute), or benefits provided by union welfare plans or by employer or employee benefit organizations.)

(7) A provision as follows:

Unpaid Premium: Upon the payment of a claim under this policy, any premium then due and unpaid or covered by any note or written order may be deducted therefrom.

(8) A provision as follows:

Cancellation: The insurer may cancel this policy at any time by written notice delivered to the insured, or mailed to his last address as shown by the records of the insurer, stating when, not less than five days thereafter, such cancellation shall be effective; and after the policy has been continued beyond its original term the insured may cancel this policy at any time by written notice delivered or mailed to the insurer, effective upon receipt or on such later date as may be specified in such notice. In the event of cancellation, the insurer will return promptly the unearned portion of any premium paid. If the insured cancels, the earned premium shall be computed by the use of the short-rate table last filed with the state official having supervision of insurance in the state where the insured resided when the policy was issued. If the insurer cancels, the earned premium shall be computed pro-rata. Cancellation shall be without prejudice to any claim originating prior to the effective date of cancellation.

(*Note: In some states by statute termination of the in force status of the policy alone may not prejudice any claim for loss arising during and out of a disability which commenced while the policy was in force. The language here is susceptible of an interpretation consistent with such statutes.*)

(9) A provision as follows:

Conformity with State Statutes: Any provision of this policy which, on its effective date, is in conflict with the statutes of the state in which the insured resides on such date is hereby amended to conform to the minimum requirements of such statutes.

(10) A provision as follows:

Illegal Occupation: The insurer shall not be liable for any loss to which a contributing cause was the insured's commission of or attempt to commit a felony or to which a contributing cause was the insured's being engaged in an illegal occupation.

(11) A provision as follows:

Intoxicants and Narcotics: The insurer shall not be liable for any loss sustained or contracted in consequence of the insured's being intoxicated or under the influence of any narcotic unless administered on the advice of a physician.

(*Note: Paragraphs* (10) *and* (11) *are suggested for states which desire such provisions.*)

(*C*) *Inapplicable or Inconsistent Provisions*

If any provision of this section is in whole or in part inapplicable to or inconsistent with the coverage provided by a particular form of policy the insurer, with the approval of the (*Commissioner*), shall omit from such policy any inapplicable provision or part of a provision, and shall modify any inconsistent provision or part of the provision in such manner as to make the provision as contained in the policy consistent with the coverage provided by the policy.

(*D*) *Order of Certain Policy Provisions*

The provisions which are the subject of subsections (A) and (B) of this section, or any corresponding provisions which are used in lieu thereof in accordance with such subsections, shall be printed in the consecutive order of the provisions in such subsections or, at the option of the insurer, any such provision may appear as a unit in any part of the policy, with other provisions to which it may be logically related, provided the resulting policy shall not be in whole or in part unintelligible, uncertain, ambiguous, abstruse, or likely to mislead a person to whom the policy is offered, delivered or issued.

(*E*) *Third Party Ownership*

The word "insured," as used in this act, shall not be construed as preventing a person other than the insured with a proper insurable interest from making application for and owning a policy covering the insured or from being entitled under such a policy to any indemnities, benefits and rights provided therein.

(*F*) *Requirements of Other Jurisdictions*

(1) Any policy of a foreign or alien insurer, when delivered or issued for delivery to any person in this state, may contain any provision which is not less favorable to the insured or the beneficiary than the provisions of this act and which is prescribed or required by the law of the state under which the insurer is organized.

(2) Any policy of a domestic insurer may, when issued for delivery in any other state or country, contain any provision permitted or required by the laws of such other state or country.

(*G*) *Filing Procedure*

The (*Commissioner*) may make such reasonable rules and regulations concerning the procedure for the filing or submission of policies subject to this act as are necessary, proper or advisable to the administration of this act. This provision shall not abridge any other authority granted the (*Commissioner*) by law.

Section 4. CONFORMING TO STATUTE.

(*A*) *Other Policy Provisions*

No policy provision which is not subject to section 3 of this act shall make a policy, or any portion thereof, less favorable in any respect to the insured or the beneficiary than the provisions thereof which are subject to this act.

(B) Policy Conflicting with This Act

A policy delivered or issued for delivery to any person in this state in violation of this act shall be held valid but shall be construed as provided in this act. When any provision in a policy subject to this act is in conflict with any provision of this act, the rights, duties and obligations of the insurer, the insured and the beneficiary shall be governed by the provisions of this act.

Section 5. APPLICATION.

(A) The insured shall not be bound by any statement made in an application for a policy unless a copy of such application is attached to or endorsed on the policy when issued as a part thereof. If any such policy delivered or issued for delivery to any person in this state shall be reinstated or renewed, and the insured or the beneficiary or assignee of such policy shall make written request to the insurer for a copy of the application, if any, for such reinstatement or renewal, the insurer shall within fifteen days after the receipt of such request at its home office or any branch office of the insurer, deliver or mail to the person making such request, a copy of such application. If such copy shall not be so delivered or mailed, the insurer shall be precluded from introducing such application as evidence in any action or proceeding based upon or involving such policy or its reinstatement or renewal.

(B) No alteration of any written application for any such policy shall be made by any person other than the applicant without his written consent, except that insertions may be made by the insurer, for administrative purposes only, in such manner as to indicate clearly that such insertions are not to be ascribed to the applicant.

(C) The falsity of any statement in the application for any policy covered by this act may not bar the right to recovery thereunder unless such false statement materially affected either the acceptance of the risk or the hazard assumed by the insurer.

(Note: Section 5, or any subsection thereof, is suggested for use in states which have no comparable statutes relating to the application.)

Section 6. NOTICE, WAIVER.

The acknowledgment by any insurer of the receipt of notice given under any policy covered by this act, or the furnishing of forms for filing proofs of loss, or the acceptance of such proofs, or the investigation of any claim thereunder still not operate as a waiver of any of the rights of the insurer in defense of any claim arising under such policy.

Section 7. AGE LIMIT.

If any such policy contains a provision establishing, as an age limit or otherwise, a date after which the coverage provided by the policy will not be effective, and if such date falls within a period for which premium is accepted by the insurer or if the insurer accepts a premium after such date, the coverage provided by the policy will continue in force subject to any right of cancellation until the end of the period for which premium has been accepted. In the event the age of the insured has been misstated and if, according to the correct age of the insured, the coverage provided by the policy would not have become effective, or would have ceased prior to the acceptance of such premium or premiums, then the liability of the insurer shall be limited to the refund, upon request, of all premiums paid for the period not covered by the policy.

Section 8. NON-APPLICATION TO CERTAIN POLICIES.

Nothing in this act shall apply to or affect (1) any policy of workmen's compensation insurance or any policy of liability insurance with or without supplementary expense coverage therein; or (2) any policy or contract of reinsurance; or (3) any blanket or group policy of insurance; or (4) life insurance, endowment or annuity contracts, or contracts supplemental thereto which contain only such provisions relating to accident and sickness insurance as (a) provide additional benefits in case of death or dismemberment or loss of sight by accident, or as (b) operate to safeguard such contracts against lapse, or to give a special surrender value or special benefit or an annuity in the event that the insured or annuitant shall become totally and permanently disabled, as defined by the contract or supplemental contract.

(*Note: This provision may, if desired, be modified in individual states so as to be consistent with current statutes of such states.*)

Section 9. VIOLATION.

Any person, partnership or corporation willfully violating any provision of this act or order of the (*Commissioner*) made in accordance with this act, shall forfeit to the people of the state a sum not to exceed $........... for each such violation, which may be recovered by a civil action. The (*Commissioner*) may also suspend or revoke the license of an insurer or agent for any such willful violation.

(*Note: This provision is to be used only in those states which do not have similar legislation now in effect.*)

Section 10. JUDICIAL REVIEW.

Any order or decision of the (*Commissioner*) under this act shall be subject to review by appeal (writ of certiorari) to the .... Court at the instance of any party in interest. The filing of the appeal (petition for such writ) shall operate as a state of any such order or decision until the Court directs otherwise. The Court may review all the facts and, in disposing of the issue before it, may modify, affirm or reverse the order or decision of the (*Commissioner*) in whole or in part.

(*Note: This provision is to be used only in those states which do not have similar legislation now in effect.*)

Section 11. REPEAL OF INCONSISTENT ACTS.

(*Note: This section should contain suitable language to repeal acts or parts of acts presently enacted and inconsistent with this act. The repealing section should contain an appropriate exception with regard to section 12 of this act.)*

Section 12. Effective Date of Act.

This act shall take effect on the .... day of ...., 19..... A policy, rider or endorsement, which could have been lawfully used or delivered or issued for delivery to any person in this state immediately before the effective date of this act may be used or delivered or issued for delivery to any such person during five years after the effective date of this act without being subject to the provisions of sections 2, 3, or 4 of this act.

I. Seventh Status Report on Overinsurance for the Subcommittee on Overinsurance of the Accident and Health Committee, National Association of Insurance Commissioners, November 22, 1963

I. INTRODUCTORY

In December 1959, the National Association of Insurance Commissioners requested that the Health Insurance Association of America undertake a study of overinsurance. In response to such request, HIAA has heretofore submitted a series of six "Status Reports on Overinsurance" to the NAIC.

The first, submitted on May 13, 1960, described the nature of the overinsurance problem and provided the findings resulting from an overinsurance survey conducted by the Health Insurance Council. *Proceedings of the National Association of Insurance Commissioners,* 1960, Vol. 11, pp. 549–64.

The second, submitted on November 23, 1960, contained a summary of court decisions permitting multiple recovery of hospital or medical expenses, some recommended principles for a new "Relation of Earnings to Insurance" provision, and a draft provision to implement such principles. *Proceedings of the National Association of Insurance Commissioners,* 1961, Vol. 1, pp. 331–38.

The third, submitted on November 22, 1961, enumerated the limitations of underwriting control of overinsurance, described the deficiencies of the "Insurance With Other Insurers" provisions, and offered the text of a new provision designed to overcome such deficiencies. *Proceedings of the National Association of Insurance Commissioners,* 1962, Vol. 1, pp. 90–96.

The fourth, submitted on June 8, 1962, provided the text of a proposed revision of the overinsurance portions of the Uniform Individual Accident and Sickness Policy Provisions Law, described in relationship between such revision and the principles contained in earlier status reports, and offered a series of illustrative hypothetical claims to show the manner in which the proposed revision would be administered. *Proceedings of the National Association of Insurance Commissioners,* 1962, Vol. 11, pp. 370–87.

The fifth, submitted on October 19, 1962 offered the views of HIAA on two questions (overinsurance criteria and premium refunds) which arose during the June 1962 NAIC meeting, as well as additional illustrative hypothetical claims. *Proceedings of the National Association of Insurance Commissioners,* 1963, Vol. 1, pp. 85–94.

The sixth, submitted on May 31, 1963, offered additional recommendations for amendments of the overinsurance provisions of the Uniform Individual Accident and Sickness Policy Provisions Law. It also provided a compilation of evidence that overinsurance is a sufficiently serious problem to justify the remedial legislation, such compilation having been requested by the NAIC at its December 1962 meetings. *Proceedings of the National Association of Insurance Commissioners,* 1963, Vol. 11.

II. RECOMMENDATIONS FOR REMEDIAL LEGISLATION

Exhibit A of this Report contains our revised recommendations for amendment of the overinsurance provisions of the Uniform Individual Accident and Sickness Policy Provisions Law. It reflects the areas of agreement reached at the July 30 and October 16 conferences between the NAIC Subcommittee on Overinsurance and an HIAA representative. It therefore differs from the amendments offered in Exhibit A of the Sixth Status Report in that the definition of "allowable expense" has been amended by the addition of "110% of" in line 57, and the reference to a pro rata return of premium has been deleted. The Instructions for Section 2 have been modified by the addition of a sentence contained in the Instructions for Section 4 but heretofore omitted by oversight from the Instructions for Section 2: "The Insurer may require, as part of the proof of claim, the information necessary to administer this provision." The Instructions for Section 2 have also been modified, as requested by the NAIC Subcommittee on Overinsurance, in three other ways:

1. The words "guaranteed renewable and noncancellable as well as guaranteed renewable" have been added in parentheses in lines 86–87 to indicate that each enacting state is to make its own decision as to the availability of Section 2 for use in policies renewable at the option of the insurer.
2. The words "except for individual policies individually underwritten" have been added to lines 90–91 as requested by the NAIC Subcommittee.
3. The words "but an insurer may at its option include a subrogation clause in its policy" have been placed in parentheses in lines 104–5 to indicate that each enacting state is to make its own decision as to whether subrogation provisions are to be permitted.

HIAA acceptance of the above modification of the definition of "allowable expense" should not be construed as a lack of continued concern regarding the objections discussed earlier. Such acceptance simply means that a majority of the industry is of the opinion that the need for effective overinsurance provisions is so immediate that acquiescence in the NAIC Subcommittee's support of such modified definition is necessary in order to have a bill for the 1964 session of the several state legislatures.

Similarly, although the attached revision of Exhibit A complies with the

NAIC Subcommittee's request to make the availability of Section 2 in contracts renewable at the option of the insurer an issue to be determined by each enacting state, it is urged that the parenthetical expression be deleted from lines 86–87 so as not to encourage refusals to renew. By reason of policies with special limitations upon the insurer's right to refuse renewal, as for example those policies the renewal of which will not be refused by reason of deterioration of health, it is no longer easy to classify all policies as noncancellable, guaranteed renewable or renewable at the option of the insurer. Even within the last named type of policy, health insurers have for many years voluntarily sought to limit refusals to renew by constricting the occasions for the exercise of such reserved right. The Subcommittee is therefore urged to reconsider its position on this point.

III. RECOMMENDATION FOR IMPLEMENTING REGULATION

At the October 16 meeting of the NAIC Subcommittee on Overinsurance, the HIAA representative was directed to submit a further modification of the Sixth Status Report which, if adopted, would require insurers electing to use either the new hospital-medical-surgical or the new loss-of-time overinsurance provision to place in the application and on the face of the policy a brief statement to the effect that the benefits of the policy could be reduced by reason of the overinsurance provision contained therein. Exhibit B of this report is offered to comply with such request. It is cast in the form of a recommended regulation for promulgation simultaneously with the enactment of Exhibit A in any particular state. It is believed that Exhibit A is responsive to the October 16 request of the NAIC Subcommittee.

The requirement contained in Exhibit B will be effective if it is confined, at the insurer's option, to the application or the policy, and need not extend to both. Many insurers use one application for several policies some of which will, and some of which will not, contain an overinsurance provision. To require the statement in the application, and thus a special application for each policy containing the overinsurance provision, would be an additional and unnecessary expense for insurers which use a statement in the policy itself as well as a "ten-day free look" provision.

Other insurers can satisfy the requirement with equal efficacy by a statement in the application rather than in the policy.

We urge that either form of compliance be permitted as indicated in Exhibit B.

Respectfully submitted,
S/d *John Hanna*
John P. Hanna
General Counsel

EXHIBIT A

Proposed Revision of Sections 3(B)(3), 3(B)(4) 3(B)(5) and 3(B)(6) of the Uniform Individual Accident and Sickness Policy Provisions Law

Section 1. (Insert reference to statutory section which contains Section 3(B)(3) of the Uniform Individual Accident and Sickness Policy Provisions Law) is amended as follows:

[OTHER INSURANCE IN THIS INSURER] *OVERINSURANCE:* If an accident or sickness or accident and sickness policy or policies previously issued by the insurer to the insured be in force concurrently herewith, making the aggregate indemnity for .... (insert type of coverage or coverages) in excess of $............ (insert maximum limit of indemnity or indemnities) the excess shall be void and all premiums paid for such excess shall be returned to the insured or to his estate.

or, in lieu thereof:

Insurance effective at any one time on the insured under *this policy* and a like policy or policies in this insurer is limited to the one [such] policy elected by the insured, his beneficiary or his estate, as the case may be, and the insurer will return all premiums paid for all other such policies.

Section 2. (Insert reference to statutory section which contains Section 3(B)(4) of the Uniform Individual Accident and Sickness Policy Provisions Law), is hereby repealed and the following is enacted in lieu thereof.

OVERINSURANCE: If, with respect to a person covered under this policy, benefits for allowable expense incurred during a claim determination period under this policy together with benefits for allowable expense during such period under all other valid coverage (without giving effect to this provision or to any "overinsurance provision" applying to such other valid coverage), exceed the total of such person's allowable expense during such period, this insurer shall be liable only for such proportionate amount of the benefits for allowable expense under this policy during such period as

(*i*) the total allowable expense during such period

bears to

(*ii*) the total amount of benefits payable during such period for such expense under this policy and all other valid coverage (without giving effect to this provision or to any "overinsurance provision" applying to such other valid coverage)

less in both (i) and (ii) any amount of benefits for allowable expense payable under other valid coverage which does not contain an "overinsurance provision." In no event shall this provision operate to increase the amount of benefits for allowable expense payable under this policy with respect to a person covered under this policy above the amount which would have been paid in the absence of this provision. This insurer may pay benefits to any insurer providing other valid coverage in the event of overpayment by such insurer. Any such payment shall discharge the liability of this insurer as fully as if the payment had been made directly to the insured, his assignee or his beneficiary. In the event that this insurer pays benefits to the insured, his assignee or his beneficiary, in excess of the amount which would have been payable if the existence of other valid coverage had been disclosed, this insurer shall have a right of action against the insured, his assignee or his beneficiary, to recover the amount which would not have been paid had there been a disclosure of the existence of the other valid coverage. The amount of other valid coverage which is on a provision of service basis shall be computed as the amount the services rendered would have cost in the absence of such coverage.

For purposes of this provision:

(*i*) "allowable expense" means 110% of any necessary, reasonable and customary item of expense which is covered, in whole or in part, as a hospital, surgical, medical or major medical expense under this policy or under any other valid coverage.

(*ii*) "claim determination period" with respect to any covered person means the initial period of . . . . (insert period of not less than thirty days) and each successive period of a like number of days, during which allowable expense covered under this policy is incurred on account of such person. The first such period begins on the date when the first such expense is incurred, and successive periods shall begin when such expense is incurred after expiration of a prior period.

or, in lieu thereof:

"claim determination period" with respect to any covered person means each . . . . (insert calendar or policy period of not less than a month) during which allowable expense covered under this policy is incurred on account of such person,

(*iii*) "overinsurance provision" means this provision and any other provision which may reduce an insurer's liability because of the existence of benefits under other valid coverage.

INSTRUCTIONS

The foregoing policy provision may be inserted in all (guaranteed renewable and non-cancellable as well as guaranteed renewable) policies providing hospital, surgical, medical or major medical benefits. The insurer may make this provision applicable to either or both (a) other valid coverage with other insurers and (b), except for individual policies individually underwritten, other valid coverage with the same insurer. The insurer shall include in this provision a definition of "other valid coverage" approved as to form by the (commissioner). Such term may include hospital, surgical, medical or major medical benefits provided by group, blanket or franchise coverage, individual and family-type coverage, Blue Cross-Blue Shield coverage and other prepayment plans, group practice and individual practice plans, uninsured benefits provided by labor-management trusteed plans, or union welfare plans, or by employer or employee benefit organizations, benefits provided under governmental programs, workmen's compensation insurance or any coverage required or provided by any other statute, and medical payments under automobile liability and personal liability policies. Other valid coverage shall not include payments made under third party liability coverage as a result of a determination of negligence (, but an insurer may at its option include a subrogation clause in its policy). The insurer may require, as part of the proof of claim, the information necessary to administer this provision.

Section 3. (Insert reference to statutory section which contains Section 3(B)(5) of the Uniform Individual Accident and Sickness Policy Provisions Law) is hereby repealed.

Section 4. (Insert reference to statutory section which contains

Section 3(B)(6) of the Uniform Individual Accident and Sickness Policy Provisions Law) is hereby repealed and the following is enacted in lieu thereof: OVERINSURANCE: After the loss-of-time benefit of this policy has been payable for 90 days, such benefit will be adjusted, as provided below, if the total amount of unadjusted loss-of-time benefits provided in all valid loss-of-time coverage upon the insured should exceed. . . . % of the insured's earned income; provided, however, that if the information contained in the application discloses that the total amount of loss-of-time benefits under this policy and under all other valid loss-of-time coverage expected to be effective upon the insured in accordance with the application for this policy exceeded . . . % of the insured's earned income at the time of such application, such higher percentage will be used in place of . . . %. Such adjusted loss-of-time benefit under this policy for any month shall be only such proportion of the loss-of-time benefit otherwise payable under this policy as

(*i*) the product of the insured's earned income and. . . . % (or, if higher, the alternative percentage described at the end of the first sentence of this provision)

bears to

(*ii*) the total amount of loss-of-time benefits payable for such month under this policy and all other valid loss-of-time coverage on the insured (without giving effect to the "overinsurance provision" in this or any other coverage)

less in both (i) and (ii) any amount of loss-of-time benefits payable under other valid loss-of-time coverage which does not contain an "overinsurance provision." In making such computation, all benefits and earnings shall be converted to a consistent (insert "weekly" if the loss-of-time benefit of this policy is payable weekly, "monthly" if such benefit is payable monthly, etc.) basis. If the numerator of the foregoing ratio is zero or is negative, no benefit shall be payable under this policy. In no event shall this provision (i) operate to reduce the total combined amount of loss-of-time benefits for such month payable under this policy and all other valid loss-of-time coverage below the lesser of $300 and the total combined amount of loss-of-time benefits determined without giving effect to any "overinsurance provision," nor (ii) operate to increase the amount of benefits payable under this policy above the amount which would have been paid in the absence of this provision, nor (iii) take into account or operate to reduce any benefit other than the loss-of-time benefit.

For purposes of this provision:

(*i*) "earned income," except where otherwise specified, means the greater of the monthly earnings of the insured at the time disability commences and his average monthly earnings for a period of two years immediately preceding the commencement of such disability, and shall not include any investment income or any other income not derived from the insured's vocational activities.

(*ii*) "overinsurance provision" shall include this provision and any other provision with respect to any loss-of-time coverage which may have the effect of reducing an insurer's liability if the total amount of loss-of-time benefits under all coverage exceeds a stated relationship to the insured's earnings.

INSTRUCTIONS. The foregoing provision may be included only in a policy which provides a loss-of-time benefit which may be payable for at least 52 weeks, which is issued on the basis of selective underwriting of each individual application, and for which the application includes a question designed to elicit information necessary either to determine the ratio of the total loss-of-time benefits of the insured to the insured's earned income or to determine that such ratio does not exceed the percentage of earnings, not less than 60%, selected by the insurer and inserted in lieu of the blank factor above. The insurer may require, as part of the proof of claim, the information necessary to administer this provision. If the application indicates that other loss-of-time coverage is to be discontinued, the amount of such other coverage shall be excluded in computing the alternative percentage in the first sentence of the overinsurance provision. The policy shall include a definition of "valid loss-of-time coverage," approved as to form by the (commissioner), which definition may include coverage provided by governmental agencies and by organizations subject to regulation by insurance law and by insurance authorities of this or any other state of the United States or of any other country or subdivision thereof, coverage provided for such insured pursuant to any disability benefits statute or any workmen's compensation or employer's liability statute, benefits provided by labor-management trusteed plans or union welfare plans or by employer or employee benefit organizations, or by salary continuance or pension programs, and any other coverage the inclusion of which may be approved by the (commissioner).

Section 5. This Act shall take effect on the .... day of ...., 19...... A policy, rider or endorsement which could have been lawfully used or delivered or issued for delivery to any person in this state immediately before the effective date of this Act may be used or delivered or issued for delivery to any such person during five years after the effective date of this Act.

EXHIBIT B

Proposed Regulation Re Overinsurance Provisions

Each individual health insurance policy, issued in this State on or after (insert the effective date contained in Section 5 of Exhibit A), which contains the overinsurance provisions authorized in (insert reference to statutory section which contains Section 3(B)(4) of the Uniform Individual Accident and Sickness Policy Provisions Law) or (insert reference to statutory section which contains Section 3(B)(6) of the Uniform Individual Accident and Sickness Policy Provisions Law) as amended by (insert session laws citation to Exhibit A) or, at the option of the insurer, the application for such policy, shall contain, or have attached to or be stamped or endorsed to add, a statement to the effect that benefits under the policy are subject to reduction if the insured has benefits under any other coverage of the type described in the overinsurance provision causing overinsurance as defined in such provision. If the insurer elects to include such statement in the policy, rather than in the application, the policy shall also contain, or have attached to or be stamped or endorsed to add, an additional statement to the effect that during a period of ten days from the date the policy is delivered to the policyholder, it may be surrendered to the insurer together with a written request for cancellation of the policy and in such event the insurer will refund any premium paid therefor including any policy fees or other charges.

J. National Association of Insurance Commissioners Model Group Life Insurance Bill

GROUP LIFE INSURANCE DEFINITION

I. No policy of group life insurance shall be delivered in this state unless it conforms to one of the following descriptions:

(1) A policy issued to an employer, or to the trustees of a fund established by an employer, which employer or trustees shall be deemed the policyholder, to insure employees of the employer for the benefit of persons other than the employer, subject to the following requirements:

(a) The employees eligible for insurance under the policy shall be all of the employees of the employer, or all of any class or classes thereof determined by conditions pertaining to their employment. The policy may provide that the term "employees" shall include the employees of one or more subsidiary corporations, and the employees, individual proprietors, and partners of one or more affiliated corporations, proprietors or partnerships if the business of the employer and of such affiliated corporations, proprietors or partnerships is under common control through stock ownership or contract. The policy may provide that the term "employees" shall include the individual proprietor or partners if the employer is an individual proprietor or a partnership. The policy may provide that the term "employees" shall include retired employees. No director of a corporate employer shall be eligible for insurance under the policy unless such person is otherwise eligible as a bona fide employee of the corporation by performing services other than the usual duties of a director. No individual proprietor or partner shall be eligible for insurance under the policy unless he is actively engaged in and devotes a substantial part of his time to the conduct of the business of the proprietor or partnership.

(b) The premium for the policy shall be paid by the policyholder, either wholly from the employer's funds or funds contributed by him, or partly from such funds and partly from funds contributed by the insured employees. No policy may be issued on which the entire premium is to be derived from funds contributed by the insured employees. A policy on which part of the premium is to be derived from funds contributed by the insured employees may be placed in force only if at least 75% of the then eligible employees, excluding any as to whom evidence of individual insurability is not satisfactory to the insurer, elect to make the required contributions. A policy on which no part of the premium is to be derived from funds contributed by the insured employees must insure all eligible employees, or all except any as to whom evidence of individual insurability is not satisfactory to the insurer.

(c) The policy must cover at least 10 employees at date of issue.

(d) The amounts of insurance under the policy must be based upon some plan precluding individual selection either by the employees or by the employer or trustees.

(2) A policy issued to a creditor, who shall be deemed the policyholder, to insure debtors of the creditor, subject to the following requirements:

(a) The debtors eligible for insurance under the policy shall be all of the debtors of the creditor whose indebtedness is repayable either (i) in installments or (ii) in one sum at the end of a period not in excess of eighteen months from the initial date of debt, or all of any class or classes thereof determined by conditions pertaining to the indebtedness or to the purchase giving rise to the indebtedness. The policy may provide that the term "debtors" shall include the debtors of one or more subsidiary corporations, and the debtors of one or more affiliated corporations, proprietors or partnerships if the business of the policyholder and of such affiliated corporations, proprietors or partnerships is under common control through stock ownership, contract or otherwise. No debtor shall be eligible unless the indebtedness constitutes an irrevocable obligation to repay which is binding upon him during his lifetime, at and from the date the insurance becomes effective upon his life.

(b) The premium for the policy shall be paid by the policyholder, either from the creditor's funds, or from charges collected from the insured debtors, or from both. A policy on which part or all of the premium is to be derived from the collection from the insured debtors of identifiable charges not required of uninsured debtors shall not include, in the class or classes of debtors eligible for insurance, debtors under obligations outstanding at its date of issue without evidence of individual insurability unless at least 75% of the then eligible debtors elect to pay the required charges. A policy on which no part of the premium is to be derived from the collection of such identifiable charges must insure all eligible debtors, or all except any as to whom evidence of individual insurability is not satisfactory to the insurer.

(c) The policy may be issued only if the group of eligible debtors is then receiving new entrants at the rate of at least 100 persons yearly, or may reasonably be expected to receive at least 100 new entrants during the first policy year, and only if the policy reserves to the insurer the right to require evidence of individual insurability if less than 75% of the new entrants become insured. The policy may exclude from the classes eligible for insurance classes of debtors determined by age.

(d) The amount of insurance on the life of any debtor shall at no time exceed the amount owed by him which is repayable in installments to the creditor, or $10,000., whichever is less. Where the indebtedness is repayable in one sum to the creditor, the insurance on the life of any debtor shall in no instance be in effect for a period in excess of eighteen months except that such insurance may be continued for an additional period not exceeding six months in the case of default, extension or recasting of the loan. The amount of the insurance on the life of any debtor shall at no time exceed the amount of the unpaid indebtedness, or $10,000., whichever is less.

(e) The insurance shall be payable to the policyholder. Such payment shall reduce or extinguish the unpaid indebtedness of the debtor to the extent of such payment."

(3) A policy issued to a labor union, which shall be deemed the policyholder, to insure members of such union for the benefit of persons other than the union or any of its officials, representatives or agents, subject to the following requirements:

(a) The members eligible for insurance under the policy shall be all of the members of the union, or all of any class or classes thereof determined by conditions pertaining to their employment, or to membership in the union, or both.

(b) The premium for the policy shall be paid by the policyholder, either wholly from the union's funds, or partly from such funds and partly from funds contributed by the insured members specifically for their insurance. No policy may be issued on which the entire premium is to be derived from funds contributed by the insured members specifically for their insurance. A policy on which part of the premium is to be derived from funds contributed by the insured members specifically for their insurance may be placed in force only if at least 75% of the then eligible members, excluding any as to whom evidence of individual insurability is not satisfactory to the insurer, elect to make the required contributions. A policy on which no part of the premium is to be derived from funds contributed by the insured members specifically for their insurance must insure all eligible members, or all except any as to whom evidence of individual insurability is not satisfactory to the insurer.

(c) The policy must cover at least 25 members at date of issue.

(d) The amounts of insurance under the policy must be based upon some plan precluding individual selection either by the members or by the union.

(4) A policy issued to the trustees of a fund established by two or more employers in the same industry or by one or more labor unions, or by one or more employers and one or more labor unions,

which trustees shall be deemed the policyholder, to insure employees of the employers or members of the unions for the benefit of persons other than the employers or the unions, subject to the following requirements:

(a) The persons eligible for insurance shall be all of the employees of the employers or all of the members of the unions, or all of any class or classes thereof determined by conditions pertaining to their employment, or to membership in the unions, or to both. The policy may provide that the term "employees" shall include retired employees, and the individual proprietor or partners if an employer is an individual proprietor or a partnership. No director of a corporate employer shall be eligible for insurance under the policy unless such person is otherwise eligible as a bona fide employee of the corporation by performing services other than the usual duties of a director. No individual proprietor or partner shall be eligible for insurance under the policy unless he is actively engaged in and devotes a substantial part of his time to the conduct of the business of the proprietor or partnership. The policy may provide that the term "employees" shall include the trustees or their employees, or both, if their duties are principally connected with such trusteeship.

(b) The premium for the policy shall be paid by the trustees wholly from funds contributed by the employer or employers of the insured persons, or by the union or unions, or by both. No policy may be issued on which any part of the premium is to be derived from funds contributed by the insured persons specifically for their insurance. The policy must insure all eligible persons, or all except any as to whom evidence of individual insurability is not satisfactory to the insurer.

(c) The policy must cover at date of issue at least 100 persons and not less than an average of five persons per employer unit; and if the fund is established by the members of an association of employers the policy may be issued only if (i) either (a) the participating employers constitute at date of issue at least 60% of those employer members whose employees are not already covered for group life insurance or (b) the total number of persons covered at date of issue exceeds 600; and (ii) the policy shall not require that, if a participating employer discontinues membership in the association, the insurance of his employees shall cease solely by reason of such discontinuance.

(d) The amounts of insurance under the policy must be based upon some plan precluding individual selection either by the insured persons or by the policyholder, employers, or unions.

II. No such policy of group life insurance may be issued to an employer, or labor union or to the trustees of a fund established in whole or in part by an employer or a labor union, which provides term insurance under any group life insurance policy or policies issued to the employer or employers of such person or to a labor union or labor unions of which such person is a member or to the trustees of a fund or funds established in whole or in part by such employer or employers or such labor union or labor unions, exceeds $20,000, unless 150% of the annual compensation of such person from his employer or employers exceeds $20,000, in which event all such term insurance shall not exceed $40,000 or 150% of such annual compensation, whichever is the lesser.

GROUP LIFE INSURANCE STANDARD PROVISIONS

No policy of group life insurance shall be delivered in this state unless it contains in substance the following provisions, or provisions which in the opinion of the Commissioner are more favorable to the persons insured, or at least as favorable to the persons insured and more favorable to the policyholder, provided, however, (a) that provisions (6) to (10) inclusive shall not apply to policies issued to a creditor to insure debtors of such creditor; (b) that the standard provisions required for individual life insurance policies shall not apply to group life insurance policies; and (c) that if the group life insurance policy is on a plan of insurance other than the term plan, it shall contain a non-forfeiture provision or provisions which in the opinion of the Commissioner is or are equitable to the insured persons and to the policyholder, but nothing herein shall be construed to require that group life insurance policies contain the same non-forfeiture provisions as are required for individual life insurance policies:

(1) A provision that the policyholder is entitled to a grace period of thirty-one days for the payment of any premium due except the first, during which grace period the death benefit coverage shall continue in force, unless the policyholder shall have given the insurer written notice of discontinuance in advance of the date of discontinuance and in accordance with the terms of the policy. The policy may provide that the policyholder shall be liable to the insurer for the payment of a pro rata premium for the time the policy was in force during such grace period.

(2) A provision that the validity of the policy shall not be contested, except for nonpayment of premiums, after it has been in force for two years from its date of issue; and that no statement made by any person insured under the policy relating to his insurability shall be used in contesting the validity of the insurance with respect to which such statement was made after such insurance has been in force prior to the contest for a period of two years during such person's lifetime nor unless it is contained in a written instrument signed by him.

(3) A provision that a copy of the application, if any, of the policyholder shall be attached to the policy when issued, that all statements made by the policyholder or by the persons insured shall be deemed representations and not warranties, and that no statement made by any person insured shall be used in any contest unless a copy of the instrument containing the statement is or has been furnished to such person or to his beneficiary.

(4) A provision setting forth the conditions, if any, under which the insurer reserves the right to require a person eligible for insurance to furnish evidence of individual insurability satisfactory to the insurer as a condition to part or all of his coverage.

(5) A provision specifying an equitable adjustment of premiums or of benefits or of both to be made in the event the age of a person in-

sured has been misstated, such provision to contain a clear statement of the method of adjustment to be used.

(6) A provision that any sum becoming due by reason of the death of the person insured shall be payable to the beneficiary designated by the person insured, subject to the provisions of the policy in the event there is no designated beneficiary, as to all or any part of such sum, living at the death of the person insured, and subject to any right reserved by the insurer in the policy and set forth in the certificate to pay at its option a part of such sum not exceeding $500 to any person appearing to the insurer to be equitably entitled thereto by reason of having incurred funeral or other expenses incident to the last illness or death of the person insured.

(7) A provision that the insurer will issue to the policyholder for delivery to each person insured an individual certificate setting forth a statement as to the insurance protection to which he is entitled, to whom the insurance benefits are payable, and the rights and conditions set forth in (8), (9) and (10) following.

(8) A provision that if the insurance, or any portion of it, on a person covered under the policy ceases because of termination of employment or of membership in the class or classes eligible for coverage under the policy, such person shall be entitled to have issued to him by the insurer, without evidence of insurability, an individual policy of life insurance without disability or other supplementary benefits, provided application for the individual policy shall be made, and the first premium paid to the insurer, within thirty-one days after such termination, and provided further that,

(a) The individual policy shall, at the option of such person be on any one of the forms, except term insurance, then customarily issued by the insurer at the age and for the amount applied for;

(b) the individual policy shall be in an amount not in excess of the amount of life insurance which ceases because of such termination, provided that any amount of insurance which shall have matured on or before the date of such termination as an endowment payable to the person insured, whether in one sum or in instalments or in the form of an annuity, shall not, for the purposes of this provision, be included in the amount which is considered to cease because of such termination; and

(c) the premium on the individual policy shall be at the insurer's then customary rate applicable to the form and amount of the individual policy, to the class of risk to which such person then belongs, and to his age attained on the effective date of the individual policy.

(9) A provision that if the group policy terminates or is amended so as to terminate the insurance of any class of insured persons, every person insured thereunder at the date of such termination whose insurance terminates and who has been so insured for at least five

years prior to such termination date shall be entitled to have issued to him by the insurer an individual policy of life insurance, subject to the same conditions and limitations as are provided by (8) above, except that the group policy may provide that the amount of such individual policy shall not exceed the smaller of (a) the amount of the person's life insurance protection ceasing because of the termination or amendment of the group policy, less the amount of any life insurance for which he is or becomes eligible under any group policy issued or reinstated by the same or another insurer within thirty-one days after such termination, and (b) $2,000.

(10) A provision that if a person insured under the group policy dies during the period within which he would have been entitled to have an individual policy issued to him in accordance with (8) or (9) above and before such an individual policy shall have become effective, the amount of life insurance which he would have been entitled to have issued to him under such individual policy shall be payable as a claim under the group policy, whether or not application for the individual policy or the payment of the first premium therefor has been made.

(11) In the case of a policy issued to a creditor to insure debtors of such creditor, a provision that the insurer will furnish to the policyholder for delivery to each debtor insured under the policy a form which will contain a statement that the life of the debtor is insured under the policy and that any death benefit paid thereunder by reason of his death shall be applied to reduce or extinguish the indebtedness.

SUPPLEMENTARY BILL RELATING TO CONVERSION PRIVILEGES

If any individual insured under a group life insurance policy hereafter delivered in this state becomes entitled under the terms of such policy to have an individual policy of life insurance issued to him without evidence of insurability, subject to making of application and payment of the first premium within the period specified in such policy, and if such individual is not given notice of the existence of such right at least 15 days prior to the expiration date of such period, then in such event the individual shall have an additional period within which to exercise such right, but nothing herein contained shall be construed to continue any insurance beyond the period provided in such policy. This additional period shall expire 15 days next after the individual is given such notice but in no event shall such additional period extend beyond 60 days next after the expiration date of the period provided in such policy. Written notice presented to the individual or mailed by the policyholder to the last known address of the individual or mailed by the insurer to the last known address of the individual as furnished by the policyholder shall constitute notice for the purpose of this paragraph.

K. Specimen Group Life Insurance Master Policy

THE ABC INSURANCE COMPANY

(herein called the Insurance Company)

In Consideration of the Application for this Policy and of the payment of premiums as stated herein, hereby insures the lives of certain Employees of

THE JOHN DOE COMPANY

(herein called the Employer)

and agrees, subject to the terms and conditions of the Policy, that immediately upon receipt of due proof in writing of the death of any insured Employee, the Insurance Company will pay the amount for which the Employee is insured to the person or persons entitled thereto under the provisions of this Policy.

This Policy takes effect on the first day of June, 1956, which is the date of issue hereof, and policy anniversaries are deemed to occur on the first day of June of each year, beginning in 1957. The Policy will terminate, as hereinafter provided, upon failure to pay any premium within the grace period allowed for payment, and under circumstances hereinafter specified it will terminate following written notice by the Insurance Company or by the Employer. Premiums are payable by the Employer in amounts determined as hereinafter provided. The first premium is due on the date the policy takes effect, and subsequent premiums are, during the continuance of the Policy, due monthly on the first day of each month thereafter. This Policy is delivered in the State of Texas and is governed by the laws of that jurisdiction.

The Sections set forth on the following pages are part of this Policy.

In Witness Whereof, The ABC Insurance Company, at its Home Office in the City of New York, New York, has caused this Policy to be executed and attested this first day of June, 1956.

Secretary ______________________ President ______________________

Attest, ______________

PLAN OF INSURANCE

The classes of Employees eligible for insurance, and the amount of insurance applicable to each classification, are set forth in the following table. Each present and future full-time Employee of such classes shall be eligible, as set forth below, to participate in the insurance; provided that if an Employee who upon termination of employment converted his previous insurance hereunder to an individual policy is re-employed and the individual policy remains in force at the time he would again become eligible, the eligibility of the Employee shall be deferred until he furnishes evidence of insurability satisfactory to the Insurance Company. No part-time Employee shall be eligible for insurance.

Employees in the service of the Employer on the effective date of the Policy shall be eligible for insurance from such date.

Employees entering the service of the Employer after the effective date of the Policy shall be eligible for insurance from the completion of three months of continuous service.

Classification	*Amount of Insurance*
Officers	*$2,500*
All other Employees	*1,000*

Each Employee becoming insured shall be insured for the amount applicable to his classification, without right to a larger or smaller amount except as provided in event of a change in classification. The Employer shall determine from time to time, without discrimination among persons in like circumstance, the classification of each individual Employee, and such determination shall be final and conclusive. The date an Employee's insurance becomes effective is determined by the section "Employees Insured."

If an insured Employee's classification changes, the Employee's insurance shall, unless otherwise stated above, be adjusted automatically to conform to the new classification on the first day on which he is both actively at work on full time and makes a contribution applicable to the new classification; provided that if thirty-one days elapse after change to a classification for which a larger amount of insurance is provided and the Employee fails to make a contribution applicable to the new classification by the first day thereafter on which he is actively at work on full time, no increase shall be allowed as a result of such change or any subsequent change unless the Employee furnishes evidence of insurability satisfactory to the Insurance Company.

Should an Employee's insurance be continued during disability, leave of absence, temporary lay-off or retirement, the amount of his insurance shall be the amount for which he was insured on his last day of work unless otherwise stated above.

ASSOCIATED COMPANIES

For the purposes of this Policy, Employees of the following subsidiaries and affiliates of the Employer shall be considered Employees of the Employer, and service with any of such subsidiaries and affiliates shall be considered service with the Employer: The Richard Roe Co.

EMPLOYEES INSURED

Each eligible Employee who makes written request to the Employer, on a form approved by the Insurance Company, to participate in the insurance and who agrees to contribute towards the payment of premiums shall, subject to the further provisions of this section, become insured as follows:

(1) If request to participate is made by the Employee on or before the date he becomes eligible, he shall be insured from such date of eligibility.

(2) If request to participate is made by the Employee after he becomes eligible but not after the end of the thirty-one day period immediately following the first day he is both eligible and actively at work on full time, he shall be insured from the xxx date of request.

(3) If request to participate is made by the Employee after the end of the thirty-one day period immediately following the first day he is both eligible and actively at work on full time, or is made after previous termination of insurance because of failure to make a contribution when due, the Employee must furnish evidence of insurability satisfactory to the Insurance Company before he may become insured. If such evidence is submitted, the Employee shall be insured from the xxx date the Insurance Company determines the evidence to be satisfactory.

In any instance when an Employee is not actively at work on full time on the date he would become insured in accordance with the above provisions, the commencement of the Employee's insurance shall be deferred until xxx return to active work on full time.

Any Employee who must furnish evidence of insurability satisfactory to the Insurance Company as a condition to becoming insured, and whose service with the Employer terminates without such evidence having been given, shall continue to be subject to the same requirement if he is subsequently re-employed.

If an Employee has made written request to the Employer, on a form approved by the Insurance Company, to participate in the insurance and has made the required contributions, the Employee's insurance shall not be invalidated by the Employer's failure, due to clerical error, to record or report such Employee for insurance.

EMPLOYEE CONTRIBUTIONS

The contributions of the individual insured Employees towards the payment of premiums shall not exceed sixty cents per month per $1,000 of insurance.

PAYMENT OF PREMIUMS

All premiums are payable by the Employer at an office of the Insurance Company or to an authorized representative, in exchange for official receipts signed by the President or the Secretary and counter-signed by the person receiving payment. Such premiums are due and payable as specified on the first page of this Policy, but upon the request of the Employer the interval of payment may be changed, with appropriate adjustment, to provide for payment annually, semi-annually, quarterly or monthly.

If premiums are payable monthly, each premium shall be equal to the product of the total amount of insurance in force on the due date of such premium and the average monthly premium rate then in effect.

If premiums are payable annually, semi-annually or quarterly, each premium due during any policy year shall be equal to the product of the total amount of insurance in force at the beginning of such year and the applicable average premium rate in effect on the due date of such premium, subject, however, to an adjustment at the end of the policy year based upon the average amount of insurance in force during the policy year. If the average amount of insurance in force exceeds the amount in force at the beginning of the policy year, the premium or premiums for such year shall be increased proportionately, and the increase over the premium or premiums actually paid shall be paid by the Employer upon demand by the Insurance Company. If the average amount of insurance in force is less than the amount in force at the beginning of the policy year, the Insurance Company shall refund to the Employer the portion of the premiums paid corresponding to the difference between the amount in force at the beginning of the policy year and the average amount in force during the policy year. The average amount of insurance in force for a twelve months' period shall be determined as one-fifth of the sum of the total amounts in force on the first and last days of such period and on the days falling respectively three months, six months and nine months after the first day of such period.

Instead of the methods of computation of premiums above provided, premiums may be computed by any method mutually agreeable to the Insurance Company and the Employer which produces approximately the same total amount.

Proper adjustment of the rate and premiums will be made if the extent of coverage is changed by amendment to this Policy.

PREMIUM RATES

The following table of individual rates shall be used in computing the amount of premiums due under this Policy, subject to the condition that upon the first policy anniversary, and upon each premium due date thereafter on which the then current premium rate basis has been in effect for at least twelve months, the Insurance Company may, by notifying the Employer, change the basis upon which the amount of further premiums, including the one then due, shall be computed.

At the issuance of this Policy the Insurance Company will determine an average annual premium rate by applying the individual rates to the amounts of insurance in force at the respective ages, nearest birthday, of all Employees then insured, and dividing the aggregate amount so obtained by the total amount of

INITIAL TABLE OF PREMIUM RATES PER $1,000 OF INSURANCE

Attained Age Nearest Birthday	*Annual Premium*	*Attained Age Nearest Birthday*	*Annual Premium*	*Attained Age Nearest Birthday*	*Annual Premium*	*Attained Age Nearest Birthday*	*Annual Premium*
15	$4.13	35	$ 6.77	55	$21.29	75	$ 97.87
16	4.17	36	7.07	56	22.86	76	105.87
17	4.24	37	7.38	57	24.56	77	114.51
18	4.29	38	7.72	58	26.41	78	123.83
19	4.37	39	8.10	59	28.43	79	133.88
20	4.43	40	8.50	60	30.62	80	144.71
21	4.52	41	8.94	61	32.99	81	156.36
22	4.61	42	9.42	62	35.59	82	168.89
23	4.70	43	9.94	63	38.39	83	182.34
24	4.80	44	10.51	64	41.45	84	196.76
25	4.92	45	11.13	65	44.76	85	212.21
26	5.04	46	11.80	66	48.36	86	228.73
27	5.17	47	12.54	67	52.26	87	246.35
28	5.32	48	13.33	68	56.49	88	265.18
29	5.49	49	14.21	69	61.09	89	285.16
30	5.66	50	15.15	70	66.07	90	306.35
31	5.84	51	16.18	71	71.46	91	328.83
32	6.05	52	17.30	72	77.30	92	352.58
33	6.27	53	18.52	73	83.63	93	377.53
34	6.51	54	19.85	74	90.47	94	403.91
						95	431.24

insurance. If premiums are payable semi-annually, quarterly or monthly, the applicable average premium rate will be determined by adding 1%, 2% or 3% to the average annual premium rate so obtained and dividing by 2, 4 or 12, respectively. Such average premium rate shall be in effect for all premiums falling due before the first policy anniversary. On each policy anniversary, and on any other premium due date on which a change in the premium rate basis has become effective, the average premium rate will be correspondingly redetermined, according to the then attained ages of the Employees insured and the basis then established for determining such rate.

GRACE IN PAYMENT OF PREMIUMS—TERMINATION OF POLICY

A grace period of thirty-one days, without interest charge, will be allowed for the payment of each premium except the first. If any premium is not paid within the days of grace this Policy shall terminate at the end of such grace period, except that the Policy shall terminate at an earlier date which is not prior to the end of the period for which premiums have been paid should the Employer make written request in advance for such earlier date of termination.

If the Policy terminates during or at the end of the grace period, the Employer shall be liable to the Insurance Company for the payment of a pro rata premium for the time the Policy was in force during such grace period.

The Insurance Company may terminate the Policy on the first policy anniversary or on any premium due date thereafter, by giving written notice to the Employer at least thirty-one days in advance, if the number of Employees insured on such policy anniversary or due date is less than fifty or less than seventy-five per cent of those eligible for insurance, or if Employees are contributing towards the payment of premiums at a rate greater than that permitted by the terms of the Policy.

TERMINATION OF INDIVIDUAL INSURANCE

The insurance on an Employee shall automatically terminate if his employment with the Employer terminates, or if he fails to make, when due, any contribution towards the payment of premiums, or if this Policy terminates. If, however, the Employee is entitled by the terms of this Policy to convert all or part of his insurance to an individual policy but dies during the thirty-one day period following termination of insurance, the amount of insurance which might otherwise have been converted will be paid as a claim under this Policy, whether or not application for conversation has been made.

Termination of employment shall, for all purposes of this Policy, be deemed to occur upon cessation of active full-time work in the classes of Employees eligible for insurance, except that an Employee who is disabled, on leave of absence, temporarily laid off, employed on a part-time basis, or retired will nevertheless be considered as still employed on a full-time basis until the Employer, acting in accordance with rules precluding individual selection, terminates the Employee's insurance by notifying the Insurance Company to that effect or by discontinuing premium payments for his insurance. Insurance shall not, however, be continued for longer than two months on an Employee who is on leave of absence or temporarily laid off, nor shall insurance be continued in any case on an Employee who is absent from work because of membership in any military, naval or air force of any country at war, declared or undeclared.

AGE CORRECTION

If premiums for the insurance on any Employee have been paid at a rate other than for his correct age, there shall be an equitable adjustment of premiums. The Employee's insurance shall remain unchanged if the amounts applicable to the individual Employees under the Plan of Insurance do not depend upon age; but if the change in age affects the Employee's insurance the amount shall be corrected accordingly and the premium adjustment shall take such correction into account.

EXTENSION OF DEATH BENEFIT

If an Employee, while less than sixty years of age and while insured under this Policy, becomes totally disabled from bodily injury or disease so as to be wholly prevented from performing any work or engaging in any occupation for remuneration or profit, and if the Employee dies within one year after discontinuance of premium payments for his insurance and while remaining continuously so disabled, then upon due proof of such disability and death the Insurance Company will pay under this section the amount of the Employee's insurance as determined by the Plan of Insurance, unless claim is otherwise established because the Employee died within thirty-one days following termination of insurance.

If the Employee has become totally disabled under the conditions stated above and then furnishes, not later than one year after discontinuance of premium payments, written proof to the Insurance Company at its Home Office that the disability is permanent as herein defined, the Employee's insurance will be extended during the further continuance of total and permanent disability until one year from the date such proof was received. Total and permanent disability shall, for the purpose of this insurance, mean total disability as described above which has existed continuously for a period of not less than nine months. The Employee's insurance will again be extended during the continuance of total and permanent disability for successive periods of one year each, provided written proof of such continuance is submitted to the Home Office of the Insurance Company within the respective three-months' period immediately preceding the beginning of each such year.

The Insurance Company shall have the right and opportunity to have physicians designated by it examine the person of the Employee when and so often as it may reasonably require during disability, but not more often than once a year after insurance has been extended for two full years. Without regard to other causes of disability and notwithstanding anything herein contained, total and permanent disability will be recognized to exist if the Employee has suffered the entire and irrecoverable loss of sight of both eyes, or the loss by severance of both hands above the wrists, or both feet above the ankles, or one hand above the wrist and one foot above the ankle.

In the event of the death of the Employee, the Insurance Company shall be liable under these provisions only if written notice of claim is given at its Home Office within one year from the date of death. Payment hereunder will be made to the person or persons entitled to receive the insurance, provided that any Beneficiary designation in an individual policy issued under the provisions of the "Conversion Privilege" shall, if different from the designation for this Policy, be considered notice of change of Beneficiary for any claim presented under this section.

If the Employee has furnished proof that he is totally and permanently disabled but nevertheless again becomes able to perform some work or to engage in some occupation for remuneration or profit, or if the Employee remains totally and permanently disabled but refuses to be examined as required above or fails to furnish within the time allowed proof of continuance of total and permanent disability, all insurance on the Employee under this section shall immediately terminate. The Employee shall thereupon be entitled to rights and benefits under the "Conversion Privilege," together with insurance protection during the thirty-one day period allowed for conversion, as if employment had then terminated, unless the Employee returns to work with the Employer during such period and is again insured under this Policy.

CONVERSION PRIVILEGE

If employment with the Employer is terminated, an Employee insured hereunder shall be entitled to convert all or part of his insurance, without evidence of insurability, to an individual policy of life insurance, provided written application and the first premium payment are made to the Insurance Company within thirty-one days from the date of termination of employment. The individual life insurance policy may be upon any of the forms then customarily being issued by the Insurance Company, except term insurance or any policy containing disability benefits, and the premium payable shall be based upon the Insurance Company's rate applicable to the class of risk to which the Employee belongs and to the age attained on the effective date of the individual policy.

If this Policy terminates after an Employee has been continuously insured by the Insurance Company, under this Policy or under this Policy and any it replaces, for at least five years immediately preceding such termination, the Employee may convert his insurance to an individual policy under the same conditions as would apply if employment had then terminated, except that the amount of the individual policy may not exceed the lesser of:

(a) The amount of the Employee's insurance at the termination of this Policy, reduced by any amount for which he may become eligible under a group life insurance policy issued, within thirty-one days after such termination, by the Insurance Company or any other insurance carrier; and

(b) $2,000.

Any individual policy issued under the provisions of this section shall take effect at the end of the thirty-one day period during which application for the policy may be made, and shall be in place of all benefits under this Policy. Conversion of insurance or payment of claim under the individual policy shall not, however, preclude the establishment of rights under the section "Extension of Death Benefit," provided all the conditions of that section are fulfilled within the required time and such rights are taken in exchange for all benefits and payments under the individual policy except for a refund of premiums.

BENEFICIARY

An Employee's insurance shall be payable at death to the person designated by him as his Beneficiary on a form furnished by or satisfactory to the Insurance Company.

The Employee may, from time to time and without the consent of his Beneficiary, change the Beneficiary by filing written notice of the change through the Employer on a form furnished by or satisfactory to the Insurance Company, whereupon an acknowledgment of the change will be furnished the Employee for attachment to his Certificate. The new designation shall take effect on the date the notice was signed, whether or not the Employee is living when the acknowledgment of the change is furnished, but without prejudice to the Insurance Company on account of any payment made by it before acknowledgment of the change.

If more than one Beneficiary is designated and in such designation the Employee has failed to specify their respective interests, the Beneficiaries shall share equally. If any designated Beneficiary predeceases the Employee, the interest of such Beneficiary shall terminate and his share shall be payable equally to such of the Beneficiaries as survive the Employee, unless the Employee has made written request to the contrary. Any amount of insurance for which there is no Beneficiary at the death of the Employee shall be payable to the estate of the Employee.

x x x x

x x x x

If a Beneficiary is a minor or is otherwise incapable of giving a valid release for any payment due, the Insurance Company may, at its option, and until claim is made by the duly appointed guardian or committee of such Beneficiary, make payment of the amount payable to such Beneficiary at a rate of not exceeding $ 50.00 per month to any relative by blood or connection by marriage of such Beneficiary, or to any other person or institution appearing to it to have assumed the custody and principal support of such Beneficiary.

INSTALLMENT SETTLEMENT

The whole or part of an Employee's insurance may be made payable to the Beneficiary in equal monthly installments extending over a fixed period not to exceed ten years, either through specification in the Plan of Insurance or by an election by the Employee in the absence of such a specification. The first installment shall be due at the Employee's death, and the amount of each installment shall be computed so as to include interest at the effective rate of 2 % per annum on the unpaid balance of the insurance, the amounts indicated in the following table being so computed. In no event, however, shall the Insurance Company be required to pay an installment of less than $ 10.00 to any one person. Such additional interest, if any, as may be authorized from time to time by the Board of Directors will be paid annually to the Beneficiary.

At the death of the Beneficiary, any installments remaining unpaid shall, unless otherwise requested by the Employee in his Beneficiary dsignation, be discounted at the effective rate of 2 % per annum compound interest and paid in one sum to the estate of the Beneficiary.

A mode of settlement other than that specified above may be arranged during the lifetime of the Employee for an amount of insurance otherwise payable in a single sum if the Employee and the Insurance Company mutually agree thereon. If, at the Employee's death, no mode of settlement has been elected for such an amount, the Beneficiary and the Insurance Company may then

Number of Years	*Monthly Installment per $1,000 Applied*
1	$84.10
2	42.46
3	28.59
4	21.65
5	17.49
6	14.72
7	12.74
8	11.25
9	10.10
10	9.18

mutually agree upon any mode of settlement, for the benefit of such Beneficiary, which would have been available to the Employee immediately prior to his death.

RECORDS—INFORMATION TO BE FURNISHED

The Insurance Company shall keep a record of the Employees insured containing, for each Employee, the essential particulars of the insurance. The Employer shall furnish periodically, on the Insurance Company's forms, such information relating to new Employees becoming insured, changes in amounts of insurance, and terminations of insurance as may be required by the Insurance Company to administer the coverage. Upon request by the Insurance Company not more often than once a year, the Employer shall furnish a statement to the Insurance Company of the ages, occupations and such other relevant data concerning the Employees in the classes eligible for insurance hereunder as may reasonably be considered to have a bearing on the administration of the coverage and on the determination of the future premium rates. The Employer's payroll and such other records as have a bearing on the insurance shall be open for inspection by the Insurance Company at any reasonable time.

DIVIDENDS

The portion, if any, of the divisible surplus of the Insurance Company accruing upon this Policy at each policy anniversary shall be determined annually by the Board of Directors of the Insurance Company and shall be credited to this Policy as a dividend on such anniversary, provided the Policy is continued in force by the payment of all premiums to such anniversary.

Any dividend under this Policy shall be (1) paid to the Employer in cash, or at the option of the Employer it may be (2) applied to the reduction of the premium then due, or (3) left to accumulate to the credit of the Employer as long as the Policy remains in force, with compound interest at the rate authorized from time to time by the Board of Directors. The Employer may withdraw dividend accumulations at any time, and if the Policy terminates any dividend accumulations then remaining with the Insurance Company shall be thereupon paid to the Employer. The Insurance Company shall, however, have the right to defer the withdrawal or payment of any dividend accumulations for as long as six months, but not exceeding the period permitted by law.

If the aggregate of any dividends should be in excess of the Employer's share of the aggregate cost, such excess shall be applied by the Employer for the sole benefit of the Employees. Payment of any dividend to the Employer shall completely discharge the liability of the Insurance Company with respect to the dividend so paid.

EMPLOYEE'S CERTIFICATE

The Insurance Company will issue to the Employer, for delivery to each Employee insured hereunder, an individual certificate which shall set forth the insurance protection to which the Employee is entitled, to whom the benefits are payable, and the provisions of the section "Conversion privilege."

NO ASSIGNMENT

An Employee's insurance shall be nonassignable.

INCONTESTABILITY

This Policy shall be incontestable, except for nonpayment of premiums, after one year from its date of issue.

THE CONTRACT

This Policy, together with the Application of the Employer, a copy of which is attached hereto and made a part hereof, constitutes the entire contract between the parties. All statements made by the Employer shall be deemed representations and not warranties, and no such statement shall avoid the insurance or be used in defense of a claim hereunder unless it is contained in the Application signed by the Employer.

This Policy may be amended at any time, without the consent of the Employees insured hereunder or of their Beneficiaries, upon written request made by the Employer and agreed to by the Insurance Company, but any such amendment shall be without prejudice to any claim arising prior to the date to which premiums have been paid. No Agent is authorized to alter or amend this Policy, to waive any conditions or restrictions contained herein, to extend the time for paying a premium, or to bind the Insurance Company by making any promise or representation or by giving or receiving any information. No change in this Policy shall be valid unless evidenced by an endorsement hereon signed by the President, a Vice President, the Secretary, the Actuary, an Associate Actuary, an Assistant Secretary or an Assistant Actuary of the Insurance Company, or by an amendment hereto signed by the Employer and by one of the aforesaid officers of the Insurance Company.

Wherever in this Policy a personal pronoun in the masculine gender is used or appears, it shall be taken to include the feminine also, unless the context clearly indicates the contrary.

L. Specimen Group Life Employee's Certificate

THE ABC INSURANCE COMPANY
(herein called the Insurance Company)

CERTIFIES that the Employee named below is insured under Group Life Insurance Policy No. G- XXX insuring certain Employees of

—THE JOHN DOE COMPANY—
(herein called the Employer)

Employee: RICHARD ROE
Certificate No. XXX Effective Date: JUNE 1, 1956.
Beneficiary: MARY ROE, WIFE OF THE EMPLOYEE
Amount of Insurance: ONE THOUSAND Dollars.

If the Employee dies while insured under the Group Policy, the amount of insurance then in force on the life of the Employee will be paid to the Beneficiary.

The Employee may, from time to time and without the consent of the Beneficiary, change the Beneficiary by filing written notice of the change through the Employer on a form furnished by or satisfactory to the Insurance Company, whereupon an acknowledgment of the change will be furnished the Employee for attachment to this Certificate. The new designation shall take effect on the date the notice was signed, whether or not the Employee is living when the acknowledgment of the change is furnished, but without prejudice to the Insurance Company on account of any payment made by it before acknowledgment of the change.

If more than one Beneficiary is designated and in such designation the Employee has failed to specify their respective interests, the Beneficiaries will share equally. If any designated Beneficiary predeceases the Employee, the interest of such Beneficiary will terminate and his share will be payable equally to such of the Beneficiaries as survive the Employee, unless the Employee has made written request to the contrary. Any amount of insurance for which there is no Beneficiary at the death of the Employee will be payable to the estate of the Employee.

If a Beneficiary is a minor or is otherwise incapable of giving a valid release for any payment due, the Insurance Company may, at its option, and until claim is made by the duly appointed guardian or committee of such Beneficiary, make payment of the amount payable to such Beneficiary at a rate not exceeding $ 50.00 per month to any relative by blood or connection by marriage of such Beneficiary, or to any other person or institution appearing to it to have assumed the custody and principal support of such Beneficiary.

The provisions of the Group Policy principally affecting the Employee's insurance are described on this and the following pages of this Certificate. All benefits described herein are governed by and are subject in every respect to the Group Policy, which alone constitutes the agreement under which payments are made.

President.

EXTENSION OF DEATH BENEFIT

If the Employee, while less than sixty years of age and while insured under the Group Policy, becomes totally disabled from bodily injury or disease so as to be wholly prevented from performing any work or engaging in any occupation for remuneration or profit, and if the Employee dies within one year after discontinuance of premium payments for his insurance and while remaining continuously so disabled, then upon due proof of such disability and death the Insurance Company will pay under this section the amount of the Employee's insurance, unless claim is otherwise established because the Employee died within thirty-one days following termination of insurance.

If the Employee has become totally disabled under the conditions stated above and then furnishes, not later than one year after discontinuance of premium payment, written proof to the Insurance Company at its Home Office that the disability is permanent as herein defined, the Employee's insurance will be extended during the further continuance of total and permanent disability until one year from the date such proof was received. Total and permanent disability will, for the purpose of the insurance, mean total disability as described above which has existed continuously for a period of not less than nine months. The Employee's insurance will again be extended during the continuance of total and permanent disability for successive periods of one year each, provided written proof of such continuance is submitted to the Home Office of the Insurance Company within the respective three months period immediately preceding the beginning of each such year.

The Insurance Company will have the right and opportunity to have physicians designated by it examine the person of the Employee when and so often as it may reasonably require during disability, but not more often than once a year after insurance has been extended for two full years. Without regard to other causes of disability and notwithstanding anything herein contained, total and permanent disability will be recognized to exist if the Employee has suffered the entire and irrecoverable loss of sight of both eyes, or the loss by severance of both hands above the wrists, or both feet above the ankles, or one hand above the wrist and one foot above the ankle.

In the event of the death of the Employee, the Insurance Company will be liable under these provisions only if written notice of claim is given at its Home Office within one year from the date of death. Payment will be made to the person or persons entitled to receive the insurance, provided that any Beneficiary designation in an individual policy issued under the provisions of the "Conversion Privilege" will, if different from the designation for the Group Policy, be considered notice of change of Beneficiary for any claim presented under this section.

If the Employee has furnished proof that he is totally and permanently disabled but nevertheless again becomes able to perform some work or to engage in some occupation for remuneration or profit, or if the Employee remains totally and permanently disabled but refuses to be examined as required above or fails to furnish within the time allowed proof of continuance of total and permanent disability, all insurance on the Employee under this section will immediately terminate. The Employee will thereupon be entitled to rights and benefits under the "Conversion Privilege," together with insurance protection during the thirty-one day period allowed for conversion, as if employment had then terminated, unless the Employee returns to work with the Employer during such period and is again insured under the Group Policy.

TERMINATION OF INSURANCE

The insurance on the Employee will automatically terminate if his employment with the Employer terminates, or if the Group Policy terminates, or (should the insurance be on a contributory basis) if he fails to make, when due, any contribution towards the payment of premiums. If, however, the Employee is entitled by the terms of the Group Policy to convert all or part of his insurance to an individual policy but dies during the thirty-one day period following termination of insurance, the amount of insurance which might otherwise have been converted will be paid as a claim under the Group Policy, whether or not application for conversion has been made.

Termination of employment will, for all purposes of the Group Policy, be deemed to occur upon cessation of active full-time work in the classes of Employees eligible for insurance; except that Employees who are disabled, employed on a part-time basis, or retired will nevertheless be considered as still employed on a full-time basis until the Employer notifies the Insurance Company to the contrary or until prior discontinuance of premium payments for their insurance, and Employees on leave of absence or temporary lay-off may, at the option of the Employer, be considered as still employed on a full-time basis for a limited period as specified in the Group Policy. The insurance may not, however, be continued on Employees who are absent from work because of membership in any military, naval or air force of any country at war, declared or undeclared.

CONVERSION PRIVILEGE

If employment with the Employer is terminated, the Employee will be entitled to convert all or part of his insurance, without evidence of insurability, to an individual policy of life insurance, provided written application and the first premium payment are made to the Insurance Company within thirty-one days from the date of termination of employment. The individual life insurance policy may be upon any of the forms then customarily being issued by the Insurance Company, except term insurance or any policy containing disability benefits, and the premium payable will be based upon the Insurance Company's rate applicable to the class of risk to which the Employee belongs and to the age attained on the effective date of the individual policy.

If the Group Policy terminates after the Employee has been continuously insured by the Insurance Company, under the Group Policy or under the Group Policy and any it replaces, for at least five years immediately preceding such termination, the Employee may convert his insurance under the Group Policy, as represented by this and any other certificates, to an individual policy under the same conditions as would apply if employment had then terminated, except that the amount of the individual policy may not exceed the lesser of:

(a) The amount of the Employee's insurance at the termination of the Group Policy, reduced by any amount for which he may become eligible under a group life insurance policy issued, within thirty-one days after such termination, by the Insurance Company or any other insurance carrier; and

(b) $2,000.

Any individual policy issued under the provisions of this section will take effect at the end of the thirty-one day period during which application for the policy may be made, and will be in place of all benefits under the Group Policy. Conversion of insurance or payment of claim under the individual policy will not, however, preclude the establishment of rights under the section "Extension of Death Benefit," provided all the conditions of that section are fulfilled within the required time and such rights are taken in exchange for all benefits and payments under the individual policy except for a refund of premiums.

INSTALLMENT SETTLEMENT

The Employee may elect that the whole or part of his insurance be made payable to the Beneficiary in equal monthly installments extending over a fixed period not to exceed ten years. The first installment will be due at the Employee's death, and the amount of each installment will be computed so as to include interest at the effective rate of 2% per annum on the unpaid balance of the insurance, the amounts indicated in the following table being so computed. In no event, however, shall the Insurance Company be required to pay an installment of less than $10.00 to any one person. Such additional interest, if any, as may be authorized from time to time by the Board of Directors will be paid annually to the Beneficiary.

Number of Years	*Monthly Installment per $1,000 Applied*
1	$84.10
2	42.46
3	28.59
4	21.65
5	17.49
6	14.72
7	12.74
8	11.25
9	10.10
10	9.18

At the death of the Beneficiary, any installments remaining unpaid will, unless otherwise requested by the Employee in his Beneficiary designation, be discounted at the effective rate of 2% per annum compound interest and paid in one sum to the estate of the Beneficiary.

A mode of settlement other than that specified above may be arranged during the lifetime of the Employee if the Employee and the Insurance Company mutually agree thereon. If, at the Employee's death, no mode of settlement has been elected for an amount payable to the Beneficiary, the Beneficiary and the Insurance Company may then mutually agree upon any mode of settlement, for the benefit of such Beneficiary, which would have been available to the Employee immediately prior to his death.

NO ASSIGNMENT

The Employee's insurance is nonassignable.

M. Model Blanket Accident and Sickness Insurance Bill

Section 1. *Blanket Accident and Sickness Insurance Defined.* Blanket accident and sickness insurance is hereby declared to be that form of accident, sickness or accident and sickness insurance covering groups of persons as enumerated in one of the following paragraphs (*a*) to (*i*) inclusive:

(*a*) Under a policy or contract issued to any common carrier or to any operator, owner or lessee of a means of transportation, who or which shall be deemed the policyholder, covering a group of persons who may become passengers defined by reference to their travel status on such common carrier or such means of transportation.

(*b*) Under a policy or contract issued to an employer, who shall be deemed the policyholder, covering any group of employees, dependents or guests, defined by reference to specified hazards incident to an activity or activities or operations of the policyholder.

(*c*) Under a policy or contract issued to a college, school or other institution of learning, a school district or districts, or school jurisdictional unit, or to the head, principal or governing board of any such educational unit, who or which shall be deemed the policyholder, covering students, teachers or employees.

(*d*) Under a policy or contract issued to any religious, charitable, recreational, educational, or civic organization, or branch thereof, which shall be deemed the policyholder, covering any group of members or participants defined by reference to specified hazards incident to an activity or activities or operations sponsored or supervised by such policyholder.

(*e*) Under a policy or contract issued to a sports team, camp or sponsor thereof, which shall be deemed the policyholder, covering members, campers, employees, officials or supervisors.

(*f*) Under a policy or contract issued to any volunteer fire department, first aid, civil defense, or other such volunteer organization, which shall be deemed the policyholder, covering any group of members or participants defined by reference to specified hazards incident to an activity or activities or operations sponsored or supervised by such policyholder.

(*g*) Under a policy or contract issued to a newspaper or other publisher, which shall be deemed the policyholder, covering its carriers.

(*h*) Under a policy or contract issued to an association, including a labor union, which shall have a constitution and by-laws and which has been organized and is maintained in good faith for purposes other than that of obtaining insurance, which shall be deemed the policyholder, covering any group of members or participants defined by reference to specified hazards incident to an activity or activities or operations sponsored or supervised by such policyholder.

(*i*) Under a policy or contract issued to cover any other risk or class of risks which, in the discretion of the Commissioner, may be properly eligible for blanket accident and sickness insurance. The discretion of the Commissioner may be exercised on an individual risk basis or class of risks, or both.

Section 2. Required Provisions. Any insurer authorized to write accident and sickness insurance in this state shall have the power to issue blanket accident and sickness insurance. No such blanket policy, except as provided in Section 5 of this Act, may be issued or delivered in this state unless a copy of the form thereof shall have been filed in accordance with Section __*__. Every such blanket policy shall contain provisions which in the opinion of the Commissioner are not less favorable to the policyholder and the individual insured than the following:

(*a*) A provision that the policy, including endorsements and a copy of the application, if any, of the policyholder and the persons insured shall constitute the entire contract between the parties, and that any statement made by the policyholder or by a person insured shall in absence of fraud, be deemed a representation and not a warranty, and that no such statements shall be used in defense to a claim under the policy, unless contained in a written application. Such person, his beneficiary, or assignee, shall have the right to make written request to the insurer for a copy of such application and the insurer shall, within 15 days after the receipt of such request at its home office or any branch office of the insurer, deliver or mail to the person making such request a copy of such application. If such copy shall not be so delivered or mailed, the insurer shall be precluded from introducing such application as evidence in any action based upon or involving any statements contained therein.

(*b*) A provision that written notice of sickness or of injury must be given to the insurer within twenty days after the date when such sickness or injury occurred. Failure to give notice within such time shall not invalidate nor reduce any claim if it shall be shown not to have been reasonably possible to give such notice and that notice was given as soon as was reasonably possible.

(*c*) A provision that the insurer will furnish either to the claimant or to the policyholder for delivery to the claimant such forms as are usually furnished by it for filing proof of loss. If such forms are not furnished before the expiration of fifteen days after giving of such notice, the claimant shall be deemed to have complied with the requirements of the

* Insert number of the section of the insurance laws applicable to the filing and approval of Accident and Sickness Policy forms.

policy as to proof of loss upon submitting, within the time fixed in the policy for filing proof of loss, written proof covering the occurrence, the character and the extent of the loss for which claim is made.

(*d*) A provision that in the case of claim for loss of time for disability, written proof of such loss must be furnished to the insurer within ninety days after the commencement of the period for which the insurer is liable, and that subsequent written proofs of the continuance of such disability must be furnished to the insurer at such intervals as the insurer may reasonably require, and that in the case of claim for any other loss, written proof of such loss must be furnished to the insurer within ninety days after the date of such loss. Failure to furnish such proof within such time shall not invalidate nor reduce any claim if it shall be shown not to have been reasonably possible to furnish such proof and that such proof was furnished as soon as was reasonably possible.

(*e*) A provision that all benefits payable under the policy other than benefits for loss of time will be payable immediately upon receipt of due written proof of such loss, and that, subject to due proof of loss, all accrued benefits payable under the policy for loss of time will be paid not less frequently than monthly during the continuance of the period for which the insurer is liable, and that any balance remaining unpaid at the termination of such period will be paid immediately upon receipt of such proof.

(*f*) A provision that the insurer at its own expense, shall have the right and opportunity to examine the person of the insured when and so often as it may reasonably require during the pendency of claim under the policy and also the right and opportunity to make an autopsy where it is not prohibited by law.

(*g*) A provision that no action at law or in equity shall be brought to recover under the policy prior to the expiration of sixty days after written proof of loss has been furnished in accordance with the requirements of the policy and that no such action shall be brought after the expiration of three years after the time written proof of loss is required to be furnished.

Section 3. *Application and Certificates Not Required.* An individual application need not be required from a person covered under a blanket accident and sickness policy or contract, nor shall it be necessary for the insurer to furnish each person a certificate.

Section 4. *Facility of Payment.* All benefits under any blanket accident and sickness policy or contract shall be payable to the person insured, or to his designated beneficiary or beneficiaries, or to his estate, except that if the person insured be a minor or otherwise not competent to give a valid release, such benefits may be made payable to his parent, guardian or other person actually supporting him. Provided further, however, that the policy may provide that all or a portion of any indemnities provided by any such policy on account of hospital, nursing, medical or surgical services may, at the option of the insurer and unless the insured requests otherwise in writing not later than the time of filing proofs of such loss, be paid directly to the hospital or person rendering such services; but the policy may not require that the service be rendered by a particular hospital or person. Payment so made shall discharge the obligation of the insurer with respect to the amount of insurance so paid.

Section 5. *Binders.* An insurer authorized to write accident and sickness insurance in this state may issue blanket accident and sickness coverages without prior approval of the policy form, provided that:

(*a*) The group is one eligible for coverage pursuant to the provisions of this Act; and

(*b*) A covering note or binder is issued to bind the insurance; and

(*c*) The covering note or binder contains in summary form: (*i*) the class or classes of persons eligible for coverage; (*ii*) the benefits to be provided; and (*iii*) the exceptions and reductions to such benefits, if any; and

(*d*) Within 30 days after the date on which the covering note or binder is issued the insurer shall submit to the Commissioner for approval a policy form drafted to provide the coverage provided by such covering note or binder and make such revisions in the policy submitted as the Commissioner may lawfully require.

(*e*) The Commissioner may exempt from the policy filing and approval requirements of Section __*__ for so long as he deems proper, any blanket accident and sickness policy or contract to which in his opinion such requirements may not practicably be applied, or may dispense with such filing and approval as, in his opinion, is not desirable nor necessary for the protection of the public.

Section 6. *Repeal of Inconsistent Act.* [Note: This section should contain suitable language to repeal acts or parts of acts presently enacted and inconsistent with this act.]

---

* Insert number of the section of the insurance laws applicable to the filing and approval of Accident and Sickness policy forms.

N. Model Franchise Accident and Health Insurance Bill

Accident and sickness insurance on a franchise plan is hereby declared to be that form of accident and sickness insurance issued to:

(1) Five or more employees of any corporation, co-partnership, or individual employer or any governmental corporation, agency or department thereof; or

(2) Ten or more members, employees, or employees of members of any trade or professional association or of a labor union or of any other association having had an active existence for at least two years where such association or union has a constitution or by-laws and is formed in good faith for purposes other than that of obtaining insurance;

where such persons, with or without their dependents, are issued the same form of an individual policy varying only as to amounts and kinds of coverage applied for by such persons under an arrangement whereby the premiums on such policies may be paid to the insurer periodically by the employer, with or without payroll deductions, or by the association or union for its members, or by some designated person acting on behalf of such employer or association or union. The term "employees" as used herein shall be deemed to include the officers, managers and employees and retired employees of the employer and the individual proprietor or partners if the employer is an individual proprietor or partnership.

O. Provisions of Disability Buy-and-Sell Agreement (Close Corporation)

1. PREAMBLE AND PURPOSE CLAUSES:

"THIS AGREEMENT made_______ between John Black, James Brown and Henry White of Home, Home State, hereinafter referred to as the Stockholders, and ABC Company of Home, Home State, hereinafter referred to as the Corporation,

WITNESSETH:

"WHEREAS, it is for the mutual protection of the Stockholders in event of the total and permanent disability of one of them to enable such a disabled Stockholder to sell his interest in the Corporation to the nondisabled Stockholders, and

"WHEREAS, the shares of stock owned by each of the Stockholders is as follows:

John Black	______ shares
James Brown	______ shares
Henry White	______ shares

"NOW, THEREFORE, in consideration of the mutual covenants and agreements set forth below, the Stockholders for themselves, their heirs, administrators, executors or assigns and the Corporation for itself and its successors, agree as follows":

2. TRANSFER OF STOCK ON TOTAL DISABILITY:

"Each Stockholder agrees that his stock in the Corporation shall be transferred to the other Stockholders who are parties to this Agreement at the time his total disability shall be deemed permanent in accordance with the provisions of this Agreement; such other Stockholders shall receive equal ownership in the stock of the Stockholder who shall be so disabled."

3. ENDORSEMENT OF SHARES:

"Each share of stock owned by a party to this Agreement shall be endorsed as follows, such endorsement to be signed by the Stockholder: "Subject to Agreement dated______, this certificate is transferable only under the terms of said Agreement.""

4. DISABILITY INSURANCE POLICIES:

"It is agreed that the funds of the Corporation shall be used to purchase and pay all premiums on the following policies of noncancellable disability insurance issued by Random Life Insurance Company of New York:

Insured	*Policy No.*	*Monthly Income*
John Black		$______
James Brown		______
Henry White		______

"Each Stockholder shall retain possession and ownership of the policy issued on his life, but agrees not to exercise any rights thereunder except in accordance with this Agreement."

5. DEFINITION OF TOTAL DISABILITY:

"Each Stockholder agrees that any Stockholder shall be considered totally disabled for the purpose of this Agreement if he meets the requirements and conditions for total disability as defined in the policy issued on his life. Such total disability shall be presumed permanent when it shall have continued without interruption for a period of ____ months."

6. SALARY DURING PERIOD OF DISABILITY:

"Each Stockholder agrees that if he shall become totally disabled as provided in the policy issued on his life, any total disability benefits under such policy shall be accepted by him in lieu of any salary he might have been receiving from the Corporation and that he will accept such benefits in lieu of such salary until benefits have been paid for not more than ____ months. Each Stockholder agrees that for said period of ____ months, the acceptance by a disabled Stockholder of disability benefits in lieu of salary shall in no way affect the stock owned by the disabled Stockholder in the Corporation."

7. PAYMENT FOR SHARES ON DISABILITY:

"Each Stockholder agrees that if a Stockholder shall have been permanently totally disabled as provided in paragraph 5, above, and the stock of such disabled Stockholder is sold and transferred after ____ months as specified in paragraph 2 above, then all benefits payable after said ____ months under the insurance policy on the life of the Stockholder shall be considered as payments to be applied against the purchase price of such disabled Stockholder's stock in the Corporation."

"The Stockholders agree that if a disabled Stockholder's stock is sold as provided in paragraph 2 above, and if such disabled Stockholder shall cease to be totally disabled before the disability insurance benefits equal the purchase price for this stock, then payments shall be made by the Corporation to the Stockholder who has been so disabled at the rate of $______ per month until the aggregate of these payments and the disability payments previously made after the disability was deemed permanent shall equal the valuation of the stock of the Stockholder who was disabled."

8. VALUATION OF STOCK:

"The Stockholders shall annually fix a valuation for the stock as soon after the close of the fiscal year of the Corporation as possible. The value so fixed shall be put in writing, signed by the parties and deposited with this agreement. If no valuation has been made for a period of over a year prior to the date on which the total disability of a Stockholder is presumed to be permanent, then the valuation of the stock on such date shall be the higher of (1) the book value of the stock based on the value of the net tangible assets as shown on its books on the date the disability is presumed permanent, or a value equal to ten times the average annual profits over a period of the last five years preceding the date the disability is presumed permanent."

9. TERMINATION OF AGREEMENT:

"This Agreement shall terminate and the stock and insurance policies subject hereto shall be released from the terms of this Agreement upon:

(*a*) Written agreement of the parties;
(*b*) The dissolution of the Corporation for any reason;
(*c*) The completion of the full purchase price for the transfer of a Stockholder's stock under this Agreement after the disability of a Stockholder."

10. DISPOSITION OF DISABILITY POLICIES ON TERMINATION:

"If this Agreement shall be terminated, each Stockholder shall have the right to assume premium payments on the policy issued on his life and to assume all rights under the policy."

11. GENERAL PROVISIONS:

"This Agreement may be amended or altered in any of its provisions and such changes shall become effective only when reduced to writing and signed by the parties hereto. This Agreement shall include any additional insurance policies that the parties may put in force under the terms of this Agreement."

12. EXECUTION:

"IN WITNESS WHEREOF, this Agreement has been executed as of the day and year first above mentioned.

____

____

____

ABC Company

By________"

P. Comparison of Five Temporary Disability Insurance Laws (Prepared as of September 30, 1963)[1]

Provision	California	New Jersey		New York		Rhode Island	Railroad
		Employed Workers	Unemployed Workers	Employed Workers	Unemployed Workers		
Name of program	Unemployment Compensation Disability Benefits	Temporary Disability Benefits--disability during employment	Temporary Disability Benefits--disability during unemployment	Disability Benefits--disability during employment	Disability Benefits--disability during unemployment	Temporary Disability Insurance	Railroad Unemployment Insurance Act, sickness and maternity benefits
Type of law	State plan, with substitution of private plans permitted; administered by employment security agency in coordination with unemployment insurance	State plan, with substitution of private plans permitted; administered by employment security agency in coordination with unemployment insurance		Private plans, with competitive State fund; special State fund for unemployed workers administered by State workmen's Compensation Board which also approves and supervises private plans. System completely separate from unemployment insurance		State plan administered by employment security agency in coordination with unemployment insurance	Government plan administered by Railroad Retirement Board in coordination with unemployment insurance
Name of agency	Department of Employment	Department of Labor and Industry, Division of Employment Security		Workmen's Compensation Board		Department of Employment Security	Railroad Retirement Board
Method of insuring	Employers insured with State fund unless and until agency approves private plan (insured or self-insured)	Employers insured with State fund unless and until agency approves private plan (insured or self-insured)		Employers must arrange for benefit payments by purchasing a policy from an insurance company or from the State insurance fund, or by self-insurance	Special State fund established for paying benefits to the unemployed	All employers insured with the State fund	All employers insured with the Government fund. Benefits paid from railroad unemployment insurance account; no separate fund for these benefits
Benefits to unemployed disabled workers	No distinction between employed and unemployed workers as to benefit formula; some difference in financial accounting	Distinctions between employed and unemployed workers as to benefit formula and financing noted in appropriate items		Distinctions between employed and unemployed workers as to benefit formula and financing noted in appropriate items		No distinction between employed and unemployed workers as to benefit formula or financing	No distinction between employed and unemployed workers as to benefit formula or financing
Definition of "unemployed"	Worker out of covered employment more than 14 days, or in noncovered employment	Worker out of covered employment for 2 weeks or more		Worker out of covered employment for 4 or more consecutive weeks and not working for remuneration or profit at time disability begins, not more than 5 days noncovered employment since termination of covered employment		None	None
Effective dates							
Contributions	May 21, 1946	June 2, 1948, for employee contributions January 1, 1949, for employer contributions		July 1, 1950, for permanent contributions	January 1, 1950; see Financing below	June 1, 1942	No additional or separate contributions
Benefits	December 1, 1946	January 1, 1949		July 1, 1950	July 1, 1950	April 1943	July 1, 1947

	also includes agricultural workers. Individual workers can elect out on religious grounds[2]			can elect out on religious grounds or on grounds that they are entitled to OASI benefits		workers can elect out on religious grounds	
Financing	Employee tax of 1 percent of wages up to $4,100 in 1962, $4,600 in 1963, $5,100 in 1964, and $5,600 in 1965 and thereafter	Employee tax of 0.50 percent of wages up to $3,000 for disability, and 0.25 percent for unemployment insurance. State plan employers pay basic 0.25 percent for temporary disability insurance modified up to 0.75 percent and down to 0.10 percent by experience rating		0.5 percent employee contribution, maximum 30 cents weekly; employer to pay additional costs, if any	January 1 to June 30, 1950, employers and employees each paid 0.1 percent on the first $60 of weekly wages, maximum 6 cents a week each. Additional amounts needed thereafter are assessed against carriers in proportion to covered payrolls	Employee tax of 1 percent of wages up to $3,600; formerly paid for unemployment insurance purposes on $3,000	Single employer contributions on wages up to $400 a month for unemployment and disability insurance. Rate based on total size of fund; ranges from 1.5 percent to 3.75 percent. (Temporary additional rate of 0.25 percent assigned 1962 and 1963.)
Administrative costs	Sum determined annually by State Director of Finance; no limit on percent of contributions	0.08 percent of wages plus assessment on employers of costs of maintaining separate accounts for experience-rating purposes		Each carrier responsible for own administrative expenses; State insurance fund as a carrier, limited to 25 percent of contributions	Necessary expense assessed against carriers including the State insurance fund in proportion to covered wages; no limit	6 percent of contributions	0.2 percent of taxable wages allowed for administration of both programs from railroad unemployment insurance administration fund
Assessments against private plans	Added administrative costs attributable to private plans with no limit; contributions to unemployment disability account at fixed rate against taxable payroll at 0.15 percent in 1962, 0.13 percent in 1963, and 0.12 percent in 1964 and thereafter	Added administrative costs attributable to private plans and to benefits to unemployed and cost of benefits to unemployed assessed against plans in proportion to covered wages, administration and benefits each limited to 0.02 percent of wages		Total administrative expenses of programs for both employed and unemployed workers (not including expense of the State as a carrier) are assessed against all carriers including the State in proportion to covered wages; no limit		No private plans	No private plans
Definition of Disability	Inability, because of physical or mental condition, to perform regular or customary work. See also Disqualifying income: Workmen's compensation	Total inability to perform duties of the employment, resulting from any accident or sickness not arising out of and in course of employment, or, if so, not compensable under workmen's compensation	Total inability to perform any work for remuneration, resulting from any accident or sickness not compensable under workmen's compensation	Inability, because of injury or sickness not arising out of and in the course of employment, to perform regular duties of his employment or any other employment his employer offers him at his regular wages	Inability, because of injury or sickness not arising out of and in the course of employment, to perform duties of any employment for which he is reasonably qualified by training and experience	Inability, because of physical or mental condition, to perform reqular or customary work. See also Disqualifying income: Workmen's compensation	Inability to work because of physical, mental, psychological or nervous injury, illness, sickness or disease. See also Disqualifying income: Workmen's compensation

[1] U.S. Department of Labor, Bureau of Employment Security, Unemployment Insurance Service, Washington, D.C.

[2] An amendment to the California law permits self-employed persons to elect coverage, on a voluntary basis, under TDI beginning September 20, 1963. All persons electing coverage under this provision contribute at the rate of 1.25 percent of the maximum amount of earnings creditable under TDI, without regard to actual self-employment earnings.

P. Comparison of Five Temporary Disability Insurance Laws (Continued)

Provision	California	New Jersey		New York		Rhode Island	Railroad
		Employed Workers	Unemployed Workers	Employed Workers	Unemployed Workers		
Payments for pregnancy	No payments for any illness or injury caused by or arising in connection with pregnancy, up to 28 days after termination of pregnancy	Limited to 4 weeks immediately before expected birth and 4 weeks immediately following termination of pregnancy		No payments for any period of disability caused by or arising in connection with pregnancy, unless that period occurs after return to covered employment for at least 2 consecutive weeks following termination of pregnancy		Limited to 14 consecutive weeks of benefits to begin 6 weeks prior to expected childbirth or with date of childbirth if such occurred more than 6 weeks prior to expected date. For unusual complications or miscarriage, duration up to statutory maximum.	Disabilities due to pregnancy not excluded from regular benefits. Special maternity benefits for a period beginning 57 days before expected date of childbirth, and ending 115 days later, or 31 days after child is born, whichever is later, but not more than 84 days benefits before childbirth. Benefits paid for each day in the maternity period. Benefits for first 14 days in maternity period, and first 14 days after childbirth at 1½ times regular rate
Other exclusions	...	No payments for any period of disability due to willfully and intentionally self-inflicted injury, or to injury sustained in perpetration of a high misdemeanor		No payments for any period of disability due to willful intention of employee to bring about injury or illness to himself or another, or to injury sustained in perpetration of an illegal act; or for disability due to any act of war occurring after June 30, 1950		...	...
Benefit formula	Differs from unemployment insurance. See below	Similar to unemployment insurance	Same as unemployment insurance	Completely different from unemployment insurance		Same as unemployment insurance	Same as unemployment insurance
Benefit year	No benefit year. Rights determined with respect to continuous period of disability established by a valid claim—"disability benefit period"	No benefit year, but maximum benefits limited in terms of any 12 consecutive months	Individual, beginning with valid claims. Valid claim either for disability during unemployment or for unemployment insurance establishes benefit year for both	No benefit year; but maximum benefit limited in terms of any 52 consecutive weeks		Individual, beginning with valid claim for disability insurance	**Uniform, beginning July 1**
Base period•	Without unexpired unemployment insurance benefit year: first 4 of last 5 calendar quarters preceding disability beginning in second or [illegible]	52 calendar weeks immediately preceding the calendar week in which the period of disability began	52 calendar weeks ending with the second week immediately preceding an individual's benefit year	No base period as used in unemployment insurance. See below for periods used for qualifying employment and weekly benefit amount		52 calendar weeks ending with the second week immediately preceding week in which benefit year begins	Calendar year preceding benefit year

	ability beginning in first month of quarter. With unexpired unemployment insurance benefit year, base period is the unemployment insurance base period						
Qualifying wages or employment	Flat qualifying requirement of $300	17 base weeks of employment. A base week is a week in which wages from 1 employer were $15 or more		4 or more consecutive weeks of covered employment (or 25 days regular part-time employment) prior to commencement of disability	2 categories of unemployed workers: (1) earned qualifying wages for unemployment insurance, or (2) if not eligible under (1) but earned $13 in covered employment in each of 20 weeks within 30 weeks preceding last day worked in covered employment[3]	20 credit weeks, or $1,200 in base period. A credit week is a week in which earnings were $20 or more	$500 in base period
Weekly benefit amount	$10 - 70, based on schedule of high-quarter wages. For almost any amount of high-quarter wages, weekly benefits will be higher for disability insurance than for unemployment insurance; after 1/1/63, the maximum weekly benefit amount is the greater of $70 and 2/3 of the average weekly wage paid by all covered employers during the second calendar quarter of each year	$10 - 50, based on schedule of average weekly wage Average wage determined by dividing wages from 1 employer during base weeks in 8 weeks preceding disability by number of such base weeks. If this is less than average using all employment, during last 8 weeks, use earnings from all employers	Average wage determined by dividing wages in all base weeks with 1 employer by number of base weeks. If not 17 base weeks with any 1 employer, average base weeks with all employers	* - 50 on basis of ½ average weekly wage for the last 8 consecutive weeks in covered employment prior to commencement of disability *No prescribed minimum--weekly benefit is average weekly wage if latter is less than $20; weekly benefit is $20 if average weekly wage is $20 to $40		$12 - 50% of the average weekly wage of all covered workers (55 percent of average weekly wage) plus $3 per dependent child up to $12. Dependents defined as children under 16 at beginning of benefit year	Daily benefit amount of $4.50 - 10.20, based on schedule of annual wages, provided not less than 60 percent of daily wages in last base period railroad employment, up to $10.20, $45-102 for 2-week registration period after the waiting period
Additional benefits	Hospital benefits of $12 a day for 20 days in any 1 benefit period. No waiting period for these benefits, or for regular benefits for hospitalized claimant	---	---	---	---	---	See Payments for pregnancy

[3] Qualifying wages required for unemployment insurance; average of at least $15 a week in 20 weeks of employment in 52 weeks preceding filing of claim, *or* average of $15 a week in 15 weeks of employment in 52 weeks and 40 weeks in 104 consecutive weeks preceding filing of claim.

P. Comparison of Five Temporary Disability Insurance Laws (Continued)

Provision	California	New Jersey		New York		Rhode Island	Railroad
		Employed Workers	Unemployed Workers	Employed Workers	Unemployed Workers		
Benefit Formula (Cont'd)							
Duration	Uniform potential 26 weeks for any one disability benefit period, $260 - 1,820. Duration independent of unemployment insurance	13 - 26 weeks, $130 - 1,300, computed as lesser of 26 x weekly benefit and 3/4 base weeks. Limit applies to benefits in any 12 consecutive-month period. Duration independent of unemployment insurance and of benefits as an unemployed disabled worker	13 - 26 weeks, $130-1,300, computed as lesser of 26 x weekly benefit and 3/4 base weeks. Duration under employment insurance and disability during unemployment limited to 150% of duration for either program separately. No benefits payable beyond 26th week of unemployment	Uniform potential 26 weeks in any 52 consecutive weeks or $520 (or less if weekly benefit is less than $20) - $1,300. Duration independent of unemployment insurance	No benefit payable beyond 26th week of unemployment	12[4] - 26 weeks. $120 - 936, computed as lesser of 26 x basic weekly benefit and 3/5 total weeks of employment in base period plus dependents' allowances, if any. Duration independent of unemployment insurance	Uniform potential 130 days (26 weeks), provided benefits not to exceed base-period wages, $585 - 1,326. Duration independent of unemployment insurance and special maternity benefits. See payments for pregnancy
Waiting period	7 consecutive days of disability at beginning of each uninterrupted period of disability. See below	7 consecutive days of disability at beginning of each uninterrupted period of disability. See below	7 consecutive days of disability or 1 week of unemployment in benefit year satisfies waiting period requirement for both unemployment insurance and disability during unemployment	7 consecutive days of disability at beginning of each uninterrupted period of disability. See below	If unemployment insurance claimant, unemployment insurance waiting period; If not qualified for unemployment insurance, 7 consecutive days of disability at beginning of each uninterrupted period of disability. See below	7 consecutive days of disability at the beginning of the benefit year	7 days in first 14-day registration period in a benefit year; benefits not paid for first 4 days of sickness in subsequent 14-day registration periods. Does not apply to special maternity benefits
Uninterrupted period of disability	Consecutive periods of disability due to the same or related cause and separated by not more than 14 days	Consecutive periods of disability due to the same or related cause and separated by not more than 14 days if the individual earned wages from his last employer during the 14-day period	---	Consecutive periods of disability caused by the same or related injury or sickness, if separated by less than 3 months		---	---
Part weeks of disability	Benefits paid for each day of disability in excess of 7 in a spell at rate	Benefits paid for each day of disability in excess of 7 in a spell at	Payment for part weeks of disability combined with employment paid	Benefits paid for each day of disability in excess of 7 in a spell: Daily benefit com-	Daily benefit com-	Benefits paid for part weeks of disability following compensable weeks at	Benefits paid for each day of disability in excess of 4 in a 14-day registration

		payment for part week rounded to next higher dollar	surance formula for partial benefits. (See also Disqualifying Income: Wages) Full week of disability and unemployment paid at full weekly rate from disability account	workdays per week	Monday through Friday	workday up to 4/5 of weekly amount, rounded to next higher dollar	
Benefit formula for private plans	Benefit rights greater than under State plan--rights at least equal in all respects, and greater in at least one	Weekly benefits and weeks of benefits at least equal to State plan and eligibility requirements no more restrictive (private plans existing at time disability law was enacted could continue throughout period of the contract; all such plans have now ended)	---	Weekly benefits and weeks of benefits at least equivalent to statutory benefits, and eligibility requirements no more restrictive; except that private plans existing at time disability law was enacted may continue throughout period of the contract, and may be extended by collective bargaining agreement without meeting statutory conditions	---	No provision for private plans	No provision for private plans
Eligibility requirements in addition to wage qualifications	Claimant withdrawn from the labor market prior to disability not eligible. Claimant neither employed nor registered at a public employment office for more than 3 months preceding beginning of period of disability must prove that unemployment is due to disability and not to withdrawal from the labor market	Must be in covered employment or out of covered employment for less than 2 weeks	If out of covered employment for 2 weeks or more, must meet unemployment insurance eligibility requirements except ability to work	Must be in covered employment or out of covered employment for not more than 4 weeks, and not more than 5 days noncovered employment since last covered employment	Out of covered employment more than 4 weeks and not working for remuneration or profit on day disability began, and not more than 5 days noncovered employment, 2 categories (see Qualifying Wages above): (1) currently claiming unemployment insurance benefits and ineligible for unemployment benefits for week solely because of disability (2) evidenced continued attachment to labor market	Claimant withdrawn from labor market prior to disability not eligible	

[4] Minimum 12 weeks for claimants who qualify with 20 weeks' work; may be less than 12 weeks for claimants who qualify only with $1,200.

P. Comparison of Five Temporary Disability Insurance Laws (Concluded)

Provision	California	New Jersey		New York		Rhode Island	Railroad
		Employed Workers	Unemployed Workers	Employed Workers	Unemployed Workers		
Disqualifying Income Workmen's compensation	If receiving or entitled to workmen's compensation for a temporary disability for same disability and week, not eligible for disability benefits unless workmen's compensation is less than disability; if so difference is payable. Benefits payable irrespective of workmen's compensation payments for permanent disability	Not eligible for any period with respect to which workmen's compensation (other than benefits for a permanent disability previously incurred) is paid or payable		Not eligible for any period with respect to which workmen's compensation (other than permanent partial benefits for a prior disability) is paid or payable		Eligible for combined workmen's compensation and disability benefits up to 85 percent of average weekly wage on last job prior to sickness, but not more than $62 exclusive of dependents' benefits. No deduction for workmen's compensation received after period to which it relates or as lump-sum payment	If receiving or entitled to receive workmen's compensation for same disability and week, not eligible disability benefits unless workmen's compensation is less than disability; if so, the difference is payable
Wages	Eligible even though receiving wages while not working provided that benefits plus wages do not exceed wages prior to disability	Eligible even though receiving wages while not working provided that benefits plus wages do not exceed wages prior to disability	If employed for part week during disability, eligible for full weekly benefit rate less wages paid or payable in excess of 20 percent of weekly benefit rate or $5.00, whichever is greater	No benefit payable for day if entitled to receive remuneration or maintenance from fund to which employer contributes in amount at least equal to benefits; does not include voluntary aid from employer	---	Eligible even though receiving regular wages or part thereof while not working	Not eligible if receiving wages
Other employer paid benefits income	---	Benefits reduced by amount of other benefit to which most recent employer contributed	---	---	---	---	Benefits reduced by amount of other benefits, excluding employer pension
Disqualification	Claimant disqualified for unemployment insurance because of a labor dispute is disqualified for disability benefits unless the disability is not connected with the dispute, and is due to an accident or requires hospitalization. Claimant disqualified for unemployment insurance for voluntary leaving, discharge for misconduct, refusal of suitable work, or willful misrepresentation is presumed dis-	Claimant disqualified for unemployment insurance because of a labor dispute is disqualified for disability benefits unless the disability began prior to the disqualification	Claimant disqualified for unemployment insurance for any cause except inability to work is disqualified for disability benefits	No benefits payable for any period during which claimant is or would be subject to suspension or disqualification under unemployment insurance law, except for inability to work		Claimant disqualified for willful false statement on a disability claim	Claimant disqualified for knowingly false or fraudulent statements in claiming benefits

	qualified for disability benefits in absence of finding of disability and of good cause for benefit payments. Claimant disqualified for willful false statement on a disability claim					
Administrative procedures						
Claims	Initial and continued claims to 17 area offices by mail	Initial and continued claims to central office by mail	Written notice of disability by or on behalf of claimant--to the employer	Written notice of disability by or on behalf of claimant--to Chairman of the Workmen's Compensation Board	Initial and continued claims to central office by mail	Initial and continued claims to 9 regional offices by mail
Medical certification of disability	Medical certification required for all initial claims, and for continued claims on request	Medical certification required for all initial claims, and for continued claims on request	Medical certification required for all initial claims, and for continued claims on request		Medical certification required for all initial claims, and for continued claims on request	Medical certification required for all initial claims, and for continued claims on request
Persons authorized to certify	Licensed physician, surgeon, optometrist, dentist, chiropodist, osteopath or chiropractor, or authorized California religious practitioner	Licensed physician, dentist, chiropodist, osteopath, chiropractor, or public health nurse	Physician authorized to render medical care under New York workmen's compensation law, except that in claim from outside State a physician licensed in the other State may certify		Licensed physician, surgeon, dentist, chiropodist, osteopath, or chiropractor	Doctor of medicine, osteopath, or dentist
Time requirements on claim or proof of disability	Initial claim and medical certification must be filed not later than 20th day following first compensable day of disability, except for good cause	Initial claim and medical certification must be filed not later than 30 days after beginning of disability, except for good cause	Notice of disability must be filed not later than 15 days, and medical certification not later than 20 days after beginning of disability, except for good cause		Initial claim must be filed not later than 30 days after beginning of disability except for good cause; medical certificate from attending physician is requested by agency on receipt of claim	Initial claim and medical certification must be filed not later than 9 days after beginning of disability
Required medical examination	Claimant may be required to submit to examination by physician designated by agency from list including all licensed physicians willing to perform such examinations. Agency pays a scheduled fee for each case	Claimant may be required to submit to examination by physician designated by agency under arrangements with county medical society. Agency pays scheduled fee for each case	Claimant may be required by employer, carrier, or Chairman of Workmen's Compensation Board to submit to examination by designated physician, not more often than once a week		Claimant may be required to submit to examination by physician designated by agency from list including all licensed physicians willing to perform such examinations. Agency pays scheduled fee for each case	Agency has designated physicians to give examinations to claimants directed by agency to report for such examinations, and pays a scheduled fee for each case
Constitution of initial and final appeals authorities	Referee; Appeals Board. Same as for unemployment insurance. Also applies to cases arising under private plans	Examiner; Board of Review. Same as for unemployment insurance. Special provision for appeal within one year from claims decision under private plan	Referee; Workmen's Compensation Board (panel of 3 members). Also applies to cases arising under private plans		Referee; Board of Review. Same as for unemployment insurance	Referee; Railroad Retirement Board

Q. Summary of Selected Provisions of Workmen's Compensation Laws, by States, 1964[1]

State	Type of Law: Whether Compulsory or Elective for Private Employment	Employer to Insure Through[2]	Medical Benefits Provided	Waiting Period[3]	Benefits for Permanent and Total Disability: Maximum Percentage of Wages	Weekly Maximum	Maximum Period	Total Maximum Stated	Maximum Total Benefit for Permanent Partial Disability[4,5]	Benefits for Total Temporary Disability: Maximum Percentage of Wages	Weekly Maximum	Maximum Period	Total Maximum Stated[5]	Maximum Death Benefit Widows and Children[6]
Alabama	Elective	Commercial	Limited[7]	7 days (temporary disability only)	55–65[8]	$38.00	400 weeks[9,10]	$15,200	$11,400 (schedule)	55–65[11]	$38.00	300 weeks	—	—
Alaska	Compulsory	Commercial	Full[12]	3 days	65	$52.65	Duration of disability	—	$20,000 (schedule) $17,000 (non-schedule)	65	$100.00	Duration of disability	$20,000	—
Arizona	Compulsory (employees may reject act)	Competitive	[13]	7 days	65	$150.00	Life	— —	—	65[14]	$150.00, plus $2.30 for each total dependent	433 weeks	—	—
Arkansas	Compulsory	Commercial	Full	7 days	65	$35.00	450 weeks	$12,500	$12,500	65	$35.00	450 weeks	$12,500	$12,500
California	Compulsory	Competitive	Full	7 days	61¾[15]	$52.50	400 weeks; thereafter, 60 per cent of average weekly earnings at time of injury, for life	—	[16]	61¾[15]	$70.00	240 weeks	$16,800	$17,500–20,500[17]
Colorado	Elective	Competitive	Limited	7 days	66⅔	$43.75	Life[18]	[18]	$11,376[18] (non-schedule)	66⅔	$43.75	Duration of disability	[18]	$13,693.75–$16,980.25
Connecticut	Compulsory	Commercial	Full	3 days	60	55 per cent of state's average production	Duration of disability	—	—	60	55 per cent of state's average production	Duration of disability	—	—

Delaware	Compulsory	Commercial	Full	3 days (no waiting period in case of amputation of a member of the body, or a part thereof, or when the injury results in hospitalization of the employee)	66⅔	$50.00[19]	Duration of disability	—	—	66⅔	$50.00	Duration of disability	—	[19]
District of Columbia	Compulsory	Commercial	Full	3 days	66⅔	$70.00[9]	Duration of disability	—	$24,000	66⅔	$70.00[9]	Duration of disability	$24,000	—
Florida	Elective	Commercial	Full	7 days	60	$42.00	Duration of disability	—	—	60	$42.00	350 weeks	—	—
Georgia	Elective	Commercial	Limited	7 days	60	$37.00	400 weeks	$12,500	$9,000 (nonschedule)	60	$37.00	400 weeks	$12,500	—
Hawaii	Compulsory	Commercial	Full	2 days (temporary total only)	66⅔	$75.00[9]	Duration of disability	[20]	$35,000	66⅔	$75.00	Duration of disability	$25,000	$25,000[21]
Idaho	Compulsory	Competitive	Full	7 days	55–60[18]	$32.00–$52.50[9]	400 weeks;[22] thereafter, $15 per week ($18 if dependent wife) plus $4–$15 for children for duration of disability	—	—	55–65[18]	$32.00–$52.00[9]	400 weeks;[23] thereafter, $15 per week ($18 if dependent wife) plus $4–$15 for children for duration of disability	—	$12,000

Q. Summary of Selected Provisions of Workmen's Compensation Laws, by States, 1964[1] (Continued)

State	Type of Law: Whether Compulsory or Elective for Private Employment	Employer to Insure Through[2]	Medical Benefits Provided	Waiting Period[3]	Benefits for Permanent and Total Disability				Maximum Total Benefit for Permanent Partial Disability[4,5]	Benefits for Total Temporary Disability				Maximum Death Benefit Widows and Children[6]
					Maximum Percentage of Wages	Weekly Maximum	Maximum Period	Total Maximum Stated		Maximum Percentage of Wages	Weekly Maximum	Maximum Period	Total Maximum Stated[5]	
Illinois	Compulsory	Commercial	Full[24]	7 days (temporary total disability only)	65–80[11]	$51.00–$61.00[11]	Life[25]	[25]	$13,500–$17,500 according to number of dependents	65–80[11]	$51.00–$61.00[11]	Duration of disability[26]	$13,500–$17,500[11]	$13,500–$17,500[17]
Indiana	Elective (compulsory to coal mining)	Commercial	Full	7 days (temporary total disability only)	60	$42.00	500 weeks	$16,500	$16,500	60	$42.00	500 weeks	$16,500	$16,500
Iowa	Elective (compulsory as to operation of coal mines or production of coal for sale)	Commercial	Full[27]	7 days (permanent total, temporary total, and temporary partial disability)	66⅔	$37.00	500 weeks	$18,500	$18,500	66⅔	$34.00–$50.00[11]	300 weeks	—	$12,000
Kansas	Elective	Commercial	Limited	7 days	60	$42.00	415 weeks	—	—	60	$42.00	415 weeks	$17,430	$15,000
Kentucky	Elective	Commercial	Limited	7 days	65	$38.00	425 weeks[28]	$16,150[28]	$13,200 (nonschedule)	65	$38.00	425 weeks[28]	$16,150	$13,600
Louisiana	Elective	Commercial	Limited	7 days	65	$35.00	400 weeks	—	—	65	$35.00	300 weeks	—	—
Maine	Elective	Commercial	Full[36]	7 days	66⅔	$42.00	500 weeks	$21,000	—	66⅔	$42.00	500 weeks	$21,000	$12,600
Maryland	Compulsory	Competitive	Full	3 days	66⅔	$48.00	Continuation of disability[29]	$30,000	$12,500	66⅔	$48.00	208 weeks	—	$15,000
Massachusetts	Compulsory	Commercial	Full	7 days	66⅔	$53; plus $6 for each total dependent[30]	Duration of disability[29]	—	$18,000	66⅔	$53; plus $6 for each total dependent[30]	Duration of disability	$16,000 plus dependents' allowances	$16,000[31]
Michigan	Compulsory	Competitive	Full	7 days	66⅔	$33.00–$57.00[11]	Duration of disability[32]	—	—	66⅔	$35.00–$57.00[11]	500 weeks	[33]	—

Minnesota....	Compulsory	Commercial	Full	7 days (temporary disability only)	66⅔	$45.00[9]	Duration of disability	[34]	—	66⅔	$45.00	350 weeks[9]	—	$17,500
Mississippi....	Compulsory	Commercial	Full	5 days	66⅔	$35.00	450 weeks	$12,500	—	66⅔	$35.00	450 weeks	$12,500	$12,500
Missouri......	Elective	Commercial	Full	3 days	66⅔	$42.50	300 weeks, thereafter, 40 per cent of wages, maximum $27.50 for duration of disability	—	—	66⅔	$47.50	400 weeks	—	$16,500
Montana.....	Elective (as to hazardous employments; compulsory as to coal-mining business)	Competitive	Limited	7 days	50–66⅔[6]	$29.00–$50.00[8]	500 weeks	—	—	50–66⅔[11]	$29.00–$50.00[11]	300 weeks	—	—
Nebraska.....	Elective	Commercial	Full	7 days	66⅔	$40.00[35]	300 weeks;[22] thereafter, 45 per cent of wages, maximum $32.00 for duration of disability	—	—	66⅔	$40.00	300 weeks;[23] thereafter, 45 per cent of wages, maximum $32.00	—	—
Nevada.......	Compulsory	State Fund	Full[36]	5 days	—	$37.50–$51.92[8]	Life	—	—	65–90[11]	$45.00–$62.31[11]	433 weeks	—	—

Q. Summary of Selected Provisions of Workmen's Compensation Laws, by States, 1964[1] (Continued)

State	Type of Law: Whether Compulsory or Elective for Private Employment	Employer to Insure Through[2]	Medical Benefits Provided	Waiting Period[3]	Benefits for Permanent and Total Disability: Maximum Percentage of Wages	Benefits for Permanent and Total Disability: Weekly Maximum	Benefits for Permanent and Total Disability: Maximum Period	Benefits for Permanent and Total Disability: Total Maximum Stated	Maximum Total Benefit for Permanent Partial Disability[4,5]	Benefits for Total Temporary Disability: Maximum Percentage of Wages	Benefits for Total Temporary Disability: Weekly Maximum	Benefits for Total Temporary Disability: Maximum Period	Benefits for Total Temporary Disability: Total Maximum Stated[5]	Maximum Death Benefit Widows and Children[6]
New Hampshire	Compulsory	Commercial	Full[37]	7 days	66⅔	$45.00	312 weeks[38]	—	$14,322	66⅔	$45.00	312 weeks[38]	—	$15,000
New Jersey	Elective	Commercial	Full	7 days	[39]	$45.00 under certain conditions benefits paid for life[39]	450 weeks[9,40]	—	—	[41]	$45.00	300 weeks	—	—
New Mexico	Elective	Commercial	Full[42]	7 days	60	$38.00	500 weeks	$20,000	$19,000	60	$38.00	500 weeks	$20,000	$20,000
New York	Compulsory	Competitive	Full	7 days	66⅔	$55.00[9]	Duration of disability	—	—	66⅔	$55.00	Duration of disability	$6,500	—
North Carolina	Elective	Commercial	Full[43]	7 days	60	$37.50	400 weeks; 500 weeks for 2 injuries in same employment[9]	$12,000	$12,000	60	$37.50	400 weeks	$12,000	$12,000
North Dakota	Compulsory (where coverage is not compulsory but employer has accepted Act voluntarily, employees may reject Act.)	State Fund	Full	5 days	80	$45.00–$60.00[11]	Life	—	—	80	$45.00–$60.00[11]	Duration of disability	—	—

Ohio	Compulsory	State Fund	Full	7 days	66⅔	$49.00	Life	—	$10,000, division A[44]	66⅔	$56.00 for the first 12 weeks, thereafter $49.00	Duration of disability	$8,000	$15,000–$18,000
Oklahoma	Compulsory	Competitive	Full	5 days	66⅔	$37.50	500 weeks	—	—	66⅔	$37.50	300 weeks; may be extended to 500 weeks	—	$13,500
Oregon	Elective	State Fund	Full	None	—	$28.85–$63.46[11]	Duration of disability	—	$6,742.50[45] (non-schedule)	50–75[11]	$32.31–$66.92[11]	Duration of disability	—	—
Pennsylvania	Elective	Competitive	Full[46]	7 days (no waiting period for schedule injury)	66⅔	$47.50	Duration of disability	—	—	66⅔	$47.50	Duration of disability	—	—
Puerto Rico	Compulsory	State Fund	Full	3 days	66⅔	$20.76	Duration of disability	—	$ 6,000	66⅔	$35.00	312 weeks	—	—
Rhode Island	Compulsory	Commercial	Full	3 days (total disability only)	60	$40.00 or $45.00[47]	Duration of disability[28]	[48]	[49]	60	$40.00 to $57.00[50]	Duration of disability[51]	[51]	[52]
South Carolina	Elective	Commercial	Full	7 days	60	$35.00	500 weeks	$10,000	$10,000	60	$35.00	500 weeks	$10,000	$10,000
South Dakota	Elective	Commercial	Limited	7 days	55	$38.00[53]	300 weeks[53]	$13,500	—	55	$38.00	312 weeks	$13,500	$10,000–$13,000[11]
Tennessee	Elective	Commercial	Limited	7 days	65	$36.00	550 weeks	$14,000	$14,000	65	$36.00	300 weeks	—	$14,000
Texas	Elective (compulsory as to motor bus companies)	Commercial	Full[54]	7 days	60	$35.00	401 weeks	—	—	60	$35.00	401 weeks	—	—

Q. Summary of Selected Provisions of Workmen's Compensation Laws, by States, 1964[1] (Continued)

State	Type of Law: Whether Compulsory or Elective for Private Employment	Employer to Insure Through[2]	Medical Benefits Provided	Waiting Period[3]	Benefits for Permanent and Total Disability: Maximum Percentage of Wages	Weekly Maximum	Maximum Period	Total Maximum Stated	Maximum Total Benefit for Permanent Partial Disability[4,5]	Benefits for Total Temporary Disability: Maximum Percentage of Wages	Weekly Maximum	Maximum Period	Total Maximum Stated[5]	Maximum Death Benefit Widows and Children[6]
Utah	Compulsory	Competitive	Full[55]	3 days	60	$40.00–$54.25[11]	260 weeks; thereafter, 45 per cent of wages during disability, maximum $40.[56]	[56]	$ 8,978[57]	60	$40.00–$54.25[11]	312 weeks	$11,204–$15,126[11]	$11,491–$14,046[11]
Vermont	Elective	Commercial	Full[58]	7 days	66⅔	$39.00, plus $2.50 for each dependent child under 21	330 weeks[22]	$12,870	—	66⅔	$39.00, plus $2.50 for each dependent child under 21	330 weeks[23]	—	$12,870
Virginia	Compulsory	Commercial	Full[59]	7 days	60	$37.00	500 weeks	$14,800	$14,800	60	$37.00	500 weeks	$14,800	$11,100
Washington	Compulsory	State Fund	Full	3 days	—	$38.08–$71.54[8]	Duration of disability	—	$8,750 (non-schedule)	—	$38.08–$71.54[11]	Duration of disability	—	—
West Virginia	Elective	State Fund	Limited	7 days	66⅔	$38.00	Life	—	[60]	66⅔	$38.00	208 weeks	—	—
Wisconsin	Compulsory	Commercial	Full	3 days	70	$64.00[9]	Life	—	—	70	$64.00[9]	Duration of disability	—	$18,286[61]
Wyoming	Compulsory	State Fund	Full	3 days (temporary total disability only)	—	$28.85–$34.62, plus $5.54 for each dependent child under 18[11,62,63]	—	$12,000–$19,000[11,62,63]	—	66⅔	$40.38–$60.00[11]	Duration of disability	—	$10,000–$17,000[11]

Q. Summary of Selected Provisions of Workmen's Compensation Laws, by States, 1964[1] (Continued)

Source: Compiled from U.S. Department of Labor, Bureau of Labor Standards, *State Workmen's Compensation Laws*, 1964 ed. and *ibid*., *Medical Care under Workmen's Compensation*, Bulletin 244 1962.

1 This table summarizes some of the specific provisions of the workmen's compensation laws of the several states. The Federal Employees Compensation Act and the Longshoremen's and Harbor Workers' Act are not included in this appendix. Many specific limits and provisions are not indicated. In general, the material presented applies. Each specific case, however, must be analyzed relative to the applicable state laws. In addition to the benefits described below, schedule benefits are payable in all cases for dismemberment. It may be noted that occupational disease is covered in full in 30 states, the District of Columbia and Puerto Rico, by schedule in 18 states, and not at all in 2 states. Moreover, the medical benefits for covered occupational disease cases differ from those available for accidenta linjury in 18 states. (See U.S. Department of Labor, Bureau of Labor Standards, *Medical Care under Workmen's Compensation*, Bulletin 244, 1962, Table 8, p. 12.)

In addition to coverage exemptions by industry and occupation, 29 states permit a numerical exemption as well.

For details, by state, see sources noted.

2 In all cases except Ohio and West Virginia, where qualified employers may substitute self-insurance for state fund, and Texas, where only commercial insurance is permitted, "commercial" means that coverage may be acquired from a commercial insurer or, if qualified, provided through self-insurance.

3 Benefits may be retroactive after a certain period has elapsed.

4 In some states the benefits do not apply if the disability is due either to silicosis or any occupational disease (see the Law in each case). The figure stated is the maximum total paid for both schedule and nonschedule injuries unless otherwise noted.

5 In addition, rehabilitation costs are borne in whole or in part in the following 26 states: Alaska, Arizona, Arkansas, Connecticut, District of Columbia, Florida, Hawaii, Maine, Maryland, Massachusetts, Minnesota, Missouri, Mississippi, Montana, New Jersey, New York, North Dakota, Ohio, Oregon, Puerto Rico, Rhode Island, Utah, Texas, Washington, West Virginia, and Wisconsin.

6 Includes multiplied totals (benefit × number of payments permitted). In addition, funeral benefits, dependents' benefits and survivors' benefits may be payable in some cases.

7 Benefits are limited to 2 years or $2,400.

8 Varies with the number of dependents. In Idaho, Oregon, Washington, and Wyoming, varies with marital status and number of dependents.

9 Additional benefits in specific cases, such as for vocational rehabilitation, constant attendant, paralysis from spinal injuries, or loss of mental faculties.

10 For specific types of disability 500 weeks may be paid.

11 Varies with the number of dependents. In Idaho, Oregon, Washington, and Wyoming varies with marital status and number of dependents; in Illinois varies according to number of dependent children under 16, or 18 when not emancipated.

12 Any state carrying the designation "full" may limit the time period over which benefits are payable. See source for details.

13 Full medical aid, in the judgment of the Arizona Industrial Commission, is authorized through a combination of the medical care and rehabilitation provisions of the law.

14 Additional benefits for dependents.

15 The California Law provides for 65 per cent of 95 per cent of actual earnings, or 61¾ per cent.

16 California: Four weeks of compensation for each 1 per cent of permanent disability, and thereafter if disability is 70 per cent or more, life pension of 1.5 per cent of average weekly each per cent of disability in excess of 60 per cent.

17 According to number of dependents.

18 If periodic disability benefits are payable to the worker under the federal OASDI, the workmen's compensation weekly benefits shall be reduced (but not below zero) by an amount approximating one half such federal benefits for such week. If disability benefits are payable under an employer pension plan, the workmen's compensation benefits shall be reduced in an amount proportional to the employer's percentage of total contributions to the plan. The total maximum for permanent and total disability from accidental injury is not limited, but a maximum of $12,598.25 is set in cases of occupational disease. The total maximum for temporary total disability from accidental injury is not limited, except that if payable in lump sum, the maximum is $13,650; in the case of occupational diseases the maximum is $13,693.75.

19 No limit on children up to age 18.

20 Hawaii: After $25,000 has been paid, benefits at the same rate are paid from special fund.

21 Hawaii: However, the dollar maximum does not apply to children under 18; nor to unmarried children over 18 for 104 weeks beyond their 18th birthday, if they are incapable of self-support; nor to an unremarried widow who is physically or mentally incapable of self-support.

22 In case total disability begins after a period of partial disability, the period of partial disability shall be deducted from the weeks specified.

23 In case total disability begins after a period of partial disability, the period of partial disability shall be deducted from the specified period for temporary total.

24 Benefits are limited in cases of silicosis or silicosis complicated with tuberculosis or asbestosis or asbestosis complicated with tuberculosis.

25 Illinois: After $13,500–$17,500 depending upon dependents, has been paid, a pension for life is paid.

26 Until the equivalent of the death benefit is paid, except in specific injury cases, limited to 64 weeks.

27 Iowa: Limited to $7,500.

28 Kentucky: If period of total disability begins after a period of partial disability, the period of partial disability shall be deducted from the 425 weeks, and the payments for partial disability shall be deducted from $16,150.

Q. Summary of Selected Provisions of Workmen's Compensation Laws, by States, 1964[1] (Continued)

29 Law expressly provides that such payments are in addition to payments for temporary total.

30 Aggregate not to exceed the average weekly wage of the employee.

31 Additional benefits for dependent child; in Massachusetts, benefits continue to children until age 18, or over age 18 if incapacitated, and to widows during periods when they are not fully self-supporting.

32 Michigan: Law states that there is a conclusive presumption that disability does not extend beyond 800 weeks, but after that time the question of permanent total disability is determined in each case in accordance with the facts.

33 Michigan: Maximum shall not exceed 500 times total weekly amount payable.

34 Minnesota: After $18,000 is paid, OASI benefits are credited against workmen's compensation benefits.

35 Available for 300 weeks; thereafter 45 per cent of wages, maximum of $32.00 weekly for duration of disability.

36 Benefits are limited in case of silicosis or asbestosis.

37 See case decisions and the New Hampshire statutes for administrative limits.

38 Thereafter, annual extensions in the discretion of the Labor Commissioner.

39 New Jersey: Benefits set in accordance with a "wage and compensation schedule."

After 450 weeks, if worker has accepted such rehabilitation as may have been ordered by the Rehabilitation Commission, and such worker is unable to earn wages equal to wages before his accident, further benefits may be paid during disability, amounting to his previous weekly compensation payment diminished by the proportion that the wages he is then able to earn bears to the wages received at the time of the accident. If his wages equal or exceed such former wages, his benefit rate shall be reduced to $5.00 a week.

40 New Jersey: Under certain conditions benefits paid for life.

41 New Jersey: Benefits set in accordance with a "wage and compensation schedule." Under this schedule, the 66⅔ per cent level is adhered to fairly closely for workers earning wages of $45 a week or less. For workers who earn more, the schedule specifies benefits which are less than 66⅔ per cent. For instance, a worker earning $60 a week is entitled to a compensation benefit of $36, or 60 per cent.

42 Limited to $15,000, accidental injury; for occupational diseases, the initial amount is $700, additional funds, unlimited as to period or amount, may be authorized by court order.

43 Limited for occupational disease; in full for accident.

44 Ohio: Employee may elect benefits under one of two plans: "A" under which benefits are 66⅔ per cent of earning capacity impairment; or "B" under which benefits are based on permanent physical impairment. Under "B" benefits are paid for a maximum of 200 weeks if disability is 90 per cent or more, and are set at 66⅔ per cent of employee's average weekly wage.

45 Schedule permanent partial injuries are compensated at the rate of $46.50 for each degree of disability, as specified in the law, but maximum weekly payments are limited by schedule.

46 Limited to six months, $450 plus six months hospitalization. May be extended by Commission review, if further care would substantially restore the worker's earning power.

47 Rhode Island: $40 if the worker is receiving benefits under the Temporary Disability Insurance Act; $45.00 if the worker is not receiving benefits under the Temporary Disability Insurance Act.

48 Rhode Island: After 1,000 weeks, or after payment of $16,000, payments to be made for life from second-injury fund.

49 Rhode Island: If employee cannot obtain suitable work and the employer cannot give him such work or show it is available elsewhere, weekly benefits for partial incapacity are paid at the same rate as for total incapacity ($45 maximum).

50 Rhode Island: $40 if the worker is receiving benefits under the Temporary Disability Insurance Act; $45 to $57, depending upon number of dependents, if the worker is not receiving benefits under the Temporary Disability Insurance Act.

51 Rhode Island: After 1,000 weeks, or after $16,000 has been paid, payments to be made from second-injury fund for period of disability. The allowance of up to $4.00 weekly for dependent children also is payable from this fund.

52 Plus $4.00 weekly for each dependent child up to age 18, unless emancipated.

53 South Dakota: Available for 300 weeks; thereafter 30 per cent of earnings, maximum of $15, for life.

54 Benefits are limited in case of silicosis or asbestosis.

55 Benefits are limited to $1,283.33 if employee is totally disabled from an occupational disease. In cases of prolonged hospitalization the Commission may increase the maximum to $1,925.01.

56 Utah: After payment of $15,800 by employer or carrier, a worker who cannot be rehabilitated receives from the combined injury fund 45 per cent of wages, for period of disability, weekly maximum $40.00.

57 Utah: The maximum, $8,978 applies in cases of accidental injury. In cases of permanent partial disability due to an occupational disease, the maximum benefits are $4,309.

58 Except for $1,000 limit on silicosis and asbestosis.

59 Medical benefits are limited to 60 days but may be extended for two years including the first 60 days.

60 West Virginia: For disability of 85 per cent to 100 per cent, benefits are payable during life.

61 Wisconsin: Additional benefits payable from Children's Fund to the widow for children under 16 years of age (13 per cent of the widow's benefit is the weekly or monthly allowance made for each dependent child), or for children over 16 if mentally or physically incapacitated.

62 Wyoming: As to the allowance for the children, the law states: ". . . there shall be credited to the account of each of such children . . . a lump sum equivalent to $24 per month ($5.54 per week), until the time when each of said children would become 18 years of age; provided that the lump sum credited to the account of all said children shall in no case exceed $7,000." The total maximum of $19,000 shown on the table includes the $7,000.

63 May be continued from age 18 to age 21 for each child incapable of self-support because of mental or physical incapacity.

The _________________ Life Insurance Company

April 17 , 1964 .

Policy No . 0 000 000

on the life of WILLIAM PENN

matured as a death claim

on April 15 , 1964 *and the sum of*

TWENTY-FIVE THOUSAND AND NO ONE-HUNDREDTHS . . .

. . . . *Dollars* ($ 25,000.00)

has become payable in accordance with the terms of the

OWNER AND BENEFICIARY DESIGNATION DATED April 1, 1964

and the Income Options, copies of which are attached hereto.

THE ____________ LIFE INSURANCE COMPANY

....

FOR SUPERVISOR OF CLAIMS

Specimen Settlement Agreement (Continued)

OWNER AND BENEFICIARY DESIGNATION

Policy No. 0000000
The _________ *Life Insurance Company*
Insured: WILLIAM PENN

I. OWNER

If no provision is inserted the owner shall be as provided on page 1.

Privileges of ownership are vested in

II. BENEFICIARY OF BENEFITS NOT RELATED TO INSURED'S DEATH

(Applicable only if this policy provides such a benefit.)

Unless otherwise provided below—any amount payable (a) as an endowment, (b) as an income or as a maturity value before the death of the insured, or (c) as a death benefit under a Family Policy upon the death of the wife or a dependent child, shall be paid as provided on page 1—and any amount which may become payable under a provision for a disability annuity shall be payable as provided in the disability agreement.

III. BENEFICIARY OF ANY BENEFIT PAYABLE BY REASON OF INSURED'S DEATH

The proceeds payable by reason of the death of the insured shall, in place of any other manner of payment, be paid as provided in the following table and in the General Provisions of IV below. (*See General Provision 3 for the order of payment under sections of the table and for requirements for payment to beneficiaries designated in a section.*)

TABLE

Beneficiaries	*Manner of Payment*
Section 1. HANNAH PENN, wife of the insured.	The proceeds shall be paid under Option D, payable monthly. *Privileges* The beneficiary shall have full privileges of withdrawal in accordance with the following General Provisions.
Section 2. Children of the insured.	Each beneficiary's share of the proceeds shall be paid under Option D, payable monthly. Any share of a beneficiary in the proceeds remaining payable under this section at the time of his death shall be paid in equal shares to such of the other beneficiaries designated in this section who are then living. Such payment shall be in one sum provided that if any portion of the share of a beneficiary is then being paid under Option D or E, the payment shall be added to such share and, in the case of Option E, so as to extend the period of payments. *Privileges* Each beneficiary shall have full privileges of withdrawal in accordance with the following General Provisions.
Section 3. The executors or administrators of that one of the foregoing beneficiaries and the insured whose death occurs last.	In one sum.

(Page)

Specimen Settlement Agreement (Continued)

(Page)

IV. GENERAL PROVISIONS

The provisions inserted in I, II and III above shall, except as may otherwise be provided therein, be subject to the following additional provisions:

1. *Definitions* "Proceeds" when applicable to any time after maturity, means the net amount payable at such time as a one sum payment or as the commuted value of any instalments certain not yet due. In applying "children", "grandchildren", "brothers" and "sisters", legally adopted children and those of the half-blood shall be included. The masculine pronoun includes the feminine and "insured" includes an annuitant.

2. *Privileges* A beneficiary who has a privilege of withdrawal may withdraw his share in any proceeds payable under a policy or option provision (or, subject to the Company's rules, may make partial withdrawals) provided that the amount withdrawable after the first payment under a provision other than Option D or E is the commuted value of his share in any instalments certain which (except for any condition that he be living when the instalments become due) would otherwise become payable to him. Such beneficiary may substitute payment under any option under which (except for any age limitation) his share could have been made payable, subject to any privileges available under the substitute option, provided that (a) substitution for a provision other than Option D or E must be made before a payment has been made under the provision to be replaced, and (b) substitution of Option B, C, FR or G by a succeeding beneficiary shall be limited to the period permitted by the Company's rules. Such beneficiary, with respect to his share, may exercise any additional privileges permitted by the Company's rules. The rules to be applied shall be those in effect at the time the privilege is exercised.

3. *Payment in accordance with the Table* *Order of Payment under Sections.* Payment shall first be made under the lowest numbered section of the table in which there is a beneficiary designated who is living or who is designated in a fiduciary capacity. Upon completion of payment to beneficiaries designated in such section in the manner provided therein and in this General Provision 3 any portion of the proceeds payable as provided in the table which then remains undistributed (unless payable under Option G), shall be paid under the next lowest numbered section in which there is a beneficiary who is living or who is designated in a fiduciary capacity and so on from section to section until all proceeds have been distributed.

Payment to All Beneficiaries in a Section. Payment shall be made to all the beneficiaries designated in the section who, when payment is due, are living or designated in a fiduciary capacity. If when proceeds or income payments first become payable under the section there is more than one such beneficiary the proceeds payable under the section shall be divided into equal shares, one for each such beneficiary.

Manner of Payment. The manner of payment under a section shall be as directed in the section, subject to the exercise of any privilege stated therein and to the limitations of General Provision 5.

Payment as an Income. Income payments to a beneficiary shall become due to him only if living on the date as of which the income payment becomes due.

4. *Payment of Accrued Interest* At the time of a change in the interval or amount of payments under Option D or E or a change from Option D or E to another option or to a one sum payment, any accrued interest shall be paid in one sum to those beneficiaries who are then living or designated in a fiduciary capacity and who are to receive such payments. Such payment shall be made without regard to any condition that the beneficiaries be living when an income payment becomes due after the date of the change. If Option D is continued without such a change, accrued interest shall be included in the next option payment.

5. *Limitations and Other Provisions Concerning Options* $1,000 shall be the minimum amount of any share of proceeds which (*a*) may be paid under an option upon maturity, reapplication of proceeds under an option or substitution of an option, or (*b*) may continue to be paid under an option upon exercise of a withdrawal privilege. A share or portion of a share which, except for the above limitation, would become or continue payable under an option shall be paid in one sum to the beneficiary or beneficiaries for whose benefit payment would have first been made or continued under the option.

Specimen Settlement Agreement (Continued)

If option payments at the interval directed would be less than $10 each, the interval shall be changed to whichever of quarterly, semi-annual or annual intervals will provide for most frequent payments of not less than $10.

Option D payments to a succeeding beneficiary shall be computed from the due date of the option payment which last became due before the date of termination of the right of the preceding beneficiary to receive option payments if Option D is continued without change in interval, otherwise from the date of such termination.

6. *Trustee and Miscellaneous Provisions* If payments or privileges are to be made or exercised in trust, the Company shall determine the rights of the trustee upon the basis of this designation, and is released of responsibility for determining the existence, modification or discharge of the trust. If the trustee or trustees named shall fail or cease to serve as trustee, such payments shall be made to and such privileges shall be exercisable by the beneficiary or owner if of legal age, otherwise his legal guardian, unless proof satisfactory to the Company is furnished of the right of a successor trustee to receive payments or exercise privileges.

If a trustee is designated to receive payments or exercise privileges for support, education and welfare of a minor beneficiary or owner named above, and the applicant while possessing the privileges of ownership executes a separate trust instrument relating to the above policy, the receipt of payments or the exercise of privileges shall be subject to the terms of the separate instrument.

The Company may in good faith rely upon proof by affidavit or other written evidence satisfactory to it in determining the identity, date of birth, death, marriage, name, address and other facts relating to any beneficiary or any person in whom a privilege of ownership is vested.

APPLICATION AMENDMENT

I hereby amend my application to The Life Insurance Company dated for a policy to be issued by the Company, and direct that the policy shall, as of the date of issue, be payable and owned as provided in the foregoing designation, which shall be included as a part of the policy.

Signed on............ April 1,.......... 19 64, at .... State of ....

....
Signature of Witness

.... WILLIAM PENN Applicant.

....
Address of Witness

(Page)

Specimen Settlement Agreement (Continued)

SECTION 7—INCOME OPTIONS

The owner may elect to have the whole or part of the proceeds upon maturity of this policy or the cash surrender value upon surrender paid under one of the following options. If at maturity no election by the owner is effective, the beneficiary, if entitled to payment of the proceeds in one sum, may make such election. The right to elect and payment under an option are subject to the limitations stated in this section. As used in an option "proceeds" means the amount of proceeds or cash surrender value elected to be paid under such option.

Option A An income for a fixed period of years not exceeding 30.

Option B An income for 20 years certain and thereafter during the life of the payee, terminating, after the certain period, with the last payment preceding death.

Option C An income for 10 years certain and thereafter during the life of the payee, terminating, after the certain period, with the last payment preceding death.

Option D An interest income on the proceeds at the guaranteed rate of 2% per year, increased by any additions as provided below.

Option E An income of a fixed amount composed of payments of principal and interest on the balance of principal retained by the Company at the guaranteed rate of 2% per year, increased by any additions as provided below, until the proceeds are exhausted, the final payment not to exceed the unpaid balance of principal plus accrued interest. Interest accrued at the time for any payment shall be paid in place of the fixed amount, if greater.

Option FR A refund life income payable during the life of the payee, terminating with the last payment preceding death; provided that after the death of the payee the income payments shall be continued (unless commuted as provided below) during any refund period necessary to make the total income paid equal the proceeds, the last payment to be the difference between the total preceding payments and the proceeds.

Option G A life income payable during the joint lifetime of two payees and the life of the survivor, terminating with the last payment preceding the death of the survivor.

Option H A monthly life income without refund payable during the life of the Insured commencing at maturity or surrender and terminating with the last payment preceding death of the Insured. The amount of the income payment shall be 103% of the monthly life income which the proceeds would purchase on the basis of the Company's published rate in use at maturity or surrender for a monthly life annuity without refund, adjusted to make the first payment immediate, and may be obtained upon application to the Company at any time after it is determinable.

The amount of the income under these options, except Option H, shall be determined from the tables stated below. The income period under an option shall commence as of the date of maturity unless the election is made after such date, in which event the period shall commence as of the date such election is received at the Home Office. In case of payment of the cash surrender value under an option the income period shall commence as of the date of surrender.

The income under Option A, B, C, FR or G shall be payable monthly in advance. The income under Option D or E shall be payable monthly, quarterly, semi-annually or annually at the end of the interval elected.

Specimen Settlement Agreement (Continued)

Election of Option—Limitations on Use Election of an option shall be in writing filed at the Home Office before payment of proceeds or cash surrender value as otherwise provided by this policy. Election by the owner shall be before maturity. Provision in this policy, a beneficiary designation, an assignment or other instrument filed with the Company directing payment under an option shall constitute an election. Consent of the Company is required to (i) an election by an owner other than the Insured or the owner designated in this policy at the date of issue, by an assignee, association, partnership or corporation or by an executor, administrator or other fiduciary, and (ii) a direction for payment under an option otherwise than to a natural person in his own right, except that consent is not required to an election by or for an authorized fiduciary if option payments will terminate within 21 years. Acceptance by the Company of an election without condition shall constitute consent.

Payment of proceeds or cash surrender value or the share of a payee therein may not be made under an option if at maturity or surrender the amount to be paid under the option (i) is less than $1,000 (ii) would produce an income of less than $10 (iii) would be payable under Option G and either payee is then under age 50 or (iv) would be payable under Option H and the Company shall have discontinued the issuance of life annuities. If, because of this limitation, payment may not be made under an option elected before maturity or surrender the amount directed to be paid under the option shall be paid in one sum to the payee to whom the first income payment under the option would otherwise be payable if the first income payment were due at maturity or surrender.

The Company may require proof of date of birth and of continued life of any person on whose life an option is based.

Commutation, Withdrawal, or Alienation The payee, except as provided below, may commute income payments still to become due under Option A, B, C, or FR during the fixed, certain or refund period, or may withdraw the principal held under Option D or E, but in no event shall there be any right to commute income payments beyond the certain or refund periods under Option B, C, or FR, or income payments under Option G or H. The Company may defer payment upon such commutation or withdrawal for a period not exceeding six months from the date of request for payment.

If an election of an option is made by the owner, no payee other than the owner (unless written consent of the owner given before maturity has been filed at the Home Office) shall have the right to commute, withdraw, anticipate, alienate or assign any payment of income or principal or interest thereunder and, to the extent permitted by law, no such payment shall be in any way subject to such payee's debts, contracts or engagements, nor to any judicial processes to levy upon or attach the same for payment thereof. The joinder by the owner with the payee, prior to maturity in an assignment of any rights under this policy shall be consent of the owner to such assignment.

The commuted value of income payments shall be calculated on the basis of compound interest at the rate of 2% per year for Option A and at the rate of 2½% per year for Options B, C and FR.

Death of Payee Upon the death of a payee entitled to payments in his own right, the commuted value of any remaining payments under the option or, in the case of Option D or E, the balance of proceeds payable thereunder, with accrued interest, shall be paid in one sum to the executors or administrators of the payee unless otherwise provided in the election and consented to by the Company.

Participation The income under Option A, the income during the certain or refund periods under Options B, C and FR and the interest under Options D and E shall be increased by such additions as may be awarded from divisible surplus by the Board of Trustees. The income under Options B and C after the certain periods, the income under Option FR after the refund period and all income under Options G and H shall not participate in divisible surplus.

Specimen Settlement Agreement (Continued)

INCOME OPTION TABLES

OPTION A

The monthly income for each $1,000 of Proceeds paid under Option A will be the amount shown below opposite the number of years selected.

Number of Years	Monthly Income	Number of Years	Monthly Income	Number of Years	Monthly Income
1	$84.09	11	$8.42	21	$4.85
2	42.46	12	7.80	22	4.67
3	28.59	13	7.26	23	4.51
4	21.65	14	6.81	24	4.36
5	17.49	15	6.42	25	4.22
6	14.72	16	6.07	26	4.10
7	12.74	17	5.77	27	3.98
8	11.25	18	5.50	28	3.87
9	10.10	19	5.26	29	3.77
10	9.18	20	5.04	30	3.68

OPTIONS D and E

At the guaranteed interest rate each $1,000 of Proceeds held at interest under Option D or E will provide income payments under Option D or interest included in Option E payments as follows:

Payable	*Amount*
Monthly	$ 1.65
Quarterly	4.96
Semi-Annually	9.95
Annually	20.00

OPTIONS B, C and FR

The monthly life income for each $1,000 of Proceeds paid under Option B, C or FR will be the amount shown below opposite the age of the Payee (in the column under the Payee's sex) at the Payee's birthday nearest the date for the first payment.

Age of Payee Nearest Birthday		Monthly Life Income		
Male	Female	Option B 20 Years Certain	Option C 10 Years Certain	Option FR With Refund
	5 and under	$2.54	$2.55	$2.52
	6	2.55	2.56	2.53
	7	2.56	2.57	2.54
	8	2.57	2.58	2.56
	9	2.59	2.60	2.57
5 and under	10	2.60	2.61	2.58
6	11	2.61	2.63	2.60
7	12	2.63	2.64	2.61
8	13	2.65	2.66	2.63
9	14	2.66	2.67	2.64
10	15	2.68	2.69	2.66
11	16	2.70	2.71	2.67
12	17	2.71	2.73	2.69
13	18	2.73	2.74	2.71
14	19	2.75	2.76	2.73
15	20	2.77	2.78	2.75
16	21	2.79	2.81	2.77
17	22	2.81	2.83	2.79
18	23	2.84	2.85	2.81
19	24	2.86	2.88	2.83
20	25	2.88	2.90	2.85
21	26	2.91	2.93	2.88
22	27	2.93	2.95	2.90
23	28	2.96	2.98	2.93
24	29	2.99	3.01	2.95
25	30	3.02	3.04	2.98
26	31	3.05	3.08	3.01
27	32	3.08	3.11	3.04
28	33	3.11	3.14	3.07
29	34	3.15	3.18	3.10
30	35	3.18	3.22	3.13
31	36	3.22	3.26	3.17
32	37	3.25	3.30	3.20
33	38	3.29	3.34	3.24
34	39	3.33	3.39	3.28
35	40	3.37	3.43	3.32
36	41	3.41	3.48	3.36
37	42	3.45	3.53	3.40
38	43	3.50	3.59	3.44
39	44	3.54	3.64	3.49
40	45	3.59	3.70	3.53
41	46	3.64	3.76	3.58
42	47	3.69	3.82	3.63
43	48	3.74	3.88	3.68
44	49	3.79	3.95	3.74

Age of Payee Nearest Birthday		Monthly Life Income		
Male	Female	Option B 20 Years Certain	Option C 10 Years Certain	Option FR With Refund
45	50	$3.84	$4.02	$3.80
46	51	3.90	4.09	3.85
47	52	3.95	4.17	3.91
48	53	4.01	4.25	3.98
49	54	4.07	4.33	4.04
50	55	4.12	4.42	4.11
51	56	4.18	4.50	4.18
52	57	4.24	4.60	4.26
53	58	4.30	4.69	4.33
54	59	4.36	4.79	4.42
55	60	4.41	4.90	4.50
56	61	4.47	5.01	4.59
57	62	4.53	5.12	4.68
58	63	4.59	5.23	4.77
59	64	4.64	5.35	4.87
60	65	4.70	5.48	4.98
61	66	4.75	5.61	5.08
62	67	4.80	5.74	5.20
63	68	4.85	5.87	5.31
64	69	4.90	6.01	5.44
65	70	4.94	6.16	5.57
66	71	4.98	6.30	5.70
67	72	5.02	6.45	5.84
68	73	5.02	6.60	5.99
69	74	5.02	6.76	6.14
70	75	5.02	6.91	6.31
71	76	5.02	7.07	6.48
72	77	5.02	7.23	6.66
73	78	5.02	7.38	6.84
74	79	5.02	7.54	7.04
75	80	5.02	7.69	7.25
76	81	5.02	7.84	7.46
77	82	5.02	7.98	7.69
78	83	5.02	8.13	7.93
79	84	5.02	8.26	8.18
80	85 and over	5.02	8.39	8.45
81		5.02	8.51	8.73
82		5.02	8.63	9.02
83		5.02	8.73	9.34
84		5.02	8.83	9.66
85 and over		5.02	8.92	10.00

Specimen Settlement Agreement (Concluded)

OPTION G

The monthly life income for each $1,000 of Proceeds paid under Option G will be the amount shown below opposite the age of one Payee (in the vertical column under such Payee's sex) and under the age of the other Payee (in the horizontal column opposite such Payee's sex) using in each case the Payee's age at the birthday nearest the date for the first payment. If no amount is shown below the age of the other Payee, reverse the Payees in using the age columns.

Age of Payee Nearest Birthday		Monthly Life Income													
Male							50	51	52	53	54	55	56	57	58
	Female	50	51	52	53	54	55	56	57	58	59	60	61	62	63
	50	$3.46													
	51	3.48	$3.51												
	52	3.51	3.54	$3.57											
	53	3.53	3.57	3.60	$3.63										
	54	3.56	3.59	3.62	3.66	$3.69									
50	55	3.58	3.62	3.65	3.69	3.72	$3.75								
51	56	3.61	3.64	3.68	3.72	3.75	3.79	$3.82							
52	57	3.63	3.67	3.71	3.75	3.78	3.82	3.86	$3.89						
53	58	3.66	3.69	3.73	3.77	3.81	3.85	3.89	3.93	$3.97					
54	59	3.68	3.72	3.76	3.80	3.84	3.89	3.93	3.97	4.01	$4.05				
55	60	3.70	3.74	3.79	3.83	3.87	3.92	3.96	4.00	4.05	4.09	$4.13			
56	61	3.72	3.77	3.81	3.86	3.90	3.95	3.99	4.04	4.09	4.13	4.18	$4.22		
57	62	3.74	3.79	3.83	3.88	3.93	3.98	4.03	4.07	4.12	4.17	4.22	4.27	$4.32	
58	63	3.76	3.81	3.86	3.91	3.96	4.01	4.06	4.11	4.16	4.21	4.26	4.31	4.36	$4.41
59	64	3.78	3.83	3.88	3.93	3.98	4.03	4.09	4.14	4.19	4.25	4.30	4.36	4.41	4.46
60	65	3.80	3.85	3.90	3.95	4.01	4.06	4.12	4.17	4.23	4.29	4.34	4.40	4.46	4.51
61	66	3.82	3.87	3.92	3.98	4.03	4.09	4.15	4.20	4.26	4.32	4.38	4.44	4.50	4.56
62	67	3.83	3.89	3.94	4.00	4.06	4.12	4.17	4.24	4.30	4.36	4.42	4.48	4.55	4.61
63	68	3.85	3.91	3.96	4.02	4.08	4.14	4.20	4.26	4.33	4.39	4.46	4.52	4.59	4.66
64	69	3.87	3.92	3.98	4.04	4.10	4.16	4.23	4.29	4.36	4.43	4.49	4.56	4.63	4.70
65	70	3.88	3.94	4.00	4.06	4.12	4.19	4.25	4.32	4.39	4.46	4.53	4.60	4.67	4.75
66	71	3.89	3.95	4.02	4.08	4.14	4.21	4.28	4.35	4.42	4.49	4.56	4.64	4.71	4.79
67	72	3.91	3.97	4.03	4.10	4.16	4.23	4.30	4.37	4.45	4.52	4.60	4.67	4.75	4.83
68	73	3.92	3.98	4.05	4.11	4.18	4.25	4.32	4.40	4.47	4.55	4.63	4.71	4.79	4.87
69	74	3.93	4.00	4.06	4.13	4.20	4.27	4.34	4.42	4.50	4.58	4.66	4.74	4.83	4.91
70	75	3.94	4.01	4.07	4.14	4.21	4.29	4.36	4.44	4.52	4.60	4.69	4.77	4.86	4.95
71	76	3.95	4.02	4.09	4.16	4.23	4.30	4.38	4.46	4.54	4.63	4.72	4.80	4.90	4.99
72	77	3.96	4.03	4.10	4.17	4.24	4.32	4.40	4.48	4.57	4.65	4.74	4.83	4.93	5.02
73	78	3.97	4.04	4.11	4.18	4.26	4.34	4.42	4.50	4.59	4.68	4.77	4.86	4.96	5.06
74	79	3.98	4.05	4.12	4.19	4.27	4.35	4.43	4.52	4.61	4.70	4.79	4.89	4.99	5.09
75	80	3.99	4.06	4.13	4.21	4.28	4.36	4.45	4.53	4.62	4.72	4.81	4.91	5.01	5.12
76	81	4.00	4.07	4.14	4.22	4.30	4.38	4.46	4.55	4.64	4.74	4.83	4.94	5.04	5.15
77	82	4.00	4.07	4.15	4.23	4.31	4.39	4.47	4.56	4.66	4.75	4.85	4.96	5.06	5.18
78	83	4.01	4.08	4.16	4.23	4.32	4.40	4.49	4.58	4.67	4.77	4.87	4.98	5.09	5.20
79	84	4.02	4.09	4.16	4.24	4.32	4.41	4.50	4.59	4.69	4.79	4.89	5.00	5.11	5.22
80	85 and over	4.02	4.09	4.17	4.25	4.33	4.42	4.51	4.60	4.70	4.80	4.91	5.01	5.13	5.25
81		4.03	4.10	4.18	4.26	4.34	4.43	4.52	4.61	4.71	4.81	4.92	5.03	5.15	5.27
82		4.03	4.11	4.18	4.26	4.35	4.44	4.53	4.62	4.72	4.83	4.93	5.05	5.16	5.29
83		4.04	4.11	4.19	4.27	4.35	4.44	4.54	4.63	4.73	4.84	4.95	5.06	5.18	5.31
84		4.04	4.11	4.19	4.27	4.36	4.45	4.54	4.64	4.74	4.85	4.96	5.07	5.20	5.32
85 and over		4.04	4.12	4.20	4.28	4.37	4.46	4.55	4.65	4.75	4.86	4.97	5.09	5.21	5.34

Age of Payee Nearest Birthday		Monthly Life Income													
Male		59	60	61	62	63	64	65	66	67	68	69	70	71	72
	Female	64	65	66	67	68	69	70	71	72	73	74	75	76	77
59	64	$4.52													
60	65	4.57	$4.63												
61	66	4.62	4.68	$4.74											
62	67	4.67	4.74	4.80	$4.86										
63	68	4.72	4.79	4.86	4.92	$4.99									
64	69	4.77	4.84	4.91	4.99	5.06	$5.13								
65	70	4.82	4.90	4.97	5.05	5.12	5.20	$5.27							
66	71	4.87	4.95	5.03	5.11	5.19	5.26	5.34	$5.42						
67	72	4.92	5.00	5.08	5.16	5.25	5.33	5.42	5.50	$5.58					
68	73	4.96	5.05	5.13	5.22	5.31	5.40	5.49	5.58	5.67	$5.75				
69	74	5.00	5.09	5.18	5.28	5.37	5.46	5.56	5.65	5.75	5.84	$5.93			
70	75	5.05	5.14	5.23	5.33	5.43	5.53	5.63	5.73	5.83	5.93	6.03	$6.13		
71	76	5.09	5.18	5.28	5.38	5.49	5.59	5.69	5.80	5.91	6.01	6.12	6.22	$6.33	
72	77	5.12	5.22	5.33	5.43	5.54	5.65	5.76	5.87	5.98	6.10	6.21	6.32	6.43	$6.55
73	78	5.16	5.27	5.37	5.48	5.59	5.71	5.82	5.94	6.06	6.18	6.30	6.42	6.54	6.66
74	79	5.20	5.30	5.41	5.53	5.65	5.76	5.88	6.01	6.13	6.26	6.38	6.51	6.64	6.77
75	80	5.23	5.34	5.46	5.57	5.69	5.82	5.94	6.07	6.20	6.33	6.47	6.60	6.74	6.87
76	81	5.26	5.38	5.49	5.62	5.74	5.87	6.00	6.13	6.27	6.41	6.55	6.69	6.84	6.98
77	82	5.29	5.41	5.53	5.66	5.79	5.92	6.06	6.19	6.34	6.48	6.63	6.78	6.93	7.08
78	83	5.32	5.44	5.57	5.70	5.83	5.97	6.11	6.25	6.40	6.55	6.71	6.86	7.02	7.18
79	84	5.34	5.47	5.60	5.73	5.87	6.01	6.16	6.31	6.46	6.62	6.78	6.94	7.11	7.28
80	85 and over	5.37	5.50	5.63	5.77	5.91	6.05	6.20	6.36	6.52	6.68	6.85	7.02	7.20	7.37
81		5.39	5.52	5.66	5.80	5.94	6.09	6.25	6.41	6.57	6.74	6.92	7.13	7.28	7.47
82		5.41	5.55	5.68	5.83	5.98	6.13	6.29	6.45	6.62	6.80	6.98	7.17	7.36	7.55
83		5.43	5.57	5.71	5.86	6.01	6.17	6.33	6.50	6.67	6.85	7.04	7.23	7.43	7.63
84		5.45	5.59	5.73	5.88	6.04	6.20	6.37	6.54	6.72	6.91	7.10	7.30	7.50	7.71
85 and over		5.47	5.61	5.75	5.91	6.06	6.23	6.40	6.58	6.76	6.95	7.15	7.36	7.57	7.79

Age of Payee Nearest Birthday		Monthly Life Income											
Male		73	74	75	76	77	78	79	80	81	82	83	84	85 and over
	Female	78	79	80	81	82	83	84	85 and over					
73	78	$6.78												
74	79	6.89	$7.02											
75	80	7.01	7.14	$7.28										
76	81	7.12	7.27	7.41	$7.56									
77	82	7.24	7.39	7.54	7.70	$7.85								
78	83	7.35	7.51	7.67	7.84	8.00	$8.16							
79	84	7.45	7.63	7.80	7.97	8.15	8.32	$8.50						
80	85 and over	7.55	7.74	7.92	8.11	8.30	8.48	8.67	$8.85					
81		7.65	7.85	8.04	8.24	8.44	8.64	8.84	9.04	$9.23				
82		7.75	7.95	8.16	8.37	8.58	8.79	9.00	9.21	9.43	$9.64			
83		7.84	8.05	8.27	8.49	8.71	8.94	9.16	9.39	9.62	9.84	$10.07		
84		7.93	8.15	8.38	8.61	8.84	9.08	9.32	9.56	9.81	10.05	10.29	$10.53	
85 and over		8.01	8.24	8.48	8.72	8.97	9.22	9.47	9.73	9.99	10.25	10.50	10.76	$11.01

S. Specifications for Beneficiary Designation and for Manner of Payment

To: ____
(life insurance company)

Please forward the proper beneficiary papers, to be executed by the owner, to put into effect under each policy listed below the following designation of beneficiary and manner of payment of proceeds:

Policies No.________ No.________ No.________ No.________

If this request applies to less than the entire proceeds, indicate the fraction________ or fixed amount $________ to which it applies. (*Please use SEPARATE request for EACH fraction or fixed amount.*)

ARTICLE 1—DESIGNATION OF BENEFICIARY

	Full Name	Relationship to Insured	Date of Birth
Primary	________	________	________
	________	________	________
Contingent	________	________	________
	________	________	________
	________	________	________

☐ and any children of the insured hereafter born.
☐ The children of a deceased child shall receive his or her parent's share.

Second Contingent ____

ARTICLE 2—"CLEAN-UP FUND"

☐ Pay $________ (or entire proceeds, if less) in one sum to the Primary Beneficiary, if living, otherwise to the executors or administrators of the insured.

☐ Hold $________ (or entire proceeds, if less) under the Interest Option for Primary and First Contingent Beneficiary, except that if the Primary Beneficiary predeceases the insured or dies within ________ months after the insured's death, proceeds or remaining funds on deposit shall be paid in one sum to insured's estate. Primary and First Contingent Beneficiaries shall have the unlimited right to withdraw proceeds or to elect any other option in the policy at any time (subject to company rules).

ARTICLE 3—MODE OF SETTLEMENT (For entire proceeds, or for balance of proceeds not payable under "Clean-up Fund" if elected under Article 2.)

Please "X" appropriate blocks and fill in necessary information for Options and Privileges desired

TO PRIMARY BENEFICIARY		TO FIRST CONTINGENT BENEFICIARY
	☐ One Sum Payment ☐	
	☐ Interest Option ☐	
________years	☐ Fixed Period Option ☐	________years
________years certain	☐ Life Income Option ☐	________years certain
	☐ Life Income "until proceeds are refunded" Option ☐	
$________to EACH beneficiary	☐ Fixed Amount Option ☐	$________to EACH beneficiary

All interest or instalment payments shall be paid:

☐	Annually	☐
☐	Semiannually	☐
☐	Quarterly	☐
☐	Monthly	☐

Option________ on________	☐ Automatic change to Option indicated on date specified ☐	Option________ on________
On________	☐ Pay proceeds in one sum on date specified ☐	On________

Beneficiary may change from Interest Option or Fixed Amount Option to:

☐ Fixed Period Option ☐
☐ Fixed Amount Option ☐
☐ Life Income Option ☐

This change may be made subject to company rules:

	☐ At any time ☐	
After________	☐ At any time after date specified ☐	After________

S. Specifications for Beneficiary Designation and for Manner of Payment

After__________
Each Primary Beneficiary may withdraw

The Beneficiary may withdraw or commute:

☐ Entire proceeds, at any time ☐
☐ Entire proceeds, after date specified ☐
☐ A limited part of the proceeds (Available only under Interest Option or Fixed Amount Option) ☐

After__________
Each First Contingent Beneficiary may withdraw

If the Primary Beneficiary dies while receiving payments under the Fixed Period or Life Income Options, continue remaining installments certain to First Contingent Beneficiary. ☐

ARTICLE 4—FAMILY MAINTENANCE OF FAMILY INCOME POLICIES:

If policy provides Family Maintenance or Family Income Benefits fill out applicable blocks below:

☐ Make monthly payments as provided in the policy and pay amount due at end of Family Maintenance or Family Income Period under Mode of Settlement designated above. ☐

NOTE: If income payments are elected, check proper box to grant or to negative the right of commutation during such income period.

- ☐ The beneficiary may at any time during said Period commute all future benefits. ☐
- ☐ The beneficiary shall have no right of commutation during said Period ☐

☐ Commute all benefits and pay entire proceeds under Mode of Settlement designated above ☐

If this portion of the Designation is not completed and if a policy provides Family Maintenance or Family Income Benefits, it will be presumed such Benefits are to be commuted at the death of the insured and such commuted value, together with the face amount of the policy, shall be paid under Mode of Settlement designated above.

ARTICLE 5—COMMON DISASTER

☐ Payment will not be made to any beneficiary until thirty days after the insured's death. If a beneficiary dies during that period, payment will be made as though he had died before the insured.

ARTICLE 6—ACCIDENTAL DEATH BENEFIT

☐ Include with and pay in same manner as policy proceeds. (Under the Fixed Period or Life Income Options, the installments are to be increased. Under the Fixed Amount Option, the installment period will be lengthened.)

☐ Pay in one sum.

ARTICLE 7—ADDITIONAL REQUESTS

☐ Spendthrift or creditor's clause.
☐ Joint and Last Survivor Annuity Option.
☐ Automatic Premium Loan Provision.
☐ Give wife power to appoint to her estate at her death any proceeds remaining with the Company to qualify policy for the marital deduction under the Federal Estate Tax Law.

☐ Please furnish cost and requirements for adding disability benefits:
- ☐ Waiver of premium.
- ☐ Monthly income.

Please furnish the following dividend information:
- ☐ Amount of accumulations or paid-up additions to date.
- ☐ Apply future dividends under the__________ dividend option.
- ☐ Advise whether current dividend accumulations can be applied to purchase paid-up additions at insured's attained age, and if so, furnish requirements.

ARTICLE 8—REMARKS (If any part of this request violates your company practice, please conform to the request as closely as your regulations will permit.)

Mail Agreement (TOGETHER WITH ANY ADDITIONAL INFORMATION AND FORMS HE MAY REQUEST) to:

Name__________
Street Address__________
City and State__________

Date__________

____
Insured or Owner

T. Mode of Settlement Designation

DESIGNATION
of Beneficiary & Mode of Settlement

Policy Number (s)____________________ Life of____________________

ARTICLE 1—This Designation cancels all prior beneficiary and mode of settlement designations under these policies. Proceeds will be paid as designated below. Proceeds shall not include amounts payable upon the death of a wife or child under a Family Plan Policy, under a Family Benefit or under Children's Insurance Benefit. The owner of the policy may change this Designation.

DESIGNATION OF BENEFICIARY Please type or print each beneficiary's full given name and relationship to insured

CLASS A—PRIMARY BENEFICIARY (Proceeds will be paid under mode of settlement designated below)

CLASS B—FIRST CONTINGENT BENEFICIARY (Proceeds will be paid under mode of settlement designated below)

☐ Pay to children of each deceased Class B beneficiary as provided in Article 5

CLASS C—SECOND CONTINGENT BENEFICIARY (Proceeds will be paid in one sum)

☐ Pay to children of each deceased Class C beneficiary as provided in Article 5

CLASS D—FINAL BENEFICIARY—Proceeds will be paid in one sum to the owner of the policy, if living, otherwise the executors or administrators of the last to die of the owner, the primary beneficiary and the first contingent beneficiary.

MODE OF SETTLEMENT

☐ "CLEAN-UP FUND"—Pay $______(or entire proceeds, if less) in one sum to the Primary Beneficiary, if living, otherwise to the executors or administrators of the insured, and pay the balance of proceeds as follows:

TO PRIMARY BENEFICIARY		Please "X" appropriate blocks and fill in necessary information for Options and Privileges desired		TO FIRST CONTINGENT BENEFICIARY
	☐	One Sum Payment	☐	
	☐	Interest - Option 1	☐	
______years	☐	Fixed Period - Option 2	☐	______years
______years certain	☐	Life Income - Option 3	☐	______years certain
	☐	Life Income - Option 3 "until proceeds are refunded" (Available on policies above #570000)	☐	
$______to EACH individual	☐	Fixed Amount - Option 4	☐	$______to EACH individual
		All interest or instalment payments shall be paid:		
	☐	Annually	☐	
	☐	Semiannually	☐	
	☐	Quarterly	☐	
	☐	Monthly	☐	
Option______ on______	☐	Automatic change to Option indicated on date specified	☐	Option______ on______
On______	☐	Pay proceeds in one sum on date specified	☐	On______
		Beneficiary may change from Option 1 or Option 4 to:		
	☐	Option 2, at any time	☐	
	☐	Option 4, at any time	☐	
		Option 3: (Use first block if policy number is below #570000)		
After______	☐	Within two years after date specified	☐	After______
	☐	At any time (Available for policies above #570000)	☐	
After______	☐	At any time after date specified (Available for policies above #570000)	☐	After______
		The Beneficiary may withdraw or commute:		
	☐	Entire proceeds, at any time	☐	
After______	☐	Entire proceeds, after date specified	☐	After______
______	☐	A limited part of the proceeds, as specified for each beneficiary in each Class (Available only under Option 1 or Option 4)	☐	______
		If the Primary Beneficiary dies while receiving payments under Option 2 or Option 3, continue remaining instalments certain to First Contingent Beneficiary	☐	

If policy provides Family Maintenance or Family Income Benefits fill out applicable blocks below:

	☐	Make monthly payments as provided in the policy and pay amount due at end of Family Maintenance or Family Income Period under Mode of Settlement designated above.	☐
NOTE: If Income payments are elected, check proper box to grant or to negative the right of commutation during such Income period.	☐	The beneficiary may at any time during said Period commute all future benefits	☐
	☐	The beneficiary shall have no right of commutation during said Period	☐
	☐	Commute all benefits and pay entire proceeds under Mode of Settlement designated above	☐

If this portion of the Designation is not completed and if a policy provides Family Maintenance or Family Income Benefits, it will be presumed such Benefits are to be commuted at the death of the insured and such commuted value, together with the face amount of the policy, shall be paid under Mode of Settlement designated above.

☐ **ARTICLE 2**—COMMON DISASTER: Payment will not be made to any beneficiary until thirty days after the insured's death. If a beneficiary dies during that period, payment will be made as though he had died before the insured.

ARTICLE 3—The provisions appearing on the other side of this form are incorporated in this Designation.

Dated______________19____ Only the Original copy should be signed____________________
Policyowner

DO NOT WRITE BELOW THIS LINE

Original signed copy dated______filed with The ______ Life Insurance Company on______.

By____________________Registrar

T. Mode of Settlement Designation

☐ **ARTICLE 4—ADDITIONAL REQUEST:** Regardless of any provision herein to the contrary,

ARTICLE 5—PAYMENT TO CHILDREN OF A DECEASED BENEFICIARY: If this Article has been elected under "Designation of Beneficiary" on the other side, and if a beneficiary in a Class is deceased at the time a share would have become available for payment or retention for his benefit had he been living, such share will be paid in one sum equally to his then living children. If a beneficiary in a Class dies after his share has become available for payment or retention for his benefit, the unpaid portion of his share, if any, will be paid in one sum equally to his children living at the time of his death.

ARTICLE 6—BENEFICIARY: The beneficiaries of each Class will receive payment in the order designated in Article 1. No payment will be made to any Class of beneficiary until all beneficiaries in all preceding Classes have died. Payments specified in Article 1 will be paid to the beneficiary if living as each payment becomes due, and when a beneficiary dies, any interest or instalment accrued since the last payment will be added to the next beneficiary's share. Unless otherwise specified, if two or more beneficiaries are designated in any one Class, a separate and equal share will be provided for each member of such Class.

When two or more beneficiaries have been designated in a Class, and one or more dies:

(a) BEFORE his share has become available for payment or retention for his benefit, such share will be paid to the beneficiaries of that Class who are living at said time for payment or retention, in the proportion that their shares as set forth in Article 1 bear to each other, and in the manner specified in that Article.

(b) AFTER his share has become available for payment or retention for his benefit, the unpaid portion of his share will be paid in one sum to the then living beneficiaries of that Class, in the proportion that their shares as set forth in Article 1 bear to each other.

(c) The provisions of Paragraphs (a) and (b) are subject to any applicable contrary provisions of Article 4 or 5.

ARTICLE 7—ASSIGNMENT: The rights of every beneficiary of each policy are subordinate to the rights of any assignee who has filed a written assignment at the Home Office of the Company, whether the assignment was made before or after the date of this Designation. If such assignment is in effect at the insured's death, the Company may, at its option, pay the entire proceeds to the assignee or may deduct from the proceeds and pay to the assignee the amount owed to the assignee, as certified in writing by the assignee or any officer or partner of the assignee, and pay only the remaining proceeds to the beneficiary.

ARTICLE 8—MINOR BENEFICIARIES: Unless provision is made by statute, or a provision is made in Article 4 for the designation of an informal trustee to act for a minor beneficiary, any payment becoming due a minor beneficiary will be made only to his legally appointed guardian, and any right, option or privilege given the minor may be exercised only by such guardian.

ARTICLE 9—RELIANCE ON AFFIDAVIT AS TO BENEFICIARIES: The Company may rely on an affidavit by any beneficiary relating to the dates of birth, death, marriage or remarriage, names and addresses and other facts concerning all beneficiaries, and the Company is hereby released from all liability in relying and acting upon the statements contained in such affidavit.

ARTICLE 10—SPENDTHRIFT CLAUSE—PROHIBITION OF COMMUTATION AND ALIENATION: Unless provided in this Designation, no beneficiary may commute, anticipate, encumber, alienate, withdraw or assign any portion of his share of the proceeds. To the extent permitted by law, no payments to a beneficiary will be subject to his debts, contracts or engagements, nor may they be levied upon or attached.

ARTICLE 11—DISTRIBUTION WHEN PAYMENTS ARE LESS THAN $10 OR PROCEEDS ARE LESS THAN $1,000: If the specified payments would amount to less than $10 each, the Company may make equivalent payments less frequently. If any share of the proceeds to be retained under an Option is less than $1,000, or if any share is reduced to less than $1,000 because of withdrawals, the Company will pay that share in one sum, regardless of any provision for payment under an Option.

ARTICLE 12—MISSTATEMENT OF AGE OF BENEFICIARIES: If the age of any beneficiary has been misstated, and if Option 3 has been elected for that beneficiary, the instalments payable will be the amount that his share of the proceeds would have provided at his correct age. The Company may adjust future payments as necessary.

ARTICLE 13—EXTENSION OF TIME FOR CERTAIN PAYMENTS AND PRIVILEGES: If a date for beginning of payments (or for the exercise of a privilege) occurs during the lifetime of a person who must die before such payments can be made (or such privilege exercised), the beginning date for such payments (or for the exercise of such privilege) shall be the date of death of such person rather than the earlier date specified.

ARTICLE 14—EFFECT OF CHANGE OF BENEFICIARY UNDER ANY POLICY: A future change of beneficiary of any policy in this Designation shall terminate the Designation with regard to that policy.

ARTICLE 15—CANCELLATION OF POLICY ENDORSEMENT REQUIREMENT: The Company is requested to waive all provisions of any policy under this Designation requiring endorsement of beneficiary changes, and to endorse any such policy as follows:

"The beneficiary of this policy has been changed according to written request filed with the Company.
"Every request for change of beneficiary shall be in writing on a form satisfactory to the Company. No change of beneficiary will take effect until the request has been filed at the Home Office of the Company, but when filed will take effect as of the date of the request, whether or not the insured is living at the time the request is filed, but without prejudice to the Company because of any payment made by it before receipt of the request at its Home Office. All provisions of the policy requiring endorsement of change of beneficiary are canceled."

ARTICLE 16—"PROCEEDS" DEFINED: The proceeds of a policy shall be:

(a) At the death of the insured, all amounts payable by reason of the insured's death under the provisions of the policy (including the commuted value of any guaranteed deferred payments).

(b) After the death of the insured, the balance of amounts under Paragraph (a) remaining with the Company, or the then commuted value of unpaid guaranteed instalments.

Proceeds shall not include surrender values, amounts payable at maturity of the policy during the insured's lifetime or any refund payable under a Receipt for Advanced Premiums. Specific amounts referred to in this Designation shall apply to the aggregate proceeds of all said policies and not to each policy separately.

ARTICLE 17—DEFINITIONS AND CONSTRUCTION OF TERMS: "Child" and "children" as used herein shall include both lawful and legally adopted sons and daughters, but not grandchildren or other descendents. "Brothers" and "Sisters" shall include half-brothers and half-sisters. Masculine terms shall apply to either sex and the singular shall include the plural. "Insured" shall mean "annuitant" when such meaning applies.

ARTICLE 18—DEFINITION OF TERM "OPTION": CONDITIONS OF WITHDRAWAL PRIVILEGES; AND PRIVILEGES TO ELECT OTHER OPTIONS: The terms "Option 1", "Option 2", "Option 3", or "Option 4" used in this Designation refer to the corresponding Option number appearing in the policy under the heading "Optional Modes of Settlement" or "Modes of Settlement at Maturity". Where any share of the proceeds is to be retained under Option 1, the interest will be paid at the rate provided in the policy. If Article 1 or Article 4 provides for more than one interest payment each year, the periodic payments shall be discounted so as to be the equivalent of interest payable at the end of the year.

No beneficiary may withdraw or commute the proceeds unless expressly provided in Article 1 or Article 4. Payment of any withdrawal or commutation may be deferred by the Company for the period permitted in the policy. The minimum amount that may be withdrawn under Option 1 or Option 4 is $100. Only the entire unpaid guaranteed instalments may be commuted under Option 2 or Option 3. Any privilege granted in this Designation to a beneficiary to elect other settlement options shall apply to the entire proceeds, or to any part of such proceeds in multiples of $1,000 or more.

Payments under Options are subject to all the terms and conditions appearing in the policy.

ARTICLE 19—MISCELLANEOUS: The furnishing by the Company or the filing with the Company of this form shall not constitute an admission that any policy under this Designation is in full force or is in effect under a Non-Forfeiture Option. Any provision or direction in this Designation which is immediately preceded or followed by a box ☐ will not be a part of this Designation unless the box is marked in such manner as to indicate clearly the election of the particular provision or direction.

U. Personal Trust Indenture*

THIS INDENTURE OF TRUST made this 16th day of July, 1963, by and between ANDERSON BRIDGE, of Waban, in the County of Middlesex and Commonwealth of Massachusetts, party of the first part, hereinafter called the Donor, and OLD COLONY TRUST COMPANY, a Massachusetts corporation, and said ANDERSON BRIDGE, the Donor, parties of the second part, hereinafter called the Trustees.

WITNESSETH THAT:

WHEREAS, the Donor has designated the Trustees as the beneficiaries of certain insurance policies upon his life, and

WHEREAS, the Donor has deposited the said policies with the trustees to be held under the terms of this Indenture of Trust, and

WHEREAS, the Donor may from time to time assign, transfer or pay over to the Trustees other property, real or personal,

NOW, THEREFORE, said Trustees do hereby declare, covenant and agree that they will hold said policies in safekeeping, and in the event of the payment to them of the proceeds, either in whole or in part, of said policies of insurance or any of them or of any other property, real or personal, they, the said Trustees, will hold the same upon the trusts hereinafter set forth, namely:

FIRST: The Trustees shall receive, hold and manage all property at any time comprising the trust estate and shall invest and reinvest the same and shall collect the income and proceeds thereof, and during the lifetime of the Donor, the Trustees shall pay to him or expend for his benefit, or in accordance with his written instructions, the net income from the trust property quarter-annually as received and available for payment, and shall also pay to him or upon his order such amounts, if any, from the principal of the trust property as he may from time to time direct in writing. In the event that in the opinion of the Trustee other than the Donor he shall be at any time mentally or physically incapacitated and unable to give directions to the Trustee other than himself, said Trustee is authorized and empowered to pay from the income and principal of the trust property such amounts, if any, for the benefit or account of the Donor or for the benefit of the Donor's wife, GOLDEN GATE BRIDGE, also known as GOLDIE BRIDGE, or for the benefit of any of the Donor's issue as it may, in its sole discretion, deem necessary or advisable for the maintenance, comfort, support and education of any of said persons.

SECOND: Upon the death of the Donor, his said wife, GOLDIE BRIDGE, shall become Co-trustee hereunder with said OLD COLONY TRUST COMPANY, and the Trustees shall thereafter deal with said trust estate, including any property that may be added thereto by reason of the will of the Donor or otherwise, as follows:

---

* The author of Chapter 58 is grateful to Endicott Smith, Esq., of the law firm of Allen, Smith & Bonner, 31 State Street, Boston, who drafted this trust which was selected, with the names obviously changed, only because it was among the trusts most recently accepted by Old Colony Trust Company from this fine draftsman.

A. If the said GOLDIE BRIDGE, wife of the Donor, shall survive him, then the Trustees shall divide the trust estate into two separate trust funds. The first trust fund, to be known as "Trust A," shall consist of an amount equal to fifty (50) per cent of the value of the Donor's "adjusted gross estate," as defined in and as finally determined for the purposes of the United States Estate Tax Law, less an amount equal to the value of all interests in property, if any, allowable as "marital deductions" for the purposes of such law, which pass or have passed to the Donor's said wife under the provisions of his will, or outside his will by operation of law or otherwise than under this trust. The Trustees shall pay to the said GOLDIE BRIDGE the net income from this trust fund at least quarter-annually during her lifetime. In addition to said income payments, the Trustees shall pay to or expend for the Donor's said wife such portions of the principal of this trust A as she from time to time requests in writing delivered to the Trustee other than herself; provided, however, that such principal payments shall not exceed in any accounting year the greater of Five Thousand Dollars ($5,000) or five (5) per cent of the value of the principal of said trust A, as determined at the beginning of each accounting year. Such annual rights of withdrawal shall be non-cumulative. The Trustee other than the Donor's said wife may also make such payments of principal to her or for her benefit as it may from time to time deem advisable for her comfort, maintenance and support, and in such event the said Trustee other than the Donor's said wife shall have the sole power of sale of any assets in this trust to make such payments. Upon the death of the Donor's said wife, the remaining balance of principal in this trust fund shall be paid to or for such person or persons as she may, by her last will making specific reference to this instrument, direct and appoint, including the right in her to appoint to her own estate, and if the Donor's said wife shall fail to direct and appoint the disposition of all or a part of the principal of this trust, that part or all of the property with respect to which there has been such failure to appoint shall be paid to the trust fund designated "Trust B," hereinafter established in the following paragraph, to be held, managed, administered and distributed as an integral part thereof.

B. The balance of said trust estate, or all thereof if the Donor's said wife shall not survive him, shall be retained by the trustees as "Trust B," and the Trustees shall pay to or apply for the benefit of any one or more than one of the group consisting of the Donor's said wife, GOLDIE BRIDGE, and such of the Donor's issue as shall be living from time to time, such amount or amounts of the net income and principal of the trust fund as the Trustee other than the Donor's said wife, in its sole discretion, may determine to be advisable for the best interests of any one or more than one of said group. Any net income which is not paid to or applied for the benefit of the members of said group may be added, in whole or in part, from time to time, in the discretion of the Trustee other than the Donor's said wife, to the principal of the trust and be invested as such. In addition, the Trustees may pay to or apply for the benefit of any one or more than one of the group consisting of the Donor's father, GEORGE WASHINGTON BRIDGE, the Donor's mother, MYSTIC RIVER BRIDGE, the Donor's father-in-law, OLD GARDEN GATE, the Donor's mother-in-law, RUSTY GATE, and SWINGING GATE, grandmother of the Donor's said wife, such amount or amounts of the income and principal of the trust fund as the Trustee other than the Donor's said wife, in its sole discretion, deems necessary for the maintenance of health and a decent manner of living of each of said persons.

Upon the death of the survivor of the Donor's said wife, GOLDIE

BRIDGE, his said father, GEORGE WASHINGTON BRIDGE, his said mother, MYSTIC RIVER BRIDGE, his said father-in-law, OLD GARDEN GATE, his said mother-in-law, RUSTY GATE, and the said SWINGING GATE, grandmother of the Donor's said wife, the Trustees shall pay to or expend for the children of the Donor and to or for the issue of any child of the Donor then deceased or of any child of the Donor who shall thereafter die, or any one or more than one of them, so much of the net income therefrom and principal thereof as the Trustees may from time to time, in their discretion, deem advisable for the reasonable comfort, support and education of such children and such issue of any deceased child of the Donor, or any one or more than one of them, until there shall be no child of the Donor living who has not attained the age of twenty-five (25) years, at which time the remaining balance of principal in the trust fund, together with any accrued and accumulated income thereon, shall be divided by the Trustees into as many equal shares as there may be children of the Donor then living, and children of his then deceased leaving issue then living, and shall hold and dispose of said shares as hereinafter set forth in paragraph 1. through 6. inclusive.

1. In the case of each share apportioned to a living child of the Donor, the Trustees shall pay to or for such child, for his or her life, the net income of the share apportioned to him or to her. In addition to said income payments, the Trustees may also pay to or expend for such child and to or for the issue of such child as shall from time to time be living, or any one or more than one of them, such part or parts of the principal of such child's share as the Trustees from time to time, in their discretion, deem advisable for the reasonable comfort, support and education of such persons, or any one or more than one of them.

2. Anything hereinbefore to the contrary notwithstanding, following the death of the survivor of the Donor and his said wife and after the division of the trust fund into shares as hereinbefore provided, any child of the Donor, at any time after attaining the age of twenty-five (25) years, may, by a request or requests in writing deposited with the Trustees, withdraw in one sum or installments up to a total of one-third (⅓) of the principal of any trust estate held hereunder for his or her benefit, valued as of the time he or she attains the age of twenty-five (25) years or at the time of the division into shares, whichever is later; and after attaining the age of thirty (30) years, may withdraw in the manner set forth above one-half (½) of the principal of any trust estate held hereunder for his or her benefit, valued as of the time he or she attains the age of thirty (30) years or at the time of the division into shares, whichever is later; and after attaining the age of thirty-five (35) years, may withdraw in the manner set forth above all or any part of the principal then remaining in his or her share, and the determination of the Trustees as to what constitutes such fractional parts and the payment thereof, whether in cash or in kind, shall be binding and conclusive on all persons. A failure or delay on the part of a child to request and receive one or more of said fractional distributions of principal, or any part thereof, shall not prejudice his or her right to request and receive a distribution representing the same fraction of the trust fund at a later date chosen by him or by her, and to request and receive also any additional fraction to which he or she is further entitled at said later date.

3. On the death of a child of the Donor, after the death of the survivor of the Donor and his said wife and after the division of the trust fund into shares as hereinbefore provided, the share of such child as it then exists shall be paid over, transferred and conveyed to or for such person or persons other than

the creditors, the estate or the creditors of the estate of such child as such child may, by his or her last will, direct and appoint, making specific reference to this instrument and this power, and in default of such appointment, such share shall be paid over and distributed, free of all trusts, to the then living issue, by right of representation, of such deceased child, or in case there are no such issue then living, to the issue then living of the Donor, by right of representation; subject, however, to the provisions hereinafter set forth in paragraphs 5. and 6., whichever shall apply.

In the exercise of the power of appointment hereinbefore provided, any child may appoint outright or in trust; may select the Trustee or Trustees if an appointment in trust is made; may create new powers of appointment in a Trustee or Trustees or in any other appointee; may, if an appointment in trust is made, establish such administrative powers for the Trustees as such child deems appropriate; may create life interests or other limited interests in an appointee with future interests in favor of other appointees; may impose lawful conditions on an appointee; may appoint by will different types of interests to selected appointees; may impose lawful spendthrift provisions; provided always, however, that no appointment shall benefit directly persons other than members of the restricted group who are the objects of this power.

4. In case a share is set aside for the issue then living of a deceased child of the Donor, the Trustees shall pay over, transfer and convey said share, free of all trusts, to such issue then living of such deceased child, by right of representation; subject, however, to the provisions hereinafter set forth in paragraph 5.

5. In the event that pursuant to the provisions of the preceding paragraph or the provisions of paragraph 3. hereof (other than pursuant to the valid exercise of the power of appointment therein provided), any portion of the trust estate becomes distributable to a person who is then under the age of thirty (30) years, and for whose benefit no share or portion of a share is held in trust hereunder, then notwithstanding anything therein contained to the contrary, the Trustees shall continue to hold the portion of the trust estate which would otherwise be distributable to such person in trust until he or she attains the age of thirty (30) years, and until such time shall pay to or expend for such person so much of the net income and principal thereof as the Trustees may from time to time deem advisable for the reasonable comfort, support, maintenance and education of such person. Upon attaining the age of thirty (30) years, the portion held in trust hereunder for such person shall be paid over and distributed, free of all trusts, to such person. In the event that any person for whom a portion of the trust estate is then held shall die prior to attaining the age of thirty (30) years, the Trustees shall, upon the death of such person, pay, transfer and convey his or her portion of the trust estate, free of all trusts, to the then living issue of such person, by right of representation, and in default of issue, in equal shares to the then living brothers and sisters of such person; provided, however, that the then living issue of a deceased brother or sister shall take, by right of representation, the share to which such deceased brother or sister would have been entitled if then living; and in default of brothers and sisters and/or issue of deceased brothers and sisters, to the then living issue of the Donor, by right of representation.

6. If property held in trust under the provisions of this article SECOND becomes distributable to a child or other issue of the Donor (other than by the valid exercise of the power of appointment given in paragraph 3. above) for whose primary benefit a share or portion of a share is then held in trust hereunder, the property otherwise so distributable to such child or such issue

shall be added to such share or portion and administered as an integral part thereof.

THIRD: If there shall be a failure of disposition of any beneficial interest created under this trust, then the beneficial interest which has failed of disposition shall be paid over and distributed, free of all trusts, as follows:

A. Twenty-five (25) per cent to the Donor's brother, HELLGATE BRIDGE, if then living and if not living, to his then living issue, by right of representation, and in default of issue, to YALE UNIVERSITY, located in New Haven, Connecticut.

B. Fifteen (15) per cent to the Donor's sister-in-law, PEARLY GATE CRASHER, if then living and if not living, to her then living issue, by right of representation, and in default of such issue, to said YALE UNIVERSITY.

C. Ten (10) per cent to the then living issue, by right of representation, of the Donor's brother-in-law, MITTA GATE, and in default of such issue, to said YALE UNIVERSITY.

D. The remaining fifty (50) per cent to SMITH COLLEGE, located in Northampton, Massachusetts.

FOURTH: In the event that the Donor's said wife and the Donor shall be killed in a common accident or as a result of a common disaster, or under such circumstances that it will be impossible to determine which of them died first, it shall be presumed that the Donor's said wife survived the Donor, and this presumption shall apply throughout this Indenture of Trust.

FIFTH: Upon the death of any beneficiary of trust fund B of Article SECOND, no undistributed or accrued income which would have been distributable to such beneficiary had such beneficiary continued to live shall be paid to the executor or administrator of the estate of such deceased beneficiary, but all such undistributed or accrued income shall be paid to the beneficiary or beneficiaries entitled to the estate next succeeding the estate of such deceased beneficiary.

SIXTH: Notwithstanding anything herein contained to the contrary, unless sooner terminated under the prior provisions hereof, the trusts of trust fund B of Article SECOND and all shares and portions thereof shall terminate twenty-one (21) years after the death of the last survivor of the Donor, his said wife, GOLDIE BRIDGE, his said father, GEORGE WASHINGTON BRIDGE, his said mother, MYSTIC RIVER BRIDGE, his said father-in-law, OLD GARDEN GATE, his said mother-in-law, RUSTY GATE, the said SWINGING GATE, grandmother of the Donor's said wife, and the issue of the Donor living at the date of this Indenture; and upon such termination and notwithstanding any of the foregoing provisions of this Indenture, the Trustees shall pay over, transfer and convey the principal of the trusts then existing under trust fund B of Article SECOND, and any undistributed income thereon, to the Donor's issue then living to whom income payments could be made under such trusts immediately prior to their termination, and if no such issue of the Donor is then living, the Trustees shall then pay the remaining principal, and any undistributed income thereon, in accordance with the provisions hereinbefore set forth in Article THIRD.

SEVENTH: The whole or any part of the income payable under the provisions of this Indenture to any minor or to any other person legally incapacitated (other than income payable to the Donor's said wife from trust A of Article SECOND hereof) may be applied by the Trustees, in their discretion, for such beneficiary's comfort, support, maintenance and education instead of being paid to such beneficiary's guardian or conservator. Any such application of income may be made at such time and in such manner as the Trustees deem advisable, whether by direct payment of such beneficiary's expenses or by payment to such beneficiary personally or to any other person deemed suitable by the Trustees; in each case the receipt of such beneficiary or other person to whom payment is made or entrusted shall be a complete discharge of the Trustees in respect thereof. The provisions of this Article SEVENTH shall also apply to any payments of principal to or applications of principal for a minor or other persons legally incapacitated, pursuant to the provisions of this Indenture, either during the continuance of any trust hereunder or on the termination of any trust hereunder.

EIGHTH: The Trustees, in addition to and not in limitation of all common law and statutory authority, shall have power, with regard to both real and personal property in the trust fund and any part thereof, to mortgage, to lease with or without option to purchase and although for a term extending beyond the termination of the trust, to sell in whole or in part at public or at private sale without the approval of any court and without liability upon any person dealing with the Trustees to see to the application of any money or other property delivered to them; to exchange property for other property; to invest in any common trust fund of which said OLD COLONY TRUST COMPANY is Trustee without giving notice to any beneficiary that such investment is to be made; to retain any security originally transferred to them and to retain and invest and reinvest in securities or properties although of a kind or in an amount which ordinarily would not be considered suitable for a trust investment, including, but without restriction, investments that yield a high rate of income or no income at all and wasting investments, intending hereby to authorize the Trustees to act in such manner as they shall believe to be for the best interests of the trust fund, regarding it as a whole, even though particular investments might not otherwise be proper; to keep any or all securities or other property in the name of some other person, firm or corporation or in their own names without disclosing their fiduciary capacity; to manage and invest separate shares or portions as a joint trust fund consisting of undivided interests; to determine what shall be charged or credited to income and what to principal notwithstanding any determination by the courts and specifically, but without limitation, to make such determination in regard to stock and cash dividends, rights and all other receipts in respect of the ownership of stock and to decide whether or not to make deductions from income for depreciation, obsolescence, amortization or waste and in what amount; to participate in such manner as they deem proper in any reorganization, merger or consolidation affecting any of the trust property; to determine who are the distributees hereunder and the proportions in which they shall take, to make payments of principal or income directly to and otherwise to deal with minors hereunder as though they were of full age; to make distributions or divisions of principal hereunder in property in kind at values determined by them; to pay, compromise or contest any claim or other matter directly affecting this fund; to employ counsel for any of the above or other purposes and to determine whether or not to act upon his advice; to receive property from any person by will or otherwise to be added to the trust estate and to be held, administered and accounted for as a part thereof; to apportion their compensation in part to principal in their discretion; and generally to do all things in relation to the trust fund which the Donor could do if living and this trust had not been executed. All such acts and decisions made by the Trustees in good faith shall be conclusive on all parties at interest. No power herein contained shall be exercised in such a way as to disqualify trust A of Article SECOND for the purposes of the marital deduction under Federal Estate Tax Law or regulations and the Trustees shall endeavor to allocate to trust A, assets, including cash, fairly representative of appreciation or depreciation in the value of all property available for allocation to said trust at the date or dates of allocation. No asset or proceeds of any asset shall be included in trust A as to which a marital deduction is not allowable, if included.

In the event that any residence owned and occupied by the Donor or his said wife at the time of the death of the survivor of them shall become an asset of any trust fund hereunder, then it is the Donor's direction that the legally appointed guardian of the Donor's children shall have the right to occupy said house so long as the youngest of the Donor's children remains a minor, without rent or liability for waste. Taxes, insurance premiums and expenses of ordinary maintenance and repair shall be paid by the Donor's Trustees out of the income from the several shares established hereunder for the Donor's said children, in such amounts as the Trustees, in their discretion, deem equitable, and in the event that such income is insufficient to pay said expenses, then the Trustees may pay such expenses from the principal of the shares established hereunder for the Donor's said children, in such amounts as the Trustees, in their discretion, deem equitable. Notwithstanding the directions hereinbefore set forth, the Trustees shall have the right to sell any such house if they deem it in the best interests of the various beneficiaries of this trust fund to do so, and no person need inquire into the authority of the Trustees to sell such real estate.

NINTH: The Donor reserves the right at any time or times to amend or revoke this trust, in whole or in part, by an instrument in writing delivered to the Trustees. If the agreement is revoked in its entirety, the revocation shall take place upon the delivery of the instrument in writing to the Trustees. Any amendment or any partial revocation shall take effect only when consented to in writing by the Trustees. The Trustees shall at any time deliver to the Donor on his written request any policy or any other property deposited hereunder.

TENTH: The interest of any beneficiary hereunder, either as to income or principal, shall not be anticipated, alienated or in any other manner assigned by such beneficiary and shall not be subject to any legal process, bankruptcy proceedings or the interference or control of creditors or others.

ELEVENTH: The Donor reserves the right by his own act alone, without the consent or approval of the Trustees, to sell, assign or hypothecate said policies or any of them, to exercise any option or privilege granted by any of said policies, including, but without limitation of the generality of the foregoing, the right to change the beneficiary of any policy, to borrow any sum in accordance with the provisions of any of said policies and to receive all payments, dividends, surrender values, benefits or privileges of any kind which may accrue on account of said policies during his lifetime. The Trustees shall assent to or join in the execution of any instrument presented to them by the Donor to enable him to exercise the rights hereinbefore reserved.

TWELFTH: No insurance company issuing any policy or policies which are or shall become subject to this declaration of trust shall be responsible for the application of any money or thing of value paid to the Trustees hereunder or for the carrying out of the provisions of this instrument or any of them.

THIRTEENTH: The Trustees shall use their best efforts to collect all sums payable thereunder whenever any policies shall, to the knowledge of the Trustees, have matured, but shall not be required to take any legal proceedings until indemnified. The Trustees shall have no responsibility, except as above specified, as to such policies nor as to the premiums thereon.

FOURTEENTH: The Trustees may, in their discretion, purchase and retain as an investment for trust fund B of Article SECOND any securities or other property, real or personal, belonging to the estate of the Donor.

The Trustees also may, in their discretion, use and apply the principal of trust fund B of Article SECOND to such extent as they deem necessary for the payment of any debt, funeral expense, administration expense or taxes, however denominated, which may be or become due or be payable from the estate of the Donor or from the estate of the Donor's said wife if she shall survive him; such payments may be made by the Trustees to the creditor or official authorized to receive and receipt for such debts, expenses or taxes upon a certificate from the Donor's executor or administrator or from the executor or administrator of the Donor's said wife to the effect that such debt, expense or tax is due and payable, and the Trustees shall be in no way bound to inquire into the legality or amount of any debt, expense or tax so certified to them by such executor or administrator.

FIFTEENTH: In addition to the powers hereinbefore conferred, the Trustees may hold, purchase, retain or maintain life insurance, annuities or other forms of insurance on the life of any beneficiary hereunder or upon the life or lives of others for the benefit of any such beneficiary or beneficiaries, and may pay all premiums and costs thereof from the income or principal of the trust estate, except that no such premiums shall at any time be paid from trust A of Article SECOND hereof.

SIXTEENTH: At any time after the trusts shall be funded in excess of Fifty Dollars ($50), the Trustees of each trust shall each year render an account of their administration of such trusts, but only if and when there be a person or persons to whom to render such account as herein provided. Any account of the Trustees shall be rendered to the person or persons entitled or eligible to receive net income and/or principal from such trusts at the time the account is rendered; provided, however, that no account shall be rendered to a person who is not of legal capacity unless he has a guardian, in which event the account shall be rendered to such guardian rather than said person; and further provided, that no account shall be rendered to a person other than the Donor, the Donor's said wife, GOLDIE, and the Donor's issue or guardian of such issue while the Donor, his said wife, GOLDIE, or any of the Donor's issue shall be living. The approval of any account at any time as hereinafter provided, by the person or a majority of the persons to whom the account is rendered as herein provided, shall, as to all matters and transactions stated therein or shown thereby, be final and binding upon all persons (whether in being or under disability or not) who have been, are then or may thereafter become entitled or eligible to share in either the principal or the net income of such trusts; provided, however, that nothing contained in this Article SIXTEENTH shall be deemed to give such person or persons acting in conjuction with the Trustees the power or right to enlarge or shift the beneficial interest of any beneficiary of such trusts. A person to whom an account is rendered as herein provided shall be deemed to have approved the same if he assents to the account in writing or if he does not communicate to the Trustees his written objection to the account within sixty (60) days after the date the account is rendered.

SEVENTEENTH: Any Trustee hereunder may resign as Trustee from the trusts hereby created at any time by giving at least thirty (30) days' written notice of his, her or its intention so to do, delivered personally or by registered mail to the Donor if living, or if he has deceased, then to the person or persons then entitled or eligible to receive the income from the trust property. During the lifetime of the Donor, he may appoint such successor Trustee or Trustees as he sees fit. If for any reason the Donor's said wife, GOLDIE BRIDGE, shall not become or remain Co-trustee under this Indenture, then said OLD COLONY TRUST COMPANY shall become or remain sole Trustee. If said OLD COLONY TRUST COMPANY shall resign as Co-trustee or as sole Trustee, then a successor Trustee may be appointed by the Donor if living, but if not living, then a successor corporate Trustee shall be appointed by the person or a majority of the persons entitled or eligible to receive income hereunder at the time such vacancy occurs, including the personal representative of any such person who is then legally incompetent. Any successor Trustee shall qualify at such time as his written acceptance is attached to this instrument. Any successor Trustee shall have all the powers, immunities and discretions conferred herein upon the original Trustees. No Trustee or successor Trustee shall be required to give any bond. No successor Trustee shall be liable or responsible in any way for any acts or defaults of any predecessor Trustee or for any loss or expense from or occasioned by anything done or neglected to be done by any predecessor Trustee; and with the consent of the Donor if he is then living, or of the Donor's said wife if she is living and the Donor is deceased, or if they both have deceased, then with the consent of the person or a majority of the persons then entitled or eligible, in the discretion of the Trustees, to receive income hereunder (including the personal representative of any such person who is then legally incompetent), any Trustee may accept the account rendered and the assets and property delivered to it by a predecessor Trustee, or the executor of the estate of the Donor or of his said wife, and shall incur no liability or responsibility to any beneficiary under this instrument by reason of so doing.

EIGHTEENTH: The trusts hereby created shall be deemed to be Massachusetts trusts and shall, in all respects, be governed by the laws of Massachusetts. The term "Trustees" or "Trustee," as used in this instrument, shall be deemed to mean, wherever the context permits, the Trustees or the Trustee for the time being of the appropriate trusts hereunder, whether original or successor, and the singular shall denote the plural and the plural shall denote the singular, wherever the context so permits. Reference herein to "children" means descendants by blood or adoption in the first degree only, and reference to "issue" means children as above described and their descendants by blood or adoption in any degree including the first degree.

IN WITNESS WHEREOF, the said ANDERSON BRIDGE has hereunto set his hand and seal, and the said OLD COLONY TRUST COMPANY, in token of its acceptance of the trust hereby created, has caused these presents to be executed and its corporate seal to be hereto affixed by its proper officer or officers thereunto duly authorized, this 16th day of July ,1963.

S/ *Anderson Bridge*
DONOR AND TRUSTEE

OLD COLONY TRUST COMPANY

S/ *A. Proper Bostonian* (SEAL)
VICE PRES.

COMMONWEALTH OF MASSACHUSETTS

Suffolk, ss

On this 16th day of July , 1963, before me personally appeared the above-named ANDERSON BRIDGE, to me known to be the person described in and who executed the foregoing instrument, and acknowledged that he executed the same as his free act and deed.

S/ *Endicott Smith*
NOTARY PUBLIC

My commission expires: July 7, 1968

V. Basic Tables for Programing*

TABLE I

AMOUNT OF PRINCIPAL NEEDED TO PRODUCE STIPULATED PERIODIC INTEREST INCOME

2½%

(First payment is made at end of first stipulated time period)

PERIODIC INCOME DESIRED	FREQUENCY OF PAYMENT			
	Annual	Semiannual	Quarterly	Monthly
$ 10	$ 400	$ 805	$ 1,615	$ 4,855
25	1,000	2,013	4,038	12,137
50	2,000	4,025	8,075	24,274
75	3,000	6,038	12,113	36,411
100	4,000	8,050	16,150	48,548

* Note: The tables in this Appendix are presented for purposes of illustration only. The underwriter who is working out specific settlement plans should use either the tables furnished by his own company or one of the published compilations of tables on different interest and mortality bases in order to apply the figures which are applicable to the specific contracts involved.

TABLE II

GUARANTEED INSTALLMENTS PER $1,000 OF PROCEEDS (2½ PER CENT)

Number of Years Payable	Annually	Semiannually	Quarterly	Monthly
1.....	$1,000.00	$503.09	$252.32	$84.28
2.....	506.17	254.65	127.72	42.66
3.....	341.60	171.86	86.19	28.79
4.....	259.33	130.47	65.43	21.86
5.....	210.00	105.65	52.99	17.70
6.....	177.12	89.11	44.69	14.93
7.....	153.65	77.30	38.77	12.95
8.....	136.07	68.46	34.33	11.47
9.....	122.40	61.58	30.88	10.32
10.....	111.47	56.08	28.13	9.39
11.....	102.54	51.59	25.87	8.64
12.....	95.11	47.85	24.00	8.02
13.....	88.83	44.69	22.41	7.49
14.....	83.45	41.98	21.06	7.03
15.....	78.80	39.64	19.88	6.64
16.....	74.73	37.60	18.86	6.30
17.....	71.15	35.79	17.95	6.00
18.....	67.97	34.20	17.15	5.73
19.....	65.13	32.77	16.43	5.49
20.....	62.58	31.48	15.79	5.27
21.....	60.28	30.33	15.21	5.08
22.....	58.19	29.27	14.68	4.90
23.....	56.29	28.32	14.20	4.74
24.....	54.55	27.44	13.76	4.60
25.....	52.95	26.64	13.36	4.46
26.....	51.48	25.90	12.99	4.34
27.....	50.12	25.21	12.65	4.22
28.....	48.87	24.59	12.33	4.12
29.....	47.70	24.00	12.04	4.02
30.....	46.61	23.45	11.76	3.93

TABLE III

Amount of Principal Needed to Provide Guaranteed Income for Varying Durations (2½ Per Cent)

Months of Income	Monthly Income			
	$10	$25	$50	$100
12.....	$ 119	$ 297	$ 593	$ 1,187
24.....	235	586	1,172	2,344
36.....	348	868	1,737	3,473
48.....	458	1,144	2,288	4,575
60.....	565	1,413	2,825	5,650
72.....	670	1,675	3,350	6,698
84.....	773	1,931	3,861	7,722
96.....	872	2,180	4,360	8,718
108.....	969	2,423	4,847	9,690
120.....	1,065	2,661	5,322	10,650
132.....	1,157	2,893	5,785	11,574
144.....	1,247	3,119	6,237	12,469
156.....	1,336	3,339	6,679	13,351
168.....	1,422	3,554	7,109	14,225
180.....	1,506	3,764	7,529	15,060
192.....	1,588	3,969	7,938	15,873
204.....	1,668	4,169	8,338	16,667
216.....	1,746	4,364	8,728	17,452
228.....	1,822	4,554	9,108	18,215
240.....	1,896	4,740	9,479	18,975
252.....	1,968	4,921	9,841	19,683
264.....	2,039	5,097	10,195	20,390
276.....	2,108	5,270	10,539	21,079
288.....	2,175	5,438	10,876	21,752
300.....	2,241	5,602	11,204	22,422
312.....	2,305	5,762	11,524	23,048
324.....	2,367	5,918	11,836	23,672
336.....	2,428	6,070	12,140	24,281
348.....	2,487	6,219	12,437	24,875
360.....	2,545	6,364	12,727	25,445

TABLE IV

Length of Period for Which Monthly Income Is Provided by Varying Principal Sums ($2\frac{1}{2}$ Per Cent)

Desired Monthly Income	$1,000		$2,000		$3,000		$4,000		$5,000		$7,500		$10,000		$12,500		$15,000		$20,000	
	Yrs.	Mos.	Yrs.	Mos.	Yrs.	Mos.	Yrs.	Mos.	Yrs.	Mos.	Yrs.	Mos.	Yrs.	Mos.	Yrs.	Mos.	Yrs.	Mos.	Yrs.	Mos.
$ 10	9	3	21	5																
15	5	11	12	11	21	5														
20	4	4	9	3	14	11	21	5												
25	3	5	7	3	11	5	16	1	21	5										
30	2	10	5	11	9	3	12	11	16	11										
40	2	1	4	4	6	9	9	3	12	0	19	8								
50	1	8	3	5	5	3	7	3	9	3	14	11	21	5						
60	1	4	2	10	4	4	5	11	7	7	12	0	16	11	22	7				
70	1	2	2	5	3	8	5	0	6	5	10	0	14	0	18	5				
75	1	1	2	3	3	5	4	8	5	11	9	3	12	11	16	11	21	5		
80			2	1	3	2	4	4	5	6	8	8	12	0	15	8	19	8		
90					2	10	3	10	4	10	7	7	10	6	13	6	16	11		
100					2	6	3	5	4	4	6	9	9	3	12	0	14	11	21	5
125					2	0	2	9	3	5	5	3	7	3	9	3	11	5	16	1
150							2	3	2	10	4	4	5	11	7	7	9	3	12	11
175							1	11	2	5	3	9	5	0	6	4	7	10	10	11
200									2	1	3	2	4	4	5	6	6	9	9	3

TABLE V

Distribution of Principal Sum as between Installment Time Option and Deferred Life Annuity under Life Income Option with Varying Periods of Guaranteed Installments ($1,000 Basis)

Age of Beneficiary: Male	Age of Beneficiary: Female	Installment Time Option: Number of Guaranteed Payments: 120	180	240	Deferred Life Annuity: Number of Guaranteed Payments: 120	180	240
30	35	$347	$488	$611	$653	$512	$389
40	45	400	559	690	600	441	310
50	55	479	658	793	521	342	207
60	65	597	785	902	403	215	98
70	75	753	911	975	247	89	25

Rate basis: 1937 Standard Annuity Table and 2½ per cent interest; male ages set back one year and female ages six years.

TABLE VI

Amount of Principal Needed to Provide Life Income of $10 per Month—at Various Ages

Age		Life Income Only	5 Years Certain and Life	10 Years Certain and Life	15 Years Certain and Life	20 Years Certain and Life
Male	Female					
25	30	$3,247	$3,247	$3,247	$3,257	$3,279
30	35	3,058	3,058	3,067	3,086	3,106
31	36	3,021	3,021	3,030	3,049	3,077
32	37	2,976	2,976	2,994	3,012	3,040
33	38	2,933	2,941	2,950	2,976	3,003
34	39	2,899	2,899	2,915	2,933	2,967
35	40	2,857	2,857	2,874	2,899	2,933
36	41	2,809	2,817	2,833	2,857	2,899
37	42	2,770	2,770	2,786	2,817	2,857
38	43	2,725	2,732	2,747	2,778	2,825
39	44	2,681	2,688	2,703	2,740	2,786
40	45	2,639	2,646	2,660	2,695	2,747
41	46	2,591	2,597	2,618	2,653	2,710
42	47	2,545	2,551	2,577	2,618	2,674
43	48	2,500	2,506	2,532	2,577	2,639
44	49	2,451	2,463	2,488	2,532	2,604
45	50	2,410	2,415	2,445	2,494	2,564
46	51	2,358	2,370	2,398	2,451	2,532
47	52	2,309	2,320	2,353	2,410	2,494
48	53	2,262	2,273	2,309	2,370	2,457
49	54	2,217	2,227	2,262	2,331	2,427
50	55	2,169	2,179	2,222	2,288	2,392
51	56	2,119	2,132	2,174	2,252	2,358
52	57	2,070	2,083	2,132	2,212	2,326
53	58	2,020	2,037	2,088	2,174	2,294
54	59	1,972	1,988	2,041	2,132	2,268
55	60	1,923	1,942	1,996	2,096	2,237
56	61	1,873	1,894	1,953	2,058	2,208
57	62	1,825	1,845	1,912	2,024	2,179
58	63	1,773	1,799	1,869	1,988	2,155
59	64	1,724	1,748	1,825	1,953	2,128
60	65	1,675	1,704	1,783	1,919	2,105
61	66	1,626	1,656	1,742	1,887	2,083
62	67	1,577	1,608	1,704	1,855	2,062
63	68	1,529	1,563	1,664	1,825	2,041
64	69	1,481	1,517	1,623	1,799	2,024
65	70	1,435	1,473	1,587	1,770	2,008
70	75	1,202	1,258	1,414	1,653	1,946

Rate basis: 1937 Standard Annuity Table and 2½ per cent interest; male ages set back one year and female ages six years; no loading.

TABLE VII

Monthly Life Income per $1,000 of Proceeds—at Various Ages

Age		Life Income Only	5 Years Certain and Life	10 Years Certain and Life	15 Years Certain and Life	20 Years Certain and Life
Male	Female					
25	30	$3.10	$3.09	$3.08	$3.07	$3.05
30	35	3.28	3.27	3.26	3.24	3.22
31	36	3.31	3.31	3.30	3.28	3.25
32	37	3.36	3.36	3.34	3.32	3.29
33	38	3.41	3.40	3.39	3.36	3.33
34	39	3.45	3.45	3.43	3.41	3.37
35	40	3.51	3.50	3.48	3.45	3.41
36	41	3.56	3.55	3.53	3.50	3.45
37	42	3.61	3.61	3.59	3.55	3.50
38	43	3.67	3.66	3.64	3.60	3.54
39	44	3.73	3.72	3.70	3.65	3.59
40	45	3.79	3.78	3.76	3.71	3.64
41	46	3.86	3.85	3.82	3.77	3.69
42	47	3.93	3.92	3.88	3.82	3.74
43	48	4.00	3.99	3.95	3.88	3.79
44	49	4.08	4.06	4.02	3.95	3.84
45	50	4.15	4.14	4.09	4.01	3.90
46	51	4.24	4.22	4.17	4.08	3.95
47	52	4.33	4.31	4.25	4.15	4.01
48	53	4.42	4.40	4.33	4.22	4.07
49	54	4.51	4.49	4.42	4.29	4.12
50	55	4.61	4.59	4.50	4.37	4.18
51	56	4.72	4.69	4.60	4.44	4.24
52	57	4.83	4.80	4.69	4.52	4.30
53	58	4.95	4.91	4.79	4.60	4.36
54	59	5.07	5.03	4.90	4.69	4.41
55	60	5.20	5.15	5.01	4.77	4.47
56	61	5.34	5.28	5.12	4.86	4.53
57	62	5.48	5.42	5.23	4.94	4.59
58	63	5.64	5.56	5.35	5.03	4.64
59	64	5.90	5.72	5.48	5.12	4.70
60	65	5.97	5.87	5.61	5.21	4.75
61	66	6.15	6.04	5.74	5.30	4.80
62	67	6.34	6.22	5.87	5.39	4.85
63	68	6.54	6.40	6.01	5.48	4.90
64	69	6.75	6.59	6.16	5.56	4.94
65	70	6.97	6.79	6.30	5.65	4.98
70	75	8.32	7.95	7.07	6.05	5.14

Rate basis: 1937 Standard Annuity Table and $2\frac{1}{2}$ per cent interest; male ages set back one year and female ages six years.

W. Reinsurance Agreement

between the ______________________ Life Insurance Company of ______________________, hereinafter referred to as the "Ceding Company," party of the first part, and

THE ______________________ LIFE INSURANCE COMPANY of ______________________

hereinafter referred to as the "________," party of the second part.

Article I. BASIS OF REINSURANCE

1. On and after the date hereof the Ceding Company's excess of Life, Waiver of Premium Disability, and Double Indemnity insurance issued directly by the Ceding Company on standard and substandard lives shall be reinsured with the ________. At the option of the Ceding Company applications for reinsurance may be on a facultative basis or reinsurance may be ceded to the ________ automatically as hereinafter provided.

Automatic Reinsurance

2. When the Ceding Company retains its maximum limit of retention on a standard risk, as shown in Schedule A attached hereto, it may cede and the ________ shall accept automatically reinsurance of Life and Waiver of Premium Disability insurance within the following limits:

Life

Ages__ to__ years, inclusive.........400% of the amount retained by the Ceding Company.

Disability

Ages__ to__ years, inclusive.........400% of the amount of Waiver of Premium Disability benefit retained by the Ceding Company in connection with an equal amount of Life coverage.

3. If the Ceding Company has for its own account its maximum limit of retention on a standard risk under previously issued policies and, therefore, is not retaining any portion of the insurance applied for in connection with the current application, and if the new examination or information in connection with it brings out no new factor which adversely affects the insurability of the risk, Life and Disability reinsurance may be ceded automatically to the ________ for amounts within the limits shown above. If, however, it is the opinion of the Ceding Company that there has been an adverse change in the insurance value of the risk since its last policy was issued, an application for the required reinsurance shall be made to the ________ upon a facultative basis.

4. Reinsurance shall not be ceded automatically to the ________ on any life if the sum of the amount of insurance already in force on the life and the amount applied for currently, in the Ceding Company and all other companies, is in excess of the following amounts:

Ages	*Amounts*
0–20	$ 500,000
21–60	1,000,000
61–65	500,000

Facultative Reinsurance

5. Applications for reinsurance of amounts in excess of those provided above, risks which the Ceding Company regards as substandard, and any risks which the Ceding Company does not care to cede to the ______ automatically or which may not be so ceded under the terms hereof, may be submitted for reinsurance upon a facultative basis.

6. Amounts less than the amount at risk upon $500 of insurance shall not be reinsured under this agreement.

Article II. MODE OF CESSION

1. When the Ceding Company desires to submit a risk to the ______ for reinsurance upon a facultative basis, an application for such reinsurance shall be made on either of the sample forms attached hereto and marked Schedule B, Part I. Copies of the original applications, all medical examinations, microscopical reports, inspection reports, and all other information which the Ceding Company may have pertaining to the insurability of the risk shall accompany the application. Upon receipt of such application, the ______ shall immediately examine the papers and shall notify the Ceding Company by telegram of its underwriting action as soon as possible.

2. Automatic reinsurance shall be effected by the Ceding Company's mailing to the ______ a preliminary notification on either of the sample forms attached hereto and marked Schedule B, Part II, showing the reinsurance being effected. The notification shall be mailed within three working days after the Ceding Company has taken final underwriting action.

3. Within five working days after the original policy has been reported delivered and paid for, the Ceding Company shall mail to the ______ a reinsurance cession in duplicate on either of the sample forms attached hereto and marked Schedule B, Part III. [Where reinsurance is ceded automatically, the Ceding Company shall complete the reinsurance cession to show the insured's race, build, sex, blood pressure if a medically examined case, occupation, and impairment, if any; but copies of the Ceding Company's papers need not be sent to the ______ unless the ______ specifically requests them.] The cession shall be completed by the ______ and one copy returned to the Ceding Company.

4. The liability of the ______ shall begin simultaneously with that of the Ceding Company and in no event shall the reinsurance of the ______ be in force and binding unless the policy issued by the Ceding Company to the insured is in force.

Article III. PLAN OF REINSURANCE

1. The Life reinsurance of the ______ shall be upon the Risk Premium Reinsurance plan for the net amount at risk under the contract issued by the Ceding Company. For the purpose of this agreement, the net amount at risk is defined as the difference between the initial amount of reinsurance and the terminal reserve on the amount reinsured (according to the Ceding Company's reserve standard), taken to the nearest dollar, except that where the original policy is issued on a level term plan for twenty years or less, or on a reducing term plan for any period of years, the reinsurance shall be for the gross amount and the terminal reserves shall be disregarded.

2. Reinsurance of Disability and Double Indemnity benefits shall be in accordance with the original forms of the Ceding Company. Copies of the Ceding Company's Waiver of Premium Disability and Double Indemnity riders shall be furnished to the ______, and the Ceding Company shall keep the ______ informed of any changes therein.

Article IV. REINSURANCE PREMIUMS

1. When the reinsurance is to be included in the experience refund account of the Ceding Company, as provided in Article V, the consideration to be paid the ______ by the Ceding Company for Life reinsurance of policies issued by the Ceding Company at standard rates shall be in accordance with the schedule of rates attached hereto and marked Schedule C, Part I, and the consideration for substandard Life reinsurance under policies accepted at a table rating shall be in accordance with the schedule of rates attached hereto and marked Schedule C, Part II. Schedule C, Part I and Schedule C, Part II shall hereinafter be referred to as "*ER*" rates.

2. When the reinsurance is *not* to be included in the experience refund account of the Ceding Company, as provided in Article V, the consideration to be paid the ______ by the Ceding Company for Life reinsurance of policies issued by the Ceding Company at standard rates shall be in accordance with the schedule of rates attached hereto and marked Schedule C, Part III, and the consideration for substandard Life reinsurance under policies accepted at a table rating shall be in accordance with the schedule of rates attached hereto and marked Schedule C, Part IV. Schedule C, Part III and Schedule C, Part IV shall hereinafter be referred to as "*NR*" rates.

3. The consideration to be paid the ______ for substandard Life reinsurance under policies accepted with flat extra premiums rather than table ratings and reinsured on the Risk Premium Reinsurance plan shall be the sum of the following:

(*a*) The standard *ER* or *NR* Risk Premium Reinsurance premiums as provided in paragraphs 1 and 2 of this Article, based upon net amounts at risk under the amount reinsured, and

(*b*) The flat extra premiums charged by the Ceding Company on the gross amount reinsured hereunder less the following commissions:

Permanent Extras (for More Than 5 Years)

First Year.	75%, except when the ______ specifies in its approval that no first year commission is to be paid.
Renewal Years.	10%

Temporary Extras (for 5 Years or Less)

First Year.	None
Renewal Years.	10%

4. For technical reasons relating to the uncertain status of deficiency reserve requirements by the various state insurance departments, the *ER* and *NR* Life reinsurance rates cannot be guaranteed for more than one year. On all reinsurance ceded at these rates, however, the ______ anticipates continuing to accept premiums on the basis of these rate schedules.

5. The consideration to be paid the ______ for reinsurance of Disability benefits and Payor benefits shall be the premiums which the Ceding Company charges the insured on the amounts reinsured less the following commissions:

First Year. 75%
Renewal Years. 10%

6. When the ______ is not required to pay state premium taxes upon reinsurance premiums received from the Ceding Company, it shall reimburse the Ceding Company for any such taxes the latter may be required to pay with respect to that part of the premiums received under the Ceding Company's original policies, which is remitted to the ______ as reinsurance premiums.

Article V. EXPERIENCE REFUND AND NON-REFUND ACCOUNTS

1. Life reinsurance ceded on the basis of the *ER* Risk Premium Reinsurance rates shall be placed in an experience refund account for the Ceding Company, and experience refunds shall be made annually by the ______ in accordance with the formula hereinafter described. The experience refund account shall include all new reinsurance on a single life so long as the total reinsurance on that Life in the ______ does not exceed the experience refund account limit of ______. The excess over the experience refund account limit and all Disability, Double Indemnity, and other supplemental benefits shall be placed in the "non-refund" account.

2. The experience refund for a given calendar year on an account eligible for such refund shall be computed by the following basic formula:

$$ER = \tfrac{1}{2}(P - E + A - C)$$

where ER = experience refund

P = earned Risk Premium Reinsurance Life premiums in the account for the calendar year, defined as the sum of one-half the premiums paid for the current calendar year plus one-half the premiums paid for the preceding calendar year.

E = an expense and contingency charge.

A = a production adjustment equal to one-half of the increase in paid reinsurance premiums for the current calendar year over the preceding calendar year.

C = claims incurred during the calendar year, including claim expenses incurred by the Ceding Company for which it is reimbursed by the______.

3. Except as provided in paragraph 6, the experience refund account will be eligible for the minimum expense and contingency charge equal to 6 per cent of the earned premiums so long as this Reinsurance Agreement is continued in force without modifying the proportion of the Ceding Company's total new reinsurance ceded to the ______; provided, however, that for any calendar year in which the *ER* account has less than five new lives entering, or less than $300 in first year reinsurance premiums paid during the calendar year, the ______ reserves the right to determine experience refunds on a basis which will produce approximately the same net costs as if reinsurance had been placed in the "non-refund" account at *NR* rates.

4. The production adjustment will apply to all calendar years after and including the calendar year in which the Ceding Company first qualifies for the 6 per cent expense and contingency charge set forth in paragraph 3 above. Until the Ceding Company so qualifies, the production adjustment will be taken as zero. If the paid premiums for a given calendar year show a decrease from those of the previous year, and the Ceding Company qualifies or has qualified for the minimum 6 per cent expense and contingency charge in some previous calendar year, the negative production adjustment will be included in the refund calculation. In no event, however, will the accumulative total of such negative adjustments exceed the total previously credited positive adjustments.

5. If the "net profit," $P - E + A - C$, is negative for a given calendar year, such negative amount will be carried forward and treated as an addition to incurred claims in calculating the experience refund for the following calendar years; provided, however, that any unrecovered balance of such negative carryover arising from a given year's experience will be dropped from the refund calculations (*a*) after two years following the year of loss if the Ceding Company qualifies for the minimum 6 per cent expense and contingency charge, and (*b*) after three years following the year of loss if the Ceding Company does not so qualify. The "first-in, first-out" principle will apply to the amortization of two or more negative carry-overs arising from the experience of different calendar years.

6. It shall be understood and agreed that the ________ reserves the right to adjust the experience refund formula in the future.

7. The ________ shall maintain for the Ceding Company a "non-refund" account to which shall be credited all premiums and against which will be charged all claims and other disbursements on reinsurance not included in the Ceding Company's experience refund account.

8. Reinsurance shall not be transferred from the "non-refund" account to the experience refund account or vice versa. At the option of the Ceding Company, however, the rule for allocating future new reinsurance between the two accounts, as provided in paragraph 1 of this Article, may be changed by mutual agreement.

Article VI. PREMIUM ACCOUNTING

1. The ________ shall send the Ceding Company each month a check list in duplicate showing all outstanding first year cases and a statement of all renewal reinsurance premiums falling due within that month.

2. Within twenty days after the close of each month, the Ceding Company shall return one copy of each statement previously received from the ________, showing the premiums for all new reinsurance in connection with policies upon which the premiums shall have been paid to the Ceding Company prior thereto, and also all renewal reinsurance premiums falling due within such month, together with any adjustments made necessary by changes in reinsurance during such month. The Ceding Company shall remit with such statement the premiums due the ________ as shown. Premiums for reinsurance hereunder shall be paid by the Ceding Company to the ________ upon an annual premium basis without regard to the manner of payment as stipulated in the contract of insurance issued by the Ceding Company.

3. Except as provided in Article VII, the payment of reinsurance premiums shall be a condition precedent to the liability of the ________ under reinsurance covered by this agreement. In the event of nonpayment of reinsurance premiums, as provided in the preceding paragraph, the ________ shall have the right to terminate the reinsurance under all policies having reinsurance premiums in arrears. If the ________ elects to exercise its right of termination, it shall give the Ceding Company 30 days' notice of its intention to terminate such reinsurance; and if all reinsurance premiums in arrears, including any which may become in arrears during the 30-day period, are not paid before the expiration of such period, the ________ shall thereupon be relieved of future liability under all policies of reinsurance under which reinsurance premiums remain unpaid. The reinsurance so terminated may be reinstated at any time within 60 days of the date of termination upon payment of all reinsurance premiums in arrears; but in the event of such reinstatement, the ________ shall have no liability in connection with any claims incurred between the date of

termination and the date of reinstatement of the reinsurance. The ________'s right to terminate reinsurance as herein provided shall be without prejudice to its right to collect premiums for the period reinsurance was in force prior to the expiration of the 30-day notice period.

Article VII. OVERSIGHTS

The ________ shall be bound as the Ceding Company is bound; and it is expressly understood and agreed that if nonpayment of premiums within the time specified or failure to comply with any terms of this contract is shown to be unintentional and the result of misunderstanding or oversight on the part of either the Ceding Company or the ________, both the Ceding Company and the ________ shall be restored to the positions they would have occupied had no such error or oversight occurred.

Article VIII. EXPENSES

The Ceding Company shall bear the expense of all medical examinations, inspection fees, and other charges incurred in connection with the original policy.

Article IX. REDUCTIONS

1. If any portion of the insurance carried by the Ceding Company on a life reinsured hereunder shall be terminated, the amount of reinsurance carried by the Ceding Company on that life shall be reduced by a like amount as of the date and time of the termination of the original insurance; if the amount of insurance terminated exceeds the total amount of reinsurance carried by the Ceding Company on the life, all such reinsurance shall be terminated. In the interpretation of this Article, the maturity of an endowment policy or the expiration of a term policy shall be considered as a termination of insurance.

2. The reduction shall be applied first to the reinsurance directly applicable to the Ceding Company's policy which is reduced or terminated, the reinsurance of the ________ being reduced by an amount which shall be the same proportion of the amount of insurance terminated that the ________'s reinsurance bore to the total amount of reinsurance under that particular policy.

3. If any portion of the terminated insurance was retained by the Ceding Company, a reduction equal to the amount of such retention shall be made in the reinsurance in force under other policies on the life, each reinsurer sharing in the reduction according to its proportion of the comparable reinsurance on the life not directly applicable to the policy of the Ceding Company which was terminated. In interpreting this paragraph, policies issued concurrently upon the same plan and at the same mortality rating shall be considered as one policy; and when the terminated policies contain Disability, Double Indemnity, or other supplementary benefits, the reduction shall be applied first to the reinsurance policies containing the same benefits and carrying the same mortality rating, the principle to be observed being always that the retention of the Ceding Company is to be maintained unchanged. It is understood, however, that in no case shall the Ceding Company be required to assume a risk for an amount in excess of its regular retention limit for the age at issue and mortality rating of the policy under which reinsurance is being terminated.

4. The ________ shall refund to the Ceding Company all unearned premiums, without interest thereon, which arise either because of reductions in reinsurance brought about as outlined in the preceding paragraphs or because the Ceding Company shall have paid the ________ a premium after its policy shall have been discontinued or to a date later than its own insured shall have paid to the Ceding Company.

Article X. INCREASE IN RETENTION

1. The reinsurance under this contract shall be maintained in force without reduction as long as the original amount of insurance carried by the Ceding Company on the life remains in force without reduction, except as provided in this Article.

2. In case the Ceding Company shall increase its maximum limits of retention, as shown in Schedule A, reductions may be made in reinsurance then in force under this contract; provided, however, that regardless of the limits established for new business, the following rules shall govern the reductions in reinsurance hereunder.

(*a*) No reduction shall be made in the reinsurance on any life unless the Ceding Company retains its maximum limit of retention for the plan, age, and mortality rating at the time the policy was issued.

(*b*) No reduction shall be made in any class of fully reinsured business or in any classes of risks for which the Ceding Company established special retention limits less than the Ceding Company's maximum retention limits for the plan, age, and mortality rating at the time the policy was issued.

(*c*) No reduction shall be made in the reinsurance of any policy until such reinsurance has been in force at least five full years.

3. The Ceding Company may elect to make any increase in retention retroactively in its application to standard business only, in which case adjustments shall be made only in reinsurance on risks on which the Ceding Company retained its maximum limit of retention at its regular standard premium rates at the time reinsurance was obtained. If, however, the Ceding Company elects to make an increase in its substandard retention limits retroactively, the new retention of the Ceding Company on each policy shall be determined by the insurance age and the mortality rating in effect on that particular policy at the date of issue.

4. In order to effect such reductions, the Ceding Company shall give written notice to the ________ of the increase in retention and thereupon the reinsurance shall be reduced by such an amount in each case as will increase the amount of total insurance to be carried by the Ceding Company at its own risk to its new maximum; but if any policy of reinsurance be so reduced, all policies of reinsurance in force in the ________ shall be similarly reduced, subject to the restrictions hereof. If there is reinsurance in other companies on risks eligible for recapture, the necessary reduction is to be applied pro rata to the total outstanding reinsurance.

5. The reduction in each individual reinsurance policy shall be effective upon the first reinsurance renewal date after the ________ has been notified of the increase in retention, provided at that time the policy has been in force for at least five full years. In all cases where the reinsurance has not been in force for five years, such reinsurance shall be continued without reduction to the fifth policy anniversaries, upon which dates the proper reductions shall be effected.

6. In the event the Ceding Company overlooks any reductions or cancellations of reinsurance which should be made on account of a retroactive increase in its retention limits, the acceptance by the ________ of reinsurance premiums under such circumstances and after the effective dates of the reductions or cancellations shall not constitute or determine a liability on the part of the ________ for such reinsurance; and the ________ shall be liable only for a refund of the premiums so received, without interest.

Article XI. EXTENDED AND PAID-UP INSURANCE

In case the original policy of the Ceding Company shall lapse and extended or paid-up insurance be granted in accordance with its provision, the Ceding Company shall notify the ________ that such extended or paid-up insurance has been granted and shall send the ________ an amended cession in duplicate showing the adjusted amounts of reinsurance; provided, however, that if the amount of extended or paid-up insurance granted under the portion of the Ceding Company's policy reinsured with the ________ is less than $500, such reinsurance shall be canceled. The reinsurance premiums shown on the amended cessions shall be calculated on the basis of the schedule of Risk Premium Reinsurance rates applicable to the reinsurance policy prior to the change. The amended cession shall be properly executed by the ________ and one copy returned to the Ceding Company.

Article XII. SETTLEMENT OF CLAIMS

1. The ________ shall be liable to the Ceding Company for the benefits covered by reinsurance hereunder to the same extent as the Ceding Company is liable to the insured for such benefits, and all reinsurance shall be subject to the terms and conditions of the particular form of policy under which the Ceding Company shall be liable. It is understood and agreed, however, that payment of a death claim by the ________ shall be made in one lump sum regardless of the mode of settlement under the policy of the Ceding Company.

2. Whenever a claim is made under a policy of the Ceding Company which has been reinsured hereunder, it shall be taken and considered by the ________ to be a claim for the amount of reinsurance on such risk, and the ________ shall abide the issue as it shall be settled by the Ceding Company and shall pay the amount of reinsurance covered by the policy of reinsurance when the Ceding Company shall settle with the claimant.

3. Any suit or claim may be contested or compromised on the part of the Ceding Company; and in case of a reduction of the claim made upon the Ceding Company, the ________ and the Ceding Company shall participate in such reduction in the ratio that each company's net liability bore to the total net liability prior to the reduction of the claim. Any unusual expenses incurred by the Ceding Company in defending or investigating any claims or taking up or rescinding any policy reinsured hereunder, aside from routine investigations and other expenses incidental to the settlement of claims, shall be shared in the same proportion.

4. In every case of loss, proofs obtained by the Ceding Company shall likewise be taken as sufficient by the ________ and copies thereof, together with a statement showing the amount paid on such claim by the Ceding Company, shall be furnished to the ________ before payment shall be demanded of it. It is agreed, however, that if the amount of the Disability or Double Indemnity benefits carried by the ________ in connection with any claim for such benefits under a policy reinsured hereunder is in excess of the amount of such benefits retained by the Ceding Company, all papers in connection with such claim shall be submitted to the ________ for its recommendation before payment is made under these benefits.

5. In the event of an increase or reduction in the amount of the Ceding Company's insurance provided by any policy or policies reinsured hereunder because of a misstatement of age being established after the death of the insured, the Ceding Company and the ________ shall share in such increase or reduction in the ratio that each company's net liability bore to the total net liability prior to the reduction under such policy or policies. The reinsurance

policy or policies of the ________ shall be rewritten from commencement on the basis of the adjusted amounts using premiums and reserves at the correct ages, and the proper adjustment for the difference in reinsurance premiums, without interest, shall be made.

6. The ________ shall return to the Ceding Company all reinsurance premiums, including those for any supplemental benefits, paid to the ________ for any period beyond the date of death of a risk reinsured hereunder. In the event of the death of a risk reinsured hereunder for Accidental Death coverage only, the ________ shall return to the Ceding Company any Accidental Death reinsurance premiums paid to the ________ for any period beyond the date of death of the risk.

Article XIII. REINSTATEMENTS

If a reinsured policy lapses for nonpayment of premium and is reinstated in accordance with its terms and the rules of the Ceding Company, the reinsurance under such policy shall be reinstated automatically by the ________. Notice of such reinstatement shall be mailed to the office of the ________ not later than the fifth working day after the reinstatement of the original policy. In connection with all such reinstatements the Ceding Company shall pay the ________ all reinsurance premiums in arrears with interest at the same rate and in like manner as the Ceding Company has received under its policy.

Article XIV. POLICY CHANGES

If any change which affects the reinsurance hereunder shall be made in the policy issued by the Ceding Company to the insured, the Ceding Company shall immediately notify the ________ of such change.

Article XV. INSPECTION OF RECORDS

The ________ shall have the right at any reasonable time to inspect, at the office of the Ceding Company, all books and documents relating to the reinsurance under this agreement.

Article XVI. INSOLVENCY

1. In the event of the insolvency of the Ceding Company, all reinsurance shall be payable directly to the liquidator, receiver, or statutory successor of said Ceding Company, without diminution because of the insolvency of the Ceding Company.

2. In the event of insolvency of the Ceding Company, the liquidator, receiver, or statutory successor shall give the ________ written notice of the pendency of a claim on a policy reinsured within a reasonable time after such claim is filed in the insolvency proceeding. During the pendency of any such claim, the ________ may investigate such claim and interpose in the name of the Ceding Company (its liquidator, receiver, or statutory successor), but at its own expense, in the proceeding where such claim is to be adjudicated, any defense or defenses which the ________ may deem available to the Ceding Company or its liquidator, receiver, or statutory successor.

3. The expense thus incurred by the ________ shall be chargeable, subject to court approval, against the Ceding Company as part of the expense of liquidation to the extent of a proportionate share of the benefit which may accrue to the Ceding Company solely as a result of the defense undertaken by the ________. Where two or more reinsurers are participating in the same claim and a majority in interest elect to interpose a defense or defenses to any such claim,

the expense shall be apportioned in accordance with the terms of the reinsurance agreement as though such expense had been incurred by the Ceding Company.

Article XVII. ARBITRATION

1. All disputes and differences between the two contracting parties upon which an amicable understanding cannot be reached are to be decided by arbitration; and the arbitrators, who shall regard this treaty from the standpoint of practical business and equity rather than from that of the strict law, are empowered to determine as to the interpretation of the treaty obligation.

2. The court of arbitrators, which is to be held in the city where the Home Office of the Ceding Company is domiciled, shall consist of three arbitrators who must be officers of life insurance companies other than the two parties to this agreement. One of the arbitrators is to be appointed by the Ceding Company, the second by the ________, and the third is to be selected by these two representatives before the beginning of the arbitration. Should one of the parties decline to appoint an arbitrator or should the two arbitrators be unable to agree upon the choice of a third, the appointment shall be left to the president of the American Life Convention.

3. The arbitrators are not bound by any rules of law. They shall decide by a majority of votes and from their written decision there can be no appeal. The cost of arbitration, including the fees of the arbitrators, shall be borne by the losing party unless the arbitrators shall decide otherwise.

Article XVIII. PARTIES TO AGREEMENT

This is an agreement solely between the ceding company and the ________. The acceptance of reinsurance hereunder shall not create any right or legal relation whatever between the ________ and the insured or the beneficiary under any policy of the Ceding Company which may be reinsured hereunder.

Article XIX. DURATION OF AGREEMENT

This agreement shall be effective as of the ______ day of ________, 19___, and shall be unlimited as to its duration but may be terminated at any time, insofar as it pertains to the handling of new business thereafter, by either party giving three months' notice of termination in writing. The ________ shall continue to accept reinsurance during the three months aforesaid and shall remain liable on all reinsurance granted under this treaty until the termination or expiry of the insurance reinsured.

IN WITNESS WHEREOF the said

________________________________ Life Insurance Company

and the said

THE ________________________________ COMPANY of ______

____________, have by their respective officers executed and delivered these presents in duplicate this ______ day of ________, 19___.

By ________________________________

____

THE ________________ LIFE INSURANCE COMPANY

By ________________________________

Vice President

____

Assistant Secretary

DOUBLE INDEMNITY ADDENDUM

to the Reinsurance Agreement between the
____________________ Life Insurance Company

and

THE ____________________ COMPANY of ______
__________ of which this Addendum is a part.

Article I.

1. On and after the date hereof all Double Indemnity insurance issued directly by the Ceding Company for amounts in excess of its own limit of retention shall be reinsured with the ______.

2. When the papers in the hands of the Ceding Company indicate that the total amount of accidental death insurance, including Principal Sum accident benefits, issued and contemplated on the life in the Ceding Company and all other companies will not be in excess of $150,000, the Ceding Company shall cede and the ______ shall accept automatically Double Indemnity reinsurance for amounts up to ______. Reinsurance of Double Indemnity issued by the Ceding Company on risks not covered by the foregoing may be submitted to the ______ upon a facultative basis. The minimum amount of Double Indemnity to be reinsured on any one life shall be $500.

3. The Double Indemnity reinsurance of the ______ shall be in accordance with the Ceding Company's original forms. Copies of the Ceding Company's present Double Indemnity riders shall be furnished the ______, and the Ceding Company shall keep the ______ informed of any changes therein.

Article II.

1. When there is Life reinsurance on the same life, the Double Indemnity reinsurance shall be included in the Life cession referred to in Article II of the above mentioned reinsurance agreement. Double Indemnity reinsurance apart from Life reinsurance shall be effected by the Ceding Company's mailing to the ______ consecutively numbered cards in accordance with the sample attached hereto and marked Schedule D. These cards shall be sent within five working days after acceptance of the risk by the Ceding Company and shall contain the name of the Insured, the place and date of birth, the occupation, the classification of the risk, and the amount of reinsurance desired.

2. If, upon receipt of a cession card, the ______ shall notice an omission in the serial numbers, the ______ shall notify the Ceding Company by mail of such omission; however, in case of any reinsurance card being delayed or lost in transit, the ______ shall nevertheless be liable for the reinsurance entered into or recorded by the Ceding Company under the number of the missing reinsurance card. In such cases the books and documents of the Ceding Company shall be prima facie evidence of the reinsurance effected under the number of the delayed or lost card.

Article III.

The consideration to be paid the ______ for Double Indemnity reinsurance shall be based upon the classification of the occupational manual of the ______ as follows:

Rates Per Thousand

Classification	*First Year*	*Renewal*
Standard	$ .25	$1.00
1½ × Standard (Medium)	.40	1.40
2 × Standard (Special)	.50	1.80
3 × Standard	.75	2.60
5 × Standard	1.25	4.20

Premiums for renewal years shall be payable as long as the reinsurance remains in force.

Article IV.

1. If the amount of insurance under the Double Indemnity provisions contained in the policies of the Ceding Company on any life reinsured hereunder shall be reduced, such reinsurance shall be reduced in like amount; if the ________ does not carry the full amount of reinsurance of Double Indemnity held by the Ceding Company on the said life, the reduction of the reinsurance hereunder shall be in the proportion that the Double Indemnity reinsurance of the ________ bears to the total amount of such reinsurance carried by the Ceding Company on such life. In no event shall any Double Indemnity reinsurance hereunder be reduced unless such insurance in force in the Ceding Company is reduced. The amount of the unearned reinsurance premiums, without interest thereon, shall be refunded to the Ceding Company.

2. It is expressly understood and agreed that the Double Indemnity reinsurance hereunder shall be subject to all the terms and conditions of the above mentioned reinsurance agreement of which this is a part which do not conflict with the terms hereof.

IT WITNESS WHEREOF the parties hereto have caused this Addendum to be executed in duplicate this ______ day of ________, 19___.

By ________________________________

THE ________________________ LIFE INSURANCE COMPANY

By ________________________________

Assistant Secretary

BINDING RECEIPT ADDENDUM

to the Reinsurance Agreement between the

________________________________ Life Insurance Company

and

THE ________________________________ COMPANY of ______

______________, of which this Addendum is a part.

1. In the event the Ceding Company, before having an opportunity to arrange the necessary reinsurance, shall become liable under a binding receipt for a death claim of an amount which, together with the amount retained by the Ceding Company under previously issued policies, if any, exceeds its own maximum limit of retention, the ________ shall accept reinsurance liability automatically for an amount equal to the greater of (*a*) the sum of the automatic Life reinsurance provided by Article I of the Reinsurance Agreement and the amount of automatic Double Indemnity reinsurance provided in the Double Indemnity Addendum to that Agreement, or (*b*) at ages 0 to 60, in-

clusive, ______ less the Ceding Company's retention limit and less the amount of Life and Double Indemnity reinsurance, if any, previously ceded by the Ceding Company to the ______.

By ______________________

THE ______________ LIFE INSURANCE COMPANY

By ______________________

Assistant Secretary

Indexes

INDEX OF NAMES

INDEX OF SUBJECTS

C

E

H

I

J

K

This book has been set on the Linotype in 10 point Caledonia leaded 2 points. Chapter numbers are in 18 point Perpetua with 18 point Caslon Open numerals, and chapter titles are in 18 point Perpetua caps. The size of the type page is 27 by 46 picas.